NEW PERSPECTIVES

Microsoft® Office 365™ & Excel 2016

COMPREHENSIVE

June Jamrich Parsons
Dan Oja
Patrick Carey

Carol A. DesJardins
St. Clair County Community College

Australia • Brazil • Mexico • Singapore • United Kingdom • United States

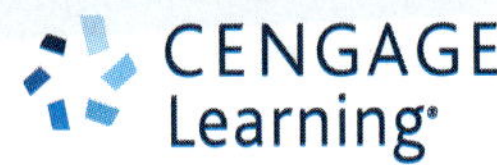

New Perspectives Microsoft® Office 365™ & Excel 2016, Comprehensive
June Jamrich Parsons, Dan Oja, Patrick Carey, Carol A. DesJardins

SVP, GM Science, Technology & Math: Balraj S. Kalsi

Senior Product Director: Kathleen McMahon

Senior Product Team Manager: Lauren Murphy

Product Team Manager: Andrea Topping

Associate Product Manager: Melissa Stehler

Senior Director, Development: Julia Caballero

Product Development Manager: Leigh Hefferon

Senior Content Developers: Kathy Finnegan, Marjorie Hunt

Developmental Editor: Robin M. Romer

Manuscript Quality Assurance: John Freitas, Chris Scriver

Product Assistant: Erica Chapman

Marketing Director: Michele McTighe

Marketing Manager: Stephanie Albracht

Marketing Coordinator: Cassie Cloutier

Production Director: Patty Stephan

Senior Content Project Managers: Jennifer Goguen McGrail, Stacey Lamodi

Manufacturing Planner: Fola Orekoya

Art Director: Diana Graham

Text Designer: Althea Chen

Composition: GEX Publishing Services

Cover Template Designer: Wing-Ip Ngan, Ink Design, Inc.

Cover image(s): BMJ/Shutterstock.com

Mac users: If you're working through this product using a Mac, some of the steps may vary. Additional information for Mac users is included with the Data Files for this product.

Library of Congress Control Number: 2016941948
Soft-cover Edition ISBN: 978-1-305-88040-5
Loose-leaf cover Edition ISBN: 978-1-337-25147-1

Cengage Learning
20 Channel Center Street
Boston, MA 02210
USA

Cengage Learning is a leading provider of customized learning solutions with employees residing in nearly 40 different countries and sales in more than 125 countries around the world. Find your local representative at **www.cengage.com.**

Cengage Learning products are represented in Canada by Nelson Education, Ltd.

To learn more about Cengage Learning, visit **www.cengage.com**

Purchase any of our products at your local college store or at our preferred online store **www.cengagebrain.com**

Printed in the United States of America
Print Number: 01 Print Year: 2016

BRIEF CONTENTS

TABLE OF CONTENTS

Productivity Apps for School and Work

OneNote
Sway
Office Mix
Edge

Corinne Hoisington

Lochlan keeps track of his class notes, football plays, and internship meetings with OneNote.
Zoe is using the annotation features of Microsoft Edge to take and save web notes for her research paper.
Nori is creating a Sway site to highlight this year's activities for the Student Government Association.
Hunter is adding interactive videos and screen recordings to his PowerPoint resume.
Statistical

Being computer literate no longer means mastery of only Word, Excel, PowerPoint, Outlook, and Access. To become technology power users, Hunter, Nori, Zoe, and Lochlan are exploring Microsoft OneNote, Sway, Mix, and Edge in Office 2016 and Windows 10.

In this Module

Learn to use productivity apps!
Links to companion **Sways**, featuring **videos** with hands-on instructions, are located on www.cengagebrain.com.

Introduction to OneNote 2016

Bottom Line
- OneNote is a note-taking app for your academic and professional life.
- Use OneNote to get organized by gathering your ideas, sketches, webpages, photos, videos, and notes in one place.

notebook | section tab | To Do tag | screen clipping | note | template | Microsoft OneNote Mobile app | sync | drawing canvas | inked handwriting | Ink to Text

As you glance around any classroom, you invariably see paper notebooks and notepads on each desk. Because deciphering and sharing handwritten notes can be a challenge, Microsoft OneNote 2016 replaces physical notebooks, binders, and paper notes with a searchable, digital notebook. OneNote captures your ideas and schoolwork on any device so you can stay organized, share notes, and work with others on projects. Whether you are a student taking class notes as shown in **Figure 1** or an employee taking notes in company meetings, OneNote is the one place to keep notes for all of your projects.

Figure 1: OneNote 2016 notebook

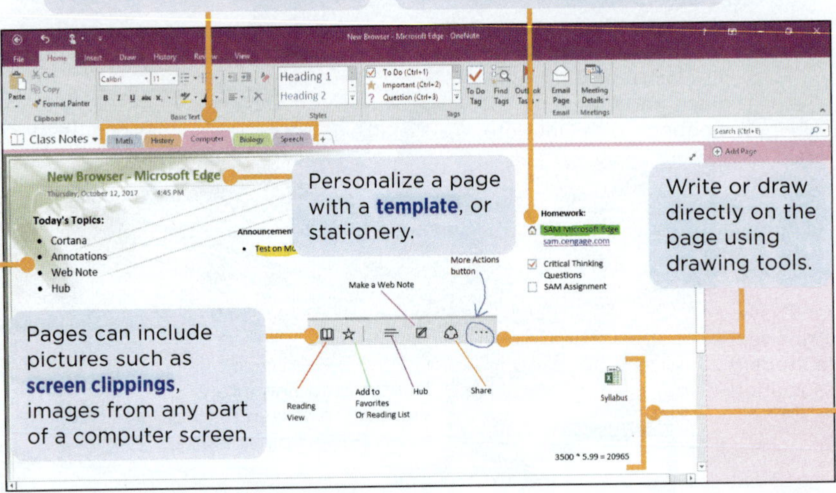

Each **notebook** is divided into sections, also called **section tabs**, by subject or topic.
Use **To Do tags**, icons that help you keep track of your assignments and other tasks.
Type on a page to add a **note**, a small window that contains text or other types of information.
Personalize a page with a **template**, or stationery.
Write or draw directly on the page using drawing tools.
Pages can include pictures such as **screen clippings**, images from any part of a computer screen.
Attach files and enter equations so you have everything you need in one place.
Class Notes
New Browser - Microsoft Edge
Today's Topics:
Cortana
Annotations
Web Note
Hub
Homework:
Critical Thinking Questions
SAM Assignment
Make a Web Note
More Actions button
Reading View
Add to Favorites Or Reading List
Hub
Share
Syllabus
3500 * 5.99 = 20965

Creating a OneNote Notebook

OneNote is divided into sections similar to those in a spiral-bound notebook. Each OneNote notebook contains sections, pages, and other notebooks. You can use OneNote for school, business, and personal projects. Store information for each type of project in different notebooks to keep your tasks separate, or use any other organization that suits you. OneNote is flexible enough to adapt to the way you want to work.

When you create a notebook, it contains a blank page with a plain white background by default, though you can use templates, or stationery, to apply designs in categories such as Academic, Business, Decorative, and Planners. Start typing or use the buttons on the Insert tab to insert notes, which are small resizable windows that can contain text, equations, tables, on-screen writing, images, audio and video recordings, to-do lists, file attachments, and file printouts. Add as many notes as you need to each page.

Learn to use OneNote!
Links to companion **Sways**, featuring **videos** with hands-on instructions, are located on www.cengagebrain.com.

Syncing a Notebook to the Cloud

OneNote saves your notes every time you make a change in a notebook. To make sure you can access your notebooks with a laptop, tablet, or smartphone wherever you are, OneNote uses cloud-based storage, such as OneDrive or SharePoint. **Microsoft OneNote Mobile app**, a lightweight version of OneNote 2016 shown in **Figure 2**, is available for free in the Windows Store, Google Play for Android devices, and the AppStore for iOS devices.

If you have a Microsoft account, OneNote saves your notes on OneDrive automatically for all your mobile devices and computers, which is called **syncing**. For example, you can use OneNote to take notes on your laptop during class, and then open OneNote on your phone to study later. To use a notebook stored on your computer with your OneNote Mobile app, move the notebook to OneDrive. You can quickly share notebook content with other people using OneDrive.

Figure 2: Microsoft OneNote Mobile app

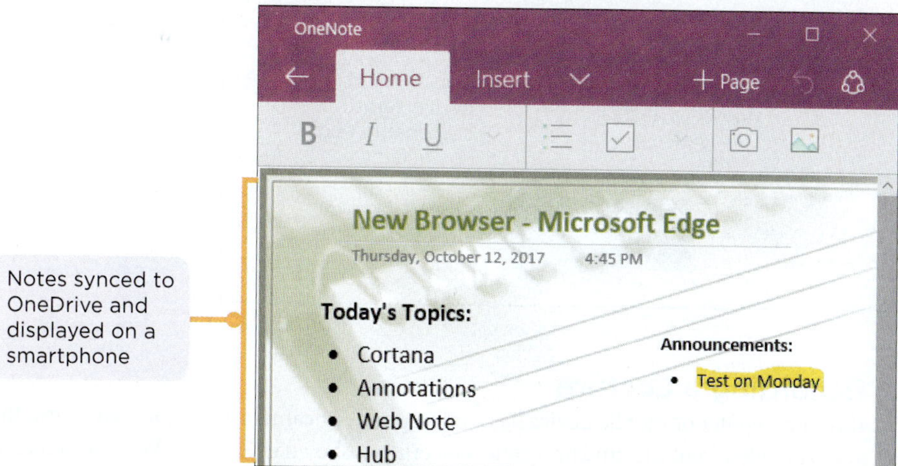

Taking Notes

Use OneNote pages to organize your notes by class and topic or lecture. Beyond simple typed notes, OneNote stores drawings, converts handwriting to searchable text and mathematical sketches to equations, and records audio and video.

OneNote includes drawing tools that let you sketch freehand drawings such as biological cell diagrams and financial supply-and-demand charts. As shown in **Figure 3**, the Draw tab on the ribbon provides these drawing tools along with shapes so you can insert diagrams and other illustrations to represent your ideas. When you draw on a page, OneNote creates a **drawing canvas**, which is a container for shapes and lines.

OneNote is ideal for taking notes during meetings, whether you are recording minutes, documenting a discussion, sketching product diagrams, or listing follow-up items. Use a meeting template to add pages with content appropriate for meetings.

Figure 3: Tools on the Draw tab

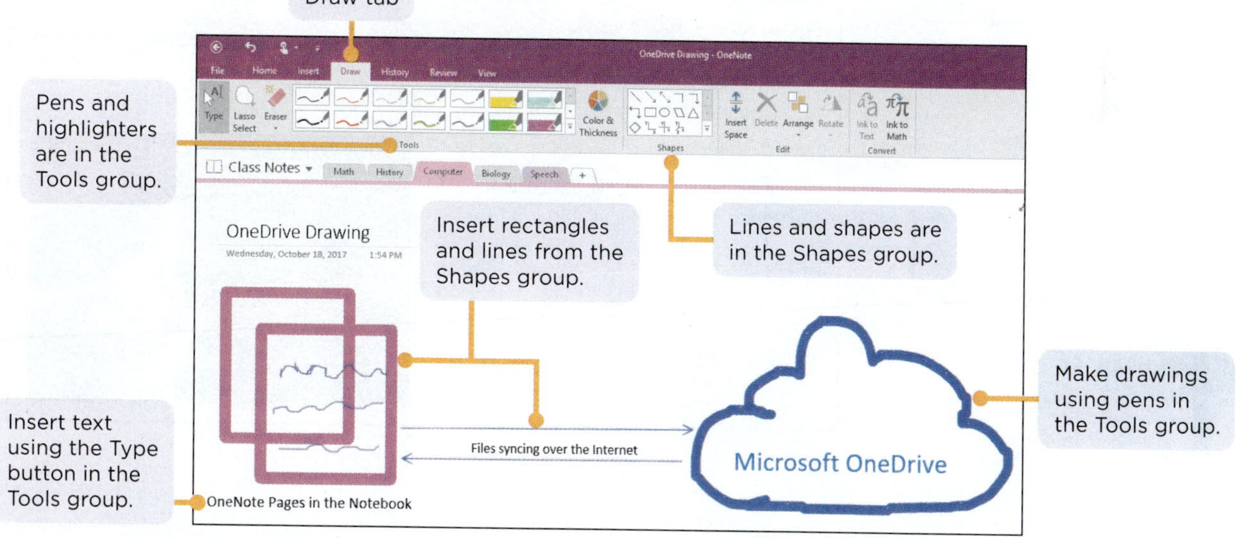

Converting Handwriting to Text

When you use a pen tool to write on a notebook page, the text you enter is called **inked handwriting**. OneNote can convert inked handwriting to typed text when you use the **Ink to Text** button in the Convert group on the Draw tab, as shown in **Figure 4**. After OneNote converts the handwriting to text, you can use the Search box to find terms in the converted text or any other note in your notebooks.

Figure 4: Converting handwriting to text

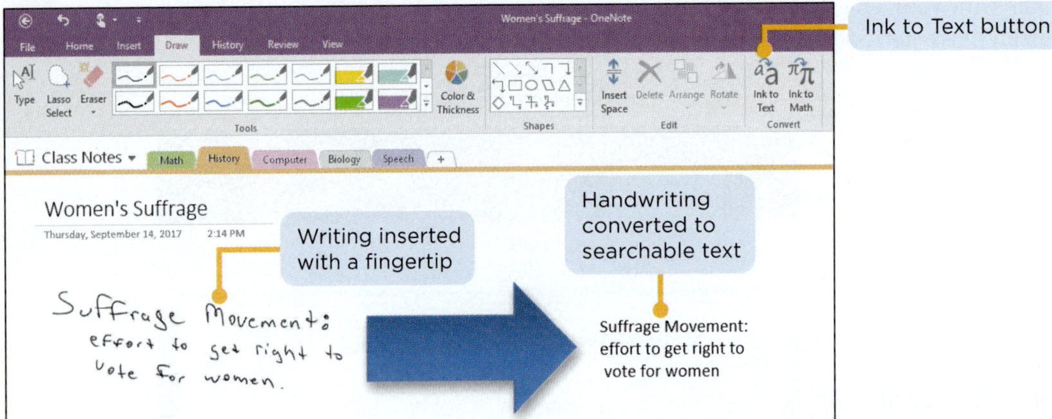

On the Job Now

Use OneNote as a place to brainstorm ongoing work projects. If a notebook contains sensitive material, you can password-protect some or all of the notebook so that only certain people can open it.

Recording a Lecture

If your computer or mobile device has a microphone or camera, OneNote can record the audio or video from a lecture or business meeting as shown in **Figure 5**. When you record a lecture (with your instructor's permission), you can follow along, take regular notes at your own pace, and review the video recording later. You can control the start, pause, and stop motions of the recording when you play back the recording of your notes.

Figure 5: Video inserted in a notebook

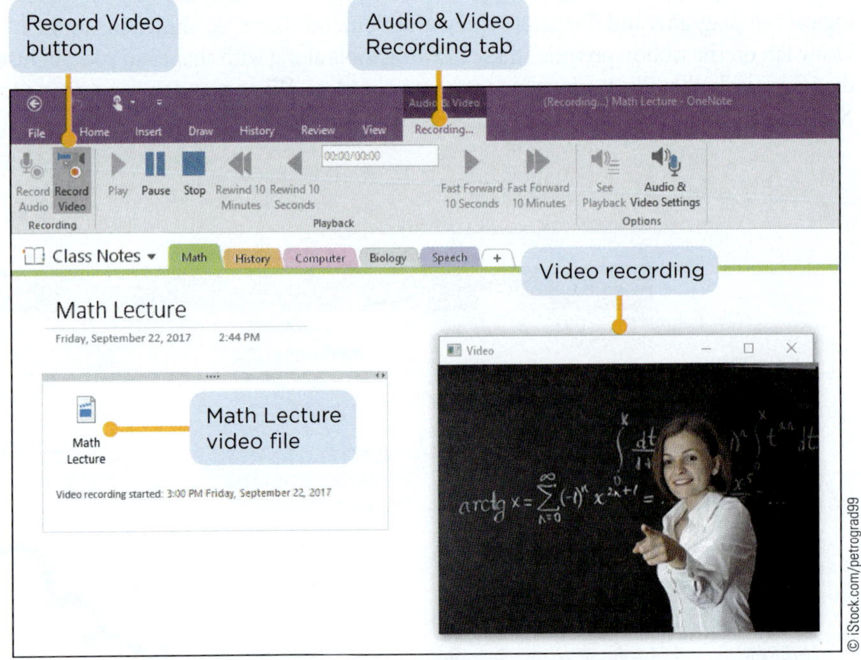

Try This Now

Learn to use OneNote!
Links to companion **Sways**, featuring **videos** with hands-on instructions, are located on www.cengagebrain.com.

1: Taking Notes for a Week

As a student, you can get organized by using OneNote to take detailed notes in your classes. Perform the following tasks:

a. Create a new OneNote notebook on your Microsoft OneDrive account (the default location for new notebooks). Name the notebook with your first name followed by "Notes," as in **Caleb Notes**.
b. Create four section tabs, each with a different class name.
c. Take detailed notes in those classes for one week. Be sure to include notes, drawings, and other types of content.
d. Sync your notes with your OneDrive. Submit your assignment in the format specified by your instructor.

2: Using OneNote to Organize a Research Paper

You have a research paper due on the topic of three habits of successful students. Use OneNote to organize your research. Perform the following tasks:

a. Create a new OneNote notebook on your Microsoft OneDrive account. Name the notebook **Success Research**.
b. Create three section tabs with the following names:
   - **Take Detailed Notes**
   - **Be Respectful in Class**
   - **Come to Class Prepared**
c. On the web, research the topics and find three sources for each section. Copy a sentence from each source and paste the sentence into the appropriate section. When you paste the sentence, OneNote inserts it in a note with a link to the source.
d. Sync your notes with your OneDrive. Submit your assignment in the format specified by your instructor.

3: Planning Your Career

Note: This activity requires a webcam or built-in video camera on any type of device.

Consider an occupation that interests you. Using OneNote, examine the responsibilities, education requirements, potential salary, and employment outlook of a specific career. Perform the following tasks:

a. Create a new OneNote notebook on your Microsoft OneDrive account. Name the notebook with your first name followed by a career title, such as **Kara - App Developer**.
b. Create four section tabs with the names **Responsibilities, Education Requirements, Median Salary**, and **Employment Outlook**.
c. Research the responsibilities of your career path. Using OneNote, record a short video (approximately 30 seconds) of yourself explaining the responsibilities of your career path. Place the video in the Responsibilities section.
d. On the web, research the educational requirements for your career path and find two appropriate sources. Copy a paragraph from each source and paste them into the appropriate section. When you paste a paragraph, OneNote inserts it in a note with a link to the source.
e. Research the median salary for a single year for this career. Create a mathematical equation in the Median Salary section that multiplies the amount of the median salary times 20 years to calculate how much you will possibly earn.
f. For the Employment Outlook section, research the outlook for your career path. Take at least four notes about what you find when researching the topic.
g. Sync your notes with your OneDrive. Submit your assignment in the format specified by your instructor.

Introduction to Sway

Sway site | responsive design | Storyline | card | Creative Commons license | animation emphasis effects | Docs.com

Bottom Line

- Drag photos, videos, and files from your computer and content from Facebook and Twitter directly to your Sway presentation.
- Run Sway in a web browser or as an app on your smartphone, and save presentations as webpages.

Expressing your ideas in a presentation typically means creating PowerPoint slides or a Word document. Microsoft Sway gives you another way to engage an audience. Sway is a free Microsoft tool available at Sway.com or as an app in Office 365. Using Sway, you can combine text, images, videos, and social media in a website called a **Sway site** that you can share and display on any device. To get started, you create a digital story on a web-based canvas without borders, slides, cells, or page breaks. A Sway site organizes the text, images, and video into a **responsive design**, which means your content adapts perfectly to any screen size as shown in **Figure 6**. You store a Sway site in the cloud on OneDrive using a free Microsoft account.

Figure 6: Sway site with responsive design

You can display a Sway presentation in a web browser.
Sway uses responsive design to make sure pages fit perfectly on any device.
The Market for Commercial Drones
Medical Defibrillator
• Ambulance drone can help heart attack victims in under 2 minutes with
The Market for Commercial Drones
Medical Defibrillator

Creating a Sway Presentation

Learn to use Sway!
Links to companion **Sways**, featuring **videos** with hands-on instructions, are located on www.cengagebrain.com.

You can use Sway to build a digital flyer, a club newsletter, a vacation blog, an informational site, a digital art portfolio, or a new product rollout. After you select your topic and sign into Sway with your Microsoft account, a **Storyline** opens, providing tools and a work area for composing your digital story. See **Figure 7**. Each story can include text, images, and videos. You create a Sway by adding text and media content into a Storyline section, or **card**. To add pictures, videos, or documents, select a card in the left pane and then select the Insert Content button. The first card in a Sway presentation contains a title and background image.

Figure 7: Creating a Sway site

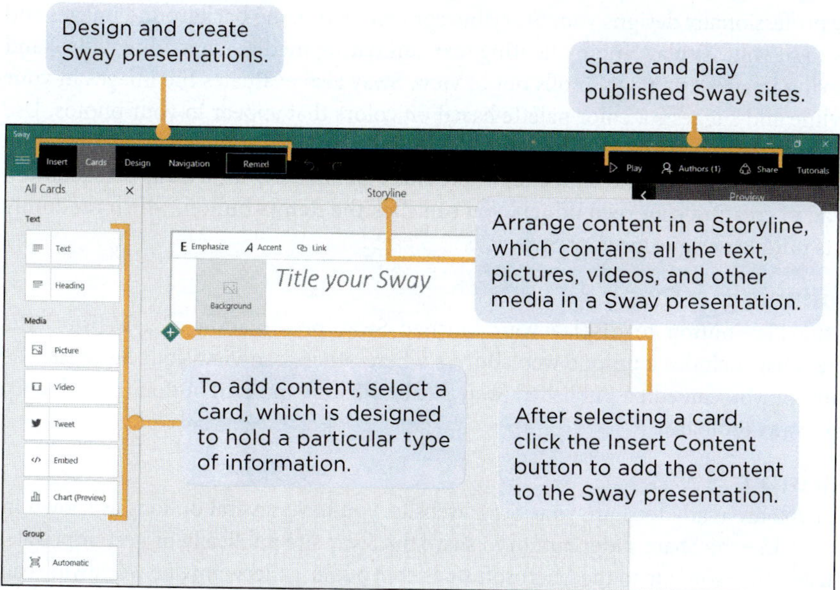

Design and create Sway presentations.
Share and play published Sway sites.
Arrange content in a Storyline, which contains all the text, pictures, videos, and other media in a Sway presentation.
To add content, select a card, which is designed to hold a particular type of information.
After selecting a card, click the Insert Content button to add the content to the Sway presentation.
Title your Sway

Adding Content to Build a Story

As you work, Sway searches the Internet to help you find relevant images, videos, tweets, and other content from online sources such as Bing, YouTube, Twitter, and Facebook. You can drag content from the search results right into the Storyline. In addition, you can upload your own images and videos directly in the presentation. For example, if you are creating a Sway presentation about the market for commercial drones, Sway suggests content to incorporate into the presentation by displaying it in the left pane as search results. The search results include drone images tagged with a **Creative Commons license** at online sources as shown in **Figure 8**. A Creative Commons license is a public copyright license that allows the free distribution of an otherwise copyrighted work. In addition, you can specify the source of the media. For example, you can add your own Facebook or OneNote pictures and videos in Sway without leaving the app.

If you have a Microsoft Word document containing an outline of your business content, drag the outline into Sway to create a card for each topic.

Figure 8: Images in Sway search results

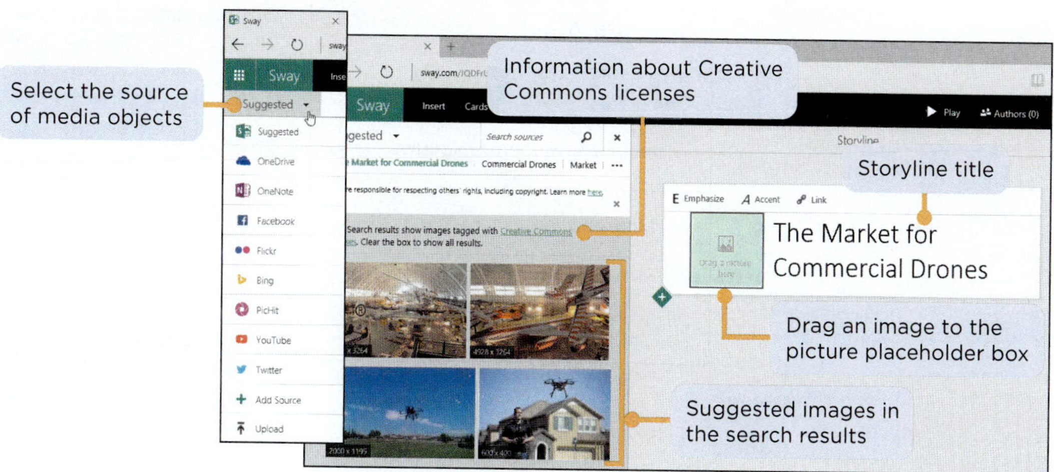

If your project team wants to collaborate on a Sway presentation, click the Authors button on the navigation bar to invite others to edit the presentation.

Designing a Sway

Sway professionally designs your Storyline content by resizing background images and fonts to fit your display, and by floating text, animating media, embedding video, and removing images as a page scrolls out of view. Sway also evaluates the images in your Storyline and suggests a color palette based on colors that appear in your photos. Use the Design button to display tools including color palettes, font choices, **animation emphasis effects**, and style templates to provide a personality for a Sway presentation. Instead of creating your own design, you can click the Remix button, which randomly selects unique designs for your Sway site.

Publishing a Sway

Use the Play button to display your finished Sway presentation as a website. The Address bar includes a unique web address where others can view your Sway site. As the author, you can edit a published Sway site by clicking the Edit button (pencil icon) on the Sway toolbar.

Sharing a Sway

When you are ready to share your Sway website, you have several options as shown in Figure 9. Use the Share slider button to share the Sway site publically or keep it private. If you add the Sway site to the Microsoft **Docs.com** public gallery, anyone worldwide can use Bing, Google, or other search engines to find, view, and share your Sway site. You can also share your Sway site using Facebook, Twitter, Google+, Yammer, and other social media sites. Link your presentation to any webpage or email the link to your audience. Sway can also generate a code for embedding the link within another webpage.

Figure 9: Sharing a Sway site

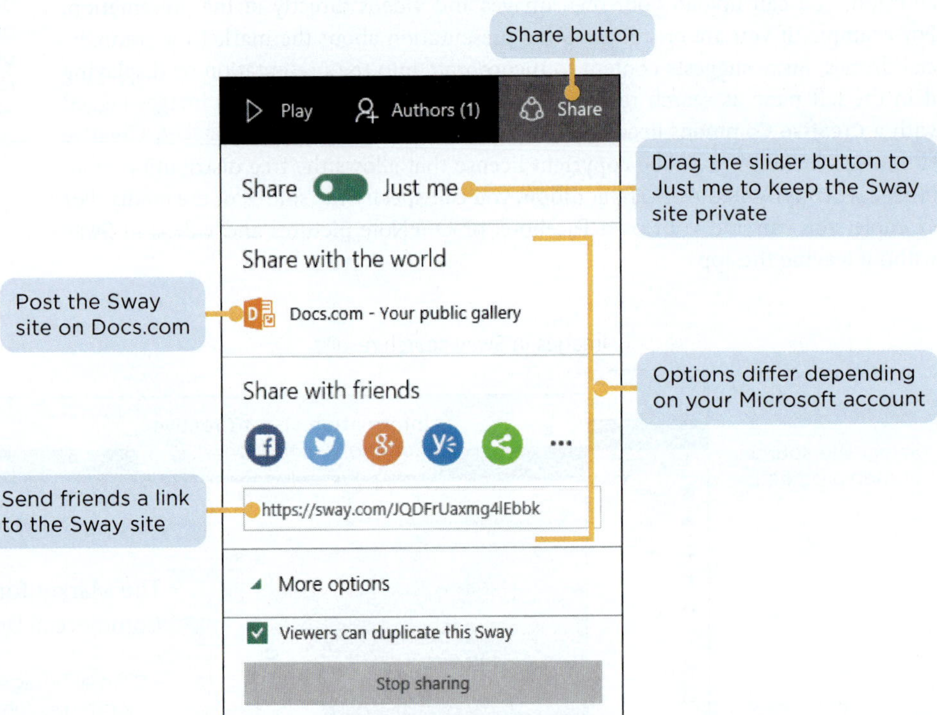

Try This Now

> **Learn to use Sway!**
> Links to companion **Sways**, featuring **videos** with hands-on instructions, are located on www.cengagebrain.com.

1: Creating a Sway Resume

Sway is a digital storytelling app. Create a Sway resume to share the skills, job experiences, and achievements you have that match the requirements of a future job interest. Perform the following tasks:

a. Create a new presentation in Sway to use as a digital resume. Title the Sway Storyline with your full name and then select a background image.
b. Create three separate sections titled **Academic Background, Work Experience**, and **Skills**, and insert text, a picture, and a paragraph or bulleted points in each section. Be sure to include your own picture.
c. Add a fourth section that includes a video about your school that you find online.
d. Customize the design of your presentation.
e. Submit your assignment link in the format specified by your instructor.

2: Creating an Online Sway Newsletter

Newsletters are designed to capture the attention of their target audience. Using Sway, create a newsletter for a club, organization, or your favorite music group. Perform the following tasks:

a. Create a new presentation in Sway to use as a digital newsletter for a club, organization, or your favorite music group. Provide a title for the Sway Storyline and select an appropriate background image.
b. Select three separate sections with appropriate titles, such as Upcoming Events. In each section, insert text, a picture, and a paragraph or bulleted points.
c. Add a fourth section that includes a video about your selected topic.
d. Customize the design of your presentation.
e. Submit your assignment link in the format specified by your instructor.

3: Creating and Sharing a Technology Presentation

To place a Sway presentation in the hands of your entire audience, you can share a link to the Sway presentation. Create a Sway presentation on a new technology and share it with your class. Perform the following tasks:

a. Create a new presentation in Sway about a cutting-edge technology topic. Provide a title for the Sway Storyline and select a background image.
b. Create four separate sections about your topic, and include text, a picture, and a paragraph in each section.
c. Add a fifth section that includes a video about your topic.
d. Customize the design of your presentation.
e. Share the link to your Sway with your classmates and submit your assignment link in the format specified by your instructor.

Introduction to Office Mix

add-in | clip | slide recording | Slide Notes | screen recording | free-response quiz

Bottom Line

- Office Mix is a free PowerPoint add-in from Microsoft that adds features to PowerPoint.
- The Mix tab on the PowerPoint ribbon provides tools for creating screen recordings, videos, interactive quizzes, and live webpages.

To enliven business meetings and lectures, Microsoft adds a new dimension to presentations with a powerful toolset called Office Mix, a free add-in for PowerPoint. (An **add-in** is software that works with an installed app to extend its features.) Using Office Mix, you can record yourself on video, capture still and moving images on your desktop, and insert interactive elements such as quizzes and live webpages directly into PowerPoint slides. When you post the finished presentation to OneDrive, Office Mix provides a link you can share with friends and colleagues. Anyone with an Internet connection and a web browser can watch a published Office Mix presentation, such as the one in **Figure 10**, on a computer or mobile device.

Figure 10: Office Mix presentation

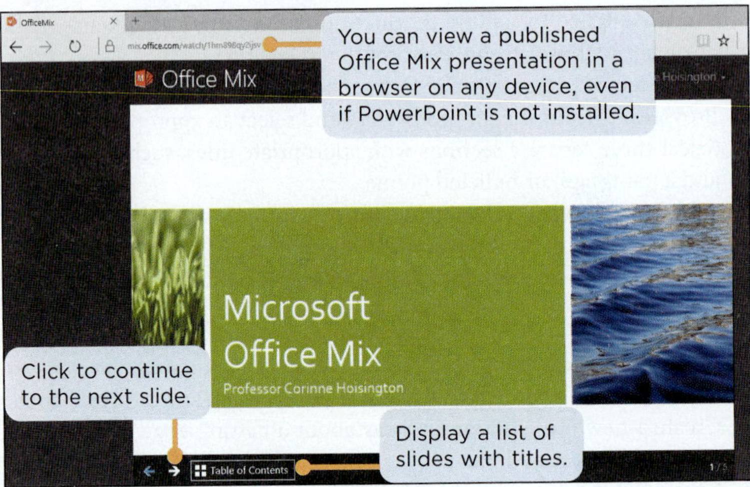

Learn to use Office Mix!

Links to companion **Sways**, featuring **videos** with hands-on instructions, are located on www.cengagebrain.com.

Adding Office Mix to PowerPoint

To get started, you create an Office Mix account at the website mix.office.com using an email address or a Facebook or Google account. Next, you download and install the Office Mix add-in (see **Figure 11**). Office Mix appears as a new tab named Mix on the PowerPoint ribbon in versions of Office 2013 and Office 2016 running on personal computers (PCs).

Figure 11: Getting started with Office Mix

Capturing Video Clips

A **clip** is a short segment of audio, such as music, or video. After finishing the content on a PowerPoint slide, you can use Office Mix to add a video clip to animate or illustrate the content. Office Mix creates video clips in two ways: by recording live action on a webcam and by capturing screen images and movements. If your computer has a webcam, you can record yourself and annotate the slide to create a **slide recording** as shown in **Figure 12**.

On the Job Now

Companies are using Office Mix to train employees about new products, to explain benefit packages to new workers, and to educate interns about office procedures.

Figure 12: Making a slide recording

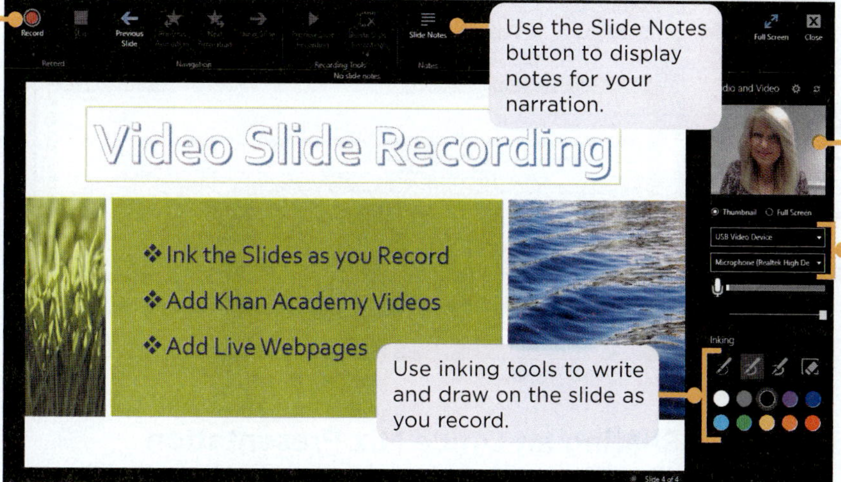

Record your voice; also record video if your computer has a camera.
Use the Slide Notes button to display notes for your narration.
For best results, look directly at your webcam while recording video.
Choose a video and audio device to record images and sound.
Use inking tools to write and draw on the slide as you record.
Video Slide Recording
Ink the Slides as you Record
Add Khan Academy Videos
Add Live Webpages

When you are making a slide recording, you can record your spoken narration at the same time. The **Slide Notes** feature works like a teleprompter to help you focus on your presentation content instead of memorizing your narration. Use the Inking tools to make annotations or add highlighting using different pen types and colors. After finishing a recording, edit the video in PowerPoint to trim the length or set playback options.

The second way to create a video is to capture on-screen images and actions with or without a voiceover. This method is ideal if you want to show how to use your favorite website or demonstrate an app such as OneNote. To share your screen with an audience, select the part of the screen you want to show in the video. Office Mix captures everything that happens in that area to create a **screen recording**, as shown in **Figure 13**. Office Mix inserts the screen recording as a video in the slide.

On the Job Now

To make your video recordings accessible to people with hearing impairments, use the Office Mix closed-captioning tools. You can also use closed captions to supplement audio that is difficult to understand and to provide an aid for those learning to read.

Figure 13: Making a screen recording

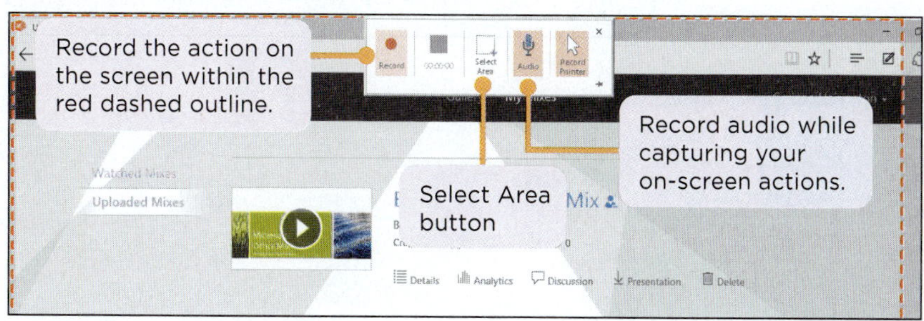

Record the action on the screen within the red dashed outline.
Record audio while capturing your on-screen actions.
Select Area button

Inserting Quizzes, Live Webpages, and Apps

To enhance and assess audience understanding, make your slides interactive by adding quizzes, live webpages, and apps. Quizzes give immediate feedback to the user as shown in **Figure 14**. Office Mix supports several quiz formats, including a **free-response quiz** similar to a short answer quiz, and true/false, multiple-choice, and multiple-response formats.

Figure 14: Creating an interactive quiz

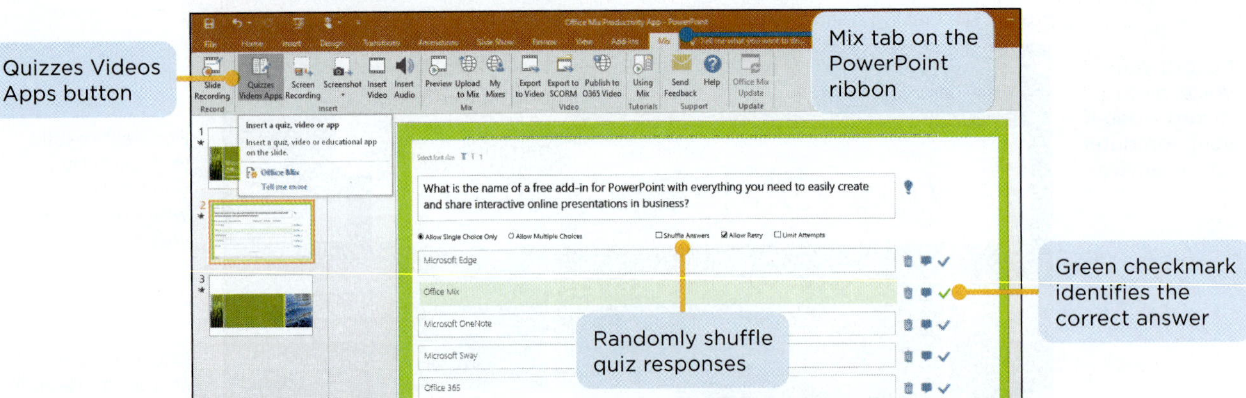

Sharing an Office Mix Presentation

When you complete your work with Office Mix, upload the presentation to your personal Office Mix dashboard as shown in **Figure 15**. Users of PCs, Macs, iOS devices, and Android devices can access and play Office Mix presentations. The Office Mix dashboard displays built-in analytics that include the quiz results and how much time viewers spent on each slide. You can play completed Office Mix presentations online or download them as movies.

Figure 15: Sharing an Office Mix presentation

Office Mix dashboard displays the quiz analytics.

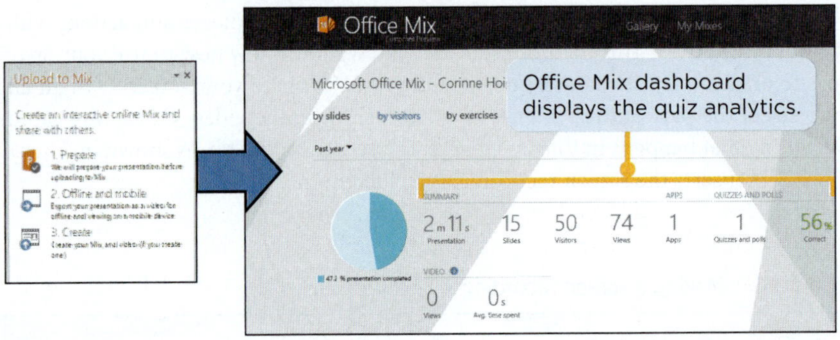

Try This Now

> **Learn to use Office Mix!**
> Links to companion **Sways**, featuring **videos** with hands-on instructions, are located on www.cengagebrain.com.

1: Creating an Office Mix Tutorial for OneNote

Note: This activity requires a microphone on your computer.

Office Mix makes it easy to record screens and their contents. Create PowerPoint slides with an Office Mix screen recording to show OneNote 2016 features. Perform the following tasks:

a. Create a PowerPoint presentation with the Ion Boardroom template. Create an opening slide with the title **My Favorite OneNote Features** and enter your name in the subtitle.
b. Create three additional slides, each titled with a new feature of OneNote. Open OneNote and use the Mix tab in PowerPoint to capture three separate screen recordings that teach your favorite features.
c. Add a fifth slide that quizzes the user with a multiple-choice question about OneNote and includes four responses. Be sure to insert a checkmark indicating the correct response.
d. Upload the completed presentation to your Office Mix dashboard and share the link with your instructor.
e. Submit your assignment link in the format specified by your instructor.

2: Teaching Augmented Reality with Office Mix

Note: This activity requires a webcam or built-in video camera on your computer.

A local elementary school has asked you to teach augmented reality to its students using Office Mix. Perform the following tasks:

a. Research augmented reality using your favorite online search tools.
b. Create a PowerPoint presentation with the Frame template. Create an opening slide with the title **Augmented Reality** and enter your name in the subtitle.
c. Create a slide with four bullets summarizing your research of augmented reality. Create a 20-second slide recording of yourself providing a quick overview of augmented reality.
d. Create another slide with a 30-second screen recording of a video about augmented reality from a site such as YouTube or another video-sharing site.
e. Add a final slide that quizzes the user with a true/false question about augmented reality. Be sure to insert a checkmark indicating the correct response.
f. Upload the completed presentation to your Office Mix dashboard and share the link with your instructor.
g. Submit your assignment link in the format specified by your instructor.

3: Marketing a Travel Destination with Office Mix

Note: This activity requires a webcam or built-in video camera on your computer.

To convince your audience to travel to a particular city, create a slide presentation marketing any city in the world using a slide recording, screen recording, and a quiz. Perform the following tasks:

a. Create a PowerPoint presentation with any template. Create an opening slide with the title of the city you are marketing as a travel destination and your name in the subtitle.
b. Create a slide with four bullets about the featured city. Create a 30-second slide recording of yourself explaining why this city is the perfect vacation destination.
c. Create another slide with a 20-second screen recording of a travel video about the city from a site such as YouTube or another video-sharing site.
d. Add a final slide that quizzes the user with a multiple-choice question about the featured city with five responses. Be sure to include a checkmark indicating the correct response.
e. Upload the completed presentation to your Office Mix dashboard and share your link with your instructor.
f. Submit your assignment link in the format specified by your instructor.

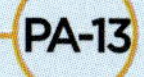

Introduction to Microsoft Edge

Reading view | Hub | Cortana | Web Note | Inking | sandbox

Bottom Line

- Microsoft Edge is the name of the new web browser built into Windows 10.
- Microsoft Edge allows you to search the web faster, take web notes, read webpages without distractions, and get instant assistance from Cortana.

Microsoft Edge is the default web browser developed for the Windows 10 operating system as a replacement for Internet Explorer. Unlike its predecessor, Edge lets you write on webpages, read webpages without advertisements and other distractions, and search for information using a virtual personal assistant. The Edge interface is clean and basic, as shown in **Figure 16**, meaning you can pay more attention to the webpage content.

Figure 16: Microsoft Edge tools

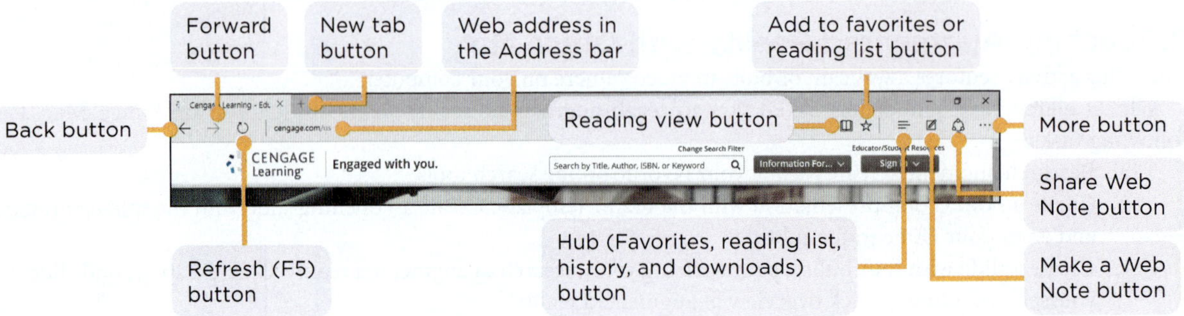

Learn to use Edge!
Links to companion **Sways**, featuring **videos** with hands-on instructions, are located on www.cengagebrain.com.

Browsing the Web with Microsoft Edge

One of the fastest browsers available, Edge allows you to type search text directly in the Address bar. As you view the resulting webpage, you can switch to **Reading view**, which is available for most news and research sites, to eliminate distracting advertisements. For example, if you are catching up on technology news online, the webpage might be difficult to read due to a busy layout cluttered with ads. Switch to Reading view to refresh the page and remove the original page formatting, ads, and menu sidebars to read the article distraction-free.

Consider the **Hub** in Microsoft Edge as providing one-stop access to all the things you collect on the web, such as your favorite websites, reading list, surfing history, and downloaded files.

On the Job Now

Businesses started adopting Internet Explorer more than 20 years ago simply to view webpages. Today, Microsoft Edge has a different purpose: to promote interaction with the web and share its contents with colleagues.

Locating Information with Cortana

Cortana, the Windows 10 virtual assistant, plays an important role in Microsoft Edge. After you turn on Cortana, it appears as an animated circle in the Address bar when you might need assistance, as shown in the restaurant website in **Figure 17**. When you click the Cortana icon, a pane slides in from the right of the browser window to display detailed information about the restaurant, including maps and reviews. Cortana can also assist you in defining words, finding the weather, suggesting coupons for shopping, updating stock market information, and calculating math.

Figure 17: Cortana providing restaurant information

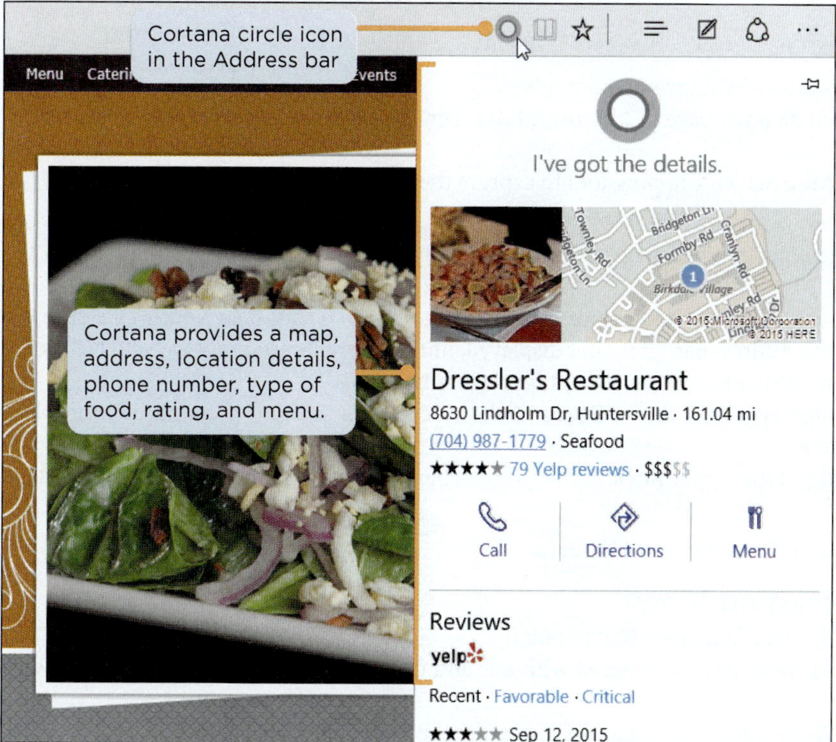

Annotating Webpages

One of the most impressive Microsoft Edge features are the **Web Note** tools, which you use to write on a webpage or to highlight text. When you click the Make a Web Note button, an **Inking** toolbar appears, as shown in **Figure 18**, that provides writing and drawing tools. These tools include an eraser, a pen, and a highlighter with different colors. You can also insert a typed note and copy a screen image (called a screen clipping). You can draw with a pointing device, fingertip, or stylus using different pen colors. Whether you add notes to a recipe, annotate sources for a research paper, or select a product while shopping online, the Web Note tools can enhance your productivity. After you complete your notes, click the Save button to save the annotations to OneNote, your Favorites list, or your Reading list. You can share the inked page with others using the Share Web Note button.

On the Job Now

To enhance security, Microsoft Edge runs in a partial sandbox, an arrangement that prevents attackers from gaining control of your computer. Browsing within the **sandbox** protects computer resources and information from hackers.

Figure 18: Web Note tools in Microsoft Edge

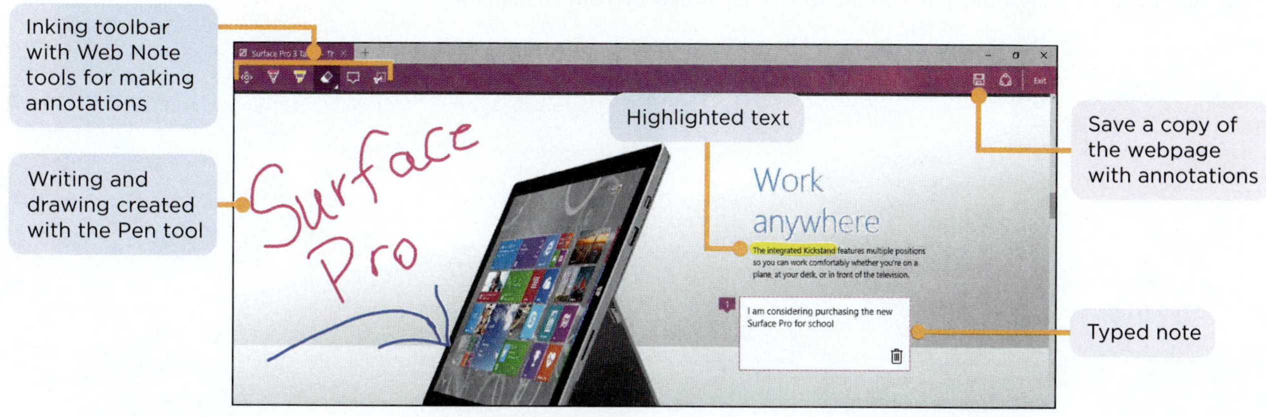

Try This Now

Learn to use Edge!
Links to companion **Sways**, featuring **videos** with hands-on instructions, are located on www.cengagebrain.com.

1: Using Cortana in Microsoft Edge

Note: This activity requires using Microsoft Edge on a Windows 10 computer.

Cortana can assist you in finding information on a webpage in Microsoft Edge. Perform the following tasks:

a. Create a Word document using the Word Screen Clipping tool to capture the following screenshots.
   - Screenshot A—Using Microsoft Edge, open a webpage with a technology news article. Right-click a term in the article and ask Cortana to define it.
   - Screenshot B—Using Microsoft Edge, open the website of a fancy restaurant in a city near you. Make sure the Cortana circle icon is displayed in the Address bar. (If it's not displayed, find a different restaurant website.) Click the Cortana circle icon to display a pane with information about the restaurant.
   - Screenshot C—Using Microsoft Edge, type **10 USD to Euros** in the Address bar without pressing the Enter key. Cortana converts the U.S. dollars to Euros.
   - Screenshot D—Using Microsoft Edge, type **Apple stock** in the Address bar without pressing the Enter key. Cortana displays the current stock quote.

b. Submit your assignment in the format specified by your instructor.

2: Viewing Online News with Reading View

Note: This activity requires using Microsoft Edge on a Windows 10 computer.

Reading view in Microsoft Edge can make a webpage less cluttered with ads and other distractions. Perform the following tasks:

a. Create a Word document using the Word Screen Clipping tool to capture the following screenshots.
   - Screenshot A—Using Microsoft Edge, open the website **mashable.com**. Open a technology article. Click the Reading view button to display an ad-free page that uses only basic text formatting.
   - Screenshot B—Using Microsoft Edge, open the website **bbc.com**. Open any news article. Click the Reading view button to display an ad-free page that uses only basic text formatting.
   - Screenshot C—Make three types of annotations (Pen, Highlighter, and Add a typed note) on the BBC article page displayed in Reading view.

b. Submit your assignment in the format specified by your instructor.

3: Inking with Microsoft Edge

Note: This activity requires using Microsoft Edge on a Windows 10 computer.

Microsoft Edge provides many annotation options to record your ideas. Perform the following tasks:

a. Open the website **wolframalpha.com** in the Microsoft Edge browser. Wolfram Alpha is a well-respected academic search engine. Type **US$100 1965 dollars in 2015** in the Wolfram Alpha search text box and press the Enter key.
b. Click the Make a Web Note button to display the Web Note tools. Using the Pen tool, draw a circle around the result on the webpage. Save the page to OneNote.
c. In the Wolfram Alpha search text box, type the name of the city closest to where you live and press the Enter key. Using the Highlighter tool, highlight at least three interesting results. Add a note and then type a sentence about what you learned about this city. Save the page to OneNote. Share your OneNote notebook with your instructor.
d. Submit your assignment link in the format specified by your instructor.

MODULE 1

Getting Started with Excel

Creating a Customer Order Report

EXCEL

OBJECTIVES

Session 1.1
- Open and close a workbook
- Navigate through a workbook and worksheet
- Select cells and ranges
- Plan and create a workbook
- Insert, rename, and move worksheets
- Enter text, dates, and numbers
- Undo and redo actions
- Resize columns and rows

Session 1.2
- Enter formulas and the SUM and COUNT functions
- Copy and paste formulas
- Move or copy cells and ranges
- Insert and delete rows, columns, and ranges
- Create patterned text with Flash Fill
- Add cell borders and change font size
- Change worksheet views
- Prepare a workbook for printing
- Save a workbook with a new filename

Case | *Game Card*

Peter Lewis is part owner of Game Card, a store in Missoula, Montana, that specializes in selling vintage board games. Peter needs to track sales data, generate financial reports, create contact lists for loyal customers, and analyze market trends. He can perform all of these tasks with **Microsoft Excel 2016**, (or just **Excel**), an application used to enter, analyze, and present quantitative data. He wants to create an efficient way of tracking the company inventory and managing customer sales. Peter asks you to use Excel to create a document in which he can enter customer purchases from the store.

STARTING DATA FILES

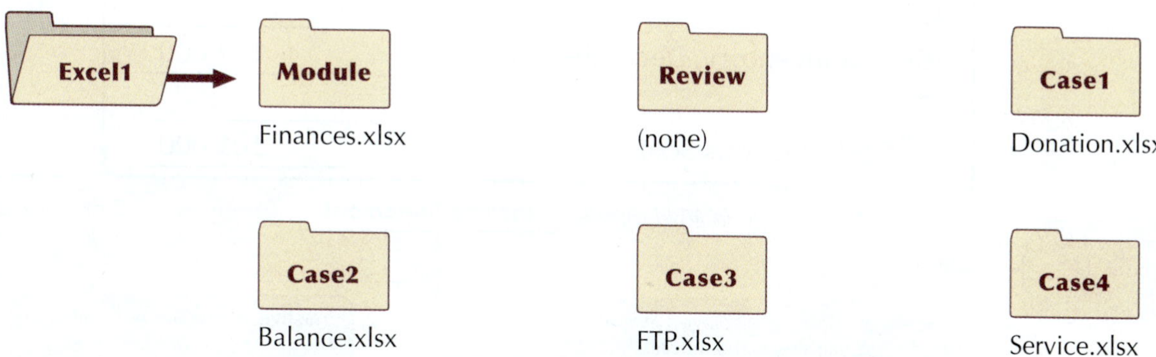

Session 1.1 Visual Overview:

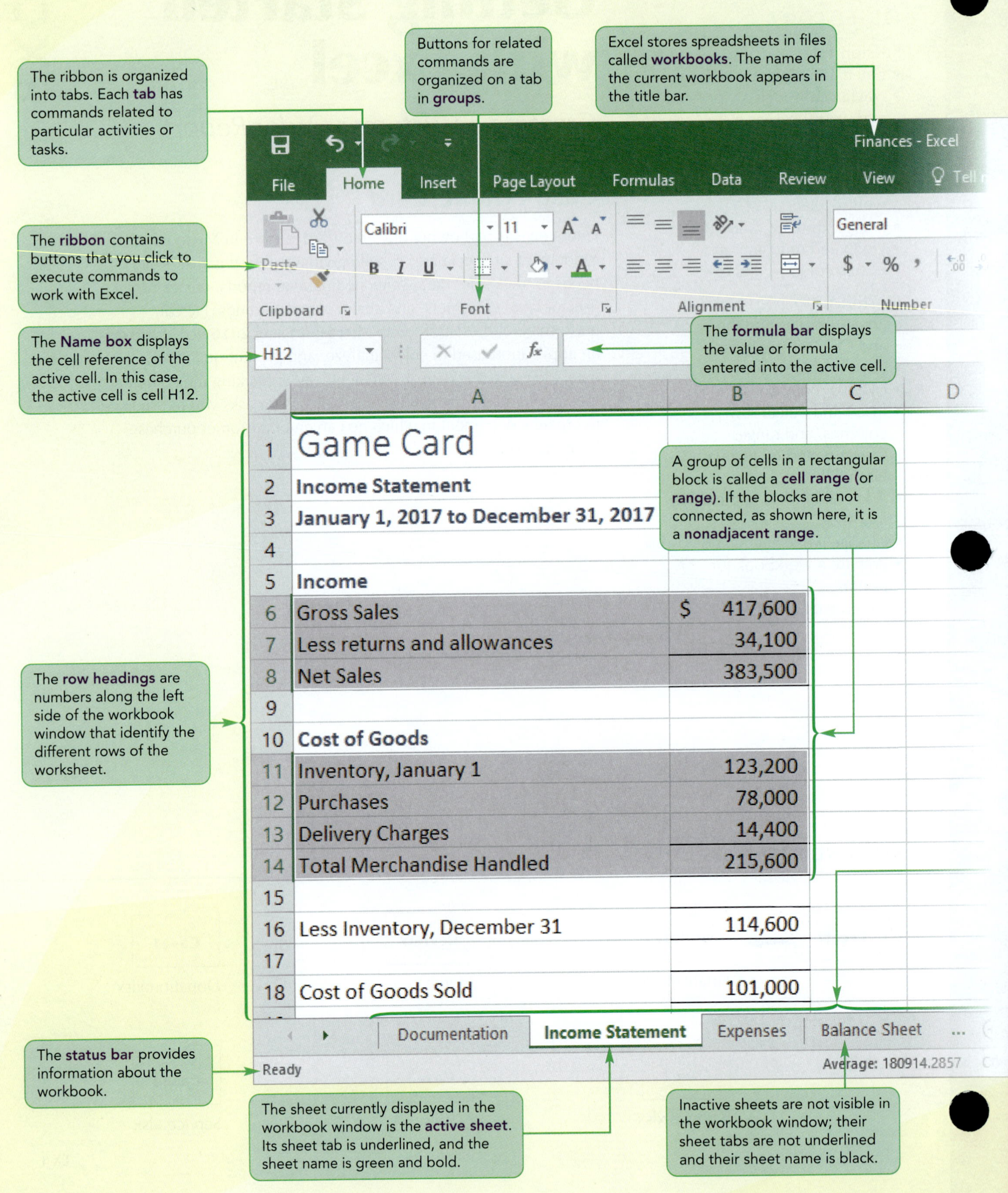

The ribbon is organized into tabs. Each tab has commands related to particular activities or tasks.
Buttons for related commands are organized on a tab in groups.
Excel stores spreadsheets in files called workbooks. The name of the current workbook appears in the title bar.
Finances - Excel
File
Home
Insert
Page Layout
Formulas
Data
Review
View
Tell
The ribbon contains buttons that you click to execute commands to work with Excel.
Paste
Calibri
11
General
Clipboard
Font
Alignment
Number
The Name box displays the cell reference of the active cell. In this case, the active cell is cell H12.
H12
The formula bar displays the value or formula entered into the active cell.
A
B
C
D
1 Game Card
2 Income Statement
3 January 1, 2017 to December 31, 2017
4
5 Income
6 Gross Sales $ 417,600
7 Less returns and allowances 34,100
8 Net Sales 383,500
9
10 Cost of Goods
11 Inventory, January 1 123,200
12 Purchases 78,000
13 Delivery Charges 14,400
14 Total Merchandise Handled 215,600
15
16 Less Inventory, December 31 114,600
17
18 Cost of Goods Sold 101,000
A group of cells in a rectangular block is called a cell range (or range). If the blocks are not connected, as shown here, it is a nonadjacent range.
The row headings are numbers along the left side of the workbook window that identify the different rows of the worksheet.
Documentation
Income Statement
Expenses
Balance Sheet
Ready
Average: 180914.2857
The status bar provides information about the workbook.
The sheet currently displayed in the workbook window is the active sheet. Its sheet tab is underlined, and the sheet name is green and bold.
Inactive sheets are not visible in the workbook window; their sheet tabs are not underlined and their sheet name is black.

The Excel Workbook

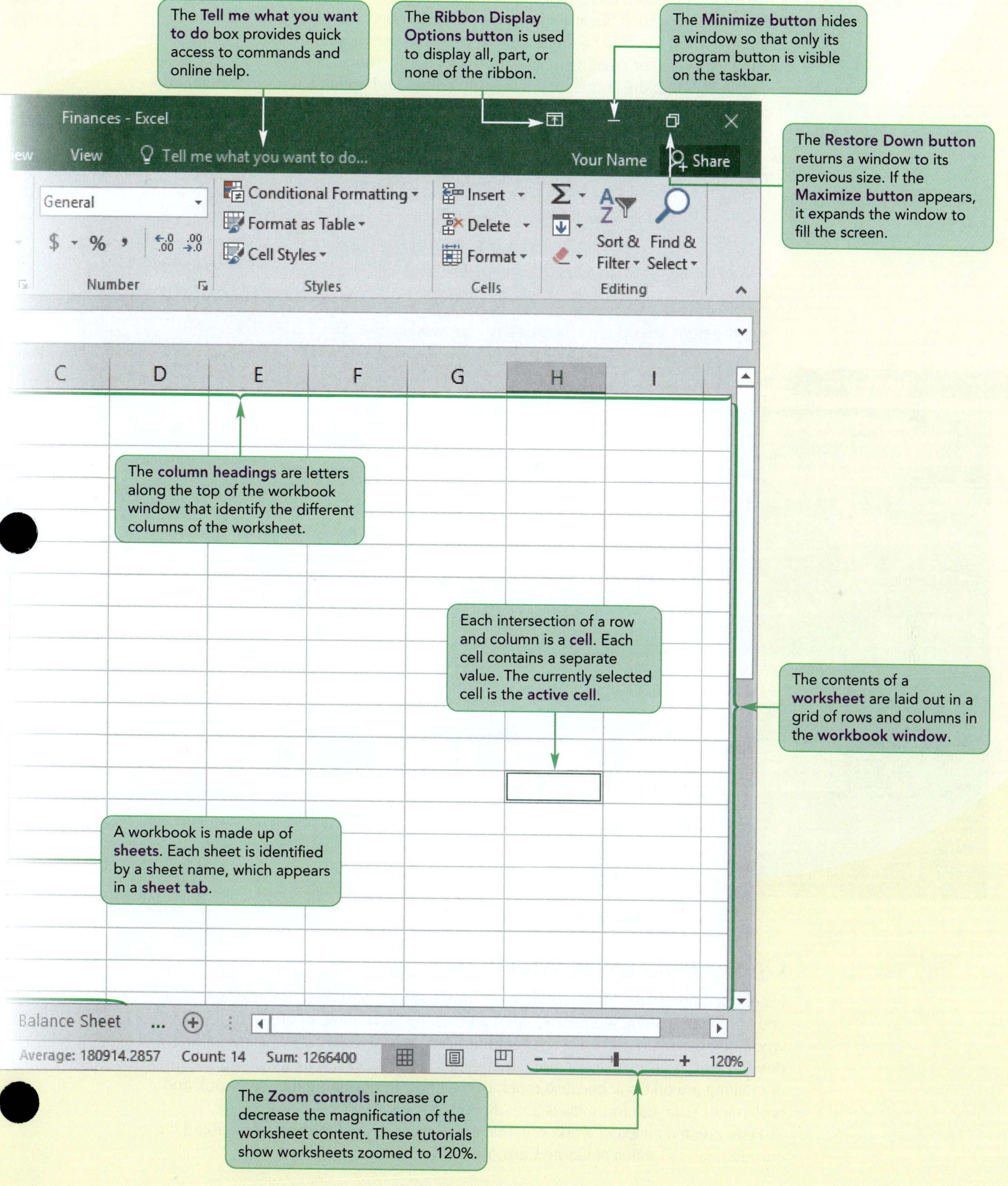

The Tell me what you want to do box provides quick access to commands and online help.
The Ribbon Display Options button is used to display all, part, or none of the ribbon.
The Minimize button hides a window so that only its program button is visible on the taskbar.
The Restore Down button returns a window to its previous size. If the Maximize button appears, it expands the window to fill the screen.
Finances - Excel
View
Tell me what you want to do...
Your Name
Share
General
Conditional Formatting
Format as Table
Cell Styles
Insert
Delete
Format
Sort & Filter
Find & Select
Number
Styles
Cells
Editing
C D E F G H I
The column headings are letters along the top of the workbook window that identify the different columns of the worksheet.
Each intersection of a row and column is a cell. Each cell contains a separate value. The currently selected cell is the active cell.
The contents of a worksheet are laid out in a grid of rows and columns in the workbook window.
A workbook is made up of sheets. Each sheet is identified by a sheet name, which appears in a sheet tab.
Balance Sheet
Average: 180914.2857 Count: 14 Sum: 1266400
120%
The Zoom controls increase or decrease the magnification of the worksheet content. These tutorials show worksheets zoomed to 120%.

Introducing Excel and Spreadsheets

A **spreadsheet** is a grouping of text and numbers in a rectangular grid or table. Spreadsheets are often used in business for budgeting, inventory management, and financial reporting because they unite text, numbers, and charts within one document. They can also be employed for personal use for planning a personal budget, tracking expenses, or creating a list of personal items. The advantage of an electronic spreadsheet is that the content can be easily edited and updated to reflect changing financial conditions.

To start Excel:

1. On the Windows taskbar, click the **Start** button. The Start menu opens.
2. Click **All Apps** on the Start menu, scroll the list, and then click **Excel 2016**. Excel starts and displays the Recent screen in Backstage view. **Backstage view** provides access to various screens with commands that allow you to manage files and Excel options. On the left is a list of recently opened workbooks. On the right are options for creating new workbooks. See Figure 1-1.

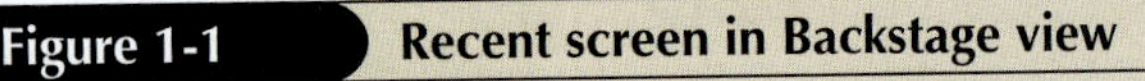

Figure 1-1 Recent screen in Backstage view

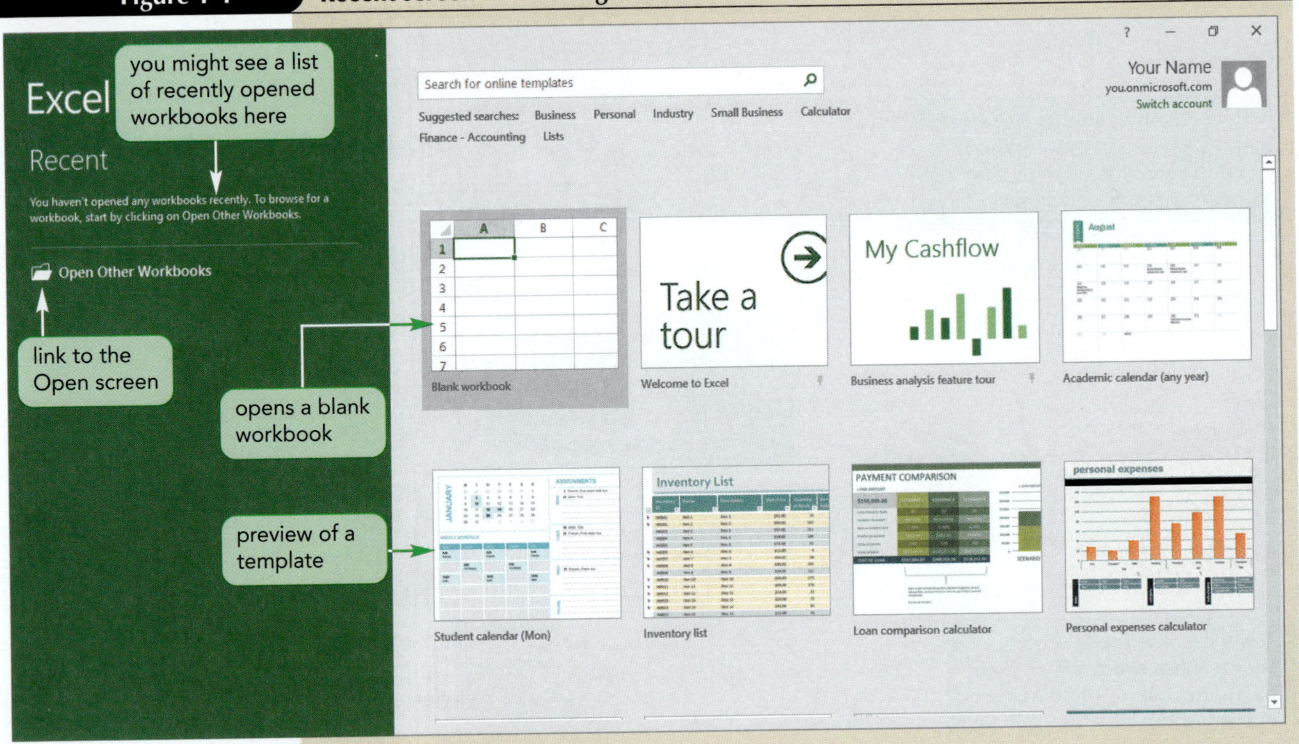

Opening an Existing Workbook

Excel documents are called workbooks. From the Recent screen in Backstage view, you can open a blank workbook, open an existing workbook, or create a new workbook based on a template. A **template** is a preformatted workbook with many design features and some content already filled in. Templates can speed up the process of creating a workbook because much of the effort in designing the workbook and entering its data and formulas is already done for you.

Peter created an Excel workbook that contains several worksheets describing the current financial status of Game Card. You will open that workbook now.

To open the Game Card financial status workbook:

1. In the navigation bar on the Recent screen, click the **Open Other Workbooks** link. The Open screen is displayed and provides access to different locations where you might store files. The Recent Workbooks list shows the workbooks that were most recently opened on your computer.
2. Click the **Browse** button. The Open dialog box appears.
3. Navigate to the **Excel1 > Module** folder included with your Data Files.

   Trouble? If you don't have the starting Data Files, you need to get them before you can proceed. Your instructor will either give you the Data Files or ask you to obtain them from a specified location (such as a network drive). If you have any questions about the Data Files, see your instructor or technical support person for assistance.
4. Click **Finances** in the file list to select it.
5. Click the **Open** button. The workbook opens in Excel.

   Trouble? If you don't see the full ribbon as shown in the Session 1.1 Visual Overview, the ribbon may be partially or fully hidden. To pin the ribbon so that the tabs and groups are fully displayed and remain visible, click the Ribbon Display Options button, and then click Show Tabs and Commands.
6. If the Excel window doesn't fill the screen, click the **Maximize** button in the upper-right corner of the title bar. See Figure 1-2.

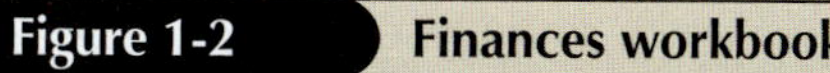

Figure 1-2 Finances workbook

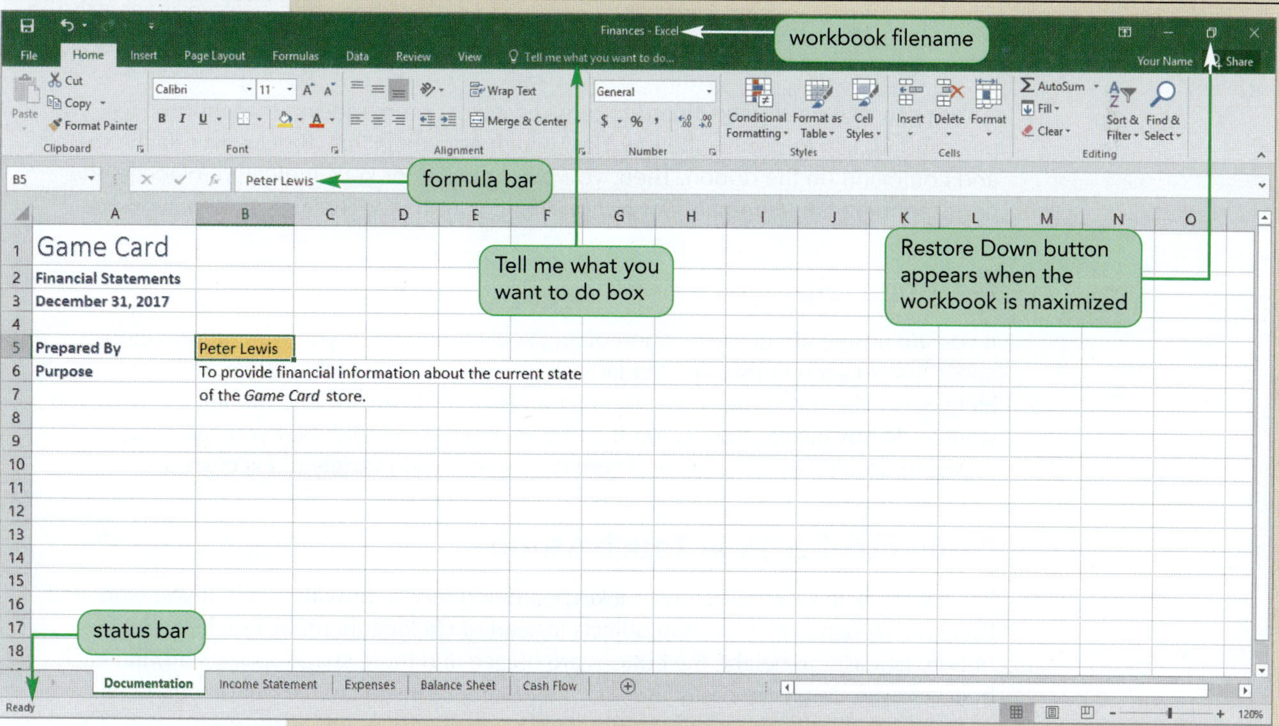

Using Keyboard Shortcuts to Work Faster

Keyboard shortcuts can help you work faster and more efficiently because you can keep your hands on the keyboard. A **keyboard shortcut** is a key or combination of keys that you press to access a feature or perform a command. Excel provides keyboard shortcuts for many commonly used commands. For example, Ctrl+S is the keyboard shortcut for the Save command, which means you hold down the Ctrl key while you press the S key to save the workbook. (Note that the plus sign is not pressed; it is used to indicate that an additional key is pressed.) When available, a keyboard shortcut is listed next to the command's name in a ScreenTip. A **ScreenTip** is a box with descriptive text about a command that appears when you point to a button on the ribbon. Figure 1-3 lists some of the keyboard shortcuts commonly used in Excel. The modules in this text show the corresponding keyboard shortcuts for accomplishing an action when available.

Figure 1-3 Excel keyboard shortcuts

Press	To	Press	To
Alt	Display the Key Tips for the commands and tools on the ribbon	Ctrl+V	Paste content that was cut or copied
Ctrl+A	Select all objects in a range	Ctrl+W	Close the current workbook
Ctrl+C	Copy the selected object(s)	Ctrl+X	Cut the selected object(s)
Ctrl+G	Go to a location in the workbook	Ctrl+Y	Repeat the last command
Ctrl+N	Open a new blank workbook	Ctrl+Z	Undo the last command
Ctrl+O	Open a saved workbook file	F1	Open the Excel Help window
Ctrl+P	Print the current workbook	F5	Go to a location in the workbook
Ctrl+S	Save the current workbook	F12	Save the current workbook with a new name or to a new location

You can also use the keyboard to quickly select commands on the ribbon. First, you press the Alt key to display the **Key Tips**, which are labels that appear over each tab and command on the ribbon. Then, you press the key or keys indicated to access the corresponding tab, command, or button while your hands remain on the keyboard.

Getting Help

If you are unsure about the function of an Excel command or you want information about how to accomplish a particular task, you can use the Help system. To access Excel Help, you either press the F1 key or enter a phrase or keyword into the Tell me what you want to do box next to the tabs on the ribbon. From this search box you can get quick access to detailed information and commands on a wide variety of Excel topics.

Using Excel 2016 in Touch Mode

You can work in Office 2016 with a keyboard and mouse or with touch. If you work with Excel on a touchscreen, you tap objects instead of clicking them. In **Touch Mode**, the ribbon increases in height, the buttons are bigger, and more space appears around each button so you can more easily use your finger or a stylus to tap the button you need.

Although the figures in these modules show the screen with Mouse Mode on, it's helpful to learn how to move between Touch Mode and Mouse Mode. You'll switch to Touch Mode and then back to Mouse Mode. If you are using a touch device, please read these steps, but do not complete them so that you remain working in Touch Mode.

To switch between Touch Mode and Mouse Mode:

1. On the Quick Access Toolbar, click the **Customize Quick Access Toolbar** button. A menu opens, listing buttons you can add to the Quick Access Toolbar as well as other options for customizing the toolbar.

   Trouble? If the Touch/Mouse Mode command on the menu has a checkmark next to it, press the Esc key to close the menu, and then skip Step 2.

2. Click **Touch/Mouse Mode**. The Quick Access Toolbar now contains the Touch/Mouse Mode button, which you can use to switch between Mouse Mode, the default display, and Touch Mode.
3. On the Quick Access Toolbar, click the **Touch/Mouse Mode** button. A menu opens listing Mouse and Touch, and the icon next to Mouse is shaded to indicate it is selected.

   Trouble? If the icon next to Touch is shaded, press the Esc key to close the menu and continue with Step 5.

4. Click **Touch**. The display switches to Touch Mode with more space between the commands and buttons on the ribbon. See Figure 1-4.

Figure 1-4 Ribbon displayed in Touch Mode

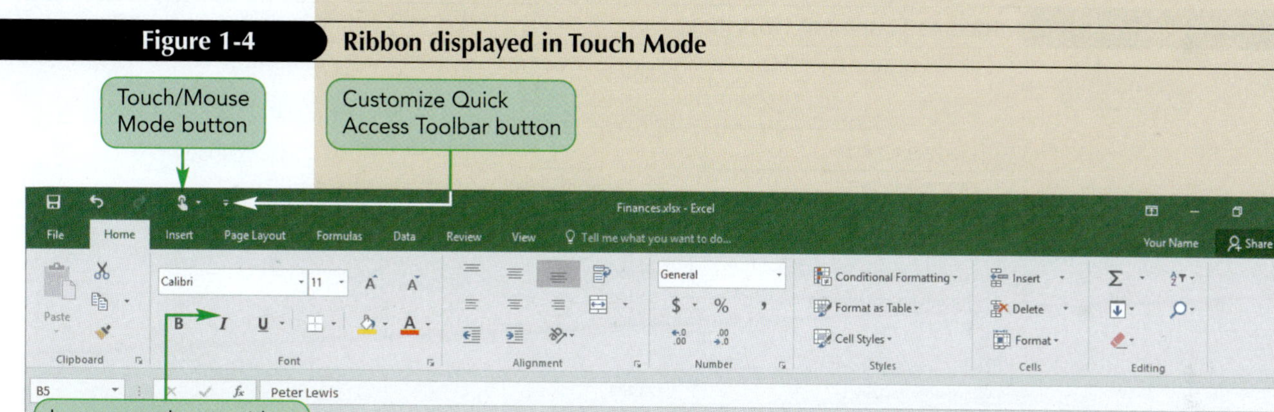

Next, you will switch back to Mouse Mode. If you are working with a touchscreen and want to use Touch Mode, skip Steps 5 and 6.

5. On the Quick Access Toolbar, click the **Touch/Mouse Mode** button, and then click **Mouse**. The ribbon returns to Mouse Mode, as shown earlier in Figure 1-2.
6. On the Quick Access Toolbar, click the **Customize Quick Access Toolbar** button, and then click **Touch/Mouse Mode** to deselect it. The Touch/Mouse Mode button is removed from the Quick Access Toolbar.

Exploring a Workbook

Workbooks are organized into separate pages called sheets. Excel supports two types of sheets: worksheets and chart sheets. A worksheet contains a grid of rows and columns into which you can enter text, numbers, dates, and formulas and display charts. A **chart sheet** contains a chart that provides a visual representation of worksheet data. The contents of a workbook are shown in the workbook window.

Changing the Active Sheet

The sheets in a workbook are identified in the sheet tabs at the bottom of the workbook window. The Finances workbook for Game Card includes five sheets labeled Documentation, Income Statement, Expenses, Balance Sheet, and Cash Flow. The sheet currently displayed in the workbook window is the active sheet, which in this case is the Documentation sheet. To make a different sheet active and visible, you click its sheet tab. You can tell which sheet is active because its name appears in bold green.

If a workbook includes so many sheets that not all of the sheet tabs can be displayed at the same time in the workbook window, you can use the sheet tab scrolling buttons to scroll through the list of tabs. Scrolling the sheet tabs does not change the active sheet; it changes only which sheet tabs are visible.

You will view the different sheets in the Finances workbook.

To change the active sheet:

1. Click the **Income Statement** sheet tab. The Income Statement worksheet becomes the active sheet, and its name is in bold green type. See Figure 1-5.

Figure 1-5 Income Statement worksheet

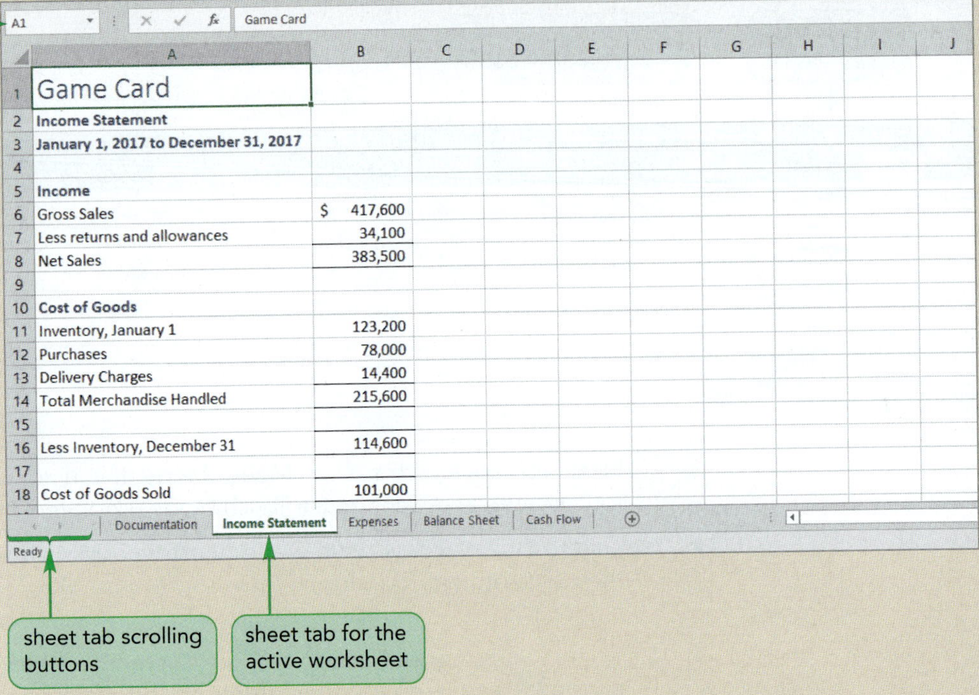

2. Click the **Expenses** sheet tab to make it the active sheet. The Expenses sheet is an example of a chart sheet containing only an Excel chart. See Figure 1-6.

Figure 1-6 Expenses chart sheet

chart sheet contains a chart but no grid of text and data

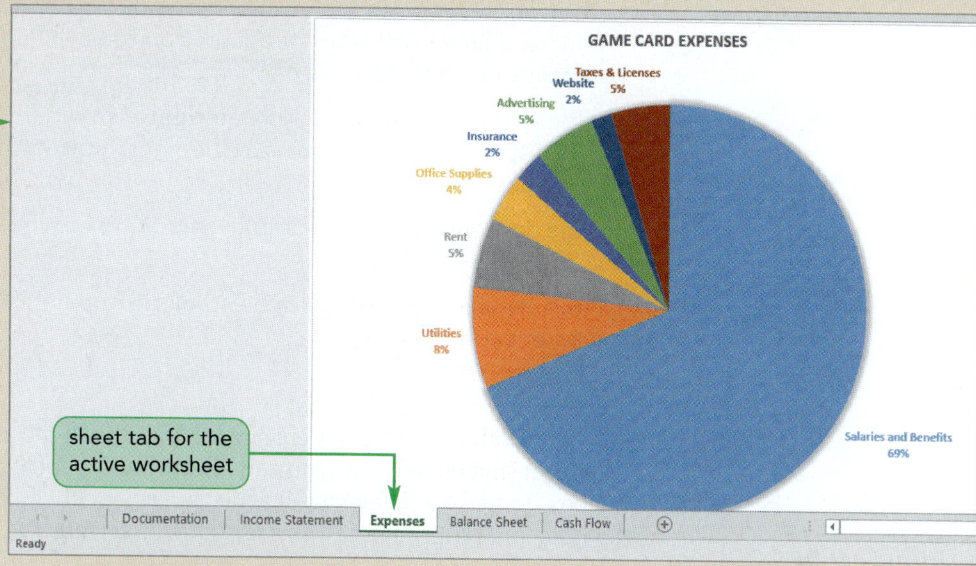

TIP

You can move to the previous or next sheet in the workbook by pressing the Ctrl+PgUp or Ctrl+PgDn keys.

3. Click the **Balance Sheet** sheet tab to make it the active sheet. Note that this sheet contains charts embedded into the grid of data values. A worksheet can contain data values, embedded charts, pictures, and other design elements.
4. Click the **Cash Flow** sheet tab. The worksheet with information about the company's cash flow is now active.
5. Click the **Income Statement** sheet tab to make the Income Statement worksheet the active sheet.

Navigating Within a Worksheet

A worksheet is organized into a grid of cells. Each cell is identified by a **cell reference**, which indicates the column and row in which the cell is located. For example, in Figure 1-5, the company name, Game Card, is in cell A1, which is the intersection of column A and row 1. The column letter always appears before the row number in any cell reference. The cell that is currently selected in the worksheet is referred to as the active cell. The active cell is highlighted with a thick green border, its cell reference appears in the Name box, and the corresponding column and row headings are highlighted. The active cell in Figure 1-5 is cell A1.

Row numbers range from 1 to 1,048,576, and column labels are letters in alphabetical order. The first 26 column headings range from A to Z. After Z, the next column headings are labeled AA, AB, AC, and so forth. Excel allows a maximum of 16,384 columns in a worksheet (the last column has the heading XFD). This means that you can create large worksheets whose content extends well beyond what is visible in the workbook window.

To move different parts of the worksheet into view, you can use the horizontal and vertical scroll bars located at the bottom and right edges of the workbook window, respectively. A scroll bar has arrow buttons that you can click to shift the worksheet one column or row in the specified direction, and a scroll box that you can drag to shift the worksheet in the direction you drag.

You will scroll the active worksheet so you can review the rest of the Game Card income statement.

To scroll through the Income Statement worksheet:

1. On the vertical scroll bar, click the **down arrow** button to scroll down the Income Statement worksheet until you see cell B36, which displays the company's net income value of $104,200.
2. On the horizontal scroll bar, click the **right arrow** button three times. The worksheet scrolls three columns to the right, moving columns A through C out of view.
3. On the horizontal scroll bar, drag the **scroll box** to the left until you see column A.
4. On the vertical scroll bar, drag the **scroll box** up until you see the top of the worksheet and cell A1.

Scrolling the worksheet does not change the location of the active cell. Although the active cell might shift out of view, you can always see the location of the active cell in the Name box. To make a different cell active, you can either click a new cell or use the keyboard to move between cells, as described in Figure 1-7.

Figure 1-7 Excel navigation keys

Press	To move the active cell
↑↓←→	Up, down, left, or right one cell
Home	To column A of the current row
Ctrl+Home	To cell A1
Ctrl+End	To the last cell in the worksheet that contains data
Enter	Down one row or to the start of the next row of data
Shift+Enter	Up one row
Tab	One column to the right
Shift+Tab	One column to the left
PgUp, PgDn	Up or down one screen
Ctrl+PgUp, Ctrl+PgDn	To the previous or next sheet in the workbook

You will use both your mouse and your keyboard to change the location of the active cell in the Income Statement worksheet.

To change the active cell:

1. Move your pointer over cell **A5**, and then click the mouse button. The active cell moves from cell A1 to cell A5. A green border appears around cell A5, the column heading for column A and the row heading for row 5 are both highlighted, and the cell reference in the Name box changes from A1 to A5.
2. Press the → key. The active cell moves one cell to the right to cell B5.
3. Press the **PgDn** key on your keyboard. The active cell moves down one full screen.
4. Press the **PgUp** key. The active cell moves up one full screen, returning to cell B5.
5. Press the **Ctrl+Home** keys. The active cell returns to the first cell in the worksheet, cell A1.

The mouse and keyboard provide quick ways to navigate the active worksheet. For larger worksheets that span several screens, you can move directly to a specific cell using the Go To command or by typing a cell reference in the Name box. You will try both of these methods.

To use the Go To dialog box and the Name box:

1. On the Home tab, in the Editing group, click the **Find & Select** button, and then click **Go To** on the menu that opens (or press the **Ctrl+G** keys). The Go To dialog box opens.
2. Type **B34** in the Reference box. See Figure 1-8.

Figure 1-8 Go To dialog box

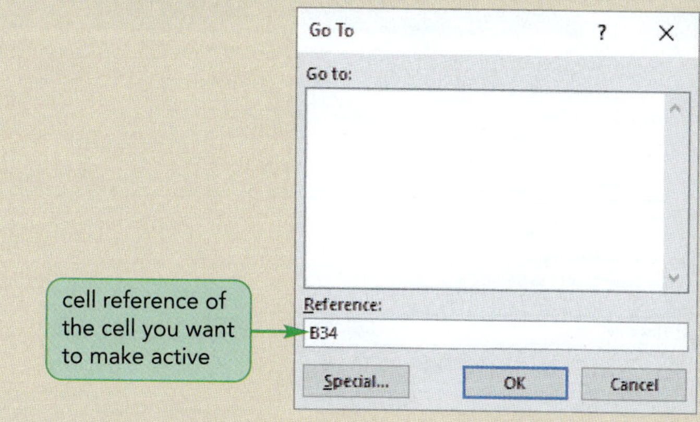

3. Click the **OK** button. Cell B34 becomes the active cell, displaying 182,000, which is the total expenses for Game Card. Because cell B34 is the active cell, its cell reference appears in the Name box.
4. Click in the Name box, type **A1**, and then press the **Enter** key. Cell A1 is again the active cell.

Selecting a Cell Range

Many tasks in Excel require you to work with a group of cells. A group of cells in a rectangular block is called a cell range (or simply a range). Each range is identified with a **range reference** that includes the cell reference of the upper-left cell of the rectangular block and the cell reference of the lower-right cell separated by a colon. For example, the range reference A1:G5 refers to all of the cells in the rectangular block from cell A1 through cell G5.

As with individual cells, you can select cell ranges using your mouse, the keyboard, or commands. You will select a range in the Income Statement worksheet.

TIP

You can also select a range by clicking its upper-left cell, holding down the Shift key as you click its lower-right cell, and then releasing the Shift key.

To select a cell range:

1. Click cell **A5** to select it, and without releasing the mouse button, drag down to cell **B8**.
2. Release the mouse button. The range A5:B8 is selected. The selected cells are highlighted and surrounded by a green border. The first cell you selected in the range, cell A5, is the active cell in the worksheet. The active cell in a selected range is white. The Quick Analysis button appears, providing options for working with the range; you will use this button in another module. See Figure 1-9.

Figure 1-9 **Range A5:B8 selected**

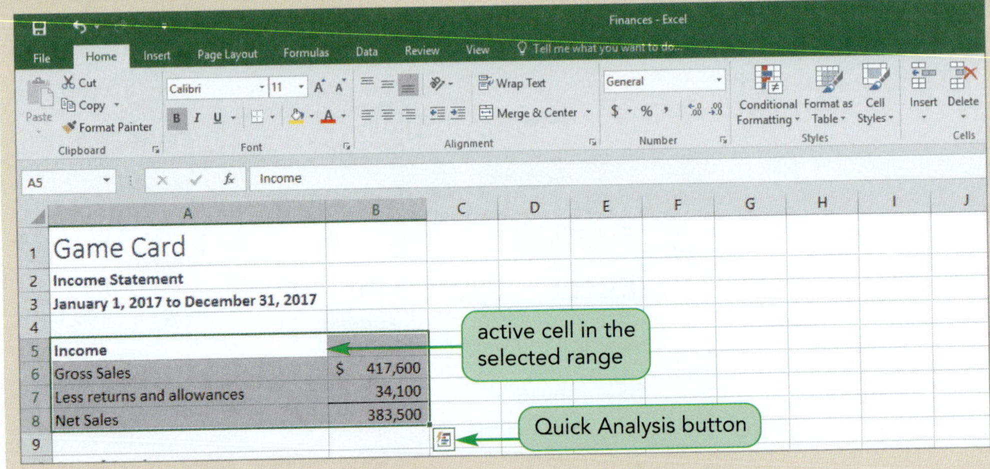

3. Click cell **A1** to deselect the range.

Another type of range is a nonadjacent range, which is a collection of separate rectangular ranges. The range reference for a nonadjacent range includes the range reference to each range separated by a comma. For example, the range reference A1:G5,A10:G15 includes two ranges—the first range is the rectangular block of cells from cell A1 to cell G5, and the second range is the rectangular block of cells from cell A10 to cell G15.

You will select a nonadjacent range in the Income Statement worksheet.

To select a nonadjacent range in the Income Statement worksheet:

1. Click cell **A5**, hold down the **Shift** key as you click cell **B8**, and then release the **Shift** key to select the range A5:B8.
2. Hold down the **Ctrl** key as you drag to select the range **A10:B14**, and then release the **Ctrl** key. The two separate blocks of cells in the nonadjacent range A5:B8,A10:B14 are selected. See Figure 1-10.

Figure 1-10 Nonadjacent range A5:B8,A10:B14 selected

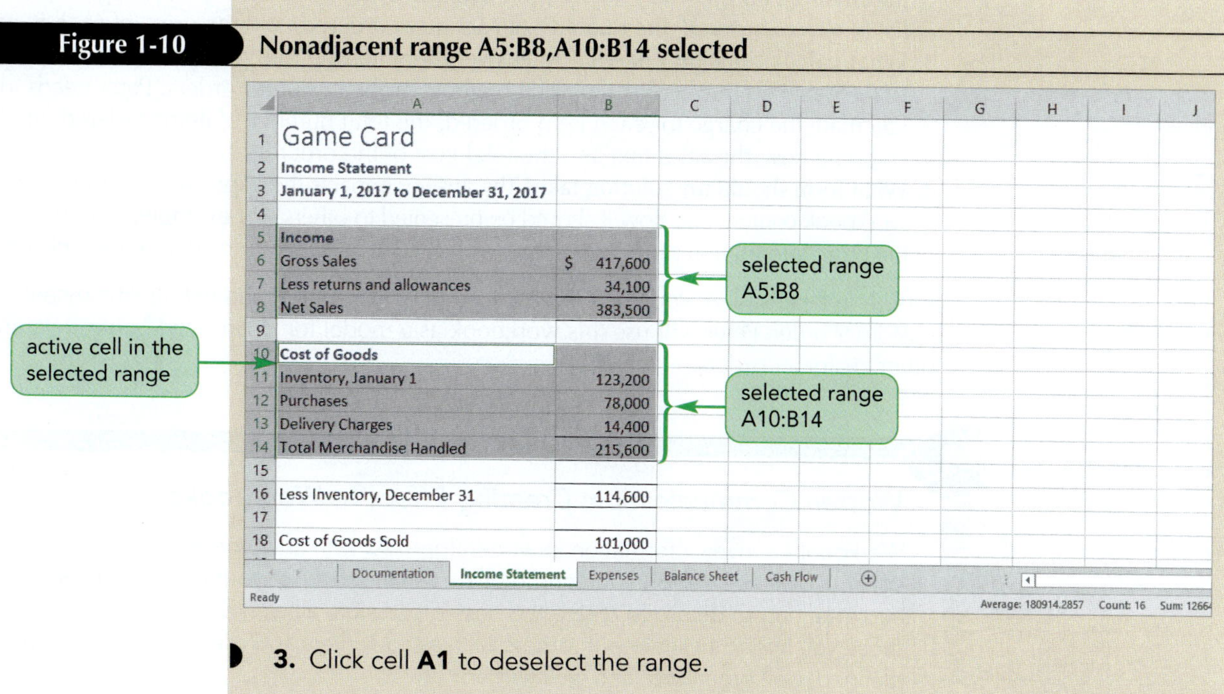

3. Click cell **A1** to deselect the range.

Closing a Workbook

Once you are finished with a workbook you can close it. When you close a workbook, a dialog box might open, asking whether you want to save any changes you may have made to the document. If you have made changes that you want to keep, you should save the workbook. Since you have finished reviewing the financial workbook for Game Card, you will close it without saving any changes you may have inadvertently made to the document contents.

To close the workbook:

1. On the ribbon, click the **File** tab to display Backstage view, and then click **Close** in the navigation bar (or press the **Ctrl+W** keys).
2. If a dialog box opens, asking whether you want to save your changes to the workbook, click the **Don't Save** button. The workbook closes without saving any changes. Excel remains opens, ready for you to create or open another workbook.

Planning a Workbook

It's good practice to plan out your workbooks before you begin creating them. You can do this by using a planning analysis sheet, which includes the following questions that help you think about the workbook's purpose and how to achieve your desired results:

1. **What problems do I want to solve?** The answer identifies the goal or purpose of the workbook. For example, Peter wants you to record customer orders and be able to analyze details from these orders.
2. **What data do I need?** The answer identifies the type of data that you need to collect and enter into the workbook. For example, Peter needs customer contact

information, an order ID number, the date the order shipped, the shipping method, a list of games ordered, the quantity of each item ordered, and the price of each item.

3. **What calculations do I need?** The answer identifies the formulas you need to apply to the data you have collected and entered. For the customer orders, Peter needs to calculate the charge for each item ordered, the total number of items ordered, the shipping cost, the sales tax, and the total cost of the order.
4. **What form should my solution take?** The answer impacts the appearance of the workbook content and how it should be presented to others. For example, Peter wants the order information stored in a single worksheet that is easy to read and prints clearly.

Based on Peter's plan, you will create a workbook containing the details of a recent customer order. Peter will use this workbook as a model for future workbooks detailing other customer orders.

PROSKILLS

Written Communication: Creating Effective Workbooks

Workbooks convey information in written form. As with any type of writing, the final product creates an impression and provides an indicator of your interest, knowledge, and attention to detail. To create the best impression, all workbooks—especially those you intend to share with others such as coworkers and clients—should be well planned, well organized, and well written.

A well-designed workbook should clearly identify its overall goal and present information in an organized format. The data it includes—both the entered values and the calculated values—should be accurate. The process of developing an effective workbook includes the following steps:

- Determine the workbook's purpose, content, and organization before you start.
- Create a list of the sheets used in the workbook, noting each sheet's purpose.
- Insert a documentation sheet that describes the workbook's purpose and organization. Include the name of the workbook author, the date the workbook was created, and any additional information that will help others to track the workbook to its source.
- Enter all of the data in the workbook. Add labels to indicate what the values represent and, if possible, where they originated so others can view the source of your data.
- Enter formulas for calculated items rather than entering the calculated values into the workbook. For more complicated calculations, provide documentation explaining them.
- Test the workbook with a variety of values; edit the data and formulas to correct errors.
- Save the workbook and create a backup copy when the project is completed. Print the workbook's contents if you need to provide a hard-copy version to others or for your files.
- Maintain a history of your workbook as it goes through different versions, so that you and others can quickly see how the workbook has changed during revisions.

By including clearly written documentation, explanatory text, a logical organization, and accurate data and formulas, you will create effective workbooks that others can use easily.

Starting a New Workbook

You create new workbooks from the New screen in Backstage view. Similar to the Recent screen that opened when you started Excel, the New screen includes templates for a variety of workbook types. You can see a preview of what the different workbooks will look like. You will create a new workbook from the Blank workbook template, in which you can add all of the content and design Peter wants for the Game Card customer order worksheet.

TIP

You can also create a new, blank workbook by pressing the Ctrl+N keys.

To start a new, blank workbook:

1. On the ribbon, click the **File** tab to display Backstage view.
2. Click **New** in the navigation bar to display the New screen, which includes access to templates for a variety of workbooks.
3. Click the **Blank workbook** tile. A blank workbook opens.

   In these modules, the workbook window is zoomed to 120% for better readability. If you want to zoom your workbook window to match the figures, complete Step 4. If you prefer to work in the default zoom of 100% or at another zoom level, read but do not complete Step 4; you might see more or less of the worksheet on your screen, but this will not affect your work in the modules.
4. If you want your workbook window zoomed to 120% to match the figures, on the Zoom slider at the bottom-right of the program window, click the **Zoom In** button [+] twice to increase the percentage to 120%. The 120% magnification increases the size of each cell but reduces the number of worksheet cells visible in the workbook window. See Figure 1-11.

Figure 1-11 Blank workbook

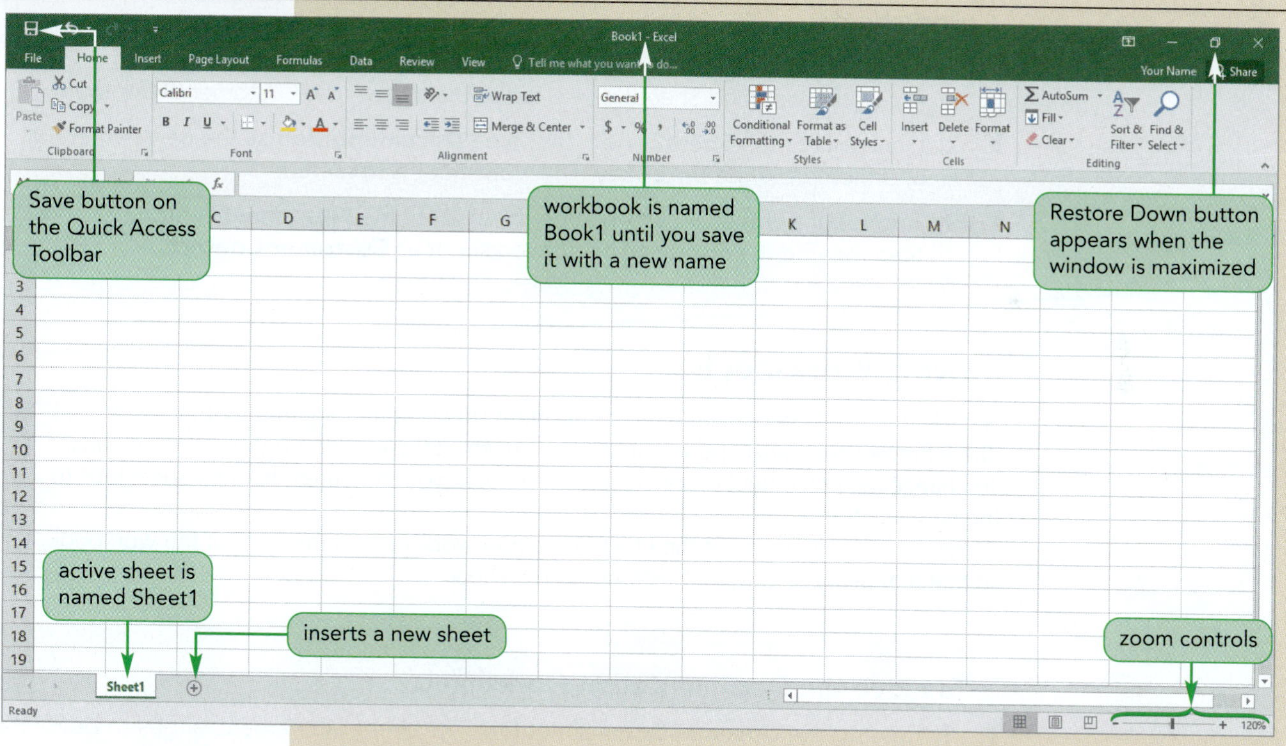

The name of the active workbook, Book1, appears in the title bar. If you open multiple blank workbooks, they are named Book1, Book2, Book3, and so forth until you save them with a more descriptive name.

Renaming and Inserting Worksheets

Blank workbooks open with a single blank worksheet named Sheet1. You can give sheets more descriptive and meaningful names. This is a good practice so that you and others can easily tell what a sheet contains. Sheet names cannot exceed 31 characters, but they can contain blank spaces and include uppercase and lowercase letters.

Because Sheet1 is not a very descriptive name, Peter wants you to rename the worksheet as Customer Order.

To rename the Sheet1 worksheet:

1. Double-click the **Sheet1** tab. The Sheet1 label in the tab is selected.
2. Type **Customer Order** as the new name, and then press the **Enter** key. The width of the sheet tab expands to fit the longer sheet name.

Many workbooks include multiple sheets so that data can be organized in logical groups. A common business practice is to include a worksheet named Documentation that contains a description of the workbook, the name of the person who prepared the workbook, and the date it was created.

Peter wants you to create two new worksheets. You will rename one worksheet as Documentation and the other worksheet as Customer Contact. The Customer Contact worksheet will be used to store the customer's contact information.

To insert and name the Documentation and Customer Contact worksheets:

1. To the right of the Customer Order sheet tab, click the **New sheet** button ⊕. A new sheet named Sheet2 is inserted to the right of the Customer Order sheet.
2. Double-click the **Sheet2** sheet tab, type **Documentation** as the new name, and then press the **Enter** key. The worksheet is renamed.
3. To the right of the Documentation sheet, click the **New sheet** button ⊕, and then rename the inserted Sheet3 worksheet as **Customer Contact**.

Moving Worksheets

A good practice is to place the most important sheets at the beginning of the workbook (the leftmost sheet tabs) and less important sheets at the end (the rightmost sheet tabs). To change the placement of sheets in a workbook, you drag them by their sheet tabs to the new location.

Peter wants you to move the Documentation worksheet to the front of the workbook, so that it appears before the Customer Order sheet.

To move the Documentation worksheet:

1. Point to the **Documentation** sheet tab. The sheet tab name changes to bold.
2. Press and hold the mouse button. The pointer changes to the move-sheet pointer, and a small arrow appears in the upper-left corner of the tab.
3. Drag to the left until the small arrow appears in the upper-left corner of the Customer Order sheet tab, and then release the mouse button. The Documentation worksheet is now the first sheet in the workbook.

TIP

To copy a sheet, hold down the Ctrl key as you drag and drop its sheet tab.

Deleting Worksheets

In some workbooks, you will want to delete an existing sheet. The easiest way to delete a sheet is by using a **shortcut menu**, which is a list of commands related to a selection that opens when you click the right mouse button. Peter asks you to include the customer's contact information on the Customer Order worksheet so all of the information is on one sheet.

To delete the Customer Contact worksheet from the workbook:

1. Right-click the **Customer Contact** sheet tab. A shortcut menu opens.
2. Click **Delete**. The Customer Contact worksheet is removed from the workbook.

Saving a Workbook

As you modify a workbook, you should save it regularly—every 10 minutes or so is a good practice. The first time you save a workbook, the Save As dialog box opens so you can name the file and choose where to save it. You can save the workbook on your computer or network or to your account on OneDrive.

To save your workbook for the first time:

1. On the Quick Access Toolbar, click the **Save** button (or press the **Ctrl+S** keys). The Save As screen in Backstage view opens.
2. Click the **Browse** button. The Save As dialog box opens.
3. Navigate to the location specified by your instructor.
4. In the File name box, select **Book1** (the suggested name) if it is not already selected, and then type **Game Card**.
5. Verify that **Excel Workbook** appears in the Save as type box.
6. Click the **Save** button. The workbook is saved, the dialog box closes, and the workbook window reappears with the new filename in the title bar.

As you modify the workbook, you will need to resave the file. Because you already saved the workbook with a filename, the next time you save, the Save command saves the changes you made to the workbook without opening the Save As dialog box.

Entering Text, Dates, and Numbers

Workbook content is entered into worksheet cells. Those cells can contain text, numbers, or dates and times. **Text data** is any combination of letters, numbers, and symbols. Text data is often referred to as a **text string** because it contains a series, or string, of text characters. **Numeric data** is any number that can be used in a mathematical calculation. **Date** and **time data** are commonly recognized formats for date and time values. For example, Excel interprets the cell entry April 15, 2017 as a date and not as text. New data is placed into the active cell of the current worksheet. As you enter data, the entry appears in both the active cell and the formula bar. By default, text is left-aligned in cells, and numbers, dates, and times are right-aligned.

Entering Text

Text is often used in worksheets to label other data and to identify areas of a sheet. Peter wants you to enter some of the information from the planning analysis sheet into the Documentation sheet.

To enter text in the Documentation sheet:

1. Go to the **Documentation** sheet, and then click the **Ctrl+Home** keys to make sure cell A1 is the active cell.
2. Type **Game Card** in cell A1. As you type, the text appears in cell A1 and in the formula bar.
3. Press the **Enter** key twice. The text is entered into cell A1, and the active cell moves down two rows to cell A3.
4. Type **Author** in cell A3, and then press the **Tab** key. The text is entered and the active cell moves one column to the right to cell B3.
5. Type your name in cell B3, and then press the **Enter** key. The text is entered and the active cell moves one cell down and to the left to cell A4.
6. Type **Date** in cell A4, and then press the **Tab** key. The text is entered, and the active cell moves one column to the right to cell B4, where you would enter the date you created the worksheet. For now, you will leave the cell for the date blank.
7. Press the **Enter** key to make cell A5 the active cell, type **Purpose** in the cell, and then press the **Tab** key. The active cell moves one column to the right to cell B5.
8. Type **To record customer game orders** in cell B5, and then press the **Enter** key. Figure 1-12 shows the text entered in the Documentation sheet.

Figure 1-12 Text entered in the Documentation sheet

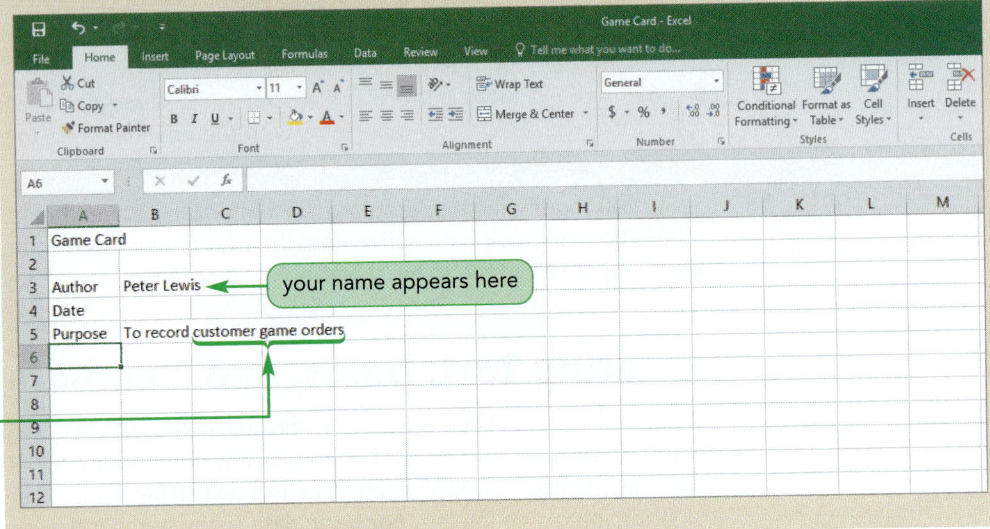

The text strings you entered in cells A1, B3, and B5 are so long that they cover the adjacent cells. Any text you enter in a cell that doesn't fit within that cell will cover the adjacent cells to the right as long as they are empty. If the adjacent cells contain data, only the text that fits into the cell is displayed. The rest of the text entry is hidden from view. The text itself is not affected. The complete text is still entered in the cell; it is just not displayed. (You will learn how to display all text in a cell in the next session.)

Undoing and Redoing an Action

As you enter data in a workbook, you might need to undo a previous action. Excel maintains a list of the actions you performed in the workbook during the current session, so you can undo most of your actions. You can use the Undo button on the Quick Access Toolbar or press the Ctrl+Z keys to reverse your most recent actions one at a time. If you want to undo more than one action, you can click the Undo button arrow and then select the earliest action you want to undo—all of the actions after the earliest action you selected are also undone.

You will undo the most recent change you made to the Documentation sheet—the text you entered into cell B5. Then you will enter more descriptive and accurate description of the worksheet's purpose.

To undo the text entry in cell B5:

1. On the Quick Access Toolbar, click the **Undo** button (or press the **Ctrl+Z** keys). The last action is reversed, removing the text you entered in cell B5.
2. In cell B5, type **To record purchases of board games from Game Card**, and then press the **Enter** key.

If you want to restore actions you have undone, you can redo them. To redo one action at a time, you can click the Redo button on the Quick Access Toolbar or press the Ctrl+Y keys. To redo multiple actions at once, you can click the Redo button arrow and then click the earliest action you want to redo. After you undo or redo an action, Excel continues the action list starting from any new changes you make to the workbook.

Editing Cell Content

As you continue to create your workbook, you might find mistakes you need to correct or entries that you want to change. To replace all of the content in a cell, you simply select the cell and then type the new entry to overwrite the previous entry. However, if you need to replace only part of a cell's content, you can work in **Edit mode**. To switch to Edit mode, you double-click the cell. A blinking insertion point indicates where the new content you type will be inserted. In the cell or formula bar, the pointer changes to an I-beam, which you can use to select text in the cell. Anything you type replaces the selected content.

Because customers can order more than just games from Game Card, Peter wants you to edit the text in cell B5. You will do that in Edit mode.

To edit the text in cell B5:

1. Double-click cell **B5** to select the cell and switch to Edit mode. A blinking insertion point appears within the text of cell B5. The status bar displays Edit instead of Ready to indicate that the cell is in Edit mode.
2. Press the **arrow keys** to move the insertion point directly to the left of the word "from" in the cell text.
3. Type **and other items** and then press the **spacebar**. The cell now reads "To record purchases of board games and other items from Game Card." See Figure 1-13.

Figure 1-13 Edited text in the Documentation sheet

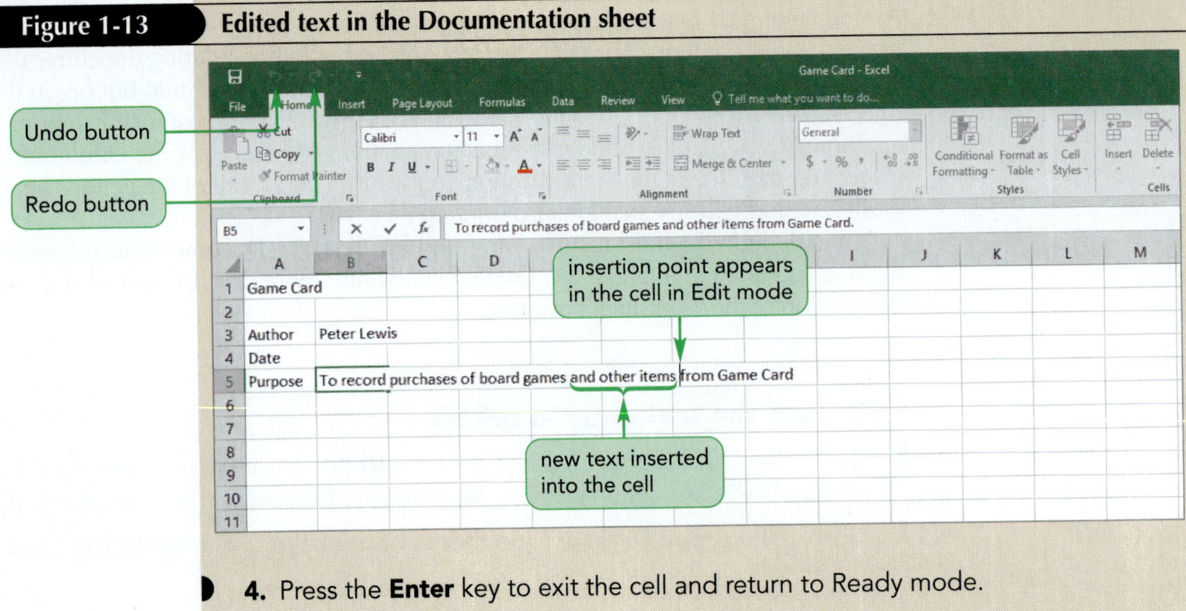

4. Press the **Enter** key to exit the cell and return to Ready mode.

Understanding AutoComplete

As you type text in the active cell, Excel tries to anticipate the remaining characters by displaying text that begins with the same letters as a previous entry in the same column. This feature, known as **AutoComplete**, helps make entering repetitive text easier. To accept the suggested text, press the Tab or Enter key. To override the suggested text, continue to type the text you want to enter in the cell. AutoComplete does not work with dates or numbers or when a blank cell is between the previous entry and the text you are typing.

Next, you will enter the contact information for Leslie Ritter, a customer from Brockton, Massachusetts, who recently placed an order with Game Card. You will enter this information on the Customer Order worksheet.

To enter Leslie Ritter's contact information:

1. Click the **Customer Order** sheet tab to make it the active sheet.
2. In cell A1, type **Customer Order** as the worksheet title, and then press the **Enter** key twice. The worksheet title is entered in cell A1, and the active cell becomes cell A3.
3. Type **Ship To** in cell A3, and then press the **Enter** key. The label is entered in the cell, and the active cell is now cell A4.
4. In the range A4:A10, enter the following labels, pressing the **Enter** key after each entry and ignoring any AutoComplete suggestions: **First Name**, **Last Name**, **Address**, **City**, **State**, **Postal Code**, and **Phone**.
5. Click cell **B4** to make that cell the active cell.
6. In the range B4:B10, enter the following contact information, pressing the **Enter** key after each entry and ignoring any AutoComplete suggestions: **Leslie**, **Ritter**, **805 Mountain St.**, **Brockton**, **MA**, **02302**, and **(508) 555-1072**. See Figure 1-14.

Figure 1-14 Customer information entered in the Customer Order worksheet

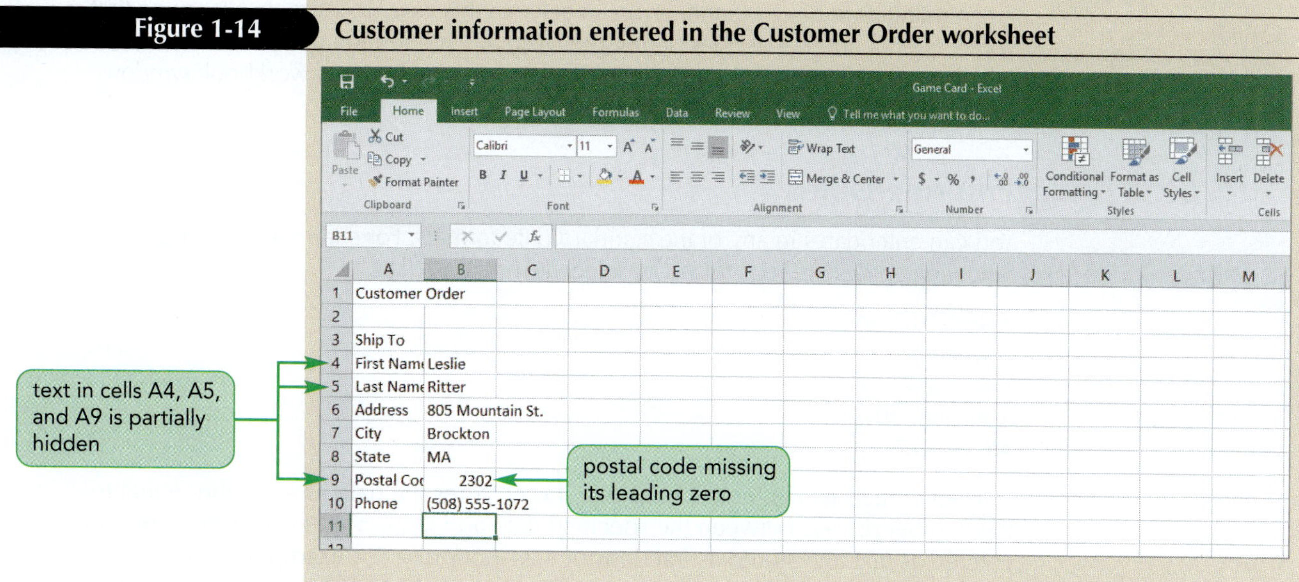

Displaying Numbers as Text

When you enter a number in a cell, Excel treats the entry as a number and ignores any leading zero. For example, in cell B9, the leading zero in the postal code 02302 is missing. Excel displays 2302 because it treats the postal code as a number, and 2302 and 02302 have the same value. To specify that a number entry should be considered text and all digits should be displayed, you include an apostrophe (') before the numbers.

To enter the postal code as text:

1. Click cell **B9** to select it. Notice that the postal code is right-aligned in the cell, unlike the other text entries, which are left-aligned—another indication that the entry is being treated as a number.
2. Type **'02302** in cell B9, and then press the **Enter** key. The text 02302 appears in cell B9 and is left-aligned in the cell, matching all of the other text entries.
3. Click cell **B9** to select it again. See Figure 1-15.

Figure 1-15 Number entered as text

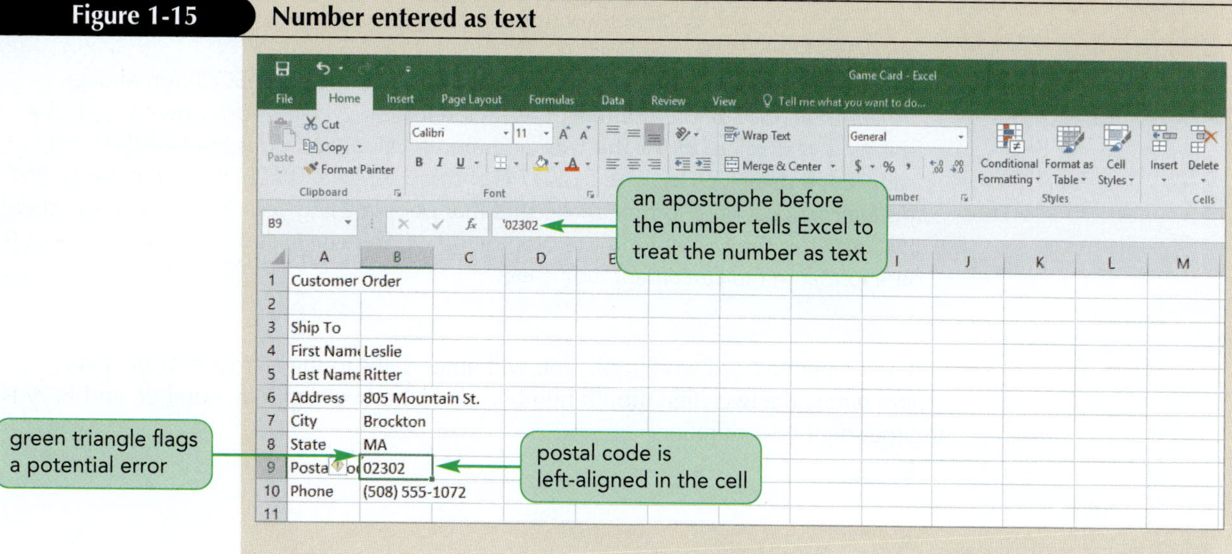

TIP

To remove a green triangle, click the cell, click the yellow caution icon that appears to the left of the cell, and then click Ignore Error.

Notice that a green triangle appears in the upper-left corner of cell B9. Excel uses green triangles to flag potential errors in cells. In this case, it is simply a warning that you entered a number as a text string. Because this is intentional, you do not have to edit the cell to fix the "error." Green triangles appear only in the workbook window and not in any printouts of the worksheet.

Entering Dates

You can enter dates in any of the standard date formats. For example, all of the following entries are recognized by Excel as the same date:

- 4/6/2017
- 4/6/17
- 4-6-2017
- April 6, 2017
- 6-Apr-17

Even though you enter a date as text, Excel stores the date as a number equal to the number of days between the specified date and January 0, 1900. Times are also entered as text and stored as fractions of a 24-hour day. For example April 4, 2017 @ 6:00 PM is stored by Excel as 42,842.75 which is 42,842 days after January 0, 1900 plus 3/4 of one day. Dates and times are stored as numbers so that Excel can easily perform date and time calculations, such as determining the elapsed time between one date and another.

Based on the default date format your computer uses, Excel might alter the format of a date after you type it. For example, if you enter the date 4/6/17 into the active cell, Excel might display the date with the four-digit year value, 4/6/2017; if you enter the text April 6, 2017, Excel might change the date format to 6-Apr-17. Changing the date or time format does not affect the underlying date or time value.

INSIGHT

International Date Formats

As business transactions become more international in scope, you may need to adopt international standards for expressing dates, times, and currency values in your workbooks. For example, a worksheet cell might contain 06/05/17. This format could be interpreted as any of the following dates: the 5th of June, 2017; the 6th of May, 2017; and the 17th of May, 2006.

The interpretation depends on which country the workbook has been designed for. You can avoid this problem by entering the full date, as in June 5, 2017. However, this might not work with documents written in foreign languages, such as Japanese, that use different character symbols.

To solve this problem, many international businesses adopt ISO (International Organization for Standardization) dates in the format *yyyy-mm-dd*, where *yyyy* is the four-digit year value, *mm* is the two-digit month value, and *dd* is the two-digit day value. So, a date such as June 5, 2017 is entered as 2017/06/05. If you choose to use this international date format, make sure that people using your workbook understand this format so they do not misinterpret the dates. You can include information about the date format in the Documentation sheet.

For the Game Card workbook, you will enter dates in the format *mm/dd/yyyy*, where *mm* is the two-digit month number, *dd* is the two-digit day number, and *yyyy* is the four-digit year number.

To enter the current date into the Documentation sheet:

1. Click the **Documentation** sheet tab to make the Documentation sheet the active worksheet.
2. Click cell **B4** to make it the active cell, type the current date in the *mm/dd/yyyy* format, and then press the **Enter** key. The date is entered in the cell.

   Trouble? Depending on your system configuration, Excel might change the date to the date format *dd-mmm-yy*. This difference will not affect your work.
3. Click the **Customer Order** sheet tab to return to the Customer Order worksheet.

The next part of the Customer Order worksheet will list the items that customer Leslie Ritter purchased from Game Card. As shown in Figure 1-16, the list includes identifying information about each item, including the item's price, and the quantity of each item ordered.

Figure 1-16 **Customer order from Leslie Ritter**

Stock ID	Category	Manufacturer	Title	Players	Price	Qty
SG71	Strategy Game	Drebeck Brothers	Kings and Jacks: A Medieval Game of Deception	4	$39.95	2
FG14	Family Game	Misty Games	Twirple, Tweedle, and Twaddle	6	$24.55	1
PG05	Party Game	Parlor Vision	Trivia Connection	8	$29.12	1
SU38	Supplies	Parlor Vision	Box of Dice (10)		$9.95	3
SG29	Strategy Game	Drebeck Brothers	Solar Warfare	2	$35.15	1

You will enter the first four columns of the order into the worksheet.

To enter the first part of the customer order:

1. In the Customer Order worksheet, click cell **A12** to make it the active cell, type **Stock ID** as the column label, and then press the **Tab** key to move to cell B12.
2. In the range B12:D12, type the following labels, pressing the **Tab** key to move to the next cell: **Category**, **Manufacturer**, and **Title**.
3. Press the **Enter** key to go to the next row of the worksheet, making cell A13 the active cell.
4. In the range A13:D17, type the Stock ID, Category, Manufacturer, and Title text for the five items purchased by Leslie Ritter listed in Figure 1-16, pressing the **Tab** key to move from one cell to the next, and pressing the **Enter** key to move to a new row. Note that the text in some cells will be partially hidden; you will fix that problem shortly. See Figure 1-17.

Figure 1-17 Partial customer order

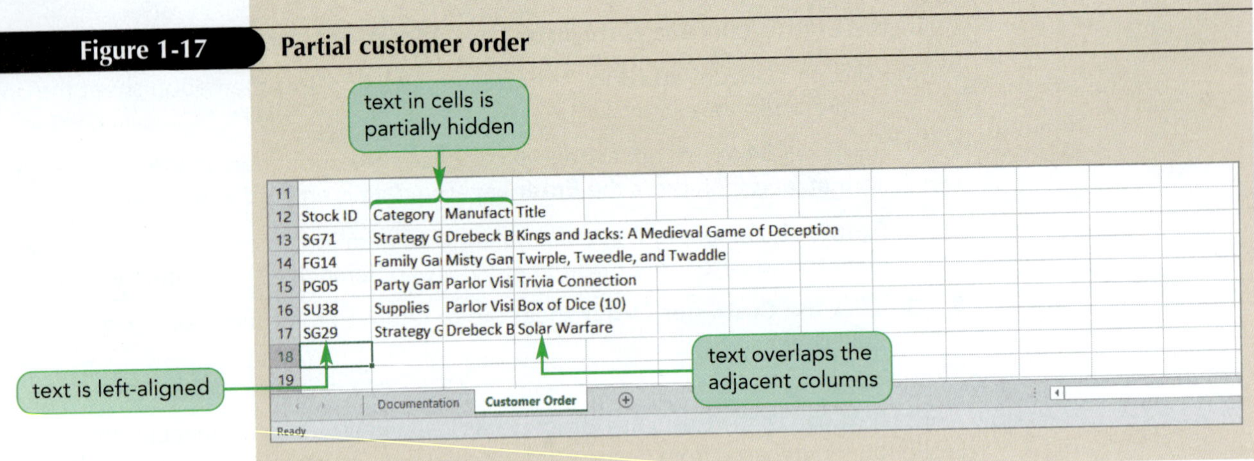

Entering Numbers

TIP

If a number exceeds its cell's width, you see ###### instead of the number. You can display the entire number by increasing the column width.

In Excel, numbers can be integers such as 378, decimals such as 1.95, or negatives such as –5.2. In the case of currency and percentages, you can include the currency symbol and percent sign when you enter the value. Excel treats a currency value such as $87.25 as the number 87.25, and a percentage such as 95% as the decimal 0.95. Much like dates, currency and percentages are formatted in a convenient way for you to read, but only the number is stored within the cell. This makes it easier to perform calculations with currency and percentage values.

You will complete Leslie Ritter's order by entering the players, price, and quantity values.

To enter the rest of the customer order:

1. In the range E12:G12, enter **Players**, **Price**, and **Qty** as the labels.
2. In cell E13, enter **4** as the number of players for the game Kings and Jacks.
3. In cell F13, enter **$39.95** as the price of the game. The game price is stored as a number but displayed with the $ symbol.
4. In cell G13, enter **2** as the quantity of the game ordered by Leslie.
5. In the range E14:G17, enter the remaining number of players, prices, and quantities shown earlier in Figure 1-16. See Figure 1-18.

Figure 1-18 Completed customer order

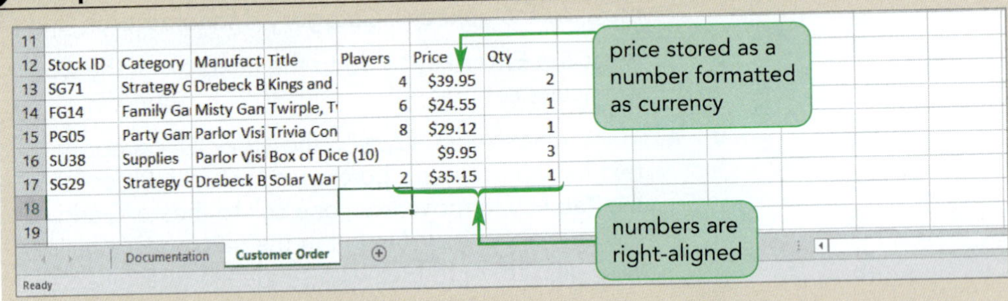

6. On the Quick Access Toolbar, click the **Save** button (or press the **Ctrl+S** keys) to save the workbook.

Resizing Columns and Rows

Much of the information in the Customer Order worksheet is difficult to read because of the hidden text. You can display all of the cell contents by changing the size of the columns and rows in the worksheet.

Changing Column Widths

Column widths are expressed as the number of characters the column can contain. The default column width is 8.43 standard-sized characters. In general, this means that you can type eight characters in a cell; any additional text is hidden or overlaps the adjacent cell. Column widths are also expressed in terms of pixels. A **pixel** is a single point on a computer monitor or printout. A column width of 8.43 characters is equivalent to 64 pixels.

INSIGHT

Setting Column Widths

On a computer monitor, pixel size is based on screen resolution. As a result, cell contents that look fine on one screen might appear very different when viewed on a screen with a different resolution. If you work on multiple computers or share your workbooks with others, you should set column widths based on the maximum number of characters you want displayed in the cells rather than pixel size. This ensures that everyone sees the cell contents the way you intended.

You will increase the width of column A so that the contact information labels in cells A4, A5, and A9 are completely displayed.

To increase the width of column A:

1. Point to the **right border** of the column A heading until the pointer changes to ✛.
2. Click and drag to the right until the width of the column heading reaches **15** characters, but do not release the mouse button. The ScreenTip that appears as you resize the column shows the new column width in characters and in pixels. See Figure 1-19.

Figure 1-19 Width of column A increased to 15 characters

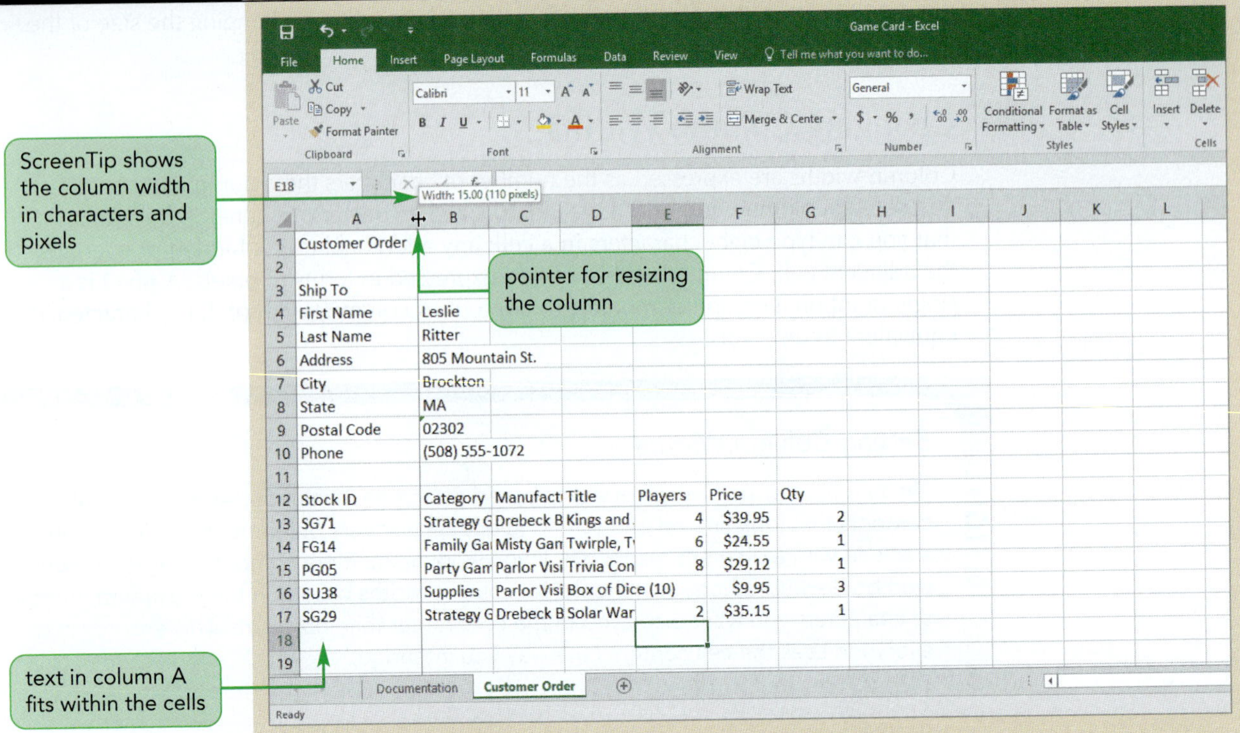

ScreenTip shows the column width in characters and pixels

pointer for resizing the column

text in column A fits within the cells

3. Release the mouse button. The width of column A expands to 15 characters, and all of the text within that column is visible within the cells.

You will increase the widths of columns B and C to 18 characters so that their complete entries are visible. Rather than resizing each column separately, you can select both columns and adjust their widths at the same time.

To increase the widths of columns B and C:

1. Click the **column B** heading. The entire column is selected.
2. Hold down the **Ctrl** key, click the **column C** heading, and then release the **Ctrl** key. Both columns B and C are selected.
3. Point to the **right border** of the column C heading until the pointer changes to ✛.
4. Drag to the right until the column width changes to **18** characters, and then release the mouse button. Both column widths increase to 18 characters and display all of the entered text.

TIP

To select adjacent columns, you can also click and drag the pointer over multiple column headings.

Using the mouse to resize columns can be imprecise and a challenge to some users with special needs. The Format command on the Home tab gives you precise control over column width and row height settings. You will use the Format command to set the width of column D to exactly 25 characters so that the hidden text is visible.

To set the width of column D using the Format command:

1. Click the **column D** heading. The entire column is selected.
2. On the Home tab, in the Cells group, click the **Format** button, and then click **Column Width.** The Column Width dialog box opens.
3. Type **25** in the Column width box to specify the new column width.
4. Click the **OK** button. The width of column D changes to 25 characters.
5. Click cell **A12** to deselect column D. Figure 1-20 shows the revised column widths for the customer order columns.

Figure 1-20 **Resized columns**

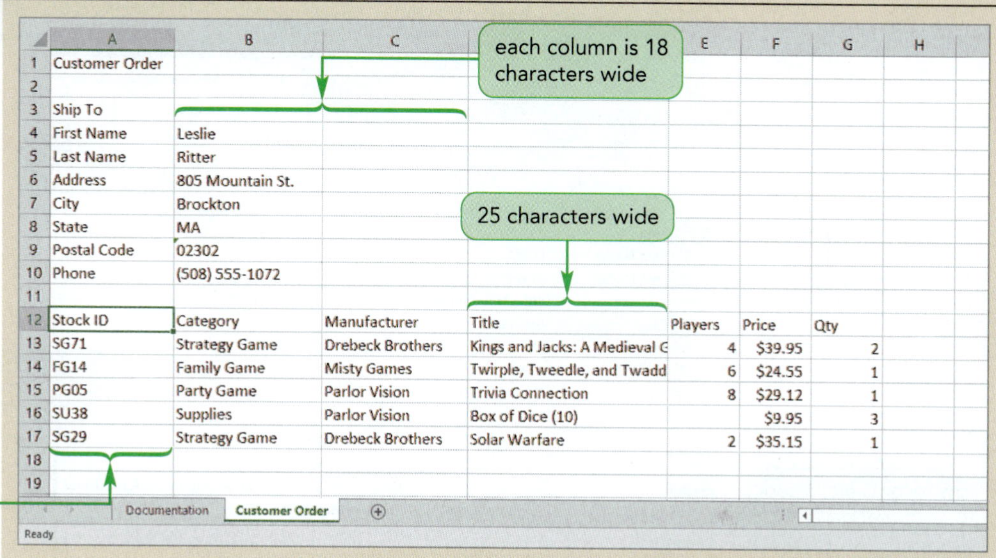

TIP

If the row or column is blank, autofitting restores its default height or width.

Notice that 25 characters is not wide enough to display all of the characters in each cell of column D. Instead of manually resizing the column width or row height to fit it to the cell contents, you can autofit the column or row. **AutoFit** changes the column width or row height to display the longest or tallest entry within the column or row. You autofit a column or a row by double-clicking the right border of the column heading or the bottom border of the row heading.

To autofit the contents of column D:

1. Point to the **right border** of column D until the pointer changes to +.
2. Double-click the **right border** of the column D heading. The width of column D increases to about 43 characters so that the longest item title is completely visible.

Wrapping Text Within a Cell

Sometimes, resizing a column width to display all of the text entered in the cells results in a cell that is too wide to read or print nicely. Another way to display long text entries is to wrap text to a new line when it would otherwise extend beyond the cell boundaries. When text wraps within a cell, the row height increases so that all of the text within the cell is displayed.

You will resize column D and then wrap the text entries in the column.

To wrap text in column D:

1. Resize the width of column D to **25** characters.
2. Select the range **D13:D17**. These cells include the titles that extend beyond the column width.
3. On the Home tab, in the Alignment group, click the **Wrap Text** button. The Wrap Text button is toggled on, and text in the selected cells that exceeds the column width wraps to a new line.
4. Click cell **A12** to make it the active cell. See Figure 1-21.

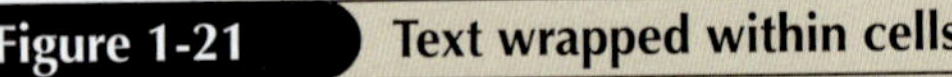
Figure 1-21 Text wrapped within cells

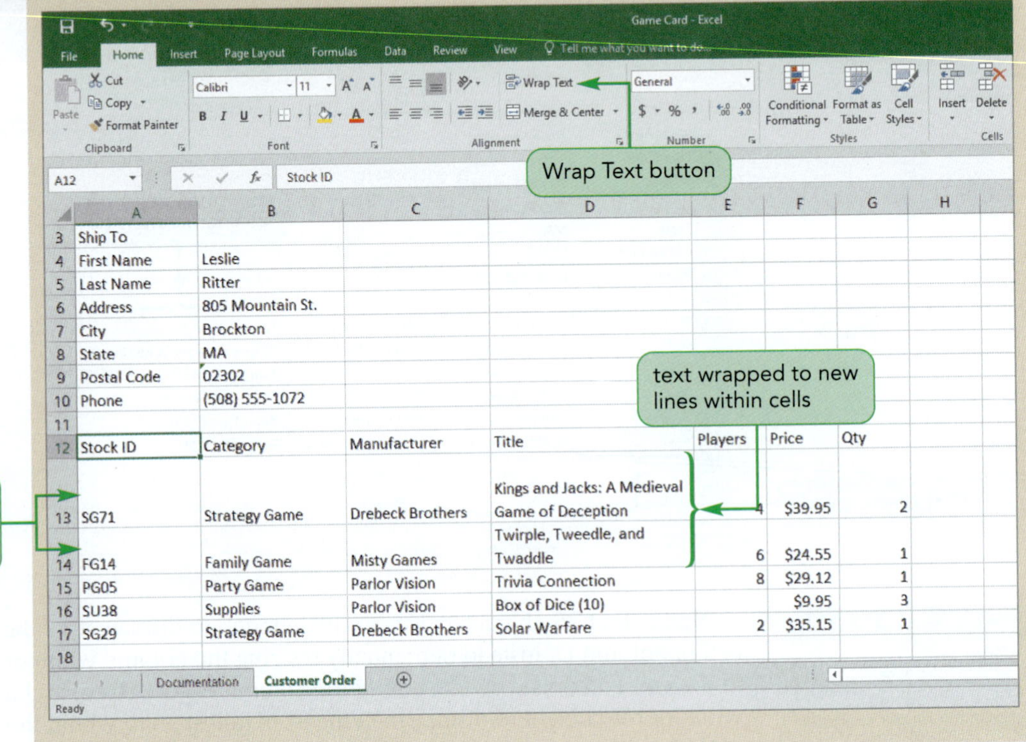

If you want to create a new line within a cell, press the Alt+Enter keys to move the insertion point to the next line within the cell. Whatever you type next will appear on the new line in the cell.

Changing Row Heights

The height of a row is measured in points or pixels. A **point** is approximately 1/72 of an inch. The default row height is 15 points, or 20 pixels. Row heights are set in the same way as column widths. You can drag the bottom border of the row heading to a new row height, specify a row height using the Format command, or autofit the row's height to match its content.

Peter notices that the height of row 13 is a little too tall for its contents. He asks you to change to it 30 points.

To change the height of row 13:

1. Point to the **bottom border** of the row 13 heading until the pointer changes to ‡.
2. Drag the **bottom border** down until the height of the row is equal to **30** points (or **40** pixels), and then release the mouse button. The height of row 13 is set to 30 points.
3. Press the **Ctrl+S** keys to save the workbook.

TIP

You can also set the row height by clicking the Format button in the Cells group on the Home tab and then using the Row Height command.

You have entered most of the data for Leslie Ritter's order at Game Card. In the next session, you will calculate the total charge for the order and print the worksheet.

REVIEW

Session 1.1 Quick Check

1. What are the two types of sheets used in a workbook?
2. What is the cell reference for the cell located in the second column and fifth row of a worksheet?
3. What is the range reference for the block of cells C2 through D10?
4. What is the reference for the nonadjacent block of cells B5 through C10 and cells B15 through D20?
5. What keyboard shortcut makes the active cell to cell A1?
6. What is text data?
7. How do you enter a number so that Excel sees it as text?
8. Cell B2 contains the entry May 3, 2017. Why doesn't Excel consider this a text entry?
9. How do you autofit a column to match the longest cell entry?

Session 1.2 Visual Overview:

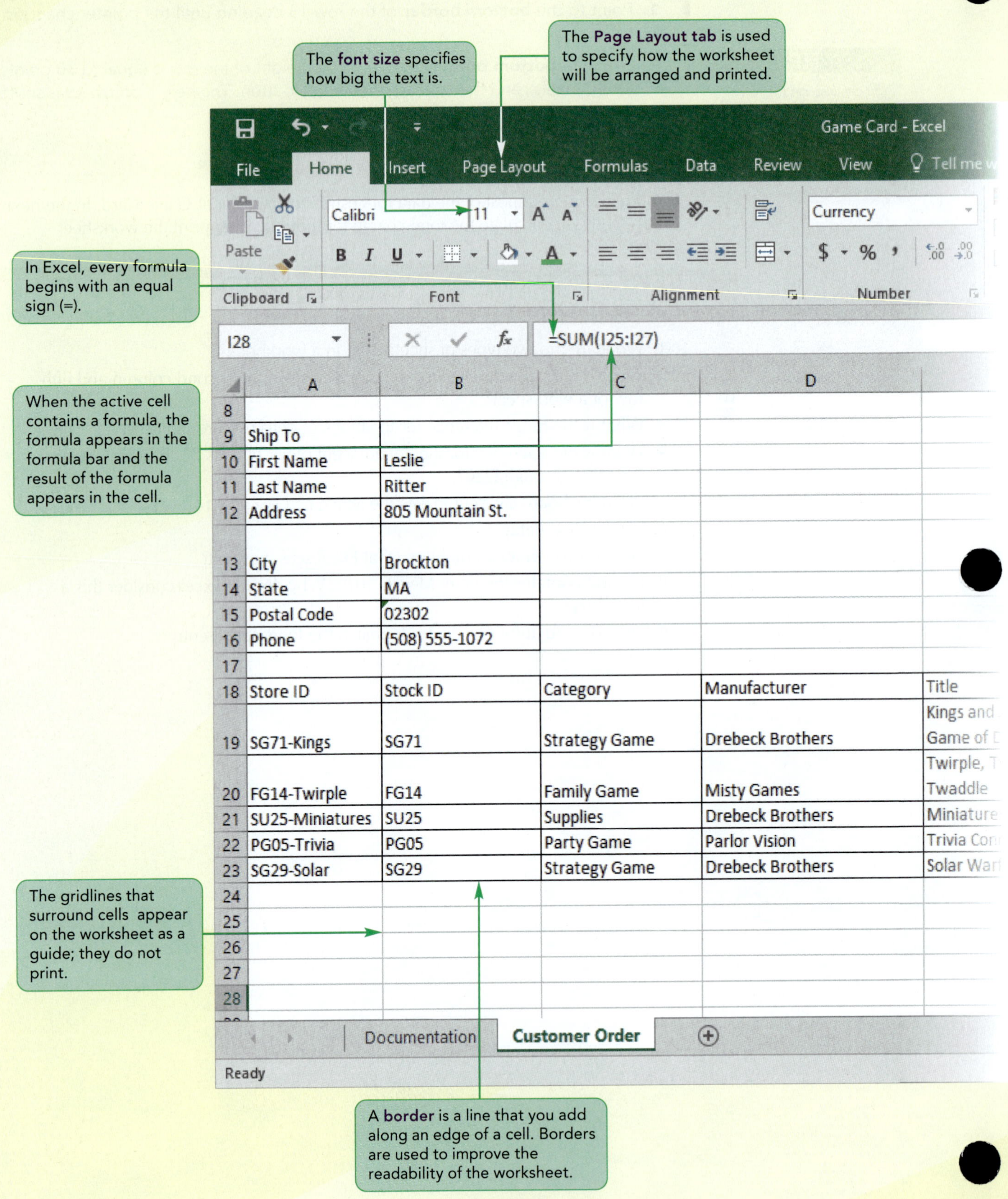
The **font size** specifies how big the text is.
The **Page Layout tab** is used to specify how the worksheet will be arranged and printed.
In Excel, every formula begins with an equal sign (=).
When the active cell contains a formula, the formula appears in the formula bar and the result of the formula appears in the cell.
The gridlines that surround cells appear on the worksheet as a guide; they do not print.
A **border** is a line that you add along an edge of a cell. Borders are used to improve the readability of the worksheet.
Game Card - Excel
File
Home
Insert
Page Layout
Formulas
Data
Review
View
Tell me
Paste
Calibri
11
Currency
Clipboard
Font
Alignment
Number
I28
=SUM(I25:I27)
Ship To
First Name
Leslie
Last Name
Ritter
Address
805 Mountain St.
City
Brockton
State
MA
Postal Code
02302
Phone
(508) 555-1072
Store ID
Stock ID
Category
Manufacturer
Title
SG71-Kings
SG71
Strategy Game
Drebeck Brothers
FG14-Twirple
FG14
Family Game
Misty Games
SU25-Miniatures
SU25
Supplies
Drebeck Brothers
PG05-Trivia
PG05
Party Game
Parlor Vision
SG29-Solar
SG29
Strategy Game
Drebeck Brothers
Documentation
Customer Order
Ready

Excel Formulas and Functions

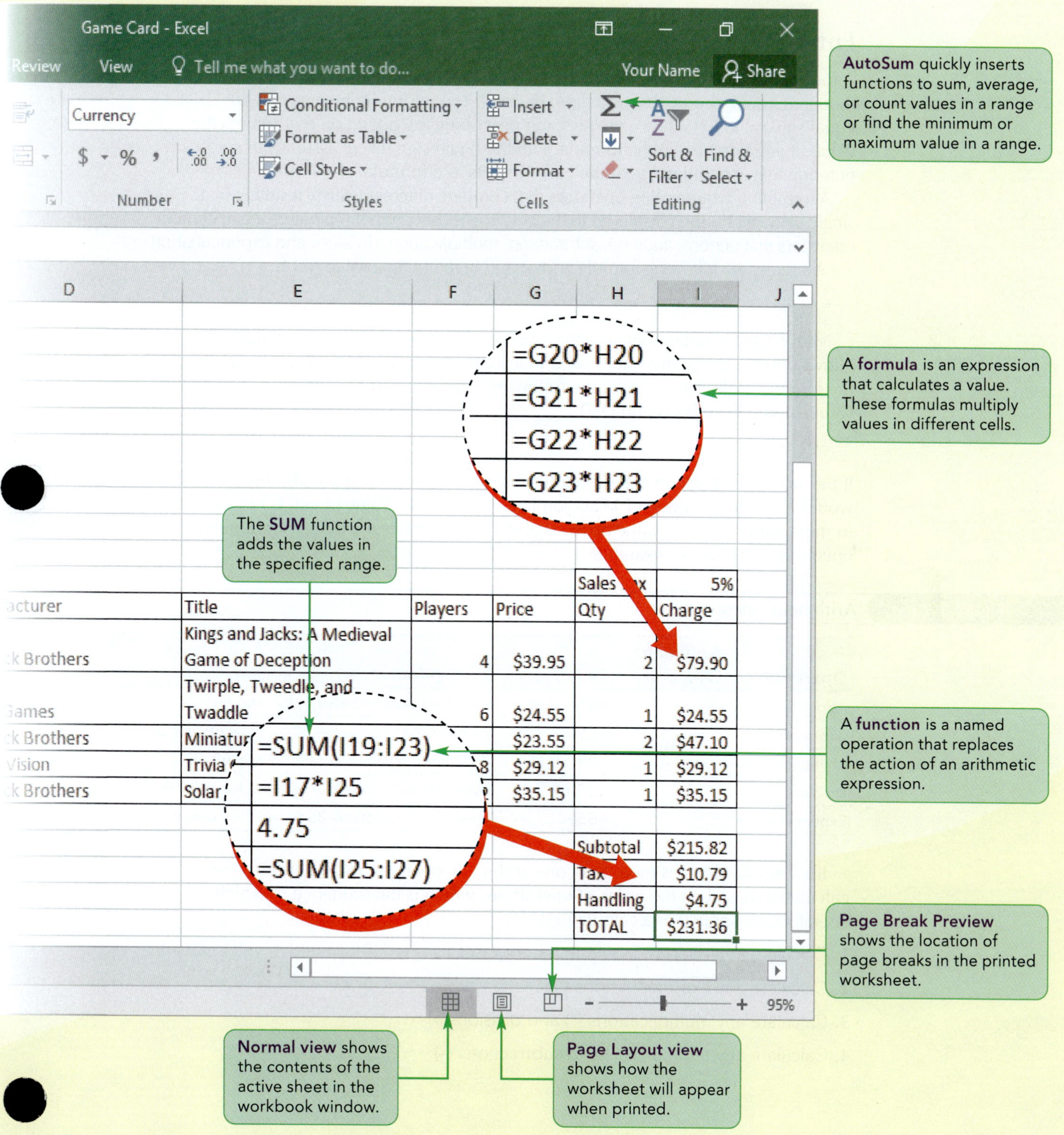

Game Card - Excel
Review
View
Tell me what you want to do...
Your Name
Share
Currency
Conditional Formatting
Format as Table
Cell Styles
Insert
Delete
Format
Sort & Filter
Find & Select
Number
Styles
Cells
Editing
=G20*H20
=G21*H21
=G22*H22
=G23*H23
=SUM(I19:I23)
=I17*I25
4.75
=SUM(I25:I27)
Sales Tax 5%
Title
Players
Price
Qty
Charge
Kings and Jacks: A Medieval Game of Deception
Twirple, Tweedle, and Twaddle
Subtotal $215.82
Tax $10.79
Handling $4.75
TOTAL $231.36
95%
AutoSum quickly inserts functions to sum, average, or count values in a range or find the minimum or maximum value in a range.
A **formula** is an expression that calculates a value. These formulas multiply values in different cells.
The **SUM** function adds the values in the specified range.
A **function** is a named operation that replaces the action of an arithmetic expression.
Page Break Preview shows the location of page breaks in the printed worksheet.
Normal view shows the contents of the active sheet in the workbook window.
Page Layout view shows how the worksheet will appear when printed.

Performing Calculations with Formulas

So far you have entered text, numbers, and dates in the worksheet. However, the main reason for using Excel is to perform calculations and analysis on data. For example, Peter wants the workbook to calculate the number of items that the customer ordered and how much revenue the order will generate. Such calculations are added to a worksheet using formulas and functions.

Entering a Formula

A formula is an expression that returns a value. In most cases, this is a number—though it could also be text or a date. In Excel, every formula begins with an equal sign (=) followed by an expression describing the operation that returns the value. If you don't begin the formula with the equal sign, Excel assumes that you are entering text and will not treat the cell contents as a formula.

A formula is written using **operators** that combine different values, resulting in a single value that is then displayed in the cell. The most common operators are **arithmetic operators** that perform addition, subtraction, multiplication, division, and exponentiation. For example, the following formula adds 3 and 8, returning a value of 11:

```
=3+8
```

Most Excel formulas contain references to cells rather than specific values. This allows you to change the values used in the calculation without having to modify the formula itself. For example, the following formula returns the result of adding the values stored in cells C3 and D10:

```
=C3+D10
```

If the value 3 is stored in cell C3 and the value 8 is stored in cell D10, this formula would also return a value of 11. If you later changed the value in cell C3 to 10, the formula would return a value of 18. Figure 1-22 describes the different arithmetic operators and provides examples of formulas.

Figure 1-22 Arithmetic operators

Operation	Arithmetic Operator	Example	Description
Addition	+	=B1+B2+B3	Adds the values in cells B1, B2, and B3
Subtraction	–	=C9-B2	Subtracts the value in cell B2 from the value in cell C9
Multiplication	*	=C9*B9	Multiplies the values in cells C9 and B9
Division	/	=C9/B9	Divides the value in cell C9 by the value in cell B9
Exponentiation	^	=B5^3	Raises the value of cell B5 to the third power

If a formula contains more than one arithmetic operator, Excel performs the calculation based on the **order of operations**, which is the sequence in which operators are applied in a calculation:

1. Calculate any operations within parentheses
2. Calculate any exponentiations (^)
3. Calculate any multiplications (*) and divisions (/)
4. Calculate any additions (+) and subtractions (–)

For example, the following formula returns the value 23 because multiplying 4 by 5 takes precedence over adding 3:

```
=3+4*5
```

If a formula contains two or more operators with the same level of priority, the operators are applied in order from left to right. In the following formula, Excel first multiplies 4 by 10 and then divides that result by 8 to return the value 5:

```
=4*10/8
```

When parentheses are used, the value inside them is calculated first. In the following formula, Excel calculates (3+4) first, and then multiplies that result by 5 to return the value 35:

```
=(3+4)*5
```

Figure 1-23 shows how slight changes in a formula affect the order of operations and the result of the formula.

Figure 1-23 **Order of operations applied to Excel formulas**

Formula	Order of Operations	Result
=50+10*5	10*5 calculated first and then 50 is added	100
=(50+10)*5	(50+10) calculated first and then 60 is multiplied by 5	300
=50/10–5	50/10 calculated first and then 5 is subtracted	0
=50/(10–5)	(10–5) calculated first and then 50 is divided by that value	10
=50/10*5	Two operators are at same precedence level, so the calculation is done left to right with 50/10 calculated first and that value is then multiplied by 5	25
=50/(10*5)	(10*5) is calculated first and then 50 is divided by that value	1

Peter wants the Customer Order worksheet to include the total amount charged for each item ordered. The charge is equal to the number of each item ordered multiplied by each item's price. You already entered this information in columns F and G. Now you will enter a formula to calculate the charge for each set of items ordered in column H.

To calculate the charge for the first item ordered:

1. If you took a break after the previous session, make sure the Game Card workbook is open and the Customer Order worksheet is active.
2. Click cell **H12** to make it the active cell, type **Charge** as the column label, and then press the **Enter** key. The label text is entered in cell H12, and cell H13 is now the active cell.
3. Type **=F13*G13** (the price of the Kings and Jacks game multiplied by the number of that game ordered). As you type the formula, a list of Excel function names appears in a ScreenTip, which provides a quick method for entering functions. The list will close when you complete the formula. You will learn more about Excel functions shortly. Also, after you type each cell reference, Excel color codes each cell reference and its cell. See Figure 1-24.

Figure 1-24 **Formula being entered in a cell**

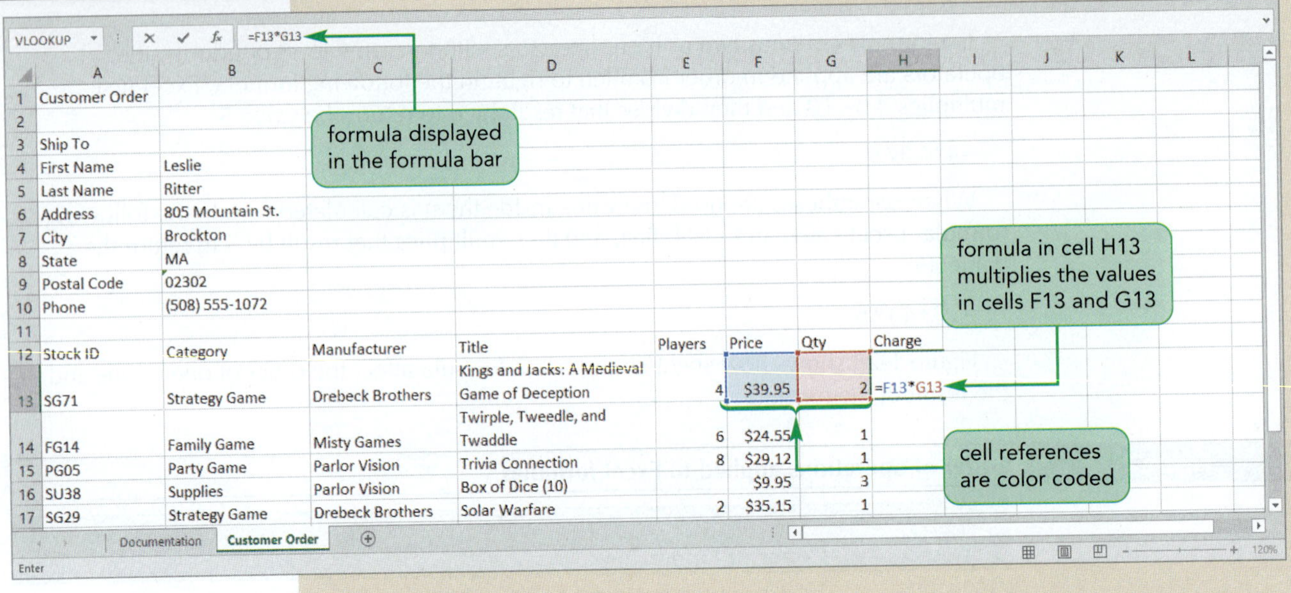

VLOOKUP =F13*G13

	A	B	C	D	E	F	G	H
1	Customer Order							
2								
3	Ship To							
4	First Name	Leslie						
5	Last Name	Ritter						
6	Address	805 Mountain St.						
7	City	Brockton						
8	State	MA						
9	Postal Code	02302						
10	Phone	(508) 555-1072						
11								
12	Stock ID	Category	Manufacturer	Title	Players	Price	Qty	Charge
13	SG71	Strategy Game	Drebeck Brothers	Kings and Jacks: A Medieval Game of Deception	4	$39.95	2	=F13*G13
14	FG14	Family Game	Misty Games	Twirple, Tweedle, and Twaddle	6	$24.55	1	
15	PG05	Party Game	Parlor Vision	Trivia Connection	8	$29.12	1	
16	SU38	Supplies	Parlor Vision	Box of Dice (10)		$9.95	3	
17	SG29	Strategy Game	Drebeck Brothers	Solar Warfare	2	$35.15	1	

Documentation | Customer Order

Enter

formula displayed in the formula bar

formula in cell H13 multiplies the values in cells F13 and G13

cell references are color coded

4. Press the **Enter** key. The formula is entered in cell H13 displaying the value $79.90. The result is displayed as currency because cell F13, which is referenced in the formula, contains a currency value.
5. Click cell **H13** to make it the active cell. Note that the cell displays the result of the formula, and the formula bar displays the formula you entered.

For the first item, you entered the formula by typing each cell reference in the expression. You can also insert a cell reference by clicking the cell as you type the formula. This technique reduces the possibility of error caused by typing an incorrect cell reference. You will use this method to enter the formula to calculate the charge for the second item on the order.

To enter a formula using the mouse:

1. Click cell **H14** to make it the active cell.
2. Type **=**. The equal sign indicates that you are entering a formula. Any cell you click from now on inserts the cell reference of the selected cell into the formula until you complete the formula by pressing the Enter or Tab key.
3. Click cell **F14**. The cell reference is inserted into the formula in the formula bar. At this point, any cell you click changes the cell reference used in the formula. The cell reference isn't locked until you type an operator.
4. Type * to enter the multiplication operator. The cell reference for cell F14 is locked in the formula, and the next cell you click will be inserted after the operator.
5. Click cell **G14** to enter its cell reference in the formula. The formula is complete.
6. Press the **Enter** key. Cell H14 displays the value $24.55, which is the charge for the second item ordered.

Be sure to type = first; otherwise, Excel will not recognize the entry as a formula.

Copying and Pasting Formulas

Sometimes you will need to repeat the same formula throughout a worksheet. Rather than retyping the formula, you can copy a formula from one cell and paste it into another cell. When you copy a formula, Excel places the formula into the **Clipboard**, which is a temporary storage location for text and graphics. When you paste, Excel takes the formula from the Clipboard and inserts it into the selected cell or range. Excel adjusts the cell references in the formula to reflect the formula's new location in the worksheet. This occurs because you usually want to copy the actions of a formula rather than the specific value the formula generates. In this case, the formula's action is to multiply the price of the item ordered by the quantity. By copying and pasting the formula, you can quickly repeat that action for every item listed in the worksheet.

You will copy the formula you entered in cell H14 to the range H15:H17 to calculate the charges on the remaining three items in Leslie Ritter's order. By copying and pasting the formula, you will save time and avoid potential mistakes from retyping the formula.

To copy and paste the formula:

1. Click cell **H14** to select the cell that contains the formula you want to copy.
2. On the Home tab, in the Clipboard group, click the **Copy** button (or press the **Ctrl+C** keys). Excel copies the formula to the Clipboard. A blinking green box surrounds the cell being copied.
3. Select the range **H15:H17**. You want to paste the formula into these cells.
4. In the Clipboard group, click the **Paste** button (or press the **Ctrl+V** keys). Excel pastes the formula into the selected cells, adjusting each formula so that the charge calculated for each ordered item is based on the corresponding values within that row. A button appears below the selected range, providing options for pasting formulas and values. See Figure 1-25.

Figure 1-25 Copied and pasted formula

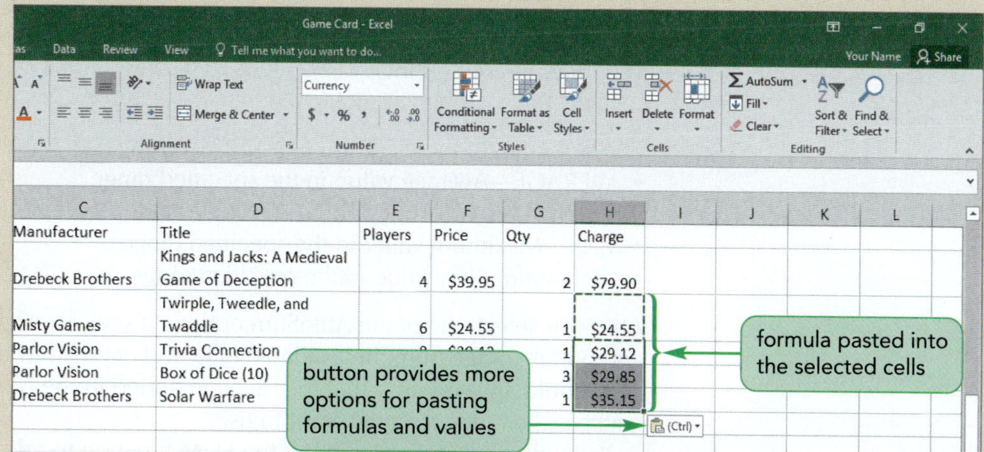

5. Click cell **H15** and verify that the formula =F15*G15 appears in the formula bar. The formula was updated to reflect the cell references in the corresponding row.
6. Click the other cells in column H, and verify that the corresponding formulas are entered in those cells.

Simplifying Formulas with Functions

In addition to cell references and operators, formulas can also contain functions. A function is a named operation that replaces the arithmetic expression in a formula. Functions are used to simplify long or complex formulas. For example, to add the values from cells A1 through A10, you could enter the following long formula:

```
=A1+A2+A3+A4+A5+A6+A7+A8+A9+A10
```

Or, you could use the SUM function to calculate the sum of those cell values by entering the following formula:

```
=SUM(A1:A10)
```

In both instances, Excel adds the values in cells A1 through A10, but the SUM function is faster and simpler to enter and less prone to a typing error. You should always use a function, if one is available, in place of a long, complex formula. Excel supports more than 300 different functions from the fields of finance, business, science, and engineering, including functions that work with numbers, text, and dates.

Introducing Function Syntax

Every function follows a set of rules, or **syntax**, which specifies how the function should be written. The general syntax of all Excel functions is

```
FUNCTION(arg1,arg2,…)
```

where `FUNCTION` is the function name, and `arg1`, `arg2`, and so forth are values used by that function. For example, the SUM function shown above uses a single argument, A1:A10, which is the range reference of the cells whose values will be added. Some functions do not require any arguments and are entered as `FUNCTION()`. Functions without arguments still require the opening and closing parentheses but do not include a value within the parentheses.

Entering Functions with AutoSum

A fast and convenient way to enter commonly used functions is with AutoSum. The AutoSum button includes options to insert the following functions into a select cell or cell range:

- SUM—Sum of the values in the specified range
- AVERAGE—Average value in the specified range
- COUNT—Total count of numeric values in the specified range
- MAX—Maximum value in the specified range
- MIN—Minimum value in the specified range

After you select one of the AutoSum options, Excel determines the most appropriate range from the available data and enters it as the function's argument. You should always verify that the range included in the AutoSum function matches the range that you want to use.

You will use AutoSum to enter the SUM function to add the total charges for Leslie Ritter's order.

To use AutoSum to enter the SUM function:

1. Click cell **G18** to make it the active cell, type **Subtotal** as the label, and then press the **Tab** key to make cell H18 the active cell.

2. On the Home tab, in the Editing group, click the **AutoSum button arrow**. The button's menu opens and displays five common functions: Sum, Average, Count Numbers, Max (for maximum), and Min (for minimum).

TIP

You can quickly insert the SUM function by pressing the Alt+= keys.

3. Click **Sum** to enter the SUM function. The formula =`SUM(H13:H17)` is entered in cell H18. The cells being summed are selected and highlighted on the worksheet so you can quickly confirm that Excel selected the appropriate range from the available data. A ScreenTip appears below the formula describing the function's syntax. See Figure 1-26.

Figure 1-26 **SUM function being entered with AutoSum button**

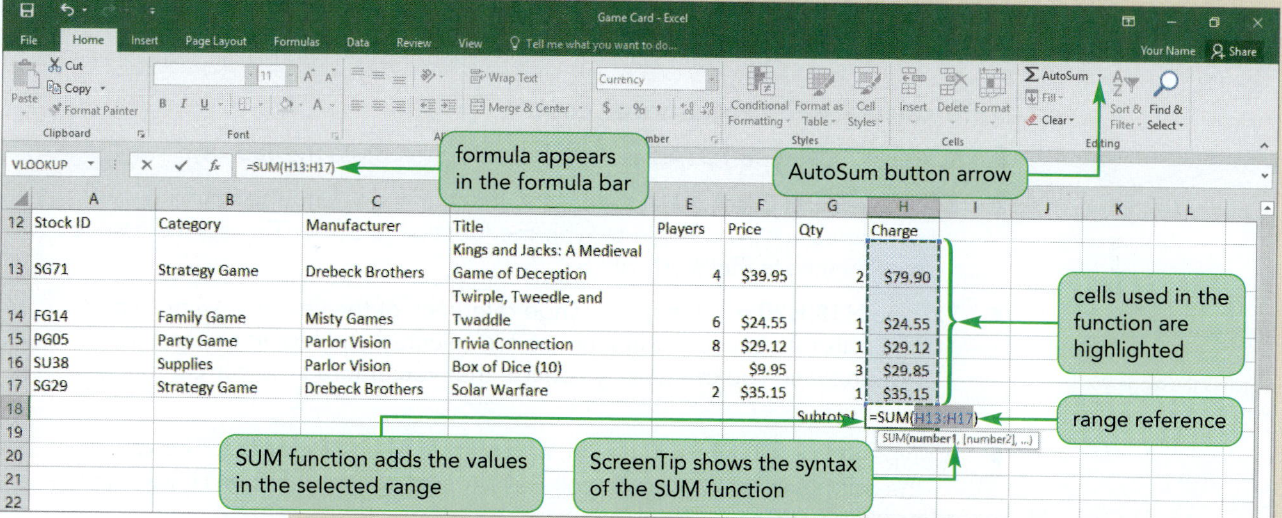

4. Press the **Enter** key to accept the formula. The subtotal of the charges on the order returned by the SUM function is $198.57.

AutoSum makes entering a commonly used formula such as the SUM function fast and easy. However, AutoSum can determine the appropriate range reference to include only when the function is adjacent to the cells containing the values you want to summarize. If you need to use a function elsewhere in the worksheet, you will have to select the range reference to include or type the function yourself.

Each purchase made at Game Card is subject to a 5 percent sales tax and, in the case of online orders, a $4.75 handling fee. You will add these to the Customer Order worksheet so you can calculate the total charge for Leslie Ritter's order.

To add the sales tax and handling fee to the worksheet:

1. Click cell **G11**, type **Sales Tax** as the label, and then press the **Tab** key to make cell H11 the active cell.
2. In cell H11, type **5%** as the sales tax rate, and then press the **Enter** key. The sales tax rate is entered in the cell and can be used in other calculations. The value is displayed with the % symbol but is stored as the equivalent decimal value 0.05.
3. Click cell **G19** to make it the active cell, type **Tax** as the label, and then press the **Tab** key to make cell H19 the active cell.
4. Type **=H11*H18** as the formula to calculate the sales tax on the customer order, and then press the **Enter** key. The formula multiplies the sales tax

value in cell H11 by the order subtotal value in cell H18. The value $9.93 is displayed in cell H19, which is 5 percent of the subtotal value of $198.57.

5. In cell G20, type **Handling** as the label, and then press the **Tab** key to make cell H20 the active cell. You will enter the handling fee in this cell.
6. Type **$4.75** as the handling fee, and then press the **Enter** key.

The last part of the customer order is to calculate the total cost by adding the subtotal, the tax, and the handling fee. Rather than using AutoSum, you will type the SUM function so you can enter the correct range reference for the function. You can type the range reference or select the range in the worksheet. Remember that you must type parentheses around the range reference.

To calculate the total order cost:

1. In cell G21, type **TOTAL** as the label, and then press the **Tab** key.
2. Type **=SUM(** in cell H21 to enter the function name and the opening parenthesis. As you begin to type the function, a ScreenTip lists the names of all functions that start with S.
3. Type **H18:H20** to specify the range reference of the cells you want to add. The cells referenced in the function are selected and highlighted on the worksheet so you can quickly confirm that you entered the correct range reference.

Make sure the cell reference in the function matches the range you want to calculate.

4. Type **)** to complete the function, and then press the **Enter** key. The value of the SUM function appears in cell H21, indicating that the total charge for the order is $213.25.
5. Click cell **H21** to select the cell and its formula. See Figure 1-27.

Figure 1-27 Total charge calculated for the order

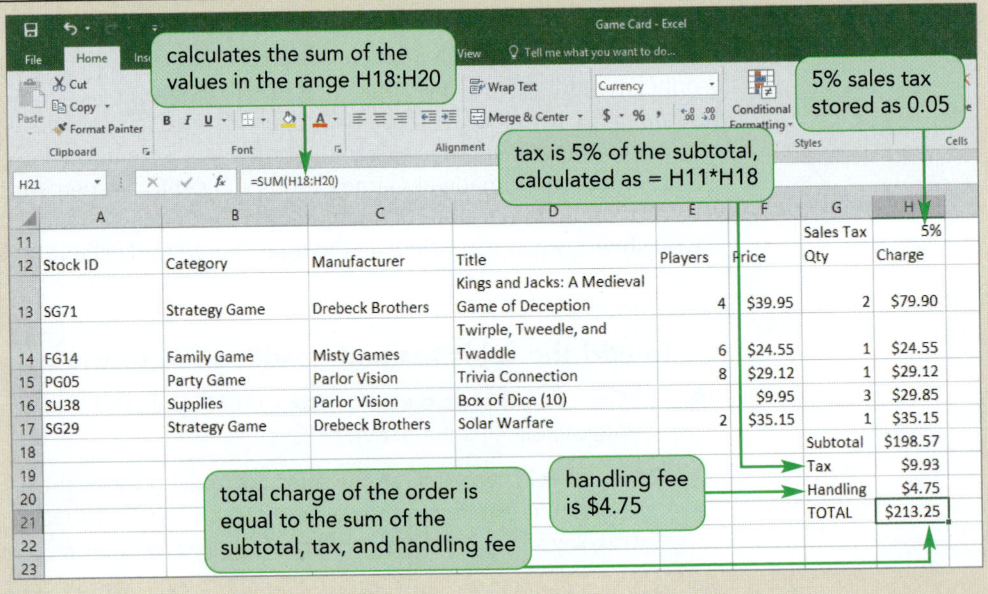

The SUM function makes it simple to quickly add the values in a group of cells.

PROSKILLS

Problem Solving: Writing Effective Formulas

You can use formulas to quickly perform calculations and solve problems. First, identify the problem you need to solve. Then, gather the data needed to solve the problem. Finally, create accurate and effective formulas that use the data to answer or resolve the problem. Follow these guidelines:

- **Keep formulas simple.** Use functions in place of long, complex formulas whenever possible. For example, use the SUM function instead of entering a formula that adds individual cells, which makes it easier to confirm that the formula is making an accurate calculation as it provides answers needed to evaluate the problem.
- **Do not hide data values within formulas.** The worksheet displays formula results, not the actual formula. For example, to calculate a 5 percent interest rate on a currency value in cell A5, you could enter the formula =0.05*A5. However, this doesn't show how the value is calculated. A better approach places the value 0.05 in a cell accompanied by a descriptive label and uses the cell reference in the formula. If you place 0.05 in cell A6, the formula =A6*A5 would calculate the interest value. Other people can then easily see the interest rate as well as the resulting interest, ensuring that the formula is solving the right problem.
- **Break up formulas to show intermediate results.** When a worksheet contains complex computations, other people can more easily comprehend how the formula results are calculated when different parts of the formula are distinguished. For example, the formula =SUM(A1:A10)/SUM(B1:B10) calculates the ratio of two sums but hides the two sum values. Instead, enter each SUM function in a separate cell, such as cells A11 and B11, and use the formula =A11/B11 to calculate the ratio. Other people can see both sums and the value of their ratio in the worksheet and better understand the final result, which makes it more likely that the best problem resolution will be selected.
- **Test formulas with simple values.** Use values you can calculate in your head to confirm that your formula works as intended. For example, using 1s or 10s as the input values lets you easily figure out the answer and verify the formula.

Finding a solution to a problem requires accurate data and analysis. With workbooks, this means using formulas that are easy to understand, clearly showing the data being used in the calculations, and demonstrating how the results are calculated. Only then can you be confident that you are choosing the best problem resolution.

Modifying a Worksheet

As you develop a worksheet, you might need to modify its content and structure to create a more logical organization. Some ways you can modify a worksheet include moving cells and ranges, inserting rows and columns, deleting rows and columns, and inserting and deleting cells.

Moving and Copying a Cell or Range

One way to move a cell or range is to select it, position the pointer over the bottom border of the selection, drag the selection to a new location, and then release the mouse button. This technique is called **drag and drop** because you are dragging the range and dropping it in a new location. If the drop location is not visible, drag the selection to the edge of the workbook window to scroll the worksheet, and then drop the selection.

You can also use the drag-and-drop technique to copy cells by pressing the Ctrl key as you drag the selected range to its new location. A copy of the original range is placed in the new location without removing the original range from the worksheet.

REFERENCE

Moving or Copying a Cell or Range

- Select the cell or range you want to move or copy.
- Move the pointer over the border of the selection until the pointer changes shape.
- To move the range, click the border and drag the selection to a new location (or to copy the range, hold down the Ctrl key and drag the selection to a new location).

or

- Select the cell or range you want to move or copy.
- On the Home tab, in the Clipboard group, click the Cut or Copy button (or right-click the selection, and then click Cut or Copy on the shortcut menu, or press the Ctrl+X or Ctrl+C keys).
- Select the cell or the upper-left cell of the range where you want to paste the content.
- In the Clipboard group, click the Paste button (or right-click the selection and then click Paste on the shortcut menu, or press the Ctrl+V keys).

Peter wants the subtotal, tax, handling, and total values in the range G18:H21 moved down one row to the range G19:H22 to set those calculations off from the list of items in the customer order. You will use the drag-and-drop method to move the range.

To drag and drop the range G18:H21:

1. Select the range **G18:H21**. These are the cells you want to move.
2. Point to the **bottom border** of the selected range so that the pointer changes to .
3. Press and hold the mouse button to change the pointer to , and then drag the selection down one row. Do not release the mouse button. A ScreenTip appears, indicating that the new range of the selected cells will be G19:H22. A dark green border also appears around the new range. See Figure 1-28.

Figure 1-28 **Range being moved**

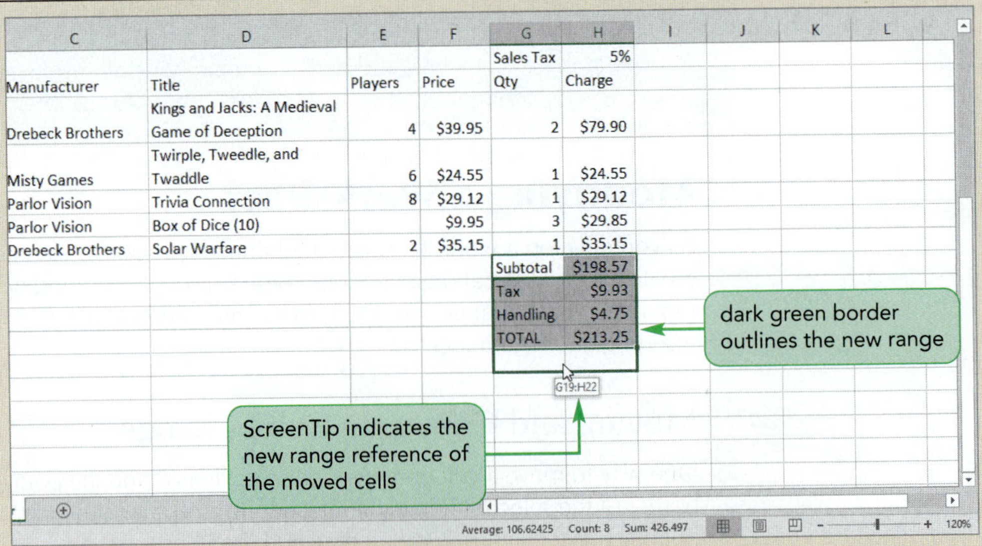

4. Make sure the ScreenTip displays the range G19:H22, and then release the mouse button. The selected cells move to their new location.

Some people find dragging and dropping a select cell range difficult and awkward, particularly if the selected range is large or needs to move a long distance in the worksheet. In those situations, it is often more efficient to cut or copy and paste the cell contents. Cutting moves the selected content, whereas copying duplicates the selected content in the new location.

Peter wants the worksheet to include a summary of the customer order starting in row 3. You will cut the customer contact information and the item listing from range A3:A22 and paste it into range A9:H28, freeing up space for the order information.

To cut and paste the customer contact information:

1. Click cell **A3** to select it.
2. Press the **Ctrl+Shift+End** keys to extend the selection to the last cell in the lower-right corner of the worksheet (cell H22).
3. On the Home tab, in the Clipboard group, click the **Cut** button (or press the **Ctrl+X** keys). The range is surrounded by a moving border, indicating that it has been cut.
4. Click cell **A9** to select it. This is the upper-left corner of the range where you want to paste the range that you cut.
5. In the Clipboard group, click the **Paste** button (or press the **Ctrl+V** keys). The range A3:H22 is pasted into the range A9:H28. Note that the cell references in the formulas were automatically updated to reflect the new location of those cells in the worksheet.

Using the COUNT Function

Sometimes you will want to know how many unique items are included in a range, such as the number of different items in the customer order. To calculate that value, you use the COUNT function

```
=COUNT(range)
```

TIP

To count cells containing non-numeric values, use the COUNTA function.

where *range* is the range of cells containing numeric values to be counted. Note that any cell in the range containing a non-numeric value is not counted in the final tally.

You will include the count of the number of different items from the order in the summary information. The summary will also display the order ID (a unique number assigned by Game Card to identify the order), the shipping date, and the type of delivery (overnight, two-day, or standard) in the freed-up space at the top of the worksheet. In addition, Peter wants the total charge for the order to be displayed with the order summary so that he does not have to scroll to the bottom of the worksheet to find that value.

To add the order summary:

1. Click cell **A3**, type **Order ID** as the label, press the **Tab** key, type **C10489** in cell B3, and then press the **Enter** key. The order ID is entered, and cell A4 is the active cell.
2. Type **Shipping Date** as the label in cell A4, press the **Tab** key, type **4/3/2017** in cell B4, and then press the **Enter** key. The shipping date is entered, and cell A5 is the active cell.
3. Type **Delivery** as the label in cell A5, press the **Tab** key, type **standard** in cell B5, and then press the **Enter** key. The delivery type is entered, and cell A6 is the active cell.

4. Type **Items Ordered** as the label in cell A6, and then press the **Tab** key. Cell B6 is the active cell. Now you will enter the COUNT function to determine the number of different items ordered.
5. In cell B6, type **=COUNT(** to begin the function.
6. With the insertion point still blinking in cell B6, select the range **G19:G23**. The range reference is entered as the argument for the COUNT function.
7. Type **)** to complete the function, and then press the **Enter** key. Cell B6 displays the value 5, indicating that five items were ordered by Leslie Ritter. Cell A7 is the active cell.
8. Type **Total Charge** as the label in cell A7, and then press the **Tab** key to make cell B7 the active cell.
9. Type **=** to start the formula, and then click cell **H28** to enter its cell reference in the formula in cell B7. The formula you created, =H28, tells Excel to display the contents of cell H28 in the current cell.
10. Press the **Enter** key to complete the formula. The total charge of $213.25 appears in cell B7. See Figure 1-29.

Figure 1-29 Customer order summary

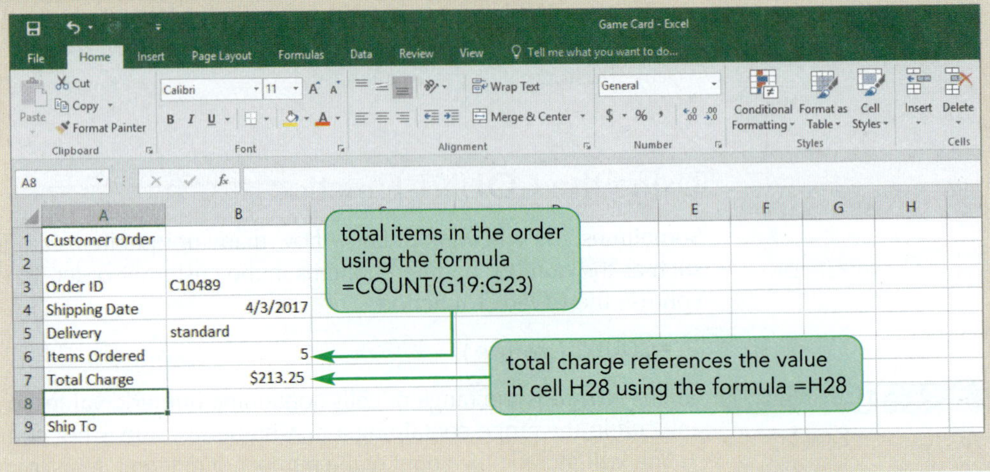

Inserting a Column or Row

You can insert a new column or row anywhere within a worksheet. When you insert a new column, the existing columns are shifted to the right, and the new column has the same width as the column directly to its left. When you insert a new row, the existing rows are shifted down, and the new row has the same height as the row above it. Because inserting a new row or column moves the location of the other cells in the worksheet, any cell references in a formula or function are updated to reflect the new layout.

REFERENCE

Inserting or Deleting a Column or Row

To insert a column or row:

- Select the column(s) or row(s) where you want to insert the new column(s) or row(s). Excel will insert the same number of columns or rows as you select to the left of the selected columns or above the selected rows.
- On the Home tab, in the Cells group, click the Insert button (or right-click a column or row heading or selected column and row headings, and then click Insert on the shortcut menu; or press the Ctrl+Shift+= keys).

To delete a column or row:

- Select the column(s) or row(s) you want to delete.
- On the Home tab, in the Cells group, click the Delete button (or right-click a column or row heading or selected column and row headings, and then click Delete on the shortcut menu; or press the Ctrl+- keys).

Peter informs you that the customer order report for Leslie Ritter is missing an item. You need to insert a new row directly above the entry for the Trivia Connection game in which you'll write the details of the missing item.

To insert a row for the missing order item:

1. Click the **row 21** heading to select the entire row.
2. On the Home tab, in the Cells group, click the **Insert** button (or press the **Ctrl+Shift+=** keys). A new row is inserted below row 20 and becomes the new row 21.
3. Enter **SU25** in cell A21, enter **Supplies** in cell B21, enter **Drebeck Brothers** in cell C21, enter **Miniatures Set (12)** in cell D21, leave cell E21 blank, enter **$23.55** in cell F21, and then enter **2** in cell G21.
4. Click cell **H20** to select the cell with the formula for calculating the item charge, and then press the **Ctrl+C** keys to copy the formula in that cell.
5. Click cell **H21** to select the cell where you want to insert the formula, and then press the **Ctrl+V** keys to paste the formula into the cell.
6. Click cell **H26**. See Figure 1-30.

TIP

You can insert multiple columns or rows by selecting that number of column or row headings, and then clicking the Insert button or pressing the Ctrl+Shift+= keys.

Figure 1-30 New row inserted into the worksheet

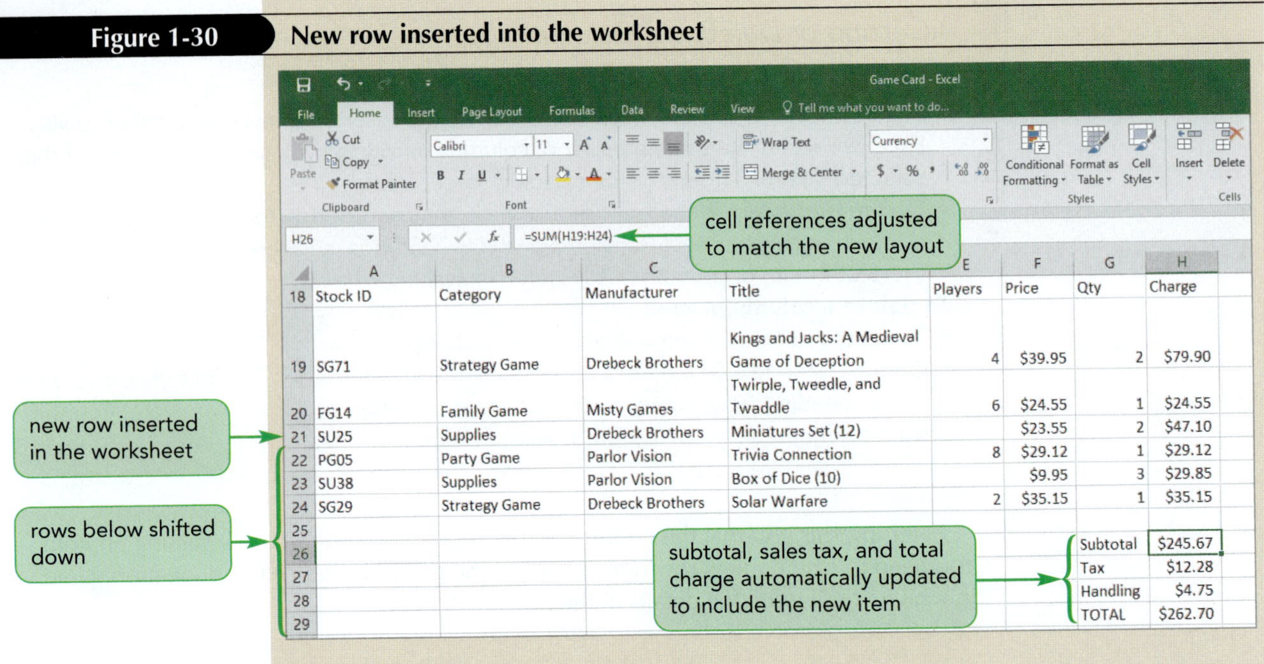

Notice that the formula in cell H26 is now =SUM(H19:H24). The range reference was updated to reflect the inserted row. Also, the tax amount increased to $12.28 based on the new subtotal value of $245.67, and the total charge increased to $262.70 because of the added item. Also, the result of the COUNT function in cell B6 increased to 6 to reflect the item added to the order.

Deleting a Row or Column

You can also delete rows or columns from a worksheet. **Deleting** removes the data from the row or column as well as the row or column itself. The rows below the deleted row shift up to fill the vacated space. Likewise, the columns to the right of the deleted column shift left to fill the vacated space. Also, all cell references in the worksheet are adjusted to reflect the change. You click the Delete button in the Cells group on the Home tab to delete selected rows or columns.

Deleting a column or row is not the same as clearing a column or row. **Clearing** removes the data from the selected row or column but leaves the blank row or column in the worksheet. You press the Delete key to clear the contents of the selected row or column, which leaves the worksheet structure unchanged.

Leslie Ritter did not order the box of dice created by Parlor Vision. Peter asks you to delete the row containing this item from the report.

To delete the row containing the box of dice from the order:

1. Click the **row 23** heading to select the entire row.
2. On the Home tab, in the Cells group, click the **Delete** button (or press the **Ctrl+-** keys). Row 23 is deleted, and the rows below it shift up to fill the space.

All of the cell references in the worksheet are again updated automatically to reflect the impact of deleting row 23. The subtotal value in cell H25 is now $215.82, which is the sum of the range H19:H23. The sales tax in cell H26 decreases to $10.79. The total cost of the order decreases to $231.36. Also, the result of the COUNT function in cell B6 decreases to 5 to reflect the item deleted from the order. As you can see, one of the great advantages of using Excel is that it modifies the formulas to reflect the additions and deletions you make to the worksheet.

Inserting and Deleting a Range

You can also insert or delete cell ranges within a worksheet. When you use the Insert button to insert a range of cells, the existing cells shift down when the selected range is wider than it is long, and they shift right when the selected range is longer than it is wide, as shown in Figure 1-31. When you use the Insert Cells command, you specify whether the existing cells shift right or down, or whether to insert an entire row or column into the new range.

Figure 1-31 Cells inserted into a worksheet

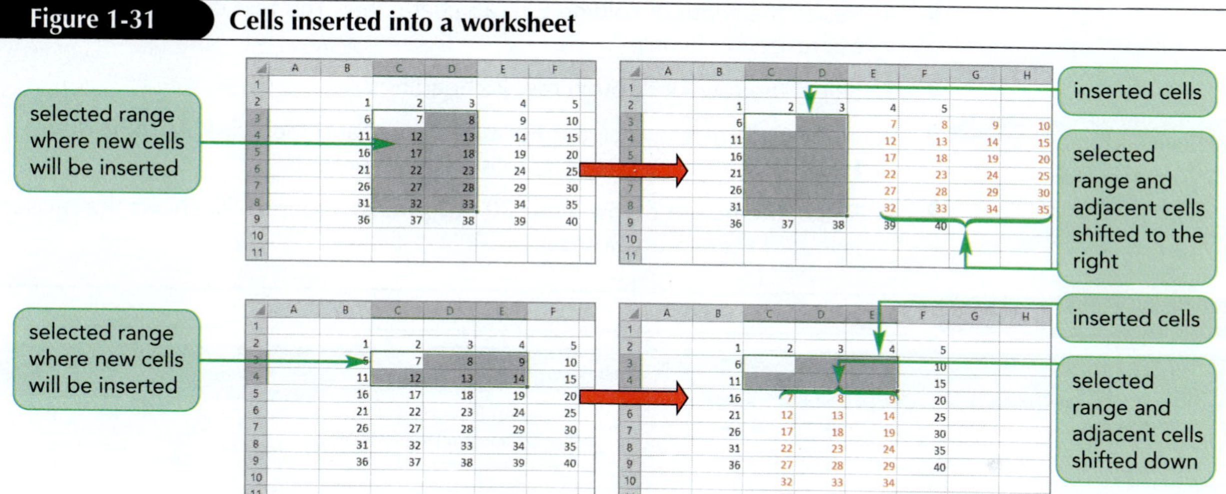

The process works in reverse when you delete a range. As with deleting a row or column, the cells adjacent to the deleted range either move up or left to fill in the space vacated by the deleted cells. The Delete Cells command lets you specify whether you want to shift the adjacent cells left or up or whether you want to delete the entire column or row.

When you insert or delete a range, cells that shift to a new location adopt the width of the columns they move into. As a result, you might need to resize columns and rows in the worksheet.

REFERENCE

Inserting or Deleting a Range

- Select a range that matches the range you want to insert or delete.
- On the Home tab, in the Cells group, click the Insert button or the Delete button.

or

- Select the range that matches the range you want to insert or delete.
- On the Home tab, in the Cells group, click the Insert button arrow and then click Insert Cells, or click the Delete button arrow and then click Delete Cells (or right-click the selected range, and then click Insert or Delete on the shortcut menu).
- Click the option button for the direction to shift the cells, columns, or rows.
- Click the OK button.

Peter wants you to insert a range into the worksheet for the ID that Game Card uses to identify the items it stocks in its store. You will insert these new cells into the range A17:A28, shifting the adjacent cells to the right.

To insert a range for the store IDs:

1. Select the range **A17:A28**.
2. On the Home tab, in the Cells group, click the **Insert button arrow**. A menu of insert options appears.
3. Click **Insert Cells**. The Insert dialog box opens.
4. Verify that the **Shift cells right** option button is selected.
5. Click the **OK** button. New cells are inserted into the selected range, and the adjacent cells move to the right. The cell contents do not fit well in the columns and rows they shifted into, so you will resize the columns and rows.
6. Resize the width of column E to **25** characters. The text is easier to read in the resized columns.
7. Select the row **19** through row **23** headings.
8. In the Cells group, click the **Format** button, and then click **AutoFit Row Height**. The selected rows autofit to their contents.
9. Resize the height of row 19 to **30 (40 pixels)**. Figure 1-32 shows the revised layout of the customer order.

TIP

You can also autofit by double-clicking the bottom border of row 23.

Figure 1-32 Range added to worksheet

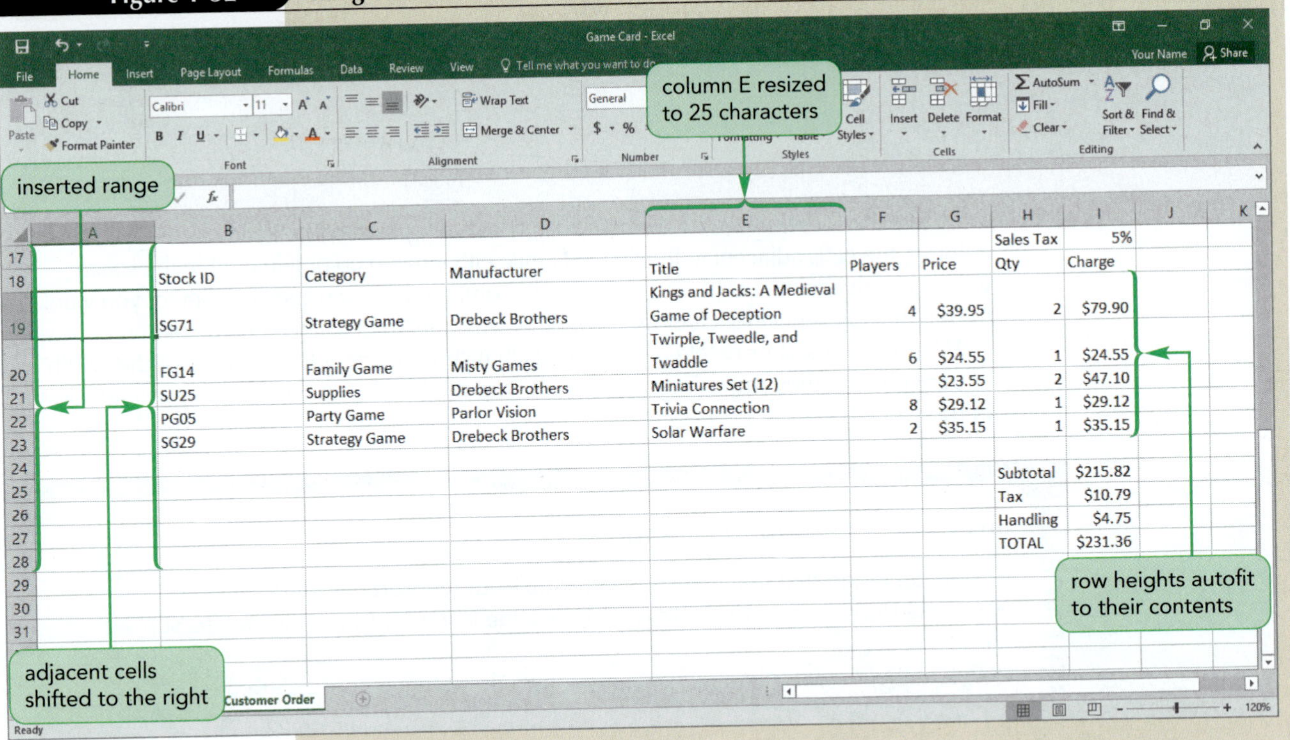

Notice that even though the customer orders will be entered only in the range A18:A23 you selected the range A17:A28 to retain the layout of the page design. Selecting the additional rows ensures that the sales tax and summary values still line up with the Qty and Charge columns. Whenever you insert a new range, be sure to consider its impact on the layout of the entire worksheet.

INSIGHT

Hiding and Unhiding Rows, Columns, and Worksheets

Workbooks can become long and complicated, filled with formulas and data that are important for performing calculations but are of little interest to readers. In those situations, you can simplify these workbooks for readers by hiding rows, columns, and even worksheets. Although the contents of hidden cells cannot be seen, the data in those cells is still available for use in formulas and functions throughout the workbook.

Hiding a row or column essentially decreases that row height or column width to 0 pixels. To a hide a row or column, select the row or column heading, click the Format button in the Cells group on the Home tab, point to Hide & Unhide on the menu that appears, and then click Hide Rows or Hide Columns. The border of the row or column heading is doubled to mark the location of hidden rows or columns.

A worksheet often is hidden when the entire worksheet contains data that is not of interest to the reader and is better summarized elsewhere in the document. To hide a worksheet, make that worksheet active, click the Format button in the Cells group on the Home tab, point to Hide & Unhide, and then click Hide Sheet.

Unhiding redisplays the hidden content in the workbook. To unhide a row or column, click in a cell below the hidden row or to the right of the hidden column, click the Format button, point to Hide & Unhide, and then click Unhide Rows or Unhide Columns. To unhide a worksheet, click the Format button, point to Hide & Unhide, and then click Unhide Sheet. The Unhide dialog box opens. Click the sheet you want to unhide, and then click the OK button. The hidden content is redisplayed in the workbook.

Although hiding data can make a worksheet and workbook easier to read, be sure never to hide information that is important to the reader.

Peter wants you to add the store ID used by Game Card to identify each item it sells. You will use Flash Fill to create these unique IDs.

Using Flash Fill

Flash Fill enters text based on patterns it finds in the data. As shown in Figure 1-33, Flash Fill generates customer names from the first and last names stored in the adjacent columns in the worksheet. To enter the rest of the names, you press the Enter key; to continue typing the names yourself, you press the Esc key.

Figure 1-33 **Text being entered with Flash Fill**

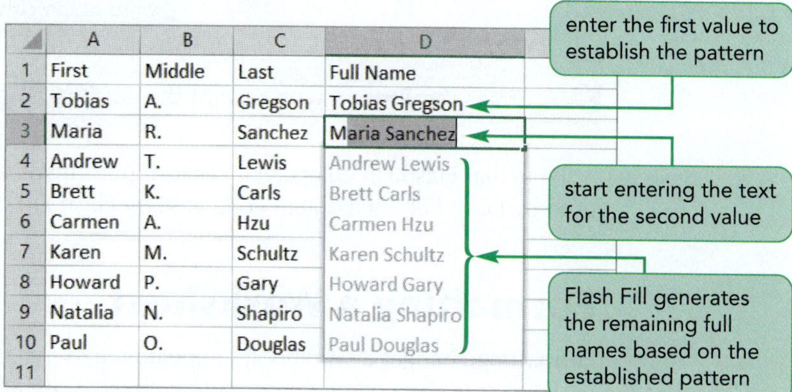

Flash Fill works best when the pattern is clearly recognized from the values in the data. Be sure to enter the data pattern in the column or row right next to the related data. The data used to generate the pattern must be in a rectangular grid and cannot have blank columns or rows.

The store IDs used by Game Card combines the Stock ID and the first name of the item. For example, the Kings and Jacks game has a Stock ID of SG71, so its Store ID is SG71-Kings. Rather than typing this for every item in the customer order, you'll use Flash Fill to complete the data entry.

To enter the Store IDs using Flash Fill:

1. Click cell **A18**, type **Store ID** as the label, and then press the **Enter** key. The label is entered in cell A18, and cell A19 is now the active cell.
2. Type **SG71-Kings** as the Store ID, and then press **Enter** to make cell A20 active.
3. Type **FG** in cell A20. As soon as you complete those two characters Flash Fill generates the remaining entries in the column based on the pattern you entered. See Figure 1-34.

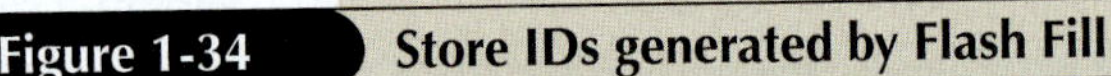

Figure 1-34 Store IDs generated by Flash Fill

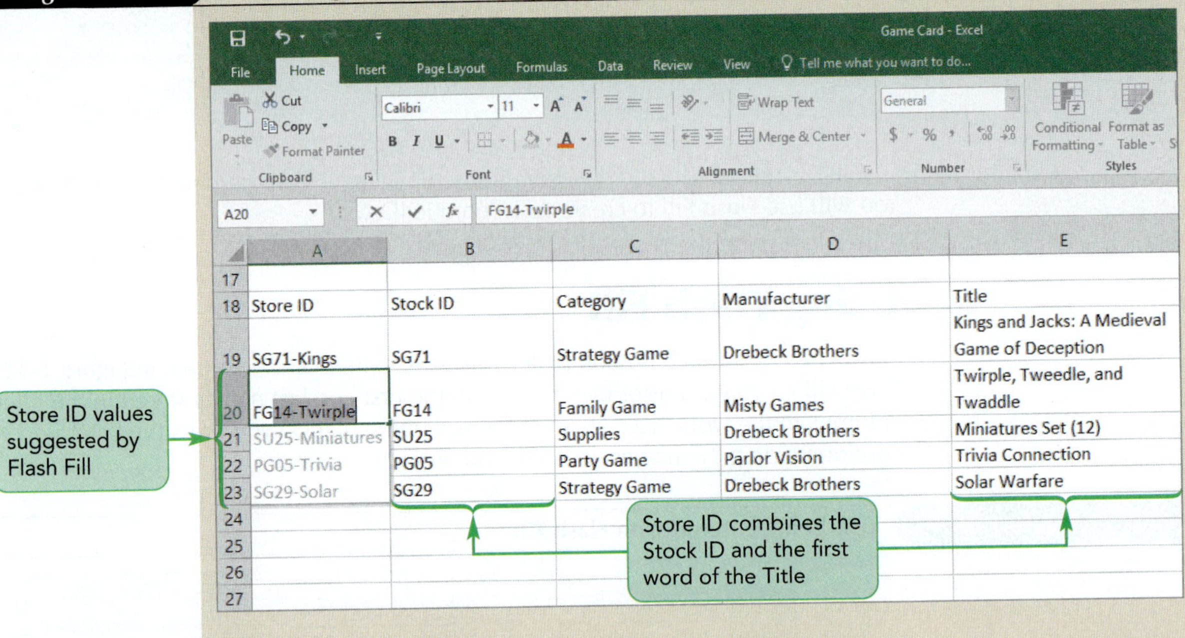

4. Press the **Enter** key to accept the suggested entries.

Note that Flash Fill enters text, not formulas. If you edit or replace an entry originally used by Flash Fill, the content generated by Flash Fill will not be updated.

Formatting a Worksheet

Formatting changes a workbook's appearance to make the content of a worksheet easier to read. Two common formatting changes are adding cell borders and changing the font size of text.

Adding Cell Borders

Sometimes you want to include lines along the edges of cells to enhance the readability of rows and columns of data. You can do this by adding a border to the left, top, right, or bottom edge of a cell or range. You can also specify the thickness of and the number of lines in the border. This is especially helpful when a worksheet is printed because the gridlines that surround the cells are not printed by default; they appear on the worksheet only as a guide.

Peter wants to add borders around the cells that contain content in the Customer Order worksheet to make the content easier to read.

To add borders around the worksheet cells:

1. Select the range **A3:B7**. You will add borders around all of the cells in the selected range.
2. On the Home tab, in the Font group, click the **Borders button arrow**, and then click **All Borders**. Borders are added around each cell in the range. The Borders button changes to reflect the last selected border option, which in this case is All Borders. The name of the selected border option appears in the button's ScreenTip.
3. Select the nonadjacent range **A9:B16,H17:I17**. You will add borders around each cell in the selected range.
4. In the Font group, click the **All Borders** button to add borders to all of the cells in the selected range.
5. Select the nonadjacent range **A18:I23,H25:I28**, and then click the **All Borders** button to add borders to all of the cells in the selected range.
6. Click cell **A28** to deselect the cells. Figure 1-35 shows the borders added to the worksheet cells.

Figure 1-35 Borders added to cells

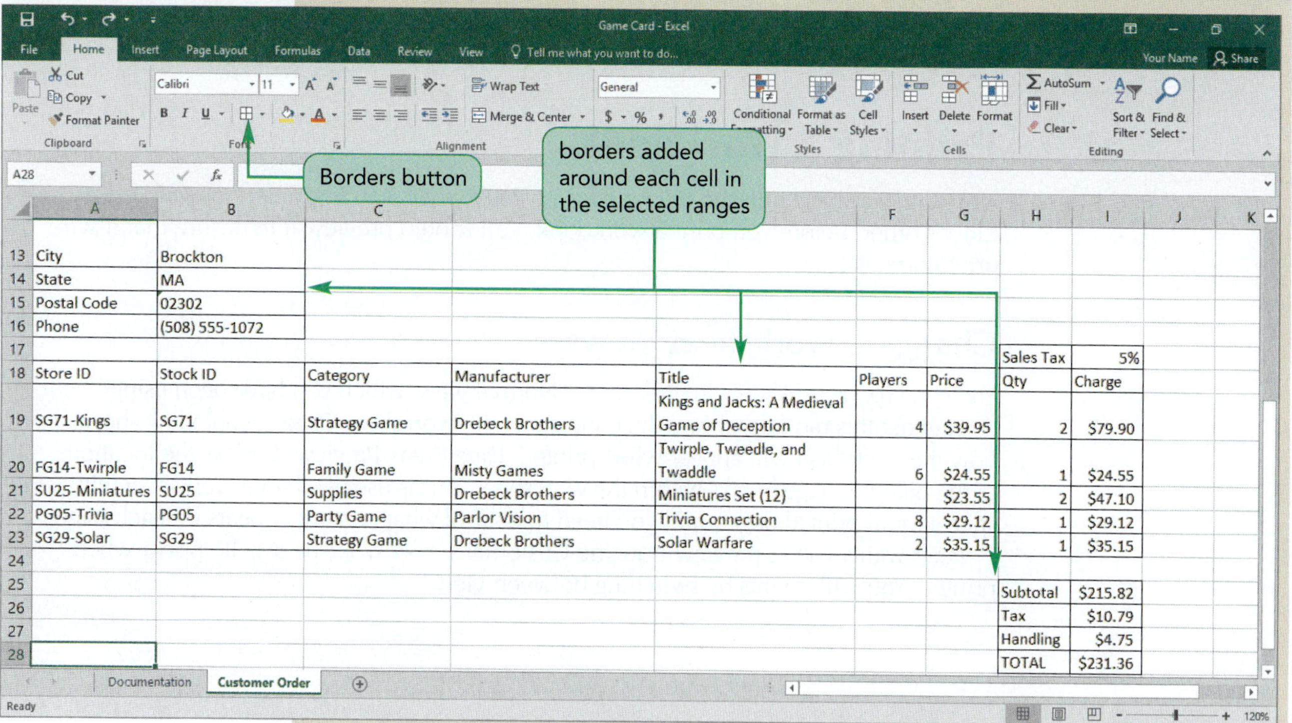

Changing the Font Size

Changing the size of text in a sheet provides a way to identify different parts of a worksheet, such as distinguishing a title or section heading from data. The size of the text is referred to as the font size and is measured in points. The default font size for worksheets is 11 points, but it can be made larger or smaller as needed. You can resize text in selected cells using the Font Size button in the Font group on the Home tab. You can also use the Increase Font Size and Decrease Font Size buttons to resize cell content to the next higher or lower standard font size.

Peter wants you to increase the size of the worksheet title to 26 points to make it more prominent.

To change the font size of the worksheet title:

1. Click cell **A1** to select the cell containing the worksheet title.
2. On the Home tab, in the Font group, click the **Font Size button arrow** 11 to display a list of font sizes, and then click **28**. The worksheet title changes to 28 points. See Figure 1-36.

Figure 1-36 Font size of the cell increased

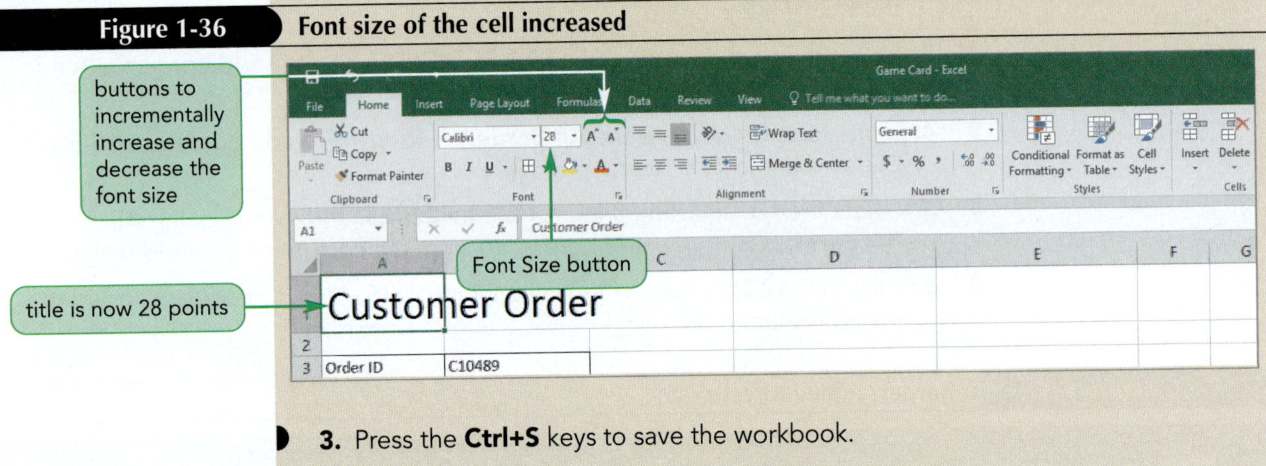

3. Press the **Ctrl+S** keys to save the workbook.

Printing a Workbook

Now that you have finished the workbook, Peter wants you to print a copy of Leslie Ritter's order. Before you print a workbook, you should preview it to ensure that it will print correctly.

Changing Worksheet Views

You can view a worksheet in three ways. Normal view, which you have been using throughout this module, shows the contents of the worksheet. Page Layout view shows how the worksheet will appear when printed. Page Break Preview displays the location of the different page breaks within the worksheet. This is useful when a worksheet will span several printed pages, and you need to control what content appears on each page.

Peter wants you to preview how the Customer Order worksheet will appear when printed. You will do this by switching between views.

To switch the Customer Order worksheet to different views:

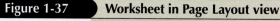

1. Click the **Page Layout** button on the status bar. The page layout of the worksheet appears in the workbook window.
2. On the Zoom slider, click the **Zoom Out** button until the percentage is **50%**. The reduced magnification makes it clear that the worksheet will spread over two pages when printed. See Figure 1-37.

Figure 1-37 Worksheet in Page Layout view

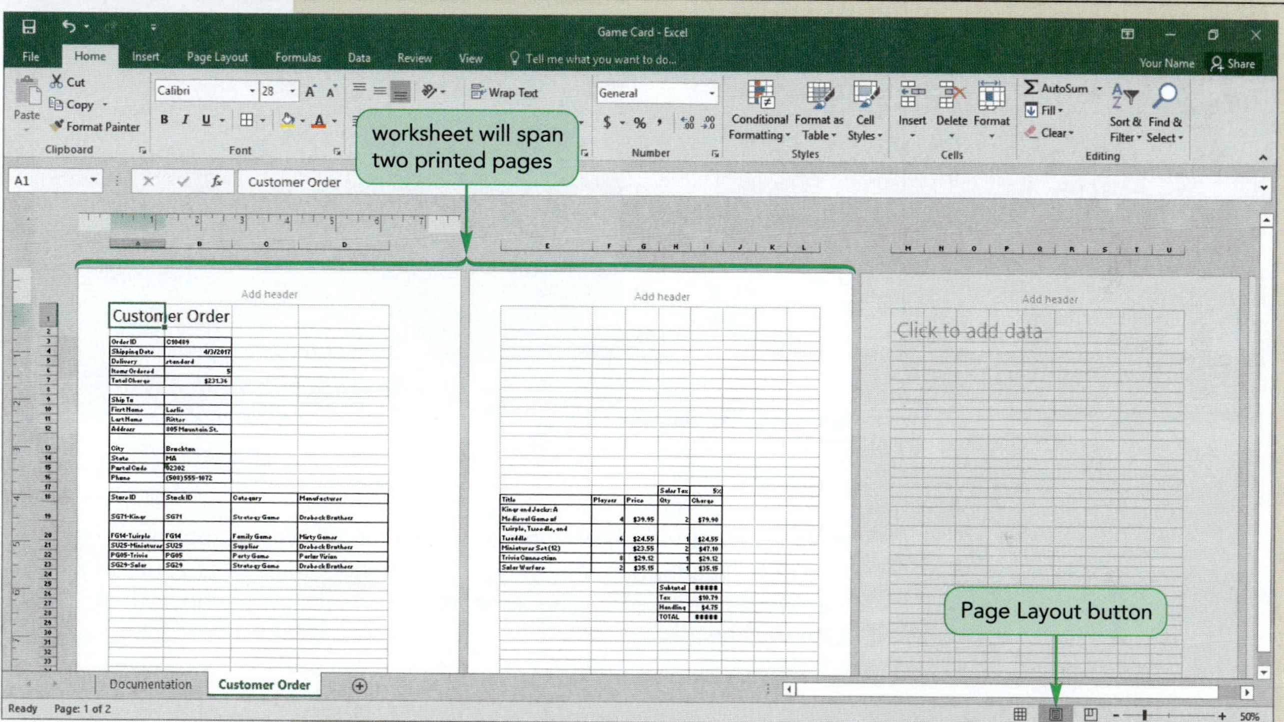

> **TIP**
> You can relocate a page break by dragging the dotted blue border in the Page Break Preview window.

3. Click the **Page Break Preview** button on the status bar. The view switches to Page Break Preview, which shows only those parts of the current worksheet that will print. A dotted blue border separates one page from another.
4. Zoom the worksheet to **70%** so that you can more easily read the contents of the worksheet. See Figure 1-38.

Figure 1-38 Worksheet in Page Break Preview

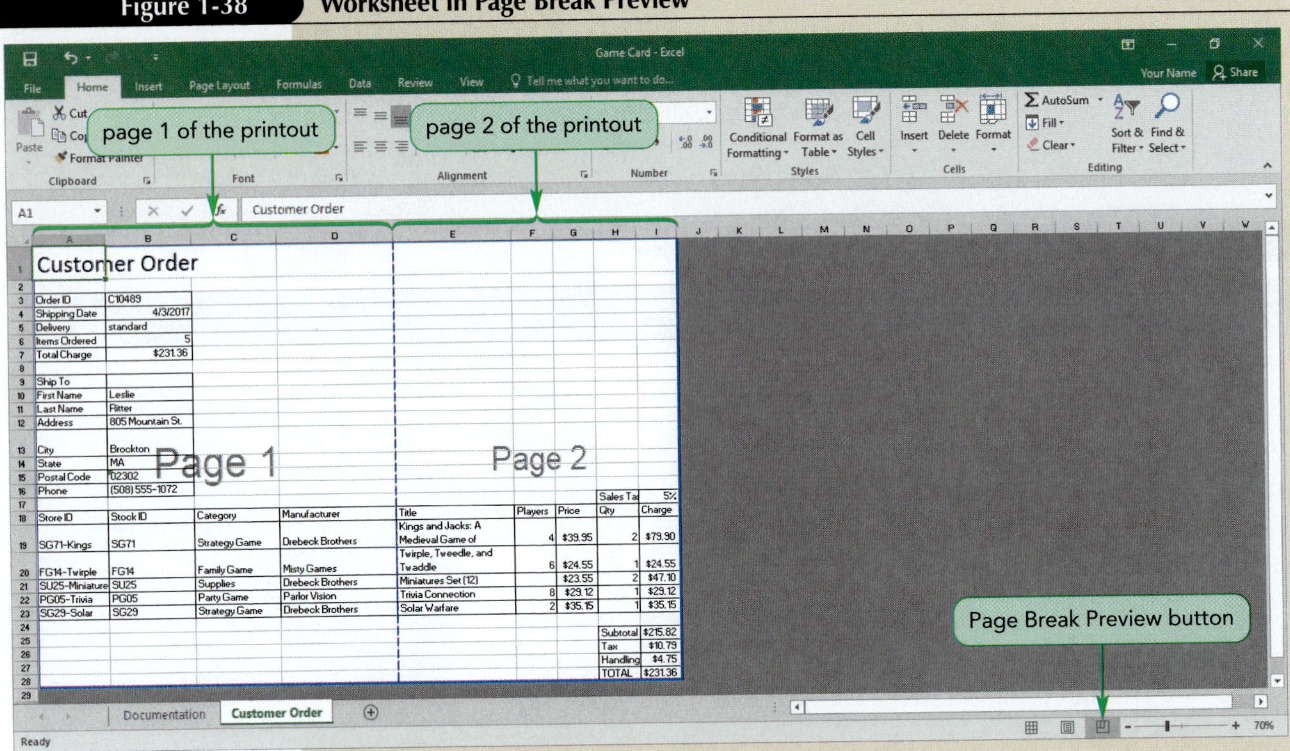

5. Click the **Normal** button on the status bar. The worksheet returns to Normal view. Notice that after viewing the worksheet in Page Layout or Page Break Preview, a dotted black line appears in Normal view to show where the page breaks occurs.

Changing the Page Orientation

Page orientation specifies in which direction content is printed on the page. In **portrait orientation**, the page is taller than it is wide. In **landscape orientation**, the page is wider than it is tall. By default, Excel displays pages in portrait orientation. Changing the page orientation affects only the active sheet or sheets.

As you saw in Page Layout view and Page Break Preview, the Customer Order worksheet will print on two pages—columns A through D will print on the first page, and columns E through I will print on the second page, although the columns that print on each page may differ slightly depending on the printer. Peter wants the entire worksheet to print on a single page, so you'll change the page orientation from portrait to landscape.

To change the page orientation of the worksheet:

1. On the ribbon, click the **Page Layout** tab. The tab includes options for changing how the worksheet is arranged.
2. In the Page Setup group, click the **Orientation** button, and then click **Landscape**. The worksheet switches to landscape orientation.
3. Click the **Page Layout** button on the status bar to switch to Page Layout view. The worksheet will still print on two pages.

Setting the Scaling Options

You can force the printout to a single page by **scaling** the printed output. There are several options for scaling your printout. You can scale the width or the height of the printout so that all of the columns or all of the rows fit on a single page. You can also scale the printout to fit the entire worksheet (both columns and rows) on a single page. If the worksheet is too large to fit on one page, you can scale the print to fit on the number of pages you select. You can also scale the worksheet to a percentage of its size. For example, scaling a worksheet to 50% reduces the size of the sheet by half when it is sent to the printer. When scaling a printout, make sure that the worksheet is still readable after it is resized. Scaling affects only the active worksheet, so you can scale each worksheet to best fit its contents.

Peter asks you to scale the printout so that all of the Customer Order worksheet fits on one page in landscape orientation.

To scale the printout of the Customer Order worksheet:

1. On the Page Layout tab, in the Scale to Fit group, click the **Width** arrow, and then click **1 page** on the menu that appears. All of the columns in the worksheet now fit on one page.

   If more rows are added to the worksheet, Peter wants to ensure that they still fit within a single sheet.

2. In the Scale to Fit group, click the **Height** arrow, and then click **1 page**. All of the rows in the worksheet now fit on one page. See Figure 1-39.

Figure 1-39 Printout scaled to fit on one page

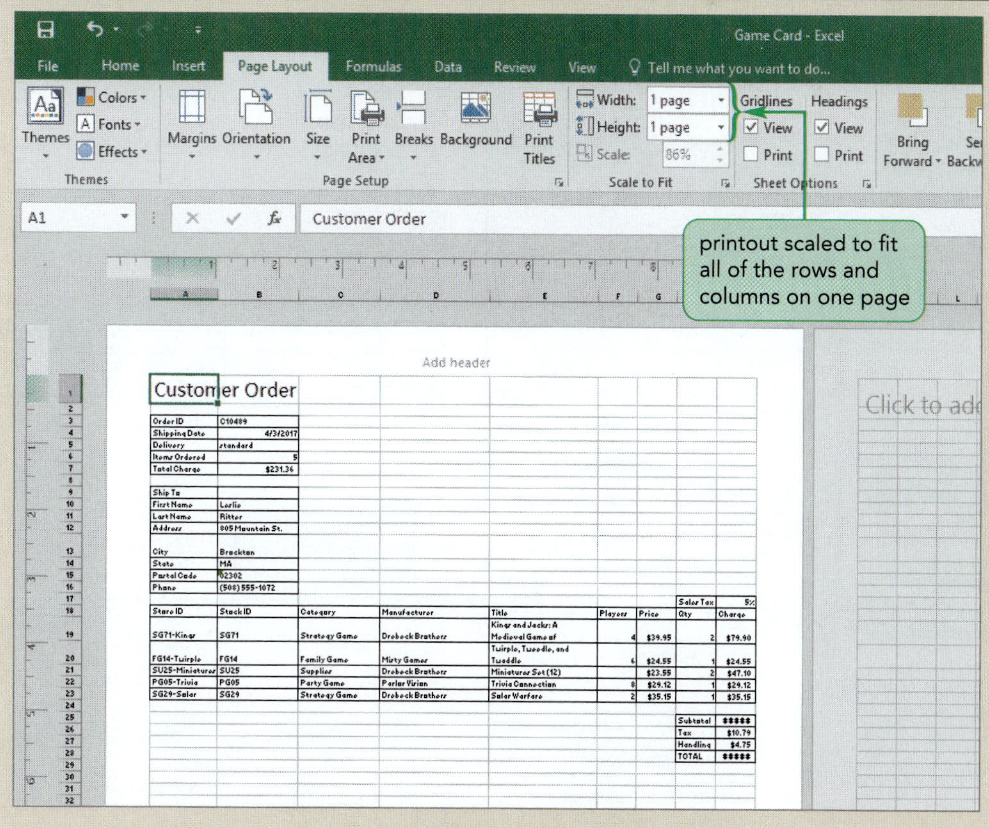

Setting the Print Options

TIP

To print the gridlines or the column and row headings, click the corresponding Print check box in the Sheet Options group on the Page Layout tab.

You can print the contents of a workbook by using the Print screen in Backstage view. The Print screen provides options for choosing where to print, what to print, and how to print. For example, you can specify the number of copies to print, which printer to use, and what to print. You can choose to print only the selected cells, only the active sheets, or all of the worksheets in the workbook that contain data. The printout will include only the data in the worksheet. The other elements in the worksheet, such as the row and column headings and the gridlines around the worksheet cells, will not print by default. The preview shows you exactly how the printed pages will look with the current settings. You should always preview before printing to ensure that the printout looks exactly as you intended and avoid unnecessary reprinting.

Peter asks you to preview and print the customer order workbook now.

Note: Check with your instructor first to make sure you should complete the steps for printing the workbook.

To preview and print the workbook:

1. On the ribbon, click the **File** tab to display Backstage view.
2. Click **Print** in the navigation bar. The Print screen appears with the print options and a preview of the Customer Order worksheet printout. See Figure 1-40.

Figure 1-40 **Print screen in Backstage view**

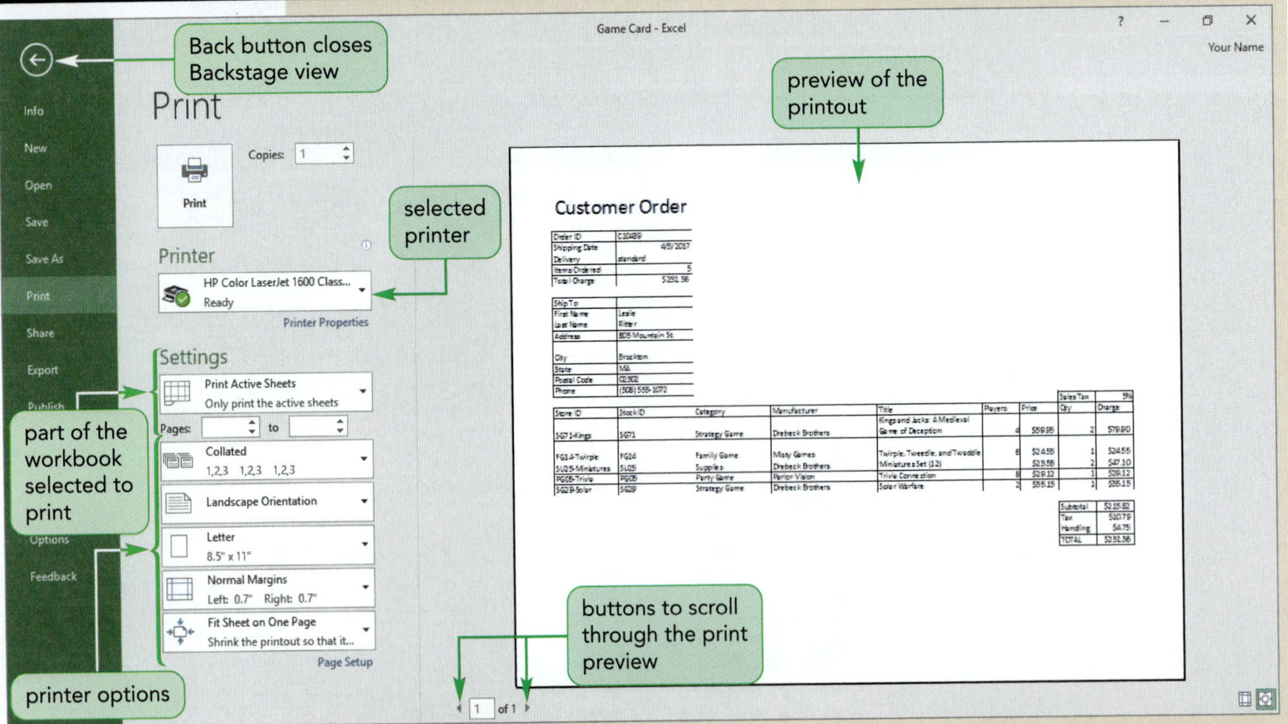

3. Click the **Printer** button, and then click the **printer** to which you want to print, if it is not already selected. By default, Excel will print only the active sheet.
4. In the Settings options, click the top button, and then click **Print Entire Workbook** to print all of the sheets in the workbook—in this case, both the Documentation and the Customer Order worksheets. The preview shows the first sheet in the workbook—the Documentation worksheet. Note that this sheet is still in the default portrait orientation.
5. Below the preview, click the **Next Page** button to view the Customer Order worksheet. As you can see, the Customer Order worksheet will print on a single page in landscape orientation.
6. If you are instructed to print, click the **Print** button to send the contents of the workbook to the specified printer. If you are not instructed to print, click the **Back** button in the navigation bar to exit Backstage view.

Viewing Worksheet Formulas

Most of the time, you will be interested in only the final results of a worksheet, not the formulas used to calculate those results. However, in some cases, you might want to view the formulas used to develop the workbook. This is particularly useful when you encounter unexpected results and you want to examine the underlying formulas, or you want to discuss your formulas with a colleague. You can display the formulas instead of the resulting values in cells.

If you print the worksheet while the formulas are displayed, the printout shows the formulas instead of the values. To make the printout easier to read, you should print the worksheet gridlines as well as the row and column headings so that cell references in the formulas are easy to find in the printed version of the worksheet.

You will look at the Customer Order worksheet with the formulas displayed.

TIP

You can also display formulas in a worksheet by clicking the Show Formulas button in the Formula Auditing group on the Formulas tab.

To display the cell formulas:

1. Make sure the Customer Order worksheet is in Page Layout view.
2. Press the **Ctrl+`** keys (the grave accent symbol ` is usually located above the Tab key). The worksheet changes to display all of the formulas instead of the resulting values. Notice that the columns widen to display all of the formula text in the cells.
3. Look at the entry in cell B4. The underlying numeric value of the shipping date (42828) is displayed instead of the formatted date value (4/3/2017). See Figure 1-41.

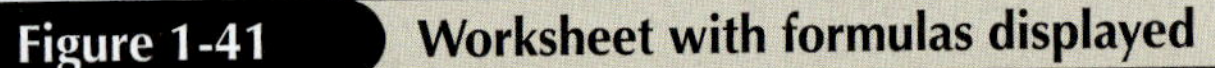

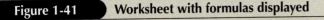

Figure 1-41 Worksheet with formulas displayed

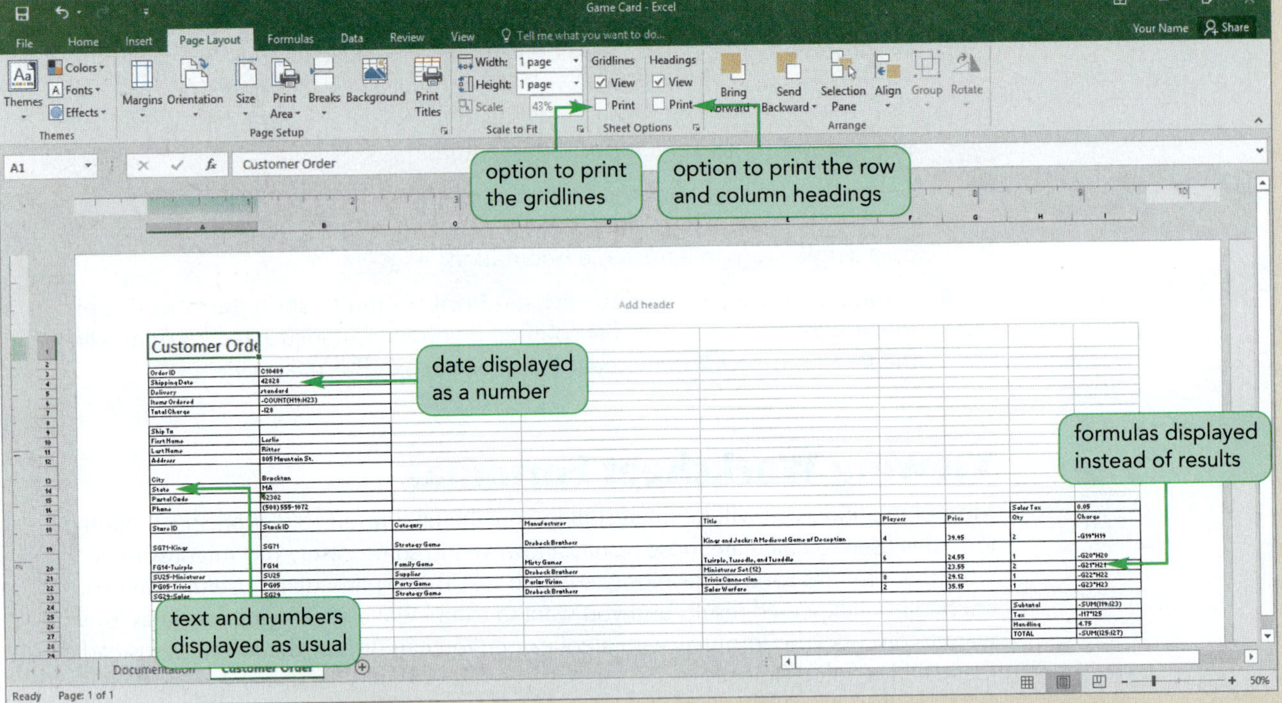

It's good practice to hide the formulas when you are done reviewing them.

4. Press the **Ctrl+`** keys to hide the formulas and display the resulting values.
5. Click the **Normal** button on the status bar to return the workbook to Normal view.

Saving a Workbook with a New Filename

Whenever you click the Save button on the Quick Access Toolbar or press the Ctrl+S keys, the workbook file is updated to reflect the latest content. If you want to save a copy of the workbook with a new filename or to a different location, you need to use the Save As command. When you save a workbook with a new filename or to a different location, the previous version of the workbook remains stored as well.

You have completed the customer order workbook for Game Card. Peter wants to use the workbook as a model for other customer order reports. You will save the workbook with a new filename to avoid overwriting the Leslie Ritter order. Then you'll clear the information related to that order, leaving the formulas intact. This new, revised workbook will then be ready for the next customer order.

To save the workbook with a new filename:

1. Press the **Ctrl+S** keys to save the workbook. This ensures that the final copy of the workbook contains the formatted version of Leslie Ritter's order.
2. On the ribbon, click the **File** tab to display Backstage view, and then click **Save As** on the navigation bar. The Save As screen is displayed.

3. Click the **Browse** button. The Save As dialog box opens so you can save the workbook with a new filename or to a new location.
4. Navigate to the location specified by your instructor.
5. In the File name box, type **Game Card Order** as the new filename.
6. Click the **Save** button. The workbook is saved with the new filename, and you are returned to the workbook window.
7. Select the range **B3:B5**, right-click the selected range to open the shortcut menu, and then click **Clear Contents** to clear the contents of the order ID, shipping date, and delivery cells.
8. Select the nonadjacent range **B10:B16,A19:H23**, and then press the **Delete** key to clear the contact information for Leslie Ritter and the list of items she ordered.
9. Select cell **I27**, and then clear the handling fee.
10. Click cell **A3** to make that cell the active cell the next time this workbook is opened.
11. Press the **Ctrl+S** keys to save the workbook.
12. Click the **Close** button on the title bar (or press the **Ctrl+W** keys). The workbook closes, and the Excel program closes.

TIP

Save the workbook with the new name before making changes to avoid inadvertently saving your edits to the wrong file.

Peter is pleased with the workbook you created. With the calculations already in place in the new workbook, he will be able to quickly enter new customer orders and see the calculated charges without having to recreate the worksheet.

REVIEW

Session 1.2 Quick Check

1. What formula would you enter to add the values in cells C1, C2, and C3? What function would you enter to achieve the same result?
2. What formula would you enter to count how many numeric values are in the range D21:D72?
3. If you insert cells into the range C1:D10, shifting the cells to the right, what is the new location of the data that was previously in cell F4?
4. Cell E11 contains the formula =SUM(D1:D20). How does this formula change if a new row is inserted above row 5?
5. Describe four ways of viewing the content of a workbook in Excel.
6. How are page breaks indicated in Page Break Preview?
7. What orientation would you use to make the printed page wider than it is tall?
8. How do you display the formulas used in a worksheet instead of the formula results?

PRACTICE

Review Assignments

There are no Data Files needed for the Review Assignment.

Game Card also buys and resells used games and gaming supplies. Peter wants to use Excel to record recent used purchases made by the store. The workbook should list every item the company has ordered, provide information about the item, and calculate the total order cost. Complete the following:

1. Create a new, blank workbook, and then save the workbook as **Game List** in the location specified by your instructor.
2. Rename the Sheet1 worksheet as **Documentation**, and then enter the data shown in Figure 1-42 in the specified cells.

Figure 1-42 Documentation sheet data

Cell	Text
A1	Game Card
A3	Author
A4	Date
A5	Purpose
B3	*your name*
B4	*current date*
B5	To record game acquisitions for Game Card

3. Set the font size of the title text in cell A1 to **28** points.
4. Add a new worksheet after the Documentation sheet, and then rename the sheet as **Game Purchases**.
5. In cell A1, enter the text **Game Purchases**. Set the font size of this text to **28** points.
6. In cell A3, enter the text **Date** as the label. In cell B3, enter the date **4/3/2017**.
7. In the range A5:F10, enter the data shown in Figure 1-43.

Figure 1-43 Game list

Purchase Number	Category	Manufacturer	Title	Players	Cost
83	Strategy Game	Drebeck Brothers	Secrets of Flight: Building an Airforce	6	$29.54
84	Family Game	Parlor Vision	Brain Busters and Logic Gaming	8	$14.21
85	Strategy Game	Aspect Gaming	Inspection Deduction	3	$18.91
86	Party Game	Miller Games	Bids and Buys	8	$10.81
87	Family Game	Aspect Gaming	Buzz Up	4	$21.43

8. Insert cells into the range A5:A10, shifting the other cells to the right.
9. In cell A5, enter **Stock ID** as the label. In cell A6, enter **SG83** as the first Stock ID, and then type **FG** in cell A7, allowing Flash Fill to enter the remaining Stock IDs.
10. Set the width of column A to **12** characters, columns B through D to **18** characters, and column E to **25** characters.
11. Wrap text in the range E6:E10 so that the longer game titles appear on multiple lines within the cells.

12. Autofit the heights of rows 5 through 10.
13. Move the game list in the range A5:G10 to the range A8:G13.
14. In cell F15, enter **TOTAL** as the label. In cell G15, enter a formula with the SUM function to calculate the sum of the costs in the range G9:G13.
15. In cell A4, enter **Total Items** as the label. In cell B4, enter a formula with the COUNT function to count the number of numeric values in the range G9:G13.
16. In cell A5, enter **Total Cost**. In cell B5, enter a formula to display the value from cell G15.
17. In cell A6, enter **Average Cost** as the label. In cell B6, enter a formula that divides the total cost of the purchased games (listed in cell B5) by the number of games purchased (listed in cell B4).
18. Add borders around each cell in the nonadjacent range A3:B6,A8:G13,F15:G15.
19. For the Game Purchases worksheet, change the page orientation to landscape and scale the worksheet to print on a single page for both the width and the height. If you are instructed to print, print the entire workbook.
20. Display the formulas in the Game Purchases worksheet. If you are instructed to print, print the entire worksheet.
21. Save and close the workbook.

APPLY

Case Problem 1

Data File needed for this Case Problem: Donation.xlsx

Henderson Pediatric Care Center Kari Essen is a fundraising coordinator for the Pediatric Care Center located in Henderson, West Virginia. Kari is working on a report detailing recent donations to the center and wants you to enter this data into an Excel workbook. Complete the following:

1. Open the **Donation** workbook located in the Excel1 > Case1 folder included with your Data Files. Save the workbook as **Donation List** in the location specified by your instructor.
2. In the Documentation sheet, enter your name in cell B3 and the date in cell B4.
3. Increase the font size of the text in cell A1 to 28 points.
4. Add a new sheet to the end of the workbook, and rename it as **Donor List**.
5. In cell A1 of the Donor List worksheet, enter **Donor List** as the title, and then set the font size to 28 points.
6. In the range A6:H13, enter the donor information shown in Figure 1-44. Enter the ZIP code data as text rather than as numbers.

Figure 1-44 **Donation list**

Last Name	First Name	Street	City	State	ZIP	Phone	Donation
Robert	Richards	389 Felton Avenue	Miami	FL	33127	(305) 555-5685	$150
Barbara	Hopkins	612 Landers Street	Caledonia	IL	61011	(815) 555-5865	$75
Daniel	Vaughn	45 Lyman Street	Statesboro	GA	30461	(912) 555-8564	$50
Parker	Penner	209 South Street	San Francisco	CA	94118	(415) 555-7298	$250
Kenneth	More	148 7th Street	Newberry	IN	47449	(812) 555-8001	$325
Robert	Simmons	780 10th Street	Houston	TX	77035	(713) 555-5266	$75
Donna	Futrell	834 Kimberly Lane	Ropesville	TX	79358	(806) 555-6186	$50

7. Set the width of columns A through D to 25 characters. Set the width of column G to 15 characters.
8. In cell A2, enter the text **Total Donors**. In cell A3, enter the text **Total Donations**. In cell A4, enter the text **Average Donation**.

9. In cell B2, enter a formula that counts how many numeric values are in the range H7:H13.
10. In cell B3, enter a formula that calculates the sum of the donations in the range H7:H13.
11. In cell B4, enter a formula that calculates the average donation by dividing the value in cell B3 by the value in cell B2.
12. Add borders around the nonadjacent range A2:B4,A6:H13.
13. Set the page orientation of the Donor List to landscape.
14. Scale the worksheet to print on a single page for both the width and the height. If you are instructed to print the worksheet, print the Donor List sheet.
15. Display the formulas in the Donor List worksheet. If you are instructed to print, print the worksheet.
16. Save and close the workbook.

CREATE

Case Problem 2

Data File needed for this Case Problem: Balance.xlsx

Scott Kahne Tool & Die Cheryl Hippe is a financial officer at Scott Kahne Tool & Die, a manufacturing company located in Mankato, Minnesota. Every month the company publishes a balance sheet, a report that details the company's assets and liabilities. Cheryl asked you to create the workbook with the text and formulas for this report. Complete the following:

1. Open the **Balance** workbook located in the Excel1 > Case2 folder included with your Data Files. Save the workbook as **Balance Sheet** in the location specified by your instructor.
2. In the Documentation sheet, enter your name in cell B3 and the date in cell B4.
3. Go to the Balance Sheet worksheet. Set the font size of the title in cell A1 to 28 points.
4. In cell A2, enter the text **Statement for March 2017**.
5. Set the width of columns A and E to 30 characters. Set the width of columns B, C, F, and G to 12 characters. Set the width of column D to 4 characters. (*Hint:* Hold down the Ctrl key as you click the column headings to select both adjacent and nonadjacent columns.)
6. Set the font size of the text in cells A4, C4, E4, and G4 to 18 points.
7. Set the font size of the text in cells A5, E5, A11, E11, A14, E15, A19, E20, and A24 to 14 points.
8. Enter the values shown in Figure 1-45 in the specified cells.

Figure 1-45 Assets and liabilities

Current Assets	Cell	Value
Cash	B6	$123,000
Accounts Receivable	B7	$75,000
Inventories	B8	$58,000
Prepaid Insurance	B9	$15,000
Long-Term Investments	**Cell**	**Value**
Available Securities	B12	$29,000
Tangible Assets	**Cell**	**Value**
Land	B15	$49,000
Building and Equipment	B16	$188,000
Less Accumulated Depreciation	B17	-$48,000
Intangible Assets	**Cell**	**Value**
Goodwill	B20	$148,000
Other Assets	B22	$14,000
Current Liabilities	**Cell**	**Value**
Accounts Payable	F6	$62,000
Salaries	F7	$14,000
Interest	F8	$12,000
Notes Payable	F9	$38,000
Long-Term Liabilities	**Cell**	**Value**
Long-Term Notes Payable	F12	$151,000
Mortgage	F13	$103,000
Stockholders' Equity	**Cell**	**Value**
Capital Stock	F16	$178,000
Retained Earnings	F17	$98,000
Comprehensive Income/Loss	F18	-$5,000

9. In cell C9, enter a formula to calculate the sum of the Current Assets in the range B6:B9.
10. In cell C12, enter a formula to display the value of B12.
11. In cell C17, enter a formula to calculate the sum of the Tangible Assets in the range B15:B17.
12. In cells C20 and C22, enter formulas to display the values of cells B20 and B22, respectively.
13. In cell C24, enter a formula to calculate the total assets in the balance sheet by adding cells C9, C12, C17, C20, and C22. Set the font size of the cell to 14 points.
14. In cell G9, enter a formula to calculate the sum of the Current Liabilities in the range F6:F9.
15. In cell G13, enter a formula to calculate the sum of the Long-Term Liabilities in the range F12:F13.
16. In cell G18, enter a formula to calculate the sum of the Stockholders' Equity in the range F16:F18.
17. In cell G20, calculate the Total Liabilities and Equity for the company by adding the values of cells G9, G13, and G18. Set the font size of the cell to 14 points.
18. Check your calculations. In a balance sheet the total assets (cell C24) should equal the total liabilities and equity (cell G20).
19. Set the page layout orientation to landscape and the Balance Sheet worksheet to print to one page for both the width and height.
20. Preview the worksheet on the Print screen in Backstage view, and then save and close the workbook.

CHALLENGE

Case Problem 3

Data File needed for this Case Problem: FTP.xslx

Succeed Gym Allison Palmer is the owner of Succeed Gym, an athletic club in Austin, Texas, that specializes in coaching men and women aspiring to participate in triathlons, marathons, and other endurance sports. During the winter, Allison runs an indoor cycling class in which she tracks the progress of each student's fitness. One measure of fitness is FTP (Functional Threshold Power). Allison has recorded FTP levels from her students over five races and wants you to use the functions described in Figure 1-46 to analyze this data so that she can track the progress of her class and of individual students.

Figure 1-46 Excel functions

Function	Description
`=AVERAGE(`*`range`*`)`	Calculates the average of the values from the specified *range*
`=MEDIAN(`*`range`*`)`	Calculates the median or midpoint of the values from the specified *range*
`=MIN(`*`range`*`)`	Calculates the minimum of the values from the specified *range*
`=MAX(`*`range`*`)`	Calculates the maximum of the values from the specified *range*

Complete the following:

1. Open the **FTP** workbook located the Excel1 > Case3 folder included with your Data Files. Save the workbook as **FTP Report** in the location specified by your instructor.
2. In the Documentation sheet, enter your name in cell B3 and the date in cell B4.
3. Go to the Race Results worksheet. Change the font size of the title in cell A1 to 28 points.
4. Set the width of column A and B to 15 characters. Set the width of column I to 2 characters.
5. In the range J4:M4, enter the labels **Median**, **Average**, **Min**, and **Max**.

Explore 6. In cell J5, use the MEDIAN function to calculate the median (midpoint) of the FTP values of races 1 through 5 for Diana Bartlett in the range D5:H5. Copy the formula in cell J5 to the range J6:J28 to calculate the median FTP values for the other riders.

Explore 7. In cell K5, use the AVERAGE function to calculate the average the FTP value for races 1 through 5 for Diana Bartlett. Copy the formula to calculate the averages for the other riders.

Explore 8. In cell L5, use the MIN function to return the minimum FTP value for Diana Bartlett. Copy the formula to calculate the minimums for the other riders.

Explore 9. In cell M5, use the MAX function to return the maximum FTP value for Diana Bartlett. Copy the formula to calculate the maximums for the other riders.

10. In the range C30:C33, enter the labels **Median**, **Average**, **Min**, and **Max** to record summary information for each of the five races.
11. In cell D30, use the MEDIAN function to calculate the median FTP value from the range D5:D28. Copy the formula to the range E30:H30 to determine the median values for the other four races.
12. In the range D31:H31, use the AVERAGE function to calculate the average FTP value for each race.
13. In the range D32:H32, use the MIN function to calculate the minimum value for each race.
14. In the range D33:H33, use the MAX function to calculate the maximum FTP value for each race.
15. Move the range A4:M33 to the range A10:M39 to create space for additional summary calculations at the top of the worksheet.

16. In the range A3:A7, enter the labels **Class Size**, **Class Average**, **Class Median**, **Class Minimum**, and **Class Maximum**.

Explore 17. In cell B3, use the COUNTA function to count the number of entries in the range A11:A34.

18. In cell B4, use the AVERAGE function to calculate the average of all FTP values in the range D11:H34.
19. In cell B5, use the MEDIAN function to calculate the median of all FTP values in the range D11:H34.
20. In cell B6, use the MIN function to calculate the minimum FTP value in the range D11:H34.
21. In cell B7, use the MAX function to calculate the maximum FTP value in the range D11:H34.
22. Set the page layout orientation for the Race Results worksheet to portrait and scale the worksheet so that its width and height fit on one page.
23. View the worksheet in Page Layout view, return to Normal view, and then save and close the workbook.

TROUBLESHOOT

Case Problem 4

Data File needed for this Case Problem: Service.xlsx

Welch Home Appliance Repair Stefan Welch is the owner of Welch Home Appliance Repair in Trenton, New Jersey. Stefan wants to use Excel to record data from his service calls to calculate the total charge on each service call and the total charges from all service calls within a given period. Unfortunately, the workbook he has created contains several errors. He has asked you to fix the errors and complete the workbook. Complete the following:

1. Open the **Service** workbook located in the Excel1 > Case4 folder included with your Data Files. Save the workbook as **Service Calls** in the location specified by your instructor.
2. In the Documentation sheet, enter your name in cell B3 and the date in cell B4.
3. Go to the Call Sheet worksheet. Insert cells in the range A7:A27, shifting the other cells to the right.
4. In cell A7, enter **Cust ID** as the label. In cell A8, enter **Jensen-5864** (the customer's last name and last four digits on the phone number) as the customer ID for Patricia Jensen. Use Flash Fill to enter in the remaining customer IDs in the column.
5. Resize the columns of the Call Sheet worksheet so that all of the column labels and the cell contents are completely displayed.

Troubleshoot 6. There is a problem with the some of the customer ZIP codes. New Jersey ZIP codes begin with a 0, and these leading zeros are not showing up in the contact information. Revise the text of the ZIP code values to correct this problem.

Troubleshoot 7. The formula in cell L8 that calculates the total number of billable hours for the first customer is not correct. Instead of showing the number of hours, it displays the value as a percentage of a day. Fix this problem by revising the formula so that it multiplies the difference between the value in K8 and J8 by 24. (*Hint:* Use parentheses to enclose the expression that calculates the difference between starting and ending times so that the difference is calculated first.)

8. Copy the formula you entered for cell L8 to calculate the total billable hours for the rest of the entries in column L.
9. The total charge for each service call is equal to the hourly rate multiplied by the number of hours plus the charge for parts. In cell O8, enter a formula to calculate the total service charge for the first customer, and then copy that formula to calculate the rest of the service charges in column O.
10. In cell B4, enter a formula that uses the COUNT function to count the total number of service calls.

Troubleshoot 11. In cell B5, Stefan entered a formula to calculate the total charges from all of the service calls. Examine the formula, and correct the expression so that it adds all of the service call charges.

12. Insert two new rows above row 5.
13. In cell A5, enter the label **Total Hours**. In cell B5, enter function to calculate the total number of hours from all of the service calls.
14. In cell A6, enter the label **Average Charge**. In cell B6, enter a formula that calculates the average charge per call by dividing the total charges by the total number of calls.
15. Add borders around the cells in the nonadjacent range A4:B7,A9:O29.
16. Set the page layout of the Call Sheet worksheet so that it prints on a single page in landscape orientation.
17. View the worksheet in Page Break Preview, return to Normal view, and then save and close the workbook.

MODULE 2

Formatting Workbook Text and Data

Creating a Sales Report

EXCEL

OBJECTIVES

Session 2.1

- Change fonts, font style, and font color
- Add fill colors and a background image
- Create formulas to calculate sales data
- Format numbers as currency and percentages
- Format dates and times
- Align, indent, and rotate cell contents
- Merge a group of cells

Session 2.2

- Use the AVERAGE function
- Apply cell styles
- Copy and paste formats with the Format Painter
- Find and replace text and formatting
- Change workbook themes
- Highlight cells with conditional formats
- Format a worksheet for printing
- Set the print area, insert page breaks, add print titles, create headers and footers, and set margins

Case | *Morning Bean*

Carol Evans is a sales manager at Morning Bean, a small but growing chain of shops specializing in coffee, tea, and other hot drinks. Carol needs to develop a workbook for the upcoming sales conference that will provide information on sales and profits for stores located in the Northwest region of the country. Carol already started the workbook by entering sales data for the previous years. She wants you to use this financial data to calculate summary statistics and then format the workbook before it's distributed to stockholders attending the conference.

STARTING DATA FILES

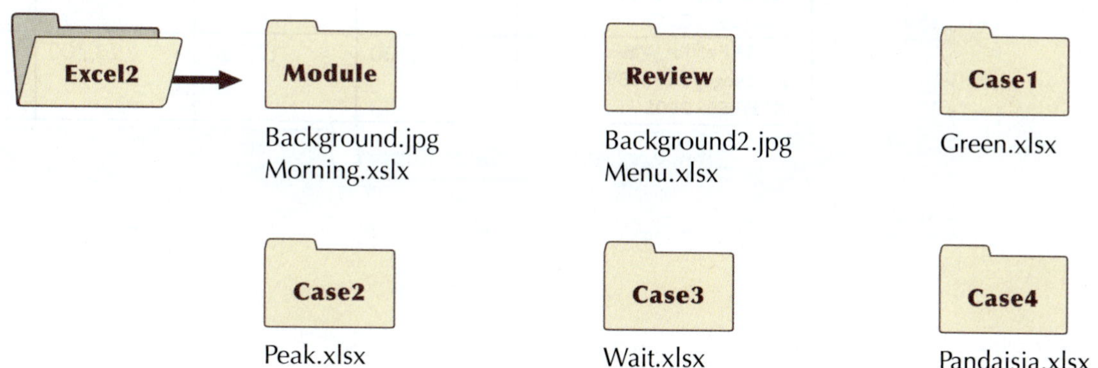

Session 2.1 Visual Overview:

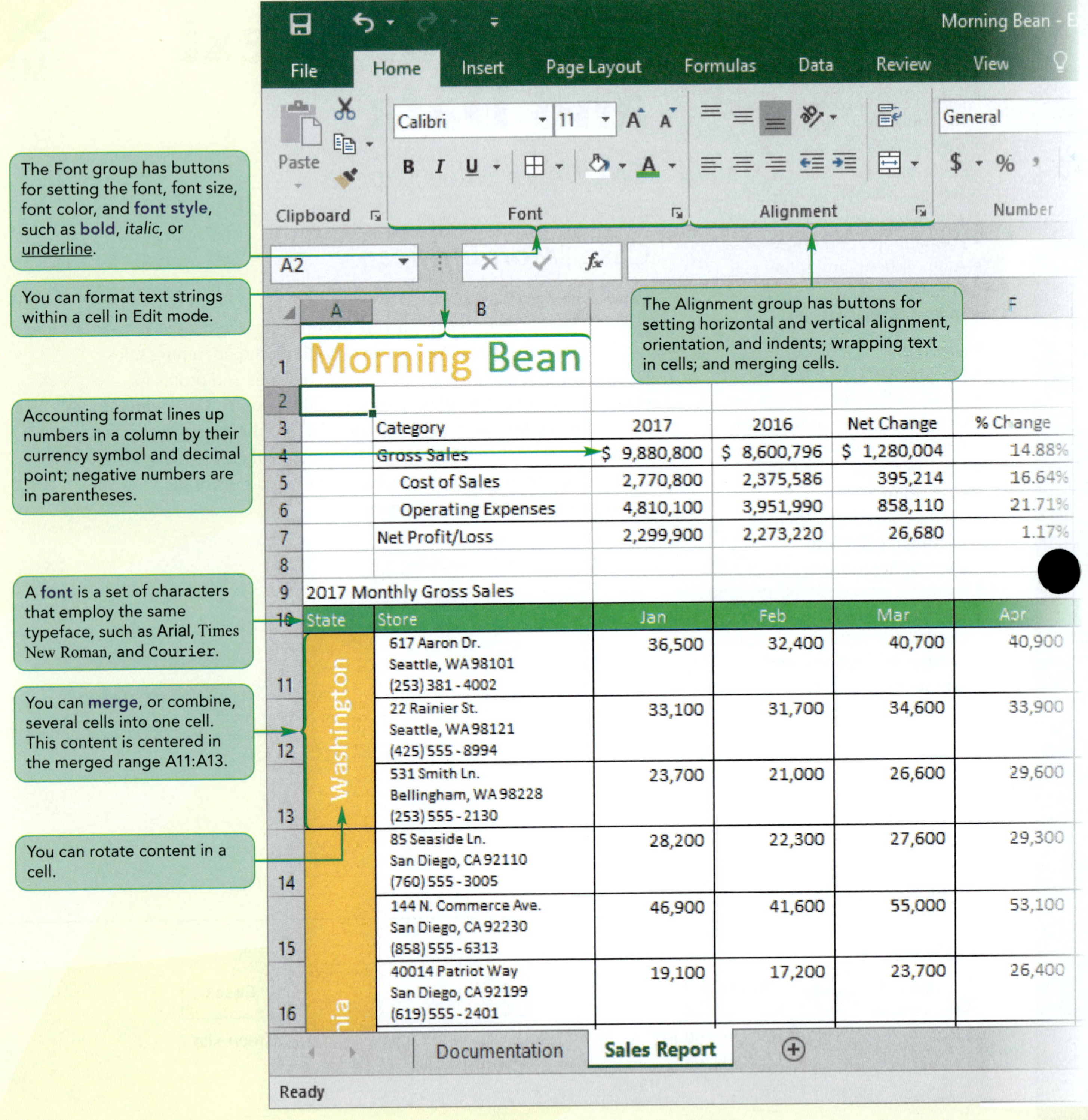

The Font group has buttons for setting the font, font size, font color, and font style, such as bold, italic, or underline.
You can format text strings within a cell in Edit mode.
Accounting format lines up numbers in a column by their currency symbol and decimal point; negative numbers are in parentheses.
A font is a set of characters that employ the same typeface, such as Arial, Times New Roman, and Courier.
You can merge, or combine, several cells into one cell. This content is centered in the merged range A11:A13.
You can rotate content in a cell.
The Alignment group has buttons for setting horizontal and vertical alignment, orientation, and indents; wrapping text in cells; and merging cells.
Morning Bean
Category
2017
2016
Net Change
% Change
Gross Sales
$ 9,880,800
$ 8,600,796
$ 1,280,004
14.88%
Cost of Sales
2,770,800
2,375,586
395,214
16.64%
Operating Expenses
4,810,100
3,951,990
858,110
21.71%
Net Profit/Loss
2,299,900
2,273,220
26,680
1.17%
2017 Monthly Gross Sales
State
Store
Jan
Feb
Mar
Apr
Washington
617 Aaron Dr. Seattle, WA 98101 (253) 381 - 4002
36,500
32,400
40,700
40,900
22 Rainier St. Seattle, WA 98121 (425) 555 - 8994
33,100
31,700
34,600
33,900
531 Smith Ln. Bellingham, WA 98228 (253) 555 - 2130
23,700
21,000
26,600
29,600
85 Seaside Ln. San Diego, CA 92110 (760) 555 - 3005
28,200
22,300
27,600
29,300
144 N. Commerce Ave. San Diego, CA 92230 (858) 555 - 6313
46,900
41,600
55,000
53,100
40014 Patriot Way San Diego, CA 92199 (619) 555 - 2401
19,100
17,200
23,700
26,400
Documentation
Sales Report
Ready

Formatting a Worksheet

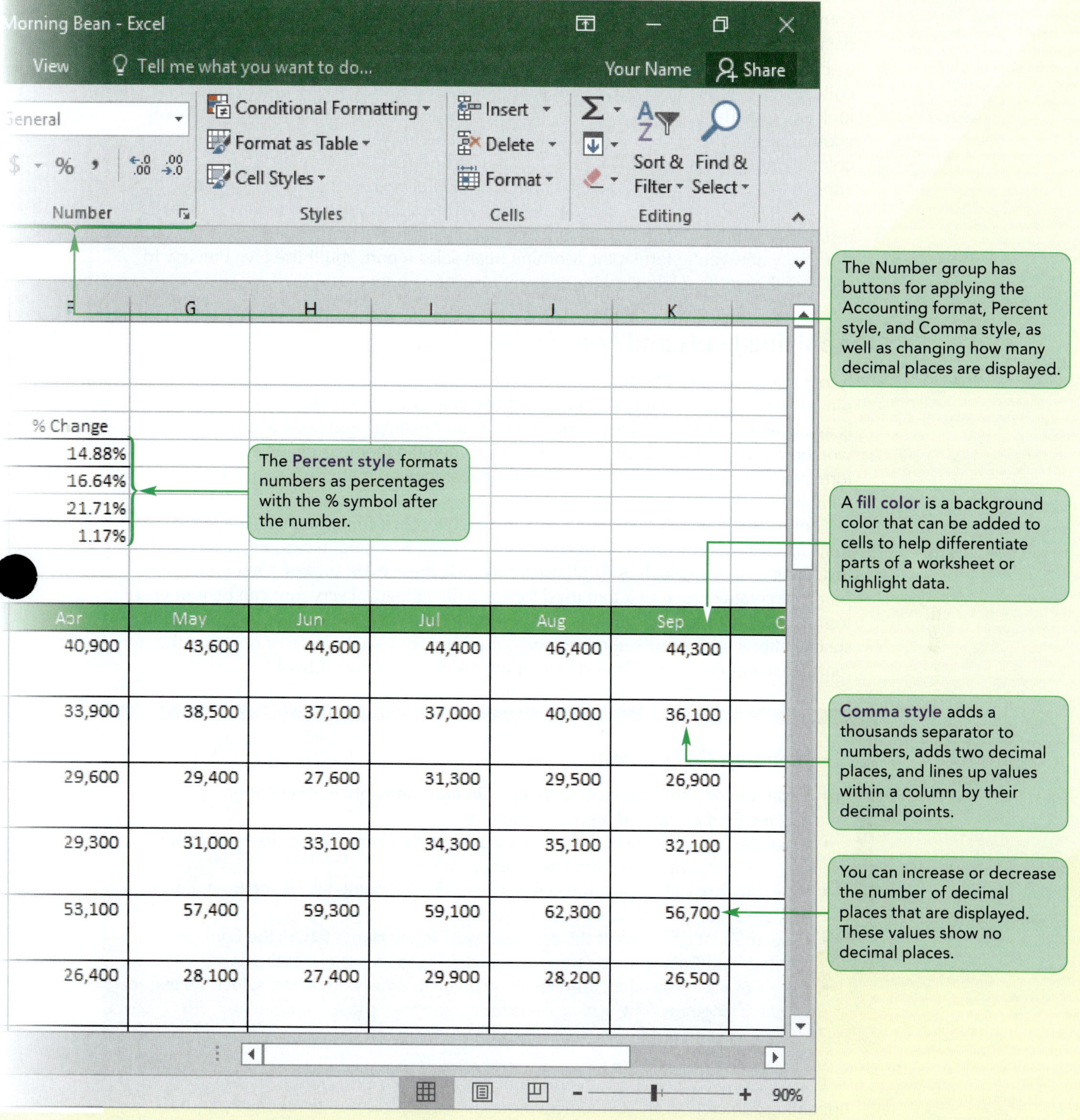

The Number group has buttons for applying the Accounting format, Percent style, and Comma style, as well as changing how many decimal places are displayed.

The **Percent style** formats numbers as percentages with the % symbol after the number.

A **fill color** is a background color that can be added to cells to help differentiate parts of a worksheet or highlight data.

Comma style adds a thousands separator to numbers, adds two decimal places, and lines up values within a column by their decimal points.

You can increase or decrease the number of decimal places that are displayed. These values show no decimal places.

Formatting Cell Text

You can improve the readability of workbooks by choosing the fonts, styles, colors, and decorative features that are used in the workbook and within worksheet cells. Formatting changes only the appearance of the workbook data—it does not affect the data itself.

Excel organizes complementary formatting options into themes. A **theme** is a collection of formatting for text, colors, and effects that give a workbook a unique look and feel. The Office theme is applied to workbooks by default, but you can apply another theme or create your own. You can also add formatting to a workbook using colors, fonts, and effects that are not part of the current theme. Note that a theme is applied to the entire workbook and can be shared between workbooks.

To help you choose the best formatting for your workbooks, **Live Preview** shows the results of each formatting option before you apply it to your workbook.

Carol wants you to format the Morning Bean sales report. You'll use Live Preview to see how the workbook looks with different formatting options.

Applying Fonts and Font Styles

A font is a set of characters that share a common appearance by employing the same typeface. Excel organizes fonts into theme and nontheme fonts. A **theme font** is associated with a particular theme and used for headings and body text in the workbook. Theme fonts change automatically when the theme is changed. Text formatted with a **nontheme font** retains its appearance no matter what theme is used with the workbook.

Fonts are classified based on their character style. **Serif fonts**, such as Times New Roman, have extra strokes at the end of each character that aid in reading passages of text. **Sans serif fonts**, such as Arial, do not include these extra strokes. Other fonts are purely decorative, such as a font used for specialized logos. Every font can be further formatted with a font style such as *italic*, **bold**, or ***bold italic***; with underline; and with special effects such as ~~strikethrough~~ and color. You can also increase or decrease the font size to emphasize the importance of the text within the workbook.

REFERENCE

Formatting Cell Content

- To set the font, select the cell or range. On the Home tab, in the Font group, click the Font arrow, and then select a font.
- To set the font size, select the cell or range. On the Home tab, in the Font group, click the Font Size arrow, and then select a font size.
- To set the font style, select the cell or range. On the Home tab, in the Font group, click the Bold, Italic, or Underline button.
- To set the font color, select the cell or range. On the Home tab, in the Font group, click the Font Color button arrow, and then select a theme or nontheme color.
- To format a text selection, double-click the cell to enter Edit mode, select the text to format, change the font, size, style, or color, and then press the Enter key.

Carol already entered the data and some formulas in her workbook for the upcoming conference. The Documentation sheet describes her workbook's purpose and content. At the top of the sheet is the company name. Carol wants you to format the name in large, bold letters using the default heading font from the Office theme.

To the format the company name:

1. Open the **Morning** workbook located in the **Excel2 > Module** folder included with your Data Files, and then save the workbook as **Morning Bean** in the location specified by your instructor.
2. In the Documentation sheet, enter your name in cell B4 and the date in cell B5.
3. Click cell **A1** to make it the active cell.
4. On the Home tab, in the Font group, click the **Font button arrow** to display a gallery of fonts available on your computer. Each name is displayed in its font. The first two fonts listed are the theme fonts for headings and body text–Calibri Light and Calibri.
5. Scroll down the Fonts gallery until you see Bauhaus 93 in the All Fonts list, and then point to **Bauhaus 93** (or another font). Live Preview shows the effect of the Bauhaus 93 font on the text in cell A1. See Figure 2-1.

Figure 2-1 Font gallery

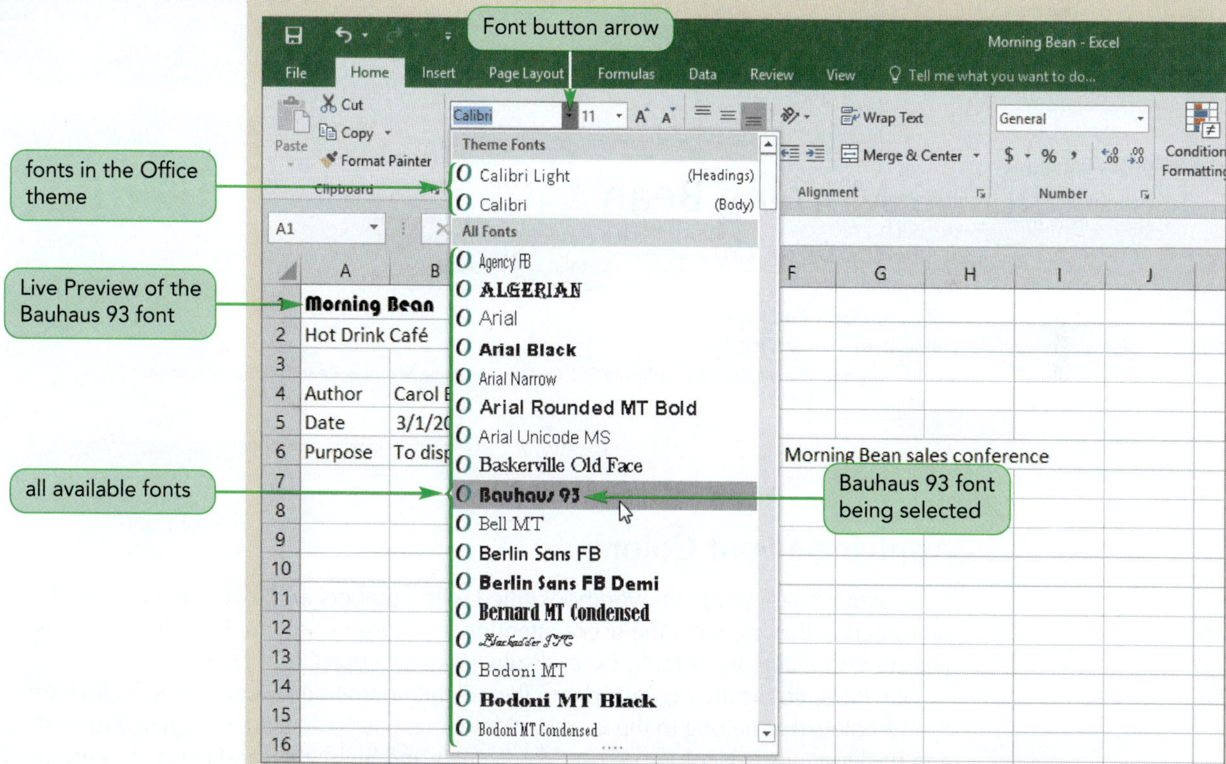

6. Point to three other fonts in the list to see the Live Preview of how the text in cell A1 would look with that font.
7. Click **Calibri Light** in the Theme Fonts list. The company name in cell A1 changes to the Calibri Light Font, the default headings font in the current theme.
8. In the Font group, click the **Font Size button arrow** [11] to display a list of font sizes, point to **26** to preview the text in that font size, and then click **26**. The company name changes to 26 points.
9. In the Font group, click the **Bold** button **B** (or press **Ctrl+B** keys). The text changes to bold.

10. Click cell **A2** to make it the active cell. The cell with the company description is selected.
11. In the Font group, click the **Font Size button arrow** [11], and then click **18**. The company description changes to 18 points.
12. In the Font group, click the **Italic** button *I* (or press the **Ctrl+I** keys). The company description in cell A2 is italicized.
13. Select the range **A4:A6**, and then press the **Ctrl+B** keys. The text in the selected range changes to bold.
14. Click cell **A7** to deselect the range. See Figure 2-2.

Figure 2-2 Formatted text in the Documentation sheet

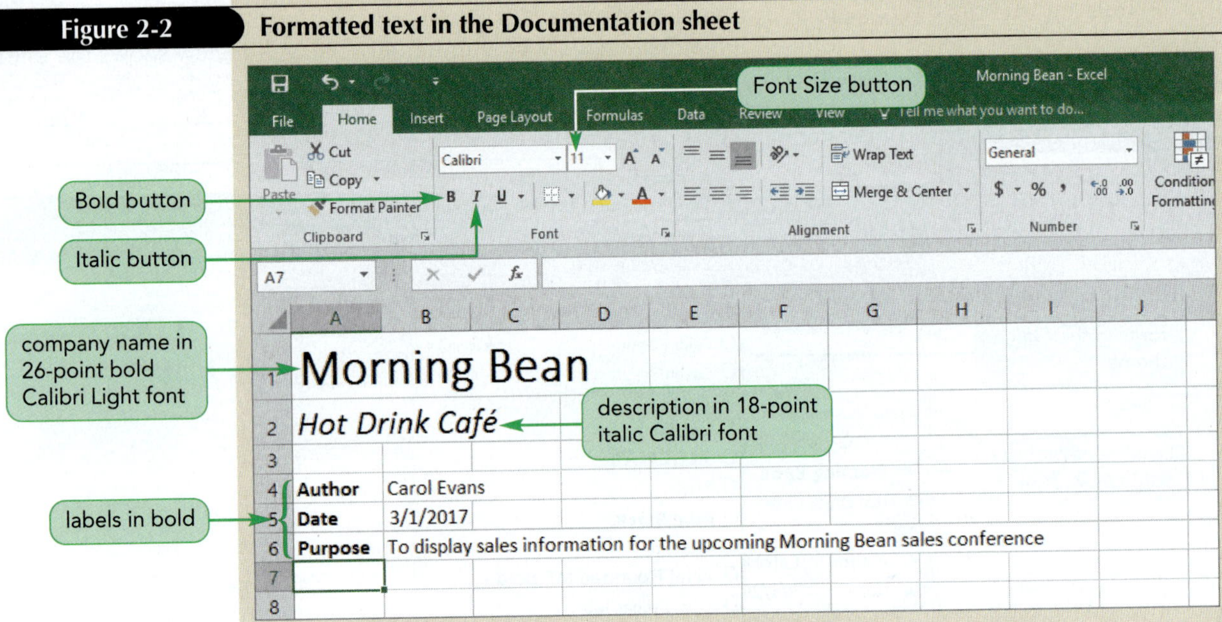

Applying a Font Color

Color can transform a plain workbook filled with numbers and text into a powerful presentation that captures the user's attention and adds visual emphasis to the points you want to make. By default, Excel displays text in a black font color.

Like fonts, colors are organized into theme and nontheme colors. **Theme colors** are the 12 colors that belong to the workbook's theme. Four colors are designated for text and backgrounds, six colors are used for accents and highlights, and two colors are used for hyperlinks (followed and not followed links). These 12 colors are designed to work well together and to remain readable in all combinations. Each theme color has five variations, or accents, in which a different tint or shading is applied to the theme color.

Ten **standard colors**—dark red, red, orange, yellow, light green, green, light blue, blue, dark blue, and purple—are always available regardless of the workbook's theme. You can open an extended palette of 134 standard colors. You can also create a custom color by specifying a mixture of red, blue, and green color values, making available 16.7 million custom colors—more colors than the human eye can distinguish. Some dialog boxes have an automatic color option that uses your Windows default text and background colors, usually black text on a white background.

INSIGHT

Creating Custom Colors

Custom colors let you add subtle and striking colors to a formatted workbook. To create custom colors, you use the **RGB Color model** in which each color is expressed with varying intensities of red, green, and blue. RGB color values are often represented as a set of numbers in the format

`(red, green, blue)`

where `red` is an intensity value assigned to red light, `green` is an intensity value assigned to green light, and `blue` is an intensity value assigned to blue light. The intensities are measured on a scale of 0 to 255—0 indicates no intensity (or the absence of the color) and 255 indicates the highest intensity. So, the RGB color value (255, 255, 0) represents a mixture of high-intensity red (255) and high-intensity green (255) with the absence of blue (0), which creates the color yellow.

To create colors in Excel using the RGB model, click the More Colors option located in a color menu or dialog box to open the Colors dialog box. In the Colors dialog box, click the Custom tab, and then enter the red, green, and blue intensity values. A preview box shows the resulting RGB color.

Carol wants the company name and description in the Documentation sheet to stand out. You will change the text in cell A1 and cell A2 to green.

To change the font color of the company name and description:

1. Select the range **A1:A2**.
2. On the Home tab, in the Font group, click the **Font Color button arrow** to display the gallery of theme and standard colors.
3. In the Standard Colors section, point to the **Green** color (the sixth color). The color name appears in a ScreenTip, and you see a Live Preview of the text with the green font color. See Figure 2-3.

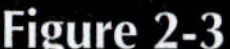

Figure 2-3 Font Color gallery

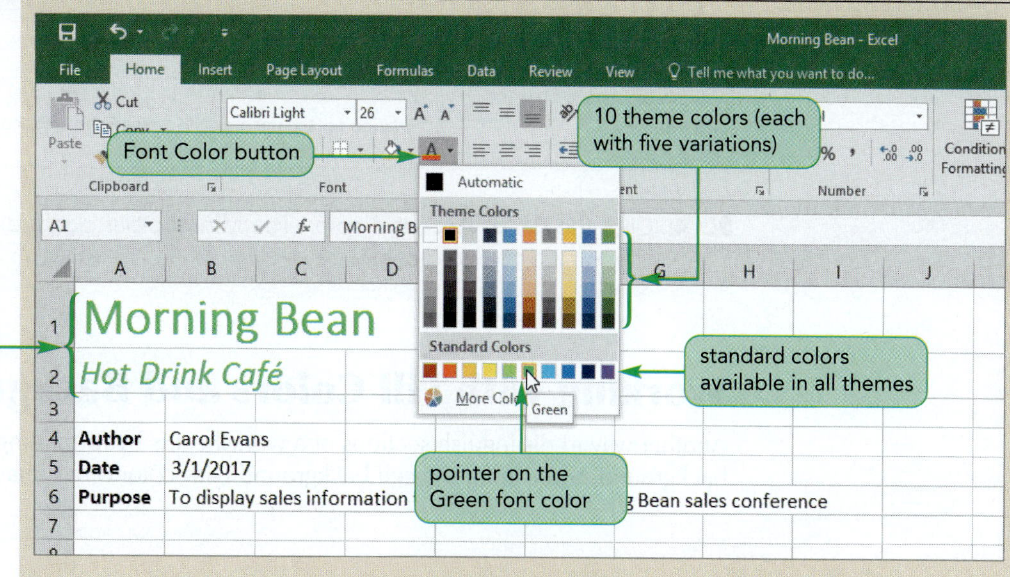

4. Click the **Green** color. The company name and description change to green.

Formatting Text Selections Within a Cell

In Edit mode, you can select and format selections of text within a cell. You can make these changes to selected text from the ribbon or from the Mini toolbar. The **Mini toolbar** contains buttons for common formatting options used for that selection. These same buttons appear on the ribbon.

Carol asks you to format the company name in cell A1 so that the text "Morning" appears in gold.

To format part of the company name in cell A1:

1. Double-click cell **A1** to select the cell and enter Edit mode (or click cell **A1** and press the **F2** key). The status bar shows Edit to indicate that you are working with the cell in Edit mode. The pointer changes to the I-beam pointer.
2. Drag the pointer over the word **Morning** to select it. A Mini toolbar appears above the selected text with buttons to change the font, size, style, and color of the selected text in the cell. In this instance, you want to change the font color.
3. On the Mini toolbar, click the **Font Color button arrow** [A], and then in the Themes Colors section, point to the **Gold, Accent 4** color (the eighth color). Live Preview shows the color of the selected text as gold. See Figure 2-4.

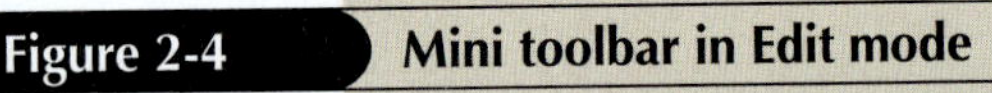

Figure 2-4 Mini toolbar in Edit mode

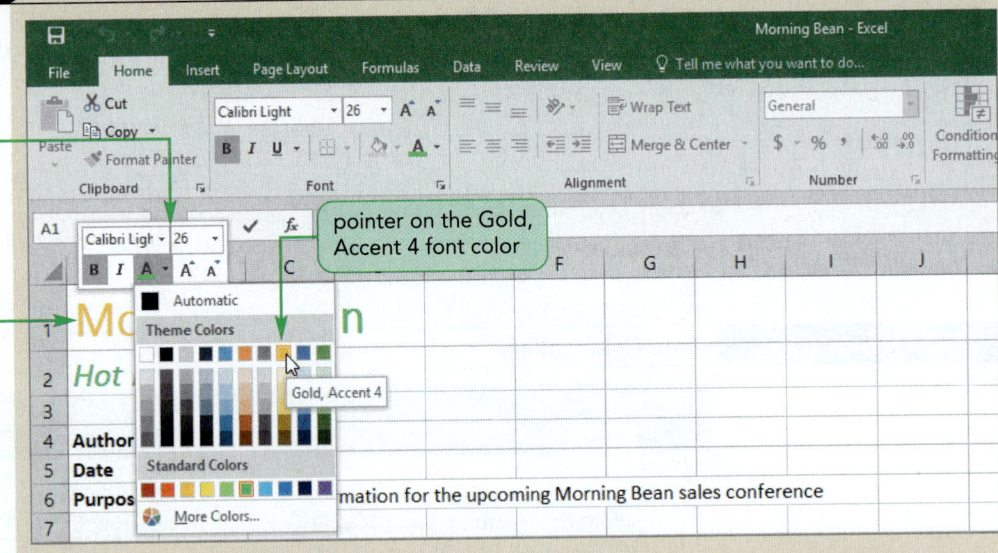

4. Click the **Gold, Accent 4** color. The Mini toolbar closes and the selected text changes to the gold color.

Working with Fill Colors and Backgrounds

Another way to distinguish sections of a worksheet is by formatting the cell background. You can fill the cell background with color or an image.

Changing a Fill Color

TIP

To change a sheet tab's color, right-click its tab, point to Tab Color, and then click a color.

By default, worksheet cells do not include any background color. But background colors, also known as fill colors, can be helpful for distinguishing different parts of a worksheet or adding visual interest. The same selection of colors used to format the color of cell text can be used to format the cell background.

INSIGHT

Using Color to Enhance a Workbook

When used wisely, color can enhance any workbook. However, when used improperly, color can distract the user, making the workbook more difficult to read. As you format a workbook, keep in mind the following tips:

- Use colors from the same theme to maintain a consistent look and feel across the worksheets. If the built-in themes do not fit your needs, you can create a custom theme.
- Use colors to differentiate types of cell content and to direct users where to enter data. For example, format a worksheet so that formula results appear in cells without a fill color and users enter data in cells with a light gray fill color.
- Avoid color combinations that are difficult to read.
- Print the workbook on both color and black-and-white printers to ensure that the printed copy is readable in both versions.
- Understand your printer's limitations and features. Colors that look good on your monitor might not look as good when printed.
- Be sensitive to your audience. About 8 percent of all men and 0.5 percent of all women have some type of color blindness and might not be able to see the text when certain color combinations are used. Red-green color blindness is the most common, so avoid using red text on a green background or green text on a red background.

Carol wants you to change the background color of the range A4:A6 in the Documentation sheet to green and the font color to white.

To change the font and fill colors in the Documentation sheet:

1. Select the range **A4:A6**.
2. On the Home tab, in the Font group, click the **Fill Color button arrow**, and then click the **Green** color (the sixth color) in the Standard Colors section.
3. In the Font group, click the **Font Color button arrow**, and then click the **White, Background 1** color (the first color) in the Theme Colors section. The labels are formatted as white text on a green background.
4. Select the range **B4:B6**, and then format the cells with the **Green** font color and the **White, Background 1** fill color.
5. Increase the width of column B to **30** characters, and then wrap the text within the selected range.
6. Select the range **A4:B6**, and then add all borders around each of the selected cells.
7. Click cell **A7** to deselect the range. See Figure 2-5.

Figure 2-5 Font and fill colors in the Documentation sheet

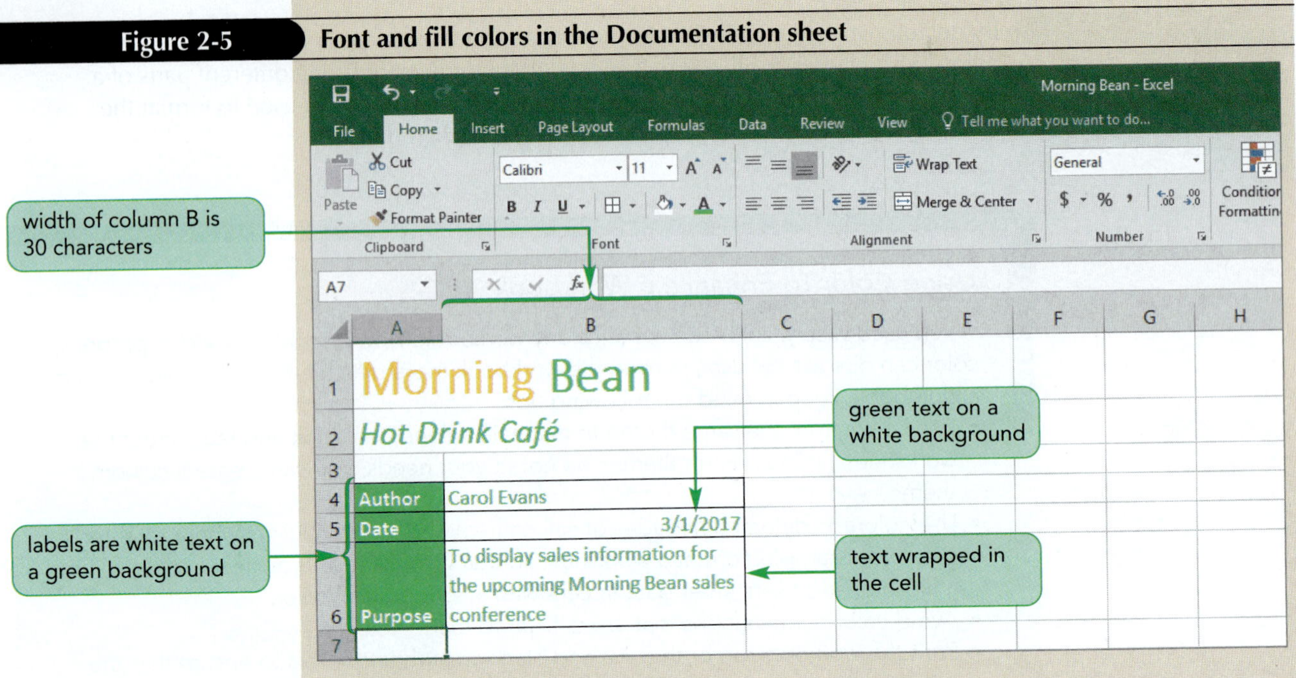

Adding a Background Image

TIP

Background images are usually visible only on the screen; by default they do not print.

Another way to add visual interest to worksheets is with a background image. Many background images are based on textures such as granite, wood, or fibered paper. The image does not need to match the size of the worksheet; a smaller image can be repeated until it fills the entire sheet. Background images do not affect any cell's format or content. Fill colors added to cells appear on top of the image, covering that portion of the image.

Carol has provided an image that she wants you to use as the background of the Documentation sheet.

To add a background image to the Documentation sheet:

1. On the ribbon, click the **Page Layout** tab to display the page layout options.
2. In the Page Setup group, click the **Background** button. The Insert Pictures dialog box opens with options to search for an image file on your computer or local network, or use the Bing Image Search tool.
3. Click the **Browse** button next to the From a file label. The Sheet Background dialog box opens.
4. Navigate to the **Excel2 > Module** folder included with your Data Files, click the **Background** JPEG image file, and then click the **Insert** button. The image is added to the background of the Documentation sheet. The Background button changes to the Delete Background button, which you can click to remove background image. See Figure 2-6.

Figure 2-6 Background image added to the Documentation sheet

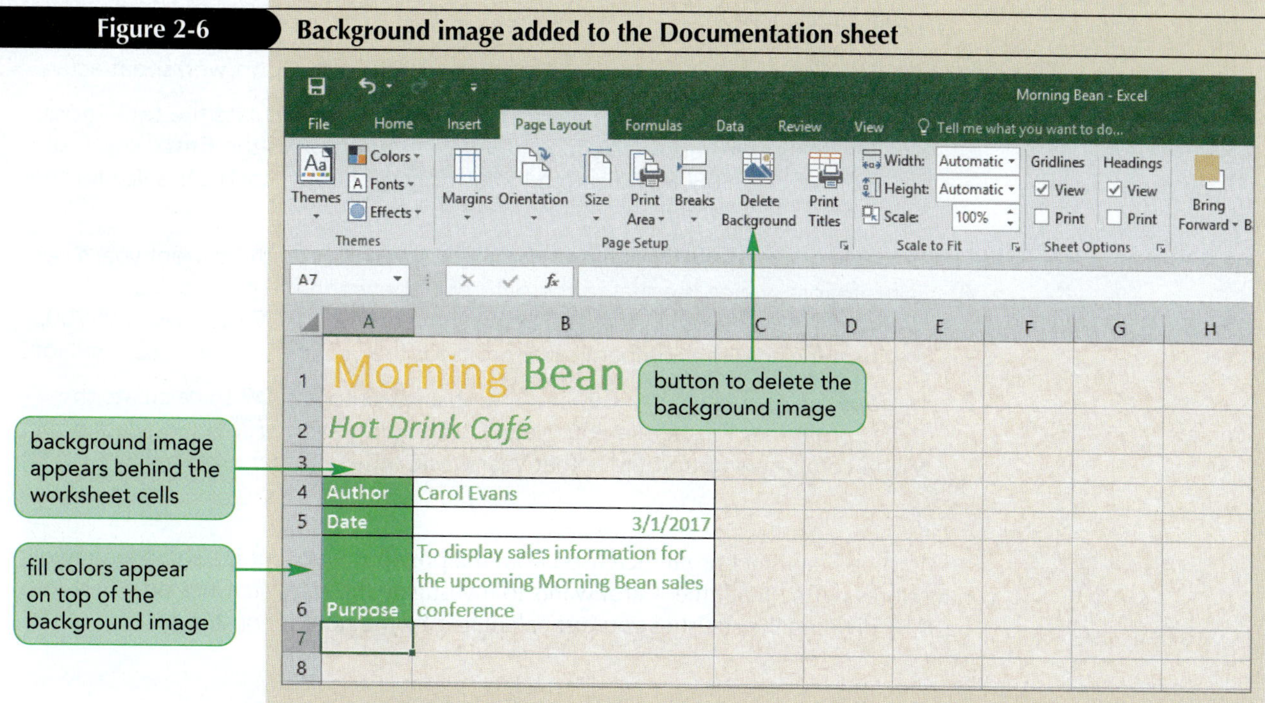

You've completed the formatting the Documentation sheet. Next, you'll work on the Sales Report worksheet.

Using Functions and Formulas to Calculate Sales Data

In the Sales Report worksheet, you will format the data on the gross sales from each of Morning Bean's 20 stores. The worksheet is divided into two areas. The table at the bottom of the worksheet displays gross sales for the past year for each month by store. The section at the top of the worksheet summarizes the sales over the past two years. Carol has compiled the following sales data:

- **Gross Sales**—the total amount of sales at all of the stores
- **Cost of Sales**—the cost of creating Morning Bean products
- **Operating Expenses**—the cost of running the individual stores including the employment and insurance costs
- **Net Profit/Loss**—the difference between the income from the gross sales and the total cost of sales and operating expenses
- **Units Sold**—the total number of menu items sold by Morning Bean during the year
- **Customers Served**—the total number of customers served by Morning Bean during the year

Carol wants you to calculate these sales statistics for the entire company and for each individual store. First, you will calculate Morning Bean's total gross sales from the past year and the company's overall net profit and loss.

To calculate Morning Bean's sales and profit/loss:

1. Click the **Sales Report** sheet tab to make the Sales Report worksheet active.
2. Click cell **C6**, type the formula **=SUM(C27:N46)** to calculate the total gross sales from all stores in the previous year, and then press the **Enter** key. Cell C6 displays 9880800, indicating that Morning Bean's total gross sales for the year were more than $9.8 million.
3. In cell **C9**, enter the formula **=C6-(C7+C8)** to calculate the current year's net profit/loss, which is equal to the difference between the gross sales and the sum of the cost of sales and operating expenses. Cell C9 displays 2299900, indicating that the company's net profit for the year was close to $2.3 million.
4. Copy the formula in cell **C9**, and then paste it into cell **D9** to calculate the net profit/loss for the previous year. Cell D9 displays 2273220, indicating that the company's net profit for that year was a little less than $2.3 million.

Morning Bean's net profit increased from the previous year, but it also opened two new stores during that time. Carol wants to investigate the sales statistics on a per-store basis by dividing the statistics you just calculated by the number of stores.

To calculate the per-store statistics:

1. In cell **C16**, enter the formula **=C6/C23** to calculate the gross sales per store for the year. The formula returns 494040, indicating each Morning Bean store had, on average, almost $500,000 in gross sales during the year.
2. In cell **C17**, enter the formula **=C7/C23** to calculate the cost of sales per store for the year. The formula returns the value 138540, indicating each Morning Bean store had a little more than $138,000 in sales cost.
3. In cell **C18**, enter the formula **=C8/C23** to calculate the operating expenses per store for the year. The formula returns the value 240505, indicating that operating expense of a typical store was a little more than $240,000.
4. In cell **C19**, enter the formula **=C9/C23** to calculate the net profit/loss per store for the year. The formula returns the value 114995, indicating that the net profit/loss of a typical store was about $115,000.
5. In cell **C21**, enter the formula **=C11/C23** to calculate the units sold per store for the year. The formula returns the value 72655, indicating that a typical store sold more than 72,000 units.
6. In cell **C22**, enter the formula **=C12/C23** to calculate the customers served per store during the year. The formula returns the value 10255, indicating that a typical store served more than 10,000 customers.
7. Copy the formulas in the range **C16:C22** and paste them into the range **D16:D22**. The cell references in the formulas change to calculate the sales data for the previous year.
8. Click cell **B24** to deselect the range. See Figure 2-7.

Figure 2-7 **Overall and per-store sales statistics**

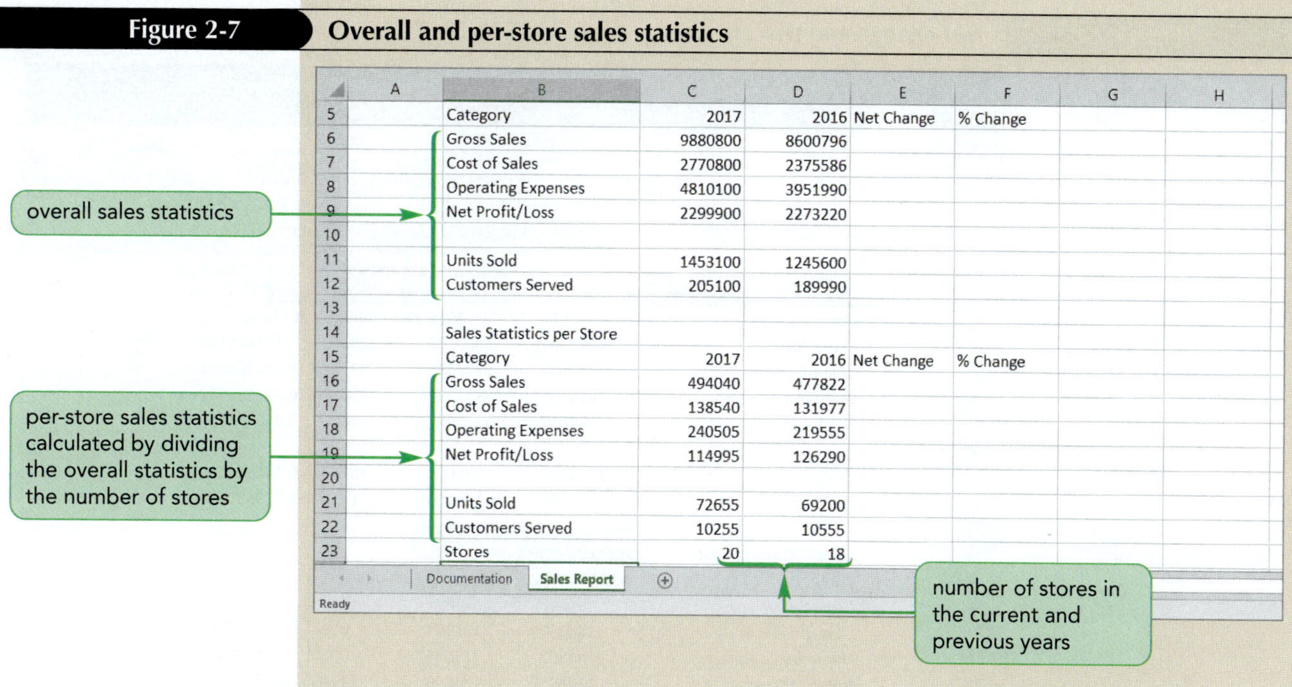

	A	B	C	D	E	F	G	H
5		Category	2017	2016	Net Change	% Change		
6		Gross Sales	9880800	8600796				
7		Cost of Sales	2770800	2375586				
8		Operating Expenses	4810100	3951990				
9		Net Profit/Loss	2299900	2273220				
10								
11		Units Sold	1453100	1245600				
12		Customers Served	205100	189990				
13								
14		Sales Statistics per Store						
15		Category	2017	2016	Net Change	% Change		
16		Gross Sales	494040	477822				
17		Cost of Sales	138540	131977				
18		Operating Expenses	240505	219555				
19		Net Profit/Loss	114995	126290				
20								
21		Units Sold	72655	69200				
22		Customers Served	10255	10555				
23		Stores	20	18				

Carol also wants to report how the company's sales and expenses have changed from the previous year to the current year. To do this, you will calculate the net change in the sales statistics as well as the percent change. The percent change is calculated using the following formula:

$$\textit{percent change} = \frac{\textit{current year value} - \textit{previous year value}}{\textit{previous year value}}$$

You will calculate the net change and percentage for all of the statistics in the Sales Report worksheet.

To calculate the net and percent changes:

1. In cell **E6**, enter the formula **=C6–D6** to calculate the difference in gross sales between the previous year and the current year. The formula returns 1280004, indicating that gross sales increased by about $1.28 million.
2. In cell **F6**, enter the formula **=(C6–D6)/D6** to calculate the percent change in gross sales from the previous year to the current year. The formula returns 0.1488239, indicating an increase in gross sales of about 14.88 percent.

   Be sure to include the parentheses as shown to calculate the percent change correctly.

   Next, you'll copy and paste the formulas in cells E6 and F6 to the rest of the sales data to calculate the net change and percent change from the previous year to the current year.
3. Select the range **E6:F6**, and then copy the selected range. The two formulas are copied to the Clipboard.
4. Select the nonadjacent range **E7:F9,E11:F12,E16:F19,E21:F23**, and then paste the formulas from the Clipboard into the selected range. The net and percent changes are calculated for the remaining sales data.
5. Click cell **B24** to deselect the range, and then scroll the worksheet up to display row 5. See Figure 2-8.

Figure 2-8 Net change and percent change from 2016 to 2017

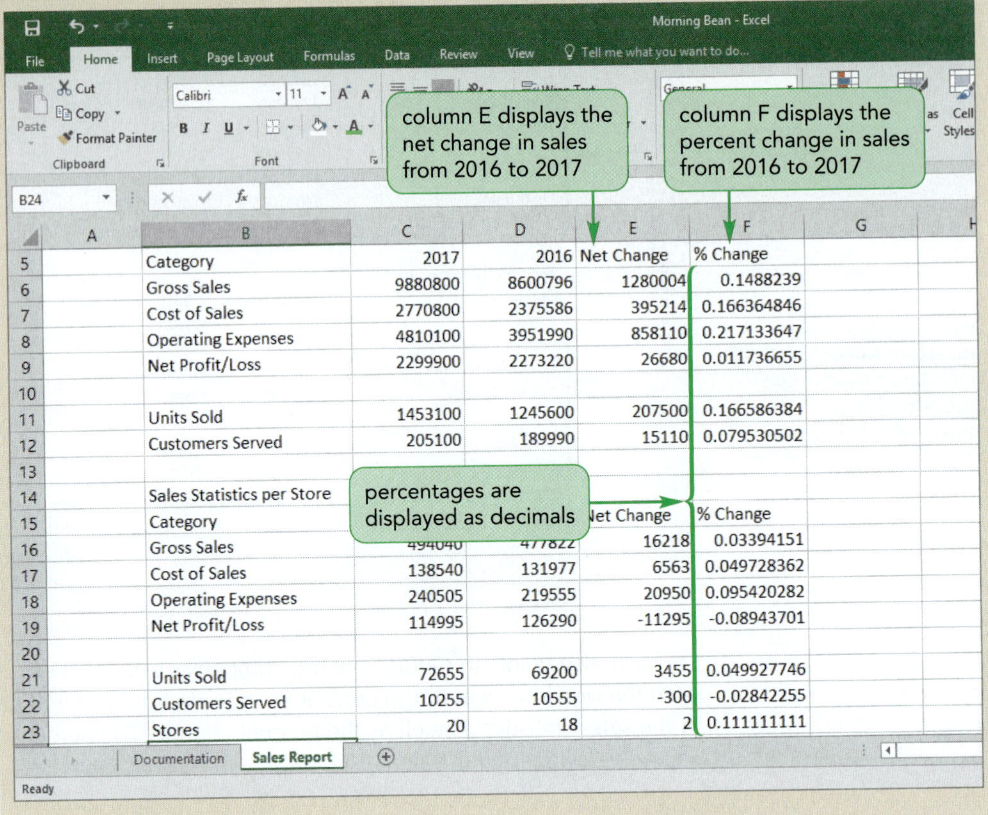

The bottom part of the worksheet contains the sales for each cafe from the current year. You will use the SUM function to calculate the total gross sales for each store during the entire year, the total monthly sales of all 20 stores, and the total gross sales of all stores and months.

To calculate different subtotals of the gross sales:

1. Click in the **Name** box to select the current cell reference, type **O26**, and then press the **Enter** key. Cell O26 is selected.
2. Type **TOTAL** as the label, and then press the **Enter** key. Cell O27 is now the active cell.
3. On the ribbon, click the **Home** tab, if necessary.
4. In the Editing group, click the **AutoSum** button, and then press the **Enter** key to accept the suggested range reference and enter the formula =SUM(C27:N27) in cell O27. The cell displays 370000, indicating gross sales in 2017 for the 85 Seaside Lane store in San Diego were $370,000.
5. Copy the formula in cell **O27**, and then paste that formula into the range **O28:O46** to calculate the total sales for each of the remaining 19 stores in the Morning Bean chain.
6. Click cell **B47**, type **TOTAL** as the label, and then press the **Tab** key. Cell C47 is now the active cell.
7. Select the range **C47:O47** so that you can calculate the total monthly sales for all of the stores.

8. On the Home tab, in the Editing group, click the **AutoSum** button to calculate the total sales for each month as well as the total sales for all months. For example, cell C47 displays 710900, indicating that monthly sales from all stores in January were $710,900.
9. Click cell **O48** to deselect the range. See Figure 2-9.

Figure 2-9 **Gross sales by store and month**

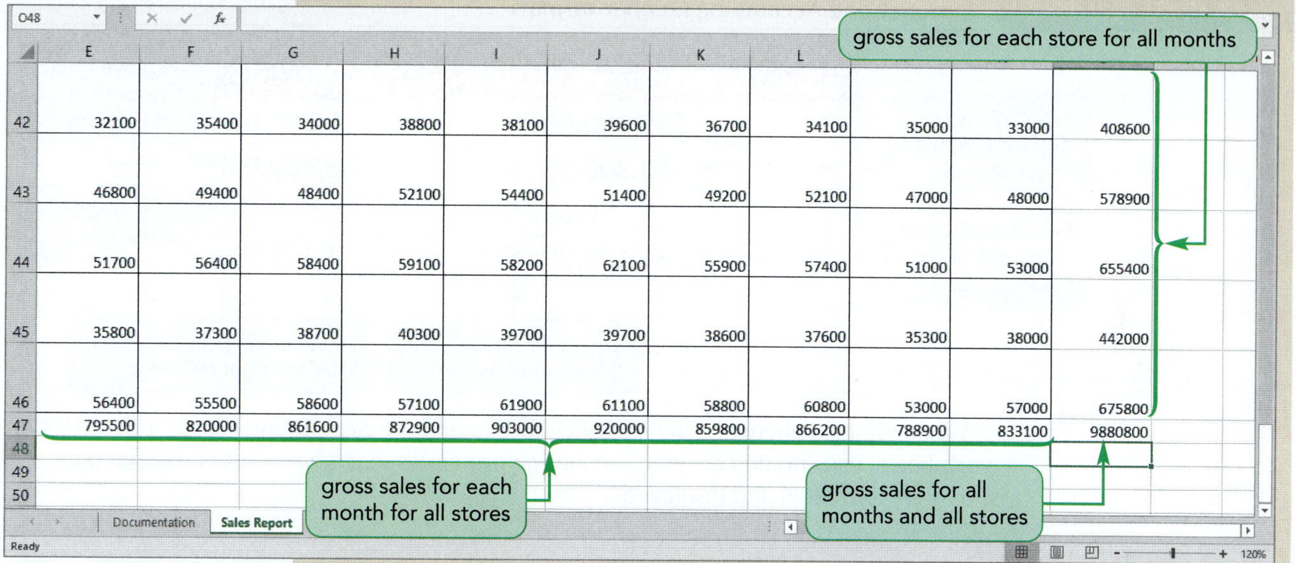

O48

	E	F	G	H	I	J	K	L			
42	32100	35400	34000	38800	38100	39600	36700	34100	35000	33000	408600
43	46800	49400	48400	52100	54400	51400	49200	52100	47000	48000	578900
44	51700	56400	58400	59100	58200	62100	55900	57400	51000	53000	655400
45	35800	37300	38700	40300	39700	39700	38600	37600	35300	38000	442000
46	56400	55500	58600	57100	61900	61100	58800	60800	53000	57000	675800
47	795500	820000	861600	872900	903000	920000	859800	866200	788900	833100	9880800
48											
49											
50											

Documentation | Sales Report

Ready

gross sales for each store for all months

gross sales for each month for all stores

gross sales for all months and all stores

The Sales Report worksheet contains a lot of information that is difficult to read in its current form. You can improve the readability of the data by adding number formats.

Formatting Numbers

The goal in formatting any workbook is to make the content easier to interpret. For numbers, this can mean adding a comma to separate thousands, setting the number of decimal places, and using percentage and currency symbols to make numbers easier to read and understand. Changing the number format does not affect the value itself, only how that value is displayed in the worksheet.

Applying Number Formats

Cells start out formatted with the **General format**, which, for the most part, displays numbers exactly as they are typed. If a value is calculated from a formula or function, the General format displays as many digits after the decimal point as will fit in the cell and rounds the last digit. Calculated values that are too large to fit into the cell are displayed in scientific notation.

The General format is fine for small numbers, but some values require additional formatting to make the numbers easier to interpret. For example, you might want to:

- Change the number of digits displayed to the right of the decimal point
- Add commas to separate thousands in large numbers
- Include currency symbols to numbers to identify the monetary unit being used
- Identify percentages using the % symbol

TIP

To apply the Currency format, click the Number Format button arrow and click Currency, or press the Ctrl+Shift+$ keys.

Excel supports two monetary formats—currency and accounting. Both formats add a thousands separator to the currency values and display two digits to the right of the decimal point. However, the **Currency format** places a currency symbol directly to the left of the first digit of the currency value and displays negative numbers with a negative sign. The **Accounting format** fixes a currency symbol at the left edge of the column, and displays negative numbers within parentheses and zero values with a dash. It also slightly indents the values from the right edge of the cell to allow room for parentheses around negative values. Figure 2-10 compares the two formats.

Figure 2-10 **Currency and Accounting number formats**

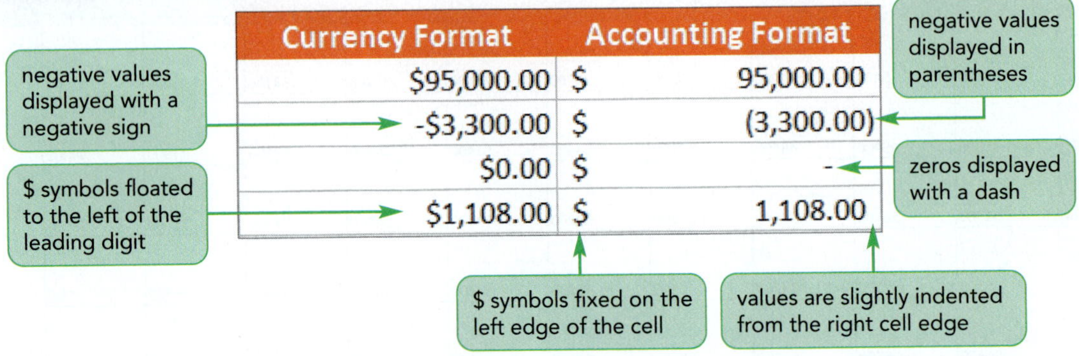

When choosing between the Currency format and the Accounting format for your worksheets, you should consider accounting principles that govern how financial data should be formatted and displayed.

PROSKILLS

Written Communication: Formatting Monetary Values

Spreadsheets commonly include monetary values. To make these values simpler to read and comprehend, keep in mind the following guidelines when formatting the currency data in a worksheet:

- **Format for your audience.** For general financial reports, round values to the nearest hundred, thousand, or million. Investors are generally more interested in the big picture than in exact values. However, for accounting reports, accuracy is important and often legally required. So, for those reports, be sure to display the exact monetary value.
- **Use thousands separators.** Large strings of numbers can be challenging to read. For monetary values, use a thousands separator to make the amounts easier to comprehend.
- **Apply the Accounting format to columns of monetary values.** The Accounting format makes columns of numbers easier to read than the Currency format. Use the Currency format for individual cells that are not part of long columns of numbers.
- **Use only two currency symbols in a column of monetary values.** Standard accounting format displays one currency symbol with the first monetary value in the column and optionally displays a second currency symbol with the last value in that column. Use the Accounting format to fix the currency symbols, lining them up within the column.

Following these standard accounting principles will make your financial data easier to read both on the screen and in printouts.

Carol wants you to format the gross sales amounts in the Accounting format so that they are easier to read.

To format the gross sales in the Accounting format:

1. Select the range **C6:E6** containing the gross sales.
2. On the Home tab, in the Number group, click the **Accounting Number Format** button $. The numbers are formatted in the Accounting format. You cannot see the format because the cells display ##########.

TIP

You can click the Accounting Number Format button arrow, and then click a different currency symbol.

The cells display ########## because the formatted numbers don't fit into the columns. One reason for this is that monetary values, by default, show both dollars and cents in the cell. However, you can increase or decrease the number of decimal places displayed in a cell. The displayed value might then be rounded. For example, the stored value 11.7 will appear in the cell as 12 if no decimal places are displayed to the right of the decimal point. Changing the number of decimal places displayed in a cell does not change the value stored in the cell.

Because the conference attendees are interested only in whole dollar amounts, Carol wants you to hide the cents values of the gross sales by decreasing the number of decimal places to zero.

To decrease the number of decimal places displayed in the gross sales:

1. Make sure the range **C6:E6** is still selected.
2. On the Home tab, in the Number group, click the **Decrease Decimal** button twice. The cents are hidden for gross sales.
3. Click cell **C4** to deselect the range. See Figure 2-11.

Figure 2-11 Formatted gross sales values

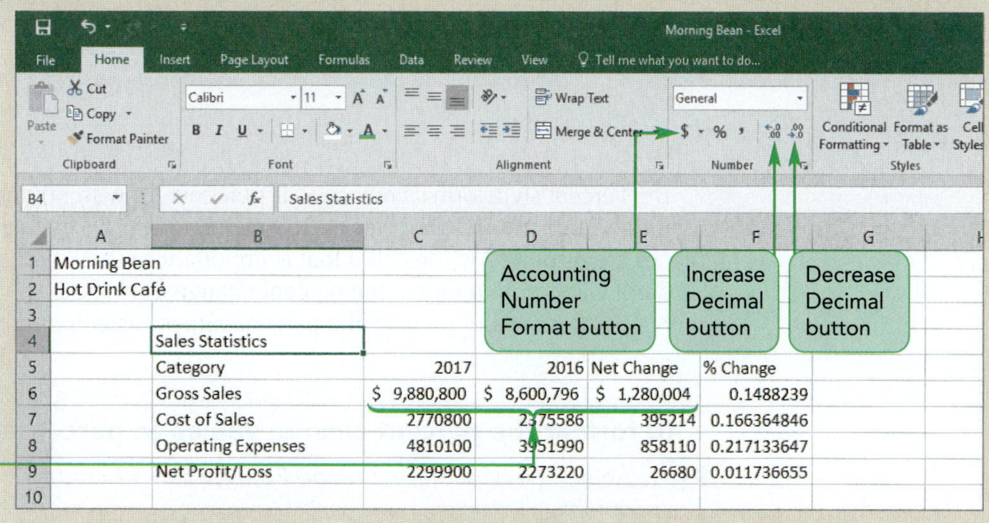

The Comma style is identical to the Accounting format except that it does not fix a currency symbol to the left of the number. The advantage of using the Comma style and the Accounting format together is that the numbers will be aligned in the column.

Carol asks you to apply the Comma style to the remaining sales statistics.

To apply the Comma style to the sales statistics:

1. Select the nonadjacent range **C7:E9,C11:E12** containing the sales figures for all stores in 2016 and 2017.
2. On the Home tab, in the Number group, click the **Comma Style** button. In some instances, the number is now too large to be displayed in the cell.
3. In the Number group, click the **Decrease Decimal** button twice to remove two decimal places. Digits to the right of the decimal point are hidden for all of the selected cells, and all of the numbers are now visible.
4. Click cell **C13** to deselect the range. See Figure 2-12.

Figure 2-12 Formatted sales values

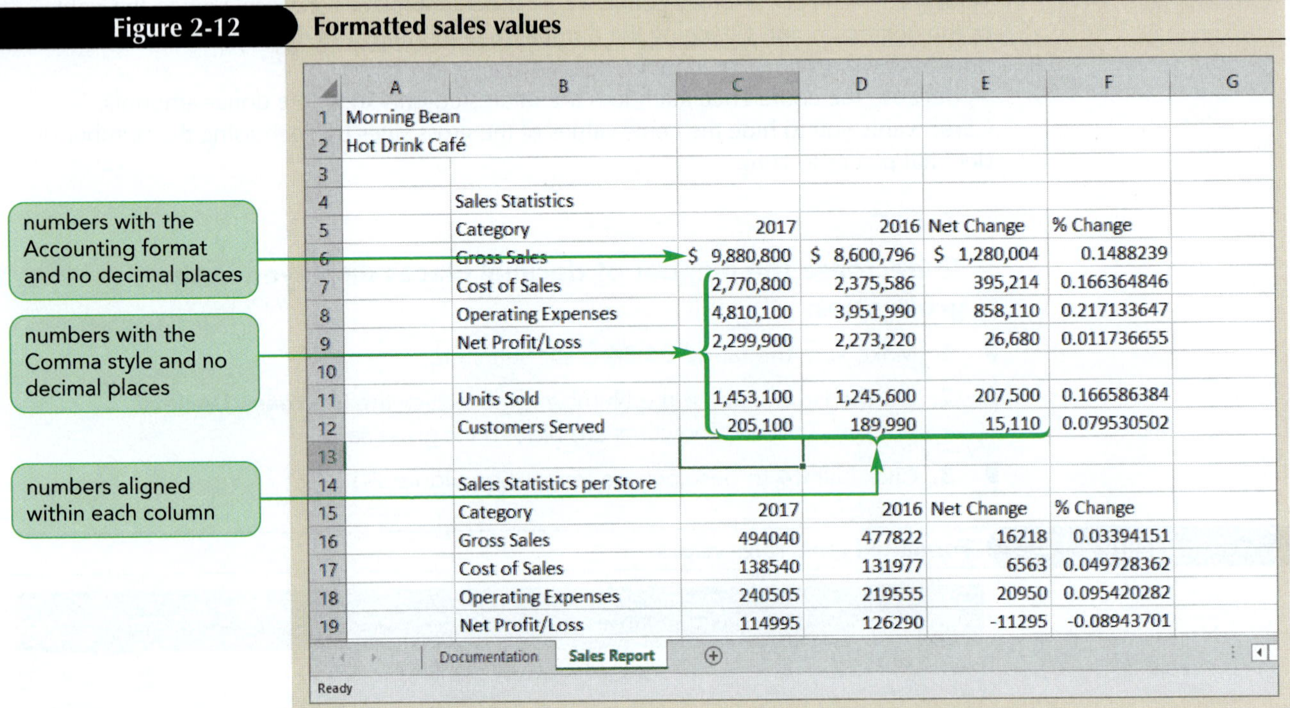

	A	B	C	D	E	F	G
1	Morning Bean						
2	Hot Drink Café						
3							
4		Sales Statistics					
5		Category	2017	2016	Net Change	% Change	
6		Gross Sales	$ 9,880,800	$ 8,600,796	$ 1,280,004	0.1488239	
7		Cost of Sales	2,770,800	2,375,586	395,214	0.166364846	
8		Operating Expenses	4,810,100	3,951,990	858,110	0.217133647	
9		Net Profit/Loss	2,299,900	2,273,220	26,680	0.011736655	
10							
11		Units Sold	1,453,100	1,245,600	207,500	0.166586384	
12		Customers Served	205,100	189,990	15,110	0.079530502	
13							
14		Sales Statistics per Store					
15		Category	2017	2016	Net Change	% Change	
16		Gross Sales	494040	477822	16218	0.03394151	
17		Cost of Sales	138540	131977	6563	0.049728362	
18		Operating Expenses	240505	219555	20950	0.095420282	
19		Net Profit/Loss	114995	126290	-11295	-0.08943701	

Documentation | Sales Report

Ready

The Percent style formats numbers as percentages with no decimal places so that a number such as 0.124 appears as 12%. You can always change how many decimal places are displayed in the cell if that is important to show with your data.

Carol wants you to format the percent change from the 2016 to 2017 sales statistics with a percent symbol to make the percent values easier to read.

To format the percent change values as percentages:

1. Select the nonadjacent range **F6:F9,F11:F12** containing the percent change values.
2. On the Home tab, in the Number group, click the **Percent Style** button % (or press the **Ctrl+Shift+%** keys). The values are displayed as percentages with no decimal places.
3. In the Number group, click the **Increase Decimal** button twice. The displayed number includes two decimal places.
4. Click cell **F13** to deselect the range. See Figure 2-13.

Figure 2-13 Formatted percent change values

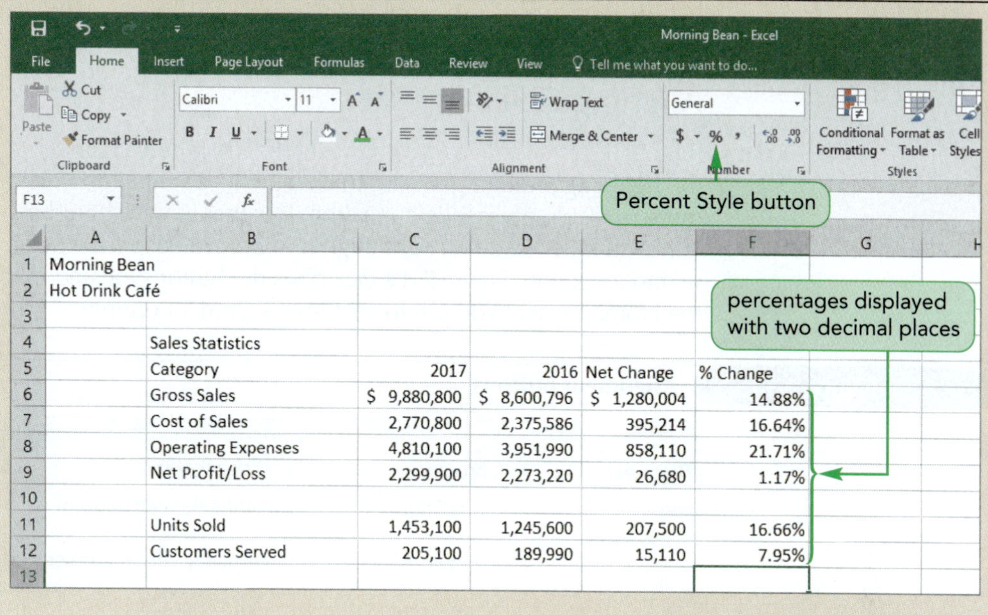

With the data reformatted, the worksheet clearly shows that Morning Bean's gross sales increased from 2016 to 2017 by almost 15 percent, but the company's net profit increased by only 1.17 percent due to increasing expenses in sales costs and operations of 16.64 percent and 21.71 percent, respectively. This type of information is very important to Morning Bean investors and to the company executives as plans are made for the upcoming year.

Formatting Dates and Times

TIP

To view the underlying date and time value, apply the General format to the cell or display the formulas instead of the formula results.

Because Excel stores dates and times as numbers and not as text, you can apply different date formats without affecting the underlying date and time value. The abbreviated format, *mm/dd/yyyy*, entered in the Documentation sheet is referred to as the **Short Date format**. You can also apply a **Long Date format** that displays the day of the week and the full month name in addition to the day of the month and the year. Other built-in formats include formats for displaying time values in 12- or 24-hour time format.

Carol asks you to change the date in the Documentation sheet to the Long Date format.

To format the date in the Long Date format:

1. Go to the **Documentation** sheet, and then select cell **B5**.
2. On the Home tab, in the Number group, click the **Number Format button arrow** to display a list of number formats, and then click **Long Date**. The date is displayed with the weekday name, month name, day, and year. Notice that the date in the formula bar did not change because you changed only the display format, not the date value.

Formatting Worksheet Cells

You can format the appearance of individual cells by modifying the alignment of text within the cell, indenting cell text, or adding borders of different styles and colors.

Aligning Cell Content

By default, text is aligned with the left edge of the cell, and numbers are aligned with the right edge. You might want to change the alignment to make the text and numbers more readable or visually appealing. In general, you should center column titles, left-align other text, and right-align numbers to keep their decimal places lined up within a column. Figure 2-14 describes the buttons located in the Alignment group on the Home tab that you use to set these alignment options.

Figure 2-14 Alignment buttons

Button	Name	Description
	Top Align	Aligns the cell content with the cell's top edge
	Middle Align	Vertically centers the cell content within the cell
	Bottom Align	Aligns the cell content with the cell's bottom edge
	Align Left	Aligns the cell content with the cell's left edge
	Center	Horizontally centers the cell content within the cell
	Align Right	Aligns the cell content with the cell's right edge
	Decrease Indent	Decreases the size of the indentation used in the cell
	Increase Indent	Increases the size of the indentation used in the cell
	Orientation	Rotates the cell content to any angle within the cell
	Wrap Text	Forces the cell text to wrap within the cell borders
	Merge & Center	Merges the selected cells into a single cell

The date in the Documentation sheet is right-aligned within cell B5 because Excel treats dates and times as numbers. Carol wants you to left-align the date from the Documentation sheet and center the column titles in the Sales Report worksheet.

To left-align the date and center the column titles:

1. In the Documentation sheet, make sure cell **B5** is still selected.
2. On the Home tab, in the Alignment group, click the **Align Left** button. The date shifts to the left edge of the cell.
3. Go to the **Sales Report** worksheet.
4. Select the range **C5:F5** containing the column titles.
5. In the Alignment group, click the **Center** button. The column titles are centered in the cells.

Indenting Cell Content

Sometimes you want a cell's content moved a few spaces from the cell's left edge. This is particularly useful to create subsections in a worksheet or to set off some entries from others. You can increase the indent to shift the contents of a cell away from the left edge of the cell, or you can decrease the indent to shift a cell's contents closer to the left edge of the cell.

Carol wants you to indent the Cost of Sales and Operating Expenses labels in the sales statistics table from the other labels because they represent expenses to the company.

To indent the expense categories:

1. Select the range **B7:B8** containing the expense categories.
2. On the Home tab, in the Alignment group, click the **Increase Indent** button twice to indent each label two spaces in its cell.

Adding Borders to Cells

Borders are another way to make financial data easier to interpret. Common accounting practices provide guidelines on when to add borders to cells. In general, a single black border should appear above a subtotal, a single bottom border should be added below a calculated number, and a double black bottom border should appear below the total.

Carol wants you to follow common accounting practices in the Sales Report worksheet. You will add borders below the column titles and below the gross sales values. You will add a top border to the net profit/loss values. Finally, you will add a top and bottom border to the Units Sold and Customers Served rows.

To add borders to the sales statistics data:

1. Select the range **B5:F5** containing the cell headings.
2. On the Home tab, in the Font group, click the **Borders button arrow**, and then click **Bottom Border**. A border is added below the column titles.
3. Select the range **B6:F6** containing the gross sales amounts.
4. In the Font group, click the **Bottom Border** button to add a border below the selected gross sales amounts.
5. Select the range **B9:F9**, click the **Borders button arrow**, and then click **Top Border** to add a border above the net profit/loss amounts.

   The Units Sold and Customers Served rows do not contain monetary values as the other rows do. You will distinguish these rows by adding a top and bottom border.

6. Select the range **B11:F12**, click the **Borders button arrow**, and then click **Top and Bottom Border** to add a border above the number of units sold and below the number of customers served.
7. Click cell **B3** to deselect the range. See Figure 2-15.

Figure 2-15 Borders, indents, and alignment added to the sales data

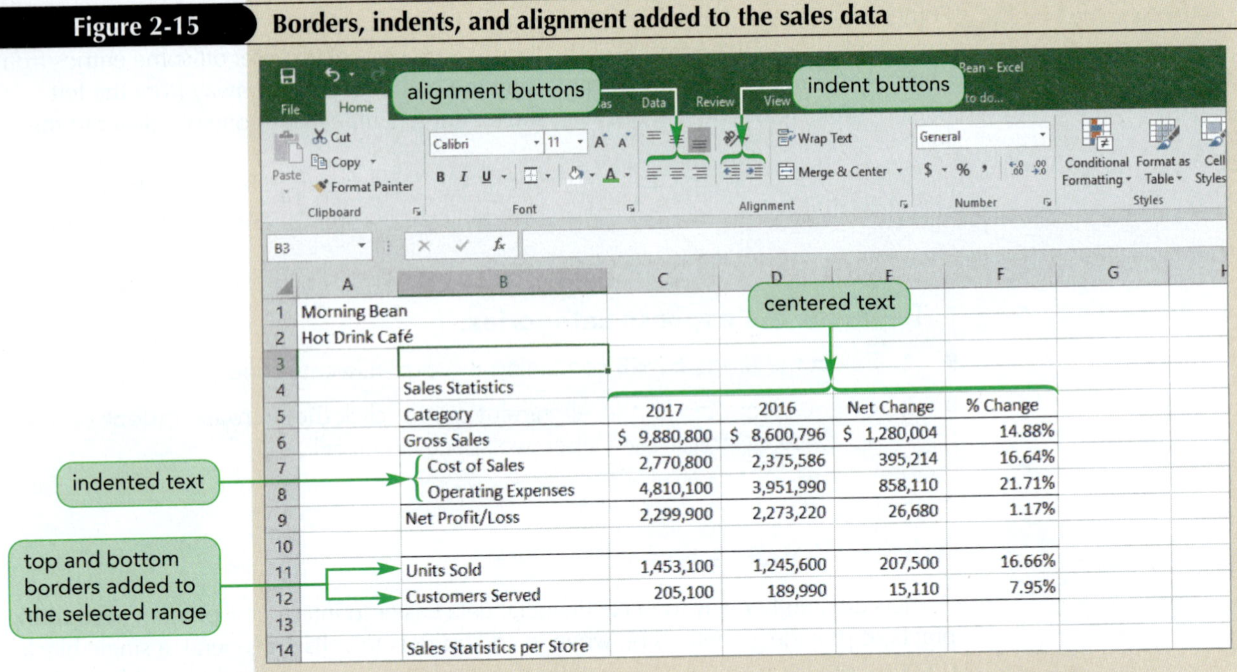

You can apply multiple formats to the same cell to create the look that best fits the data. For example, one cell might be formatted with a number format, alignments, borders, indents, fonts, font sizes, and so on. The monthly sales data needs to be formatted with number styles, alignments, indents, and borders. You'll add these formats now.

To format the monthly sales table:

1. Click in the **Name** box, type **C27:O47**, and then press the **Enter** key. The range C27:O47, containing the monthly gross sales for each store, is selected.
2. On the Home tab, in the Number group, click the **Comma Style** button to add a thousands separator to the values.
3. In the Number group, click the **Decrease Decimal** button twice to hide the cents from the sales results.
4. In the Alignment group, click the **Top Align** button to align the sales numbers with the top of each cell.
5. Select the range **C26:O26** containing the labels for the month abbreviations and the TOTAL column.
6. In the Alignment group, click the **Center** button to center the column labels.
7. Select the range **B27:B46** containing the store addresses.
8. Reduce the font size of the store addresses to **9** points.
9. In the Alignment group, click the **Increase Indent** button to indent the store addresses.
10. In the Alignment group, click the **Top Align** button to align the addresses at the top of each cell.
11. Select the range **B47:O47** containing the monthly totals.
12. In the Font group, click the **Borders button arrow**, and then click **All Borders** to add borders around each monthly totals cell.

13. Select the range **O26:O46** containing the annual totals for each restaurant, and then click the **All Borders** button to add borders around each restaurant total.

14. Click cell **A24** to deselect the range. See Figure 2-16.

Figure 2-16 Formatted monthly gross sales

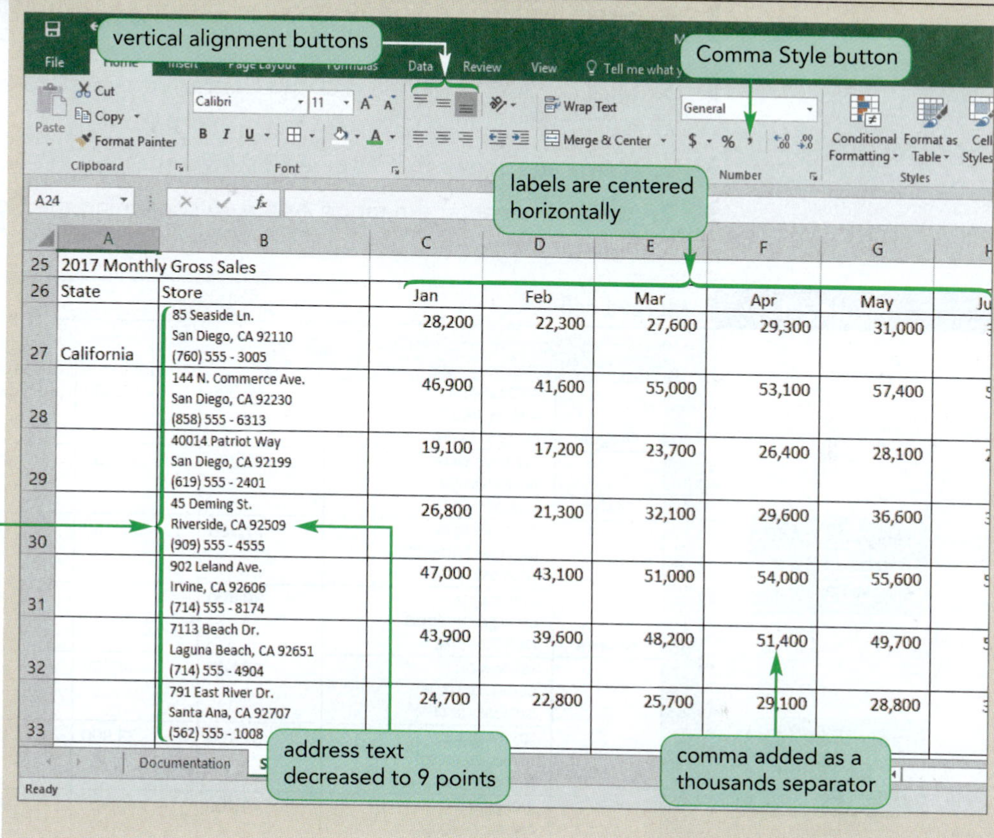

Merging Cells

You can merge, or combine, several cells into one cell. A merged cell contains two or more cells with a single cell reference. When you merge cells, only the content from the upper-left cell in the range is retained. The cell reference for the merged cell is the upper-left cell reference. So, if you merge cells A1 and A2, the merged cell reference is cell A1. After you merge cells, you can align the content within the merged cell. The Merge & Center button in the Alignment group on the Home tab includes the following options:

- **Merge & Center**—merges the range into one cell and horizontally centers the content
- **Merge Across**—merges each row in the selected range across the columns in the range
- **Merge Cells**—merges the range into a single cell but does not horizontally center the cell content
- **Unmerge Cells**—reverses a merge, returning the merged cell to a range of individual cells

The first column of the monthly sales data lists the states in which Morning Bean has stores. You will merge the cells for each state name into a single cell.

To merge the state name cells:

1. Select the range **A27:A33** containing the cells for the California stores. You will merge these seven cells into a single cell.

2. On the Home tab, in the Alignment group, click the **Merge & Center** button. The range A27:A33 merges into one cell with the cell reference A27, and the text is centered and bottom-aligned within the cell.
3. Select the range **A34:A36**, and then click the **Merge & Center** button to merge and center the cells for stores in the state of Washington.
4. Select the range **A37:A40**, and then merge and center the cells for the Oregon stores.
5. Click cell **A41**, and then click the **Center** button to center the Idaho text horizontally in the cell.
6. Merge and center the range **A42:A43** containing the Nevada cells.
7. Merge and center the range **A44:A46** containing the Colorado cells. See Figure 2-17.

Figure 2-17 **Merged cells**

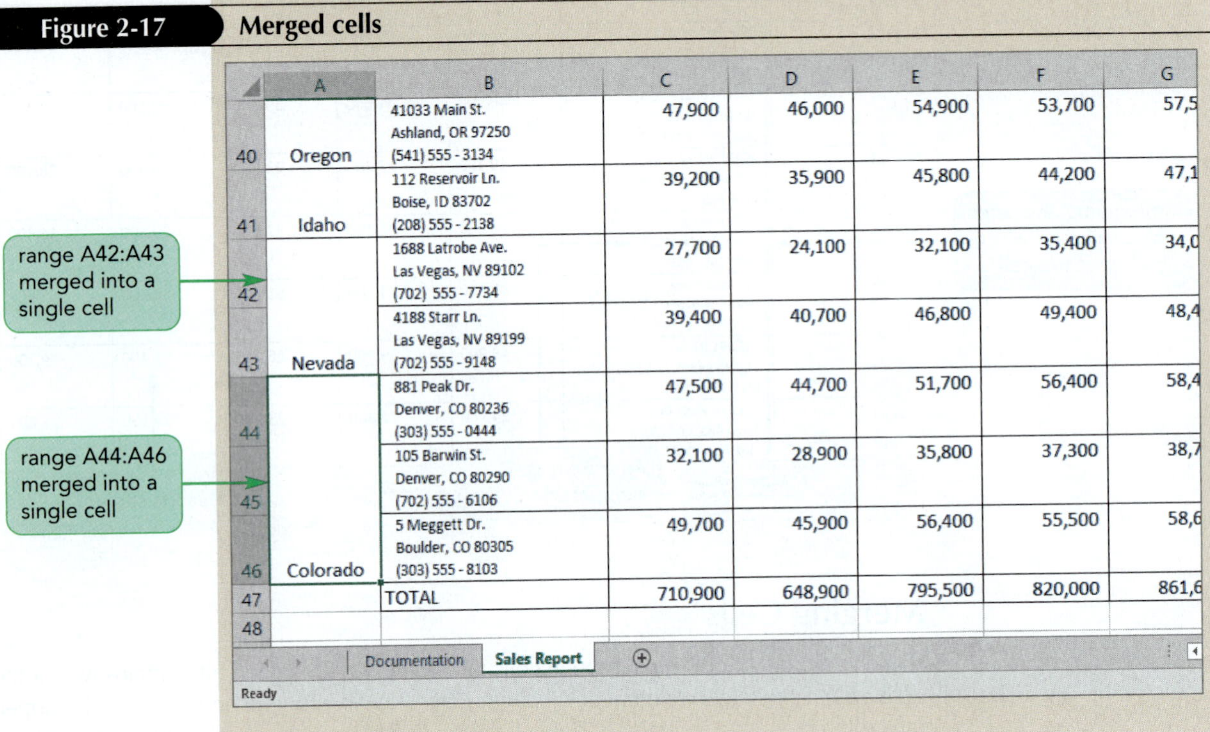

	A	B	C	D	E	F	G
40	Oregon	41033 Main St. Ashland, OR 97250 (541) 555 - 3134	47,900	46,000	54,900	53,700	57,5
41	Idaho	112 Reservoir Ln. Boise, ID 83702 (208) 555 - 2138	39,200	35,900	45,800	44,200	47,1
42		1688 Latrobe Ave. Las Vegas, NV 89102 (702) 555 - 7734	27,700	24,100	32,100	35,400	34,0
43	Nevada	4188 Starr Ln. Las Vegas, NV 89199 (702) 555 - 9148	39,400	40,700	46,800	49,400	48,4
44		881 Peak Dr. Denver, CO 80236 (303) 555 - 0444	47,500	44,700	51,700	56,400	58,4
45		105 Barwin St. Denver, CO 80290 (702) 555 - 6106	32,100	28,900	35,800	37,300	38,7
46	Colorado	5 Meggett Dr. Boulder, CO 80305 (303) 555 - 8103	49,700	45,900	56,400	55,500	58,6
47		TOTAL	710,900	648,900	795,500	820,000	861,6
48							

The merged cells make it easier to distinguish restaurants in each state. Next, you will rotate the cells so that the state name rotates up the merged cells.

Rotating Cell Contents

Text and numbers are displayed horizontally within cells. However, you can rotate cell text to any angle to save space or to provide visual interest to a worksheet. The state names at the bottom of the merged cells would look better and take up less room if they were rotated vertically within their cells. Carol asks you to rotate the state names.

To rotate the state names:

1. Select the merged cell **A27**.
2. On the Home tab, in the Alignment group, click the **Orientation** button to display a list of rotation options, and then click **Rotate Text Up**. The state name rotates 90 degrees counterclockwise.

3. In the Alignment group, click the **Middle Align** button to vertically center the rotated text in the merged cell.
4. Select the merged cell range **A34:A46**, and then repeat Steps 2 and 3 to rotate and vertically center the rest of the state names in their cells.
5. Reduce the width of column A to **7** characters because the rotated state names take up less space.
6. Select cell **A47**. See Figure 2-18.

Figure 2-18 Rotated cell content

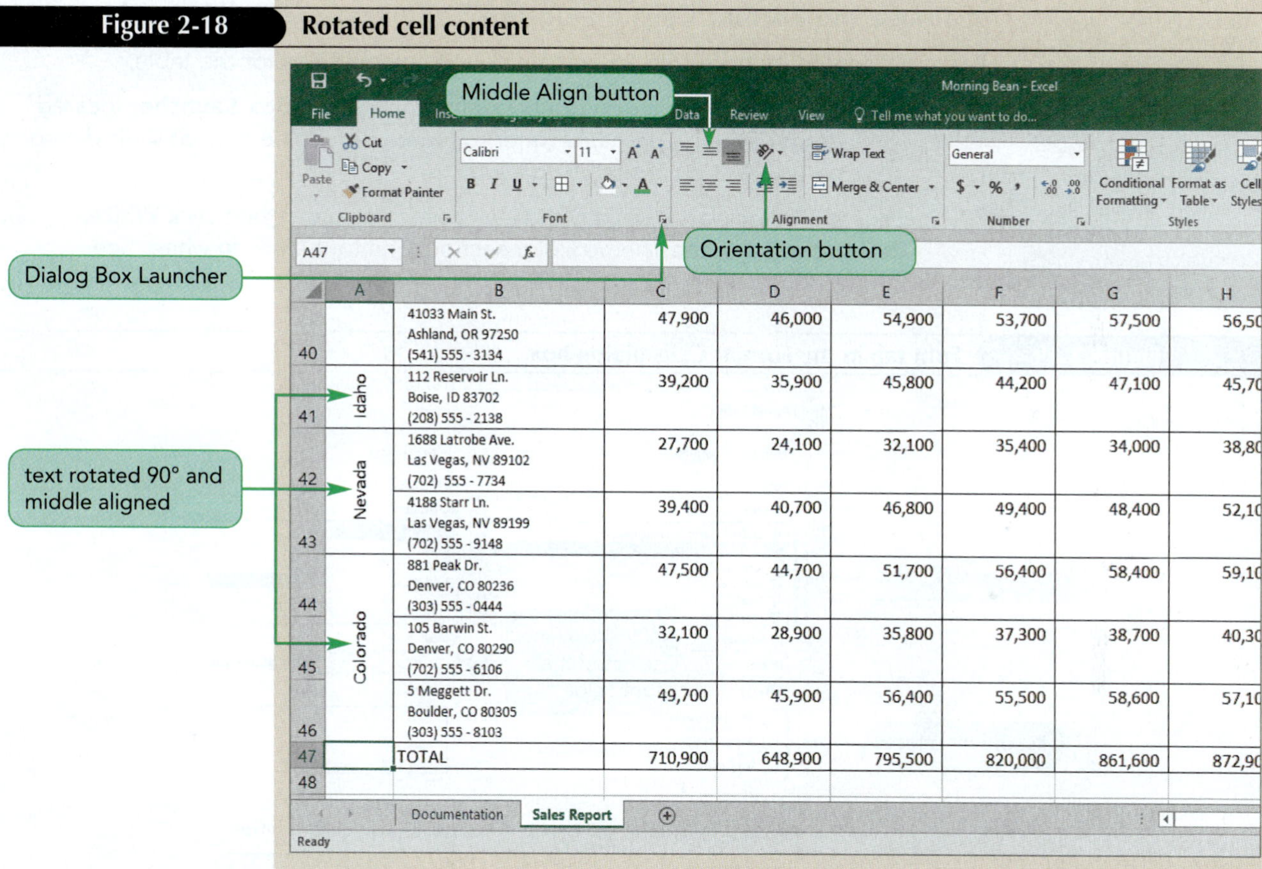

In addition to using the ribbon to apply formatting to a worksheet, you can also use the Format Cells dialog box to apply formatting.

Exploring the Format Cells Dialog Box

The buttons on the Home tab provide quick access to the most commonly used formatting choices. For more options, you can use the Format Cells dialog box. You can apply the formats in this dialog box to the selected worksheet cells. The Format Cells dialog box has six tabs, each focusing on a different set of formatting options, as described below:

- **Number**—provides options for formatting the appearance of numbers, including dates and numbers treated as text such as telephone or Social Security numbers
- **Alignment**—provides options for how data is aligned within a cell
- **Font**—provides options for selecting font types, sizes, styles, and other formatting attributes such as underlining and font colors

- **Border**—provides options for adding and removing cell borders as well as selecting a line style and color
- **Fill**—provides options for creating and applying background colors and patterns to cells
- **Protection**—provides options for locking or hiding cells to prevent other users from modifying their contents

Although you have applied many of these formats from the Home tab, the Format Cells dialog box presents them in a different way and provides more choices. You will use the Font and Fill tabs to format the column titles with a white font on a green background.

To use the Format Cells dialog box to format the column titles:

1. Select the range **A26:O26** containing the column titles for the table.
2. On the Home tab, in the Font group, click the **Dialog Box Launcher** located to the right of the group name (refer to Figure 2-18). The Format Cells dialog box opens with the Font tab displayed.
3. Click the **Color** box to display the available colors, and then click **White, Background 1** in the Theme Color section. The font is set to white. See Figure 2-19.

TIP

Clicking the Dialog Box Launcher in the Font, Alignment, or Number group opens the Format Cells dialog box with that tab displayed.

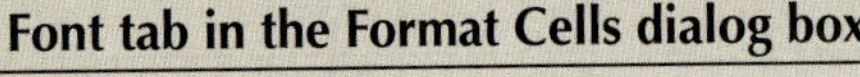

Figure 2-19 Font tab in the Format Cells dialog box

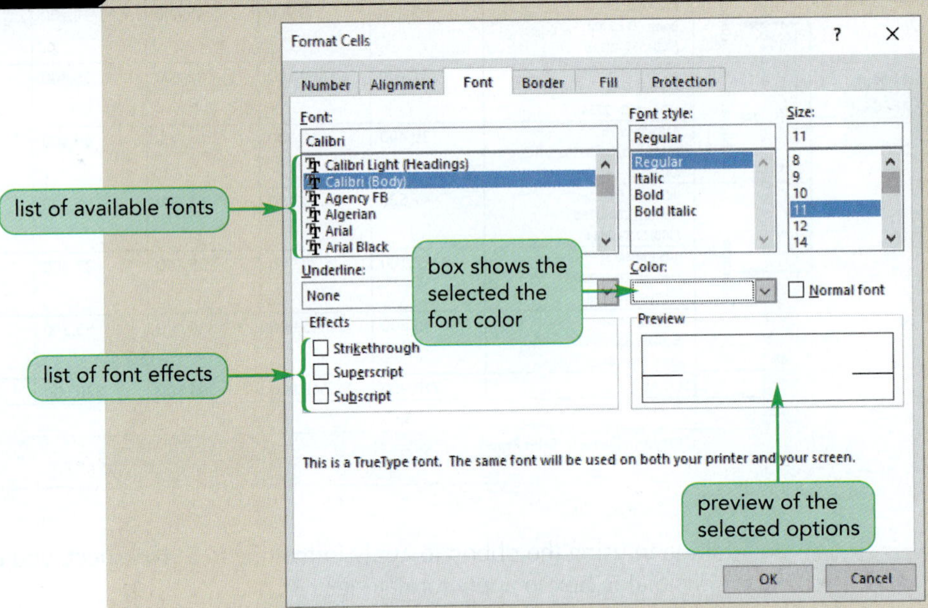

4. Click the **Fill** tab to display background options.
5. In the Background Color section, click the **green** standard color (the sixth color in the last row). The background is set to green, as you can see in the Sample box.
6. Click the **OK** button. The dialog box closes, and the font and fill options you selected are applied to the column titles.

You will also use the Format Cells dialog box to change the appearance of the row titles. You'll format them to be displayed in a larger white font on a gold background.

To format the row titles:

1. Select the range **A27:A46** containing the rotated state names.
2. Right-click the selected range, and then click **Format Cells** on the shortcut menu. The Format Cells dialog box opens with the last tab used displayed—in this case, the Fill tab.
3. In the Background Color section, click the **gold** theme color (the eighth color in the first row). Its preview is shown in the Sample box.
4. Click the **Font** tab to display the font formatting options.
5. Click the **Color** box, and then click the **White, Background 1** theme color to set the font color to white.
6. In the Size box, click **14** to set the font size to 14 points.
7. In the Font style box, click **Bold** to change the font to boldface.
8. Click the **OK** button. The dialog box closes, and the font and fill formats are applied to the state names.
9. Scroll up and click cell **A24** to deselect the A27:A46 range. See Figure 2-20.

Figure 2-20 Formatted worksheet cells

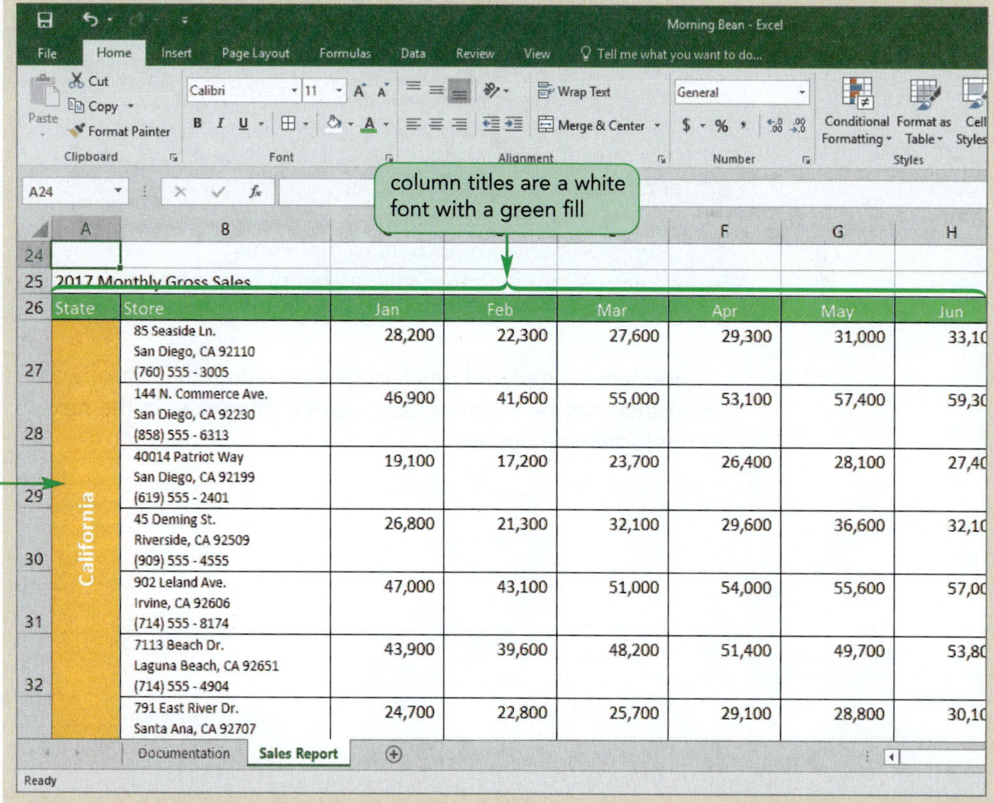

10. Save the workbook.

With the formats you have added to the Sales Report worksheet, readers will be able to more easily read and interpret the large table of store sales.

PROSKILLS

Written Communication: Formatting Workbooks for Readability and Appeal

Designing a workbook requires the same care as designing any written document or report. A well-formatted workbook is easy to read and establishes a sense of professionalism with readers. Do the following to improve the appearance of your workbooks:

- **Clearly identify each worksheet's purpose.** Include column or row titles and a descriptive sheet name.
- **Include only one or two topics on each worksheet.** Don't crowd individual worksheets with too much information. Place extra topics on separate sheets. Readers should be able to interpret each worksheet with a minimal amount of horizontal and vertical scrolling.
- **Place worksheets with the most important information first in the workbook.** Position worksheets summarizing your findings near the front of the workbook. Position worksheets with detailed and involved analysis near the end as an appendix.
- **Use consistent formatting throughout the workbook.** If negative values appear in red on one worksheet, format them in the same way on all sheets. Also, be consistent in the use of thousands separators, decimal places, and percentages.
- **Pay attention to the format of the printed workbook.** Make sure your printouts are legible with informative headers and footers. Check that the content of the printout is scaled correctly to the page size and that page breaks divide the information into logical sections.

Excel provides many formatting tools. However, too much formatting can be intrusive, overwhelm data, and make the document difficult to read. Remember that the goal of formatting is not simply to make a "pretty workbook" but also to accentuate important trends and relationships in the data. A well-formatted workbook should seamlessly convey your data to the reader. If the reader is thinking about how your workbook looks, it means he or she is not thinking about your data.

You have completed much of the formatting that Carol wants in the Sales Report worksheet for the Morning Bean sales conference. In the next session, you will explore other formatting options.

REVIEW

Session 2.1 Quick Check

1. What is the difference between a serif font and a sans serif font?
2. What is the difference between a theme color and a standard color?
3. A cell containing a number displays #######. Why does this occur, and what can you do to fix it?
4. What is the General format?
5. Describe the differences between Currency format and Accounting format.
6. The range B3:B13 is merged into a single cell. What is its cell reference?
7. How do you format text so that it is set vertically within the cell?
8. Where can you access all the formatting options for worksheet cells?

Session 2.2 Visual Overview:

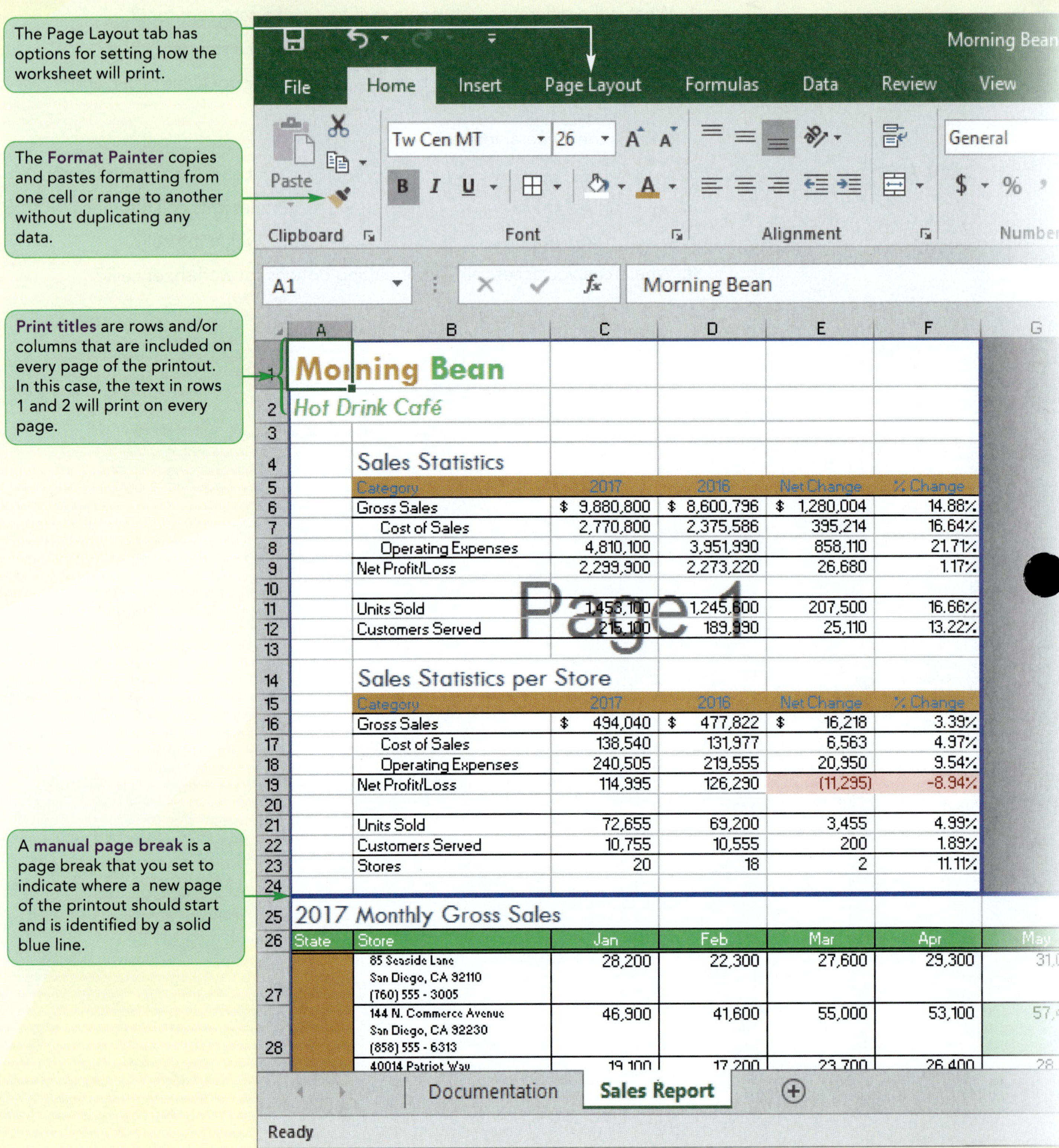

The Page Layout tab has options for setting how the worksheet will print.
The Format Painter copies and pastes formatting from one cell or range to another without duplicating any data.
Print titles are rows and/or columns that are included on every page of the printout. In this case, the text in rows 1 and 2 will print on every page.
A manual page break is a page break that you set to indicate where a new page of the printout should start and is identified by a solid blue line.
Morning Bean
File
Home
Insert
Page Layout
Formulas
Data
Review
View
Paste
Clipboard
Tw Cen MT
26
Font
Alignment
General
Number
A1
Morning Bean
Hot Drink Café
Sales Statistics
Category
2017
2016
Net Change
% Change
Gross Sales $ 9,880,800 $ 8,600,796 $ 1,280,004 14.88%
Cost of Sales 2,770,800 2,375,586 395,214 16.64%
Operating Expenses 4,810,100 3,951,990 858,110 21.71%
Net Profit/Loss 2,299,900 2,273,220 26,680 1.17%
Units Sold 1,453,100 1,245,600 207,500 16.66%
Customers Served 215,100 189,990 25,110 13.22%
Page 1
Sales Statistics per Store
Category
2017
2016
Net Change
% Change
Gross Sales $ 494,040 $ 477,822 $ 16,218 3.39%
Cost of Sales 138,540 131,977 6,563 4.97%
Operating Expenses 240,505 219,555 20,950 9.54%
Net Profit/Loss 114,995 126,290 (11,295) -8.94%
Units Sold 72,655 69,200 3,455 4.99%
Customers Served 10,755 10,555 200 1.89%
Stores 20 18 2 11.11%
2017 Monthly Gross Sales
State
Store
Jan
Feb
Mar
Apr
85 Seaside Lane
San Diego, CA 92110
(760) 555 - 3005
28,200 22,300 27,600 29,300
144 N. Commerce Avenue
San Diego, CA 92230
(858) 555 - 6313
46,900 41,600 55,000 53,100
Documentation
Sales Report
Ready

Designing a Printout

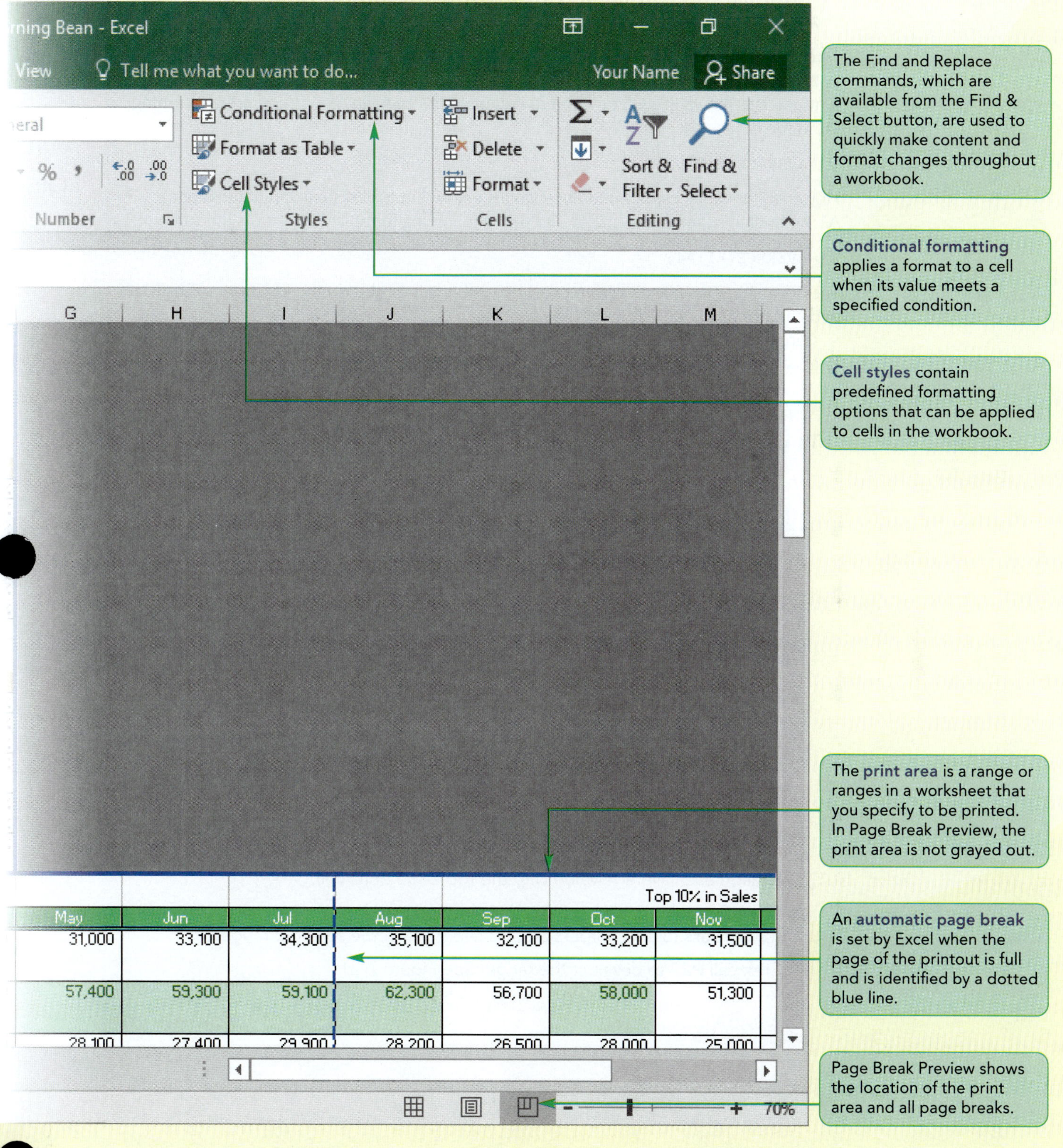

The Find and Replace commands, which are available from the Find & Select button, are used to quickly make content and format changes throughout a workbook.

Conditional formatting applies a format to a cell when its value meets a specified condition.

Cell styles contain predefined formatting options that can be applied to cells in the workbook.

The **print area** is a range or ranges in a worksheet that you specify to be printed. In Page Break Preview, the print area is not grayed out.

An **automatic page break** is set by Excel when the page of the printout is full and is identified by a dotted blue line.

Page Break Preview shows the location of the print area and all page breaks.

Calculating Averages

The **AVERAGE function** calculates the average value from a collection of numbers. It has the syntax

```
AVERAGE(number1,number2,number3,...)
```

where *number1*, *number2*, *number3*, and so forth are either numbers or cell references to the cells or a range where the numbers are stored. For example, the following formula uses the AVERAGE function to calculate the average of 1, 2, 5, and 8, returning the value 4:

```
=AVERAGE(1,2,5,8)
```

However, functions usually reference values entered in a worksheet. So, if the range A1:A4 contains the values 1, 2, 5, and 8, the following formula also returns the value 4:

```
=AVERAGE(A1:A4)
```

The advantage of using cell references is that the values used in the function are visible and can be easily edited.

Carol wants you to calculate the average monthly sales for each of the 20 Morning Bean stores. You will use the AVERAGE function to calculate these values.

To calculate the average monthly sales for each store:

1. If you took a break after the previous session, make sure the Morning Bean workbook is open and the Sales Report worksheet is active.
2. In cell **P26**, enter **AVERAGE** as the column title. The cell is formatted with a green fill and white font color, matching the other column titles.
3. In cell **P27**, enter the formula **=AVERAGE(C27:N27)** to calculate the average of the monthly gross sales values entered in the range C27:N27. The formula returns the value 30,833, which is the average monthly gross sales for the store on 85 Seaside Lane in San Diego, California.
4. Copy the formula in cell **P27**, and then paste the copied formula in the range **P28:P47** to calculate the average monthly gross sales for each of the remaining Morning Bean stores as well as the average monthly sales from all stores. The average monthly gross sales for individual stores range from $25,408 to $56,317. The monthly gross sales from all stores is $823,400.
5. Select the range **P27:P47**. You will format this range of sales statistics.
6. On the Home tab, in the Alignment group, click the **Top Align** button to align each average value with the top edge of its cell.
7. In the Font group, click the **Borders button arrow**, then click **All Borders** to add borders around every cell in the selected range.
8. Click cell **P27** to deselect the range. See Figure 2-21.

Figure 2-21 Average sales results

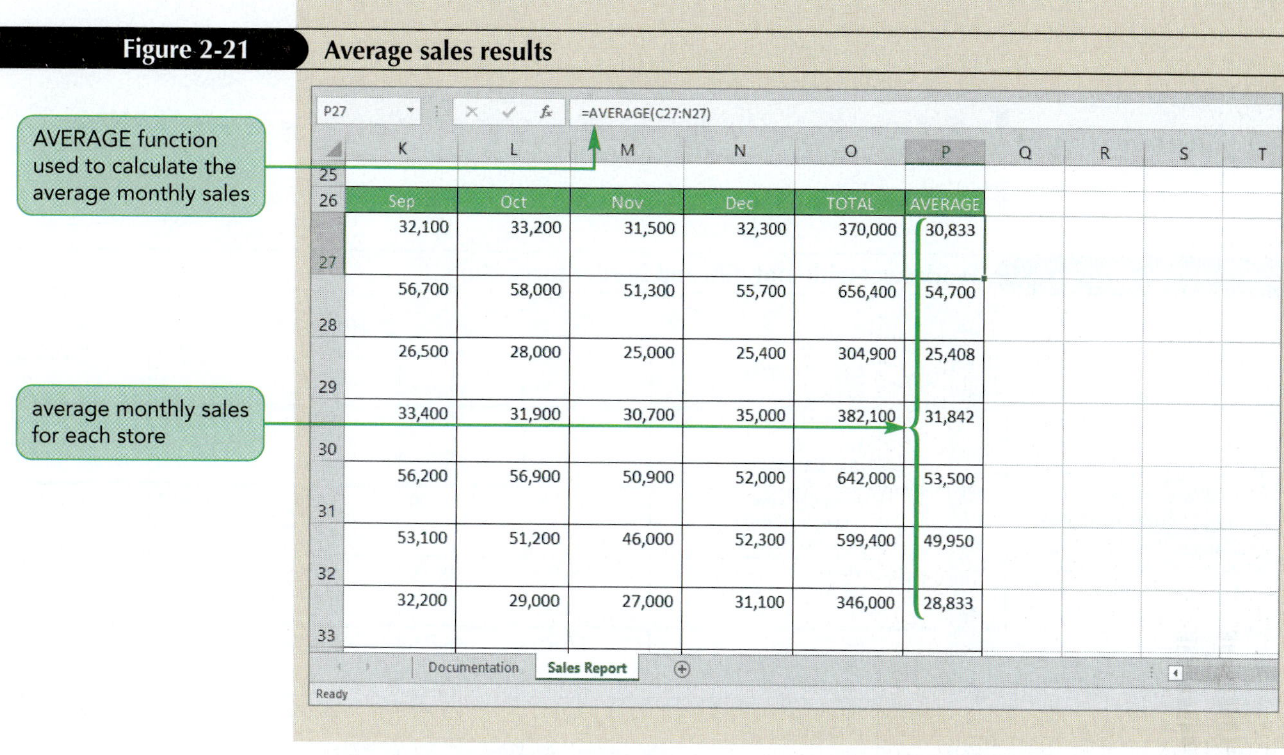

With so many values in the data, Carol wants you to insert double borders around the sales values for each state. The Border tab in the Format Cells dialog box provides options for changing the border style and color and placement.

To add a double border to the state results:

1. Select the range **A27:N33** containing the California monthly sales totals.
2. Open the Format Cells dialog box, and then click the **Border** tab.
3. In the Line section, click the **double line** in the lower-right corner of the Style box.
4. In the Presets section, click the **Outline** option. The double border appears around the selected cells in the Border preview. See Figure 2-22.

Figure 2-22 Border tab in the Format Cells dialog box

selected border option
selected border style
selected border color
preview of the selected border style

Format Cells

Number | Alignment | Font | Border | Fill | Protection

Line
Style:
None
Color:
Automatic

Presets
None Outline Inside

Border
Text Text
Text Text

The selected border style can be applied by clicking the presets, preview diagram or the buttons above.

OK Cancel

5. Click the **OK** button. The selected border is applied to the California monthly sales.
6. Repeat Steps 2 through 5 to apply double borders to the ranges **A34:N36**, **A37:N40**, **A41:N41**, **A42:N43**, and **A44:N46**.
7. Click cell **A48** to deselect the range. See Figure 2-23.

Figure 2-23 **Worksheet with font, fill, and border formatting**

double borders around each state's sales row

	A	B	C	D	E	F	G
40		41033 Main St. Ashland, OR 97250 (541) 555 - 3134	47,900	46,000	54,900	53,700	57,500
41	Idaho	112 Reservoir Ln. Boise, ID 83702 (208) 555 - 2138	39,200	35,900	45,800	44,200	47,100
42	Nevada	1688 Latrobe Ave. Las Vegas, NV 89102 (702) 555 - 7734	27,700	24,100	32,100	35,400	34,000
43		4188 Starr Ln. Las Vegas, NV 89199 (702) 555 - 9148	39,400	40,700	46,800	49,400	48,400
44	Colorado	881 Peak Dr. Denver, CO 80236 (303) 555 - 0444	47,500	44,700	51,700	56,400	58,400
45		105 Barwin St. Denver, CO 80290 (702) 555 - 6106	32,100	28,900	35,800	37,300	38,700
46		5 Meggett Dr. Boulder, CO 80305 (303) 555 - 8103	49,700	45,900	56,400	55,500	58,600
47		TOTAL	710,900	648,900	795,500	820,000	861,600
48							

Documentation | Sales Report

Ready

Another way to format worksheet cells is with styles.

Applying Cell Styles

A workbook often contains several cells that store the same type of data. For example, each worksheet might have a cell displaying the sheet title, or a range of financial data might have several cells containing totals and averages. It is good design practice to apply the same format to worksheet cells that contain the same type of data.

One way to ensure that similar data is displayed consistently is with styles. A **style** is a collection of formatting options that include a specified font, font size, font styles, font color, fill color, and borders. The Cell Styles gallery includes a variety of built-in styles that you can use to format titles and headings, different types of data such as totals or calculations, and cells that you want to emphasize. For example, you can use the Heading 1 style to display sheet titles in a bold, blue-gray, 15-point Calibri font with no fill color and a blue bottom border. You can then apply the Heading 1 style to all titles in the workbook. If you later revise the style, the appearance of any cell formatted with that style is updated automatically. This saves you the time and effort of reformatting each cell individually.

You already used built-in styles when you formatted data in the Sales Report worksheet with the Accounting, Comma, and Percent styles. You can also create your own cell styles by clicking New Cell Style at the bottom of the Cell Styles gallery.

REFERENCE

Applying a Cell Style

- Select the cell or range to which you want to apply a style.
- On the Home tab, in the Styles group, click the Cell Styles button.
- Point to each style in the Cell Styles gallery to see a Live Preview of that style on the selected cell or range.
- Click the style you want to apply to the selected cell or range.

Carol wants you to add more color and visual interest to the Sales Report worksheet. You'll use the styles in the Cell Styles gallery to do this.

To apply cell styles to the Sales Report worksheet:

1. Click cell **B4** containing the text "Sales Statistics."
2. On the Home tab, in the Styles group, click the **Cell Styles** button. The Cell Styles gallery opens.
3. Point to the **Heading 1** style in the Titles and Headings section. Live Preview shows cell B4 in a 15-point, bold font with a solid blue bottom border. See Figure 2-24.

Figure 2-24 **Cell Styles gallery**

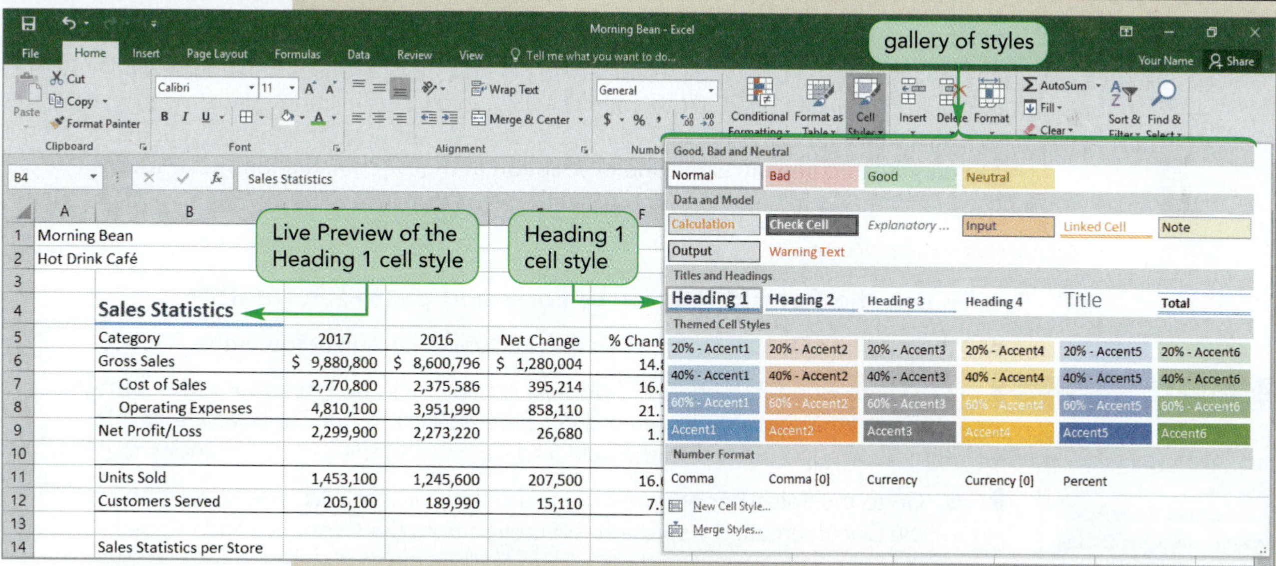

4. Move the pointer over different styles in the Cell Styles gallery to see cell B4 with a Live Preview of each style.
5. Click the **Title** style. The Title style—18-point, Blue-Gray, Text 2 Calibri Light font—is applied to cell B4.
6. Select the range **B5:F5** containing the column titles for the Sales Statistics data.
7. In the Styles group, click the **Cell Styles** button, and then click the **Accent4** style in the Themed Cell Styles section of the Cell Styles gallery.
8. Click cell **A25** containing the text "2017 Monthly Gross Sales," and then apply the **Title** cell style to the cell.

9. Click cell **A3**. See Figure 2-25.

Figure 2-25 Cell styles applied to the worksheet

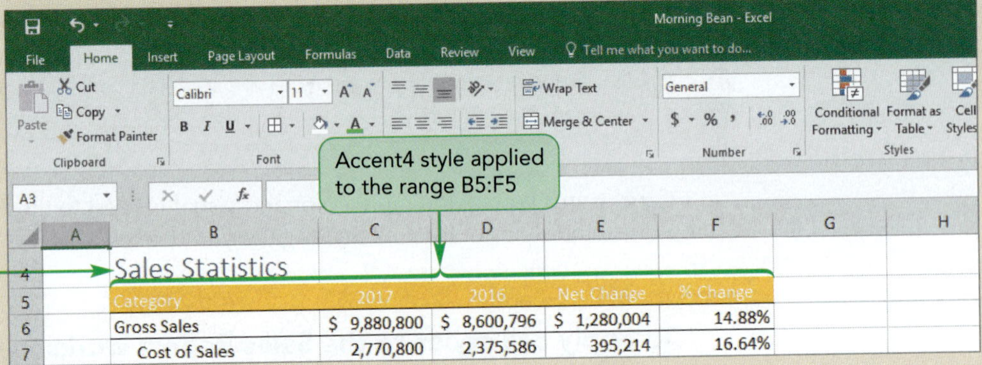

Copying and Pasting Formats

Large workbooks often use the same formatting on similar data throughout the workbook, sometimes in widely scattered cells. Rather than repeating the same steps to format these cells, you can copy the format of one cell or range and paste it to another.

Copying Formats with the Format Painter

The Format Painter provides a fast and efficient way of copying and pasting formats, ensuring that a workbook has a consistent look and feel. The Format Painter does not copy formatting applied to selected text within a cell, and it does not copy data.

Carol wants the Sales Report worksheet to use the same formats you applied to the Morning Bean company name and description in the Documentation sheet. You will use the Format Painter to copy and paste the formats.

TIP

To paste the same format multiple times, double-click the Format Painter button. Click the button again or press the Esc key to turn it off.

To use the Format Painter to copy and paste a format:

1. Go to the **Documentation** worksheet, and then select the range **A1:A2**.
2. On the Home tab, in the Clipboard group, click the **Format Painter** button. The formats from the selected cells are copied to the Clipboard, a flashing border appears around the selected range, and the pointer changes to ✚🖌.
3. Go to the **Sales Report** worksheet, and then click cell **A1**. The formatting from the Documentation worksheet is removed from the Clipboard and applied to the range A1:A2. Notice that gold font color you applied to the text selection "Morning" was not included in the pasted formats.
4. Double-click cell **A1** to enter Edit mode, select **Morning**, and then change the font color to the **Gold, Accent 4** theme color. The format for the company title now matches what you applied earlier in the Documentation sheet.
5. Press the **Enter** key to exit Edit mode and select cell A2.

You can use the Format Painter to copy all of the formats within a selected range and then apply those formats to another range that has the same size and shape by clicking the upper-left cell of the range. Carol wants you to copy all of the formats that you applied to the Sales Statistics data to the sales statistics per store data.

To copy and paste multiple formats:

1. Select the range **B4:F12** in the Sales Report worksheet.
2. On the Home tab, in the Clipboard group, click the **Format Painter** button.
3. Click cell **B14**. All of the number formats, cell borders, fonts, and fill colors are pasted in the range B14:F22.
4. Select the range **C23:E23**. You'll format this data.
5. On the Home tab, in the Number group, click the **Comma Style** button, and then click the **Decrease Decimal** button twice to remove the decimal places to the right of the decimal point. The numbers are now vertically aligned in their columns.
6. Click cell **F23**.
7. In the Number group, click the **Percent Style** button to change the number to a percentage, and then click the **Increase Decimal** button twice to display two decimal places in the percentage. The value is now formatted to match the other percentages.
8. Click cell **B24**. See Figure 2-26.

TIP

If the range you paste the formats in is bigger than the range you copied, Format Painter will repeat the copied formats to fill the pasted range.

Figure 2-26 Formatting copied and pasted between ranges

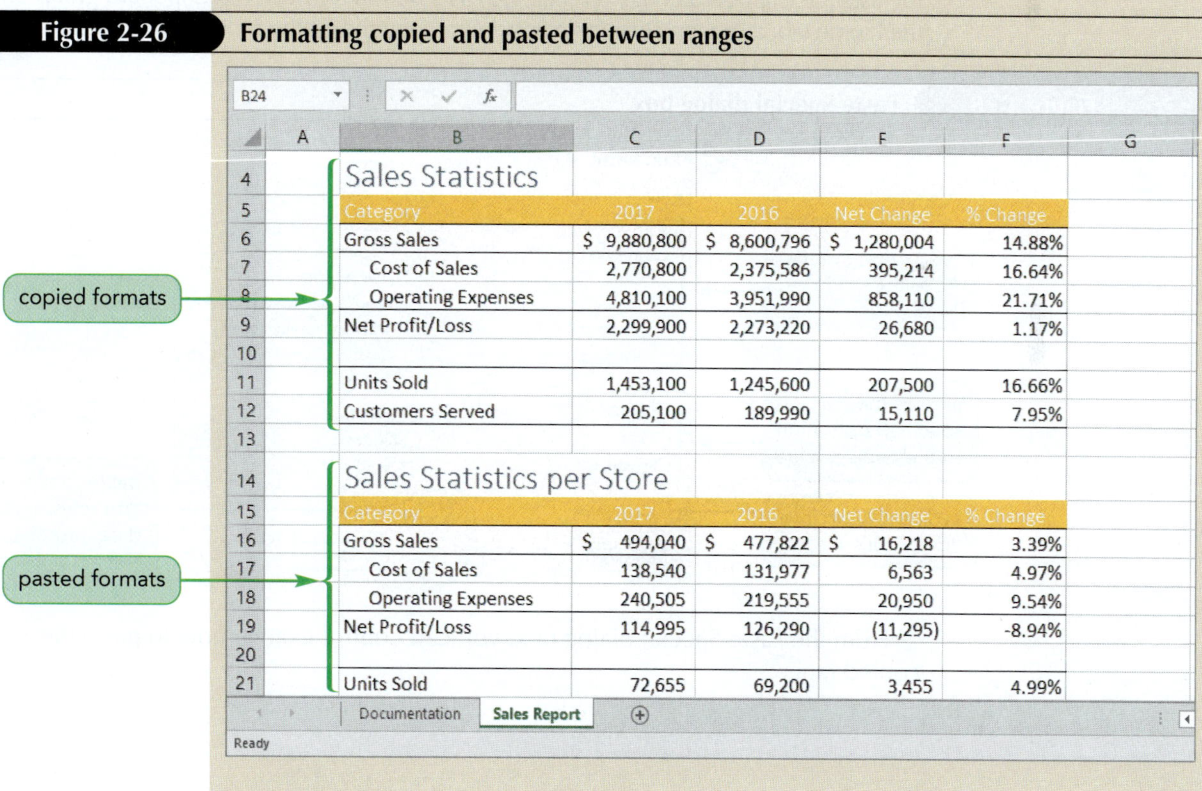

	A	B	C	D	E	F
4		Sales Statistics				
5		Category	2017	2016	Net Change	% Change
6		Gross Sales	$ 9,880,800	$ 8,600,796	$ 1,280,004	14.88%
7		Cost of Sales	2,770,800	2,375,586	395,214	16.64%
8		Operating Expenses	4,810,100	3,951,990	858,110	21.71%
9		Net Profit/Loss	2,299,900	2,273,220	26,680	1.17%
10						
11		Units Sold	1,453,100	1,245,600	207,500	16.66%
12		Customers Served	205,100	189,990	15,110	7.95%
13						
14		Sales Statistics per Store				
15		Category	2017	2016	Net Change	% Change
16		Gross Sales	$ 494,040	$ 477,822	$ 16,218	3.39%
17		Cost of Sales	138,540	131,977	6,563	4.97%
18		Operating Expenses	240,505	219,555	20,950	9.54%
19		Net Profit/Loss	114,995	126,290	(11,295)	-8.94%
20						
21		Units Sold	72,655	69,200	3,455	4.99%

Copying Formats with the Paste Options Button

Another way to copy and paste formats is with the Paste Options button, which provides options for pasting only values, only formats, or some combination of values and formats. Each time you paste, the Paste Options button appears in the lower-right corner of the pasted cell or range. You click the Paste Options button to open a list of pasting options, shown in Figure 2-27, such as pasting only the values or only the formatting. You can also click the Transpose button to paste the column data into a row, or to paste the row data into a column.

Figure 2-27 Paste Options button

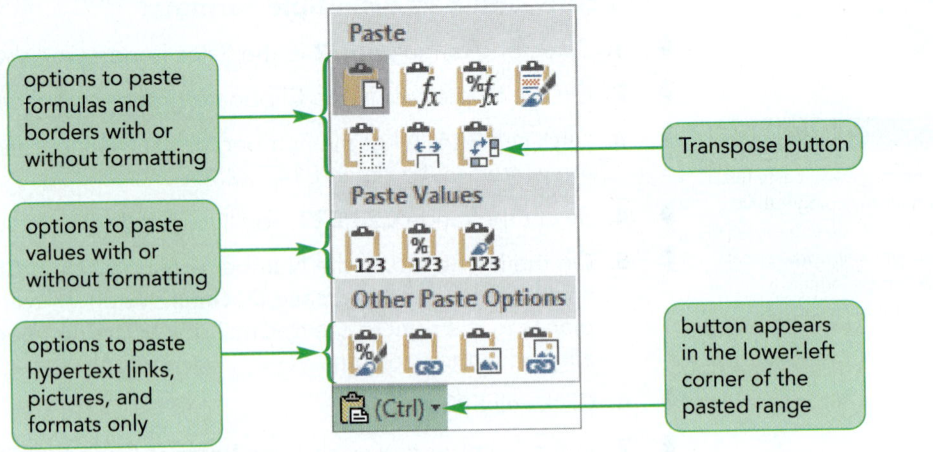

Copying Formats with Paste Special

The Paste Special command provides another way to control what you paste from the Clipboard. To use Paste Special, select and copy a range, select the range where you want to paste the Clipboard contents, click the Paste button arrow in the Clipboard group on the Home tab, and then click Paste Special to open the dialog box shown in Figure 2-28.

Figure 2-28 Paste Special dialog box

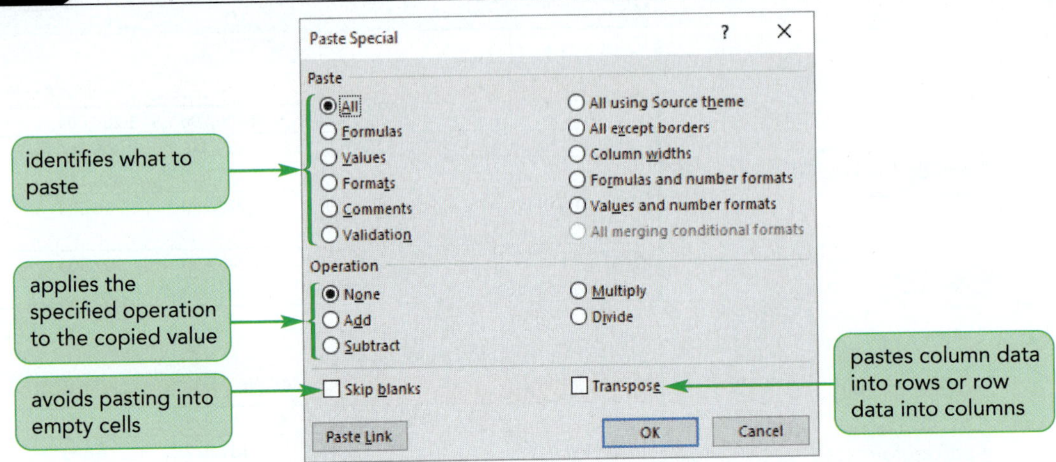

From the Paste Special dialog box, you can control exactly how to paste the copied range.

Finding and Replacing Text and Formats

The Find and Replace commands let you make content and design changes to a worksheet or the entire workbook quickly. The Find command searches through the current worksheet or workbook for the content or formatting you want to locate, and the Replace command then substitutes it with the new content or formatting you specify.

The Find and Replace commands are versatile. You can find each occurrence of the search text one at a time and decide whether to replace it. You can highlight all occurrences of the search text in the worksheet. Or, you can replace all occurrences at once without reviewing them.

Carol wants you to replace all the street title abbreviations (such as Ave.) in the Sales Report with their full names (such as Avenue). You will use Find and Replace to make these changes.

To find and replace the street title abbreviations:

1. On the Home tab, in the Editing group, click the **Find & Select** button, and then click **Replace** (or press the **Ctrl+H** keys). The Find and Replace dialog box opens.
2. Type **Ave.** in the Find what box.
3. Press the **Tab** key to move the insertion point to the Replace with box, and then type **Avenue**. See Figure 2-29.

Figure 2-29 Find and Replace dialog box

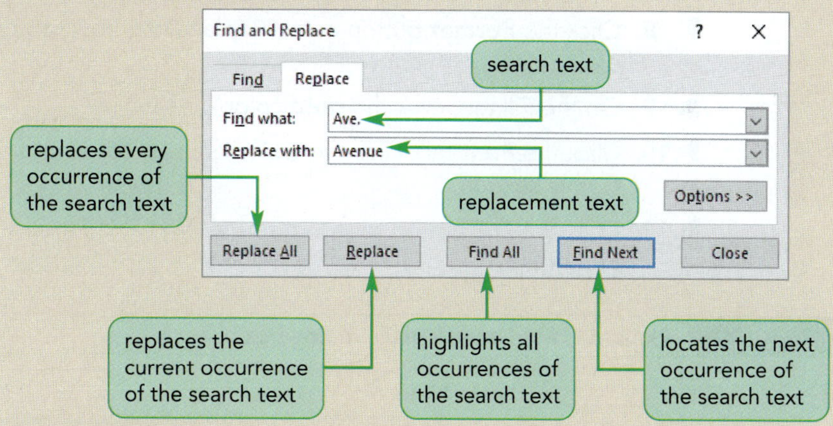

4. Click the **Replace All** button to replace all occurrences of the search text without reviewing them. A dialog box opens, reporting that three replacements were made in the worksheet.
5. Click the **OK** button to return to the Find and Replace dialog box.

   Next, you will replace the other street title abbreviations.
6. Repeat Steps 2 through 5 to replace all occurrences of each of the following: **St.** with **Street**, **Ln.** with **Lane,** and **Dr.** with **Drive**.
7. Click the **Close** button to close the Find and Replace dialog box.
8. Scroll through the Sales Report worksheet to verify that all street title abbreviations were replaced with their full names.

The Find and Replace dialog box can also be used to replace one format with another or to replace both text and a format simultaneously. Carol wants you to replace all occurrences of the white text on a gold fill in the Sales Report worksheet with blue text on a gold fill. You'll use the Find and Replace dialog box to make this formatting change.

To replace white text with blue text:

1. On the Home tab, in the Editing group, click the **Find & Select** button, and then click **Replace** (or press the **Ctrl+H** keys). The Find and Replace dialog box opens.
2. Delete the search text from the Find what and Replace with boxes, leaving those two boxes empty. By not specifying a text string to find and replace, the dialog box will search through all cells regardless of their content.
3. Click the **Options** button to expand the dialog box.
4. Click the **Format** button in the Find what row to open the Find Format dialog box, which is similar to the Format Cells dialog box you used earlier to format a range.
5. Click the **Font** tab to make it active, click the **Color** box, and then click the **White, Background 1** theme color.
6. Click the **Fill** tab, and then in the Background Color section, click the **gold** color (the eighth color in the first row).
7. Click the **OK** button to close the Find Format dialog box and return to the Find and Replace dialog box.
8. Click the **Format** button in the Replace with row to open the Replace Format dialog box.
9. On the Fill tab, click the **gold** color.
10. Click the **Font** tab, click the **Color** box, and then click **Blue** in the Standard Colors section.
11. Click the **OK** button to return to the Find and Replace dialog box. See Figure 2-30.

Figure 2-30 Expanded Find and Replace dialog box

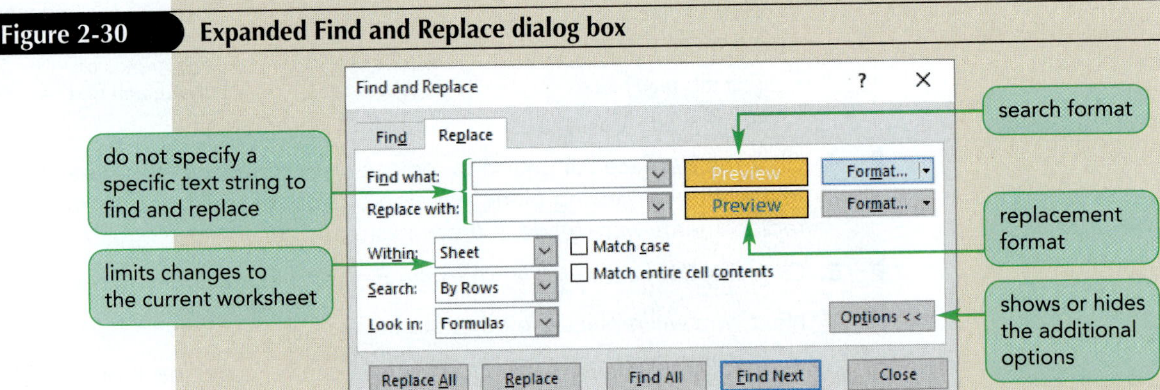

12. Click the **Replace All** button to replace all occurrences of white text on a gold fill in the Sales Report worksheet with blue text on a gold fill. A dialog box opens, reporting that 16 replacements were made.
13. Click the **OK** button to return to the Find and Replace dialog box.

It is a good idea to clear the find and replace formats after you are done so that they won't affect any future searches and replacements. Carol asks you to remove the formats from the Find and Replace dialog box.

To clear the options from the Find and Replace dialog box:

1. In the Find and Replace dialog box, click the **Format button arrow** in the Find what row, and then click **Clear Find Format**. The search format is removed.
2. Click the **Format button arrow** in the Replace with row, and then click **Clear Replace Format**. The replacement format is removed.
3. Click the **Close** button. The Find and Replace dialog box closes.

Another way to make multiple changes to the formats used in your workbook is through themes.

Working with Themes

Recall that a theme is a coordinated selection of fonts, colors, and graphical effects that are applied throughout a workbook to create a specific look and feel. When you switch to a different theme, the theme-related fonts, colors, and effects change throughout the workbook to reflect the new theme. The appearance of nontheme fonts, colors, and effects remains unchanged no matter which theme is applied to the workbook.

Most of the formatting you have applied to the Sales Report workbook is based on the Office theme. Carol wants you to change the theme to see how it affects the workbook's appearance.

To change the workbook's theme:

1. On the ribbon, click the **Page Layout** tab.
2. In the Themes group, click the **Themes** button. The Themes gallery opens. Office—the current theme—is the default.
3. Point to different themes in the Themes gallery using Live Preview to preview the impact of each theme on the fonts and colors used in the worksheet.
4. Click the **Droplet** theme to apply that theme to the workbook. See Figure 2-31.

Figure 2-31 Live Preview of the Droplet theme

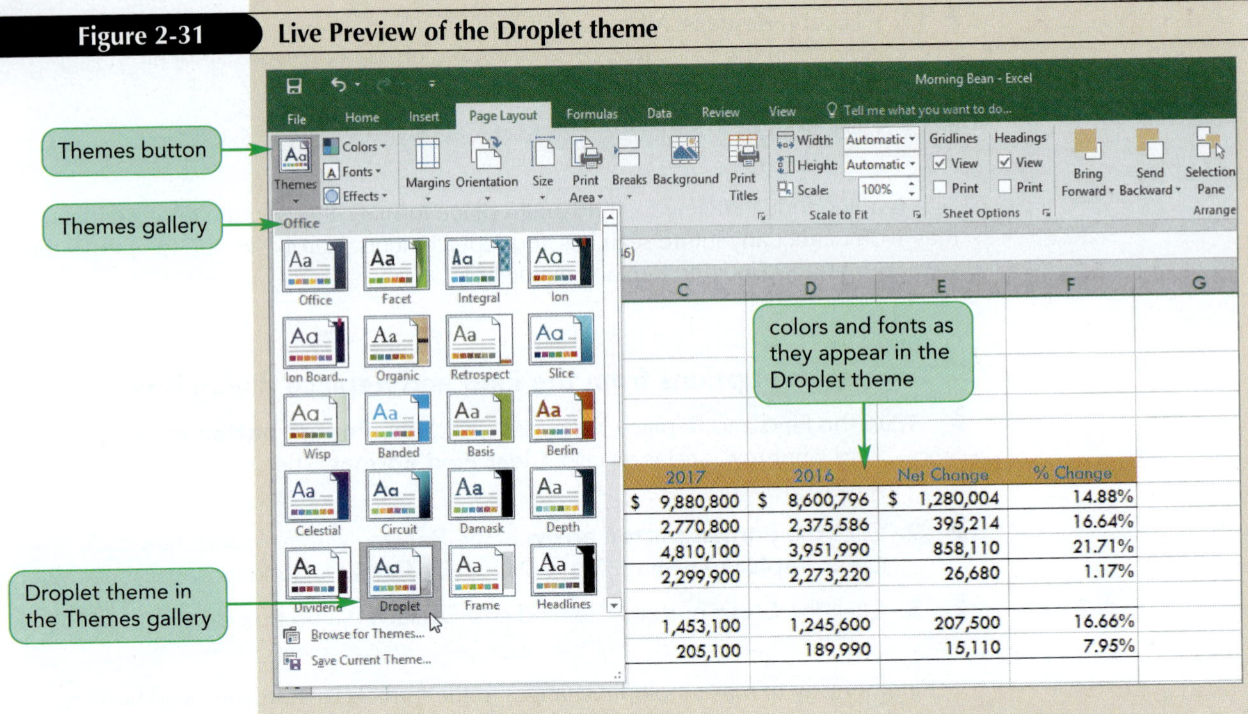

Changing the theme made a significant difference in the worksheet's appearance. The most obvious changes to the worksheet are the fill colors and the fonts. Only formatting options directly tied to a theme change when you select a different theme. Any formatting options you selected that were not theme-based remain unaffected by the change. For example, using a standard color or a nontheme font will not be affected by the choice of theme. In the Sales Report worksheet, the standard green color used for the font of the company description and the fill of the column title cells in the 2017 Monthly Gross Sales data didn't change because that green is not a theme color.

INSIGHT

Sharing Styles and Themes

Using a consistent look and feel for all the files you create in Microsoft Office is a simple way to project a professional image. This consistency is especially important when a team is collaborating on a set of documents. When all team members work from a common set of style and design themes, readers will not be distracted by inconsistent or clashing formatting.

To quickly copy the styles from one workbook to another, open the workbook with the styles you want to copy, and then open the workbook in which you want to copy those styles. On the Home tab, in the Styles group, click the Cell Styles button, and then click Merge Styles. The Merge Styles dialog box opens, listing the currently open workbooks. Select the workbook with the styles you want to copy, and then click the OK button to copy those styles into the current workbook. If you modify any styles, you must copy the styles to the other workbook; Excel does not update styles between workbooks.

Because other Office files, including those created with Word or PowerPoint, use the same file format for themes, you can create one theme to use with all your Office files. To save a theme, click the Themes button in the Themes group on the Page Layout tab, and then click Save Current Theme. The Save Current Theme dialog box opens. Select a save location, type a name in the File name box, and then click the Save button. If you saved the theme file in a default Theme folder, the theme appears in the Themes gallery and affects any Office file that uses that theme.

Highlighting Data with Conditional Formats

Conditional formatting is often used to help analyze data. Conditional formatting applies formatting to a cell when its value meets a specified condition. For example, conditional formatting can be used to format negative numbers in red and positive numbers in black. Conditional formatting is dynamic, which means that the formatting can change when the cell's value changes. Each conditional format has a set of rules that define how the formatting should be applied and under what conditions the format will be changed.

REFERENCE

Highlighting Cells with Conditional Formatting

- Select the range in which you want to highlight cells.
- On the Home tab, in the Styles group, click the Conditional Formatting button, point to Highlight Cells Rules or Top/Bottom Rules, and then click the appropriate rule.
- Select the appropriate options in the dialog box.
- Click the OK button.

Excel has four types of conditional formatting—data bars, highlighting, color scales, and icon sets. In this module, you will use conditional formatting to highlight cells.

Highlighting Cells Based on Their Values

Cell highlighting changes the cell's font color or fill color based on the cell's value, as described in Figure 2-32. You can enter a value or a cell reference if you want to compare other cells with the value in a certain cell.

Figure 2-32 Highlight Cells rules

Rule	Highlights Cell Values
Greater Than	Greater than a specified number
Less Than	Less than a specified number
Between	Between two specified numbers
Equal To	Equal to a specified number
Text that Contains	That contain specified text
A Date Occurring	That contain a specified date
Duplicate Values	That contain duplicate or unique values

Carol wants to highlight important trends and sales values in the Sales Report worksheet. She asks you to highlight sales statistics that show a negative net change or negative percent change from the previous year to the current year. You will use conditional formatting to highlight the negative values in red.

To highlight negative values in red:

1. In the Sales Report worksheet, select the range **E6:F12,E16:F22** containing the net and percent changes overall and per store from the previous year to the current year.

2. On the ribbon, click the **Home** tab.
3. In the Styles group, click the **Conditional Formatting** button, and then point to **Highlight Cells Rules** to display a menu of the available rules.
4. Click **Less Than**. The Less Than dialog box opens so you can select the value and formatting to highlight negative values.
5. Make sure the value in the first box is selected, and then type **0** so that cells in the selected range that contain values that are less than 0 are formatted with a light red fill and dark red text. Live Preview shows the conditional formatting applied to the cells with negative numbers. See Figure 2-33.

TIP

To create a format, click the right box arrow, then click Custom Format to open the Format Cells dialog box.

Figure 2-33 **Live Preview of the Less Than conditional format**

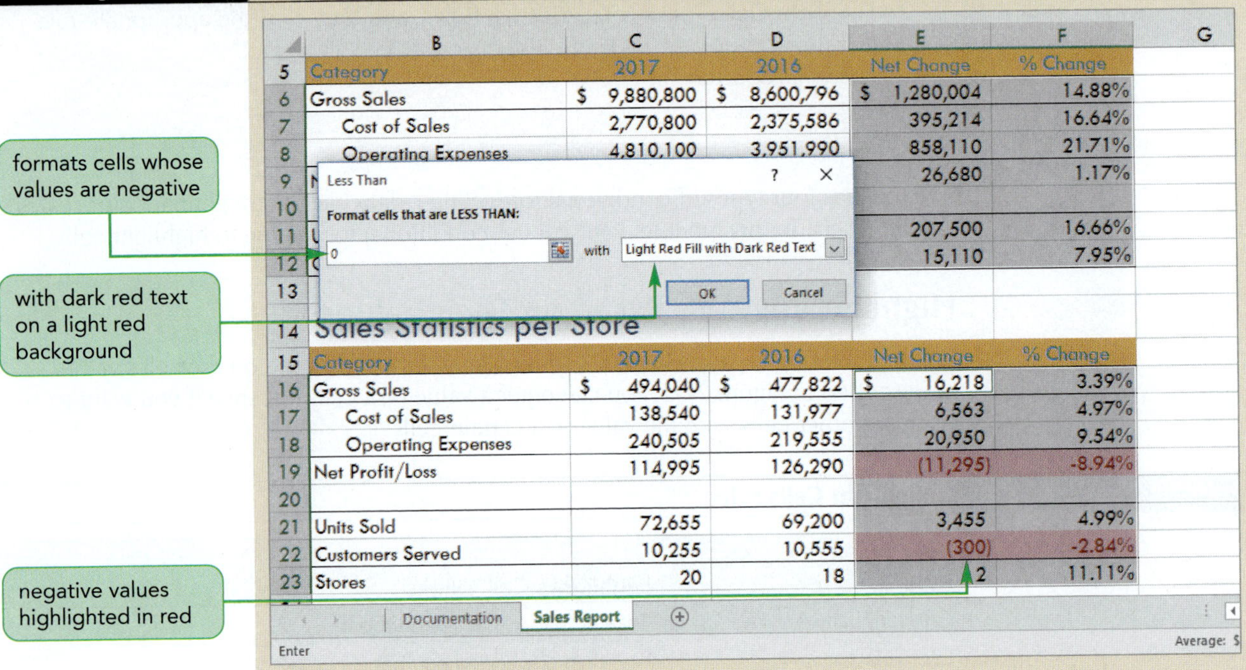

6. Click the **OK** button to apply the highlighting rule.

The conditional formatting highlights that Morning Bean showed a decline from the previous year to the current year for two statistics: The net profit per store declined $11,295 or 8.94 percent, and the number of customers served per store declined by 300 persons or 2.84 percent. These declines occurred because the two new stores that Morning Bean opened in 2017 are still finding a market, resulting in lower profit and customer served per store for the entire franchise.

Conditional formatting is dynamic, which means that changes in the values affect the format of those cells. The total number of customers served in 2017 was incorrectly entered in cell C12 as 205,100. The correct value is 215,100. You will make this change and view its impact on the cells highlighted with conditional formatting.

To view the impact of changing values on conditional formatting:

1. Click cell **C12** to select it.
2. Type **215,100** as the new value, and then press the Enter key. The conditional formatting changes based on the new value. See Figure 2-34.

Figure 2-34 Cells with conditional formatting

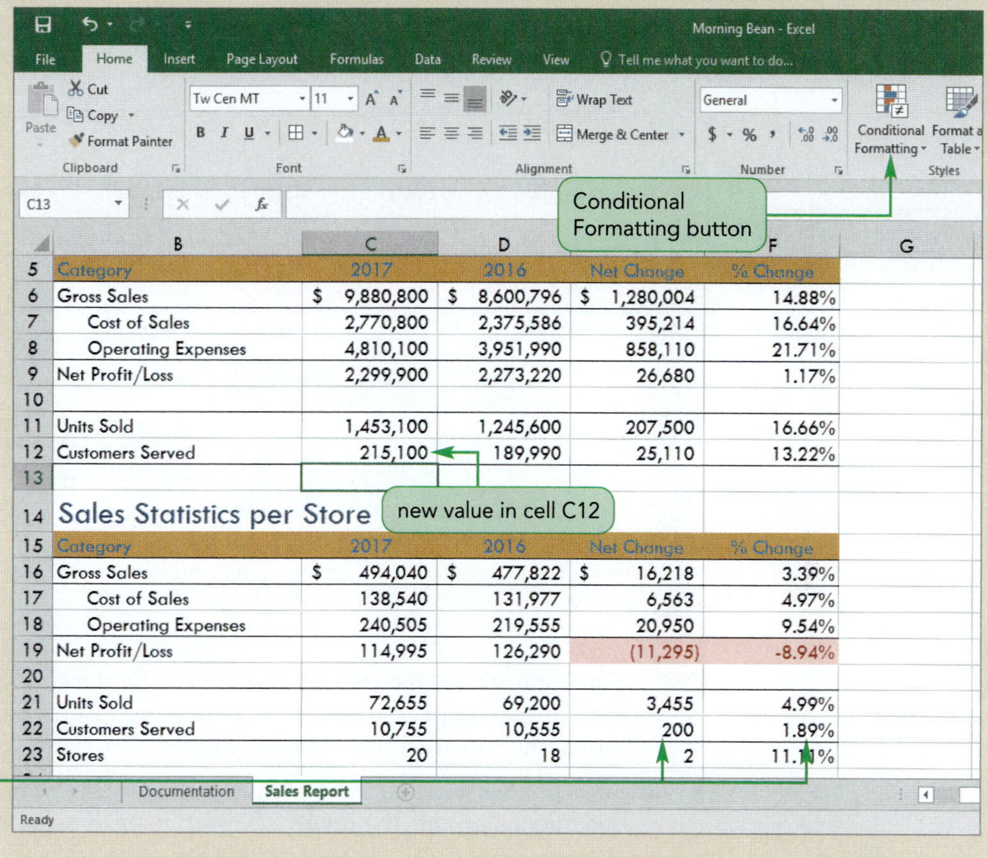

By changing the value in cell C12 to 215,100, the net change in customers served per store in cell E22 is now 200 and the percentage change in cell F22 is now 1.89%. Because both of these values are now positive, the cells are no longer highlighted in red.

Highlighting Cells with a Top/Bottom Rule

Another way of applying conditional formatting is with the Quick Analysis tool. The **Quick Analysis tool**, which appears whenever you select a range of cells, provides access to the most common tools for data analysis and formatting. The Formatting category includes buttons for the Greater Than and Top 10% conditional formatting rules. You can highlight cells based on their values in comparison to other cells. For example, you can highlight cells with the 10 highest or lowest values in a selected range, or you can highlight the cells with above-average values in a range.

Carol wants to know which stores and which months rank in the top 10 percent of sales. She wants to use this information to identify the most successful stores and learn which months those stores show the highest sales volume. You'll highlight those values using the Quick Analysis tool.

To use a Top/Bottom Rule to highlight stores with the highest average sales:

1. Select the range **C27:N46** containing the monthly sales values for each of the 20 Morning Bean stores.
2. Click the **Quick Analysis** button, and then point to **Top 10%**. Live Preview formats the cells in the top 10 percent with red font and a red fill. See Figure 2-35.

Figure 2-35 Quick Analysis tool applying conditional formatting

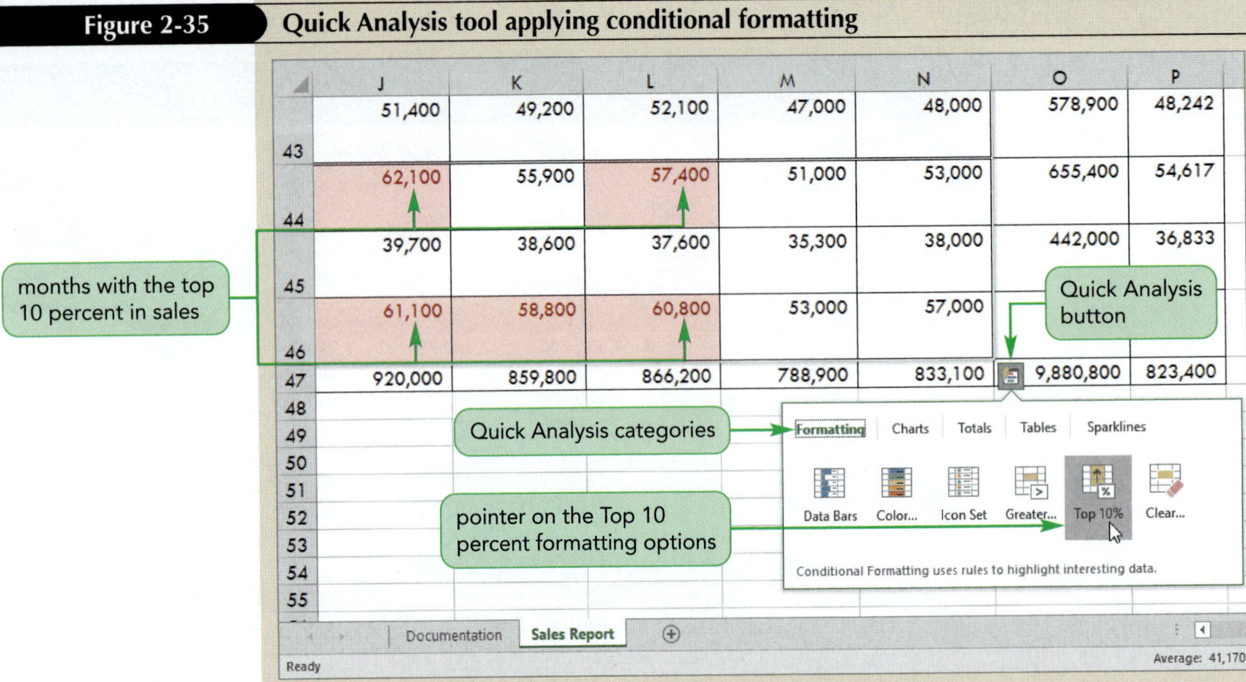

Carol doesn't like the default format used by the Quick Analysis tool because red is usually applied to negative values and results. Instead, she wants to format the top 10 percent values in green.

3. Press the **Esc** key to close the Quick Analysis tool without applying the conditional format. The range C27:N46 remains selected.

   Trouble? If the conditional formatting was applied to the worksheet, press the Ctrl+Z keys to undo the format, and then continue with Step 4.

4. On the Home tab, in the Styles group, click the **Conditional Formatting** button, and then point to **Top/Bottom Rules** to display a list of available rules.
5. Click **Top 10%** to open the Top 10% dialog box.
6. Click the **with** arrow box and click **Green Fill with Dark Green Text** to apply green to cells with sales value in the top 10 percent. See Figure 2-36.

Figure 2-36 Top 10% dialog box

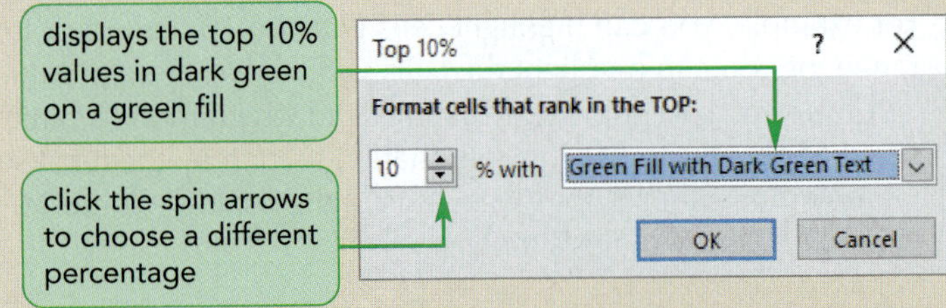

7. Click the **OK** button, and then click cell **A24** to deselect the cells. Monthly sales that rank in the top 10 percent are formatted with green.
8. Zoom the worksheet to **40%** so you can view all of the monthly gross sales and more easily see the sales pattern. See Figure 2-37.

Figure 2-37 Top 10 percent highlighted with green conditional formatting

top 10 percent sales occur between May and October and are found in six stores

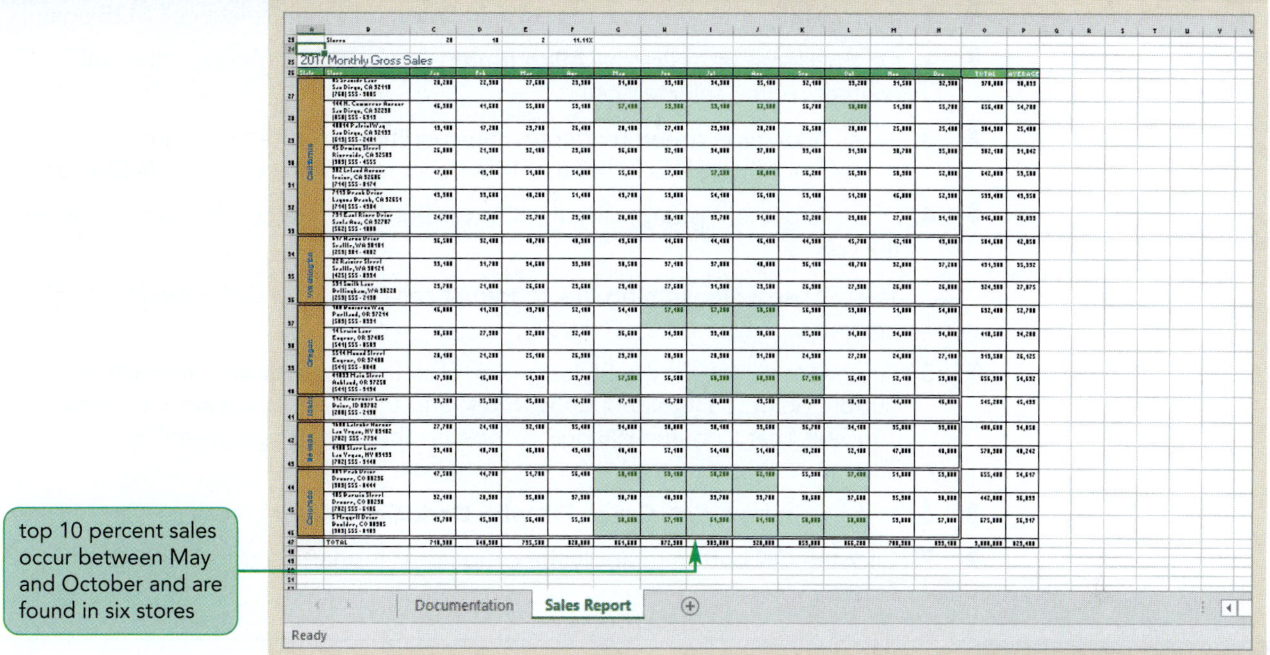

9. Return the zoom to **120%** or whatever zoom is appropriate for your monitor.

The top 10 percent in monthly sales comes from six stores located in San Diego, Irvine, Portland, Ashland, Denver, and Boulder. The highest sales appear to be centered around the months from May to October. This information will be valuable to Carol as she compares the sales performance of different stores and projects monthly cash flows for the company.

Other Conditional Formatting Options

To create dynamic conditional formats that are based on cell values rather than a constant value, you can enter a cell reference in the conditional format dialog box. For example, you can highlight all cells whose value is greater than the value in cell B10. For this type of conditional format, enter the formula =$B$10 in the conditional formatting dialog box. Note that the $ character keeps the cell reference from changing if that formula moves to another cell.

You can remove a conditional format at any time without affecting the underlying data by selecting the range containing the conditional format, clicking the Conditional Formatting button, and then clicking the Clear Rules command. A menu opens, providing options to clear the conditional formatting rules from the selected cells or the entire worksheet. You can also click the Quick Analysis button that appears in the lower-right corner of the selected range and then click the Clear Format button in the Formatting category. Note that you might see only "Clear..." as the button name.

Creating a Conditional Formatting Legend

When you use conditional formatting to highlight cells in a worksheet, the purpose of the formatting is not always immediately apparent. To ensure that everyone knows why certain cells are highlighted, you should include a **legend**, which is a key that identifies each format and its meaning.

Carol wants you to add a legend to the Sales Report worksheet to document the two conditional formatting rules you created in the worksheet.

To create a conditional formatting legend:

1. In cell **M25**, enter the text **Top 10% in Sales**, and then select cell **M25** again.
2. On the Home tab, click the **Align Right** button to right-align the cell contents of the selected cell.
3. In cell **N25**, type **green** to identify the conditional formatting color you used to highlight the values in the top 10 percent, and then select cell **N25** again.
4. In the Alignment group, click the **Center** button to center the contents of the cell.

   You will use a highlighting rule to format cell N25 using dark green text on a green fill.

5. On the Home tab, in the Styles group, click the **Conditional Formatting** button, point to **Highlight Cells Rules**, and then click **Text that Contains**. The Text That Contains dialog box opens. The text string "green" is automatically entered into the left input box.
6. In the right box, click **Green Fill with Dark Green Text**.
7. Click the **OK** button to apply the conditional formatting to cell N25. See Figure 2-38.

Figure 2-38 Conditional formatting legend

legend explains the purpose of the conditional formatting

	J	K	L	M	N	O	P	Q
22								
23								
24								
25				Top 10% in Sales	green			
26	Aug	Sep	Oct	Nov	Dec	TOTAL	AVERAGE	
	35,100	32,100	33,200	31,500	32,300	370,000	30,833	
27	62,300	56,700	58,000	51,300	55,700	656,400	54,700	
28	28,200	26,500	28,000	25,000	25,400	304,900	25,408	
29	37,800	33,400	31,900	30,700	35,000	382,100	31,842	
30	60,800	56,200	56,900	50,900	52,000	642,000	53,500	
31	56,100	53,100	51,200	46,000	52,300	599,400	49,950	

Documentation | Sales Report

Ready

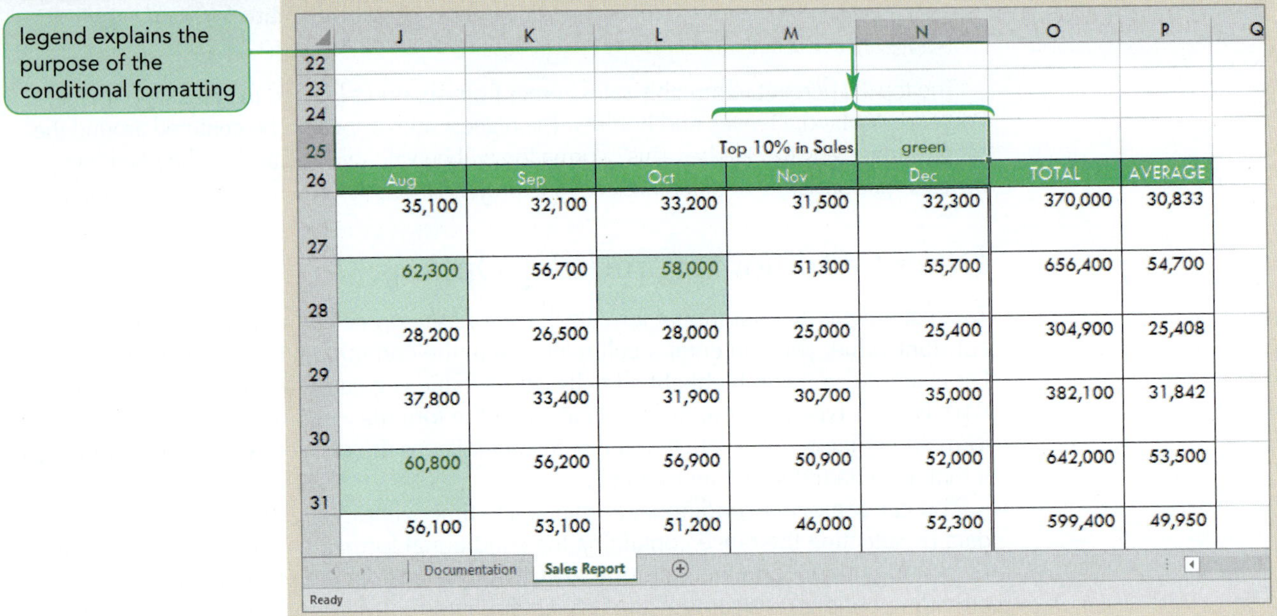

You've completed formatting the appearance of the workbook for the computer screen. Next you'll explore how to format the workbook for the printer.

PROSKILLS

Written Communication: Using Conditional Formatting Effectively

Conditional formatting is an excellent way to highlight important trends and data values to clients and colleagues. However, be sure to use it judiciously. Overusing conditional formatting might obscure the very data you want to emphasize. Keep in mind the following tips as you make decisions about what to highlight and how it should be highlighted:

- **Document the conditional formats you use.** If a bold, green font means that a sales number is in the top 10 percent of all sales, include that information in a legend in the worksheet.
- **Don't clutter data with too much highlighting.** Limit highlighting rules to one or two per data set. Highlights are designed to draw attention to points of interest. If you use too many, you will end up highlighting everything—and, therefore, nothing.
- **Use color sparingly in worksheets with highlights.** It is difficult to tell a highlight color from a regular fill color, especially when fill colors are used in every cell.
- **Consider alternatives to conditional formats.** If you want to highlight the top 10 sales regions, it might be more effective to simply sort the data with the best-selling regions at the top of the list.

Remember that the goal of highlighting is to provide a strong visual clue to important data or results. Careful use of conditional formatting helps readers to focus on the important points you want to make rather than distracting them with secondary issues and facts.

Formatting a Worksheet for Printing

You should format any worksheets you plan to print so that they are easy to read and understand. You can do this using the print settings, which enable you to set the page orientation, the print area, page breaks, print titles, and headers and footers. Print settings can be applied to an entire workbook or to individual sheets. Because other people will likely see your printed worksheets, you should format the printed output as carefully as you format the electronic version.

Carol wants you to format the Sales Report worksheet so she can distribute the printed version at the upcoming sales conference.

Using Page Break Preview

Page Break Preview shows only those parts of the active sheet that will print and how the content will be split across pages. A dotted blue border indicates a page break, which separates one page from another. As you format the worksheet for printing, you can use this view to control what content appears on each page.

Carol wants to know how the Sales Report worksheet would print in portrait orientation and how many pages would be required. You will look at the worksheet in Page Break Preview to find these answers.

To view the Sales Report worksheet in Page Break Preview:

1. Click the **Page Break Preview** button on the status bar. The worksheet switches to Page Break Preview.
2. Change the zoom level of the worksheet to **30%** so you can view the entire contents of this large worksheet. See Figure 2-39.

Figure 2-39 Sales Report worksheet in Page Break preview

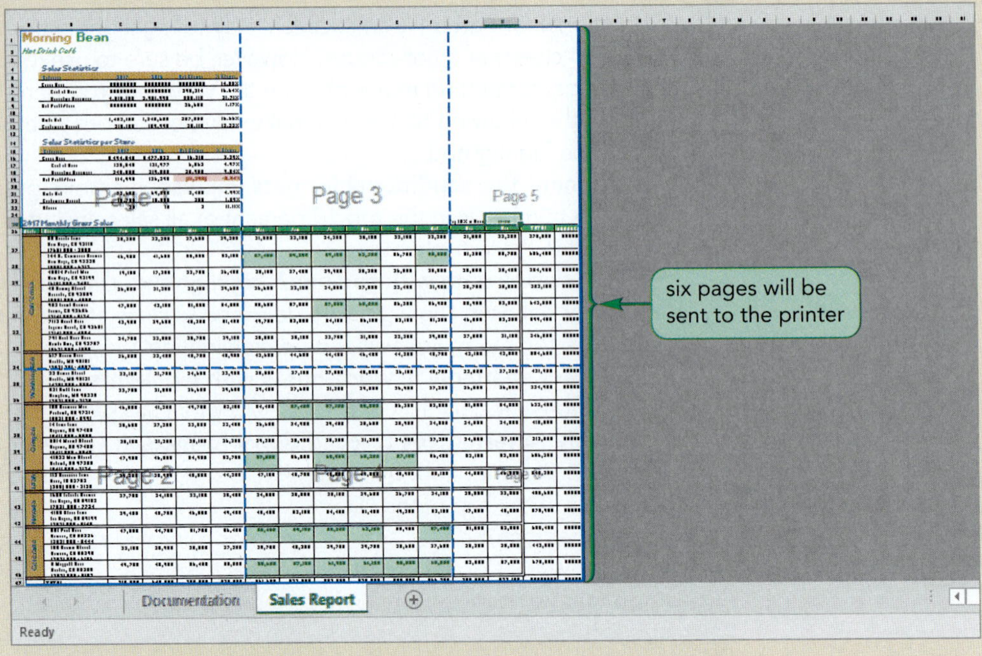

Trouble? If you see a different page layout or the worksheet is split onto a different number of pages, don't worry. Each printer is different, so the layout and pages might differ from what is shown in Figure 2-39.

Page Break Preview shows that a printout of the Sales Report worksheet requires six pages in portrait orientation, and that pages 3 and 5 would be mostly blank. Note that each printer is different, so your Page Break Preview might show a different number of pages. With this layout, each page would be difficult to interpret because the data is separated from the descriptive labels. Carol wants you to fix the layout so that the contents are easier to read and understand.

Defining the Print Area

By default, all cells in a worksheet containing text, formulas, or values are printed. If you want to print only part of a worksheet, you can set a print area, which is the region of the worksheet that is sent to the printer. Each worksheet has its own print area. Although you can set the print area in any view, Page Break Preview shades the areas of the worksheet that are not included in the print area, making it simple to confirm what will print.

Carol doesn't want the empty cells in the range G1:P24 to print, so you will set the print area to exclude those cells.

To set the print area of the Sales Report worksheet:

1. Change the zoom level of the worksheet to **80%** to make it easier to select cells and ranges.
2. Select the nonadjacent range **A1:F24,A25:P47** containing the cells with content.
3. On the ribbon, click the **Page Layout** tab.

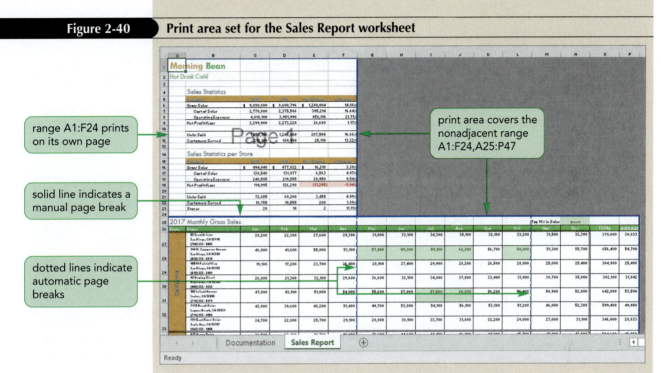

4. In the Page Setup group, click the **Print Area** button, and then click **Set Print Area**. The print area changes to cover only the nonadjacent range A1:F24,A25:P47. The rest of the worksheet content is shaded to indicate that it will not be part of the printout.
5. Click cell **A1** to deselect the range.
6. Change the zoom level to **50%** so you can view more of the worksheet. See Figure 2-40.

Figure 2-40 **Print area set for the Sales Report worksheet**

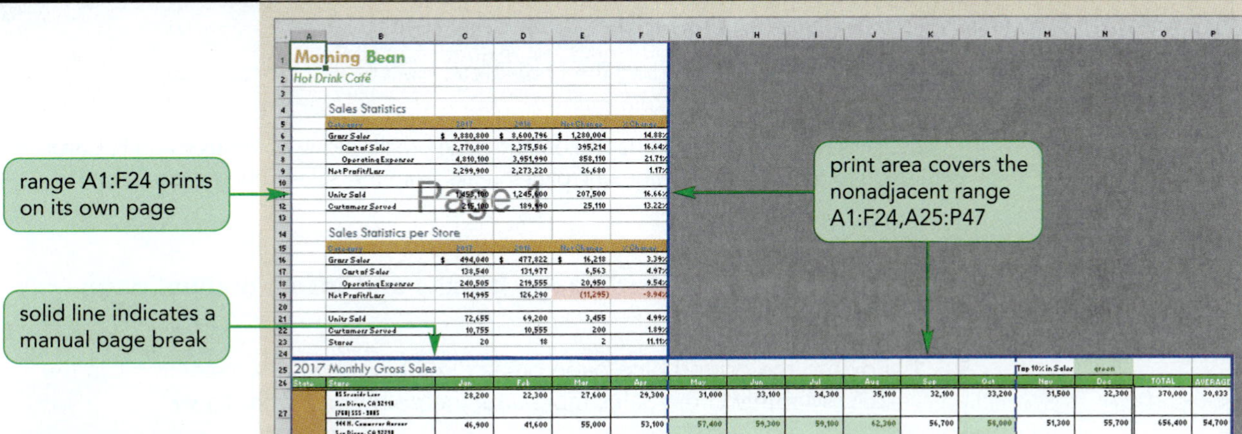

Inserting Page Breaks

Often, the contents of a worksheet will not fit onto a single printed page. When this happens, Excel prints as much of the content that fits on a single page without resizing, and then inserts automatic page breaks to continue printing the remaining worksheet content on successive pages. The resulting printouts might split worksheet content in awkward places, such as within a table of data.

TIP

When you remove a page break, Excel will automatically rescale the printout to fit into the allotted pages.

To split the printout into logical segments, you can insert manual page breaks. Page Break Preview identifies manual page breaks with a solid blue line and automatic page breaks with a dotted blue line. When you specify a print area for a nonadjacent range, as you did for the Sales Report worksheet, you also insert manual page breaks around the adjacent ranges. So a manual page break already appears in the print area you defined (see Figure 2-40). You can remove a page break in Page Break Preview by dragging it out of the print area.

REFERENCE

Inserting and Removing Page Breaks

To insert a page break:

- Click the first cell below the row where you want to insert a page break, click a column heading, or click a row heading.
- On the Page Layout tab, in the Page Setup group, click the Breaks button, and then click Insert Page Break.

To remove a page break:

- Select any cell below or to the right of the page break you want to remove.
- On the Page Layout tab, in the Page Setup group, click the Breaks button, and then click Remove Page Break.

or

- In Page Break Preview, drag the page break line out of the print area.

The Sales Report worksheet has automatic page breaks along columns F and L. Carol wants you to remove these automatic page breaks from the Sales Report worksheet.

To remove the automatic page breaks and insert manual page breaks:

1. Point to the dotted blue page break directly to the right of column L in the 2017 Monthly Gross Sales table until the pointer changes to ↔.
2. Drag the page break to the right and out of the print area. The page break is removed from the worksheet.
3. Point to the page break that is located in column F so that the pointer changes to ↔, and then drag the page break to the right and out of the print area.
4. Click the **I** column heading to select the entire column. You will add a manual page break between columns H and I to split the monthly gross sales data onto two pages so the printout will be larger and easier to read.
5. On the Page Layout tab, in the Page Setup group, click the **Breaks** button, and then click **Insert Page Break**. A manual page break is added between columns H and I, forcing the monthly gross sales onto a new page after the June data.
6. Click cell **A1** to deselect the column. The printout of the Sales Report worksheet is now limited to three pages. However, the gross sales data in the range A25:P47 is split across pages. See Figure 2-41.

Figure 2-41 Manual page break in the print area

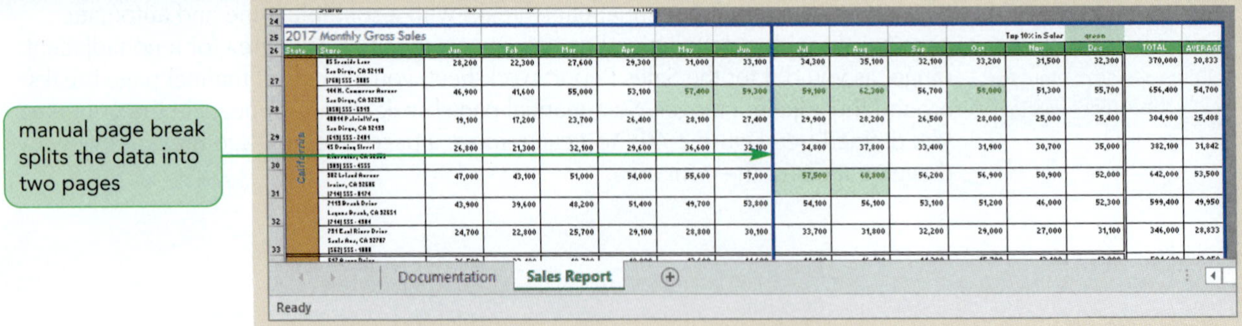

manual page break splits the data into two pages

Adding Print Titles

It is a good practice to include descriptive information such as the company name, logo, and worksheet title on each page of a printout in case a page becomes separated from the other pages. You can repeat information, such as the company name, by specifying which rows or columns in the worksheet act as print titles. If a worksheet contains a large table, you can print the table's column headings and row headings on every page of the printout by designating those columns and rows as print titles.

In the Sales Report worksheet, the company name appears on the first page of the printout but does not appear on subsequent pages. Also, the descriptive row titles for the monthly sales table in column A do not appear on the third page of the printout. You will add print titles to fix these issues.

TIP

You can also open the Page Setup dialog box by clicking the Dialog Box Launcher in the Page Setup group on the Page Layout tab.

To set the print titles:

1. On the Page Layout tab, in the Page Setup group, click the **Print Titles** button. The Page Setup dialog box opens with the Sheet tab displayed.
2. In the Print titles section, click the **Rows to repeat at top** box, move the pointer over the worksheet, and then select the range **A1:A2**. A flashing border appears around the first two rows of the worksheet to indicate that the contents of the first two rows will be repeated on each page of the printout. The row reference $1:$2 appears in the Rows to repeat at top box.
3. Click the **Columns to repeat at left** box, and then select columns A and B from the worksheet. The column reference $A:$B appears in the Columns to repeat at left box. See Figure 2-42.

Figure 2-42 Sheet tab in the Page Setup dialog box

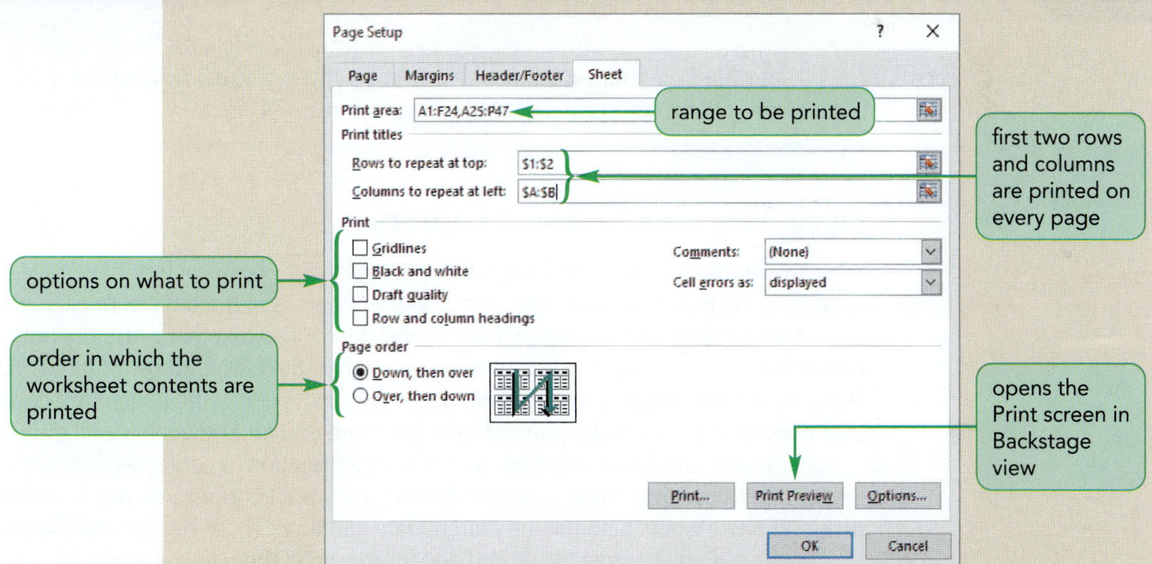

You will next rescale the worksheet so that it doesn't appear too small in the printout.

4. In the Page Setup dialog box, click the **Page** tab.
5. In the Scaling section, change the Adjust to amount to **60%** of normal size.
6. Click the **Print Preview** button to preview the three pages of printed material on the Print screen in Backstage view.

7. Verify that each of the three pages has the Morning Bean title at the top of the page and that the state and store names appear in the leftmost columns of pages 2 and 3. See Figure 2-43.

Figure 2-43 Print titles on page 3 of the printout

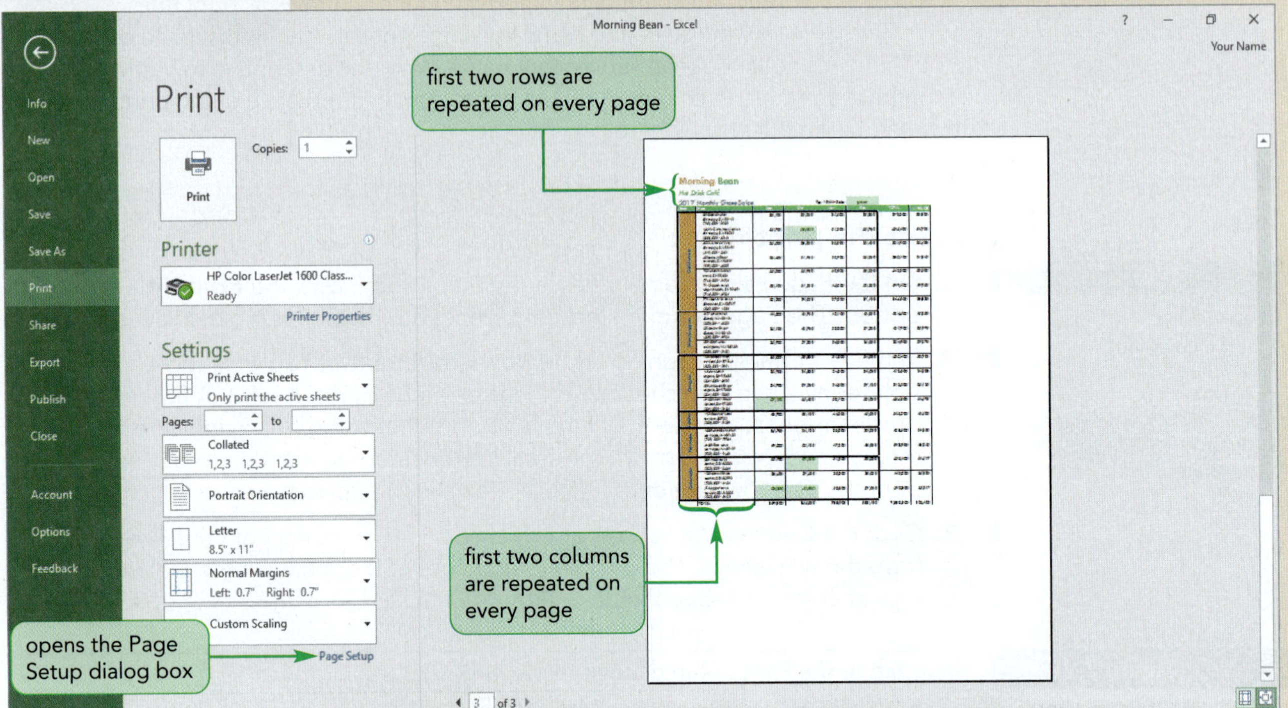

Trouble? If your printout doesn't fit on three pages, reduce the scaling factor from 60 percent to a slightly lower percentage until it does fit on three pages.

Designing Headers and Footers

You can also use headers and footers to repeat information on each printed page. A **header** appears at the top of each printed page; a **footer** appears at the bottom of each printed page. Headers and footers contain helpful and descriptive text that is usually not found within the worksheet, such as the workbook's author, the current date, or the workbook's filename. If the printout spans multiple pages, you can display the page number and the total number of pages in the printout to help ensure you and others have all the pages.

Each header and footer has three sections—a left section, a center section, and a right section. Within each section, you type the text you want to appear, or you insert elements such as the worksheet name or the current date and time. These header and footer elements are dynamic; if you rename the worksheet, for example, the name is automatically updated in the header or footer. Also, you can create one set of headers and footers for even and odd pages, and you can create another set for the first page in the printout.

Carol wants the printout to display the workbook's filename in the header's left section, and the current date in the header's right section. She wants the center footer to display the page number and the total number of pages in the printout, and the right footer to display your name as the workbook's author.

To set up the page header:

1. Near the bottom of the Print screen, click the **Page Setup** link. The Page Setup dialog box opens.
2. Click the **Header/Footer** tab to display the header and footer options.
3. Click the **Different first page** check box to select it. This lets you create one set of headers and footers for the first page, and one set for the rest of the pages.
4. Click the **Custom Header** button to open the Header dialog box. The dialog box contains two tabs—Header and First Page Header—because you selected the Different first page option.
5. On the Header tab, in the Left section box, type **Filename:**, press the **spacebar**, and then click the **Insert File Name** button. The code `&[File]`, which displays the filename of the current workbook, is added to the left section of the header.
6. Press the **Tab** key twice to move to the right section of the header, and then click the **Insert Date** button. The code `&[Date]` is added to the right section of the header. See Figure 2-44.

TIP

You can create or edit headers and footers in Page Layout view by clicking in the header/footer section and using the tools on the Design tab.

Figure 2-44 Header dialog box

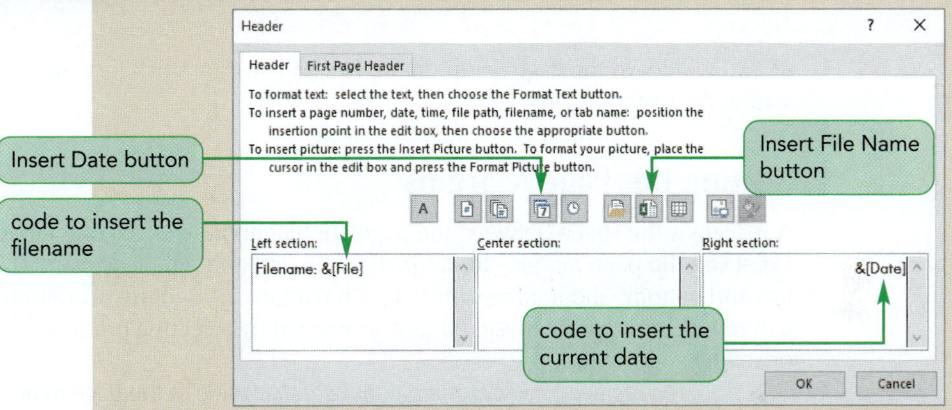

7. Click the **OK** button to return to the Header/Footer tab in the Page Setup dialog box.

You did not define a header for the first page of the printout, so no header information will be added to that page. Next, you will format the footer for all pages of the printout.

To create the page footer:

1. On the Header/Footer tab of the Page Setup dialog box, click the **Custom Footer** button. The Footer dialog box opens.
2. On the Footer tab, click the **Center section** box, type **Page**, press the **spacebar**, and then click the **Insert Page Number** button. The code `&[Page]`, which inserts the current page number, appears after the label "Page."
3. Press the **spacebar**, type **of**, press the **spacebar**, and then click the **Insert Number of Pages** button. The code `&[Pages]`, which inserts the total number of pages in the printout, is added to the Center section box. See Figure 2-45.

Figure 2-45 Footer dialog box

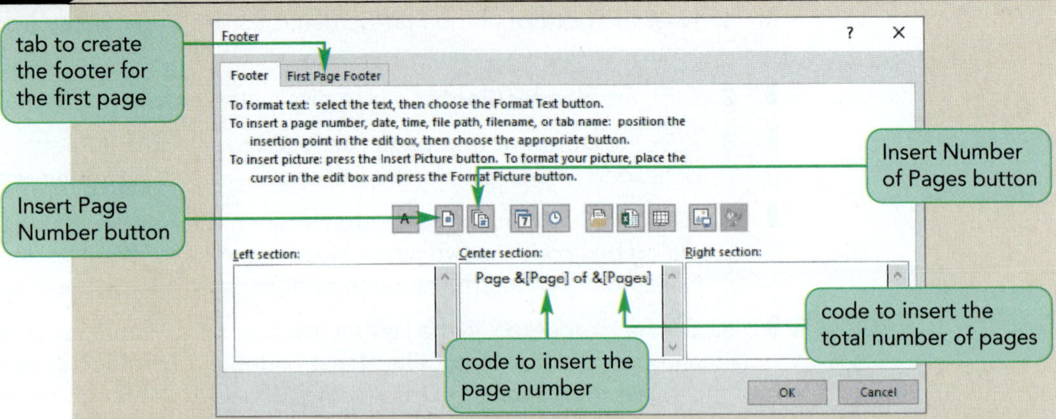

4. Click the **First Page Footer** tab so you can create the footer for the first page of the printout.
5. Click the **Right section** box, type **Prepared by:**, press the **spacebar**, and then type your name.
6. Click the **OK** button to return to the Page Setup dialog box.

You will leave the Page Setup dialog box so you can finish formatting the printout by setting the page margins.

Setting the Page Margins

A **margin** is the space between the page content and the edges of the page. By default, Excel sets the page margins to 0.7 inch on the left and right sides, and 0.75 inch on the top and bottom; and it allows for 0.3-inch margins around the header and footer. You can reduce or increase these margins as needed by selecting predefined margin sizes or setting your own.

Carol's reports need a wider margin along the left side of the page to accommodate the binding. She asks you to increase the left margin for the printout from 0.7 inch to 1 inch.

TIP

To select preset margins, click the Margins button in the Page Setup group on the Page Layout tab.

To set the left margin:

1. Click the **Margins** tab in the Page Setup dialog box to display options for changing the page margins.
2. Double-click the **Left** box to select the setting, and then type **1** to increase the size of the left margin to 1 inch. See Figure 2-46.

Figure 2-46 **Margins tab in the Page Setup dialog box**

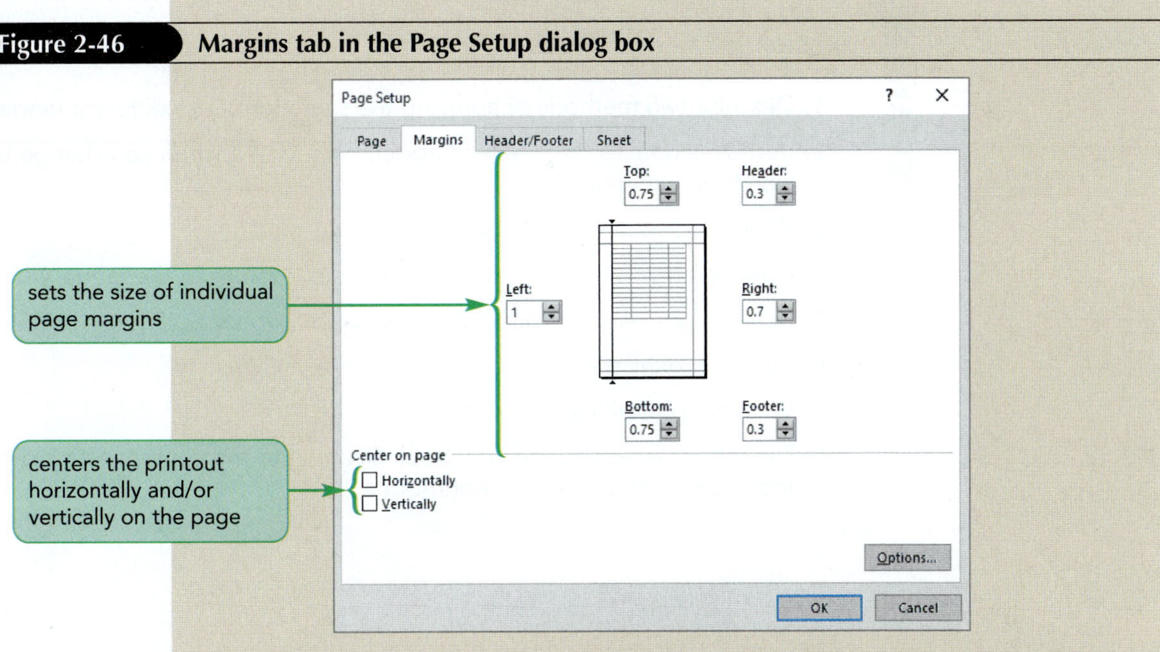

3. Click the **OK** button to close the dialog box. You can see the margin change in the preview on the Print screen in Backstage view.

Now that you have formatted the printout, you can print the final version of the worksheet.

To save and print the workbook:

1. With the workbook still in the Print screen in Backstage view, click the first box in the Settings section, and then click **Print Entire Workbook**.

   Both the Sales Report worksheet and the Documentation sheet appear in the preview. As you can see, the printout will include a header with the filename and date on every page except the first page and a footer with your name on the first page and the page number along with the total number of pages on subsequent pages.

2. If you are instructed to print, print the entire workbook.
3. Click the **Back** button from the Backstage View navigation bar to return to the workbook window.
4. Click the **Normal** button on the status bar to return the view of the workbook to normal.
5. Save the workbook, and then close it.

Carol is pleased with the worksheet's appearance and the layout of the printout. The formatting has made the contents easier to read and understand.

REVIEW

Session 2.2 Quick Check

1. Describe two methods of applying the same format to different ranges.
2. Red is a standard color. What happens to red text when you change the workbook's theme?
3. What is a conditional format?
4. How would you highlight the top 10 percent values of the range A1:C20?
5. How do you insert a manual page break in a worksheet?
6. What is a print area?
7. What are print titles?
8. Describe how to add the workbook filename to the center section of the footer on every page of the printout.

PRACTICE

Review Assignments

Data Files needed for the Review Assignments: Menu.xlsx, Background2.jpg

Carol created a workbook that tracks the sales of individual items from the Morning Bean menu to share at an upcoming conference. She has already entered most of the financial formulas but wants you to calculate some additional values. She also asks you to format the workbook so that it will look professional and be easy to read and understand. Complete the following:

1. Open the **Menu** workbook located in the Excel2 > Review folder included with your Data Files, and then save the workbook as **Menu Sales** in the location specified by your instructor.
2. In the Documentation sheet, enter your name in cell B4 and the date in cell B5.
3. Change the theme of the workbook to Retrospect.
4. Make the following formatting changes to the Documentation sheet:
   a. Set the background image to the **Background2** JPEG file located in the Excel2 > Review folder.
   b. Format the text in cell A1 in a 26-point bold Calibri Light.
   c. In cell A1, change the font color of the word "Morning" to the Orange, Accent 1 theme color and change the font color of the word "Bean" to the Brown, Accent 3 theme color.
   d. Format the text in cell A2 in 18-point, italic, and change the font color to the Brown, Accent 3 theme color.
   e. Format the range A4:A6 with the Accent 3 cell style.
   f. Change the font color of the range B4:B6 to the Brown, Accent 3 theme color, and change the fill color to the White, Background 1 theme color.
   g. In cell B5, format the date in the Long Date format and left-align the cell contents.
5. Use the Format Painter to copy the formatting in the range A1:A2 in the Documentation sheet and paste it to the same range in the Menu Items worksheet. Change the font colors in cell A1 of the Menu Items worksheet to match the colors used in cell A1 of the Documentation sheet.
6. Apply the Title cell style to cells B4, B12, and A20.
7. Make the following changes to the Units Sold table in the range B5:F10:
   a. Apply the Accent3 cell style to the headings in the range B5:F5. Center the headings in the range C5:F5.
   b. In cell C6, use the SUM function to calculate the total number of specialty drinks sold by the company (found in the range C22:N31 in the Units Sold per Month table). In cell C7, use the SUM function to calculate the total number of smoothies sold (in the range C32:N36). In cell C8, use the SUM function calculate the total number of sandwiches sold (in the range C37:N41). In cell C9, calculate the total number of soups sold (in the range C42:N45).
   c. In cell C10, use the SUM function to calculate the total units sold from all menu types in 2017 (based on the range C6:C9). Copy the formula to cell D10 to calculate the total units sold in 2016.
   d. In each cell of the range E6:E10, calculate the change in units sold between the 2017 and 2016 values. In each cell of the range F6:F10, calculate the percent change from 2016 to 2017. (*Hint*: The percent change is the net change divided by the 2016 value.)
   e. Format the range C6:E10 with the Comma style and no decimal places.
   f. Format the range F6:F10 with the Percent style and two decimal places.
   g. Add a top border to the range B10:F10.
8. Make the following changes to the Gross Sales table in the range B13:F18:
   a. In cells C18 and D18, use the SUM function to calculate the totals of the 2017 and 2016 sales.
   b. In the range E14:F18, enter formulas to calculate the net change and the percent change in sales.
   c. Use the Format Painter to copy the formatting from the range B5:F10 to the range B13:F18.
   d. Format the ranges C14:E14 and C18:E18 with Accounting format and no decimal places.

9. Make the following changes to the Units Sold per Month table in the range A21:O46:
   a. In the range O22:O45, use the SUM function to calculate the total units sold for each menu item. In the range C46:O46, use the SUM function to calculate the total items sold per month and overall.
   b. Format the headings in the range A21:O21 with the Accent3 cell style. Center the headings in the range C21:O21.
   c. Format the units sold values in the range C22:O46 with the Comma style and no decimal places.
   d. Change the fill color of the subtotals in the range O22:O45,C46:N46 to the White, Background 1, Darker 15% theme color (the first color in the third row).
   e. Merge each of the menu categories in the ranges A22:A31, A32:A36, A37:A41, and A42:A45 into single cells. Rotate the text of the cells up, and middle-align the cell contents.
   f. Format cell A22 with the Accent1 cell style. Format cell A32 with the Accent2 cell style. Format cell A37 with the Accent3 cell style. Format cell A42 with the Accent4 cell style. Change the font size of these four merged cells to 14 points.
   g. Add thick outside borders around each category of menu item in the ranges A22:O31, A32:O36, A37:O41, and A42:O45.
10. Use conditional formatting to highlight negative values in the range E6:F10,E14:F18 with a light red fill with dark red text to highlight which menu categories showed a decrease in units sold or gross sales from 2016 to 2017.
11. Use conditional formatting to format cells that rank in the top 10 percent of the range C22:N45 with a green fill with dark green text to highlight the menu items and months that are in the top 10 percent of units sold.
12. Create a legend for the conditional formatting you added to the worksheet. In cell O20, enter the text **Top Sellers**. Add thick outside borders around the cell, and then use conditional formatting to display this text with a green fill with dark green text.
13. Set the following print formats for the Menu Items worksheet:
   a. Set the print area to the nonadjacent range A1:F19,A20:O46.
   b. Switch to Page Break Preview, and then remove any automatic page breaks in the Units Sold per Month table. Insert a manual page break to separate the June and July sales figures. The printout of the Menu Sales worksheet should fit on three pages.
   c. Scale the printout to 70 percent.
   d. Create print titles that repeat the first three rows at the top of the sheet and the first two columns at the left of the sheet.
   e. Increase the left margin of the printout from 0.7 inch to 1 inch.
   f. Create headers and footers for the printout with a different first page.
   g. For the first page header, print **Prepared by** followed by your name in the right section. For every other page, print **Filename:** followed by the filename in the left section and the date in the right section. (*Hint*: Use the buttons in the Header dialog box to insert the filename and date.)
   h. For every footer, including the first page, print **Page** followed by the page number and then **of** followed by the total number of pages in the printout in the center section.
   i. Preview the printout to verify that the company name and description appear on every page of the Menu Items worksheet printout and that the menu category and menu item name appear on both pages with the Units Sold table. If you are instructed to print, print the entire workbook in portrait orientation.
14. Save the workbook, and then close it.

APPLY

Case Problem 1

Data File needed for this Case Problem: Green.xlsx

Green Clean Homes Sean Patel is developing a business plan for Green Clean Homes, a new professional home cleaning service in Toledo, Ohio. As part of his business plan, Sean needs to predict the company's annual income and expenses. You will help him finalize and format the Excel workbook containing the projected income statement. Complete the following:

1. Open the **Green** workbook located in the Excel2 > Case1 folder, and then save the workbook as **Green Clean** in the location specified by your instructor.
2. In the Documentation sheet, enter your name in cell B3 and the date in cell B4.
3. Display the date in cell B4 in the Long Date format and left-aligned.
4. Change the theme of the workbook to Facet.
5. Make the following formatting changes to the Documentation sheet:
   a. Merge and center cells A1 and B1.
   b. Apply the Accent2 cell style to the merged cell A1 and to the range A3:A5.
   c. In cell A1, set the font size to 22 points and bold the text. Italicize the word "Clean" in the company name.
   d. Add borders around each cell in the range A3:B5. Top-align the text in the range A3:B5.
   e. Change the font color of the text in the range B3:B5 to Dark Green, Accent 2.
6. In the Income Statement worksheet, merge and center the range A1:C1, and then apply the Accent2 cell style to the merged cell. Change the font size to 24 points and the text style to bold. Italicize the word "Clean" within the company name.
7. Make the following changes to the Income Statement worksheet:
   a. Format the range A3:C3 with the Heading 1 cell style.
   b. Format the range A4:C4,A9:C9 with the 40% - Accent1 cell style.
   c. Format cell B5 in the Accounting style with no decimal places.
   d. Format cell B6 and the range B10:B17 in the Comma style with no decimal places.
8. Add the following calculations to the workbook:
   a. In cell C7, calculate the gross profit, which is equal to the gross sales minus the cost of sales.
   b. In cell C18, calculate the company's total operating expenses, which is equal to the sum of the values in the range B10:B17. Format the value in the Accounting format with no decimal places.
   c. In cell C20, calculate the company's operating profit, which is equal to its gross profit minus its total operating expenses.
   d. In cell C21, calculate the company's incomes taxes by multiplying its total operating profit by the corporate tax rate (cell G25). Format the value in the Accounting format with no decimal places.
   e. In cell C22, calculate the company's net profit, which is equal to the total operating profit minus the income taxes.
9. Finalize the formatting of the Projected Income statement by adding the following:
   a. Add a bottom border to the ranges A6:C6, A17:C17, and A20:C20. Add a single top border and a double bottom border to the range A22:C22.
   b. Indent the expenses categories in the range A10:A17 twice.
10. Format the Financial Assumptions section as follows:
    a. Add borders around all of the cells in the range E4:G25.
    b. Format the range E3:G3 with the Heading 1 cell style.
    c. Merge the cells in the ranges E4:E7, E9:E13, E14:E15, E16:E18, and E20:E22.
    d. Top-align and left-align the range E4:E25.
    e. Change the fill color of the range E4:F25 to Green, Accent 1, Lighter 60%.

11. Use conditional formatting to highlight the net profit (cell C22) if its value is less than $50,000 with a light red fill with dark red text.
12. Change the value in cell G9 from 4 to **5**. Observe the impact that hiring another cleaner has on the projected net profit for the company in cell C22.
13. Format the printed version of the Income Statement worksheet as follows:
    a. Add a manual page break between columns D and E.
    b. For the first page, add a header that prints **Prepared by** followed by your name in the left section of the header and the current date in the right section of the header. Do not display header text on any other page.
    c. For every page, add a footer that prints the workbook filename in the left section, **Page** followed by the page number in the center section, and the worksheet name in the right section.
    d. Set the margins to 1 inch on all four sides of the printout, and center the contents of the worksheet horizontally within the printed page.
14. If you are instructed to print, print the entire contents of the workbook in portrait orientation.
15. Save and close the workbook.

APPLY

Case Problem 2

Data File needed for this Case Problem: Peak.xlsx

Peak Bytes Peter Taylor is an engineer at Peak Bytes, an Internet service provider located in Great Falls, Montana. Part of Peter's job is to track the over-the-air connection speeds from the company's transmitters. Data from an automated program recording Internet access times has been entered into a workbook, but the data is difficult to interpret. He wants you to edit the workbook so that the data is easier to read and the fast and slow connection times are quickly visible. He also wants the workbook to provide summary statistics on the connection speeds. Complete the following:

1. Open the **Peak** workbook located in the Excel2 > Case2 folder, and then save the workbook as **Peak Bytes** in the location specified by your instructor.
2. In the Documentation sheet, enter your name in cell B3 and the date in cell B4.
3. Apply the Banded theme to the workbook.
4. Format the Documentation sheet as follows:
    a. Apply the Title cell style to cell A1. Change the font style to bold and the font size to 24 points.
    b. Add borders around the range A3:B5.
    c. Apply the Accent4 cell style to the range A3:A5.
    d. Top-align the contents in the range A3:B5.
5. In the Speed Test worksheet, move the data from the range A1:D97 to the range A12:D108.
6. Copy cell A1 from the Documentation sheet, and paste it into cell A1 of the Speed Test worksheet.
7. In cell A2, enter **Internet Speed Test Results**. Apply the Heading 1 cell style to the range A2:D2.
8. In cell A4, enter **Date** and format it using the Accent4 cell style. In cell B4, enter **4/8/2017** and format it using the Long Date format. Add a border around the cells in the range A4:B4.
9. Format the data in the Speed Test worksheet as follows:
    a. In the range A13:A108, format the numeric date and time values with the Time format. (*Hint*: The Time format is in the Number Format box in the Number group on the Home tab.)
    b. In the range C13:D108, show the numbers with three decimal places.
    c. In the range A12:D12, apply the Accent4 cell style and center the text.
    d. In the range A12:D108, add borders around all of the cells.
10. Create a table of summary statistics for the Internet Speed Test as follows:
    a. Copy the headings in the range B12:D12, and paste them into the range B6:D6.
    b. In cell A7, enter **Average**. In cell A8, enter **Minimum**. In cell A9, enter **Maximum**. Format the range A7:A9 with the Accent4 cell style.

   c. In cell B7, use the AVERAGE function to calculate the average ping value of the values in the range B13:B108. In cell B8, use the MIN function to calculate the minimum ping value of the values in the range B13:B108. In cell B9, use the MAX function to calculate the maximum ping value of the values in the range B13:B108.
   d. Copy the formulas from the range B7:B9 to the range C7:D9 to calculate summary statistics for the download and upload speeds from the Internet test.
   e. Format the values in the range B7,C7:D9 to show two decimal places.
   f. Add borders around all of the cells in the range A6:D9.
11. Use conditional formatting to highlight ping values greater than 70 in the range B13:B108 with a light red fill with dark red text to highlight times when the Internet usually appears to be slow.
12. Use conditional formatting to highlight upload values less than 3.5 in the range C13:C108 with a light red fill with dark red text.
13. Use conditional formatting to highlight download values less than 2 in the range D13:D108 with a light red fill with dark red text.
14. In cell D11, enter the text **Slow Connection**. Use conditional formatting to display this text string with a light red fill with dark red text. Center the text, and add a border around cell D11.
15. Set the print titles to repeat the first 12 rows at the top of every page of the printout.
16. For the first page of the printout, add a header that prints **Prepared by** followed by your name in the left section of the header and the current date in the right section of the header. Do not display header text on any other page.
17. For every page, add a footer that prints the workbook filename in the left section, **Page** followed by the page number followed by **of** followed by the number of pages in the center section, and then the worksheet name in the right section.
18. If you are instructed to print, print the entire contents of the workbook in portrait orientation.
19. Save and close the workbook.

CHALLENGE

Case Problem 3

Data File needed for this Case Problem: Wait.xlsx

YuriTech Kayla Schwartz is the customer service manager at YuriTech, an electronics and computer firm located in Scottsdale, Arizona. Kayla is analyzing the calling records for technical support calls to YuriTech to determine which times are understaffed, resulting in unacceptable wait times. She has compiled several months of data and calculated the average wait times in one-hour intervals for each day of the week. You will format Kayla's workbook to make it easier to determine when YuriTech should hire more staff to assist with customer support requests. Complete the following:

1. Open the **Wait** workbook located in the Excel2 > Case3 folder, and then save the workbook as **Wait Times** in the location specified by your instructor.
2. In the Documentation sheet, enter your name in cell B3 and the date in cell B4.
3. Apply the Ion theme to the workbook.
4. Format the Documentation sheet as follows:
   a. Format the title in cell A1 using a 36-point Impact font with the Purple, Accent 6 font color.
   b. Format the range A3:A5 with the Accent6 cell style.
   c. Add a border around the cells in the range A3:B5. Wrap the text within each cell, and top-align the cell text.
5. Copy the format you used in cell A1 of the Documentation sheet, and paste it to cell A1 of the Wait Times worksheet.

6. Format the text in cell A2 with 14-point bold font and the Purple, Accent6 font color.
7. In the range A14:H39, format the average customer wait times for each hour and day of the week data as follows:
   a. Merge and center the range A14:H14, and apply the Title cell style to the merged contents.
   b. Change the number format of the data in the range B16:H39 to show one decimal place.
   c. Format the column and row labels in the range A15:H15,A16:A39 with the Accent6 cell style. Center the column headings in the range B15:H15.
8. In cell B5, enter the value **22** as an excellent wait time. In cell B6, enter **34** as a good wait time. In cell B7, enter **45** as an acceptable wait time. In cell B8, enter **60** as a poor wait time. In cell B9, enter **78** as a very poor wait time. In cell B10, enter **90** as an unacceptable wait time.
9. In the range A4:C10, apply the following formats to the wait time goals:
   a. Merge and center the range A4:C4, and apply the Accent6 cell style to the merged cells.
   b. Add borders around the cells in the range A4:C10.
10. In cell E4, enter the label **Average Wait Time (All Days)**. In cell E7, enter the label **Average Wait Time (Weekdays)**. In cell E10, enter the label **Average Wait Time (Weekends)**.
11. Merge and center the range E4:F6, wrap the text in the merged cell, center the cell content both horizontally and vertically, and then apply the Accent6 cell style to the merged cell.
12. Copy the format from the merged cell E4:F6 to cells E7 and E10.
13. In cell G4, enter a formula to calculate the average of the wait times in the range B16:H39. In cell G7, enter a formula to calculate the average weekday wait times in the range C16:G39. In cell G10, calculate the average weekend rate times in the range B16:B39,H16:H39.
14. Merge and center the ranges G4:G6, G7:G9, and G10:G12, and then center the calculated averages vertically within each merged cell.
15. Add borders around the cells in the range E4:G12.
16. Change the fill color of the range A5:C5 to a medium green, the fill color of the range A6:C6 to a light green, the fill color of the range A7:C7 to a light gold, the fill color of the range A8:C8 to a light red, and the fill color of the range A9:C9 to a medium red. Format the range A10:C10 with white text on a black background.

Explore 17. Use conditional formatting to highlight cells with custom formats as follows:
   a. Select the range G4:G12,B16:H39. Use conditional formatting to highlight cells with values less than 22 with a custom format that matches the fill color used in the range A5:C5.
   b. Use conditional formatting to highlight cells with values greater than 90 in the range G4:G12,B16:H39 with a custom format of a white font on a black fill.
   c. Use conditional formatting to highlight cells with values between 22 and 34 in the range G4:G12,B16:H39 with a custom format that matches the fill color used in the range A6:C6.
   d. Use conditional formatting to highlight cells with values between 34 and 60 in the range G4:G12,B16:H39 with a light gold fill color that matches the cells in the range A7:C7.
   e. Use conditional formatting to highlight cells with values between 60 and 78 in the range G4:G12,B16:H39 with light red, matching the fill color of the cells in the range A8:C8.
   f. Use conditional formatting to highlight cells with values between 78 and 90 in the range G4:G12,B16:H39 with medium red, matching the fill color of the cells in the range A9:C9.

18. In cell A41, enter the label **Notes** and then format it with the Title cell style.
19. Merge the range A42:H50. Top- and left-align the contents of the cell. Turn on text wrapping within the merged cell. Add a thick outside border to the merged cell.
20. Within the merged cell in the range A42:H50, summarize your conclusions about the wait times. Answer whether the wait times are within acceptable limits on average for the entire week, on weekdays, and on weekends. Also indicate whether there are times during the week that customers are experience very poor to unacceptable delays.
21. Format the printed version of the Wait Times worksheet as follows:
   a. Scale the sheet so that it fits on a single page in portrait orientation.
   b. Center the sheet on the page horizontally and vertically.

c. Add the header **Prepared by** followed by your name in the right section.
d. Add a footer that prints the filename in the left section, the worksheet name in the center section, and the date in the right section.

22. If you are instructed to print, print the entire contents of the workbook.
23. Save and close the workbook.

CREATE

Case Problem 4

Data File needed for this Case Problem: Pandaisia.xlsx

Pandaisia Chocolates Anne Ambrose is the owner and head chocolatier of Pandaisia Chocolates, a chocolate shop located in Essex, Vermont. Anne has asked you to create an Excel workbook in which she can enter customer orders. She wants the workbook to be easy to use and read. The final design of the order form is up to you. One possible solution is shown in Figure 2-47.

Figure 2-47 Pandaisia Chocolates order form

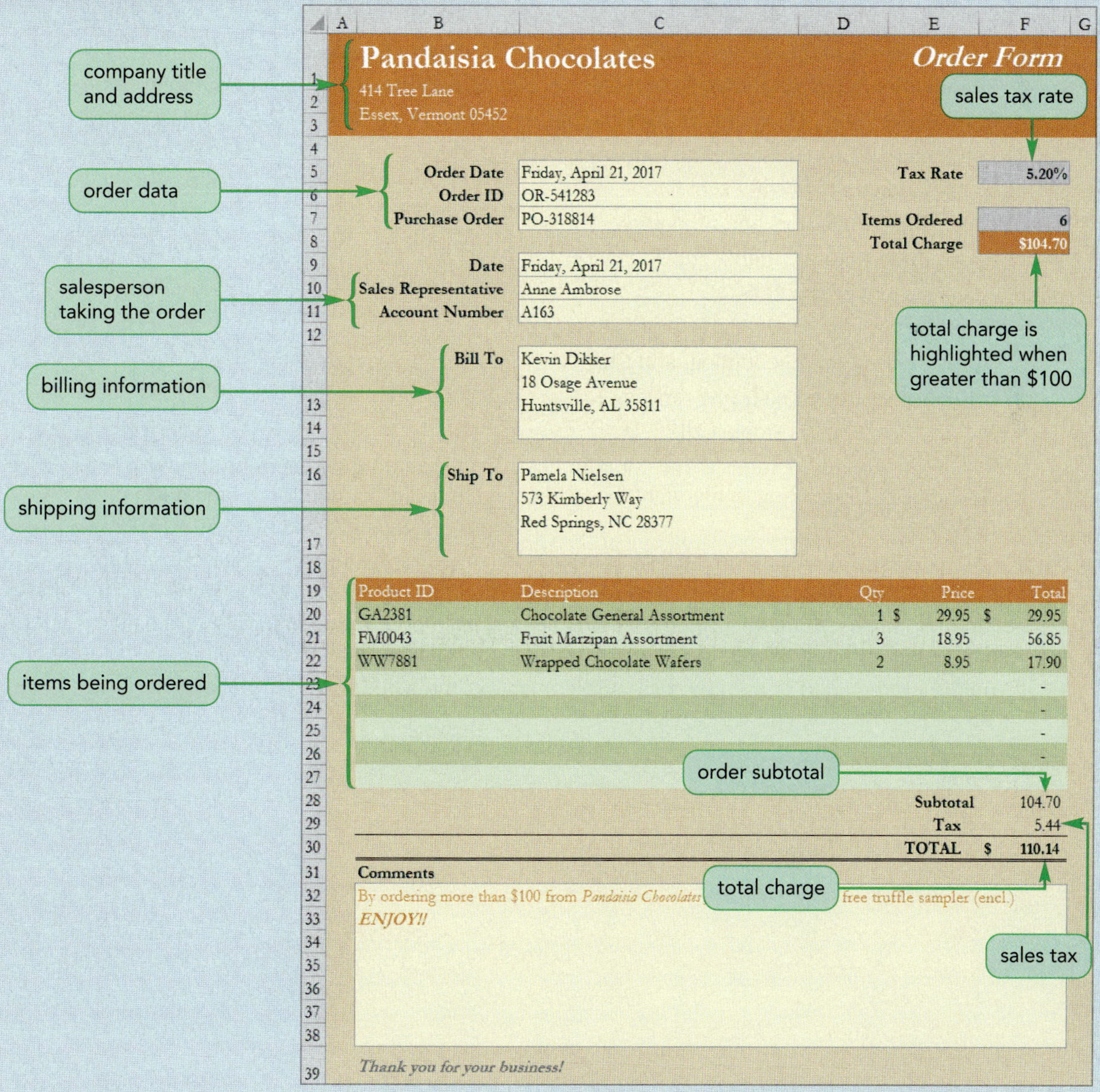

Complete the following:

1. Open the **Pandaisia** workbook located in the Excel2 > Case3 folder, and then save the workbook as **Pandaisia Order** in the location specified by your instructor.
2. In the Documentation sheet, enter your name in cell B3 and the date in cell B4.
3. Insert a worksheet named **Order Form** after the Documentation worksheet.
4. Enter the following information in the order form:
   - The title and address of Pandaisia Chocolates
   - The order date, order ID, and purchase order ID
   - The date, sales representative, and account number for the order
   - The billing address of the order
   - The shipping address of the order
   - A table listing every item ordered including the item's product ID, description, quantity ordered, price, and total charge for the item(s)
   - A comment box where Anne can insert additional information about the order
5. Include formulas in the order form to do the following:
   a. For each item ordered, calculate the cost of the item(s), which is equal to the quantity multiplied by the price.
   b. Calculate the subtotal of the costs for every item ordered by the customer.
   c. Calculate the sales tax for the order, which is equal to 5.2 percent times the subtotal value.
   d. Calculate the total cost of the order, which is equal to the subtotal plus the sale tax.
6. Format the order form by doing the following:
   a. Apply a different built-in Excel theme.
   b. Change the font colors and fill colors.
   c. Format a text string within a cell.
   d. Align content within cells.
   e. Format dates with the Long Date format.
   f. Apply the Percent, Accounting, and Currency formats as appropriate.
   g. Add borders around cells and ranges.
   h. Merge a range into a single cell.
7. Pandaisia Chocolates includes a free complimentary truffle sample for every order over $100. Use conditional formatting to highlight the total charge in bold colored font when it is greater than $100.
8. Test your order form by entering the data shown in Figure 2-47. Confirm that the charge on your order matches that shown in the figure.
9. Set up the print version of the order form so that it prints in portrait orientation on a single sheet. Add a header and/or footer that includes your name, the date, and the name of the workbook.
10. If you are instructed to print, print the entire contents of the workbook.
11. Save and close the workbook.

MODULE 3

Performing Calculations with Formulas and Functions

Calculating Farm Yield and Revenue

EXCEL

OBJECTIVES

Session 3.1
- Document formulas and data values
- Explore function syntax
- Insert functions from the Formula Library
- Perform a what-if analysis

Session 3.2
- AutoFill series and formulas
- Use relative and absolute cell references
- Use the Quick Analysis tool
- Work with dates and Date functions
- Find values with Lookup functions
- Work with Logical functions

Case | *Wingait Farm*

Jane Wingait is the owner and operator of Wingait Farm, a small farm located outside of Cascade, Iowa. Jane's cash crop is corn, and she has planted almost 140 acres of the sweet corn variety for the past 11 years. Near harvest time every year Jane samples and analyzes a portion of her crop to estimate her farm's total yield for the year. She wants you to help her design an Excel workbook that will calculate her corn yield. As Jane prepares for next year's crop, she also wants to use Excel to track her corn's growth from planting to harvesting. As you create the workbook, you will explore how Jane can use Excel formulas to help her in running her farm.

STARTING DATA FILES

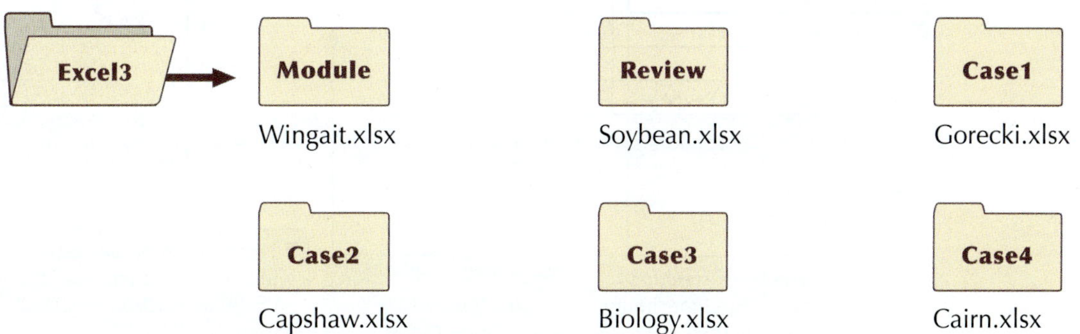

Session 3.1 Visual Overview:

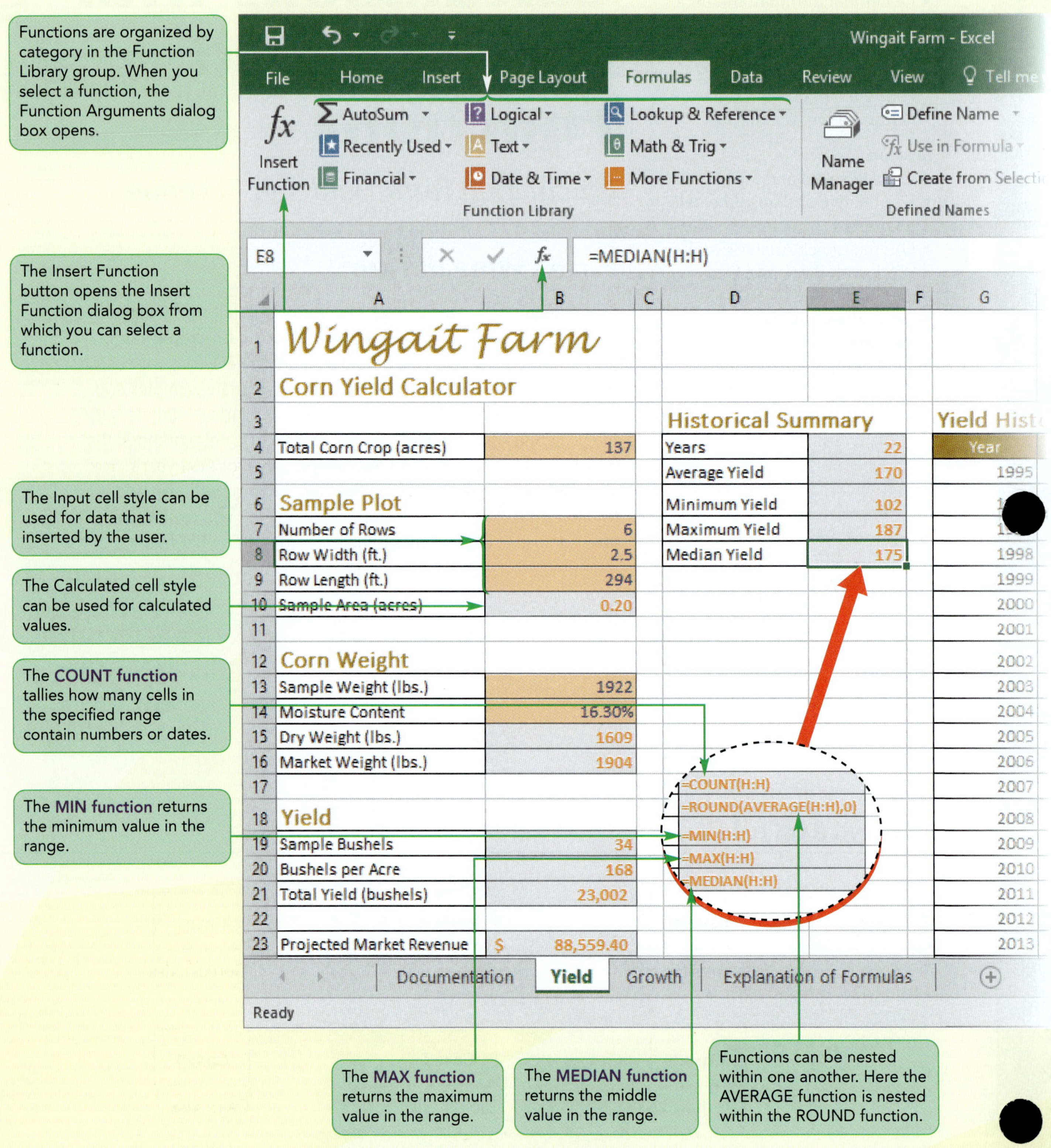
Functions are organized by category in the Function Library group. When you select a function, the Function Arguments dialog box opens.
Wingait Farm - Excel
File
Home
Insert
Page Layout
Formulas
Data
Review
View
Tell me
Insert Function
AutoSum
Recently Used
Financial
Logical
Text
Date & Time
Lookup & Reference
Math & Trig
More Functions
Function Library
Name Manager
Define Name
Use in Formula
Create from Selection
Defined Names
The Insert Function button opens the Insert Function dialog box from which you can select a function.
E8
=MEDIAN(H:H)
Wingait Farm
Corn Yield Calculator
Total Corn Crop (acres) 137
Sample Plot
Number of Rows 6
Row Width (ft.) 2.5
Row Length (ft.) 294
Sample Area (acres) 0.20
Corn Weight
Sample Weight (lbs.) 1922
Moisture Content 16.30%
Dry Weight (lbs.) 1609
Market Weight (lbs.) 1904
Yield
Sample Bushels 34
Bushels per Acre 168
Total Yield (bushels) 23,002
Projected Market Revenue $ 88,559.40
Historical Summary
Years 22
Average Yield 170
Minimum Yield 102
Maximum Yield 187
Median Yield 175
Yield History
Year
1995
1998
1999
2000
2001
2002
2003
2004
2005
2006
2007
2008
2009
2010
2011
2012
2013
=COUNT(H:H)
=ROUND(AVERAGE(H:H),0)
=MIN(H:H)
=MAX(H:H)
=MEDIAN(H:H)
Documentation
Yield
Growth
Explanation of Formulas
Ready
The Input cell style can be used for data that is inserted by the user.
The Calculated cell style can be used for calculated values.
The COUNT function tallies how many cells in the specified range contain numbers or dates.
The MIN function returns the minimum value in the range.
The MAX function returns the maximum value in the range.
The MEDIAN function returns the middle value in the range.
Functions can be nested within one another. Here the AVERAGE function is nested within the ROUND function.

Formulas and Functions

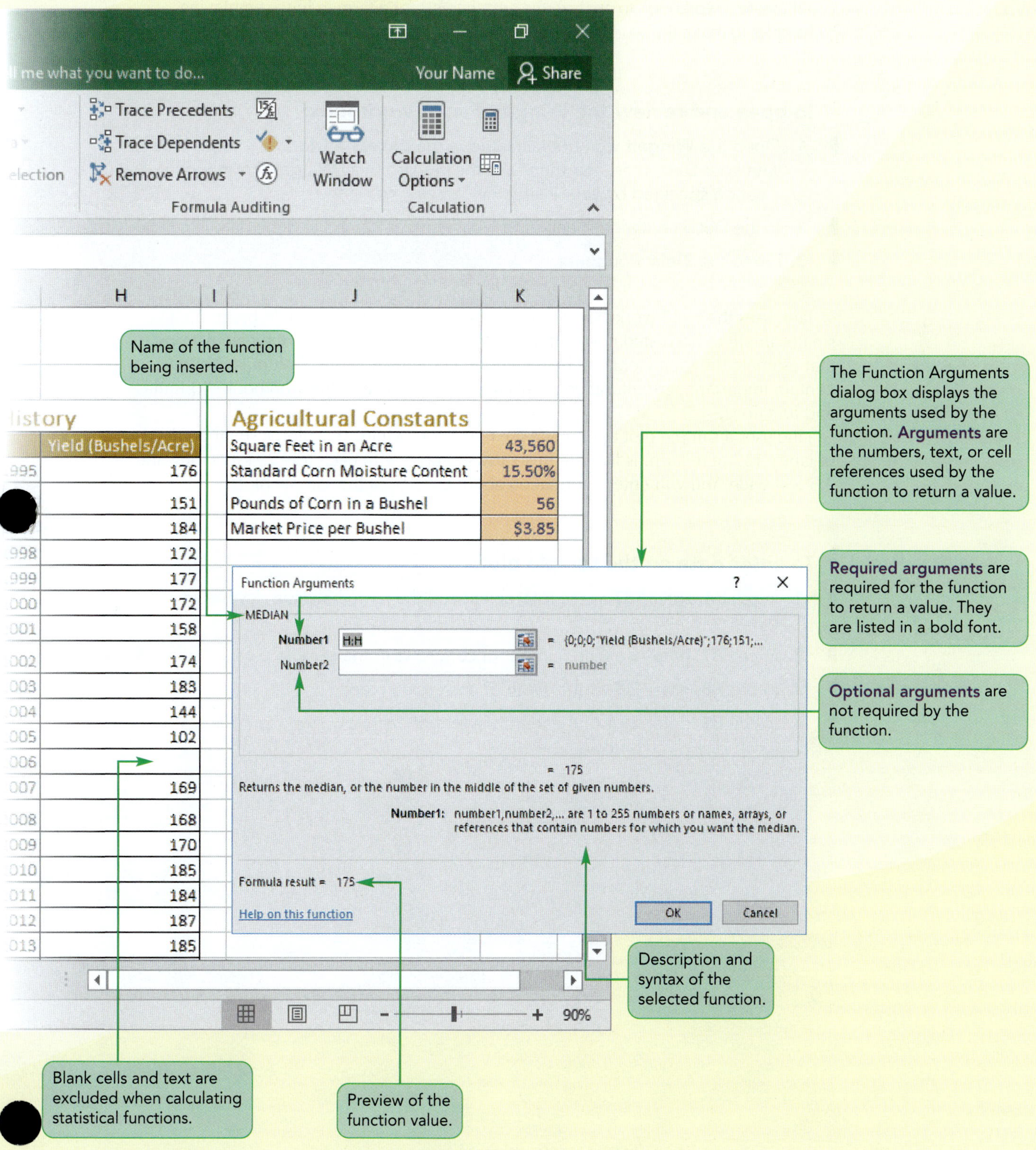

Making Workbooks User-Friendly

Excel is a powerful application for interpreting a wide variety of data used in publications from financial reports to scientific articles. To be an effective tool for data analysis, a workbook needs to be easy to use and interpret. This includes defining any technical terms in the workbook and explaining the formulas used in the analysis. In this module, you'll create a workbook to analyze the corn harvest for a farm in Iowa, employing techniques to make the workbook easily accessible to other users.

To open and review the Wingait Farms workbook:

1. Open the **Wingait** workbook located in the **Excel3 > Module** folder included with your Data Files, and then save the workbook as **Wingait Farm** in the location specified by your instructor.
2. In the Documentation sheet, enter your name in cell B3 and the date in cell B4.
3. Go to the **Yield** worksheet.

Jane uses the Yield worksheet to project her farm's entire corn yield based on a small sample of harvested corn. Information about the sample and the calculations that estimate the total yield will be entered in columns A and B. Columns D and E contain important agricultural constants that Jane will use in the workbook's formulas and functions.

Jane uses a sample plot to estimate the farm's total yield. This plot, a small portion of Jane's 137-acre farm, is laid out in six rows of corn with each row 294 feet long and 2.5 feet wide. You will enter information about the size of the sample plot.

To enter data on the sample plot:

1. In cell **B4**, enter **137** as the total acreage of the farm that Jane devotes to sweet corn.
2. In cell **B7**, enter **6** as the number of corn rows in the sample plot.
3. In cell **B8**, enter **2.5** as the width of each row in feet.
4. In cell **B9**, enter **294** as the length in feet of each row. See Figure 3-1.

Figure 3-1 Sample plot data entered

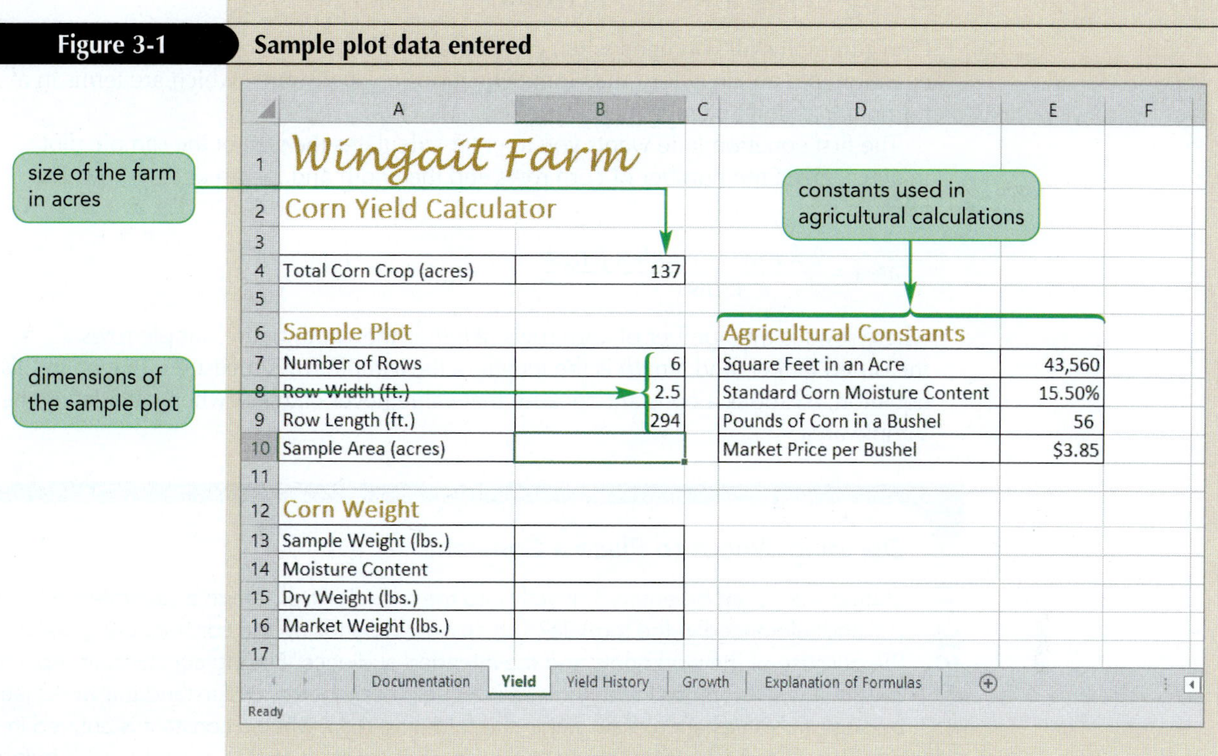

The width and length of the sample rows are measured in feet, but Jane needs the total area expressed in acres. To calculate the area of the sample being tested, you need to refer to the agricultural equations that Jane documented for you.

Documenting Formulas

Documenting the contents of a workbook helps to avoid errors and confusion. It also makes it easier for others to interpret the analysis in the workbook. For workbooks that include many calculations, such as the Wingait Farm workbook, it is helpful to explain the formulas and terms used in the calculations. Such documentation also can serve as a check that the equations are accurate.

Jane has included explanations of equations you'll use in developing her workbook. Before proceeding, you'll review this documentation.

To review the documentation in Wingait Farm workbook:

1. Go to the **Explanation of Formulas** worksheet.
2. Read the worksheet contents, reviewing the descriptions of common agricultural constants and formulas. As you continue developing the Wingait Farm workbook, you'll learn about these terms and formulas in more detail.
3. Go to the **Yield** worksheet.

Using Constants in Formulas

One common skill you need when creating a workbook is being able to translate an equation into an Excel formula. Some equations use **constants**, which are terms in a formula that don't change their value.

The first equation Jane wants you to enter calculates the size of the sample plot in acres, given the number of corn rows and the width and length of each row. The formula is

$$area = \frac{2 \times rows \times width \times length}{43560}$$

where *rows* is the number of corn rows, *width* is the width of the sample rows measured in feet, and *length* is the length of the sample rows measured in feet. In this equation, 43560 is a constant because that value never changes when calculating the sample area.

INSIGHT

Deciding Where to Place a Constant

Should a constant be entered directly into the formula or placed in a separate worksheet cell and referenced in the formula? The answer depends on the constant being used, the purpose of the workbook, and the intended audience. Placing constants in separate cells that you reference in the formulas can help users better understand the worksheet because no values are hidden within the formulas. Also, when a constant is entered in a cell, you can add explanatory text next to each constant to document how it is being used in the formula. On the other hand, you don't want a user to inadvertently change the value of a constant and throw off all the formula results. You will need to evaluate how important it is for other people to immediately see the constant and whether the constant requires any explanation for other people to understand the formula.

To convert the area equation to an Excel formula, you'll replace the *row*, *width*, and *length* values with references to the cells B7, B8, and B9, and you'll replace 43560 with a reference to cell E7. These cells provide the number of rows in the sample plot, the row width in feet, the row length in feet, and the number of square feet in one acre of land.

To calculate the area of the sample plot:

1. In cell **B10**, enter the formula **=2*B7*B8*B9/E7** to calculate the area of the sample plot. The formula returns 0.202479339.

   Trouble? If your result differs from 0.202479339, you probably entered the formula incorrectly. Edit the formula you entered in cell B10 as needed so that the numbers and cell references match those shown in the formula in Step 1.

   Jane does not need to see the acreage of the sample plot with eight decimal places.

2. Click cell **B10**, and then decrease the number of decimal places to **2**. The area of the sample plot is displayed as 0.20 acres. See Figure 3-2.

TIP

Decreasing the number decimals places rounds the displayed value; the stored value remains unchanged.

Figure 3-2 Calculated size of the sample plot in acres

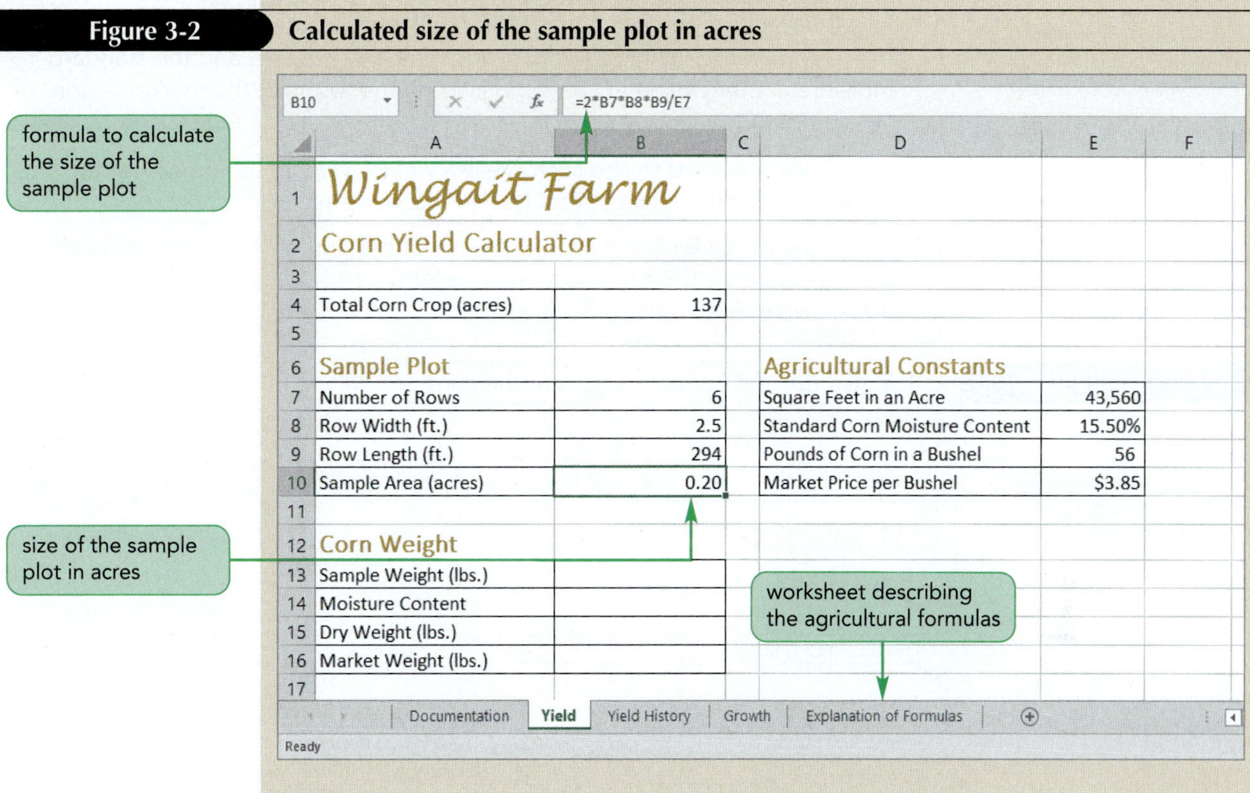

When Jane harvests the corn from the sample plot, she measures the total weight of the corn, which includes its moisture content. She then analyzes the corn to determine what percentage of its weight is due to moisture. The total weight of the corn is 1,922 pounds of which 16.3 percent is moisture. To sell the corn, Jane needs to calculate the dry weight of the corn without the moisture. She can do this with the formula

$$\textit{dry weight} = \textit{total weight} \times (1 - \textit{moisture})$$

where *total weight* is the weight of the corn and *moisture* is the percentage of the weight due to moisture. Market prices for corn are standardized at a moisture percentage of 15.5 percent, so to get the correct market weight of her corn, Jane uses the following formula:

$$\textit{market weight} = \frac{\textit{dry weight}}{1 - 0.155}$$

You will enter these two formulas in Jane's workbook to calculate the market weight of the corn she harvested from the sample plot.

To calculate the market weight of the corn:

1. In cell **B13**, enter **1922** as the total weight of the corn sample.
2. In cell **B14**, enter **16.3%** as the moisture content.
3. In cell **B15**, enter the formula **=B13*(1-B14)** to calculate the dry weight of the corn kernels. Based on the formula, the dry weight of the corn harvested from the sample plot is 1608.714 pounds.

Because the expression requires dividing by two terms, you must enclose those terms within parentheses.

4. In cell **B16**, enter the formula **=B15/(1-E8)** to calculate the market weight of the corn kernels using the dry weight value in cell B15 and the standard moisture content value in cell E8. Based on the formula, the market weight of the corn is 1903.80355 pounds.

   Jane does not need to see such precise weight values, so you will reduce the number of decimal places displayed in the worksheet.

5. Select the range **B15:B16**, and then format the numbers with no decimals places to display the dry and market weights of 1609 and 1904 pounds, respectively. See Figure 3-3.

Figure 3-3 Calculated dry and market weights of the corn

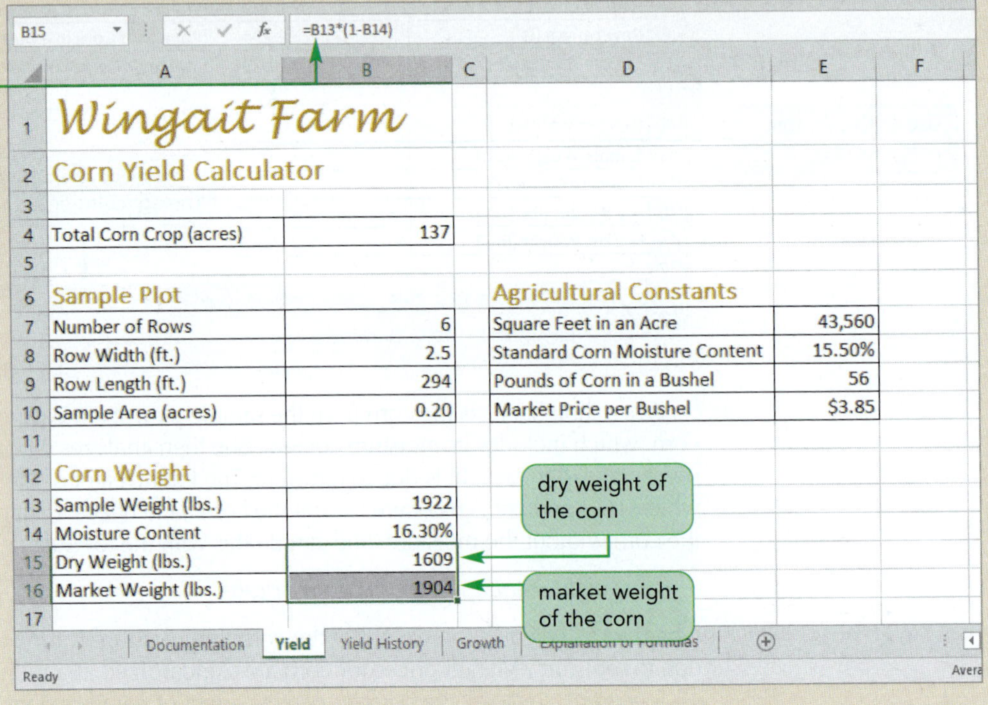

Corn is not sold by the pound but rather by the bushel where 1 bushel contains 56 pounds of corn. You will calculate the number of bushels of corn in the sample plot and then use this number to estimate the farm's total yield and revenue.

To project the farm's total yield and revenue:

1. In cell **B19**, enter the formula **=B16/E9** to convert the market weight to bushels. In this case, the market weight is equal to 33.99649197 bushels.
2. In cell **B19**, format the number with no decimals places. The number is rounded to 34 bushels.
3. In cell **B20**, enter the formula **=B19/B10** to divide the number of bushels in the sample plot by the size of the plot in acres. Based on this calculation, this year's crop has yielded 167.901042 bushels per acre.

4. In cell **B20**, format the number with no decimals places. This year's crop yielded about 168 bushels per acre.

   Assuming that the rest of the farm is as productive as the sample plot, you can calculate the total bushels that the farm can produce by multiplying the bushels per acre by the total acreage of the farm.

5. In cell **B21**, enter the formula **=B20*B4** to multiply the bushels per acre by the total acreage of the farm. Assuming that the rest of the farm is as productive as the sample plot, the total bushels that the farm can produce is 23002.44275 bushels.
6. Format cell B21 using the Comma style with no decimal places. Cell B21 displays 23,002.
7. In cell **B23**, enter the formula **=B21*E10** to calculate the revenue Jane can expect by selling all of the farm's corn at the market price of $3.85 per bushel.
8. Format cell B23 with the Accounting style. The formula result is displayed as $88,559.40. See Figure 3-4.

Figure 3-4 Projected yield and revenue from the corn harvest

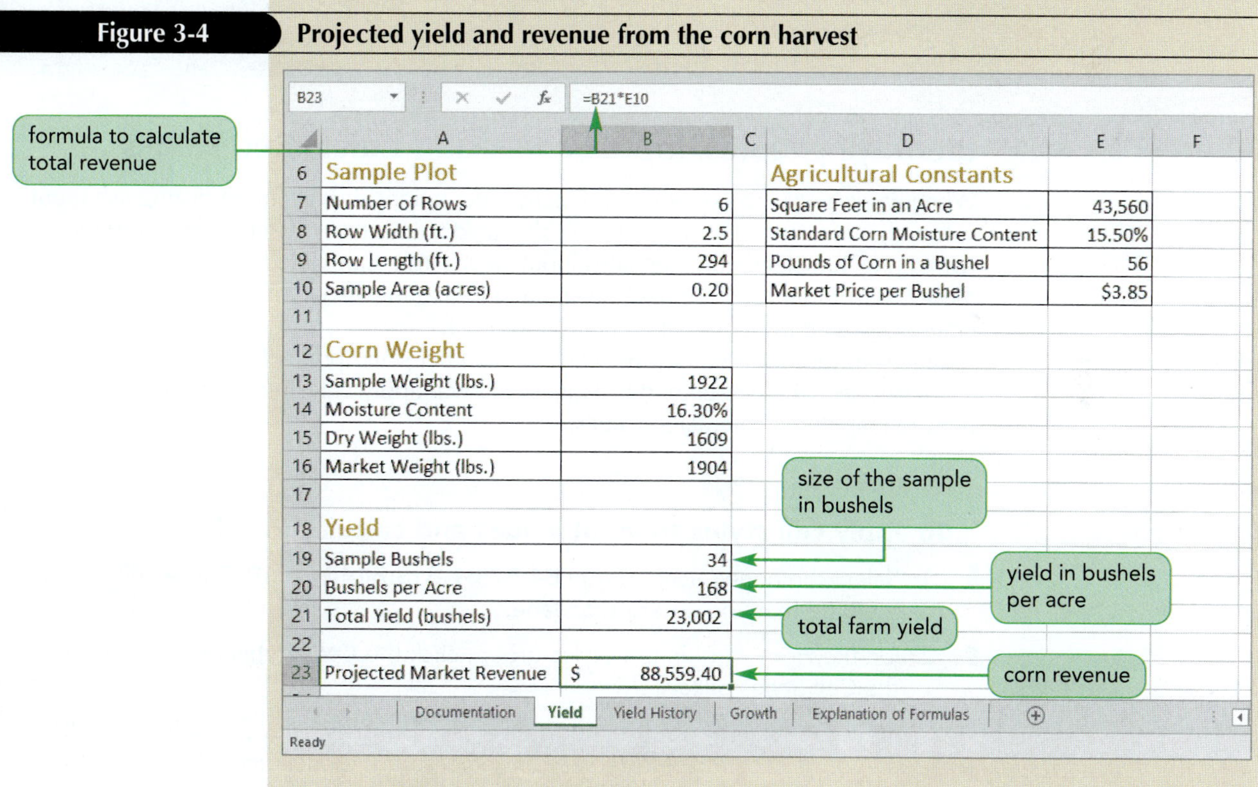

Based on your calculations, Jane projects an income of almost $90,000 from this year's corn crop.

PROSKILLS

Written Communication: Displaying Significant Digits

Excel stores numbers with up to 15 digits and displays as many digits as will fit into the cell. So even the result of a simple formula such as =10/3 will display 3.33333333333333 if the cell is wide enough.

A number with 15 digits is difficult to read, and calculations rarely need that level of accuracy. Many scientific disciplines, such as chemistry or physics, have rules for specifying exactly how many digits should be displayed with any calculation. These digits are called **significant digits** because they indicate the accuracy of the measured and calculated values. For example, an input value of 19.32 has four significant digits.

The rules are based on several factors and vary from one discipline to another. Generally, a calculated value should display no more digits than are found in any of the input values. For example, because the input value 19.32 has four significant digits, any calculated value based on that input should have no more than four significant digits. Showing more digits would be misleading because it implies a level of accuracy beyond that which was actually measured.

Because Excel displays calculated values with as many digits as can fit into a cell, you need to know the standards for your profession and change the display of your calculated values accordingly.

Identifying Notes, Input Values, and Calculated Values

When worksheets involve notes and many calculations, it is useful to distinguish input values that are used in formulas from calculated values that are returned by formulas. Formatting that clearly differentiates input values from calculated values helps others more easily understand the worksheet. Such formatting also helps prevent anyone from entering a value in a cell that contains a formula.

Jane wants to be sure that whenever she and her staff update the workbook, they can easily see where to enter data values. You will apply cell styles to distinguish between input and calculated values.

To apply cell styles to input values and calculated values:

1. Select the nonadjacent range **B4,B7:B9,B13:B14,E7:E10**. These cells contain the data that you entered for Jane.
2. On the Home tab, in the Styles group, click the **Cell Styles** button to open the Cell Styles gallery.
3. In the Data and Model section, click the **Input** cell style. The selected cells are formatted with a light blue font on an orange background, identifying those cells as containing input values.
4. Select the nonadjacent range **B10,B15:B16,B19:B21,B23**. These cells contain the formulas for calculating the weight, yield, and revenue values.
5. Format the selected cells with the **Calculation** cell style located in the Data and Model section of the Cell Styles gallery. The cells with the calculated values are formatted with a bold orange font on a light gray background.
6. Click cell **D12** to deselect the range. See Figure 3-5.

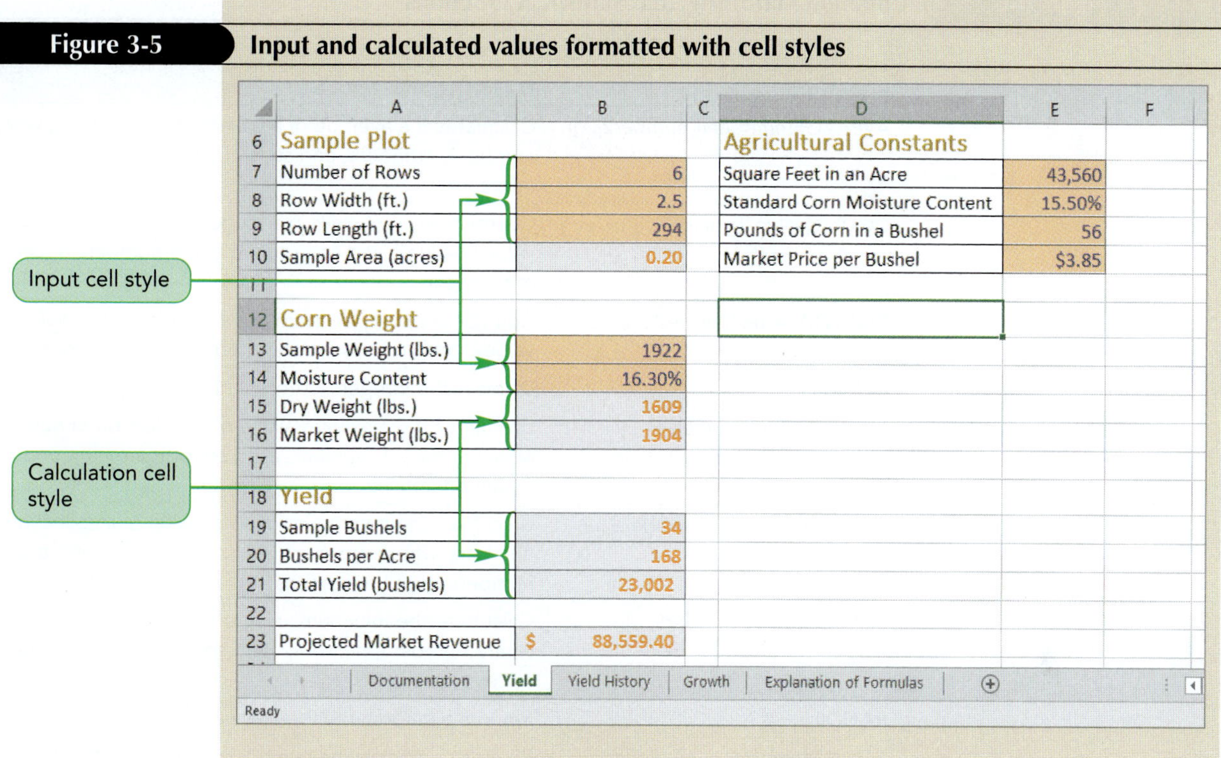

Input cell style
Calculation cell style
A
B
C
D
E
F
6 Sample Plot
7 Number of Rows 6
8 Row Width (ft.) 2.5
9 Row Length (ft.) 294
10 Sample Area (acres) 0.20
12 Corn Weight
13 Sample Weight (lbs.) 1922
14 Moisture Content 16.30%
15 Dry Weight (lbs.) 1609
16 Market Weight (lbs.) 1904
18 Yield
19 Sample Bushels 34
20 Bushels per Acre 168
21 Total Yield (bushels) 23,002
23 Projected Market Revenue $ 88,559.40
Agricultural Constants
Square Feet in an Acre 43,560
Standard Corn Moisture Content 15.50%
Pounds of Corn in a Bushel 56
Market Price per Bushel $3.85
Documentation
Yield
Yield History
Growth
Explanation of Formulas
Ready

Figure 3-5 Input and calculated values formatted with cell styles

Using Excel Functions

Excel functions can be used in place of long and complicated formulas to simplify your worksheet. Jane wants to compare the estimated yield for this year's crop to historic trends. To make that comparison, you'll work with some Excel functions.

Understanding Function Syntax

Before you use functions, you should understand the function syntax. Recall that the syntax of an Excel function follows the general pattern

```
FUNCTION(argument1,argument2,...)
```

where `FUNCTION` is the name of the function, and `argument1`, `argument2`, and so forth are arguments used by the function. An argument can be any type of value including text, numbers, cell references, or even other formulas or functions. Not all functions require arguments.

TIP

Optional arguments are always placed last in the argument list.

Some arguments are optional and can be included with the function or omitted altogether. Most optional arguments will have default values, so that if you omit an argument value, Excel will automatically apply the default. The convention is to show optional arguments within square brackets along with the argument's default value (if any), as

```
FUNCTION(argument1[,argument2=value2,...])
```

where `argument1` is a required argument, `argument2` is optional, and `value2` is the default value for argument2. As you work with specific functions, you will learn which arguments are required and which are optional as well as any default values associated with those optional arguments.

Figure 3-6 describes some of the more commonly used Math, Trig, and Statistical functions and provides the syntax of those functions, including any optional arguments.

Figure 3-6 Common Math, Trig, and Statistical functions

Function	Description
AVERAGE(*number1*[,*number2*,...])	Calculates the average of a collection of numbers, where *number1*, *number2*, and so forth are numbers or cell references
COUNT(*value1*[,*value2*,...])	Counts how many cells in a range contain numbers, where *value1*, *value2*, and so forth are either numbers or cell references
COUNTA(*value1*[,*value2*,...])	Counts how many cells are not empty in ranges *value1*, *value2*, and so forth including both numbers and text entries
INT(*number*)	Displays the integer portion of *number*
MAX(*number1*[,*number2*,...])	Calculates the maximum value of a collection of numbers, where *number1*, *number2*, and so forth are either numbers or cell references
MEDIAN(*number1*[,*number2*,...])	Calculates the median, or middle, value of a collection of numbers, where *number1*, *number2*, and so forth are either numbers or cell references
MIN(*number1*[,*number2*,...])	Calculates the minimum value of a collection of numbers, where *number1*, *number2*, and so forth are either numbers or cell references
RAND()	Returns a random number between 0 and 1
ROUND(*number*,*num_digits*)	Rounds *number* to the number of digits specified by *num_digits*
SUM(*number1*[,*number2*,...])	Adds a collection of numbers, where *number1*, *number2*, and so forth are either numbers or cell references

Entering the COUNT function

The following COUNT function is used by Excel to count how many cells in a range contain numbers. The COUNT function syntax is

```
COUNT(value1[,value2,…])
```

where ***value1*** is either a cell reference, range reference, or a number, and ***value2*** and so on are optional arguments that provide additional cell references, range references, or numbers. There are no default values for the optional arguments.

The COUNT function does not include blank cells or cells that contain text in its tally. For example, the following function counts how many cells in the range A1:A10, the range C1:C5, and cell E5 contain numbers or dates:

```
COUNT(A1:A10,C1:C5,E5)
```

The COUNT function is especially helpful when data in the ranges are regularly updated.

INSIGHT

Counting Text

Excel has another important function for counting cells—the **COUNTA function**. This function counts the number of cells that contain any entries, including numbers, dates, or text. The syntax of the COUNTA function is

```
COUNTA(value1[,value2,...])
```

where `value1` is the first item or cell reference containing the entries you want to count. The remaining optional value arguments are used primarily when you want to count entries in nonadjacent ranges. The COUNTA function should be used for text data or for data in which you need to include blanks as part of the total.

You'll use the COUNT function to tally how many years of data are included in the corn yield history.

To count the number of years in the corn yield history:

1. Go to the **Yield History** worksheet, and then click cell **B5**. You'll enter the COUNT function in this cell.
2. Type **=COUNT(** to begin entering the COUNT function. The first argument, which is the only required argument, is the cell or range reference for the cells to be counted.

   The yield values are stored in the range E5:E27. Instead of referencing this range, you will use column E as the argument for the COUNT function because Jane plans to add data to this column each year as she continues to track the farm's annual corn yield.
3. Click the **E** column heading to select the entire column. The column reference E:E is inserted into the function as the first argument.
4. Type **)** to end the function, and then press the **Enter** key. The formula =COUNT(E:E) is entered in cell B5 and returns 22, which is the number of years for which Jane has corn yield data.

Nesting the ROUND and AVERAGE Functions

One function can be placed inside, or **nested**, within another function. When a formula contains more than one function, Excel first evaluates the innermost function and then moves outward to evaluate the next function. The inner function acts as an argument value for the outer function. For example, the following expression nests the AVERAGE function within the ROUND function.

```
ROUND(AVERAGE(A1:A100),0)
```

TIP

The ROUND function changes the value stored in the cell, not the number of decimal places displayed in the cell.

Excel first uses the AVERAGE function to calculate the average of the values in the range A1:A100 and then uses the ROUND function to round that average to the nearest integer (where the number of digits to the right of the decimal point is 0.)

One challenge of nested functions is being sure to include all of the parentheses. You can check this by counting the number of opening parentheses and making sure that number matches the number of closing parentheses. Excel also displays each level of nested parentheses in different colors to make it easier for you to match the opening and closing parentheses. If the number of parentheses doesn't match, Excel will not accept the formula and will provide a suggestion for how to rewrite the formula so the number of opening and closing parentheses does match.

Jane wants you to analyze the corn yield history at Wingait Farm. You'll use the COUNT function to tally the number of years in the historical sample and then use the AVERAGE function to calculate the average yield during those years. Because Jane doesn't need the exact corn yield values, you'll use the ROUND function to round that calculated average to the nearest integer.

To analyze the corn yield history:

1. Click cell **B6**. You want to enter the nested function in this cell.
2. Type **=ROUND(** to begin the formula with the ROUND function.
3. Type **AVERAGE(E:E)** to enter the AVERAGE function as the first argument of the ROUND function.
4. Type **,** (a comma) to separate the first and second arguments.
5. Type **0)** to specify the number of decimal places to include in the results. In this case, Jane doesn't want to include any decimal places.
6. Press the **Enter** key. The nested functions first calculate the average value of the numbers in column E and then round that number to the nearest integer. The formula returns 170, which is the average annual yield of Wingait Farm in bushels per acre rounded to the nearest integer. See Figure 3-7.

Figure 3-7 Nested functions calculate the average annual yield

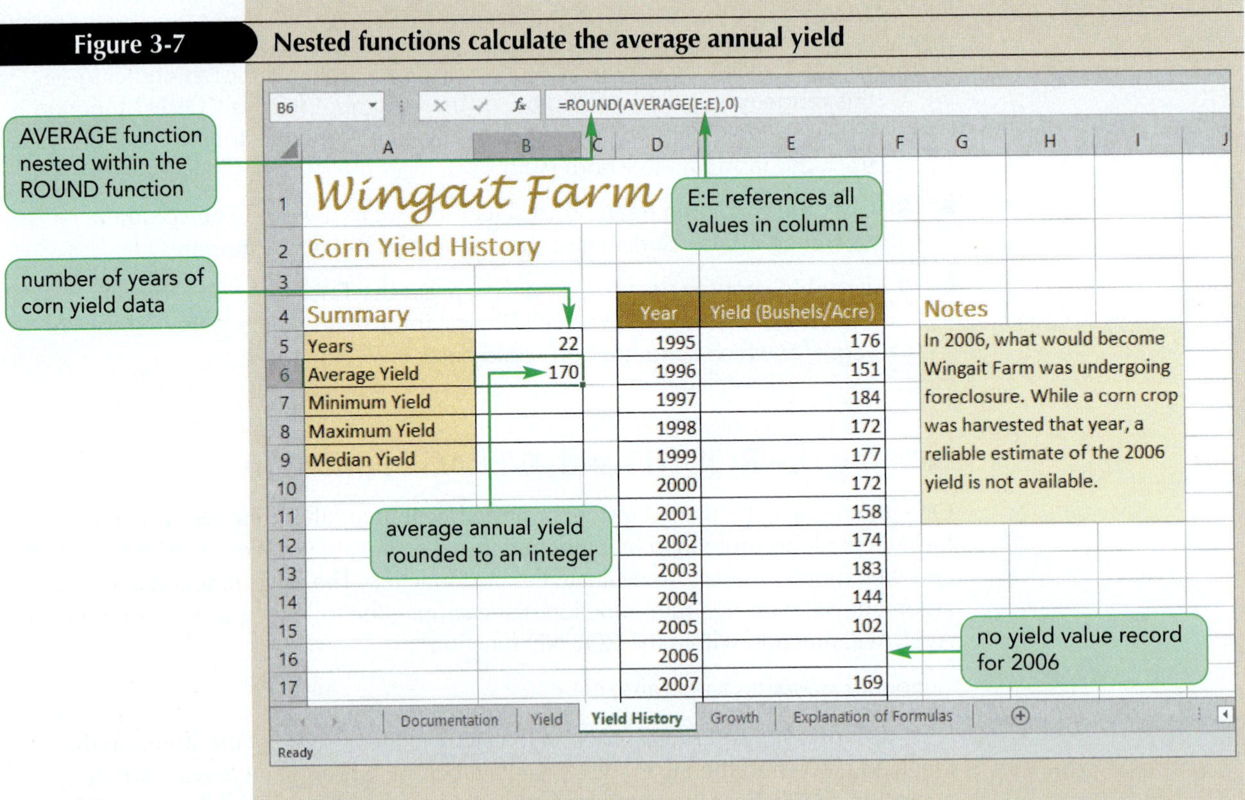

Based on values from 22 seasons of data, Jane expects her farm to yield 170 bushels of corn per acre each year.

Note that in 2006, no data on corn yield was available. Excel ignores nonnumeric data and blank cells when calculating statistical functions such as COUNT and AVERAGE. So, the count and average values in cells B5 and B6 represent only those years containing recorded corn yields. Keep in mind that a blank cell is not the same as a zero value in worksheet calculations. Figure 3-8 shows how function results differ when a zero replaces a blank in the selected range.

Figure 3-8 **Calculations with blank cells and zero values**

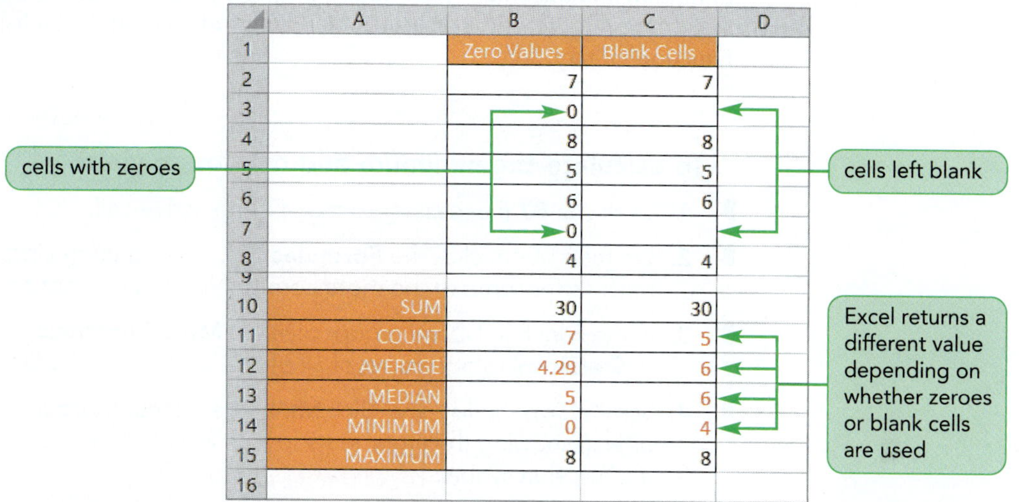

Whether you use a blank or zero depends on what you're trying to measure. For example, if Jane were to calculate average hours worked per day at the Wingait farm store, she could enter 0 for the holidays on which the store is closed, or she could enter a blank and thus calculate the average only for days in which the store is open.

Using the Function Library and the Insert Function Dialog Box

With so many Excel functions, it can difficult to locate the function you want to use for a particular application. Excel organizes its function into the 13 categories described in Figure 3-9. These function categories are available in the Function Library group on the Formulas tab and in the Insert Function dialog box.

Figure 3-9 **Excel function categories**

Category	Description
Compatibility	Functions from Excel 2010 or earlier, still supported to provide backward compatibility
Cube	Retrieve data from multidimensional databases involving online analytical processing (OLAP)
Database	Retrieve and analyze data stored in databases
Date & Time	Analyze or create date and time values and time intervals
Engineering	Analyze engineering problems
Financial	Analyze information for business and finance
Information	Return information about the format, location, or contents of worksheet cells
Logical	Return logical (true-false) values
Lookup & Reference	Look up and return data matching a set of specified conditions from a range
Math & Trig	Perform math and trigonometry calculations
Statistical	Provide statistical analyses of data sets
Text	Return text values or evaluate text
Web	Provide information on web-based connections

Once you select a function either from the Function Library or the Insert Function dialog box, the Function Arguments dialog box opens, listing all of the arguments associated with that function. Required arguments are in bold type; optional arguments are in normal type.

Jane wants to know the range of annual corn yields, so she asks you to calculate the minimum and maximum yield values from the past 23 years. Because minimums and maximums are statistical measures, you will find them in the Statistics category in the Function Library.

To calculate the minimum and maximum yield:

1. Click cell **B7** if necessary to make it the active cell.
2. On the ribbon, click the **Formulas** tab. The Function Library group has buttons for some of the more commonly used categories of functions.
3. In the Function Library group, click the **More Functions** button, and then point to **Statistical** to open a list of all of the functions in the Statistical category.
4. Scroll down the list, and click **MIN**. The Function Arguments dialog box opens, showing the arguments for the MIN function and a brief description of the function syntax.
5. With the entry for the Number1 argument highlighted, click the **E** column heading to select the entire column and insert the cell reference **E:E** into the Number1 input box. See Figure 3-10.

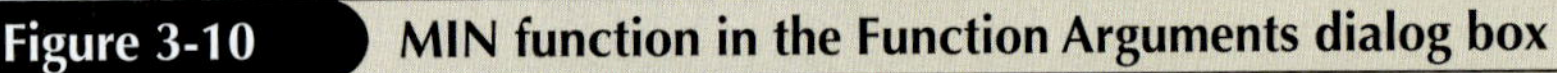

Figure 3-10 MIN function in the Function Arguments dialog box

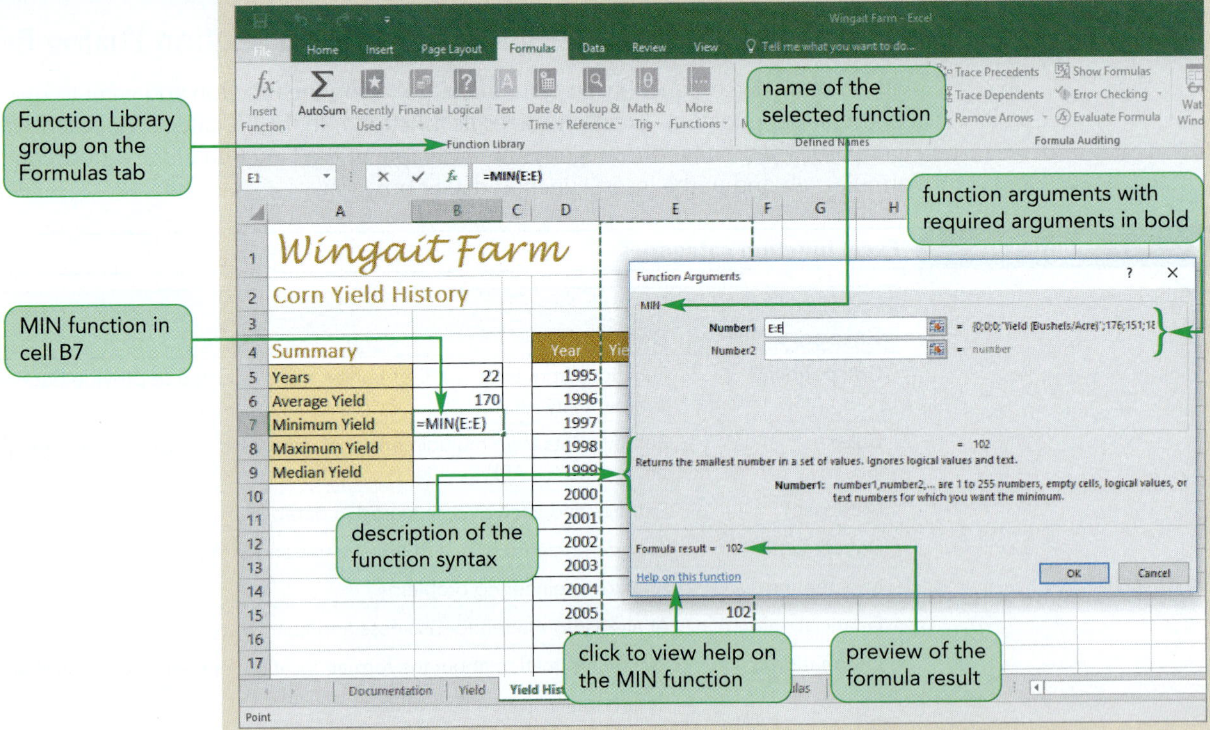

Trouble? You can click and drag the title bar in the Function Arguments dialog box to move it out of the way of the column E heading.

6. Click the **OK** button to insert the formula =MIN(E:E) into cell B7. The formula returns 102, which is the minimum value in column E.
7. Click cell **B8**, and then repeat Steps 3 through 6, selecting the **MAX** function from the Statistical category. The formula =MAX(E:E) entered in cell B8, and returns 187, which is the maximum value in column E. See Figure 3-11.

Figure 3-11 **Results of the MIN and MAX functions**

formula to calculate the maximum value in column E

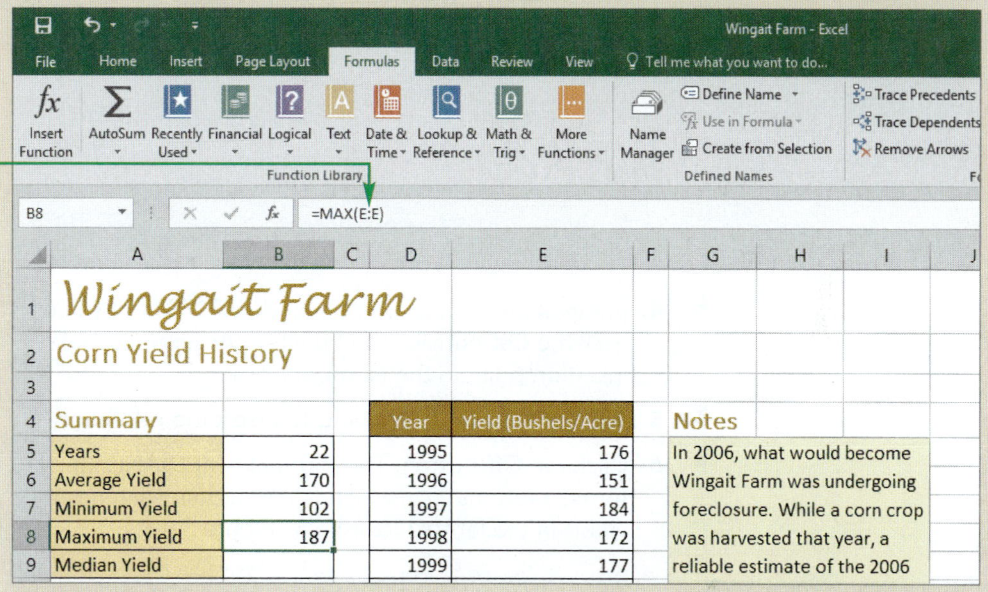

Note that like the COUNT and AVERAGE functions, the MIN and MAX functions ignore cells with text or blank cells in the selected range.

The average is one way of summarizing data from a sample. However, averages are susceptible to the effects of extremely large or extremely small values. For example, imagine calculating the average net worth of 10 people when one of them is a billionaire. An average would probably not be a good representation of the typical net worth of that group. To avoid the effect of extreme values, statisticians often use the middle, or median, value in the sample.

Jane wants you to include the median corn yield value from the farm's history. Rather than inserting the function from the Function Library, you'll search for this function in the Insert Function dialog box.

To find the median corn yield:

1. Click cell **B9** to make it the active cell.
2. Click the **Insert Function** button f_x located to the left of the formula bar. The Insert Function dialog box opens.
3. In the Search for a function box, type **middle value** as the search description, and then click the **Go** button. A list of functions matching that description appears in the Select a function box. See Figure 3-12.

Figure 3-12 Search results in the Insert Function dialog box

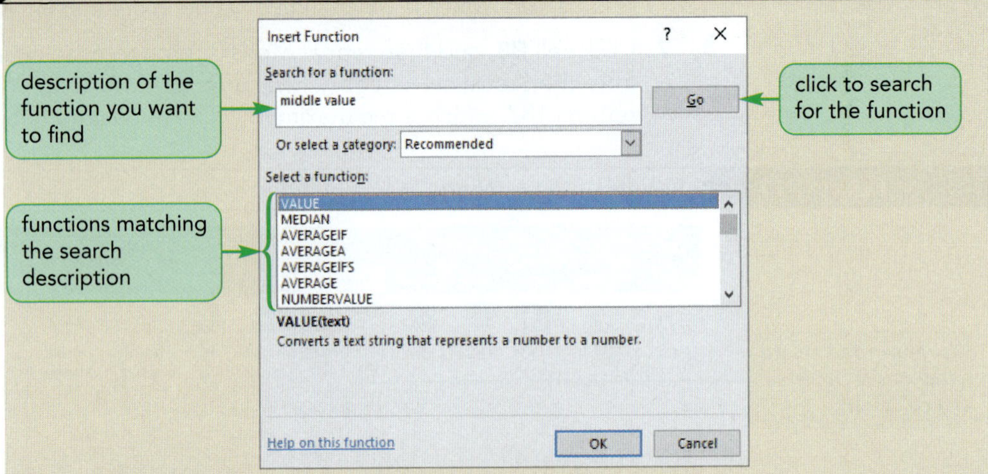

4. In the Select a function box, click **MEDIAN** to select that function, and then click the **OK** button. The Function Arguments dialog box opens with the insertion point in the Number1 box.
5. Click the **E** column heading to insert the reference E:E in the Number1 box.
6. Click the **OK** button. The formula =MEDIAN(E:E) is entered in cell B9. The formula returns 175, which is the middle value from the list of annual corn yields in the farm's history. See Figure 3-13.

Figure 3-13 Median function finds the middle corn yield value

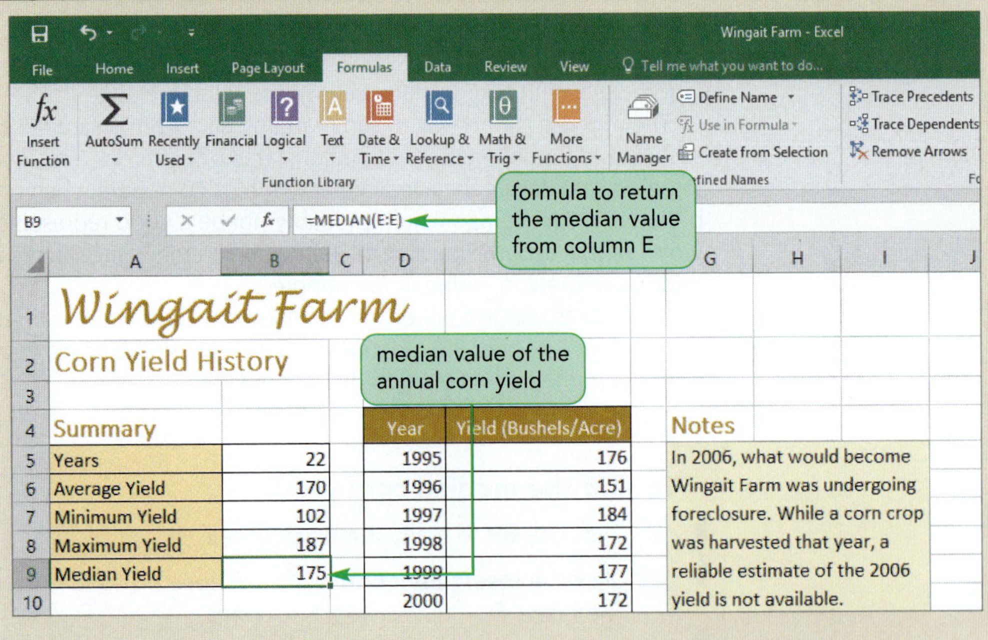

The median estimate of 175 bushels per acre is higher than the average value of 170 bushels per acre. This is due in part to the extremely low yield of 102 bushels per acre in 2005, which brought the overall average value down. Because of this, 175 bushels per acre might be a more reliable estimate of the farm's productivity.

INSIGHT

Methods of Rounding

For cleaner and neater workbooks, you will often want to round your values. There is little need for a large corporation to show revenue to the nearest cents at the annual stockholders' convention. Excel provides several methods for rounding data values. One method is to decrease the number of decimal places displayed in the cell, leaving the underlying value unchanged but rounding the displayed value to a specified number of digits.

Another approach is to use the ROUND function, which rounds the value itself to a specified number of digits. The ROUND function also accepts negative values for the number of digits in order to round the value to the nearest multiple of 10, 100, 1000, and so forth. The formula

```
=ROUND(5241,-2)
```

returns a value of 5200, rounding the value to the nearest hundred. For rounding to the nearest of multiple of a given number, use the function

```
MROUND(number,multiple)
```

where ***number*** is the number to be rounded and ***multiple*** is the multiple that the number should be rounded to. For example, the formula

```
=MROUND(5241,25)
```

rounds 5241 to the nearest multiple of 25, returning 5250. Remember though that when you use these rounding methods, you should always have access to the original, unrounded data, in case you need to audit your calculations in the future.

Next Jane wants to explore how to increase the farm's corn revenue in future seasons. You can explore the possibilities with a what-if analysis.

Performing What-If Analyses

A **what-if analysis** explores the impact that changing input values has on calculated values. For example, Jane wants to increase the farm's total revenue from corn, which you calculated as $88,559.40 for the current year, to at least $100,000. The most obvious way to increase the farm's corn revenue is to plant and then harvest more corn. Jane asks you to perform a what-if analysis to determine how many acres of corn would be needed to generate $100,000 of income, assuming conditions remain the same as the current year in which the farm yielded 168 bushels per acre at a selling price of $3.85 per bushel.

Using Trial and Error

One way to perform a what-if analysis is with **trial and error** where you change one or more of the input values to see how they affect the calculated results. Trial and error requires some guesswork as you estimate which values to change and by how much. You will use the trial and error to study the impact of changing the cornfield acreage on the total revenue generated for the farm.

To use trial and error to find how many acres of corn will generate $100,000 revenue:

1. Go to the **Yield** worksheet containing calculations for determining the farm's current corn revenue.

2. In cell **B4**, change the farm acreage from 137 to **150**. Cell B23 shows that with 150 acres of corn sold at $3.85 per bushel, the farm's revenue from corn sales would increase from $88,559.40 to $96,962.85.
3. In cell **B4**, change the farm acreage from 150 to **175**. Cell B23 shows that if the farm plants 175 acres of corn, the revenue would increase to $113,123.33.
4. In cell **B4**, change the farm acreage back to **137**, which is the current acreage of corn on Wingait Farm.

To find the exact acreage that would result in $100,000 of revenue, you would have to continue trying different values in cell B4, gradually closing in on the correct value. This is why the method is called "trial and error." For some calculations, trial and error can be a very time-consuming way to locate the exact input value. A more direct approach to this problem is to use Goal Seek.

Using Goal Seek

TIP

Goal Seek can be used only with calculated numbers, not with text.

Goal Seek automates the trial-and-error process by allowing you to specify a value for a calculated item, which Excel uses to determine the input value needed to reach that goal. In this case, because Jane wants $100,000 of revenue, the question that Goal Seek answers is: "How many acres of corn are needed to generate $100,000?" Goal Seek starts by setting the calculated value and automatically works backward to determine the correct input value.

REFERENCE

Performing What-If Analysis and Goal Seek

To perform a what-if analysis by trial and error:
- Change the value of a worksheet cell (the input cell).
- Observe its impact on one or more calculated cells (the result cells).
- Repeat until the desired results are achieved.

To perform a what-if analysis using Goal Seek:
- On the Data tab, in the Forecast group, click the What-If Analysis button, and then click Goal Seek.
- Select the result cell in the Set cell box, and then specify its value (goal) in the To value box.
- In the By changing cell box, specify the input cell.
- Click the OK button. The value of the input cell changes to set the value of the result cell.

You will use Goal Seek to find how much acreage Wingait Farms must plant with corn to achieve $100,000 of revenue.

To use Goal Seek to find how many acres of corn will generate $100,000 revenue:

1. On the ribbon, click the **Data** tab.
2. In the Forecast group, click the **What-If Analysis** button, and then click **Goal Seek**. The Goal Seek dialog box opens.

3. With Set cell box selected, click cell **B23** in the Yield worksheet. The cell reference $B$23 appears in the Set cell box. The set cell is the calculated value you want Goal Seek to change to meet your goal. (You'll learn about $ symbols in cell references in the next session.)
4. Press the **Tab** key to move the insertion point to the To value box, and then type **100000** indicating that you want Goal Seek to set the value in cell B23 value to 100,000.
5. Press the **Tab** key to move the insertion point to the By changing cell box.

   There are often many possible input values you can change to meet a goal. In this case, you want to change the size of the farm acreage in cell B4.
6. Click cell **B4**. The cell reference $B$4 appears in the By changing cell box. See Figure 3-14.

Figure 3-14 Goal Seek dialog box

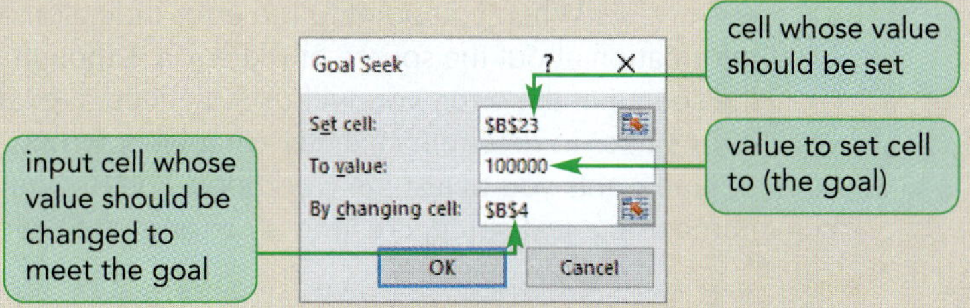

7. Click the **OK** button. The Goal Seek dialog box closes, and the Goal Seek Status dialog box opens, indicating that Goal Seek found a solution.
8. Click the **OK** button. The value in cell B4 changes to 154.6984204, and the value of cell B23 changes to $100,000.

If Jane increases the acreage devoted to corn production to almost 155 acres, the farm would produce a total revenue from corn of $100,000, assuming a yield of 168 bushels per acre sold at $3.85 per bushel. If the yield or market price increases, the revenue would also increase.

Interpreting Error Values

As you add formulas and values to a workbook, you might make a mistake such as mistyping a formula or entering data as the wrong type. When such errors occur, Excel displays an error value in the cell. An **error value** indicates that some part of a formula is preventing Excel from returning a value. Figure 3-15 lists the common error values you might see in place of calculated values from Excel formulas and functions. For example, the error value #VALUE! indicates that the wrong type of value is used in a function or formula.

Figure 3-15 Excel error values

Error Value	Description
#DIV/0!	The formula or function contains a number divided by 0.
#NAME?	Excel doesn't recognize text in the formula or function, such as when the function name is misspelled.
#N/A	A value is not available to a function or formula, which can occur when a workbook is initially set up prior to entering actual data values.
#NULL!	A formula or function requires two cell ranges to intersect, but they don't.
#NUM!	Invalid numbers are used in a formula or function, such as text entered in a function that requires a number.
#REF!	A cell reference used in a formula or function is no longer valid, which can occur when the cell used by the function was deleted from the worksheet.
#VALUE!	The wrong type of argument is used in a function or formula. This can occur when you reference a text value for an argument that should be strictly numeric.

Error values themselves are not particularly descriptive or helpful. To help you locate the error, an error indicator appears in the upper-left corner of the cell with the error value. When you point to the error indicator, a ScreenTip appears with more information about the source of the error. Although the ScreenTips provide hints as to the source of the error, you will usually need to examine the formulas in the cells with error values to determine exactly what went wrong.

Jane wants you to test the workbook. You'll change the value of cell B4 from a number to a text string, creating an error in the Yield worksheet.

To create an error value:

1. In cell **B4**, enter the text string **137 acres**. After you press the Enter key, the #VALUE! error value appears in cells whose formulas use the value in cell B4 either directly or indirectly, indicating that the wrong type of argument is used in a function or formula. In the Yield worksheet, the value in cell B4 affects the values of cells B21 and B23. See Figure 3-16.

Figure 3-16 Error value in the worksheet

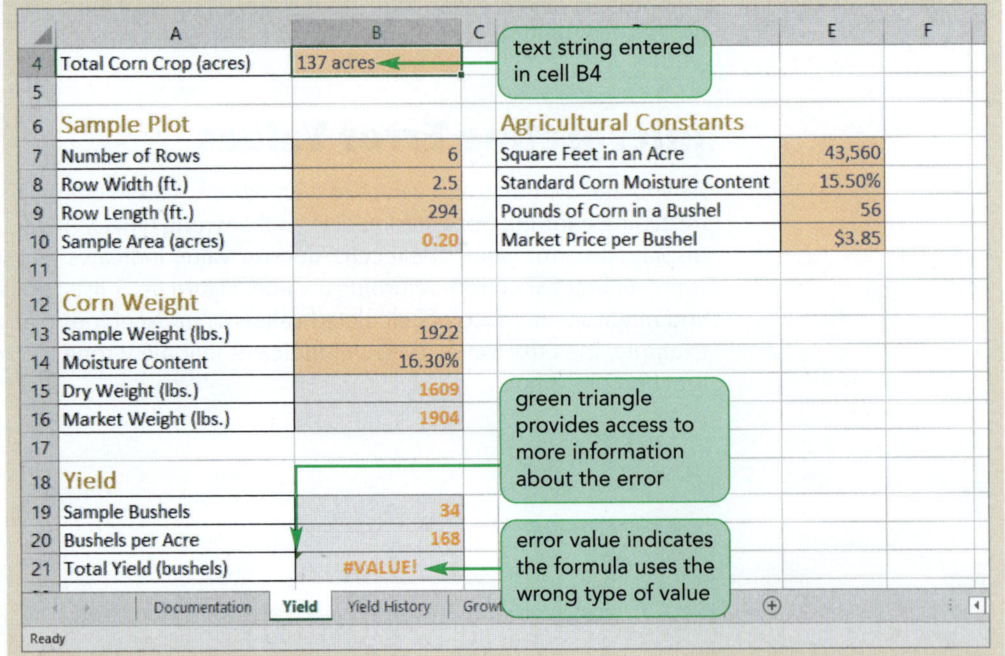

	A	B	C	D	E	F
4	Total Corn Crop (acres)	137 acres				
5						
6	Sample Plot			Agricultural Constants		
7	Number of Rows	6		Square Feet in an Acre	43,560	
8	Row Width (ft.)	2.5		Standard Corn Moisture Content	15.50%	
9	Row Length (ft.)	294		Pounds of Corn in a Bushel	56	
10	Sample Area (acres)	0.20		Market Price per Bushel	$3.85	
11						
12	Corn Weight					
13	Sample Weight (lbs.)	1922				
14	Moisture Content	16.30%				
15	Dry Weight (lbs.)	1609				
16	Market Weight (lbs.)	1904				
17						
18	Yield					
19	Sample Bushels	34				
20	Bushels per Acre	168				
21	Total Yield (bushels)	#VALUE!				

Documentation | Yield | Yield History | Growt

Ready

2. Click cell **B21**, and then point to the button that appears to the left of the cell. A ScreenTip appears, providing useful information about the cause of the error value. In this case, the ScreenTip is, "A value used in the formula is of the wrong data type."
3. Click cell **B4**, enter **137** to change the value back to the current acreage that Wingait Farm devotes to corn. After you press the Enter key, the error values disappear, the total yield in cell B21 returns to 23,002, and the projected revenue in cell B23 returns to $88,559.40.
4. Save the workbook.

So far, you have used formulas and functions to analyze the current and past season's crop yield at Wingait Farm. In the next session, you'll use additional formulas and functions to analyze the growth of Wingait Farm's corn crop from planting to harvesting.

REVIEW

Session 3.1 Quick Check

1. Convert the following equation into an Excel formula where the *radius* value is stored in cell E31 and the value of π is stored in cell D12:

$$area = \pi \times radius^2$$

2. In Excel, the PI() function returns the decimal value of π. Rewrite your answer for the previous formula using this function.
3. Write a formula to round the value in cell A5 to the fourth decimal place.
4. Write a formula to return the middle value from the values in the range Y1:Y100.
5. The range of a set of values is defined as the maximum value minus the minimum value. Write a formula to calculate the range of values in the range Y1:Y100 and then to round that value to the nearest integer.
6. Explain the difference between the COUNT function and the COUNTA function.
7. Stephen is entering hundreds of temperature values into an Excel worksheet for a climate research project, and he wants to speed up data entry by leaving freezing point values as blanks rather than typing zeroes. Explain why this will cause complications if he later tries to calculate the average temperature from those data values.
8. What is the difference between a what-if analysis by trial and error and by Goal Seek?
9. Cell B2 contains the formula =SUME(A1:A100) with the name of the SUM function misspelled as SUME. What error value will appear in the cell?

Session 3.2 Visual Overview:

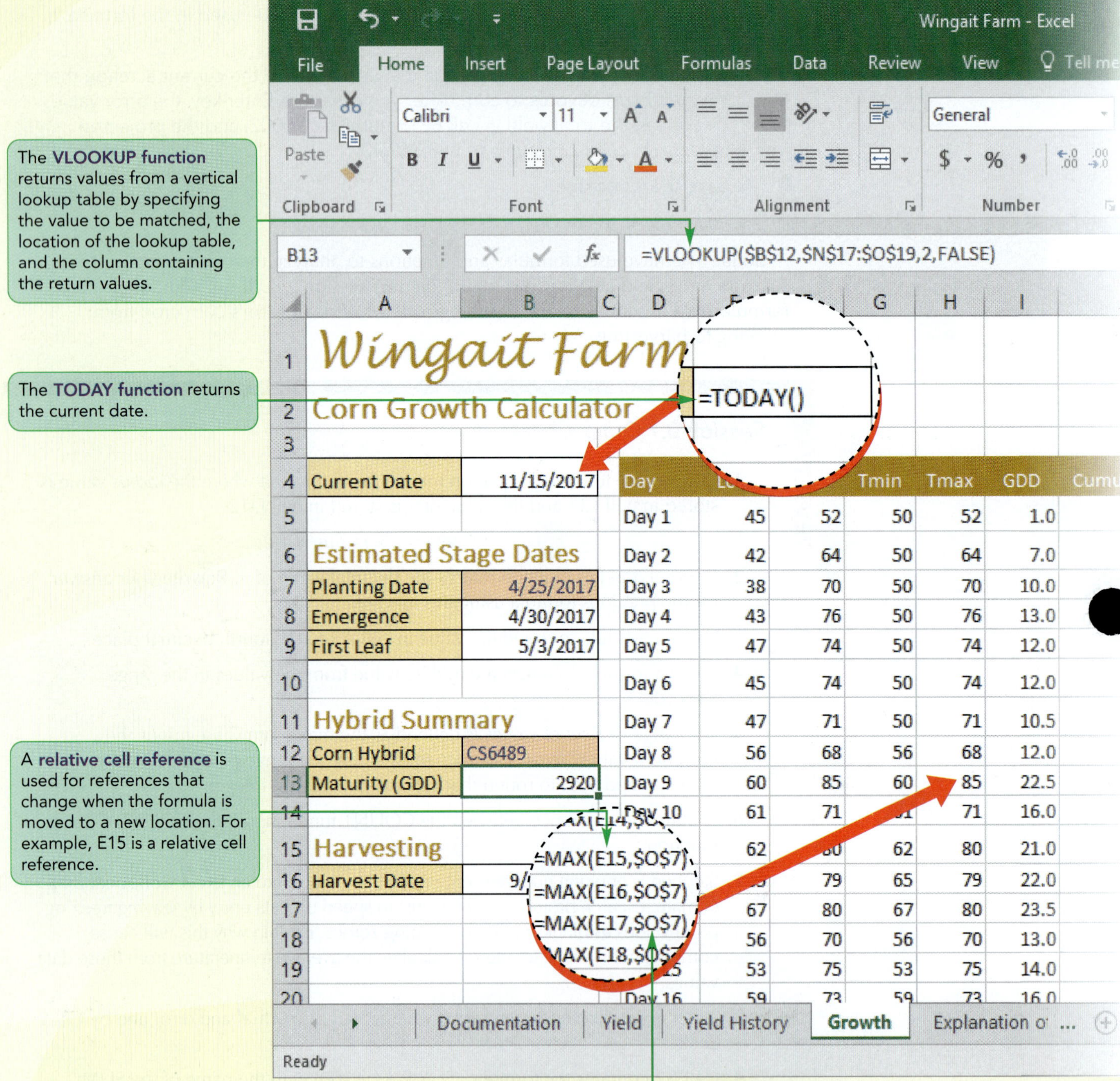

An **absolute cell reference** is used for references that do not change when the formula is moved to a new location. Absolute references have "$" before the row and column components. For example, $O$7 is an absolute cell reference.

Cell References and Formulas

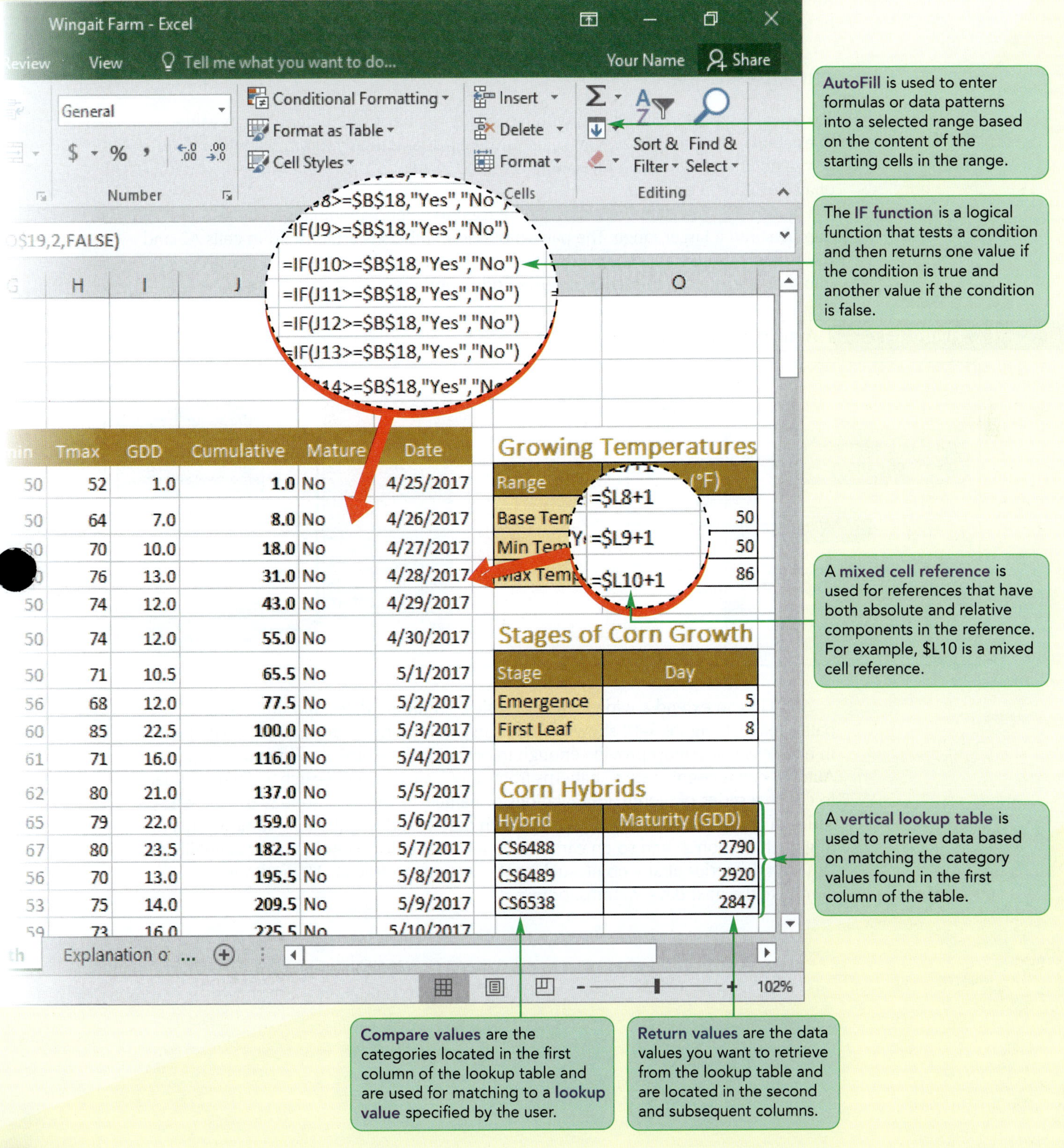

AutoFill is used to enter formulas or data patterns into a selected range based on the content of the starting cells in the range.

The **IF function** is a logical function that tests a condition and then returns one value if the condition is true and another value if the condition is false.

A **mixed cell reference** is used for references that have both absolute and relative components in the reference. For example, $L10 is a mixed cell reference.

A **vertical lookup table** is used to retrieve data based on matching the category values found in the first column of the table.

Compare values are the categories located in the first column of the lookup table and are used for matching to a **lookup value** specified by the user.

Return values are the data values you want to retrieve from the lookup table and are located in the second and subsequent columns.

AutoFilling Formulas and Data

One way to efficiently enter long columns or rows of data values and formulas is with AutoFill. AutoFill extends formulas or data patterns that were entered in a selected cell or range into adjacent cells. AutoFill is faster than copying and pasting.

Filling a Series

To extend a series of data values with a particular pattern, you enter enough values to establish the pattern, next you select those cells, and then you drag the fill handle across additional cells. The **fill handle** is the box that appears in the lower-right corner of a selected cell or range.

Figure 3-17 shows how AutoFill can be used to extend an initial series of odd numbers into a larger range. The pattern of odd numbers is established in cells A2 and A3. When the user drags the fill handle over the range A4:A9, Excel extends the series into those cells using the same pattern of odd numbers.

Figure 3-17 AutoFill used to extend a series

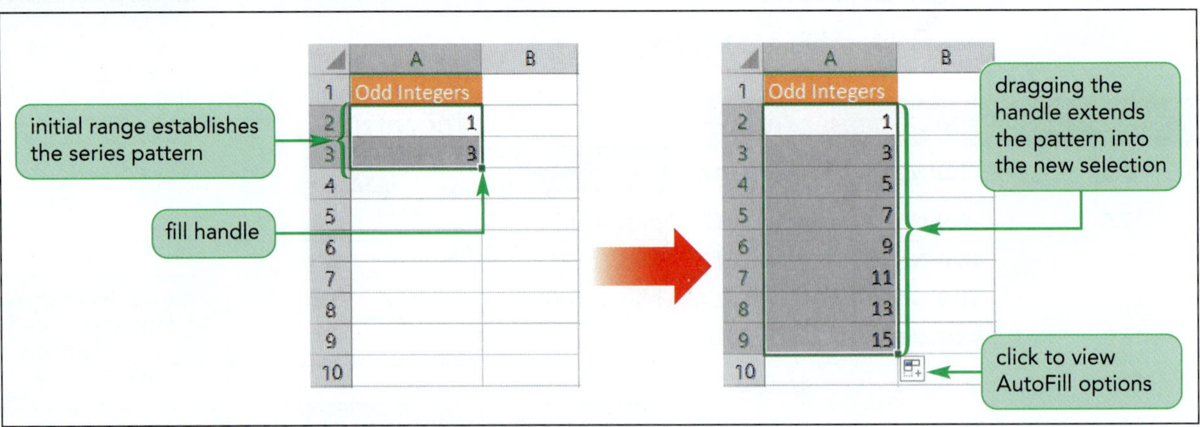

AutoFill can extend a wide variety of series, including dates and times and patterned text. Figure 3-18 shows some examples of series that AutoFill can generate. In each case, you must provide enough information for AutoFill to identify the pattern. AutoFill can recognize some patterns from only a single entry—such as Jan or January to create a series of month abbreviations or names, or Mon or Monday to create a series of the days of the week. A text pattern that includes text and a number such as Region 1, Region 2, and so on can also be automatically extended using AutoFill. You can start the series at any point, such as Weds, June, or Region 10, and AutoFill will complete the next days, months, or text.

Figure 3-18 Series patterns extended with AutoFill

Type	Initial Values	Extended Values
Numbers	1, 2, 3	4, 5, 6, ..
	2, 4, 6	8, 10, 12, ...
Dates and Times	Jan	Feb, Mar, Apr, ...
	January	February, March, April, ...
	15-Jan, 15-Feb	15-Mar, 15-Apr, 15-May, ...
	12/30/2017	12/31/2017, 1/1/2018, 1/2/2018, ...
	12/31/2017, 1/31/2018	2/29/2018, 3/31/2018, 4/30/2018, ...
	Mon	Tue, Wed, Thu, ...
	Monday	Tuesday, Wednesday, Thursday, ...
	11:00AM	12:00PM, 1:00PM, 2:00PM, ...
Patterned Text	1st period	2nd period, 3rd period, 4th period, ...
	Region 1	Region 2, Region 3, Region 4, ...
	Quarter 3	Quarter 4, Quarter 1, Quarter 2, ...
	Qtr3	Qtr4, Qtr1, Qtr2, ...

With AutoFill, you can quickly fill a range with a series of numbers, dates and times, and patterned text.

REFERENCE

Creating a Series with AutoFill

- Enter the first few values of the series into a range.
- Select the range, and then drag the fill handle of the selected range over the cells you want to fill.
- To copy only the formats or only the formulas, click the Auto Fill Options button and select the appropriate option.

or

- Enter the first few values of the series into a range.
- Select the entire range into which you want to extend the series.
- On the Home tab, in the Editing group, click the Fill button, and then click Down, Right, Up, Left, Series, or Justify to set the direction in which you want to extend the series.

Jane wants you to complete the worksheet she started to explore the growth of the Wingait Farm corn crop from planting through harvesting. You need to create a column that labels each day of corn growth starting with Day 1, Day2, and so forth through the end of the season. You will create these labels using AutoFill.

To use AutoFill to extend a series of labels:

TIP

You can also fill a series down by selecting the entire range including the initial cell(s) that establish the pattern, and then pressing the Ctrl+D keys.

1. If you took a break after the previous session, make sure the Wingait Farm workbook is open.
2. Go to the **Growth** worksheet.
3. In cell **D5**, enter the text string **Day 1**. This is the initial label in the series.
4. Click cell **D5** to select the cell, and then drag the **fill handle** (located in the bottom-right corner of the cell) down over the range **D5:D163**.

5. Release the mouse button. AutoFill enters the labels Day1 through Day 159 in the selected range. See Figure 3-19.

Figure 3-19 **Farm Day pattern extended with AutoFill**

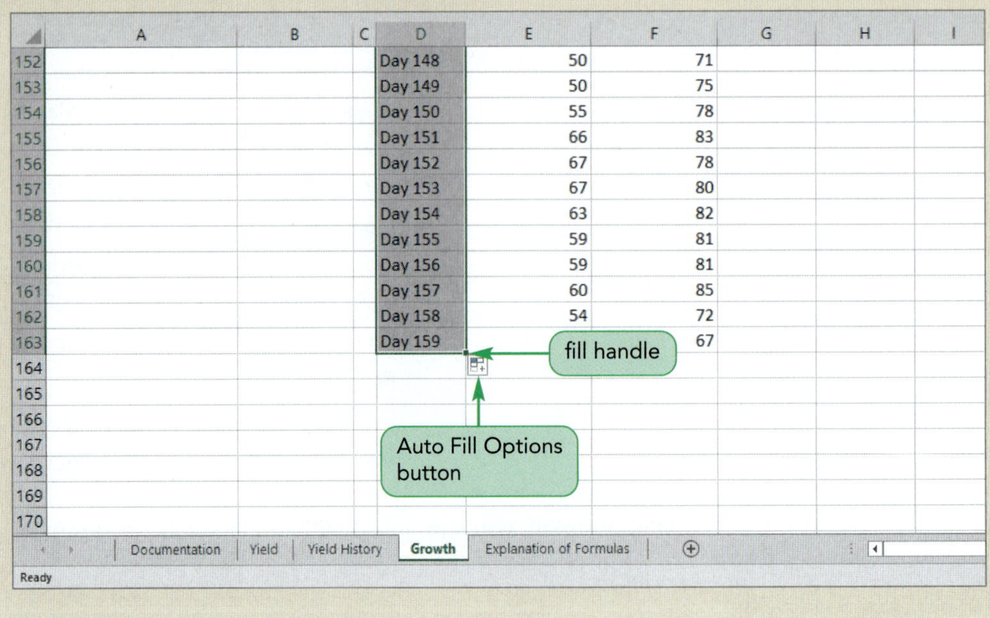

Exploring Auto Fill Options

By default, AutoFill copies both the content and the formatting of the original range to the selected range. However, sometimes you might want to copy only the content or only the formatting. The Auto Fill Options button that appears after you release the mouse button lets you specify what is copied. Figure 3-20 shows the Auto Fill Options menu for an extended series of patterned text.

Figure 3-20 **Auto Fill Options menu**

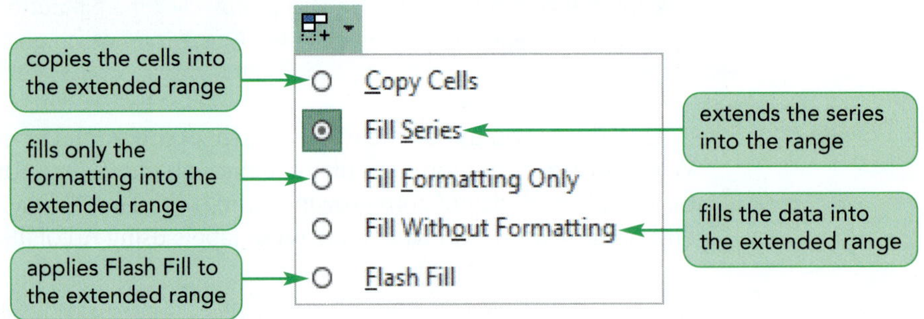

The Copy Cells option copies both the cell content and formatting but does not extend a series based on the initial values. The Fill Series option (the default) extends the initial series values into the new range. Other options allow you to fill in the values with or without the formatting used in the initial cells. Additional options (not shown in Figure 3-20) are provided when extending date values, allowing AutoFill to extend the initial dates by days, weekdays, months, or years.

The Series dialog box provides other options for how AutoFill is applied. To open the Series dialog box, click the Fill button in the Editing group on the Home tab, and then click Series. You can specify a linear or growth series for numbers; a date series for dates that increase by day, weekday, month, or year; or an AutoFill series for patterned text. With numbers, you can also specify the step value (how much each number increases over the previous entry) and a stop value (the endpoint for the entire series). See Figure 3-21.

Figure 3-21 **Series dialog box**

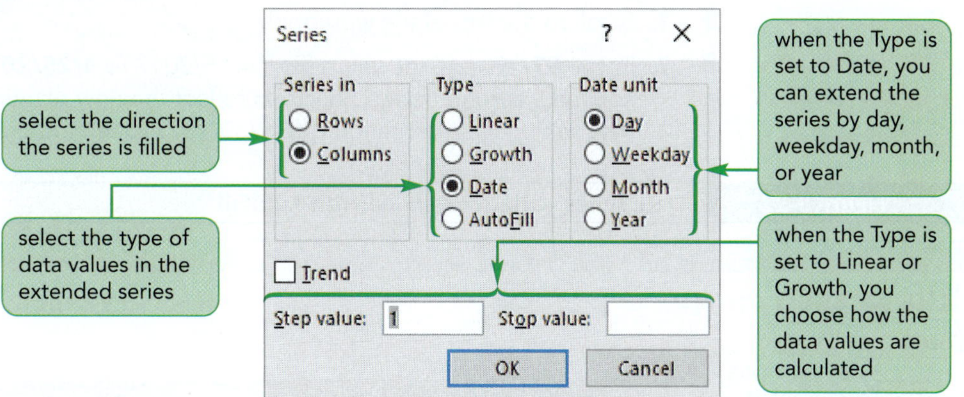
Series
?
X
Series in
Rows
Columns
Type
Linear
Growth
Date
AutoFill
Date unit
Day
Weekday
Month
Year
Trend
Step value:
1
Stop value:
OK
Cancel
select the direction the series is filled
select the type of data values in the extended series
when the Type is set to Date, you can extend the series by day, weekday, month, or year
when the Type is set to Linear or Growth, you choose how the data values are calculated

Filling Formulas

You can also use AutoFill to extend formulas into a range. AutoFill copies the formula in the initial cell or range into the extended range. Excel modifies the cell references in the formulas based on the location of the cells in the extended range.

Jane wants the Growth worksheet to include the date of each growing day starting from the planting date and extending to the last day of recorded data. Because dates are stored as numbers, you can fill in the calendar days by adding 1 to the date displayed in the previous row. Jane wants to use the date 4/15/2017 as the starting date of when the farm began planting corn.

To copy the formula with the dates for the growing season with AutoFill:

1. In cell **B7**, enter the date **4/15/2017** as the starting date of when the farm began planting corn.
2. In cell **L5**, enter the formula **=B7**. After you press the Enter key, cell L5 displays 4/15/2017, which is the first date of the growing season for corn.
3. In cell **L6**, enter the formula **=L5+1** to add one day to the date in cell L5. After you press the Enter key, the date 4/16/2017 appears in cell L6.
4. Click cell **L6** to select it, and then drag the fill handle over the range **L6:L163**. AutoFill copies the formula in cell L6 to the range L7:L163, increasing the date value by one day in each row.

AutoFill extends the formulas to display the date 4/16/2017 in cell L6 through the date 9/20/2017 in cell L163. Each date is calculated by increasing the value in the cell one row above it by one day. The formulas for these calculations are= L5+1 in cell L6, =L6+1 in cell L7, and so forth up to =L162+1 in cell L163.

Jane wants you to change the planting date to 4/25/2017, which is closer to the final date for planting corn at Wingait Farm.

To change the planting date:

1. Scroll to the top of the workbook.
2. In cell **B7**, change the value from 4/15/2017 to **4/25/2017**. The dates in column L automatically change to reflect the new planting date with the last date in the column changing to 9/30/2017. See Figure 3-22.

Figure 3-22 Date series pattern extended with AutoFill

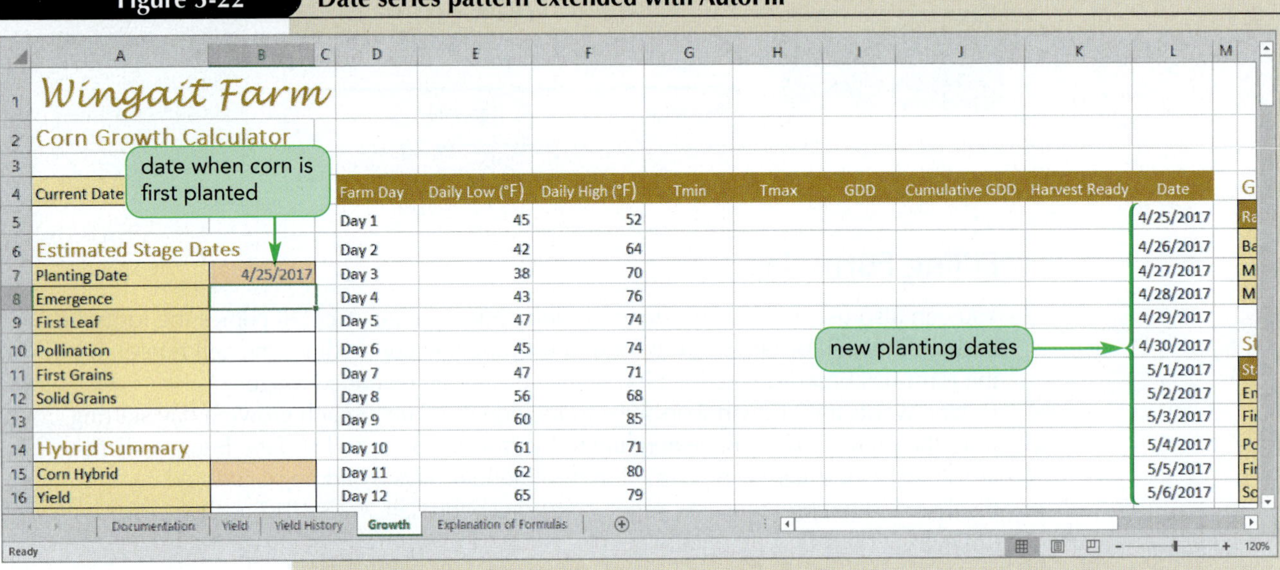

Jane wants to know when the corn crop will reach different stages of growth. In the range N11:O16 of the Growth worksheet, Jane created a table listing the number of days after planting that different growth milestones are reached. For example, the sprouts of the corn plant are often visible five days after planting (cell O12), the first small leaf appears eight days after planting (cell O13), and so forth. You will use the values in the range O12:O16 to estimate the calendar dates for when the first sprouts emerge, the first leaf appears, the corn begins to pollinate, the corn shows its first grains, and finally when the corn shows its solid grains or kernels.

To display the dates for corn growth milestones:

1. In cell **B8**, enter the formula **=B7+O12** to add the number of days until emergence to the planting date. The date 4/30/2017, which is the estimated date when the first corn sprouts will appear, is displayed in cell B8.
2. Click cell **B8** to select it, and then drag the fill handle over the range **B8:B12** to fill in the dates for the other growth milestones. See Figure 3-23.

Figure 3-23 **Formula extended with AutoFill**

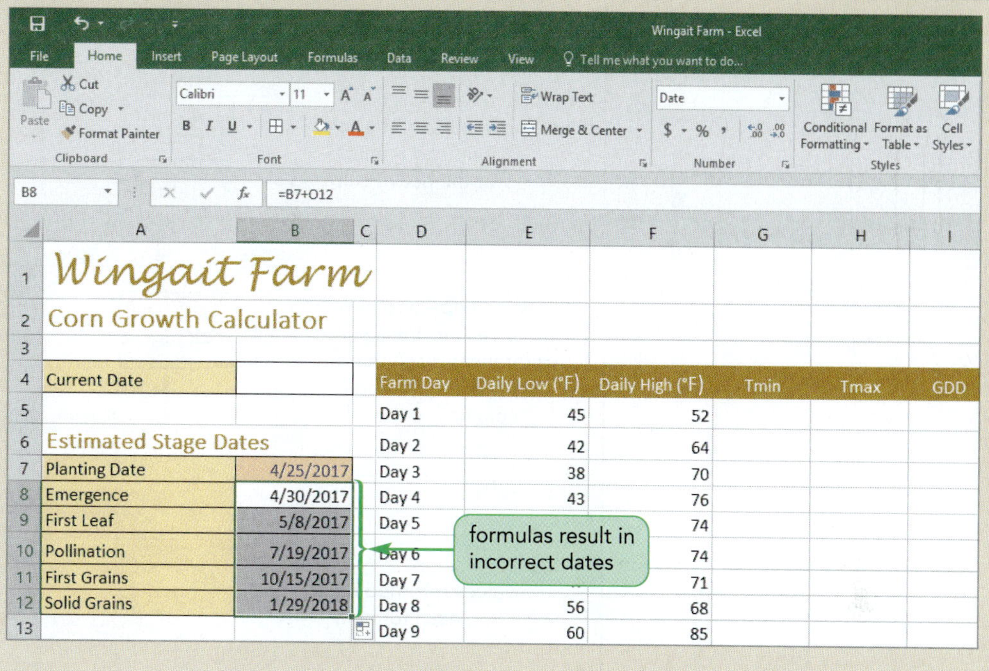

Something is wrong with the formulas that calculate the milestone dates. For example, the date for when the first corn kernels appear is January of the next year. To understand why the formulas resulted in incorrect dates, you need to look at the cell references.

Exploring Cell References

Excel has three types of cell references: relative, absolute, and mixed. Each type of cell reference in a formula is affected differently when the formula is copied and pasted to a new location.

Understanding Relative References

So far, all of the cell references you have worked with are relative cell references. When a formula includes a relative cell reference, Excel interprets the reference to each cell relative to the position of the cell containing the formula. For example, if cell A1 contains the formula =B1+B2, Excel interprets that formula as "Add the value of the cell one column to the right (B1) to the value of the cell one column to the right and one row down (B2)".

This relative interpretation of the cell reference is retained when the formula is copied to a new location. If the formula in cell A1 is copied to cell A3 (two rows down in the worksheet), the relative references also shift two rows down, resulting in the formula =B3+B4.

Figure 3-24 shows another example of how relative references change when a formula is pasted to new locations in the worksheet. In this figure, the formula =A3 entered in cell D6 displays 10, which is the number entered in cell A3. When pasted to a new location, each of the pasted formulas contains a reference to a cell that is three rows up and three rows to the left of the current cell's location.

Figure 3-24 **Formulas using relative references**

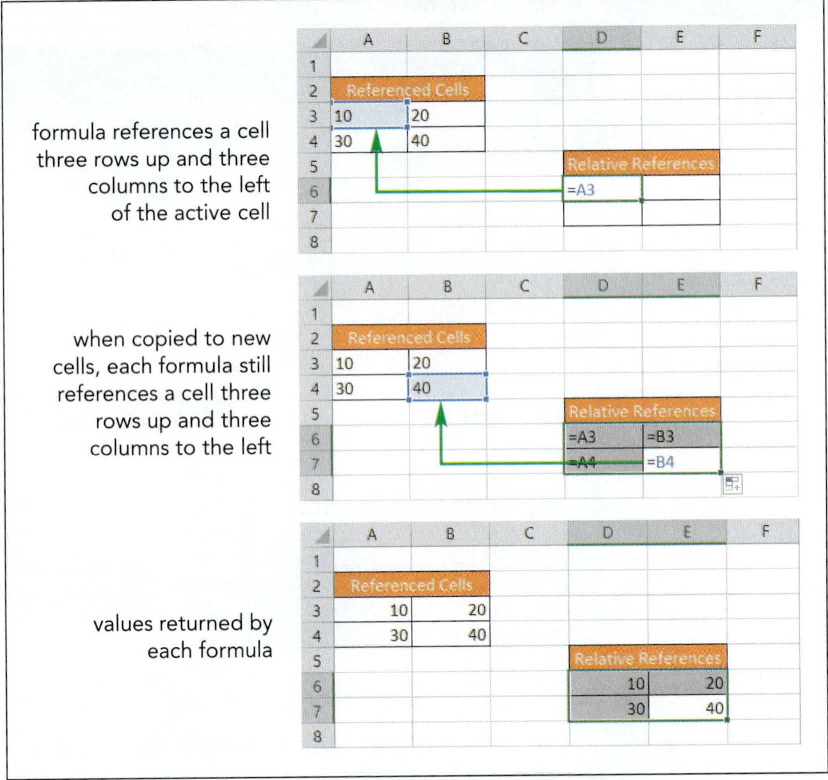
formula references a cell three rows up and three columns to the left of the active cell
Referenced Cells
10
20
30
40
Relative References
=A3
when copied to new cells, each formula still references a cell three rows up and three columns to the left
=A3
=B3
=A4
=B4
values returned by each formula
10
20
30
40

This explains what happened when you used AutoFill to copy the formula =B7+O12 in cell B8 into the range B9:B12. The formula in cell B9 became =B8+O13, the formula in cell B10 became =B9+O14, the formula in cell B11 became =B10+O15, and the formula in cell B12 became =B11+O16. In each case, the stage days were added to the date in the previous row, not the original planting date entered in cell B7. As a result, date calculation for the appearance of the first solid grains was pushed out to January of the following year.

To correct this, you need a cell reference that remains fixed on cell B7 no matter where the formula is pasted. This can be accomplished with an absolute reference.

Understanding Absolute References

An absolute reference is used for a cell reference that remains fixed even when that formula is copied to a new cell. Absolute references include $ (a dollar sign) before each column and row designation. For example, B8 is a relative reference to cell B8, while $B$8 is an absolute reference to that cell.

Figure 3-25 shows an example of how copying a formula with an absolute reference results in the same cell reference being pasted in different cells regardless of their position compared to the location of the original copied cell. In this example, the formula =$A$3 will always reference cell A3 no matter where the formula is copied to.

Figure 3-25 Formulas using absolute references

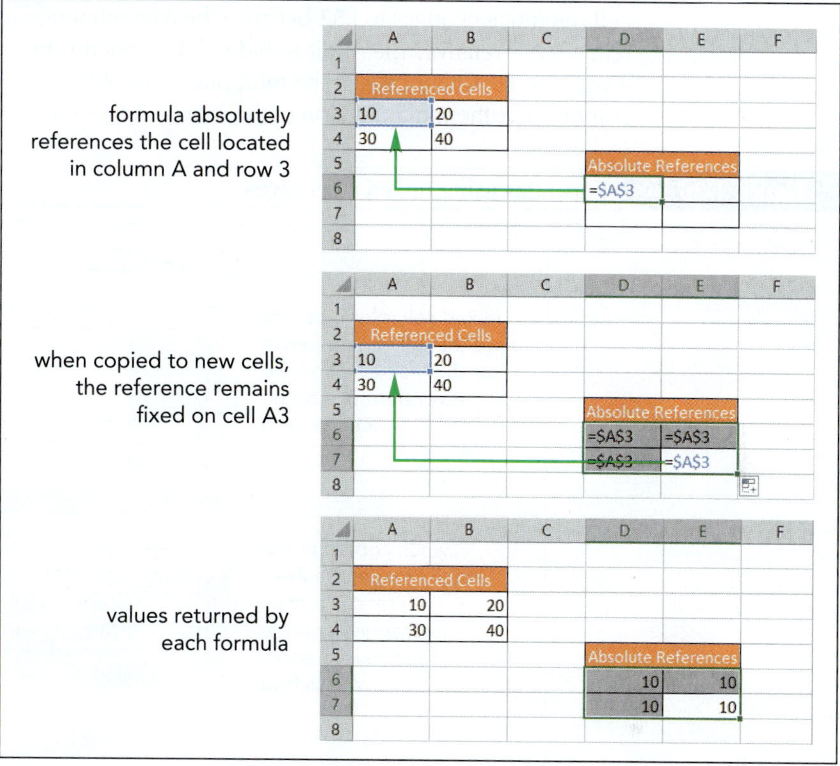
formula absolutely references the cell located in column A and row 3
Referenced Cells
10
20
30
40
Absolute References
=$A$3
when copied to new cells, the reference remains fixed on cell A3
Referenced Cells
=$A$3
=$A$3
=$A$3
=$A$3
values returned by each formula
Absolute References
10
10
10
10

Sometimes, you'll want only one part of the cell reference to remain fixed. This requires a mixed cell reference.

Understanding Mixed References

A mixed cell reference contains both relative and absolute components. For example, a mixed reference for cell A2 can be either $A2 where the column component is absolute and the row component is relative, or it can be entered as A$2 with a relative column component and a fixed row component. A mixed reference "locks" only one part of the cell reference. When you copy and paste a cell with a mixed reference to a new location, the absolute portion of the cell reference remains fixed, and the relative portion shifts along with the new location of the pasted cell.

Figure 3-26 shows an example of using mixed references to complete a multiplication table. The first cell in the table, cell B3, contains the formula =$A3*B$2, which multiplies the first column entry (cell A3) by the first row entry (cell B2), returning 1. When this formula is copied to another cell, the absolute portions of the cell references remain unchanged, and the relative portions of the references change. For example, if the formula is copied to cell E6, the first mixed cell reference changes to $A6 because the column reference is absolute and the row reference is relative, and the second cell reference changes to E$2 because the row reference is absolute and the column reference is relative. The result is that cell E6 contains the formula =$A6*E$2 and returns a value of 16. Other cells in the multiplication table are similarly modified so that each entry returns the multiplication of the intersection of the row and column headings.

Figure 3-26 Formulas using mixed references

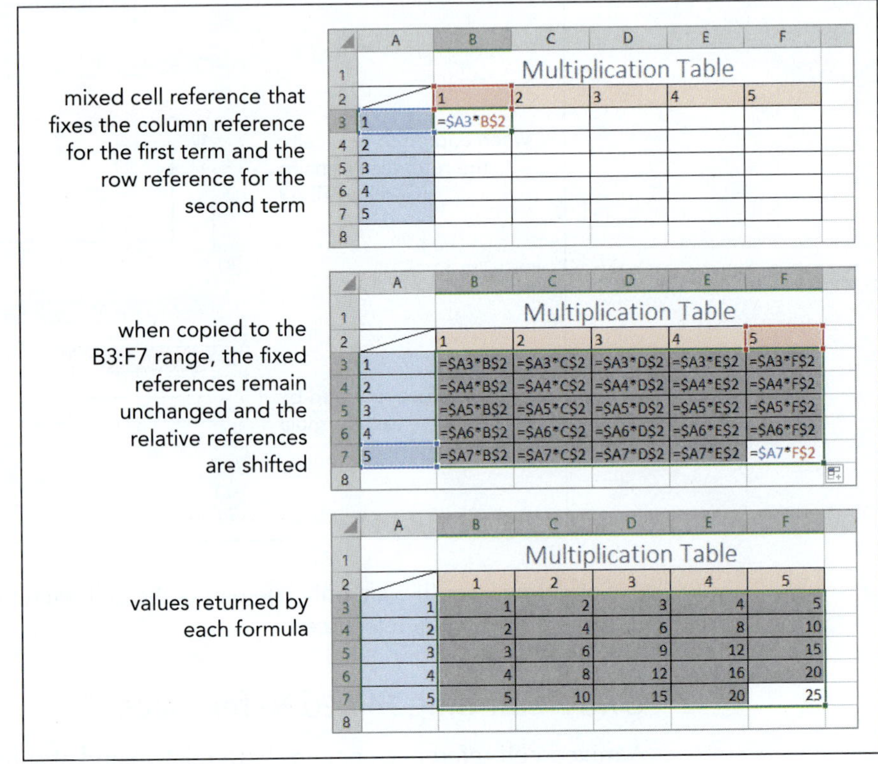
mixed cell reference that fixes the column reference for the first term and the row reference for the second term
Multiplication Table
=$A3*B$2
when copied to the B3:F7 range, the fixed references remain unchanged and the relative references are shifted
Multiplication Table
Multiplication Table
values returned by each formula

Changing Cell References in a Formula

You can quickly switch a cell reference from relative to absolute or mixed. Rather than retyping the formula, you can select the cell reference in Edit mode and then press the F4 key. As you press the F4 key, Excel cycles through the different reference types—starting with the relative reference, followed by the absolute reference, then to a mixed reference with an absolute row component followed by a mixed reference with an absolute column component.

To calculate the correct stage dates in the Growth worksheet, you will change the formula in cell B8 to use an absolute reference to cell B7 and then use AutoFill to copy that formula into range B9:B12.

To correct the stage dates formulas with absolute cell references:

1. Double-click cell **B8** to select it and enter Edit mode.
2. In cell B8, double-click the **B7** reference to select it, and then press the **F4** key. Excel changes the formula in cell B8 to =$B$7+O12.
3. Press the **Enter** key to enter the formula and exit Edit mode.
4. Click cell **B8** to select it, and then drag the fill handle over the range **B8:B12**. Figure 3-27 shows the revised dates for the different stages of corn growth.

Figure 3-27 Stage dates calculated with absolute cell references

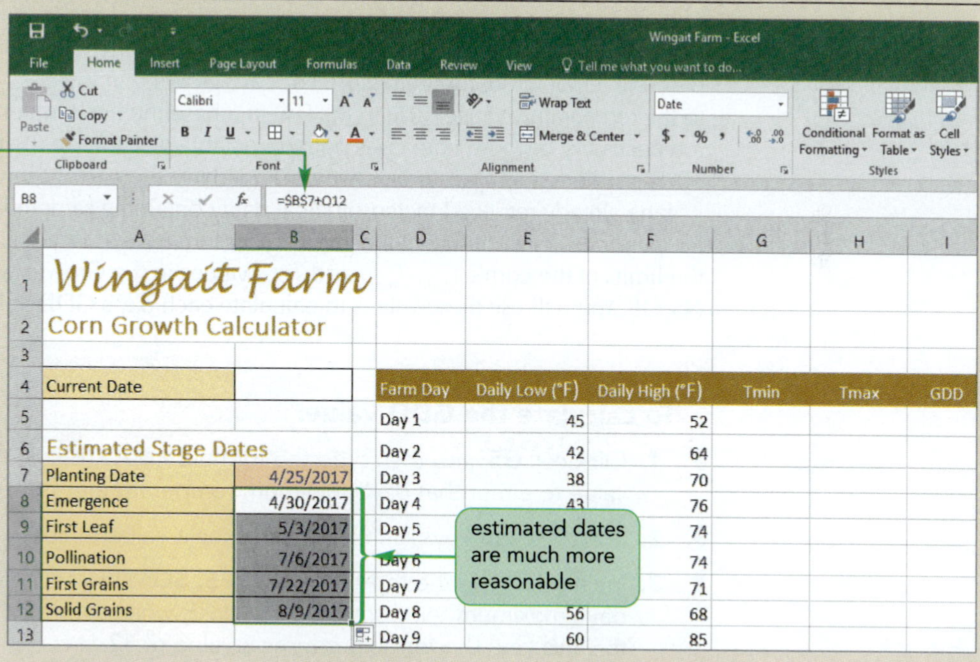

The revised dates for the different stages of the corn maturation are much more reasonable. For example, the date on which solid grains first appear is 8/9/2017, which is more in line with Jane's experience.

PROSKILLS

Problem Solving: When to Use Relative, Absolute, and Mixed References

Part of effective workbook design is knowing when to use relative, absolute, and mixed references. Use relative references when you want to apply the same formula with input cells that share a common layout or pattern. Relative references are commonly used when copying a formula that calculates summary statistics across columns or rows of data values. Use absolute references when you want your copied formulas to always refer to the same cell. This usually occurs when a cell contains a constant value, such as a tax rate, that will be referenced in formulas throughout the worksheet. Mixed references are seldom used other than when creating tables of calculated values such as a multiplication table in which the values of the formula or function can be found at the intersection of the rows and columns of the table.

Calendar days are one way of predicting crop growth, but Jane knows that five days of hot weather will result in more rapid growth than five mild days. A more accurate method to estimate growth is to calculate the crop's Growing Degree Days (GDD), which take into account the range of daily temperatures to which the crop is exposed. GDD is calculated using the formula

$$GDD = \frac{T_{max} + T_{min}}{2} - T_{base}$$

where T_{max} is the daily high temperature, T_{min} is the daily low temperature, and T_{base} is a baseline temperature for the region. For corn growing in Iowa, T_{min} and T_{max} are limited to the temperature range 50°F to 86°F with a baseline line temperature of 50°F. The limits are necessary because corn does not appreciably grow when the temperature falls below 50°F, nor does a temperature above 86°F increase the rate of growth.

Jane already retrieved meteorological data containing sample low and high temperatures for each day of the growing season in the Cascade, Iowa, region. She stored the limits of the corn's T_{min}, T_{max}, and T_{base} values in the Growth worksheet in the range N5:O8. You will use these values to calculate each day's GDD value for corn growth.

To calculate the GDD value:

1. Click cell **G5**, and then type the formula **=MAX(E5, $O$7)** to set the T_{min} value to either that day's minimum temperature or to 50°F, whichever is larger.
2. Press the **Tab** key. The formula returns a value of 50.
3. In cell H5, type the formula **=MIN(F5, $O$8)** to set the T_{max} value to that day's maximum temperature or to 86°F, whichever is smaller, and then press the **Tab** key. The formula returns a value of 52.
4. In cell I5, enter the formula **=(G5+H5)/2-$O$6** to calculate that day's GDD value using the T_{base} value of 50°F stored in cell O6. The formula returns 1.0, indicating that the GDD value for that day is 1.

   Next you'll use AutoFill to copy these formulas into the range G5:I163. Because you used absolute references in the formulas, the copied formulas will continue to reference cells O7, O8, and O6 in the extended range.
5. Select the range **G5:I5**, and then drag the fill handle down to row **163**. Figure 3-28 shows the first several rows of GDD values for the corn crop's history.

Figure 3-28 GDD values for the corn crop

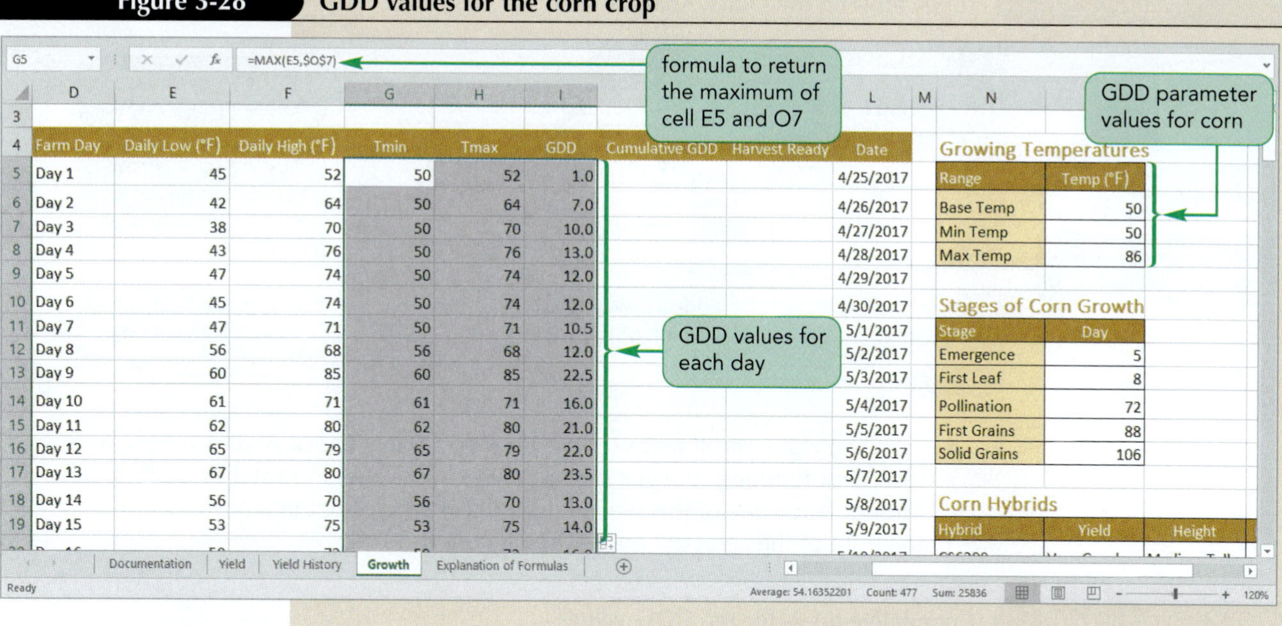

The first GDD values range between 1 and 22.5, but in July and August, GDD routinely reach the upper 20s and lower 30s, indicating that those hot days result in rapid corn growth.

Summarizing Data with the Quick Analysis Tool

The Quick Analysis tool can generate columns and rows of summary statistics and formulas that can be used for analyzing data. GDD is cumulative, which means that as the crop gains more Growing Degree Days, it continues to grow and mature. Jane needs you to calculate a running total of the GDD value for each day in the season. You will enter this calculation using the Quick Analysis tool.

To calculate a running total of GDD:

1. Select the range **I5:I163** containing the GDD values for day of the growing season.
2. Click the **Quick Analysis** button in the lower-right corner of the select range (or press the **Ctrl+Q** keys) to display the menu of Quick Analysis tools.
3. Click **Totals** from the list of tools. The Quick Analysis tools that calculate summary statistics for the selected data appear. See Figure 3-29.

Figure 3-29 Totals tools on the Quick Analysis tool

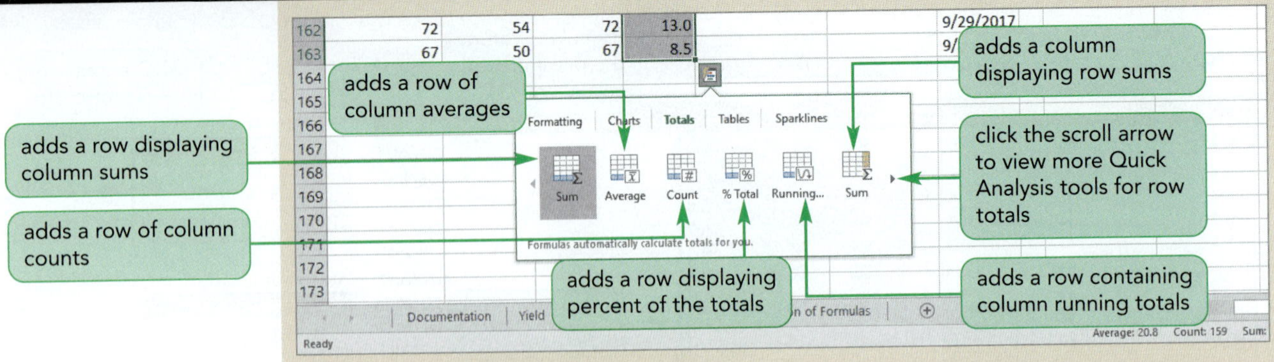

4. Click the **right scroll arrow** ▶ to view additional Quick Analysis tools, and then click **Running** (the last icon in the list). The running total of GDD values through each day of the season appears in a bold font in a new column J to the right of the selected range. See Figure 3-30.

Figure 3-30 Cumulative totals for the GDD values

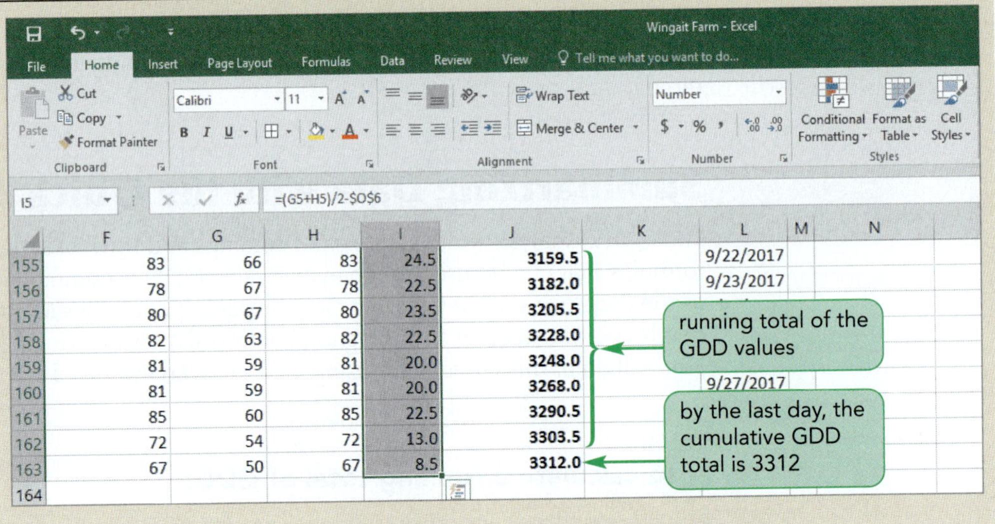

	F	G	H	I	J
155	83	66	83	24.5	**3159.5**
156	78	67	78	22.5	**3182.0**
157	80	67	80	23.5	**3205.5**
158	82	63	82	22.5	**3228.0**
159	81	59	81	20.0	**3248.0**
160	81	59	81	20.0	**3268.0**
161	85	60	85	22.5	**3290.5**
162	72	54	72	13.0	**3303.5**
163	67	50	67	8.5	**3312.0**

Based on the running total in column J, Jane projects that by 9/30/2017, the corn crop will have a total of 3312 Growing Degree Days. To create the running total, the Quick Analysis tool added the following formula to cell J5 and then copied that formula over the range J5:J163:

```
=SUM($I$5:I5)
```

Note that this formula uses a combination of absolute and relative cell references. When copied to cell J6 the formula becomes

```
=SUM($I$5:I6)
```

and when copied to J7 the formula is

```
=SUM($I$5:I7)
```

In this formula, the starting cell of the range used with the SUM function is fixed at cell I5, but the ending cell is relative, causing the number of rows in the range to expand to match the cell selection. For the last date in row 163, the formula becomes:

```
=SUM($I$5:I163)
```

This approach shows how a combination of absolute and relative cell references expands the capability of Excel to create formulas for a variety of ranges.

Working with Dates and Date Functions

Excel has several functions that work with dates and times. These functions are particularly useful in workbooks that involve production schedules and calendars. Figure 3-31 describes some of the commonly used date and time functions.

Figure 3-31 Date functions

Function	Description
DATE(*year*,*month*,*day*)	Creates a date value for the date represented by the *year*, *month*, and *day* arguments
DAY(*date*)	Extracts the day of the month from *date*
MONTH(*date*)	Extracts the month number from *date* where 1=January, 2=February, and so forth
YEAR(*date*)	Extracts the year number from *date*
NETWORKDAYS(*start*,*end*[,*holidays*])	Calculates the number of whole working days between *start* and *end*; to exclude holidays, add the optional *holidays* argument containing a list of holiday dates to skip
WEEKDAY(*date*[,*return_type*])	Calculates the weekday from *date*, where 1=Sunday, 2=Monday, and so forth; to choose a different numbering scheme, set *return_type* to 1 (1=Sunday, 2=Monday, ...), 2 (1=Monday, 2=Tuesday, ...), or 3 (0=Monday, 1=Tuesday, ...)
WORKDAY(*start*,*days*[,*holidays*])	Returns the workday after *days* workdays have passed since the *start* date; to exclude holidays, add the optional *holidays* argument containing a list of holiday dates to skip
NOW( )	Returns the current date and time
TODAY( )	Returns the current date

Many workbooks include the current date so that any reports generated by the workbook are identified by date. To display the current date, you can use the TODAY function:

```
TODAY()
```

TIP

To display the current date and time, which is updated each time the workbook is reopened, use the NOW function.

Note that although the TODAY function doesn't have any arguments, you still must include the parentheses for the function to work. The date displayed by the TODAY function is updated automatically whenever you reopen the workbook or enter a new calculation.

Jane wants the Growth worksheet to show the current date each time it is used or printed. You will use the TODAY function to display the current date in cell B4.

To display the current date:

1. Scroll to the top of the worksheet, and then click cell **B4**.
2. On the ribbon, click the **Formulas** tab.
3. In the Function Library group, click the **Date & Time** button to display the date and time functions.
4. Click **TODAY**. The Function Arguments dialog box opens and indicates that the TODAY function requires no arguments.

5. Click the **OK** button. The formula =TODAY() is entered in cell B4, and the current date is displayed in the cell.

Note that Excel automatically formats cells containing the TODAY function to display the value in Short Date format.

INSIGHT

Date Calculations with Working Days

Businesspeople are often more interested in workdays rather than in all of the days of the week. For example, to estimate a delivery date in which packages are not shipped or delivered on weekends, it is more useful to know the date of the next weekday rather than the date of the next day.

To display the date of a weekday that is a specified number of weekdays past a start date, Excel provides the **WORKDAY function**

```
WORKDAY(start,days[,holidays])
```

where ***start*** is a start date, ***days*** is the number of workdays after that starting date, and ***holidays*** is an optional list of holiday dates to skip. For example, if cell A1 contains the date 12/20/2018, a Thursday, the following formula displays the date 1/2/2019, a Wednesday that is nine working days later:

```
=WORKDAY(A1,9)
```

The optional ***holidays*** argument references a series of dates that the WORKDAY function will skip in performing its calculations. So, if both 12/25/2018 and 1/1/2019 are entered in the range B1:B2 as holidays, the following function will return the date 1/4/2019, a Friday that is nine working days, excluding the holidays, after 12/20/2018:

```
=WORKDAY(A1,9,B1:B2)
```

To reverse the process and calculate the number of working days between two dates, use the NETWORKDAYS function

```
NETWORKDAYS(start,end[,holidays])
```

where ***start*** is the starting date and ***end*** is the ending date. So, if cell A1 contains the date 12/20/2018 and cell A2 contains the date 1/3/2019, the following function returns 9, indicating that there are nine working days between the start and ending, excluding the holidays specified in the range B1:B2:

```
=NETWORKDAYS(A1,A2,B1:B2)
```

For international applications in which the definition of working day differs between one country and another, Excel supports the WORKDAY.INTL function. See Excel Help for more information.

Corn seed is sold in a wide variety of hybrids used to create corn of different quality, size, resistance to parasites, and growth rates. Jane wants the Growth worksheet to display data about the corn hybrid she chose for Wingait Farm. You can retrieve that data using a lookup function.

Using Lookup Functions

A **lookup function** retrieves values from a table of data that match a specified condition. For example, a lookup function can be used to retrieve a tax rate from a tax table for a given annual income or to retrieve shipping rates for different delivery options.

The table that stores the data you want to retrieve is called a **lookup table**. The first row or column of the table contains compare values, which are the values that are being looked up. If the compare values are in the first row, the table is a **horizontal lookup table**; if the compare values are in the first column, the table is a vertical lookup table. The remaining rows or columns contain the return values, which are the data values being retrieved by the lookup function.

Figure 3-32 shows the range N19:Q27 in the Growth worksheet containing information about different corn hybrids. This information is a vertical lookup table because the first column of the table containing the names of the hybrids stores the compare values. The remaining columns containing type of yield, height of the corn stalk, and GDD units until the hybrid reaches maturity are the return values. To look up the Growing Degree Days required until the corn hybrid CS6478 reaches maturity, Excel scans the first column of the lookup table until it finds the entry for CS6478. Excel then moves to the right to the column containing information that needs to be returned.

Figure 3-32 Finding an exact match from a lookup table

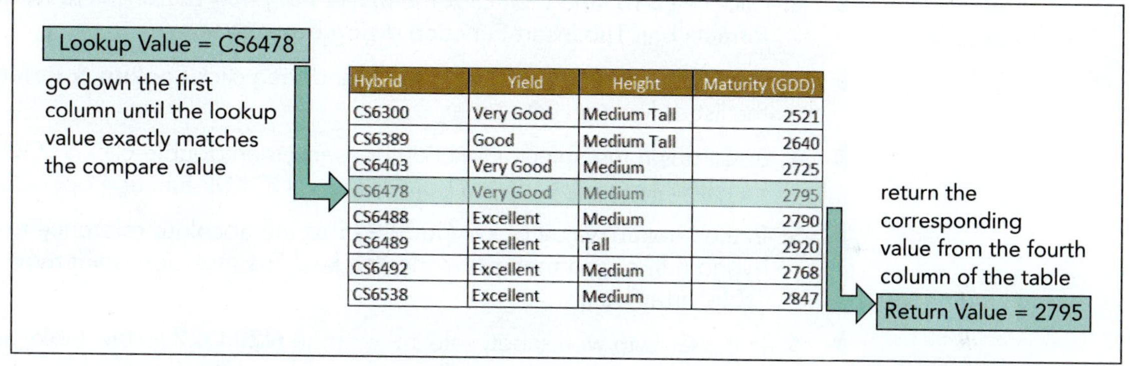
Lookup Value = CS6478
go down the first column until the lookup value exactly matches the compare value
return the corresponding value from the fourth column of the table
Return Value = 2795

Hybrid	Yield	Height	Maturity (GDD)
CS6300	Very Good	Medium Tall	2521
CS6389	Good	Medium Tall	2640
CS6403	Very Good	Medium	2725
CS6478	Very Good	Medium	2795
CS6488	Excellent	Medium	2790
CS6489	Excellent	Tall	2920
CS6492	Excellent	Medium	2768
CS6538	Excellent	Medium	2847

Lookup tables can be constructed for exact match or approximate match lookups. In an **exact match lookup**, the lookup value must exactly match one of the compare values in the first row or column of the lookup table. Figure 3-32 is an exact match lookup because the name of the corn hybrid must match one of the compare values in the table. An **approximate match lookup** is used when the lookup value falls within a range of compare values. You will work with exact match lookups in this module.

Finding an Exact Match with the VLOOKUP Function

To retrieve the return value from a vertical lookup table, you use the VLOOKUP function

```
VLOOKUP(comp_value,table_array,col_index_num[,range_lookup=TRUE])
```

where *comp_value* is the compare value to find in the first column of the lookup table, *table_array* is the range reference to the lookup table, and *col_index_num* is the number of the column in the lookup table that contains the return value. Keep in mind that *col_index_num* refers to the number of the column within the lookup table, not the worksheet column. So, a *col_index_num* of 2 refers to the lookup table's second column. Finally, *range_lookup* is an optional argument that specifies whether the lookup should be done as an exact match or an approximate match. For an exact match, you set the *range_lookup* value to FALSE. For approximate match lookups, you set the *range_lookup* value to TRUE. The default is to assume an approximate match.

For example, the following formula performs an exact match lookup using the text "CS6478" as the compare value and the data in the range N20:Q27 (shown in Figure 3-32) as the lookup table:

```
=VLOOKUP("CS6478",N20:Q27,4,FALSE)
```

TIP

If the VLOOKUP function cannot find the lookup value in the lookup table, it returns the #N/A error value.

The function looks through the compare values in the first column of the table to locate the "CS6478" entry. When the exact entry is found, the function returns the corresponding value in the fourth column of the table, which in this case is 2795.

Jane wants you to retrieve information about the CS6478 hybrid she uses at Wingait Farm and then display that information in the range B16:B18 on the Growth worksheet. You'll use a VLOOKUP function to retrieve yield information about the hybrid.

To use the VLOOKUP function to find yield information for hybrid CS6478:

1. In cell **B15**, enter the hybrid **CS6478**.
2. Click cell **B16**, and then click the **Insert Function** button to the left of the formula bar. The Insert Function dialog box opens.
3. Click the **Or select a category** box, and then click **Lookup & Reference** in the list of function categories.
4. Scroll down the Select a function box, and then double-click **VLOOKUP**. The Function Arguments dialog box for the VLOOKUP function opens.
5. In the Lookup_value box, type **$B$15** as the absolute reference to the hybrid name, and then press the **Tab** key. The insertion point moves to the Table_array box.
6. In the Growth worksheet, select the range **N20:Q27** as the Table_array value, press the **F4** key to change the range reference to the absolute reference **$N$20:$Q$27**.
7. Press the **Tab** key. The insertion point moves to the Col_index_num box. Yield information is stored in the second column of the lookup table.
8. Type **2** in the Col_index_num box to return information from the second column of the lookup table, and then press the **Tab** key. The insertion point moves to the Range_lookup box.
9. Type **FALSE** in the Range_lookup box to perform an exact match lookup. See Figure 3-33.

TIP

Exact matches are not case sensitive, so the lookup values False, false, and FALSE are considered the same.

Figure 3-33 Function Arguments dialog box for the VLOOKUP function

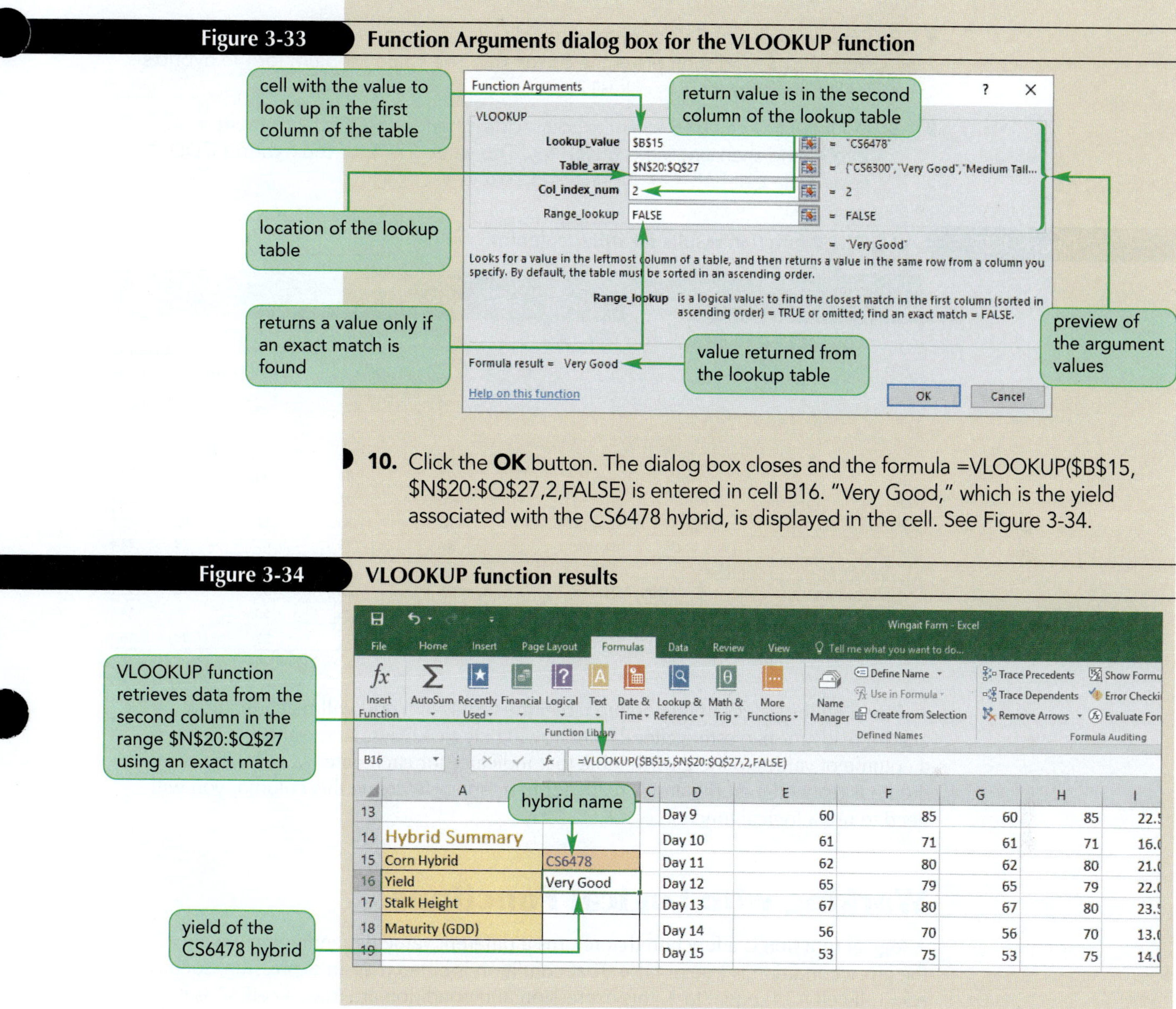
cell with the value to look up in the first column of the table
return value is in the second column of the lookup table
location of the lookup table
returns a value only if an exact match is found
preview of the argument values
value returned from the lookup table
Function Arguments
VLOOKUP
Lookup_value $B$15 = "CS6478"
Table_array $N$20:$Q$27 = {"CS6300","Very Good","Medium Tall...
Col_index_num 2 = 2
Range_lookup FALSE = FALSE
= "Very Good"
Looks for a value in the leftmost column of a table, and then returns a value in the same row from a column you specify. By default, the table must be sorted in an ascending order.
Range_lookup is a logical value: to find the closest match in the first column (sorted in ascending order) = TRUE or omitted; find an exact match = FALSE.
Formula result = Very Good
Help on this function
OK
Cancel

10. Click the **OK** button. The dialog box closes and the formula =VLOOKUP($B$15, $N$20:$Q$27,2,FALSE) is entered in cell B16. "Very Good," which is the yield associated with the CS6478 hybrid, is displayed in the cell. See Figure 3-34.

Figure 3-34 VLOOKUP function results

VLOOKUP function retrieves data from the second column in the range $N$20:$Q$27 using an exact match
hybrid name
yield of the CS6478 hybrid
Wingait Farm - Excel
File Home Insert Page Layout Formulas Data Review View Tell me what you want to do...
B16
=VLOOKUP($B$15,$N$20:$Q$27,2,FALSE)
Hybrid Summary
Corn Hybrid CS6478
Yield Very Good
Stalk Height
Maturity (GDD)

Jane wants to see the stalk height and the GDD information about the hybrid CS6478. You will use AutoFill to copy the VLOOKUP function into the other cells in the Hybrid Summary table.

To display other information about the hybrid CS6478:

1. Click cell **B16** to select it, and then drag the fill handle over the range **B16:B18** to copy the VLOOKUP formula into cells B17 and B18. The text "Very Good" appears in cells B17 and B18, because the formula is set up to retrieve text from the second column of the lookup table.

   You need to edit the formulas in cells B17 and B18 to retrieve information from the third and fourth columns of the lookup table, respectively.

2. Double-click cell **B17** to enter into Edit mode, change the third argument from 2 to **3**, and then press the **Enter** key. The value Medium for the hybrid's stalk height appears in cell B17.

3. Double-click cell **B18** to enter Edit mode, change the third argument from 2 to **4**, and then press the **Enter** key. The value 2795 for the hybrid's GDD appears in cell B18. See Figure 3-35.

Figure 3-35 **VLOOKUP function results for other columns**

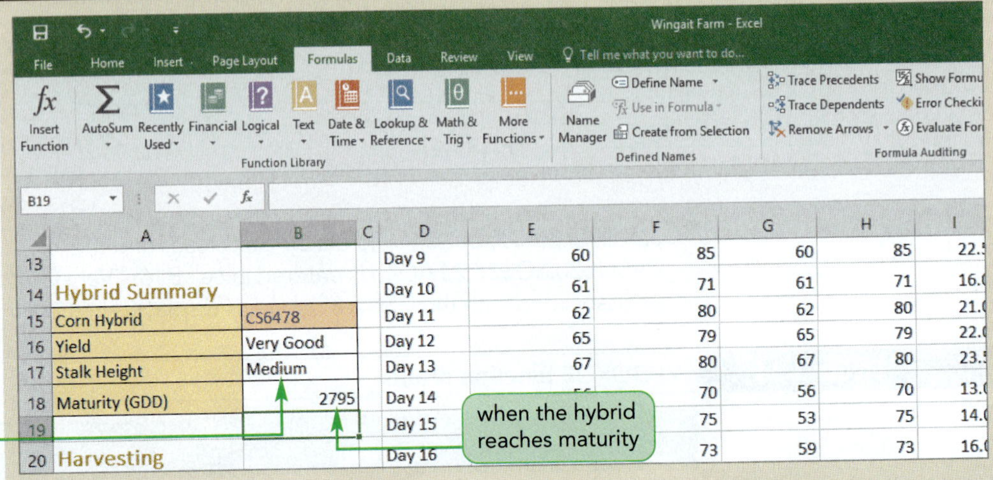

Based on the values in the lookup table, the CS6478 hybrid will reach maturity and be ready for harvesting after 2795 Growing Degree Days. Jane wants you to add a column of values to the growth table that indicates for each date, whether the corn crop has reached maturity and is ready for harvesting. To create this column, you will need to use a logical function.

Working with Logical Functions

A **logical function** is a function that returns a different value depending on whether the given condition is true or false. That condition is entered as an expression, such as A5=3. If cell A5 is equal to 3, this expression and condition are true; if cell A5 is not equal to 3, this expression and condition are false. The most commonly used logical function is the IF function. The syntax of the IF function is

```
IF(condition,value_if_true,value_if_false)
```

where `condition` is an expression that is either true or false, `value_if_true` is the value returned by the function if the expression is true, and `value_if_false` is the value returned if the expression is false.

The value returned by the IF function can be a number, text, a date, a cell reference, or a formula. For example, the following formula tests whether the value in cell A1 is equal to the value in cell B1, returning 100 if those two cells are equal and 50 if they're not.

```
=IF(A1=B1,100,50)
```

TIP

To apply multiple logical conditions, you can nest one IF function within another.

In many cases, you will use cell references instead of values in the IF function. The following formula, for example, uses cell references, returning the value of cell C1 if A1 equals B1; otherwise, it returns the value of cell C2:

```
=IF(A1=B1,C1,C2)
```

The = symbol in these formulas is a **comparison operator** that indicates the relationship between two parts of the logical function's condition. Figure 3-36 describes other comparison operators that can be used within logical functions.

Figure 3-36 **Logical comparison operators**

Operator	Expression	Tests
=	A1 = B1	If the value in cell A1 is equal to the value in cell B1
>	A1 > B1	If the value in cell A1 is greater than the value in cell B1
<	A1 < B1	If the value in cell A1 is less than the value in cell B1
>=	A1 >= B1	If the value in cell A1 is greater than or equal to the value in cell B1
<=	A1 <= B1	If the value in cell A1 is less than or equal to the value in cell B1
<>	A1 <> B1	If the value in cell A1 is not equal to the value in cell B1

The IF function also works with text. For example, the following formula tests whether the value of cell A1 is equal to "yes":

```
=IF(A1="yes","done","restart")
```

If the condition is true (the value of cell A1 is equal to "yes"), then the formula returns the text "done"; otherwise, it returns the text "restart".

For each date in the growth record of the corn crop, Jane wants to know whether the cumulative GDD value is greater than or equal to the GDD value on which the hybrid reaches maturity and is ready for harvesting. If the crop is ready for harvesting, she wants the cell to display the text "Yes"; otherwise, it should display the text "No". You'll use the IF function to do this.

To enter the IF function to specify whether the corn is ready for harvesting:

1. Click cell **K5** to select it. You'll enter the IF function in this cell.
2. On the Formulas tab, in the Function Library group, click the **Logical** button to display the list of logical functions, and then click **IF**. The Function Arguments dialog box for the IF function opens.
3. In the Logical_test box, enter the expression **J5>=$B$18** to test whether the cumulative GDD value is greater than the maturity value in cell B18.
4. Press **Tab** key to move the insertion point to the Value_if_true box, and then type **"Yes"** as the value if the logical test is true.
5. Press **Tab** key to move the insertion point to the Value_if_false box, and then type **"No"** as the value if the logical test is false. See Figure 3-37.

Figure 3-37 Function Arguments dialog box for the IF function

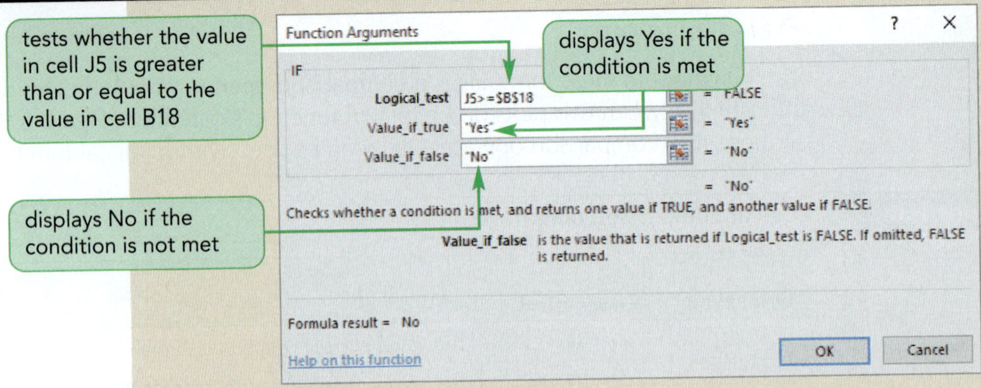
tests whether the value in cell J5 is greater than or equal to the value in cell B18
displays Yes if the condition is met
displays No if the condition is not met
Function Arguments
IF
Logical_test J5>=$B$18 = FALSE
Value_if_true "Yes" = "Yes"
Value_if_false "No" = "No"
= "No"
Checks whether a condition is met, and returns one value if TRUE, and another value if FALSE.
Value_if_false is the value that is returned if Logical_test is FALSE. If omitted, FALSE is returned.
Formula result = No
Help on this function
OK
Cancel

6. Click the **OK** button. The formula =IF(J5>=$B$18,"Yes","No") is entered in cell K5. The cell displays the text "No," indicating that the crop is not harvest ready on this day (a logical result because this is the day when the farm starts planting the corn).
7. Click cell **K5**, and then drag fill handle to select the range **K5:K163**. The formula with the IF function is applied to the remaining days of the growing season. As shown in Figure 3-38, by the end of the growing season, the crop is ready for harvesting because the cumulative GDD value for the hybrid CS6478 has exceeded 2795.

Figure 3-38 IF function evaluates whether the crop is harvest ready

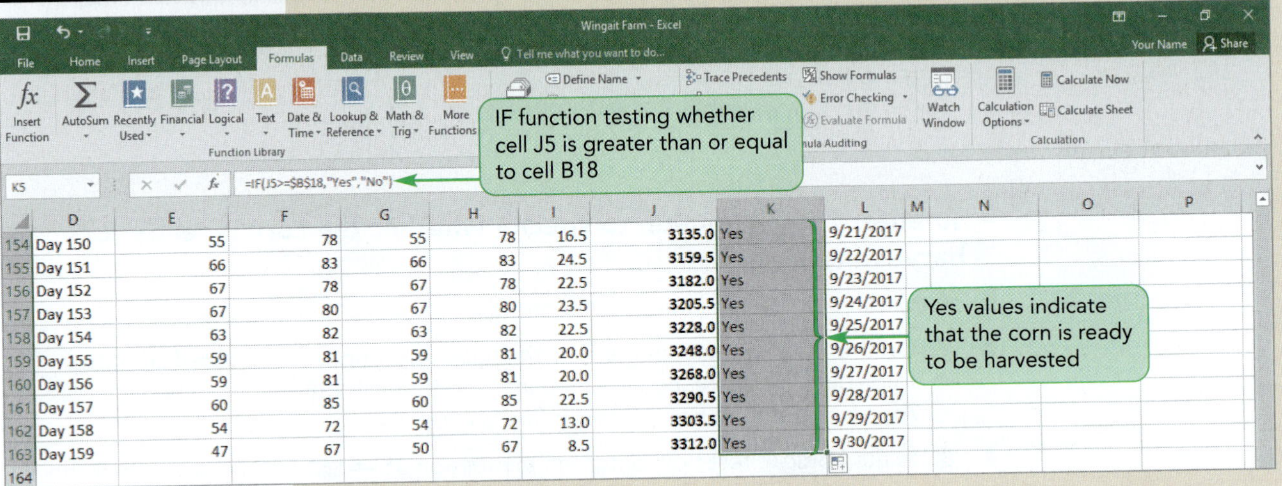
IF function testing whether cell J5 is greater than or equal to cell B18
Yes values indicate that the corn is ready to be harvested
=IF(J5>=$B$18,"Yes","No")

By scrolling up and down the Growth worksheet you can locate the row in which the value in the Harvest Ready column switches from No to Yes. For this data, the switch occurs in row 138 where the cumulative GDD value is equal to 2814, exceeding the minimum GDD value required for this particular hybrid to reach maturity.

Rather than scrolling through the worksheet, Jane wants the worksheet to display the calendar date on which the crop reaches maturity and is ready for harvesting. You can obtain this information by using columns K and L as a lookup table. Recall that Excel scans a lookup table from the top to the bottom and stops when it reaches the first value in the compare column that matches the lookup value. You can use this fact to find the first location in column K where the Harvest Ready value is equal to "Yes" and then apply the VLOOKUP function to return the corresponding calendar date in column L.

To display the harvest date for the corn crop:

1. Near the top of the worksheet, click cell **B21** to select it.
2. Click the **Insert Function** button fx to the left of the formula bar. The Insert Function dialog box opens.
3. Click the **Or select a category box arrow**, and then click **Most Recently Used** to display a list of the functions you have used most recently.
4. Double-click **VLOOKUP** in the list. The Function Arguments dialog box for the VLOOKUP function opens.
5. In the Lookup_value box, type **"Yes"** and then press the **Tab** key. The insertion point moves to the Table_array box.
6. Select the **K** and **L** column headings to insert the reference K:L in the Table_array box, and then press the **Tab** key. The insertion point moves to the Col_index_num box.
7. Type **2** in the Col_index_num box to retrieve the value from the second column in the lookup table, and then press the **Tab** key. The insertion point moves to the Range_lookup box.
8. Type **FALSE** in the Range_lookup box to apply an exact match lookup. See Figure 3-39.

Use FALSE to perform an exact match lookup.

Figure 3-39 Function Arguments for the VLOOKUP function

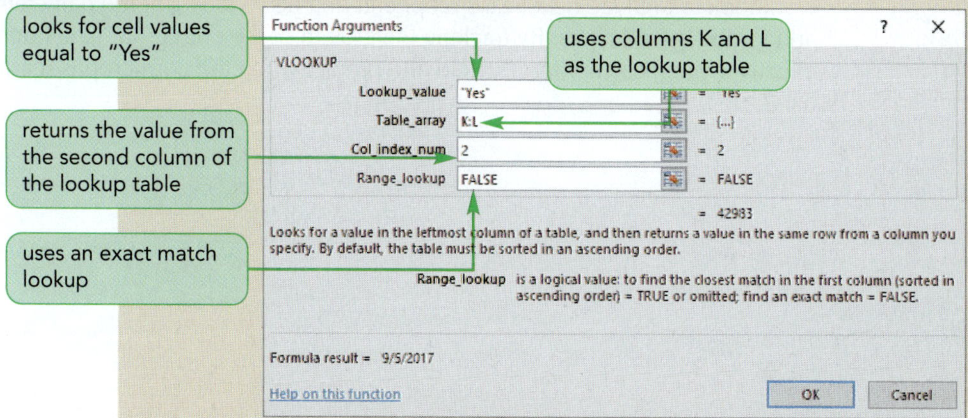
looks for cell values equal to "Yes"
uses columns K and L as the lookup table
returns the value from the second column of the lookup table
uses an exact match lookup
Function Arguments
VLOOKUP
Lookup_value "Yes" = "Yes"
Table_array K:L = {...}
Col_index_num 2 = 2
Range_lookup FALSE = FALSE
= 42983
Looks for a value in the leftmost column of a table, and then returns a value in the same row from a column you specify. By default, the table must be sorted in an ascending order.
Range_lookup is a logical value: to find the closest match in the first column (sorted in ascending order) = TRUE or omitted; find an exact match = FALSE.
Formula result = 9/5/2017
Help on this function
OK
Cancel

9. Click the **OK** button. The formula =VLOOKUP("Yes",K:L,2,FALSE) is entered in cell B21. The cell displays 9/5/2017, which is the date when the corn crop has reached maturity and is ready for harvesting to begin.

Jane can view the impact of different hybrids on the harvest date by changing the value of cell B15.

10. Click cell **B15**, and then change the corn hybrid from CS6478 to **CS6489**. The results from the lookup and IF functions in the worksheet change to reflect the corn hybrid CS6489. This hybrid has excellent yield and tall stalks and is ready for harvesting on 9/10/2017, five days later than the corn hybrid CS6478. See Figure 3-40.

Figure 3-40 Summary and harvesting data for the hybrid CS6489

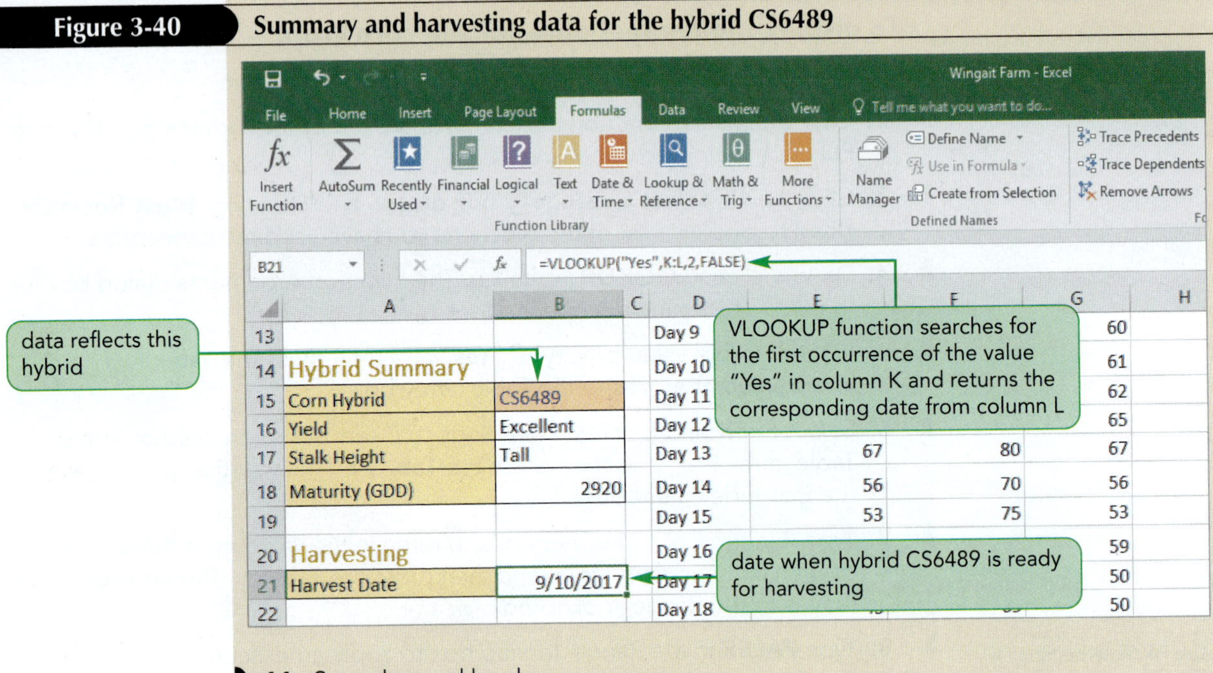

11. Save the workbook.

You've completed your work on the Wingait Farm workbook. Jane will use this workbook to analyze next year's crop, entering new values for the daily temperatures and for the hybrid types. By tracking the growth of the corn crop, Jane hopes to more effectively increase her farm's yield and predict when the corn crop is ready for harvesting.

INSIGHT

Managing Error Values with the IF Function

An error value does not mean that you must correct the cell's formula or function. Some error values appear simply because you have not yet entered any data into the workbook. For example, if you use the VLOOKUP function without a lookup value, the #N/A error value appears because Excel cannot look up an empty value. However, as soon as you enter a lookup, the #N/A error value disappears, replaced with the result of the VLOOKUP function.

Error values of this type can make your workbook difficult to read and can confuse other users. One way to avoid error values resulting from missing input values is to nest formulas within an IF function. For example, the following formula first tests whether a value has been entered into cell B2 before attempting to use that cell as a lookup value in the VLOOKUP function:

```
=IF(B2="","",VLOOKUP(B2,$E1:$G$10,3,FALSE)
```

Note that "" is used to represent an empty text string or value. If the IF condition is true because no value has been entered into cell B2, the formula will return an empty text string instead of an error value, but if B2 has a value, the VLOOKUP function is applied using cell B2 as the lookup value. The result is a cleaner workbook that is easier for other people to read and use.

Jane appreciates all of the work you have done in developing the Wingait Farm workbook. She will continue to study the document and get back to you with future projects at the farm.

REVIEW

Session 3.2 Quick Check

1. If 4/30/2017 and 5/31/2017 are the initial values, what are the next two values AutoFill will insert?
2. You need to reference cell Q57 in a formula. What is its relative reference? What is its absolute reference? What are the two mixed references?
3. If cell R10 contains the formula =R1+R2, which is then copied to cell S20, what formula is entered in cell S20?
4. If cell R10 contains the formula =$R1+R$2, which is then copied to cell S20, what formula is entered in cell S20?
5. Explain how to use the Quick Analysis tool to calculate a running total of the values in the range D1:D10.
6. Write the formula to display the current date in the worksheet.
7. Write the formula to display a date that is four workdays after the date in cell A5. Do not assume any holidays in your calculation.
8. Write the formula to perform an exact match lookup with the lookup value from cell G5 using a vertical lookup table located in the range A1:F50. Return the value from the third column of the table.
9. If cell Q3 is greater than cell Q4, you want to display the text "OK"; otherwise, display the text "RETRY". Write the formula that accomplishes this.

PRACTICE

Review Assignments

Data File needed for the Review Assignments: Soybean.xlsx

Another cash crop grown at Wingait Farm is soybeans. Jane wants you to create a workbook for the soybean crop similar to the workbook you created for the corn crop. The workbook should estimate the total yield and revenue from a small plot sample and compare that yield to the farm's historic norms. The workbook should also track the soybean growth from planting to harvest. Complete the following:

1. Open the **Soybean** workbook located in the Excel3 > Review folder, and then save the workbook as **Soybean Crop** in the location specified by your instructor.
2. In the Documentation worksheet, enter your name in cell B3 and the date in cell B4.
3. The size of the soybean crop is **72** acres. Enter this value in cell B4 of the Yield worksheet.
4. The soybean sample comes from a plot of **4** rows each **7.5** inches wide and **21** inches long. Enter these values in the range B7:B9.
5. Within the plot, the farm has harvested **400** soybean pods with an average of **2.5** soybeans per pod. Enter these values in the B14:B15 range.
6. Apply the Input cell style to cells B4, B7:B9, and B14:B15.
7. Using the equations described in the Formulas worksheet, enter the following calculations:
   a. In cell B10, calculate the area of the plot sample in inches.
   b. In cell B11, convert the sample area to acres by dividing the value in cell B10 by the number of square inches in an acre (cell H4). Display the result to four decimal places.
   c. In cell B16, calculate the total number of seeds harvested in the sample.
   d. In cell B17, calculate the weight of the sample in pounds by dividing the number of seeds by the number of seeds in one pound (cell H5). Display the value to two decimal places.
   e. In cell B18, convert the weight to bushels by dividing the weight in pounds by the number of pounds of soybeans in one bushel (cell H6). Display the value to four decimal places.
   f. In cell B19, estimate the farm's soybean yield in bushels per acre by dividing the number of bushels in the plot sample by the area of the sample in acres. Display the value as an integer.
8. Calculate the following values for soybean yield and revenue:
   a. In cell B20, calculate the farm's average soybean yield using the values in column E. Use the ROUND function to round that average value to the nearest integer.
   b. In cell B21, calculate the farm's median soybean yield from the values in column E.
   c. In cell B24, calculate the farm's total production of soybeans in bushels by multiplying the bushels per acre value by the total number of acres that the farm devotes to soybeans. Display the value as an integer.
   d. In cell B25, calculate the total revenue from the soybean crop by multiplying the total bushels harvested by the current price per bushel (cell H7). Display the value using the Accounting format style.
9. Apply the Calculation style to the range B10:B11,B16:B21,B24:B25.
10. Use Goal Seek to determine what value in cell B4 (the number of acres devoted to soybeans) will result in a total soybean revenue of $40,000.
11. In the Growth worksheet, in cell B5, enter a formula with a function to display the current date.
12. Use AutoFill to insert the text strings Day 1 through Day 112 in the range D5:D116.
13. In cell G5, calculate the Growing Degree Days (GDD) for the first day of the season using the formula described in the Formulas worksheet and the temperature range values in the range L6:M9. (*Hint*: Use the same formula used in the tutorial for corn, but enter the T_{min}, T_{max}, and *base* values directly in the formula. Be sure to use absolute references for the temperature range values.)
14. Copy the formula in cell G5 to the range G5:G112.

15. Use the Quick Analysis tool to calculate the cumulative total of the GDD values from the range G5:G112, placing those values in the range H5:H112.
16. In cell B9, enter **5/12/2017**, which is the date the farm will start planting the soybean crop.
17. In cell J5, enter a formula to display the date from cell B9. In cell J6, enter a formula to increase the date in cell J5 by one day. Copy the formula in cell J6 to the range J6:J112 to enter the dates for the growing season.
18. In cell B8, enter **M070** as the maturity group for the current soybean hybrid.
19. In cell B10, use the VLOOKUP function to retrieve the cumulative GDD value for the M070 hybrid. (*Hint:* The range L12:M21 displays the cumulative GDD for each maturity group.)
20. In cell I5, enter an IF function that tests whether the cumulative GDD value in cell H5 is greater than the maturity value in cell B10. Use an absolute reference to cell B10. If the condition is true, return the text string "Ready"; otherwise, return the text "Not Ready". Copy the formula to the range I5:I112.
21. In cell B11, insert a VLOOKUP function using the values in the columns I and J that returns the date on which the Harvest Ready value is first equal to the text string "Ready".
22. In cell B12, calculate the number of days between planting and harvesting by subtracting the planting date (cell B9) from the harvest date (cell B11).
23. Save and close the workbook.

APPLY

Case Problem 1

Data File needed for this Case Problem: Gorecki.xlsx

Gorecki Construction Stefan Gorecki is the owner of Gorecki Construction, a small construction firm in Chester, Pennsylvania. He wants to use Excel to track his company's monthly income and expenses and then use that information to create a monthly budget. Stefan has already entered the raw data values but has asked to you to complete the workbook by adding the formulas and functions to perform the calculations. Complete the following:

1. Open the **Gorecki** workbook located in the Excel3 > Case1 folder, and then save the workbook as **Gorecki Budget** in the location specified by your instructor.
2. In the Documentation worksheet, enter your name in cell B3 and the date in cell B4.
3. The budget values are entered based on the end-of-month values. In the Monthly Budget worksheet, enter the date **31-Jan-18** in cell E4 and **28-Feb-18** in cell F4. Use AutoFill to fill in the remaining end-of-month date in the range G4:P4.
4. Calculate the company's total monthly income by selecting the range E6:P7 and using the Quick Analysis tool to insert the SUM function automatically into the range E8:P8.
5. Calculate the company's total cost of goods sold by selecting values in range E10:P11 and using the Quick Analysis tool to insert the SUM function automatically into the range E12:P12.
6. In the range E14:P14, calculate the company's monthly gross profit, which is equal to the difference between the monthly income and the monthly cost of goods sold.
7. Select the expenses entered in the range E17:P26, and use the Quick Analysis tool to insert the sum of the monthly expenses into the range E27:P27.
8. In the range E29:P29, calculate the company's net income equal to the difference between its gross profit and its total expenses.
9. Select the values in the range E29:P29, and then use the Quick Analysis tool to insert a running total of the company's net income into the range E30:P30.
10. Calculate the year-end totals for all financial categories by selecting the range E6:P29 and using the Quick Analysis tool to insert the sum of each row into the range Q6:Q29. Delete the content of any cells that do not contain financial figures.

11. Stefan wants the monthly averages of each financial category to be displayed in range B6:B29. Select cell B6, and then enter a formula that contains a nested function that first calculates the average of the values in the range E6:P6 and then uses the ROUND function to round that average to the nearest 10 dollars. (*Hint*: Use –1 for the value of the num_digits argument.) Use AutoFill to extend formula over the range B6:B29, deleting any cells corresponding to empty values.
12. Save and close the workbook.

APPLY

Case Problem 2

Data File needed for this Case Problem: Capshaw.xlsx

Capshaw Family Dentistry Carol Lemke is a new receptionist at Capshaw Dentistry in East Point, Georgia. She wants to get a rough estimate of what her take-home pay would be after deductions for federal and local taxes. She asks you to set up an Excel worksheet to perform the wage calculations for a sample two-week period. Carol already entered the work schedule and several tables containing the federal and state tax rates but needs you to insert the formulas. (*Note:* The tax rate tables and formulas used in this example are a simplified version of the tax code and should not be used to calculate actual taxes.) Complete the following:

1. Open the **Capshaw** workbook located in the Excel3 > Case2 folder, and then save the workbook as **Capshaw Wages** in the location specified by your instructor.
2. In the Documentation worksheet, enter your name in cell B3 and the date in cell B4.
3. In the Work Schedule worksheet, enter the following information in the range B5:B9: Name **Carol Lemke**; Hourly Rate **$16.25**; Federal Marital Status **Single**; State Marital Status **Single**; and Withholding Allowances **1**
4. In cell D6, enter the date **4/10/2017**. Use AutoFill to fill in the next day weekdays in the range D6:D15. (*Hint*: Click the AutoFill options button after dragging the fill handle, and then select the Fill Weekdays option button.)
5. In cell G6, calculate the total hours worked on the first day, which is equal to the difference between cell F6 and cell E6 multiplied by 24.
6. Carol will get overtime wages when she works more than eight hours in a day. Calculate the non-overtime hours in cell H6 by using the MIN function to return the minimum of the value in cell G6 and the value 8.
7. In cell I6, calculate the amount of overtime hours by using the IF function to test whether cell G6 is greater than 8. If it is, return the value cell G6 minus 8; otherwise, return the value 0.
8. In cell J6, calculate the salary due on the first day. The salary due is equal to the Straight Time worked multiplied by the hourly rate in cell B6 plus the Overtime multiplied by the hourly rate times 1.5 (Carol will receive time-and-a-half for each overtime hour.) Use an absolute reference to cell B6.
9. Select the range G6:J6, and then use AutoFill to copy the formulas into the range G7:J15 to calculate the salary for each of the ten days in the table.
10. In cell B11, calculate the total straight time hours worked by summing the values in column H. In cell B12, calculate the total overtime hours by summing the values in column I. In cell B13, calculate the total hours worked by summing the value in column G. In cell B14, calculate the total payments by summing the values in column J.
11. In cell B17, calculate the amount of federal tax by multiplying the Total Pay value in cell B14 by the appropriate federal tax rate for an employee with the marital status in cell B7 and withholding allowances in cell B9. (*Hint*: Use the VLOOKUP function with an exact match lookup for the lookup table in the range L6:W8. For the Col_index_num argument, use the value of cell B9 plus 2.)
12. In cell B18, calculate the Social Security tax equal to the value of cell B14 multiplied by the tax rate in cell M16.

13. In cell B19, calculate the Medicare tax equal to the value of cell B14 multiplied by the tax rate in cell M17.
14. In cell B20, calculate the amount of Georgia state tax by multiplying the value of cell B14 by the appropriate state tax rate in the range L12:W14 lookup table using the state marital status in cell B8 and the withholding allowance in cell B9. (*Hint*: Use the same type of VLOOKUP function as you did in Step 10 to retrieve the correct state tax rate.)
15. In cell B22, calculate the total deduction from pay by summing the values in the range B17:B20. In cell B23, calculate the withholding rate by dividing cell B22 by the total pay in cell B14.
16. In cell B24, calculate the take-home pay from subtracting the total withholding in cell B22 from cell B14.
17. Carol wants her take-home pay for the two weeks that she works in the sample schedule to be $1000. Use Goal Seek to find the hourly rate in cell B6 that will result in a take-home pay value of $1000.
18. Save and close the workbook.

CHALLENGE

Case Problem 3

Data File needed for this Case Problem: Biology.xlsx

Biology 221 Daivi Emani teaches biology and life sciences at Milford College in White Plains, New York. She wants to use Excel to track the test scores and calculate final averages for the students in her Biology 221 class. She has already entered the homework, quiz, and final exam scores for 66 students. The overall score is based on weighted average of the individual scores with homework accounting for 10 percent of the final grade, each of three quizzes accounting for 20 percent, and the final exam accounting for 30 percent. To calculate a weighted average you can use the SUMPRODUCT function

```
SUMPRODUCT(array1,array2)
```

where *array1* is the range containing the weights assigned to each score and *array2* is the range containing the scores themselves.

Daivi also wants you to calculate each student's rank in the class based on the student's weighted average. Ranks are calculated using the RANK function

```
RANK(number,ref[,order=0])
```

where *number* is the value to be ranked, *ref* is a reference to the range containing the values against which the ranking is done, and *order* is an optional argument that specifies whether to rank in descending order or ascending order. The default order value is 0 to rank the values in descending order.

Finally, you will create formulas that will look up information on a particular student based on that student's ID so that Daivi doesn't have to scroll through the complete class roster to find a particular student. Complete the following:

1. Open the **Biology** workbook located in the Excel3 > Case3 folder, and then save the workbook as **Biology Grades** in the location specified by your instructor.
2. In the Documentation worksheet, enter your name in cell B3 and the date in cell B4.
3. In the Biology Grades worksheet, in cell B5, calculate the number of students in the class by using the COUNTA function to count up the student IDs in the H column and subtracting 1 from that value (so as to not include cell H2 in the count).
4. In the range B8:F8, enter the weight values **10%**, **20%**, **20%**, **20%**, and **30%**.
5. In the range B9:F9, calculate the average of the numbers in columns K, L, M, N, and O.
6. In the range B10:F10, calculate the minimum values in the corresponding student score columns.

7. In the range B11:F11, use the MEDIAN function to calculate the midpoint of each of the student scores.
8. In the range B12:F12, calculate the maximum values for each of the student scores.

Explore 9. In cell P3, use the SUMPRODUCT function to calculate the weighted average of the scores for the first student in the list. Use an absolute reference to the range B8:F8 for the `array1` argument, and use the relative reference to the student scores in the range K3:O3 for the `array2` argument.

Explore 10. In cell Q3, use the RANK function to calculate the first student's rank in class. Use cell P3 for the `number` argument and column P for the `ref` argument. You do not to specify a value for the `order` argument.

11. Calculate the weighted average and ranks for all of the students by using AutoFill to copy the formulas in the range P3:Q3 to the range P3:Q68.
12. In cell B15, enter the student ID **602-1-99** for Lawrence Fujita.
13. In cell B16, use the VLOOKUP function with the student ID from cell B15 to look up the first name of the student matching that ID. Use the range H:Q as the reference to the lookup table, and retrieve the third column from the table.
14. In the range B17:B24, use lookup functions to retrieve the other data for the student ID entered in cell B15.
15. Test the VLOOKUP function by adding other student IDs in cell B15 to confirm that you can retrieve the record for any student in class based on his or her student ID.
16. Manuel Harmon was not able to take the final exam because of a family crisis. Daivi is scheduling a makeup exam for him. A weighted average of 92.0 will give Manuel an A for the course. Use Goal Seek to determine what grade he would need on the final to get an A for the course.
17. Save and close the workbook.

CHALLENGE

Case Problem 4

Data File needed for this Case Problem: Cairn.xlsx

Cairn Camping Supplies Diane Cho is the owner of Cairn Camping Supplies, a small camping store she runs out of her home in Fort Smith, Arkansas. To help her manage her inventory and orders, she wants to develop an Excel worksheet for recording orders. The worksheet needs to calculate the cost of each order, including the cost of shipping and sales tax. Shipping costs vary based on whether the customer wants to use standard, three-day, two-day, or overnight shipping. Diane will also offer free shipping for orders that are more than $250. The shipping form worksheet will use lookup functions so that Diane can enter each product's ID code and have the name and price of the product automatically entered into the form. To keep the worksheet clean without distracting error values when no input values have been entered, you'll use IF functions to test whether the user has entered a required value first before applying a formula using that value. Complete the following:

1. Open the **Cairn** workbook located in the Excel3 > Case4 folder, and then save the workbook as **Cairn Camping** in the location specified by your instructor.
2. In the Documentation worksheet, enter your name in cell B3 and the date in cell B4.
3. In the Order Form worksheet, enter the following sample order data: Customer **Dixie Kaufmann**; Order Number **381**; Order Date **4/5/2018**; Street **414 Topeak Lane**; City **Fort Smith**; State **AK**; ZIP **72914**; Phone **(479) 555-2081**; and Delivery Type **3 Day**.

Explore 4. In cell B17, calculate the number of delivery days for the order. Insert an IF function that first tests whether the value in cell B16 is equal to an empty text string (""). If it is, return an empty text string; otherwise, apply a lookup function to retrieve the lookup value from the table in the range F5:H8 using the value of cell B16 as the lookup value.

Explore 5. In cell B18, estimate the date of weekday delivery by inserting an IF function that tests whether cell B16 is equal to an empty text string. If it is, return an empty text string, otherwise apply the WORKDAY function using the values in cell B6 as the starting date and cell B17 as the number of days.

6. In cell D13, enter **p4981** as the initial item ordered by the customer. In cell G13, enter **2** as the number of items ordered.
7. In cell E13, enter an IF function that tests whether the value in cell D13 is equal to an empty text string. If true, return an empty text string. If false, apply the VLOOKUP function to return the name of the product ID entered into cell D13.
8. In cell F13, enter another IF function that tests whether the value in cell D13 is equal to an empty text string. If true, return an empty text string. If false, return the price of the product ID entered in cell D13.
9. In cell H13, enter another IF function to test whether the value in cell D13 is equal to an empty text string. If true, return an empty text string; otherwise, calculate the value of the price of the item multiplied by the number of items ordered.
10. Copy the formula in the range E13:F13 to the range E13:F20. Use AutoFill to copy the formula from cell H13 into the range H13:H20.
11. In cell H22, calculate the sum of the values in the range H13:H20.
12. In cell H23, calculate the sales tax equal to the total cost of the items ordered multiplied by the sales tax rate in cell G10.
13. In cell H24, calculate the shipping cost of the order by inserting an IF function that tests whether the value of cell B16 is an empty text string. If it is, return the value 0; otherwise, use a lookup function to return the shipping cost for the indicated shipping method.
14. In cell H25, insert an IF function that tests whether the value of cell H22 is greater than 250 (the minimum order needed to qualify for free shipping). If it is, return a value of cell H24; otherwise, return a value of 0.
15. In cell H27, calculate the total cost of the order by summing the values in the range H22:H24 and subtracting the value of cell H25.
16. Complete the customer order by adding the following items: Item **t7829** and Qty **1**; Item **led7331** and Qty **3**; and Item **sb8502** and Qty **5**.
17. Confirm that your worksheet correctly calculates the total cost, and then save your workbook.
18. Save the workbook as **Cairn Order Form** in the location specified by your instructor.
19. Create a blank order form sheet by deleting the input values in the ranges B4:B6, B9:B13, B16, D13:D16, G13:G16. Do *not* delete any formulas in the worksheet. Confirm that the worksheet does not show any error values when the input data is removed.
20. Save and close the workbook.

EXCEL

MODULE 4

Analyzing and Charting Financial Data

Preparing a Business Plan

OBJECTIVES

Session 4.1
- Use the PMT function to calculate a loan payment
- Create an embedded pie chart
- Apply styles to a chart
- Add data labels to a pie chart
- Format a chart legend
- Create a clustered column chart
- Create a stacked column chart

Session 4.2
- Create a line chart
- Create a combination chart
- Format chart elements
- Modify the chart's data source
- Create a histogram and Pareto chart
- Add sparklines to a worksheet
- Format cells with data bars

Case | *Backspace Gear*

Haywood Mills is the owner of Backspace Gear, a new business in Kennewick, Washington, that manufactures backpacks for work, school, travel, and camping. Haywood has been working from a small shop making specialized packs for friends and acquaintances and wants to expand his business and his customer base. To do that, he needs to secure a business loan. Part of the process of securing a loan is to present a business plan that shows the current state of the market and offers projections about the company's future growth and earnings potential.

In addition to financial tables and calculations, Haywood's presentation needs to include charts and graphics that show a visual picture of the company's current financial status and where he hopes to take it. Haywood has asked for your help in creating the Excel charts and financial calculations he needs to include in his business plan.

STARTING DATA FILES

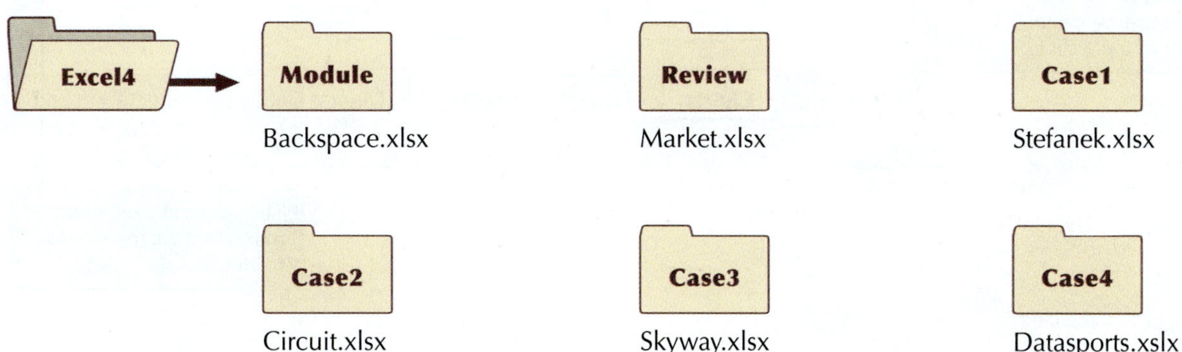

Session 4.1 Visual Overview:

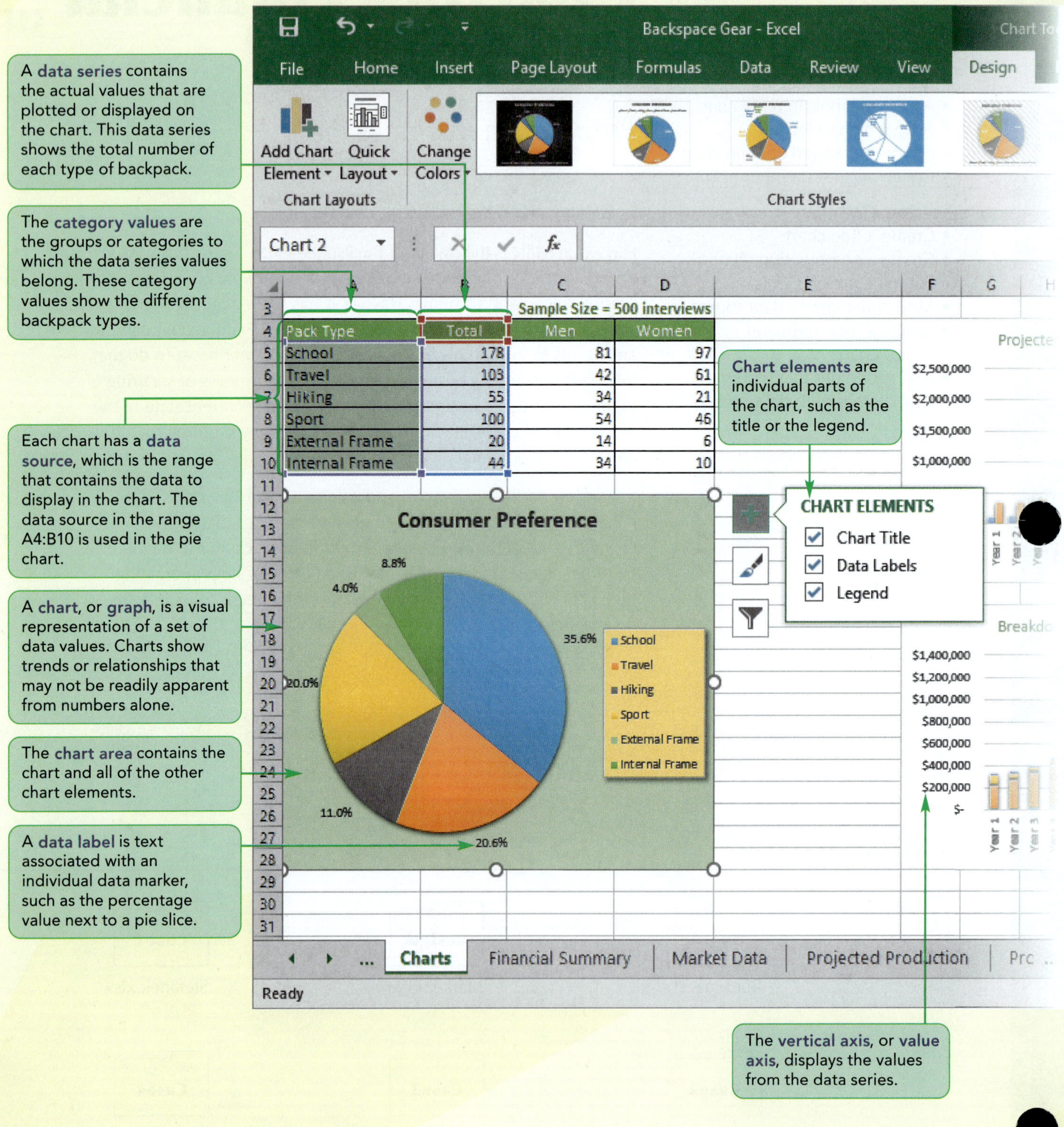
A data series contains the actual values that are plotted or displayed on the chart. This data series shows the total number of each type of backpack.
The category values are the groups or categories to which the data series values belong. These category values show the different backpack types.
Each chart has a data source, which is the range that contains the data to display in the chart. The data source in the range A4:B10 is used in the pie chart.
A chart, or graph, is a visual representation of a set of data values. Charts show trends or relationships that may not be readily apparent from numbers alone.
The chart area contains the chart and all of the other chart elements.
A data label is text associated with an individual data marker, such as the percentage value next to a pie slice.
Chart elements are individual parts of the chart, such as the title or the legend.
The vertical axis, or value axis, displays the values from the data series.
Backspace Gear - Excel
File
Home
Insert
Page Layout
Formulas
Data
Review
View
Design
Add Chart Element
Quick Layout
Change Colors
Chart Layouts
Chart Styles
Chart 2
Sample Size = 500 interviews
Pack Type
Total
Men
Women
School 178 81 97
Travel 103 42 61
Hiking 55 34 21
Sport 100 54 46
External Frame 20 14 6
Internal Frame 44 34 10
Consumer Preference
8.8%
4.0%
35.6%
20.0%
11.0%
20.6%
School
Travel
Hiking
Sport
External Frame
Internal Frame
CHART ELEMENTS
Chart Title
Data Labels
Legend
$2,500,000
$2,000,000
$1,500,000
$1,000,000
$1,400,000
$1,200,000
$1,000,000
$800,000
$600,000
$400,000
$200,000
$-
Charts
Financial Summary
Market Data
Projected Production
Ready

Chart Elements

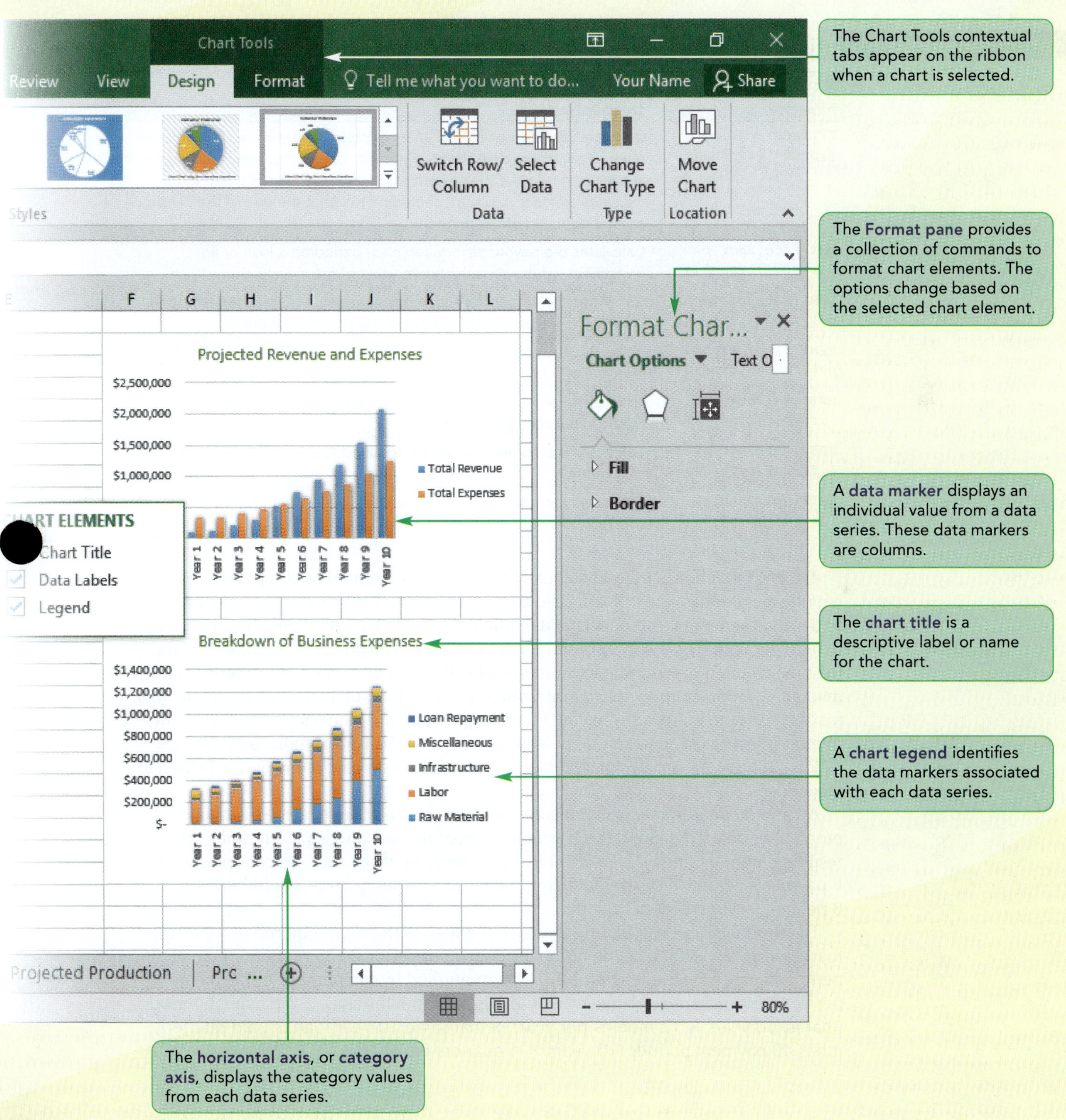

Chart Tools
Review
View
Design
Format
Tell me what you want to do...
Your Name
Share
Switch Row/ Column
Select Data
Change Chart Type
Move Chart
Styles
Data
Type
Location
Format Char...
Chart Options
Text O
Fill
Border
Projected Revenue and Expenses
$2,500,000
$2,000,000
$1,500,000
$1,000,000
Total Revenue
Total Expenses
Year 1
Year 2
Year 3
Year 4
Year 5
Year 6
Year 7
Year 8
Year 9
Year 10
CHART ELEMENTS
Chart Title
Data Labels
Legend
Breakdown of Business Expenses
$1,400,000
$1,200,000
$1,000,000
$800,000
$600,000
$400,000
$200,000
$-
Loan Repayment
Miscellaneous
Infrastructure
Labor
Raw Material
Projected Production
Prc ...
80%
The Chart Tools contextual tabs appear on the ribbon when a chart is selected.
The Format pane provides a collection of commands to format chart elements. The options change based on the selected chart element.
A data marker displays an individual value from a data series. These data markers are columns.
The chart title is a descriptive label or name for the chart.
A chart legend identifies the data markers associated with each data series.
The horizontal axis, or category axis, displays the category values from each data series.

Introduction to Financial Functions

Financial functions are used to analyze loans, investments, and business statistics. Figure 4-1 lists some of the many Excel financial functions that are often used in business applications.

Figure 4-1 Financial functions for loans and investments

Function	Description
FV(*rate*,*nper*,*pmt* [,*pv*=0][,*type*=0])	Calculates the future value of an investment, where *rate* is the interest rate per period, *nper* is the total number of periods, *pmt* is the payment in each period, *pv* is the present value of the investment, and *type* indicates whether payments should be made at the end of the period (0) or the beginning of the period (1)
PMT(*rate*,*nper*,*pv* [,*fv*=0][,*type*=0])	Calculates the payments required each period on a loan or an investment, where *fv* is the future value of the investment
IPMT(*rate*,*per*,*nper*, *pv*[,*fv*=0][,*type*=0])	Calculates the amount of a loan payment devoted to paying the loan interest, where *per* is the number of the payment period
PPMT(*rate*,*per*,*nper*, *pv*[,*fv*=0][,*type*=0])	Calculates the amount of a loan payment devoted to paying off the principal of a loan
PV(*rate*,*nper*,*pmt* [,*fv*=0][,*type*=0])	Calculates the present value of a loan or an investment based on periodic, constant payments
NPER(*rate*,*pmt*,*pv* [,*fv*=0][,*type*=0])	Calculates the number of periods required to pay off a loan or an investment
RATE(*nper*,*pmt*,*pv* [,*fv*=0][,*type*=0])	Calculates the interest rate of a loan or an investment based on periodic, constant payments

The **PMT function** is used to calculate the payments required to completely repay a mortgage or other type of loan. Before you can use the PMT function, you need to understand some of the concepts and definitions associated with loans. The cost of a loan to the borrower is largely based on three factors—the principal, the interest, and the time required to repay the loan. **Principal** is the amount of the loan. **Interest** is the amount added to the principal by the lender. You can think of interest as a kind of "user fee" because the borrower is paying for the right to use the lender's money. Generally, interest is expressed at an annual percentage rate, or APR. For example, an 8 percent APR means that the annual interest rate on the loan is 8 percent of the amount owed to the lender.

An annual interest rate is divided by the number of payments per year (often monthly or quarterly). So, if the 8 percent annual interest rate is paid monthly, the resulting monthly interest rate is 1/12 of 8 percent, or about 0.67 percent per month. If payments are made quarterly, then the interest rate per quarter would be 1/4 of 8 percent, or 2 percent per quarter.

The third factor in calculating the cost of a loan is the time required to repay the loan, which is specified as the number of payment periods. The number of payment periods is based on the length of the loan multiplied by the number of payments per year. For example, a 10-year loan that is paid monthly has 120 payment periods (that is, 10 years × 12 months per year). If that same 10-year loan is paid quarterly, it has 40 payment periods (10 years × 4 quarters per year).

Using the PMT Function

To calculate the costs associated with a loan, such as the one that Haywood needs to fund the startup costs for Backspace Gear, you need the following information:

- The annual interest rate
- The number of payment periods per year
- The length of the loan in terms of the total number of payment periods
- The amount being borrowed
- When loan payments are due

The PMT function uses this information to calculate the payment required in each period to pay back the loan. The PMT function syntax is

```
PMT(rate,nper,pv[,fv=0][,type=0])
```

where `rate` is the interest rate for each payment period, `nper` is the total number of payment periods required to repay the loan, and `pv` is the present value of the loan or the amount that needs to be borrowed. The PMT function has two optional values—`fv` and `type`. The `fv` value is the future value of the loan. Because the intent with most loans is to repay them completely, the future value is equal to 0 by default. The `type` value specifies when the interest is charged on the loan, either at the end of the payment period (`type=0`), which is the default, or at the beginning of the payment period (`type=1`).

For example, you can use the PMT function to calculate the monthly payments required to repay a car loan of $15,000 over a five-year period at an annual interest rate of 9 percent. The `rate`, or interest rate per period value, is equal to 9 percent divided by 12 monthly payments, or 0.75 percent per month. The `nper`, or total number of payments value, is equal to 12 × 5 (12 monthly payments over five years) or 60 payments. The `pv`, or present value of the loan, is 15,000. In this case, because the loan will be repaid completely and payments will be made at the end of the month, you can accept the defaults for the `fv` and `type` values. The resulting PMT function can be written as

```
PMT(0.09/12, 5*12, 15000)
```

returning the value –311.38, or a monthly loan payment of $311.38. The PMT function returns a negative value because the monthly loan payments are treated as an expense to the borrower.

Rather than entering the argument values directly in the PMT function, you should include the loan terms in worksheet cells that are referenced in the function. This makes it clear what values are being used in the loan calculation. It also makes it easier to perform a what-if analysis exploring other loan options.

Haywood wants to borrow $150,000 to help start up his new business at a 6 percent annual interest rate. He plans to repay the loan in 10 years with monthly payments. You will calculate the amount of his monthly loan payment.

To enter the terms of the loan:

1. Open the **Backspace** workbook located in the **Excel4 > Module** folder included with your Data Files, and then save the workbook as **Backspace Gear** in the location specified by your instructor.
2. In the Documentation sheet, enter your name in cell B3 and the date in cell B4.
3. Go to the **Business Loan** worksheet. You'll use this worksheet to calculate the monthly payments that will be due on Haywood's loan.
4. In cell **B4**, enter **$150,000** as the loan amount.
5. In cell **B5**, enter **6.00%** as the annual interest rate.

6. In cell **B6**, enter **12** as the number of payments per year, indicating that the loan will be repaid monthly.
7. In cell **B7**, enter the formula **=B5/B6** to calculate the interest rate per period. In this case, the 6 percent interest rate is divided by 12 payments per year, returning a monthly interest rate of 0.50 percent.
8. In cell **B8**, enter **10** as the number of years in the loan.
9. In cell **B9**, enter **=B6*B8** to multiply the number of payments per year by the number of years in the loan, returning a value of 120 payments needed to repay the loan.

Next, you will use the PMT function to calculate the monthly payment needed to repay the loan in 10 years.

To calculate the monthly payment:

1. Select cell **B11** to make it the active cell. You will enter the PMT function in this cell.
2. On the ribbon, click the **Formulas** tab.
3. In the Function Library group, click the **Financial** button, and then scroll down and click **PMT** in the list of financial functions. The Function Arguments dialog box opens.
4. With the insertion point in the Rate box, click cell **B7** in the worksheet to enter the reference to the cell with the interest rate per month.
5. Click in the **Nper** box, and then click cell **B9** in the worksheet to enter the reference to the cell with the total number of monthly payments required to repay the loan.
6. Click in the **Pv** box, and then click cell **B4** in the worksheet to enter the reference to the cell with the present value of the loan. See Figure 4-2.

TIP

For the Rate argument, you must enter the interest rate per payment, not the annual interest rate.

Figure 4-2 Function Arguments dialog box for the PMT function

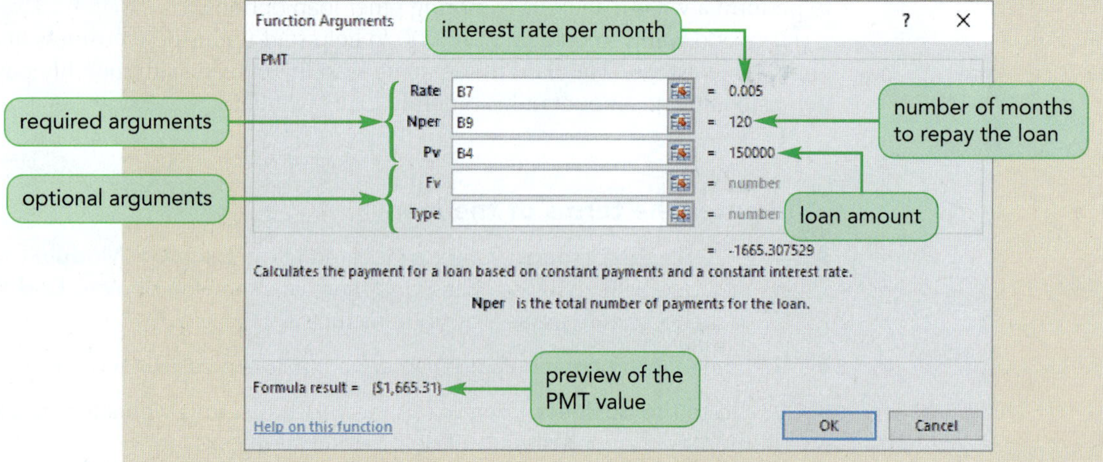

7. Click the **OK** button. The monthly payment amount ($1,665.31) appears in cell B11. The number is displayed in parentheses and in a red font to indicate a negative value because that is the payment that Backspace Gear must make rather than income it receives.
8. In cell B12, enter the formula **=B6*B11** to multiply the number of payments per year by the monthly payment amount, calculating the total payments for the entire year. The annual payments would be ($19,983.69), shown as a negative number to indicate money being paid out.
9. Select cell **B11**. The calculations for the business loan are complete. See Figure 4-3.

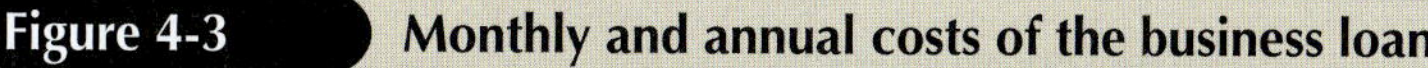

Figure 4-3 Monthly and annual costs of the business loan

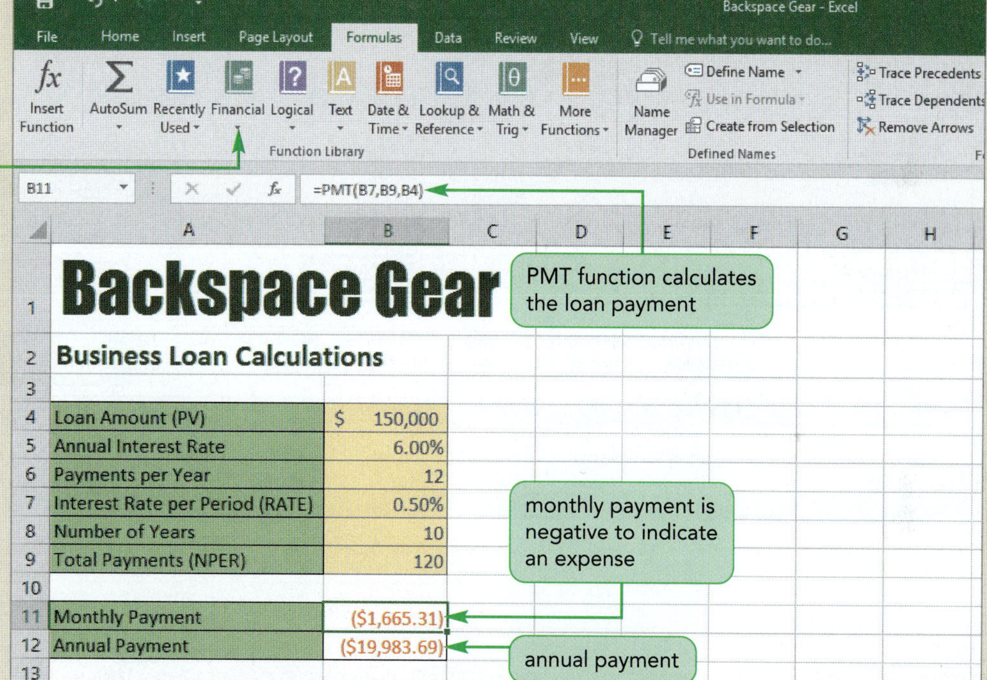

Haywood wants to see the financial impact of taking out a larger loan.

10. In cell **B4**, change the loan amount to **250,000**. With a loan of that size, the monthly payment increases to $2,775.51, and the annual total increases to $33,306.15.

    Although a larger loan might help the business get off the ground, Haywood does not want the company to take such a large debt.

11. In cell **B4**, return the loan amount to **150,000**.

Based on your analysis, Backspace Gear would spend about $20,000 a year repaying the $150,000 business loan over the next 10 years. Haywood wants this information included in the Projected Cash Flow worksheet, which estimates Backspace Gear's annual revenue, expenses, and cash flow for the first 10 years of its operation. You will enter that amount as an expense for each year, completing the projected cash flow calculations.

To enter the loan repayment amount in the cash flow projection:

1. Go to the **Projected Cash Flow** worksheet, and review the estimated annual revenue, expenses, and cash flow for the next decade.
2. In cell **B20**, enter **20,000** as the projected yearly amount of the loan repayment. Because the projected cash flow is a rough estimate of the projected income and expenses, it is not necessary to include the exact dollar-and-cents cost of the loan.
3. Copy the annual loan payment in cell **B20** into the range **C20:K20** to enter the projected annual loan payment in each year of the cash flow projections. See Figure 4-4.

Figure 4-4 **Completed Projected Cash Flow worksheet**

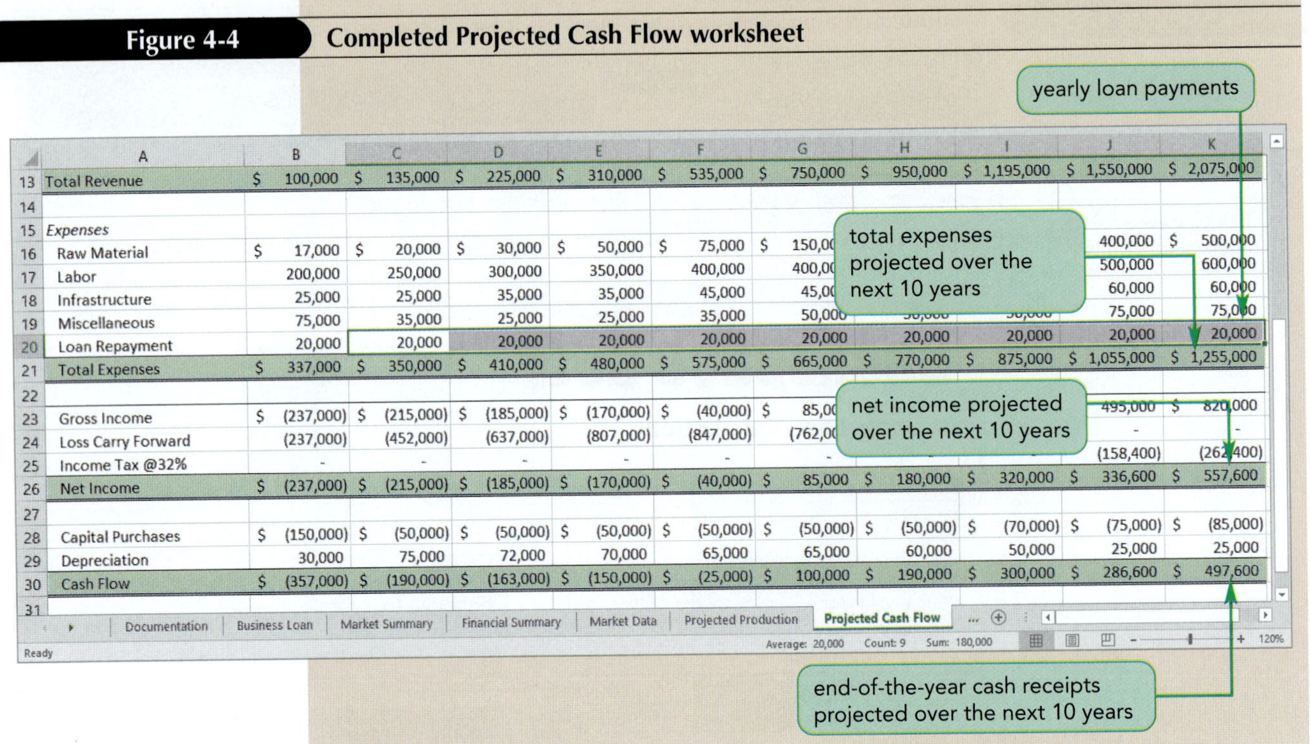

	A	B	C	D	E	F	G	H	I	J	K
13	Total Revenue	$ 100,000	$ 135,000	$ 225,000	$ 310,000	$ 535,000	$ 750,000	$ 950,000	$ 1,195,000	$ 1,550,000	$ 2,075,000
14											
15	*Expenses*										
16	Raw Material	$ 17,000	$ 20,000	$ 30,000	$ 50,000	$ 75,000	$ 150,0	[illegible]	[illegible]	400,000	$ 500,000
17	Labor	200,000	250,000	300,000	350,000	400,000	400,0	[illegible]	[illegible]	500,000	600,000
18	Infrastructure	25,000	25,000	35,000	35,000	45,000	45,0	[illegible]	[illegible]	60,000	60,000
19	Miscellaneous	75,000	35,000	25,000	25,000	35,000	50,000	[illegible]	[illegible]	75,000	75,000
20	Loan Repayment	20,000	20,000	20,000	20,000	20,000	20,000	20,000	20,000	20,000	20,000
21	Total Expenses	$ 337,000	$ 350,000	$ 410,000	$ 480,000	$ 575,000	$ 665,000	$ 770,000	$ 875,000	$ 1,055,000	$ 1,255,000
22											
23	Gross Income	$ (237,000)	$ (215,000)	$ (185,000)	$ (170,000)	$ (40,000)	$ 85,0	[illegible]	[illegible]	495,000	$ 820,000
24	Loss Carry Forward	(237,000)	(452,000)	(637,000)	(807,000)	(847,000)	(762,0	[illegible]	[illegible]	-	-
25	Income Tax @32%	-	-	-	-	-	-	[illegible]	[illegible]	(158,400)	(262,400)
26	Net Income	$ (237,000)	$ (215,000)	$ (185,000)	$ (170,000)	$ (40,000)	$ 85,000	$ 180,000	$ 320,000	$ 336,600	$ 557,600
27											
28	Capital Purchases	$ (150,000)	$ (50,000)	$ (50,000)	$ (50,000)	$ (50,000)	$ (50,000)	$ (50,000)	$ (70,000)	$ (75,000)	$ (85,000)
29	Depreciation	30,000	75,000	72,000	70,000	65,000	65,000	60,000	50,000	25,000	25,000
30	Cash Flow	$ (357,000)	$ (190,000)	$ (163,000)	$ (150,000)	$ (25,000)	$ 100,000	$ 190,000	$ 300,000	$ 286,600	$ 497,600
31											

After including the projected annual loan payments, the Projected Cash Flow worksheet shows that Backspace Gear's projected net income at the end of the tenth year would be about $560,000, assuming all of the other projections are accurate. Based on these figures, the company should have almost $500,000 in cash at that time.

INSIGHT

Using Functions to Manage Personal Finances

Excel has many financial functions to manage personal finances. The following list can help you determine which function to use for the most common personal finance calculations:

- To determine how much an investment will be worth after a series of monthly payments at some future time, use the FV (future value) function.
- To determine how much you have to spend each month to repay a loan or mortgage within a set period of time, use the PMT (payment) function.
- To determine how much of your monthly loan payment is used to pay the interest, use the IPMT (interest payment) function.
- To determine how much of your monthly loan payment is used for repaying the principal, use the PPMT (principal payment) function.
- To determine the largest loan or mortgage you can afford given a set monthly payment, use the PV (present value) function.
- To determine how long it will take to pay off a loan with constant monthly payments, use the NPER (number of periods) function.

For most loan and investment calculations, you need to enter the annual interest rate divided by the number of times the interest is compounded during the year. If interest is compounded monthly, divide the annual interest rate by 12; if interest is compounded quarterly, divide the annual rate by four. You must also convert the length of the loan or investment into the number of payments per year. If you will make payments monthly, multiply the number of years of the loan or investment by 12.

Now that you have calculated the cost of the business loan and determined its impact on future cash flows, your next task is to summarize Haywood's business proposal for Backspace Gear. An effective tool for summarizing complex scientific and financial data is a chart.

Getting Started with Excel Charts

Charts show trends or relationships in data that are easier to see than by looking at the actual numbers. Creating a chart is a several-step process that involves choosing the chart type, selecting the data to display in the chart, and formatting the chart's appearance.

REFERENCE

Creating a Chart

- Select the range containing the data you want to chart.
- On the Insert tab, in the Charts group, click the Recommended Charts button or a button representing the general chart type, and then click the chart you want to create (or click the Quick Analysis button, click the Charts category, and then click the chart you want to create).
- On the Chart Tools Design tab, in the Location group, click the Move Chart button, select whether to embed the chart in a worksheet or place it in a chart sheet, and then click the OK button.

Excel provides 59 types of charts organized into the 10 categories described in Figure 4-5. Within each chart category are chart variations called **chart subtypes**. You can also design your own custom chart types to meet the specific needs of your reports and projects.

Figure 4-5 **Excel chart types and subtypes**

Chart Category	Description	Chart Subtypes
Column or Bar	Compares values from different categories. Values are indicated by the height of the columns or the length of a bar.	2-D Column, 3-D Column, 2-D Bar, 3-D Bar
Hierarchy	Displays data that is organized into a hierarchy of categories where the size of the groups is based on a number.	Treemap, Sunburst
Waterfall or Stock	Displays financial cash flow values or stock market data.	Waterfall, Stock
Line	Compares values from different categories. Values are indicated by the height of the lines. Often used to show trends and changes over time.	2-D Line, 3-D Line, 2-D Area, 3-D Area
Statistic	Displays a chart summarizing the distribution of values from a sample population.	Histogram, Pareto, Box and Whisker
Pie	Compares relative values of different categories to the whole. Values are indicated by the areas of the pie slices.	2-D Pie, 3-D Pie, Doughnut
X Y (Scatter)	Shows the patterns or relationship between two or more sets of values. Often used in scientific studies and statistical analyses.	Scatter, Bubble
Surface or Radar	Compares three sets of values in a three-dimensional chart.	Surface, Radar
Combo	Combines two or more chart types to make the data easy to visualize, especially when the data is widely varied.	Clustered Column-Line, Clustered Column-Line on Secondary Axis, Stacked Area-Clustered Column
PivotChart	Creates a chart summarizing data from a PivotTable.	*none*

Sometimes more than one chart can be used for the same data. Figure 4-6 presents the same labor cost data displayed as a line chart, a bar chart, and column charts. The column charts are shown with both a 2-D subtype that has two-dimensional, or flat, columns and a 3-D subtype that gives the illusion of three-dimensional columns. The various charts and chart subtypes are better suited for different data. You should choose the one that makes the data easiest to interpret.

Figure 4-6 **Same data displayed as different chart types**

Line chart

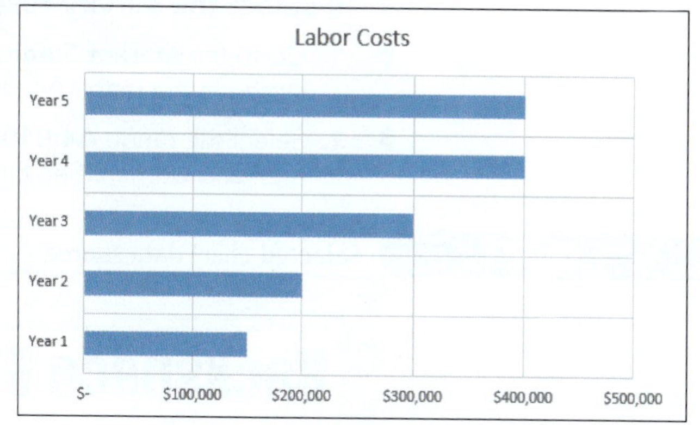

Bar chart

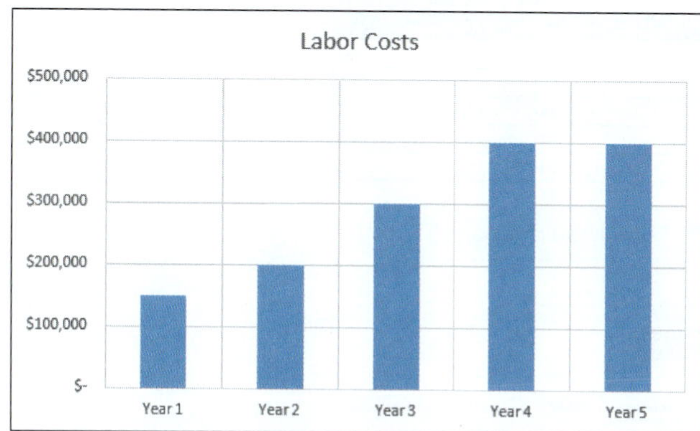

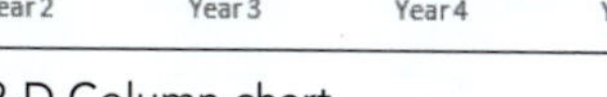

2-D Column chart

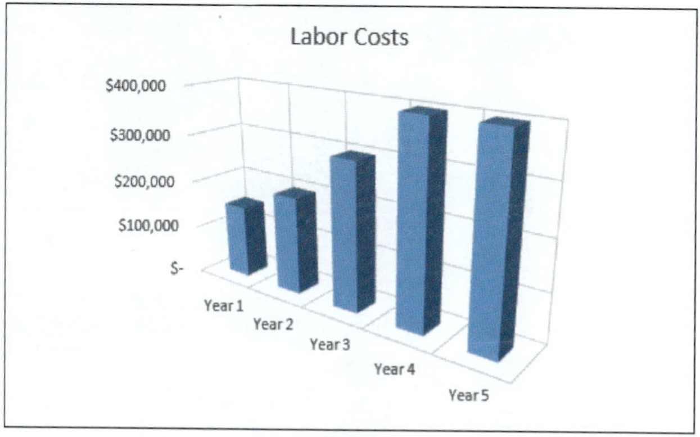

3-D Column chart

Creating a Pie Chart

> **TIP**
>
> Don't include row or column totals in the pie chart data because Excel will treat those totals as another category.

The first chart you will create is a **pie chart**, which is a chart in the shape of a circle divided into slices like a pie. Each slice represents a single value from a data series. Larger data values are represented with bigger pie slices. The relative sizes of the slices let you visually compare the data values and see how much each contributes to the whole. Pie charts are most effective with six or fewer slices and when each slice is large enough to view easily.

Selecting the Data Source

The data displayed in a chart comes from the chart's data source, which includes one or more data series and a series of category values. A data series contains the actual values that are plotted on the chart, whereas the category values provide descriptive labels for each data series and are used to group those series. Category values are usually located in the first column or first row of the data source. The data series are usually placed in subsequent columns or rows. However, you can select category and data values from anywhere within a workbook.

Over the next 10 years Backspace Gear plans to produce school, travel, hiking, sport, external frame (for camping), and internal frame (for camping) packs. Haywood conducted a consumer survey of 500 adults to determine which of these will likely have the greatest demand in the Washington area. You will use the survey results, which Hayward entered in the Market Summary worksheet, as the data source for a pie chart.

To select the survey results as the pie chart's data source:

1. Go to the **Market Summary** worksheet. A summary of the survey results is stored in the range A4:D10.
2. Select the range **A4:B10** containing the overall results of the survey for both men and women. See Figure 4-7.

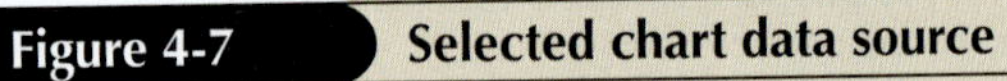

Figure 4-7 Selected chart data source

Backspace Gear

Market Summary

Sample Size = 500 interviews

Pack Type	Total	Men	Women
School	178	81	97
Travel	103	42	61
Hiking	55	34	21
Sport	100	54	46
Ext. Frame	20	14	6
Int. Frame	44	34	10

The selected data source covers two columns. The category values are located in the first column, and the data series that you will chart is located in the second column. When the selected range is taller than it is wide, Excel assumes that the category values and data series are laid out in columns. Conversely, a data source that is wider than it is tall is assumed to have the category values and data series laid out in rows. Note that the first row in this selected data source contains labels that identify the category values (Pack Type) and the data series name (Total).

Charting with the Quick Analysis Tool

After you select a data source, the Quick Analysis tool appears. The Charts category contains a list of chart types that are often appropriate for the selected data source. For the market survey results, a pie chart provides the best way to compare the preferences for the six types of packs that Backspace Gear plans to produce. You will use the Quick Analysis tool to generate the pie chart for Haywood.

TIP

You can also insert a chart by selecting a chart type in the Charts group on the Insert tab.

To create a pie chart with the Quick Analysis tool:

1. With the range A4:B10 still selected, click the **Quick Analysis** button in the lower-right corner of the selected range (or press the **Ctrl+Q** keys) to open the Quick Analysis tool.
2. Click the **Charts** category. The chart types you will most likely want to use with the selected data source are listed. See Figure 4-8.

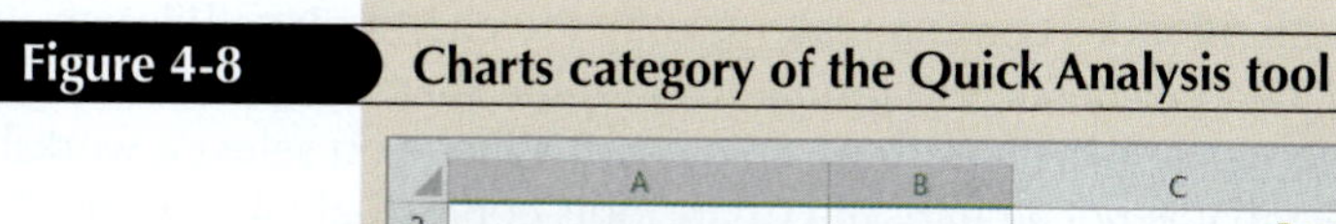

Figure 4-8 **Charts category of the Quick Analysis tool**

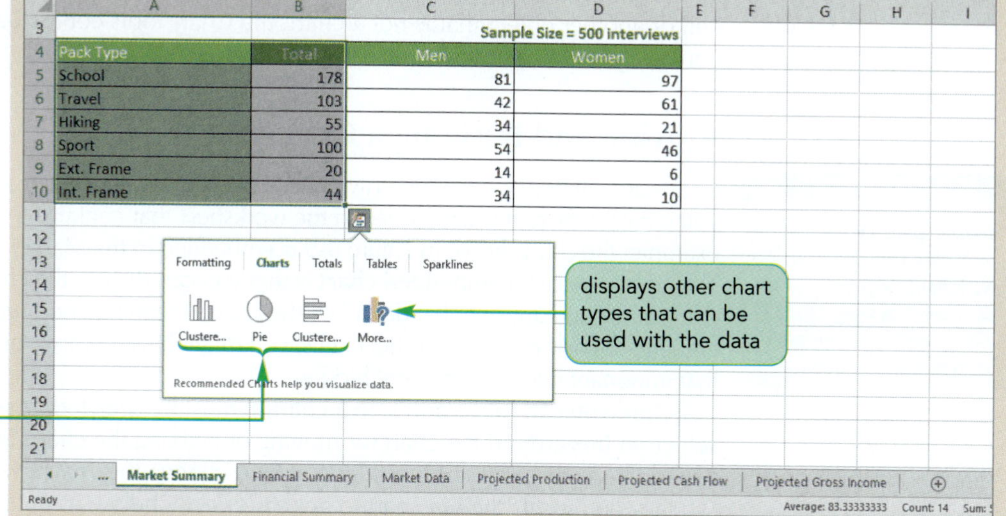

3. Click **Pie**. A pie chart appears in the Market Summary worksheet. Each slice is a different size based on its value in the data series. The biggest slice represents the 178 people in the survey who selected a school pack as their most likely purchase from Backspace Gear. The smallest slice of the pie represents the 20 individuals who selected the external frame pack. See Figure 4-9.

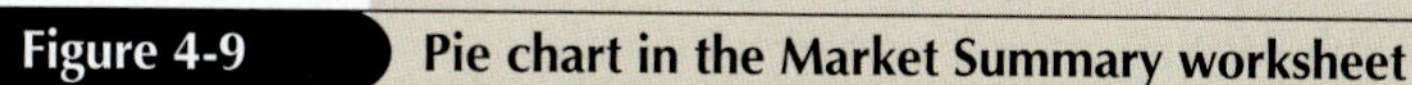

Figure 4-9 **Pie chart in the Market Summary worksheet**

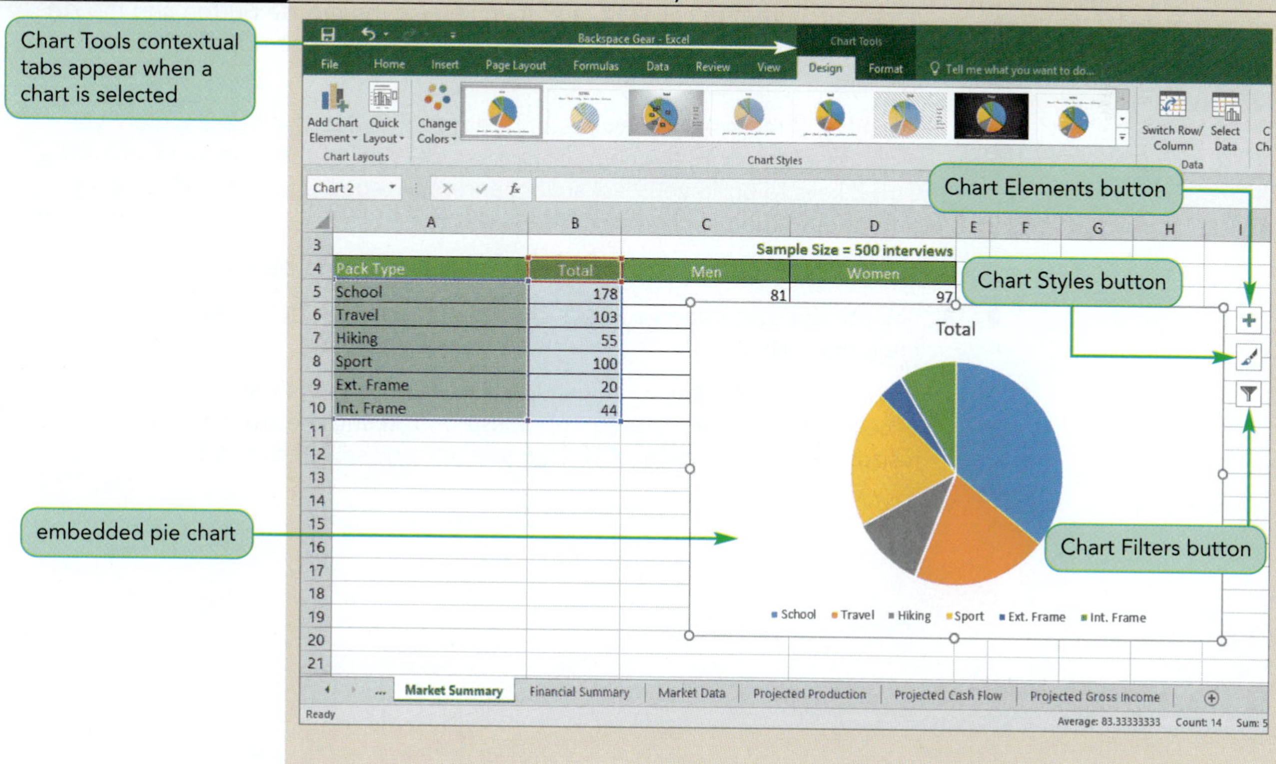

When you create or select a chart, two Chart Tools contextual tabs appear on the ribbon. The Design tab provides commands to specify the chart's overall design. The Format tab supplies the tools needed to format the graphic shapes found in the chart, such as the chart's border or the slices from a pie chart. When you select a worksheet cell or another object that is not a chart, the Chart Tools contextual tabs disappear until you reselect the chart.

Moving and Resizing a Chart

TIP

You can print an embedded chart with its worksheet, or you can print only the selected embedded chart without its worksheet.

Charts are either placed in their own chart sheets or embedded in a worksheet. When you create a chart, it is embedded in the worksheet that contains the data source. For example, the chart shown in Figure 4-9 is embedded in the Market Summary worksheet. The advantage of an **embedded chart** is that you can display the chart alongside its data source and any text that describes the chart's meaning and purpose. Because an embedded chart covers worksheet cells, you might have to move or resize the chart so that important information is not hidden.

Before you can move or resize a chart, it must be selected. A selected chart has a **selection box** around the chart for moving or resizing the chart. **Sizing handles**, which appear along the edges of the selection box, change the chart's width and height.

Haywood wants the pie chart to appear directly below its data source in the Market Summary worksheet. You will move and resize the chart to fit this location.

To move and resize the survey results pie chart:

1. Point to an empty area of the selected chart. The pointer changes to ✥ and "Chart Area" appears in a ScreenTip.
2. Hold down the **Alt** key, drag the chart until its upper-left corner snaps to the upper-left corner of cell **A12**, and then release the mouse button and the **Alt** key. The upper-left corner of the chart is aligned with the upper-left corner of cell A12.

   Be sure to drag the chart from an empty part of the chart area so the entire chart moves, not just chart elements within the chart.

   Trouble? If the pie chart resizes or does not move to the new location, you probably didn't drag the chart from an empty part of the chart area. Press the Ctrl+Z keys to undo your last action, and then repeat Steps 1 and 2, being sure to drag the pie chart from the chart area.

   The chart moves to a new location, but it still needs to be resized.
3. Point to the sizing handle in the lower-right corner of the selection box until the pointer changes to ⤡.
4. Hold down the **Alt** key, drag the sizing handle up to the lower-right corner of cell **D26**, and then release the mouse button and the **Alt** key. The chart resizes to cover the range A12:D26 and remains selected. See Figure 4-10.

Figure 4-10 Moved and resized pie chart

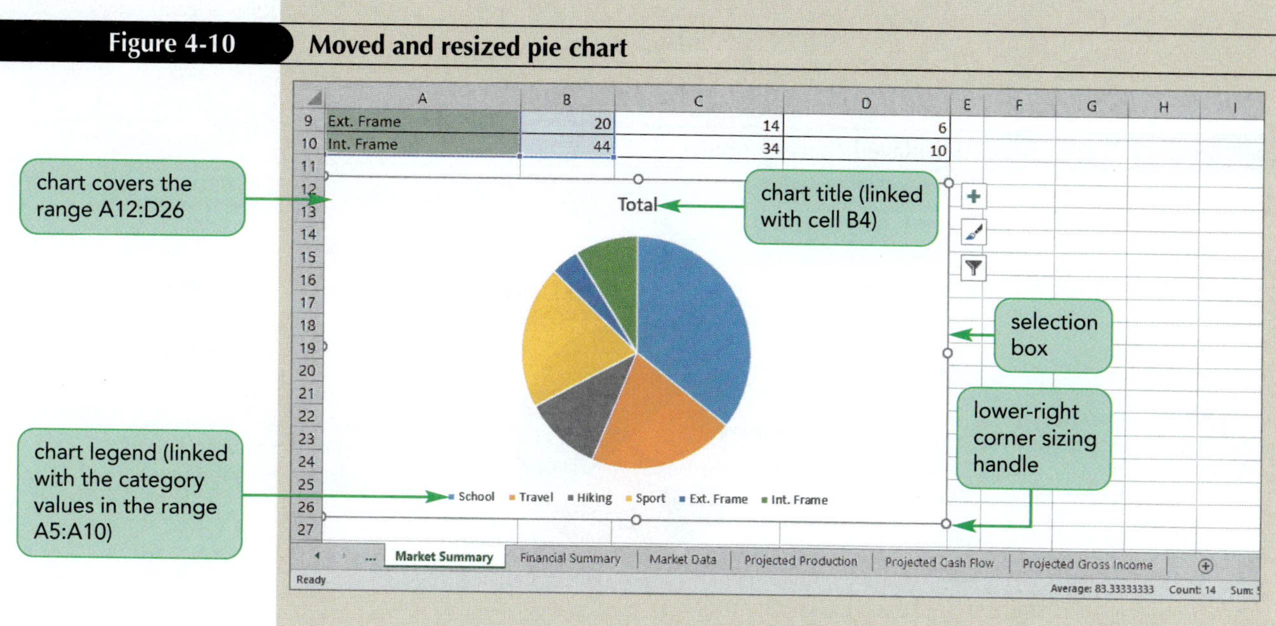

Note that three buttons appear to the right of the selected chart: the Chart Elements button [+], the Chart Styles button, and the Chart Filters button. You will use these to modify the chart's appearance.

Working with Chart Elements

Every chart contains elements that can be formatted individually. For example, a pie chart has three elements—the chart title, the chart legend identifying each pie slice, and data labels that provide a data value associated with each slice. The Chart Elements button [+] that appears to the right of the selected chart lists the elements that can be added or removed from the chart. When you add or remove a chart element, the other elements resize to fit in the unoccupied space in the chart. Live Preview shows how changing an element will affect the chart's appearance so that you can experiment with different formats before applying them.

Haywood doesn't want the pie chart to include a title because the text in cell B4 and the data in the range A5:B10 sufficiently explain the chart's purpose. However, he does want to display the data values next to the pie slices. You will remove the chart title element and add the data labels element.

TIP

You can also add and remove chart elements with the Add Chart Element button in the Chart Layouts group on the Chart Tools Design tab.

To remove the chart title and add data labels:

1. With the pie chart still selected, click the **Chart Elements** button [+]. A menu of chart elements that are available for the pie chart opens. As the checkmarks indicate, only the chart title and the chart legend are displayed in the pie chart.
2. Click the **Chart Title** check box to deselect it. The chart title is removed from the pie chart, and the chart elements resize to fill the space.
3. Point to the **Data Labels** check box. Live Preview shows how the chart will look when the data labels show a count of responses within each category.

4. Click the **Data Labels** check box to select it. The data labels are added to the chart. See Figure 4-11.

Figure 4-11 **Displayed chart elements**

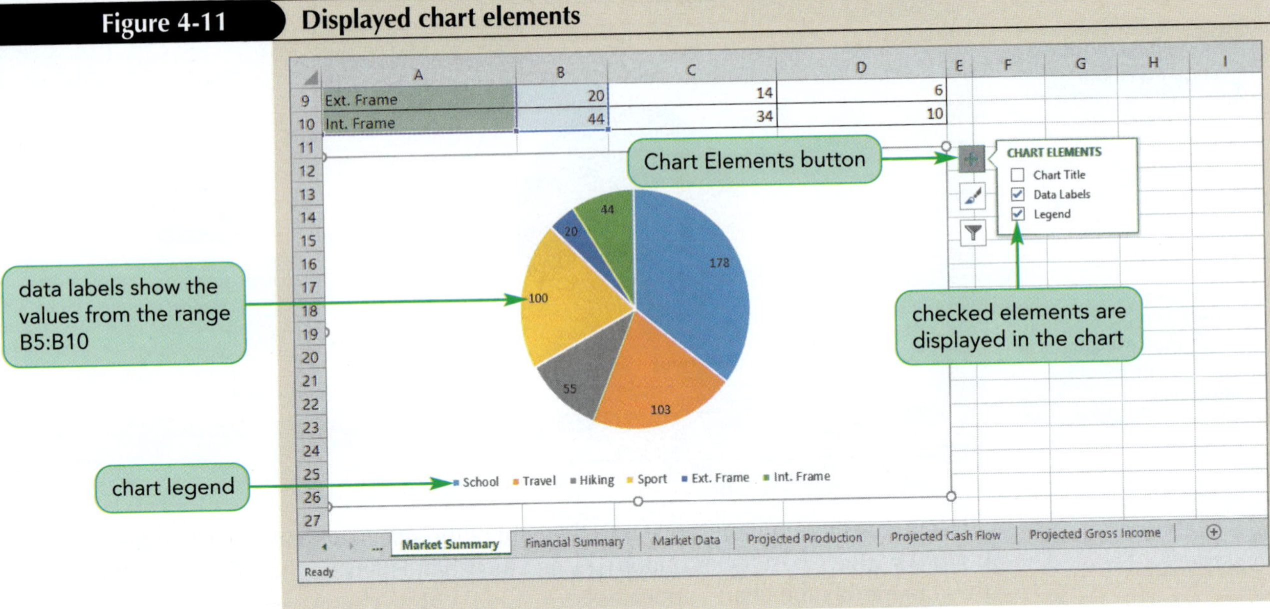

Choosing a Chart Style

Chart elements can be formatted individually or as a group using one of the many built-in Excel chart styles. In the pie chart you just created, the format of the chart title, the location of the legend, and the colors of the pie slices are all part of the default pie chart style. You can quickly change the appearance of a chart by selecting a different style from the Chart Styles gallery. Live Preview shows how a chart style will affect the chart.

Haywood wants the pie slices to have a raised, three-dimensional look. You will explore different chart styles to find a style that best fulfills his request.

To choose a different chart style for the backpack production pie chart:

TIP

You can also select a chart style from the Chart Styles gallery in the Chart Styles group on the Chart Tools Design tab.

1. Click the **Chart Styles** button next to the selected pie chart. The Chart Styles gallery opens.
2. Point to different styles in the gallery. Live Preview shows the impact of each chart style on the pie chart's appearance.
3. Scroll to the bottom of the gallery, and then click the **Style 12** chart style. The chart style is applied to the pie chart. See Figure 4-12.

Figure 4-12 Chart Styles gallery

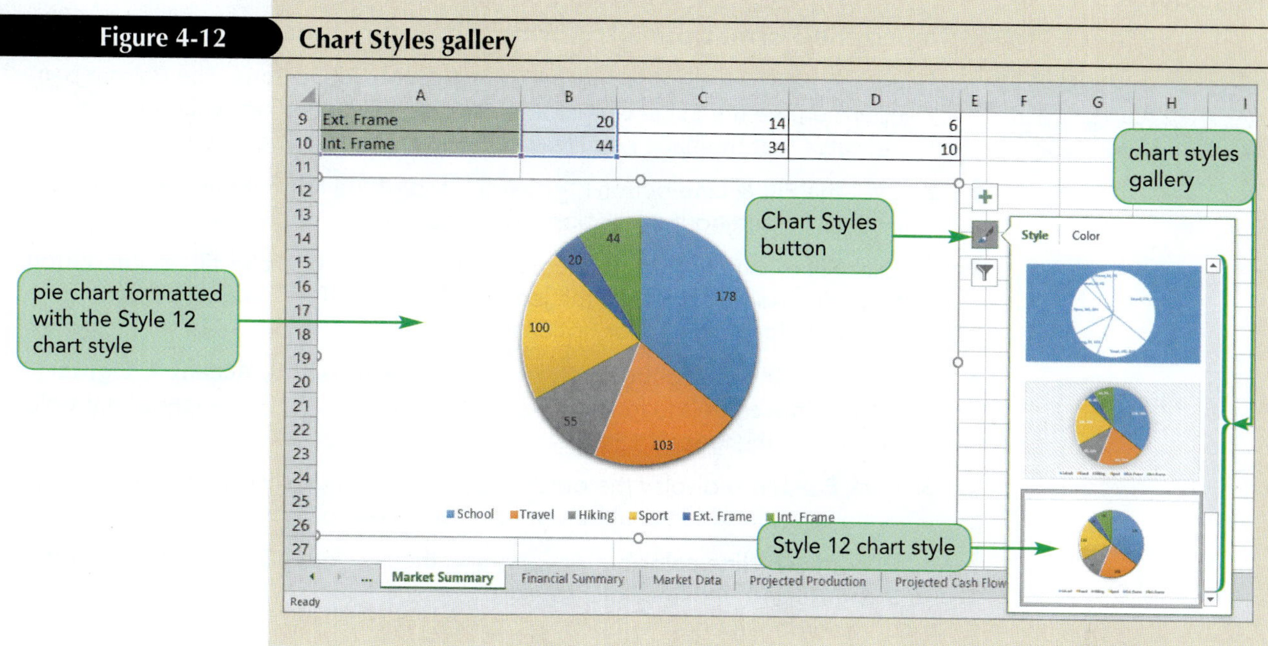

Formatting a Chart Legend

You can fine-tune a chart style by formatting individual chart elements. Using the Chart Elements button, you can open a submenu for each element that includes formatting options, such as the element's location within the chart. You can also open a Format pane, which has more options for formatting the selected chart element.

The default location for the pie chart legend is alongside the chart's bottom edge. Haywood thinks the chart would look better if the legend were aligned with the right edge of the chart. You'll make that change.

To format the pie chart legend:

1. With the pie chart still selected, click the **Chart Elements** button [+].
2. Point to **Legend** in the Chart Elements menu, and then click the **right arrow** icon next to the Legend entry, displaying a submenu of formatting options for that chart element.
3. Point to **Left** to see a Live Preview of the pie chart with the legend aligned along the left side of the chart area.
4. Click **Right** to place the legend along the right side of the chart area. The pie shifts to the left to make room for the legend.

The Chart Elements button also provides access to the Format pane, which has more design options for the selected chart element. Haywood wants you to add a drop shadow to the legend similar to the pie chart's drop shadow, change the fill color to a light gold, and add a light gray border. You'll use the Format pane to make these changes.

TIP

You can also double-click any chart element to open its Format pane.

To use the Format pane to format the chart legend:

1. On the Legend submenu for the entry, click **More Options**. The Format pane opens on the right side of the workbook window. The Format Legend title indicates that the pane contains options relating to chart legend styles.
2. Click the **Fill & Line** button near the top of the Format pane to display options for setting the fill color and border style of the legend.
3. Click **Fill** to expand the fill options, and then click the **Solid fill** option button to apply a solid fill color to the legend. Color and Transparency options appear below the fill color options.
4. Click the **Fill Color** button, and then click the **Gold, Accent 4, Lighter 40%** theme color (the fourth color in the eighth column) to apply a light gold fill color to the legend.
5. Click **Border** to display the border options, and then click the **Solid line** option button. Additional border options appear below the border options.
6. Click the **Outline color** button, and then click the **Gray - 50%, Accent 3, Lighter 40%** theme color (the fourth color in the seventh column) to add a gray border around the legend.
7. At the top of the Format Legend pane, click the **Effects** button to display options for special visual effects.
8. Click **Shadow** to display the shadow options, and then next to the **Presets** button, click to display the Shadow gallery. See Figure 4-13.

Figure 4-13 Formatted chart legend

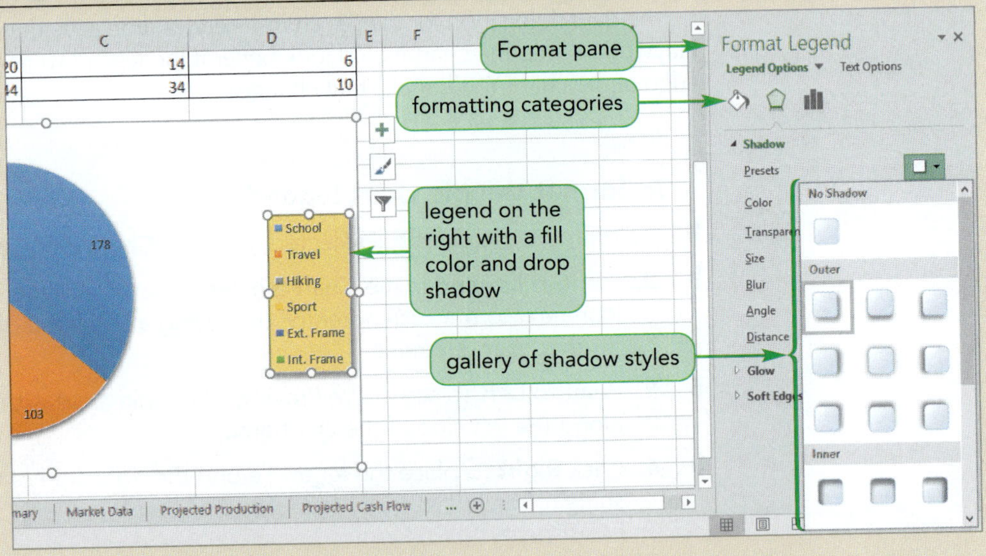

9. Click the **Offset Diagonal Bottom Right** button in the first row and first column to apply the drop shadow effect to the legend.

Formatting Pie Chart Labels

You can modify the content and appearance of data labels, selecting what the labels contain as well as where the labels are positioned. Data labels are placed where they best fit to keep the chart nicely proportioned, but you can change their location. From the Format pane, you can center the labels on the pie slices, place them outside of the slices, or set them as data callouts with each label placed in a text bubble and connected to its slice with a callout line. You can also change the text and number styles used in the data labels. You can also drag and drop individual data labels, placing them anywhere within the chart. When a data label is placed far from its pie slice, a **leader line** is added to connect the data label to its pie slice.

The pie chart data labels display the number of potential customers interested in each pack type, but this information also appears on the worksheet directly above the chart. Haywood wants to include data labels that add new information to the chart—in this case, the percentage that each pack type received in the survey. You'll change the label options.

TIP

You can also format chart elements using the formatting buttons on the Home tab or on the Chart Tools Format tab.

To display percentage labels in the pie chart:

1. At the top of the Format pane, click the **Legend Options** arrow to display a menu of chart elements, and then click **Series "Total" Data Labels** to display the formatting options for data labels. The title of the Format pane changes to Format Data Labels and includes formatting options for data labels. Selection boxes appear around every data label in the pie chart.
2. Near the top of the Format Data Labels pane, click the **Label Options** button, and then click **Label Options**, if necessary, to display the options for the label contents and position. Data labels can contain series names, category names, values, and percentages.
3. Click the **Percentage** check box to add the percentage associated with each pie slice to the pie chart.
4. Click the **Value** check box to deselect it, removing the data series values from the data labels and showing only the percentages. For example, the pie chart shows that 35 percent of the survey responders indicated a willingness to buy Backspace Gear packs designed for school use.
5. Click the **Outside End** option button to move the labels outside of the pie slices. The labels are easier to read in this location.
6. Scroll down the Format pane, and then click **Number** to show the number formatting options for the data labels.
7. Click the **Category** box to display the number formats, and then click **Percentage**.
8. In the Decimal places box, select **2**, type **1**, and then press the **Enter** key. The percentages are displayed with one decimal place. See Figure 4-14.

Figure 4-14 Formatted data labels

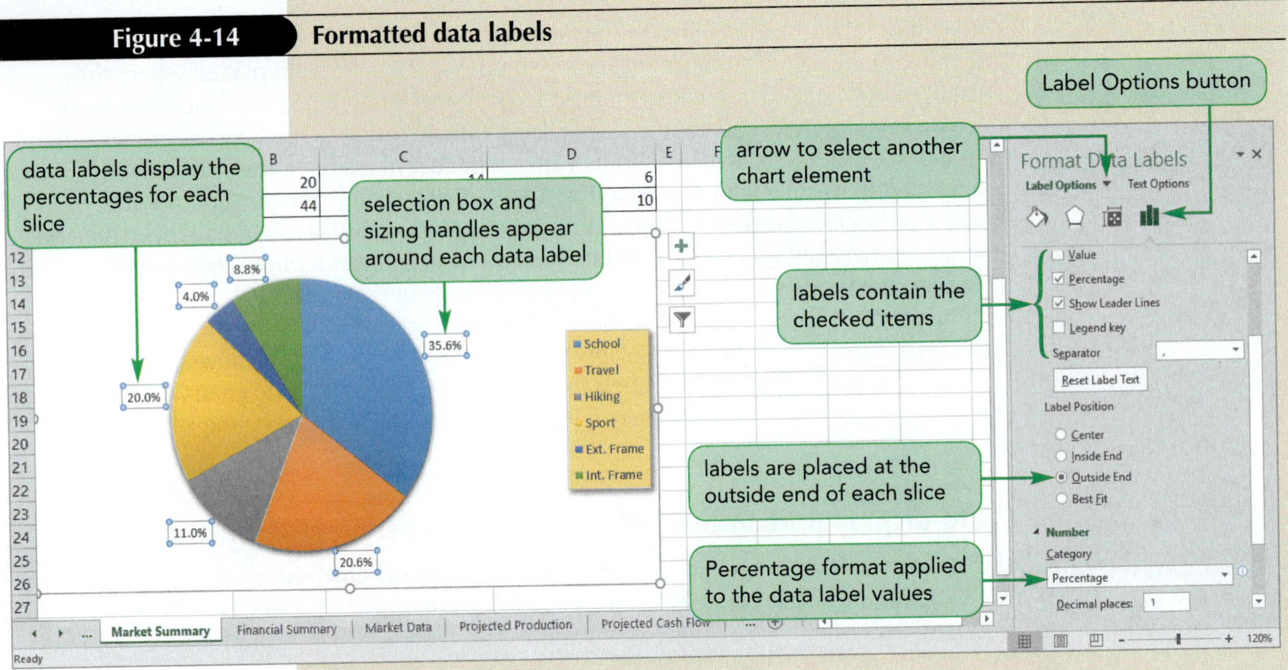

Changing the Pie Slice Colors

A pie slice is an example of a data marker representing a single data value from a data series. You can format the appearance of individual data markers to make them stand out from the others. Pie slice colors should be as distinct as possible to avoid confusion. Depending on the printer quality or the monitor resolution, it might be difficult to distinguish between similarly colored slices. If data labels are displayed within the slice, you also need enough contrast between the slice color and the data label color to make the text readable.

Haywood is concerned that the dark blue color of the Ext. Frame slice will be too dark when printed. He wants you to change it to a light shade of green.

To change the color of a pie slice:

1. Click any pie slice to select all of the slices in the pie chart.
2. Click the **Ext. Frame** slice, which is the darker blue slice that represents 4.0% percent of the pie. Only that slice is selected, as you can see from the sizing handles that appear at each corner of the slice.
3. On the ribbon, click the **Home** tab.
4. In the Font group, click the **Fill Color button arrow**, and then click the **Green, Accent 6, Lighter 40%** theme color (the fourth color in the last column) of the gallery. The pie slice changes to a light green, and the chart legend automatically updates to reflect that change.

You can also change the colors of all the pie slices by clicking the Chart Styles button next to the selected chart, clicking the Color heading, and then selecting a color scheme.

INSIGHT

Exploding a Pie Chart

Pie slices do not need to be fixed within the pie. An **exploded pie chart** moves one slice away from the others as if someone were taking the piece away from the pie. Exploded pie charts are useful for emphasizing one category above all of the others. For example, to emphasize the fact that Backspace Gear will be producing more school packs than any other type of pack, you could explode that single slice, moving it away from the other slices.

To explode a pie slice, first click the pie to select all of the slices, and then click the single slice you want to move. Make sure that a selection box appears around only that slice. Drag the slice away from the pie to offset it from the others. You can explode multiple slices by selecting each slice in turn and dragging them away. To explode all of the slices, select the entire pie and drag the pointer away from the pie's center. Each slice will be exploded and separated from the others. Although you can explode more than one slice, the resulting pie chart is rarely effective as a visual aid to the reader.

Formatting the Chart Area

The chart's background, which is called the chart area, can also be formatted using fill colors, border styles, and special effects such as drop shadows and blurred edges. The chart area fill color used in the pie chart is white, which blends in with the worksheet background. Haywood wants you to change the fill color to a medium green to match the worksheet's color scheme and to make the chart stand out better.

TIP

You can select any chart element using the Chart Elements box in the Current Selection group on the Chart Tools Format tab.

To change the chart area color:

1. Click a blank area within the chart, not containing either a pie slice or the chart legend. The chart area is selected, which you can verify because the Format pane title changes to "Format Chart Area."
2. On the Home tab, in the Font group, click the **Fill Color button arrow**, and then click the **Green, Accent 6, Lighter 60%** theme color (the last color in the third row). The chart area fill color is now medium green. See Figure 4-15.

Figure 4-15 Chart area fill color

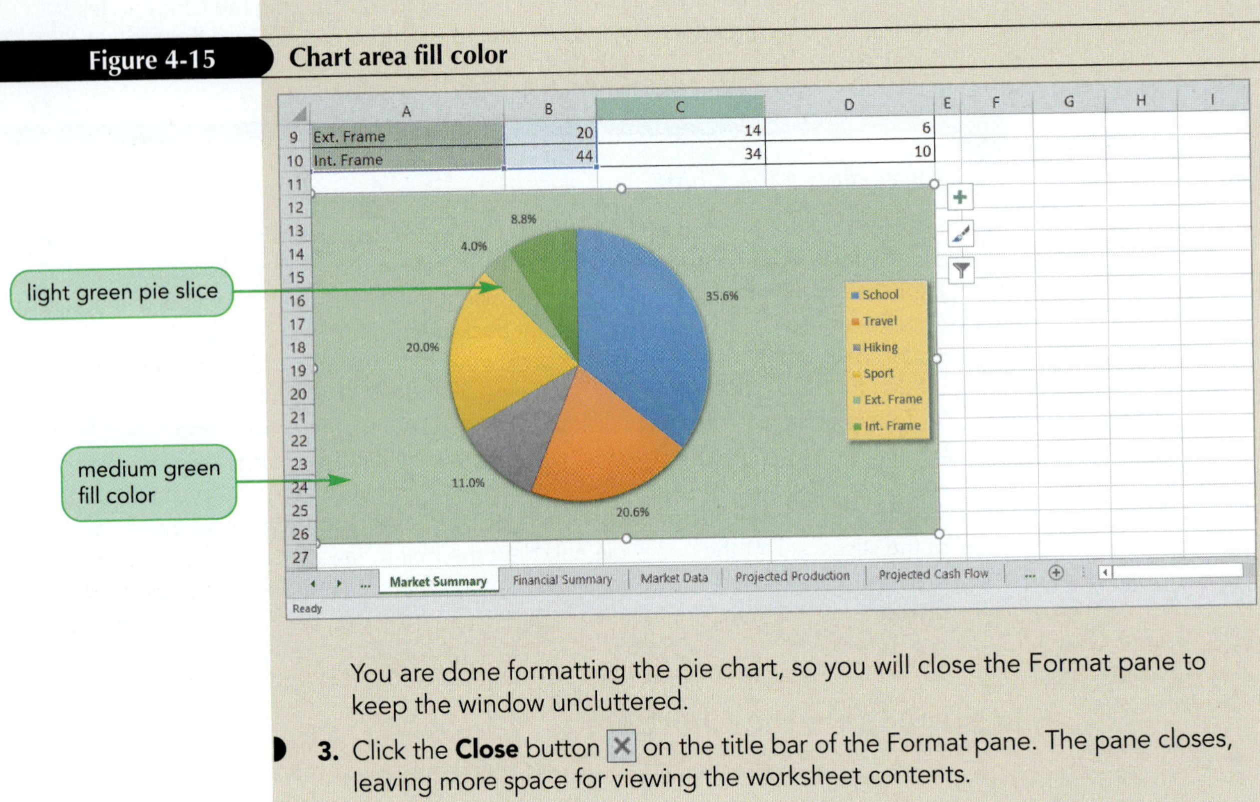

You are done formatting the pie chart, so you will close the Format pane to keep the window uncluttered.

3. Click the **Close** button on the title bar of the Format pane. The pane closes, leaving more space for viewing the worksheet contents.

Performing What-If Analyses with Charts

Because a chart is linked to its data source, any changes in the data source values will be automatically reflected in the chart. For the Market Survey pie chart, the chart title is linked to the text in cell B4, the size of the pie slices is based on the production goals in the range B5:B10, and the category names are linked to the category values in the range A5:A10. Any changes to these cells affect the chart's content and appearance. This makes charts a powerful tool for data exploration and what-if analysis.

Haywood wants to see how the pie chart would change if the survey results were updated.

To apply a what-if analysis to the pie chart:

1. In cell **B7**, enter **100** to change the number of individuals who expressed an interest in Backspace hiking packs to 100. The Hiking slice automatically increases in size, changing from 11 percent to 18.3 percent. The size of the remaining slices and their percentages are reduced to compensate.
2. In cell **B7**, restore the value to **55**. The pie slices return to their initial sizes, and the percentages return to their initial values.

   Haywood wants you to change the category names "Ext. Frame" and "Int. Frame" to "External Frame" and "Internal Frame."

3. Click cell **A9**, and then change the text to **External Frame**.

4. Click cell **A10**, and then change the text to **Internal Frame**. The legend text in the pie chart automatically changes to reflect the new text.

Another type of what-if analysis is to **filter** the data source, which limits the data to fewer values. For example, the pie chart shows the survey results for all six types of packs that Backspace Gear will manufacture, but you can filter the pie chart so that it shows only the packs you select.

Haywood wants you to filter the pie chart so that it compares only the packs used for school, travel, and sport.

To filter the pie chart to show only three packs:

1. Click the pie chart to select it.
2. Click the **Chart Filters** button next to the chart to open a menu listing the chart categories.
3. Click the **Hiking**, **External Frame**, and **Internal Frame** check boxes to deselect them, leaving only the School, Travel, and Sport check boxes selected.
4. At the bottom of the Chart Filters menu, click the **Apply** button. Excel filters the chart, showing only the three marked pack types. After filtering the data, the chart shows that 46.7 percent of the survey respondents would buy the School pack out of the choice of school, travel, and sport packs. See Figure 4-16.

Figure 4-16 Filtered pie chart

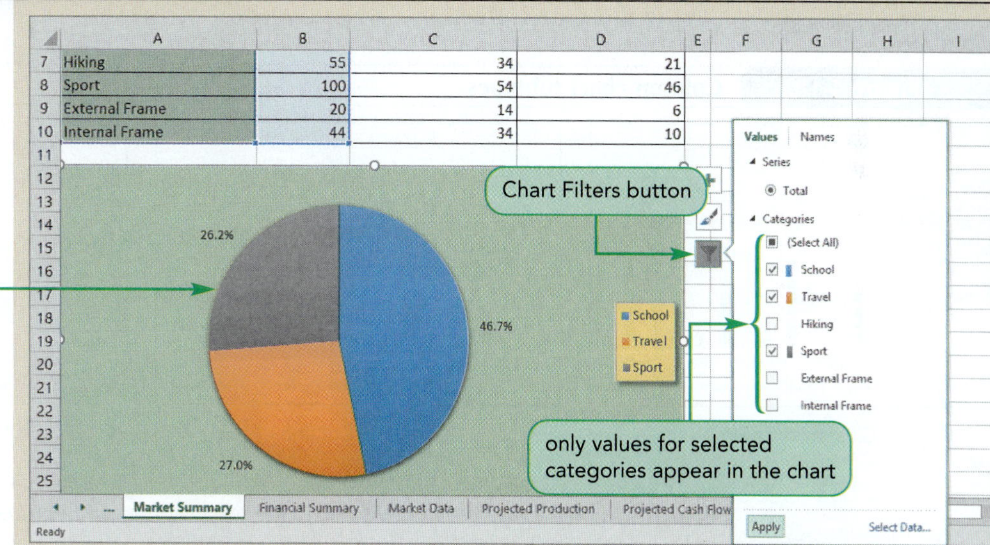

5. In the Categories section of the Chart Filters menu, double-click the **Select All** check box to reselect all six pack types.
6. Click the **Apply** button to update the chart's appearance.
7. Press the **Esc** key to close the menu, leaving the chart selected.

The pie chart is complete. Next you'll create column charts to examine Haywood's proposed production schedule for the next years.

Creating a Column Chart

A **column chart** displays data values as columns with the height of each column based on the data value. A column chart turned on its side is called a **bar chart**, with the length of the bar determined by the data value. It is better to use column and bar charts than pie charts when the number of categories is large or the data values are close in value. Figure 4-17 displays the same data as a pie chart and a column chart. As you can see, it's difficult to determine which pie slice is biggest and by how much. It is much simpler to make those comparisons in a column or bar chart.

Figure 4-17 **Data displayed as a pie chart and a column chart**

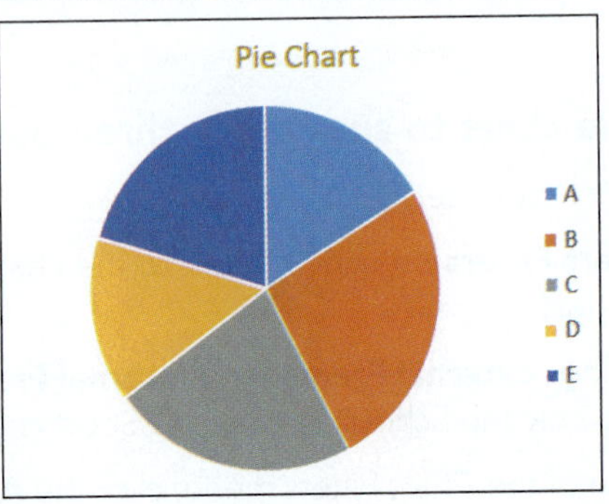

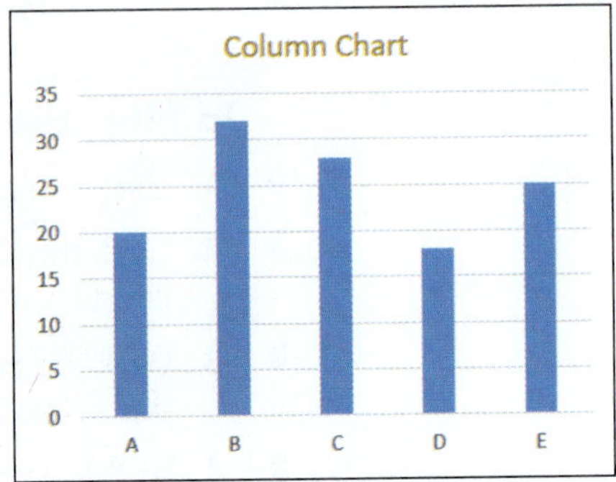

Comparing Column Chart Subtypes

Unlike pie charts, which can show only one data series, column and bar charts can display multiple data series. Figure 4-18 shows three examples of column charts in which four data series named School, Travel, Hiking, and Sport are plotted against one category series (Years).

Figure 4-18 **Column chart subtypes**

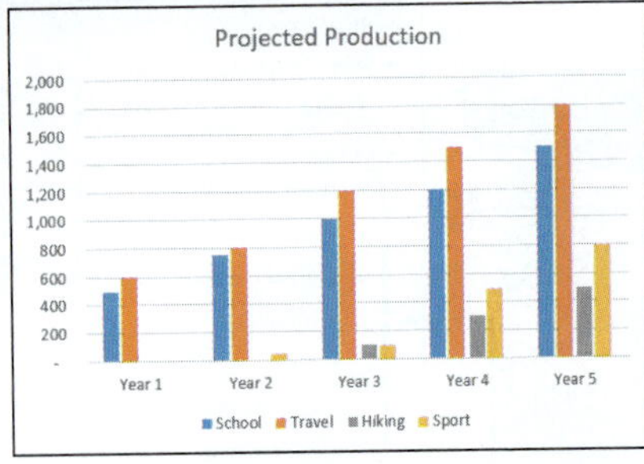

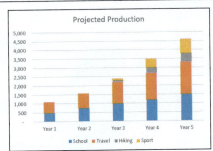

Clustered Column

Stacked Column

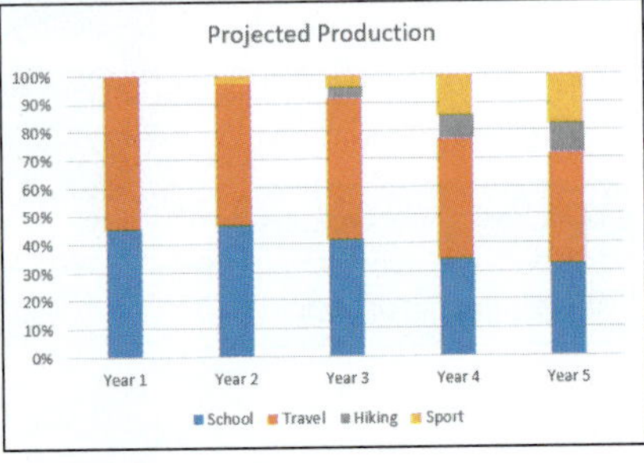

100% Stacked Column

The **clustered column chart** displays the data series in separate columns side by side so that you can compare the relative heights of the columns in the three series. The clustered column chart in Figure 4-18 compares the number of packs produced in year 1 through year 5. Note that Backspace Gear mostly produces school and travel packs in years 1 through 3 with hiking and sport packs production increasing in years 4 and 5.

The **stacked column chart** places the data series values within combined columns showing how much is contributed by each series. The stacked column chart in Figure 4-18 gives information on the total number of packs produced each year and how each year's production is split among the four types of packs.

Finally, the **100% stacked column chart** makes the same comparison as the stacked column chart except that the stacked sections are expressed as percentages. As you can see from the 100% stacked column chart in Figure 4-18, school and travel packs account for about 100% of the production in year 1 and steadily decline to 70% of the production in year 5 as Backspace Gear introduces hiking and sport packs.

Creating a Clustered Column Chart

The process for creating a column chart is the same as for creating a pie chart: selecting the data source and choosing a chart type and subtype. After the chart is embedded in the worksheet, you can move and resize the chart as well as change the chart's design, layout, and format.

Haywood wants his business plan to show the projected revenue and expenses for Backspace Gear's first 10 years. Because this requires comparing the data series values, you will create a clustered column chart.

To create a clustered column chart showing projected revenue and expenses:

1. Go to the **Projected Cash Flow** worksheet.
2. Select the nonadjacent range **A4:K4,A13:K13,A21:K21** containing the Year categories in row 4, the Total Revenue data series in row 13, and the Total Expenses data series in row 21. Because you selected a nonadjacent range, the Quick Analysis tool is not available.
3. On the ribbon, click the **Insert** tab. The Charts group contains buttons for inserting different types of charts.
4. In the Charts group, click the **Recommended Charts** button. The Insert Chart dialog box opens with a gallery of suggested charts for the selected data. See Figure 4-19.

TIP

You can also open the Insert Chart dialog box to see the chart types recommended for the selected data source.

Figure 4-19 Recommended Charts tab in the Insert Chart dialog box

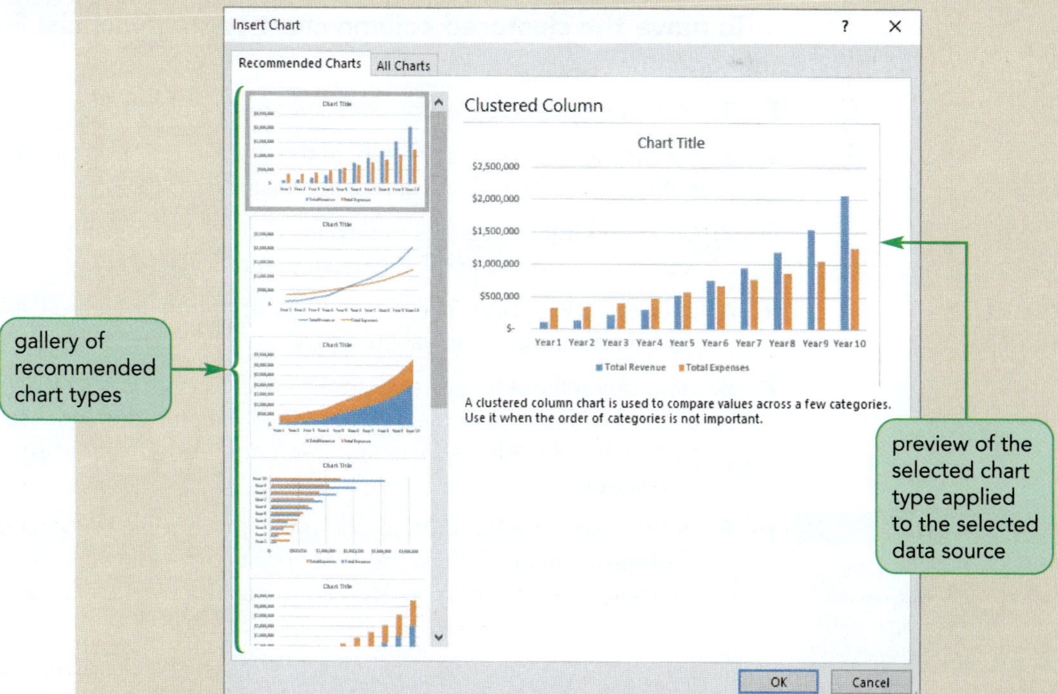

5. Make sure the **Clustered Column** chart is selected, and then click the **OK** button. The clustered column chart is embedded in the Projected Cash Flow worksheet.
6. Click the **Chart Styles** button next to the selected column chart.

7. In the Style gallery, scroll down, and click the **Style 14** chart style to format the columns with drop shadows.
8. Click the **Chart Styles** button again to close the Style gallery.

Next, you will move the chart to a new location in the workbook.

INSIGHT

Changing a Chart Type

After creating a chart, you can easily switch the chart to a different chart type without having to recreate the chart from scratch. For example, if the data in a column chart would be more effective presented as a line chart, you can change its chart type rather than creating a new chart. Clicking the Change Chart Type button in the Type group on the Chart Tools Design tab opens a dialog box similar to the Insert Chart dialog box, from which you can select a new chart type.

Moving a Chart to a Different Worksheet

The Move Chart dialog box provides options for moving charts between worksheets and chart sheets. You can also cut and paste a chart from one location to another. Haywood wants you to move the column chart of the projected revenue and expenses to the Financial Summary worksheet.

To move the clustered column chart to the Financial Summary worksheet:

1. Make sure the clustered column chart is still selected.
2. On the Chart Tools Design tab, in the Location group, click the **Move Chart** button. The Move Chart dialog box opens.
3. Click the **Object in** arrow to display a list of the worksheets in the active workbook, and then click **Financial Summary**.
4. Click the **OK** button. The chart moves from the Projected Cash Flow worksheet to the Financial Summary worksheet and remains selected.
5. Hold down the **Alt** key as you drag the chart so that its upper-left corner is aligned with the upper-left corner of cell **E4**, and then release the mouse button and the **Alt** key. The upper-left corner of the chart snaps to the worksheet.
6. Hold down the **Alt** key as you drag the lower-right sizing handle of the clustered column chart to the lower-right corner of cell **L20**, and then release the mouse button and the **Alt** key. The chart now covers the range E4:L20.

TIP

To set an exact chart size, enter the height and width values in the Size group on the Chart Tools Format tab.

The revenue and expenses chart shows that Backspace Gear will produce little revenue during its first few years as it establishes itself and its customer base. It is only during year 6 that the revenue will outpace the expenses. After that, Haywood anticipates that the company's revenue will increase rapidly while expenses grow at a more moderate pace.

Editing a Chart Title

When a chart has a single data series, the name of the data series is used for the chart title. When a chart has more than one data series, *Chart Title* appears as the temporary title of the chart. You can replace the placeholder text with a more descriptive title and add a custom format.

Haywood wants you to change the chart title of the clustered column chart to "Projected Revenue and Expenses."

To change the title of the column chart:

1. At the top of the column chart, click **Chart Title** to select the placeholder text.
2. Type **Projected Revenue and Expenses** as the new title, and then press the **Enter** key. The new title is entered into the chart, and the chart title element remains selected.
3. On the ribbon, click the **Home** tab, and then use the buttons in the Font group to remove the bold from the chart title, change the font to **Calibri Light**, change the font size to **16** points, and then change the font color to the **Green, Accent 6, Darker 25%** theme color. See Figure 4-20.

Figure 4-20 Clustered column chart

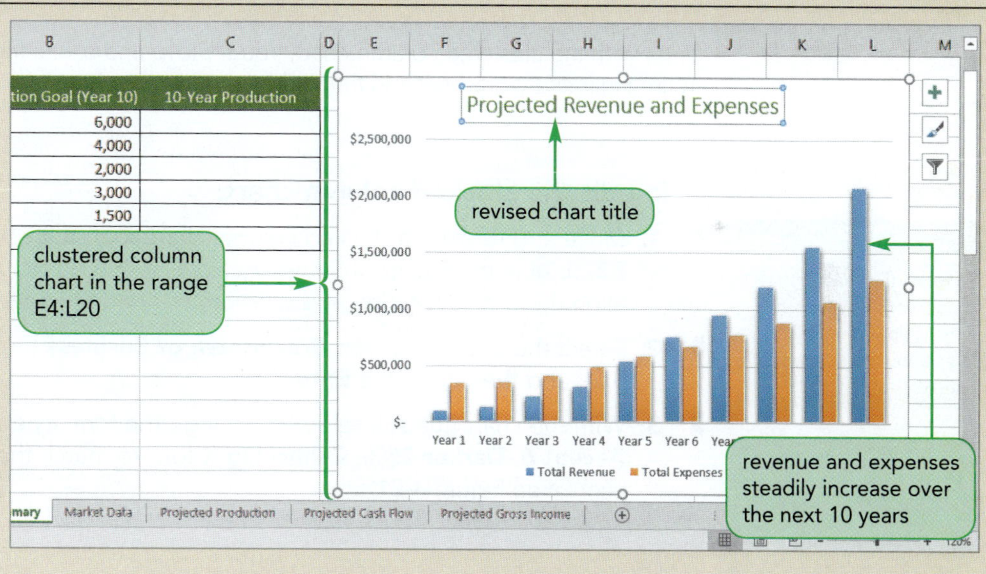

Creating a Stacked Column Chart

The next chart that Haywood wants added to the Financial Summary worksheet is a chart that projects the expenses incurred by the company over the next 10 years broken down by category. Because this chart looks at how different parts of the whole vary across time, that information would be better displayed in a stacked column chart. You will create this chart based on the data located in the Projected Cash Flow worksheet.

To create a stacked column chart:

1. Return to the **Projected Cash Flow** worksheet, and then select the nonadjacent range **A4:K4,A16:K20** containing the year categories and five data series for different types of expenses.
2. On the ribbon, click the **Insert** tab.
3. In the Charts group, click the **Insert Column or Bar Chart** button. A list of column and bar chart subtypes appears.
4. Click the **Stacked Column** icon (the second chart in the 2-D Column section). The stacked column chart is embedded in the Projected Cash Flow worksheet.
5. With the chart still selected, click the **Chart Styles** button, and then apply the **Style 11** chart style (the last style in the gallery).

   You'll move this chart to the Financial Summary worksheet.
6. On the Chart Tools Design tab, in the Location group, click the **Move Chart** button. The Move Chart dialog box opens.
7. Click the **Object in** arrow, and then click **Financial Summary**.
8. Click the **OK** button. The stacked column chart is moved to the Financial Summary worksheet.

As with the clustered column chart, you'll move and resize the stacked column chart in the Financial worksheet and then add a descriptive chart title.

To edit the stacked column chart:

TIP

To retain the chart's proportions as you resize it, hold down the Shift key as you drag the sizing handle.

1. Move and resize the stacked column chart so that it covers the range **E22:L38** in the Financial Summary worksheet. Use the Alt key to help you align the chart's location and size with the underlying worksheet grid.
2. Select the chart title, type **Breakdown of Business Expenses** as the new title, and then press the **Enter** key.
3. With the chart title still selected, change the font style to a nonbold **Green, Accent 6, Darker 25%**; **Calibri Light** font to match the clustered column chart. See Figure 4-21.

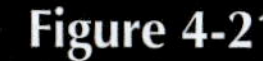

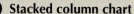

Figure 4-21 **Stacked column chart**

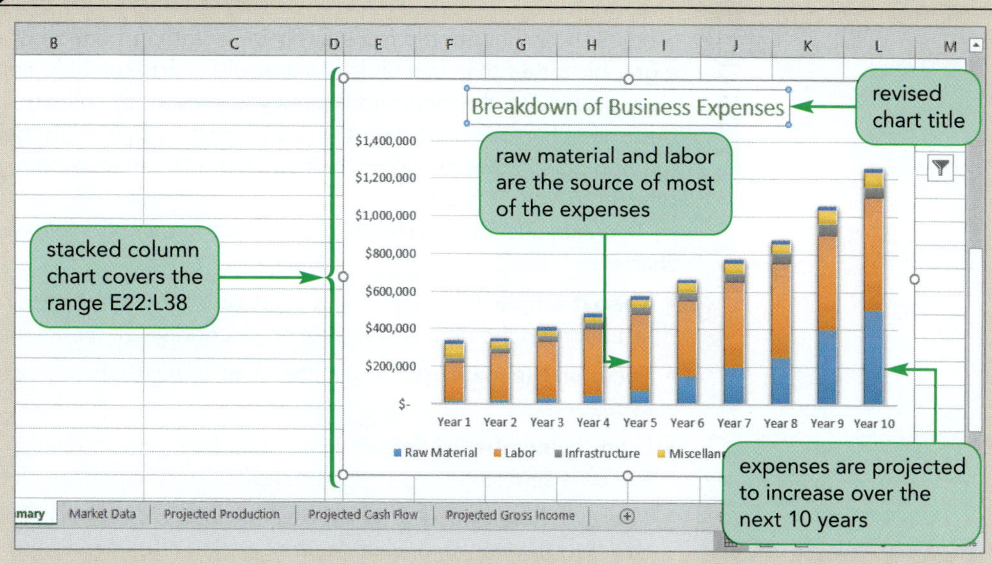

The chart clearly shows that the company's main expenses over the next 10 years will come from the raw material and labor costs. General maintenance, miscellaneous, and the business loan repayment constitute a smaller portion of the company's projected expenses. The overall yearly expense of running the company is expected to increase from about $337,000 in year 1 to $1,255,000 by year 10.

PROSKILLS

Written Communication: Communicating Effectively with Charts

Studies show that people more easily interpret information when it is presented as a graphic rather than in a table. As a result, charts can help communicate the real story underlying the facts and figures you present to colleagues and clients. A well-designed chart can illuminate the bigger picture that might be hidden by viewing only the numbers. However, poorly designed charts can mislead readers and make it more difficult to interpret data.

To create effective and useful charts, keep in mind the following tips as you design charts:

- **Keep it simple.** Do not clutter a chart with too many graphical elements. Focus attention on the data rather than on decorative elements that do not inform.
- **Focus on the message.** Design the chart to highlight the points you want to convey to readers.
- **Limit the number of data series.** Most charts should display no more than four or five data series. Pie charts should have no more than six slices.
- **Choose colors carefully.** Display different data series in contrasting colors to make it easier to distinguish one series from another. Modify the default colors as needed to make them distinct on the screen and in the printed copy.
- **Limit your chart to a few text styles.** Use a maximum of two or three different text styles in the same chart. Having too many text styles in one chart can distract attention from the data.

The goal of written communication is always to inform the reader in the simplest, most accurate, and most direct way possible. When creating worksheets and charts, everything in the workbook should be directed toward that end.

So far, you have determined monthly payments by using the PMT function and created and formatted a pie chart and two column charts. In the next session, you'll continue your work on the business plan by creating line charts, combination charts, histograms, sparklines, and data bars.

REVIEW

Session 4.1 Quick Check

1. You want to apply for a $225,000 mortgage. The annual interest on the loan is 4.8 percent with monthly payments. You plan to repay the loan in 20 years. Write the formula to calculate the monthly payment required to completely repay the loan under those conditions.
2. What function do you use to determine how many payment periods are required to repay a loan?
3. Why does the PMT function return a negative value when calculating the monthly payment due on a loan or mortgage?
4. What three chart elements are included in a pie chart?
5. A data series contains values grouped into 10 categories. Would this data be better displayed as a pie chart or a column chart? Explain why.
6. A research firm wants to create a chart that displays the total population growth of a county over a 10-year period broken down by five ethnicities. Which chart type best displays this information? Explain why.
7. If the research firm wants to display the changing ethnic profile of the county over time as a percentage of the county population, which chart type should it use? Explain why.
8. If the research firm is interested in comparing the numeric sizes of different ethnic groups over time, which chart should it use? Explain why.
9. If the research firm wants to display the ethnic profile of the county only for the current year, which chart should it use? Explain why.

Session 4.2 Visual Overview:

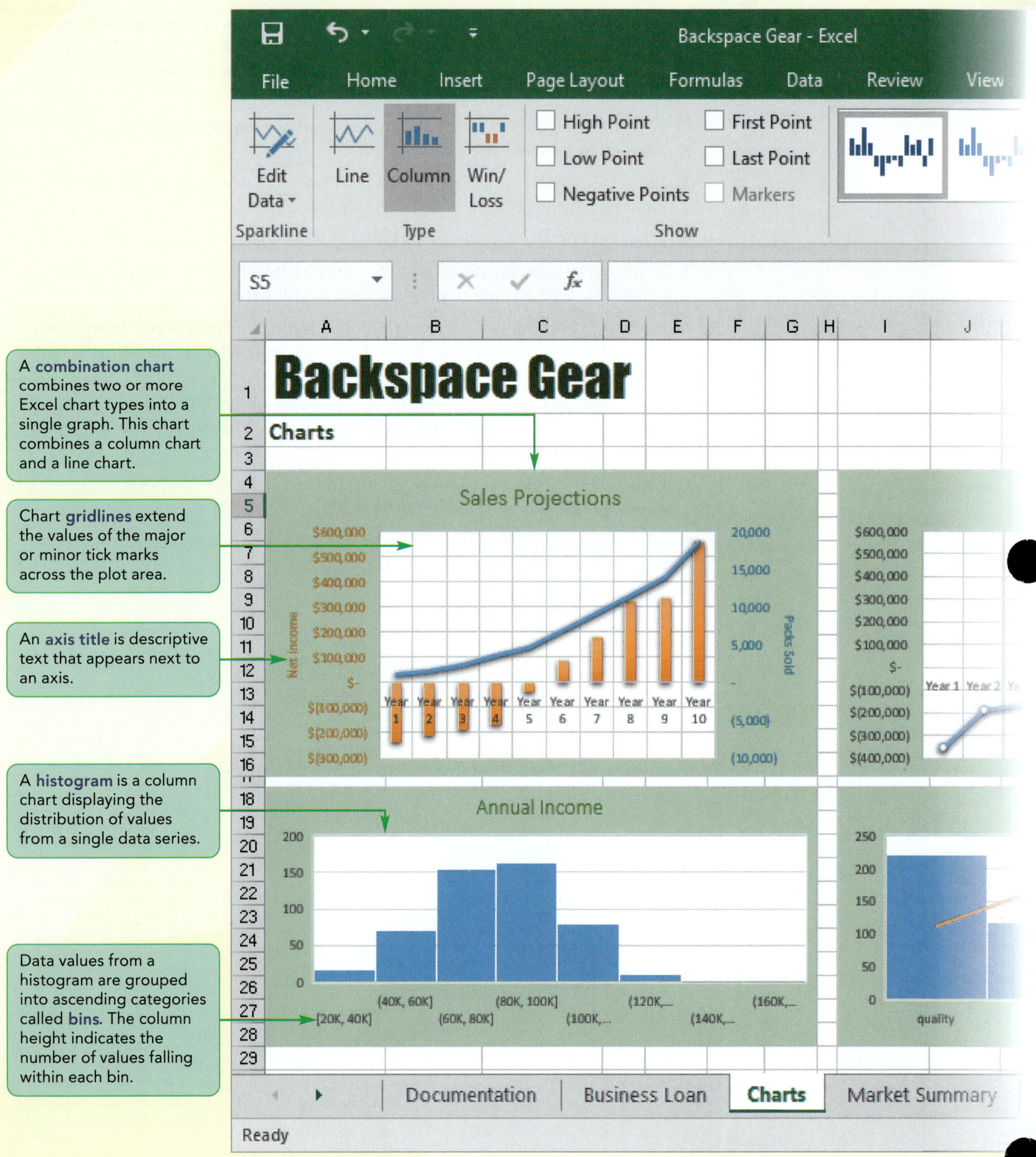

A **combination chart** combines two or more Excel chart types into a single graph. This chart combines a column chart and a line chart.

Chart **gridlines** extend the values of the major or minor tick marks across the plot area.

An **axis title** is descriptive text that appears next to an axis.

A **histogram** is a column chart displaying the distribution of values from a single data series.

Data values from a histogram are grouped into ascending categories called **bins**. The column height indicates the number of values falling within each bin.

Charts, Sparklines, and Data Bars

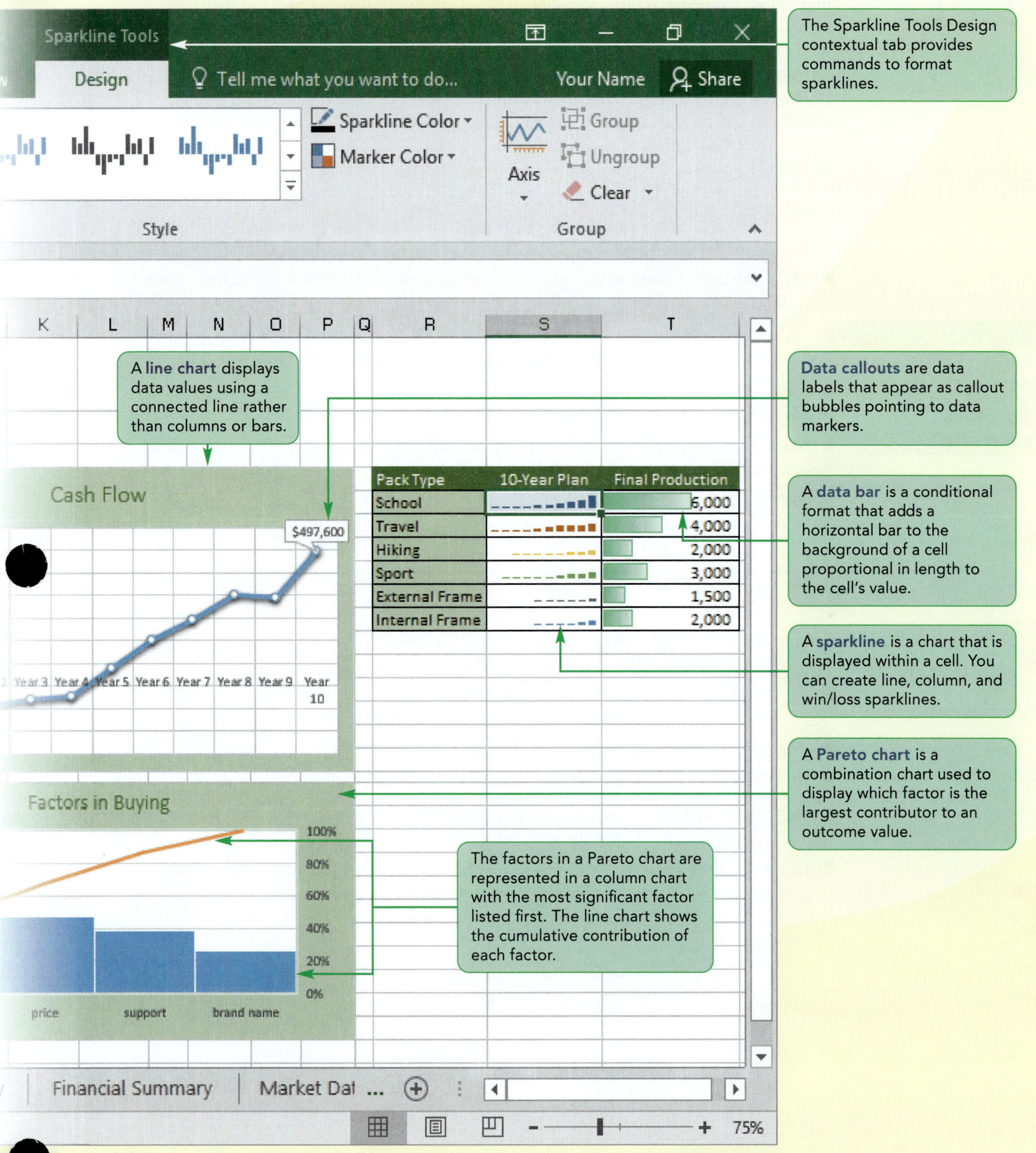

Sparkline Tools
Design
Tell me what you want to do...
Your Name
Share
Sparkline Color
Marker Color
Axis
Group
Ungroup
Clear
Style
Group
The Sparkline Tools Design contextual tab provides commands to format sparklines.
A line chart displays data values using a connected line rather than columns or bars.
Data callouts are data labels that appear as callout bubbles pointing to data markers.
Cash Flow
$497,600
Year 3 Year 4 Year 5 Year 6 Year 7 Year 8 Year 9 Year 10
Pack Type
10-Year Plan
Final Production
School 5,000
Travel 4,000
Hiking 2,000
Sport 3,000
External Frame 1,500
Internal Frame 2,000
A data bar is a conditional format that adds a horizontal bar to the background of a cell proportional in length to the cell's value.
A sparkline is a chart that is displayed within a cell. You can create line, column, and win/loss sparklines.
A Pareto chart is a combination chart used to display which factor is the largest contributor to an outcome value.
Factors in Buying
100%
80%
60%
40%
20%
0%
price
support
brand name
The factors in a Pareto chart are represented in a column chart with the most significant factor listed first. The line chart shows the cumulative contribution of each factor.
Financial Summary
Market Dat ...
75%

Creating a Line Chart

Line charts are typically used when the data consists of values drawn from categories that follow a sequential order at evenly spaced intervals, such as historical data that is recorded monthly, quarterly, or yearly. Like column charts, a line chart can be used with one or more data series. When multiple data series are included, the data values are plotted on different lines with varying line colors.

Haywood wants to use a line chart to show Backspace Gear's potential cash flow over the next decade. Cash flow examines the amount of cash flowing into and out of a business annually; it is one measure of a business's financial health and ability to make its payments.

TIP

When charting table values, do not include the summary totals because they will be treated as another category.

To create a line chart showing the projected cash flow:

1. If you took a break at the end of the previous session, make sure the Backspace Gear workbook is open.
2. Go to the **Projected Cash Flow** worksheet, and select the nonadjacent range **A4:K4,A30:K30** containing the Year categories from row 4 and the Cash Flow data series from row 30.
3. On the ribbon, click the **Insert** tab.
4. In the Charts group, click the **Recommended Charts** button. The Insert Chart dialog box opens, showing different ways to chart the selected data.
5. Click the second chart (the Line chart), and then click the **OK** button. The line chart of the year-end cash flow values is embedded in the Projected Cash Flow worksheet.
6. On the Home tab, in the Clipboard group, click the **Cut** button (or press the **Ctrl+X** keys). The selected line chart moves to the Clipboard.
7. Go to the **Financial Summary** worksheet, and then click cell **A12**. You want the upper-left corner of the line chart in cell A12.
8. In the Clipboard group, click the **Paste** button (or press the **Ctrl+V** keys). The line chart is pasted into the Financial Summary worksheet.
9. Resize the line chart to cover the range **A12:C24**.
10. On the ribbon, click the **Chart Tools Design** tab.
11. In the Chart Styles group, click the **Style 15** chart style (the last style in the style gallery) to format the line chart with a raised 3-D appearance.
12. Format the chart title with the same nonbold **Green, Accent 6, Darker 25%**; **Calibri Light** font style you applied to the two column charts. See Figure 4-22.

Figure 4-22 Line chart showing the projected cash flow

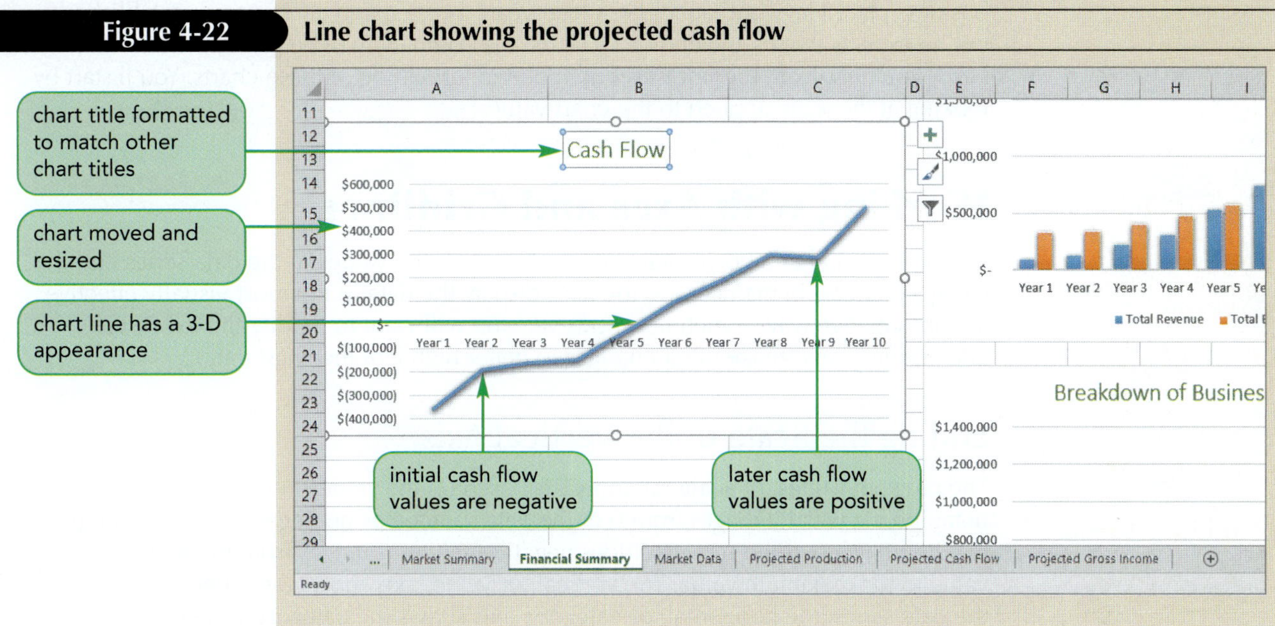

The line chart shows that Backspace Gear will have a negative cash flow in its early years and that the annual cash flow will increase throughout the decade, showing a positive cash flow starting in its sixth year.

INSIGHT

Line Charts and Scatter Charts

Line charts can sometimes be confused with XY (scatter) charts, but they are very different chart types. A line chart is more like a column chart that uses lines instead of columns. In a line chart, the data series are plotted against category values. These categories are assumed to have some sequential order. If the categories represent dates or times, they must be evenly spaced in time. For example, the Cash Flow line chart plotted the cash flow values against categories that ranged sequentially from year 1 to year 10.

A scatter chart has no category values. Instead, one series of data values is plotted against another. For example, if you were analyzing the relationship between height and weight among high school students, you would use a scatter chart because both weight and height are data values. On the other hand, if you charted weight measures against height categories (Short, Average, Tall), a line chart would be more appropriate.

Scatter charts are more often used in statistical analysis and scientific studies in which the researcher attempts to find a relationship between one variable and another. For that purpose, Excel includes several statistical tools to augment scatter charts, such as trendlines that provide the best fitting line or curve to the data. You can add a trendline by right-clicking the data series in the chart, and then clicking Add Trendline on the shortcut menu. From the Format Trendline pane that opens you can select different types of trendlines, including exponential and logarithmic lines as well as linear (straight) lines.

You have created three charts that provide a visual picture of the Backspace Gear business plan. Haywood anticipates lean years as the company becomes established, but he expects that by the end of 10 years, the company will be profitable and stable. Next, you'll look at other tools to fine-tune the formatting of these charts. You'll start by looking at the scale applied to the chart values.

Working with Axes and Gridlines

A chart's vertical and horizontal axes are based on the values in the data series and the category values. In many cases, the axes display the data in the most visually effective and informative way. Sometimes, however, you will want to modify the axes' scale, add gridlines, and make other changes to better highlight the chart data.

Editing the Scale of the Vertical Axis

The range of values, or **scale**, of an axis is based on the values in the data source. The default scale usually ranges from 0 (if the data source has no negative values) to the maximum value. If the scale includes negative values, it ranges from the minimum value to the maximum value. The vertical, or value, axis shows the range of values in the data series; the horizontal, or category, axis shows the category values.

Excel divides the scale into regular intervals, which are marked on the axis with **tick marks** and labels. For example, the scale of the vertical axis for the Projected Revenue and Expenses chart (shown in Figure 4-20) ranges from $0 up to $2,500,000 in increments of $500,000. Having more tick marks at smaller intervals could make the chart difficult to read because the tick mark labels might start to overlap. Likewise, having fewer tick marks at larger intervals could make the chart less informative. **Major tick marks** identify the main units on the chart axis while **minor tick marks** identify the smaller intervals between the major tick marks.

Some charts involve multiple data series that have vastly different values. In those instances, you can create dual axis charts. You can plot one data series against a **primary axis**, which usually appears along the left side of the chart, and the other against a **secondary axis**, which is usually placed on the right side of the chart. The two axes can be based on entirely different scales.

By default, no titles appear next to the value and category axes. This is fine when the axis labels are self-explanatory. Otherwise, you can add descriptive axis titles. In general, you should avoid cluttering a chart with extra elements such as axis titles when that information is easily understood from other parts of the chart.

Haywood thinks the value axis scale for the Projected Revenue and Expenses chart needs more tick marks and asks you to modify the axis so that it ranges from $0 to $2,500,000 in intervals of $250,000.

To change the scale of the vertical axis:

1. Click the **Projected Revenue and Expenses** chart to select it.
2. Double-click the vertical axis. The Format Axis pane opens with the Axis Options list expanded.

   Trouble? If you don't see the Axis Options section on the Format Axis pane, click the Axis Options button near the top of the pane.

   The Bounds section provides the minimum and maximum boundaries of the axis, which in this case are set from 0.0 to 2.5E6 (which stands for 2,500,000). Note that minimum and maximum values are set to Auto, which means that Excel automatically set these boundaries based on the data values.

TIP

To return a scale value to Auto, click the Reset button next to the value in the Format pane.

The Units section provides the intervals between the major tick marks and between minor tick marks. The major tick mark intervals, which are currently 500,000, are also set automatically by Excel.

3. In the Units section, click in the **Major** box, delete the current value, type **250000** as the new interval between major tick marks, and then press the **Enter** key. The scale of the value axis changes. See Figure 4-23.

Figure 4-23 **Formatted value axis**

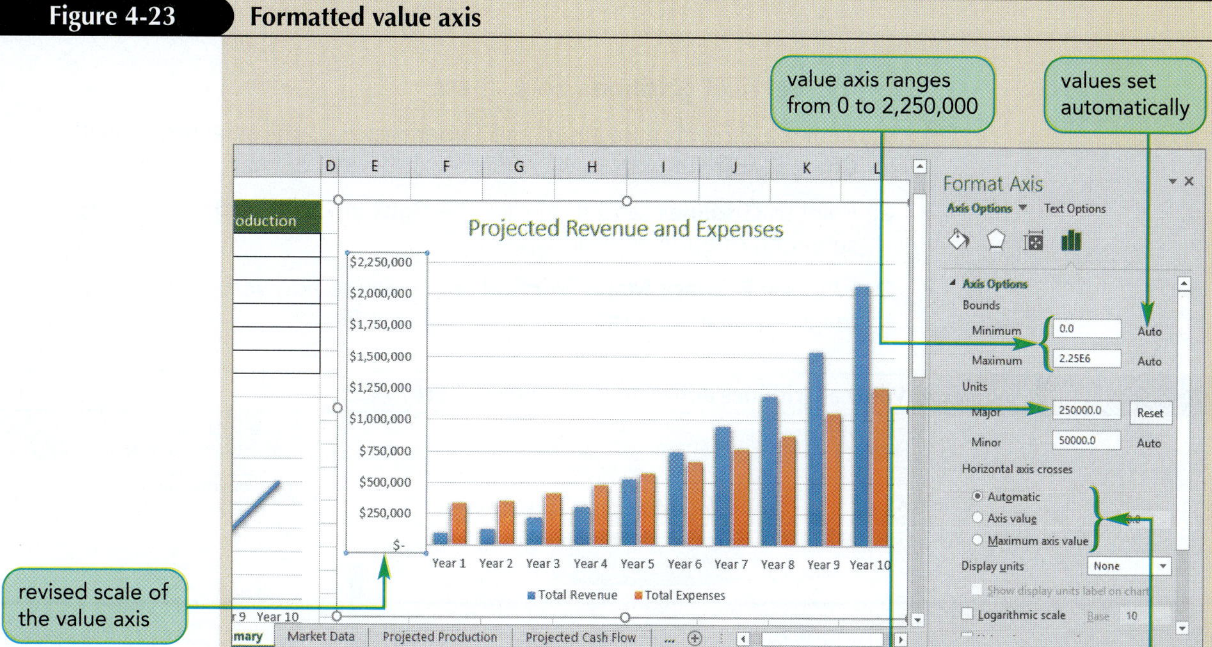

The revised axis scale makes it easier to determine the values displayed in the column chart.

INSIGHT

Displaying Unit Labels

When a chart involves large numbers, the axis labels can take up a lot of the available chart area and be difficult to read. You can simplify the chart's appearance by displaying units of measure more appropriate to the data values. For example, you can display the value 20 to represent 20,000 or 20,000,000. This is particularly useful when space is at a premium, such as in an embedded chart confined to a small area of the worksheet.

To display a units label, you double-click the axis to open the Format pane displaying options to format the axis. Select the units type from the Display units box. You can choose unit labels to represent values measured in the hundreds up to the trillions. Excel will modify the numbers on the selected axis and add a label so that readers will know what the axis values represent.

Adding Gridlines to a Chart

Gridlines are horizontal and vertical lines that help you compare data and category values in a chart. Depending on the chart style, gridlines may or may not appear in a chart, though you can add or remove them separately. Gridlines are placed at the major tick marks on the axes, or you can set them to appear at the minor tick marks.

The chart style used for the two column charts and the line chart includes horizontal gridlines. Haywood wants you to add vertical gridlines to the Projected Revenue and Expenses chart to help further separate one set of year values from another.

To add vertical gridlines to a chart:

1. With the Projected Revenue and Expenses chart still selected, click the **Chart Elements** button + to display the menu of chart elements.
2. Point to **Gridlines**, and then click the **right arrow** that appears to open a submenu of gridline options.
3. Click the **Primary Major Vertical** check box to add vertical gridlines at the major tick marks on the chart. See Figure 4-24.

Figure 4-24 Vertical gridlines added to the column chart

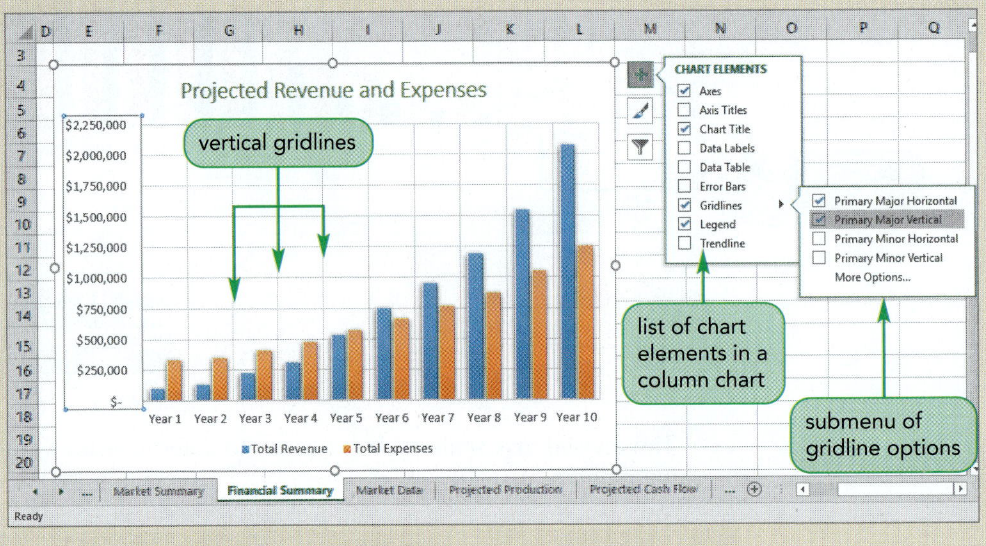

4. Click the **Chart Elements** button + to close the Chart Elements menu.

Working with Column Widths

Category values do not have the scale options used with data values. However, you can set the spacing between one column and another in your column charts. You can also define the width of the columns. As with the vertical axis, the default spacing and width are set automatically by Excel. A column chart with several categories will naturally make those columns thinner and more tightly packed.

Haywood thinks that the columns in the Projected Revenue and Expenses chart are spaced too closely, making it difficult to distinguish one year's values from another. He wants you to increase the gap between the columns.

To format the chart columns:

1. Make sure the Projected Revenue and Expenses chart is still selected and the Format pane is still open.
2. Click the **Axis Options arrow** at the top of the Format pane, and then click **Series "Total Revenue"** from the list of chart elements. The Format pane title changes to "Format Data Series," and all of the columns in the chart that show total revenue values are selected.
3. In the Format pane, click the **Series Options** button to display the list of series options.

   Series Overlap sets the amount of overlap between columns of different data series. Gap Width sets the amount of space between one group of columns and the next.

4. Drag the **Gap Width** slider until **200%** appears in the Gap Width box. The gap between groups of columns increases, and the individual column widths decrease to make room for the larger gap. See Figure 4-25.

TIP

You can use the up and down spin arrows in the Gap Width box to fine-tune the gap width in 1 percent increments.

Figure 4-25 **Gap width between columns**

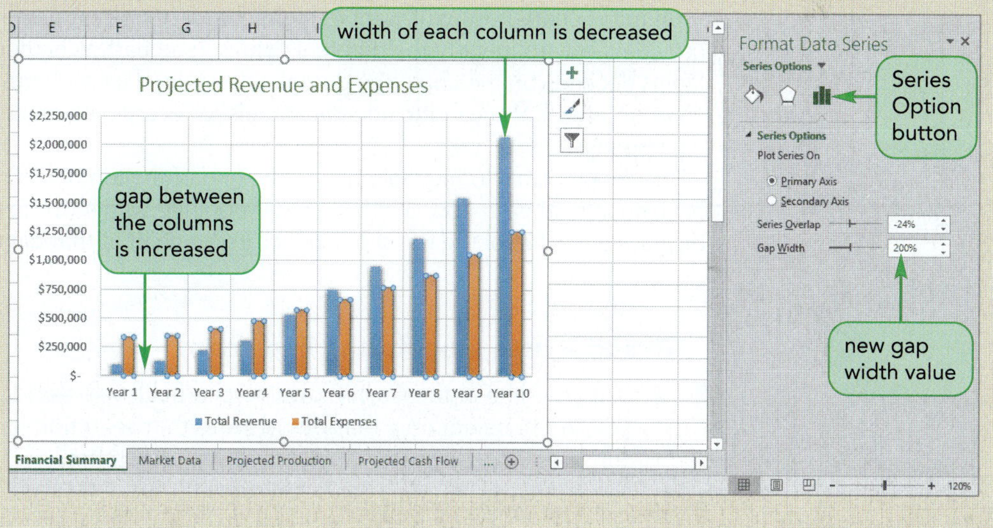

Formatting Data Markers

Each value from a data series is represented by a data marker. In pie charts, the data markers are the individual pie slices. In column charts, the columns are the data markers. In a line chart, the data markers are the points connected by the line. Depending on the line chart style, these data marker points can be displayed or hidden.

In the Cash Flow line chart, the data marker points are hidden, and only the line connecting them is visible. Haywood wants you to display these data markers and change their fill color to white so that they stand out, making the chart easier to understand.

To display and format the line chart data markers:

1. Scroll to view the Cash Flow line chart, and then double-click the line within the chart. The Format pane changes to the Format Data Series pane.
2. Click the **Fill & Line** button at the top of the Format pane.

   You can choose to display the format options for lines or data markers.
3. Click **Marker**, and then click **Marker Options** to expand the list of options for the line chart data markers. Currently, the None option button is selected to hide the data markers.
4. Click the **Automatic** option button to automatically display the markers.

   The data markers are now visible in the line chart, but they have a blue fill color. You will change this fill color to white.
5. Click **Fill** to expand the list of fill options, if necessary.
6. Click the **Solid fill** option button, click the **Color** button, and then click the **White, Background 1** theme color. The fill color for the data markers in the line chart changes to white.

In many charts, you will want to highlight an important data point. Data labels provide a way to identify the different values in a chart. Whether you include data labels depends on the chart, the complexity of the data and presentation, and the chart's purpose. You can include data labels for every data marker or just for individual data points.

Haywood wants to highlight that at the end of the tenth year, the company should have an annual cash flow of almost $500,000. He wants you to add a data label that displays the value of the last data marker in the chart at that data point.

To add a data label to the line chart:

1. With the line in the Cash Flow line chart still selected, click the last point on the line to select only that point. Note that selection handles appear around this data marker but not around any of the others.
2. Click the **Chart Elements** button next to the line chart, and then click the **Data Labels** check box to select it. The data label appears above only the selected data marker.
3. Click the **Data Labels** arrow to display a menu of data label positions and options, and then click **Data Callout**. The data label is changed to a data callout box that includes both the category value and the data value, displaying "Year 10, $497,600." You will modify this callout to display only the data value.
4. On the Data Labels menu, click **More Options**. The Format pane title changes to "Format Data Label."
5. Click the **Label Options** button, and then click **Label Options**, if necessary, to expand the list of those options.
6. Click the **Category Name** check box to deselect it. The data callout now displays only $497,600. See Figure 4-26.

Figure 4-26 Formatted data markers and data label

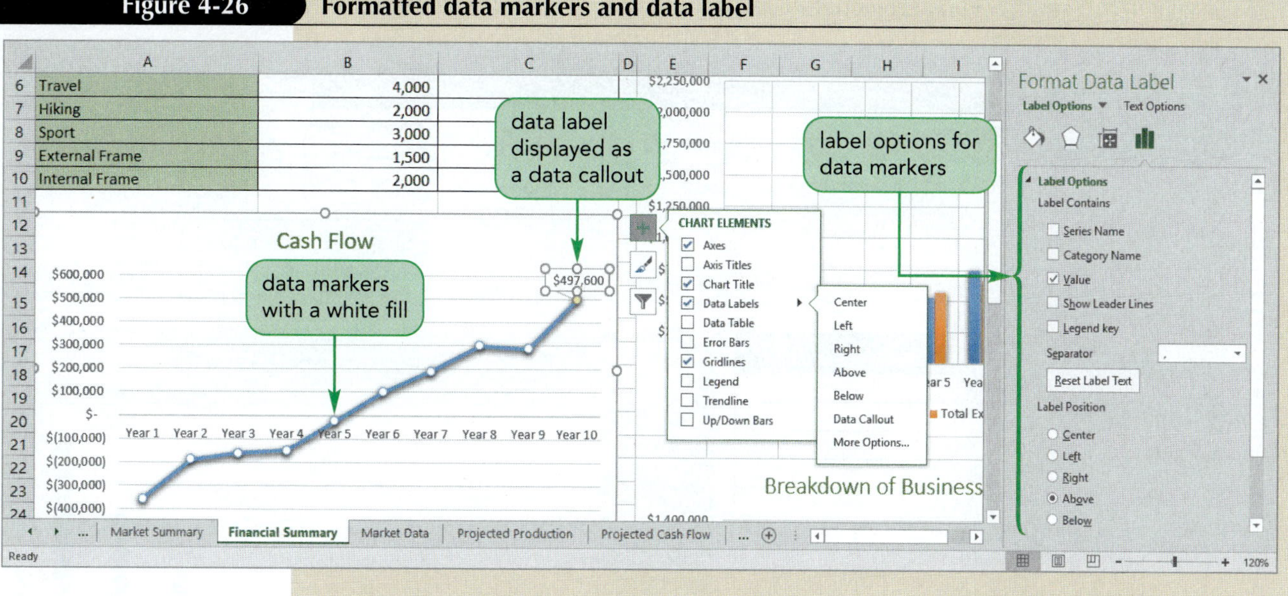

Formatting the Plot Area

The chart area covers the entire background of the chart, whereas the **plot area** includes only that portion of the chart in which the data markers, such as the columns in a column chart, have been placed or plotted. You can format the plot area by changing its fill and borders and by adding visual effects. Changes to the plot area are often made in conjunction with the chart area.

Haywood wants you to format the chart area and plot area of the Projected Revenue and Expenses chart. You will set the chart area fill color to a light green to match the pie chart background color you applied in the last session, and you will change the plot area fill color to white.

To change the fill colors of the chart and plot areas:

1. Click the **Projected Revenue and Expenses** chart to select it.
2. On the ribbon, click the **Chart Tools Format** tab.
3. In the Current Selection group, click the **Chart Elements arrow** to display a list of chart elements in the current chart, and then click **Chart Area**. The chart area is selected in the chart.
4. In the Shape Styles group, click the **Shape Fill button arrow**, and then click the **Green, Accent 6, Lighter 60%** theme color in the third row and last column. The entire background of the chart changes to light green.
5. In the Current Selection group, click the **Chart Elements arrow**, and then click **Plot Area** to select that chart element.
6. Change the fill color of the plot area to the **White, Background 1** theme color. See Figure 4-27.

Figure 4-27 Final Projected Revenue and Expenses chart

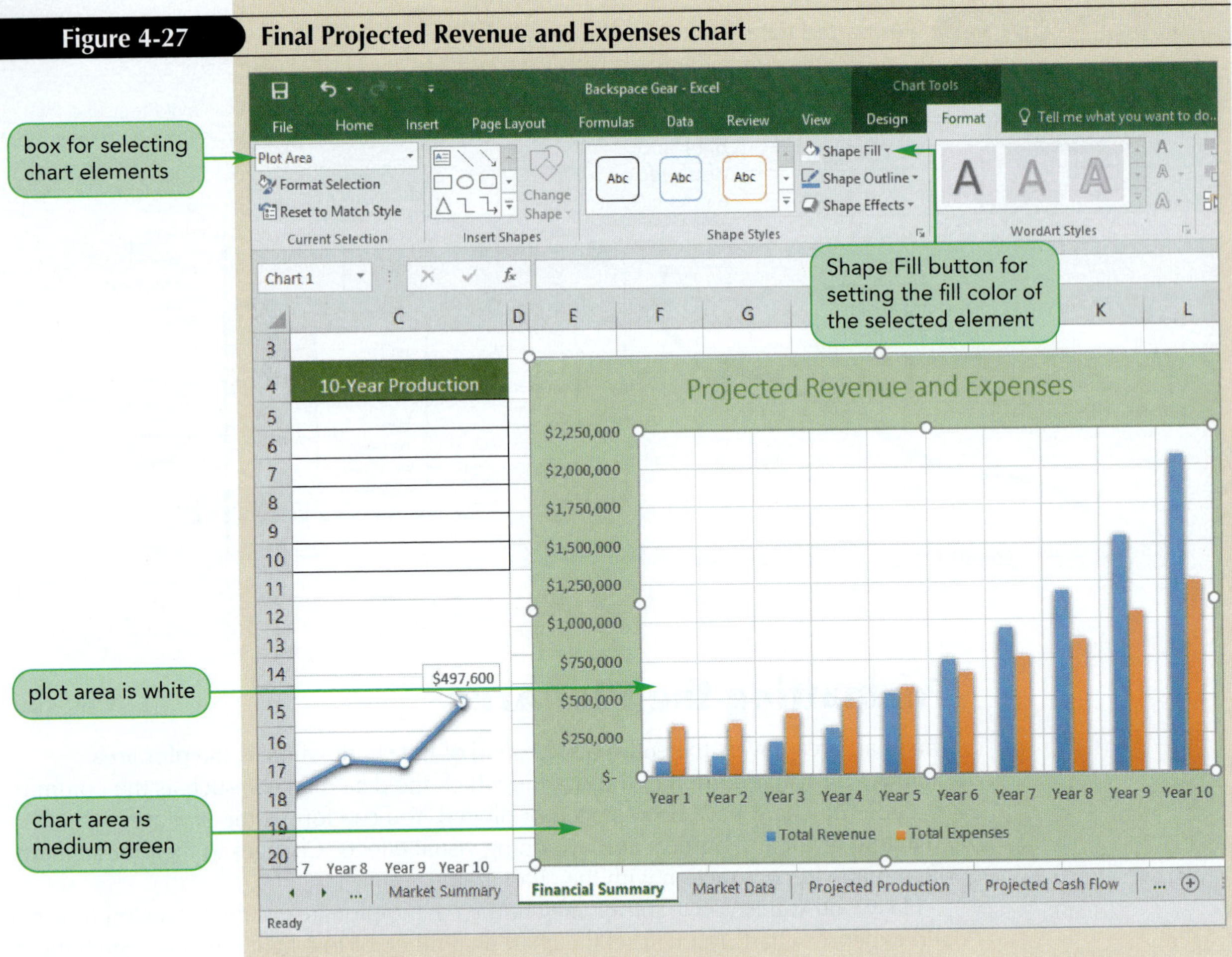

Haywood wants to apply the same general design applied to the Breakdown of Business Expenses column chart and the Cash Flow line chart. You will add vertical gridlines to each chart and then change the chart area fill color to light green and the plot area fill color to white.

To format the other charts:

1. Click the **Breakdown of Business Expenses** column chart to select it.
2. Select the **chart area**, and then set the fill color of the chart area to **Green, Accent 6, Lighter 60%** theme color.
3. Select the **plot area**, and then change the fill color to the **White, Background 1** theme color.

   Next, you'll add vertical gridlines to the chart. You can also use the Chart Tools Design tab to add chart elements such as gridlines.
4. On the ribbon, click the **Chart Tools Design** tab.
5. In the Chart Layouts group, click the **Add Chart Element** button, scroll down the chart elements, point to **Gridlines**, and then click **Primary Major Vertical** on the submenu. Vertical gridlines are added to the chart. See Figure 4-28.

Figure 4-28 **Final Business Expenses chart**

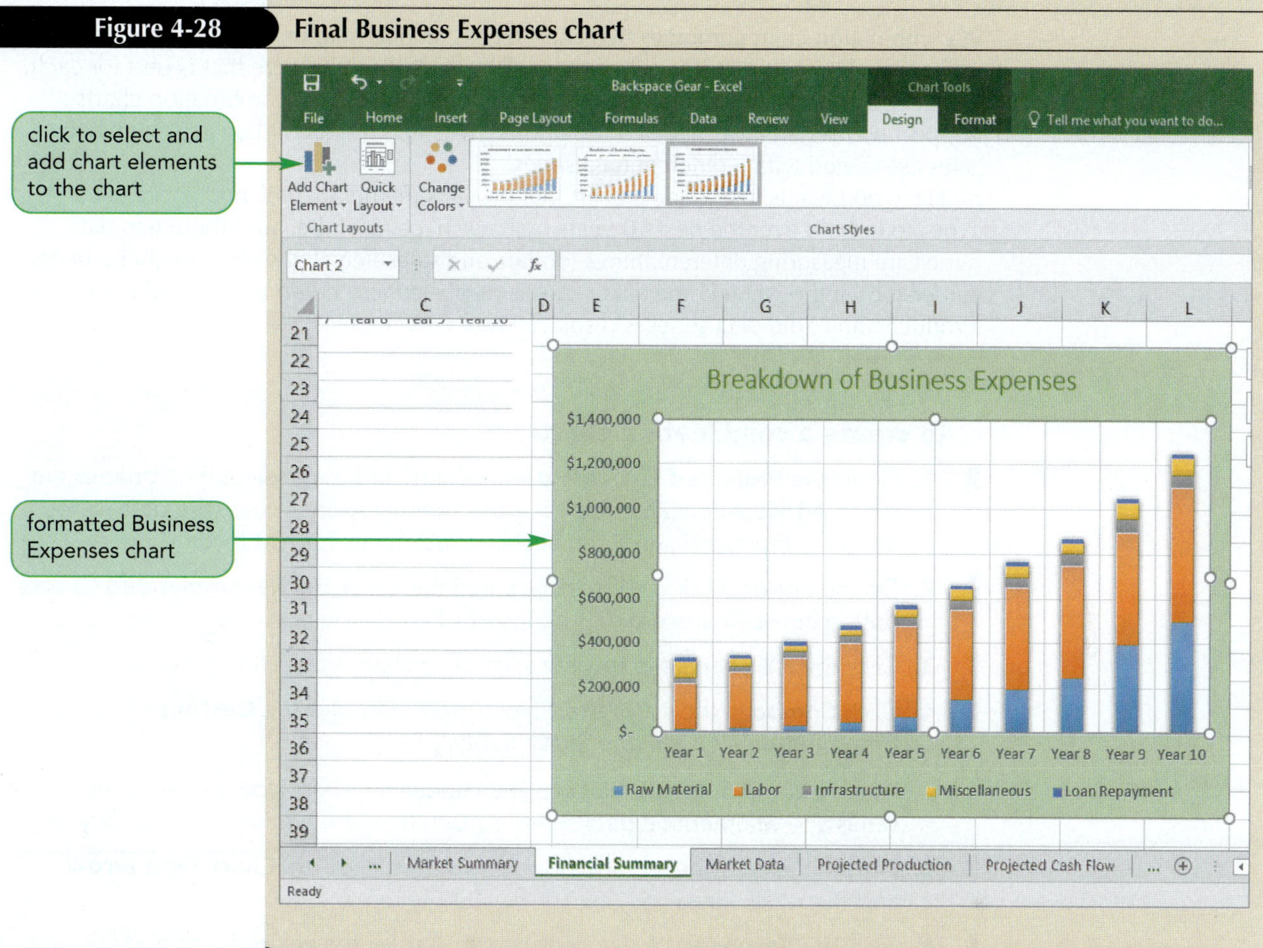

6. Select the **Cash Flow** line chart, and then repeat Steps 2 through 5 to set the chart area fill color to light green, set the plot area fill color to white, and add major gridlines to the chart's primary axis.

The Breakdown of Business Expenses column chart and the Cash Flow line chart are now formatted with the same design.

INSIGHT

Overlaying Chart Elements

An embedded chart takes up less space than a chart sheet. However, it can be challenging to fit all of the chart elements into that smaller space. One solution is to overlay one element on top of another. The most commonly overlaid elements are the chart title and the chart legend. To overlay the chart title, click the Chart Title arrow from the list of Chart Elements and select Centered Overlay from the list of position options. Excel will place the chart title on top of the plot area, freeing up more space for other chart elements. Chart legends can also be overlaid by opening the Format pane for the legend and deselecting the Show the legend without overlapping the chart check box in the Legend Options section. Other chart elements can be overlaid by dragging them to new locations in the chart area and then resizing the plot area to recover the empty space.

Don't overuse the technique of overlaying chart elements. Too much overlaying of chart elements can make your chart difficult to read.

Creating a Combination Chart

A combination chart combines two chart types, such as a column chart and a line chart, enabling you to display two sets of data using the chart type that is best for each. Because the two data series might have vastly different values, combination charts support two vertical axes labeled the primary axis and the secondary axis, with each axes associated with a different data series.

Haywood wants to include a chart that projects the net income and packs of all types to be sold over the next 10 years by Backspace Gear. Because these two data series are measuring different things (dollars and sales items), the chart might be better understood if the Net Income data series is displayed as a column chart and the Packs Produced and Sold data series is displayed as a line chart.

To create a combination chart:

1. Go to the **Projected Cash Flow** worksheet, and then select the nonadjacent range **A4:K5,A26:K26** containing the Year category values, the data series for Packs Produced and Sold, and the data series for Net Income.
2. On the ribbon, click the **Insert** tab, and then click the **Recommended Charts** button in the Charts group. The Insert Chart dialog box opens.
3. Click the **All Charts** tab to view a list of all chart types and subtypes.
4. Click **Combo** in the list of chart types, and then click the **Custom Combination** subtype (the fourth subtype).

   At the bottom of the dialog box, you choose the chart type for each data series and whether that data series is plotted on the primary or secondary axis.
5. For the Packs Produced and Sold data series, click the **Chart Type arrow**, and then click **Line**.
6. Click the **Secondary Axis** check box to display the values for that series on a secondary axis.
7. For the Net Income data series, click the **Chart Type arrow**, and then click **Clustered Column**. See Figure 4-29.

Figure 4-29 Custom Combination chart in the Insert Chart dialog box

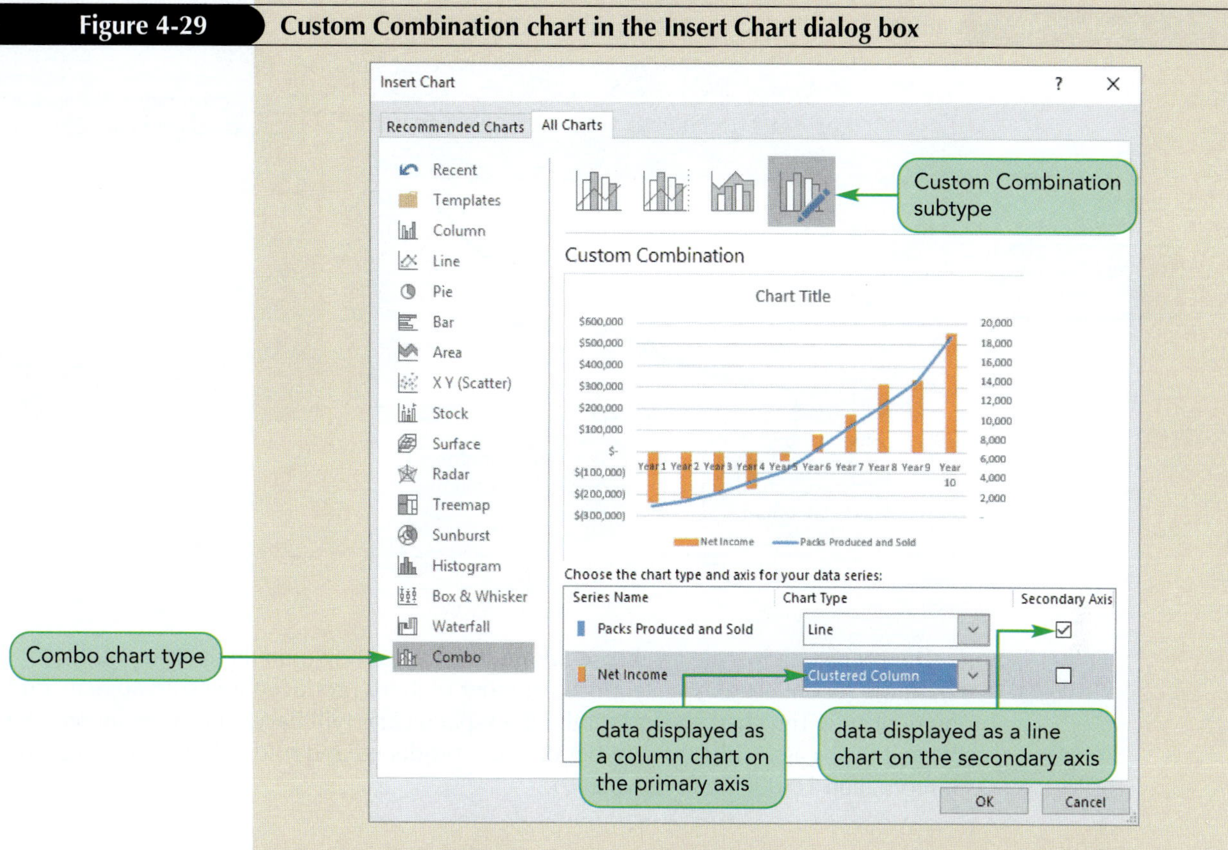

8. Click the **OK** button. The combination chart is embedded in the Projected Cash Flow worksheet.
9. Format the combination chart with the **Style 8** chart style to give both the line and the columns a raised 3-D effect.

Haywood wants the combo chart moved to the Financial Summary worksheet and formatted to match the style used for the other charts.

To move and format the combo chart:

1. Move the combination chart to the **Financial Summary** worksheet, and then resize it cover the range **A26:C38**.
2. Change the title of the combination chart to **Sales Projections**, and then format the title in the same nonbold **Green, Accent 6, Darker 25%**; **Calibri Light** font you used with the other chart titles.
3. Remove the **Legend** chart element from the combination chart.
4. Add **Primary Major Vertical** gridlines to the combination chart.
5. Change the fill color of the plot area to the **White, Background 1** theme color, and then change the fill color of the chart area to the same **Green, Accent 6, Lighter 60%** theme color as the other charts. See Figure 4-30.

Figure 4-30 **Initial Sales Projections combination chart**

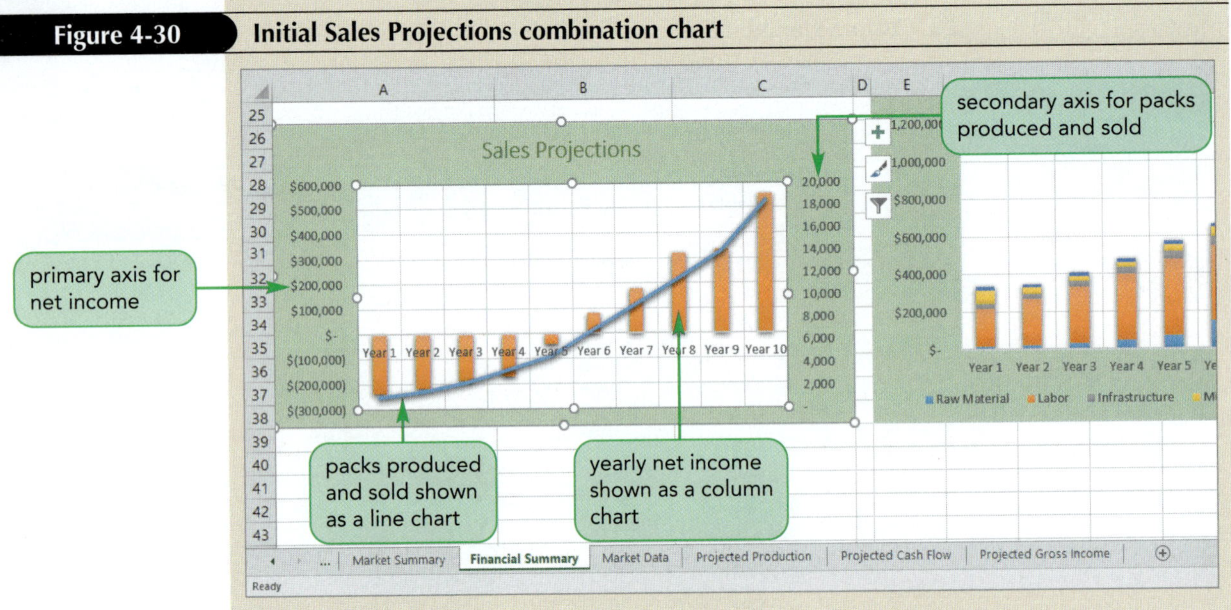

The primary axis scale for the net income values is shown on the left side of the chart; the secondary axis scale for the number of items produced and sold appears on the right side. The chart shows that the Backspace Gear will have a negative income for the first five years, while the number of packs produced and sold will increase steadily to more than 18,000 items by year 10.

Working with Primary and Secondary Axes

With a primary and secondary axis, combo charts can be confusing to the reader trying to determine which axis is associated with each data series. It is helpful to add an axis title to the chart with descriptive text that appears next to the axis values. As with other chart elements, you can add, remove, and format axis titles.

Haywood wants you to edit the Sales Projections chart to include labels describing what is being measured by the primary and secondary axes.

To add titles to the primary and second axes:

1. Click the **Chart Elements** button [+] next to the combination chart, and then click the **Axis Titles** check box to select it. Titles with the placeholders "Axis Title" are added to the primary and secondary axes.
2. Click the left axis title to select it, type **Net Income** as the descriptive title, and then press the **Enter** key.
3. With the left axis title selected, change the font color to the **Orange, Accent 2, Darker 25%** theme color to match the color of the columns in the chart.
4. Select the numbers on the left axis scale, and then change the font color to the **Orange, Accent 2, Darker 25%** theme color. The left axis title and scale are now the same color as the columns that reference that axis.

5. Select the **right axis** title, type **Packs Sold** as the descriptive title, and then press the **Enter** key.
6. With the right axis title still selected, change the font color to the **Blue, Accent 1, Darker 25%** theme color to match the color of the line in the chart.
7. On the Home tab, in the Alignment group, click the **Orientation** button, and then click **Rotate Text Down** to change the orientation of the right axis title.
8. Select the numbers on the right axis scale, and then change the font color to the **Blue, Accent 1, Darker 25%** theme color. The right axis title and scale are now the same color as the line that references that axis.
9. Click the horizontal axis title to select it, and then press the **Delete** key. The placeholder is removed from the chart, freeing up more space for other chart elements. See Figure 4-31.

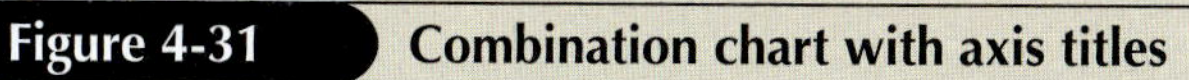

Figure 4-31 Combination chart with axis titles

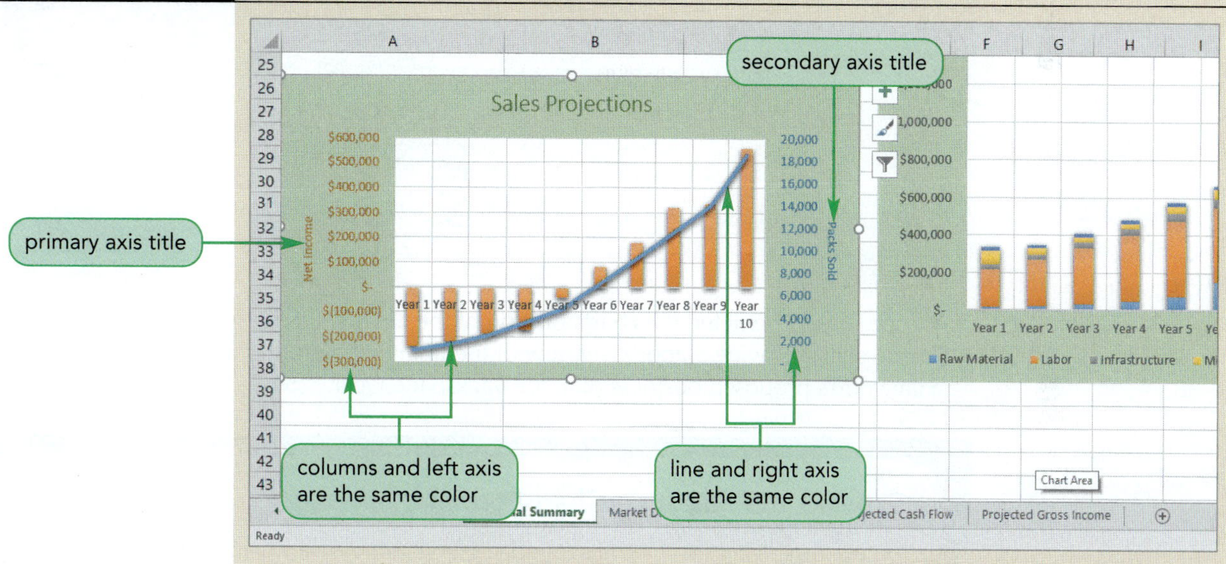

Haywood is concerned that the line chart portion of the graph makes it look as if the number of packs produced and sold was negative for the first five years. This is because the secondary axis scale, which is automatically generated by Excel, goes from a minimum of 0 to a maximum of 20,000. You will change the scale so that the 0 tick mark for Packs Sold better aligns with the $0 for Net Income.

To modify the secondary axis scale:

1. Double-click the secondary axis scale to select it and open the Format pane.
2. Click the **Axis Options** button, if necessary, to display the list of axis options.

3. In Axis Options section, click the **Minimum** box, change the value from 0.0 to **–10000**, and then press the **Enter** key. The secondary axis scale is modified. The Packs Sold scale is now better aligned with the Net Income scale, providing a clearer picture of the data.
4. Close the Format pane, and then press the **Esc** key to deselect the secondary axis. See Figure 4-32.

Figure 4-32 **Final combination chart**

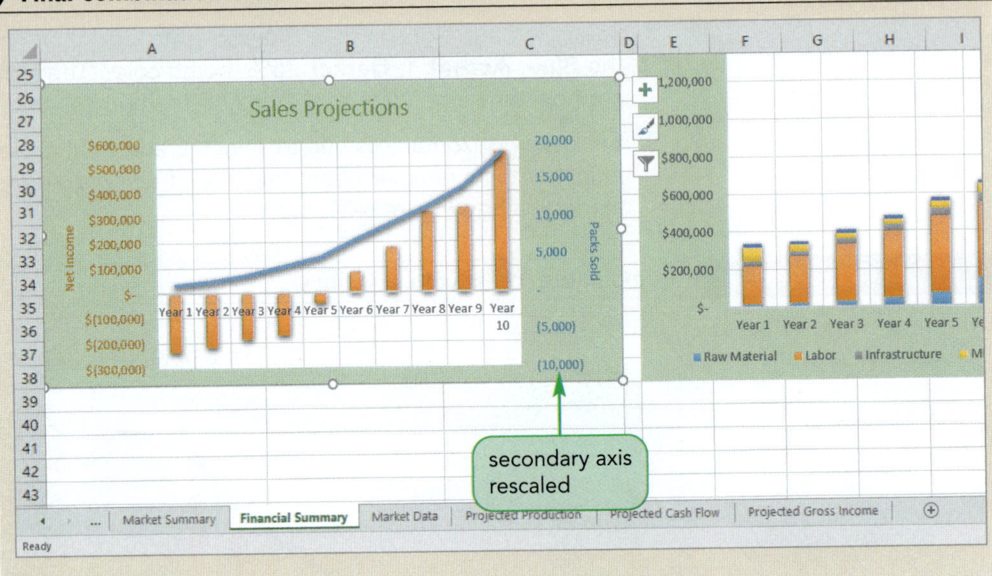

You have completed the charts portion of the Financial Summary worksheet. These charts provide a good overview of the financial picture of the first 10 years of Haywood's proposed business plan for Backspace Gear.

INSIGHT

Copying and Pasting a Chart Format

You will often want to use the same design over and over again for the charts in your worksheet. Rather than repeating the same commands, you can copy the formatting from one chart to another. To copy a chart format, first select the chart with the existing design that you want to replicate, and then click the Copy button in the Clipboard group on the Home tab (or press the Ctrl+C keys). Next, select the chart that you want to format, click the Paste button arrow in the Clipboard group, and then click Paste Special to open the Paste Special dialog box. In the Paste Special dialog box, select the Formats option button, and then click the OK button. All of the copied formats from the original chart—including fill colors, font styles, axis scales, and chart types—are then pasted into the new chart. Be aware that the pasted formats will overwrite any formats previously used in the new chart.

Editing a Chart Data Source

Excel automates most of the process of creating and formatting a chart. However, sometimes the rendered chart does not appear the way you expected. One situation where this happens is when the selected cells contain numbers you want to treat as categories but Excel treats them as a data series. When this happens, you can modify the data source to specify exactly which ranges should be treated as category values and which ranges should be treated as data values.

REFERENCE

Modifying a Chart's Data Source

- Click the chart to select it.
- On the Chart Tools Design tab, in the Data group, click the Select Data button.
- In the Legend Entries (Series) section of the Select Data Source dialog box, click the Add button to add another data series to the chart, or click the Remove button to remove a data series from the chart.
- Click the Edit button in the Horizontal (Category) Axis Labels section to select the category values for the chart.

The Projected Gross Income worksheet contains a table that projects the company's gross income for the next 10 years. Haywood wants you to create a simple line chart of this data.

To create the line chart:

1. Go to the **Projected Gross Income** worksheet, and then select the range **A4:B14**.
2. On the ribbon, click the **Insert** tab.
3. In the Charts group, click the **Insert Line or Area Chart** button.
4. In the 2-D Line charts section, click the **Line** subtype (the first subtype in the first row) to create a 2-D line chart.
5. Move the chart over the range **D2:J14**. See Figure 4-33.

Figure 4-33 Line chart with Year treated as a data series

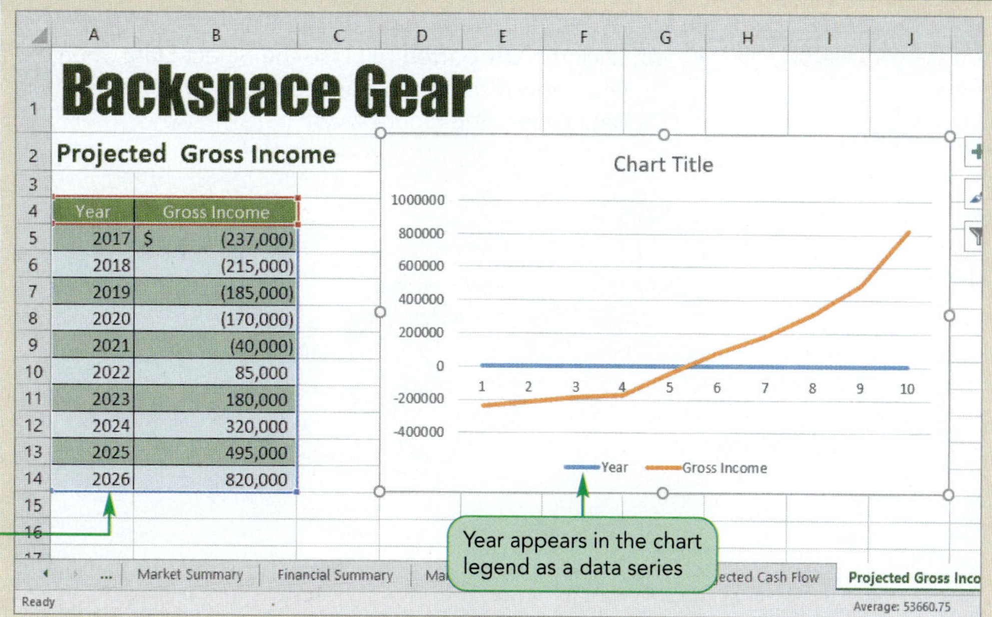

The line chart is incorrect because the Year values from the range A5:A14 are treated as another data series rather than category values. The line chart actually doesn't even have category values; the values are charted sequentially from the first value to the tenth. You can correct this problem from the Select Data dialog box by identifying the data series and category values to use in the chart.

To edit the chart's data source:

1. On the Chart Tools Design tab, in the Data group, click the **Select Data** button. The Select Data Source dialog box opens. Note that Year is selected as a legend entry and the category values are simply the numbers 1 through 10. See Figure 4-34.

Figure 4-34 **Select Data Source dialog box**

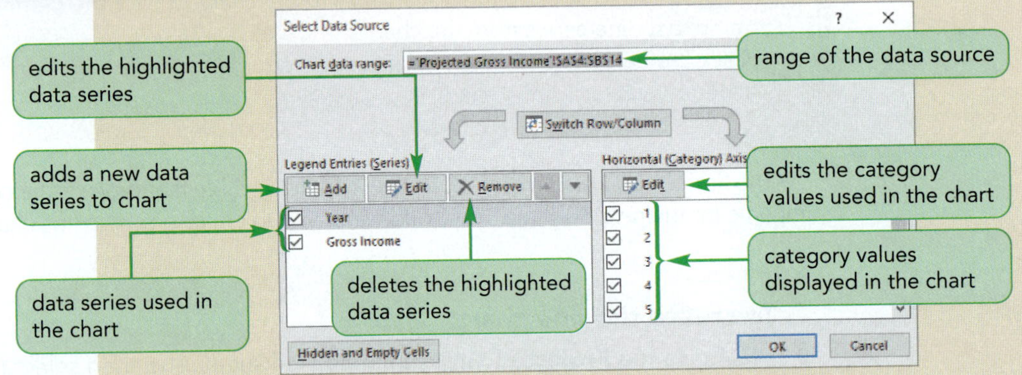

TIP

To organize a data series in rows, click the Switch Row/Column button.

2. With Year selected (highlighted in gray) in the list of legend entries, click the **Remove** button. Year is removed from the line chart.
3. Click the **Edit** button for the Horizontal (Category) Axis Labels. The Axis Labels dialog box opens. You'll specify that Year should be used as the category values.

Make sure you insert a completely new range for the category values rather than simply adding to the category values already in use.

4. Select the range **A5:A14** containing the years as the axis label range, and then click the **OK** button. The Year values now appear in the list of Horizontal (Category) Axis Labels.
5. Click the **OK** button to close the Select Data Source dialog box. The line chart now displays Year as the category values and Gross Income as the only data series. See Figure 4-35.

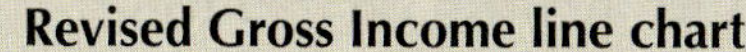

Figure 4-35 Revised Gross Income line chart

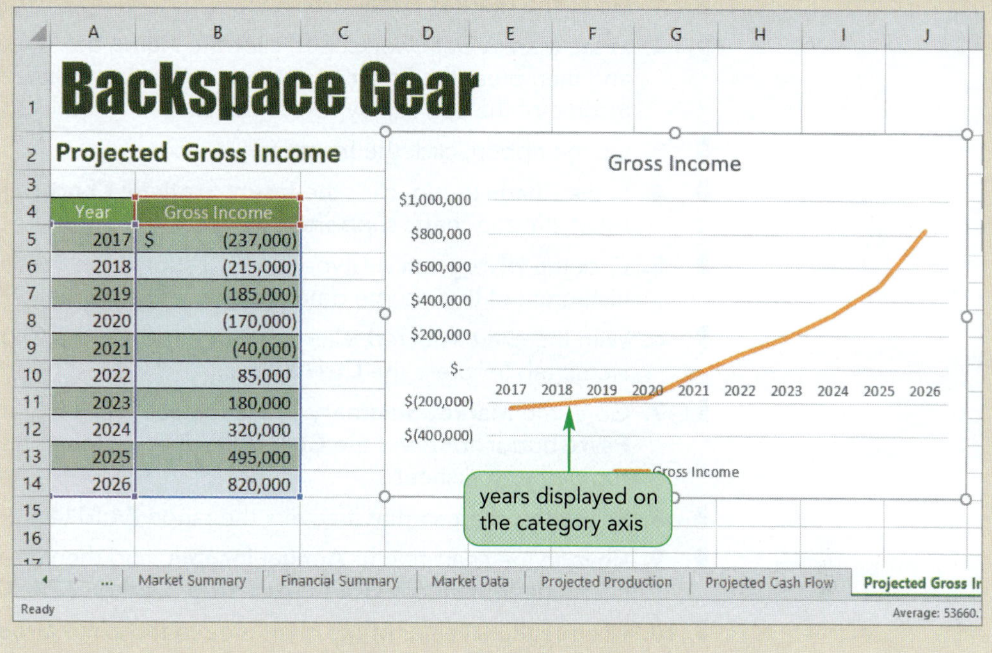

The Select Data Source dialog box is also useful when you want to add more data series to a chart. For example, if Haywood wanted to include other financial estimates in an existing chart, he could add the data series to the existing chart rather than creating a new chart. To add a data series to a chart, select the chart, click the Select Data button in the Data group on the Chart Tools Design tab to open the Select Data Source dialog box, click the Add button, and then select the range for the data series.

Exploring Other Chart Types

Excel provides many chart types tailored to specific needs in finance, statistics, science, and project management. One chart that is often used in finance and statistics is the histogram.

Creating a Histogram

A histogram is a column chart displaying the distribution of values from a single data series. For example, a professor might create a histogram to display the distribution of scores from a midterm exam. There is no category series for a histogram; instead, the data values are automatically grouped into ascending categories, or bins, with the histogram displaying the number of data points falling within the bin. So a histogram of midterm exam scores might consist of four bins corresponding to exam scores of 60 to 70, 70 to 80, 80 to 90, and 90 to 100. The number and placement of the bins is arbitrary and is chosen to best indicate the shape of the distribution.

You will use a histogram chart to summarize data from the market survey. Part of the survey included demographic information such as the respondent's gender and annual income. Haywood wants a histogram displaying the income distribution for Backspace Gear's most likely customers, which will help him better market Backspace Gear to its core customer base.

To create a histogram of income distribution:

1. Go to the **Market Data** worksheet.
2. In the Market Data worksheet, click the **Name** box, type the range **E6:E506**, and then press the **Enter** key to select the data values containing the annual income of the 500 survey respondents.
3. On the ribbon, click the **Insert** tab.
4. In the Charts group, click the **Insert Statistic Chart** button to display a list of statistic charts supported by Excel.
5. Click the **Histogram** subtype (the first subtype in the Histogram section). The histogram of the income data appears in the Market Data worksheet.
6. With the chart selected, click the **Cut** button in the Clipboard group on the Home tab (or press the **Ctrl+X** keys).
7. Go to the **Market Summary** worksheet, click cell **F4**, and then click the **Paste** button (or press the **Ctrl+V** keys) to paste the histogram chart at the top of the worksheet.
8. Resize the chart so that it covers the range **F4:M14**.
9. Change the chart title to **Annual Income**, and then change the color of the chart title to nonbold **Green, Accent 6, Darker 25%**; **Calibri Light** font.
10. Change the fill color of the chart area to the same **Green, Accent 6, Lighter 60%** theme color used with other charts, and then change the plot area fill color to the **White, Background 1** theme color. See Figure 4-36.

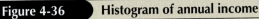

Figure 4-36 Histogram of annual income

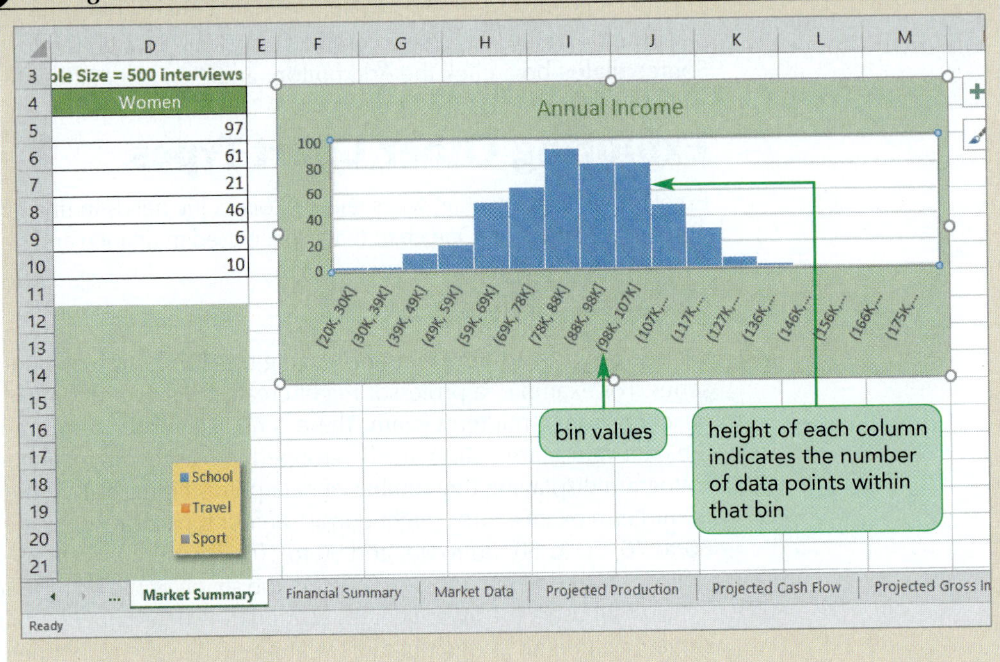

The histogram shows that most of the respondents are clustered around incomes of \$59,000 to \$100,000 per year. The lowest incomes are in the \$20,000 to \$30,000 range with some very few respondents having incomes around \$175,000. Excel created the histogram with 17 bins. The number of bins is used to cover the range of values from the smallest income value up to the largest. This can result in odd-sized ranges. Haywood suggests that you change the width of each bin to 20,000. You can modify the bins by editing the values in the horizontal axis of the histogram chart.

To modify the bins used in the histogram:

1. Double-click the horizontal axis values to select them and open the Format Axis pane.
2. Click the **Axis Options** button near the top of the Format pane, and then click **Axis Options** to expand the list. Excel displays a list of options to set the size and number of bins used in the histogram.
3. Click the **Bin width** option button, change the width of the bins from the default value of 9700 to **20000**, and then press the **Tab** key. See Figure 4-37.

TIP

To combine bin values, set the Overflow bin and Underflow bin values in Axis Options section.

Figure 4-37 Histogram with new bin widths

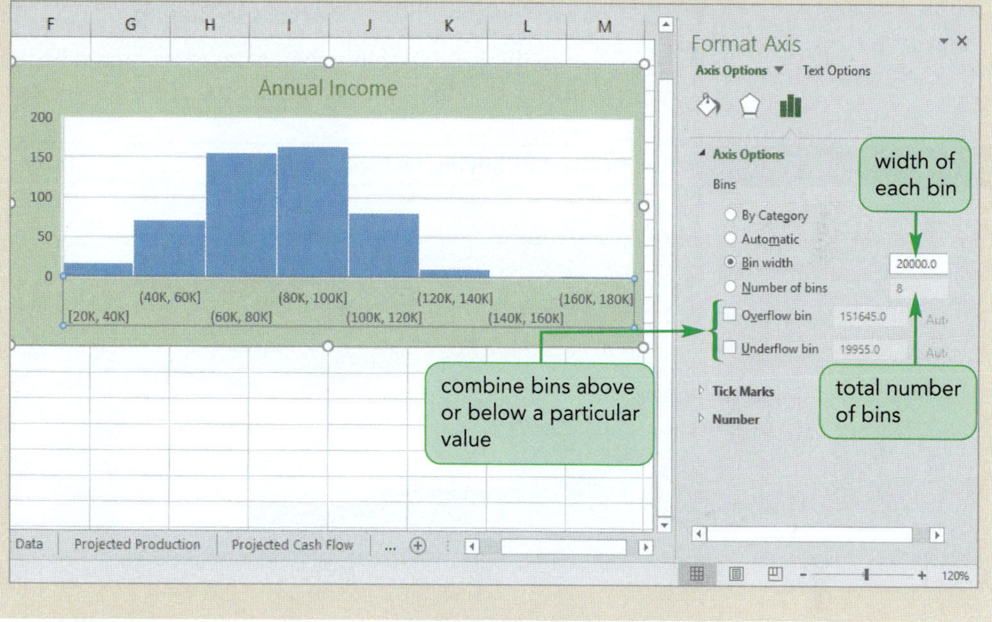

By changing the bin widths, you made the histogram easier to read and interpret. The distribution of the income values shows that there are a couple of outlying incomes in the 160,000 to 180,000 range, but almost all of the annual incomes are reported in the 60,000 to 100,000 range.

Creating a Pareto Chart

Another important statistical chart is the Pareto chart, which is used to indicate which factors are the largest contributors to an outcome value. Pareto charts are often used in quality control studies to isolate the most significant factors in the failure of a manufacturer process. They can also be used with market research to indicate which factor and combination of factors is the most crucial buying decision. Pareto charts appear as combination charts, combining a column chart and a line chart. The column chart lists the individual factors sorted from the most significant factor to the least significant. The line chart provides the cumulative percentage that each factor contributes to the whole.

Haywood's market survey asked respondents to list which one of the following factors was most important in choosing their pack: brand name, customer support, price, and quality. He wants you display this information in a Pareto chart that shows the factor that was listed most often in the survey results followed by the factor that was listed second-most often in the survey results, and so forth.

To create a Pareto chart showing buying factors:

1. Go to the **Market Data** worksheet, and then select the range **H5:I8** containing the total responses in each of the four categories: brand name, support, price, and quality.
2. On the ribbon, click the **Insert** tab.
3. In the Charts group, click the **Insert Statistic Chart** button, and then click the **Pareto** subtype (the second subtype in the Histogram section). The Pareto chart is inserted into the worksheet.
4. Move the Pareto chart to the **Market Summary** worksheet, and then resize it to cover the range **F16:M26**.
5. Change the chart title to **Factors in Buying**.
6. Change the format of the chart title, chart area fill color, and plot area fill color to match the other charts on the sheet. See Figure 4-38.

Figure 4-38 Pareto chart of buying factors

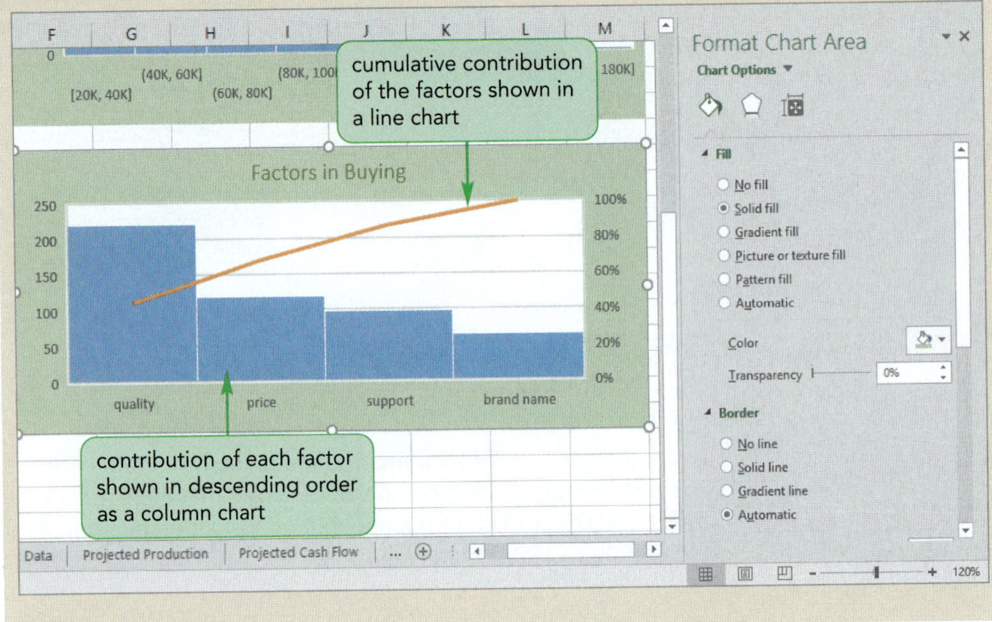

The Pareto chart quickly shows that quality is the most important factor in making a purchase for more than 200 of the respondents. The next most important factor is price, followed by support. Brand name is the least important factor. The line chart shows the cumulative effect of the four factors as a percentage of the whole. About 70 percent of the people in the survey listed quality or price as the most important factor in making a purchase, and about 90 percent listed quality, price, or customer support. Brand name, by comparison, had little impact on the respondent's buying decision, which is good for a new company entering the market.

Using a Waterfall Chart

A **waterfall chart** is used to track the effect of adding and subtracting values within a sum. Waterfall charts are often used to show the impact of revenue and expenses in profit and loss statements. The waterfall chart in Figure 4-39 is based on Backspace Gear's year 10 revenue and expenses projections.

Figure 4-39 Waterfall chart of Year 10 cash flow

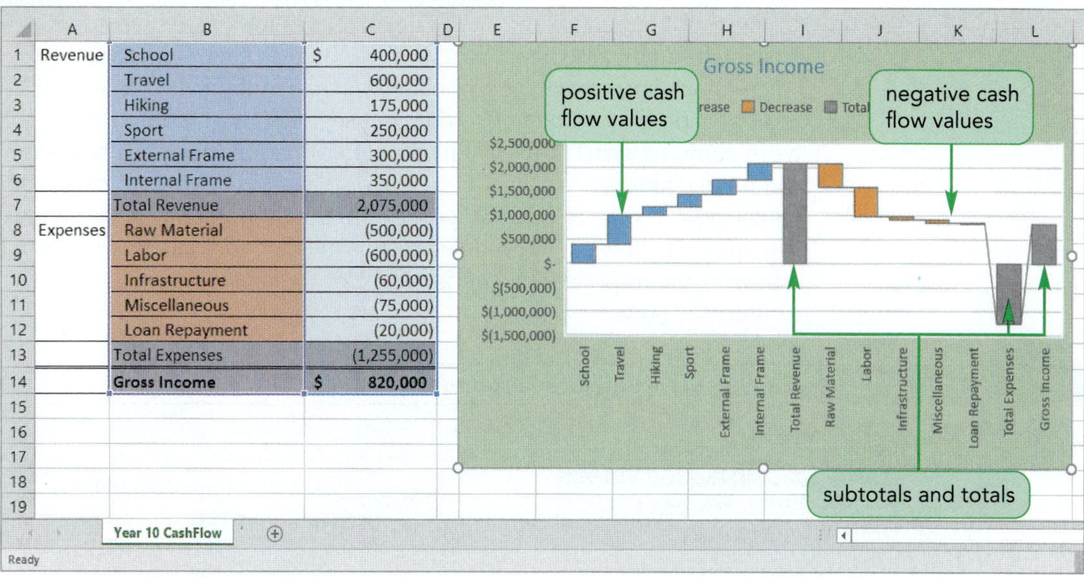

In waterfall charts, every positive value that adds to the total is represented by an increasing step, whereas negative values that subtract from the total are represented by decreasing steps. Subtotals such as the Total Revenue, Total Expenses, and Gross Income values are displayed in gray. The steps and colors in the chart show how each revenue and expense value contributes to the final gross income value.

Using a Hierarchical Chart

Hierarchy charts are like pie charts in that they show the relative contribution of groups to a whole. Unlike pie charts, a hierarchy chart also shows the organizational structure of the data with subcategories displayed within main categories. Excel supports two types of hierarchical charts: treemap charts and sunburst charts.

In a **treemap chart** each category is placed within a rectangle, and subcategories are nested as rectangles within those rectangles. The rectangles are sized to show the relative proportions of the two groups based on values from a data series. The treemap chart in Figure 4-40 measures the responses from the market survey broken down by gender and backpack type.

Figure 4-40 Treemap chart of preferences

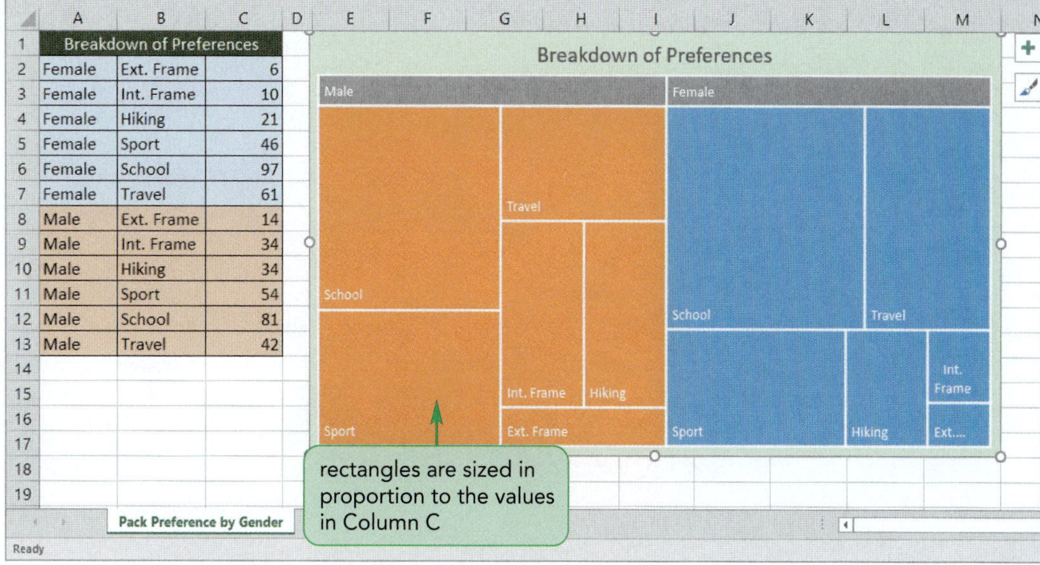

The size of the rectangles demonstrates how men and women in the survey differ in the types of packs they are likely to purchase. Men are more likely than women to purchase internal frame and hiking packs as indicated by the larger size of those rectangles in the treemap chart. Women, on the other hand, were more likely than men to purchase packs for school and travel. From this information, Haywood can tailor his product marketing to different segments of the population.

A **sunburst chart** conveys this same information through a series of concentric rings with the upper levels of the hierarchy displayed in the innermost rings. The size of the rings indicates the relative proportions of the different categories and subcategories. Figure 4-41 shows market survey results in a sunburst chart with three levels of rings showing the responses by gender, backpack category, and finally backpack type within category.

Figure 4-41 **Sunburst chart of backpack preferences**

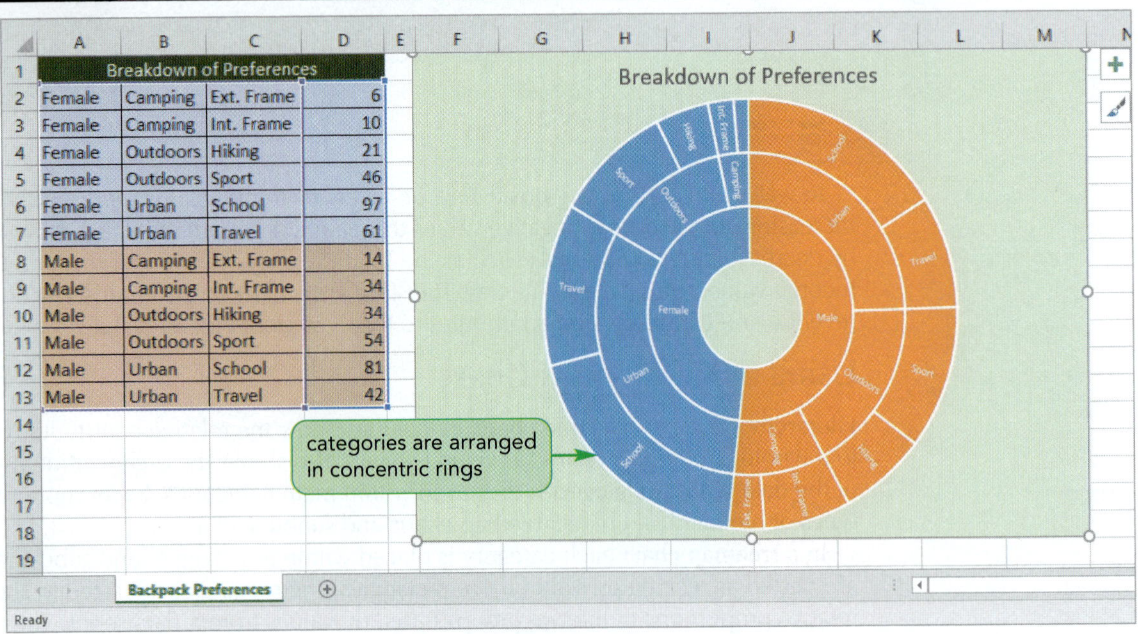

Sunburst charts are better than treemap charts at conveying information from multiple levels of nested categories and are better at displaying the relative sizes of the groups within each category level.

PROSKILLS

Decision Making: Choosing the Right Chart

Excel supports a wide variety of charts and chart styles. To decide which type of chart to use, you must evaluate your data and determine the ultimate purpose or goal of the chart. Consider how your data will appear in each type of chart before making a final decision.

- In general, pie charts should be used only when the number of categories is small and the relative sizes of the different slices can be easily distinguished. If you have several categories, use a column or bar chart.
- Line charts are best for categories that follow a sequential order. Be aware, however, that the time intervals must be a constant length if used in a line chart. Line charts will distort data that occurs at irregular time intervals, making it appear that the data values occurred at regular intervals when they did not.
- Pie, column, bar, and line charts assume that numbers are plotted against categories. In science and engineering applications, you will often want to plot two numeric values against one another. For that data, use **XY scatter charts**, which show the pattern or relationship between two or more sets of values. XY scatter charts are also useful for data recorded at irregular time intervals.

If you still can't find the right chart to meet your needs, you can create a custom chart based on the built-in chart types. Third-party vendors also sell software to allow Excel to create chart types that are not built into the software.

Creating Sparklines

Data can be displayed graphically without charts by using sparklines and data bars. A sparkline is a graphic that is displayed entirely within a worksheet cell. Because sparklines are compact in size, they don't include chart elements such as legends, titles, or gridlines. The goal of a sparkline is to convey the maximum amount of information within a very small space. As a result, sparklines are useful when you don't want charts to overwhelm the rest of your worksheet or take up valuable page space.

You can create the following types of sparklines in Excel:

- A line sparkline for highlighting trends
- A column sparkline for column charts
- A win/loss sparkline for highlighting positive and negative values

Figure 4-42 shows examples of each sparkline type. The line sparklines show the sales history from each department and across all four departments of a computer manufacturer. The sparklines provide enough information for you to examine the sales trend within and across departments. Notice that although total sales rose steadily during the year, some departments, such as Printers, showed a sales decline midway through the year.

Figure 4-42 **Types of sparklines**

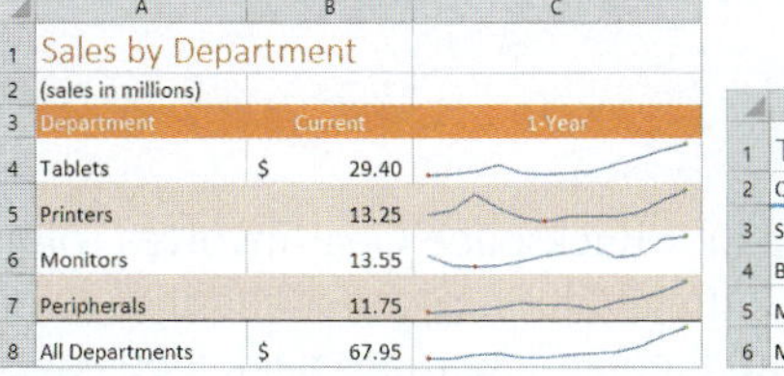

line sparklines

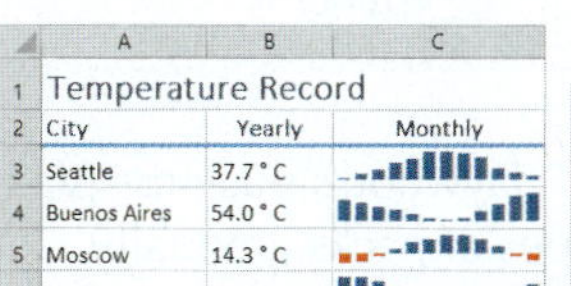

column sparklines

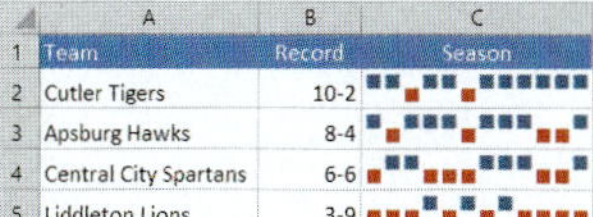

win/loss sparklines

The column sparklines present a record of monthly temperature averages for four cities. Temperatures above 0 degrees Celsius are presented in blue columns; temperatures below 0 degrees Celsius are presented in red columns that extend downward. The height of each column is related to the magnitude of the value it represents.

Finally, the win/loss sparklines reveal a snapshot of the season results for four sports teams. Wins are displayed in blue; losses are in red. From the sparklines, you can quickly see that the Cutler Tigers finished their 10–2 season with six straight wins, and the Liddleton Lions finished their 3–9 season with four straight losses.

INSIGHT

Edward Tufte and Chart Design Theory

Any serious study of charts will include the works of Edward Tufte, who pioneered the field of information design. One of Tufte's most important works is *The Visual Display of Quantitative Information*, in which he laid out several principles for the design of charts and graphics.

Tufte was concerned with what he termed as "chart junk," in which a proliferation of chart elements—chosen because they look "nice"—confuse and distract the reader. One measure of chart junk is Tufte's data-ink ratio, which is the amount of "ink" used to display quantitative information compared to the total ink required by the chart. Tufte advocated limiting the use of nondata ink. Nondata ink is any part of the chart that does not convey information about the data. One way of measuring the data-ink ratio is to determine how much of the chart you can erase without affecting the user's ability to interpret the chart. Tufte would argue for high data-ink ratios with a minimum of extraneous elements and graphics.

To this end, Tufte helped develop sparklines, which convey information with a high data-ink ratio within a compact space. Tufte believed that charts that can be viewed and comprehended at a glance have a greater impact on the reader than large and cluttered graphs, no matter how attractive they might be.

To create a set of sparklines, you first select the data you want to graph, and then select the range where you want the sparklines to appear. Note that the cells in which you insert the sparklines do not need to be blank because the sparklines are part of the cell background and do not replace any content.

REFERENCE

Creating and Editing Sparklines

- On the Insert tab, in the Sparklines group, click the Line, Column, or Win/Loss button.
- In the Data Range box, enter the range for the data source of the sparkline.
- In the Location Range box, enter the range into which to place the sparkline.
- Click the OK button.
- On the Sparkline Tools Design tab, in the Show group, click the appropriate check boxes to specify which markers to display on the sparkline.
- In the Group group, click the Axis button, and then click Show Axis to add an axis to the sparkline.

Haywood's business plan for Backspace Gear involves rolling out the different types of packs gradually, starting with the school and travel packs, which have the most consumer interest, and then adding more pack types over the first five years. The company won't start producing all six types of packs until year 6. Haywood suggests that you add a column sparkline to the Financial Summary worksheet that indicates this production plan.

To create column sparklines that show projected production:

1. Go to the **Financial Summary** worksheet, and then select the range **C5:C10**. This is the location range into which you will insert the sparklines.
2. On the ribbon, click the **Insert** tab.
3. In the Sparklines group, click the **Column** button. The Create Sparklines dialog box opens. The location range is already entered because you selected it before opening the dialog box.
4. With the insertion point in the Data Range box, click the **Projected Production** sheet tab, and then select the data in the range **B5:K10**. This range contains the data you want to chart in the sparklines.
5. Click the **OK** button. The Create Sparklines dialog box closes, and the column sparklines are added to the location range in the Financial Summary worksheet. See Figure 4-43.

Figure 4-43 Column sparklines of projected production for pack type

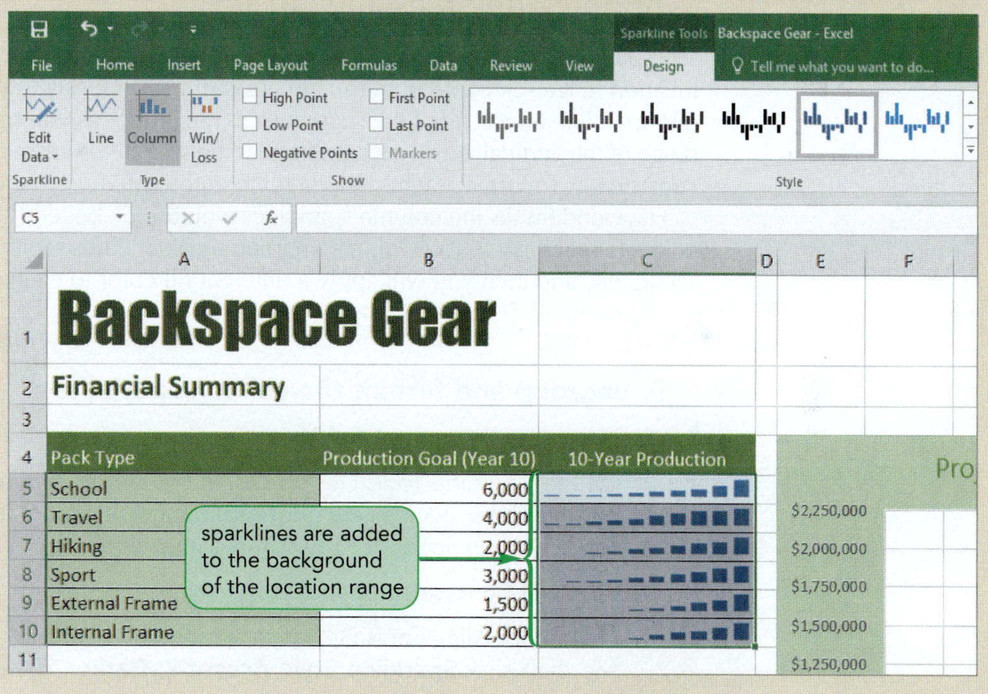

The column sparklines make it clear how the different product lines are placed into production at different times—school and travel packs first, and other models later in the production cycle. Each product, once it is introduced, is steadily produced in greater quantities as the decade progresses.

Formatting the Sparkline Axis

Because of their compact size, you have few formatting options with sparklines. One thing you can change is the scale of the vertical axis. The vertical axis will range from the minimum value to the maximum value. By default, this range is defined differently for each cell to maximize the available space. But this can be misleading. For example, the column sparklines in Figure 4-43 seem to show that Backspace Gear will be producing the same amount of each product line by the end of year 10 because the heights of the last columns are all the same. You can change the vertical axis scale to be the same for the related sparklines.

To set the scale of the column sparklines:

1. On the Financial Summary worksheet, make sure the range **C5:C10** is still selected. Because the sparklines are selected, the Sparkline Tools contextual tab appears on the ribbon.
2. On the Sparkline Tools Design tab, in the Group group, click the **Axis** button, and then click **Custom Value** in the Vertical Axis Maximum Value Options section. The Sparkline Vertical Axis Setting dialog box opens.
3. Select the value in the box, and then type **6000**. You do not have to set the vertical axis minimum value because Excel assumes this to be 0 for all of the column sparklines.
4. Click the **OK** button. The column sparklines are now based on the same vertical scale, with the height of each column indicating the number of packs produced per year.

Working with Sparkline Groups

The sparklines in the location range are part of a single group. Clicking any cell in the location range selects all of the sparklines in the group. Any formatting you apply to one sparkline affects all of the sparklines in the group, as you saw when you set the range of the vertical axis. This ensures that the sparklines for related data are formatted consistently. To format each sparkline differently, you must first ungroup them.

Haywood thinks the column sparklines would look better if they used different colors for each pack. You will first ungroup the sparklines so you can format them separately, and then you will apply a different fill color to each sparkline.

To ungroup and format the column sparklines:

1. Make sure the range **C5:C10** is still selected.
2. On the Sparkline Tools Design tab, in the Group group, click the **Ungroup** button. The sparklines are ungrouped, and selecting any one of the sparklines will no longer select the entire group.
3. Click cell **C6** to select it and its sparkline.
4. On the Sparkline Tools Design tab, in the Style group, click the **More** button, and then click **Sparkline Style Accent 2, Darker 25%** (the second style in the second row) in the Style gallery.
5. Click cell **C7**, and then change the sparkline style to **Sparkline Style Accent 4, (no dark or light)** (the fourth style in the third row) in the Style gallery.
6. Click cell **C8**, and then change the sparkline style to **Sparkline Style Accent 6, (no dark or light)** (the last style in the third row) in the Style gallery.
7. Click cell **C9**, and then change the sparkline style to **Sparkline Style Dark #1** (the first style in the fifth row) in the Style gallery.
8. Click cell **C10**, and then click **Sparkline Style Colorful #2** (the second style in the last row) in the Style gallery.
9. Click cell **A4** to deselect the sparklines. See Figure 4-44.

Figure 4-44 Sparklines formatted with different styles

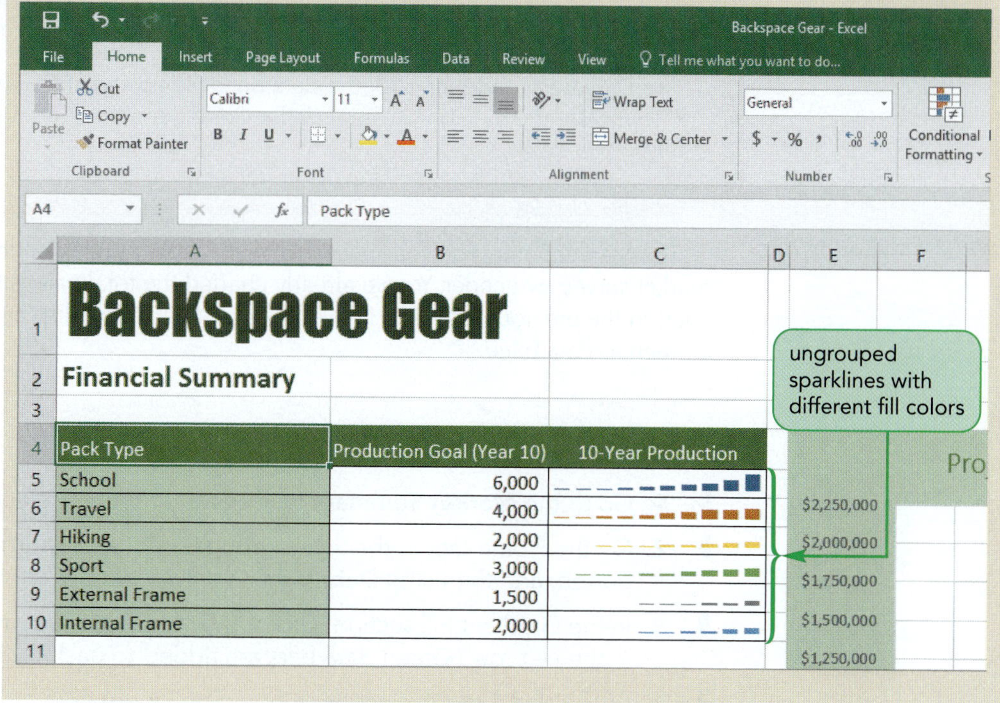

To regroup sparklines, you select all of the cells in the location range containing the sparklines and then click the Group button in the Group group on the Sparkline Tools Design tab. Be aware that regrouping sparklines causes them to share a common format, so you will lose any formatting applied to individual sparklines.

The Sparkline Color button applied a single color to the entire sparkline. You can also apply colors to individual markers within a sparkline by clicking the Marker Color button. Using this button, you can set a distinct color for negative values, maximum values, minimum values, first values, and last values. This is useful with line sparklines that track data across a time range in which you might want to identify the maximum value within that range or the minimum value.

Creating Data Bars

A data bar is a conditional format that adds a horizontal bar to the background of a cell containing a number. When applied to a range of cells, the data bars have the same appearance as a bar chart, with each cell containing one bar. The lengths of data bars are based on the value of each cell in the selected range. Cells with larger values have longer bars; cells with smaller values have shorter bars. Data bars are dynamic, changing as the cell's value changes.

Data bars differ from sparklines in that the bars are always placed in the cells containing the value they represent, and each cell represents only a single bar from the bar chart. By contrast, a column sparkline can be inserted anywhere within the workbook and can represent data from several rows or columns. However, like sparklines, data bars can be used to create compact graphs that can be easily integrated alongside the text and values stored in worksheet cells.

REFERENCE

Creating Data Bars

- Select the range containing the data you want to chart.
- On the Home tab, in the Styles group, click the Conditional Formatting button, point to Data Bars, and then click the data bar style you want to use.
- To modify the data bar rules, click the Conditional Formatting button, and then click Manage Rules.

The Market Summary worksheet contains a table of pack preferences from the market survey by gender. You've already charted the total values from this table as a pie chart in the previous session. Haywood suggests that you display the totals for men and women as data bars.

To add data bars to the worksheet:

1. Go to the **Market Summary** worksheet, and then select the range **C5:D10**.
2. On the Home tab, in the Styles group, click the **Conditional Formatting** button, and then click **Data Bars**. A gallery of data bar styles opens.
3. In the Gradient Fill section, click the **Green Data Bar** style (the second style in the first row.) Green data bars are added to each of the selected cells.
4. Click cell **A4** to deselect the range. See Figure 4-45.

Figure 4-45 **Data bars added to the Market Summary worksheet**

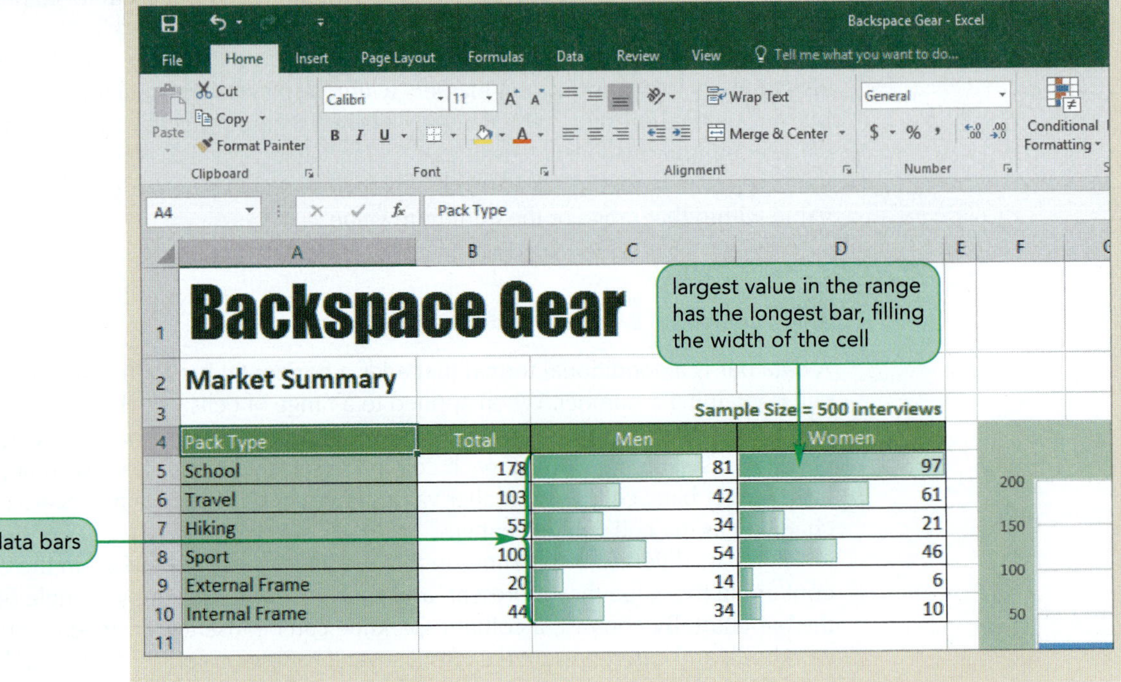

The data bars make it easy to compare the popularity of the different pack types among men and women. The bars clearly show that school packs are most popular followed by either the travel packs or the sport packs.

Modifying a Data Bar Rule

The lengths of the data bars are determined based on the values in the selected range. The cell with the largest value contains a data bar that extends across the entire width of the cell, and the lengths of the other bars in the selected range are determined relative to that bar. In some cases, this will result in the longest data bar overlapping its cell's data value, making it difficult to read. You can modify the length of the data bars by altering the rules of the conditional format.

TIP

With negative values, the data bars originate from the center of the cell—negative bars extend to the left, and positive bars extend to the right.

The longest data bar is in cell D5, representing a count of 97 respondents. The length of every other data bar is proportional to this length. However, because it is the longest, it also overlaps the value of the cell. You will modify the data bar rule, setting the maximum length to 120 so that the bar no longer overlaps the cell value.

To modify the data bar rule:

1. Select the range **C5:D10** containing the data bars.
2. On the Home tab, in the Styles group, click the **Conditional Formatting** button, and then click **Manage Rules**. The Conditional Formatting Rules Manager dialog box opens, displaying all the rules applied to any conditional format in the workbook.
3. Make sure **Current Selection** appears in the Show formatting rules for box. You'll edit the rule applied to the current selection—the data bars in the Market Summary worksheet.
4. Click the **Edit Rule** button to open the Edit Formatting Rule dialog box.

   You want to modify this rule so that the maximum value for the data bar is set to 120. All data bar lengths will then be defined relative to this value.
5. In the Type row, click the **Maximum arrow**, and then click **Number**.
6. Press the **Tab** key to move the insertion point to the Maximum box in the Value row, and then type **120**. See Figure 4-46.

Figure 4-46 Edit Formatting Rule dialog box

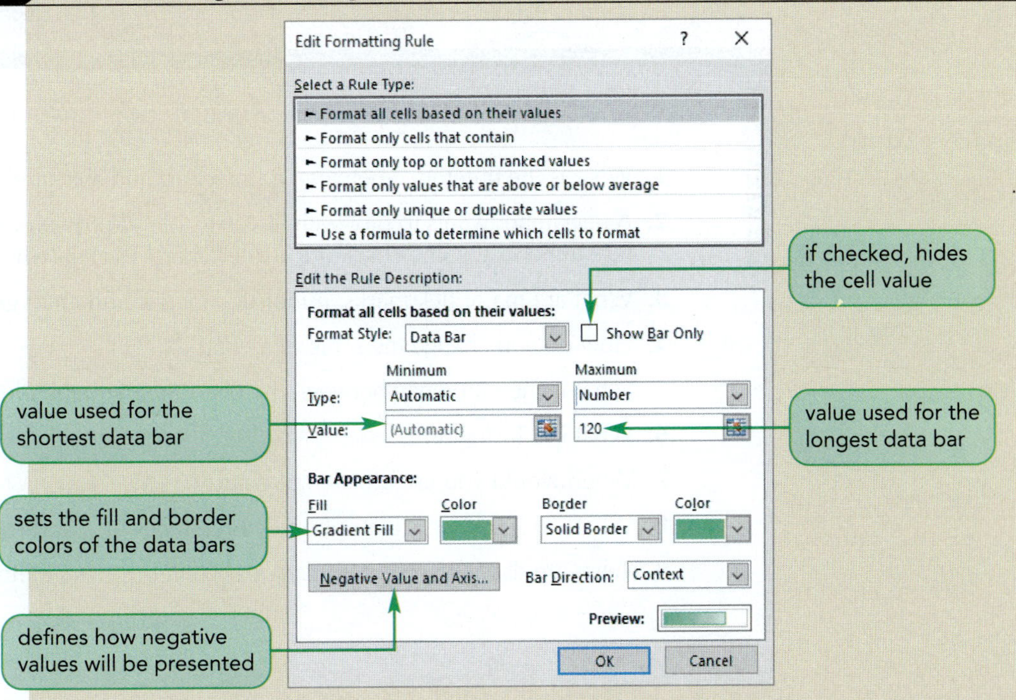

7. Click the **OK** button in each dialog box, and then select cell **A4**. The lengths of the data bars are reduced so that no cell values are obscured. See Figure 4-47.

Figure 4-47 **Revised data bars**

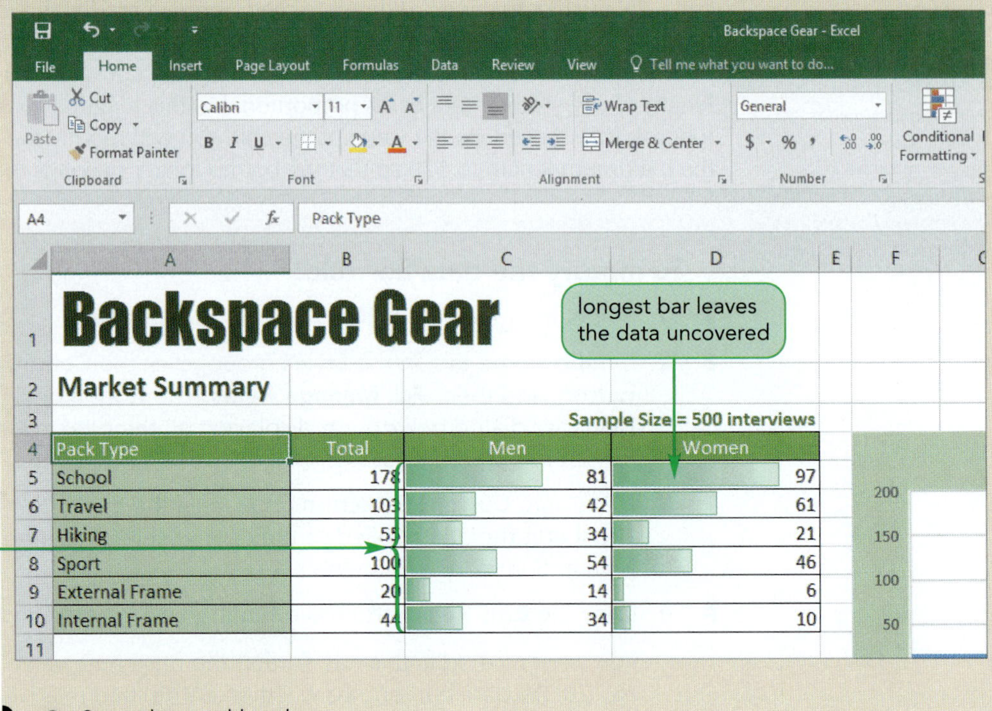

8. Save the workbook.

You have finished your work on the Backspace Gear workbook. Haywood is pleased with the charts you created and feels that they provide useful visuals for anyone considering his business proposal.

REVIEW

Session 4.2 Quick Check

1. What is the difference between a line chart and a scatter chart?
2. A researcher wants to plot weight versus blood pressure. Should the researcher use a line chart or a scatter chart? Explain why.
3. What are major tick marks, minor tick marks, and chart gridlines?
4. How do you change the scale of a chart axis?
5. What is the difference between the chart area and the plot area?
6. What is a histogram?
7. When would you use a waterfall chart?
8. What are sparklines? Describe the three types of sparklines.
9. What are data bars? How do data bars differ from sparklines?

PRACTICE

Review Assignments

Data File needed for the Review Assignments: Market.xlsx

Haywood is creating another workbook that will have market survey data on competing manufacturers as well as more demographic data on potential Backspace Gear customers. He wants you to add charts to his workbook that show this data graphically. Complete the following:

1. Open the **Market** workbook located in the Excel4 > Review folder included with your Data Files, and then save the workbook as **Market Analysis** in the location specified by your instructor.
2. In the Documentation worksheet, enter your name in cell B3 and the date in cell B4.
3. In the Business Loan worksheet, enter the data values and formulas required to calculate the monthly payment on a business loan of **$225,000** at **6.2%** annual interest to be repaid in **15 years**. Calculate both the monthly payment and the size of the annual payment.
4. In the Market Analysis worksheet, use the data in the range A4:B9 to create a pie chart in the range A11:C24 that shows information about competitors in the Northwest region.
5. Apply the Style 11 chart style to the pie chart, and then move the legend to the left side of the chart. Place the data labels on the inside end of each pie slice.
6. In the Market Tables worksheet, create a clustered column chart of the data in the range A5:F10 to show how many units each competitor sold in the Northwest region in the past five years.
7. Move the chart to the Market Analysis worksheet, and then resize it to cover the range E4:L13. Change the chart title to **Units Sold**. Apply the Style 9 chart style to the chart. Add both primary major horizontal and vertical gridlines. Change the fill color of the chart area to the Gold Accent 4, Lighter 80% theme color and the fill color of the plot area to white. Move the legend to the right side of the chart area.
8. In the Market Tables worksheet, use the data in the range A5:F10 to create a stacked column chart. Move the chart to the Market Analysis worksheet, and then resize it to cover the range E15:L24.
9. Change the chart title to **Total Units Sold**. Format the chart with the same fill colors and gridlines you used the clustered column chart. Move the legend to the right side of the chart.
10. In the Market Tables worksheet, select the nonadjacent range A5:F5,A11:F11,A29:F29, and then create a combination chart with Total Units as a clustered column chart and Total Revenue as a line chart displayed on the secondary axis.
11. Move the chart to the Market Analysis worksheet, and then resize it to cover the range E26:L40. Change the chart title to **Units Sold and Revenue**. Format the chart with the same fill colors and gridlines you used the clustered column chart. Remove the chart legend.
12. Add axis titles to the primary and secondary vertical axes with the title **Total Units** on the primary axis and **Total Revenue** on the secondary axis. Rotate the secondary axis text down. Change the color of the scales and axis titles for the primary and secondary axes to match the color of the clustered column chart and the line chart.
13. Change the scale of the Total Revenue axis to go from $3,500,000 to $5,000,000 in intervals of $250,000.
14. In the Market Tables worksheet, select the range A23:A28,F23:F28 containing the final year revenue for each brand, and then create a Pareto chart based on this data. Move the chart to the Market Analysis worksheet, and then resize it to cover the range A26:C40.
15. Change the chart title to **Market Revenue (2017)**. Format the chart with the same fill colors and gridlines you used the clustered column chart.
16. In the Survey Data worksheet, create a histogram of the distribution of customer ages in the range E7:E506. Change the chart title to **Age Distribution**. Resize the chart to cover the range G4:P22 in the Survey Data worksheet.
17. Change the width of the histogram bins to **5** units.

18. In the Market Analysis worksheet, add gradient fill orange data bars to the values in the range B5:B9. Set the maximum value of the data bars to **0.6**.
19. In the range C5:C9, insert line sparklines based on the data in the range B15:F19 of the Market Tables worksheet to show how the competitors' share of the market has changed over the past five years.
20. Save the workbook, and then close it.

APPLY

Case Problem 1

Data File needed for this Case Problem: Stefanek.xlsx

Stefanek Budget Edmund and Lydia Stefanek of Little Rock, Arkansas, are using Excel to track their family budget to determine whether they can afford the monthly loan payments that would come with the purchase of a new house. The couple is considering a $285,000 mortgage at a 4.30 percent interest rate to be paid back over 25 years. They want to know the impact that this mortgage will have on their budget. Complete the following:

1. Open the **Stefanek** workbook located in the Excel4 > Case1 folder included with your Data Files, and then save the workbook as **Stefanek Budget** in the location specified by your instructor.
2. In the Documentation worksheet, enter your name in cell B3 and the date in cell B4.
3. In the Budget worksheet, in the range B3:B8, enter the parameters for a **$285,000** mortgage at **4.3%** annual interest paid back over **25 years**. Calculate the interest rate per month and the total number of payments.
4. In cell B10, calculate the amount of the monthly payment needed to pay back the mortgage.
5. In the range C15:N15, calculate the total income from Edmund and Lydia's monthly salaries.
6. In the range C22:N22, use an absolute reference to insert the monthly mortgage payment you calculated in cell B10.
7. In the range C24:N24, calculate Edmund and Lydia's total expenses per month.
8. In the range C25:N25, calculate the couple's monthly net income by adding their income and their expenses. (Note that expenses are entered as negative values.)
9. In the range C28:C40, calculate the averages for the income and expenses from the 12-month budget.
10. In the range C28:C40, add data bars to the values. Note that negative data bars are displayed to the left of the center point in the cell, whereas positive data bars are displayed to the right.
11. In the range D28:D40, insert line sparklines using the values from the range C13:N25 to show how the different budget entries change throughout the year.
12. Create a pie chart of the income values in the range B28:C29 to show the breakdown of the family income between Edmund and Lydia. Resize the chart to cover the range E27:I40. Change the chart title to **Income** and apply the Style3 chart style to chart.
13. Create a pie chart of the expenses values in the range B31:C38. Resize the chart to cover the range J27:N40. Change the chart title to **Expenses** and apply the Style3 chart style to the chart. Change the position of the data labels to data callouts. If any data labels appear to overlap, select one of the overlapping data labels, and drag it to another position.
14. Save the workbook, and then close it.

APPLY

Case Problem 2

Data File needed for this Case Problem: Circuit.xlsx

Circuit Realty Alice Cho works at Circuit Realty in Tempe, Arizona. She wants to use Excel to summarize the home listings in the Tempe area. Alice has already inserted some of the new listings into an Excel workbook including descriptive statistics about the homes and their prices. She wants your help in summarizing this data using informative charts. Complete the following:

1. Open the **Circuit** workbook located in the Excel4 > Case2 folder included with your Data Files, and then save the workbook as **Circuit Realty** in the location specified by your instructor.
2. In the Documentation worksheet, enter your name in cell B3 and the date in cell B4.
3. In the Housing Tables worksheet, using the data in the range A4:B8, create a 2-D pie chart of the number of listings by region. Move the pie chart to the Summary worksheet in the range A4:E15. Change the chart title to **Listings by Region**. Add data labels showing the percentage of listings in each region, displaying the data labels outside the pie slices.
4. In the Housing Tables worksheet, using the range A10:B14, create a pie chart of the listings by the number of bedrooms. Move the pie chart to the Summary worksheet in the range A17:E28. Change the chart title to **Listings by Bedrooms**. Add data labels showing the percentage of listings in each category outside the pie slices.
5. In the Housing Tables worksheet, using the range A16:B22, create a pie chart of the listings by the number of bathrooms. Move the pie chart to the Summary worksheet in the range A30:E341. Change the chart title to **Listings by Bathrooms** and format the pie chart to match the two other pie charts.
6. In the Housing Tables worksheet, using the data in the range D4:E8, create a column chart showing the average home price in four Tempe regions. Move the chart to the Summary worksheet in the range G4:L15. Change the chart title to **Average Price by Region**.
7. In the Housing Tables worksheet, using the data in the range D10:E15, create a column chart of the average home price by age of the home. Move the chart to the Summary worksheet in the range G17:L28. Change the chart title to **Average Price by Home Age**.
8. In the Housing Tables worksheet, using the data in the range D17:E24, create a column chart of the average home price by house size. Move the chart to the Summary worksheet in the range G30:L41. Change the chart title to **Average Price by Home Size**.
9. In the Listings worksheet, create a histogram of all of the home prices in the range H4:H185. Move the histogram to the Summary worksheet in the range N4:U17. Change the chart title to **Home Prices**. Set the scale of the vertical axis to go from **0** to **50**. Set the number of bins to **6**. Set the overflow bin value to **350,000** and the underflow bin value to **150,000**.
10. Create a histogram of the distribution of home prices in each of the four regions, as follows:
    a. Use the data from the range H52:H107 in the Listings worksheet to create the North Region histogram. Place the chart in the range N18:U28 of the Summary worksheet. Change the chart title to **North Region**.
    b. Use the data from the range H5:H51 in the Listings worksheet to create the East Region histogram. Place the chart in the range N29:U39 of the Summary worksheet. Change the chart title to **East Region**.
    c. Use the data from the range H108:H143 in the Listings worksheet to create the South Region histogram. Place the chart in the range N40:U50 of the Summary worksheet. Change the chart title to **South Region**.
    d. Use the data from the range H144:H185 in the Listings worksheet to create the West Region histogram. Place the chart in the range N51:U61 of the Summary worksheet. Change the chart title to **West Region**.
11. The four regional histograms should use a common scale. For each histogram, set the scale of the vertical axis from **0** to **20**, set the number of bins to **6**, set the overflow bin value to **350,000**, and the underflow bin value to **150,000**.

12. In the Price History worksheet, use the data in the range A4:C152 to create a combination chart. Display the Average Price as a line chart on the primary axis and display the Foreclosure values as a column chart on the secondary axis. Move the chart to the Summary worksheet in the range A43:L61. Change the chart title to **Average Home Price and Foreclosure Rates**.
13. Add axis titles to the combination chart, naming the left axis **Average Home Price** and the right axis **Foreclosure (per 10,000)**. Change the horizontal axis title to **Date**. Change the minimum value on the left axis to **100,000**.
14. Change the color of the primary axis and axis title to match the color of the line in the line chart. Change the color of the secondary axis and axis title to match the color used in the column chart. Remove the chart legend.
15. Save the workbook, and then close it.

CHALLENGE

Case Problem 3

Data File needed for this Case Problem: Skyway.xlsx

Skyway Funds Kristin Morandi is an accounts assistant at Skyway Funds, a financial consulting firm in Monroe, Louisiana. Kristin needs to summarize information on companies that are held in stock by the firm's clients. You will help her develop a workbook that will serve as a prototype for future reports. She wants the workbook to include charts of the company's financial condition, structure, and recent stock performance. Stock market charts should display the stock's daily opening; high, low, and closing values; and the number of shares traded for each day of the past few weeks. The volume of shares traded should be expressed in terms of millions of shares. Complete the following:

1. Open the **Skyway** workbook located in the Excel4 > Case3 folder included with your Data Files, and then save the workbook as **Skyway Funds** in the location specified by your instructor.
2. In the Documentation worksheet, enter your name in cell B3 and the date in cell B4.
3. In the Overview worksheet, add green data bars with a gradient fill to the employee numbers in the range B15:B19. Set the maximum value of the data bars to **20,000**.
4. Add a pie chart of the shareholder data in the range A22:B24. Resize and position the chart to cover the range A26:B37. Do not display a chart title. Add data labels to the pie chart, and then move the legend to the left edge of the chart area.
5. In the Income Statement worksheet, create a 3-D column chart of the income and expenses data from the last three years in the range A4:D4,A7:D7,A13:D13,A20:D20.
6. Move the chart to the range D6:I20 of the Overview worksheet. Change the chart title to **Income and Expenses (Thousands of Dollars)**. Remove the chart legend.

Explore 7. Double-click the horizontal axis values to open the Format Axis pane. Expand the Axis Options list, and click the Categories in reverse order check box in the Axis position section to display the year value in reverse order so that 2015 is listed first.

Explore 8. Add the data table chart element with legend keys showing the actual figures used in the column chart. (*Hint*: Use the Chart Elements button to add the data table to the chart, and use the data table submenu to show the legend keys.)

9. In the Balance Sheet worksheet, create a 3-D stacked column chart of the data in the range A4:D4,A7:D11 to show the company's assets over the past three years. Move the chart to the Overview worksheet covering the range D21:I37. Change the chart title to **Assets (Thousands of Dollars)**. Remove the chart legend.

Explore 10. Use the Switch Row/Column button in the Data group on the Chart Tools Design tab to switch the categories used in the chart from the asset categories to the year values. Display the values on the horizontal axis in reverse order, and add a data table chart element with legend keys to the chart.

11. Repeat Steps 9 and 10 to create a stacked column chart of the company's liabilities in the range A4:D4,A15:D18 in the Balance Sheet worksheet. Place the chart in the range J21:P37 of the Overview worksheet. Change the chart title to **Liabilities (Thousands of Dollars).**
12. Create a line chart of the company's net cash flow using the data in the range A4:D4,A26:D26 of the Cash Flow worksheet. Place the chart in the range J6:P20 of the Overview worksheet. Display the values in the horizontal axis in reverse order. Change the chart title to **Net Cash Flow (Thousands of Dollars)**.
13. **Explore** In the Stock History worksheet, select the data in the range A4:F9, and then insert a Volume-Open-High-Low-Close chart that shows the stock's volume of shares traded, opening value, high value, low value, and closing value for the previous five days on the market. Move the chart to the Overview worksheet in the range A39:D54.
14. Change the chart title to **5-Day Stock Chart**. Remove the chart gridlines and the chart legend. Change the scale of the left vertical axis to go from **0** to **8**.
15. In the Stock History worksheet, create another Volume-Open-High-Low-Close chart for the 1-year stock values located in the range A4:F262. Move the chart to the Overview worksheet in the range E39:J54. Change the chart title to **1-Year Stock Chart**. Remove the chart legend and gridlines.
16. Create a stock chart for all of the stock market data in the range A4:F2242 of the Stock History worksheet. Move the chart to the range K39:P54 of the Overview worksheet. Change the chart title to **All Years Stock Chart** and remove the chart legend and gridlines.
17. Save the workbook, and then close it.

CREATE

Case Problem 4

Data File needed for this Case Problem: Datasports.xlsx

Datasports Diane Wilkes runs the Datasports website for sports fans who are interested in the statistics and data that underlie sports. She is developing a series of workbooks in which she can enter statistics and charts for recent sporting events. She wants your help designing the charts and graphics that will appear in the workbook for college basketball games. She has already created a sample workbook containing the results of a hypothetical game between the University of Maryland and the University of Minnesota. She wants you to design and create the charts. For each chart, you need to:

- Include a descriptive chart title.
- Add horizontal and vertical gridlines.
- Add and remove chart elements to effectively illustrate the data.
- Change the colors and format of chart elements to create an attractive chart.
- Insert chart data labels as needed to explain the data.
- Resize and position charts to create an attractive and effective workbook.

Complete the following:

1. Open the **Datasports** workbook located in the Excel4 > Case4 folder included with your Data Files, and then save the workbook as **Datasports Report** in the location specified by your instructor.
2. In the Documentation worksheet, enter your name in cell B3 and the date in cell B4.
3. Create two column charts, as follows, and place them in the Game Report worksheet:
    a. Use the data in the range A6:A19,I6:I19 of the Box Score worksheet to chart the points scores by the University of Maryland players.
    b. Use the data in the range A23:A32,I23:I32 of the Box Score worksheet to chart the points score by the Minnesota players.

4. Add a line chart to the Game Report worksheet tracking the changing score of the game from its beginning to its end. Use the data in the range B5:D47 of the Game Log worksheet as the chart's data source.
5. Add eight pie charts to the Game Report worksheet in comparing the Maryland and Minnesota results for points, field goal percentage, free throw percentage, 3-point field goals, assists, rebounds, turnovers, and blocked shots. Use the data in the Box Score worksheet as the data source for these pie charts.
6. In the Game Log worksheet, in the range E6:E47, calculate the value of the Minnesota score minus the value of the Maryland score.
7. Add data bars to the values in the range E6:E47 showing the score difference as the game progresses. The format of the data bars is up to you.
8. In the Season Record worksheet, in the ranges C6:C19 and G6:G19, enter **–1** for every game that the team lost and **1** for every game that the team won.
9. In the Game Report worksheet, create two sparklines, as follows:
   a. In cell D6, insert a Win/Loss sparkline using the values from the range C6:C19 of the Season Record worksheet to show a graphic of Maryland's conference wins and losses.
   b. In cell D7, insert a Win/Loss sparkline using the values from the range G6:G19 of the Season Record worksheet to show a graphic of Minnesota's wins and losses.
10. Save the workbook, and then close it.

MODULE 5

Working with Excel Tables, PivotTables, and PivotCharts

Tracking Sales Data

OBJECTIVES

Session 5.1
- Explore a structured range of data
- Freeze rows and columns
- Plan and create an Excel table
- Rename and format an Excel table
- Add, edit, and delete records in an Excel table
- Sort data

Session 5.2
- Filter data using filter buttons
- Filter an Excel table with a slicer
- Insert a Total row to summarize an Excel table
- Split a worksheet into two panes
- Insert subtotals into a range of data
- Use the Outline buttons to show or hide details

Session 5.3
- Create and modify a PivotTable
- Apply PivotTable styles and formatting
- Filter a PivotTable
- Insert a slicer to filter a PivotTable
- Insert a recommended PivotTable
- Create a PivotChart

Case | *Victoria's Veggies*

Victoria Calderon has a very large backyard farm in Watertown, Wisconsin, and a passion for local, organic, fresh vegetables. Five years ago, she started selling organic vegetables harvested from her backyard farm at a roadside stand in front of her home. Over the years, she expanded from selling fresh vegetables to individual customers to supplying restaurants, group homes, and residential care facilities. As the stand has become more popular, Victoria has hired staff to help during the busy selling times. To better accommodate both her individual customers and business clients, six months ago, she opened Victoria's Veggies as a storefront. She stocks the store with vegetables grown in her own backyard farm and supplements her supply with fresh vegetables that she purchases from the year-round farmers market in Madison.

Victoria wants to use the June data to analyze the current state of Victoria's Veggies storefront operations. Victoria has entered the June sales data into an Excel workbook and wants you to help her analyze the data. You'll work with the data as an Excel table so you can easily edit, sort, and filter the data. You'll also summarize the data using the Subtotals command, a PivotTable, and a PivotChart.

STARTING DATA FILES

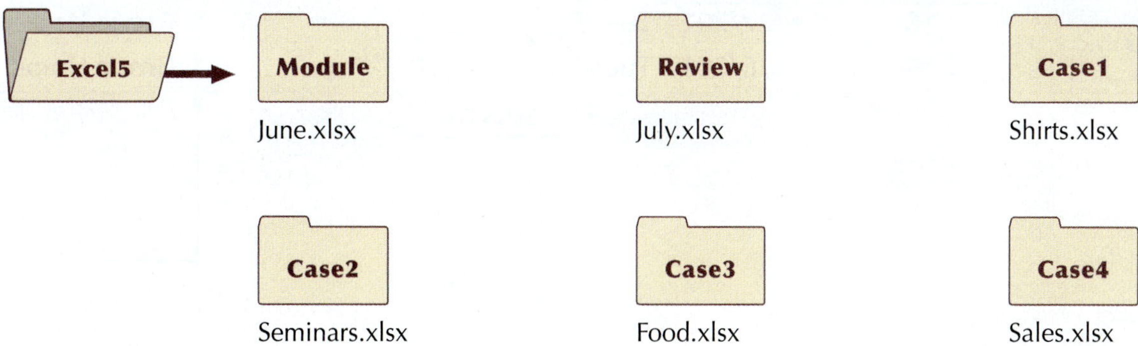

Session 5.1 Visual Overview:

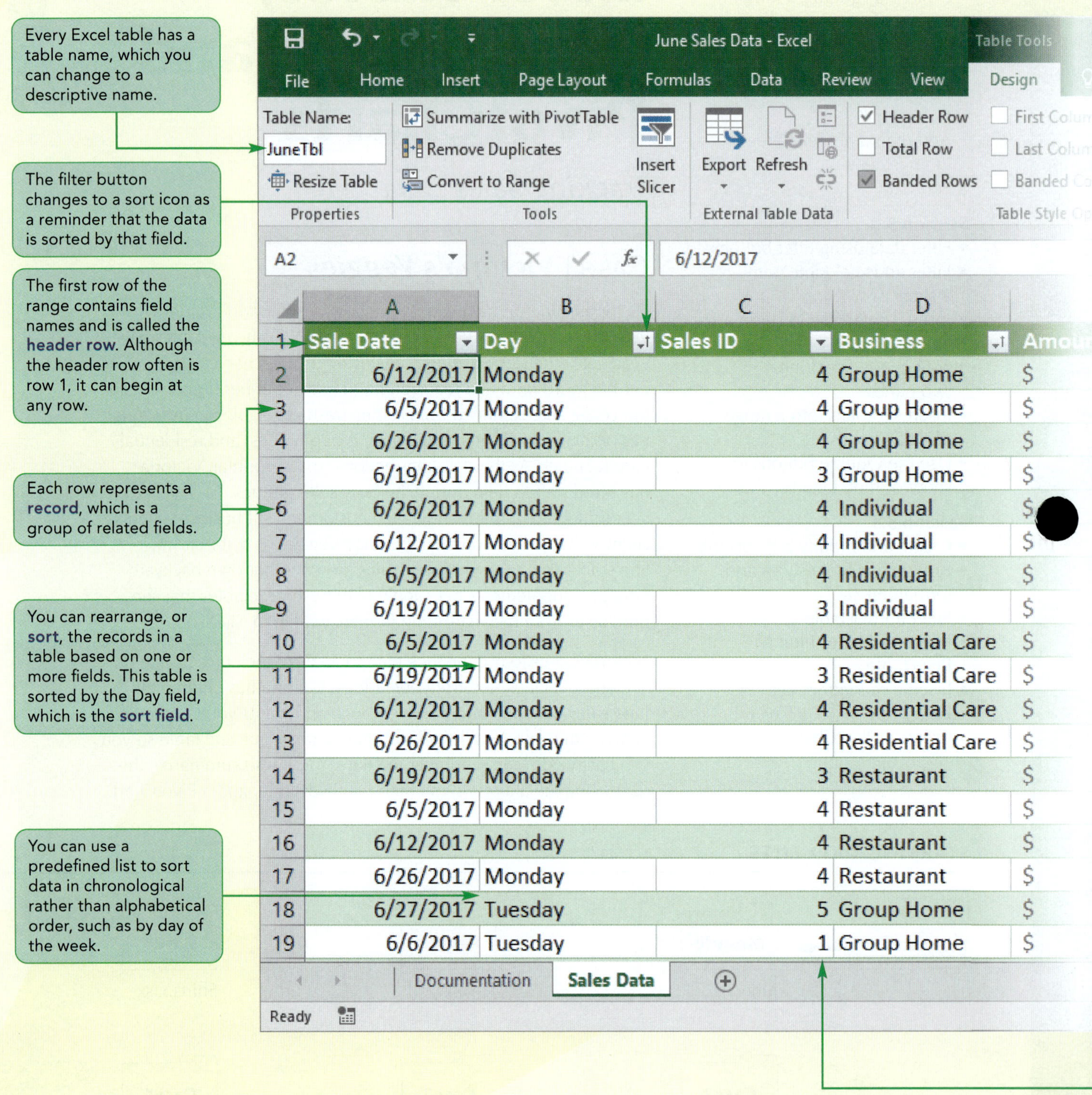
Every Excel table has a table name, which you can change to a descriptive name.
The filter button changes to a sort icon as a reminder that the data is sorted by that field.
The first row of the range contains field names and is called the header row. Although the header row often is row 1, it can begin at any row.
Each row represents a record, which is a group of related fields.
You can rearrange, or sort, the records in a table based on one or more fields. This table is sorted by the Day field, which is the sort field.
You can use a predefined list to sort data in chronological rather than alphabetical order, such as by day of the week.
June Sales Data - Excel
Table Tools
File
Home
Insert
Page Layout
Formulas
Data
Review
View
Design
Table Name:
JuneTbl
Resize Table
Properties
Summarize with PivotTable
Remove Duplicates
Convert to Range
Tools
Insert Slicer
Export
Refresh
External Table Data
Header Row
Total Row
Banded Rows
A2
6/12/2017
Sale Date
Day
Sales ID
Business
Documentation
Sales Data
Ready

Elements of an Excel Table

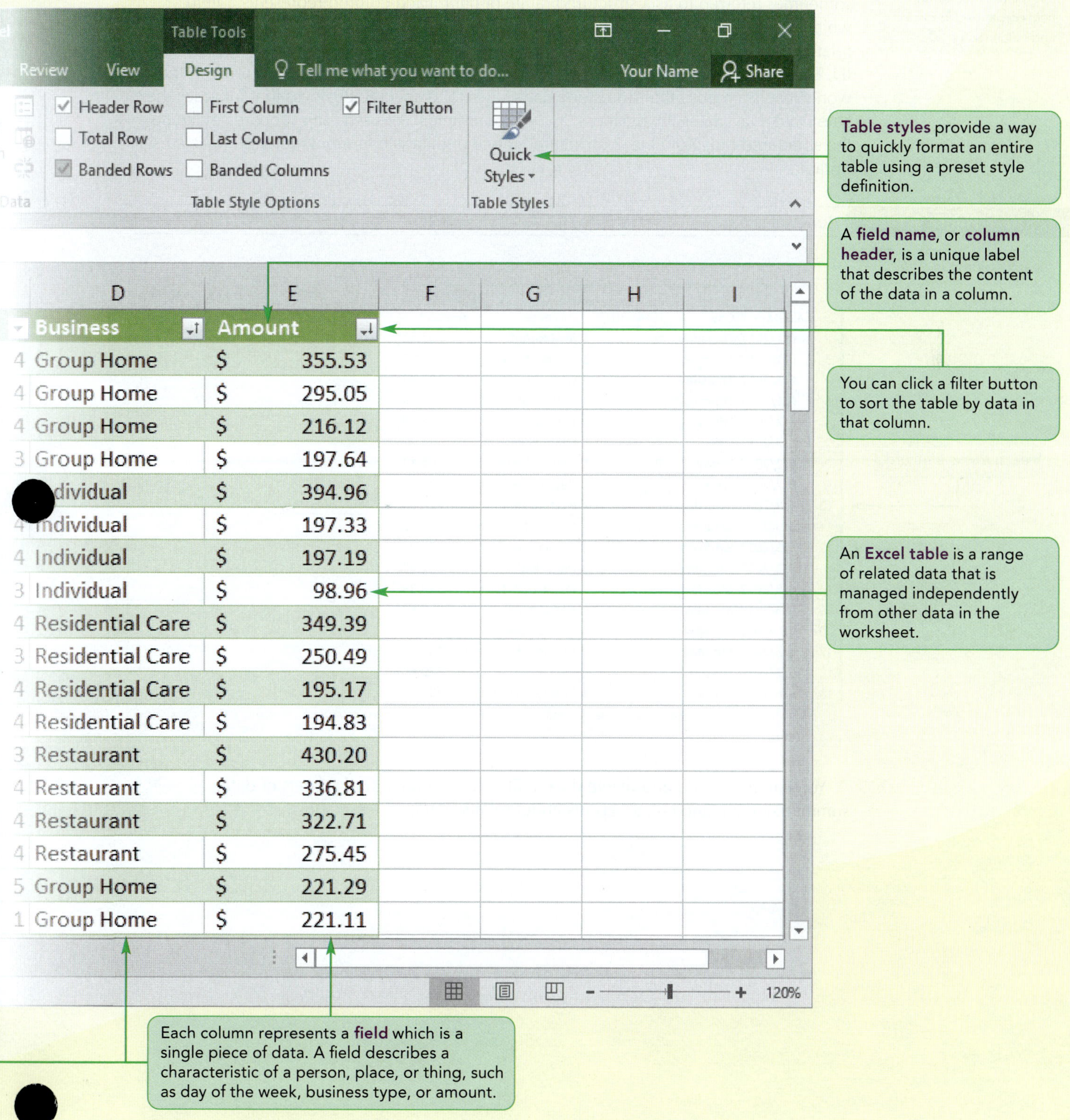
Table Tools
Review View Design Tell me what you want to do... Your Name Share
Header Row First Column Filter Button
Total Row Last Column
Banded Rows Banded Columns
Table Style Options
Quick Styles
Table Styles
D E F G H I
Business Amount
Group Home $ 355.53
Group Home $ 295.05
Group Home $ 216.12
Group Home $ 197.64
Individual $ 394.96
Individual $ 197.33
Individual $ 197.19
Individual $ 98.96
Residential Care $ 349.39
Residential Care $ 250.49
Residential Care $ 195.17
Residential Care $ 194.83
Restaurant $ 430.20
Restaurant $ 336.81
Restaurant $ 322.71
Restaurant $ 275.45
Group Home $ 221.29
Group Home $ 221.11
120%
Table styles provide a way to quickly format an entire table using a preset style definition.
A **field name**, or **column header**, is a unique label that describes the content of the data in a column.
You can click a filter button to sort the table by data in that column.
An **Excel table** is a range of related data that is managed independently from other data in the worksheet.
Each column represents a **field** which is a single piece of data. A field describes a characteristic of a person, place, or thing, such as day of the week, business type, or amount.

Planning a Structured Range of Data

TIP

In Excel, a range of data is any block of cells, whereas a structured range of data has related records and fields organized in rows and columns.

A worksheet is often used to manage related data, such as lists of clients, products, or transactions. For example, the June sales for Victoria's Veggies that Victoria entered in the Sales Data worksheet, which is shown in Figure 5-1, are a collection of related data. Related data that is organized in columns and rows, such as the June sales, is sometimes referred to as a structured range of data. Each column represents a field, which is a single piece of data. Each row represents a record, which is a group of related fields. In the Sales Data worksheet, the columns labeled Sale Date, Day, Sales ID, Business, and Amount are fields that store different pieces of data. Each row in the worksheet is a record that stores one day's sales for a specific business that includes the Sale Date, Day, Sales ID, Business, and Amount fields. All of the sales records make up the structured range of data. A structured range of data is commonly referred to as a list or table.

Figure 5-1 **June sales data**

each column is a field
each row is a record

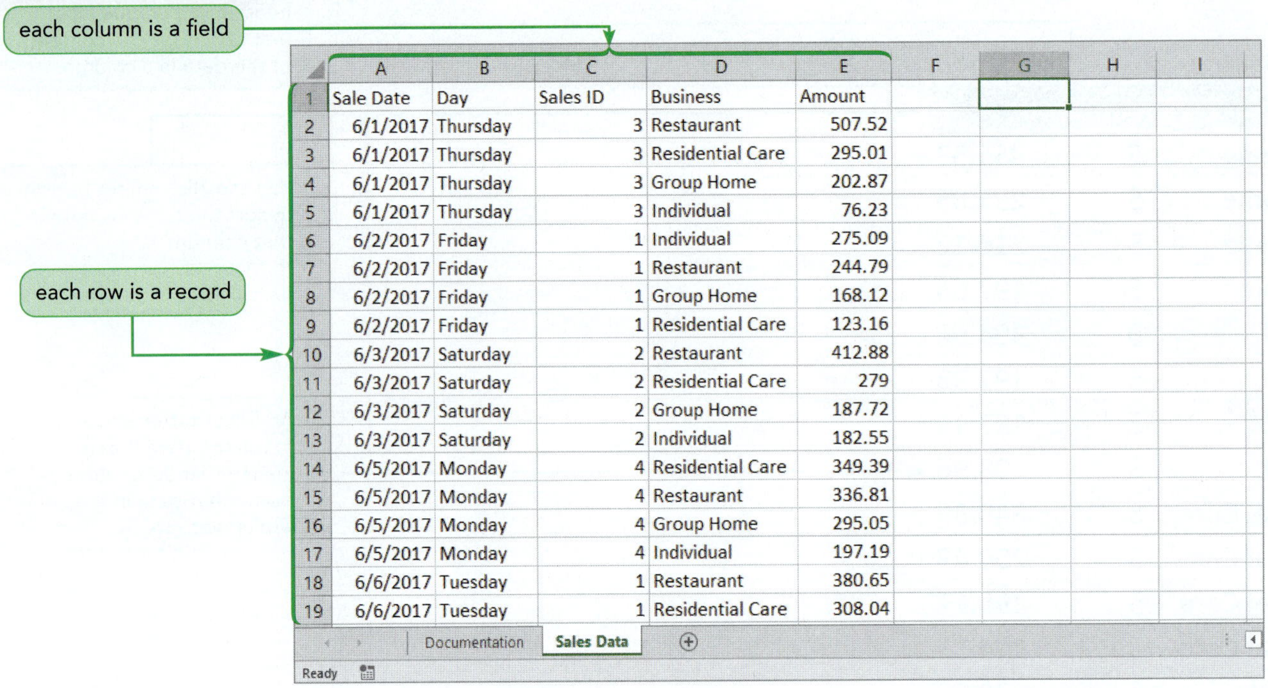

	A	B	C	D	E
1	Sale Date	Day	Sales ID	Business	Amount
2	6/1/2017	Thursday	3	Restaurant	507.52
3	6/1/2017	Thursday	3	Residential Care	295.01
4	6/1/2017	Thursday	3	Group Home	202.87
5	6/1/2017	Thursday	3	Individual	76.23
6	6/2/2017	Friday	1	Individual	275.09
7	6/2/2017	Friday	1	Restaurant	244.79
8	6/2/2017	Friday	1	Group Home	168.12
9	6/2/2017	Friday	1	Residential Care	123.16
10	6/3/2017	Saturday	2	Restaurant	412.88
11	6/3/2017	Saturday	2	Residential Care	279
12	6/3/2017	Saturday	2	Group Home	187.72
13	6/3/2017	Saturday	2	Individual	182.55
14	6/5/2017	Monday	4	Residential Care	349.39
15	6/5/2017	Monday	4	Restaurant	336.81
16	6/5/2017	Monday	4	Group Home	295.05
17	6/5/2017	Monday	4	Individual	197.19
18	6/6/2017	Tuesday	1	Restaurant	380.65
19	6/6/2017	Tuesday	1	Residential Care	308.04

Documentation
Sales Data
Ready

You can easily add and delete data, edit data, sort data, find subsets of data, summarize data, and create reports about related data.

PROSKILLS

Decision Making: The Importance of Planning

Before you create a structured range of data, you should create a plan. Planning involves gathering relevant information about the data and deciding your goals. The end results you want to achieve will help you determine the kind of data to include in each record and how to divide that data into fields. Specifically, you should do the following to create an effective plan:

- Spend time thinking about how you will use the data.
- Consider what reports you want to create for different audiences (supervisors, customers, directors, and so forth) and the fields needed to produce those reports.
- Think about the various questions, or queries, you want answered and the fields needed to create those results.

This information is often documented in a **data definition table**, which lists the fields to be maintained for each record, a description of the information each field will include, and the type of data (such as numbers, text, or dates) stored in each field. Careful and thorough planning will help you avoid having to redesign a structured range of data later.

Before creating the list of sales, Victoria carefully considered what information she needs and how she wants to use it. Victoria plans to use the data to track daily sales for each business type, which she has identified as group home, individual, residential care, and restaurant. She wants to be able to create reports that show specific lists of sales, such as all the sales for a specific date, day of the week, or Sales ID. Based on this information, Victoria developed the data definition table shown in Figure 5-2.

Figure 5-2 **Data definition table for the sales data**

Data Definition Table			
Field	**Description**	**Data Type**	**Notes**
Sale Date	Date of the sale	Date	Use the *mm/dd/yyyy* format
Day	Day of the week	Text	Monday, Tuesday, Wednesday, ...
Sales ID	Salesperson ID	Number	1=Victoria, 2=Miguel, 3=Michelle, 4=Sandy, 5=James
Business	Type of business for the sale	Text	Group Home, Individual, Residential Care, and Restaurant
Amount	Sales total for a specific transaction date and business type	Number	Use the Accounting format and show two decimal places

After you determine the fields and records you need, you can enter the data in a worksheet. You can then work with the data in many ways, including the following common operations:

- Add, edit, and delete data in the range.
- Sort the data range.
- Filter to display only rows that meet specified criteria.
- Insert formulas to calculate subtotals.
- Create summary tables based on the data in the range (usually with PivotTables).

You'll perform many of these operations on the sales data.

INSIGHT

Creating an Effective Structured Range of Data

For a range of data to be used effectively, it must have the same structure throughout. Keep in mind the following guidelines:

- **Enter field names in the top row of the range.** This clearly identifies each field.
- **Use short, descriptive field names.** Shorter field names are easier to remember and enable more fields to appear in the workbook window at once.
- **Format field names.** Use formatting to distinguish the header row from the data. For example, apply bold, color, and a different font size.
- **Enter the same kind of data in a field.** Each field should store the smallest bit of information and be consistent from record to record. For example, enter Los Angeles, Tucson, or Chicago in a City field, but do not include states, such as CA, AZ, or IL, in the same column of data.
- **Separate the data from the rest of the worksheet.** The data, which includes the header row, should be separated from other information in the worksheet by at least one blank row and one blank column. The blank row and column enable Excel to accurately determine the range of the data.

Victoria created a workbook and entered the sales data for June based on the plan outlined in the data definition table. You'll open this workbook and review its structure.

To open and review Victoria's workbook:

1. Open the **June** workbook located in the **Excel5 > Module** folder included with your Data Files, and then save the workbook as **June Sales Data** in the location specified by your instructor.
2. In the Documentation worksheet, enter your name in cell B3 and the date in cell B4.
3. In the range A7:D13, review the data definition table. This table, which is shown in Figure 5-2, describes the different fields that are used in the Sales Data worksheet.
4. Go to the **Sales Data** worksheet. This worksheet, which is shown in Figure 5-1, contains data about the vegetable store's sales. Currently, the worksheet includes 101 sales records. Each sale record is a separate row (rows 2 through 102) and contains five fields (columns A through E). Row 1, the header row, contains labels that describe the data in each column.
5. Scroll the worksheet to row **102**, which is the last record.

When you scroll the worksheet, the first column headers in row 1 are no longer visible. Without seeing the column headers, it is difficult to know what the data entered in each column represents.

Freezing Rows and Columns

You can select rows and columns to remain visible in the workbook window as you scroll the worksheet. **Freezing** a row or column lets you keep the headers visible as you work with the data in a large worksheet. You can freeze the top row, freeze the first column, or freeze the rows and columns above and to the left of the selected cell. If you freeze the top row, row 1 remains on the screen as you scroll, leaving column headers visible and making it easier to identify the data in each record.

Victoria wants to see the column headers as she scrolls the sales records. You'll freeze row 1, which contains the column headers.

TIP

To freeze the columns and rows above and to the left of the selected cell, click the Freeze Panes button, and then click Freeze Panes.

To freeze row 1 of the worksheet:

1. Press the **Ctrl+Home** keys to return to cell A1. You want to freeze row 1.
2. On the ribbon, click the **View** tab.
3. In the Window group, click the **Freeze Panes** button, and then click **Freeze Top Row**. A horizontal line appears below the column labels to indicate which row is frozen.
4. Scroll the worksheet to row **102**. This time, the column headers remain visible as you scroll. See Figure 5-3.

Figure 5-3 Top row of the worksheet is frozen

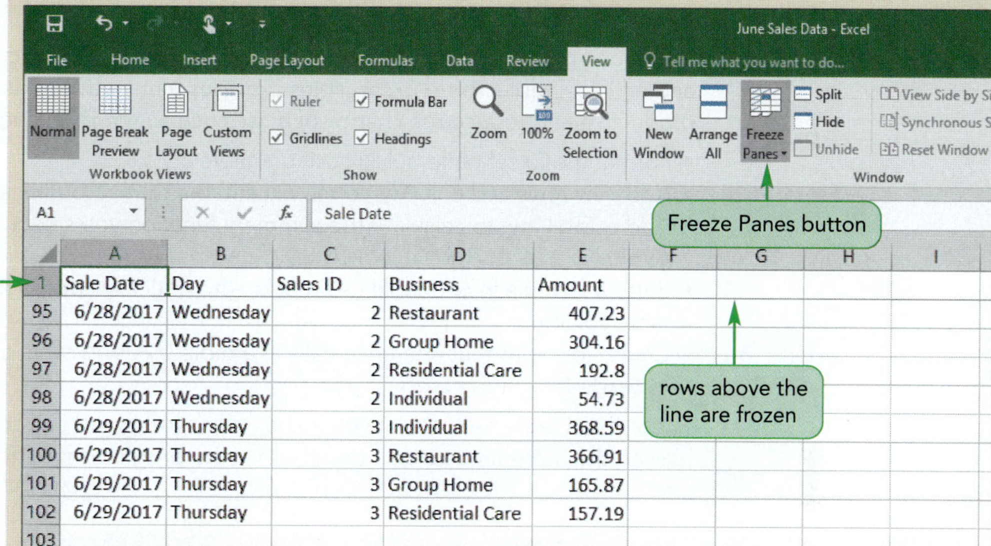

5. Press the **Ctrl+Home** keys. Cell A2, the cell directly below the frozen row, becomes the active cell.

After you freeze panes, the first option on the Freeze Panes button menu changes to Unfreeze Panes. This option releases the frozen panes so that all the columns and rows in the worksheet shift when you scroll. Victoria wants you to use a different method to keep the column headers visible, so you will unfreeze the top row of the worksheet.

To unfreeze the top row of the worksheet:

1. On the View tab, in the Window group, click the **Freeze Panes** button. The first Freeze Panes option is now Unfreeze Panes.
2. Click **Unfreeze Panes**. The headers are no longer frozen, and the horizontal line below the column headers is removed. You can now scroll all the rows and columns in the worksheet.

Creating an Excel Table

You can convert a structured range of data, such as the sales data in the range A1:E102, to an Excel table. An Excel table makes it easier to identify, manage, and analyze the groups of related data. When a structured range of data is converted into an Excel table, you see the following:

- A filter button in each cell of the header row
- The range formatted with a table style
- A sizing handle (a small triangle) in the lower-right corner of the last cell of the table
- The Table Tools Design tab on the ribbon

You can create more than one Excel table in a worksheet. Although you can leave the sales data as a structured range of data and still perform all of the tasks in this section, creating an Excel table helps you to be more efficient and accurate.

INSIGHT

Saving Time with Excel Tables

Although you can perform the same operations for both a structured range of data and an Excel table, using Excel tables provides many advantages to help you be more productive and reduce the chance of error, such as the following:

- Format the Excel table quickly using a table style.
- Add new rows and columns to the Excel table that automatically expand the range.
- Add a Total row to calculate the summary function you select, such as SUM, AVERAGE, COUNT, MIN, or MAX.
- Enter a formula in one table cell that is automatically copied to all other cells in that table column.
- Create formulas that reference cells in a table by using table and column names instead of cell addresses.

These Excel table features let you focus on analyzing and understanding the data, leaving the more time-consuming tasks for the program to perform.

Victoria wants you to create an Excel table from the sales data in the Sales Data worksheet. You'll be able to work with the Excel tables to analyze Victoria's data effectively.

To create an Excel table from the sales data:

1. If necessary, select any cell in the range of sales data to make it the active cell.
2. On the ribbon, click the **Insert** tab.
3. In the Tables group, click the **Table** button. The Create Table dialog box opens. The range of data you want to use for the table is selected in the worksheet, and a formula with its range reference, =$A$1:$E$102, is entered in the dialog box.
4. Verify that the **My table has headers** check box is selected. The headers are the field names entered in row 1. If the first row did not contain field names, the My table has headers check box would be unchecked, and Excel would insert a row of headers with the names Column1, Column2, and so on.

5. Click the **OK** button. The dialog box closes, and the range of data is converted to an Excel table, which is selected. Filter buttons appear in the header row, the sizing handle appears in the lower-right corner of the last cell of the table, the table is formatted with a predefined table style, and the Table Tools Design tab appears on the ribbon. See Figure 5-4.

Figure 5-4 Excel table with the sales data

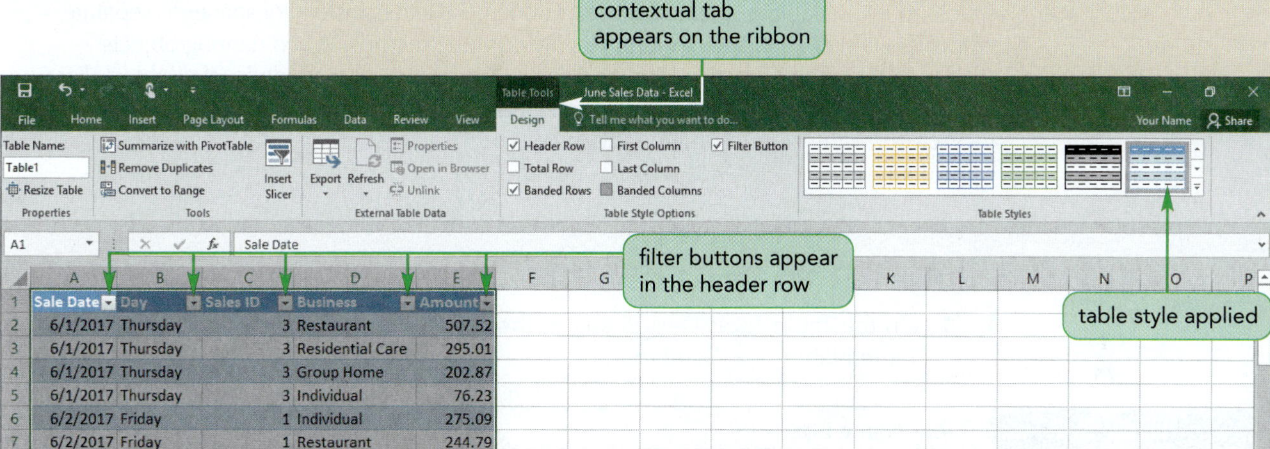
contextual tab appears on the ribbon
filter buttons appear in the header row
table style applied

6. Select any cell in the table, and then scroll down the table. The field names in the header row replace the standard lettered column headings (A, B, C, and so on) as you scroll, so you don't need to freeze panes to keep the header row visible. See Figure 5-5.

Figure 5-5 Sales table scrolled

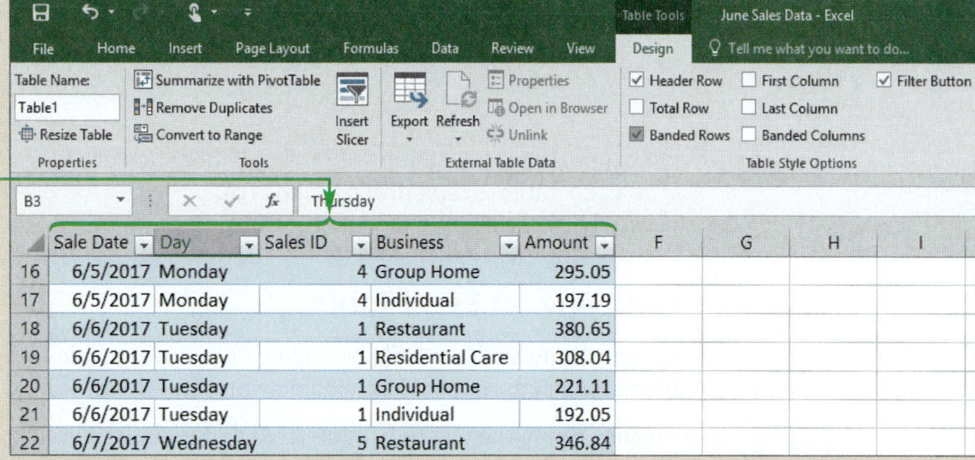
header row replaces column headings

7. Press the **Ctrl+Home** keys to make cell A1 the active cell. The column headers return to the standard display, and the Excel table header row scrolls back into view as row 1.

Renaming an Excel Table

Each Excel table in a workbook must have a unique name. Excel assigns the name Table1 to the first Excel table created in a workbook. Any additional Excel tables you create in the workbook are named consecutively as Table2, Table3, and so forth. You can assign a more descriptive name to a table, making it easier to identify a particular table by its content. Descriptive names are especially useful when you create more than one Excel table in the same workbook because they make it easier to reference the different Excel tables.

TIP

If you copy a worksheet that contains a table, Excel adds the next consecutive number at the end of the table name to create a unique table name.

Table names must start with a letter or an underscore but can use any combination of letters, numbers, and underscores for the rest of the name. Table names cannot include spaces, but you can use an underscore or uppercase letters instead of spaces to separate words in a table name, such as June_Records or JuneRecords. When naming objects such as tables, a best practice is to include an abbreviation that identifies that object. For example, table names often end with the letters *Tbl*, such as June_Records_Tbl or JuneTbl.

Victoria wants you to rename the Excel table you just created from the June sales data.

To rename the Table1 table:

1. On the Table Tools Design tab, in the Properties group, select **Table1** in the Table Name box. See Figure 5-6.

Figure 5-6 Table Name box

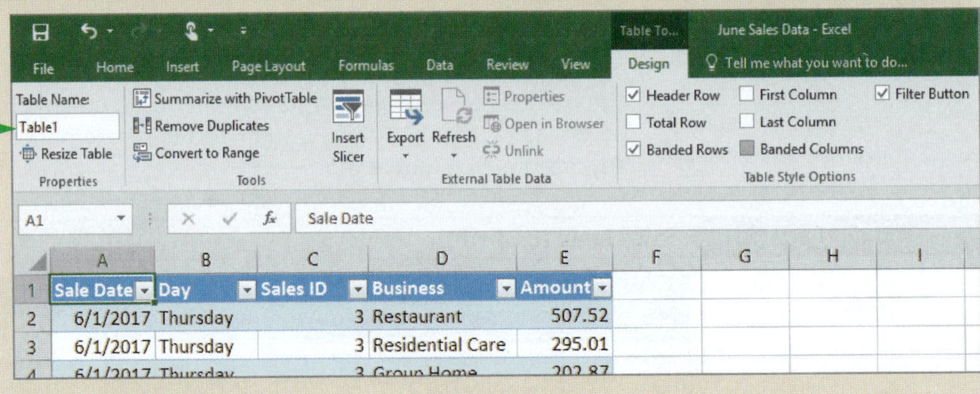

2. Type **JuneTbl** as the descriptive name, and then press the **Enter** key. The Excel table is renamed as "JuneTbl."

Modifying an Excel Table

You can modify an Excel table by adding or removing table elements or by changing the table's formatting. For every Excel table, you can display or hide the following elements:

- **Header row**—The first row of the table that includes the field names
- **Total row**—A row at the bottom of the table that applies a function to the column values
- **First column**—Formatting added to the leftmost column of the table
- **Last column**—Formatting added to the rightmost column of the table
- **Banded rows**—Formatting added to alternating rows so that even and odd rows are different colors, making it simpler to distinguish records
- **Banded columns**—Formatting added to alternating columns so they are different colors, making it simpler to distinguish fields
- **Filter buttons**—Buttons that appear in each column of the header row and open a menu with options for sorting and filtering the table data

You can also modify a table by applying a table style. As with other styles, a table style formats all of the selected table elements with a consistent, unified design. You can change the font, fill, alignment, number formats, column widths and row heights, and other formatting of selected cells in the table the same way you would for other cells in the worksheet.

Victoria wants the JuneTbl table to have a format that makes the table easier to read. You will apply a table style and make other formatting changes to the table.

To format the JuneTbl table:

1. On the Table Tools Design tab, in the Table Styles group, click the **More** button. A gallery of table styles opens.
2. In the Table Styles gallery, in the Medium section, click **Table Style Medium 7**. The table now has a green style.
3. In the Table Style Options group, click the **Banded Rows** check box. The alternating row colors disappear. The table is more challenging to read this way, so you will reapply the banded rows formatting.
4. In the Table Style Options group, click the **Banded Rows** check box to select it. The alternating row colors reappear.
5. Change the width of columns A through E to **15** characters. The entire column headers and all of the values are now visible.
6. Select the **Amount** column, and then change the values to the **Accounting** format. See Figure 5-7.

TIP

To display or hide alternating column colors, click the Banded Columns check box in the Table Style Options group.

Figure 5-7 Modified JuneTbl table

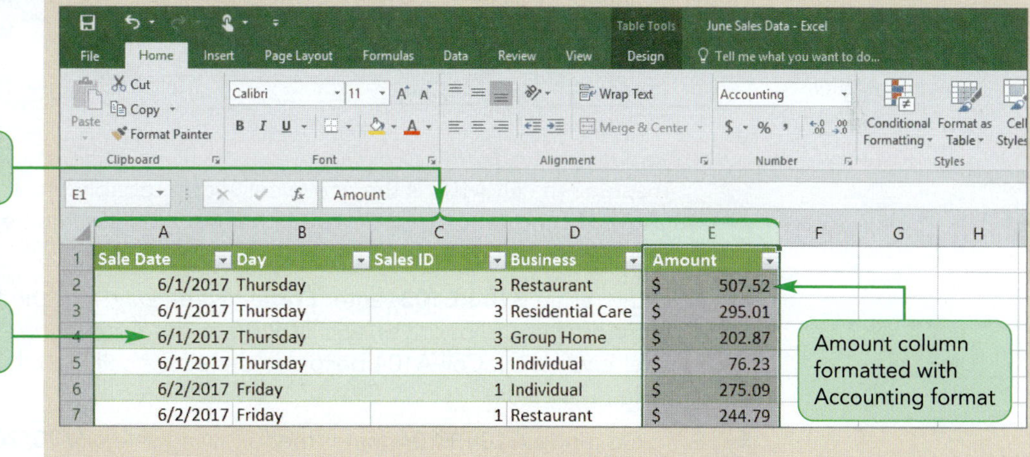

7. Select cell **A1** to make it the active cell.

Maintaining Data in an Excel Table

As you develop a worksheet with an Excel table, you may need to add new records to the table, find and edit existing records in the table, and delete records from the table. Victoria wants you to make several changes to the data in the JuneTbl table.

Adding Records

As you maintain data in an Excel table, you often need to add new records. You add a record to an Excel table in a blank row. The simplest and most convenient way to add a record to an Excel table is to enter the data in the first blank row below the last record. You can then sort the data to arrange the table in the order you want. If you want the record in a specific location, you can also insert a row within the table for the new record.

The sales records for June 30 are missing from the JuneTbl table. Victoria asks you to add to the table four new records that contain the missing data.

To add four records to the JuneTbl table:

1. Press the **End** key, and then press the ↓ key to make cell A102 the active cell. This cell is in the last row of the table.
2. Press the ↓ key to move the active cell to cell A103, which is in the first blank row below the table.
3. In cell A103, type **6/30/2017**, and then press the **Tab** key. Cell B103 in the Day column becomes the active cell. The table expands to include a new row with the same formatting as the rest of the table. The AutoCorrect Options button appears so you can undo the table formatting if you hadn't intended the new data to be part of the existing table. The sizing handle moves to the lower-right corner of cell E103, which is now the cell in the lower-right corner of the table. See Figure 5-8.

TIP

You can drag the sizing handle to add columns or rows to the Excel table or delete them from it.

Figure 5-8 New row added to the JuneTbl table

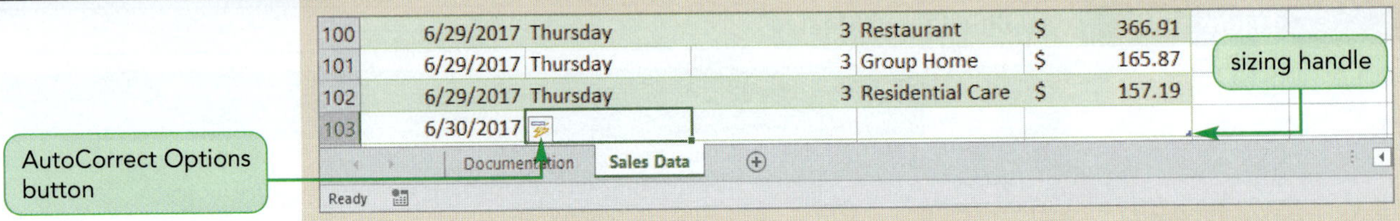
100 6/29/2017 Thursday 3 Restaurant $ 366.91
101 6/29/2017 Thursday 3 Group Home $ 165.87
102 6/29/2017 Thursday 3 Residential Care $ 157.19
103 6/30/2017
Documentation
Sales Data
Ready
sizing handle
AutoCorrect Options button

Trouble? If cell A104 is the active cell, you probably pressed the Enter key instead of the Tab key. Click cell B103, and then continue entering the data in Step 4.

4. In the range **B103:E103**, enter **Friday** as the Day, **1** as the Sales ID, **Individual** as the Business, and **309.00** as the Amount, pressing the **Tab** key after each entry. Cell A104 becomes the active cell, and the table expands to include row 104.
5. In the range **A104:E104**, enter the following sales: **6/30/2017**, **Friday**, **1**, **Restaurant**, and **464.12**.
6. In the range **A105:E105**, enter the following sales: **6/30/2017**, **Friday**, **1**, **Group Home**, and **431.12**.
7. In the range **A106:E106**, enter the following sales: **6/30/2017**, **Friday**, **1**, **Residential Care**, and **225.02**.
8. Press the **Enter** key. The records are added to the table. See Figure 5-9.

Figure 5-9 Records added to the JuneTbl table

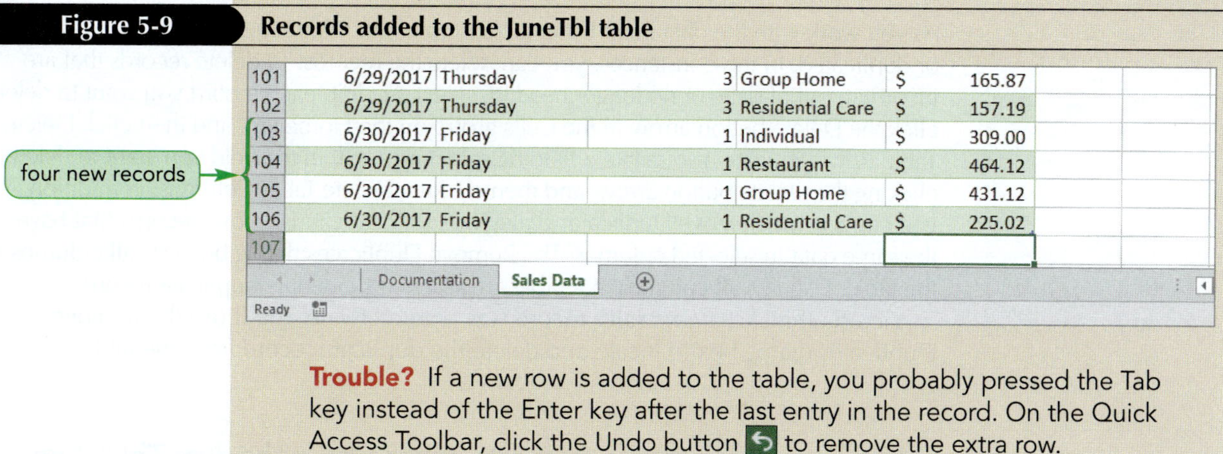

Trouble? If a new row is added to the table, you probably pressed the Tab key instead of the Enter key after the last entry in the record. On the Quick Access Toolbar, click the Undo button to remove the extra row.

Finding and Editing Records

Although you can manually scroll through the table to find a specific record, often a quicker way to locate a record is to use the Find command. When using the Find or Replace command, it is best to start at the top of a worksheet to ensure that all cells in the table are searched. You edit the data in a table the same way as you edit data in a worksheet cell.

Victoria wants you to update the June 20 Residential Care sales amount. You'll use the Find command to locate the record, which is currently blank. Then, you'll edit the record in the table to change the amount to $309.00.

To find and edit the 6/20/2017 Residential Care record:

1. Press the **Ctrl+Home** keys to make cell A1 the active cell so that all cells in the table will be searched.
2. On the Home tab, in the Editing group, click the **Find & Select** button, and then click **Find** (or press the **Ctrl+F** keys). The Find and Replace dialog box opens.
3. In the Find what box, type **6/20/2017**, and then click the **Find Next** button. Cell A67, which contains the record for an Individual, is selected. This is not the record you want.
4. Click the **Find Next** button three times to display the record for Residential Care on 6/20/2017.
5. Click the **Close** button. The Find and Replace dialog box closes.
6. Press the **Tab** key four times to move the active cell to the Amount column, type **309**, and then press the **Enter** key. The record is updated to reflect the $309.00 amount.
7. Press the **Ctrl+Home** keys to make cell A1 the active cell.

Deleting a Record

As you work with the data in an Excel table, you might find records that are outdated or duplicated. In these instances, you can delete the records. To delete records that are incorrect, out of date, or no longer needed, select a cell in each record you want to delete, click the Delete button arrow in the Cells group on the Home tab, and then click Delete Table Rows. You can also delete a field by selecting a cell in the field you want to delete, clicking the Delete button arrow, and then clicking Delete Table Columns. In addition, you can use the Remove Duplicates dialog box to locate and remove records that have the same data in selected columns. The Remove Duplicates dialog box lists all columns in the table. Usually, all columns in a table are selected to identify duplicate records.

Victoria thinks that one sales record was entered twice. You'll use the Remove Duplicates dialog box to locate and delete the duplicate record from the table.

To find and delete the duplicate record from the JuneTbl table:

1. Scroll to row **56**, and observe that the entries in row 56 and row 57 are exactly the same. One of these records needs to be deleted.
2. On the ribbon, click the **Table Tools Design** tab.
3. In the Tools group, click the **Remove Duplicates** button. The Remove Duplicates dialog box opens, and all of the columns in the table are selected. Excel looks for repeated data in the selected columns to determine whether any duplicate records exist. If duplicates are found, all but one of the records are deleted. See Figure 5-10.

Figure 5-10 Remove Duplicates dialog box

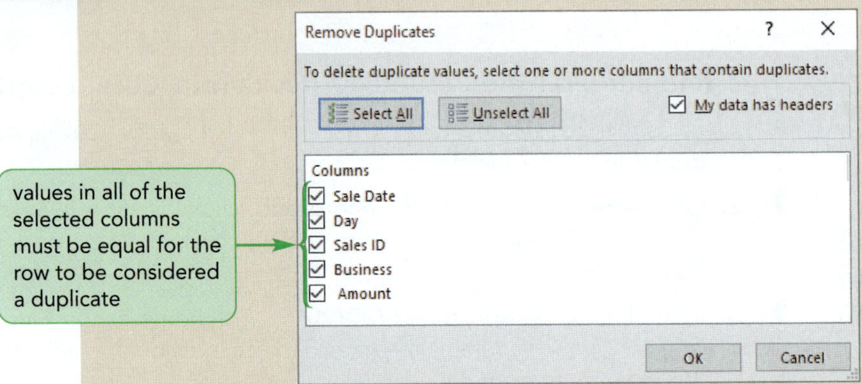

You want to search all of the columns in the table for duplicated data so that you don't inadvertently delete a record that has duplicate values in the selected fields but a unique value in the deselected field.

4. Click the **OK** button. A dialog box opens, reporting "1 duplicate values found and removed; 104 unique values remain."
5. Click the **OK** button.

   Trouble? If you deleted records you did not intend to delete, you can reverse the action. On the Quick Access Toolbar, click the Undo button, and then repeat Steps 3 through 5.

6. Press the **Ctrl+Home** keys to make cell A1 the active cell.

Sorting Data

The records in an Excel table initially appear in the order they were entered. As you work, however, you may want to view the same records in a different order. For example, Victoria might want to view the sales by business or day of the week. You can sort data in ascending or descending order. **Ascending order** arranges text alphabetically from A to Z, numbers from smallest to largest, and dates from oldest to newest. **Descending order** arranges text in reverse alphabetical order from Z to A, numbers from largest to smallest, and dates from newest to oldest. In both ascending and descending order, blank cells are placed at the end of the table.

Sorting One Column Using the Sort Buttons

You can quickly sort data with one sort field using the Sort A to Z button or the Sort Z to A button. Victoria wants you to sort the sales in ascending order by the Business column. This will rearrange the table data so that the records appear in alphabetical order by Business.

To sort the JuneTbl table in ascending order by the Business column:

1. Select any cell in the Business column. You do not need to select the entire JuneTbl table, which consists of the range A1:E105. Excel determines the table's range when you click any cell in the table.
2. On the ribbon, click the **Data** tab.
3. In the Sort & Filter group, click the **Sort A to Z** button. The data is sorted in ascending order by Business. The Business filter button changes to show that the data is sorted by that column. See Figure 5-11.

TIP

You can also use the Sort & Filter button in the Editing group on the Home tab.

Figure 5-11 JuneTbl table sorted by the Business field

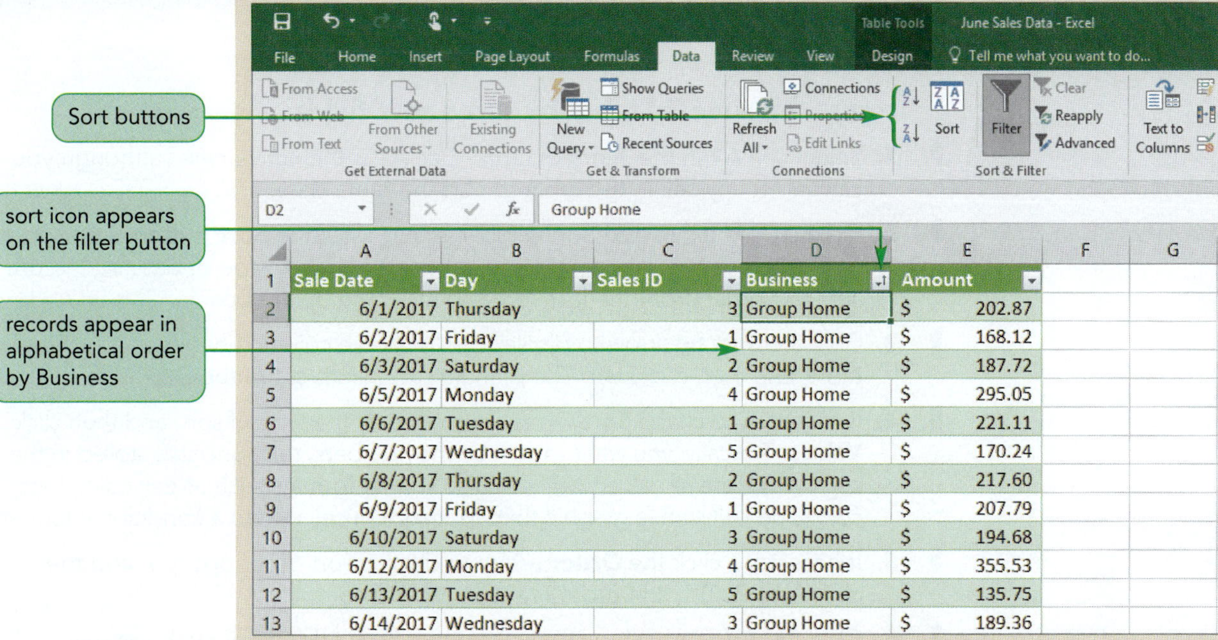
Sort buttons
sort icon appears on the filter button
records appear in alphabetical order by Business

	A	B	C	D	E
1	Sale Date	Day	Sales ID	Business	Amount
2	6/1/2017	Thursday	3	Group Home	$ 202.87
3	6/2/2017	Friday	1	Group Home	$ 168.12
4	6/3/2017	Saturday	2	Group Home	$ 187.72
5	6/5/2017	Monday	4	Group Home	$ 295.05
6	6/6/2017	Tuesday	1	Group Home	$ 221.11
7	6/7/2017	Wednesday	5	Group Home	$ 170.24
8	6/8/2017	Thursday	2	Group Home	$ 217.60
9	6/9/2017	Friday	1	Group Home	$ 207.79
10	6/10/2017	Saturday	3	Group Home	$ 194.68
11	6/12/2017	Monday	4	Group Home	$ 355.53
12	6/13/2017	Tuesday	5	Group Home	$ 135.75
13	6/14/2017	Wednesday	3	Group Home	$ 189.36

Trouble? If the data is sorted in the wrong order, you might have clicked in a different column than the Business column. Repeat Steps 1 through 3.

Sorting Multiple Columns Using the Sort Dialog Box

Sometimes one sort field is not adequate for your needs. For example, Victoria wants to arrange the JuneTbl table so that the sales are ordered first by Day (Monday, Tuesday, and so forth), then by Business for each day of the week, and then by Amount (highest to lowest). You must sort by more than one column to accomplish this. The first sort field is called the **primary sort field**, the second sort field is called the **secondary sort field**, and so forth. Although you can include up to 64 sort fields in a single sort, you typically will use one to three sort fields. In this case, the Day field is the primary sort field, the Business field is the secondary sort field, and the Amount field is the tertiary sort field. When you have more than one sort field, you should use the Sort dialog box to specify the sort criteria.

REFERENCE

Sorting Data Using Multiple Sort Fields

- Select any cell in a table or range.
- On the Data tab, in the Sort & Filter group, click the Sort button.
- If necessary, click the Add Level button to insert the Sort by row.
- Click the Sort by arrow, select the column heading for the primary sort field, click the Sort On arrow to select the type of data, and then click the Order arrow to select the sort order.
- For each additional column to sort, click the Add Level button, click the Then by arrow, select the column heading for the secondary sort field, click the Sort On arrow to select the type of data, and then click the Order arrow to select the sort order.
- Click the OK button.

Victoria wants to see the sales sorted by day, and then within day by business, and then within business by amount, with the highest amounts appearing before the smaller ones for each business. This will make it easier for Victoria to evaluate sales on specific days of the week in each business.

To sort the JuneTbl table by three sort fields:

1. Select cell **A1** in the JuneTbl table. Cell A1 is the active cell—although you can select any cell in the table to sort the table data.
2. On the Data tab, in the Sort & Filter group, click the **Sort** button. The Sort dialog box opens. Any sort specifications (sort field, type of data sorted on, and sort order) from the last sort appear in the dialog box.
3. Click the **Sort by** arrow to display the list of the column headers in the JuneTbl table, and then click **Day**. The primary sort field is set to the Day field.
4. If necessary, click the **Sort On** arrow to display the type of sort, and then click **Values**. Typically, you want to sort by the numbers, text, or dates stored in the cells, which are all values. You can also sort by formats such as cell color, font color, and cell icon (a graphic that appears in a cell due to a conditional format).
5. If necessary, click the **Order** arrow to display sort order options, and then click **A to Z**. The sort order is set to ascending.
6. Click the **Add Level** button. A Then by row is added below the primary sort field.
7. Click the **Then by** arrow and click **Business**, and then verify that **Values** appears in the Sort On box and **A to Z** appears in the Order box.

8. Click the **Add Level** button to add a second Then by row.
9. Click the second **Then by** arrow, click **Amount**, verify that **Values** appears in the Sort On box, click the **Order** arrow, and then click **Largest to Smallest** to specify a descending sort order for the Amount values. See Figure 5-12.

Figure 5-12 Sort dialog box with three sorted fields

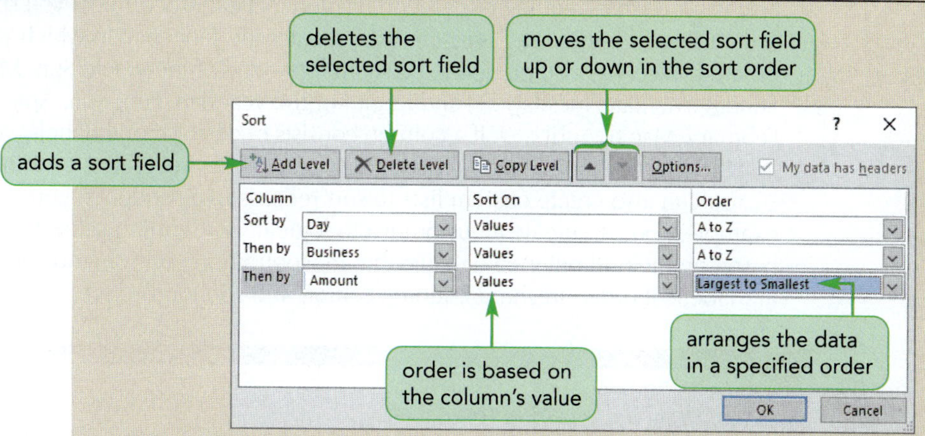

10. Click the **OK** button. Excel sorts the table records first in ascending order by the Day field, then within each Day in ascending order by the Business field, and then within each Business in descending order by the Amount field. For example, the first 20 records are Friday sales. Of these records, the first five are Group Home, the next five are Individual, and so on. Finally, the Friday Group Home sales are arranged from highest to lowest in the Amount column. See Figure 5-13.

Figure 5-13 Sales sorted by Day, then by Business, and then by Amount

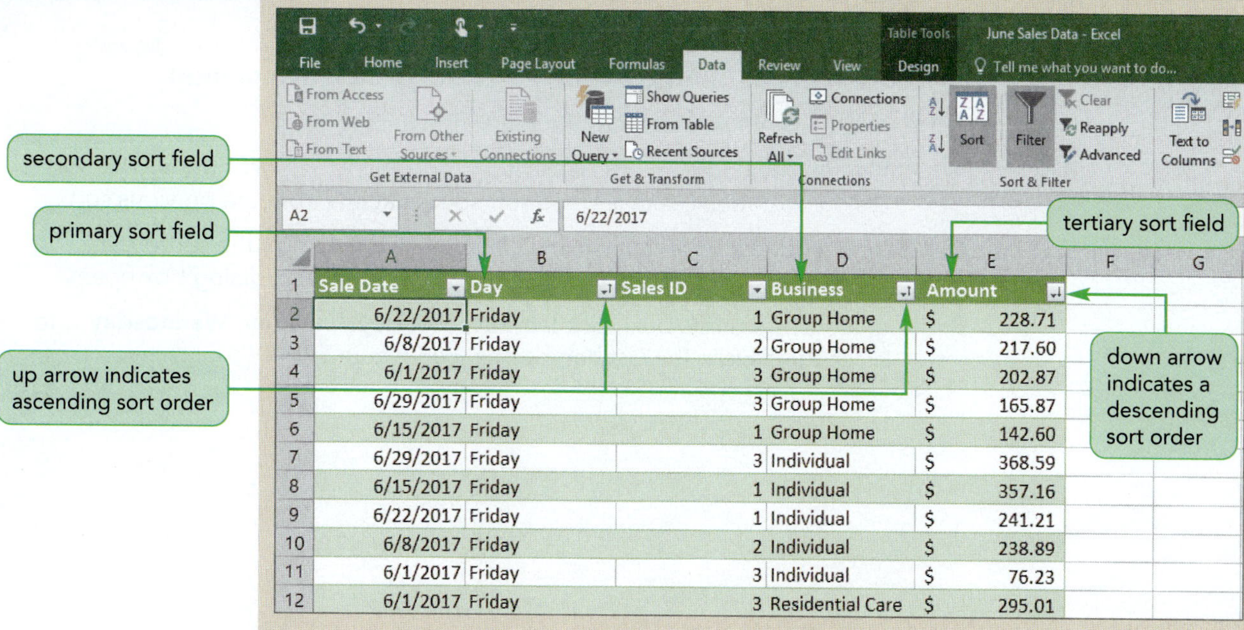

11. Scroll the table to view the sorted table data.

The table data is sorted in alphabetical order by the day of the week—Friday, Monday, Saturday, and so forth. This default sort order for fields with text values is not appropriate for days of the week. Instead, Victoria wants you to base the sort on chronological rather than alphabetical order. You'll use a custom sort list to set up the sort order Victoria wants.

Sorting Using a Custom List

Text is sorted in ascending or descending alphabetical order unless you specify a different order using a custom list. A **custom list** indicates the sequence in which you want data ordered. Excel has two predefined custom lists—day-of-the-week (Sun, Mon, Tues, … and Sunday, Monday, Tuesday, …) and month-of-the-year (Jan, Feb, Mar, Apr, … and January, February, March, April, …). If a column consists of day or month labels, you can sort them in their correct chronological order using one of these predefined custom lists.

You can also create custom lists to sort records in a sequence you define. For example, you can create a custom list to logically order high school or college students based on their admittance date (freshman, sophomore, junior, and senior) rather than alphabetical order (freshman, junior, senior, and sophomore).

REFERENCE

Sorting Using a Custom List

- On the Data tab, in the Sort & Filter group, click the Sort button.
- Click the Order arrow, and then click Custom List.
- If necessary, in the List entries box, type each entry for the custom list (in the desired order) and press the Enter key, and then click the Add button.
- In the Custom lists box, select the predefined custom list.
- Click the OK button.

You'll use a predefined custom list to sort the records by the Day column in chronological order rather than alphabetical order.

To use a predefined custom list to sort the Day column:

1. Make sure the active cell is in the JuneTbl table.
2. On the Data tab, in the Sort & Filter group, click the **Sort** button. The Sort dialog box opens, showing the sort specifications from the previous sort.
3. In the Sort by Day row, click the **Order** arrow to display the sort order options, and then click **Custom List**. The Custom Lists dialog box opens.
4. In the Custom lists box, click **Sunday**, **Monday**, **Tuesday**, **Wednesday**... to place the days in the List entries box. See Figure 5-14.

Figure 5-14 Custom Lists dialog box

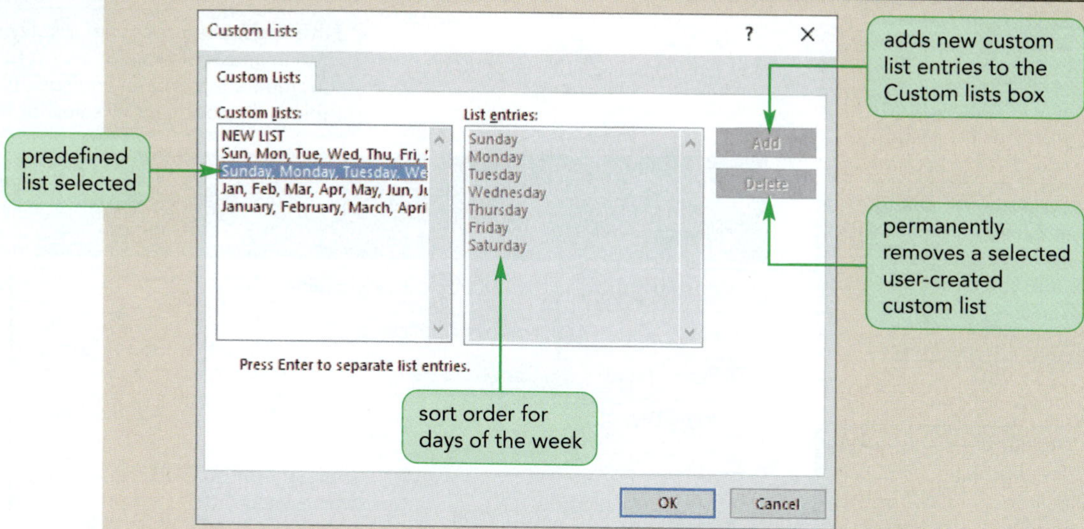

5. Click the **OK** button to return to the Sort dialog box. The custom sort list—Sunday, Monday, Tuesday, Wednesday…—appears in the Order box.
6. Click the **OK** button. The table is sorted based on the predefined custom list.
7. Scroll the sorted table to verify that the sales are sorted by their chronological day order—Sunday, Monday, Tuesday, Wednesday, Thursday, Friday, Saturday. No sales appear for Sundays because Victoria's Veggies is closed on that day.

So far, you created an Excel table for the sales and then named and formatted the table. You updated the table by adding, editing, and deleting records. You also sorted the records and used a predefined custom list to sort the Day field by its chronological order. In the next session, you will continue to work with the JuneTbl table.

REVIEW

Session 5.1 Quick Check

1. In Excel, what is the difference between a range of data and a structured range of data?
2. Explain the difference between a field and a record.
3. What is the purpose of the Freeze Panes button in the Window group on the View tab? Why is this feature helpful?
4. What three elements indicate that a range of data is an Excel table?
5. How can you quickly find and delete duplicate records from an Excel table?
6. If you sort table data from the most recent purchase date to the oldest purchase date, in what order have you sorted the data?
7. An Excel table of college students tracks each student's first name, last name, major, and year of graduation. How can you order the table so that students graduating in the same year appear together in alphabetical order by the students' last names?
8. An Excel table of sales data includes the Month field with the values Jan, Feb, Mar, … Dec. How can you sort the data so the sales data is sorted by Month in chronological order (Jan, Feb, Mar, … Dec)?

Session 5.2 Visual Overview:

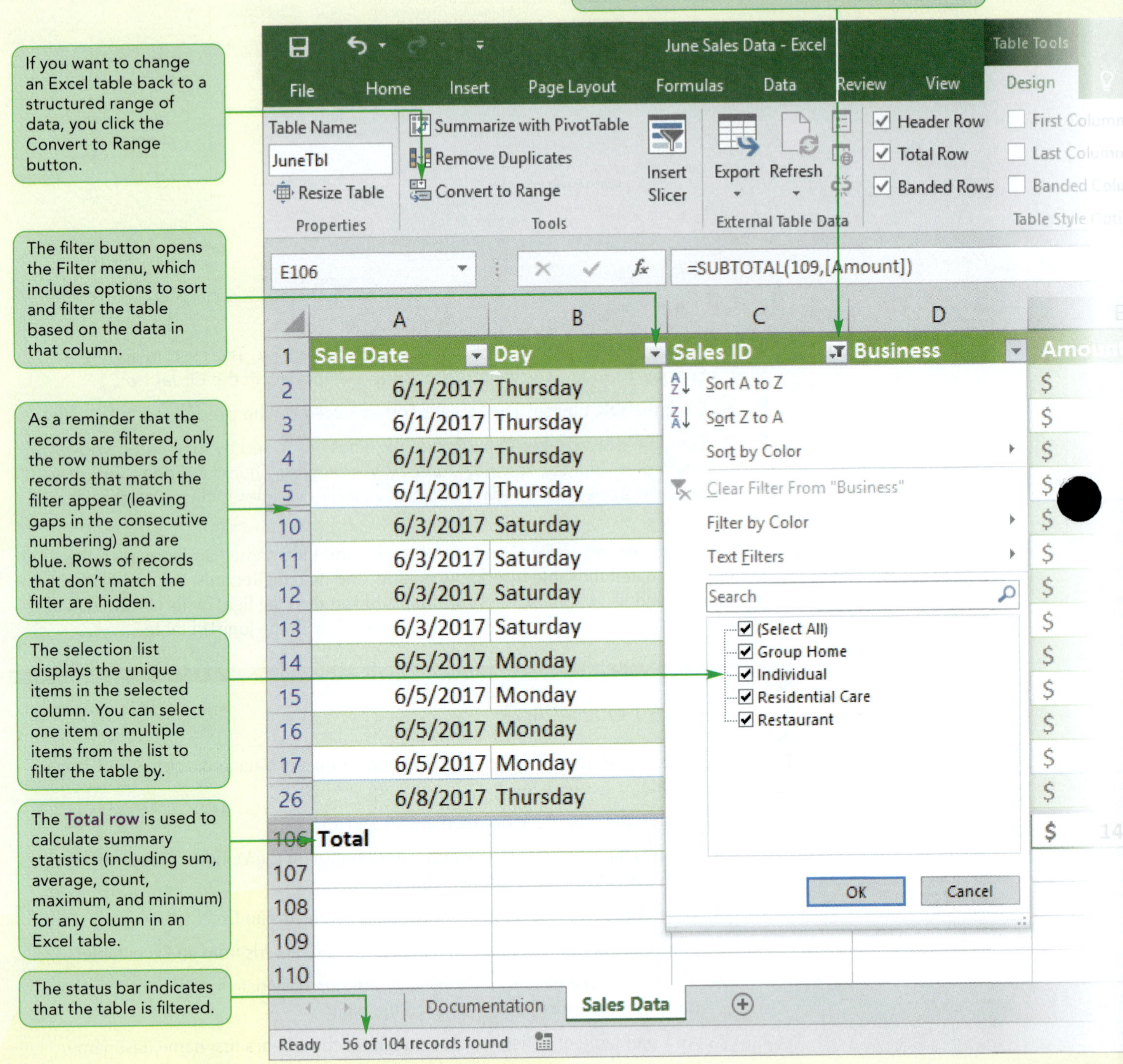

Filtering is the process of displaying a subset of rows in an Excel table or a structured range of data that meets the criteria you specify. In this case, the table is filtered to show sales for Sales ID 2, 3 & 4.
If you want to change an Excel table back to a structured range of data, you click the Convert to Range button.
The filter button opens the Filter menu, which includes options to sort and filter the table based on the data in that column.
As a reminder that the records are filtered, only the row numbers of the records that match the filter appear (leaving gaps in the consecutive numbering) and are blue. Rows of records that don't match the filter are hidden.
The selection list displays the unique items in the selected column. You can select one item or multiple items from the list to filter the table by.
The **Total row** is used to calculate summary statistics (including sum, average, count, maximum, and minimum) for any column in an Excel table.
The status bar indicates that the table is filtered.
June Sales Data - Excel
Table Tools
File
Home
Insert
Page Layout
Formulas
Data
Review
View
Design
Table Name:
JuneTbl
Resize Table
Properties
Summarize with PivotTable
Remove Duplicates
Convert to Range
Tools
Insert Slicer
Export
Refresh
External Table Data
Header Row
Total Row
Banded Rows
First Column
Last Column
Banded Columns
E106
=SUBTOTAL(109,[Amount])
Sale Date
Day
Sales ID
Business
Sort A to Z
Sort Z to A
Sort by Color
Clear Filter From "Business"
Filter by Color
Text Filters
Search
(Select All)
Group Home
Individual
Residential Care
Restaurant
OK
Cancel
6/1/2017 Thursday
6/3/2017 Saturday
6/5/2017 Monday
6/8/2017 Thursday
Total
Documentation
Sales Data
Ready
56 of 104 records found

Filtering Table Data

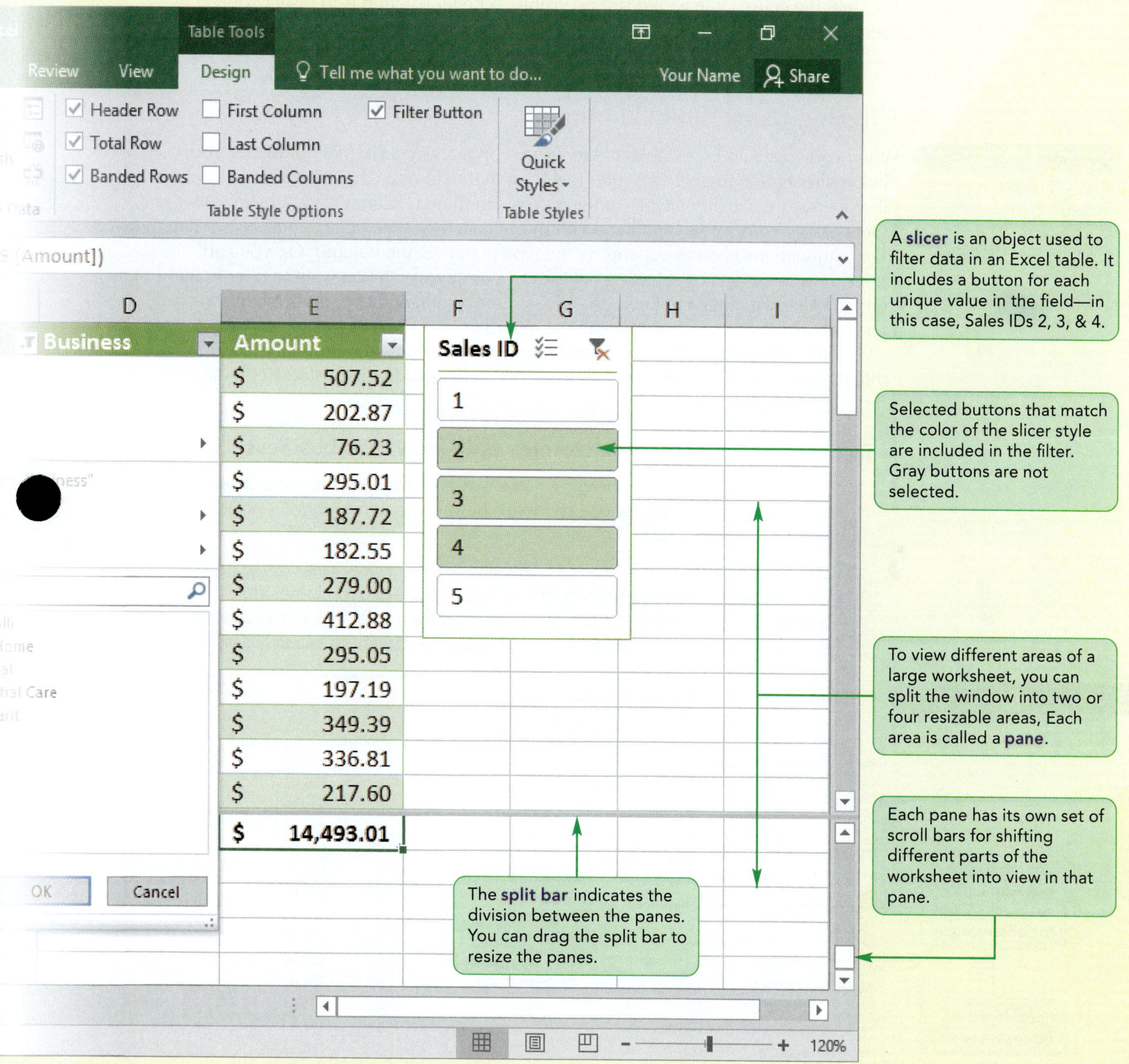
Table Tools
Review
View
Design
Tell me what you want to do...
Your Name
Share
Header Row
Total Row
Banded Rows
First Column
Last Column
Banded Columns
Filter Button
Table Style Options
Quick Styles
Table Styles
D
E
F
G
H
I
Business
Amount
Sales ID
1
2
3
4
5
$ 507.52
$ 202.87
$ 76.23
$ 295.01
$ 187.72
$ 182.55
$ 279.00
$ 412.88
$ 295.05
$ 197.19
$ 349.39
$ 336.81
$ 217.60
$ 14,493.01
OK
Cancel
120%
A slicer is an object used to filter data in an Excel table. It includes a button for each unique value in the field—in this case, Sales IDs 2, 3, & 4.
Selected buttons that match the color of the slicer style are included in the filter. Gray buttons are not selected.
To view different areas of a large worksheet, you can split the window into two or four resizable areas, Each area is called a pane.
Each pane has its own set of scroll bars for shifting different parts of the worksheet into view in that pane.
The split bar indicates the division between the panes. You can drag the split bar to resize the panes.

Filtering Data

Victoria wants to analyze the sales data to determine if she could close Victoria's Veggies to individual customers one day during the week and use that time for buying and planning. She wants to see a list of all of the individual sales and then narrow that list to see only those days with sales less than or equal to $200. Although you could sort the sales by Business and Amount to group the records of interest to Victoria, the entire table would still be visible. A better solution is to display only the specific records you want. Filtering temporarily hides any records that do not meet the specified criteria. After data is filtered, you can sort, copy, format, chart, and print it.

Filtering Using One Column

TIP

To show or hide filter buttons for an Excel table or a structured range of data, click the Filter button in the Sort & Filter group on the Data tab.

When you create an Excel table, a filter button appears in each column header. You click a filter button to open the Filter menu for that field. You can use options on the Filter menu to create three types of filters. You can filter a column of data by its cell colors or font colors. You can filter a column of data by a specific text, number, or date filter, although the choices depend on the type of data in the column. Or, you can filter a column of data by selecting the exact values by which you want to filter in the column. After you filter a column, the Clear Filter command becomes available so you can remove the filter and redisplay all the records.

Victoria wants to see the sales for only individual customers. You'll filter the JuneTbl table to show only those records with the value Individual in the Business column.

To filter the JuneTbl table to show only individual business:

1. If you took a break after the previous session, make sure the June Sales Data workbook is open, the Sales Data worksheet is the active sheet, and the JuneTbl table is active.
2. Click the **Business** filter button 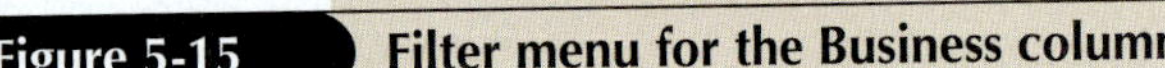. The Filter menu opens, as shown in Figure 5-15, listing the unique entries in the Business field—Group Home, Individual, Residential Care, and Restaurant. All of the items are selected, but you can set which items to use to filter the data. In this case, you want to select Individual.

Figure 5-15 Filter menu for the Business column

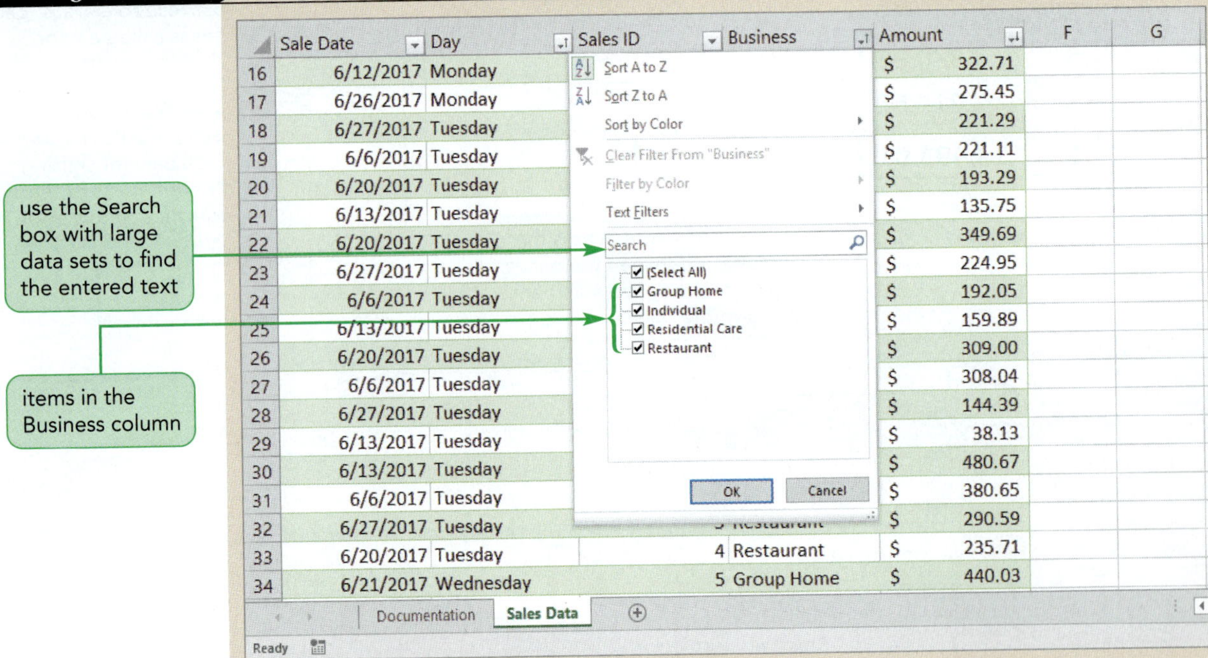

3. Click the **(Select All)** check box to remove the checkmarks from all of the Business items.
4. Click the **Individual** check box to select it. The filter will show only records that match the checked item and will hide records that contain the unchecked items.
5. Click the **OK** button. The filter is applied. The status bar lists the number of Individual rows found in the entire table—in this case, 26 of the 104 records in the table are displayed. See Figure 5-16.

Figure 5-16 JuneTbl table filtered to show only Individual business

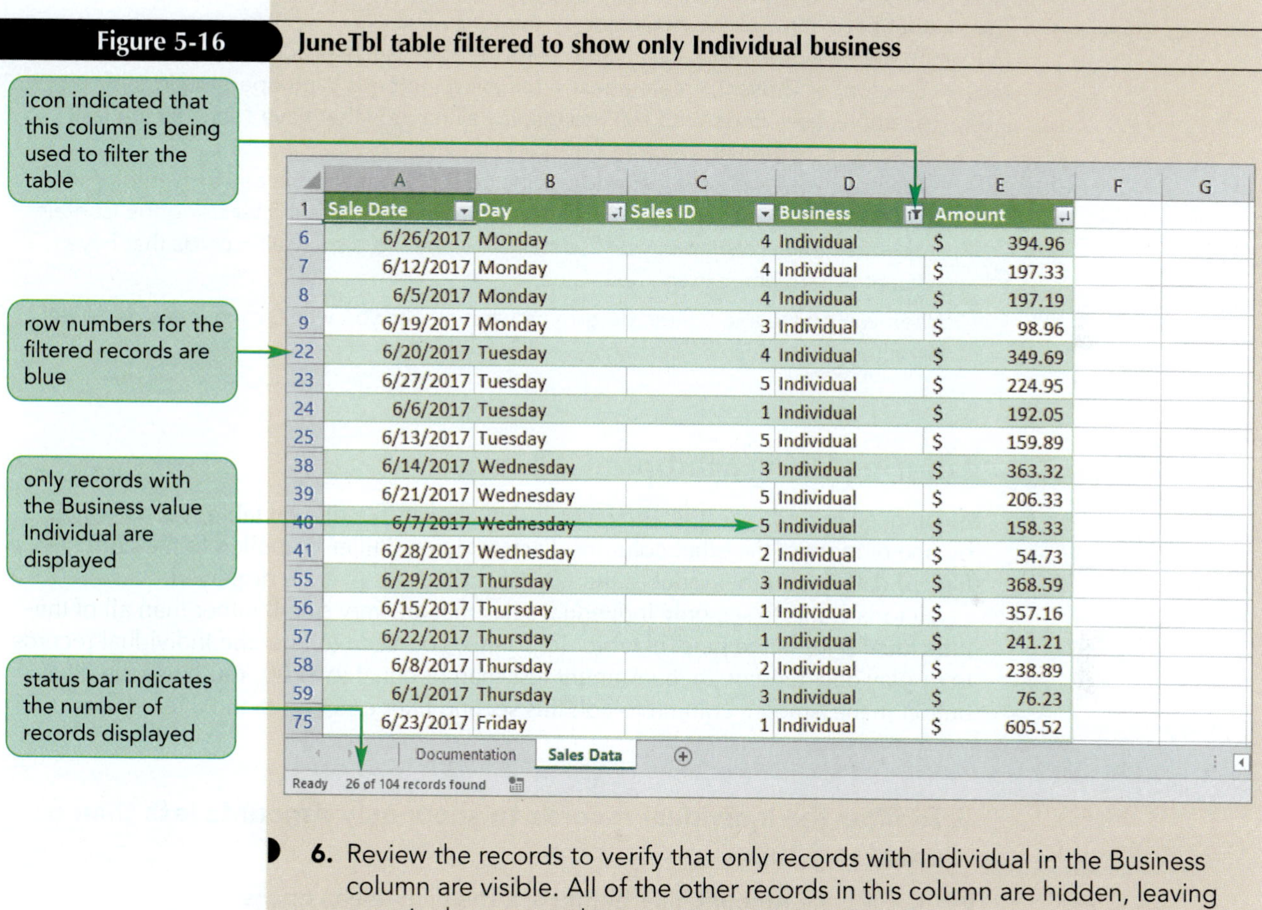
icon indicated that this column is being used to filter the table
row numbers for the filtered records are blue
only records with the Business value Individual are displayed
status bar indicates the number of records displayed
Documentation
Sales Data
Ready
26 of 104 records found

	A	B	C	D	E	F	G
1	Sale Date	Day	Sales ID	Business	Amount		
6	6/26/2017	Monday	4	Individual	$ 394.96		
7	6/12/2017	Monday	4	Individual	$ 197.33		
8	6/5/2017	Monday	4	Individual	$ 197.19		
9	6/19/2017	Monday	3	Individual	$ 98.96		
22	6/20/2017	Tuesday	4	Individual	$ 349.69		
23	6/27/2017	Tuesday	5	Individual	$ 224.95		
24	6/6/2017	Tuesday	1	Individual	$ 192.05		
25	6/13/2017	Tuesday	5	Individual	$ 159.89		
38	6/14/2017	Wednesday	3	Individual	$ 363.32		
39	6/21/2017	Wednesday	5	Individual	$ 206.33		
40	6/7/2017	Wednesday	5	Individual	$ 158.33		
41	6/28/2017	Wednesday	2	Individual	$ 54.73		
55	6/29/2017	Thursday	3	Individual	$ 368.59		
56	6/15/2017	Thursday	1	Individual	$ 357.16		
57	6/22/2017	Thursday	1	Individual	$ 241.21		
58	6/8/2017	Thursday	2	Individual	$ 238.89		
59	6/1/2017	Thursday	3	Individual	$ 76.23		
75	6/23/2017	Friday	1	Individual	$ 605.52		

6. Review the records to verify that only records with Individual in the Business column are visible. All of the other records in this column are hidden, leaving gaps in the row numbers.
7. Point to the **Business** filter button. A ScreenTip—Business: Equals "Individual"—describes the filter applied to the column.

The Filter menu includes options to Sort by Color and Filter by Color. These options enable you to filter and sort data using color, one of many cell attributes. Victoria could use specific cell background colors for certain sales in the JuneTbl table. For example, she might want to highlight dates when the store could have used an additional employee. So cells in the Sale Date column for busy days would be formatted with yellow as a reminder. You could click the Sort by Color option to display a list of available colors by which to sort and then click the specific color so that all the records for the days when she needed more help in the store (formatted with yellow) would appear together. Similarly, you could click the Filter by Color option to display a submenu with the available colors by which to filter, and then click a color.

INSIGHT

Exploring Text Filters

You can use different text filters to display the records you want. If you know only part of a text value or if you want to match a certain pattern, you can use the Begins With, Ends With, and Contains operators to filter a text field to match the pattern you specify. The following examples are based on a student directory table that includes First Name, Last Name, Address, City, State, and Zip fields:

- To find a student named Smith, Smithe, or Smythe, create a text filter using the Begins With operator. In this example, use "Begins With Sm" to display all records that have "Sm" at the beginning of the text value.
- To Find anyone whose Last Name ends in "son" (such as Robertson, Anderson, Dawson, or Gibson), create a text filter using the Ends With operator. In this example, use "Ends With son" to display all records that have "son" as the last characters in the text value.
- To find anyone whose street address includes "Central" (such as 101 Central Ave., 1024 Central Road, or 457 SW Willow Central), create a text filter using the Contains operator. In this example, use "Contains Central" to display all records that have "Central" anywhere in the text value.

When you create a text filter, determine what results you want. Then, consider what text filter you can use to best achieve those results.

Filtering Using Multiple Columns

If you need to further restrict the records that appear in a filtered table, you can filter by one or more of the other columns. Each additional filter is applied to the currently filtered data and further reduces the number of records that are displayed.

Victoria wants to see only individual sales that are very small, rather than all of the individual sales in the JuneTbl table. To do this, you need to filter the Individual records to display only those with the Amount less than or equal to $200. You'll use the filter button in the Amount column to add this second filter criterion to the filtered data.

To filter the Individual records to show only Amounts less than or equal to $200:

1. Click the **Amount** filter button [▾]. The Filter menu opens.
2. Click the **(Select All)** check box to remove the checkmarks from all of the check boxes.
3. Click the check boxes for all of the amounts that are less than or equal to $200, starting with the **54.73** check box and ending with the **$197.33** check box. The ten check boxes are selected.
4. Click the **OK** button. The JuneTbl table is further filtered and shows the ten records in June for Individual sales that are less than or equal to $200. See Figure 5-17.

Figure 5-17 JuneTbl table filtered to show Individual business with amounts less than $200

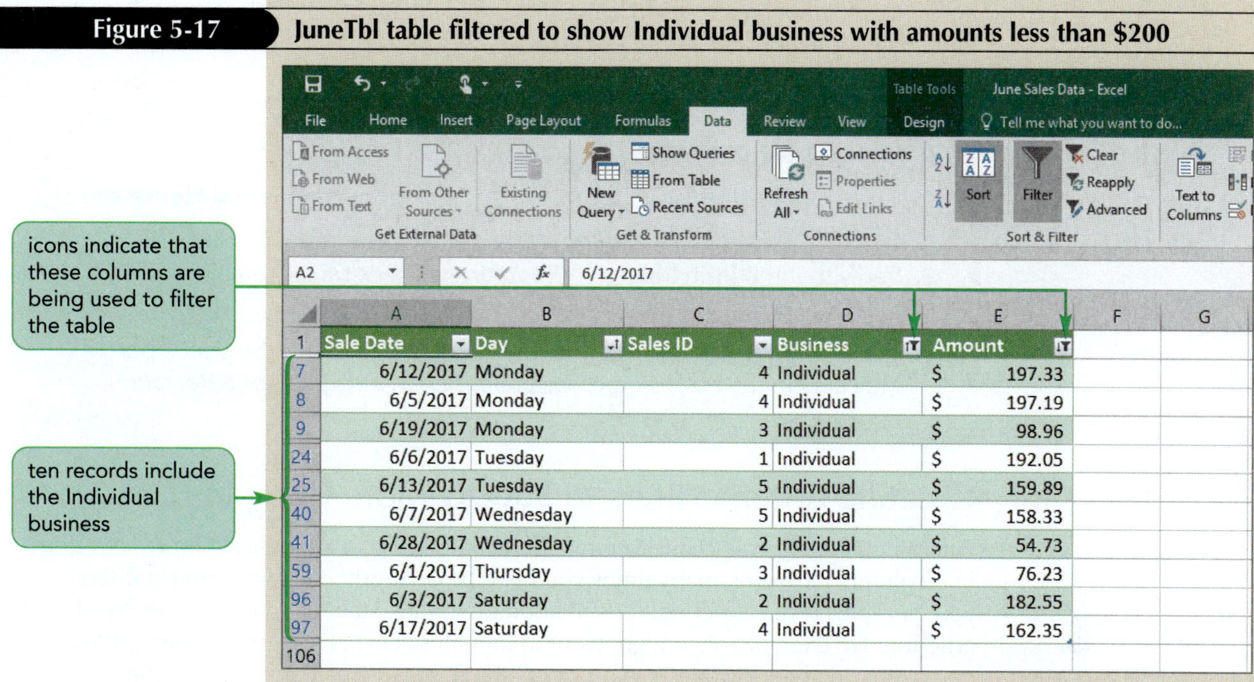
icons indicate that these columns are being used to filter the table
ten records include the Individual business

	A Sale Date	B Day	C Sales ID	D Business	E Amount
7	6/12/2017	Monday	4	Individual	$ 197.33
8	6/5/2017	Monday	4	Individual	$ 197.19
9	6/19/2017	Monday	3	Individual	$ 98.96
24	6/6/2017	Tuesday	1	Individual	$ 192.05
25	6/13/2017	Tuesday	5	Individual	$ 159.89
40	6/7/2017	Wednesday	5	Individual	$ 158.33
41	6/28/2017	Wednesday	2	Individual	$ 54.73
59	6/1/2017	Thursday	3	Individual	$ 76.23
96	6/3/2017	Saturday	2	Individual	$ 182.55
97	6/17/2017	Saturday	4	Individual	$ 162.35

Clearing Filters

When you want to redisplay all of the data in a filtered table, you need to **clear** (or remove) the filters. When you clear a filter from a column, any other filters are still applied. For example, in the JuneTbl table, you would see all the Individual sales if you cleared the filter from the Amount field. To redisplay all of the sales in the table, you need to clear both the Amount filter and the Business filter. You will do this now to redisplay the entire table of sales.

To clear the filters to show all the records in the JuneTbl table:

1. Click the **Amount** filter button, and then click **Clear Filter From "Amount"**. The Amount filter is removed from the table. The table shows only Individual sales because the Business filter is still in effect.
2. Click the **Business** filter button, and then click **Clear Filter From "Business"**. The Business filter is removed, and all of the records in the JuneTbl table are displayed.

Selecting Multiple Filter Items

You can often find the information you need by selecting a single filter item from a list of filter items. Sometimes, however, you need to specify a more complex set of criteria to find the records you want. Earlier, you selected one filter item for the Business column and one filter item for the Amount column to display the records whose Business field value equals Individual *and* whose Amount field value equals less than or equal to $200. A record had to contain both values to be displayed. Now you want the Business column to display records whose Business field value equals Individual *or* Restaurant. The records must have one of these values to be displayed. You do this by selecting two filter items from the list of filter items. For example, checking the Individual and Restaurant check boxes in the Business filter items creates the filter "Business equals Individual" *or* "Business equals Restaurant."

Victoria wants a list of all Individual and Restaurant sales on days when their sales are greater than or equal to $400. You'll create a filter with multiple items selected to find this information.

To select multiple filter items:

1. Click the **Business** filter button, and then click the **Group Home** and **Residential Care** check boxes to remove the checkmarks.
2. Verify that the **Individual** and **Restaurant** check boxes remain checked. Selecting more than one item creates a multiselect filter.
3. Click the **OK** button. The JuneTbl table is filtered, and the status bar indicates that 52 of 104 records are either an Individual or a Restaurant.

Creating Criteria Filters to Specify More Complex Criteria

Filter items enable you to filter a range of data or an Excel table based on exact values in a column. However, many times you need broader criteria. With **criteria filters**, you can specify various conditions in addition to those that are based on an equals criterion. For example, you might want to find all sales that are greater than $400 or that occurred after 6/15/2017. You use criteria filters to create these conditions.

The types of criteria filters available change depending on whether the data in a column contains text, numbers, or dates. Figure 5-18 shows some of the options for text, number, and date criteria filters.

Figure 5-18 **Options for text, number, and date criteria filters**

Filter	Criteria	Records Displayed
Text	Equals	Exactly match the specified text
	Does Not Equal	Do not exactly match the specified text
	Begins With	Begin with the specified text
	Ends With	End with the specified text
	Contains	Have the specified text anywhere
	Does Not Contain	Do not have the specified text anywhere
Number	Equals	Exactly match the specified number
	Greater Than or Equal to	Are greater than or equal to the specified number
	Less Than	Are less than the specified number
	Between	Are greater than or equal to and less than or equal to the specified numbers
	Top 10	Are the top or bottom 10 (or the specified number)
	Above Average	Are greater than the average
Date	Today	Have the current date
	Last Week	Are in the prior week
	Next Month	Are in the month following the current month
	Last Quarter	Are in the previous quarter of the year (quarters defined as Jan, Feb, Mar; Apr, May, June; and so on)
	Year to Date	Are since January 1 of the current year to the current date
	Last Year	Are in the previous year (based on the current date)

You can use these criteria filters to find the answers to complex questions that you ask about data.

PROSKILLS

Problem Solving: Using Filters to Find Appropriate Data

Problem solving often requires finding information from a set of data to answer specific questions. When you're working with a range of data or an Excel table that contains hundreds or thousands of records, filters help you find that information without having to review each record in the table. For example, a human resources manager can use a filter to narrow the search for a specific employee out of the 2500 working at the company knowing only that the employee's first name is Elliot.

Filtering limits the data to display only the specific records that meet the criteria you set, enabling you to more effectively analyze the data. The following examples further illustrate how filtering can help people to quickly locate the data they need to answer a particular question:

- A customer service representative can use a filter to search a list of 10,000 products to find all products priced between $500 and $1000.
- A donations coordinator can use a filter to prepare a report that shows the donations received during the first quarter of the current year.
- An academic dean can use a filter to retrieve the names of all students with GPAs below 2.0 (probation) or above 3.5 (high honors).
- A professor who has 300 students in a psychology class can use a filter to develop a list of potential student assistants for next semester from the names the professor has highlighted in blue because their work was impressive. Filtering by the blue color generates a list of students to interview.
- The author of a guide to celebrity autographs can use a filter to determine whether an entry for a specific celebrity already exists in an Excel table and, if it does, determine whether the entry needs to be updated. If the entry does not exist, the author will know to add the autograph data to the table.

As these examples show, filtering is a useful tool for locating the answers to a wide variety of questions. You then can use this information to help you resolve problems.

Victoria wants you to display the records for sales to individuals or restaurants that are greater than $400. You'll modify the filtered JuneTbl table to add a criteria filter that includes records for Individual or Restaurant with Amounts greater than $400.

To add a number filter that shows sales amounts greater than $400:

1. Click the **Amount** filter button, and then point to **Number Filters**. A menu opens, displaying the comparison operators available for columns of numbers.
2. Click **Greater Than**. The Custom AutoFilter dialog box opens. The upper-left box displays *is greater than*, which is the comparison operator you want to use to filter the Amount column. You enter the value you want to use for the filter criteria in the upper-right box, which, in this case, is $400.
3. Type **400** in the upper-right box. See Figure 5-19. You use the lower set of boxes if you want the filter to meet a second condition. You click the And option button to display rows that meet both criteria. You click the Or option button to display rows that meet either of the two criteria. You only want to set one criterion for this filter, so you'll leave the lower boxes empty.

Figure 5-19 Custom AutoFilter dialog box

Custom AutoFilter ? X
Show rows where:
Amount
is greater than | 400
(•) And ( ) Or
Use ? to represent any single character
Use * to represent any series of characters
OK Cancel

column being filtered
operator for the first condition
criterion for the first condition
logical operators used when there are two conditions
boxes to specify a second condition

4. Click the **OK** button. The status bar indicates that 14 of 104 records were found. The 14 records that appear in the JuneTbl table are either Individual or Restaurant and have an Amount greater than $400.

Next, you'll sort the filtered data to show the largest Amount first. Although you can sort the data using Sort buttons, as you did earlier, these sort options are also available on the Filter menu. If you want to perform a more complex sort, you still need to use the Sort dialog box.

To sort the filtered table data:

1. Click the **Amount** filter button. The Filter menu opens. The sort options are at the top of the menu.
2. Click **Sort Largest to Smallest**. The filtered records are sorted in descending order. The filtered table now displays records for individuals and restaurants with daily sales greater than $400 sorted in descending order. See Figure 5-20.

Figure 5-20 Filtered and sorted JuneTbl table

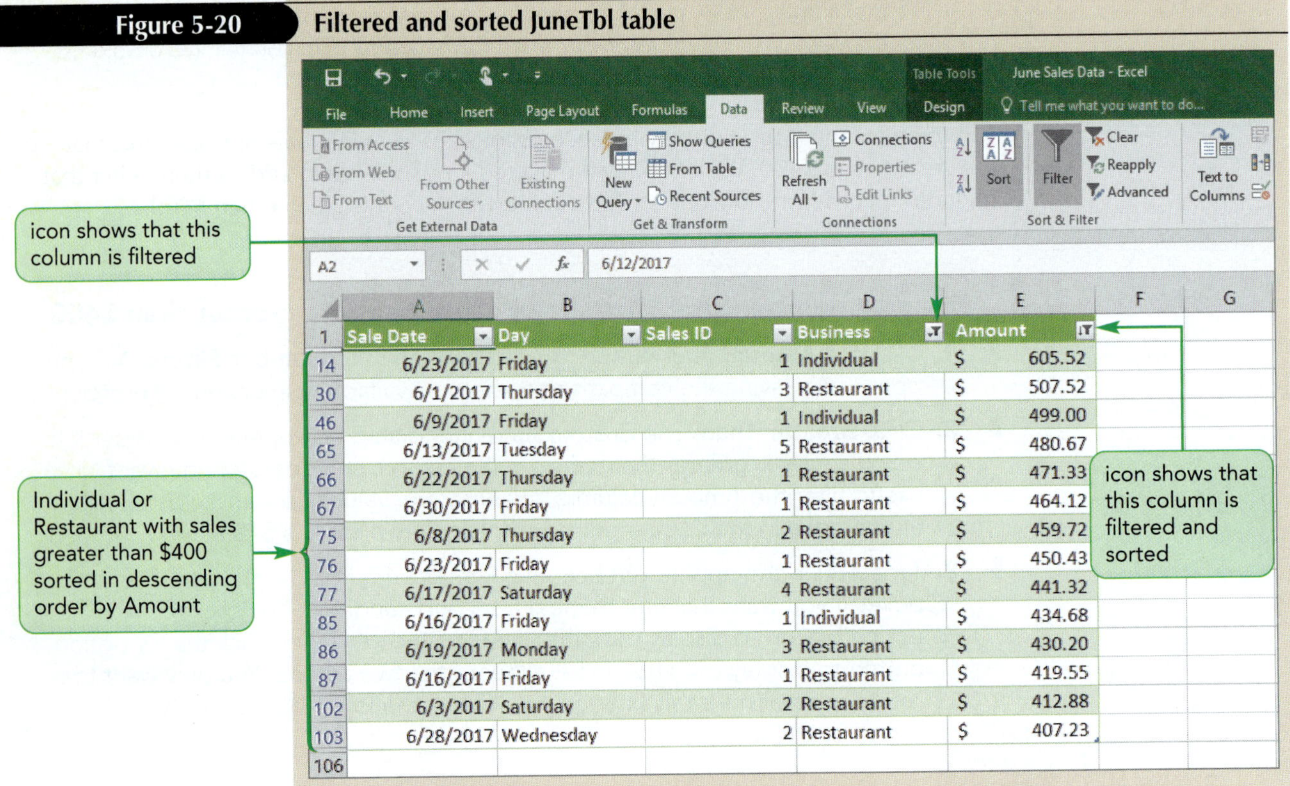

	Sale Date	Day	Sales ID	Business	Amount
14	6/23/2017	Friday	1	Individual	$ 605.52
30	6/1/2017	Thursday	3	Restaurant	$ 507.52
46	6/9/2017	Friday	1	Individual	$ 499.00
65	6/13/2017	Tuesday	5	Restaurant	$ 480.67
66	6/22/2017	Thursday	1	Restaurant	$ 471.33
67	6/30/2017	Friday	1	Restaurant	$ 464.12
75	6/8/2017	Thursday	2	Restaurant	$ 459.72
76	6/23/2017	Friday	1	Restaurant	$ 450.43
77	6/17/2017	Saturday	4	Restaurant	$ 441.32
85	6/16/2017	Friday	1	Individual	$ 434.68
86	6/19/2017	Monday	3	Restaurant	$ 430.20
87	6/16/2017	Friday	1	Restaurant	$ 419.55
102	6/3/2017	Saturday	2	Restaurant	$ 412.88
103	6/28/2017	Wednesday	2	Restaurant	$ 407.23
106					

Victoria will use this data to help her decide which days she may need to hire additional workers. You need to restore the entire table of JuneTbl, which you can do by clearing all the filters at one time.

To clear all the filters from the JuneTbl table:

1. On the ribbon, click the **Data** tab, if necessary.
2. In the Sort & Filter group, click the **Clear** button. All of the records are redisplayed in the table.

Creating a Slicer to Filter Data in an Excel Table

TIP

You can insert a Timeline to filter PivotTable data by time periods. On the PivotTable Tools Analyze tab, in the Filter group, click Insert Timeline, select the field, and then click the OK button. Use the scrollbar to select the time period.

Another way to filter an Excel table is with slicers. You can create a slicer for any field in the Excel table. You also can create more than one slicer for a table. Every slicer consists of an object that contains a button for each unique value in that field. For example, a slicer created for the Day field would include six buttons—one for each day of the week that Victoria's Veggies is open. One advantage of a slicer is that it clearly shows what filters are currently applied—the buttons for selected values are a different color. However, a slicer can take up a lot of space or hide data if there isn't a big enough blank area near the table. You can format the slicer and its buttons, changing its style, height, and width.

Victoria wants to be able to quickly filter the table to show sales for a specific Sales ID. You will add a slicer for the Sales ID field so she can do this.

To add the Sales ID slicer to the JuneTbl table:

1. On the ribbon, click the **Table Tools Design** tab.
2. In the Tools group, click the **Insert Slicer** button. The Insert Slicers dialog box opens, listing every available field in all tables in the workbook. You can select any or all of the fields.
3. Click the **Sales ID** check box to insert a checkmark, and then click the **OK** button. The Sales ID slicer appears on the worksheet. All of the slicer buttons are selected, indicating that every Sales ID is included in the table.
4. Drag the **Sales ID** slicer to the right of the JuneTbl table, placing its upper-left corner in cell G1.
5. If the Slicer Tools Options tab does not appear on the ribbon, click the **Sales ID** slicer to select it. The Slicer Tools Options tab appears on the ribbon and is selected.
6. In the Size group, enter **1.9"** in the Height box and **1.25"** in the Width box. The slicer is resized, eliminating the extra space below the buttons and to the right of the labels.
7. In the Slicer Styles group, click the **More** button, and then click **Slicer Style Dark 6**. The slicer colors now match the formatting of the Excel table. See Figure 5-21.

Figure 5-21 JuneTbl table with the Sales ID slicer

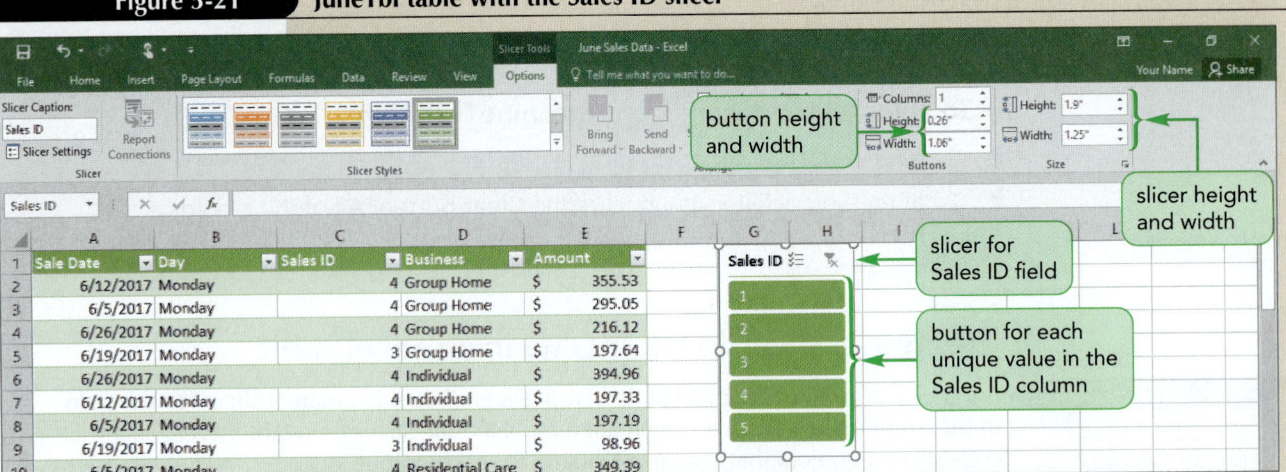

You can use the slicer to quickly filter records in an Excel table. Just click the slicer button corresponding to the data you want to display in the table. If you want to show more than one Sales ID, hold down the Ctrl key as you click the buttons that correspond to the additional data you want to show.

Victoria wants you to filter the JuneTbl table to display sales for Sales ID 1 and Sales ID 5. You will use the Sales ID slicer to do this.

To filter the JuneTbl table using the Sales ID slicer:

1. On the Sales ID slicer, click the **1** button. Only Sales ID 1 data appears in the JuneTbl table. All of the other buttons are gray, indicating that these Sales IDs are not included in the filtered data.
2. Press and hold the **Ctrl** key, click the **5** button, and then release the **Ctrl** key. Sales for Sales ID 5 are now added to the JuneTbl filtered table. See Figure 5-22.

Figure 5-22 **JuneTbl table filtered to show Sales IDs 1 and 5**

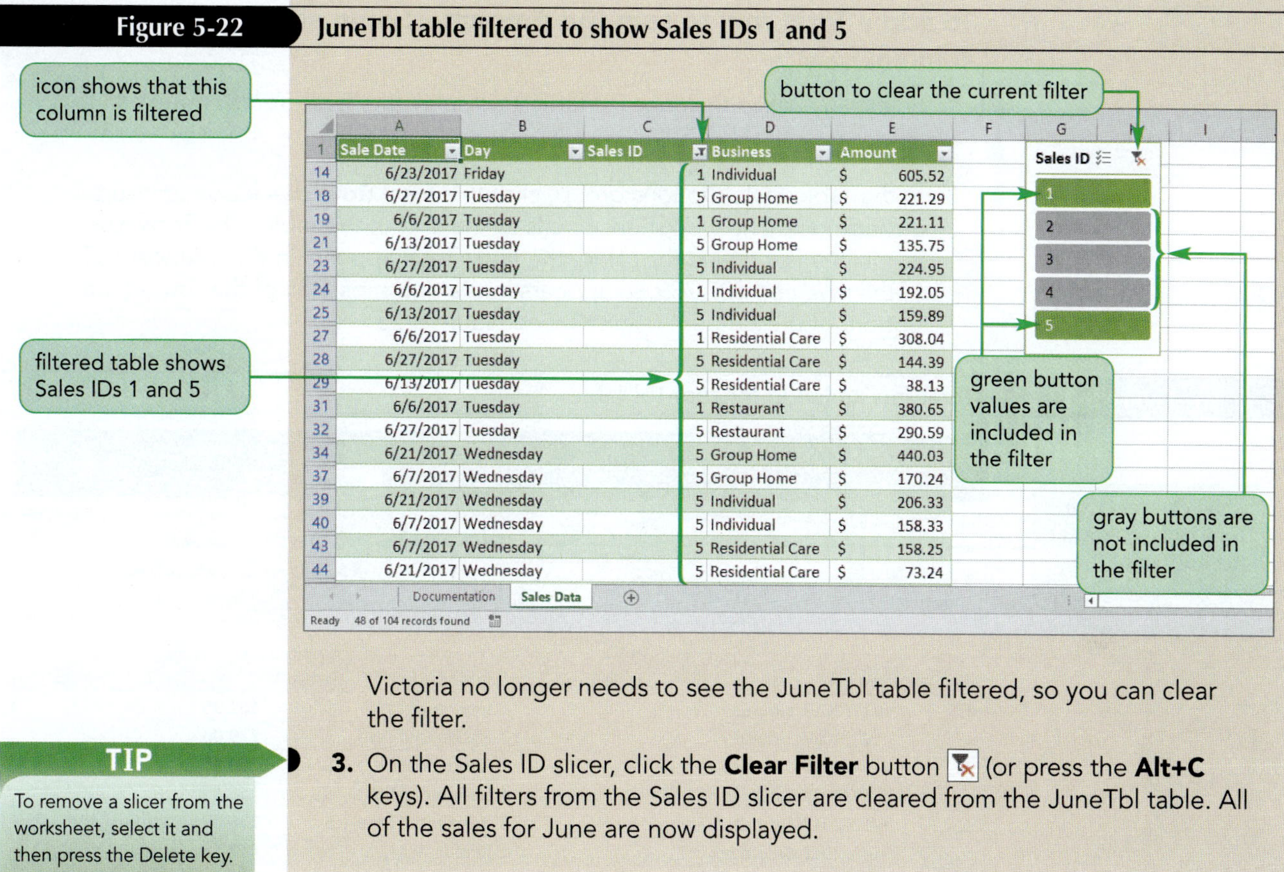

	Sale Date	Day	Sales ID	Business	Amount
14	6/23/2017	Friday	1	Individual	$ 605.52
18	6/27/2017	Tuesday	5	Group Home	$ 221.29
19	6/6/2017	Tuesday	1	Group Home	$ 221.11
21	6/13/2017	Tuesday	5	Group Home	$ 135.75
23	6/27/2017	Tuesday	5	Individual	$ 224.95
24	6/6/2017	Tuesday	1	Individual	$ 192.05
25	6/13/2017	Tuesday	5	Individual	$ 159.89
27	6/6/2017	Tuesday	1	Residential Care	$ 308.04
28	6/27/2017	Tuesday	5	Residential Care	$ 144.39
29	6/13/2017	Tuesday	5	Residential Care	$ 38.13
31	6/6/2017	Tuesday	1	Restaurant	$ 380.65
32	6/27/2017	Tuesday	5	Restaurant	$ 290.59
34	6/21/2017	Wednesday	5	Group Home	$ 440.03
37	6/7/2017	Wednesday	5	Group Home	$ 170.24
39	6/21/2017	Wednesday	5	Individual	$ 206.33
40	6/7/2017	Wednesday	5	Individual	$ 158.33
43	6/7/2017	Wednesday	5	Residential Care	$ 158.25
44	6/21/2017	Wednesday	5	Residential Care	$ 73.24

Victoria no longer needs to see the JuneTbl table filtered, so you can clear the filter.

TIP

To remove a slicer from the worksheet, select it and then press the Delete key.

3. On the Sales ID slicer, click the **Clear Filter** button (or press the **Alt+C** keys). All filters from the Sales ID slicer are cleared from the JuneTbl table. All of the sales for June are now displayed.

Using the Total Row to Calculate Summary Statistics

The Total row is used to calculate summary statistics (including sum, average, count, maximum, and minimum) for any column in an Excel table. The Total row is inserted immediately after the last row of data in the table. A double-line border is inserted to indicate that the following row contains totals, and the label Total is added to the leftmost cell of the row. By default, the Total row adds the numbers in the last column of the Excel table or counts the number of records if the data in the last column contains text. When you click in each cell of the Total row, an arrow appears that you can click to open a list of the most commonly used functions. You can also select other functions by opening the Insert Functions dialog box.

Victoria wants to see the total amount of sales in June and the total number of records being displayed. You will add a Total row to the JuneTbl table and then use the SUM and COUNT functions to calculate these statistics for Victoria.

To add a Total row to sum the Amount column and count the Day column:

1. Select any cell in the JuneTbl table to display the Table Tools contextual tab.
2. On the ribbon, click the **Table Tools Design** tab.
3. In the Table Style Options group, click the **Total Row** check box to insert a checkmark. The worksheet scrolls to the end of the table. The Total row is now the last row in the table, the label Total appears in the leftmost cell of the row, and $27,739.26 appears in the rightmost cell of the row (at the bottom of the Amount column). See Figure 5-23.

Figure 5-23 Total row added to the JuneTbl table

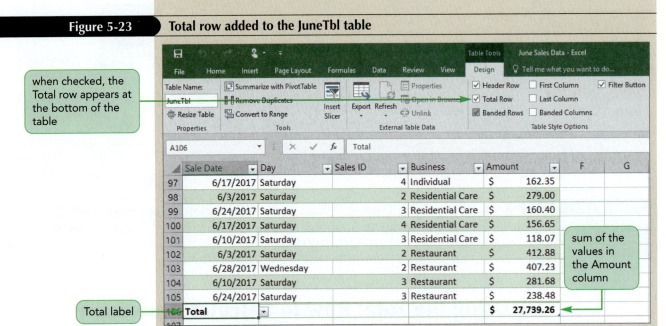

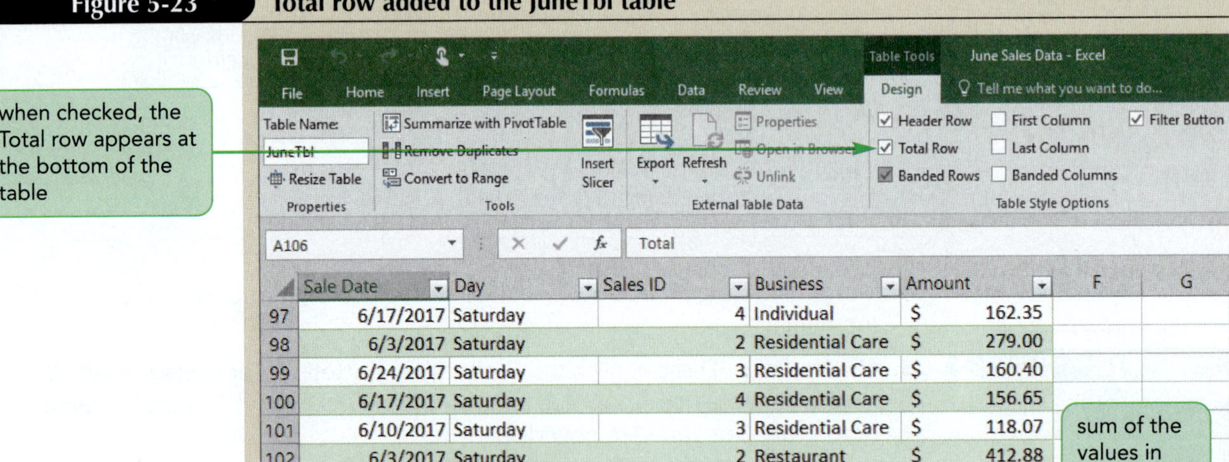

Next, you will use the COUNT function to add the number of records displayed.

4. Click cell **B106** (the Day cell in the Total row), and then click the **arrow** button ▾ to display a list of functions. None is the default function in all columns except the last column. See Figure 5-24.

Figure 5-24 Total row functions

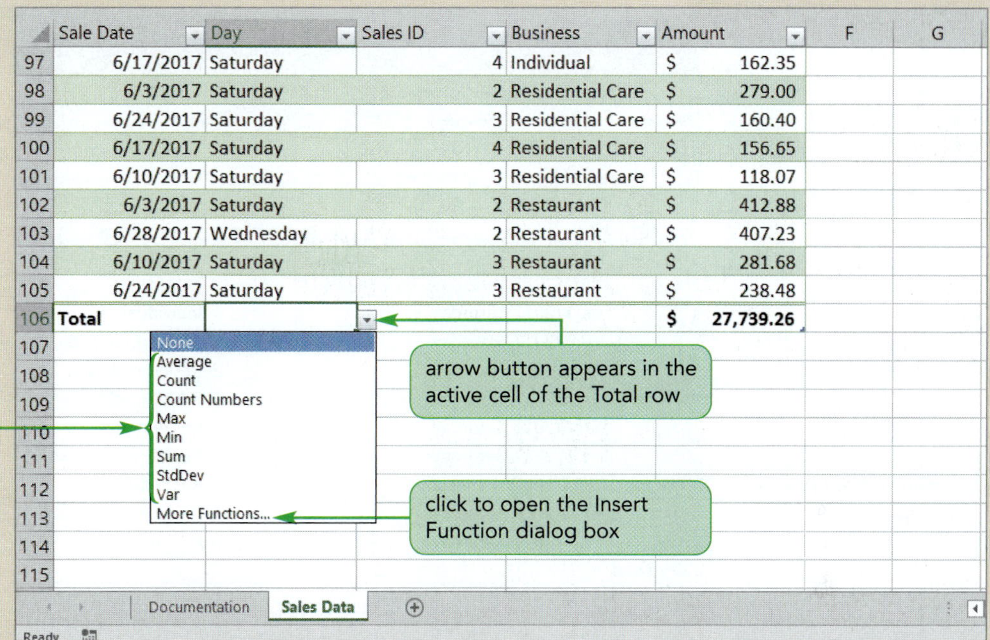

TIP

When you select Sum, Count, or Average, Excel uses the SUBTOTAL function to calculate the summary statistic in the Total row.

5. Click **Count**. The number 104, which is the number of records in the JuneTbl table, appears in the cell.

As you add, edit, or delete data in the table, the Total row values change. This also happens if you filter the table to show only some of the table data. Victoria wants the total sales to include sales from all seasonal employees (Sales IDs 2 through 4). You will filter the table to exclude Sales IDs 1 and 5, displaying the total Amount for Sales IDs 2 through 4 only. The COUNT function will also change to show only the number of transactions for the filtered data.

To filter sales by excluding sales from Sales ID 1 and Sales ID 5:

1. Press the **Ctrl+Home** keys to make cell A1 the active cell.
2. On the Sales ID slicer, click the **2** slicer button, press and hold the **Ctrl** key as you click the **3** and **4** slicer buttons, and then release the **Ctrl** key. The JuneTbl table is filtered to display sales for the seasonal employees in June.
3. Scroll to the end of the table. The Total row shows that the 56 records contain total sales of $14,393.01. See Figure 5-25.

Figure 5-25 Summary statistics in the filtered table

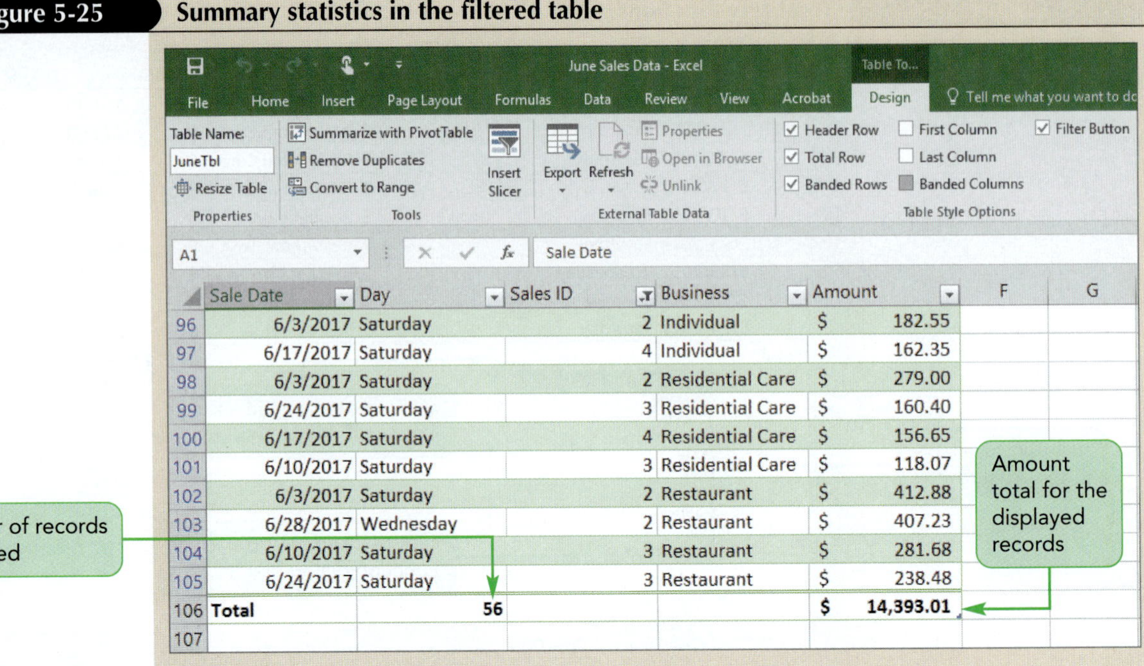

Splitting the Worksheet Window into Panes

You can split the worksheet window into two or four separate panes. This allows you to easily view data from several areas of the worksheet at the same time. Each pane has its own scroll bars so you can navigate easily within one pane or display different parts of the worksheet. You can move between panes using the mouse. To create two panes, select a cell in row 1 to split the worksheet vertically, or select a cell in column A to split the worksheet horizontally; to create four panes, select any other cell in the worksheet.

Victoria wants to view the JuneTbl summary totals at the same time she views the data on individual sales. You will divide the worksheet into two horizontal panes to view the sales records in the top pane and the totals in the bottom pane.

To split the Sales Data worksheet window into panes:

1. Press the **Ctrl+Home** keys to make cell A1 at the top of the table the active cell.
2. Select the cell in column A that is two rows above the last row visible on your screen.
3. On the ribbon, click the **View** tab.
4. In the Window group, click the **Split** button. The worksheet window splits into two panes. Each pane has its own set of scroll bars. The active cell is in the bottom pane below the split bar. See Figure 5-26.

Figure 5-26 **Worksheet split into two panes**

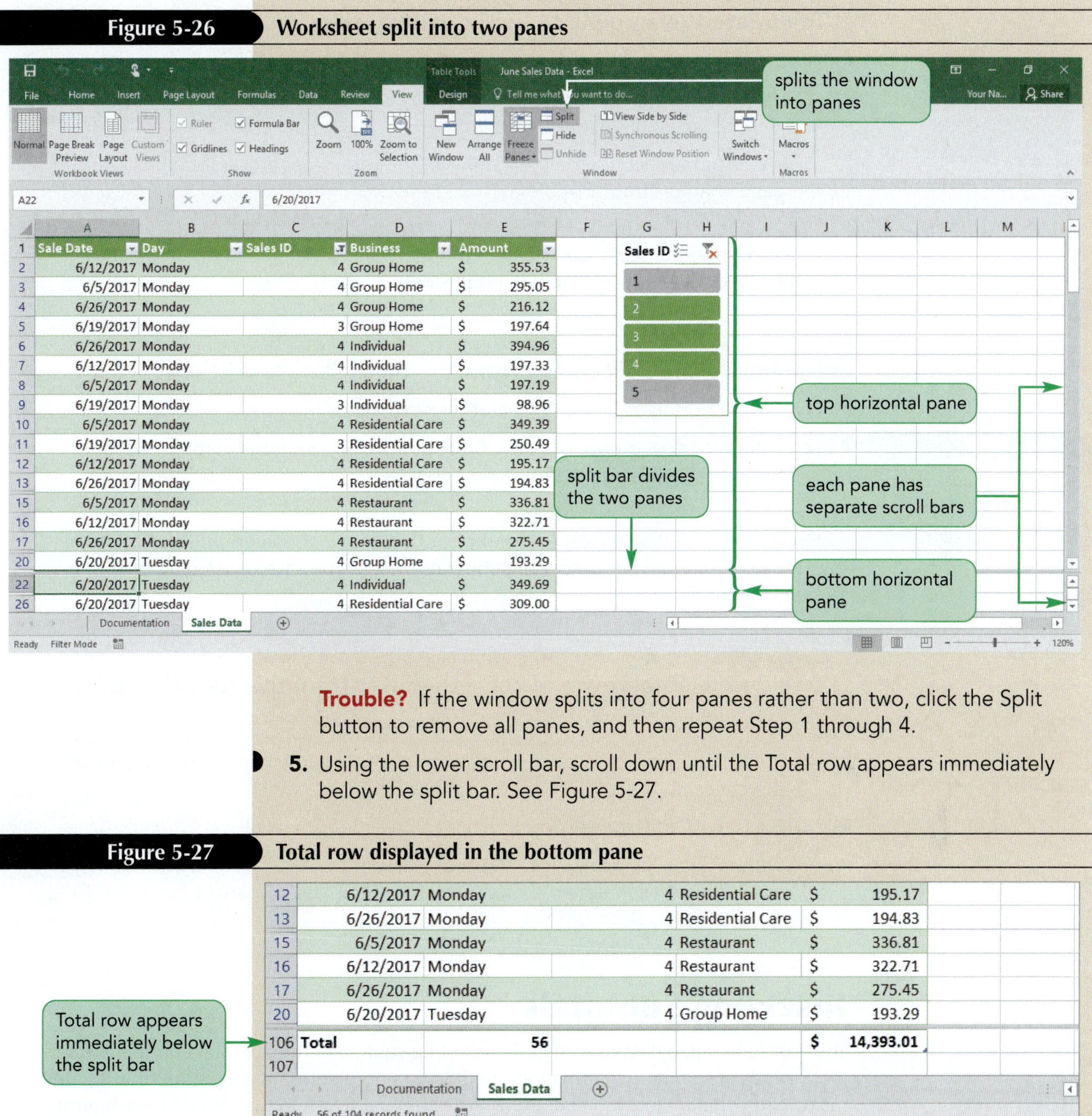

Trouble? If the window splits into four panes rather than two, click the Split button to remove all panes, and then repeat Step 1 through 4.

5. Using the lower scroll bar, scroll down until the Total row appears immediately below the split bar. See Figure 5-27.

Figure 5-27 **Total row displayed in the bottom pane**

Victoria discovered a data entry error in the sales amount for Individual on 6/28/2017. It was entered as $54.73; the correct amount is $154.73. You will change the amount.

To update the amount of the Individual sales on 6/28/2017:

1. Select any cell in the top pane.
2. Use the Find command to locate the **6/28/2017** sales for **Individual**. The amount is $54.73.
3. In the Amount column, enter **154.73**. The total sales amount in the bottom pane changes from $14,393.01 to $14,493.01.

When you want to see a worksheet in a single pane, you remove the split panes from the worksheet window. You will do this now.

To remove the split panes from the Sales Data worksheet

1. On the ribbon, click the **View** tab, if necessary.
2. In the Window group, click the **Split** button. The split bar is removed, and the worksheet is again a single window.

TIP

You can also double-click the split bar to remove the panes.

Now, you will hide the Total row and clear the filter. If you later redisplay the Total row, the functions you last used will appear even after you save, close, and then reopen the workbook.

To hide the Total row and clear the filter from the JuneTbl table:

1. On the ribbon, click the **Table Tools Design** tab.
2. In the Table Style Options group, click the **Total Row** check box to remove the checkmark. The Total row is no longer visible.
3. Press the **Ctrl+Home** keys to make cell A1 the active cell.
4. On the Sales ID slicer, click the **Clear Filter** button to remove the filters from the JuneTbl table. All of the sales for June are displayed.

Inserting Subtotals

You can summarize data in a range by inserting subtotals. The Subtotal command offers many kinds of summary information, including counts, sums, averages, minimums, and maximums. The Subtotal command inserts a subtotal row into the range for each group of data and adds a grand total row below the last row of data. Because Excel inserts subtotals whenever the value in a specified field changes, you need to sort the data so that records with the same value in a specified field are grouped together *before* you use the Subtotal command. The Subtotal command cannot be used in an Excel table, so you must first convert the Excel table to a normal range.

REFERENCE

Calculating Subtotals for a Range of Data

- Sort the data by the column for which you want a subtotal.
- If the data is in an Excel table, on the Table Tools Design tab, in the Tools group, click the Convert to Range button, and then click the Yes button to convert the Excel table to a range.
- On the Data tab, in the Outline group, click the Subtotal button.
- Click the At each change in arrow, and then click the column that contains the group you want to subtotal.
- Click the Use function arrow, and then click the function you want to use to summarize the data.
- In the Add subtotal to box, click the check box for each column that contains the values you want to summarize.
- To calculate another category of subtotals, click the Replace current subtotals check box to remove the checkmark, and then repeat the previous three steps.
- Click the OK button.

Victoria wants to create a report that shows all the vegetable store's sales sorted by Sale Date with the total amount of the sales for each date. She also wants to see the total amount for each sale date after the last item of that date. The Subtotal command is a simple way to provide the information Victoria needs. First, you will sort the sales by Sale Date, then you will convert the Excel table to a normal range, and finally you will calculate subtotals in the Amount column for each Sale Date grouping to produce the results Victoria needs.

Be sure to sort the table and convert the table to a range before calculating subtotals.

To sort the sales and convert the table to a range:

1. Click the **Sale Date** filter button, and then click **Sort Oldest to Newest** on the Filter menu. The JuneTbl table is sorted in ascending order by the Sale Date field. This ensures one subtotal is created for each date.
2. On the Table Tools Design tab, in the Tools group, click the **Convert to Range** button. A dialog box opens, asking if you want to convert the table to a normal range.
3. Click the **Yes** button. The Excel table is converted to a range, and the Home tab is selected on the ribbon. You can tell the table data is now a normal range because the filter buttons, the Table Tools Design tab, and the slicer disappear.

Next, you'll calculate the subtotals.

To calculate the sales amount subtotals for each date:

1. On the ribbon, click the **Data** tab.
2. In the Outline group, click the **Subtotal** button. The Subtotal dialog box opens. See Figure 5-28.

Figure 5-28 Subtotal dialog box

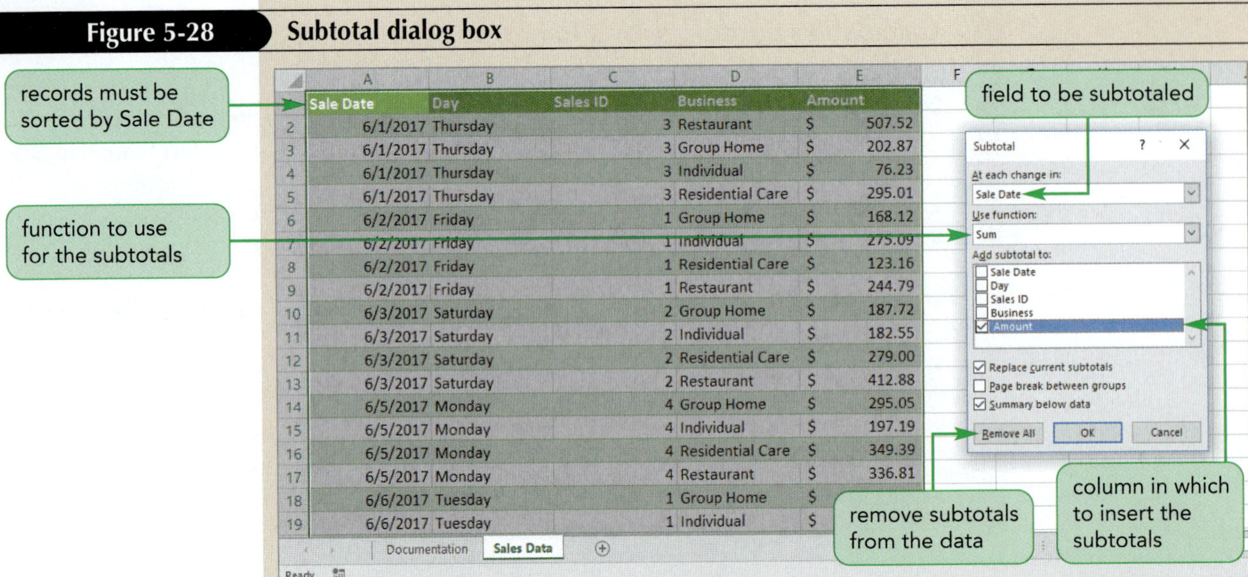

3. If necessary, click the **At each change in** arrow, and then click **Sale Date**. This is the column you want Excel to use to determine where to insert the subtotals; it is the column you sorted. A subtotal will be calculated at every change in the Sale Date value.
4. If necessary, click the **Use function** arrow, and then click **Sum**. The Use function list provides several options for subtotaling data, including counts, averages, minimums, maximums, and products.
5. In the Add subtotal to box, make sure only the **Amount** check box is checked. This specifies the Amount field as the field to be subtotaled.

   If the data already included subtotals, you would check the Replace current subtotals check box to replace the existing subtotals or uncheck the option to display the new subtotals on separate rows above the existing subtotals. Because the data has no subtotals, it makes no difference whether you select this option.
6. Make sure the **Summary below data** check box is checked. This option places the subtotals below each group of data instead of above the first entry in each group and places the grand total at the end of the data instead of at the top of the column just below the row of column headings.
7. Click the **OK** button. Excel inserts rows below each Sale Date group and displays the subtotals for the amount of each Sale Date in the Amount column. A series of Outline buttons appear to the left of the worksheet so you can display or hide the detail rows within each subtotal.

   Trouble? If each item has a subtotal following it, or repeating subtotals appear for the same item, you probably forgot to sort the data by Sale Date. Click the Undo button on the Quick Access Toolbar, sort the data by Sale Date, and then repeat Steps 1 through 7.
8. Scroll through the data to see the subtotals below each category and the grand total at the end of the data. See Figure 5-29.

Figure 5-29 Subtotals and grand total added to the sales data

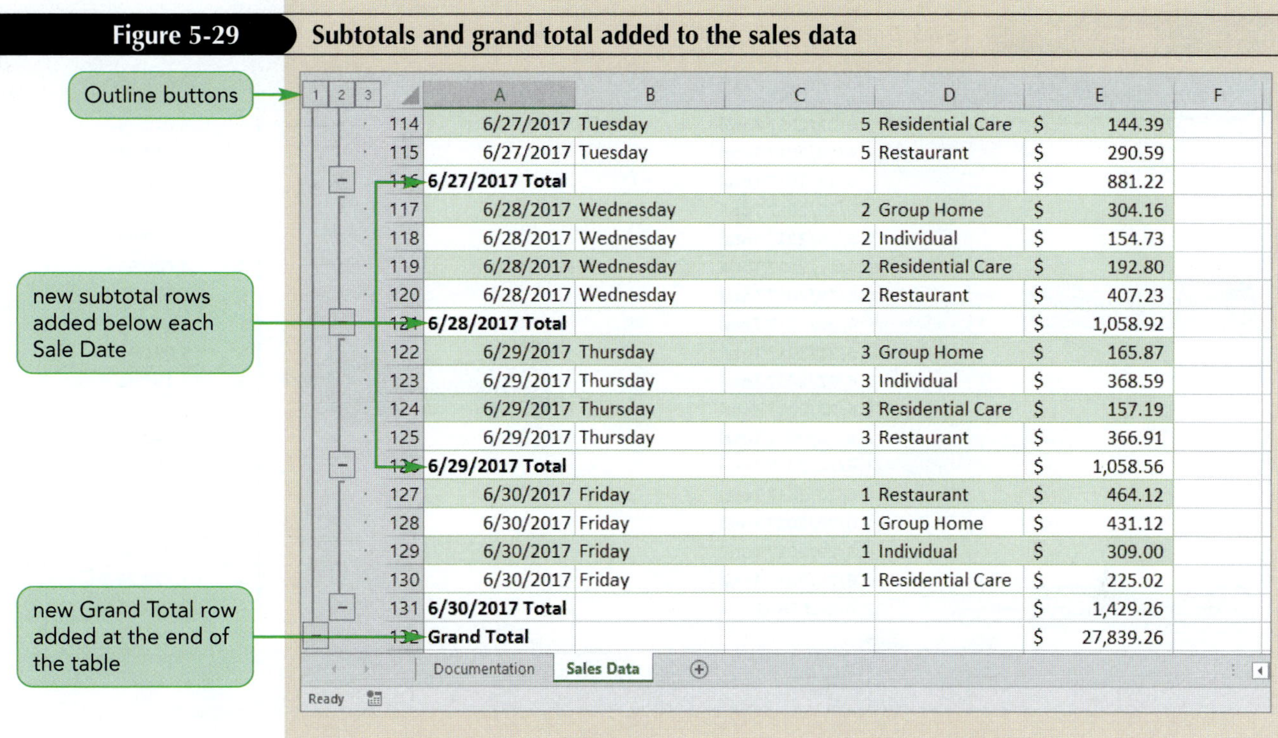

	A	B	C	D	E	F
114	6/27/2017	Tuesday	5	Residential Care	$ 144.39	
115	6/27/2017	Tuesday	5	Restaurant	$ 290.59	
116	6/27/2017 Total				$ 881.22	
117	6/28/2017	Wednesday	2	Group Home	$ 304.16	
118	6/28/2017	Wednesday	2	Individual	$ 154.73	
119	6/28/2017	Wednesday	2	Residential Care	$ 192.80	
120	6/28/2017	Wednesday	2	Restaurant	$ 407.23	
121	6/28/2017 Total				$ 1,058.92	
122	6/29/2017	Thursday	3	Group Home	$ 165.87	
123	6/29/2017	Thursday	3	Individual	$ 368.59	
124	6/29/2017	Thursday	3	Residential Care	$ 157.19	
125	6/29/2017	Thursday	3	Restaurant	$ 366.91	
126	6/29/2017 Total				$ 1,058.56	
127	6/30/2017	Friday	1	Restaurant	$ 464.12	
128	6/30/2017	Friday	1	Group Home	$ 431.12	
129	6/30/2017	Friday	1	Individual	$ 309.00	
130	6/30/2017	Friday	1	Residential Care	$ 225.02	
131	6/30/2017 Total				$ 1,429.26	
132	Grand Total				$ 27,839.26	

Using the Subtotal Outline View

The Subtotal feature "outlines" the worksheet so you can control the level of detail that is displayed. The three Outline buttons at the top of the outline area, shown in Figure 5-29, allow you to show or hide different levels of detail in the worksheet. By default, the highest level is active; in this case, Level 3. Level 3 displays the most detail—the individual sales records, the subtotals, and the grand total. Level 2 displays the subtotals and the grand total but not the individual records. Level 1 displays only the grand total.

Victoria wants you to isolate the different subtotal sections so that she can focus on them individually. You will use the Outline buttons to prepare a report for Victoria that includes only subtotals and the grand total.

To use the Outline buttons to hide records:

1. Click the **Level 2 Outline** button [2], and then scroll to view the daily subtotals and grand total. The individual sales records are hidden; only the subtotals for each Sale Date and the grand total are displayed. See Figure 5-30.

Figure 5-30 Level 2 outline

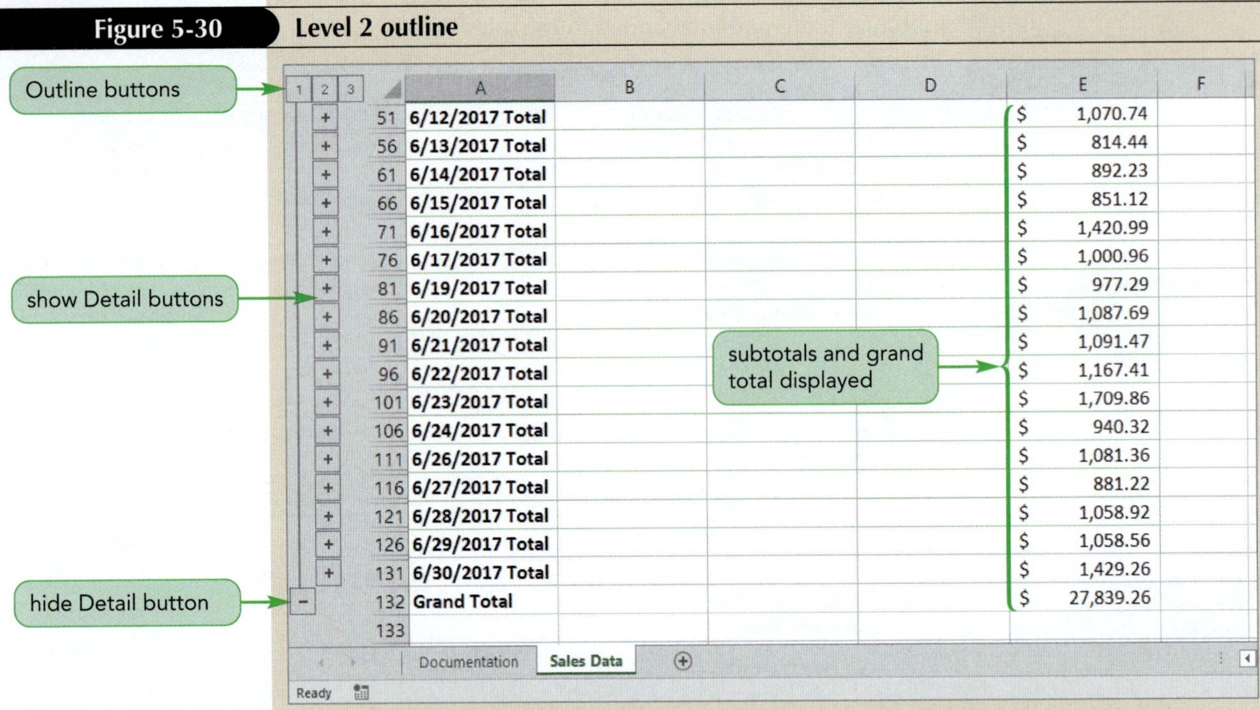

Outline buttons
show Detail buttons
hide Detail button
subtotals and grand total displayed
1 2 3
A B C D E F
51 6/12/2017 Total $ 1,070.74
56 6/13/2017 Total $ 814.44
61 6/14/2017 Total $ 892.23
66 6/15/2017 Total $ 851.12
71 6/16/2017 Total $ 1,420.99
76 6/17/2017 Total $ 1,000.96
81 6/19/2017 Total $ 977.29
86 6/20/2017 Total $ 1,087.69
91 6/21/2017 Total $ 1,091.47
96 6/22/2017 Total $ 1,167.41
101 6/23/2017 Total $ 1,709.86
106 6/24/2017 Total $ 940.32
111 6/26/2017 Total $ 1,081.36
116 6/27/2017 Total $ 881.22
121 6/28/2017 Total $ 1,058.92
126 6/29/2017 Total $ 1,058.56
131 6/30/2017 Total $ 1,429.26
132 Grand Total $ 27,839.26
133
Documentation
Sales Data
Ready

TIP

To collapse the outline and hide the rows with details, click the Hide Detail button.

2. Click the **Show Detail** button [+] to the left of 6/30/2017 to expand the outline and show the details of daily sales by unhiding rows for this date. Sales for each Business on 6/30/2017 are now displayed.
3. Click the **Level 1 Outline** button [1]. The individual sales records and the subtotals for each Sale Date are hidden. Only the grand total remains visible.
4. Click the **Level 3 Outline** button [3], and then scroll up. All the records along with the subtotals and the grand total are visible.

Victoria has completed her review of the daily sales report for June. She asks you to remove the subtotals from the data.

To remove the subtotals from the Sales Data worksheet:

1. On the Data tab, in the Outline group, click the **Subtotal** button. The Subtotal dialog box opens.
2. Click the **Remove All** button. The subtotals are removed from the data, and only the records appear in the worksheet.

   You'll reset the JuneTbl Excel table.
3. Make sure the active cell is a cell within the normal range of data.
4. On the ribbon, click the **Insert** tab.
5. In the Tables group, click the **Table** button. The Create Table dialog box opens.
6. Click the **OK** button to create the Excel table, and then click any cell in the table. The table structure is active.
7. On the Table Tools Design tab, in the Properties group, type **JuneTbl** in the Table Name box, and then press the **Enter** key. The Excel table is again named JuneTbl.

In this session, you filtered the table data, inserted a Total row, and determined totals and subtotals for the data. In the next session, you will work with PivotTables and PivotCharts to gather information to help Victoria with staffing and storefront opening decisions.

REVIEW

Session 5.2 Quick Check

1. Explain filtering.
2. How can you display a list of economics majors with a GPA less than 2.5 from an Excel table with records for 1000 students?
3. An Excel table includes records for 500 employees. What can you use to calculate the average salary of employees in the finance department?
4. What is a slicer, and how does it work?
5. If you have a list of employees that includes fields for gender and salary, among others, how can you determine the average salary for females using the Total row feature?
6. Explain the relationship between the Sort and Subtotal commands.
7. After you display subtotals, how can you use the Outline buttons?

Session 5.3 Visual Overview:

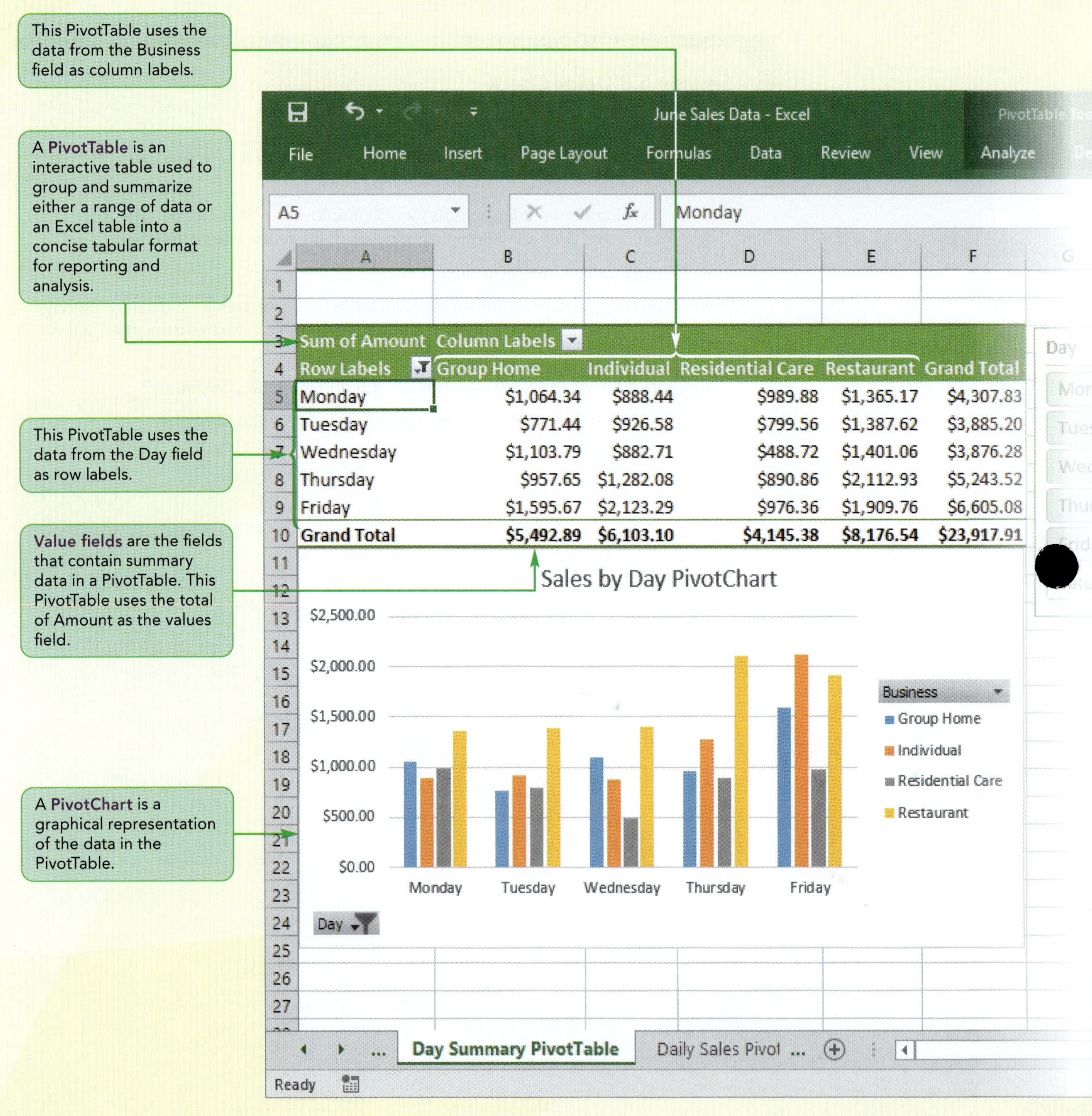
This PivotTable uses the data from the Business field as column labels.
A PivotTable is an interactive table used to group and summarize either a range of data or an Excel table into a concise tabular format for reporting and analysis.
This PivotTable uses the data from the Day field as row labels.
Value fields are the fields that contain summary data in a PivotTable. This PivotTable uses the total of Amount as the values field.
A PivotChart is a graphical representation of the data in the PivotTable.
June Sales Data - Excel
File
Home
Insert
Page Layout
Formulas
Data
Review
View
Analyze
A5
Monday
Sales by Day PivotChart
$2,500.00
$2,000.00
$1,500.00
$1,000.00
$500.00
$0.00
Monday
Tuesday
Wednesday
Thursday
Friday
Business
Group Home
Individual
Residential Care
Restaurant
Day
Day Summary PivotTable
Daily Sales Pivot ...
Ready

Sum of Amount	Column Labels				
Row Labels	Group Home	Individual	Residential Care	Restaurant	Grand Total
Monday	$1,064.34	$888.44	$989.88	$1,365.17	$4,307.83
Tuesday	$771.44	$926.58	$799.56	$1,387.62	$3,885.20
Wednesday	$1,103.79	$882.71	$488.72	$1,401.06	$3,876.28
Thursday	$957.65	$1,282.08	$890.86	$2,112.93	$5,243.52
Friday	$1,595.67	$2,123.29	$976.36	$1,909.76	$6,605.08
Grand Total	**$5,492.89**	**$6,103.10**	**$4,145.38**	**$8,176.54**	**$23,917.91**

PivotTable and PivotChart

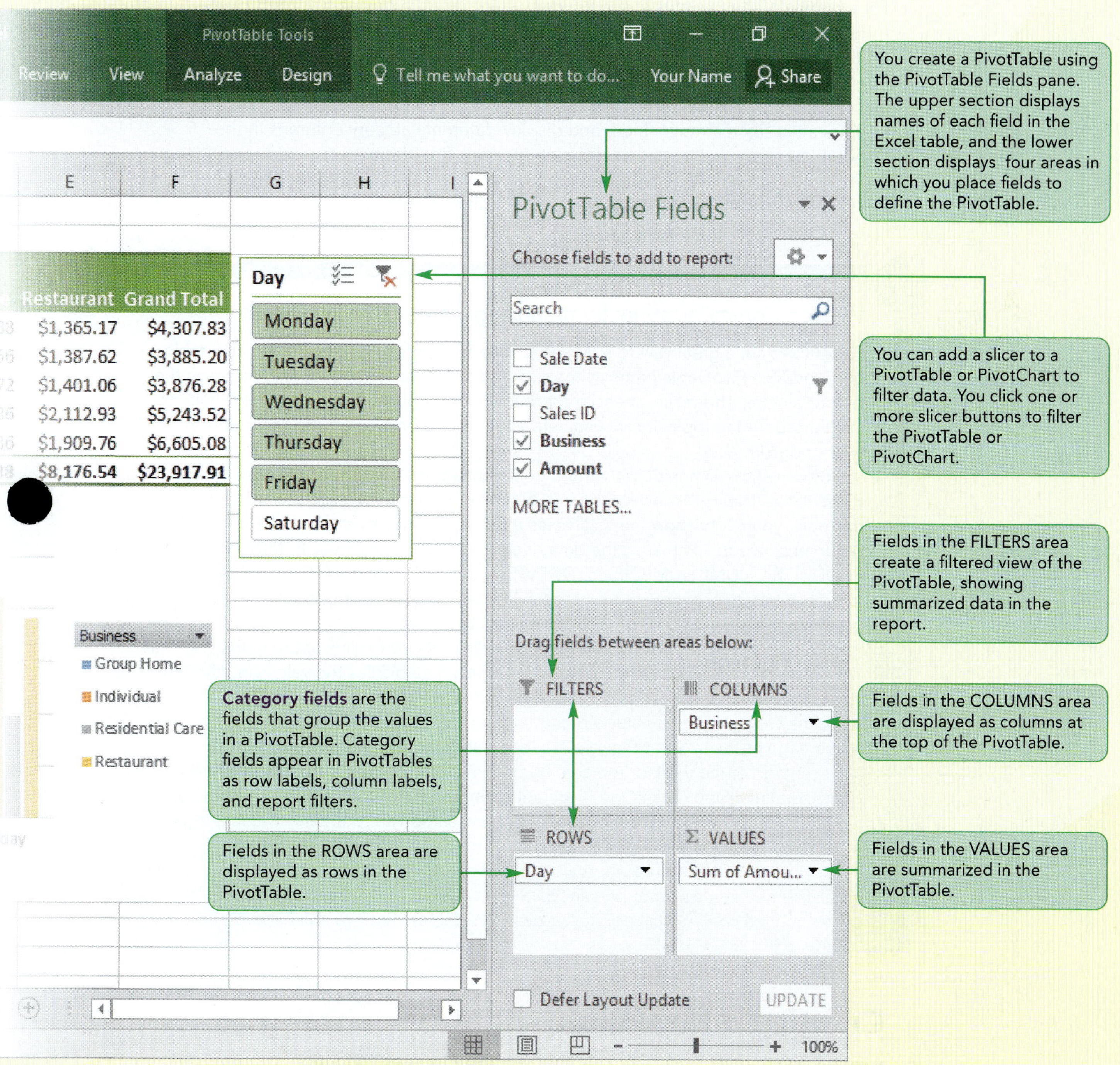
PivotTable Tools
Review View Analyze Design
Tell me what you want to do...
Your Name Share
E F G H I
Restaurant Grand Total
$1,365.17 $4,307.83
$1,387.62 $3,885.20
$1,401.06 $3,876.28
$2,112.93 $5,243.52
$1,909.76 $6,605.08
$8,176.54 $23,917.91
Day
Monday
Tuesday
Wednesday
Thursday
Friday
Saturday
Business
Group Home
Individual
Residential Care
Restaurant
PivotTable Fields
Choose fields to add to report:
Search
Sale Date
Day
Sales ID
Business
Amount
MORE TABLES...
Drag fields between areas below:
FILTERS
COLUMNS
Business
ROWS
Day
VALUES
Sum of Amou...
Defer Layout Update
UPDATE
100%
You create a PivotTable using the PivotTable Fields pane. The upper section displays names of each field in the Excel table, and the lower section displays four areas in which you place fields to define the PivotTable.
You can add a slicer to a PivotTable or PivotChart to filter data. You click one or more slicer buttons to filter the PivotTable or PivotChart.
Fields in the FILTERS area create a filtered view of the PivotTable, showing summarized data in the report.
Category fields are the fields that group the values in a PivotTable. Category fields appear in PivotTables as row labels, column labels, and report filters.
Fields in the COLUMNS area are displayed as columns at the top of the PivotTable.
Fields in the ROWS area are displayed as rows in the PivotTable.
Fields in the VALUES area are summarized in the PivotTable.

Analyzing Data with PivotTables

An Excel table can contain a wealth of information. However, when the table contains large amounts of detailed data, it often becomes more difficult to obtain a clear, overall view of that information. You can use a PivotTable to help organize the data into a meaningful summary. A PivotTable groups data into categories and then uses functions such as COUNT, SUM, AVERAGE, MAX, and MIN to summarize that data. For example, Victoria wants to see the daily sales for each business (Group Home, Individual, Residential Care, and Restaurant) grouped by week. Although there are several ways to generate the information Victoria needs, you can use a PivotTable like the one shown in the Session 5.3 Visual Overview to generate this information quickly and present it concisely.

You can easily rearrange, hide, and display different category columns in the PivotTable to provide alternative views of the data. This ability to "pivot" the table—for example, change row headings to column positions and vice versa—gives the PivotTable its name and makes it a powerful analytical tool.

PROSKILLS

Written Communication: Summarizing Data with a PivotTable

PivotTables are a great way to summarize data from selected fields of an Excel table or range. The PivotTable omits all the detailed data, enabling readers to focus on the bigger picture. This makes it easier for readers to understand the results and gain insights about the topic. It can also help you back up or support specific points in written documents.

You can show summaries in written documents based on function results in PivotTables. The SUM function is probably the most frequently used function. For example, you might show the total sales for a region. However, you can use many other functions to summarize the data, including COUNT, AVERAGE, MIN, MAX, PRODUCT, COUNT NUMBERS, STDDEV, STDDEVP, VAR, and VARP. Using these functions, you might show the average sales for a region, the minimum price of a product, or a count of the number of students by major.

When you write a report, you want supporting data to be presented in the way that best communicates your points. With PivotTables, you display the values in different views. For example, to compare one item to another item in the PivotTable, you can show the values as a percentage of a total. You can display the data in each row as a percentage of the total for the row. You can also display the data in each column as a percentage of the total for the column or display the data as a percentage of the grand total of all the data in the PivotTable. Viewing data as a percentage of the total is useful for analyses such as comparing product sales with total sales within a region or comparing expense categories to total expenses for the year.

As you can see, PivotTables provide great flexibility in how you analyze and display data. This makes it easier to present data in a way that highlights and supports the points you are communicating, making your written documents much more effective.

Creating a PivotTable

A useful first step in creating a PivotTable is to plan its layout. Figure 5-31 shows the PivotTable that Victoria wants you to create. As you can see in the figure, the PivotTable will show the total Amount of the sales organized by Sales ID, Sale Date, and Business.

Figure 5-31 PivotTable plan

Sales ID	XXXX					
Total Sales						
Sale Date		Group Home	Individual	Residential Care	Restaurant	Total
Total						

You are ready to create the PivotTable summarizing the total sales for Victoria.

REFERENCE

Creating a PivotTable

- Click in the Excel table (or select the range of data for the PivotTable).
- On the Insert tab, in the Tables group, click the PivotTable button.
- Click the Select a table or range option button, and then verify the reference in the Table/Range box.
- Click the New Worksheet option button, or click the Existing Worksheet option button and specify a cell.
- Click the OK button.
- Click the check boxes for the fields you want to add to the PivotTable (or drag fields to the appropriate box in the layout section).
- If needed, drag fields to different boxes in the layout section.

When you create a PivotTable, you need to specify where to find the data for the PivotTable. The data can be in an Excel table or range in the current workbook or an external data source such as an Access database file. You also must specify whether to place the PivotTable in a new or an existing worksheet. If you place the PivotTable in an existing worksheet, you must also specify the cell in which you want the upper-left corner of the PivotTable to appear.

To create the PivotTable that will provide the information Victoria needs, you will use the JuneTbl table and place the PivotTable in a new worksheet.

To create a PivotTable using the JuneTbl table:

1. If you took a break after the previous session, make sure the June Sales Data workbook is open, the Sales Data worksheet is the active sheet, and the JuneTbl table is active.
2. On the ribbon, click the **Insert** tab.
3. In the Tables group, click the **PivotTable** button. The Create PivotTable dialog box opens. See Figure 5-32.

TIP

You can also click the Summarize with PivotTable button in the Tools group on the Table Tools Design tab.

Figure 5-32 Create PivotTable dialog box

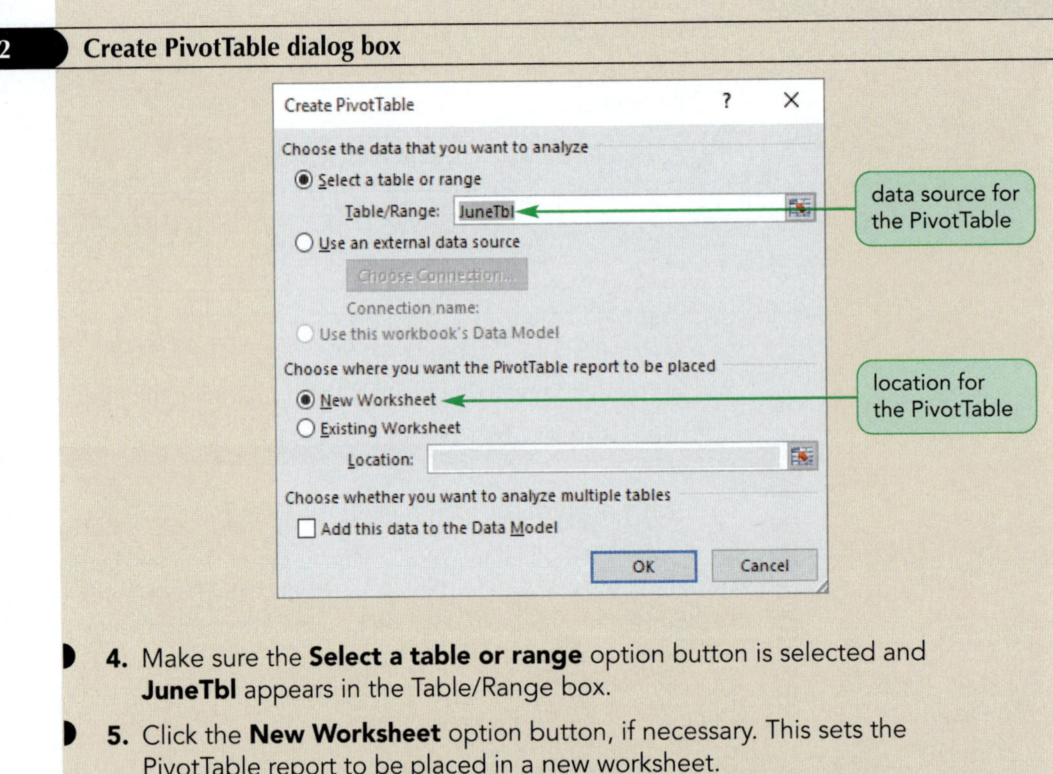

4. Make sure the **Select a table or range** option button is selected and **JuneTbl** appears in the Table/Range box.
5. Click the **New Worksheet** option button, if necessary. This sets the PivotTable report to be placed in a new worksheet.
6. Click the **OK** button. A new worksheet, Sheet1, is inserted to the left of the Sales Data worksheet. On the left is the empty PivotTable report area, where the finished PivotTable will be placed. On the right is the PivotTable Fields task pane, which you use to build the PivotTable. The PivotTable Tools tabs appear on the ribbon. See Figure 5-33.

Figure 5-33 Empty PivotTable report

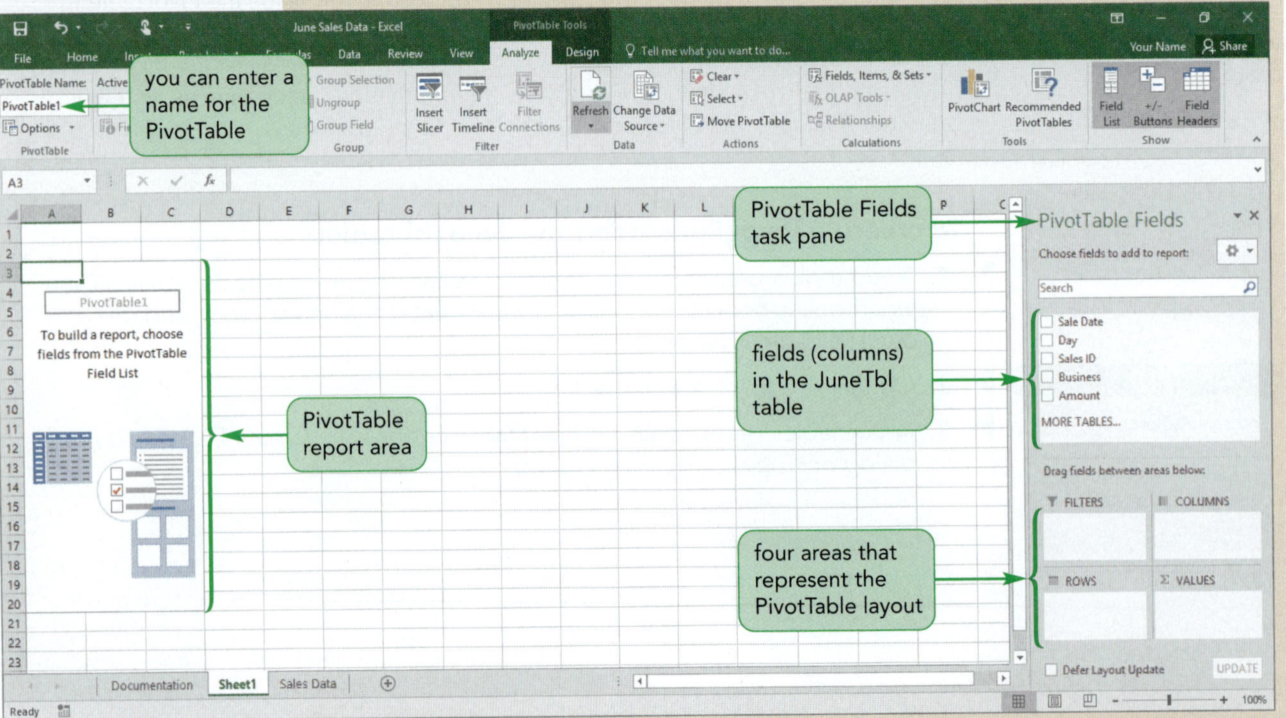

Trouble? If the PivotTable Fields task pane is not displayed, you need to display it. On the PivotTable Tools Analyze tab, in the Show group, click the Field List button.

Adding Fields to a PivotTable

To display data in a PivotTable, you add fields to the PivotTable. In PivotTable terminology, fields that contain summary data are Values fields, and fields that group the values in the PivotTable are Category fields. Category fields appear in PivotTables as row labels, column labels, and filters. You add fields to a PivotTable from the PivotTable Fields task pane, which is divided into two sections. The upper section lists the names of each field in the data source, which is the JuneTbl table, in this case. You select a field check box or drag the field into the lower section to add that field to the FILTERS, ROWS, COLUMNS, or VALUES area (described in Figure 5-34). The placement of fields in the area boxes determines the layout of the PivotTable.

Figure 5-34 **Layout areas for a PivotTable**

Area	Description
ROWS	Fields placed in this area appear as Row Labels on the left side of the PivotTable. Each unique item in this field is displayed in a separate row. Row fields can be nested.
COLUMNS	Fields placed in this area appear as Column Labels on the top of the PivotTable. Each unique item in this field is displayed in a separate column. Column fields can be nested.
FILTERS	Fields placed in this area appear as top-level filters above the PivotTable. These fields are used to select one or more items to display in the PivotTable.
VALUES	Fields placed in this area are numbers that are summarized in the PivotTable.

TIP

By default, Excel uses the COUNT function for nonnumeric fields placed in the VALUES area.

Typically, fields with text or nonnumeric data are placed in the ROWS area. Fields with numeric data are most often placed in the VALUES area and by default are summarized with the SUM function. If you want to use a different function, click the field button in the VALUES area, click Value Field Settings to open the Value Field Settings dialog box, select a different function such as AVERAGE, COUNT, MIN, MAX, and so on, and then click the OK button. You can move fields between the areas at any time to change how data is displayed in the PivotTable. You can also add the same field to the VALUES area more than once so you can calculate its sum, average, and count in one PivotTable.

Victoria wants to see the total value of sales by Sales ID. Then, within each Sales ID, she wants to see total sales for each Day. Finally, she wants each Day further divided to display sales for each Business. You'll add fields to the PivotTable so that the Sales ID, Sale Date, and Business fields are row labels, and the Amount field is the data to be summarized as the Values field.

To add fields to the PivotTable:

1. In the PivotTable Fields task pane, drag **Sales ID** from the upper section to the ROWS area in the lower section. The Sales ID field appears in the ROWS area, and the unique values in the Sales ID field—1, 2, 3, 4, and 5—appear in the PivotTable report area. See Figure 5-35.

Figure 5-35 PivotTable with the Sales ID field values as row labels

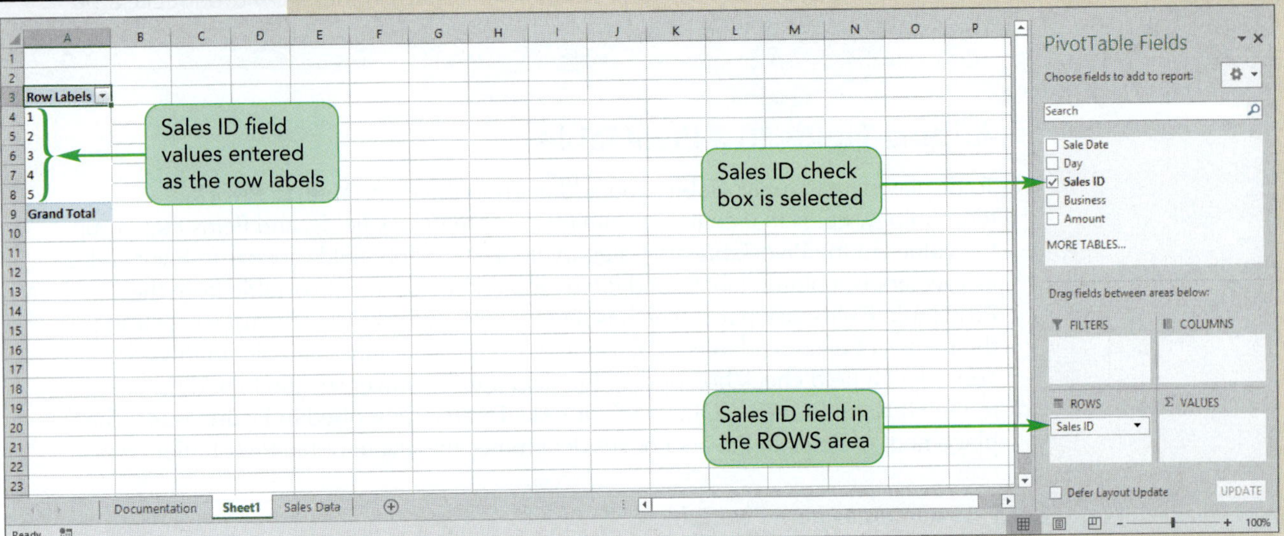

Trouble? If the Sales ID field appears in the VALUES area, you probably checked the Sales ID field, which places fields with numeric values in the VALUES area. Drag the Sales ID field from the VALUES area to the ROWS area.

2. In the PivotTable Fields task pane, click the **Amount** check box. The Sum of Amount button is placed in the VALUES box because the field contains numeric values. The PivotTable groups the items from the JuneTbl table by Sales ID and calculates the total Amount for each week. The grand total appears at the bottom of the PivotTable. See Figure 5-36.

Figure 5-36 PivotTable shows the sum of the Amounts field for each Sales ID

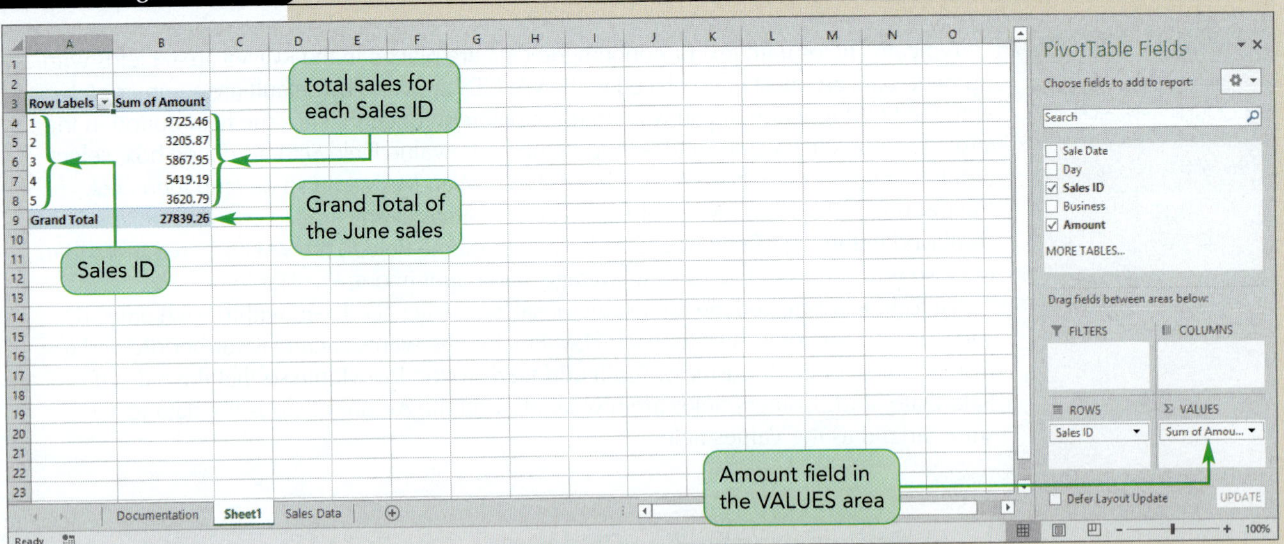

Next, you'll add the Sale Date and Business fields to the PivotTable.

3. In the PivotTable Fields task pane, click the **Sale Date** check box. The Sale Date field appears in the ROWS area box below the Sales ID field, and the unique items in the Sale Date field are indented below each Sales ID field item in the PivotTable report.

Trouble? If the PivotTable Fields task pane is not visible, the active cell is probably not in the PivotTable. Click any cell within the PivotTable to redisplay the PivotTable Fields task pane. If the PivotTable Fields task pane is still not visible, click the PivotTable Tools Analyze tab, and then click the Field List button in the Show group.

4. In the PivotTable Fields task pane, click the **Business** check box. The Business field appears in the ROWS area below the Sale Date field, and its unique items are indented below the Sales ID and Sale Date fields already in the PivotTable. See Figure 5-37.

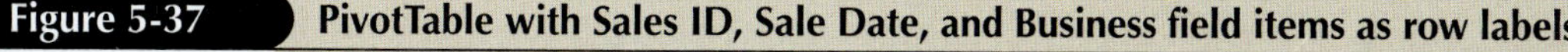

Figure 5-37 PivotTable with Sales ID, Sale Date, and Business field items as row labels

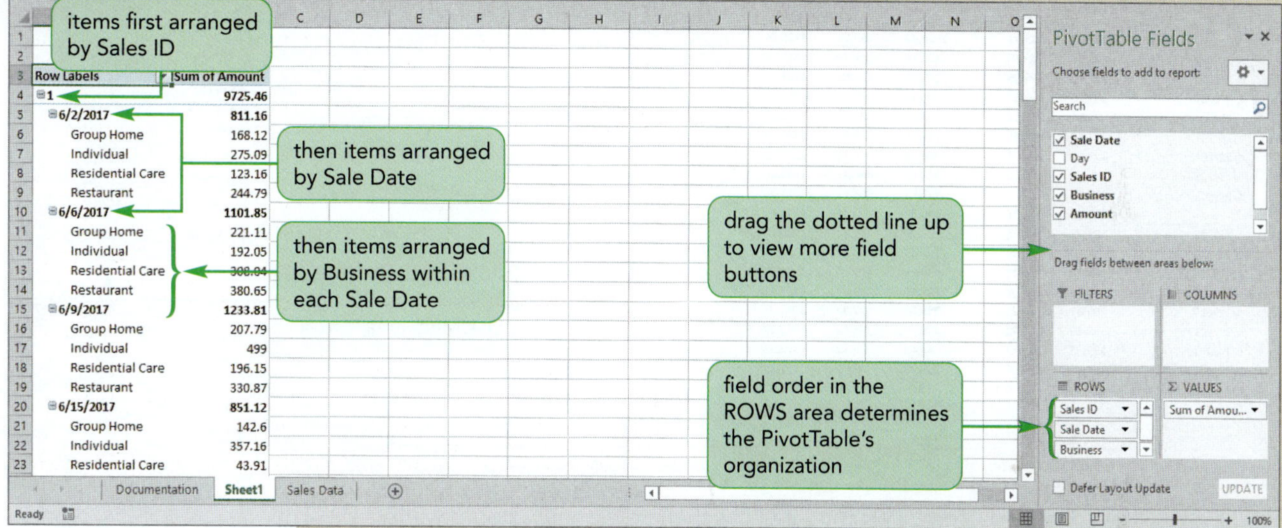

Trouble? If the Business field button is not visible in the ROWS area, drag the dotted line above the "Drag fields between areas below" label up until the Business field button is visible.

If a PivotTable becomes too detailed or confusing, you can always remove one of its fields. In the PivotTable Fields task pane, click the check box of the field you want to remove. The field is then deleted from the PivotTable and the area box.

Changing the Layout of a PivotTable

You can add, remove, and rearrange fields to change the PivotTable's layout. Recall that the benefit of a PivotTable is that it summarizes large amounts of data into a readable format. After you create a PivotTable, you can view the same data in different ways. Each time you make a change in the areas section of the PivotTable Fields task pane, the PivotTable layout is rearranged. This ability to "pivot" the table—for example, change row headings to column positions and vice versa—makes the PivotTable a powerful analytical tool.

Based on Victoria's PivotTable plan that is shown in Figure 5-31, the Business field items should be positioned as columns instead of rows in the PivotTable. You'll move the Business field now to produce the layout Victoria wants.

To move the Business field to the COLUMNS area:

1. In the PivotTable Fields task pane, locate the **Business** field button in the ROWS area.
2. Drag the **Business** field button from the ROWS area to the COLUMNS area. The PivotTable is rearranged so that the Business field is a column label instead of a row label. See Figure 5-38.

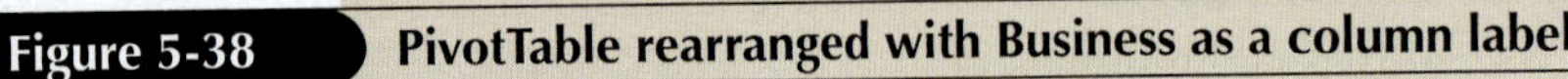

Figure 5-38 PivotTable rearranged with Business as a column label

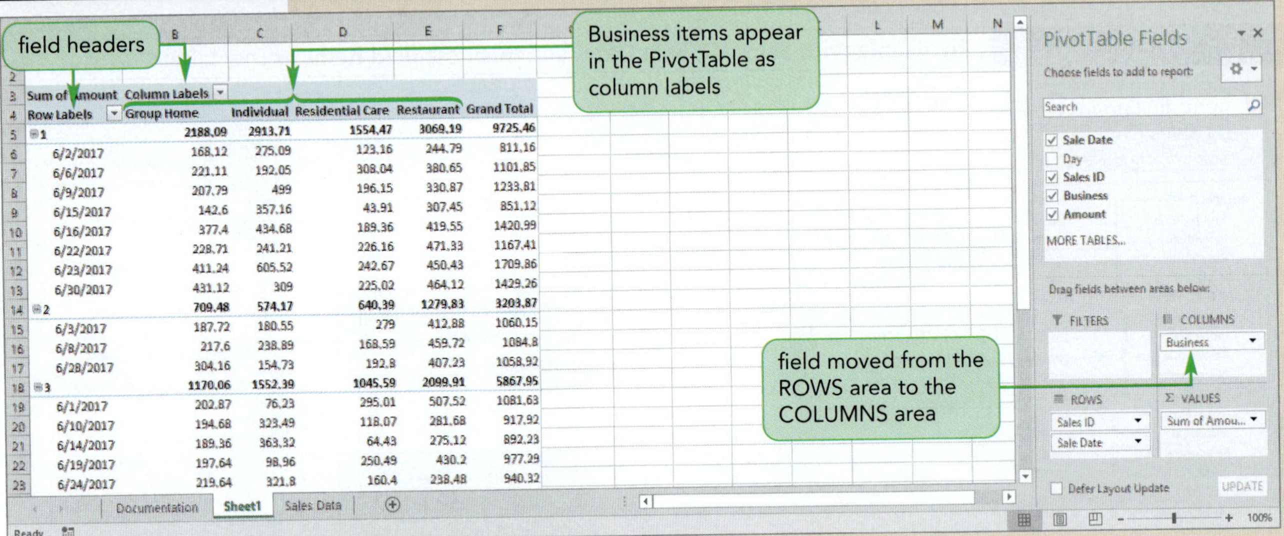

The PivotTable now has the layout that Victoria wants.

INSIGHT

Choosing a Report Layout

There are three different report layouts available for PivotTables. The report layout shown in Figure 5-38, which is referred to as the Compact Form, is the default layout. It places all fields from the ROWS area in a single column and indents the items from each field below the outer fields. In the Outline Form layout, each field in the ROWS area takes a column in the PivotTable. The subtotal for each group appears above every group. The Tabular Form layout displays one column for each field and leaves space for column headers. A total for each group appears below each group. To select a different report layout, click the Report Layout button in the Layout group on the PivotTable Tools Design tab.

Formatting a PivotTable

Like worksheet cells and Excel tables, you can quickly format a PivotTable report using one of the built-in styles available in the PivotTable Styles gallery. As with cell and table styles, you can point to any style in the gallery to see a Live Preview of the PivotTable with that style. You also can modify the appearance of PivotTables by adding or removing banded rows, banded columns, row headers, and column headers.

Victoria wants you to apply the Pivot Style Medium 14 style, which makes each group in the PivotTable stand out and makes subtotals in the report easier to find.

To apply the Pivot Style Medium 14 style to the PivotTable:

1. Make sure the active cell is in the PivotTable.
2. On the ribbon, click the **PivotTable Tools Design** tab.
3. In the PivotTable Styles group, click the **More** button to open the PivotTable Styles gallery.
4. Move the pointer over each style to see the Live Preview of the PivotTable report with that style.
5. Click the **Pivot Style Medium 14** style (the last style in the second row of the Medium section). The style is applied to the PivotTable.

You can format cells in a PivotTable the same way that you format cells in a worksheet. This enables you to further customize the look of the PivotTable by changing the font, color, alignment, and number formats of specific cells in the PivotTable. Victoria wants the numbers in the PivotTable to be quickly recognized as dollars. You'll change the total Amount values in the PivotTable to the Currency style.

To format the Amount field in the PivotTable as currency:

1. In the VALUES area of the PivotTable Fields task pane, click the **Sum of Amount** button. A shortcut menu opens with options related to that field.
2. Click the **Value Field Settings** button on the shortcut menu. The Value Field Settings dialog box opens. See Figure 5-39.

Figure 5-39 Value Field Settings dialog box

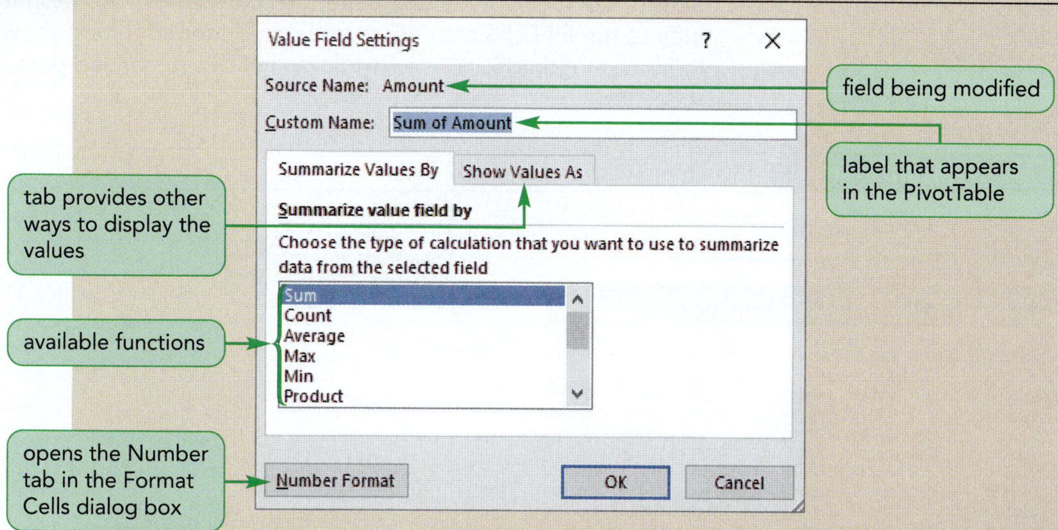

3. In the Custom Name box, type **Total Sales** as the label for the field. You will leave Sum as the summary function for the field; however, you could select a different function.
4. Click the **Number Format** button. The Format Cells dialog box opens. This is the same dialog box you have used before to format numbers in worksheet cells.

TIP

You can also right-click in the PivotTable data area and click Number Format or Format Cells to quickly format the PivotTable.

5. In the Category box, click **Currency**. You will use the default number of decimal places, currency symbol, and negative number format.
6. Click the **OK** button. The numbers in the PivotTable will be formatted as currency with two decimal places.
7. Click the **OK** button. The Value Field Settings dialog box closes. The PivotTable changes to reflect the label you entered, and the number format for the field changes to currency.

Filtering a PivotTable

As you analyze the data in a PivotTable, you might want to show only a portion of the total data. You can do this by filtering the PivotTable. Filtering a field lets you focus on a subset of items in that field.

Adding a Field to the FILTERS Area

You can drag one or more fields to the FILTERS area of the PivotTable Fields task pane to change what values are displayed in the PivotTable. A field placed in the FILTERS area provides a way to filter the PivotTable so that it displays summarized data for one or more items or all items in that field. For example, placing the Sales ID field in the FILTERS area allows you to view or print the total sales for all Sales IDs, a specific Sales ID such as 1, or multiple Sales IDs such as 2 through 5.

Victoria wants you to move the Sales ID field from the ROWS area to the FILTERS area so that she can focus on specific subsets of the sales.

To add the Sales ID field to the FILTERS area:

1. In the PivotTable Fields task pane, drag the **Sales ID** button from the ROWS area to the FILTERS area. By default, the Filter field item shows "(All)" to indicate that the PivotTable displays all the summarized data associated with the Sales ID field. See Figure 5-40.

Figure 5-40 PivotTable with the Sales ID filter

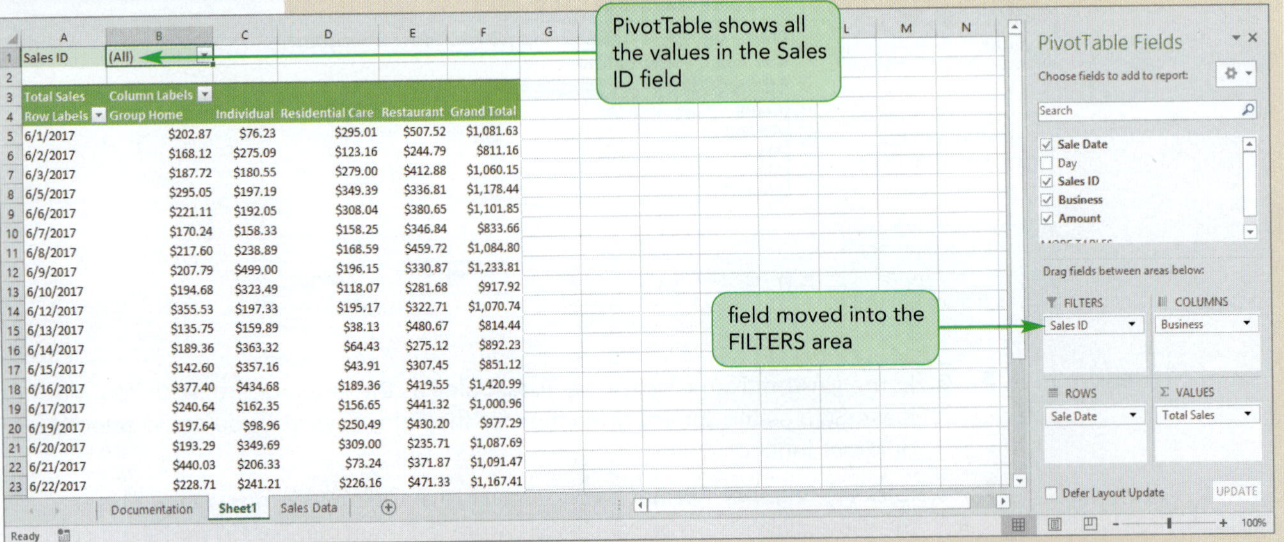

Sales ID	(All)				
Total Sales	Column Labels				
Row Labels	Group Home	Individual	Residential Care	Restaurant	Grand Total
6/1/2017	$202.87	$76.23	$295.01	$507.52	$1,081.63
6/2/2017	$168.12	$275.09	$123.16	$244.79	$811.16
6/3/2017	$187.72	$180.55	$279.00	$412.88	$1,060.15
6/5/2017	$295.05	$197.19	$349.39	$336.81	$1,178.44
6/6/2017	$221.11	$192.05	$308.04	$380.65	$1,101.85
6/7/2017	$170.24	$158.33	$158.25	$346.84	$833.66
6/8/2017	$217.60	$238.89	$168.59	$459.72	$1,084.80
6/9/2017	$207.79	$499.00	$196.15	$330.87	$1,233.81
6/10/2017	$194.68	$323.49	$118.07	$281.68	$917.92
6/12/2017	$355.53	$197.33	$195.17	$322.71	$1,070.74
6/13/2017	$135.75	$159.89	$38.13	$480.67	$814.44
6/14/2017	$189.36	$363.32	$64.43	$275.12	$892.23
6/15/2017	$142.60	$357.16	$43.91	$307.45	$851.12
6/16/2017	$377.40	$434.68	$189.36	$419.55	$1,420.99
6/17/2017	$240.64	$162.35	$156.65	$441.32	$1,000.96
6/19/2017	$197.64	$98.96	$250.49	$430.20	$977.29
6/20/2017	$193.29	$349.69	$309.00	$235.71	$1,087.69
6/21/2017	$440.03	$206.33	$73.24	$371.87	$1,091.47
6/22/2017	$228.71	$241.21	$226.16	$471.33	$1,167.41

Next, you'll filter the summarized report to show only sales for Sales ID 2.

2. In cell B1, click the **filter** button [▼]. The Filter menu opens, showing the field items displayed.

3. In the Filter menu, click **2**, and then click the **OK** button. The PivotTable displays the total Amount of sales on dates associated with Sales ID 2. The filter button changes to indicate that the PivotTable is currently filtered. See Figure 5-41.

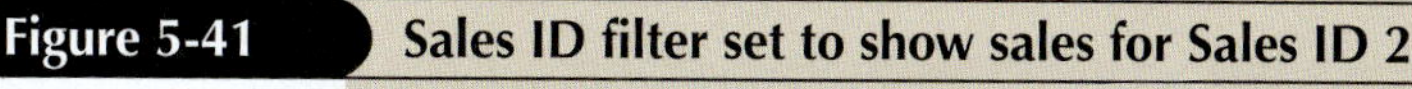

Figure 5-41 Sales ID filter set to show sales for Sales ID 2

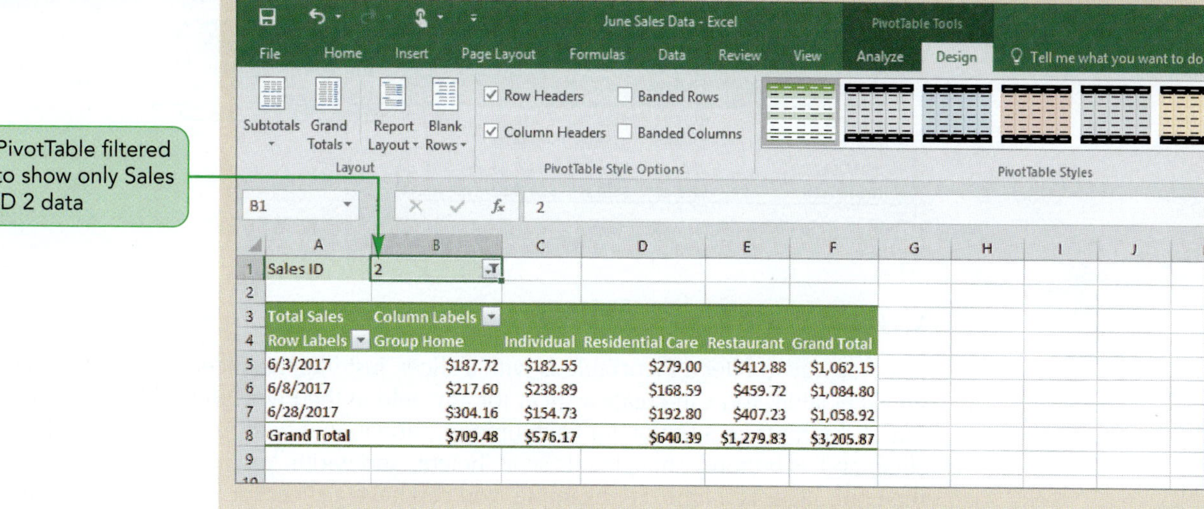

Filtering PivotTable Fields

Another way that you can filter field items in the PivotTable is by using the Filter menu, which you open by clicking the Row Labels filter button or the Column Labels filter button. You then check or uncheck items to show or hide them, respectively, in the PivotTable.

Victoria wants to exclude Residential Care from the analysis. She asks you to remove the Residential Care sales from the PivotTable.

To filter Residential Care from the Business column labels:

1. In the PivotTable, click the **Column Labels** filter button [▼]. The Filter menu opens, listing the items in the Business field.

2. Click the **Residential Care** check box to remove the checkmark. The Select All check box is filled with black indicating that all items are not selected.

3. Click the **OK** button. The Residential Care column is removed from the PivotTable. The PivotTable includes sales from only Group Home, Individual, and Restaurant. See Figure 5-42. You can show the hidden objects by clicking the Column Labels filter button and checking the Residential Care check box.

Figure 5-42 PivotTable report filtered by Business

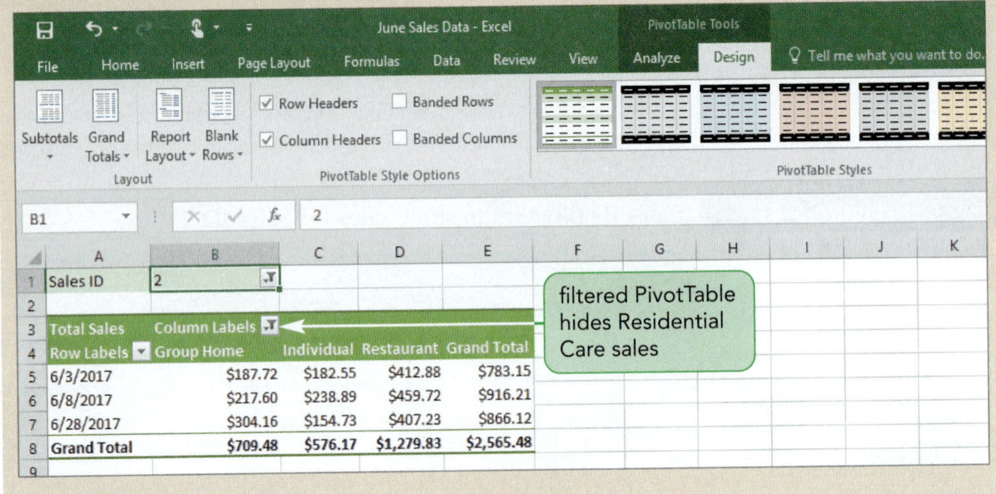

Creating a Slicer to Filter a PivotTable

Another way to filter a PivotTable is with a slicer, just like the slicer you created to filter an Excel table. You can create a slicer for any field in the PivotTable Fields task pane. The slicer contains a button for each unique value in that field. You can format the slicer and its buttons, changing its style, height, and width. You also can create more than one slicer at a time. For example, you can have a slicer for Sales ID that has a button for each unique Sales ID value and a second slicer for Business. This allows you to filter a PivotTable report so that it displays the sales amount for Sales ID 2, Group Home, Individual, and Restaurant by clicking the corresponding slicer buttons.

Victoria wants flexibility in how she views the data in the PivotTable, so she asks you to add a slicer for the Sales ID field to the current PivotTable.

To add the Sales ID slicer to the PivotTable:

1. On the ribbon, click the **PivotTable Tools Analyze** tab.
2. In the Filter group, click the **Insert Slicer** button. The Insert Slicers dialog box opens, displaying a list of available PivotTable fields. You can select any or all of the fields.
3. Click the **Sales ID** check box to insert a checkmark, and then click the **OK** button. The Sales ID slicer appears on the worksheet. Because the PivotTable is already filtered to display only the results for Sales ID 2, the 2 button is selected. The other slicer buttons are white because those weeks have been filtered and are not part of the PivotTable.
4. If the Slicer Tools Options tab does not appear on the ribbon, click the **Sales ID** slicer to select it.
5. On the Slicer Tools Options tab, in the Size group, change the height to **1.9"** and change the width to **1.25"**. The slicer object is resized, eliminating the extra space below the buttons and to the right of the labels.
6. In the Slicer Styles group, click the **More** button, and then click **Slicer Style Dark 6**. The slicer colors now match the PivotTable.
7. Drag the **Sales ID** slicer to the right of the PivotTable, placing its upper-left corner in cell G3. See Figure 5-43.

Figure 5-43 Sales ID slicer

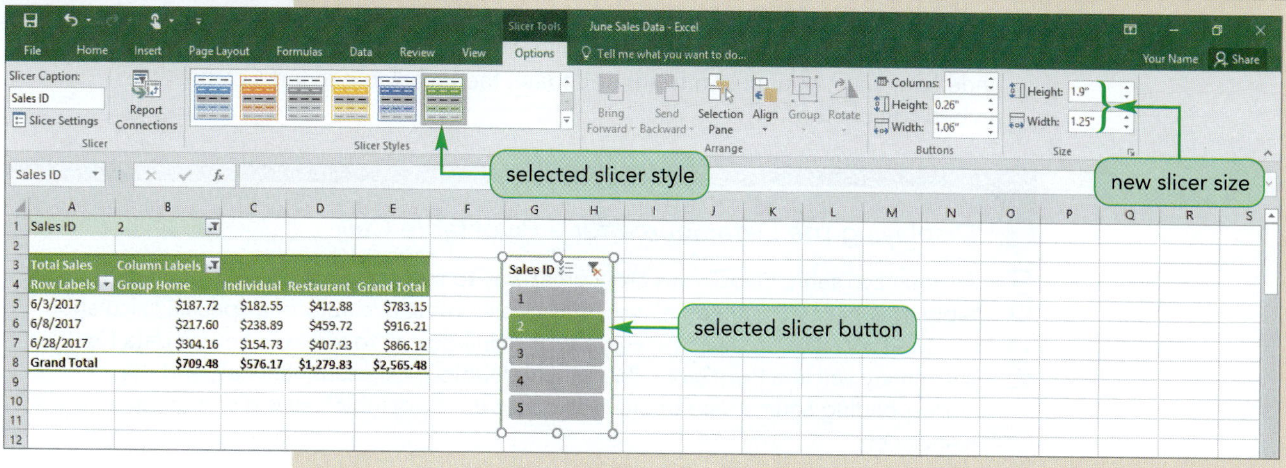

Victoria wants you to display the results of the PivotTable for all the seasonal employees in June—Sales IDs 2, 3, and 4. You can do this quickly using the Sales ID slicer.

To filter the PivotTable using the Sales ID slicer:

1. Press and hold the **Ctrl** key, click the **3** button, and then release the **Ctrl** key. Sales ID 3 data also appears on the PivotTable.
2. Press and hold the **Ctrl** key, click the **4** button, and then release the **Ctrl** key. Data for Sales ID 4 is added to the PivotTable.
3. Click the **Sales ID 2** slicer button. Only the sales for Sales ID 2 are displayed in the PivotTable.

TIP

To remove all filters from the PivotTable, click the Clear Filter button in the upper-right corner of the slicer.

After you have finished creating a PivotTable, you can hide the PivotTable Fields task pane so that it won't appear when a cell is selected in the PivotTable. You can also assign more descriptive names to the PivotTable as well as the worksheet that contains the PivotTable.

To hide the PivotTable Fields task pane and rename the PivotTable and worksheet:

1. Click in the PivotTable to display the PivotTable Tools contextual tabs on the ribbon.
2. Click the **PivotTable Tools Analyze** tab.
3. In the Show group, click the **Field List** button. The PivotTable Fields task pane is hidden and won't reappear when a cell in the PivotTable is selected.
4. In the PivotTable group, select the name in the PivotTable Name box, type **SalesIDSummary** as the descriptive PivotTable name, and then press the **Enter** key.
5. Rename the worksheet as **Sales ID Summary PivotTable**.

Refreshing a PivotTable

You cannot change data directly in a PivotTable. Instead, you must edit the data source on which the PivotTable is created. However, PivotTables are not updated automatically when the source data for the PivotTable is updated. After you edit the underlying data, you must **refresh**, or update, the PivotTable report to reflect the revised calculations.

INSIGHT

Displaying the Data Source for a PivotTable Cell

As you have seen, PivotTables are a great way to summarize the results of an Excel table. However, at some point, you may question the accuracy of a specific calculation in your PivotTable. In these cases, you can "drill down" to view the source data for a summary cell in a PivotTable. You simply double-click a summary cell, and the corresponding source data of the records for the PivotTable cell is displayed in a new worksheet.

The sales entry for Individual on 6/3/2017 should have been $180.55 (not $182.55 as currently listed). You'll edit the record in the JuneTbl table, which is the underlying data source for the PivotTable. This one change will affect the PivotTable in several locations—the Amount for Individual on 6/3/2017 (currently $182.55), the Grand Total for Individual (currently $576.17), the Grand Total for 6/3/2017 (currently $783.15), and the overall Grand Total for Sales ID 2 (currently $2,565.48).

To update the JuneTbl table and refresh the PivotTable:

1. Go to the **Sales Data** worksheet, and then find the Individual sales for 6/3/2017. The amount is $182.55.
2. Click the record's **Amount** cell, and then enter **180.55**. The sales Amount is updated in the table. You'll return to the PivotTable report to see the effect of this change.
3. Go to the **Sales ID Summary PivotTable** worksheet. The Amount for Individual on 6/3/2017 is still $182.55, the Grand Total for Individual is still $576.17, the Grand Total for 6/3/2017 is still $783.15, and the overall Grand Total is still $2,565.48.

   The PivotTable was not automatically updated when the data in its source table changed, so you need to refresh the PivotTable.
4. Click any cell in the PivotTable.
5. On the ribbon, click the **PivotTable Tools Analyze** tab.
6. In the Data group, click the **Refresh** button (or press the **Alt+F5** keys). The PivotTable report is updated. The totals are now $180.55, $574.17, $781.15, and $2,563.48. See Figure 5-44.

Figure 5-44 Refreshed PivotTable

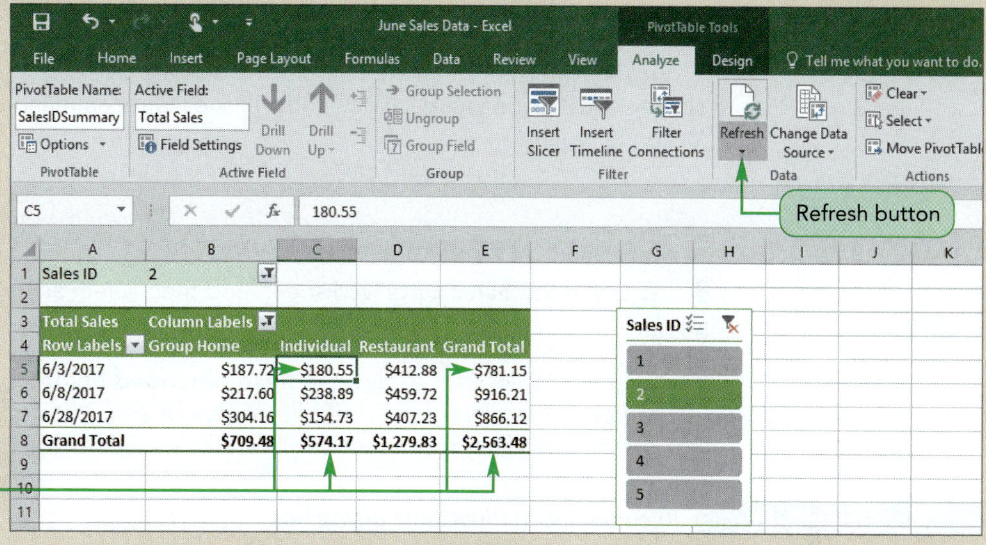

PivotTables provide an efficient way to display and analyze data. Like with charts, if a value displayed in the PivotTable is incorrect, you must update the data itself and then refresh the PivotTable to show that new data.

INSIGHT

Creating Different Types of PivotTables

This module only scratched the surface of the variety of PivotTables you can create. Here are a few more examples:

- Most PivotTable summaries are based on numeric data; Excel uses SUM as the default calculation. If your analysis requires a different calculation, you can select any of the 11 built-in summary calculations. For example, you could build a report that displays the minimum, maximum, and average sales for each week in June.
- You can use PivotTables to combine row label and column label items into groups. If items are numbers or dates, they can be grouped automatically using the Grouping dialog box, or they can be grouped manually using the Ctrl key to select items in a group and then clicking Group Selection from the shortcut menu. For example, you can manually combine Saturday and Sunday sales into a Weekend group, combine Monday through Friday sales into a Weekday group, and then display total sales by these groups within the PivotTable. Over time, you will also be able to group the Sale Date field to summarize daily sales by month, quarter, and year.
- You can develop PivotTables that use the percent of row, percent of column, or percent of total calculation to view each item in the PivotTable as a percent of the total in the current row, current column, or grand total. For example, you can display the total weekly sales as a percent of the total monthly sales.
- You can develop PivotTables that display how the current month/quarter/year compares to the previous month/quarter/year. For example, you can compare this month's sales for each Business to the corresponding sales for the previous month to display the difference between the two months.

Being able to enhance PivotTables by changing summary calculations, consolidating data into larger groups, and creating custom calculations based on other data in the VALUES area gives you flexibility in your analysis.

Creating a Recommended PivotTable

The Recommended PivotTables dialog box shows previews of PivotTables based on the source data, which lets you see different options for how to create the PivotTable. You can then choose the one that best meets your needs.

Victoria wants to summarize sales by days of the week so she can gain insights into staffing and ordering for each day. You will see if a recommended PivotTable meets Victoria's request.

To create a recommended PivotTable:

1. Go to the **Sales Data** worksheet, and then select any cell in the Excel table.
2. On the ribbon, click the **Insert** tab.
3. In the Tables group, click the **Recommended PivotTables** button. The Recommended PivotTables dialog box opens. You can select a PivotTable from the list of recommended PivotTables. See Figure 5-45.

Figure 5-45 Recommended PivotTable dialog box

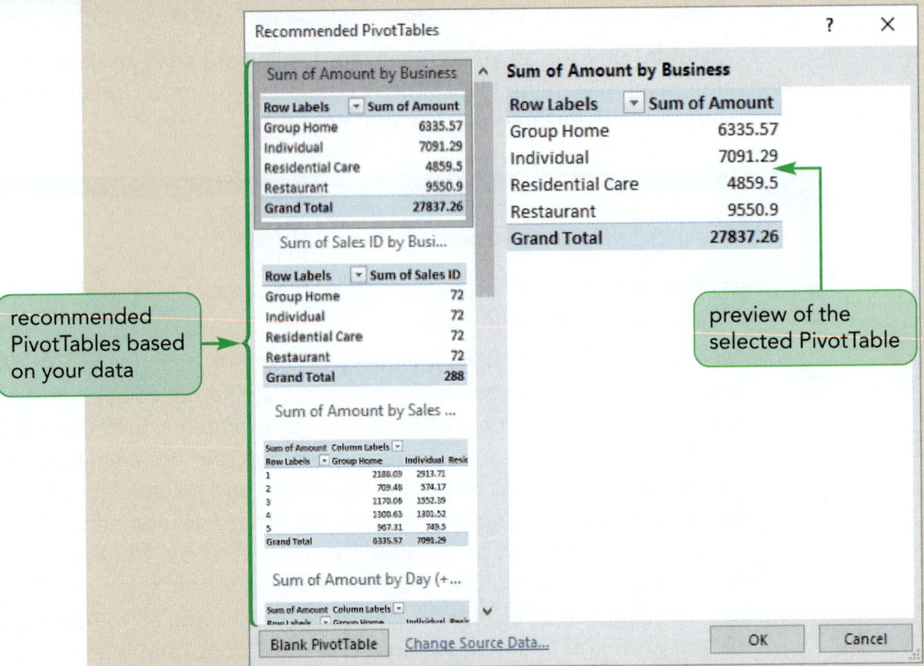

The Sum of Amount by Day PivotTable meets Victoria's request.

4. Click **Sum of Amount by Day** (the sixth PivotTable in the left pane). An enlarged version of the selected PivotTable is displayed in the right pane of the dialog box.
5. Click the **OK** button. A PivotTable of the sales by day appears in a new worksheet. See Figure 5-46.

Figure 5-46 PivotTable of sales by day

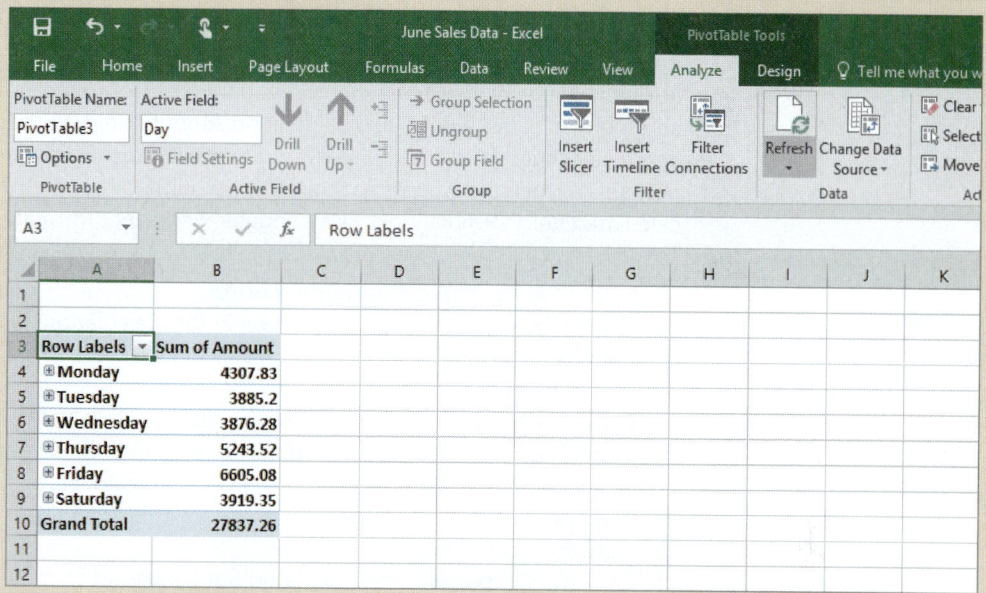

6. In the PivotTable Fields task pane, in the VALUES area, click the **Sum of Amount** button, and then click **Value Field Settings** on the shortcut menu. The Value Field Settings dialog box opens.
7. Click the **Number Format** button. The Format Cells dialog box opens.
8. In the Category box, click **Currency**, and then click the **OK** button.
9. In the Value Field Settings dialog box, click the **OK** button. The numbers in the PivotTable are formatted as currency with two decimal places.
10. On the ribbon, click the **PivotTable Tools Design** tab.
11. In the PivotTable Styles group, click the **More** button to open the PivotTable Styles gallery, and then click the **Pivot Style Medium 14** style. The style is applied to the PivotTable.
12. Rename the worksheet as **Daily Sales PivotTable**.

Victoria will use the summary of sales by days of the week in the Daily Sales PivotTable worksheet to evaluate staffing and ordering for each day.

INSIGHT

Adding a Calculated Field to a PivotTable Report

Occasionally, you might need to display more information than a PivotTable is designed to show, but it doesn't make sense to alter your data source to include this additional information. For example, you might want to include a field that shows an 8 percent sales tax on each value in an Amount field. In these instances, you can add a calculated field to the PivotTable. A **calculated field** is a formula you define to generate PivotTable values that otherwise would not appear in the PivotTable. The calculated field formula looks like a regular worksheet formula.

To add a calculated field to a PivotTable, complete the following steps:

1. Select any cell in the PivotTable report.
2. On the PivotTable Tools Analyze tab, in the Calculations group, click the Fields, Items & Sets button, and then click Calculated Field. The Insert Calculated Field dialog box opens.
3. In the Name box, type a name for the field, such as Sales Tax.
4. In the Formula box, enter the formula for the field. To use data from another field, click the field in the Fields box, and then click Insert Field. For example, to calculate an 8 percent sales tax on each value in the Amount field, enter =Amount*8%.
5. Click the Add button.
6. Click the OK button. The calculated field is added to the PivotTable's data area and to the PivotTable Fields task pane.

As you can see, you can use calculated fields to include additional information in a PivotTable.

Creating a PivotChart

A PivotChart is a graphical representation of the data in a PivotTable. You can create a PivotChart from a PivotTable. A PivotChart allows you to interactively add, remove, filter, and refresh data fields in the PivotChart similar to working with a PivotTable. PivotCharts can have all the same formatting as other charts, including layouts and styles. You can move and resize chart elements or change formatting of individual data points.

Victoria wants you to add a PivotChart next to the Sum of Amount by Day PivotTable. You will prepare a clustered column chart next to the PivotTable.

TIP

You can also create a PivotChart based directly on an Excel table, which creates both a PivotTable and a PivotChart.

To create and format the PivotChart:

1. In the Daily Sales PivotTable worksheet, select any cell in the PivotTable.
2. On the ribbon, click the **PivotTable Tools Analyze** tab.
3. In the Tools group, click the **PivotChart** button. The Insert Chart dialog box opens.
4. If necessary, click the **Clustered Column** chart (the first chart subtype for Column charts), and then click the **OK** button. A PivotChart appears next to the PivotTable, and the task pane changes to the PivotChart Fields task pane.

   Trouble? If you selected the wrong PivotChart, delete the PivotChart you just created, and then repeat Steps 1 through 4.
5. To the right of the PivotChart, click the **Chart Elements** button [+], and then click the **Legend** check box to remove the checkmark. The legend is removed from the PivotChart. You do not need a legend because the PivotChart has only one data series.

6. Click the PivotChart chart title, type **Sales by Day** as the new title, and then press the **Enter** key. The PivotChart displays the descriptive name.
7. To the right of the PivotChart, click the **Chart Styles** button, click **Color** at the top of the gallery, and then in the Colorful section, click **Color 4**. The columns change to green, the first color in that palette.
8. Drag the PivotChart so its upper-left corner is in cell **D3**. The PivotChart is aligned with the PivotTable. See Figure 5-47.

Figure 5-47 PivotChart added to the PivotTable report

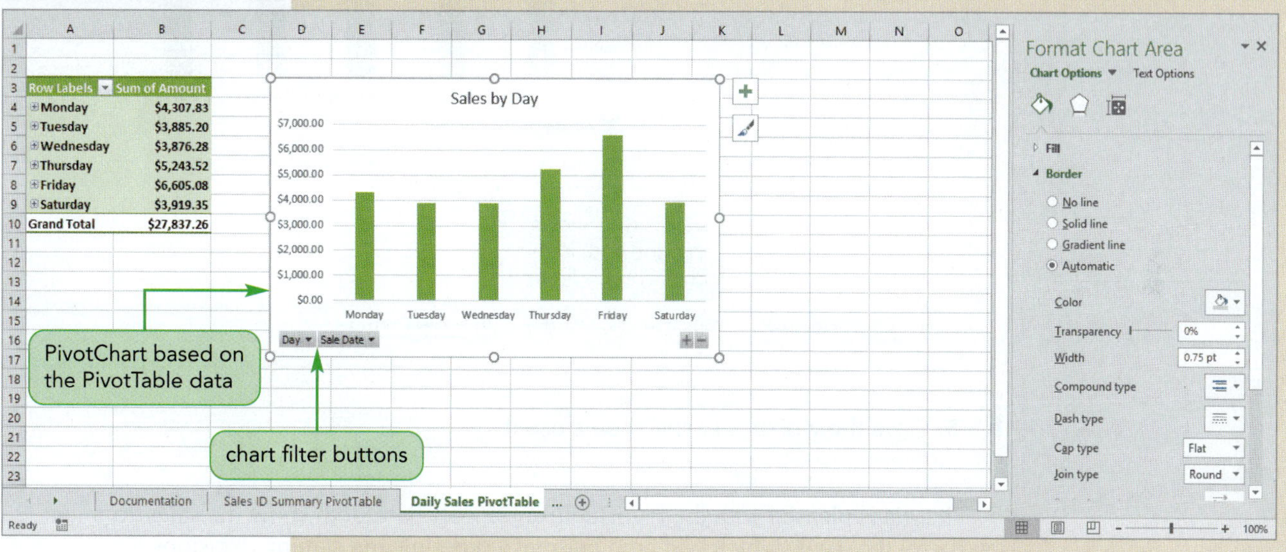

The PivotChart Tools contextual tabs enable you to work with and format the selected PivotChart the same way as an ordinary chart. A PivotChart and its associated PivotTable are linked. When you modify one, the other also changes. You can quickly display different views of the PivotChart by using the chart filter buttons on the PivotChart to filter the data.

Victoria wants you to display sales for only Monday through Friday. You will filter the PivotChart to display only those items.

To filter the PivotChart to display sales for Monday through Friday:

1. Make sure the PivotChart is selected, and then click the **Day** filter button in the lower-left corner of the PivotChart. The Filter menu opens.
2. Click the **Saturday** check box to remove its checkmark. Only the weekdays remain selected.
3. Click the **OK** button. The PivotChart updates to display only sales for weekdays. The PivotTable is automatically filtered to display the same results.
4. Select cell **A1**. See Figure 5-48.

Figure 5-48 **Filtered PivotChart**

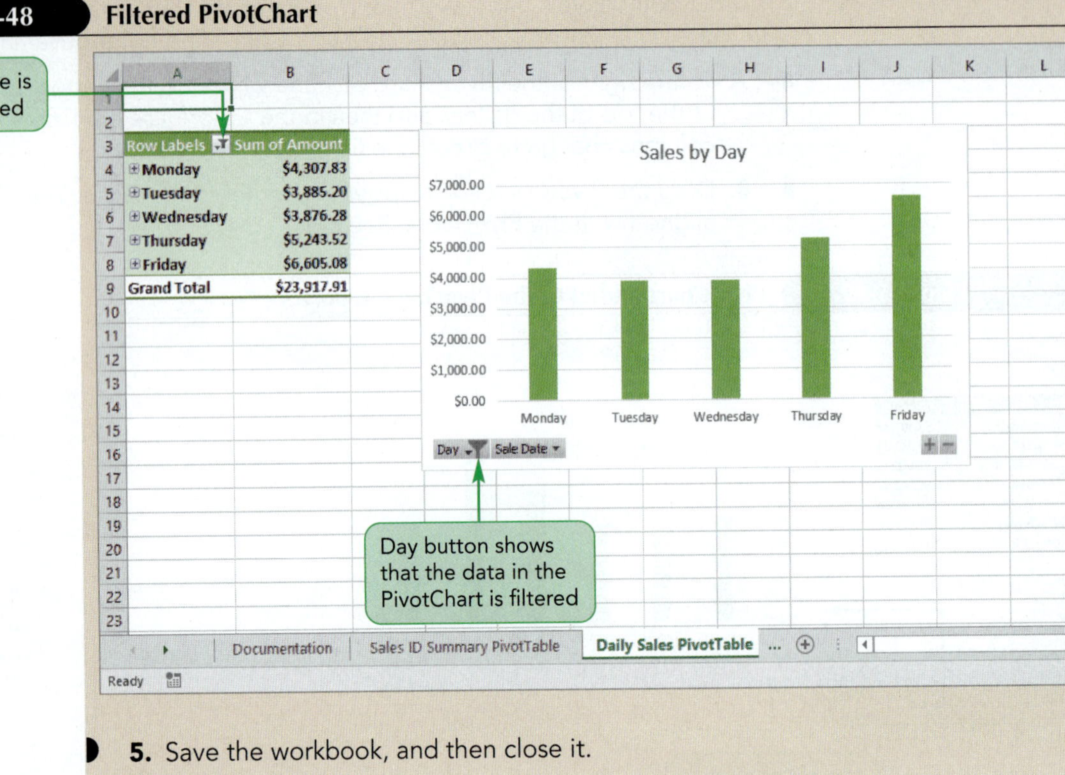

5. Save the workbook, and then close it.

Victoria is pleased with the PivotTable and PivotChart. Both show the sales arranged by day of the week, which will help her make ordering and staffing decisions.

REVIEW

Session 5.3 Quick Check

1. What is a PivotTable?
2. How do you add fields to a PivotTable?
3. How are fields such as region, state, and country most likely to appear in a PivotTable?
4. How are fields such as revenue, costs, and profits most likely to appear in a PivotTable?
5. A list of college students includes a code to indicate the student's gender (male or female) and a field to identify the student's major. Would you use a filter or a PivotTable to (a) create a list of all females majoring in history and (b) count the number of males and females in each major?
6. An Excel table of professional baseball player data consists of team name, player name, position, and salary. What area of a PivotTable report would be used for the Team name field if you wanted to display the average salaries by position for all teams or an individual team?
7. After you update data in an Excel table, what must you do to a PivotTable that is based on that Excel table?
8. What is a PivotChart?

PRACTICE

Review Assignments

Data File needed for the Review Assignments: July.xlsx

Victoria needs to analyze the sales for July. She entered this data into a new workbook and wants you to sort and filter the data, as well as create summary reports using the Subtotal command, PivotTables, and PivotCharts. Complete the following:

1. Open the **July** workbook located in the Excel5 > Review folder included with your Data Files, and then save the workbook as **July Sales Data** in the location specified by your instructor.
2. In the Documentation worksheet, enter your name and the date.
3. In the Sales Data worksheet, freeze the top row so that the headers remain on the screen as you scroll.
4. Make a copy of the Sales Data worksheet, and then rename the copied worksheet as **July Data**. (*Hint*: To make a copy of a worksheet, press and hold the Ctrl key as you drag the sheet tab to the right of the Sales Data sheet tab.)
5. In the July Data worksheet, unfreeze the top row.
6. Create an Excel table for the sales data in the July Data worksheet.
7. Format the Excel table with Table Style Medium 4, and then change the Amount field to the Accounting format with two decimal places.
8. Rename the Excel table as **JulyTbl**.
9. Make the following changes to the JulyTbl table:
   a. Add a record for 7/31/2017, Monday, 4, Group Home, 256.52.
   b. Edit the record for Individual on 7/27/2017 by changing the Amount from 462.74 to 492.05.
   c. Remove any duplicate records.
10. Make a copy of the July Data worksheet, and then rename the copied worksheet as **Sort by Sale Date**. In the Sort by Sale Date worksheet, sort the JulyTbl table by Sale Date, displaying the newest sales first, and then by Amount, displaying the largest amounts first.
11. Make a copy of the July Data worksheet, and then rename the copied worksheet as **Sort by Day**. In the Sort by Day worksheet, sort the sales data by Day (use the custom list order of Sunday, Monday,... for the chronological sort), then by Business (A to Z), and then by Amount (smallest to largest).
12. Make a copy of the July Data worksheet, and then rename the copied worksheet as **Filter to Omit Restaurant**. In the Filter to Omit Restaurant worksheet, filter the JulyTbl table to display the sales for all businesses except Restaurant.
13. In the Filter to Omit Restaurant worksheet, insert the Total row to calculate the average amount of sales for the filtered data. Change the label in the Total row to **Average**. Sort the filtered data by descending order by Amount.
14. Split the Filter to Omit Restaurant worksheet into two panes above the last row of the table. Display the sales records in the top pane, and display only the Total row in the bottom pane.
15. Make a copy of the July Data worksheet, and then rename the copied worksheet as **Filter by Sales ID**. In the Filter by Sales ID worksheet, insert a slicer for the Sales ID column. Move the slicer to row 1. Format the slicer with Slicer Style Light 3. Change the slicer's height to 1.9" and its width to 1.25". Use the slicer to display sales for Sales ID 3 and Sales ID 5.
16. Make a copy of the July Data worksheet, and then rename the copied worksheet as **July Subtotals**. In the July Subtotals worksheet, convert the JulyTbl Table to a range, and then sort the range by the Business column in ascending order.
17. In the July Subtotals worksheet, use the Subtotal command to calculate the total sales for each business in the Amount column. Display only the subtotal results. Widen columns as needed so that all of the data is visible.

18. Based on the JulyTbl table in the July Data worksheet, create a PivotTable in a new worksheet that shows the total sales Amount by Day. Format the data area with the Currency format. Rename the worksheet with the PivotTable as **PivotTableChart Sales by Day**.
19. In the PivotTableChart Sales by Day worksheet, insert a Clustered Column PivotChart based on the PivotTable you created. Move the PivotChart to row 3. Remove the legend. Change the PivotChart title to **Sales by Day of Week**.
20. Based on the JulyTbl table in the July Data worksheet, create a PivotTable in a new worksheet that shows Amount by Sale Date. Add the Business field to the FILTERS area. Format the PivotTable with Pivot Style Medium 4. Format the Amount field with the Accounting format with two decimal places. Rename that worksheet as **PivotTable by Sale Date**.
21. In the PivotTable by Sale Date worksheet, insert a slicer for the Business field of the PivotTable. Change the slicer height to 1.6" and the width to 1.5". Format the slicer with Slicer Style Dark 3. Move the slicer to row 3.
22. Use the slicer to filter the PivotTable to display only the Restaurant and Group Home sales.
23. Based on the JulyTbl table in the July Data worksheet, create the Recommended PivotTable Sum of Amount by Sales ID and Business. Rename the worksheet as **Recommended PivotTable**.
24. Save the workbook, and then close it.

APPLY

Case Problem 1

Data File needed for this Case Problem: Shirts.xlsx

Go Sports Anton Aliyev is the store manager for Go Sports, a sports clothing store in Middletown, Ohio. In addition to its clothing inventory, the store will print logos provided by local sports teams on T-shirts, jerseys, or sweatshirts purchased at the store. Anton uses Excel for a variety of tasks, including pricing and inventory. He wants you to create an Excel table from information about current products and then analyze this data. Complete the following:

1. Open the **Shirts** workbook located in the Excel5 > Case1 folder included with your Data Files, and then save the workbook as **Shirts Inventory** in the location specified by your instructor.
2. In the Documentation worksheet, enter your name and the date.
3. In the Shirts worksheet, create an Excel table using all of the data in the worksheet. Rename the table as **ShirtsTbl**. Format the table with Table Style Medium 9. Change the Price data to the Currency format showing no decimal places. Change the In Stock data to the Number format with no decimals.
4. Make a copy of the Shirts worksheet, and then rename the copied worksheet as **Sort by Style**. (*Hint*: Press the Ctrl key as you drag and drop the Shirts sheet tab to the right of the Shirts sheet tab to make a copy of the worksheet.)
5. In the Sort by Style worksheet, sort the data in ascending order by Style, and then in descending order by In Stock.
6. Filter the ShirtsTbl table by Size to remove the youth extra small (yxsm) and ladies extra small (lxsm) sizes.
7. Insert a Total row that shows the total shirts In Stock. Change the Total row label to **Total Shirts**.
8. Split the worksheet window into two horizontal panes. Place the split bar two rows above the bottom row of the worksheet. In the top pane, display the shirt data. In the bottom pane, display only the Total row.
9. Make a copy of the Shirts worksheet, and then rename the copied worksheet as **Filter by Color**. In the Filter by Color worksheet, filter the ShirtsTbl table to display only T-shirt style.

10. Insert a slicer for Color, position the slicer so its upper-left corner is in cell G1, resize the slicer's height to 1.8" and its width to 1.2", and then format the slicer with Slicer Style Dark 1.
11. Use the Color slicer to further filter the ShirtsTbl table to display only blue T-shirts and white T-shirts.
12. Filter the ShirtsTbl table so that it displays only blue and white T-shirts with a price greater than $10. Sort the filtered data in ascending order by Price and then in descending order by In Stock.
13. Make a copy of the Shirts worksheet, and then rename the copied worksheet as **Subtotals**. Convert the table to a range because the Subtotal command cannot be used with an Excel table. Sort the table in ascending order by Style. Use the Subtotal command to display the minimum In Stock for each Style.
14. Based on the ShirtsTbl table in the Shirts worksheet, insert a PivotTable in a new worksheet that calculates the total In Stock for each Style and Color. Display both Style and Color in rows. Use the Value Field Settings dialog box to rename Sum of In Stock as **Total Inventory**. Apply the Pivot Style Medium 9 style to the PivotTable. Rename the worksheet as **PivotTable by Style and Color**.
15. In the PivotTable by Style and Color worksheet, insert a PivotChart with the Clustered Column chart subtype. Place the PivotChart to the right of the PivotTable. Remove the legend. Filter the PivotChart to exclude any white shirts. Change the chart title to **Inventory by Style and Color**.
16. Based on the ShirtsTbl table in the Shirts worksheet, insert a PivotTable in a new worksheet that displays the total In Stock and count of Item IDs by Style and Color. Place Style in the FILTERS area. Rename the worksheet as **PivotTable by Style**.
17. In the PivotTable by Style worksheet, format the PivotTable with Pivot Style Medium 2 style. In the Value Field Settings dialog box, rename the Count of Item ID as **Number of Shirts** and change the Number format to Number with no decimal places. Change the Number format of the Sum of In Stock to the Number format with no decimal places.
18. In the PivotTable, change the Style filter to show only Jersey.
19. Save the workbook, and then close it.

APPLY

Case Problem 2

Data File needed for this Case Problem: Seminars.xlsx

Collegiate Seminars Phillip Cunningham is the new manager of Collegiate Seminars in McLean, Virginia. To help him better understand the current schedule, he created an Excel table that tracks the data he has collected about currently scheduled seminars, including topic, type, instructor, length, location, cost, and maximum enrollment. He asks you to analyze this data. Complete the following:

1. Open the **Seminars** workbook located in the Excel5 > Case2 folder included with your Data Files, and then save the workbook as **Seminar Bookings** in the location specified by your instructor.
2. In the Documentation worksheet, enter your name and the date.
3. In the Seminars worksheet, create an Excel table, and then name it **SeminarsTbl**. Format the Cost column with the Accounting format and no decimal places. Format the SeminarsTbl table with the table style of your choice.
4. Make a copy of the Seminars worksheet, and then rename the copied worksheet as **Sort by Type**. (*Hint*: Press the Ctrl key, and drag the Seminars sheet tab to the right of the Seminars sheet tab to make a copy of the worksheet.) Sort the SeminarsTbl table in ascending order by Type, then in descending order by Cost.

5. Use conditional formatting to highlight all Seminars with a cost greater than $950 with yellow fill with dark yellow text.
6. Make a copy of the Seminars worksheet, and then rename the copied worksheet as **Filter by Location**. Insert a slicer to filter by Location. Place the slicer to the right of the top of the SeminarsTbl table. Select a slicer style that matches the style you used to format the SeminarsTbl table. Resize the slicer's height and width to improve its appearance.
7. Use the slicer to filter the SeminarsTbl table to display only Seminars at the Downtown location.
8. Expand the filter to also display Beltway seminars in the SeminarsTbl table. Sort the filtered table in ascending order by cost.
9. Make a copy of the Seminars worksheet, and then rename the copied worksheet as **Filter Top 25%**. Filter the SeminarsTbl table to display Seminars whose Costs are in the top 25 percent. (*Hint*: Use the Top 10 number format.) Sort the data in descending order by Cost.
10. Use the Total row to include the average cost at the bottom of the table, and then change the Total row label to **Average**. Remove the entry in the Max column of the Total row.
11. Make a copy of the Seminars worksheet, and then rename the copied worksheet as **Subtotals**. Use the Subtotal command to display the total cost for each Topic in the Cost column. Make sure your table is sorted in the correct sequence for the required subtotals, and remember to convert the table to a range before subtotaling.
12. Based on the SeminarsTbl table in the Seminars worksheet, create a PivotTable in a new worksheet that totals cost by Type and Topic. Place the Type field in the COLUMNS area. Format the cost in the PivotTable with the Accounting format and no decimal places. Format the PivotTable with the style of your choice. Rename the worksheet as **PivotTable by Type**.
13. Insert a slicer to filter the PivotTable by Type. Resize the slicer object and buttons as needed, and then select a slicer style that matches the PivotTable. Use the slicer to filter the PivotTable to display totals for Graduate and Undergrad.
14. Based on the SeminarsTbl table in the Seminars worksheet, create a PivotTable in a new worksheet that calculates average Cost by Location and the count of Seminar IDs. Format the average cost to the Accounting format with no decimal places. Apply the same PivotTable style to this PivotTable. Rename the worksheet as **PivotTable for Average Cost**.
15. Save the workbook, and then close it.

TROUBLESHOOT

Case Problem 3

Data File needed for this Case Problem: Food.xlsx

Food for All Samuel Hamilton started Food for All in Lake Charles, Louisiana, three years ago in response to a growing number of residents who encountered unexpected challenges with being able to feed themselves and their families. The food bank has been very successful providing healthy food for the town residents. Samuel is considering expanding the food bank's reach to include several other towns in the area and needs to analyze current donations to see whether it can support the expansion. Samuel tracks donations in Excel. He has entered donation data for the first quarter of the year in a worksheet and wants you to analyze the data. Complete the following:

1. Open the **Food** workbook located in the Excel5 > Case3 folder included with your Data Files, and then save the workbook as **Food Bank** in the location specified by your instructor.
2. In the Documentation sheet, enter your name and the date.

Troubleshoot 3. Samuel wants to view donations with values that are either less than $10 or greater than $100. He tried filtering the donations in the Donation Amount Filter worksheet, but it's not working as expected. Review the custom Number filter in the worksheet, and fix the problems.

4. In the Donations worksheet, create an Excel table, and then rename the table as **DonationsTbl**. Format the DonationsTbl table using the table style of your choice.
5. In the DonationsTbl table, format the Value column so that it is clear that this field contains dollars.
6. Find the record that has a year of 3018. Correct the year so that it is **2017**.
7. Make a copy of the Donations worksheet, and then rename the copied worksheet as **Sorted Donations**. (*Hint*: Press the Ctrl key and drag the sheet tab to the right of the current sheet tab to make a copy of the worksheet.) In the Sorted Donations worksheet, sort the data in ascending order by Zip and then in ascending order by Date.
8. Using conditional formatting, highlight all of the records in the sorted table that are the type Food with the format of your choice.
9. Make a copy of the Donations worksheet, and then rename the copied worksheet as **Filtered Donations**. Filter the DonationsTbl table to display records that have not been sent a receipt. Sort the data by Zip in ascending order and then by Value in descending order.
10. Insert a Total row that calculates the total of the Value column for the filtered data and the count of the Receipt column. Remove any totals that appear for other columns. Make sure that the columns are wide enough to display the values.

Troubleshoot 11. In the Donation Type Subtotal worksheet, Samuel is trying to include subtotals that show the total Value for each donation Type. However, the subtotal for each type appears more than once. Fix this report so it shows only one subtotal for each type.

12. Based on the DonationsTbl table in the Donations worksheet, create a PivotTable in a new worksheet that displays the Count of Value and the average Value of the donations by Type. Place the Type field in the ROWS area of the PivotTable. Apply the PivotTable style that matches the DonationsTbl table style. Format the Average values using the Accounting format. Change the labels above the average donations to **Average**, and change the label above the count of donations to **Number**.
13. Insert a slicer to filter the PivotTable by Type, and then use the slicer to filter Food from the PivotTable. Format the slicer to match the PivotTable style. Resize and position the slicer appropriately. Rename the worksheet as **PivotTable by Type**.
14. Based on the DonationsTbl table in the Donations worksheet, create a PivotTable in a new worksheet that shows the Total Value by Zip. Format the Sum of Value so that it is more readable. Apply a PivotTable style to match the style of the DonationsTbl table. Rename the worksheet as **PivotTable Value by Zip**.
15. Based on the PivotTable in the PivotTable Value by Zip worksheet, create a PivotChart using the Clustered column chart type. Move the PivotChart to row 3. Change the chart title to **Donations by Zip**. Change the fill color of the bars to a color that matches the style in the PivotTable. Remove the legend.
16. Filter the PivotChart to hide the donations in the ZIP code 70611.
17. Save the workbook, and then close it.

CREATE

Case Problem 4

Data File needed for this Case Problem: Sales.xlsx

BePresent BePresent is a social networking consulting group in Yuma, Arizona, that plans, implements, and tracks social networking campaigns to help small-business owners create a strong presence on the Internet. Sales manager Alana Laidlaw regularly creates reports about the response rates for the social networking campaigns. She asks you to help her analyze data about the performance of the past year's introductory campaigns. Complete the following:

1. Open the **Sales** workbook located in the Excel5 > Case4 folder included with your Data Files, and then save the workbook as **Intro Sales** in the location specified by your instructor.
2. In the Documentation sheet, enter your name and the date.
3. In the Campaigns worksheet, create an Excel table. Rename the table as **CampaignsTbl**. Format the Responses column in the Number format with no decimal places using the comma separator. Apply a table style of your choice.
4. Make a copy of the Campaigns worksheet, and then rename the copied worksheet as **Sorted Campaigns**. (*Hint*: Press the Ctrl key, and drag the Campaigns sheet tab to the right of the Campaigns sheet tab to make a copy of the worksheet.) Sort the table in ascending order by Type of social media, then in chronological order by Month (January, February, March,…), and then in ascending order by Name.
5. Make a copy of the Campaigns worksheet, and then rename the copied worksheet as **Filter with Total Row**. Insert a slicer for the Type field. Move the slicer to row 1. Match the slicer style with the style you selected for the CampaignsTbl table. Resize the slicer height and width to eliminate any excess space.
6. Display the records for Facebook campaigns that occurred from January through June. Sort the filtered data in descending order of Responses.
7. Add a Total row to the table that calculates the average number of Responses for the filtered data. Change the label in the Total row to **Average**.
8. Make a copy of the Campaigns worksheet, and then rename the copied worksheet as **Campaign Subtotals**. Include subtotals that calculate the total Responses per Month and the total Responses per Type of Social Media. (*Hint*: Remember to sort the data, and then add two sets of subtotals. When you use the Subtotal command the second time, do not replace existing subtotals.)
9. Make a copy of the Campaigns worksheet, and then rename the copied worksheet as **Bottom 15 Campaigns**. Use the Top Number filter to display the 15 campaigns with the lowest Responses (each row represents a campaign). Sort the filtered table so that the lowest Responses appear first.
10. Based on the CampaignsTbl table in the Campaigns worksheet, create the PivotTable and the PivotChart shown in Figure 5-49 in a new worksheet to summarize the social media responses. Rename the worksheet as **PivotTableChart by Month**.

Figure 5-49 PivotTable and PivotChart of social media responses

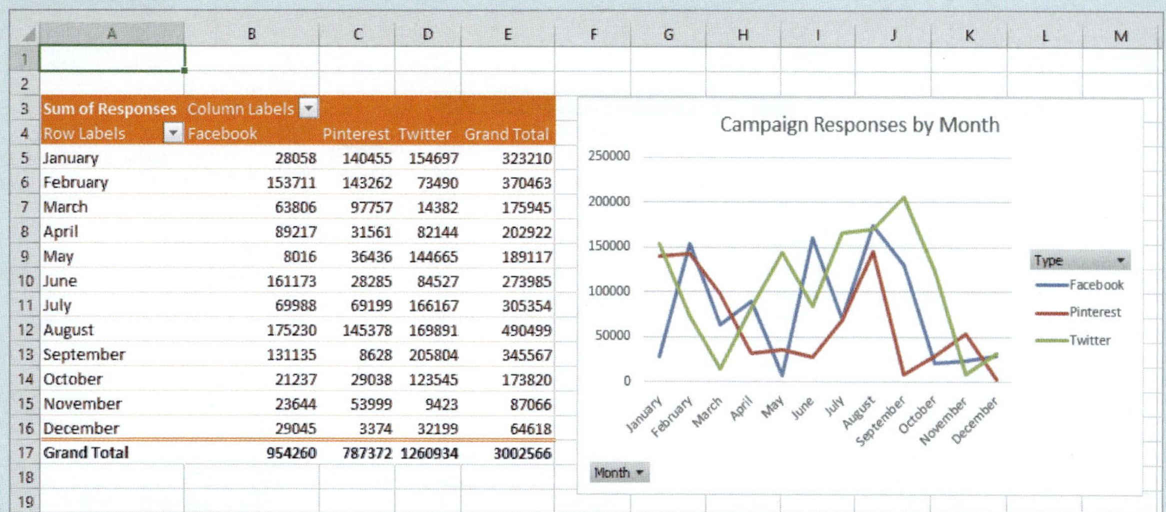

Sum of Responses	Column Labels			
Row Labels	Facebook	Pinterest	Twitter	Grand Total
January	28058	140455	154697	323210
February	153711	143262	73490	370463
March	63806	97757	14382	175945
April	89217	31561	82144	202922
May	8016	36436	144665	189117
June	161173	28285	84527	273985
July	69988	69199	166167	305354
August	175230	145378	169891	490499
September	131135	8628	205804	345567
October	21237	29038	123545	173820
November	23644	53999	9423	87066
December	29045	3374	32199	64618
Grand Total	954260	787372	1260934	3002566

11. Based on the CampaignsTbl table in the Campaigns worksheet, create the PivotTable shown in Figure 5-50 in a new worksheet to calculate the sum of Responses categorized by Description and Type using Month as a filter. Insert slicers for Type and Month. Format the slicers to coordinate with the PivotTable, resize the slicers as needed, and then position them next to the PivotTable. Rename the worksheet as **PivotTable Response Analysis**.

Figure 5-50 PivotTable displaying sales analyzing social media responses

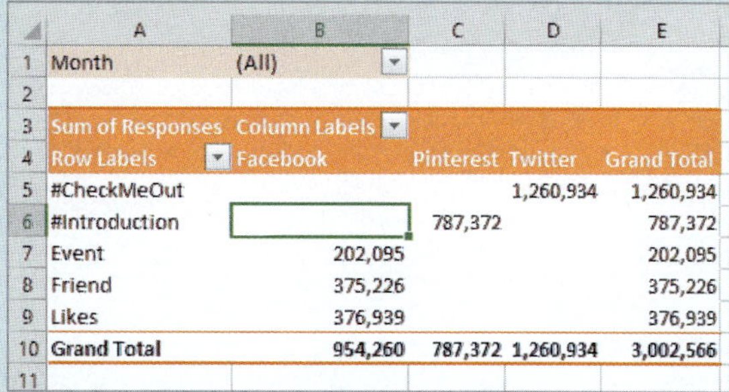

Month	(All)			
Sum of Responses	Column Labels			
Row Labels	Facebook	Pinterest	Twitter	Grand Total
#CheckMeOut			1,260,934	1,260,934
#Introduction		787,372		787,372
Event	202,095			202,095
Friend	375,226			375,226
Likes	376,939			376,939
Grand Total	954,260	787,372	1,260,934	3,002,566

12. Based on the CampaignsTbl table in the Campaigns worksheet, create the PivotTable and slicers shown in Figure 5-51 in a new worksheet, displaying total Responses, by Name with Month as a filter. Include a second calculation that displays each of the Reponses by Name as a percentage of the total Responses. (*Hint*: In the Value Field Settings dialog box, use the Show Values As tab to show values as a percentage of the column total.) Format the PivotTable and slicers with matching styles, and adjust the height and width of the slicers as needed to improve their appearance. Rename the worksheet as **PivotTable Response by Name**.

Figure 5-51 PivotTable displaying Responses by Name

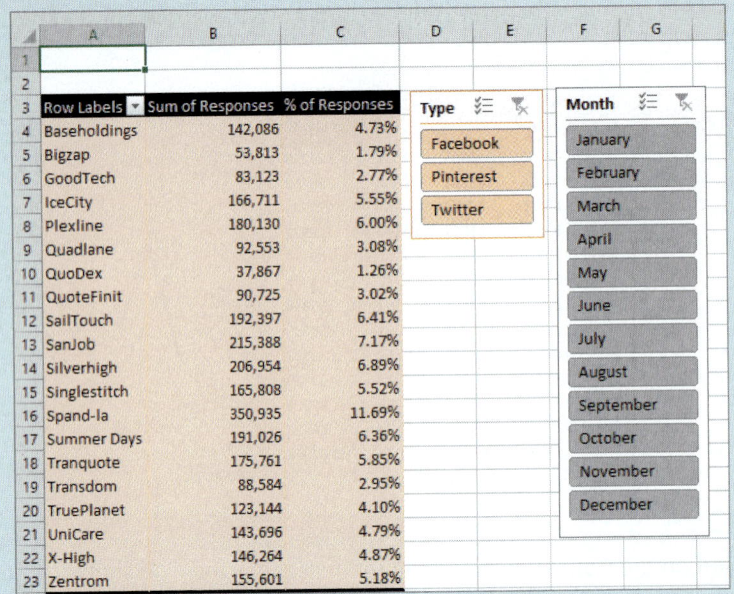

Row Labels	Sum of Responses	% of Responses
Baseholdings	142,086	4.73%
Bigzap	53,813	1.79%
GoodTech	83,123	2.77%
IceCity	166,711	5.55%
Plexline	180,130	6.00%
Quadlane	92,553	3.08%
QuoDex	37,867	1.26%
QuoteFinit	90,725	3.02%
SailTouch	192,397	6.41%
SanJob	215,388	7.17%
Silverhigh	206,954	6.89%
Singlestitch	165,808	5.52%
Spand-la	350,935	11.69%
Summer Days	191,026	6.36%
Tranquote	175,761	5.85%
Transdom	88,584	2.95%
TruePlanet	123,144	4.10%
UniCare	143,696	4.79%
X-High	146,264	4.87%
Zentrom	155,601	5.18%

13. Save the workbook, and then close it.

MODULE 6

Managing Multiple Worksheets and Workbooks

Summarizing Rental Income Data

OBJECTIVES

Session 6.1
- Create a worksheet group
- Format and edit multiple worksheets at once
- Create cell references to other worksheets
- Consolidate information from multiple worksheets using 3-D references
- Create and print a worksheet group

Session 6.2
- Create a link to data in another workbook
- Create a workbook reference
- Learn how to edit links

Session 6.3
- Insert a hyperlink in a cell
- Create a workbook based on an existing template
- Create a custom workbook template

Case | *Reveries Urban Centers*

Reveries Urban Centers is a rental agency with three locations in Michigan—Jackson, Fint, and Petosky. The agency specializes in innovative leasing of empty retail spaces to meet other community needs, including child care centers, medical clinics, religious centers, and music practice rooms, in addition to retail stores. Timothy Root is the COO (chief operating officer). Aubrette Caron manages the Jackson rental center, Gordon Warren manages the Petosky rental center, and Tammy Hernandez manages the Flint rental center.

As COO, Timothy is responsible for analyzing rental income at all locations. Each rental center tracks the rental amounts and types for each quarter in a workbook, which is sent to Timothy to consolidate and analyze. Timothy has received the workbooks with the quarterly rental income data for the past year from all three locations. You will create a worksheet in each workbook that summarizes the rental income totals.

STARTING DATA FILES

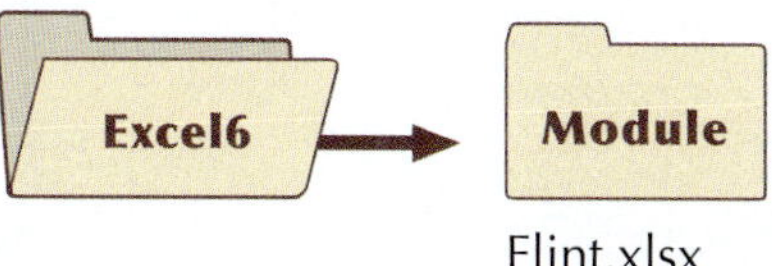

Module
Flint.xlsx
Michigan.xlsx
Petosky.xlsx
UCMemo.docx
UCTotals.xlsx

Review
FlintMI.xlsx
JacksonMI.xlsx
Midland.xlslx
NewUC.xlsx
NewUCMemo.docx
PetoskyMI.xlsx

Case1
Tea.xlsx

Case2
Barstow.xlsx
Carlsbad.xlsx
GoodieBag.xlsx
SanDiego.xlsx

Case3
RoomGroom.xlsx

Case4
Delaware.xlsx
ELSSummary.xlsx
ELSTemplate.xltx
Maryland.xlsx
NewMD.xlsx
Virginia.xlsx

Session 6.1 Visual Overview:

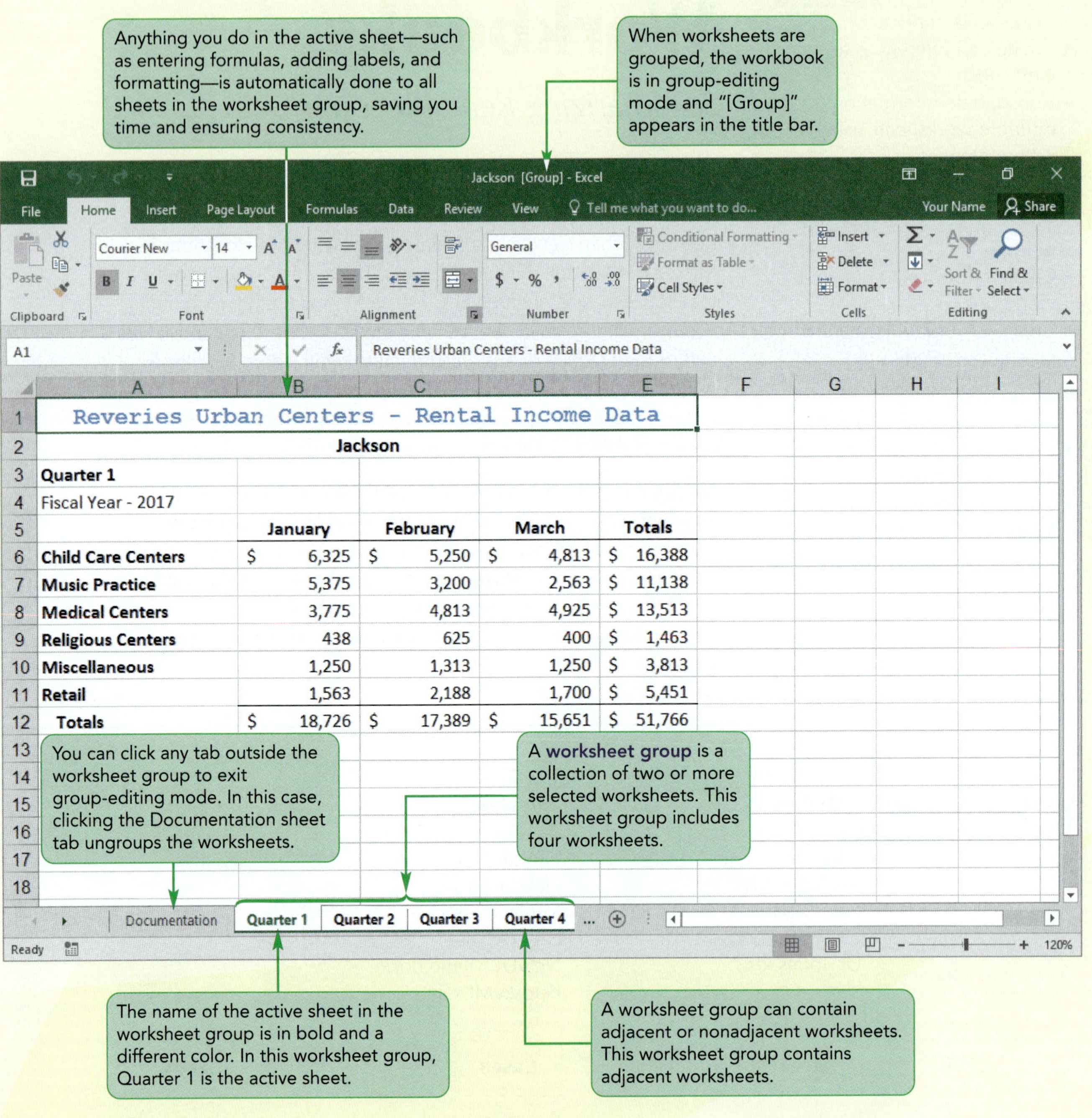
Anything you do in the active sheet—such as entering formulas, adding labels, and formatting—is automatically done to all sheets in the worksheet group, saving you time and ensuring consistency.
When worksheets are grouped, the workbook is in group-editing mode and "[Group]" appears in the title bar.
Jackson [Group] - Excel
Reveries Urban Centers - Rental Income Data
Jackson
Quarter 1
Fiscal Year - 2017
January February March Totals
Child Care Centers $ 6,325 $ 5,250 $ 4,813 $ 16,388
Music Practice 5,375 3,200 2,563 $ 11,138
Medical Centers 3,775 4,813 4,925 $ 13,513
Religious Centers 438 625 400 $ 1,463
Miscellaneous 1,250 1,313 1,250 $ 3,813
Retail 1,563 2,188 1,700 $ 5,451
Totals $ 18,726 $ 17,389 $ 15,651 $ 51,766
You can click any tab outside the worksheet group to exit group-editing mode. In this case, clicking the Documentation sheet tab ungroups the worksheets.
A worksheet group is a collection of two or more selected worksheets. This worksheet group includes four worksheets.
Documentation
Quarter 1
Quarter 2
Quarter 3
Quarter 4
The name of the active sheet in the worksheet group is in bold and a different color. In this worksheet group, Quarter 1 is the active sheet.
A worksheet group can contain adjacent or nonadjacent worksheets. This worksheet group contains adjacent worksheets.

Worksheet Groups and 3-D References

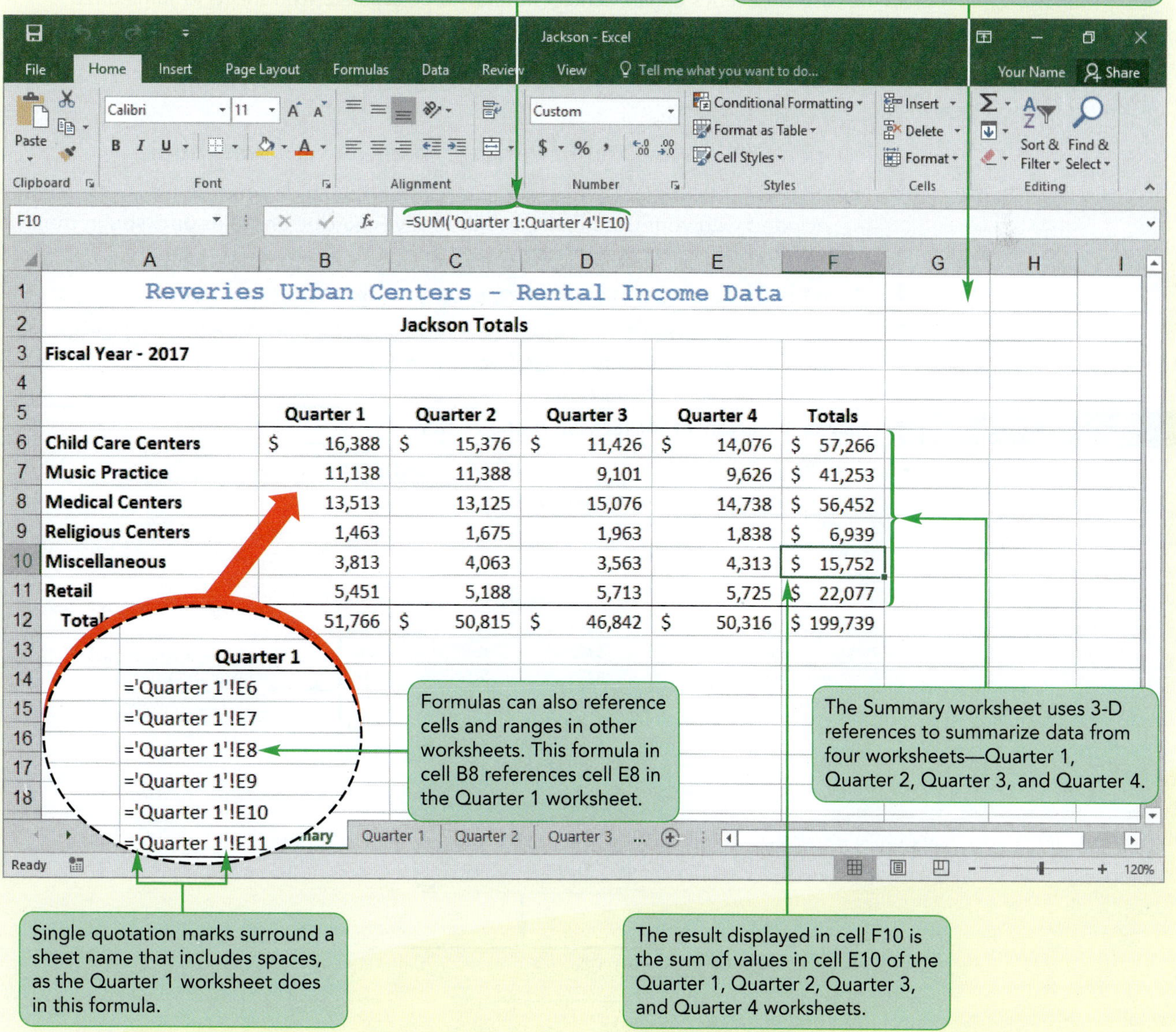
A 3-D reference is a reference to the same cell or range in multiple worksheets in the same workbook. This 3-D reference refers to cell E10 in Quarter1:Quarter 4 worksheets.
When two or more worksheets have identical row and column layouts, as the quarterly worksheets in this workbook do, you can enter formulas with 3-D references to summarize those worksheets in another worksheet.
Jackson - Excel
File
Home
Insert
Page Layout
Formulas
Data
Review
View
Tell me what you want to do...
Your Name
Share
Paste
Calibri
11
Custom
Conditional Formatting
Format as Table
Cell Styles
Insert
Delete
Format
Sort & Filter
Find & Select
Clipboard
Font
Alignment
Number
Styles
Cells
Editing
F10
=SUM('Quarter 1:Quarter 4'!E10)
Reveries Urban Centers - Rental Income Data
Jackson Totals
Fiscal Year - 2017
Quarter 1
Quarter 2
Quarter 3
Quarter 4
Totals
Child Care Centers
$ 16,388
$ 15,376
$ 11,426
$ 14,076
$ 57,266
Music Practice
11,138
11,388
9,101
9,626
$ 41,253
Medical Centers
13,513
13,125
15,076
14,738
$ 56,452
Religious Centers
1,463
1,675
1,963
1,838
$ 6,939
Miscellaneous
3,813
4,063
3,563
4,313
$ 15,752
Retail
5,451
5,188
5,713
5,725
$ 22,077
Total
51,766
$ 50,815
$ 46,842
$ 50,316
$ 199,739
Quarter 1
='Quarter 1'!E6
='Quarter 1'!E7
='Quarter 1'!E8
='Quarter 1'!E9
='Quarter 1'!E10
='Quarter 1'!E11
Formulas can also reference cells and ranges in other worksheets. This formula in cell B8 references cell E8 in the Quarter 1 worksheet.
The Summary worksheet uses 3-D references to summarize data from four worksheets—Quarter 1, Quarter 2, Quarter 3, and Quarter 4.
Quarter 1
Quarter 2
Quarter 3
Ready
120%
Single quotation marks surround a sheet name that includes spaces, as the Quarter 1 worksheet does in this formula.
The result displayed in cell F10 is the sum of values in cell E10 of the Quarter 1, Quarter 2, Quarter 3, and Quarter 4 worksheets.

Grouping Worksheets

Workbook data is often placed in several worksheets. Using multiple worksheets makes it easier to group and summarize data. For example, a company such as Reveries Urban Centers with locations in different cities within a geographic region can place income information for each site in a separate worksheet. Rather than scrolling through one large and complex worksheet that contains data for all locations, users can access collection information for a specific location simply by clicking a sheet tab in the workbook.

Using multiple worksheets enables you to place summarized data first. Managers interested only in an overall picture can view the first worksheet of summary data without looking at the details available in the other worksheets. Others, of course, might want to view the supporting data in the individual worksheets that follow the summary worksheet. In the case of Reveries Urban Centers, Timothy used separate worksheets to summarize the rental income for the Jackson location for each quarter of the 2017 fiscal year.

You will open Timothy's workbook and review the current information.

To open and review the Reveries Urban Centers workbook:

1. Open the **Michigan** workbook located in the **Excel6 > Module** folder included with your Data Files, and then save the document as **Jackson** in the location specified by your instructor.
2. In the Documentation worksheet, enter your name and the date.
3. Go to the **Quarter 1** worksheet, and then view the rental income in Jackson for the first quarter of the year. See Figure 6-1.

Figure 6-1 Quarter 1 worksheet for Jackson rental center

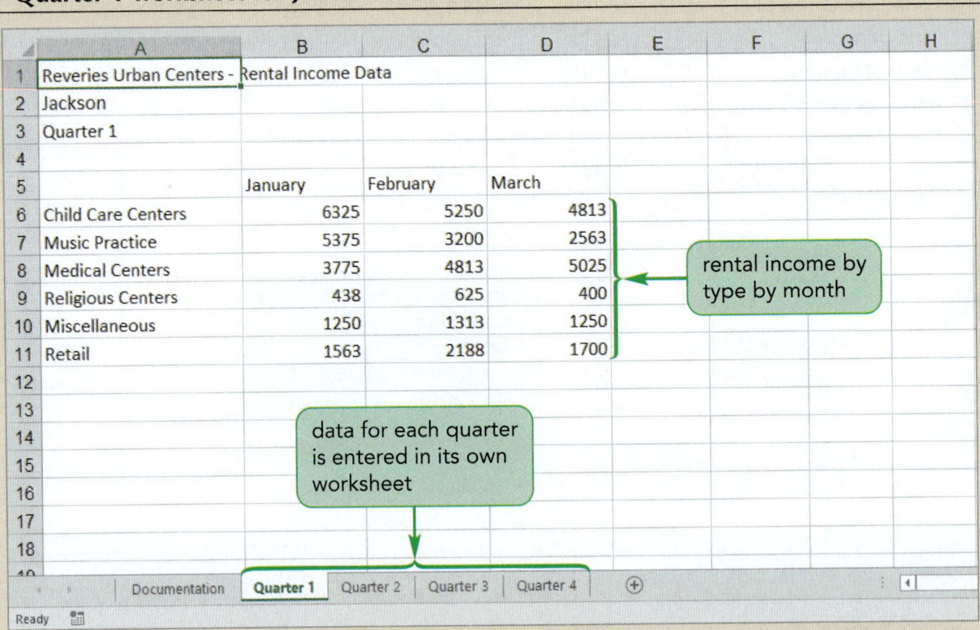

	A	B	C	D
1	Reveries Urban Centers - Rental Income Data			
2	Jackson			
3	Quarter 1			
4				
5		January	February	March
6	Child Care Centers	6325	5250	4813
7	Music Practice	5375	3200	2563
8	Medical Centers	3775	4813	5025
9	Religious Centers	438	625	400
10	Miscellaneous	1250	1313	1250
11	Retail	1563	2188	1700

4. Review the **Quarter 2**, **Quarter 3**, and **Quarter 4** worksheets. The layout for all four worksheets is identical.

Timothy didn't enter any formulas in the workbook. You need to enter formulas to calculate the total rental income for each column (columns B through D) and each row (rows 6 through 11) in all four worksheets. Rather than retyping the formulas in each worksheet, you can enter them all at once by creating a worksheet group.

A worksheet group, like a range, can contain adjacent or nonadjacent worksheets. In group-editing mode, most editing tasks that you complete in the active worksheet also affect the other worksheets in the group. By forming a worksheet group, you can:

- **Enter or edit data and formulas.** Changes made to content in the active worksheet are also made in the same cells in all the worksheets in the group. You can also use the Find and Replace commands with a worksheet group.
- **Apply formatting.** Changes made to formatting in the active worksheet are also made to all the worksheets in the group, including changing row heights or column widths and applying conditional formatting.
- **Insert or delete rows and columns.** Changes made to the worksheet structure in the active worksheet are also made to all the worksheets in the group.
- **Set the page layout options.** Changes made to the page layout settings in one worksheet also apply to all the worksheets in the group, such as changing the orientation, scaling to fit, and inserting headers and footers.
- **Apply view options.** Changes made to the worksheet view such as zooming, showing and hiding worksheets, and so forth are also made to all the worksheets in the group.
- **Print all the worksheets.** You can print all of the worksheets in the worksheet group at the same time.

Worksheet groups save you time and help improve consistency among the worksheets because you can perform an action once, yet affect multiple worksheets.

REFERENCE

Grouping and Ungrouping Worksheets

- To select an adjacent group, click the sheet tab of the first worksheet in the group, press and hold the Shift key, click the sheet tab of the last worksheet in the group, and then release the Shift key.
- To select a nonadjacent group, click the sheet tab of one worksheet in the group, press and hold the Ctrl key, click the sheet tabs of the remaining worksheets in the group, and then release the Ctrl key.
- To ungroup the worksheets, click the sheet tab of a worksheet that is not in the group (or right-click the sheet tab of one worksheet in the group, and then click Ungroup Sheets on the shortcut menu).

In the Jackson workbook, you'll group an adjacent range of worksheets—the Quarter 1 worksheet through the Quarter 4 worksheet.

To group the quarterly worksheets:

1. Click the **Quarter 1** sheet tab to make the worksheet active. This is the first worksheet you want to include in the group.
2. Press and hold the **Shift** key, and then click the **Quarter 4** sheet tab. This is the last worksheet you want to include in the group.
3. Release the **Shift** key. The four selected sheet tabs are white, the green border extends across the bottom of the four selected sheet tabs, and the sheet tab labels—Quarter 1 through Quarter 4—are in bold, indicating they are all selected. The text "[Group]" appears in the title bar to remind you that a worksheet group is selected in the workbook. See Figure 6-2.

TIP

If you cannot see the sheet tab of a worksheet you want to include in a group, use the sheet tab scroll buttons to display it.

Figure 6-2 **Grouped worksheets**

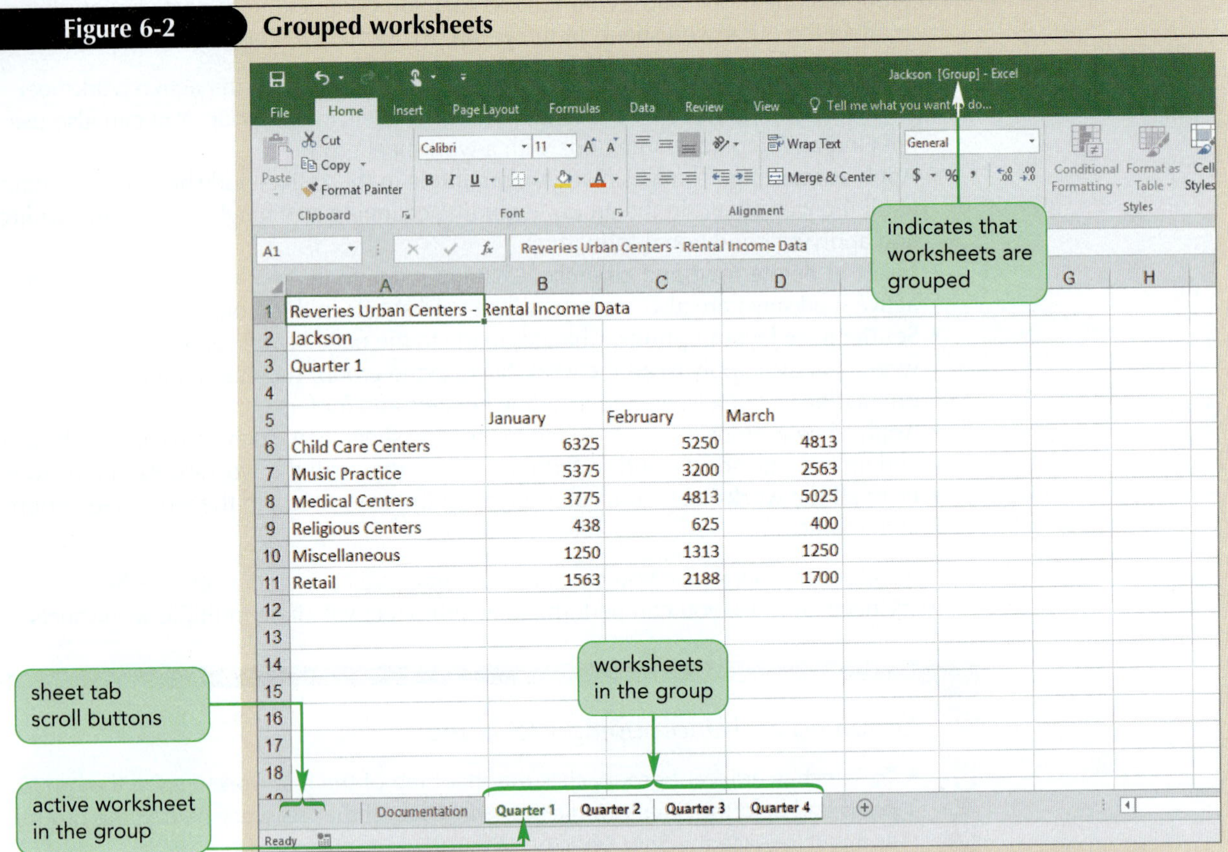

You can change which worksheet in a worksheet group is active. Just click the sheet tab of the worksheet you want to make active. If a worksheet group includes all the worksheets in a workbook, you cannot change which worksheet is the active sheet because clicking a sheet tab ungroups the worksheets.

To change the active sheet in the grouped quarterly worksheets:

1. Click the **Quarter 2** sheet tab to make the worksheet active. The Quarter 2 worksheet is now the active worksheet in the group.
2. Click the **Quarter 4** sheet tab. The Quarter 4 worksheet is now the active worksheet in the group.

Entering Headings and Formulas in a Worksheet Group

When you enter a formula in the active worksheet (in this case, the Quarter 4 worksheet), the formula is entered in the same cells in all the worksheets in the group. The grouped worksheets must have the exact same organization and layout (rows and columns) in order for this to work. Otherwise, any formulas you enter in the active worksheet will be incorrect in the other worksheets in the group and could overwrite existing data.

With the quarterly worksheets grouped, you will enter formulas to calculate the rental income totals for each month.

To enter formulas to calculate the rental income totals in the worksheet group:

1. Select cell **B12**. You want to enter the formula in cell B12 in each of the four worksheets in the group.
2. On the Home tab, in the Editing group, click the **AutoSum** button, and then press the **Enter** key. The formula =SUM(B6:B11) is entered in cell B12 in each worksheet, adding the total rental income at the Jackson rental center for the first month of each quarter. For Quarter 4, the October total of rental income shown in cell B12 is 15426.
3. Copy the formula in cell B12 to the range **C12:D12**. The formula calculates the rental income for the other months in each quarter. For Quarter 4, the rental incomes are 16427 in November and 18413 in December.
4. In cell **E6**, enter a formula with the SUM function to add the total rental income for Child Care Centers for each quarter at the Jackson rental center. The formula =SUM(B6:D6) adds the monthly rental income for Child Care Centers. In Quarter 4, the rental income was 14076.
5. Copy the formula in cell E6 to the range **E7:E12** to calculate the rental income for Music Practice, Medical Centers, Religious Centers, Miscellaneous, and Retail, as well as the grand total of rental income at the Jackson rental center for the quarter. For Quarter 4, the Jackson site had 9626 in rental income for Music Practice, 14738 for Medical Centers, 1838 for Religious Centers, 4313 for Miscellaneous, 5675 for Retail, and 50266 overall.
6. In cells **A12** and **E5**, enter **Totals** as the labels.
7. Click the **Quarter 3** sheet tab, and then click cell **B12** to make it the active cell. The formula =SUM(B6:B11), which adds the rental income for July, appears in the formula bar, and the formula result 15014 appears in the cell. See Figure 6-3.

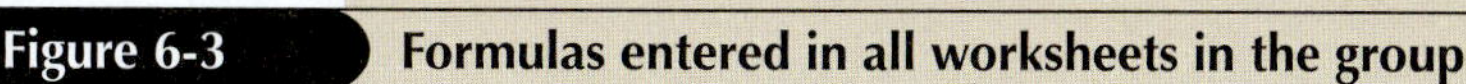

Figure 6-3 Formulas entered in all worksheets in the group

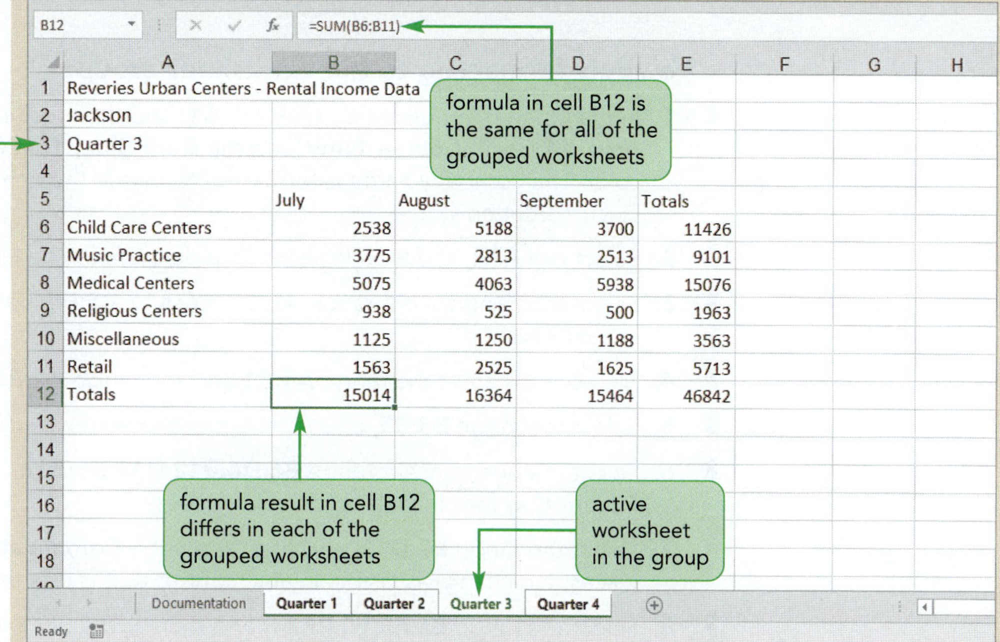

	A	B	C	D	E
1	Reveries Urban Centers - Rental Income Data				
2	Jackson				
3	Quarter 3				
4					
5		July	August	September	Totals
6	Child Care Centers	2538	5188	3700	11426
7	Music Practice	3775	2813	2513	9101
8	Medical Centers	5075	4063	5938	15076
9	Religious Centers	938	525	500	1963
10	Miscellaneous	1125	1250	1188	3563
11	Retail	1563	2525	1625	5713
12	Totals	15014	16364	15464	46842

The formulas and labels you entered in the Quarter 4 worksheet were entered in the Quarter 1, 2, and 3 worksheets at the same time.

8. Click the **Quarter 2** sheet tab. Cell B12 is the active cell. The formula =SUM(B6:B11), which adds the rental income for April, appears in the formula bar, and the formula result 18938 appears in the cell.
9. Click the **Quarter 1** sheet tab. Cell B12 is the active cell. The formula =SUM(B6:B11), which adds the rental income for January, appears in the formula bar, and the formula result 18726 appears in the cell.

The grouped worksheets made it quick to enter the formulas needed to calculate the rental incomes for each quarter.

INSIGHT

Editing Grouped Worksheets

When you enter, edit, or format cells in a worksheet group, the changes you make to one worksheet are automatically applied to the other worksheets in the group. For example, if you delete a value from one cell, the content is also deleted from the same cell in all the worksheets in the group. Be cautious when editing a worksheet that is part of a group. If the layout and structure of the other grouped worksheets are not exactly the same, you might inadvertently overwrite data in some of the worksheets. Also, remember to ungroup the worksheet group after you finish entering data, formulas, and formatting. Otherwise, changes you intend to make in one worksheet will be made to all the worksheets in the group, potentially producing incorrect results.

Formatting a Worksheet Group

As when inserting formulas and text, any formatting changes you make to the active worksheet are applied to all worksheets in the group. Timothy wants you to format the quarterly worksheets, which are still grouped, so that they are easier to read and understand.

To apply formatting to the worksheet group:

1. In the Quarter 1 worksheet, click cell **A1**, and then format the cell with **bold**, **14**-point, **Courier New**, and the **Dark Blue, Text 2, Lighter 40%** font color. The company name is formatted to match the company name on the Documentation worksheet.
2. Select cell **A12**, and then increase its indent once. The label shifts to the right.
3. Select the nonadjacent range **A2:A3,A6:A12,B5:E5**, and then bold the text in the headings.
4. Merge and center the range **A1:E1** and the range **A2:E2**.
5. Select the range **B5:E5**, and then center the text.
6. Select the nonadjacent range **B6:D6,B12:D12,E6:E12**, and then apply the **Accounting** format with no decimal places.
7. Select the range **B7:D11**, and then apply the **Comma style** with no decimal places. No change is visible in any number that is less than 1000.
8. Select the range **B5:E5,B11:E11**, and then add a bottom border.
9. Select cell **A1**. All the worksheets in the group are formatted.

10. Go to each worksheet in the group and review the formatting changes, and then go to the **Quarter 1** worksheet. See Figure 6-4.

Figure 6-4 Formatting applied to the worksheet group

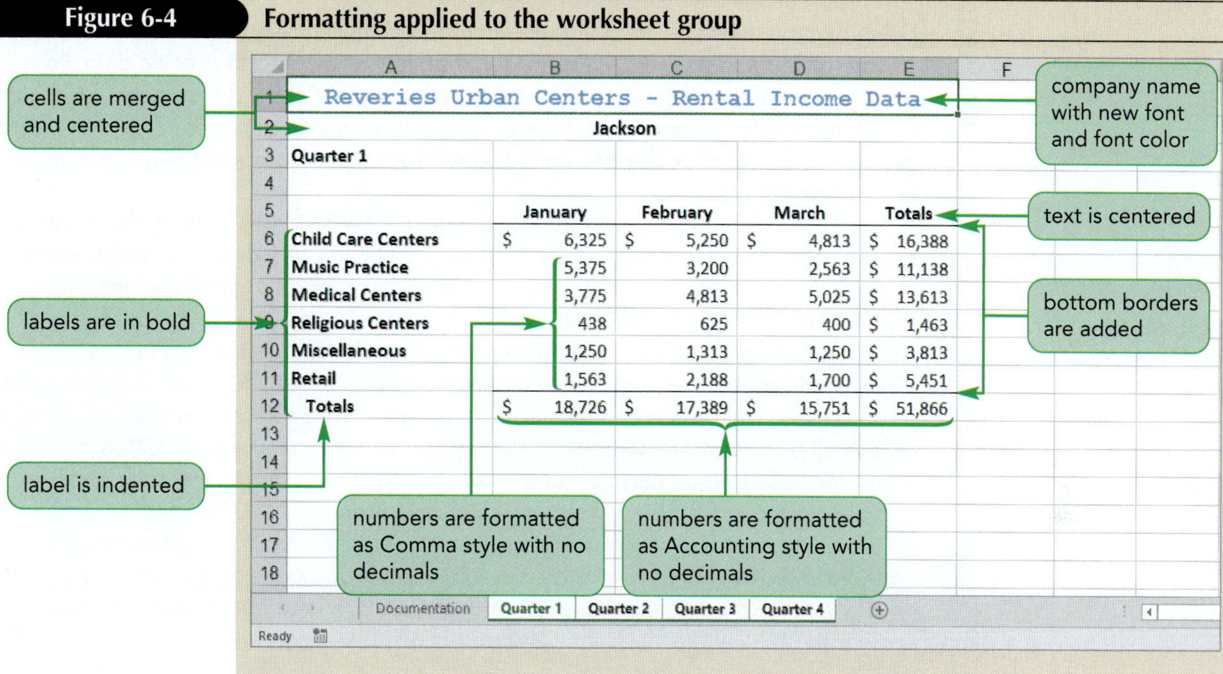

Ungrouping Worksheets

When you ungroup the worksheets, each worksheet functions independently again. If you forget to ungroup the worksheets, any changes you make in one worksheet will be applied to all the worksheets in the group. So be sure to ungroup worksheets when you are finished making changes that apply to multiple worksheets. To ungroup worksheets, click the sheet tab of a worksheet that is not part of the group. If a worksheet group includes all of the sheets in a workbook, click any of the sheet tabs to ungroup the worksheets.

You will ungroup the quarterly worksheets so you can work in each worksheet separately.

Be sure to ungroup the worksheets; otherwise, any changes you make will affect all worksheets in the group.

To ungroup the quarterly worksheets:

1. Click the **Documentation** sheet tab. The worksheets are ungrouped because the Documentation worksheet was not part of the worksheet group. The text "[Group]" no longer appears in the Excel title bar.
2. Verify that the worksheets are ungrouped and the word "[Group]" no longer appears in the title bar.

Timothy wants you to include a new Summary worksheet in the workbook. You'll start working on that next.

PROSKILLS

Written Communication: Using Multiple Worksheets with Identical Layouts

Using multiple worksheets to organize complex data can help make that data simpler to understand and analyze. It also makes it easier to navigate to specific data. For example, a workbook that contains data about a variety of products, stores, or regions could use a different worksheet for each rental type, store, or region. This arrangement provides a way to view discrete units of data that can be combined and summarized in another worksheet.

When you use multiple worksheets to organize similar types of data, the worksheets should have identical layouts. You can quickly group the worksheets with the identical layouts, and then enter the formulas, formatting, and labels in all of the grouped worksheets at once. This helps to ensure consistency and accuracy among the worksheets as well as make it faster to create the different worksheets needed.

Using multiple worksheets with identical layouts enables you to use 3-D references to quickly summarize the data in another worksheet. The summary worksheet provides an overall picture of the data that is detailed in the other worksheets. Often, managers are more interested in this big-picture view. However, the supporting data is still available in the individual worksheets when a deeper analysis is needed.

So, when you are working with a large and complex worksheet filled with data, consider the different ways to organize it in multiple worksheets. Not only will you save time when entering and finding data, but also the data becomes more understandable, and connections and results become clearer.

Working with Multiple Worksheets

As you develop a workbook, you might need to add a worksheet that has the same setup as an existing worksheet. Rather than starting from scratch, you can copy that worksheet as a starting point. For example, Timothy wants the workbook to include a Summary worksheet that adds the annual rental income from the quarterly worksheets. The formulas you create in the Summary worksheet will reference cells in each quarterly worksheet using 3-D references. You can then group the completed worksheets to develop a consistent page setup in all worksheets and then print them all at once.

Copying Worksheets

Often, after spending time developing a worksheet, you can use it as a starting point for creating another, saving you time and energy compared to developing a new worksheet from scratch. Copying a worksheet duplicates all the values, formulas, and formats into the new worksheet, leaving the original worksheet intact. You can then edit, reformat, and enter new content as needed to create the exact worksheet you need.

REFERENCE

Copying Worksheets

- Select the sheet tabs of the worksheets you want to copy.
- Right-click the sheet tabs, and then click Move or Copy on the shortcut menu.
- Click the To book arrow, and then click the name of an existing workbook or click (new book) to create a new workbook for the worksheets.
- In the Before sheet box, click the worksheet before which you want to insert the new worksheet.
- Click the Create a copy check box to insert a checkmark to copy the worksheets.
- Click the OK button.

or

- Select the sheet tabs of the worksheets you want to copy.
- Press and hold the Ctrl key as you drag the selected sheet tabs to a new location in the sheet tabs, and then release the Ctrl key.

Timothy wants you to create the Summary worksheet to provide an overall picture of the data in the detailed quarterly worksheets. The Summary worksheet needs the same formatting and structure as the quarterly worksheets. To ensure consistency among worksheets, you will copy the Quarter 1 worksheet to the beginning of the workbook and then modify its contents.

TIP

You can move or copy a worksheet group within a workbook by dragging one of the group's sheet tabs and dropping it in the new location.

To copy the Quarter 1 worksheet and create the Summary worksheet:

1. Click the **Quarter 1** sheet tab, and then press and hold the **Ctrl** key as you drag the worksheet to the left of the Documentation worksheet. The pointer changes to ⧉ and a triangle indicates the drop location.
2. Release the mouse button, and then release the **Ctrl** key. An identical copy of the Quarter 1 worksheet appears in the new location. The sheet tab shows "Quarter 1 (2)" to indicate that this is the copied sheet.
3. Rename the Quarter 1 (2) worksheet as **Summary**.
4. Drag the **Summary** worksheet between the Documentation worksheet and the Quarter 1 worksheet to make it the second worksheet in the workbook.

Timothy wants the Summary worksheet to show the rental income for each rental type by quarter and the total rental income for each rental type and quarter. You will modify the Summary worksheet to do this now.

To modify the Summary worksheet:

1. Make sure the **Summary** worksheet is the active sheet.
2. In cell **A2**, enter **Jackson Totals**. The new title reflects this worksheet's content.
3. In cell **A3**, enter **2017**. This is the year to which the summary refers.
4. Clear the contents of the cells in the range **B6:E11**. You removed the rental incomes and the formulas in column E, though the formatting remains intact.
5. Insert a new column **C** into the worksheet. The column appears between the January and February labels and has the same formatting as the January column.

6. In the range **B5:E5**, enter **Quarter 1**, **Quarter 2**, **Quarter 3**, and **Quarter 4** as the new labels.
7. Copy the formula in cell B12 to cell **C12**. See Figure 6-5.

Figure 6-5 Summary Worksheet created from the Quarter 1 worksheet

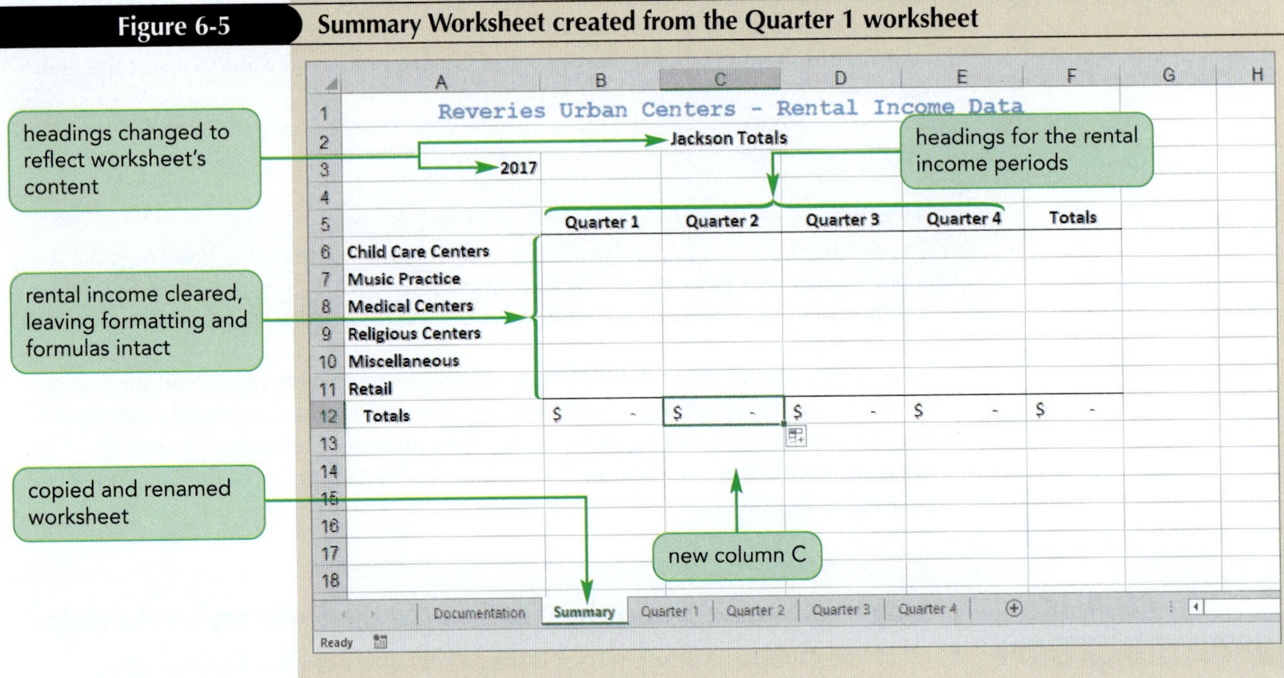

Referencing Cells and Ranges in Other Worksheets

When you use multiple worksheets to organize related data, you can reference a cell or a range in another worksheet in the same workbook. For example, the Summary worksheet references cells in the four quarterly worksheets to calculate the total rental income for the entire year. The syntax to reference a cell or a range in a different worksheet is

```
=SheetName!CellRange
```

where *SheetName* is the worksheet's name as listed on the sheet tab and *CellRange* is the reference for the cell or range in that worksheet. An exclamation mark (!) separates the worksheet reference from the cell or range reference. For example, you could enter the following formula in the Summary worksheet to reference cell D10 in the Quarter1 worksheet:

```
=Quarter1!D10
```

If the worksheet name contains spaces, you must enclose the name in single quotation marks. For example, the following formula references cell D10 in the Quarter 1 worksheet:

```
='Quarter 1'!D10
```

You can use these references to create formulas that reference cells in different locations in different worksheets. For example, to add rental income from two worksheets—cell C9 in the Quarter 1 worksheet and cell C9 in the Quarter 2 worksheet—you would enter the following formula:

```
='Quarter 1'! C9+'Quarter 2'!C9
```

You could type the formula directly in the cell, but it is faster and more accurate to use your mouse to select cells to enter their references to other worksheets.

REFERENCE

Entering a Formula with References to Another Worksheet

- Select the cell where you want to enter the formula.
- Type = and begin entering the formula.
- To insert a reference from another worksheet, click the sheet tab for the worksheet, and then click the cell or select the range you want to reference.
- When the formula is complete, press the Enter key.

Timothy wants you to enter a formula in cell A4 in each quarterly worksheet that displays the fiscal year entered in cell A3 in the Summary worksheet. All four quarterly worksheets will use the formula =Summary!A3 to reference the fiscal year in cell A3 of the Summary worksheet.

To enter the formula that references the Summary worksheet:

1. Click the **Quarter 1** sheet tab, press and hold the **Shift** key, and then click the **Quarter 4** sheet tab. The Quarter 1 through Quarter 4 worksheets are grouped.
2. Select cell **A4**. This is the cell in which you want to enter the formula to display the fiscal year.
3. Type = to begin the formula, click the **Summary** sheet tab, and then click cell **A3**. The reference to cell A3 in the Summary worksheet is added to the formula in cell A4 in the grouped worksheets.
4. On the formula bar, click the **Enter** button ✓. The formula =Summary!A3 is entered in cell A4 in each the worksheet in the group. The formula appears in the formula bar and 2017 appears in cell A4. See Figure 6-6.

Figure 6-6 Formula with a worksheet reference

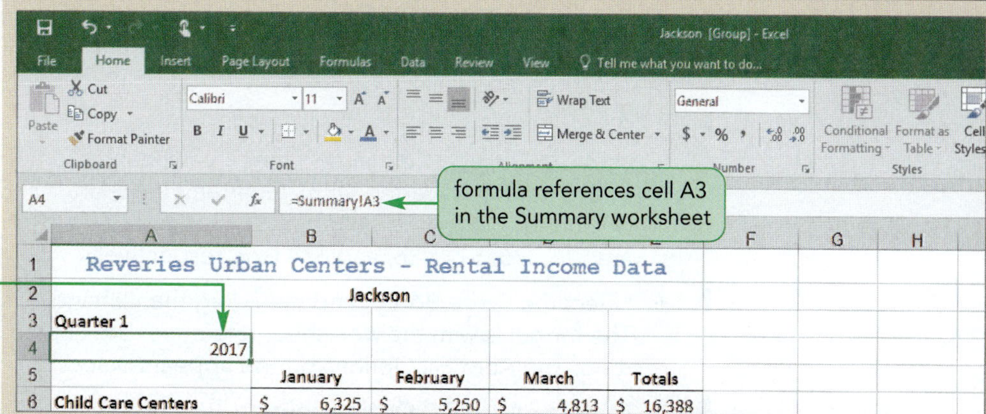

5. Go to each worksheet in the group and verify that the formula =Summary!A3 appears in the formula bar and 2017 appears in cell A4.
6. Go to the **Summary** worksheet. The quarterly worksheets are ungrouped.
7. In cell **A3**, enter **Fiscal Year - 2017**. The descriptive label in cell A3 is entered in the Summary worksheet and is also displayed in the quarterly worksheets because of the formula you entered.

8. Go to the **Quarter 1** through **Quarter 4** worksheets and verify that the label "Fiscal Year - 2017" appears in cell A4 in each worksheet. See Figure 6-7.

Figure 6-7 **Edited content displayed in the cell with the worksheet reference**

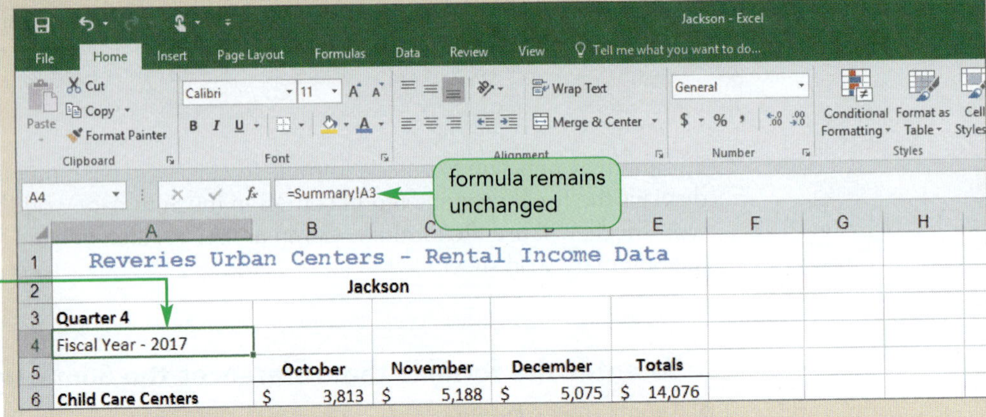

The Summary worksheet needs to include the quarterly totals for each category. You will use formulas that reference the totals in the quarterly worksheets to calculate those totals.

To enter worksheet references for the quarterly totals:

1. Go to the **Summary** worksheet, and then select cell **B6.**
2. Type **=** to begin the formula.
3. Click the **Quarter 1** sheet tab, and then click cell **E6**. The cell is selected and added to the formula.
4. Click the **Enter** button ✓ on the formula bar to complete the formula and return to the Summary worksheet. Cell B6 remains selected, and the formula ='Quarter 1'!E6 appears in the formula bar. The formula result showing the rental income from Child Care Centers in the first quarter of 2017—$16,388—appears in cell B6.
5. Repeat Steps 2 through 4 to enter formulas with worksheet references in cells **C6**, **D6**, and **E6** that add the rental income from Child Care Centers in Quarter 2 (='Quarter 2'!E6), Quarter 3 (='Quarter 3'!E6), and Quarter 4 (='Quarter 4'!E6). The quarterly rental income totals from Child Care Centers are $15,376, $11,426, and $14,076, respectively.
6. Select the range **B6:E6**, and then drag the fill handle over the range **B7:E11**. The formulas with the worksheet references are copied to the rest of the item rows. The Auto Fill Options button appears below the copied range.
7. Click the **Auto Fill Options** button, and then click the **Fill Without Formatting** option button. You didn't copy the formatting in this case because you want to keep the Accounting format in the range B7:E11 and the bottom border formatting in the range B11:E11. The total values for the year appear in the range.
8. Click cell **B6** to deselect the range. The Summary worksheet now shows the 2017 totals for each rental type in Jackson by quarter and for all rental income in 2017. See Figure 6-8.

Figure 6-8 Rental income totals for Jackson in 2017

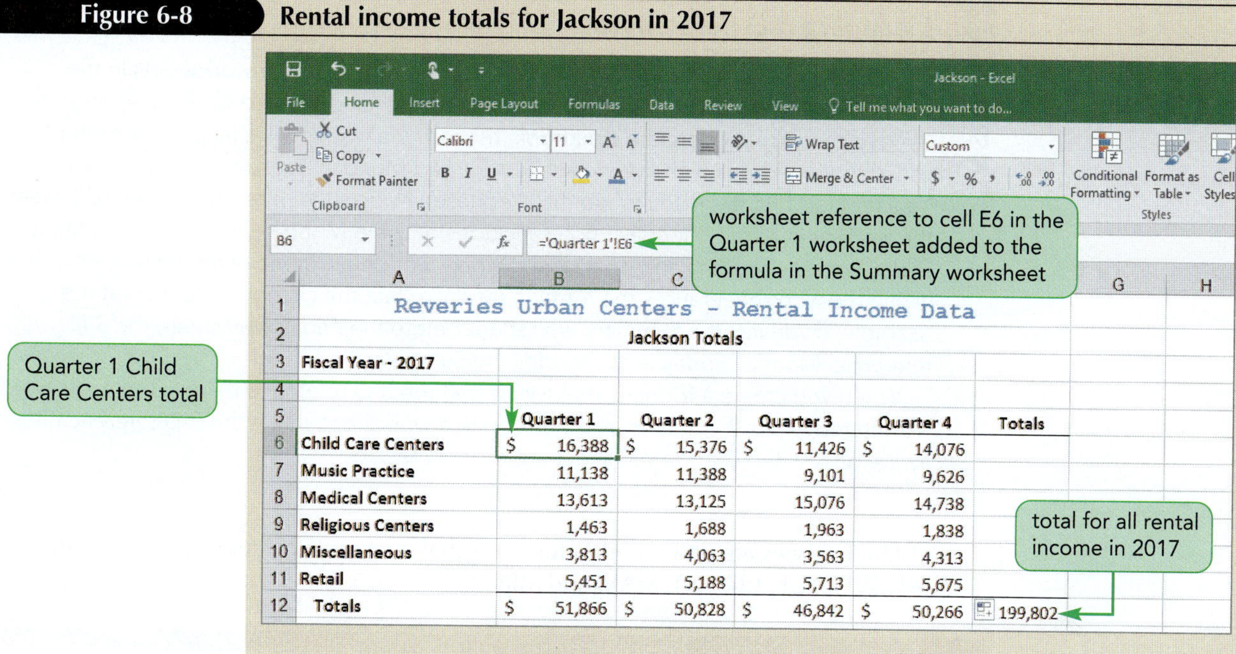

Using 3-D References to Add Values Across Worksheets

Timothy wants you to calculate the rental income for each type of rental for the year and display the totals for the fiscal year in the Summary worksheet. To calculate the totals for the year, you can add the results from each quarterly worksheet and place the sum in the Summary worksheet. For example, in cell B6 of the Summary worksheet, you can enter the following formula:

```
='Quarter 1'!E6+'Quarter 2'!E6+'Quarter 3'!E6+'Quarter 4'!E6
```

This formula calculates the total rental income for Child Care Centers by adding the values in cell E6 in each of the quarterly worksheets. Continuing this approach for the entire worksheet would be time consuming and error prone.

Instead, when two or more worksheets have *identical* row and column layouts, as the quarterly worksheets in the Jackson workbook do, you can enter formulas with 3-D references to summarize those worksheets in another worksheet. The 3-D reference specifies not only the range of rows and columns but also the range of worksheet names in which the cells appear. The general syntax of a 3-D reference is

```
WorksheetRange!CellRange
```

where *WorksheetRange* is the range of worksheets you want to reference and is entered as *FirstSheetName*:*LastSheetName* with a colon separating the first and last worksheets in the worksheet range. If the sheet names include spaces, they are surrounded by ' ' (single quotation marks). *CellRange* is the same cell or range in each of those worksheets that you want to reference. An exclamation mark (`!`) separates the worksheet range from the cell or range. For example, the following formula adds the values in cell D11 in the worksheets between Monday and Friday, including Monday and Friday:

```
=SUM(Monday:Friday!D11)
```

If worksheets named Monday, Tuesday, Wednesday, Thursday, and Friday are included in the workbook, the worksheet range Monday:Friday references all five worksheets. Although the Tuesday, Wednesday, and Thursday worksheets aren't specifically mentioned in this 3-D reference, all worksheets positioned within the starting and ending names are included in the calculation.

INSIGHT

Managing 3-D References

The results of a formula using a 3-D reference reflect the current worksheets in the worksheet range. If you move a worksheet outside the referenced worksheet range or remove a worksheet from the workbook, the formula results will change. For example, consider a workbook with five worksheets named Monday, Tuesday, Wednesday, Thursday, and Friday. If you move the Wednesday worksheet after the Friday worksheet, the worksheet range 'Monday:Friday' includes only the Monday, Tuesday, Thursday, and Friday worksheets. Similarly, if you insert a new worksheet or move an existing worksheet within the worksheet range, the formula results reflect the change. To continue the example, if you insert a Summary worksheet before the Friday worksheet, the 3-D reference 'Monday:Friday' also includes the Summary worksheet.

When you create a formula, make sure that the 3-D reference reflects the appropriate worksheets. Also, if you later insert or delete a worksheet within the 3-D reference, be aware of how the change will affect the formula results.

3-D references are often used in formulas that contain Excel functions, including SUM, AVERAGE, COUNT, MAX, and MIN.

REFERENCE

Entering a Function That Contains a 3-D Reference

- Select the cell where you want to enter the formula.
- Type = to begin the formula, type the name of the function, and then type (to indicate the beginning of the argument.
- Click the sheet tab for the first worksheet in the worksheet range, press and hold the Shift key, and then click the tab for the last worksheet in the worksheet range.
- Select the cell or range to reference, and then press the Enter key.

In the Jackson workbook, Timothy wants to use 3-D references in the Summary worksheet to add the total rental income for each type of rental for the year. You will begin by entering a formula to add the total rental income for Child Care Centers in the first quarter. Then, you'll copy this formula to calculate the total rental income for Music Practice, Medical Centers, Religious Centers, Miscellaneous, and Retail in the first quarter.

To use a 3-D reference to enter the total rental income for Child Care Centers:

1. In the Summary worksheet, select cell **F6**, and then type **=SUM(** to begin the formula.
2. Click the **Quarter 1** sheet tab, press and hold the **Shift** key, click the **Quarter 4** sheet tab, and then release the **Shift** key. The quarterly worksheets are grouped to create the worksheet range.
3. In the Quarter 1 worksheet, click cell **E6**. Cell E6 is selected in each quarterly worksheet and added to the function. Notice that the worksheet names are enclosed in single quotation marks because the worksheet names include spaces. See Figure 6-9.

Figure 6-9 3-D reference added to the SUM function

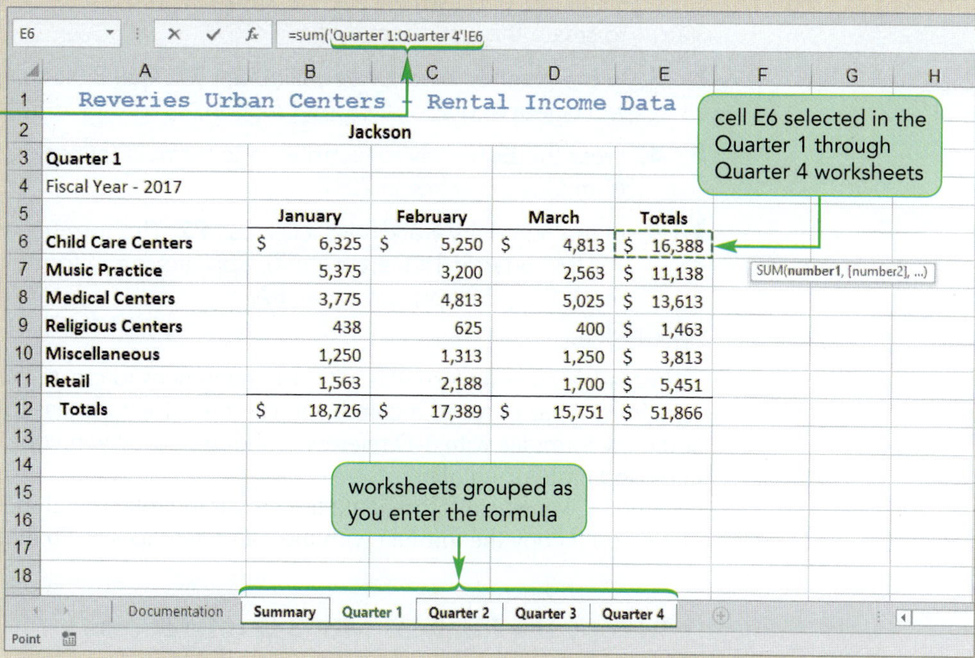

4. Press the **Enter** key. The completed formula in the Summary worksheet adds the total rental income for Child Care Centers in 2017.
5. In the Summary worksheet, select cell **F6**. The formula with the 3-D reference, =SUM('Quarter 1:Quarter 4'!E6), appears in the formula bar. The formula result—$57,266—appears in the cell. See Figure 6-10.

Figure 6-10 3-D reference used in the SUM function

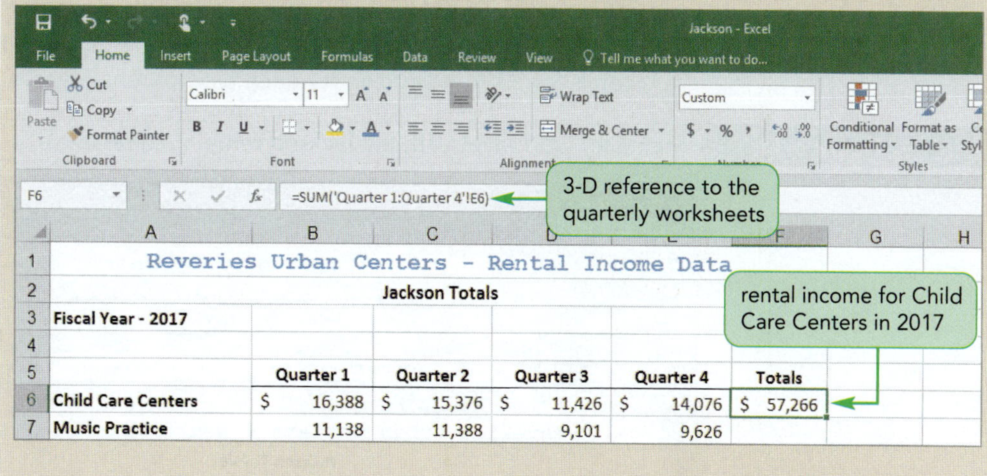

The next formula will add the total rental income for Music Practice in the first quarter.

To calculate the total rental income for Music Practice:

1. In the Summary worksheet, click cell **F7**, and then type **=SUM(** to begin the formula.

2. Click the **Quarter 1** sheet tab, press and hold the **Shift** key, click the **Quarter 4** sheet tab, and then release the **Shift** key. The quarterly worksheets are grouped to create the worksheet range.
3. In the Quarter 1 worksheet, click cell **E7**. Cell E7 is selected in each quarterly worksheet and added to the function.
4. Press the **Enter** key to complete the formula that adds the total rental income from Music Practice in 2017.
5. In the Summary worksheet, click cell **F7**. The formula with the 3-D reference, =SUM('Quarter 1:Quarter 4'!E7), appears in the formula bar, and the formula result $41,253 appears in cell F7.

Instead of entering formulas with 3-D references to create the totals for the remaining types of rental income, you can copy the formulas to the rest of the range. You copy formulas with 3-D references the same way you copy other formulas—using copy and paste or AutoFill.

Timothy wants you to calculate the remaining total rental incomes by rental type in 2017. You'll copy the formula with the 3-D references to do that.

To copy the formulas with 3-D references:

1. In the Summary worksheet, make sure cell **F7** is selected. This cell contains the formula with the 3-D reference you already entered.
2. Drag the fill handle over the range **F8:F11**. The formulas are copied for the rest of the rental income totals. The Auto Fill Options button appears below the copied range.
3. Click the **Auto Fill Options** button, and then click the **Fill Without Formatting** option button. You don't want to copy the formatting in this case because you want to keep the bottom border formatting in cell F11. The total values for the year appear in the range.
4. Select cell **B6** to deselect the range. The Summary worksheet now shows the totals for 2017 in Jackson for each type of rental income. See Figure 6-11.

Figure 6-11 Summary worksheet with the Jackson rental income totals

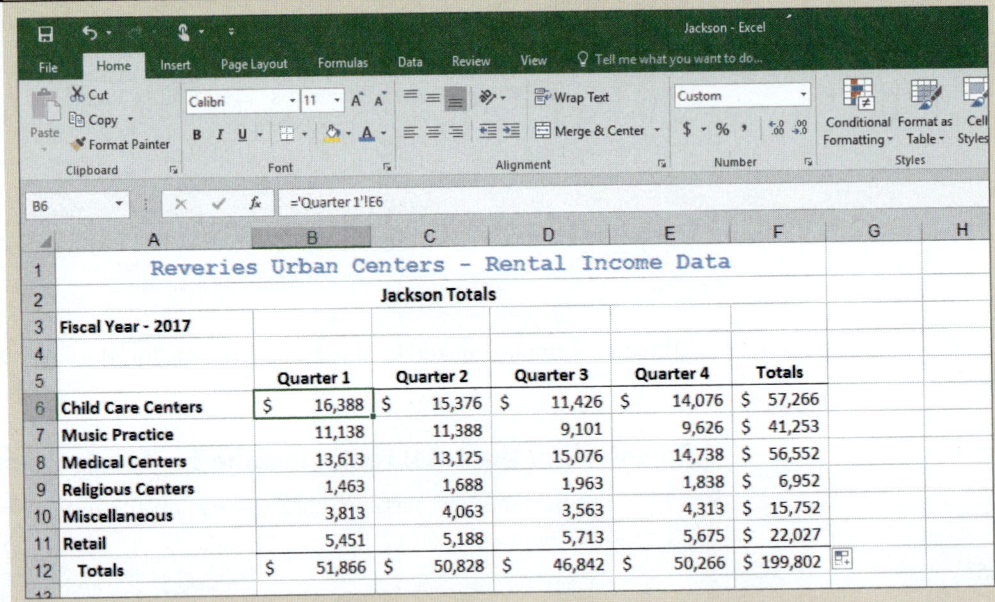

Jackson - Excel

B6 =’Quarter 1’!E6

	A	B	C	D	E	F
1	Reveries Urban Centers - Rental Income Data					
2	Jackson Totals					
3	Fiscal Year - 2017					
4						
5		Quarter 1	Quarter 2	Quarter 3	Quarter 4	Totals
6	Child Care Centers	$ 16,388	$ 15,376	$ 11,426	$ 14,076	$ 57,266
7	Music Practice	11,138	11,388	9,101	9,626	$ 41,253
8	Medical Centers	13,613	13,125	15,076	14,738	$ 56,552
9	Religious Centers	1,463	1,688	1,963	1,838	$ 6,952
10	Miscellaneous	3,813	4,063	3,563	4,313	$ 15,752
11	Retail	5,451	5,188	5,713	5,675	$ 22,027
12	Totals	$ 51,866	$ 50,828	$ 46,842	$ 50,266	$ 199,802

One benefit of summarizing data using formulas with 3-D references, like any other formula, is that if you change the value in one worksheet, the results of formulas that reference that cell reflect the change.

Timothy has discovered an error in the Jackson rental income data. In May, the rental income from Religious Centers was $425, not $438. You will correct the rental income.

To change the rental income in the Quarter 2 worksheet:

1. In the Summary worksheet, note that the rental income for Religious Centers in Quarter 2 is 1,688.
2. Go to the **Quarter 2** worksheet.
3. In cell **C9**, enter **425**. The total rental income for Religious Centers for Quarter 2 is now $1,675.

   The results in the Summary worksheet are also updated because of the 3-D references in the formulas.
4. Go to the **Summary** worksheet. The total rental income for Religious Centers in Quarter 2 is now 1,675. The Quarter 2 total is now $50,815, the 2017 total for Religious Centers is now $6,939, and the total rental income for 2017 is $199,789. See Figure 6-12.

Figure 6-12 Summary worksheet with updated Quarter 2 data

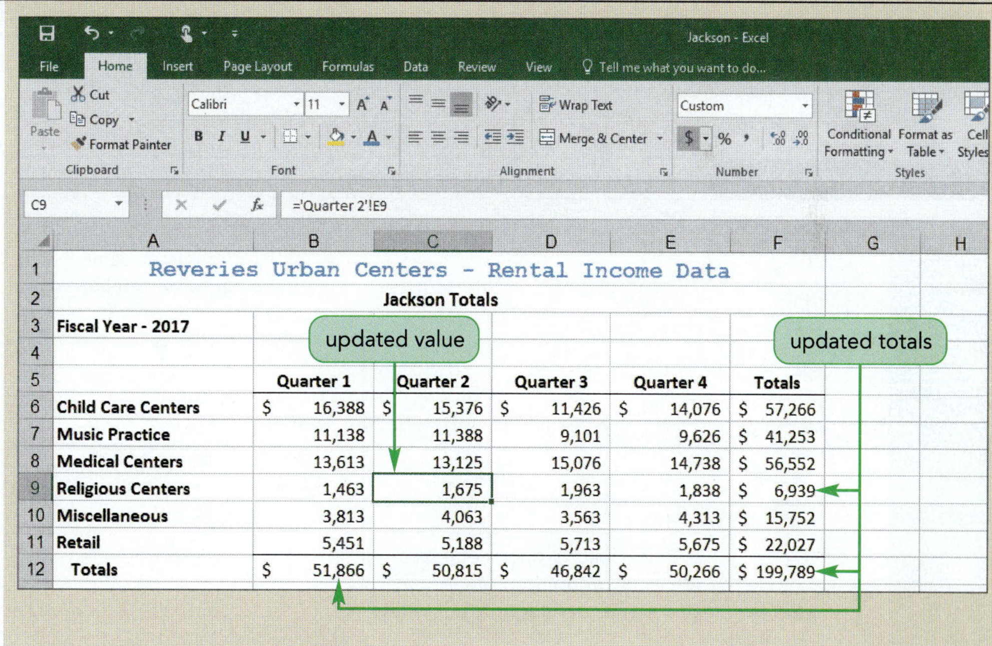

	A	B	C	D	E	F
1	Reveries Urban Centers - Rental Income Data					
2	Jackson Totals					
3	Fiscal Year - 2017					
4						
5		Quarter 1	Quarter 2	Quarter 3	Quarter 4	Totals
6	Child Care Centers	$ 16,388	$ 15,376	$ 11,426	$ 14,076	$ 57,266
7	Music Practice	11,138	11,388	9,101	9,626	$ 41,253
8	Medical Centers	13,613	13,125	15,076	14,738	$ 56,552
9	Religious Centers	1,463	1,675	1,963	1,838	$ 6,939
10	Miscellaneous	3,813	4,063	3,563	4,313	$ 15,752
11	Retail	5,451	5,188	5,713	5,675	$ 22,027
12	Totals	$ 51,866	$ 50,815	$ 46,842	$ 50,266	$ 199,789

Printing a Worksheet Group

When you create a worksheet group, you apply the same page layout settings to all of the worksheets in the group at the same time. You can also print all of the worksheets in the group at once. The process for printing a worksheet group is the same as for printing a single worksheet, except that you must first group the worksheets you want to print.

Timothy wants a printed copy of the five rental income worksheets to include in his report. Each page should have the same setup. Because the layout will be the same for all the quarterly worksheets in the Jackson workbook, you can speed the page layout setup by creating a worksheet group before selecting settings.

Be sure to include all five worksheets in the group so you can apply page layout settings and print the worksheets at once.

To preview the Summary and quarterly worksheets with a custom header and footer:

1. Group the **Summary, Quarter 1**, **Quarter 2**, **Quarter 3**, and **Quarter 4** worksheets. The five worksheets are grouped.
2. On the ribbon, click the **Page Layout** tab.
3. In the Page Setup group, click the **Dialog Box Launcher**. The Page Setup dialog box opens with the Page tab active.
4. Click the **Margins** tab, and then click the **Horizontally** check box in the Center on page section to insert a checkmark. The printed content will be centered horizontally on the page.
5. Click the **Header/Footer** tab, click the **Custom Header** button to open the Header dialog box, click in the **Center section** box, click the **Insert Sheet Name** button to add the &[Tab] code in the section box, and then click the **OK** button. A preview of the header appears in the upper portion of the dialog box.
6. Click the **Custom Footer** button to open the Footer dialog box, type your name in the Left section box, click in the Right section box, click the **Insert Date** button to add the &[Date] code in the section box, and then click the **OK** button. A preview of the footer appears in the center of the dialog box.
7. Click the **Print Preview** button. The preview of the Summary worksheet, the first worksheet in the group, appears on the Print screen in Backstage view. See Figure 6-13.

Figure 6-13 Preview of the worksheet group

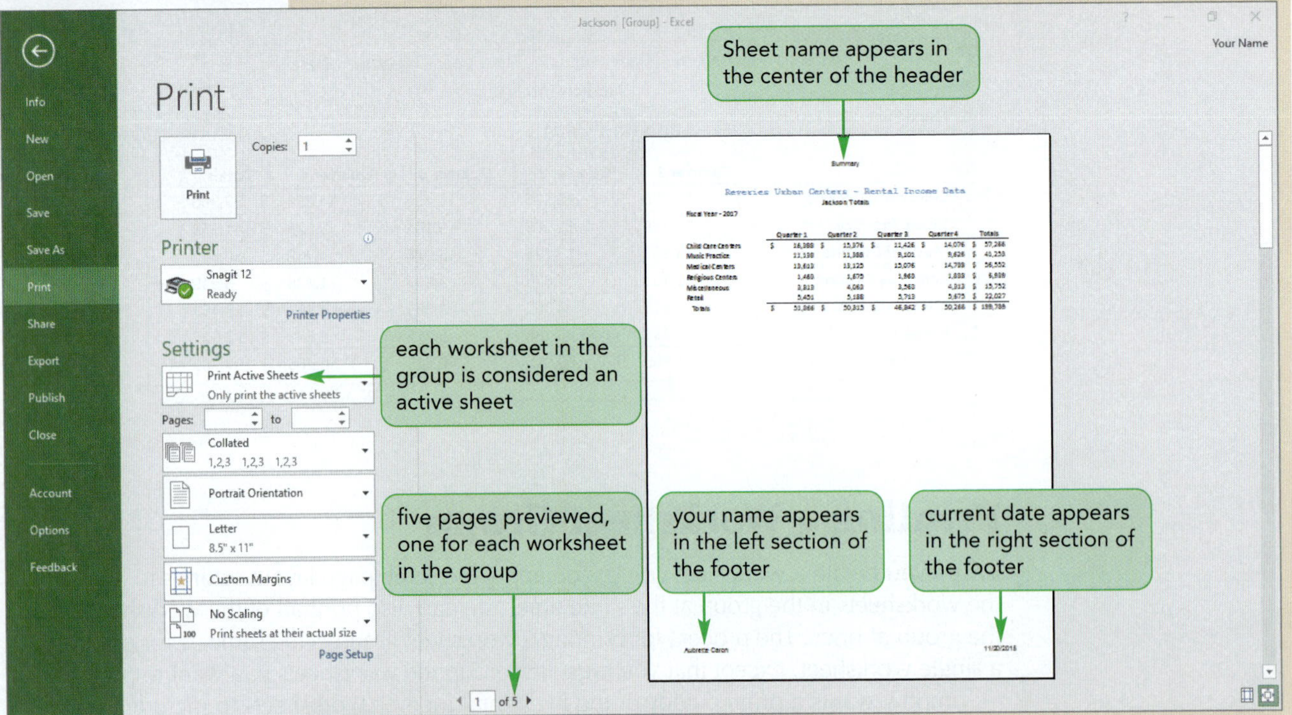
Sheet name appears in the center of the header
each worksheet in the group is considered an active sheet
five pages previewed, one for each worksheet in the group
your name appears in the left section of the footer
current date appears in the right section of the footer
Print
Printer
Settings
Print Active Sheets
Only print the active sheets
Collated
Portrait Orientation
Letter
Custom Margins
No Scaling
Print sheets at their actual size
Page Setup

8. Below the preview, click the **Next Page** button four times to view the other worksheets in the group. Each page has the same page layout, but the header shows the sheet tab names.

   Trouble? If only one page appears in the preview, the worksheets are not grouped. Click the Back button to exit Backstage view, and then repeat Steps 1 through 8.

9. Click the **Back** button to exit Backstage view without printing the worksheet group.
10. Go to the **Documentation** worksheet to ungroup the worksheets, and then go to the **Summary** worksheet.

In this session, you consolidated the data in Reveries Urban Centers Jackson workbook into a Summary worksheet so that Timothy can quickly see the collection totals for the rental income totals for each rental type. In the next session, you will help Timothy determine the annual totals for the other Reveries Urban Centers—Flint and Petosky.

REVIEW

Session 6.1 Quick Check

1. What is a worksheet group?
2. How do you select an adjacent worksheet group? How do you select a nonadjacent worksheet group? How do you deselect a worksheet group?
3. What formula would you enter in the Summary worksheet to reference cell C8 in the Quarter 2 worksheet?
4. What is the 3-D reference to cell E6 in the adjacent Summary 1, Summary 2, and Summary 3 worksheets?
5. Explain what the formula =AVERAGE(Sheet1:Sheet4!B1) calculates.
6. If you insert a new worksheet named Sheet5 after Sheet4, how would you change the formula =MIN(Sheet1:Sheet4!B1) to include Sheet5 in the calculation?
7. If you insert a new worksheet named Sheet5 before Sheet4, how would you change the formula =SUM(Sheet1:Sheet4!B1) to include Sheet5 in the calculation?
8. How do you apply the same page layout to all of the worksheets in a workbook at one time?

Session 6.2 Visual Overview:

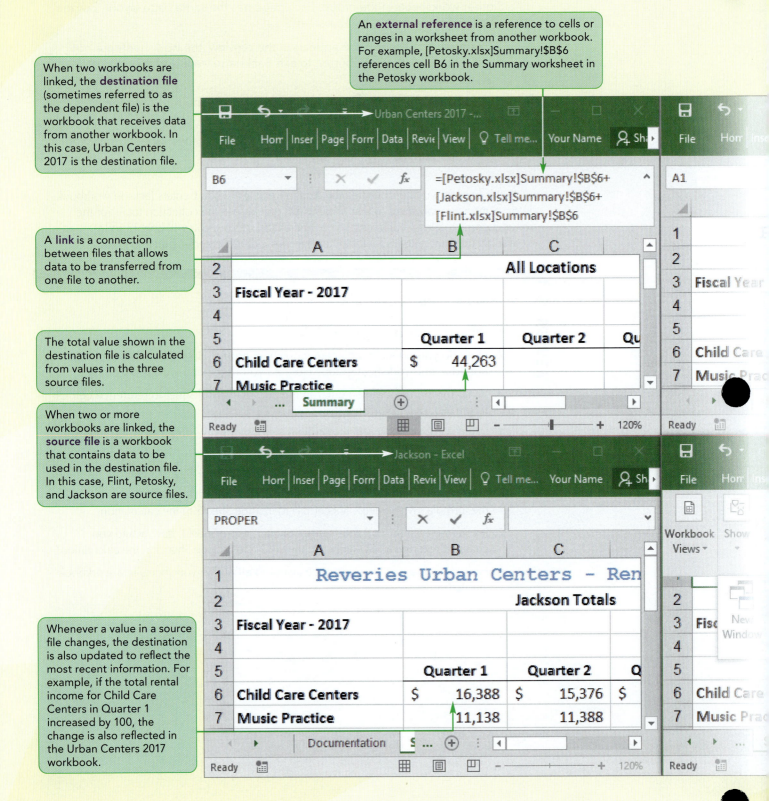

An **external reference** is a reference to cells or ranges in a worksheet from another workbook. For example, [Petosky.xlsx]Summary!$B$6 references cell B6 in the Summary worksheet in the Petosky workbook.

When two workbooks are linked, the **destination file** (sometimes referred to as the dependent file) is the workbook that receives data from another workbook. In this case, Urban Centers 2017 is the destination file.

A **link** is a connection between files that allows data to be transferred from one file to another.

The total value shown in the destination file is calculated from values in the three source files.

When two or more workbooks are linked, the **source file** is a workbook that contains data to be used in the destination file. In this case, Flint, Petosky, and Jackson are source files.

Whenever a value in a source file changes, the destination is also updated to reflect the most recent information. For example, if the total rental income for Child Care Centers in Quarter 1 increased by 100, the change is also reflected in the Urban Centers 2017 workbook.

Links and External References

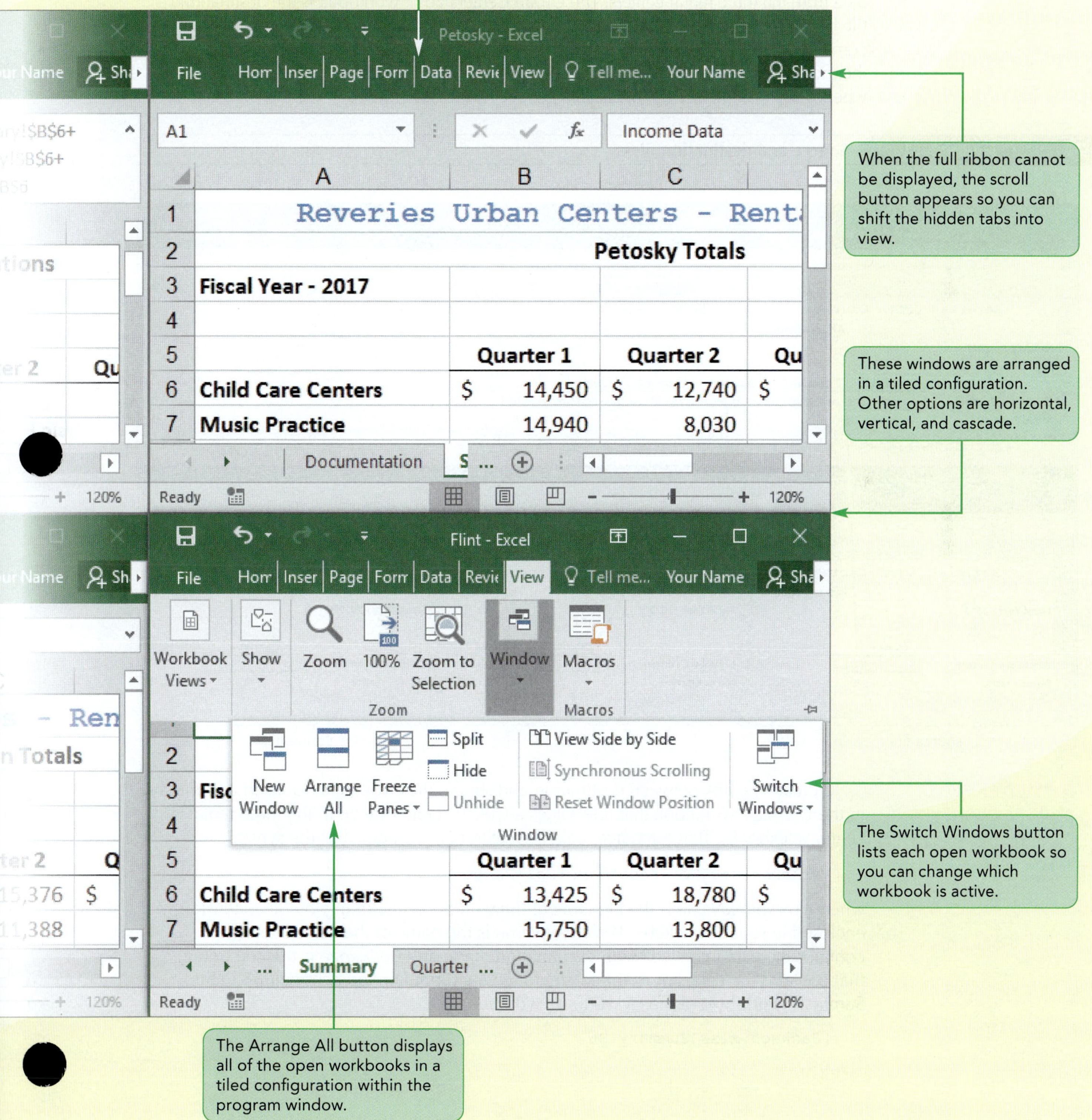
You can collapse the ribbon to make more space available for viewing the worksheet. This is helpful when you tile a workbook.
When the full ribbon cannot be displayed, the scroll button appears so you can shift the hidden tabs into view.
These windows are arranged in a tiled configuration. Other options are horizontal, vertical, and cascade.
The Switch Windows button lists each open workbook so you can change which workbook is active.
The Arrange All button displays all of the open workbooks in a tiled configuration within the program window.
Petosky - Excel
Reveries Urban Centers - Rent
Petosky Totals
Fiscal Year - 2017
Quarter 1
Quarter 2
Child Care Centers
Music Practice
Flint - Excel
New Window
Arrange All
Freeze Panes
Split
Hide
Unhide
View Side by Side
Synchronous Scrolling
Reset Window Position
Switch Windows
Window
Summary

Linking Workbooks

When creating formulas in a workbook, you can reference data in other workbooks. To do so, you must create a link between the workbooks. When two files are linked, the source file contains the data, and the destination file (sometimes called the dependent file) receives the data. For example, Timothy wants to create a company-wide workbook that summarizes the annual totals from each of the three Reveries Urban Centers. In this case, the Petosky, Flint, and Jackson workbooks are the source files because they contain the data from the three rental centers. The Urban Centers 2017 workbook is the destination file because it receives the data from the three rental center workbooks to calculate the company totals for 2017. The Urban Centers 2017 workbook will always have access to the most recent information in the rental center workbooks because it can be updated whenever any of the linked values change. See Figure 6-14.

Figure 6-14 Source and destination files

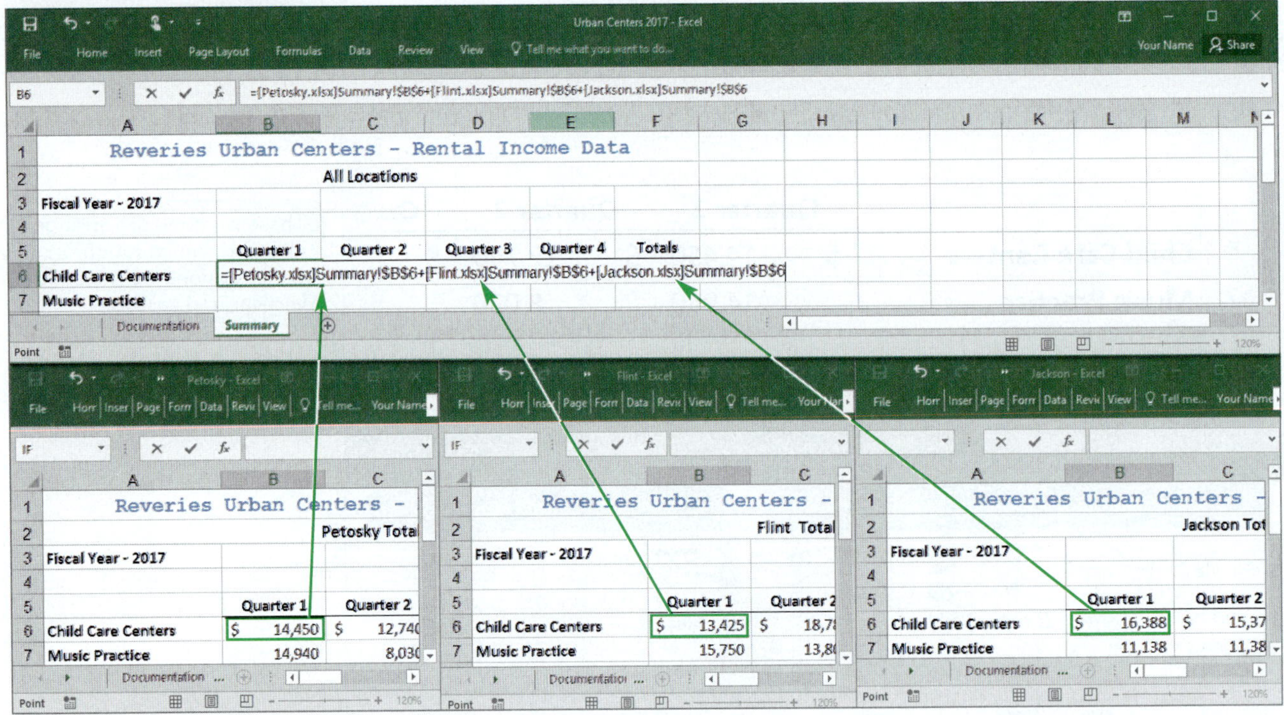

To create the link between destination and source files, you need to insert a formula in the UCTotals workbook that references a specific cell or range in the three rental center workbooks. That reference, called an external reference, has the syntax

```
[WorkbookName]WorksheetName!CellRange
```

where *WorkbookName* is the filename of the workbook (including the file extension) enclosed in square brackets; *WorksheetName* is the name of the worksheet that contains the data followed by an exclamation mark; and *CellRange* is the cell or range that contains the data. For example, the following formula references cell B6 in the Summary worksheet of the Jackson.xlsx workbook:

```
=[Jackson.xlsx]Summary!B6
```

TIP

When you click cells to include in formulas with external references, Excel enters all of the required punctuation, including quotation marks.

If the workbook name or the worksheet name contains one or more spaces, you must enclose the entire workbook name and worksheet name in single quotation marks. For example, the following formula references cell B6 in the Summary worksheet of the Flint 2017.xlsx workbook:

```
='[Flint 2017.xlsx]Summary'!B6
```

When the source and destination workbooks are stored in the same folder, you need to include only the workbook name in the external reference. However, when the source and destination workbooks are located in different folders, the workbook reference must include the file's complete location (also called the path). For example, if the destination file is stored in C:\Rental Income and the source file is stored in C:\Rental Income\Local Data, the complete reference in the destination file would be:

```
='C:\Rental Income\Local Data\[Flint.xlsx]Summary'!B6
```

The single quotation marks start at the beginning of the path and end immediately before the exclamation mark.

PROSKILLS

Decision Making: Understanding When to Link Workbooks

More than one person is usually involved in developing information that will be used in an organization's decision-making process. If each person has access to only part of the data, everyone's ability to see the whole picture and make good decisions is limited. Linking workbooks provides one way to pull together all of the data being compiled by different people or departments to support the decision-making process.

When deciding whether to link workbooks, consider the following questions:

- **Can separate workbooks have the same purpose and structure?** With linked workbooks, each workbook can focus on a different store, branch office, or department with the same products or expenditure types and reporting periods (such as weekly, monthly, and quarterly).
- **Is a large workbook too unwieldy to use?** A large workbook can be divided into smaller workbooks for each quarter, division, or product and then linked to provide the summary information.
- **Can information from different workbooks be summarized?** Linked workbooks provide a way to quickly and accurately consolidate information from multiple source workbooks, and the summary worksheet will always contain the most current information even when information is later updated.
- **Are source workbooks continually updated?** With linked workbooks, an outdated source workbook can be replaced and the destination workbook will then reflect the latest information.
- **Will the source workbooks be available to the destination workbook?** If the person who is working with the destination workbook cannot access the source workbooks, then the destination workbook cannot be updated.

If you can answer yes to these questions, then linked workbooks are the way to go. Creating linked workbooks can help you analyze data better, leading to better decision making. It also provides greater flexibility as data becomes more expansive and complex. However, keep in mind that workbooks with many links can take a long time to open and update.

Navigating Multiple Workbooks

When you create external reference formulas, you'll need to move between open workbooks. The Switch Windows button in the Window group on the View tab lists each open workbook so you can change which workbook is active. Another method is to click the Excel button on the taskbar and then click the thumbnail of the workbook you want to make active.

Timothy received workbooks from the Flint and Petosky managers that are similar to the one you helped prepare. These three rental income workbooks (named Petosky, Flint, and Jackson) contain the rental income for 2017. Timothy wants to create a company-wide workbook that summarizes the annual totals from each rental center workbook. You'll combine the three rental center workbooks into one rental center summary workbook. First you need to open the workbooks that you want to reference. Then you'll switch between them to make each Summary worksheet the active sheet in preparation for creating the external references.

To open the regional workbooks and switch between them:

1. If you took a break after the previous session, make sure the Jackson workbook is open and the Summary worksheet is active.
2. Open the **UCTotals** workbook located in the **Excel6 > Module** folder included with your Data Files, and then save the workbook as **Urban Centers 2017** in the location specified by your instructor.
3. In the Documentation worksheet of the Urban Centers 2017 workbook, enter your name and the date.
4. Open the **Petosky** workbook located in the **Excel6 > Module** folder included with your Data Files, and then go to the **Summary** worksheet.
5. Open the **Flint** workbook located in the **Excel6 > Module** folder included with your Data Files, and then go to the **Summary** worksheet. All three location workbooks have the same active sheet.
6. On the ribbon, click the **View** tab.
7. In the Window group, click the **Switch Windows** button. A menu lists the names of all the workbooks that are currently open.
8. Click **Urban Centers 2017** to make that the active workbook, and then go to the **Summary** worksheet. The Summary worksheet is the active sheet in each workbook.

Arranging Multiple Workbooks

Rather than continually switching between open workbooks, you can display all the open workbooks on your screen at the same time. This way, you can easily click among the open workbooks to create links as well as quickly compare the contents of worksheets in different workbooks. You can arrange workbooks in the following layouts:

- **Tiled**—divides the open workbooks evenly on the screen
- **Horizontal**—divides the open workbooks into horizontal bands
- **Vertical**—divides the open workbooks into vertical bands
- **Cascade**—layers the open workbooks on the screen

The layout you select will depend on the contents being displayed and your purpose.

REFERENCE

Arranging Workbooks

- On the View tab, in the Window group, click the Arrange All button.
- Select the layout in which you want to arrange the open workbooks.
- When arranging multiple workbooks, uncheck the Windows of active workbook option. When arranging multiple worksheets within one workbook, check this option.
- Click the OK button.

Currently, the four workbooks are open, but only one is visible. You'll make all the workbooks visible by displaying the workbooks in the tiled arrangement.

To tile the open workbooks:

1. On the ribbon, click the **View** tab.
2. In the Window group, click the **Arrange All** button. The Arrange Windows dialog box opens so you can select the layout arrangement you want.
3. Click the **Tiled** option button, if necessary. The Tiled option will arrange the four Reveries Urban Centers workbooks evenly on the screen.
4. Click the **OK** button. The four open workbooks appear in a tiled layout.
5. Click in the **Urban Centers 2017** workbook to make it the active workbook, if necessary. In the tiled layout, the active workbook contains the active cell.
6. In the Summary worksheet, click cell **B6** to make it the active cell.

   The ribbon appears in each window, taking up a lot of the workbook space. To see more of the worksheets, you will collapse the ribbon in each window to show only the ribbon tabs.

7. In each window, click the **Collapse the Ribbon** button in the lower-right corner of the ribbon (or press the **Ctrl+F1** keys). Only the ribbon tabs are visible in each window. If the ribbon includes more tabs than can be displayed, a ribbon scroll button appears to the right of the last visible tab, which you can click to display the other tabs. See Figure 6-15.

TIP

You can click the Windows of active workbook check box to tile the sheets in the current workbook on the screen.

Figure 6-15 **Four workbooks arranged in a tiled layout**

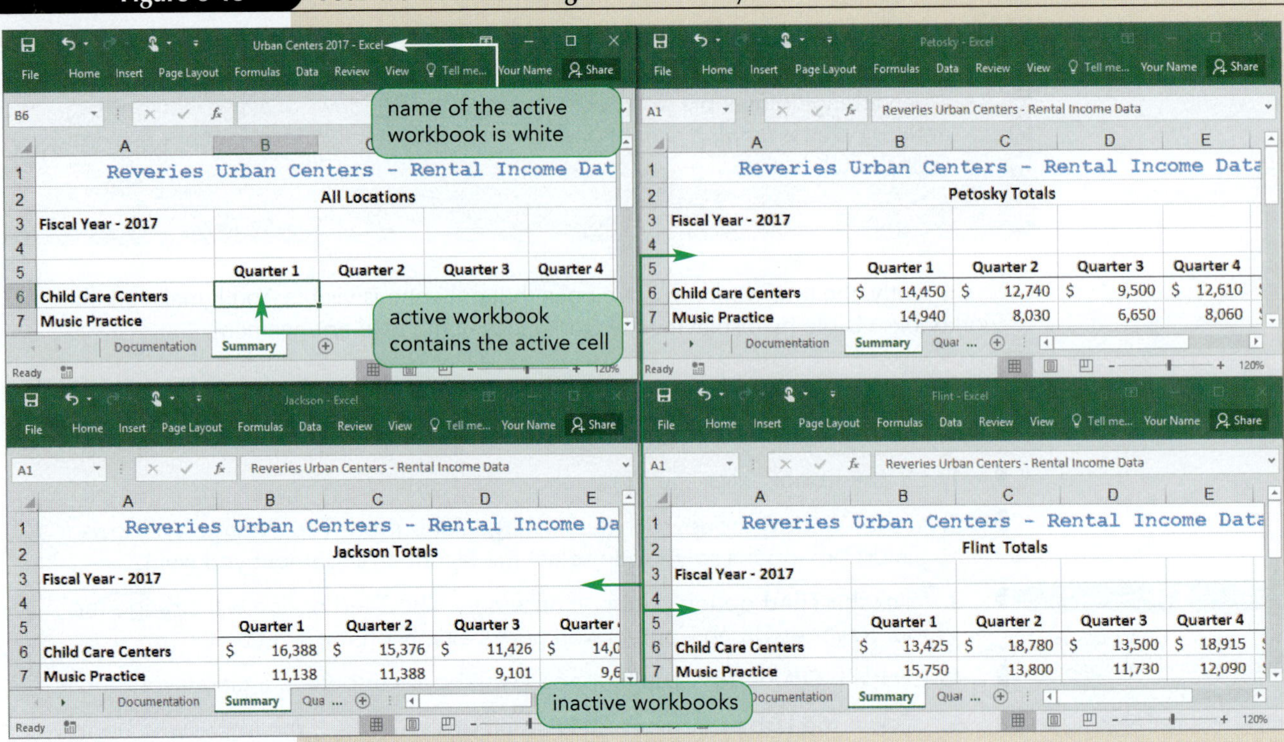
name of the active workbook is white
active workbook contains the active cell
inactive workbooks

Creating Formulas with External References

A formula can include a reference to another workbook (called an external reference), which creates a set of linked workbooks. The process for entering a formula with an external reference is the same as for entering any other formula using references within the same worksheet or workbook. You can enter the formulas by typing them or using the point-and-click method. In most situations, you will use the point-and-click method to switch between the source files and the destination files so that Excel enters the references to the workbook, worksheet, and cell using the correct syntax.

You need to enter the external reference formulas in the Urban Centers 2017 workbook to summarize the rental center totals into one workbook for Timothy. You'll start by creating the formula that adds the total rental income for Child Care Centers in Petosky, Flint, and Jackson for Quarter 1 of 2017. You cannot use the SUM function with 3-D references here because you are referencing multiple workbooks, and 3-D references can be used only to reference multiple worksheets in the same workbook.

To create the formula with external references to add the total rental income for Child Care Centers:

1. In the Urban Centers 2017 workbook, in the Summary worksheet, make sure cell **B6** is the active cell, and then type = to begin the formula.

As you create the formula, be sure to verify each external reference before going to the next step.

2. Click anywhere in the **Petosky** workbook to make the Petosky workbook active and place the formula in its formula bar, and then click cell **B6** in the Summary worksheet. The external reference to cell B6 in the Summary worksheet of the Petosky workbook—[Petosky.xlsx]Summary!$B$6—is added to the formula in the Urban Centers 2017 workbook. See Figure 6-16.

Figure 6-16 Formula with an external cell reference

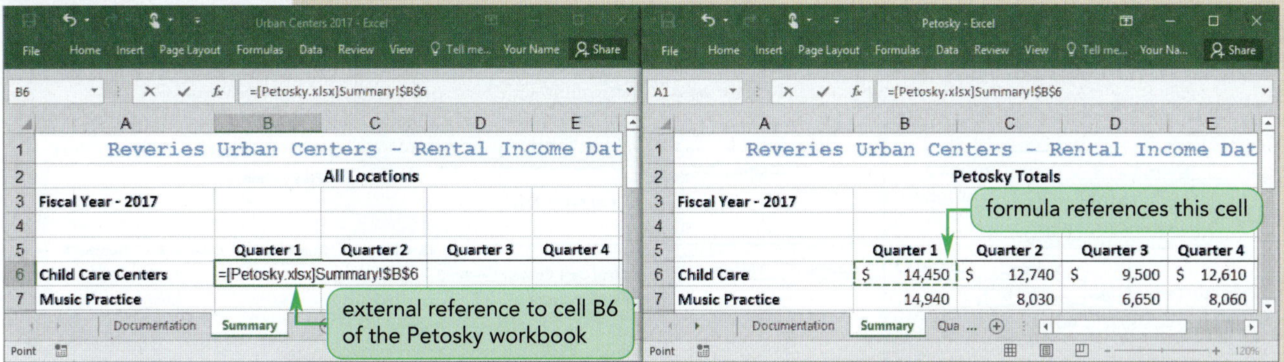

The reference created in a 3-D reference is an absolute cell reference, which does not change when the formula is copied. The formula remains in the formula bar of both the Urban Centers 2017 and Petosky workbooks until you make another workbook active. At that time, the formula will appear in the Urban Centers 2017 workbook and the active worksheet.

3. Type **+**. The Urban Centers 2017 workbook becomes active, and you can continue entering the formula. You need to create an external reference to the Flint workbook.
4. Click anywhere in the **Flint** workbook, click cell **B6** in the Summary worksheet, and then type **+**. The formula in the Urban Centers 2017 workbook includes the external reference to the cell that contains the total rental income for Child Care Centers in Flint during Quarter 1.
5. Click anywhere in the **Jackson** workbook, click cell **B6** in the Summary worksheet, and then press the **Enter** key. The formula with three external references is entered in the Summary worksheet in the Urban Centers 2017 workbook.
6. In the Urban Centers 2017 workbook, in the Summary worksheet, click cell **B6**. The complete formula is too long to appear in the formula bar of the tiled window. You will expand the formula bar so that it can display the full formula.
7. At the right edge of the formula bar, click the **Expand Formula Bar** button (or press the **Ctrl+Shift+U** keys). The complete formula is now visible in the formula bar, and the Collapse Formula Bar button appears at the right edge of the formula bar, which you can click to return the formula bar to a single line. The formula results in cell B6 show that the Child Care Centers had rental income of 44263 during Quarter 1 in the three rental centers—$14,450 in Petosky, $13,425 in Flint, and $16,388 in Jackson. See Figure 6-17.

Figure 6-17 Total rental income for Child Care Centers from Petosky, Flint, and Jackson in Quarter 1

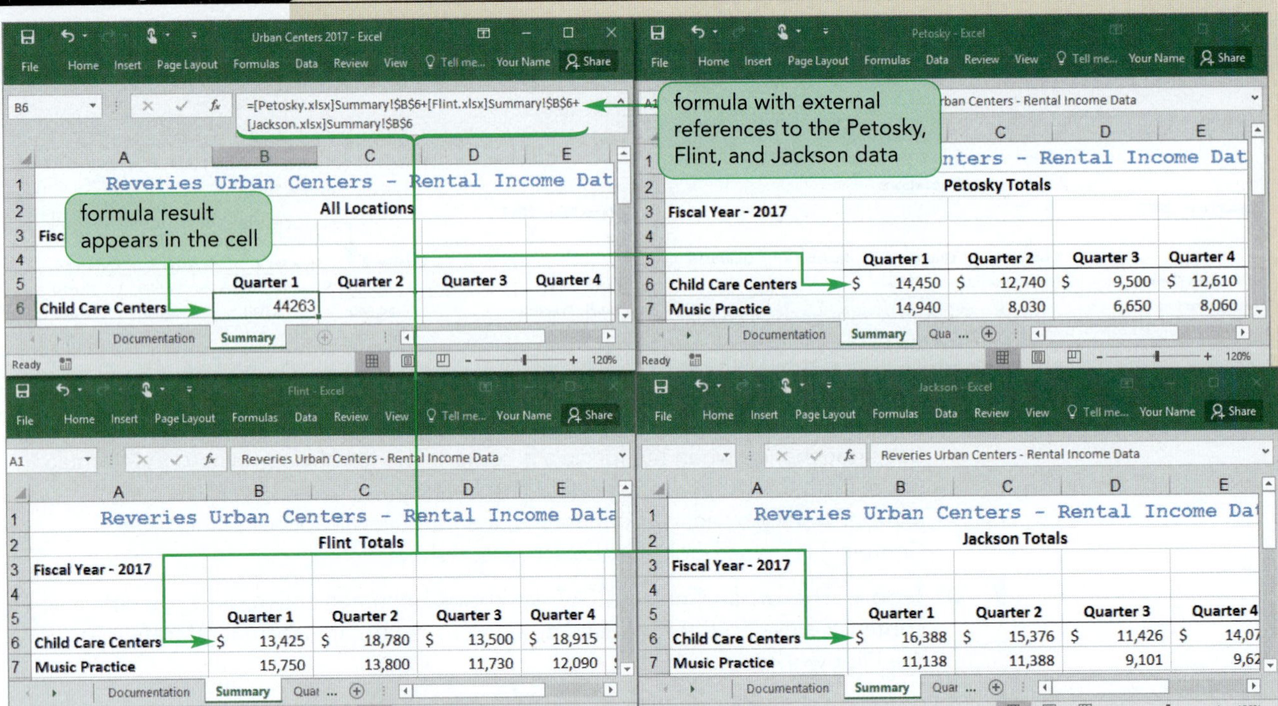

Trouble? If 44263 doesn't appear in cell B6 in the Summary worksheet in the Urban Centers 2017 workbook, you might have clicked an incorrect cell for an external reference in the formula. Repeat Steps 1 through 6 to correct the formula.

You'll use the same process to enter the external reference formula for cells C6, D6, and E6, which contain the total rental income for Child Care Centers in Quarter 2, Quarter 3, and Quarter 4, respectively. These formulas will calculate the total amounts from all three locations.

To create the remaining external reference formulas:

1. In the Urban Centers 2017 workbook, in the Summary worksheet, select cell **C6,** and then type **=** to begin the formula.
2. Click the **Petosky** workbook, click cell **C6** in the Summary worksheet, and then type **+**. The formula in the Urban Centers 2017 workbook includes the external reference to cell C6 in the Summary worksheet in the Petosky workbook.
3. Click the **Flint** workbook, click cell **C6** in the Summary worksheet, and then type **+**. The formula includes an external reference to cell C6 in the Summary worksheet in the Flint workbook.
4. Click the **Jackson** workbook, click cell **C6** in the Summary worksheet, and then press the **Enter** key. The external reference formula is complete.
5. In the Urban Centers 2017 workbook, in the Summary worksheet, click cell **C6**. Cell C6 displays 46896—the total rental income for Child Care Centers in Quarter 2 in Petosky, Flint, and Jackson, and the following formula appears in the formula bar: =[Petosky.xlsx]Summary!$C$6+[Flint.xlsx]Summary!$C$6 +[Jackson.xlsx]Summary!$C$6.

Next, you'll enter the external reference formulas in cells D6 and E6 to add the total rental income in Quarter 3 and Quarter 4.

6. Repeat Steps 1 through 4 to enter the formula from cell **D6** in the Summary worksheet in the Urban Centers 2017 workbook. The formula result displayed in cell D6 is 34426—the total rental income for Child Care Centers during Quarter 3 in Petosky, Flint, and Jackson.
7. Repeat Steps 1 through 4 to enter the formula from cell **E6** in the Summary worksheet in the Urban Centers 2017 workbook. The formula result displayed in cell E6 is 45601—the total rental income for Child Care Centers during Quarter 4 in Petosky, Flint, and Jackson.

You need to enter the remaining formulas for the other types of rental income. Rather than creating the rest of the external reference formulas manually, you can copy the formulas in row 6 and paste them in rows 7 through 11. The formulas created using the point-and-click method contain absolute references. Before you copy them to other cells, you need to change them to use mixed references because the rows in the formula need to change.

To edit the external reference formulas to use mixed references:

1. Maximize the Urban Centers 2017 workbook, click the **Ribbon Display Options** button in the title bar, and then click **Show Tabs and Commands** (or press the **Ctrl+F1** keys) to pin the ribbon to show both the tabs and the commands. The other workbooks are still open but are not visible.
2. At the right edge of the formula bar, click the **Collapse Formula Bar** button (or press the **Ctrl+Shift+U** keys) to reduce the formula bar to one line.
3. In the Summary worksheet, double-click cell **B6** to enter Edit mode and display the formula in the cell.
4. Click in the first absolute reference in the formula, and then press the **F4** key twice to change the absolute reference $B$6 to the mixed reference $B6.
5. Edit the other two absolute references in the formula to be mixed references with absolute column references and relative row references.
6. Press the **Enter** key, and then select cell **B6**. The formula is updated to include mixed references, but the formula results aren't affected. Cell B6 still displays 44263, which is correct. See Figure 6-18.

TIP

You can also create the mixed reference by deleting the $ symbol from the row references in the formula.

Figure 6-18 External reference formula with mixed references

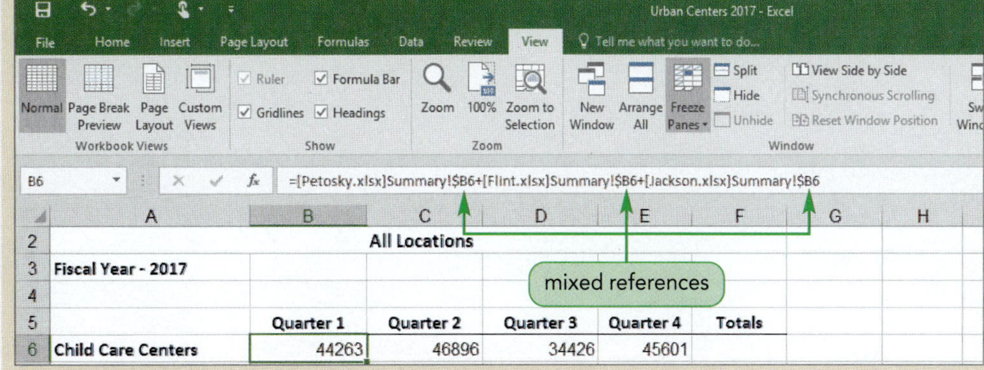

7. Edit the formulas in cells **C6**, **D6**, and **E6** to change the absolute references to the mixed references **$C6**, **$D6**, and **$E6**, respectively. The formulas are updated, but the cells in the range C6:E6 still correctly display 46896, 34426, and 45601, respectively.

With the formulas corrected to include mixed references, you can now copy the external reference formulas in the range B6:E6 to the other rows. Then you'll enter the SUM function to total the values in each row and column.

To copy and paste the external reference formulas:

1. Select the range **B6:E6**, and then drag the fill handle to select the range **B7:E11**. The formulas are copied to the range B7:E11, and the formula results appear in the cells. The Auto Fill Options button appears in the lower-right corner of the selected range, but you do not need to use it.

   Trouble? If all of the values in the range B7:E11 are the same as those in the range B6:E6, you didn't change the absolute cell references to mixed cell references in the formulas in the range B6:E6. Repeat Steps 3 through 7 in the previous set of steps, and then repeat Step 1 in this set of steps.

2. In cell **B12**, enter the SUM function to add the range **B6:B11**. The total rental income is 163016 in Quarter 1.
3. Copy the formula in cell **B12** to the range **C12:E12**. The total rental income is 152010 in Quarter 2, 144197 in Quarter 3, and 153921 in Quarter 4.
4. In cell **F6**, enter the SUM function to add the range B6:E6. The total rental income is 171186 for Child Care Centers at all rental centers in 2017.
5. Copy the formula in cell **F6** to the range **F7:F12**. The total for Music Practice is 132303, Medical Centers is 170087, Religious Centers is 20304, Miscellaneous is 44752, and Retail is 74512, with a grand total of 613144 for the year.
6. Format the nonadjacent range **B6:E6,F6:F11,** and **B12:F12** with the **Accounting** style and no decimal places.
7. Format the range **B7:E11** with the **Comma** style and no decimal places.
8. Format the range **B11:F11** with a bottom border, and then select cell **A1** to deselect the range. See Figure 6-19.

Figure 6-19 Completed summary of rental income data

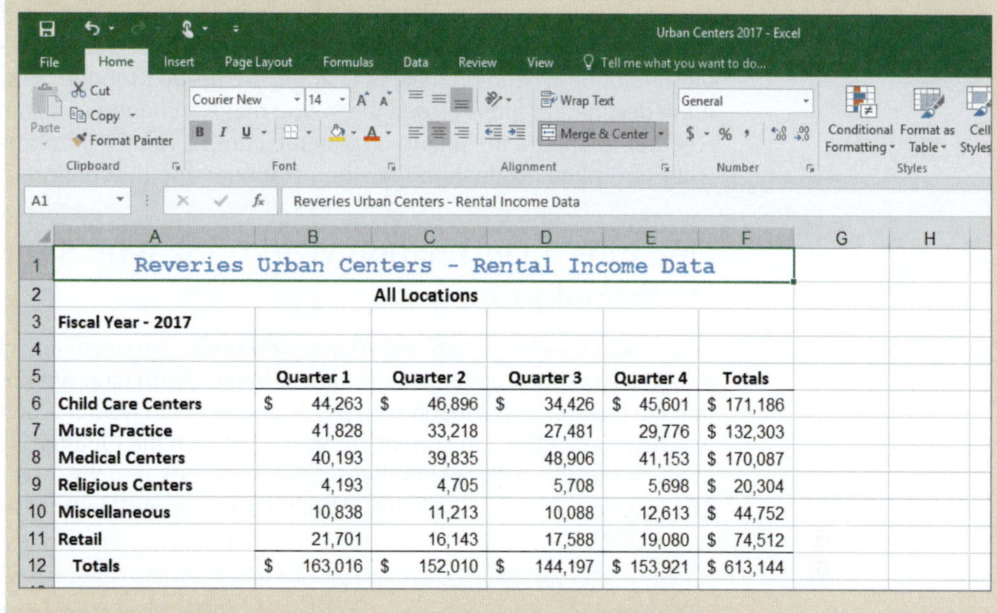

	A	B	C	D	E	F
1	Reveries Urban Centers - Rental Income Data					
2	All Locations					
3	Fiscal Year - 2017					
4						
5		Quarter 1	Quarter 2	Quarter 3	Quarter 4	Totals
6	Child Care Centers	$ 44,263	$ 46,896	$ 34,426	$ 45,601	$ 171,186
7	Music Practice	41,828	33,218	27,481	29,776	$ 132,303
8	Medical Centers	40,193	39,835	48,906	41,153	$ 170,087
9	Religious Centers	4,193	4,705	5,708	5,698	$ 20,304
10	Miscellaneous	10,838	11,213	10,088	12,613	$ 44,752
11	Retail	21,701	16,143	17,588	19,080	$ 74,512
12	Totals	$ 163,016	$ 152,010	$ 144,197	$ 153,921	$ 613,144

Timothy is pleased; the summary results match his expectations.

INSIGHT

Managing Linked Workbooks

As you work with a linked workbook, you might need to replace a source file or change where you stored the source and destination files. However, replacing or moving a file can affect the linked workbook. Keep in mind the following guidelines to manage your linked workbooks:

- If you rename a source file, the destination workbook won't be able to find it. A dialog box opens, indicating "This workbook contains one or more links that cannot be updated." Click the Continue button to open the workbook with the most recent values, or click the Change Source button in the Edit Links dialog box to specify the new name of that linked source file.
- If you move a source file to a different folder, the link breaks between the destination and source files. Click the Change Source button in the Edit Links dialog box to specify the new location of the linked workbook.
- If you receive a replacement source file, you can swap the original source file with the replacement file. No additional changes are needed.
- If you receive a destination workbook but the source files are not included, Excel will not be able to find the source files, and a dialog box opens with the message "This workbook contains one or more links that cannot be updated." Click the Continue button to open the workbook with the most recent values, or click the Break Link button in the Edit Links dialog box to replace the external references with the existing values.
- If you change the name of a destination file, you can open that renamed version destination file without affecting the source files or the original destination file.

Updating Linked Workbooks

When workbooks are linked, it is important that the data in the destination file accurately reflects the contents of the source file. When data in a source file changes, you want the destination file to reflect those changes. If both the source and destination files are open when you make a change, the destination file is updated automatically. If the destination file is closed when you make a change in a source file, you choose whether to update the link to display the current values or continue to display the older values from the destination file when you open the destination file.

Updating a Destination Workbook with Source Workbooks Open

When both the destination and source workbooks are open, any changes you make in a source workbook automatically appear in the destination workbook. Timothy tells you that the Jackson rental income for Medical Centers in March is actually $100 less than was recorded. After you correct the March value in the Quarter 1 worksheet, the amount in the Summary worksheet of the Jackson workbook and the total in the Urban Centers 2017 workbook will also change if both the source and destination files are open.

To update the source workbook with the destination file open:

1. Maximize the **Petosky**, **Flint**, and **Jackson** workbooks, and show the ribbon tabs and commands in each workbook.
2. Make the **Jackson** workbook active, and then go to the **Quarter 1** worksheet. You'll update the rental income for Medical Centers in March.
3. In cell **D8**, enter 4925. Jackson's rental income is updated, and the total rental income for March changes to $15,651.
4. Go to the **Summary** worksheet in the Jackson workbook, and then verify that the total rental income for Medical Centers in Quarter 1 (cell B8) is 13,513, the total rental income for Medical Centers in 2017 (cell F8) is $56,452, the total rental income in Quarter 1 (cell B12) is $51,766, and the total rental income in 2017 (cell F12) is $199,689. See Figure 6-20.

Figure 6-20 Summary worksheet in the Jackson workbook with revised Quarter 1 data

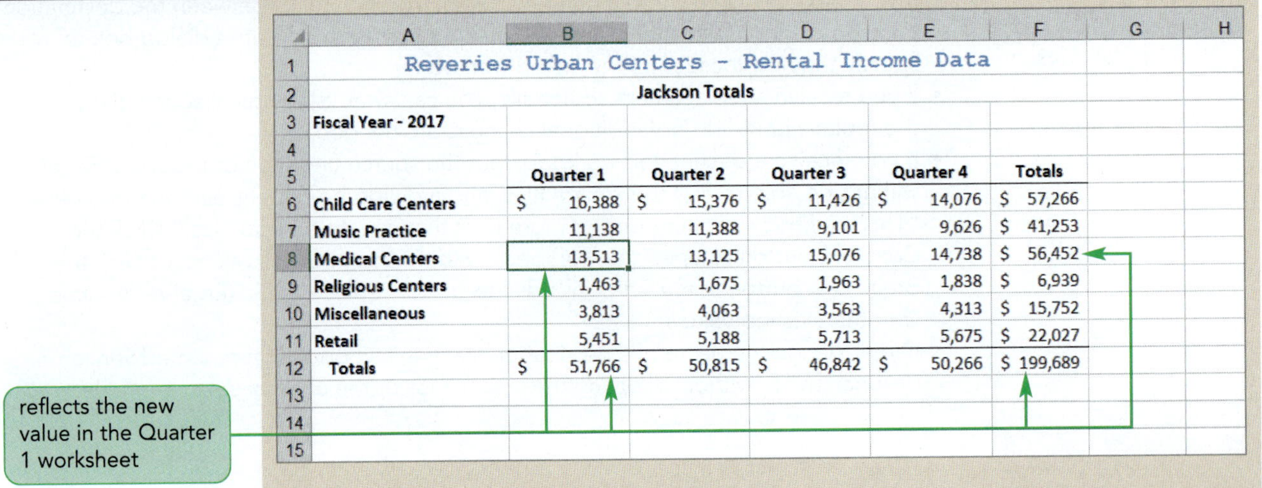

	A	B	C	D	E	F	G	H
1	Reveries Urban Centers - Rental Income Data							
2			Jackson Totals					
3	Fiscal Year - 2017							
4								
5		Quarter 1	Quarter 2	Quarter 3	Quarter 4	Totals		
6	Child Care Centers	$ 16,388	$ 15,376	$ 11,426	$ 14,076	$ 57,266		
7	Music Practice	11,138	11,388	9,101	9,626	$ 41,253		
8	Medical Centers	13,513	13,125	15,076	14,738	$ 56,452		
9	Religious Centers	1,463	1,675	1,963	1,838	$ 6,939		
10	Miscellaneous	3,813	4,063	3,563	4,313	$ 15,752		
11	Retail	5,451	5,188	5,713	5,675	$ 22,027		
12	Totals	$ 51,766	$ 50,815	$ 46,842	$ 50,266	$ 199,689		
13								
14								
15								

reflects the new value in the Quarter 1 worksheet

5. Make the **Urban Centers 2017** workbook active, and then verify in the Summary worksheet that the rental income for Medical Centers in Quarter 1 (cell B8) is 40,093, the total rental income for Medical centers in 2017 (cell F8) is $169,987, the total rental income in Quarter 1 (cell B12) is $162,916, and the total rental income in 2017 (cell F12) is $613,044, reflecting the new value you entered in the Jackson workbook. Because both the destination and source files are open, Excel updated the destination file automatically. See Figure 6-21.

Figure 6-21 **Summary worksheet in the Urban Centers 2017 workbook with the revised Quarter 1 data**

	A	B	C	D	E	F	G	H
1	Reveries Urban Centers - Rental Income Data							
2	All Locations							
3	Fiscal Year - 2017							
4								
5		Quarter 1	Quarter 2	Quarter 3	Quarter 4	Totals		
6	Child Care Centers	$ 44,263	$ 46,896	$ 34,426	$ 45,601	$ 171,186		
7	Music Practice	41,828	33,218	27,481	29,776	$ 132,303		
8	Medical Centers	40,093	39,835	48,906	41,153	$ 169,987		
9	Religious Centers	4,193	4,705	5,708	5,698	$ 20,304		
10	Miscellaneous	10,838	11,213	10,088	12,613	$ 44,752		
11	Retail	21,701	16,143	17,588	19,080	$ 74,512		
12	Totals	$ 162,916	$ 152,010	$ 144,197	$ 153,921	$ 613,044		
13								
14								
15								

reflects the new value in the Jackson worksheet

6. Save the Jackson and Urban Centers 2017 workbooks.

Updating a Destination Workbook with Source Workbooks Closed

When you save a workbook that contains external reference formulas, such as the Urban Centers 2017 workbook, Excel stores the most recent results of those formulas in the destination file. Source files, such as the Petosky, Flint, and Jackson workbooks, are often updated while the destination file is closed. In that case, the values in the destination file are not updated at the same time the source files are updated. The next time you open the destination file, the cells containing external reference formulas still display the old values. Therefore, some of the values in the edited source workbooks are different from the values in the destination workbook.

To update the destination workbook with the current data, you must specify that you want the update to occur. As part of the Excel security system that attempts to protect against malicious software, links to other workbooks are not updated without your permission. When you open a workbook with external reference formulas (the destination file), a dialog box appears, notifying you that the workbook contains links to an external source that could be unsafe. You then can choose to update the content, which allows the external reference formulas to function and updates the links in the destination workbook, or you can choose not to update the links, which lets you continue working with the data you have. The old values in the destination workbook are displayed and the links to the source files have an unknown status.

Timothy realizes that the Jackson workbook needs a second correction. In Quarter 4, the total rental income for Retail in December was $1,925 not $1,875 as currently entered in the Jackson workbook. He asks you to increase the rental income for Retail in December by $50. As a result, the totals in the Summary worksheet in the Jackson workbook and the rental income in the Urban Centers 2017 workbook will both increase by $50. You'll edit the source file, the Jackson workbook, while the destination file is closed.

To update the source workbook with the destination file closed:

1. Close the Petosky, Flint, and Urban Centers 2017 workbooks. The Jackson workbook remains open.
2. In the Jackson workbook, go to the **Quarter 4** worksheet.
3. In cell **D11**, enter 1,925. The rental income from Retail in Quarter 4 increases to $5,725.
4. Go to the **Summary** worksheet. The rental income from Retail for Quarter 4 (cell E11) is 5,725, the rental income from Retail for 2017 (cell F11) is $22,077, the total rental income for Quarter 4 (cell E12) is $50,316, and the total rental income in 2017 (cell F12) is $199,739. See Figure 6-22.

Figure 6-22 Revised Retail rental income for Quarter 4 in the Jackson workbook

	A	B	C	D	E	F	G	H
1	Reveries Urban Centers - Rental Income Data							
2			Jackson Totals					
3	Fiscal Year - 2017							
4								
5		Quarter 1	Quarter 2	Quarter 3	Quarter 4	Totals		
6	Child Care Centers	$ 16,388	$ 15,376	$ 11,426	$ 14,076	$ 57,266		
7	Music Practice	11,138	11,388	9,101	9,626	$ 41,253		
8	Medical Centers	13,513	13,125	15,076	14,738	$ 56,452		
9	Religious Centers	1,463	1,675	1,963	1,838	$ 6,939		
10	Miscellaneous	3,813	4,063	3,563	4,313	$ 15,752		
11	Retail	5,451	5,188	5,713	5,725	$ 22,077		
12	Totals	$ 51,766	$ 50,815	$ 46,842	$ 50,316	$ 199,739		
13								
14								
15								

reflects changes made to Retail rental income in Quarter 4

5. Save the Jackson workbook, and then close it.

Now you'll open the destination file (the Urban Centers 2017 workbook). The rental income from the source workbooks won't be updated until you specify that it should. When the destination file is open and the source files are closed, the complete file path is included as part of the external reference formula that appears in the formula bar.

To open and update the destination workbook:

1. Open the **Urban Centers 2017** workbook, and then go to the **Summary** worksheet, if necessary. The value in cell E11 has *not* changed; it is still 19,080. A dialog box appears, indicating that the workbook contains links to one or more external sources that could be unsafe. See Figure 6-23.

Figure 6-23 Dialog box warning of possible unsafe links

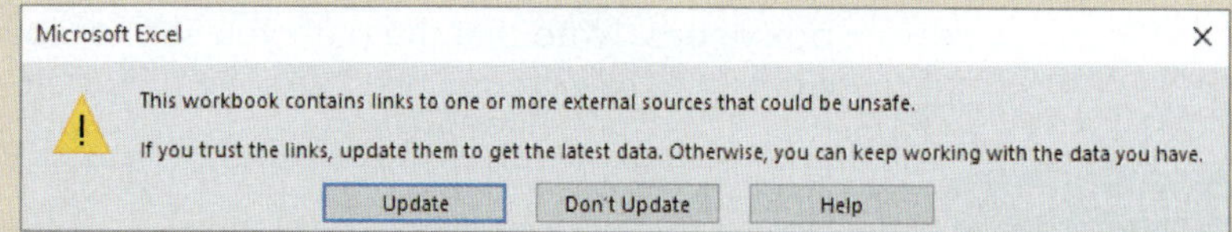

   Trouble? If the Message Bar appears below the ribbon with "SECURITY WARNING Automatic update of links has been disabled," click the Enable Content button. The values in the destination workbook are updated. Continue with Step 3.

   You want the current values in the source files to appear in the destination workbook.

2. In the dialog box, click the **Update** button. The values in the destination file are updated. The total rental income from Retail in Quarter 4, shown in cell E11 of the Urban Centers 2017 workbook, increased to 19,130, the rental income from Retail for 2017 (cell F11) is $74,562, the total Quarter 4 rental income (cell E12) is $153,971, and the grand total of all rental income in 2017 (cell F12) increased to $613,094.
3. Click cell **E11**, and then look at the complete file path for each external reference in the formula. The full path appears because the source workbooks are closed. Note that the path you see will match the location where you save your workbooks.
4. Save the workbook.

Managing Links

When workbooks are linked, the Edit Links dialog box provides ways to manage the links. You can review the status of the links and update the data in the files. You can repair **broken links**, which are references to files that have been moved since the link was created. Broken links appear in the dialog box as having an unknown status. You can also open the source file and break the links, which converts all external reference formulas to their most recent values.

After the fiscal year audit is completed and the source workbooks are final, Timothy will archive the summary workbook and move the files to an off-site storage location as part of his year-end backup process. You will save a copy of the Urban Centers 2017 workbook and then break the links to the source files in the copy.

To save a copy of the Urban Centers 2017 workbook and open the Edit Links dialog box:

1. Save the Urban Centers 2017 workbook as **Urban Centers Audited 2018** in the location specified by your instructor. The Urban Centers 2017 workbook closes, and the Urban Centers Audited 2018 workbook remains open.
2. On the ribbon, click the **Data** tab.
3. In the Connections group, click the **Edit Links** button. The Edit Links dialog box opens. Note that the path you see for source files will match the location where you save your workbooks. See Figure 6-24.

Figure 6-24 Edit Links dialog box

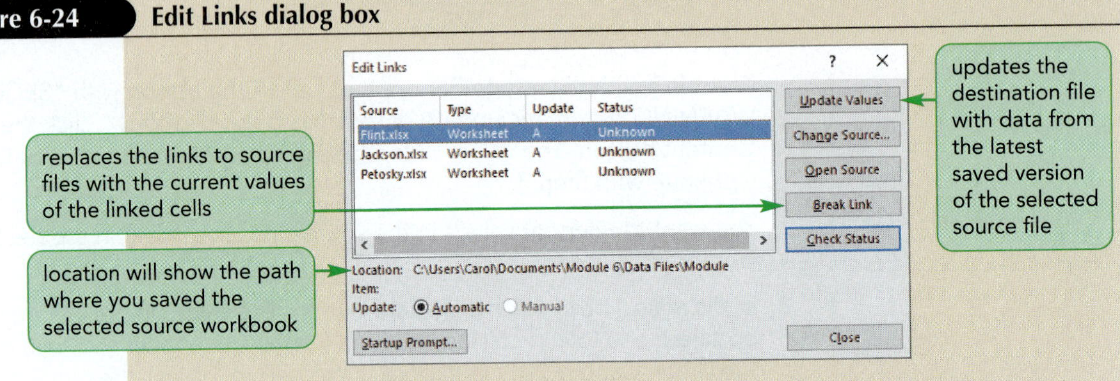

The Edit Links dialog box lists all of the files to which the destination workbook is linked so that you can update, change, open, or remove the links. You can see that the destination workbook—Urban Centers Audited 2018—has links to the Flint, Jackson, and Petosky workbooks. The dialog box shows the following information about each link:

- **Source**—indicates the file to which the link points. The Urban Centers Audited 2018 workbook contains three links pointing to the Flint.xlsx, Jackson.xlsx, and Petosky.xlsx workbooks.
- **Type**—identifies the type of each source file. In this case, the type is an Excel worksheet, but it could also be a Word document, a PowerPoint presentation, or some other type of file.
- **Update**—specifies the way values are updated from the source file. The letter *A* indicates the link is updated automatically when you open the workbook or when both the source and destination files are open simultaneously. The letter *M* indicates the link must be updated manually by the user, which is useful when you want to see the older data values before updating to the new data. To manually update the link and see the new data values, click the Update Values button.
- **Status**—shows whether Excel successfully accessed the link and updated the values from the source document (status is OK), or Excel has not attempted to update the links in this session (status is Unknown). The status of the three links in the Urban Centers Audited 2018 workbook is Unknown.

Timothy wants you to break the links so that the Urban Centers Audited 2018 workbook contains only the updated values (and is no longer affected by changes in the source files). Then he wants you to save the Urban Centers Audited 2018 workbook for him to archive. This allows Timothy to store a "snapshot" of the data at the end of the fiscal year.

To convert all external reference formulas to their current values:

1. In the Edit Links dialog box, click the **Break Link** button. A dialog box opens, alerting you that breaking links in the workbook permanently converts formulas and external references to their existing values.
2. Click the **Break Links** button. No links appear in the Edit Links dialog box.
3. Click the **Close** button. The Urban Centers Audited 2018 workbook now contains values instead of formulas with external references.
4. Select cell **B6**. The value $44,263 appears in the cell and the formula bar; the link (the external reference formula) was replaced with the data value. All of the cells in the range B6:E11 contain values rather than external reference formulas.
5. Save the Urban Centers Audited 2018 workbook, and then close it. The Urban Centers 2017 workbook contains external reference formulas, and the Urban Centers Audited 2018 workbook contains current values.

TIP

You cannot undo the break link action. To restore the links, you must reenter the external reference formulas.

In this session, you worked with multiple worksheets and workbooks, summarizing data and linking workbooks. This ensures that the data in the summary workbook is accurate and remains updated with the latest data in the source files. In the next session, you will create templates and hyperlinks.

REVIEW

Session 6.2 Quick Check

1. What is the external reference to the range B6:F6 in the Grades worksheet in the Grade Book workbook located in the Course folder on drive D?
2. What is a source file?
3. What is a destination file?
4. What are the layouts that you can use to arrange multiple workbooks?
5. How are linked workbooks updated when both the destination and source files are open?
6. How are linked workbooks updated when the source file is changed and the destination file is closed?
7. How would you determine what workbooks a destination file is linked to?
8. What happens to an external reference formula in a cell after you break the links in the worksheet?

Session 6.3 Visual Overview:

This Weekly Time Sheet workbook was created from one of the templates available from Office.com. Microsoft provides many templates that you can download.

A template is a workbook with labels, formats, and formulas already built into it with data removed. In other words, a template includes everything but the variable data.

A template can use any Excel feature, including formatting, formulas, and charts. The template used to create this workbook includes labels, formatting, and formulas.

Variable data is entered in the workbook created from the template. In this workbook, employee data was entered to fill out the weekly time record.

The formulas to calculate the total hours worked and total pay were included in the template.

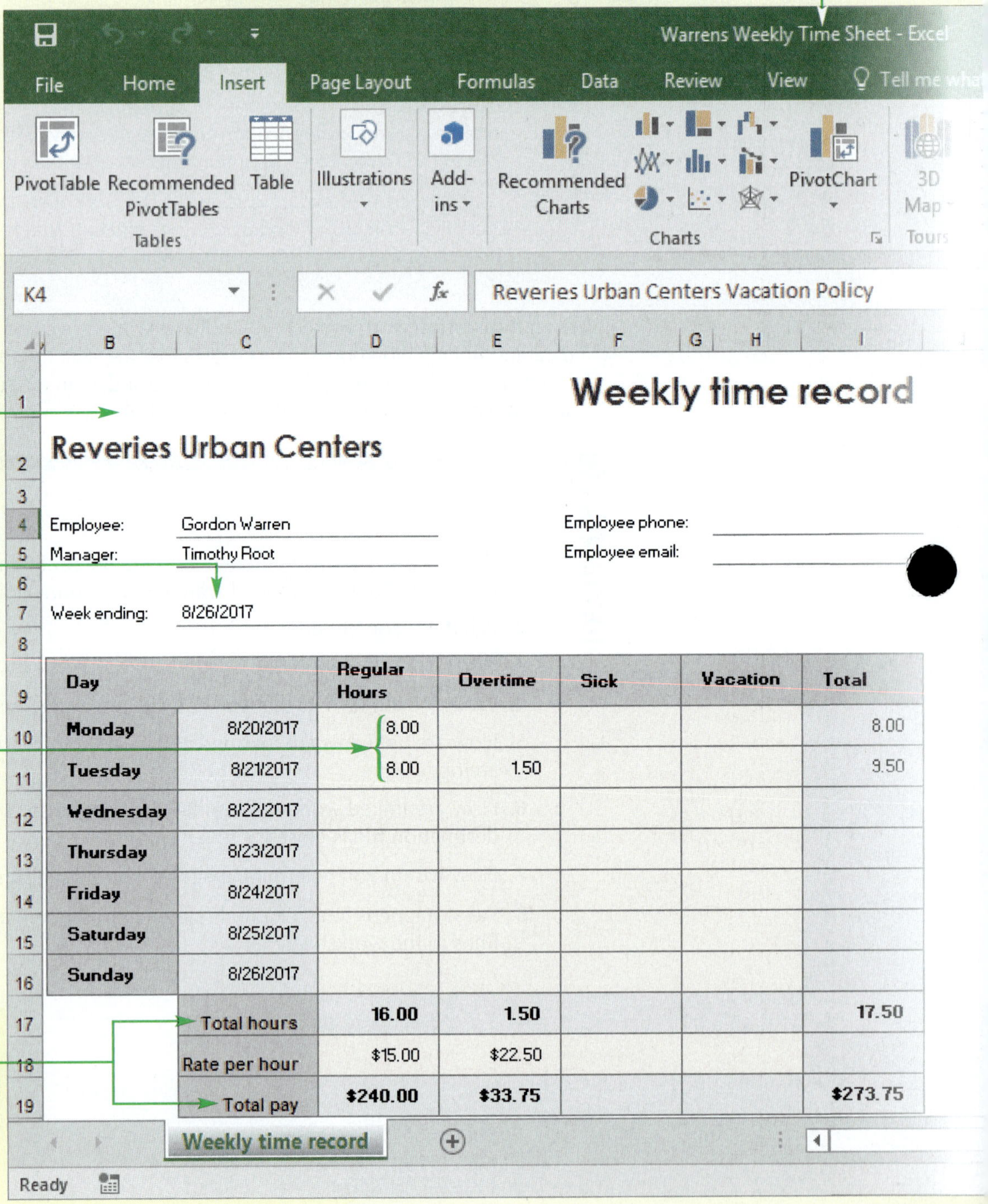

Day		Regular Hours	Overtime	Sick	Vacation	Total
Monday	8/20/2017	8.00				8.00
Tuesday	8/21/2017	8.00	1.50			9.50
Wednesday	8/22/2017					
Thursday	8/23/2017					
Friday	8/24/2017					
Saturday	8/25/2017					
Sunday	8/26/2017					
	Total hours	16.00	1.50			17.50
	Rate per hour	$15.00	$22.50			
	Total pay	$240.00	$33.75			$273.75

Templates and Hyperlinks

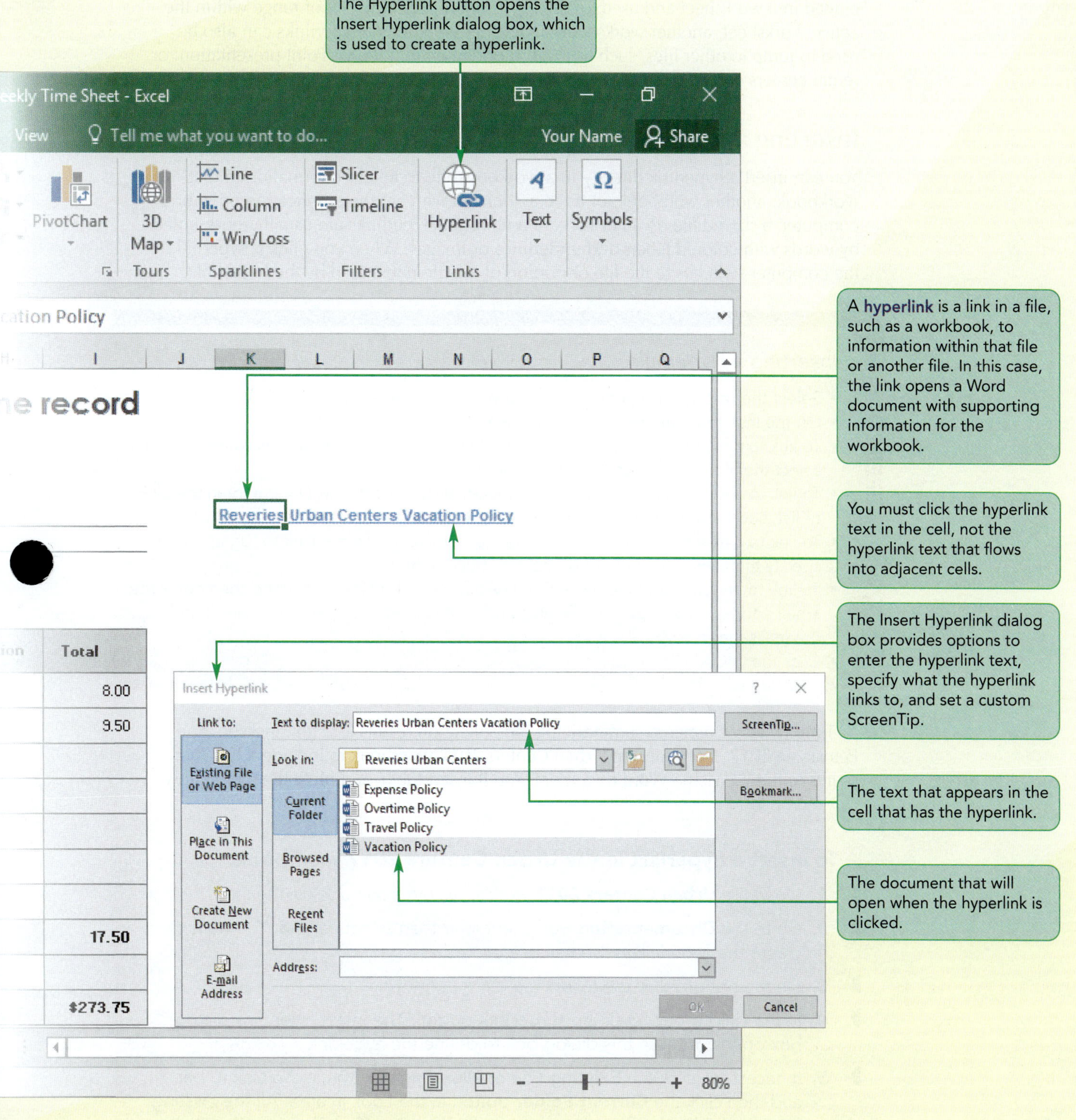

Creating a Hyperlink

A hyperlink is a link in a file, such as a workbook, to information within that file or another file. Although hyperlinks are most often found on webpages, they can also be placed in a worksheet and used to quickly jump to a specific cell or range within the active worksheet, another worksheet, or another workbook. Hyperlinks can also be used to jump to other files, such as a Word document or a PowerPoint presentation, or rental centers on the web.

Inserting a Hyperlink

You can insert a hyperlink directly in a workbook file to link to information in that workbook, another workbook, or a file associated with another application on your computer, a shared file on a network, or a website. Hyperlinks are usually represented by words with colored letters and underlines or images. When you click a hyperlink, the computer switches to the file or portion of the file referenced by the hyperlink.

REFERENCE

Inserting a Hyperlink

- Select the text, graphic, or cell in which you want to insert the hyperlink.
- On the Insert tab, in the Links group, click the Hyperlink button.
- To link to a file or webpage, click Existing File or Web Page in the Link to list, and then select the file or webpage from the Look in box.
- To link to a location in the current workbook, click Place in This Document in the Link to list, and then select the worksheet, cell, or range in the current workbook.
- To link to a new document, click Create New Document in the Link to list, and then specify the filename and path of the new document.
- To link to an email address, click E-mail Address in the Link to list, and then enter the email address of the recipient (such as name@example.com) and a subject line for the message.
- Click the OK button.

Timothy wrote a memo summarizing the collection results for Flint, Jackson, and Petosky in 2017. He wants the Urban Centers 2017 workbook to include a link that points to the UCMemo Word document. You'll insert the hyperlink to the memo now.

To insert a hyperlink in the Urban Centers 2017 workbook:

1. Open the **Urban Centers 2017** workbook, but don't update the links.
2. Go to the **Documentation** worksheet, and then select cell **A8**. You want to create the hyperlink in this cell.
3. On the ribbon, click the **Insert** tab.
4. In the Links group, click the **Hyperlink** button. The Insert Hyperlink dialog box opens. You use this dialog box to define the hyperlink.
5. If necessary, click the **Existing File or Web Page** button in the Link to bar, and then click the **Current Folder** button in the Look in area. All the existing files and folders in the current folder are displayed. See Figure 6-25, which shows the Excel6 > Module folder included with your Data Files.

Figure 6-25 Insert Hyperlink dialog box

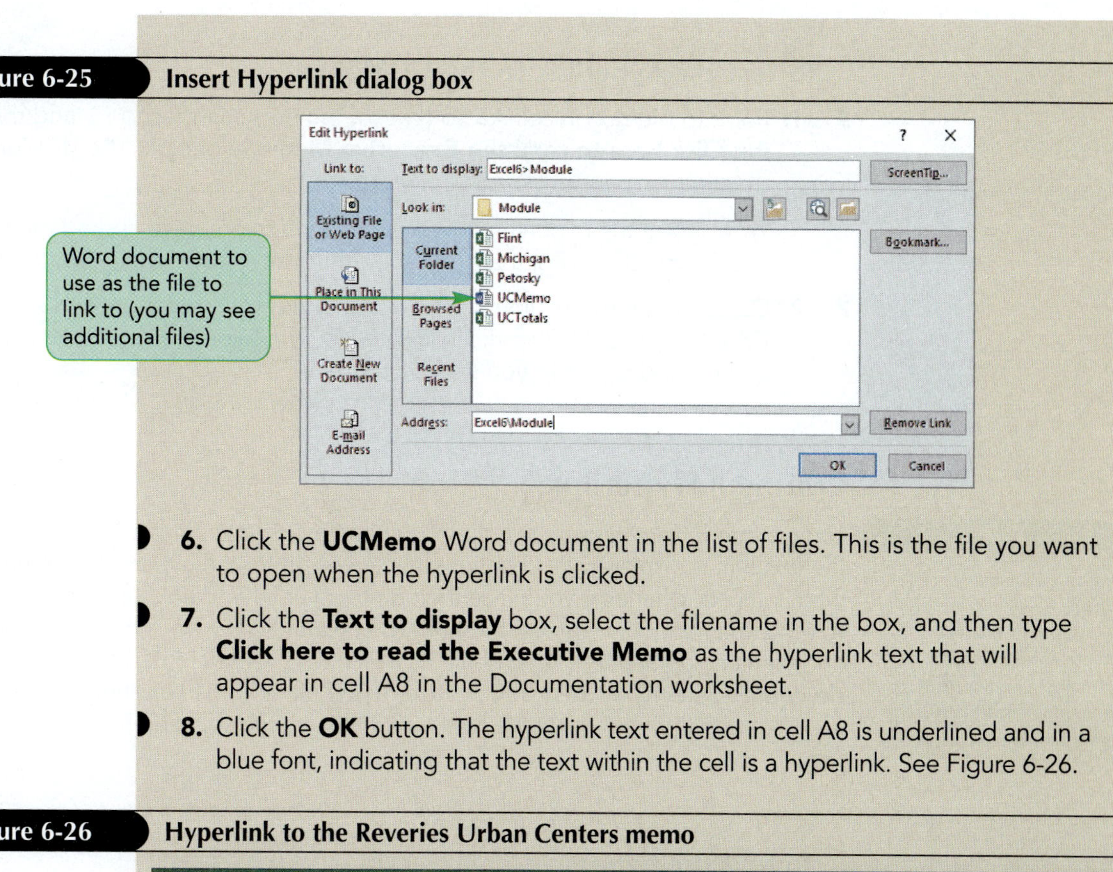

6. Click the **UCMemo** Word document in the list of files. This is the file you want to open when the hyperlink is clicked.
7. Click the **Text to display** box, select the filename in the box, and then type **Click here to read the Executive Memo** as the hyperlink text that will appear in cell A8 in the Documentation worksheet.
8. Click the **OK** button. The hyperlink text entered in cell A8 is underlined and in a blue font, indicating that the text within the cell is a hyperlink. See Figure 6-26.

Figure 6-26 Hyperlink to the Reveries Urban Centers memo

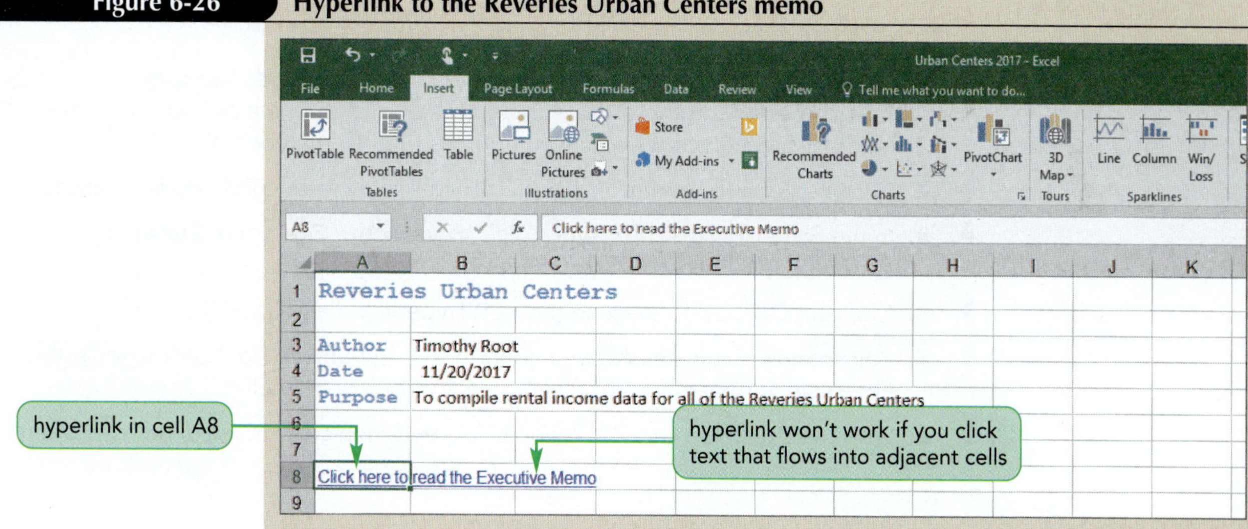

You will test the hyperlink that you just created to ensure it works correctly. To use a hyperlink in a worksheet, you must click the text inside the cell that contains the link. If you click white space in the cell or any text that flows into an adjacent cell, the hyperlink does not work.

To test the hyperlink to the UCMemo:

1. Point to the text in cell **A8** so that the pointer changes to 👆, and then click the **Click here to read the Executive Memo** hyperlink. The UCMemo document opens in Word.

   Trouble? If the hyperlink doesn't work, you might have clicked the text that overflows cell A8. Point to the text within cell A8, and then click the hyperlink.

2. Close the Word document and Word. The Documentation worksheet in the Urban Centers 2017 workbook is active. The hyperlink in cell A8 changed color to indicate that you used the link.

Editing a Hyperlink

TIP

You can right-click a hyperlink cell and then click Clear Contents to delete a hyperlink or click Remove Hyperlink to delete the hyperlink but keep the text.

You can modify an existing hyperlink by changing its target file or webpage, modifying the text that is displayed, or changing the ScreenTip for the hyperlink. ScreenTips, which appear whenever you place the pointer over a hyperlink, provide additional information about the target of the link. The default ScreenTip is the folder location and filename of the file you will link to, which isn't very helpful. You can insert a more descriptive ScreenTip when you create a hyperlink or edit an existing hyperlink.

Timothy wants you to edit the hyperlink to the memo so that it has a more descriptive ScreenTip.

To edit the hyperlink:

1. In the Documentation worksheet, right-click cell **A8**, and then click **Edit Hyperlink** on the shortcut menu. The Edit Hyperlink dialog box opens; it has the same layout and information as the Insert Hyperlink dialog box.
2. Click the **ScreenTip** button. The Set Hyperlink ScreenTip dialog box opens.
3. In the ScreenTip text box, type **Click to view the Executive Summary for 2017**, and then click the **OK** button.
4. Click the **OK** button to close the Edit Hyperlink dialog box.
5. Point to the text in cell **A8** and confirm that the ScreenTip "Click to view the Executive Summary for 2017" appears just below the cell.
6. Save the Urban Centers 2017 workbook, and then close it. Excel remains open.

Using Templates

If you want to create a new workbook that has the same format as an existing workbook, you could save the existing workbook with a new name and replace the values with new data or blank cells. The potential drawback to this method is that you might forget to rename the original file and overwrite data you intended to keep. A better method is to create a template workbook that includes all the text (row and column labels), formatting, and formulas but does not contain any data. The template workbook is a model from which you create new workbooks. When you create a new workbook from a template, an unnamed copy of the template opens. You can then enter data as well as modify the existing content or structure as needed. Any changes or additions you make to the new workbook do not affect the template file; the next time you create a workbook based on the template, the original text, formatting, and formulas will be present.

Teamwork: Using Excel Templates

A team working together will often need to create the same types of workbooks. Rather than each person or group designing a different workbook, each team member should create a workbook from the same template. The completed workbooks will then all have the same structure with identical formatting and formulas. Not only does this ensure consistency and accuracy, it also makes it easier to compile and summarize the results. Templates help teams work better together and avoid misunderstandings.

For example, a large organization may need to collect the same information from several regions. By creating and distributing a workbook template, each region knows what data to track and where to enter it. The template already includes the formulas, so the results are calculated consistently. If you want to review the formulas that are in the worksheet, you can display them using the Show Formula command in the Formula Auditing group on the Formulas tab or by pressing the Ctrl+` keys.

The following are just some of the advantages of using a template to create multiple workbooks with the same features:

- Templates save time and ensure consistency in the design and content of workbooks because all labels, formatting, and formulas are entered once.
- Templates ensure accuracy because formulas can be entered and verified once, and then used with confidence in all workbooks.
- Templates standardize the appearance and content of workbooks.
- Templates prevent data from being overwritten when an existing workbook is inadvertently saved with new data rather than saved as a new workbook.

If you are part of a team that needs to create the same type of workbook repeatedly, it's a good idea to use a template to both save time and ensure consistency in the design and content of the workbooks.

Creating a Workbook Based on an Existing Template

The Blank workbook template that you have used to create new, blank workbooks contains no text or formulas, but it includes formatting—General format applied to numbers, Calibri 11-point font, text left-aligned in cells, numbers and formula results right-aligned in cells, column widths set to 8.38 characters, one worksheet inserted in the workbook, and so forth.

Excel has many other templates available. Some are automatically installed on your hard drive when you install Excel. Other templates are available to download from the Office.com site or other sites that you can find by searching the web. These templates provide commonly used worksheet formats that can save you the time of creating the template yourself. Some of the task-specific templates available from the Office.com site include:

- **Family monthly budget planner**—builds projections and actual expenditures for items such as housing, transportation, and insurance
- **Inventory list**—tracks the cost and quantity reorder levels of inventory
- **Sports team roster**—organizes a list with each player's name, phone number, email address, and so forth
- **Employee time sheet**—creates an online time card to track employees' work hours
- **Expense report**—creates an expense report to track employee expenses for reimbursement

Using a template to create a new workbook lets you focus on the unique content for that workbook.

REFERENCE

Creating a Workbook Based on a Template

- On the ribbon, click the File tab, and then click New in the navigation bar.
- On the New screen, click a template category for the type of workbook you want to create (or type a keyword in the Search for online templates box, and then press the Enter key).
- Click the template you want to create, then click the Create button.
- Save the workbook based on the template with a new filename.

Gordon Warren, manager for the Petosky rental center, uses the Weekly time sheet template to submit his work hours to Timothy. You'll download this template and enter Gordon's most recent hours. *If you don't have an Internet connection, you should read but not complete the steps involving creating and using the online template.*

To create a workbook based on the Weekly time sheet template:

1. On the ribbon, click the **File** tab.
2. Click **New** in the navigation bar. The New screen in Backstage view shows the available templates on your computer and template categories on Office.com.
3. Click in the **Search for online templates** box, type **time sheets**, and then press the **Enter** key. All of the available time sheet templates are displayed. See Figure 6-27.

Figure 6-27 New screen with available time sheet templates

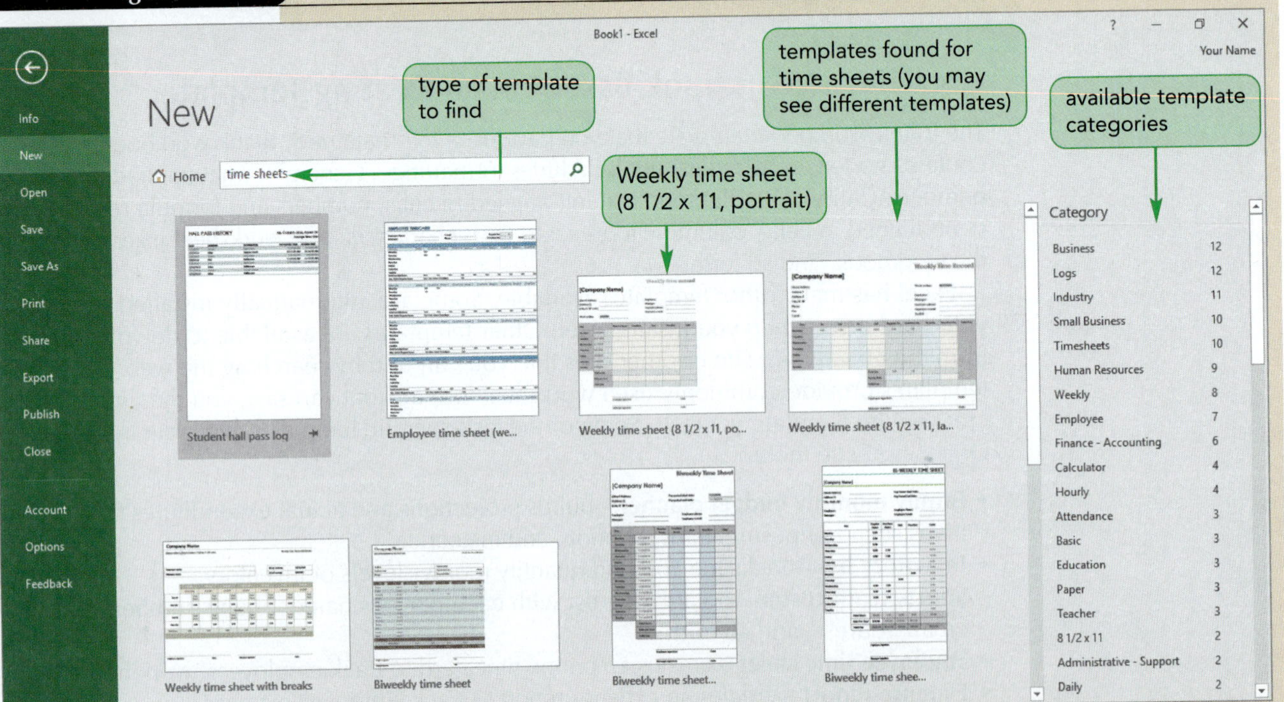

4. Click **Weekly time sheet (8 1/2 × 11, portrait)**. A preview of a worksheet based on the selected template appears in the center of the screen. If this is not the template you need, you can scroll through the time sheets by clicking the left or right arrow button. See Figure 6-28.

Figure 6-28 Weekly time sheet preview

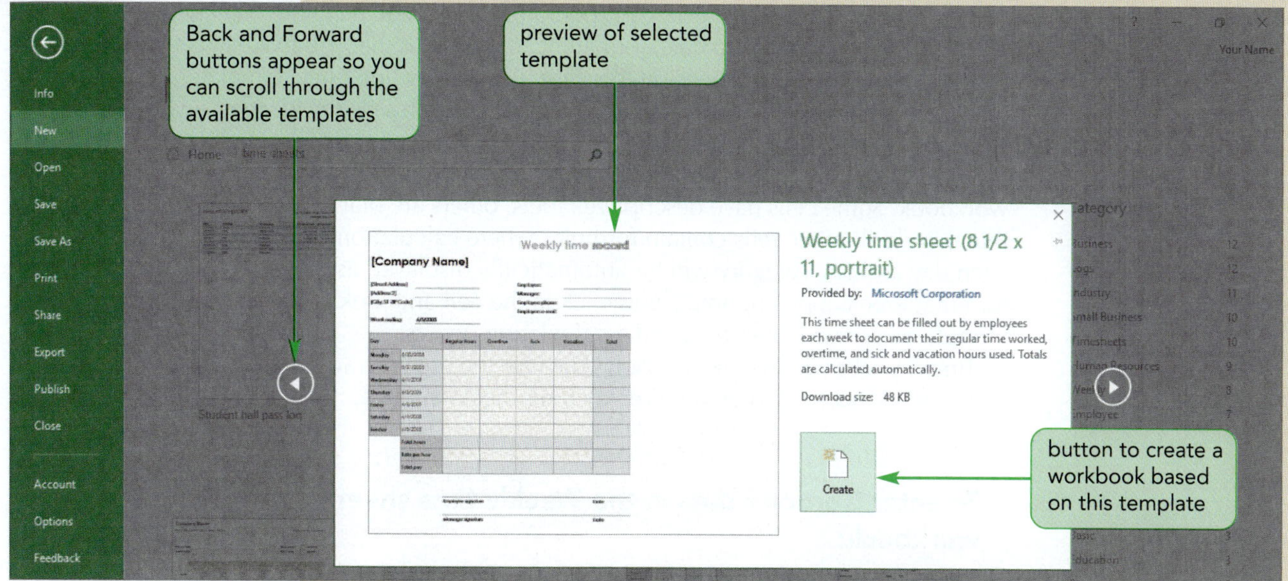
Back and Forward buttons appear so you can scroll through the available templates
preview of selected template
button to create a workbook based on this template
Weekly time sheet (8 1/2 x 11, portrait)
Provided by: Microsoft Corporation
This time sheet can be filled out by employees each week to document their regular time worked, overtime, and sick and vacation hours used. Totals are calculated automatically.
Download size: 48 KB
Create

5. Click the **Create** button. A new workbook based on the selected template opens. See Figure 6-29.

Figure 6-29 Workbook created from the Weekly time sheet template

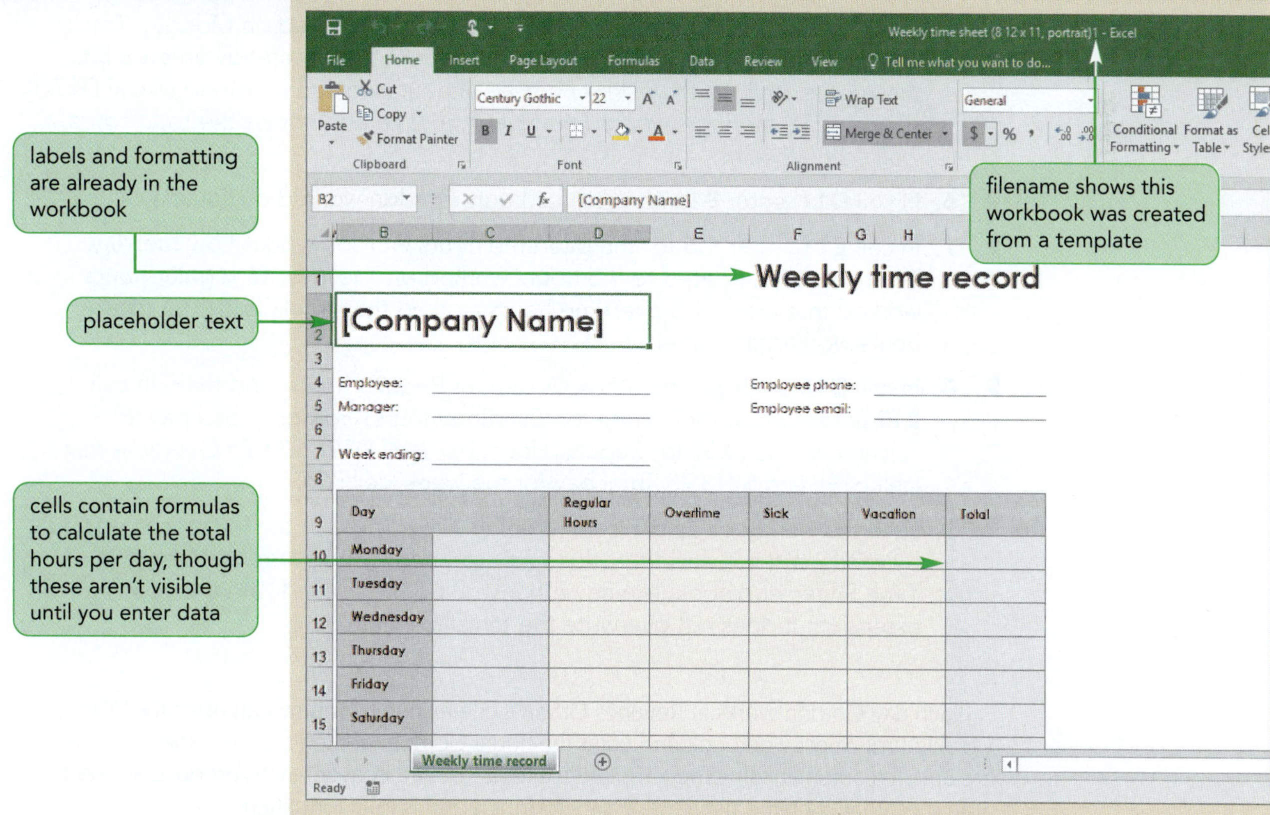
labels and formatting are already in the workbook
placeholder text
cells contain formulas to calculate the total hours per day, though these aren't visible until you enter data
filename shows this workbook was created from a template
Weekly time sheet (8 12 x 11, portrait)1 - Excel
Weekly time record
[Company Name]
Employee:
Manager:
Week ending:
Employee phone:
Employee email:
Day
Regular Hours
Overtime
Sick
Vacation
Total
Monday
Tuesday
Wednesday
Thursday
Friday
Saturday
Weekly time record

A workbook based on a specific template always displays the name of the template followed by a sequential number. Just as a blank workbook that you open is named Book1, Book2, and so forth, the workbook based on the Weekly time sheet template is named "Weekly time sheet (8 ½ x 11, portrait)1" in the title bar, not "Weekly time sheet." Any changes or additions to data, formatting, or formulas that you make affect only this workbook and not the template (in this case, the Weekly time sheet template). When you save the workbook, the Save As screen opens so you can save the workbook with a new name and to the location you specify.

Look at the labels and formatting already included in the Weekly time sheet workbook. Some cells have descriptive labels, others are blank so you can enter data in them, and still other cells contain formulas where calculations for total hours worked each day and pay category will be automatically displayed as data is entered. The formulas aren't apparent unless you click in the cell and look at the cell contents in the formula bar, or you enter data and a calculation occurs.

Timothy asks you to enter Gordon's data for the previous week in the Weekly time record worksheet based on the Weekly time sheet template.

To enter Gordon's data in the Weekly time sheet (8 ½ x 11, portrait)1 workbook:

1. In cell **B2,** enter **Reveries Urban Centers** as the company name, and then format the text in **18** point font size.
2. In cell **C4,** enter **Gordon Warren** as the employee.
3. In cell **C5,** enter **Timothy Root** as the manager.
4. In cell **C7**, enter **8/26/2017** as the week ending date.
5. In cell **D10**, enter **8** for the regular hours Gordon worked on Monday. Totals appear in cells I10, D17, and I17 because formulas are already entered into these cells. Cell I10 shows the number of hours worked on Monday, cell D17 shows 8 regular hours worked that week, and cell I17 shows the total hours worked that week.
6. In cell **D11**, enter **8** for the regular hours Gordon worked on Tuesday.
7. In cell **E11**, enter **1.5** for the overtime hours Gordon worked on Tuesday. The totals are updated to 9.5 hours worked on Tuesday, 16 regular hours worked that week, 1.5 overtime hours worked that week, and 17.5 total hours worked that week.
8. In cell **D18** enter $15 for Warren's rate for Regular hours, and then, in cell **E18** enter $22.50 for his rate for Overtime hours. Gordon's total pay is calculated—$240.00 for Regular Hours pay (cell D19), $33.75 Overtime pay (cell E19), and $273.75 Total pay for the week (cell I19).
9. Save the workbook as **Warrens Weekly Time Sheet** in the location specified by your instructor, and then close the workbook. The Warrens Weekly Time Sheet workbook, like any other workbook, is saved with the .xlsx file extension. It does not overwrite the template file.

Each day Gordon works at Reveries Urban Centers, he or Timothy can open the Warrens Weekly Time Sheet workbook and enter the hours Gordon worked that day. The total hours are updated automatically. The template makes it fast and convenient to produce a weekly time sheet that contains all the necessary formulas and is fully formatted.

Creating a Custom Workbook Template

A **custom template** is a workbook template you create that is ready to run with the formulas for all calculations included as well as all formatting and labels. A template can use any Excel feature, including formulas and charts. To create a custom template, you build the workbook with all the necessary labels, formatting, and data, and then you save the workbook as a template. The template includes everything but the variable data. You can also create a template from a chart or chart sheet.

When you save a workbook as an Excel template file, the save location in the Save As dialog box defaults to the Templates folder. Although template files are usually stored in the Templates folder, you can store template files in any folder. However, custom template files stored in the Templates folder are available on the New screen in Backstage view.

All template files have the .xltx file extension. This extension differentiates template files from workbook files, which have the .xlsx file extension. After you have saved a workbook in a template format, you can make the template accessible to other users.

REFERENCE

Creating a Custom Template

- Prepare the workbook—enter values, text, and formulas as needed; apply formatting; and replace data values with zeros or blank cells.
- On the ribbon, click the File tab, and then click Save As in the navigation bar.
- Click the Browse button to open the Save As dialog box.
- In the File name box, enter the template name.
- Click the Save as type button, and then click Excel Template.
- If you don't want to save the template in the Custom Office Templates folder, select another folder in which to save the template file.
- Click the Save button.

or

- Create the chart you want to use for the template.
- Right-click the chart, and then click Save as Template.
- In the Save Chart Template dialog box, enter a filename, then select a folder in which to save the template file if you don't want to store it in the Charts subfolder of the Templates folder.
- Click the Save button.

The three rental income workbooks for 2017 have the same format. Timothy wants to use this workbook format for rental income data and analysis for next year. He asks you to create a template from one of the rental center workbooks. You'll save the Jackson workbook as a template file to use as the basis for the custom template.

To save the Jackson workbook as a template:

1. Open the **Jackson** workbook you created in this Module.
2. On the ribbon, click the **File** tab to open Backstage view, and then in the navigation bar, click **Save As**. The Save As screen appears.
3. Select the location where you are saving the files for this Module.
4. In the File name box, type **Urban Centers Template** as the template name.

5. Click the **Save as type** button, and then click **Excel Template**. The save location changes to the Custom Office Templates folder on your computer. You want to save the template in the same location as the other files you created in this Module.
6. Navigate to the location where you are storing the files you create in this Module.
7. Click the **Save** button. The Urban Centers Template is saved in the location you specified.

Make sure you change the save location so you can easily find and use the template file later in the next set of steps.

TIP

You can use a fill color or cell style to differentiate input cells from other cells in the worksheet.

When you create a template from an existing workbook, you should remove any values and text that will change in each workbook created from the custom template. Be careful not to delete the formulas. Also, you should make sure that all of the formulas work as intended, the numbers and text are entered correctly, and the worksheet is formatted appropriately.

Next, you will clear the data from the template file, so that the input cells are ready for new data. You will leave the formulas that you already entered. You will also add placeholder text to the template to remind users what labels they need to enter.

To prepare a custom template from the Urban Centers Template:

1. With the Urban Centers Template open, group the **Quarter 1** through **Quarter 4** worksheets. The worksheet group includes the four quarterly worksheets but not the Summary and Documentation worksheets.
2. Select the range **B6:D11.** This range includes the rental income data. You want to delete these values.
3. Right-click the selected range, and then click **Clear Contents** on the shortcut menu. The data values are cleared from the selected range in each of the quarterly worksheets, but the formulas and formatting remain intact. The cleared cells are blank. The ranges E6:E12 and B12:D12 display dashes, representing zeros, where there are formulas.
4. Change the fill color of the selected range to the **Dark Blue, Text 2, Lighter 80%** theme color. The blue fill color indicates where users should enter data for rental income in the quarterly worksheets.
5. In cell **A2,** enter **[Center Name]** as the placeholder text to remind users to enter the correct rental center name.
6. Go to the **Summary** worksheet. The quarterly worksheets are ungrouped, and dashes, representing zeros, appear in the cells in the ranges B6:F12, which contain formulas.
7. In cell **A2**, enter **[Center Name]** as the placeholder text to remind users to enter the correct rental center name.
8. In cell **A3,** enter **[Enter Fiscal Year - yyyy]**. This text will remind users to enter the year.
9. Group the **Summary** through **Quarter 4** worksheets, and then make sure column A is wide enough to see the entire contents of cell A3. See Figure 6-30.

Figure 6-30 Worksheet modified to be used as a custom template

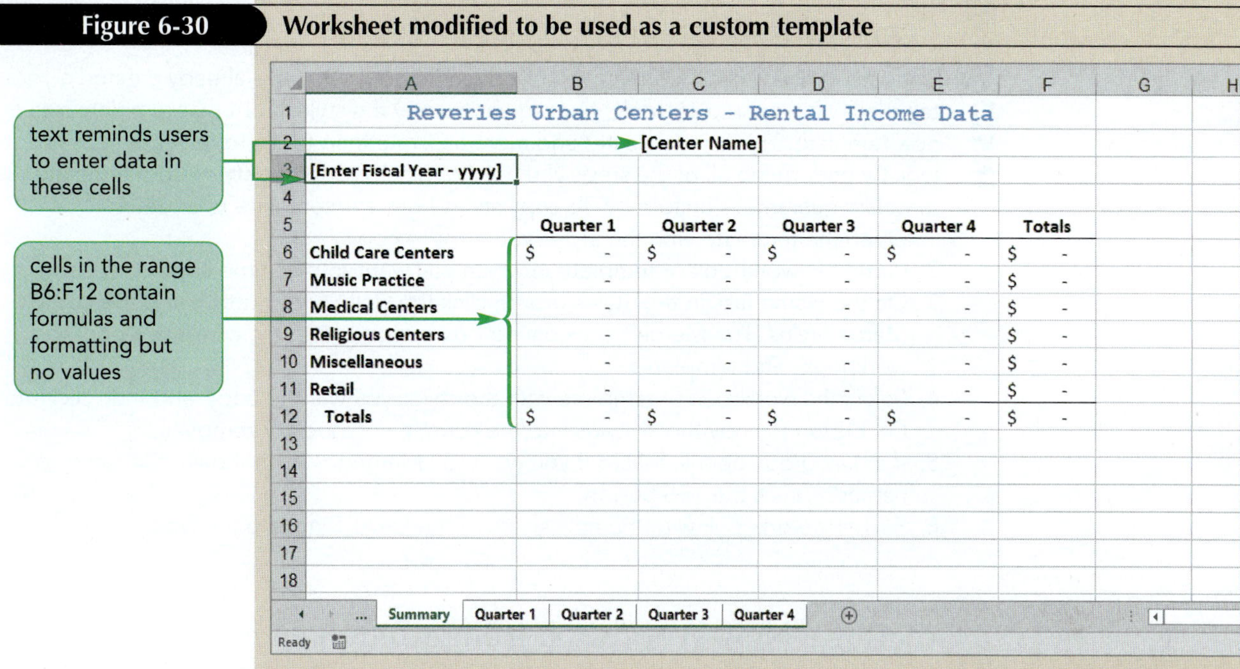

10. Go to the **Documentation** worksheet, and then delete your name and the date from the range B3:B4.
11. In cell **B5**, enter **To compile the rental income for [Center Name]**. The Documentation worksheet is updated to reflect the purpose of the workbook.
12. Save the Urban Centers Template, and then close it.

Timothy will use the Urban Centers Template file to create the workbooks to track next year's rental income for each rental center and then distribute the workbooks to each rental center manager. By basing these new workbooks on the template file, Timothy has a standard workbook with identical formatting and formulas for each manager to use. He also avoids the risk of accidentally changing the workbook containing the 2017 data when preparing for 2018.

INSIGHT

Copying Styles from One Template to Another

Consistency is a hallmark of professional documents. If you have already created a template with a particular look, you can easily copy the styles from that template into a new template. This is much faster and more accurate than trying to recreate the same look by performing all of the steps you used originally. Copying styles from template to template guarantees uniformity. To copy styles from one template to another:

1. Open the template with the styles you want to copy.
2. Open the workbook or template in which you want to place the copied styles.
3. On the Home tab, in the Styles group, click the Cell Styles button, and then click Merge Styles. The Merge Styles dialog box opens, listing the currently open workbooks and templates.
4. Select the workbook or template with the styles you want to copy, and then click the OK button to copy those styles into the current workbook or template.
5. If a dialog box opens, asking if you want to "Merge Styles that have the same names?", click the YES button.
6. Save the workbook with the new styles as the Excel Template file type.

Creating a New Workbook from a Template

A template file has special properties that allow you to open it, make changes, and save it in a new location. Only the data must be entered because the formulas are already in the template file. The original template file is not changed by this process. After you have saved a template, you can access the template from the New screen in Backstage view or in the location you saved it.

Timothy wants all Reveries Urban Centers locations to collect rental income data in the same format and submit the workbooks to the central office for analysis. He wants you to create a workbook for fiscal year 2018 based on the Urban Centers Template file. You will enter Jackson as the rental center name where indicated on all of the worksheets and then enter test data for January.

TIP

To create a copy of workbook based on a template stored in the Custom Office Templates folder, click the File tab, click New in the navigation bar, click Personal below the Search for online templates box, and then click the template.

To create a new workbook based on the Reveries Urban Centers Template file:

1. On the taskbar, click the **File Explorer** button. The File Explorer window opens.
2. Navigate to the location where you stored the template file.
3. Double-click the **Urban Centers Template** file. A new workbook opens named "Urban Centers Template1" to indicate this is the first copy of the Urban Centers workbook created during the current Excel session.
4. Go to the **Summary** worksheet, in cell **A2** replace [Center Name] with **Jackson Total**, and then, in cell **A3**, enter **Fiscal Year – 2018**.
5. Group the **Quarter 1** through **Quarter 4** worksheets, and then in cell **A2**, replace [Center Name] with **Jackson**.
6. Go to the **Documentation** worksheet to ungroup the worksheets.
7. In cell **B5**, replace [Center Name] with **Jackson.**
8. Go to the **Quarter 1** worksheet. The text "Fiscal Year - 2018" appears in cell A4.
9. In each cell in the range **B6:B11**, which has the blue fill color, enter **100**.
10. Review the totals in the range E6:E11 (the cells that contain formulas to sum each column). See Figure 6-31.

Figure 6-31 New workbook based on the Reveries Urban Centers template file

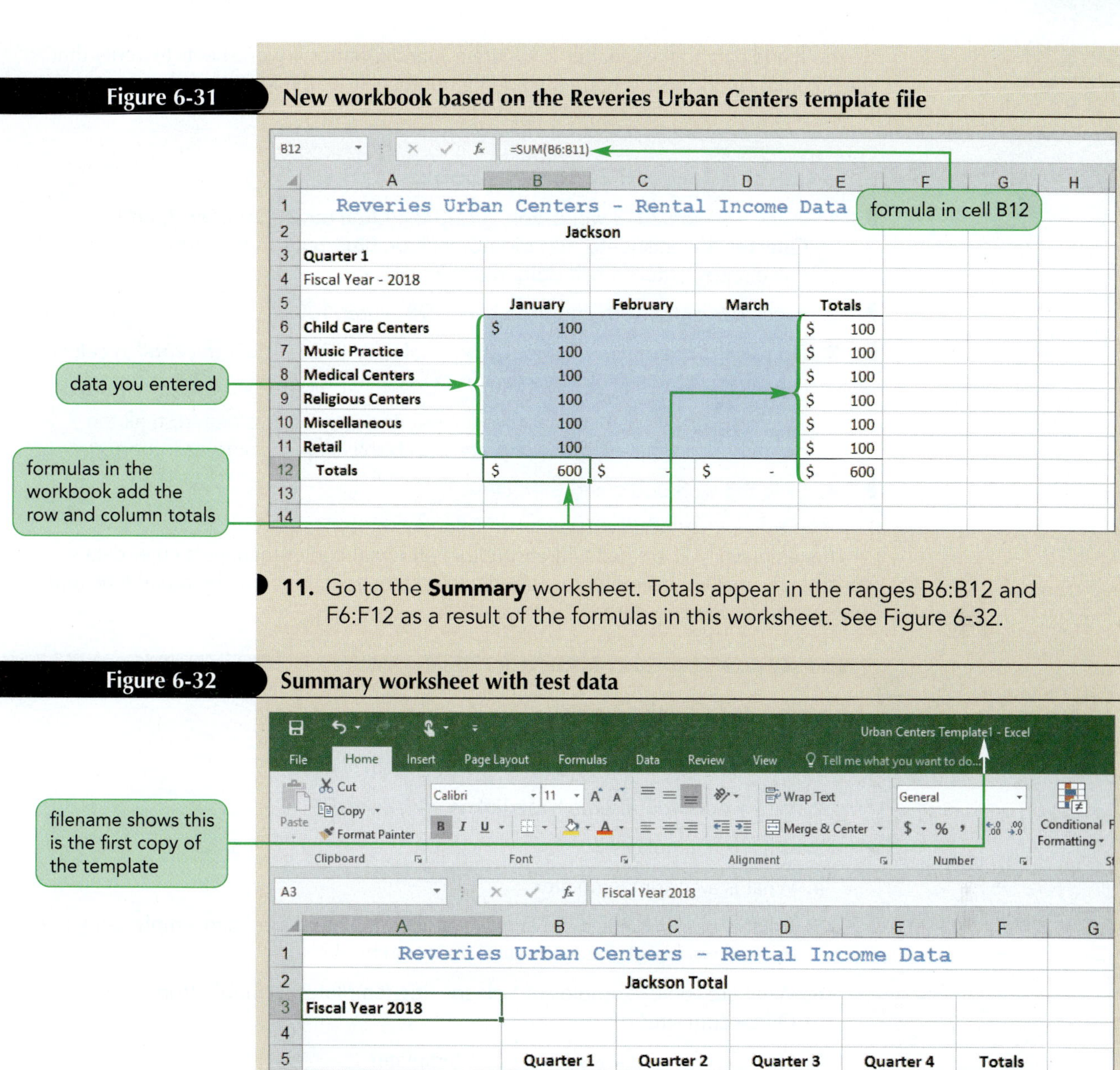

11. Go to the **Summary** worksheet. Totals appear in the ranges B6:B12 and F6:F12 as a result of the formulas in this worksheet. See Figure 6-32.

Figure 6-32 Summary worksheet with test data

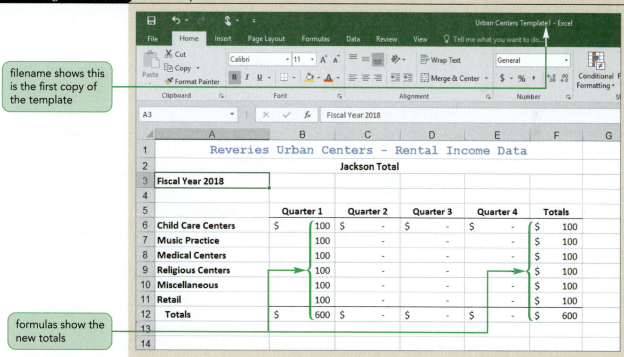

12. Save the workbook as **Jackson 2018** in the location specified by your instructor. The workbook is saved with the .xlsx file extension. The original template file is not changed.

Make sure the Save as type box shows Excel Workbook so that you create a new workbook file without overwriting the template.

You'll add data to the Quarter 2, Quarter 3, and Quarter 4 worksheets to verify that the Summary worksheet is correctly adding numbers from the four worksheets.

To test the Jackson 2018 workbook:

1. In the Jackson 2018 workbook, group the **Quarter 2, Quarter 3**, and **Quarter 4** worksheets. You did not include Quarter 1 in this group because you already entered test data in this worksheet.
2. In cell **C6**, enter **100**, and then in cell **D8**, enter **100**.
3. Go to the **Summary** worksheet. The total in cell F6 is $400, the total in cell F8 is $400, and the total for the year in cell F12 is $1,200.

   The formulas in the Summary worksheet correctly add values from all the quarterly worksheets. The template workbook is functioning as intended.
4. Save the workbook, and then close it.

The templates you created will ensure that all rental center managers enter data consistently, making it simpler for Timothy to add the rental income by rental type and time period for Reveries Urban Centers.

REVIEW

Session 6.3 Quick Check

1. How do you insert a hyperlink into a worksheet cell?
2. Why would you insert a hyperlink in a worksheet?
3. What is a template?
4. What is a custom template?
5. What is one advantage of using a custom template rather than simply using the original workbook file to create a new workbook?
6. What are some examples of task-specific templates available from the Office.com site?
7. How do you save a workbook as a template?
8. How do you create a workbook based on a template that is not saved in the Custom Office Templates folder?

PRACTICE

Review Assignment

Data Files needed for the Review Assignments: Midland.xlsx, NewUCMemo.docx, NewUC.xlsx, JacksonMI.xlsx, PetoskyMI.xlsx, FlintMI.xlsx.

Reveries Urban Centers opened a new rental center in Midland, Michigan, on January 1, 2017. Michael Verhallen, the manager of the Midland rental center, collected the year's rental income in a workbook provided by Timothy Root at the central office. Before Michael can send the completed workbook to Timothy for the year-end reporting, he needs you to summarize the results and format the worksheets. Complete the following:

1. Open the **Midland** workbook located in the Excel6 > Review folder included with your Data Files, and then save the workbook as **Midland MI** in the location specified by your instructor.
2. In the Documentation worksheet, enter your name and the date, and then review the worksheets in the workbook.
3. Create a worksheet group that contains the Quarter 1 through Quarter 4 worksheets.
4. In the worksheet group, in the range B12:D12, enter formulas that sum the values in each column, and then in the range E6:E12, enter formulas that sum the values in each row.
5. Format the quarterly worksheets as specified below:
   a. In cell E5 and cell A12, enter the label **Totals**.
   b. Increase the indent of cell A12 by one.
   c. In the range A2:A3, A6:A12;B5:E5, bold the text.
   d. Merge and center the range A1:E1 and the range A2:E2.
   e. In the range B5:E5, center the text.
   f. Add a bottom border to the range B5:E5 and the range B11:E11.
   g. Format the range B6:D6,B12:D12,E6:E12 with the Accounting style and no decimal places.
   h. Format the range B7:E11 with the Comma style and no decimal places.
6. Ungroup the worksheets, make a copy of the Quarter 1 worksheet, rename it as **Summary**, and then place it after the Documentation worksheet.
7. In the Summary worksheet, make the following changes:
   a. In cell A2, change the heading to **Midland Total**.
   b. Change cell A3 to **Fiscal Year - 2017**.
   c. Insert a column between columns B and C.
   d. In the range B5:E5, change the headings to **Quarter 1**, **Quarter 2**, **Quarter 3**, and **Quarter 4**, respectively.
   e. Make sure that the text in the range B5:F5 is centered.
   f. Clear the contents of the range B6:F11.
8. Complete the formulas in the Summary worksheet, as follows, using the Fill Without Formatting paste option so that you can keep the bottom border on the range B11:F11.
   a. In the range B6:E11, create formulas that reference cells in other worksheets to display the quarterly totals for the rental income by type. For example, the formula in cell B6 will reference cell E6 in the Quarter 1 worksheet.
   b. In the range F6:F11, create formulas that use 3-D cell references to calculate the total for each type of rental income.
   c. Copy the formula from cell B12 to cell C12.
9. Change the March rental income for medical centers to **1976**, and then verify that the total rental income for Medical Centers in Quarter 1 in the Summary worksheet is $5,214, the total rental income in Quarter 1 is $19,538, the total rental income for medical centers in 2017 is $22,186, and the total rental income for 2017 is $82,286.
10. Group the Quarter 1 through Quarter 4 worksheets, and then enter a formula in cell A4 that references cell A3 in the Summary worksheet.

11. In cell A8 of the Documentation worksheet, insert a hyperlink that points to the **NewUCMemo** located in the Module6 > Review folder included with your Data Files. Make sure the text to display is **Click here to read Midland Executive Memo**.
12. Edit the hyperlink to use the ScreenTip **Midland Rental Center Summary for 2017**.
13. Save the Midland MI workbook, and leave it open.
14. Open the **NewUC** workbook located in the Excel6 > Review folder included with your Data Files, and then save the workbook as **New Urban Centers** in the location specified by your instructor. In the Documentation worksheet enter your name and the date. Open the **JacksonMI**, **PetoskyMI**, and **FlintMI** workbooks located in the Excel6 > Review folder included with your Data Files.
15. Make the New Urban Centers the active workbook, and then arrange the workbooks in a tiled layout. The New Urban Centers is the full height of the screen on the left with the remaining four taking the rest the screen. In each workbook, hide the ribbon so you can see as much data in the Summary worksheet as possible.
16. In the Summary worksheet of the New Urban Centers workbook, enter external reference formulas to create a set of linked workbooks to summarize the totals for JacksonMI, PetoskyMI, Midland MI, and FlintMI. Format the Summary worksheet in the New UC Totals workbook so that the numbers are readable and the range B11:F11 has a bottom border.
17. Maximize the New Urban Centers and Midland MI worksheets, making sure that the ribbon is displayed. Save the New Urban Centers workbook, and leave it open. Close the JacksonMI, PetoskyMI, and FlintMI workbooks.
18. In the New Urban Centers workbook, break the links. Select a cell, and notice that the formula has been replaced with a value. Save the workbook as **New UC Audited 2018**.
19. Create headers and footers for the Summary worksheet. Display the name of the workbook and the name of the worksheet on separate lines in the right section of the header. Display your name and the date on separate lines in the right section of the footer. Save the New UC Audited 2018 workbook, and then close it.
20. Use the Midland MI workbook to create an Excel template with the filename **Midland MI Template** in the location specified by your instructor.
21. Create a new workbook based on the Midland MI Template file, and then save the workbook as **Midland MI 2018** in the location specified by your instructor. In the Documentation worksheet, enter your name and the date.
22. In the Summary worksheet, enter **2018** as the fiscal year in cell A3. The Center Name should be Midland in all worksheets. In the Quarter 1 worksheet, enter **500** in each cell in the range B6:D11. In the Quarter 2 worksheet, enter **1000** in each cell in the range B6:D11. Confirm that the values entered in this step are correctly totaled in the Summary worksheet.
23. Save the Midland MI 2018 workbook, and then close it.

APPLY

Case Problem 1

Data File needed for this Case Problem: Tea.xlsx

Paige's Tea Room Paige's Tea Room has three locations: Atlanta, Georgia; Naples, Florida; and New Orleans, Louisiana. Paige Sapienza is the chief of operations and supervises the ongoing business operations of the three tea rooms. She uses Excel to summarize annual sales data from each location in separate workbooks. She wants you to total the sales by type of tea and location for each quarter and then format each worksheet. Paige also wants you to calculate sales for all of the locations and types of tea. Complete the following:

1. Open the **Tea** workbook located in the Excel6 > Case1 folder included with your Data Files, and then save the document as **Tea Room** in the location specified by your instructor.
2. In the Documentation worksheet, enter your name and the date.
3. Group the Atlanta, Naples, and New Orleans worksheets.

4. In the grouped worksheets, calculate the quarterly totals in the range B12:E12 and the types of tea totals in the range F4:F12.
5. In cells A12 and F3, enter **Totals** as the labels.
6. Improve the look of the quarterly worksheets using the formatting of your choice. Ungroup the worksheets.
7. Place a copy of one of the location worksheets between the Documentation and Atlanta worksheets, and then rename the new worksheet as **Summary Sales**.
8. In the Summary Sales worksheet, delete the values in the range B4:E11, and then change the label in cell A2 to **Summary Sales**.
9. In the range B4:E11, enter formulas that add the sales in the corresponding cells of the four quarterly worksheets. Use 3-D references to calculate the sum of each tea type per quarter.
10. Set up the Summary Sales and the three location worksheets for printing. Each worksheet should be centered horizontally, display the name of the worksheet centered in the header, and display your name and the current date on separate lines in the right section of the footer.
11. Make sure that any grouped worksheets have been ungrouped, and then save the Tea Room workbook.
12. Save the workbook as an Excel template with the name **Tea Room Template** in the location specified by your instructor.
13. In the Documentation worksheet, clear your name and date. In each of the location worksheets, clear the sales data but not the formulas. Save and close the Tea Room Template.
14. Create a new workbook based on the **Tea Room Template** file, and then save the workbook as **Tea Room 2017** in the location specified by your instructor.
15. In the Documentation worksheet, enter your name and the date.
16. In the three location worksheets, in the range B4:E11, enter **10**. Verify that the formulas in the three location worksheets and the Summary Sales worksheet summarize the data accurately.
17. Save the workbook, and then close it.

TROUBLESHOOT

Case Problem 2

Data Files needed for this Case Problem: Barstow.xlsx, SanDiego.xlsx, Carlsbad.xlsx, GoodieBag.xlsx

Clara's Goodie Bags Clara Perry founded Clara's Goodie Bags to create unique party favor packages for private and corporate events. The first retail location opened on July 1, 2016, in Barstow, California. The San Diego location opened in 2017, and recently the Carlsbad location was added. Each location uses an Excel workbook to track the number of goodie bags sold in major categories—wedding, birthday, holiday, graduation, retirement, and custom. Clara wants you to use the workbooks to prepare a report showing the number of goodie bags sold by quarter and location for each category. Complete the following:

1. Open the **Barstow** workbook located in the Excel6 > Case2 folder included with your Data Files, and then save the workbook as **Barstow 2017** in the location specified by your instructor.
2. In the Documentation worksheet, enter your name and the date.
3. In the Barstow worksheet, calculate the total number of goodie bags sold in each category in the range B8:G8, and the total number sold each quarter in the range H4:H8.
4. Improve the look of the worksheet by using the formatting of your choice including a bottom border in the range A7:H7 and appropriate number formats for the total numbers of grab bags sold.
5. Save the Barstow 2017 workbook, and leave it open.
6. Repeat Steps 1 through 5 for the **SanDiego** and **Carlsbad** workbooks, naming them **San Diego 2017** and **Carlsbad 2017**, respectively.
7. Open the **GoodieBag** workbook located in the Excel6 > Case2 folder included with your Data Files, and then save the workbook as **Goodie Bags 2017** in the location specified by your instructor.

8. In the Documentation worksheet, enter your name and the date.
9. Rename Sheet1 as **Summary**. In cell A2, enter **Summary Sales** as the label.

Troubleshoot 10. The quarterly totals in the Goodie Bag 2017 Summary worksheet are not displaying the correct results. Make any necessary corrections to the formulas so that they add the correct cells from the Barstow 2017, San Diego 2017, and Carlsbad 2017 workbooks.

11. Insert formulas to calculate the totals for the range B8:G8 and the range H4:H8.

Troubleshoot 12. The Documentation worksheet in the Goodie Bag 2017 workbook includes hyperlinks in the range A9:A11 for each city's corresponding workbook (Barstow 2017, San Diego 2017, and Carlsbad 2017 located in the folder where you saved the workbooks). The text displayed for each hyperlink does not match its source file. Edit the hyperlinks so that each hyperlink points to its corresponding location workbook.

13. Add appropriate text for the ScreenTip to each hyperlink. Test each hyperlink.
14. Prepare each workbook for printing. For all worksheets except the Documentation worksheet, display the workbook name and the worksheet name on separate lines in the right section of the header and display your name and the current date on separate lines in the right section of the footer. Change the orientation so that each workbook will print on one page.
15. Save and close all of the workbooks.

APPLY

Case Problem 3

Data File needed for this Case Problem: RoomGroom.xlsx

Room and Groom Room and Groom has been kenneling and grooming small, medium, and large cats and dogs in Topeka, Kansas, since June 2010. The standard kennel program includes access to the outside fenced play area, healthy meals, and private rooms. With the deluxe kennel program, the animal also has a daily playtime with a kennel employee, daily treats, and music or video playing in its room. Grooming services can occur during a kennel stay or as a standalone service. Samuel Wooten, the manager of Room and Groom, has been tracking the kennel and grooming services by month for the past year. Samuel wants you to analyze the data he has collected and create some preliminary charts. Complete the following:

1. Open the **RoomGroom** workbook located in the Excel6 > Case3 folder included with your Data Files, and then save the workbook as **RoomGroom 2017** in the location specified by your instructor.
2. In the Documentation worksheet, enter your name and the date.
3. Group the 12 monthly worksheets to ensure consistency in headings and for ease in entering formulas. Enter the heading **Total** in cells A11 and E4. For each month (January through December), enter formulas to calculate the total for each type of visit (the range B11:D11) and the total for each type of animal (the range E5:E11).
4. Improve the formatting of the monthly worksheets using the formatting of your choice. Be sure to include a bottom border in the ranges A4:E4 and A10:E10. Ungroup the worksheets.
5. In the Service by Month worksheet, in the range B5:B16, enter formulas with worksheet references to display the total grooming services for each month (the formulas will range from =January!B11 through =December!B11). Copy these formulas to the range C5:C16 (Room-Standard) and the range D5:D16 (Room-Deluxe).
6. In cells A17 and E4, enter the label **Total**. In the range B17:D17, enter formulas to add the total for each type of service, and then in the range E5:E17, enter formulas to add the total services each month by animal type.
7. Add a bottom border to the ranges A4:E4 and A16:E16. Improve the formatting of the Service by Month worksheet using the formatting of your choice.

8. Create a bar chart or a column chart that compares the types of services by month (the range A4:D16). Include an appropriate chart title and a legend. Format the chart so that it is attractive and effective. Position the chart below the data.
9. In the Service by Animal worksheet, in the range B5:D10, enter formulas using 3-D cell references to sum the services for the year for each animal. For example, in cell B5, the formulas for Small Dog Groom would be =SUM(January:December!B5).
10. In cells A11 and E4, enter the label **Total**. In the range B11:D11, enter formulas to add the total by type of service, and then in the range E5:E11, enter formulas to add the total services and total services by animal type.
11. Add a bottom border to the ranges A4:E4 and A10:E10. Improve the formatting of the Service by Animal worksheet using the formatting of your choice.
12. Create a pie chart based on the annual total for each animal type. Include an appropriate chart title and a legend. Format the chart so that it is attractive and effective. Position the pie chart below the data in the Service by Animal worksheet.
13. Group all of the worksheets except Documentation. Prepare the workbook for printing by displaying the workbook name and the worksheet name on separate lines in the right section of the header. Display your name and the current date on separate lines in the right section of the footer.
14. Save the workbook, and then close it.

Case Problem 4

Data Files needed for this Case Problem: Maryland.xlsx, Delaware.xlsx, Virginia.xlsx, ELSSummary.xlsx, NewMD.xlsx, ELSTemplate.xltx

Economic Landscape Supplies Economic Landscape Supplies (ELS), a distributor of landscaping supplies, has offices in Delaware, Virginia, and Maryland. In December, each office submits a workbook that contains worksheets for all salespersons in that state. Each salesperson's worksheet contains the current year's sales by month and the projected increase that they will need to meet. Kyle Walker, the chief financial officer (CFO), wants you to calculate each salesperson's projected monthly sales based on the current sales and the projected increase. After you have added this information to each workbook, Kyle wants you to consolidate the information from the three workbooks into a single workbook. Complete the following:

1. Open the **Maryland** workbook located in the Excel6 > Case4 folder included with your Data Files, and then save the workbook as **ELS Maryland** in the location specified by your instructor.
2. In the Documentation worksheet, enter your name and the date.
3. Repeat Steps 1 and 2, opening the **Delaware** and **Virginia** workbooks and saving them as **ELS Delaware** and **ELS Virginia**, respectively.
4. Complete each salesperson worksheets in workbooks by doing the following:
   a. Group the Salesperson worksheets.
   b. Calculate the 2018 Projected Sales for each month by multiplying the 2017 Gross Sales by the Projected Increase. (*Hint*: Remember to use absolute cell references to the Project Increase cell.)
   c. Enter **Total** in cell A16, and then enter formulas to sum the totals of the 2017 Gross Sales and 2018 Projected Sales.
   d. Display all of the monthly sales numbers (the range B4:C15) with a comma and no decimal places. Display the total row values (the range B16:C16) with a dollar sign. Leave the Projected Increase value in cell B19 as formatted.
   e. Bold the ranges A4:A16 and B3:C3. Wrap the text and center the range B3:C3. Make sure all of the data and the headings are visible.
   f. Ungroup the worksheets.

5. In each of the state workbooks, do the following:
   a. Make a copy of the first salesperson's worksheet, rename it as **Summary**, and then place it after the Documentation worksheet.
   b. In cell A2, change the salesperson name to **Summary** and then clear the 2017 Gross Sales and 2018 Projected Sales data, leaving the formulas for the totals.
   c. Clear the label and data from the range A19:B19.
   d. In the range B4:C15, create 3-D reference formulas to calculate the total of each month's 2017 Gross Sales and 2018 Projected Sales. Widen columns as needed so you can see the totals.
   e. Group all worksheets except the Documentation worksheet. Prepare the workbook for printing by displaying the workbook name and the worksheet name on separate lines in the right section of the header. Display your name and the current date on separate lines in the right section of the footer.
   f. Ungroup the worksheets, and then save the workbook.
6. Open the **ELSSummary** workbook located in the Excel6 > Case4 folder included with your Data Files, and then save the workbook as **ELS Summary 2017** in the location specified by your instructor. Enter your name and date in the Documentation worksheet.
7. Make sure the three ELS state workbooks are open with the Summary worksheet active.
8. In the range B4:C15, enter external reference formulas to create a set of linked workbooks to summarize the 2017 Gross Sales and 2018 Projected Sales.
9. In cell A16, enter **Total**. In the range B16:C16, enter formulas to total the 2017 Gross Sales and 2018 Projected Sales.
10. Bold the range A4:A16. Bold, wrap text, and center the range B3:C3. Display all the monthly sales numbers with a comma and no decimal places. Display the total values (the range B16:C16) with a dollar sign and no decimal places.
11. Prepare the Summary worksheet for printing with the workbook name and the worksheet name on separate lines in the right section of the header. Display your name and the date on separate lines in the right section of the footer.
12. Save the Summary workbook.

Explore 13. The office manager for the Maryland ELS location found a newer workbook for that location's sales and commissions and has submitted it to you. Close the ELS Maryland workbook that you have been working with, open the **New MD** workbook located in the Excel6 > Case4 folder included with your Data Files, and then save the workbook as **New ELS Maryland** in the location specified by your instructor. Use Update Links to update the totals on the Summary worksheet in the ELS Summary 2017 workbook. The Totals before the update are 2017 Gross Sales $5,323,750 and 2018 Projected Sales $5,730,424. The totals after the update are 2017 Gross Sales $5,406,750 and 2018 Projected Sales $5,682,700.

14. Save and close all of the open workbooks.

Explore 15. Open the template named **ELSTemplate** located in the Excel6 > Case4 folder included with your Data Files, save the template as **ELS Template Revised** in the location specified by your instructor, and then change the company name in cell A1 of all the worksheets to **ELS**. Change the font for the company name to Bookman Old Style. Save the template.

16. Create a new workbook from the ELS Template Revised template. In the Documentation worksheet, enter your name and date.
17. In the Salesperson worksheet, enter **10,000** for each month's 2017 Gross Sales and Projected Increase of 1.20. Verify that the formulas are working correctly.
18. Save the workbook as **ELS Test** in a location specified by your instructor, and then close it.

MODULE 7

Developing an Excel Application

Creating a Registration Receipt

EXCEL

OBJECTIVES

Session 7.1
- Create an application
- Create, edit, and delete defined names for cells and ranges
- Paste a list of defined names as documentation
- Use defined names in formulas
- Add defined names to existing formulas

Session 7.2
- Create validation rules for data entry
- Protect the contents of worksheets and workbooks
- Add, edit, and delete comments

Session 7.3
- Learn about macro viruses and Excel security features
- Add the Developer tab to the ribbon
- Create and run a macro
- Edit a macro using the Visual Basic Editor
- Assign a macro to a keyboard shortcut and a button
- Save and open a workbook in macro-enabled format

Case | *Rockport Youth Center*

The Rockport Youth Center in Rockport, Indiana, offers classes and activities to school-age children. Each fall, the Center mails a brochure with the upcoming winter activities to households with students in grades 3 through 6 in the Rockport area. This winter's weekly activities include First Friday (games, pizza, and drinks), Kids Game Night (board games, video games, and snacks), Kids in the Kitchen (hands-on cooking), and Modern Manners (more than please and thank you). The brochure includes a registration form that guardians complete and return with their payment. The manager, Stephen Maynard, wants to automate the registration process, which will include capturing the data, calculating the charges, printing a receipt, and collecting the data for the shirts that participants will receive.

Many of these tasks can be accomplished in Excel. But without validating data entry, protecting cells with formulas from accidental deletion, and reducing repetitious keystrokes and mouse clicks, too many opportunities for errors exist. The Center relies on volunteers to assist with registration. To accommodate the volunteers' varying skill levels and reduce errors, Stephen wants to create a custom interface for this project that does not rely exclusively on the ribbon, galleries, and so forth. You will help Stephen create a unique Excel application to resolve these issues and help ensure accurate data entry.

STARTING DATA FILES

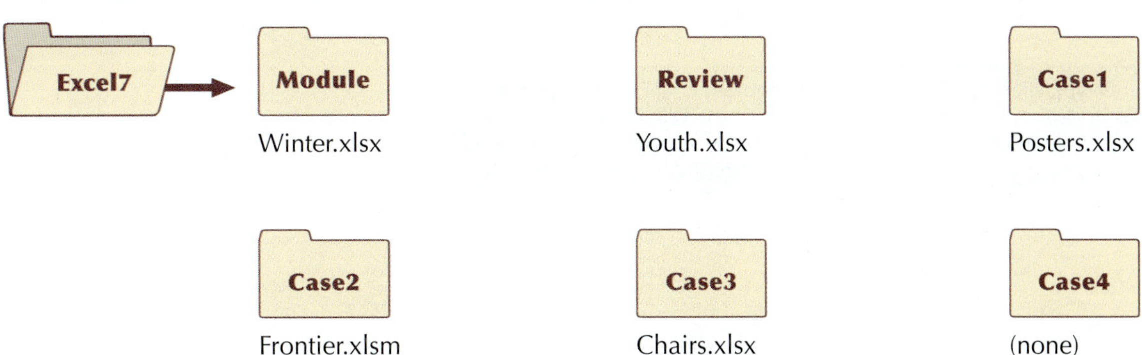

Session 7.1 Visual Overview:

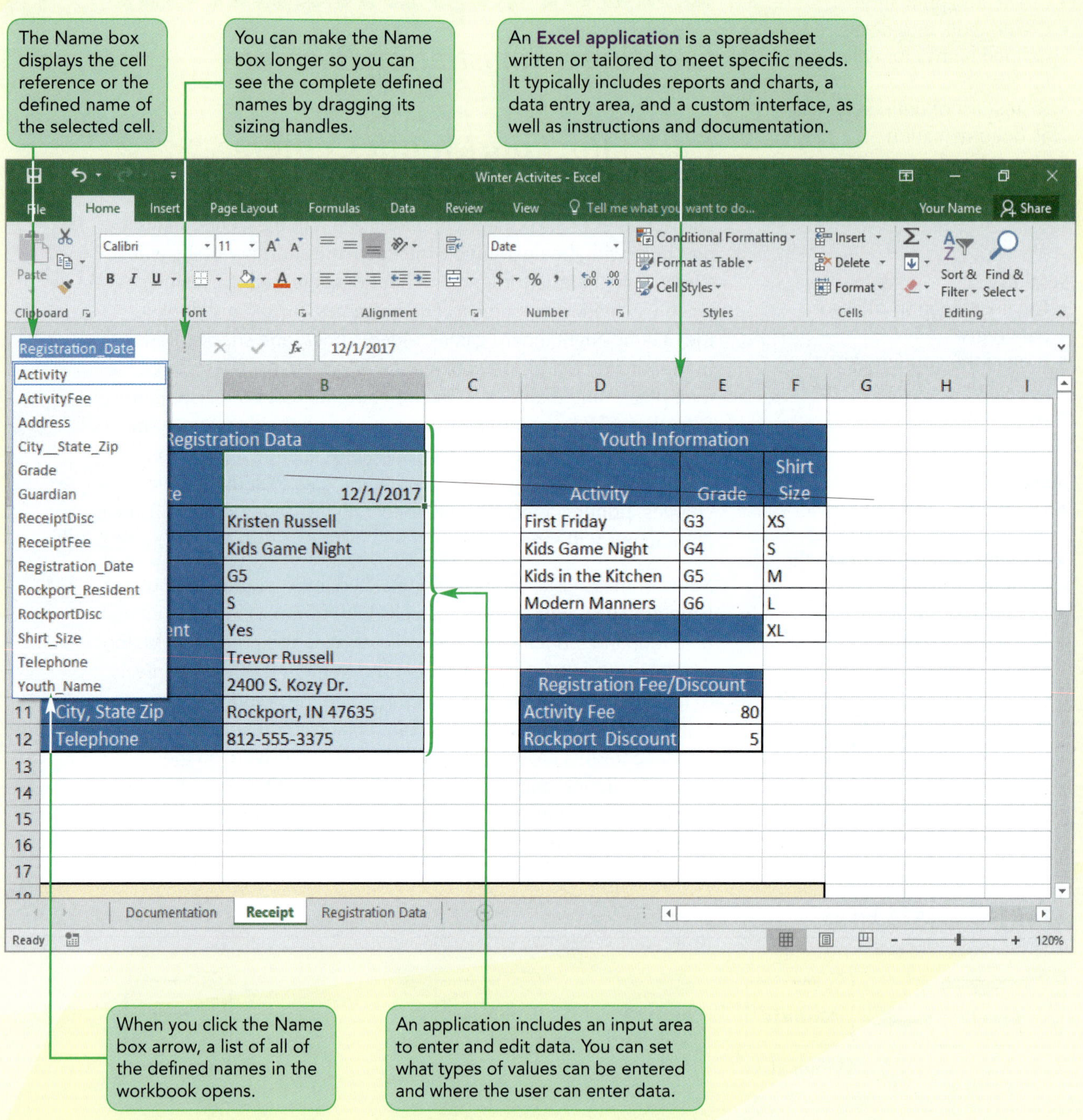

Excel Application and Defined Names

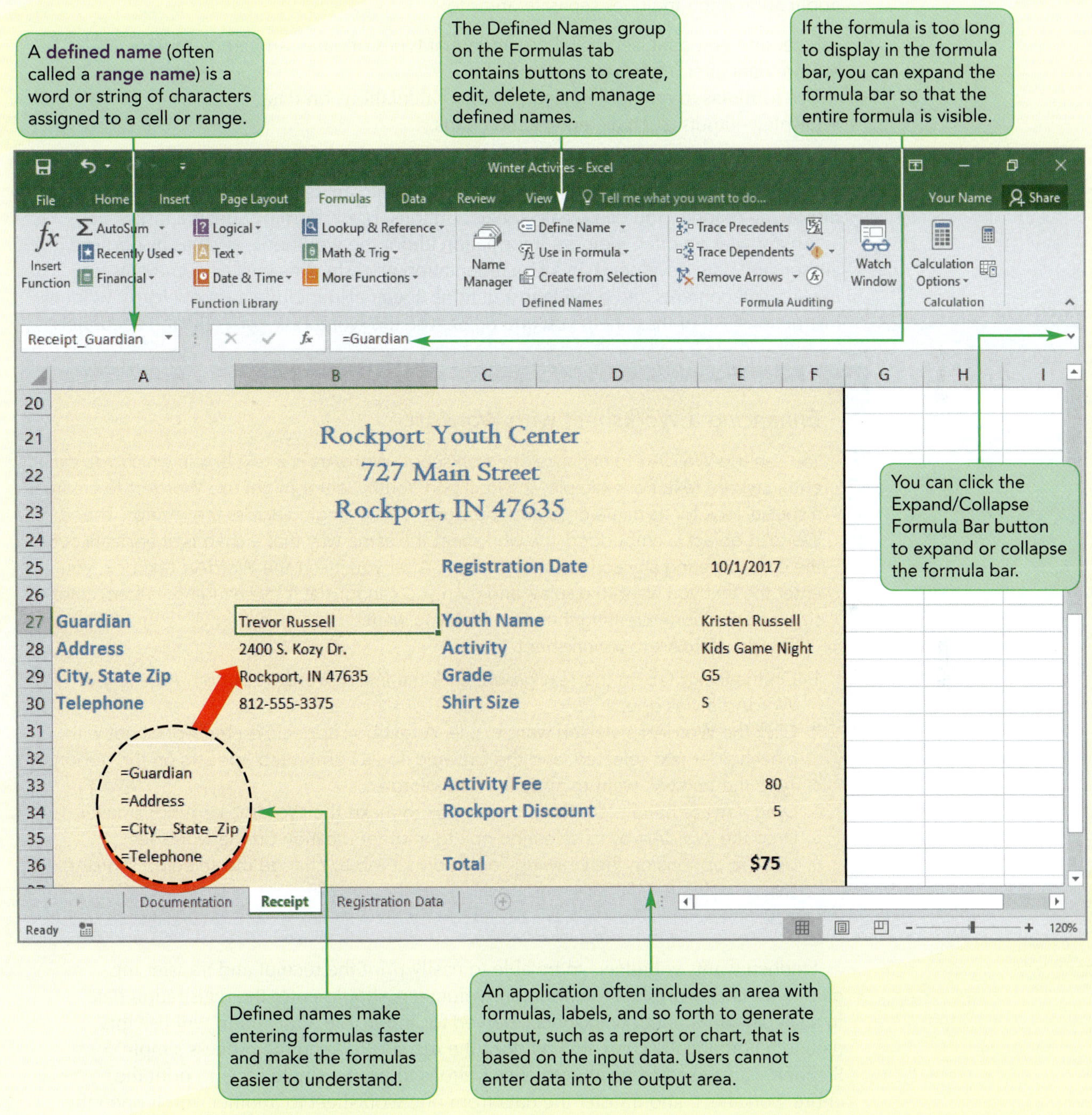

Planning an Excel Application

An Excel application is a spreadsheet written or tailored to meet specific needs, such as creating a receipt for winter activities registrations. Planning an Excel application includes designing how the worksheet(s) will be organized. You can include different areas for each function, depending on the complexity of the project. For example, an application often includes separate areas to:

- Enter and edit data (setting where and what types of data can be entered).
- Store data after it has been entered.
- Use formulas to manipulate and perform calculations on data.
- Display outputs, such as reports and charts.

Excel applications can be set up to help users understand how they will interact with the project. For example, you can have separate areas for inputting data and displaying outputs. You can create special buttons for performing specific tasks.

An application often includes information about the workbook, such as its purpose, author, and date developed, in a Documentation worksheet as well as comments to explain cell contents and provide instructions. It can also include a set of clearly written instructions. All of these help you and others use the workbook correctly and accurately.

INSIGHT

Enhancing a Worksheet with WordArt

You can use WordArt to enhance any worksheet. **WordArt** is a text box in which you can enter stylized text. For example, the Rockport Youth Center might use WordArt to create a special look for its name or to add the word "PAID" angled across the receipt. The WordArt object is embedded in a worksheet the same way that a chart is; it appears over the cells, covering any content they contain. After you insert the WordArt text box, you enter the text you want to display, and then you can format it by changing its font, color, size, and position—creating the exact look you want.

To add WordArt to a worksheet:

1. On the Insert tab, in the Text group, click the Insert WordArt button. A gallery of WordArt styles opens.
2. Click the WordArt style you want to use. A text box appears on the worksheet with placeholder text selected, and the Drawing Tools Format tab appears on the ribbon.
3. Type the text you want to appear in the WordArt.
4. Drag a resize handle on the selection box to make the WordArt larger or smaller.
5. Drag the WordArt by its selection box to another location on the worksheet.
6. Use the options on the Drawing Tools Format tab to change the selected WordArt's shape, style, text, fill, size, and position.

Stephen wants volunteers to be able to easily print the receipt and transfer the data to another worksheet. In addition, volunteers should enter the registration data in a specific area of the worksheet reserved for input. The application will use this data to automatically generate and print the receipt. To keep the process simple, Stephen wants users to be able to click buttons to print a single receipt, print the entire worksheet, and transfer the data from one worksheet to another. You'll open the workbook Stephen created.

To open and review the Winter workbook:

1. Open the **Winter** workbook located in the **Excel7 > Module** folder included with your Data Files, and then save the workbook as **Winter Activities** in the location specified by your instructor.
2. In the Documentation worksheet, enter your name and the date.
3. Review the contents of each worksheet, and then go to the **Receipt** worksheet. See Figure 7-1.

Figure 7-1 Input area of the Receipt worksheet

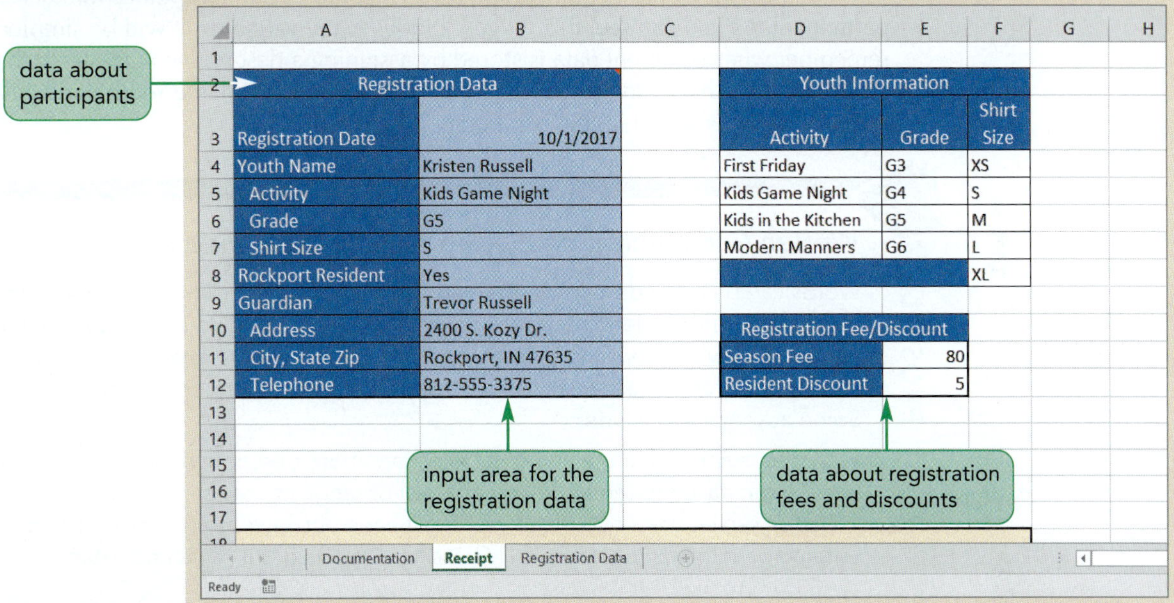

	A	B	C	D	E	F	G	H
1								
2	Registration Data			Youth Information				
3	Registration Date	10/1/2017		Activity	Grade	Shirt Size		
4	Youth Name	Kristen Russell		First Friday	G3	XS		
5	Activity	Kids Game Night		Kids Game Night	G4	S		
6	Grade	G5		Kids in the Kitchen	G5	M		
7	Shirt Size	S		Modern Manners	G6	L		
8	Rockport Resident	Yes				XL		
9	Guardian	Trevor Russell						
10	Address	2400 S. Kozy Dr.		Registration Fee/Discount				
11	City, State Zip	Rockport, IN 47635		Season Fee	80			
12	Telephone	812-555-3375		Resident Discount	5			

Documentation | Receipt | Registration Data

Ready

data about participants

input area for the registration data

data about registration fees and discounts

TIP

Larger and more complex applications often place the input and output areas in separate worksheets.

In addition to the Documentation worksheet, the Winter Activities workbook includes two other worksheets—Receipt and Registration Data. The Receipt worksheet contains input, output, and transfer areas. The input area is divided into the following three parts:

- Registration Data includes items that change for each registration, such as youth name, activity, grade, shirt size, guardian name, address, telephone, and whether the student is a Rockport resident.
- Youth Information is the list of codes for the different activities, grades, and shirt sizes.
- Registration Fee/Discount includes costs that will not change, such as activity fee ($80/youth) and Rockport resident discount ($5/youth).

The output section contains formulas and labels used to generate the receipt based on data in the input section. The receipt in the output section will be printed. The transfer section gathers selected data from the receipt in one area before the data is transferred to the Registration Data worksheet for storage. The transfer section makes it simpler and easier to identify the data to be moved to the Registration Data worksheet for storage and future analysis.

Naming Cells and Ranges

So far, you have referred to a cell or range by its column and row location except when you entered formulas in an Excel table. Cell and range references do not indicate what data is stored in those cells. Instead, you can use a defined name to assign a meaningful, descriptive name to a cell or range. For example, if the range D1:D100 contains sales data for 100 transactions, you can use the defined name Sales to refer to the range of sales data.

A defined name enables you to quickly navigate within a workbook to the cell or range with the defined name. You can also use defined names to create more descriptive formulas. However, keep in mind that the defined name includes only the specified range. Any cells you insert within that range are then included with the defined name, but any cells you insert outside the range with the defined name are not included in the defined name.

In the Receipt worksheet, the range B3:B12 contains the data values for each participant. As you can see, this range includes many variables. It will be simpler to remember where different data is stored by assigning a descriptive name to each cell or range rather than using its cell address. For example, the name YouthName better identifies what is stored in the cell than cell B4.

PROSKILLS

Written Communication: Saving Time with Defined Names

Words can be more descriptive than numbers. This is especially true in cell references. Instead of using the letter and number references for cells, you can create defined names to provide more intuitive references. Defined names have several advantages over cell references, especially as a worksheet becomes longer and more complex. Some advantages include:

- Names, such as TaxRate and TotalSales, are more descriptive than cell references, making it easier to remember what a cell or range contains.
- Names can be used in formulas, making it easier for users to understand the calculations being performed. For example, =GrossPay−Deductions is more understandable than =C15−C16.
- When you move a named cell or range within a worksheet, its name moves with it. Any formulas that contain the name automatically reference the new location.
- In a formula, referencing a named cell or range is the same as referencing the cell or range's absolute reference. So, if you move a formula that includes a defined name, the reference remains pointed to the correct cell or range.

By using defined names, you'll often save time, and everyone reviewing the worksheet will have a clearer understanding of what a formula is calculating.

Creating defined names for cells or ranges makes it easier to create and understand the formulas in a workbook. When you define a name for a cell or range, keep in mind the following rules:

- The name must begin with a letter or _ (an underscore).
- The name can include letters and numbers as well as periods and underscores but not other symbols or spaces. To distinguish multiword names, use an underscore between the words or capitalize the first letter of each word. For example, the names Net_Income and NetIncome are valid, but Net Income and Net-Income are not.
- The name cannot be a valid cell address (such as FY2017), a function name (such as Average), or a reserved word (such as Print_Area).
- The name can include as many as 255 characters, although short, meaningful names of 5 to 15 characters are more practical.
- The name is not case sensitive. For example, both Sales and SALES refer to the same cell or range.

REFERENCE

Creating a Defined Name for a Cell or Range

- Select the cell or range to which you want to assign a name.
- Click in the Name box, type the name, and then press the Enter key (or on the Formulas tab, in the Defined Names group, click the Define Name button, type a name in the Name box, and then click the OK button).

or

- Select the range with labels to which you want to assign a name.
- On the Formulas tab, in the Defined Names group, click the Create from Selection button.
- Specify whether to create the ranges based on the top row, bottom row, left column, or right column in the list.
- Click the OK button.

Using the Name Box to Create Defined Names

The Name box is a quick way to create a defined name for a selected cell or range. Stephen wants you to create defined names for cells and ranges in the Receipt worksheet. You'll start by using the Name box to define some of these names.

To create defined names for the input area using the Name box:

1. Select cell **E11**, and then click the **Name box** to the left of the formula bar. The cell reference for the active cell, E11 is selected in the Name box.
2. Type **ActivityFee** and then press the **Enter** key. Cell E11 remains active, and ActivityFee appears in the Name box instead of the cell reference. See Figure 7-2.

Figure 7-2 **Defined name for cell E11**

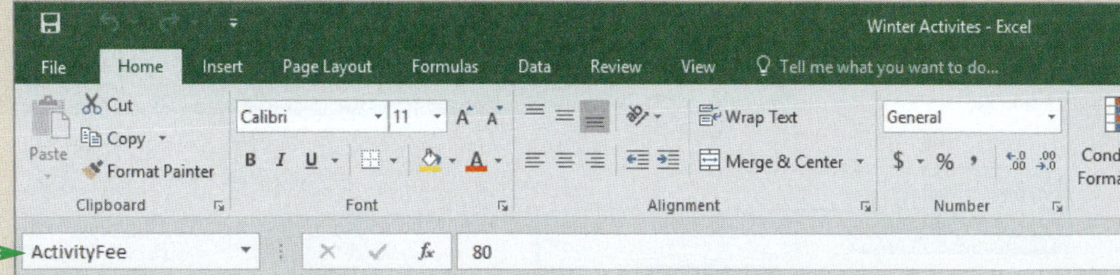

Trouble? If ActivityFee appears in cell E11, you did not click the Name box before typing the name. On the Quick Access Toolbar, click the Undo button, and then repeat Steps 1 and 2.

3. Select cell **E12**, click the **Name box** to select the cell reference, type **RockportDisc** and then press the **Enter** key. Cell E12 remains active, and RockportDisc appears in the Name box instead of the cell reference.
4. Select the range **D2:F8**. The cell reference for the active cell in the range appears in the Name box.
5. Click the **Name box**, type **YouthInfo** and then press the **Enter** key. The name YouthInfo is assigned to the range D2:F8.
6. Select the range **A40:F40**, click the **Name box**, type **TransferArea** and then press the **Enter** key. The name TransferArea is assigned to the range A40:F40.

7. Select cell **E33**, click the **Name box** to select the cell reference, type **RecActivityFee** and then press the **Enter** key. Cell E33 remains active, and RecActivityFee appears in the Name box instead of the cell reference.
8. Select cell **E34**, click the **Name box** to select the cell reference, type **RecRockportDisc** and then press the **Enter** key. Cell E34 remains active, and RecRockportDisc appears in the Name box instead of the cell reference.

Selecting Cells and Ranges by Their Defined Names

The Name box displays all of the defined names in a workbook. You can click a name in the Name box list to quickly select the cell or range referenced by that name. Stephen wants you to verify that defined names are associated with the correct cell or range. You'll view the defined names you added to the workbook, and then use them to select cells and ranges.

To select cells and ranges with the Name box:

1. Click the **Name box arrow** to open a list of defined names in the workbook. Six names appear in the list.

   If the names are longer than the Name box, you can make the Name box wider so that the full names are visible by performing Steps 2 and 3. Otherwise, skip to Step 4.
2. Press the **Esc key** to close the Name box.
3. On the right side of the Name box, drag the sizing handle (the three vertical dots) to the right until you can see the full names.
4. Click the **Name box arrow** to display the list of defined names. See Figure 7-3.

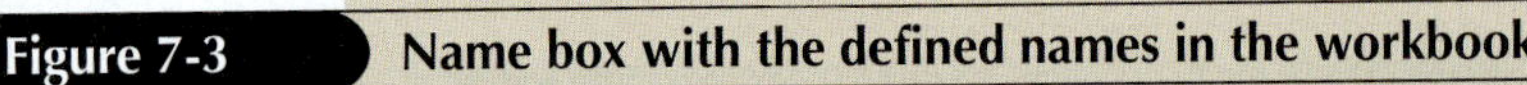

Figure 7-3 Name box with the defined names in the workbook

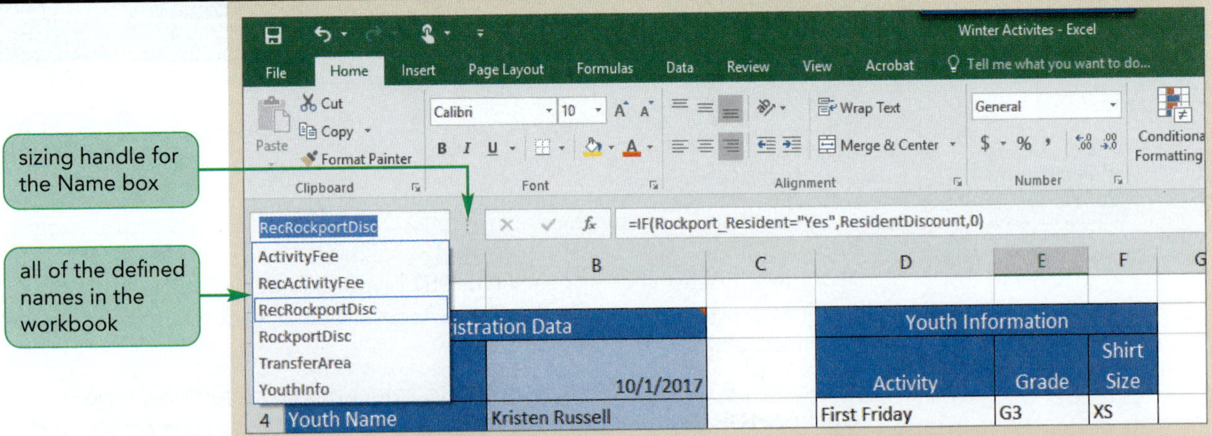

5. Click **ActivityFee**. Cell E11 becomes the active cell.
6. Click the **Name box arrow**, and then click **YouthInfo**. The range D2:F8 is selected in the worksheet.
7. Repeat Step 6 to select the **RockportDisc**, **RecRockportDisc**, **RecActivityFee**, and **TransferArea** defined names in the Name box to confirm that they select their associated cell or range.

Creating Defined Names by Selection

You can quickly define names without typing them if the data is organized as a structured range of data with labels in the first or last column or in the top or bottom row. The defined names are based on the row or column labels. For example, the Registration Data area contains labels in column A that can be used as the defined names for the corresponding cells in column B. Any blank space or parenthesis in a label is changed to an underscore (_) in the defined name.

Stephen wants you to create names for each cell in the Registration Data area using the labels in the range A3:A12 to name the cells in the range B3:B12.

Select only the range A3:B12; otherwise, formulas you create later in this module will not work.

To create defined names by selection for the registration data:

1. Select the range **A3:B12**. Column A contains the labels you want to use as the defined names, and column B contains the cells you want to name.
2. On the ribbon, click the **Formulas** tab.
3. In the Defined Names group, click the **Create from Selection** button. The Create Names from Selection dialog box opens.
4. Make sure only the **Left column** check box contains a checkmark. The labels in the left column will be used to create the defined names. See Figure 7-4.

Figure 7-4 Create Names from Selection dialog box

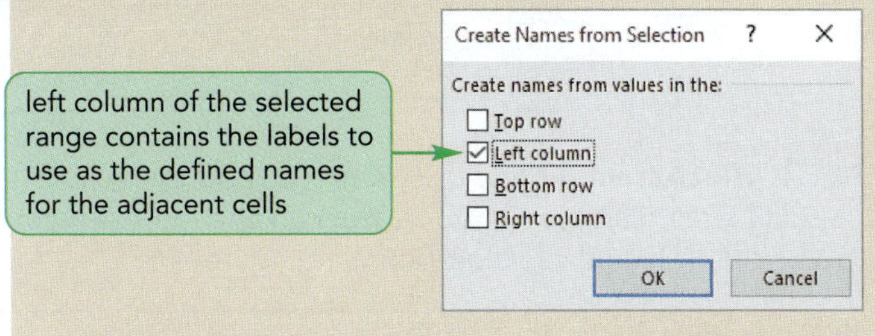

5. Click the **OK** button. Each cell in the range B3:B12 is named based on its corresponding label in column A. For example, cell B3 is named Registration_Date based on the Registration Date label in cell A3.
6. Click the **Name box arrow** to see the 16 defined names in the list. Notice that underscores have replaced spaces in the names.
7. Press the **Esc** key to close the list of defined names.

Editing and Deleting Defined Names

Although you can use the Name box to verify that the names were created, the Name Manager dialog box lists all of the names currently defined in the workbook, including Excel table names. In addition to the name, it identifies the current value for that name as well as the worksheet and cell or range it references. You can use the Name Manager dialog box to create a new name, edit or delete existing names, and filter the list of names.

The names RecActivityFee and RecRockportDisc define the location of these two cells on the worksheet. Although the names are descriptive, they are also fairly long. Stephen wants you to use the shorter names ReceiptFee and ReceiptDisc, respectively, which still reflect the stored data in each cell. Stephen also decides that the TransferArea and YouthInfo defined names are not needed, so you will delete them.

To edit and delete defined names with the Name Manager dialog box:

1. On the Formulas tab, in the Defined Names group, click the **Name Manager** button (or press the **Ctrl+F3** keys). The Name Manager dialog box opens, listing the 16 defined names in the workbook. See Figure 7-5.

Figure 7-5 Name Manager dialog box

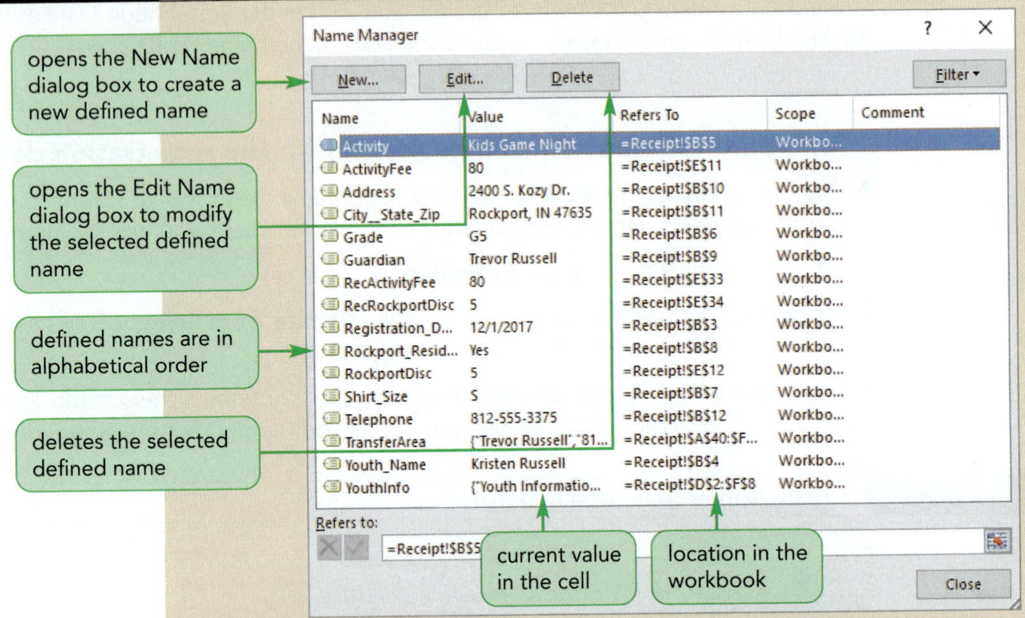
opens the New Name dialog box to create a new defined name
opens the Edit Name dialog box to modify the selected defined name
defined names are in alphabetical order
deletes the selected defined name
current value in the cell
location in the workbook

2. Click **RecActivityFee** in the Name list, and then click the **Edit** button. The Edit Name dialog box opens. You can change the name and its referenced cell or range in this dialog box. See Figure 7-6.

Figure 7-6 Edit Name dialog box

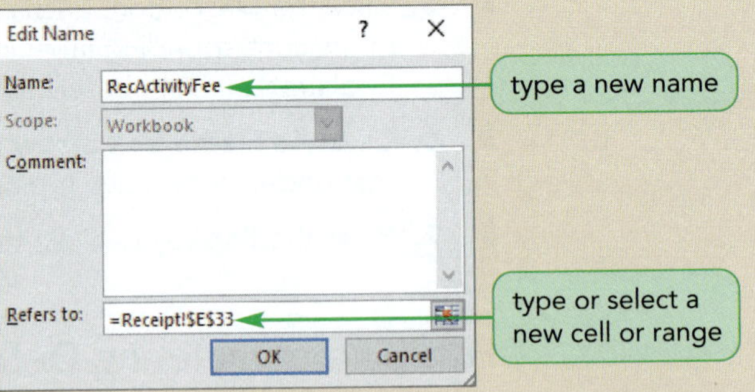
type a new name
type or select a new cell or range

3. In the Name box, type **ReceiptFee** to create a shorter defined name, and then click the **OK** button. The edited name appears in the list in the Name Manager dialog box.
4. Repeat Steps 2 and 3 to rename the RecRockportDisc defined name as **ReceiptDisc**.
5. Click **TransferArea**, and then click the **Delete** button. A dialog box opens to confirm that you want to delete the selected defined name.
6. Click the **OK** button. The name is removed from the list.

7. Repeat Steps 5 and 6 to delete the **YouthInfo** name.
8. Click the **Close** button. The Name Manager dialog box closes.

Using the Paste Names Command

When a workbook contains many defined names, it can be helpful to list all of the defined names and their corresponding cell addresses in the workbook's documentation. You can generate a list of names using the Paste Names command.

To create a list of the defined names in the Documentation worksheet:

1. Go to the **Documentation** worksheet.
2. In cell **B10**, enter **Defined Names**, and then format the label with bold.
3. Select cell **B11**. This is the upper-left cell of the range where you want to paste the list of defined names.
4. On the Formulas tab, in the Defined Names group, click the **Use in Formula** button, and then click **Paste Names** (or press the **F3** key). The Paste Name dialog box opens. You can paste any selected name, or you can paste the entire list of names.
5. Click the **Paste List** button. The defined names and their associated cell references are pasted into the range B11:C24.
6. Click cell **A10** to deselect the range. See Figure 7-7. Only some names in the pasted list of defined names include underscores in place of spaces. The names with underscores were created using the Create from Selection button; you entered the names without underscores in the Name box.

Figure 7-7 **Defined names in the Winter Activities workbook**

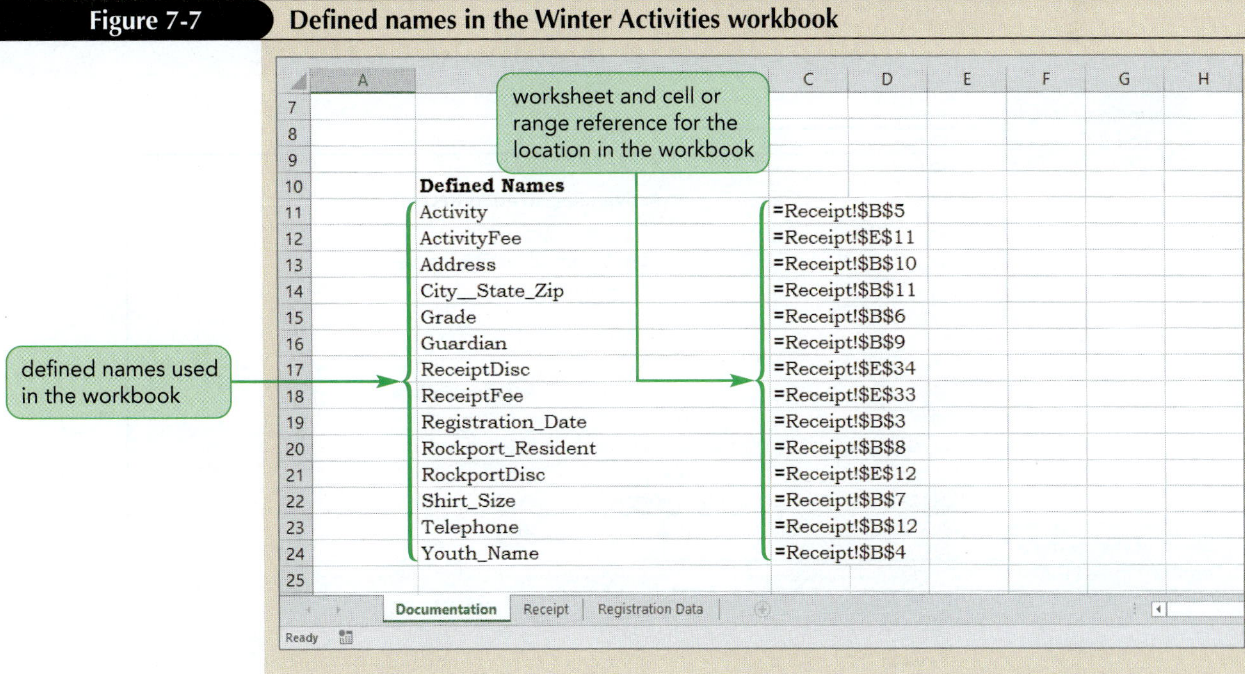

If you edit a defined name or add a new defined name, the list of defined names and their addresses in the Documentation worksheet is not updated. You must paste the list again to update the names and locations. Usually, it is a good idea to wait until the workbook is complete before pasting defined names in the Documentation worksheet.

Using Defined Names in Formulas

You can create more descriptive formulas by using defined names instead of cell or range references in formulas. For example, in the following formulas, the defined name Sales replaces the range reference D1:D100 in a formula to calculate average sales:

Range reference =AVERAGE(D1:D100)
Defined name =AVERAGE(Sales)

Keep in mind that range references in formulas are not updated with their defined names. So, if you enter a range reference in a formula, its corresponding defined name does *not* automatically replace the range reference in the formula.

Stephen wants you to enter the formulas required to generate the receipt. You'll start by entering formulas to display the registration date, the guardian's name, and the guardian's address entered in the Registration Data area in the receipt.

To enter formulas to display the guardian's name and address on the receipt:

1. Go to the **Receipt** worksheet.
2. In cell **B27**, enter **=B9**. Trevor Russell, the guardian's name, appears in the cell.
3. In cell **B28**, enter **=B10**. 2400 S. Kozy Dr., the guardian's street address, appears in the cell.
4. In cell **B29**, enter **=B11**. The guardian's city, state, and Zip code—Rockport, IN 47635—appear in the cell.
5. Select cell **B29**. The formula =B11 appears in the formula bar. See Figure 7-8.

Figure 7-8 Formula to display the City, State and Zip data

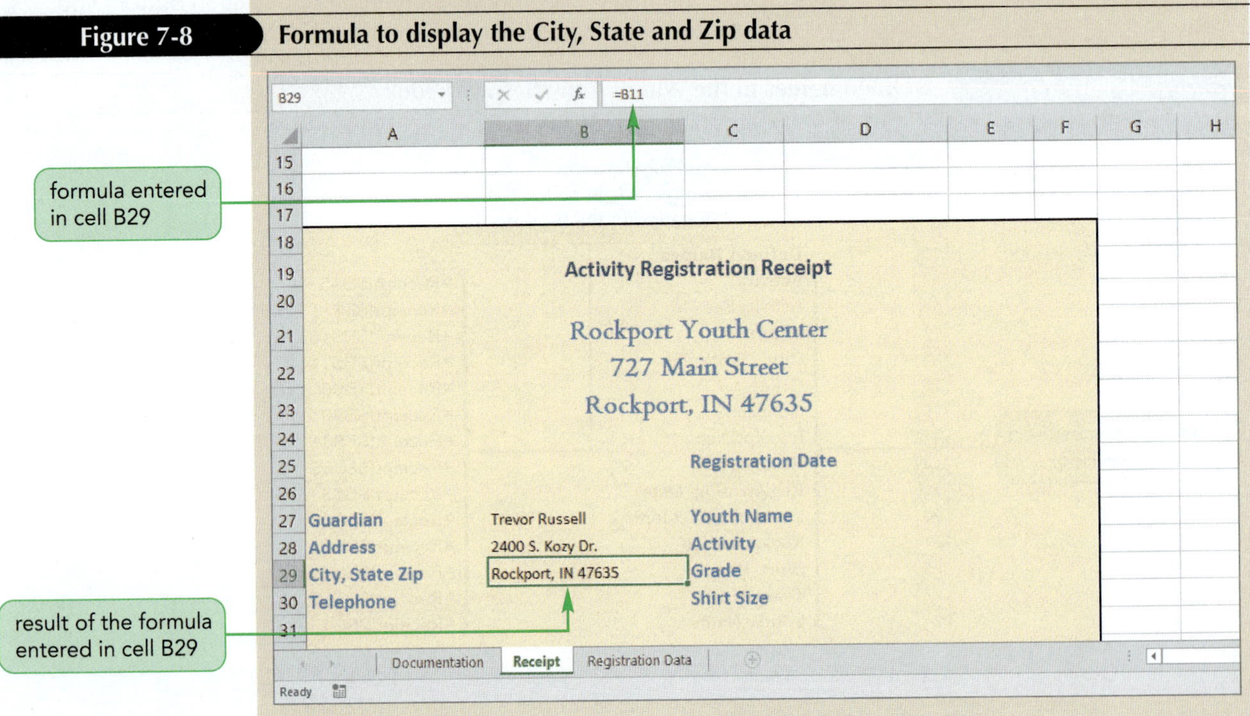

You entered these formulas using cell addresses rather than defined names. Although you defined names for cells B9, B10, and B11, the names do not automatically replace the cell addresses in the formula when you type the cell addresses.

Entering Formulas with Defined Names

Defined names make formulas simpler to enter and understand. To use a defined name in a formula, you enter the formula as usual. As you type a defined name in a formula, the Formula AutoComplete box appears, listing functions and defined names that begin with the letters you typed. As you type additional letters, the list narrows. You can double-click the name you want in the Formula AutoComplete box or press the Tab key to enter the selected name. You can also just continue to type the rest of the name.

Stephen wants you to use named cells and ranges in the remaining formulas. You'll enter these now.

To enter defined names in formulas:

1. In cell **B30**, type **=T** to display a list of functions and defined names that begin with the letter T.
2. Type **el** to narrow the list to the defined name =Telephone.
3. Press the **Tab** key to enter the defined name in the formula, and then press the **Enter** key. The guardian's telephone number appears in the cell.
4. Select cell **B30**. The data from cell B12 appears in the cell, and the formula with the defined name =Telephone appears in the formula bar.
5. In cell **E25**, enter **=Reg** to list the defined name =Registration_Date, press the **Tab** key to insert the defined name in the formula, and then press the **Enter** key.
6. Select cell **E25**. The data from cell B3, 10/1/2017, appears in the cell, and the formula with the defined name =Registration_Date appears in the formula bar. See Figure 7-9.

Figure 7-9 Formula with a defined name

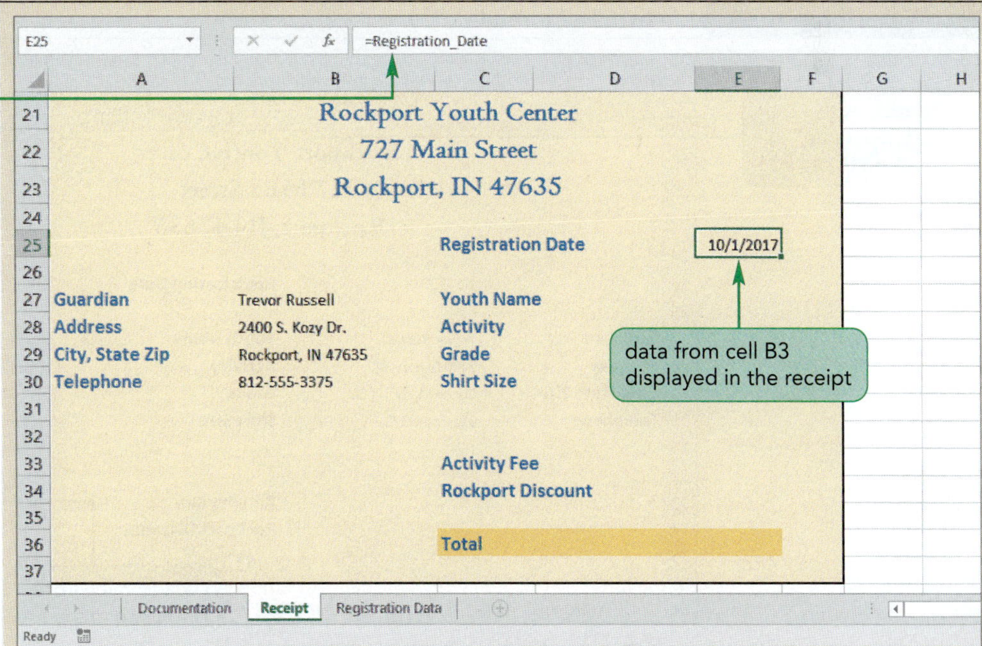

Trouble? If the date is displayed as an integer, you need to reformat the cell as a date. On the ribbon, click the Home tab. In the Number group, click the Number Format box arrow, and then click Short Date. AutoFit column E so that the date is displayed.

You can also use the point-and-click method to create a formula with defined names. When you click a cell or select a range, Excel substitutes the defined name for the cell reference in the formula. You'll use this method to enter formulas that display the youth name, activity, grade, and shirt size from the Registration Data area in the Activity Registration Receipt area.

To enter formulas with defined names using the point-and-click method:

1. Select cell **E27**, type **=**, and then click cell **B4**. The formula uses the defined name Youth_Name rather than the cell reference B4.
2. Press the **Enter** key. Kristen Russell, which is the name of the participant, appears in cell E27.
3. In cell **E28**, type **=**, and then click cell **B5**. The formula uses the defined name Activity rather than the cell reference B5.
4. Press the **Enter** key. Kids Game Night appears in cell E28.
5. In cell **E29**, type **=**, click cell **B6**, and then press the **Enter** key. The grade code, G5, appears in cell E29, and the formula with the defined name =Grade appears in the formula bar.
6. In cell **E30**, type **=**, click cell **B7**, and then press the **Enter** key. The participant's shirt size, S for small, appears in cell E30, and the formula with the defined name =Shirt_Size appears in the formula bar.
7. In cell **E33**, type **=**, click cell **E11**, and then click the **Enter** button ✓ on the formula bar. The activity fee, 80, appears in cell E33 and the formula with the defined name =ActivityFee appears in the formula bar. See Figure 7-10.

Figure 7-10 **ActivityFee formula**

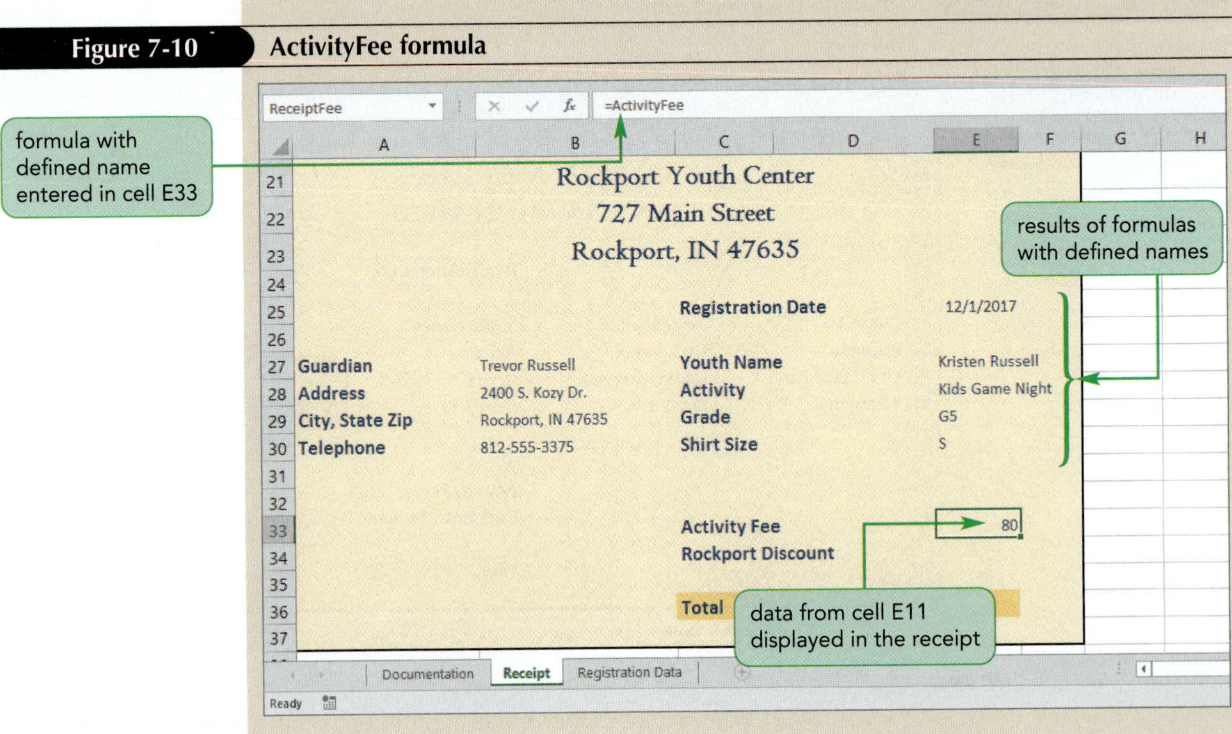

Next, Stephen wants you to enter the formula to calculate the total registration paid based on the data in the Registration Fee/Discount area. All participants pay the activity fee ($80). Rockport residents receive a $5 discount. You will need to use an IF function to determine whether the participant will receive the $5 discount.

To enter the IF function to calculate the registration total:

1. Select cell **E34**. The defined name ReceiptDisc appears in the Name box.
2. On the Formulas tab, in the Function Library group, click the **Logical** button, and then click **IF**. The Function Arguments dialog box opens.
3. In the Logical_test box, type **Rockport_Resident="Yes"**. This logical test evaluates whether the youth qualifies for the Rockport resident discount. If the value in cell B8 equals Yes, then the condition is true. TRUE appears to the right of the Logical_test box, indicating that this youth qualifies for the Rockport resident discount of $5.

   Trouble? If an error value appears to the right of the Logical_test box, you probably mistyped the formula. If the error value is #NAME?, you mistyped the defined name or didn't include quotation marks around the word "Yes." If the error value is Invalid, you used single quotation marks (') around the word "Yes." Edit the content in the Logical_test box as needed.

TIP

You must use quotation marks around text in the IF function.

4. In the Value_if_true box, type **RockportDisc**—the defined name for cell E12, which has the value 5. This discount amount will be added to the receipt if the logical test is true.
5. In the Value_if_false box, type **0** to indicate that no discount will be applied if the value in cell B8 does not equal Yes. See Figure 7-11.

Figure 7-11 Completed IF Function Arguments dialog box

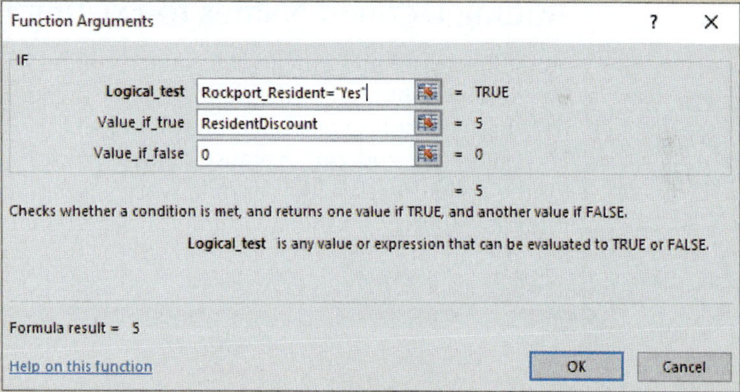

6. Click the **OK** button to enter the IF function in cell E34. In this case, cell E34 displays 5 because the participant is a Rockport resident.
7. In cell **E36**, enter the formula **=ReceiptFee-ReceiptDisc** to calculate the registration total, which is $75. See Figure 7-12.

Figure 7-12 Receipt with all formulas entered

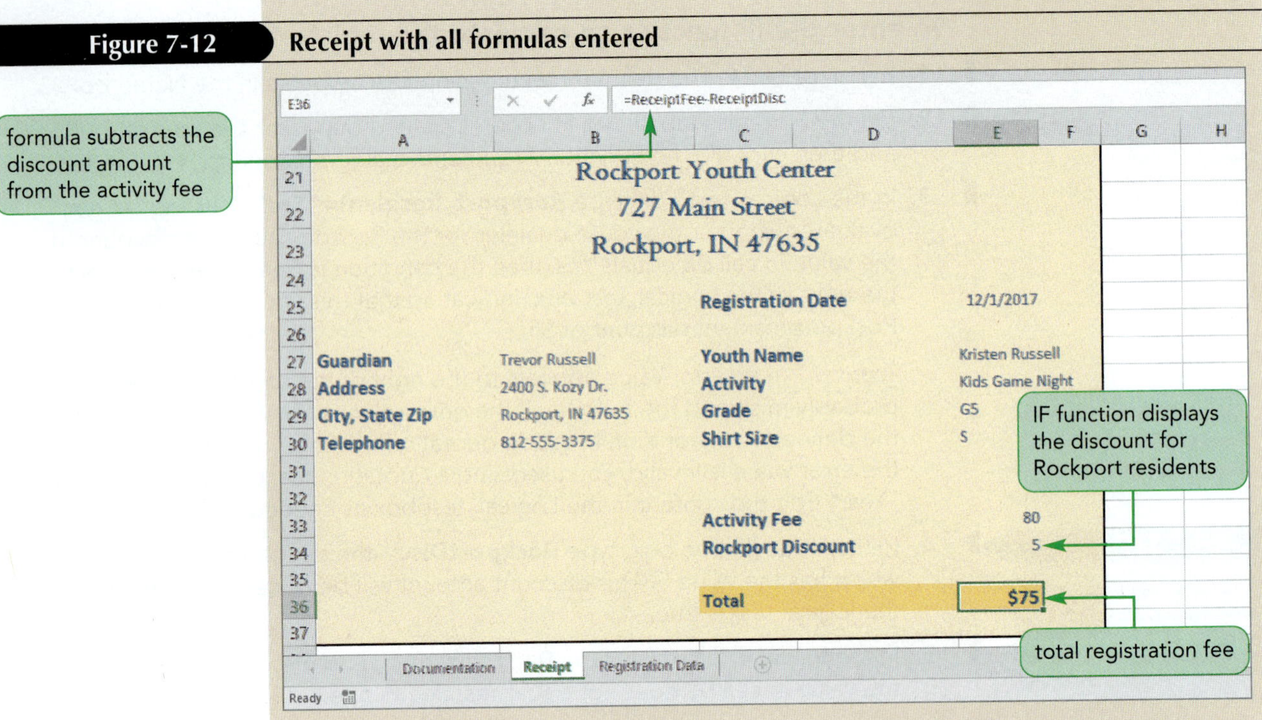

Adding Defined Names to Existing Formulas

Sometimes you might name cells after creating formulas in the worksheet. Other times you might not use the defined names when you create formulas (as with the first three formulas you created in the receipt for the guardian; guardian address; and city, state, and zip). Because defined names are not automatically substituted for the cell addresses in a formula, you can replace cell addresses in existing formulas in the worksheet with their defined names to make the formulas more understandable.

REFERENCE

Adding Defined Names to Existing Formulas

- On the Formulas tab, in the Defined Names group, click the Define Name button arrow, and then click Apply Names (if the cell reference and defined name are in the same worksheet).
- In the Apply Names dialog box, select the names you want to apply.
- Click the OK button.

or

- Edit the formula by selecting the cell reference and typing the defined name or clicking the appropriate cell.

In the formulas you created to display the guardian's name, address, and city state zip in the receipt, Stephen wants you to use defined names instead of cell references. This will make the formulas much clearer to anyone who looks at the worksheet.

To add defined names to existing formulas in the receipt:

1. On the Formulas tab, in the Defined Names group, click the **Define Name button arrow**, and then click **Apply Names**. The Apply Names dialog box opens. See Figure 7-13.

Figure 7-13 Apply Names dialog box

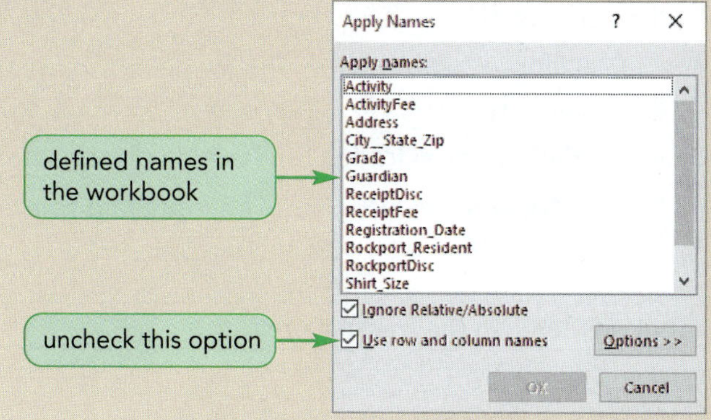

You want to select only the names you need for the existing formulas with cell references.

2. If any name is selected in the Apply names list, click that name to deselect it.
3. In the Apply names list, click **Address, City_State_Zip**, and **Guardian**. The three names you want to apply to the formulas are selected.
4. Make sure that the **Use row and column names** check box is unchecked. If you leave this checked, the formula will contain too many characters and return an error.
5. Click the **OK** button. The three selected names are applied to the formulas.
6. Click cell **B27** and verify that the formula changed to =Guardian.
7. Click cell **B28** and verify that the formula changed to =Address.
8. Click cell **B29** and verify that the formula changed to =City__State_Zip. The formulas now use the defined names in the files.

TIP

You can also select a cell that contains a formula, click the Use in Formula button in the Defined Names group, click the name to replace the cell reference, and then press the Enter key.

Stephen wants to store the following items in the Registration Data worksheet—guardian, telephone, youth name, activity, grade, and shirt size. Displaying this data in the Transfer Area enables you to copy and paste all of these items to the Registration Data worksheet at once. You'll enter formulas to display the appropriate items in this section of the worksheet.

To enter formulas to display data in the Transfer Area:

1. In cell **A40**, enter **=Guardian**. The formula displays the guardian name (Trevor Russell).
2. In cell **B40**, enter **=Telephone**. The formula displays the telephone number (812-555-3375).
3. In cell **C40**, enter **=Youth_Name**. The formula displays the name of the youth (Kristen Russell).
4. In cell **D40**, enter **=Activity**. The formula displays the Activity of the youth (Kids Game Night).
5. In cell **E40**, enter **=Grade**. The formula displays the youth Grade (G5).
6. In cell **F40**, enter **=Shirt_Size**. The formula displays the Shirt Size (S). See Figure 7-14.

Figure 7-14 Formulas entered in the Transfer Area

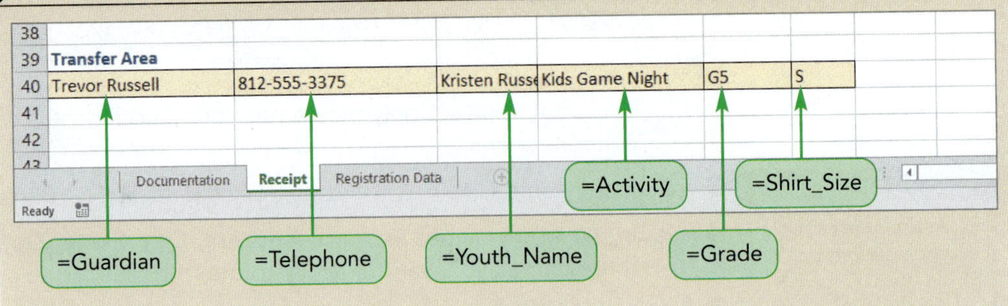

The worksheet contains all of the formulas required to create the receipt based on the registration data. Because Stephen relies on volunteers to enter registration data into the worksheet and print receipts, he wants to be sure the values entered are correct. You will continue to work on Stephen's application by creating validation checks, which are designed to prevent users from inserting incorrect data values. You will also protect cells so that volunteers cannot accidentally overwrite or delete the formulas. You'll complete both of these tasks in the next session.

REVIEW

Session 7.1 Quick Check

1. What is an Excel application?
2. What areas of a worksheet should you consider including in an Excel application?
3. What are two advantages of using defined names in workbooks?
4. What are three ways to create a defined name?
5. Is Annual Sales a valid defined name? Explain why or why not.
6. How do you select a cell or range using its defined name?
7. In the Report workbook, the defined name "Expenses" refers to a list of expenses in the range D2:D100. Currently, the total expenses are calculated by the formula =SUM(D2:D100). Change this formula to use the defined name.
8. How do you add defined names to existing formulas?

Session 7.2 Visual Overview:

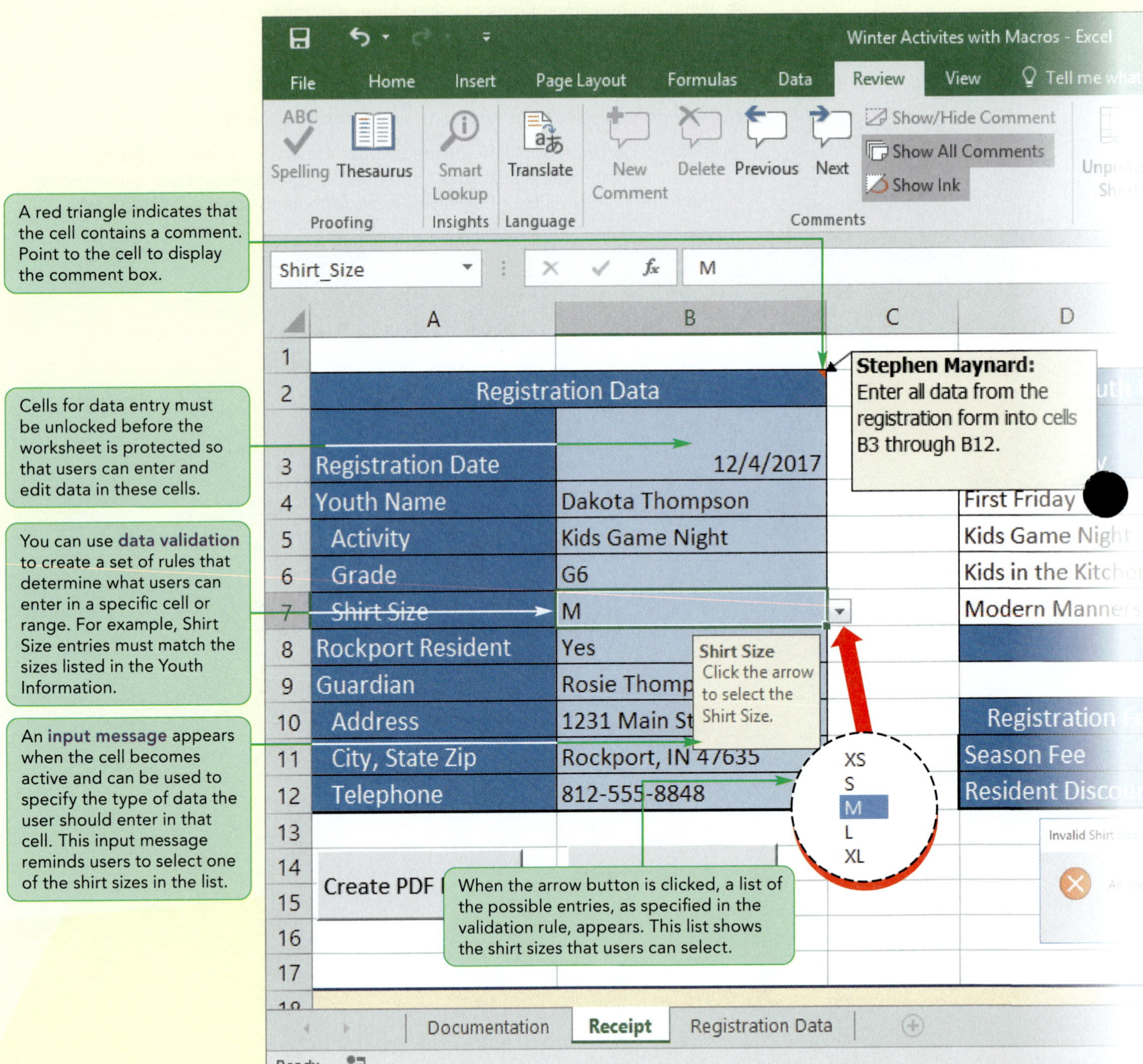
A red triangle indicates that the cell contains a comment. Point to the cell to display the comment box.
Cells for data entry must be unlocked before the worksheet is protected so that users can enter and edit data in these cells.
You can use data validation to create a set of rules that determine what users can enter in a specific cell or range. For example, Shirt Size entries must match the sizes listed in the Youth Information.
An input message appears when the cell becomes active and can be used to specify the type of data the user should enter in that cell. This input message reminds users to select one of the shirt sizes in the list.
When the arrow button is clicked, a list of the possible entries, as specified in the validation rule, appears. This list shows the shirt sizes that users can select.
Winter Activites with Macros - Excel
File
Home
Insert
Page Layout
Formulas
Data
Review
View
Tell me what y
Spelling
Thesaurus
Smart Lookup
Translate
New Comment
Delete
Previous
Next
Show/Hide Comment
Show All Comments
Show Ink
Proofing
Insights
Language
Comments
Shirt_Size
M
Stephen Maynard:
Enter all data from the registration form into cells B3 through B12.
Registration Data
Registration Date
12/4/2017
Youth Name
Dakota Thompson
Activity
Kids Game Night
Grade
G6
Shirt Size
M
Rockport Resident
Yes
Guardian
Rosie Thomp
Address
1231 Main St
City, State Zip
Rockport, IN 47635
Telephone
812-555-8848
Shirt Size
Click the arrow to select the Shirt Size.
XS
S
M
L
XL
First Friday
Kids Game Nigh
Kids in the Kitch
Modern Manne
Registration Fe
Season Fee
Resident Discou
Create PDF
Documentation
Receipt
Registration Data
Ready

Data Validation and Protection

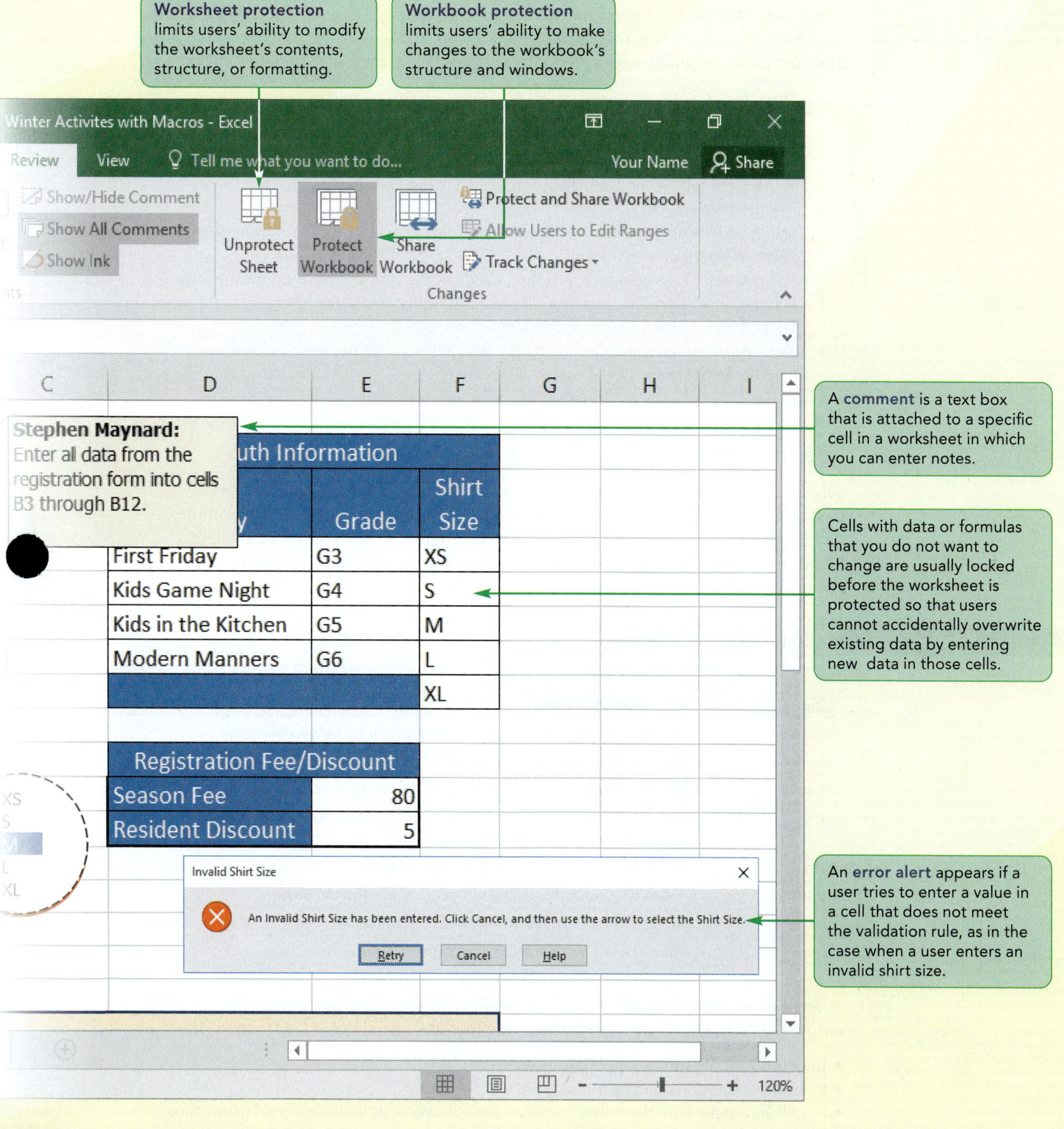
Worksheet protection limits users' ability to modify the worksheet's contents, structure, or formatting.
Workbook protection limits users' ability to make changes to the workbook's structure and windows.
Winter Activites with Macros - Excel
Review
View
Tell me what you want to do...
Your Name
Share
Show/Hide Comment
Show All Comments
Show Ink
Unprotect Sheet
Protect Workbook
Share Workbook
Protect and Share Workbook
Allow Users to Edit Ranges
Track Changes
Changes
C
D
E
F
G
H
I
Stephen Maynard:
Enter all data from the registration form into cells B3 through B12.
uth Information
Grade
Shirt Size
First Friday
G3
XS
Kids Game Night
G4
S
Kids in the Kitchen
G5
M
Modern Manners
G6
L
XL
Registration Fee/Discount
Season Fee
80
Resident Discount
5
XS
S
M
L
XL
Invalid Shirt Size
An Invalid Shirt Size has been entered. Click Cancel, and then use the arrow to select the Shirt Size.
Retry
Cancel
Help
120%
A **comment** is a text box that is attached to a specific cell in a worksheet in which you can enter notes.
Cells with data or formulas that you do not want to change are usually locked before the worksheet is protected so that users cannot accidentally overwrite existing data by entering new data in those cells.
An **error alert** appears if a user tries to enter a value in a cell that does not meet the validation rule, as in the case when a user enters an invalid shirt size.

Validating Data Entry

TIP

Each cell can have only one validation rule. Any subsequent validation rule replaces the existing rule.

When collecting data, accuracy is important. To ensure that correct data is entered and stored in a worksheet, you can use data validation. Each **validation rule** defines criteria for the data that can be entered and stored in a cell or range. You can also add input and error alert messages for the user to that cell or range. You specify the validation criteria, the input message, and the error alert for the active cell in the Data Validation dialog box.

REFERENCE

Validating Data

- On the Data tab, in the Data Tools group, click the Data Validation button.
- Click the Settings tab.
- Click the Allow arrow, click the type of data allowed in the cell, and then enter the validation criteria for that data.
- Click the Input Message tab, and then enter a title and text for the input message.
- Click the Error Alert tab, and then, if necessary, click the Show error alert after invalid data is entered check box to insert a checkmark.
- Select an alert style, and then enter the title and text for the error alert message.
- Click the OK button.

Specifying Validation Criteria

When you create a validation rule, you specify the type of data that is allowed as well as a list or range of acceptable values (called **validation criteria**). For example, you might specify integers between 1 and 100 or a list of codes such as Excellent, Good, Fair, and Poor. Figure 7-15 describes the types of data you can allow and the acceptable values for each type.

Figure 7-15 **Allow options for validation**

Type	Acceptable Values
Any value	Any number, text, or date; removes any existing data validation
Whole Number	Integers only; you can specify the range of acceptable integers
Decimal	Any type of number; you can specify the range of acceptable numbers
List	Any value in a range or entered in the Data validation dialog box separated by commas
Date	Dates only; you can specify the range of acceptable dates
Time	Times only; you can specify the range of acceptable times
Text Length	Text limited to a specified number of characters
Custom	Values based on the results of a logical formula

Stephen wants you to add the following six validation rules to the workbook to help ensure that volunteers enter valid data in the Receipt worksheet:

- In cell B3, make sure a valid date is entered.
- In cell B4, specify an input message.
- In cell B5, make sure the value is one of the following activities—First Friday, Kids Game Night, Kids in the Kitchen, or Modern Manners.
- In cell B6, make sure the value is one of the following grades—G3, G4, G5, or G6.
- In cell B7, make sure the value is one of the following shirt sizes—XS, S, M, L, or XL.
- In cell B8, make sure the Rockport resident value is Yes or No.

Cell B3, which contains the Registration Date, requires the date that the registration was submitted, which is not necessary the date the registration is entered in the system. Stephen wants to be sure everyone enters a valid date in this cell. You will define the validation rule for the Registration Date.

To create the validation rule for the Registration Date cell:

1. If you took a break after the previous session, make sure the Winter Activities workbook is open and the Receipt worksheet is active.
2. Select cell **B3**. You will enter a date validation rule to ensure that a valid date is entered in this cell.
3. On the ribbon, click the **Data** tab.
4. In the Data Tools group, click the **Data Validation** button. The Data Validation dialog box opens with the Settings tab displayed. You use the Settings tab to enter the validation rule for the active cell.
5. On the Settings tab, click the **Allow arrow**, and then click **Date**. The Data Validation dialog box expands to display the options specific to dates.
6. Click the **Ignore blank** check box to deselect it. You want to ensure that cell B3 is not left blank and require users to enter a date value in the cell.
7. If necessary, click the **Data arrow**, and then click **greater than or equal to.** The dialog box reflects the selected criteria.
8. Enter **1/1/2017** in the Start date box to provide an example of what to look for when checking the cell. You cannot use data validation to simply check for the presence of data. You must provide an example for checking. See Figure 7-16.

TIP

To apply a validation rule to multiple cells, select the range and then create the validation rule.

Figure 7-16 Settings tab in the Data Validation dialog box

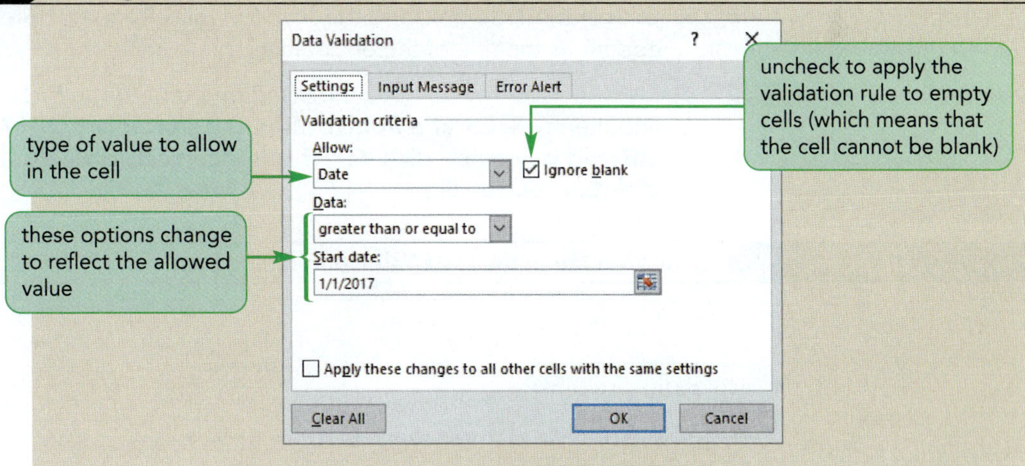

If you wanted to create a validation rule that checks if the date is the current date, you would select "equal to" in the Data list and then enter =TODAY() in the Date box. Then, a user cannot enter any date other than the current date. Stephen wants to check only for the presence of a date because sometimes the registration form is submitted on a different day than its data is entered.

Creating an Error Alert Style and Message

An error alert determines what happens after a user tries to make an invalid entry in a cell that has a validation rule defined. The three error alert styles are Stop, Warning, and Information. The Stop alert prevents the entry from being stored in the cell. The Warning alert prevents the entry from being stored in the cell unless the user overrides the rejection and decides to continue using the data. The Information alert accepts the data value entered but allows the user to choose to cancel the data entry.

Stephen wants to display an error alert if a volunteer enters data that violates the validation rule. Although the registration date is usually equal to the current date, a user might forget to enter the date. To account for this possibility, Stephen wants you to create a Warning error alert that appears when a user does not enter a registration date or enters a date prior to 1/1/2017. The user can then verify the date entered. If the entry is correct, the user can accept the entry. If the entry is incorrect, the user can reenter the correct date.

You'll create the Warning error alert for the Registration Date cell.

To create the Warning error alert for the Registration Date cell:

1. Make sure cell **B3** is still the active cell and the Data Validation dialog box is still open.
2. In the Data Validation dialog box, click the **Error Alert** tab. You use this tab to select the type of error alert and enter the message you want to appear.
3. Make sure that the **Show error alert after invalid data is entered** check box is selected. If unchecked, the error alert won't appear when an invalid value is entered in the cell.
4. Click the **Style arrow**, and then click **Warning**. This style allows the user to accept the invalid value, return to the cell and reenter a valid value, or cancel the data entry and restore the previous value to the cell.
5. Click in the **Title** box, and then type **Invalid Registration Date**. This text will appear as the title of the error alert box.
6. Press the **Tab** key to move the insertion point to the Error message box, and then type **Enter a Registration Date after 1/1/2017. If the date you entered is correct, click Yes. If it is incorrect, click No. If you are not sure, click Cancel.** See Figure 7-17.

TIP

You can change between showing and hiding the input and error alert messages as needed for new and experienced users.

Figure 7-17 Error Alert tab in the Data Validation dialog box

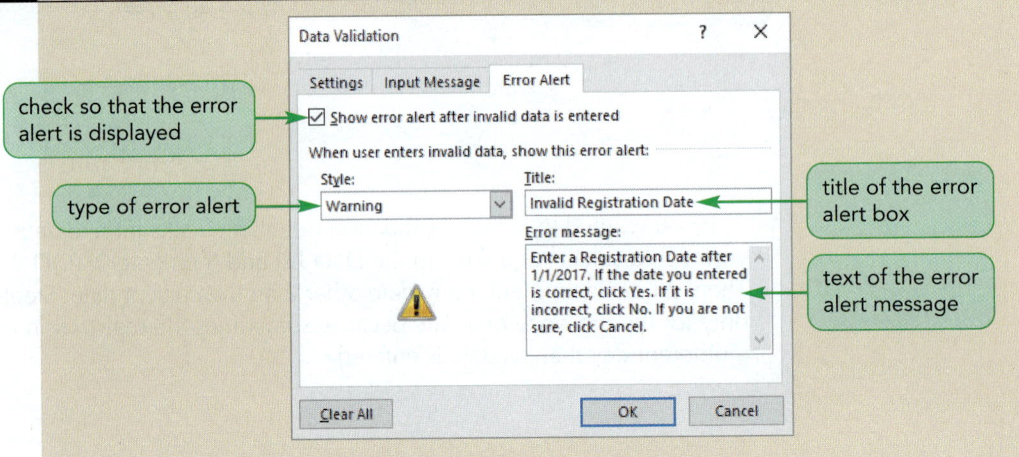

7. Click the **OK** button. The Data Validation dialog box closes.

Creating an Input Message

One way to reduce the chance of a data-entry error is to display an input message when a user makes the cell active. An input message provides additional information about the type of data allowed for that cell. Input messages appear as ScreenTips next to the cell when the cell is selected. You can add an input message to a cell even if you don't set up a rule to validate the data in that cell.

Stephen wants volunteers to see that they must enter a value for the Youth Name in cell B4. An input message will minimize the chance of a volunteer skipping this cell, so you will create an input message for cell B4.

To create an input message for the Youth Name cell:

1. Select cell **B4**. You will create an input message for this cell.
2. On the Data tab, in the Data Tools group, click the **Data Validation** button. The Data Validation dialog box opens.
3. Click the **Input Message** tab. You enter the input message title and text on this tab.
4. Verify that the **Show input message when cell is selected** check box contains a checkmark. If you uncheck this option, you cannot enter a new input message, and any existing input message will not be displayed when the selected cell becomes active.
5. Click in the **Title** box, and then type **Youth Name**. This title will appear in bold at the top of the ScreenTip above the text of the input message.
6. Press the **Tab** key to move the insertion point to the Input message box, and then type **Enter the youth's first and last name**. See Figure 7-18.

TIP

The maximum number of characters allowed in the Title box is 32.

Figure 7-18 Input Message tab in the Data Validation dialog box

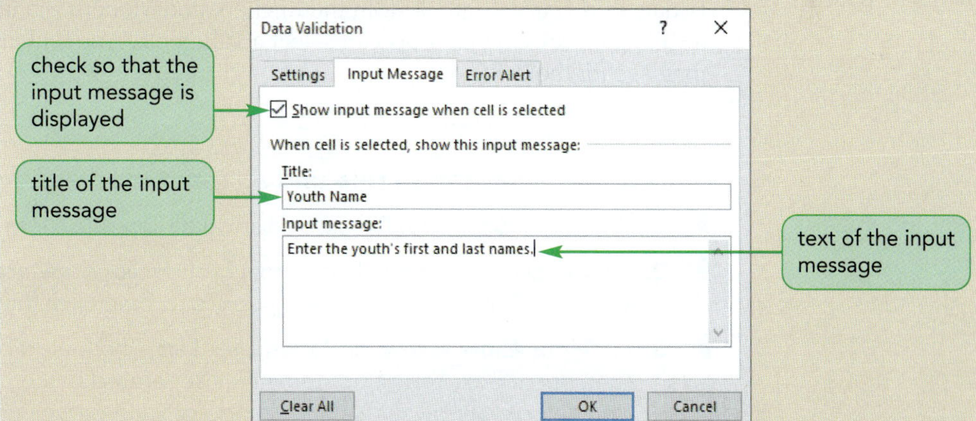

7. Click the **OK** button. The Data Validation dialog box closes. The input message appears in a ScreenTip because the cell is active. See Figure 7-19.

Figure 7-19 Input message for the Youth Name cell

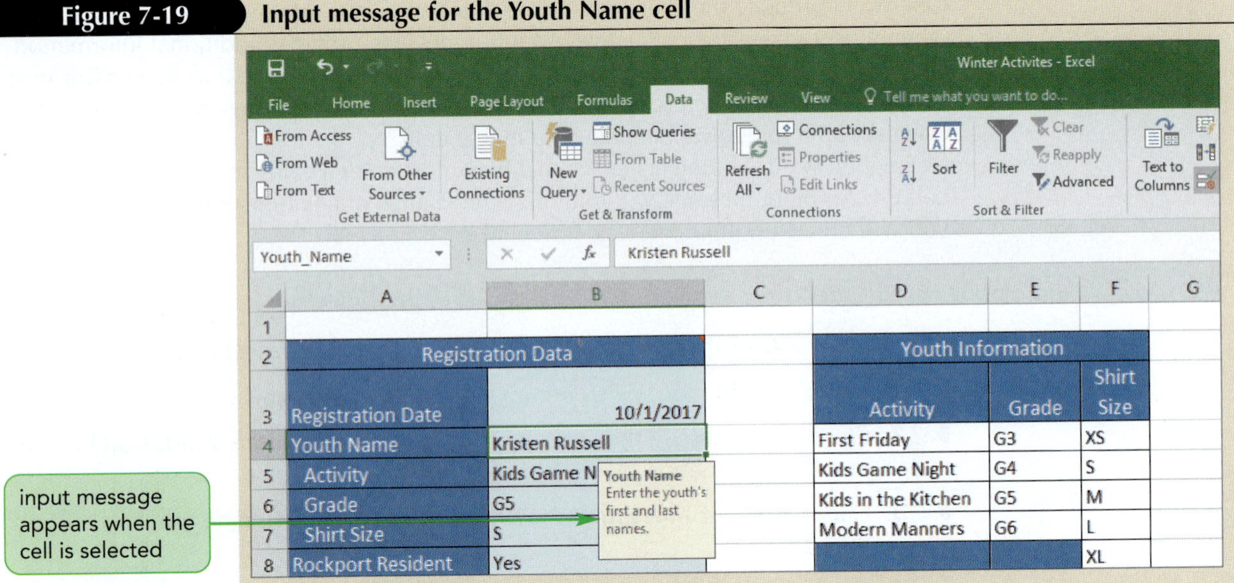

Creating a List Validation Rule

You can use the data validation feature to restrict a cell to accept only entries that are on a list you create. You can create the list of valid entries in the Data Validation dialog box, or you can use a list of valid entries in a single column or row. Once you create a list validation rule for a cell, a list box with the possible values appears when the user selects the cell.

Stephen wants you to use list validation rules for the Activity, Grade, and Shirt Size cells to ensure that users select a valid entry. The Activity has four possible values—First Friday, Kids Game Night, Kids in the Kitchen, and Modern Manners. You will create a validation rule so that users can select a valid entry. You will also create an input message for the cell.

To create a validation rule and an input message for the Activity cell:

1. Select cell **B5**. You will create a list validation rule for this cell.
2. On the Data tab, in the Data Tools group, click the **Data Validation** button to open the Data Validation dialog box, and then click the **Settings** tab.
3. Click the **Allow arrow**, and then click **List**. The dialog box expands to display the Source box. You can enter values separated by commas directly in the Source box, or you can select a range of valid entries in the worksheet.
4. Next to the Source box, click the **Collapse** button so you can see the entire worksheet.
5. Select the range **D4:D7**, which contains the four valid entry values, and then click the **Expand** button. The Data Validation dialog box returns to its full size, and =$D$4:$D$7 appears in the Source box. See Figure 7-20.

Figure 7-20 Activity List validation rule settings

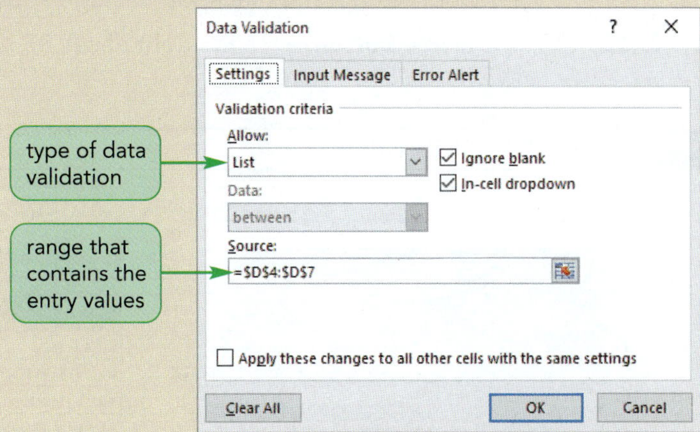

Next, you'll create an input message and an error alert.

6. Click the **Input Message** tab, click in the **Title** box, and then type **Activity** to enter the title of the input message.
7. Click in the **Input message** box, and then type **Click the arrow to select the Activity.** to enter the text of the input message.
8. Click the **Error Alert** tab, and then make sure that **Stop** appears in the Style box. You want to prevent a user from entering a value that is not included in the list of values you specified.
9. In the Title text box, type **Invalid Activity** to enter the title of the error alert.
10. In the Error message box, type **An invalid Activity has been entered. Click Cancel, and then use the arrow to select a valid Activity.** as the error message. See Figure 7-21.

Figure 7-21 Stop error alert for the Activity cell

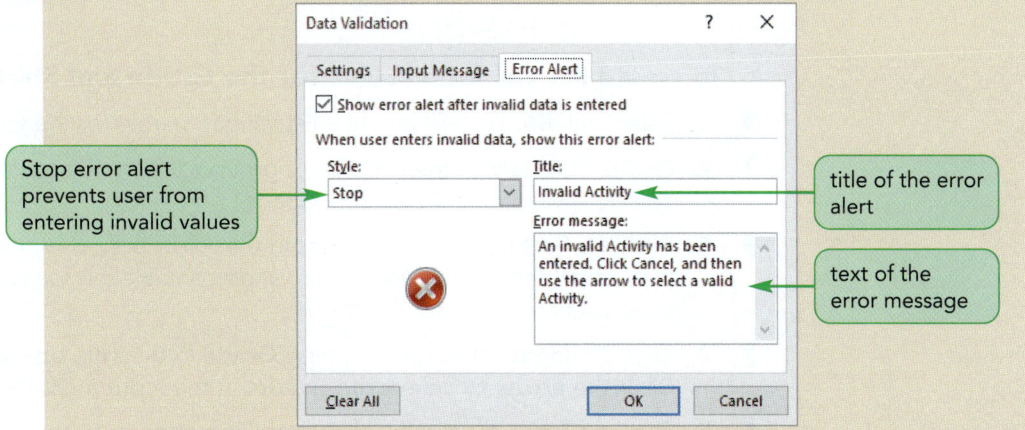

11. Click the **OK** button. The Data Validation dialog box closes, an arrow appears to the right of cell B5, and the input message appears in a ScreenTip.
12. Click the **arrow button** ▾ to the right of cell B5 to view the list of valid Activity entries. See Figure 7-22.

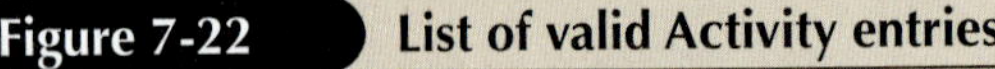

Figure 7-22 List of valid Activity entries

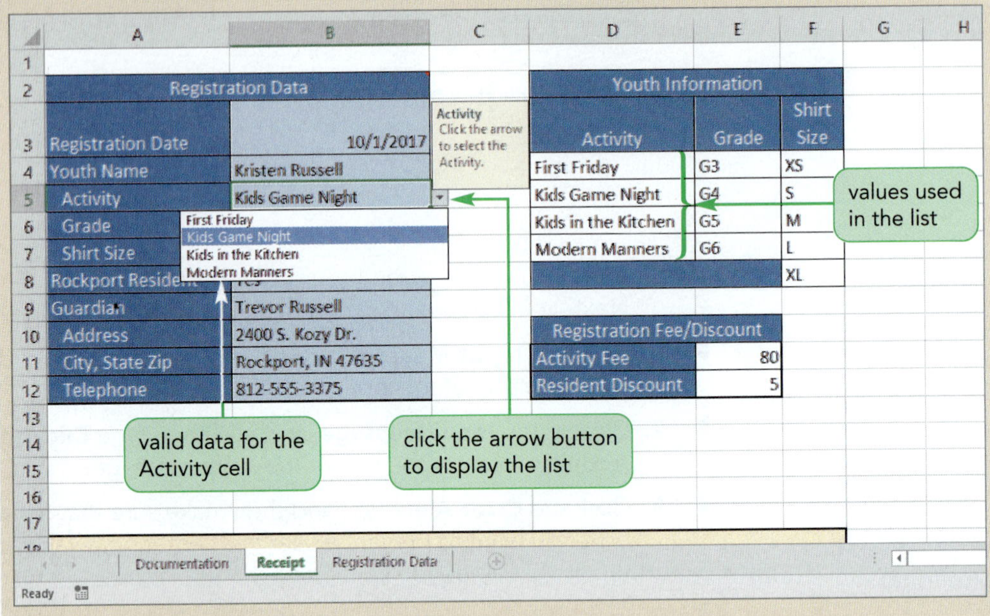

13. Press the **Esc** key to close the list.

Next, Stephen wants you to enter a list validation rule for cells B6 and B7, which specify the participant's Grade (G3, G4, G5, or G6) and Shirt Size (XS, S, M, L, or XL), respectively. Both rules will include an error alert.

To create list validation rules for the Grade and Shirt Size cells:

1. Select cell **B6**. You will create a list validation rule for the Grade cell.
2. On the Data tab, in the Data Tools group, click the **Data Validation** button. The Data Validation dialog box opens.
3. Click the **Settings** tab, select **List** in the Allow box, click the **Source** box, and then select the range **E4:E7**. This range contains the four values you want to allow users to select for Grade.
4. Click the **Input Message** tab, type **Grade** in the Title box, and then type **Click the arrow to select the Grade.** in the Input message box.
5. Click the **Error Alert** tab, verify that **Stop** appears in the Style box, type **Invalid Grade** in the Title box, and then type **An invalid Grade has been entered. Click Cancel, and then use the arrow to select the Grade.** in the Error message box.
6. Click the **OK** button. The dialog box closes, an arrow button appears to the right of cell B6, and the input message appears in a ScreenTip.
7. Select cell **B7** so you can create the validation rule for the Shirt Size cell.

8. In the Data Tools group, click the **Data Validation** button to open the Data Validation dialog box, and then click the **Settings** tab.
9. Select **List** in the Allow box, click the **Source** box, and then select the range **F4:F8**. This range contains the five values you want to allow users to select for the Shirt Size.
10. Click the **Input Message** tab, type **Shirt Size** in the Title box, and then type **Click the arrow to select the Shirt Size**. in the Input message box.
11. Click the **Error Alert** tab, make sure that **Stop** appears in the Style box, type **Invalid Shirt Size** in the Title box, and then type **An invalid Shirt Size has been entered. Click Cancel, and then use the arrow to select the Shirt Size.** in the Error message box.
12. Click the **OK** button. An arrow button appears to the right of cell B7, and the input message appears in a ScreenTip.

Stephen also wants you to enter a validation rule for cell B8 to limit the Rockport Resident cell to either Yes or No. This rule will also include an input message and an error alert. To specify the entries that the list includes, you will type each entry separated by commas in the Source box on the Settings tab in the Data Validation dialog box.

To create a list validation rule for the Rockport Resident cell:

1. Select cell **B8** so you can create a validation rule for the Rockport Resident cell.
2. On the Data tab, in the Data Tools group, click the **Data Validation** button. The Data Validation dialog box opens.
3. Click the **Settings** tab, select **List** in the Allow box, click the **Source** box, and then type **Yes, No** in the Source box. You typed the items for the list because they are not already entered in any range of the worksheet. See Figure 7-23.

Figure 7-23 List validation rule for the Rockport Resident cell

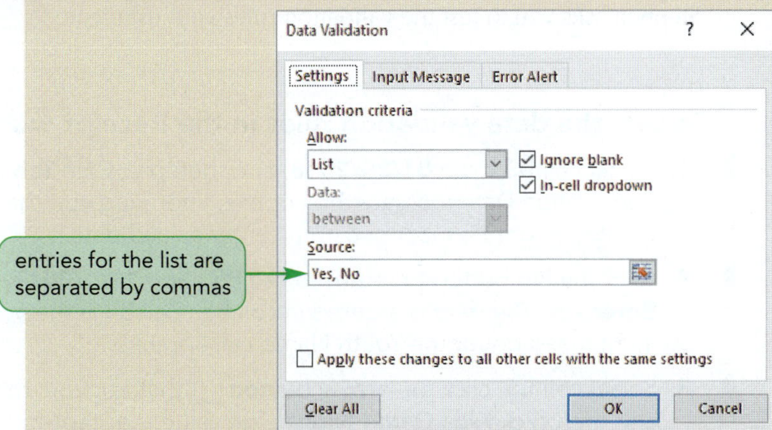

4. Click the **Input Message** tab, type **Rockport Resident** in the Title box, and then type **Click the arrow to select the correct response.** in the Input message box.

5. Click the **Error Alert** tab, make sure that **Stop** appears in the Style box, type **Invalid Rockport Resident** in the Title box, and then type **An invalid response for Rockport Resident has been entered. Click Cancel, and then use the arrow to select the response.** in the Error message box.
6. Click the **OK** button. An arrow button appears to the right of cell B8, and the input message appears in a ScreenTip.

You can edit an existing validation rule, input message, or error alert at any time by selecting the cell with the current validation rule and then opening the Data Validation dialog box. You can also add or remove an input message or error alert to an existing validation rule. Stephen notices that the Registration Date cell does not have an input message. For consistency, he wants you to add one now.

To create an input message for the Registration Date cell:

1. Select cell **B3**.
2. On the Data tab, in the Data Tools group, click the **Data Validation** button.
3. Click the **Settings** tab. The validation rule you created earlier is displayed.
4. Click the **Input Message** tab, type **Registration Date** in the Title box, and then type **Enter the date listed on the registration form.** in the Input message box.
5. Click the **OK** button. The input message is added to the Registration Date cell.

Testing Data Validation Rules

After you create validation rules, you should test them. You do this by entering incorrect values that violate the validation rules. Keep in mind that the only way an error occurs in cells that have a list validation is if an incorrect entry is typed or pasted in the cell. Entering invalid data will ensure that validation rules work as expected.

Stephen asks you to test the validation rules you just created.

To test the data validation rules in the Receipt worksheet:

1. Select cell **B3**, type **01/30/2016**, and then press the **Tab** key. The Invalid Registration Date message box opens, informing you that the value you entered might be incorrect. You'll enter a valid date.
2. Click the **No** button to return to cell B3, type **12/1/2017**, and then press the **Enter** key. The date is entered in cell B3. Cell B4 is the active cell, and the input message for the Youth Name cell appears.
3. Select cell **B5**, click the **arrow button** that appears to the right of cell B5, and then click **Kids Game Night**. The value is accepted.

   The only way an error occurs in cells that have a list validation is if an incorrect entry is typed or copied in the cell. You will try typing in cell B6.
4. In cell **B6**, type **5** and then press the **Enter** key. The Invalid Grade message box opens.
5. Click the **Cancel** button to close the message box and return to the original value in the cell.

6. Click the **arrow** button ▾ to the right of cell B6, and then click **G5**. The Grade is entered correctly as fifth grade.
7. In cell **B7**, type **M** and then press the **Enter** key. An error alert does not appear because M for medium is a valid entry.
8. In cell **B7**, type **SM** for small and then press the **Enter** key. The Invalid Shirt Size message appears.
9. Click the **Cancel** button, click the **arrow** button ▾ to the right of cell B7, and then click **S** in the validation list. The Shirt Size cell is entered as S for small.
10. Select cell **B8**, click the **arrow** button ▾ to the right of cell B8, and then click **Yes** for Rockport Resident.

TIP

If you click the Retry button in the error alert dialog box, you must press the Esc key to return to the original cell value.

The validation rules that you entered for cells B3 through B8 work as intended.

INSIGHT

Using the Circle Invalid Data Command

Validation rules come into play only during data entry. If you add validation rules to a workbook that already contains data with erroneous values, Excel does not determine if any existing data is invalid.

To ensure the entire workbook contains valid data, you need to also verify any data previously entered in the workbook. You can use the Circle Invalid Data command to find and mark cells that contain invalid data. Red circles appear around any data that does not meet the validation criteria, making it simple to scan a worksheet for errors. After you correct the data in a cell, the circle disappears.

To display circles around invalid data, perform the following steps:

1. Apply validation rules to an existing cell range, a worksheet, or a workbook.
2. On the Data tab, in the Data Tools group, click the Data Validation button arrow, and then click Circle Invalid Data. Red circles appear around cells that contain invalid data.
3. To remove the circle from a single cell, enter valid data in the cell.
4. To hide all circles, on the Data tab, in the Data Tools group, click the Data Validation button arrow, and then click Clear Validation Circles.

To ensure an error-free workbook, you should use the Circle Invalid Data command to verify data entered before you set up the validation criteria or to verify data in a workbook you inherited from someone else, such as a coworker.

Protecting a Worksheet and a Workbook

Another way to minimize data-entry errors is to limit access to certain parts of the workbook. Worksheet protection prevents users from changing cell contents, such as editing formulas in a worksheet. Workbook protection also prevents users from changing the workbook's association, such as inserting or deleting worksheets in the workbook. You can even keep users from viewing the formulas used in the workbook.

Stephen wants to protect the contents of the Receipt and Registration Data worksheets. He wants volunteers to have access only to the range B3:B12 in the Receipt worksheet, where new receipt data is entered. He also wants to prevent volunteers from editing the contents of any cells in the Registration Data worksheet.

Locking and Unlocking Cells

Every cell in a workbook has a **locked property** that determines whether changes can be made to that cell. The locked property has no impact as long as the worksheet is unprotected. However, after you protect a worksheet, the locked property controls whether the cell can be edited. You unlock a cell by turning off the locked property. By default, the locked property is turned on for each cell, and worksheet protection is turned off.

So, unless you unlock cells in a worksheet *before* protecting the worksheet, all of the cells in the worksheet will be locked, and you won't be able to make any changes in the worksheet. Usually, you will want to protect the worksheet but leave some cells unlocked. For example, you might want to lock cells that contain formulas and formatting so they cannot be changed, but unlock cells in which you want to enter data.

To protect some—but not all—cells in a worksheet, you first turn off the locked property of cells in which data can be entered. Then, you protect the worksheet to activate the locked property for the remaining cells.

In the Receipt worksheet, Stephen wants users to be able to enter data in the range B3:B12 but not in any other cell. To do this, you must unlock the cells in the range B3:B12.

To unlock the cells in the range B3:B12:

1. In the Receipt worksheet, select the range **B3:B12**. You want to unlock the cells in this range before you protect the worksheet.
2. On the ribbon, click the **Home** tab.
3. In the Cells group, click the **Format** button, and then click **Format Cells** (or press the **Ctrl+1** keys). The Format Cells dialog box opens. The locked property is on the Protection tab.
4. Click the **Protection** tab, and then click the **Locked** check box to remove the checkmark. See Figure 7-24.

TIP

Click the Format button in the Cells group, then click Lock Cell to add or remove the locked property for selected cells.

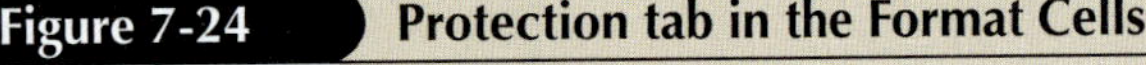

Figure 7-24 Protection tab in the Format Cells dialog box

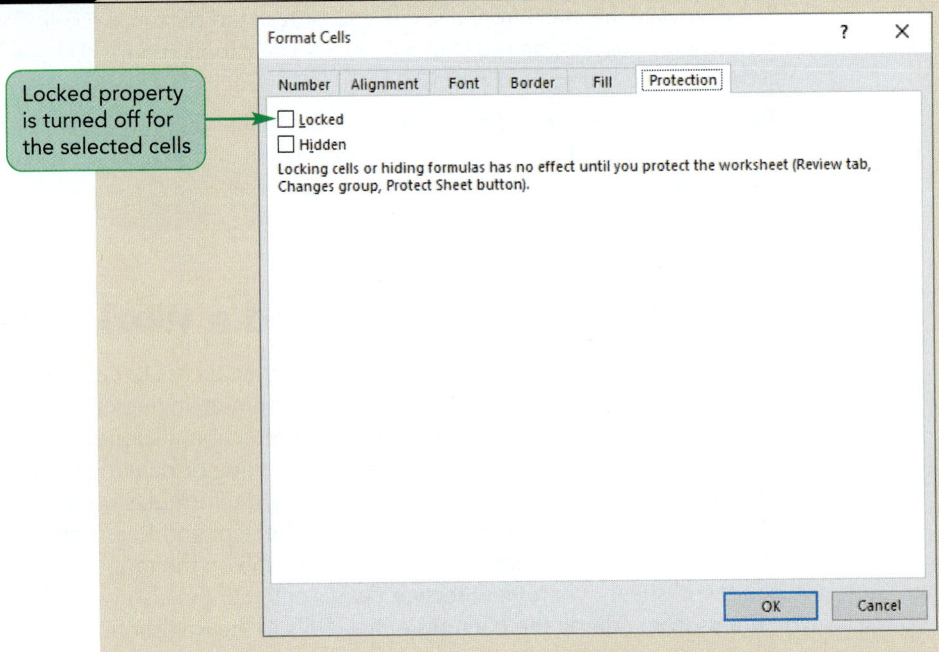

5. Click the **OK** button. The cells in the range B3:B12 are unlocked.
6. Select cell **A1** to deselect the range.

Protecting a Worksheet

When you set up worksheet protection, you specify which actions are still available to users in the protected worksheet. For example, you can choose to allow users to insert new rows or columns or to delete rows and columns. You can limit the user to selecting only unlocked cells or allow the user to select any cell in the worksheet. These choices remain active as long as the worksheet is protected.

A protected worksheet can always be unprotected. You can also add a password to the protected worksheet that users must enter in order to turn off the protection. Passwords are case sensitive, which means the uppercase and lowercase letters are considered different letters. If you are concerned that users will turn off protection and make changes to formulas, you should use a password; otherwise, it is probably best to not specify a password. Keep in mind that if you forget the password, it is very difficult to remove the worksheet protection.

REFERENCE

Protecting a Worksheet

- Select the cells and ranges to unlock so that users can enter data in them.
- On the Home tab, in the Cells group, click the Format button, and then click Format Cells (or press the Ctrl+1 keys).
- In the Format Cells dialog box, click the Protection tab.
- Click the Locked check box to remove the checkmark, and then click the OK button.
- On the Review tab, in the Changes group, click the Protect Sheet button.
- Enter a password (optional).
- Select all of the actions you want to allow users to take when the worksheet is protected.
- Click the OK button.

Stephen wants to protect the Receipt and Registration Data worksheets, but he doesn't want a password specified. You will enable worksheet protection that will allow users to select any cell in the worksheets but enter data only in the unlocked cells.

To protect the Receipt worksheet:

1. On the ribbon, click the **Review** tab.
2. In the Changes group, click the **Protect Sheet** button. The Protect Sheet dialog box opens. See Figure 7-25.

Figure 7-25 Protect Sheet dialog box

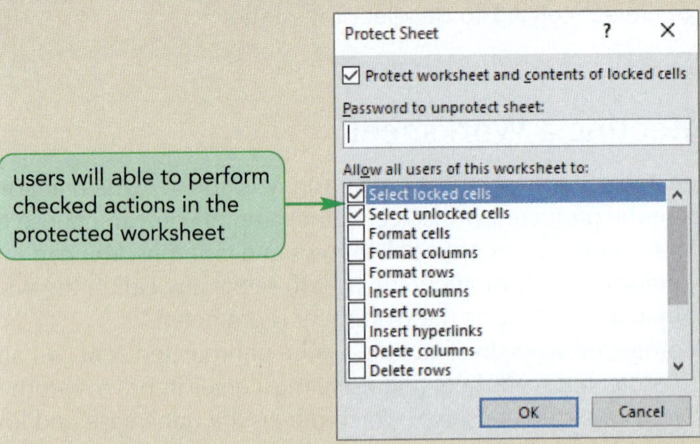

TIP

Keep passwords in a safe place. Remember, passwords are case sensitive. If you forget the password, it is very difficult to remove the worksheet protection.

You will leave the Password to unprotect sheet box blank because you do not want to use a password. By default, users can select both locked and unlocked cells, which constitute all of the cells in the worksheet, but they can enter or edit values only in unlocked cells.

3. Click the **OK** button. The Protect Sheet dialog box closes, and the Protect Sheet button changes to the Unprotect Sheet button.

Any time you modify a worksheet, you should test the worksheet to ensure that changes work as intended. You'll test the protection you added to the Receipt worksheet by trying to edit a locked cell and then trying to edit an unlocked cell.

To test the Receipt worksheet protection:

1. Select cell **B14**, and then type **1**. As soon as you press any key, a dialog box opens, indicating that the cell is protected and cannot be modified. See Figure 7-26.

Figure 7-26 Cell protection error message

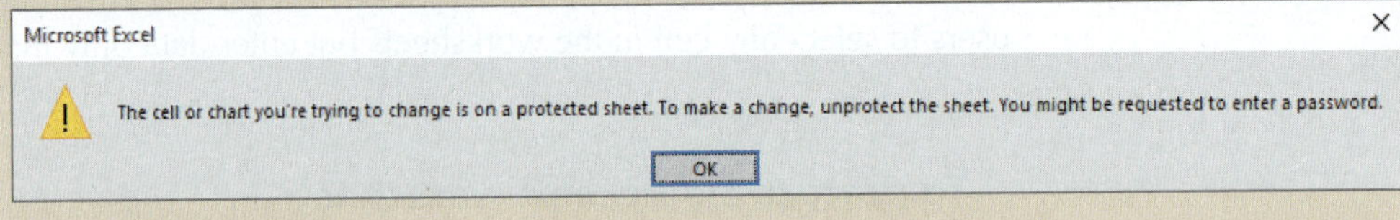

2. Click the **OK** button.
3. Click cell **B8**, type **No**, and then press the **Enter** key. The Rockport Resident cell is updated because you allowed editing in the range B3:B12.

   A user can enter and edit values in any cell in the range B3:B12. Although users can select any cell in the worksheet, they cannot make an entry in any other cell outside of that range.

4. On the Quick Access Toolbar, click the **Undo** button to return the Rockport Resident cell to Yes.

You will repeat this process to protect all of the cells in the Registration Data worksheet. Then you will test to see what would happen if someone tried to edit one of the cells. Because you did not unlock any cells in the Registration Data worksheet, no cells may be edited.

To protect and test the Registration Data worksheet:

1. Go to the **Registration Data** worksheet.
2. On the Review tab, in the Changes group, click the **Protect Sheet** button. The Protect Sheet dialog box opens.
3. Click the **OK** button to accept the default set of user actions.
4. Select cell **A2**, and then type **B**. A dialog box opens, indicating that the cell is protected and cannot be modified. All of the cells in this worksheet are protected because no cells have been unlocked.
5. Click the **OK** button to close the dialog box.

Protecting a Workbook

Worksheet protection applies only to the contents of a worksheet, not to the worksheet itself. To keep a worksheet from being modified, you need to protect the workbook. You can protect both the structure and the windows of a workbook. Protecting the structure prevents users from renaming, deleting, hiding, or inserting worksheets. Protecting the windows prevents users from moving, resizing, closing, or hiding parts of the Excel window. The default is to protect only the structure of the workbook, not the windows used to display it.

You can also add a password to the workbook protection. However, the same guidelines apply as for protecting worksheets. Add a password only if you are concerned that others might unprotect the workbook and modify it. If you add a password, keep in mind that it is case sensitive and you cannot unprotect the workbook without it.

REFERENCE

Protecting a Workbook

- On the Review tab, in the Changes group, click the Protect Workbook button.
- Click the check boxes to indicate whether you want to protect the workbook's structure, windows, or both.
- Enter a password (optional).
- Click the OK button.

The contents of the Receipt and Registration Data worksheets, with the exception of the range B3:B12 in the Receipt worksheet, cannot be changed. However, a volunteer could inadvertently rename or delete the protected worksheet. To keep the worksheets themselves from being modified, you will protect the workbook. Stephen doesn't want users to be able to change the structure of the workbook, so you will set workbook protection for the structure but not the window.

To protect the Winter Activities workbook:

1. On the Review tab, in the Changes group, click the **Protect Workbook** button. The Protect Structure and Windows dialog box opens. See Figure 7-27.

Figure 7-27 Protect Structure and Windows dialog box

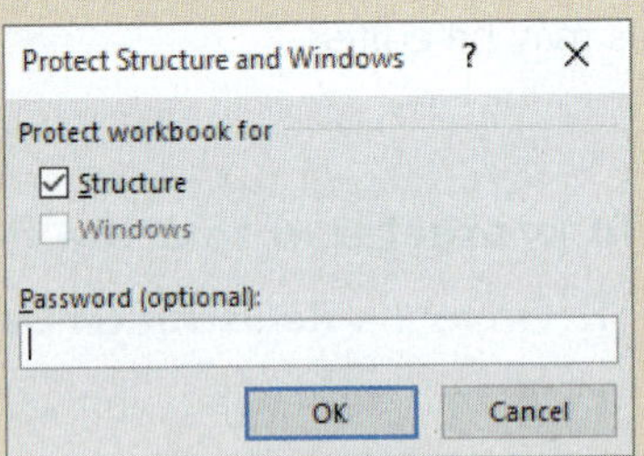

2. Make sure the **Structure** check box is checked and the **Password** box is blank. The Windows check box is unavailable and unchecked.
3. Click the **OK** button to protect the workbook without specifying a password.
4. Right-click the **Registration Data** sheet tab. On the shortcut menu, notice that the Insert, Delete, Rename, Move or Copy, Tab Color, Hide, and Unhide commands are gray. This indicates that the options for modifying the worksheets are no longer available for the Registration Data worksheet.
5. Press the **Esc** key to close the shortcut menu.

Unprotecting a Worksheet and a Workbook

You can turn off worksheet protection at any time. This is often referred to as *unprotecting* the worksheet. You must unprotect a worksheet to edit its contents. If you assigned a password when you protected the worksheet, you would need to enter the password to remove worksheet protection. Likewise, you can unprotect the workbook. If you need to insert a new worksheet or rename an existing worksheet, you can unprotect the protected workbook, make the changes to the structure, and then reapply workbook protection.

At this point, Stephen wants you to make additional changes to the Receipt worksheet, so you'll turn off worksheet protection in that worksheet. Later, when the worksheet is complete, Stephen can turn worksheet protection back on.

TIP

To remove workbook protection, click the Protect Workbook button in the Changes group on the Review tab.

To turn off worksheet protection for the Receipt worksheet:

1. Go to the **Receipt** worksheet.
2. On the Review tab, in the Changes group, click the **Unprotect Sheet** button. Worksheet protection is removed from the Receipt worksheet. The button changes back to the Protect Sheet button.

Inserting Comments

Comments are often used in workbooks to: (a) explain the contents of a particular cell, such as a complex formula; (b) provide instructions to users; and (c) share ideas and notes from several users collaborating on a project. The username for your installation of Excel appears in bold at the top of the comments box. If you collaborate on a workbook, the top of the comment boxes would show the name of each user who created that comment. A small red triangle appears in the upper-right corner of a cell with a comment. The comment box appears when you point to a cell with a comment.

REFERENCE

Inserting a Comment

- Select the cell to which you want to attach a comment.
- Right-click the selected cell, and then click Insert Comment on the shortcut menu (or press the Shift+F2 keys; or on the Review tab, in the Comments group, click the New Comment button).
- Type the comment into the box.
- Click a cell to hide the comment.

Stephen wants you to insert a note in cell A2 about entering data from the order form into the input section.

TIP

You can also add a comment by right-clicking the cell and then clicking Insert Comment on the shortcut menu.

To insert a comment in cell A2:

1. In the Receipt worksheet, select cell **A2**.
2. On the Review tab, in the Comments group, click the **New Comment** button (or press the **Shift+F2** keys). A comment box opens to the right of cell A2. The username for your installation of Excel appears in bold at the top of the box. An arrow points from the box to the small red triangle that appears in the upper-right corner of the cell.
3. Type **Enter all data from the Registration form into cells B3 through B11.** in the comment box. A selection box with sizing handles appears around the comment box. If the box is too small or too large for the comment, you can drag a sizing handle to increase or decrease the size of the box. See Figure 7-28.

Figure 7-28 Comment added to cell A2

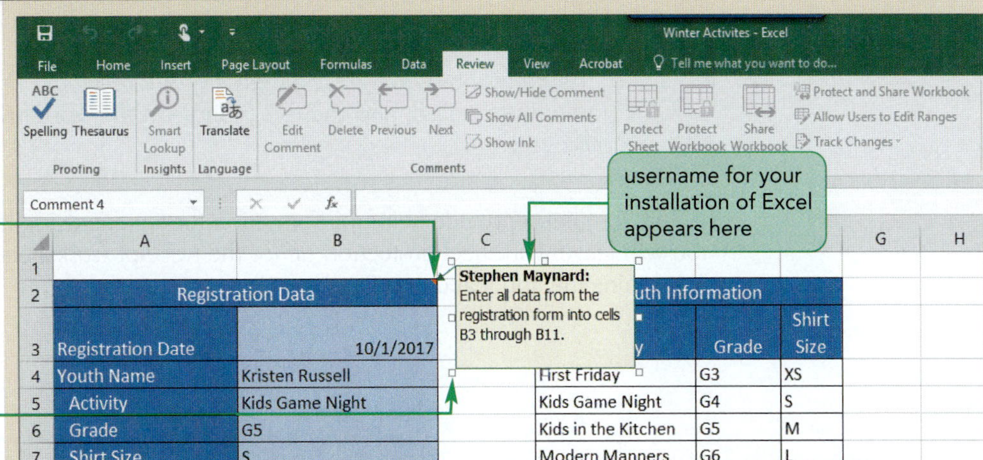

4. Click cell **B12** to hide the comment. The comment disappears. A small red triangle remains in the upper-right corner of cell A2 to indicate this cell contains a comment.

   Trouble? If the comment box did not disappear, comments are set to be displayed in the worksheet. On the Review tab, in the Comments group, click the Show All Comments button to deselect it.

5. Point to cell **A2**. The comment appears.

You can now edit your comments and enter a note in cell E34 explaining how the IF functions are used to determine whether to give the discount for Rockport Resident.

To edit comments in the input area:

1. Click cell **A2**.
2. On the Review tab, in the Comments group, click the **Edit Comment** button. The comment appears with the insertion point at the end of the comment text, so you can edit the incorrect cell reference.
3. Select **B11** in the comment box, and then type **B12**. The comment in cell A2 now correctly references the range B3:B12.
4. Select any other cell to hide the comment, and then point to cell **A2** to view the edited comment.
5. Click cell **E34**, and then on the Review tab, in the Comments group, click the **New Comment** button. A comment box opens to the right of cell E34.
6. In the comment box, type **This IF function determines whether to allow the Rockport Resident discount.**
7. Select cell **E35** to hide the comment. A small red triangle remains in the upper-right corner of cell E34 to indicate it contains a comment.
8. Point to cell **E34** to see the comment.

TIP

To keep an active cell's comment displayed, click the Show/Hide Comment button in the Comments group on the Review tab. Click the button again to hide the active cell's comment.

Stephen decides that the volunteers don't need to know how the Rockport Resident discount is calculated. You'll delete the comment in cell E34.

To edit and delete comments:

1. Select cell **E34**.
2. On the Review tab, in the Comments group, click the **Delete** button. The comment is deleted, and the red triangle in the upper-right corner of cell E34 is removed.

The comments provide helpful information for anyone using the Receipt worksheet. You will leave worksheet protection off for the Receipt worksheet while you finish developing the application for Stephen.

PROSKILLS

Written Communication: Documenting a Spreadsheet

Providing documentation for a spreadsheet is important because it provides instructions on the spreadsheet's use, defines technical terms, explains complex formulas, and identifies assumptions. By documenting a spreadsheet, you help users work more effectively. In addition, documentation helps you recall what is in the spreadsheet that might otherwise be forgotten months or years from now. Furthermore, when someone else becomes responsible for modifying the spreadsheet in the future, the documentation will help that person get up to speed quickly.

You can create a Documentation worksheet to provide an overview, definitions, assumptions, and instructions on how to use various parts of a workbook. Excel also offers a variety of tools to help you document spreadsheets, including:

- Defined names and structured references to make formulas easier to create and understand
- Data validation, including input messages specifying what to enter in a cell and error messages providing instructions on what to do if the data entered is incorrect
- Cell comments to explain complex formulas, give reminders, and so on
- Formula mode to view all formulas in a worksheet at one time

Providing documentation will help users better understand the application, which will save time and minimize frustration.

In this session, you used data validation to help ensure that all values entered in the Receipt worksheet are valid. You created validation rules that included input messages and error alert messages. You learned how to protect and unprotect both the worksheet and the workbook. In addition, you used comments to add notes to specific cells. In the next session, you'll automate some of the steps in the application by recording macros.

REVIEW

Session 7.2 Quick Check

1. Why would you want to validate data?
2. What is the purpose of the input message in the Data Validation command?
3. Describe the three types of error alert messages Excel can display when a user violates a validation rule.
4. What is a locked cell? What are unlocked cells?
5. What is the difference between worksheet protection and workbook protection?
6. Can you rename a protected worksheet? Explain why or why not.
7. Give two reasons for adding a comment to a worksheet cell.

Session 7.3 Visual Overview:

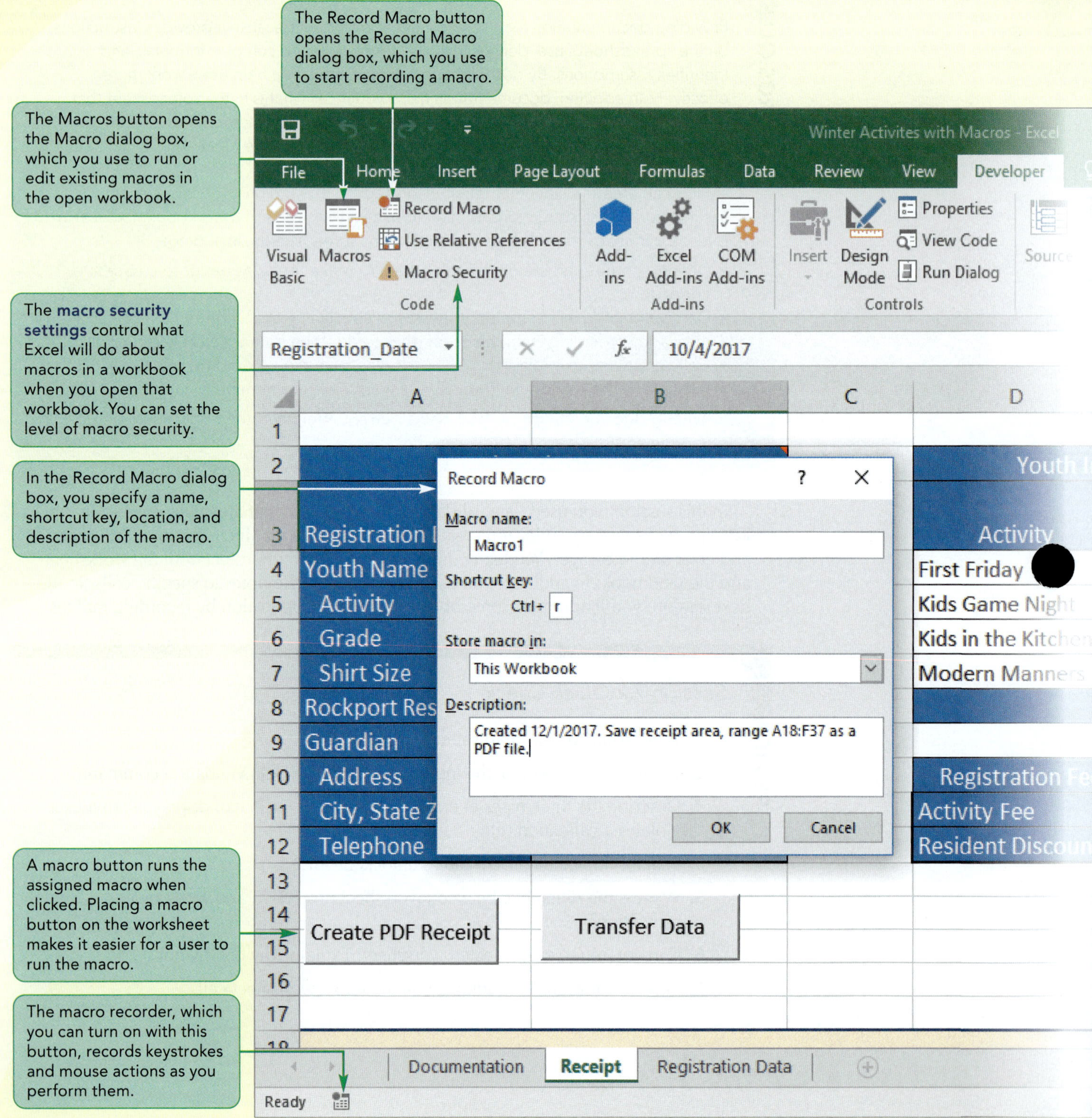

The Record Macro button opens the Record Macro dialog box, which you use to start recording a macro.
The Macros button opens the Macro dialog box, which you use to run or edit existing macros in the open workbook.
The macro security settings control what Excel will do about macros in a workbook when you open that workbook. You can set the level of macro security.
In the Record Macro dialog box, you specify a name, shortcut key, location, and description of the macro.
A macro button runs the assigned macro when clicked. Placing a macro button on the worksheet makes it easier for a user to run the macro.
The macro recorder, which you can turn on with this button, records keystrokes and mouse actions as you perform them.
Winter Activites with Macros - Excel
File
Home
Insert
Page Layout
Formulas
Data
Review
View
Developer
Visual Basic
Macros
Record Macro
Use Relative References
Macro Security
Code
Add-ins
Excel Add-ins
COM Add-ins
Add-ins
Insert
Design Mode
Properties
View Code
Run Dialog
Controls
Registration_Date
10/4/2017
Record Macro
Macro name:
Macro1
Shortcut key:
Ctrl+ r
Store macro in:
This Workbook
Description:
Created 12/1/2017. Save receipt area, range A18:F37 as a PDF file.
OK
Cancel
Registration
Youth Name
Activity
Grade
Shirt Size
Rockport Res
Guardian
Address
City, State Z
Telephone
Activity
First Friday
Kids Game Night
Kids in the Kitchen
Modern Manners
Activity Fee
Resident Discount
Create PDF Receipt
Transfer Data
Documentation
Receipt
Registration Data
Ready

Working with Macros

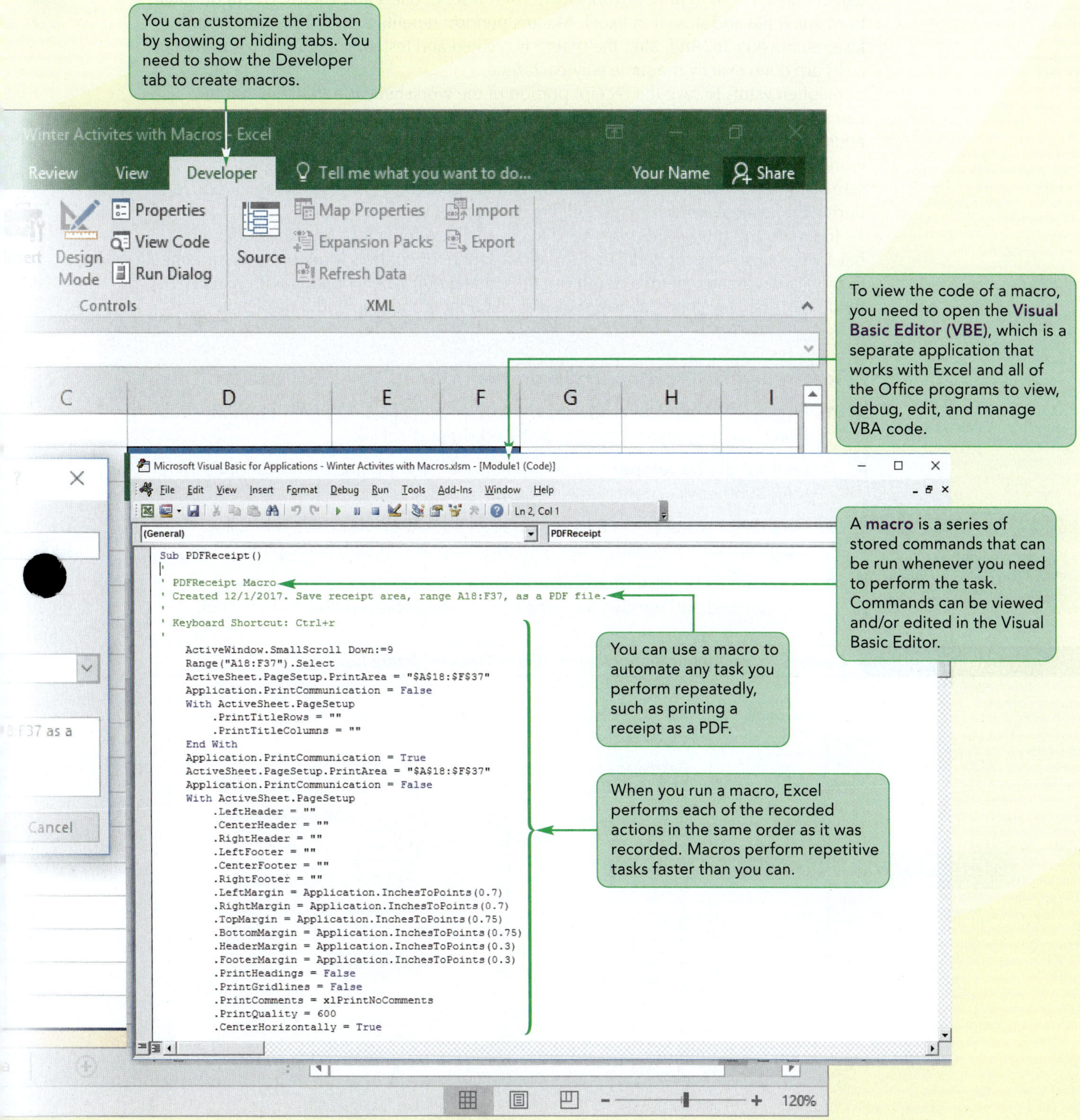

You can customize the ribbon by showing or hiding tabs. You need to show the Developer tab to create macros.
Winter Activites with Macros - Excel
Review
View
Developer
Tell me what you want to do...
Your Name
Share
Properties
View Code
Run Dialog
Design Mode
Source
Map Properties
Expansion Packs
Refresh Data
Import
Export
Controls
XML
C
D
E
F
G
H
I
Microsoft Visual Basic for Applications - Winter Activites with Macros.xlsm - [Module1 (Code)]
File Edit View Insert Format Debug Run Tools Add-Ins Window Help
Ln 2, Col 1
(General)
PDFReceipt
Sub PDFReceipt()
' PDFReceipt Macro
' Created 12/1/2017. Save receipt area, range A18:F37, as a PDF file.
' Keyboard Shortcut: Ctrl+r
ActiveWindow.SmallScroll Down:=9
Range("A18:F37").Select
ActiveSheet.PageSetup.PrintArea = "$A$18:$F$37"
Application.PrintCommunication = False
With ActiveSheet.PageSetup
.PrintTitleRows = ""
.PrintTitleColumns = ""
End With
Application.PrintCommunication = True
ActiveSheet.PageSetup.PrintArea = "$A$18:$F$37"
Application.PrintCommunication = False
With ActiveSheet.PageSetup
.LeftHeader = ""
.CenterHeader = ""
.RightHeader = ""
.LeftFooter = ""
.CenterFooter = ""
.RightFooter = ""
.LeftMargin = Application.InchesToPoints(0.7)
.RightMargin = Application.InchesToPoints(0.7)
.TopMargin = Application.InchesToPoints(0.75)
.BottomMargin = Application.InchesToPoints(0.75)
.HeaderMargin = Application.InchesToPoints(0.3)
.FooterMargin = Application.InchesToPoints(0.3)
.PrintHeadings = False
.PrintGridlines = False
.PrintComments = xlPrintNoComments
.PrintQuality = 600
.CenterHorizontally = True
Cancel
120%
To view the code of a macro, you need to open the Visual Basic Editor (VBE), which is a separate application that works with Excel and all of the Office programs to view, debug, edit, and manage VBA code.
A macro is a series of stored commands that can be run whenever you need to perform the task. Commands can be viewed and/or edited in the Visual Basic Editor.
You can use a macro to automate any task you perform repeatedly, such as printing a receipt as a PDF.
When you run a macro, Excel performs each of the recorded actions in the same order as it was recorded. Macros perform repetitive tasks faster than you can.

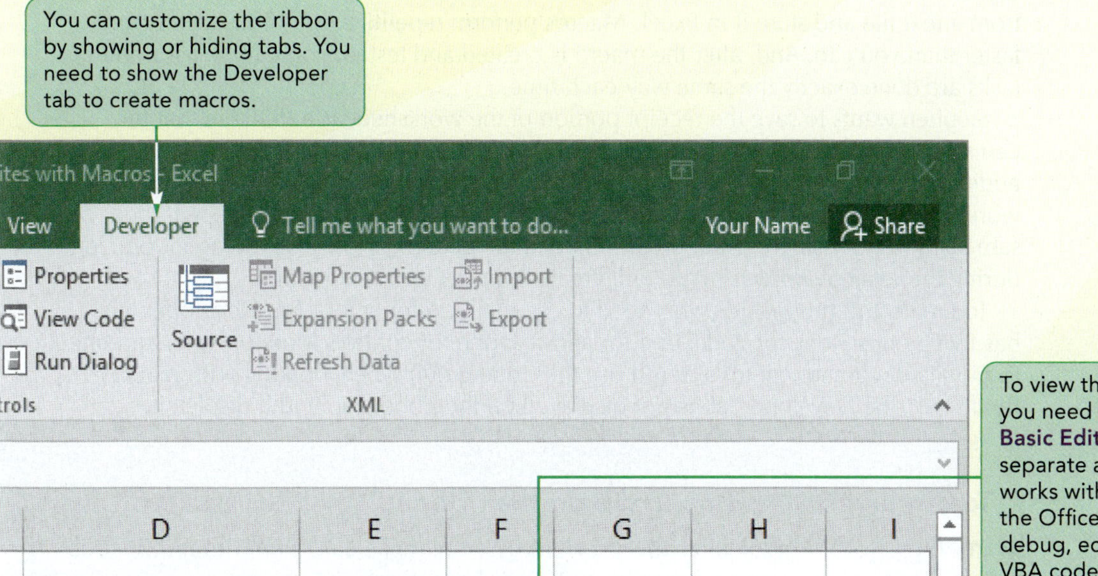

Automating Tasks with Macros

Using a macro, you can automate any task you perform repeatedly. For example, you can create a macro to print a worksheet, insert a set of dates and values, or import data from a text file and store it in Excel. Macros perform repetitive tasks consistently and faster than you can. And, after the macro is created and tested, you can be assured the tasks are done exactly the same way each time.

Stephen wants to save the receipt portion of the worksheet as a PDF file that he can send as an attachment to the guardian in an email confirming the registration. In addition, Stephen wants data from the receipt to be transferred to the Registration Data worksheet. He wants to simplify these tasks so volunteers don't need to repeat the same actions for each registration and reduce the possibility of errors being introduced during the repetitive process. You will create a macro for each action.

To create and run macros, you need to use the Developer tab. The Developer tab has five groups—one for code, one for add-ins, one for controls, one for XML, and one to modify document controls. You'll use the Code group when working with macros. By default, the Developer tab is not displayed on the ribbon, so you'll display it.

To display the Developer tab on the ribbon:

1. If you took a break after the previous session, make sure the Winter Activities workbook is open and the Receipt worksheet is active.
2. Look for the **Developer** tab on the ribbon. If you do not see it, continue with Step 3; otherwise, continue with Step 7.
3. On the ribbon, click the **File** tab to open Backstage view, and then click **Options** in the navigation bar. The Excel Options dialog box opens.
4. In the left pane, click **Customize Ribbon**. The different commands and tabs you can add and remove from the ribbon are displayed. See Figure 7-29.

TIP

You can also right-click the ribbon and click Customize the Ribbon to add a tab.

Figure 7-29 Customize the Ribbon options in the Excel Options dialog box

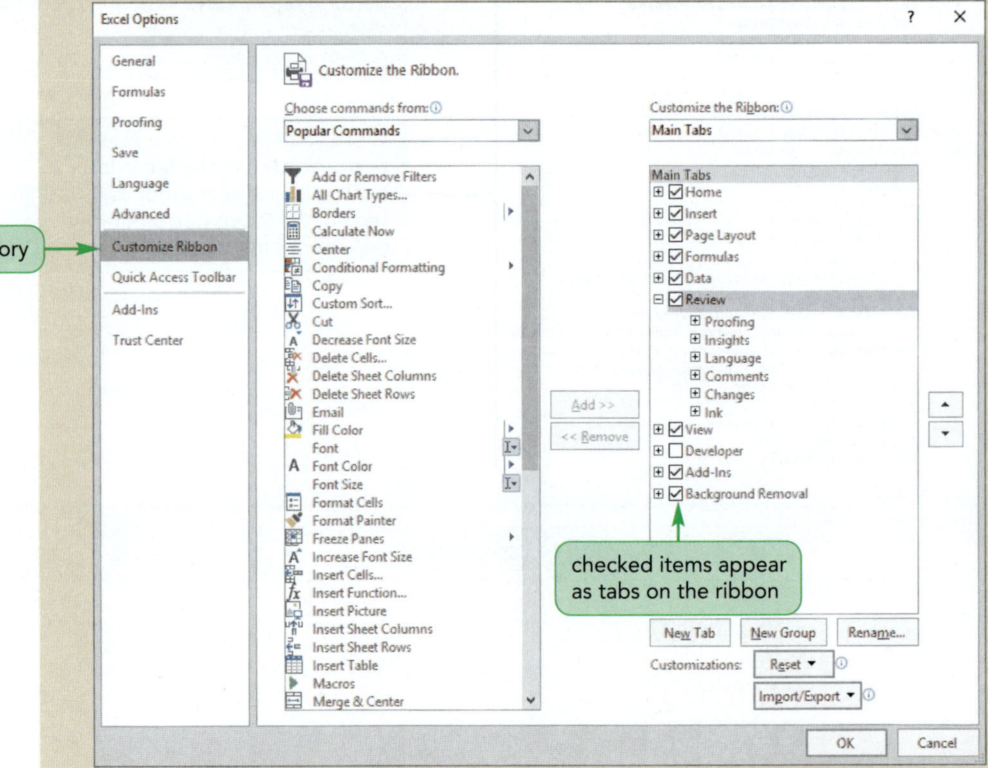

5. In the right pane, click the **Developer** check box to insert a checkmark.
6. Click the **OK** button. The Developer tab appears on the ribbon.
7. On the ribbon, click the **Developer** tab. See Figure 7-30.

Figure 7-30 Developer tab on the ribbon

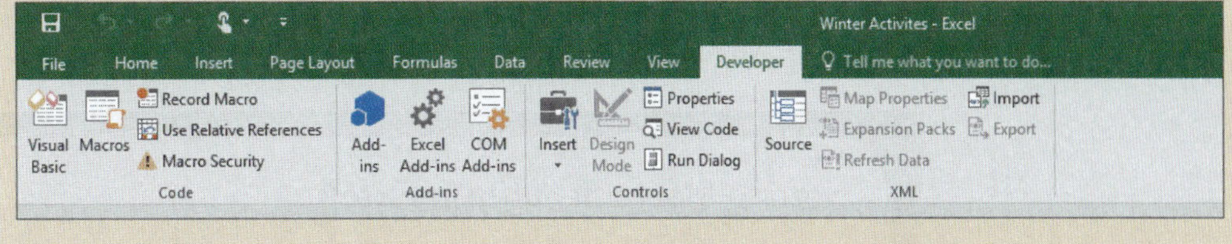

Protecting Against Macro Viruses

Viruses can be and have been attached as macros to files created in Excel and other Office programs. A **virus** is a computer program designed to copy itself into other programs with the intention of causing mischief or harm. When unsuspecting users open these infected workbooks, Excel automatically runs the attached virus-infected macro. **Macro viruses** are a type of virus that uses a program's own macro programming language to distribute the virus. Macro viruses can be destructive and can modify or delete files that may not be recoverable. Because it is possible for a macro to contain a virus, Microsoft Office 2016 provides several options from which you can choose to set a security level you feel comfortable with.

Macro Security Settings

The macro security settings control what Excel will do about macros in a workbook when you open that workbook. For example, one user may choose to run macros only if they are "digitally signed" by a developer who is on a list of trusted sources. Another user might want to disable all macros in workbooks and see a notification when a workbook contains macros. The user can then elect to enable the macros. Excel has four macro security settings, which are described in Figure 7-31.

Figure 7-31 Macro security settings

Setting	Description
Disable all macros without notification	All macros in all workbooks are disabled and no security alerts about macros are displayed. Use this setting if you don't want macros to run.
Disable all macros with notification	All macros in all workbooks are disabled, but security alerts appear when the workbook contains a macro. Use this default setting to choose on a case-by-case basis whether to run a macro.
Disable all macros except digitally signed macros	The same as the "Disable all macros with notification" setting except any macro signed by a trusted publisher runs if you have already trusted the publisher. Otherwise, security alerts appear when a workbook contains a macro.
Enable all macros	All macros in all workbooks run. Use this setting temporarily in such cases as when developing an application that contains macros. This setting is not recommended for regular use.

You set macro security in the Trust Center. The **Trust Center** is a central location for all of the security settings in Office. By default, all potentially dangerous content, such as macros and workbooks with external links, is blocked without warning. If content is blocked, the Message Bar (also called the trust bar) opens below the ribbon, notifying you that some content was disabled. You can click the Message Bar to enable that content.

You can place files you consider trustworthy in locations you specify; the file paths of these locations are stored as Trusted Locations in the Trust Center. Any workbook opened from a trusted location is considered safe, and content such as macros will work without the user having to respond to additional security questions in order to use the workbook.

REFERENCE

Setting Macro Security in Excel

- On the Developer tab, in the Code group, click the Macro Security button.
- Click the option button for the macro setting you want.
- Click the OK button.

or

- Click the File tab, and then click Options in the navigation bar (or right-click the ribbon, and then click Customize the Ribbon on the shortcut menu).
- Click the Trust Center category, and then click the Trust Center Settings button.
- Click the Macro Settings category, and then click the option button for a macro setting.
- Click the OK button.

Stephen wants the workbook to have some protection against macro viruses, so he asks you to set the security level to "Disable all macros with notification." When you open a file with macros, this macro security level disables the macros and displays a security alert, allowing you to enable the macros if you believe the workbook comes from a trusted source. After the macros are enabled, you can run them.

To set the macro security level:

1. On the Developer tab, in the Code group, click the **Macro Security** button. The Trust Center dialog box opens with the Macro Settings category displayed.
2. In the Macro Settings section, click the **Disable all macros with notification** option button if it is not already selected. See Figure 7-32.

Figure 7-32 Macro Settings in the Trust Center dialog box

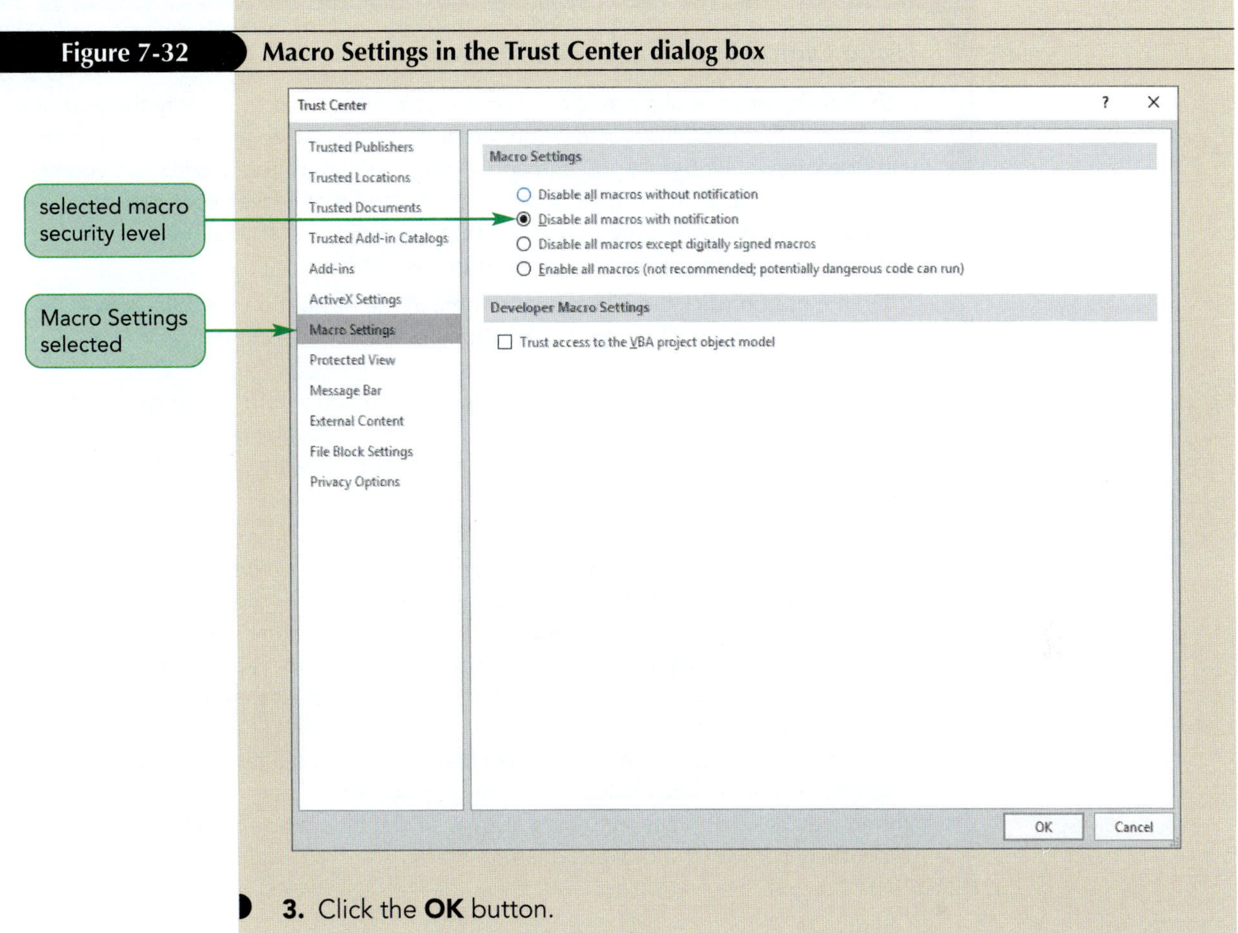

3. Click the **OK** button.

Each time you open a workbook that contains a macro detected by the Trust Center, the macro is disabled, and a Message Bar containing the SECURITY WARNING that macros have been disabled appears below the ribbon. If you developed the workbook or trust the person who sent you the workbook, click the Enable Content button to run the macros in the workbook. If you do not click the Enable Content button, you cannot run the macros in the workbook, but you can use the rest of the workbook.

INSIGHT

Using Digital Signatures with Macros

A **digital signature** is like a seal of approval. It is often used to identify the author of a workbook that contains macros. You add a digital signature as the last step before you distribute a file. Before you can add a digital signature to a workbook, you need to obtain a digital ID (also called a digital certificate) that proves your identity. Digital certificates are typically issued by a certificate authority. After you have a digital certificate, do the following to digitally sign a workbook:

1. On the ribbon, click the File tab, and then, in the navigation bar, click Info.
2. On the Info screen, click the Protect Workbook button, and then click Add a Digital Signature.
3. If the Get a Digital ID dialog box opens, asking if you would like to get a digital ID from a Microsoft Partner, click the Yes button. Your browser opens to a website with information about digital signature providers and available digital IDs.
4. Read the information.
5. Select a provider, and follow the steps to obtain a digital ID from that provider.

By digitally signing a workbook that contains a macro you intend to publicly distribute, you assure others of the identity of the creator of the macro and that the macro has not been altered since the digital signature was created. When you open a digitally signed file, you can see who the author is and decide whether the information in the file is authentic and whether you trust that the macros in the workbook are safe to run.

The digital signature is removed any time a file with a digital signature is saved. This ensures that no one (including the original workbook author) can open a digitally signed file, make changes to the workbook, save the workbook, and then send the file to another user with the digital signature intact.

Recording a Macro

You can create an Excel macro in one of two ways: You can use the macro recorder to record keystrokes and mouse actions as you perform them, or you can enter a series of commands in the **Visual Basic for Applications (VBA)** programming language. The macro recorder can record only those actions you perform with the keyboard or mouse. The macro recorder is a good choice for creating simple macros. For more sophisticated macros, you might need to write VBA code directly in the Visual Basic Editor (VBE).

For Stephen's application, the actions you need to perform can all be done with the keyboard and the mouse, so you will use the macro recorder to record the two macros. One macro will save the receipt as a PDF file, which is a file format created by Adobe Systems for document exchange. The second macro will transfer data from the Receipt worksheet to the Registration Data worksheet.

Decision Making: Planning and Recording a Macro

Planning and practice help to ensure you create an error-free macro. First, decide what you want to accomplish. Then, consider the best way to achieve those results. Next, practice the keystrokes and mouse actions before you actually record the macro. This may seem like extra work, but it reduces the chance of error when you actually record the macro. As you set up the macro, consider the following:

- Choose a descriptive name that helps you recognize the macro's purpose.
- Weigh the benefits of selecting a shortcut key against its drawbacks. Although a shortcut key is an easy way to run a macro, you are limited to one-letter shortcuts, which can make it difficult to remember the purpose of each shortcut key. In addition, the macro shortcut keys will override the standard Office shortcuts for the workbook.
- Store the macro with the current workbook unless the macro can be used with other workbooks.
- Include a description that provides an overview of the macro and perhaps your name and contact information.

Good decision making includes thinking about what to do and what not to do as you progress to your goals. This is true when developing a macro as well.

Each macro must have a unique name that begins with a letter. The macro name can contain up to 255 characters, including letters, numbers, and the underscore symbol. The macro name cannot include spaces or special characters. It is helpful to use a descriptive name that describes the macro's purpose.

Macro shortcut keys are used to run a macro directly from the keyboard. You can assign a shortcut key to run the macro by selecting the Ctrl key plus a letter or the Ctrl+Shift keys plus a letter. If you use the same set of shortcut keys that are already assigned to a default Excel shortcut, the new shortcut you create overrides the default Excel shortcut for the open workbook. For example, using the Ctrl+p keys to run a macro overrides the default Excel 2016 shortcut for opening the Print screen while the workbook containing the macro is open. Some people find macro shortcut keys a quick way to run a macro; others dislike them because they override the original function of the shortcut key. It's a personal preference.

A macro needs to be stored somewhere. By default, the macro is stored in the current workbook, making the macro available in only that workbook when it is open. Another option is to store the macro in the **Personal Macro workbook**, a hidden workbook named Personal.xlsb that opens whenever you start Excel, making the macro available any time you use Excel. The Personal Macro workbook stores commonly used macros that apply to many workbooks. It is most convenient for users on stand-alone computers. Finally, you can store the macro in a new workbook. Keep in mind that the new workbook must be open in order to use the macro. For example, an accountant might store a set of macros that help with end-of-the-month tasks in a separate workbook.

You can also add a description of the macro to briefly explain what it does. The description can also include the name of the person to contact and the date it was created.

REFERENCE

Recording a Macro

- On the Developer tab, in the Code group, click the Record Macro button.
- Enter a name for the macro.
- Specify a shortcut key (optional).
- Specify the location to store the macro.
- Enter a description of the macro (optional).
- Click the OK button to start the macro recorder.
- Perform the tasks you want to automate.
- Click the Stop Recording button.

Stephen provided you with the following outline of the actions needed for the macro to save the receipt as a PDF file:

1. Set the range A18:F37 as the print area for the Activity Registration Receipt range.
2. Create the PDF file, and name it "Receipt."
3. Remove the horizontal centering from the page.
4. Remove the print area.
5. Make cell A1 the active cell.

You'll record the steps for this macro using a macro named PDFReceipt that is assigned a keyboard shortcut, has a description, and is stored in the Winter Activities workbook. Practice these steps before recording the macro. Once you feel comfortable with the steps, you can start the macro recorder.

To start the macro recorder:

Save the workbook before recording a macro in case you make a mistake and need to restart.

1. Save the **Winter Activities** workbook. If you make a mistake when recording the macro, you can close the workbook without saving, reopen the workbook, and then record the macro again.
2. On the Developer tab, in the Code group, click the **Record Macro** button. The Record Macro dialog box opens. The Macro name box displays a default name for the macro that consists of the word "Macro" followed by a number that is one greater than the number of macros already recorded in the workbook during the current Excel session. See Figure 7-33.

Figure 7-33 Record Macro dialog box

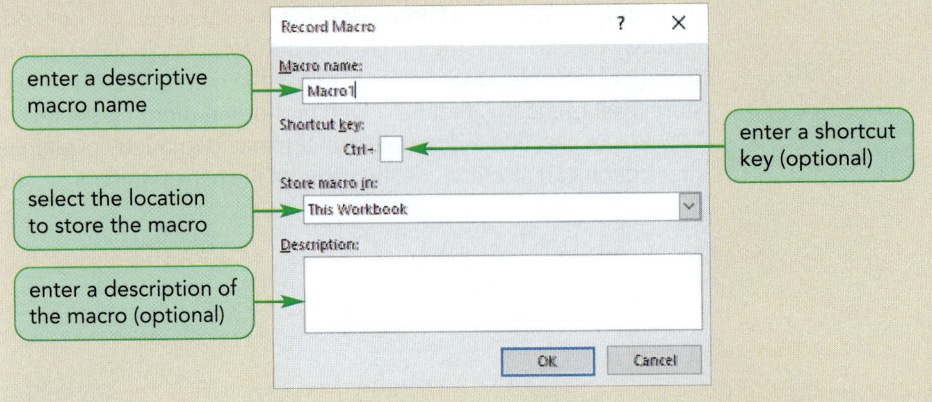

3. In the Macro name box, type **PDFReceipt** to change the selected default name to a more descriptive one, and then press the **Tab** key.
4. In the Shortcut key box, type **r** to set the Ctrl+r keys as the shortcut to run the macro from the keyboard, and then press the **Tab** key.
5. Verify that the Store macro in box is set to **This Workbook** to store the macro in the Winter Activities workbook, and then press the **Tab** key.
6. In the Description box, type **Created 12/1/2017. Save receipt area, range A18:F37, as a PDF file.** to enter notes about the macro.
7. Click the **OK** button. The workbook enters macro record mode. The Record Macro button changes to the Stop Recording button, which also appears on the status bar.

From this point on, *every* mouse click and keystroke you perform will be recorded and stored as part of the PDFReceipt macro. For that reason, it is very important to follow the instructions in the next steps precisely. Take your time as you perform each step, reading the entire step carefully first. After you finish recording the keystrokes, click the Stop Recording button to turn off the macro recorder.

To record the PDFReceipt macro:

1. Select the range **A18:F37**. This range contains the receipt that you want to print.
2. On the ribbon, click the **Page Layout** tab.
3. In the Page Setup group, click the **Print Area** button, and then click **Set Print Area**. The receipt is set as the print area.
4. In the Page Setup group, click the **Dialog Box Launcher** to open the Page Setup dialog box.
5. In the Page Setup dialog box, click the **Margins** tab, click the **Horizontally** check box to select it, and then click the **OK** button. The receipt is centered on the page.
6. On the ribbon, click the **File** tab to open Backstage view, and then click **Export** in the navigation bar.
7. On the Export screen, make sure **Create PDF/XPS Document** is selected in the left pane, and then click the **Create PDF/XPS** button in the right pane. The Publish as PDF or XPS dialog box opens, which is similar to the Save As dialog box.
8. In the File name box, type **Receipt** to replace the suggested filename.
9. Make sure the folder is set to the location specified by your instructor.
10. Click the **Publish** button. The receipt is saved as a PDF file, and automatically opens in a PDF reader, such as Windows Reader, Adobe Reader, or Adobe Acrobat, depending on which program is installed on your computer.

    Trouble? If the receipt doesn't open, you probably don't have a PDF reader installed on your computer. Continue with Step 14.

    Trouble? If a dialog box asking how you want to open this file opens, you need to specify an app to use. Select an app, and then click the OK button. Continue with Step 11.

11. Close the PDF file. You should now see the Receipt worksheet in the Winter Activities workbook.
12. On the Page Layout tab, in the Page Setup group, click the **Print Area** button, and then click **Clear Print Area**.
13. In the Page Setup group, click the Dialog Box Launcher to open the Page Setup dialog box, click the **Margins** tab, click the **Horizontally** check box so that the printout is no longer centered on the page, and then click the **OK** button.
14. In the Receipt worksheet, click cell **A1**.

    You have completed all of the steps in the PDFReceipt macro. You'll turn off the macro recorder.

Be sure to turn off the macro recorder; otherwise, you'll continue to record your keystrokes and mouse clicks, leading to unintended consequences.

15. Click the **Stop Recording** button on the status bar. The macro recorder turns off, and the button changes to the Record Macro button.

    Trouble? If you made a mistake while recording the macro, close the Winter Activities workbook without saving. If you created the Receipt file, delete the Receipt PDF file that you created. Reopen the workbook, and then repeat all of the steps beginning with the "To start the macro recorder" steps.

The process for saving a workbook that contains a macro is different from saving one that does not contain a macro. If you need to save the workbook before you complete this session, refer to the "Saving a Workbook with Macros" section later in this session.

Running a Macro

After you record a macro, you should run it to test whether it works as intended. Running a macro means Excel performs each of the steps in the same order as when it was recorded. To run the macro you created, you can either use the shortcut key you specified or select the macro in the Macro dialog box. The Macro dialog box lists all of the macros in the open workbooks. From this dialog box, you can select and run a macro, edit the macro with VBA, run the macro one step at a time so you can determine in which step an error occurs, or delete it.

REFERENCE

Running a Macro

- Press the shortcut key assigned to the macro.

or

- On the Developer tab, in the Code group, click the Macros button.
- Select the macro from the list of macros.
- Click the Run button.

You will test the PDFReceipt macro by running it.

To run the PDFReceipt macro:

1. On the ribbon, click the **Developer** tab.
2. In the Code group, click the **Macros** button. The Macro dialog box opens, listing all of the macros in the open workbooks. See Figure 7-34.

Figure 7-34 Macro dialog box

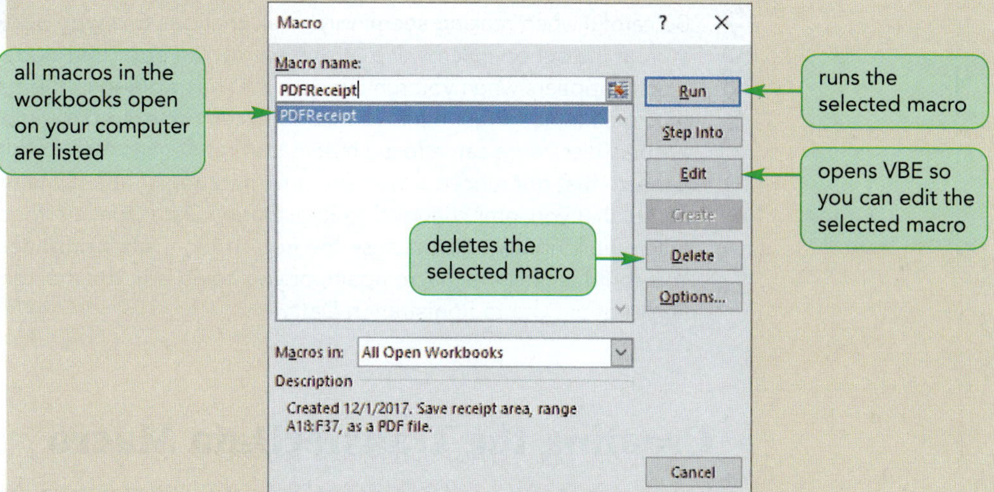

3. Verify that **PDFReceipt** is selected in the Macro name box, and then click the **Run** button. The PDFReceipt macro runs. The receipt is saved as a PDF file, and the file is opened in the PDF reader installed on your computer.

4. Close the PDF reader installed on your computer. No print area is selected, and cell A1 is the active cell in the Receipt worksheet.

   Trouble? If the PDFReceipt macro did not run properly, you might have made a mistake in the steps while recording the macro. On the Developer tab, in the Code group, click the Macros button. Select the PDFReceipt macro, and then click the Delete button. Click the OK button to confirm the deletion, and then repeat all of the steps beginning with the "To start the macro recorder" steps.

   Next, you will test the shortcut keys you used for the PDFReceipt macro.

5. Press the **Ctrl+r** keys. The PDFReceipt macro runs. The receipt is saved as a PDF file. No print area is selected, and cell A1 in the Receipt worksheet is the active cell.

6. Close the PDF reader installed on your computer.

   Trouble? If your macro doesn't end on its own, you need to end it. Press the Ctrl+Break keys to stop the macro from running.

The macro works as expected, printing the receipt as a PDF file.

INSIGHT

How Edits Can Affect Macros

Be careful when making seemingly small changes to a workbook, as these can have a great impact on macros. If a run-time error (an error that occurs while running a macro) appears when you run a macro that has worked in the past, some part of the macro code no longer makes sense to Excel. For example, simply adding a space to a worksheet name can affect a macro that references the worksheet. If you recorded a macro that referenced a worksheet named RegistrationData (no spaces in the name) that you later changed to Registration Data (space added to the name), the macro no longer works because the RegistrationData worksheet no longer exists. You could record the macro again, or you could edit the macro in VBA by changing RegistrationData to Registration Data.

Creating the TransferData Macro

You need to record one more macro. The data you entered earlier in the input section of the Receipt worksheet was never added to the Registration Data worksheet. Stephen wants to add this data to the next available blank row in the Registration Data worksheet. You'll record another macro to do this. You may want to practice the following steps before recording the macro:

1. Go to the Registration Data worksheet.
2. Turn off worksheet protection in the Registration Data worksheet.
3. Switch to the Receipt worksheet.
4. Select and copy the Transfer Area to the Clipboard.
5. Go to the Registration Data worksheet.
6. Go to cell A1, and then go to the last row in the Registration Data area.
7. Turn on Use Relative References. The Use Relative Reference button controls how Excel records the act of selecting a range in the worksheet. By default, the macro will select the same cells regardless of which cell is first selected because the macro records a selection using absolute cell references. If you want a macro to select cells regardless of the position of the active cell when you run the macro, set the macro recorder to record relative cell references.
8. Move down one row.
9. Turn off Use Relative References.
10. Paste values to the Registration Data worksheet.
11. Go to cell A1.
12. Turn on worksheet protection.
13. Switch to the Receipt worksheet, and then make cell B3 the active cell.

You may want to practice these steps before recording the macro. Stephen wants you to name this new macro "TransferData" and assign the Ctrl+t keys as the shortcut.

To record the TransferData macro:

1. Click the **Record Macro** button on the status bar to open the Record Macro dialog box, type **TransferData** in the Macro name box, type **t** in the Shortcut key box, store the macro in this workbook, type **Created 12/1/2017. Copy values in the Transfer Area in the Receipt worksheet to the Registration Data worksheet.** in the Description box, and then click the **OK** button. The macro recorder is on.
2. Go to the **Registration Data** worksheet.
3. Click the **Review** tab on the ribbon, and then click the **Unprotect Sheet** button in the Changes group to turn off protection.
4. Go to the **Receipt** worksheet, and then select the range **A40:F40** in the Transfer Area.
5. Click the **Home** tab on the ribbon, and then click the **Copy** button in the Clipboard group.
6. Click the **Registration Data** sheet tab, click cell **A1**, and then press the **Ctrl+↓** keys to go to the last row with values.
7. Click the **Developer** tab on the ribbon.
8. In the Code group, click the **Use Relative References** button. Relative references ensure that the receipt data being transferred is inserted in the next blank row (in this case, row 3) and not always in row 3 in the Registration Data worksheet.
9. Press the **↓** key to move to the first blank cell in the worksheet.
10. On the Developer tab, in the Code group, click the **Use Relative References** button. The Use Relative References button is toggled off.
11. On the ribbon, click the **Home** tab.
12. In the Clipboard group, click the **Paste button arrow**, and then click the **Values** button in the Paste Values section. This option pastes the values rather than the formulas from the Transfer Area.

    Trouble? If #REF! appears in row 3 of the Registration Data worksheet, you clicked the Paste button instead of the Paste Values button. Stop the macro recorder. Delete the macro, and begin recording the macro again.
13. Click cell **A1**, and then click the **Review** tab on the ribbon.
14. In the Changes group, click the **Protect Sheet** button. The Protect Sheet dialog box opens.
15. In the Protect Sheet dialog box, click the **OK** button.
16. Click the **Receipt** sheet tab, and then click cell **B3**.
17. Click the **Stop Recording** button on the status bar. The macro recorder turns off, and the button changes to the Record Macro button.

TIP

You can also turn off the macro recorder by clicking the Stop Recording button in the Code group on the Developer tab.

You have completed recording the TransferData macro. Next, you'll test whether it works. Stephen has a new registration to add to the worksheet. You'll enter this data as you test the TransferData macro.

To test the TransferData macro:

1. In the range **B3:B12**, enter the following data, pressing the **Enter** key after each entry:

   12/5/2017

   Will Lang

   First Friday

   G5

   L

   No

   Sandy Lang

   115 N. 7th St.

   Chrisney, IN 47611

   812-555–3444

2. Press the **Ctrl+t** keys. The TransferData macro runs, and the data transfers to the Registration Data worksheet.
3. Go to the **Registration Data** worksheet, and then verify that the data for Sandy Lang appears in row 4.
4. Go to the **Receipt** worksheet.

The TransferData macro makes it easy for the entered data to be transferred to the Registration Data worksheet.

Fixing Macro Errors

If a macro does not work correctly, you can fix it. Sometimes you'll find a mistake when you test a macro you just created. Other times you might not discover that error until later. No matter when you find an error in a macro, you have the following options:

- Rerecord the macro using the same macro name.
- Delete the recorded macro, and then record the macro again.
- Run the macro one step at a time to locate the problem, and then use one of the previous methods to correct the problem.

You can delete or edit a macro by opening the Macro dialog box (shown earlier in Figure 7-34), selecting the macro from the list, and then clicking the appropriate button. To rerecord the macro, simply restart the macro recorder, and enter the same macro name you used earlier. Excel overwrites the previous version of the macro.

Working with the Visual Basic Editor

To view the code of a macro, you need to open the Visual Basic Editor, which is a separate application that works with Excel and all of the Office programs to view, debug, edit, and manage VBA code. The VBE consists of several components, including the Code window that contains the VBA code, the Project Explorer window that displays a treelike diagram consisting of every open workbook, and a menu bar with menus of commands you use to edit, debug, and run VBA statements. You can access the Visual Basic Editor through the Macro dialog box or the Visual Basic button in the Code group on the Developer tab.

REFERENCE

Editing a Macro

- On the Developer tab, in the Code group, click the Macros button, select the macro in the Macro name list, and then click the Edit button (or on the Developer tab, in the Code group, click the Visual Basic button).
- Use the Visual Basic Editor to edit the macro code.
- Click File on the menu bar, and then click Close and Return to Microsoft Excel.

You can also use the Visual Basic Editor to copy a macro from one workbook to another. Do the following:

1. Set the security level on your computer to enable all macros.
2. Open both the workbook that contains the module you want to copy and the workbook that you want to copy the module to.
3. On the ribbon, click the Developer tab, and then in the Code group, click the Visual Basic button (or press the Alt+F11 keys) to open the Visual Basic Editor.
4. In the Visual Basic Editor, on the Standard toolbar, click the Project Explorer button (or press the Ctrl+R keys) to open the Project pane.
5. In the Project pane, drag the module that you want to copy to the destination workbook.
6. Close the Visual Basic Editor, and save the workbook with the copied module.
7. Return the security level to its original setting.

Stephen wants the PDFReceipt macro to stop in cell B3 of the Receipt worksheet. Right now, the macro stops with cell A1 selected. Although you can delete the PDFReceipt macro and record it again, it is simpler to edit the existing macro. You will edit the VBA command in the macro.

To view the code for the PDFReceipt macro:

1. On the ribbon, click the **Developer** tab.
2. In the Code group, click the **Macros** button. The Macro dialog box opens.
3. Click **PDFReceipt** in the Macro name list, and then click the **Edit** button. The Visual Basic Editor opens as a separate program, consisting of three windows—the Project Explorer, Properties, and the Code window.
4. If the Code window is not maximized, click the **Maximize** button on the Code window title bar. The Code window contains the VBA code generated by the macro recorder. You will see the beginning of the PDFReceipt sub. See Figure 7-35 (your window may differ).

Figure 7-35 Visual Basic for Applications Editor window

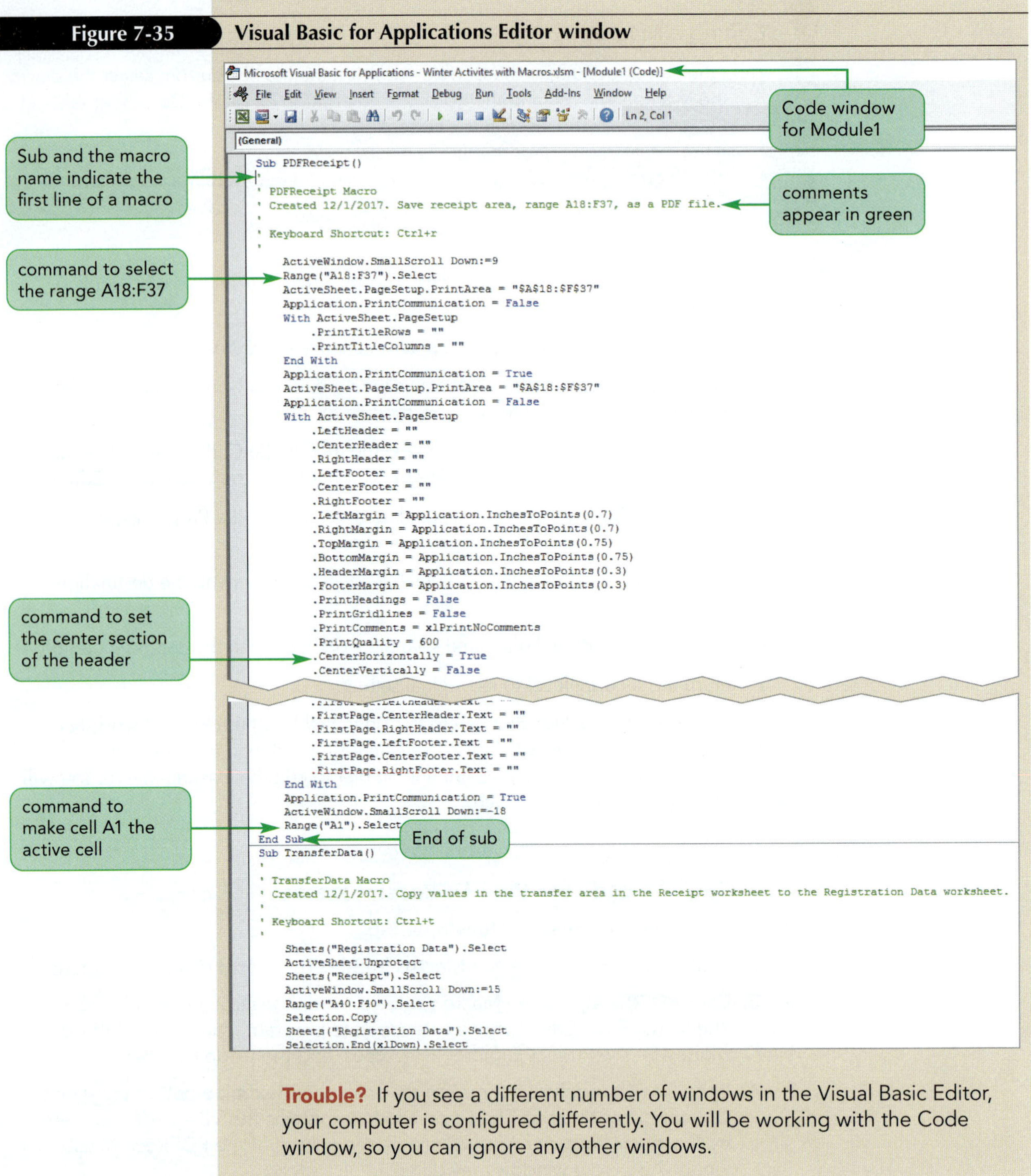

Trouble? If you see a different number of windows in the Visual Basic Editor, your computer is configured differently. You will be working with the Code window, so you can ignore any other windows.

Understanding the Structure of Macros

The VBA code in the Code window lists all of the actions you performed when recording the PDFReceipt macro. In VBA, macros are called **sub procedures**. Each sub procedure begins with the keyword *Sub* followed by the name of the sub procedure and a set of parentheses. In the example in Figure 7-35, the code begins with

```
Sub PDFReceipt()
```

which provides the name of this sub procedure—PDFReceipt—the name you gave the macro. The parentheses are used to include any arguments in the procedure. These arguments pass information to the sub procedure and have roughly the same purpose as the arguments in an Excel function. If you write your own VBA code, sub procedure arguments are an important part of the programming process. However, they are not used when you create macros with the macro recorder.

Following the `Sub PDFReceipt()` statement are comments about the macro taken from the macro name, shortcut key, and description you entered in the Record Macro dialog box. Each line appears in green and is preceded by an apostrophe ('). The apostrophe indicates that the line is a comment and does not include any actions Excel needs to perform.

After the comments is the body of the macro, a listing of all of the commands performed by the PDFReceipt macro as written in the VBA language. Your list of commands might look slightly different, depending on the exact actions you performed when recording the macro. Even though you might not know VBA, some of the commands are easy to interpret. For example, near the top of the PDFReceipt macro, you should see the command:

```
Range("A18:F37").Select
```

which tells Excel to select the range A18:F37. Several lines below this command you see the following command, which centers the worksheet horizontally on the page:

```
.CenterHorizontally = True
```

At the bottom of the macro is the following statement, which indicates the end of the PDFReceipt sub procedure:

```
End Sub
```

A Code window can contain several sub procedures, with each procedure separated from the others by the `Sub ProcedureName()` statement at the beginning, and the `End Sub` statement at the end. Sub procedures are organized into **modules**. As was shown in Figure 7-35, all of the macros that have been recorded are stored in the Module1 module.

Editing a Macro Using the Visual Basic Editor

The Visual Basic Editor provides tools to assist you in writing error-free code. As you type a command, the editor will provide pop-up windows and text to help you insert the correct code.

Stephen wants you to edit the following command in the PDFReceipt sub procedure, which sets the active cell to cell A1:

```
Range("A1").Select
```

You'll change the command to

```
Range("B3").Select
```

to change the active cell from cell A1 to cell B3.

To edit a command in the macro:

1. Scroll down the Code window to the line immediately before `End Sub` in the PDFReceipt macro.
2. In the line with the command `Range("A1").Select`, select **A1**, and then type **B3**. The command in the macro is edited to select a different cell. See Figure 7-36.

Figure 7-36 Edited Macro

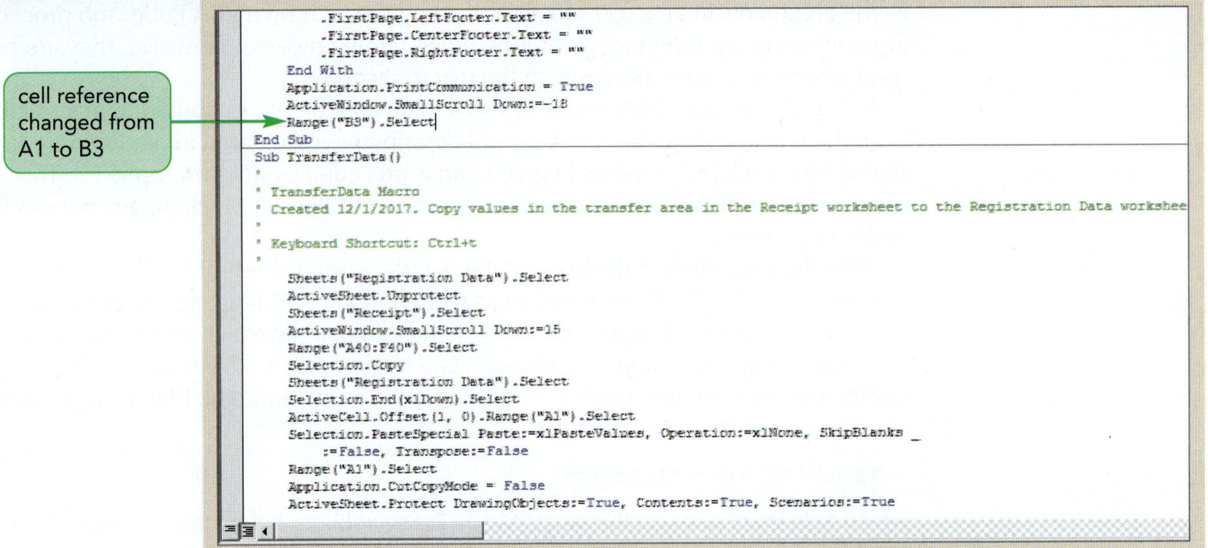

cell reference changed from A1 to B3

```
            .FirstPage.LeftFooter.Text = ""
            .FirstPage.CenterFooter.Text = ""
            .FirstPage.RightFooter.Text = ""
        End With
        Application.PrintCommunication = True
        ActiveWindow.SmallScroll Down:=-18
        Range("B3").Select
    End Sub
    Sub TransferData()
    '
    ' TransferData Macro
    ' Created 12/1/2017. Copy values in the transfer area in the Receipt worksheet to the Registration Data workshee
    '
    ' Keyboard Shortcut: Ctrl+t
    '
        Sheets("Registration Data").Select
        ActiveSheet.Unprotect
        Sheets("Receipt").Select
        ActiveWindow.SmallScroll Down:=15
        Range("A40:F40").Select
        Selection.Copy
        Sheets("Registration Data").Select
        Selection.End(xlDown).Select
        ActiveCell.Offset(1, 0).Range("A1").Select
        Selection.PasteSpecial Paste:=xlPasteValues, Operation:=xlNone, SkipBlanks _
            :=False, Transpose:=False
        Range("A1").Select
        Application.CutCopyMode = False
        ActiveSheet.Protect DrawingObjects:=True, Contents:=True, Scenarios:=True
```

3. On the menu bar, click **File**, and then click **Close and Return to Microsoft Excel** (or press the **Alt+Q** keys). The Visual Basic Editor closes, and the Winter Activities workbook is displayed.

Stephen wants you to test the macro. You'll check to see whether cell B3 is the active cell once the macro has run.

To test the edited PDFReceipt macro:

1. Press the **Ctrl+r** keys. The PDFReceipt macro runs.

   Trouble? If a Microsoft Visual Basic message box appears with a run-time error, click the End button, click the Macros button, click PDFReceipt in the Macro name box, and then click the Edit button. In the Code window, find the line you edited (one line above `End Sub`), and then change it to `Range("B3").Select`. On the menu bar, click File, and then click Close and Return to Microsoft Excel.

2. Close your PDF reader. Cell B3 is the active cell in the Receipt worksheet.

Creating Macro Buttons

Another way to run a macro is to assign it to a button placed directly in the worksheet. A macro button is often a better way to run a macro than shortcut keys. Clicking a button (with a descriptive label) is often more intuitive and simpler for users than trying to remember different combinations of keystrokes.

REFERENCE

Creating a Macro Button

- On the Developer tab, in the Controls group, click the Insert button.
- In the Form Controls section, click the Button (Form Control) button.
- Click the worksheet where you want the macro button to be located, drag the pointer until the button is the size and shape you want, and then release the mouse button.
- In the Assign Macro dialog box, select the macro you want to assign to the button.
- With the button still selected, type a new label.

Stephen wants you to add two macro buttons to the Receipt worksheet—one for each of the macros you've created. You will create the macro buttons in the blank range A14:A16 so they don't cover any existing data.

To insert a macro button in the worksheet:

1. Scroll until the range **A14:A16** of the Receipt worksheet is completely visible.
2. On the Developer tab, in the Controls group, click the **Insert** button. The Form Controls appear, with a variety of objects that can be placed in the worksheet. You'll insert the Button form control. See Figure 7-37.

Figure 7-37 **Form Controls**

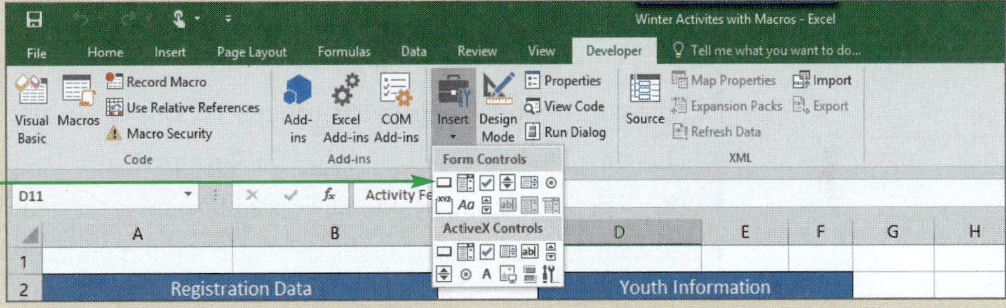

Trouble? If the Insert button is unavailable, the worksheet is protected. Click the Review tab. In the Changes group, click the Unprotect Sheet button to unprotect the Receipt worksheet, and then repeat Step 2.

3. In the Form Controls section, click the **Button (Form Control)** button, and then point to cell **A14**. The pointer changes to +.
4. Click and drag the pointer over the range **A14:A16**, and then release the mouse button. The Assign Macro dialog box opens with the button's default name in the Macro name box. See Figure 7-38.

Figure 7-38 Assign Macro dialog box

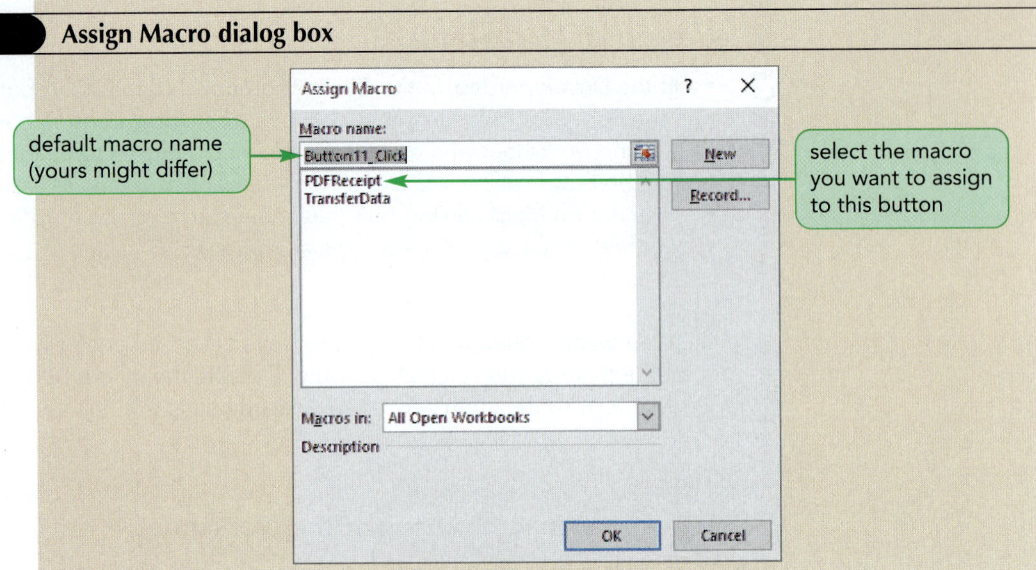

From the Assign Macro dialog box, you can assign a macro to the button. After you assign a macro to the button, the button appears with a default label. You can change the default label to a descriptive one that will indicate which macro will run when the button is clicked.

Stephen wants you to assign the PDFReceipt macro to this new button and then rename the button with a label that reflects the PDFReceipt macro.

To assign the PDFReceipt macro to the new button:

1. In the Macro name box, click **PDFReceipt**.
2. Click the **OK** button. The PDFReceipt macro is assigned to the selected button.
3. With the sizing handles still displayed around the button, type **Create PDF Receipt** (do not press the Enter key). The new label replaces the default label.

   Trouble? If no sizing handles appear around the button, the button is not selected. Right-click the button, click Edit Text to place the insertion point within the button, and then repeat Step 3.

   Trouble? If a new line appeared in the button, you pressed the Enter key after entering the label. Press the Backspace key to delete the line, and then continue with Step 4.
4. Click any cell in the worksheet to deselect the macro button.

At this point, if you click the Create PDF Receipt button, the PDFReceipt macro will run. Before you test the Create PDF Receipt button, you will add the other button.

To add a Transfer Data macro button to the Receipt worksheet:

1. On the Developer tab, in the Controls group, click the **Insert** button, and then click the **Button (Form Control)** button.
2. Drag the pointer over the range **B14:B16**.
3. In the Assign Macro dialog box, click **TransferData** in the Macro name box, and then click the **OK** button.
4. Type **Transfer Data** as the button label, and then click any cell in the worksheet to deselect the button. See Figure 7-39.

TIP

To move or resize a macro button, right-click it, press the Esc key, and then drag a sizing handle or the selection box.

Figure 7-39 Macro buttons on the Receipt worksheet

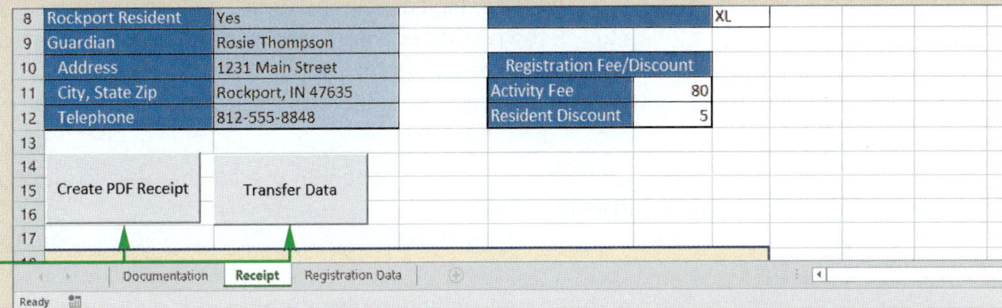

Trouble? If the macro buttons on your screen do not match the size and location of the buttons shown in the figure, right-click a button to select it, press the Esc key to close the shortcut menu, and then resize or reposition the button on the worksheet as needed.

You have completed the application, so you will reset worksheet protection.

5. On the ribbon, click the **Review** tab.
6. In the Changes group, click the **Protect Sheet** button. The Protect Sheet dialog box opens.
7. Click the **OK** button to turn on worksheet protection.

You have completed the Create PDF Receipt and Transfer Data macro buttons.

INSIGHT

Creating a Macro Button with Pictures or Shapes

You are not restricted to using the control buttons on the Developer tab for macro buttons. A macro can also be assigned to a picture or shape. For example, sometimes you might want to assign to an arrow a macro that takes you to another worksheet.

1. On the Insert tab, in the Illustrations group, click the button for the picture, online picture, or shape you want to use for a macro button.
2. Drag the pointer over the range where you want to insert the picture or shape on the worksheet.
3. Resize and position the picture or shape as needed.
4. Right-click the picture or shape, and then click Edit Text on the shortcut menu to add a name to the button.
5. Change the style, fill, and outline of the picture or shape as needed.
6. Right-click the picture or shape, and then click Assign Macro on the shortcut menu. The Assign Macro dialog box opens.
7. In the Macro name box, select the macro you want to assign to the button, and then click the OK button.

No matter what picture or shape you use for the macro button, the macro runs when the button is clicked.

Stephen has a new activity registration to add to the worksheet. You'll enter this data and then test the Create PDF Receipt and TransferData macro buttons.

To test the macro buttons:

1. In the range **B3:B12**, enter the following subscriber order:

   12/4/2017

   Dakota Thompson

   Kids Game Night

   G6

   M

   Yes

   Rosie Thompson

   1231 Main St.

   Rockport, IN 47635

   812-555-8848

2. Click the **Create PDF Receipt** button to save the current receipt as a PDF file. See Figure 7-40.

Figure 7-40 **PDF file created from the PDFReceipt macro**

Activity Registration Receipt

Rockport Youth Center
727 Main Street
Rockport, IN 47635

		Registration Date	10/4/2017
Guardian	Rosie Thompson	Youth Name	Dakota Thompson
Address	1231 Main Street	Activity	Kids Game Night
City, State Zip	Rockport, IN 47635	Grade	G6
Telephone	812-555-8848	Shirt Size	M
		Season Fee	80
		Resident Discount	5
		Total	$75

3. Close your PDF reader to return to the Receipt worksheet.
4. Click the **Transfer Data** button to transfer data to the Registration Data worksheet. Excel inserts the new transaction in the table.
5. Go to the **Registration Data** worksheet and make sure the data was transferred. See Figure 7-41.

Figure 7-41 **Data transferred to the Registration Data worksheet with the TransferData macro**

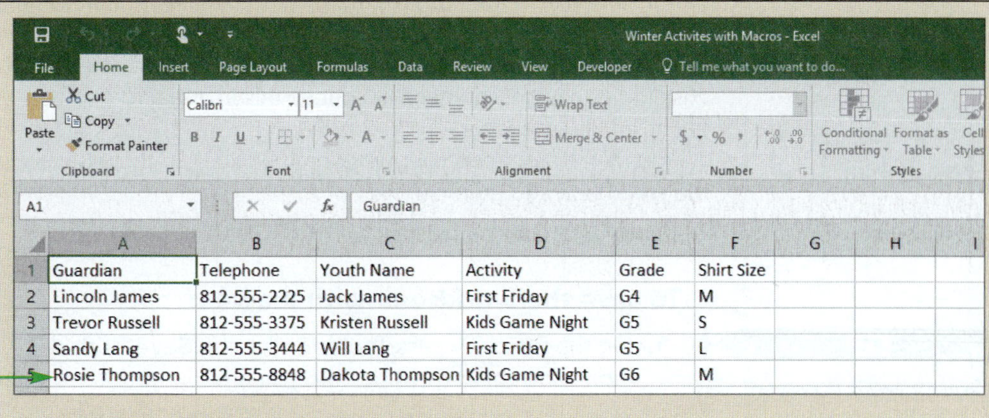

	A	B	C	D	E	F
1	Guardian	Telephone	Youth Name	Activity	Grade	Shirt Size
2	Lincoln James	812-555-2225	Jack James	First Friday	G4	M
3	Trevor Russell	812-555-3375	Kristen Russell	Kids Game Night	G5	S
4	Sandy Lang	812-555-3444	Will Lang	First Friday	G5	L
5	Rosie Thompson	812-555-8848	Dakota Thompson	Kids Game Night	G6	M

The macro buttons make it simpler to create the receipt and transfer the data from the Receipt worksheet into the Registration Data worksheet.

INSIGHT

Making Data Entry Easier with a Data Form

When a lot of data needs to be entered, consider creating a data form. A data form is a dialog box that lists the labels and entry boxes from an Excel table or structured range of data in a worksheet. Data forms can be helpful when people who are unfamiliar with Excel need to enter the data. They can also be useful when a worksheet is very wide and requires repeated horizontal scrolling.

To create a data form, do the following:

1. Make sure each column in the structured range of data or the Excel table has column headers. These headers become the labels for each field on the form.
2. Add the Form button to the Quick Access Toolbar. Click the Customize Quick Access Toolbar button, and then click More Commands. In the Quick Access Toolbars options, click the Choose commands from arrow, click Commands Not in the Ribbon, click the Form button in the box, click the Add button, and then click the OK button. The Form button appears on the Quick Access Toolbar.
3. Select the range or table for which you want to create the data form.
4. On the Quick Access Toolbar, click the Form button. The data form opens with the selected fields ready for data entry.
5. Enter data in each box, and then click the New button to add the complete record to end of the range or table and create a new record.
6. Click the Close button to close the data form.

Saving a Workbook with Macros

When you save a workbook that contains macros, a dialog box opens indicating that the workbook you are trying to save contains features that cannot be saved in a macro-free workbook. The default Excel workbook does not allow macros to be stored as part of the file. If you want to save the workbook without the macros, click the Yes button. The workbook will be saved as a macro-free workbook, which means the macros you created will be lost. If you want to save the workbook with the macros, click the No button, and then save the workbook as a new file—one that allows macros to be saved as part of the file. The default Excel Workbook format, which is a macro-free workbook, has the .xlsx file extension. You need to change this to a macro-enabled workbook, which has the .xlsm file extension.

You have completed your work on the Excel application, so you will save and close the workbook and then exit Excel.

TIP

To move the Quick Access Toolbar below the ribbon, click the Customize Quick Access Toolbar button, and then click Show Below the Ribbon.

To save the workbook with macros:

1. On the Quick Access Toolbar, click the **Save** button. A dialog box opens indicating that the workbook you are trying to save contains features that cannot be saved in a macro-free workbook. See Figure 7-42.

Figure 7-42 Macro warning dialog box

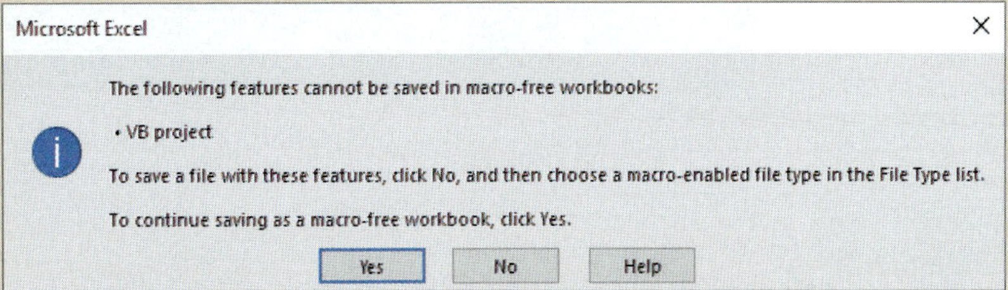

2. Click the **No** button. The Save As dialog box opens so you can save the workbook as a macro-enabled workbook.
3. Navigate to the location where you saved the files you created in this module.
4. In the File name box, type **Winter Activities with Macros** so you can easily determine which workbook contains macros.
5. Click the **Save as type** button, and then click **Excel Macro-Enabled Workbook**.
6. Click the **Save** button. The workbook is saved with the macros.
7. Close the workbook.

Opening a Workbook with Macros

TIP

After you enable the content, the filename is added to a list of trusted files and the SECURITY WARNING will not reappear as long as the workbook name or location is not changed

When you open a file with macros, Excel checks the opening workbook to see if it contains any macros. The response you see is based on the security level set on the computer. Earlier, you disabled all macros with notification. Therefore, all of the macros will be disabled when the workbook opens. When the workbook opens the first time, a SECURITY WARNING appears in the Message Bar providing the option to enable the macros so they can be run, or to open the workbook with the macros disabled. If you know a workbook contains macros that you or a coworker created, you can enable them, which adds the filename to a list of trusted files so that you won't see the SECURITY WARNING when you open this file again. If you do not click the Enable Content button, the macros remain disabled and unavailable during the current session, but the other features of the workbook are still available.

You'll open the Winter Activities with Macros workbook and enable the macros.

To open the Winter Activities with Macros workbook and enable the macros:

1. Open the **Winter Activities with Macros** workbook. The workbook opens, and "SECURITY WARNING Macros have been disabled." appears in the Message Bar below the ribbon. See Figure 7-43.

Figure 7-43 SECURITY WARNING in the Message Bar

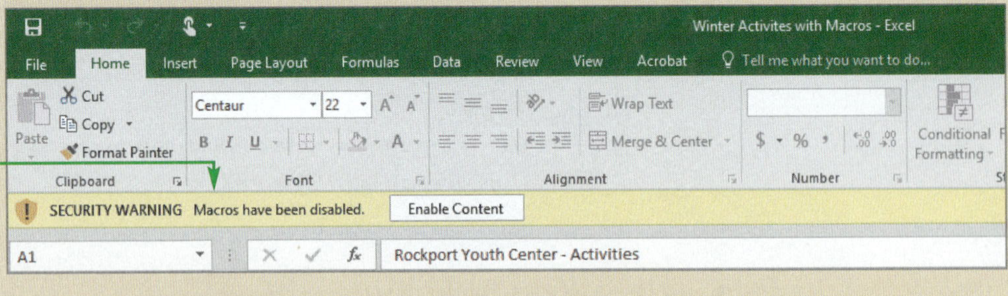

2. In the Message Bar, click the **Enable Content** button. The macros in the workbook are available for use.
3. Go to the **Receipt** worksheet.

Removing a Tab from the Ribbon

If you decide you don't want a tab displayed on the ribbon, you can remove it. Now that the macros are completed, Stephen doesn't need the Developer tab to appear on the ribbon. You will remove it.

To remove the Developer tab from the ribbon:

1. Right-click any tab on the ribbon, and then click **Customize the Ribbon** on the shortcut menu. The Excel Options dialog box opens with the Customize Ribbon options displayed.
2. In the right box listing the Main Tabs, click the **Developer** check box to remove the checkmark.
3. Click the **OK** button. The Developer tab is removed from the ribbon.
4. Save the workbook, and then close it.

Stephen is pleased with your work on the Winter Activities workbook. The workbook protection and macros will streamline the data-entry process for volunteers.

REVIEW

Session 7.3 Quick Check

1. Which tab must be displayed on the ribbon in order to record a macro?
2. What types of actions should you record as a macro?
3. Describe two ways of creating a macro.
4. What are the three places in which you can store a macro?
5. Identify two ways to run a macro.
6. What are the steps to edit a macro?
7. How do you insert a macro button into a worksheet?
8. What happens when you save a workbook with the .xlsx extension and it contains a macro?

PRACTICE

Review Assignments

Data File needed for the Review Assignments: Youth.xlsx

The Rockport Youth Center also runs half-day Winter Youth Events, Hip-Hop Dance, Secret Agent Day, and Zombietron Workshop, for boys and girls in grades 1 through 5. Stephen wants you to automate the registration process for the Winter Youth Events so it is similar to the process you created for the Winter Activities registration. Complete the following:

1. Open the **Youth** workbook located in the Excel7 > Review folder included with your Data Files, and then save the workbook as **Youth Events** in the location specified by your instructor.
2. In the Documentation worksheet, enter your name and the date.
3. In the Receipt worksheet, define names as follows:
   a. Create defined names from selection using the range A3:B11 to name all of the input cells.
   b. Change the defined name Address to **Street_Address**.
   c. Use the Name box to create the defined name **Youth_Info** for the range D2:E8 and the defined name **Events** for the range A13:B16.
4. In the Documentation worksheet, in the range B9:B19, paste the list of defined names.
5. In the Receipt worksheet, in the range B3:B11, create the data validation rules, input messages, and error alerts shown in Figure 7-44.

Figure 7-44 Validation rules for the range B3:B11

Cell(s)	Settings	Input Message	Error Alert
B3	Registration Date must be >=1/1/2017	Title: Registration Date Message: Enter the date on the registration form.	Style: Stop Title: Invalid Registration Date Message: The registration date must be present and >=1/1/2017.
B4	Any value	Title: Youth Name Message: Please enter the full name of the youth participant.	
B5	List Source (range A14:A16 in the Receipt worksheet)	Title: Event Message: Click the arrow to select the Event.	Style: Stop Title: Invalid Event Message: Use the arrow to select the Event.
B6	List Source (range D4:D8 in the Receipt worksheet)	Title: Grade Message: Click the arrow to select the Grade.	Style: Stop Title: Invalid Grade Message: Use the arrow to select the Grade.
B7	List Source (range E4:E8 in the Receipt worksheet)	Title: Shirt Size Message: Click the arrow to select the Shirt Size.	Style: Stop Title: Invalid Shirt Size Message: Use the arrow to select the Shirt Size.
B8:B11	Any value	Title: Guardian contact information Message: Please enter the Guardian contact information.	

6. In the range B3:B11, enter the data shown in Figure 7-45.

Figure 7-45 Registration data

Registration Date	10/1/2017
Youth Name	Henry Boardman
Event	Zombietron Workshop
Grade	G5
Shirt Size	L
Guardian	Sharon Boardman
Address	3642 Washington Ave.
City State Zip	Rockport, IN 47635
Telephone	812-555-1234

7. Enter the following formulas for the transfer area in the specified cells using the defined names you created earlier:
   a. Cell A40: **=Guardian**
   b. Cell B40: **=Telephone**
   c. Cell C40: **=Youth_Name**
   d. Cell D40: **=Event**
   e. Cell E40: **=Grade**
   f. Cell F40: **=Shirt_Size**
8. Enter the following formulas in the specified cells to add information to the registration receipt:
   a. Cell B27: **=Guardian**
   b. Cell B28: **=Street_Address**
   c. Cell B29: **=City_State_Zip**
   d. Cell B30: **=Telephone**
   e. Cell E25: **=Registration_Date**
   f. Cell E27: **=Youth_Name**
   g. Cell E28: **=Event**
   h. Cell E29: **=Grade**
   i. Cell E30: **=Shirt_Size**
9. Make sure that column E displays the date in the short date format and is wide enough to see the entire date.
10. In cell E36, enter a formula with a nested IF function. If the event is Hip-Hop Dance, the fee will be the value in cell B14; otherwise, if the event is Secret Agent Day, the fee will be the value in B15; otherwise, it will be the value in cell B16.
11. Unlock the input cells on the Receipt worksheet so that the user can enter data only in the range B3:B11.
12. Protect the Documentation and Registration Data worksheets so that the user cannot enter data. Do not use a password. The Receipt worksheet remains unprotected.
13. Add the Developer tab to the ribbon.
14. Save the workbook. If you have any trouble as you record the macros, you can close the workbook without saving, open the workbook that you saved, and start with Step 15.
15. Create a macro named **PDFEvent** with **Ctrl+e** as the shortcut key. Store the macro in the current workbook. Type **Created 12/7/2017. Save receipt area, range A18:F37, as a PDF file.** as the description. Record the following steps to create the PDFEvent macro:
   a. Make the Receipt worksheet the active sheet.
   b. Select the range A18:F37, and then set the selected range as the print area.
   c. Open the Page Setup dialog box. On the Margins tab make sure that the print area is centered horizontally on the page.

d. Export the worksheet to create a PDF/XPS document with the filename **Event Receipt** saved in the location specified by your instructor.
e. Close the PDF file.
f. Clear the print area.
g. Open the Page Setup dialog box. On the Margins tab, uncheck the Horizontally check box.
h. In the Receipt worksheet, make cell A1 the active cell.

16. Create a macro named **TransferData** with **Ctrl+d** as the shortcut key. Store the macro in the current workbook. Type **Created 12/7/2017. Copy values in the transfer area of the Receipt worksheet to the Registration Data worksheet.** in the macro description. Record the following steps to create the TransferData macro:
    a. Remove worksheet protection from the Registration Data worksheet.
    b. Make the Receipt worksheet the active worksheet.
    c. Select the range A40:F40 and then copy it to the Clipboard.
    d. Go to the Registration Data worksheet.
    e. Click cell A1, and then press the Ctrl+↓ keys to go to the last row with values.
    f. On the Developer tab, in the Code group, click the Use Relative References button.
    g. Move down one row.
    h. On the Developer tab, in the Code group, click the Use Relative References button.
    i. Paste the values you copied in the Registration Data worksheet.
    j. Click cell A1.
    k. Turn on worksheet protection for the Registration Data worksheet.
    l. Go to the Receipt worksheet, and then make cell B3 the active cell.
17. Test each macro using the shortcut keys you assigned to it.
18. In the Receipt worksheet, create the following macro buttons:
    a. For the PDFEvent macro, create a macro button over the range D10:D11 with the label **Print PDF Receipt**.
    b. For the TransferData macro, create a macro button over the range D12:D13 with the label **Transfer Data**.
19. Turn on cell protection for the Receipt worksheet.
20. Test the PDFEvent and TransferData macro buttons.
21. Edit the PDFEvent macro. Scroll to the last lines of the macro and in the line with the command `Range("A1").select`, change A1 to B3.
22. Remove the Developer tab from the ribbon.
23. Save the workbook as **Youth Events with Macros**, a macro-enabled workbook, and then close the workbook.

APPLY

Case Problem 1

Data File needed for this Case Problem: Posters.xlsx

Vintage Posters Ernest Loden collects vintage posters. He started his collection with circus posters but has since expanded his collection to include posters of cars, movies, and music. Ernest needs to keep track of his collection for insurance purposes. He has started to design a worksheet to enter this information, but he needs your help to set up data validation rules and record macros to update his inventory with the new posters. Complete the following:

1. Open the **Posters** workbook located in the Excel7 > Case1 folder included with your Data Files, and then save the workbook as **Vintage Posters** in the location specified by your instructor.
2. In the Documentation worksheet, enter your name and the date.

3. In the Input worksheet, create defined names from selection using the range A2:B9 to name all of the input cells.
4. In the Data Tables worksheet, paste the list of defined names in the range A9:B16.
5. In the Input worksheet, create the validation rules for cells B2, B4, B7, B8, and B9, as shown in Figure 7-46.

Figure 7-46 Validation rules for the cells B2, B4, B7, B8, and B9

Cell	Validation	Input Message	Error Alert
B2	Date Date Purchased >=1/1/2017	Title: Date Purchased Message: Enter the date purchased.	Stop Title: Invalid Date Purchased Message: You must enter a date >= 1/1/2017
B4	List Source (range A2:A5 in the Data Tables worksheet)	Title: Category Message: Click the arrow to select the Category.	Type: Stop Title: Invalid Category Message: Use the arrow to select the Category.
B7	List Source (Antique, Collectable, Print)	Title: Classification Message: Click the arrow to select the Classification.	Type: Stop Title: Invalid Classification Message: Use the arrow to select the Classification.
B8	List Source (range C2:C6 in the Data Tables worksheet)	Title: Location Message: Click the arrow to select the Location.	Type: Stop Title: Invalid Location Message: Use the arrow to select the Location.
B9	Text length Data between 0 and 100	Title: Comments Message: Enter additional comments about the poster here. Comments are restricted to 100 characters.	Type: Warning Title: Invalid Comments Message: You have exceeded 100 characters.

6. In the range B2:B9, enter the following data:
   - Cell B2: **12/5/2017**
   - Cell B3: **Frank Sinatra Pop Music Star**
   - Cell B4: **Music**
   - Cell B5: **28″ x 24″**
   - Cell B6: **9.99**
   - Cell B7: **Print**
   - Cell B8: **Loft**
   - Cell B9: **Fabric Poster**
7. Enter the following formulas for the specified cells in the transfer area:
   - Cell A12: **=Date_Purchased**
   - Cell B12: **=Brief_Description**
   - Cell C12: **=Category**
   - Cell D12: **=Size**
   - Cell E12: **=Purchase_Price**
   - Cell F12: **=Classification**
   - Cell G12: **=Location**
   - Cell H12: **=Comments**

8. Unlock the input cells in the Input worksheet so that a user can enter data only in the range B2:B9.
9. Protect the Documentation, Data, and Data Tables worksheets so that the user cannot enter data. Do not use a password. The Input worksheet will remain unprotected.
10. Add the Developer tab to the ribbon.
11. Save the workbook so that you can return to Step 12 and rerecord the macros if you have trouble.
12. Create a macro named **TransferData** with **Ctrl+t** as the shortcut key. Store the macro in the current workbook. Type **Created 12/1/2017. Copy values in the transfer area of the Input worksheet to the Data worksheet.** as the description. Record the following steps to create the TransferData macro:
    a. Go to the Data worksheet, and turn off the worksheet protection.
    b. Make the Input worksheet the active worksheet.
    c. Select the transfer area, and then copy it to the Clipboard.
    d. Go to the Data worksheet, select cell A1, and then go to the last row with values. (*Hint*: Press the Ctrl+down arrow keys.)
    e. On the Developer tab, turn on Use Relative References.
    f. Move down one row.
    g. Turn off Use Relative References.
    h. Paste the contents the Clipboard to the Data worksheet using the Values option.
    i. Go to cell A1.
    j. Turn on the worksheet protection.
    k. Go to the Input worksheet, and then make cell B2 the active cell.
13. Create a macro named **ClearInput** with **Ctrl+i** as the shortcut key. Store the macro in the current workbook. Type **Created 12/1/2017. Clear the values in the input area, range B2:B9, of the Input worksheet.** in the macro description. Record the following steps to create the ClearInput macro:
    a. In the Input worksheet, select the range B2:B9.
    b. Delete the data from the selected cells.
    c. Make cell B2 the active cell.
14. Test the macros using the shortcut keys you assigned to each of them. The Transfer Area will show zeros after the ClearInput macro has been run.
15. In the Input worksheet, create a macro button for each macro to the right of the Vintage Poster Input form. Enter labels that describe the corresponding macro. Protect the Input worksheet. Do not use a password.
16. Remove the Developer tab from the ribbon.
17. Re-enter the data from Step 6, and then test the macro buttons.
18. Save your workbook as **Vintage Posters with Macros**, a macro-enabled workbook, and then close the workbook.

TROUBLESHOOT

Case Problem 2

Data File needed for this Case Problem: Frontier.xlsm

Frontier School's Out Event Frontier School in Pineville, Missouri, is being sold to developers who plan to convert the 1949 building into a boutique shopping center. Originally serving kindergarten through 12th grade, changing demographics and more schooling options have led to the school district plan to close the school and sell the building and surrounding property. Lourdes Dreyer, president of the school's alumni association, is planning a School's Out Event at the old school. The event will include Building Tours, Breakfast with Principal Sanderson (the school principal for the past 30 years), Lunch with the Teachers and Staff who are still in the area, and a silent auction of school memorabilia. Lourdes has created a workbook to record the breakfast and lunch reservations for. She asks you to finish creating the application that will enable volunteers to enter the reservations for the event and tally a final count of attendees for the caterer. Complete the following:

1. Open the macro-enabled **Frontier** workbook located in the Excel7 > Case2 folder included with your Data Files, and then save the macro-enabled workbook as **Frontier School** in the location specified by your instructor.
2. In the Documentation worksheet, enter your name and the date. Review the formulas, defined names, and data validation information in the Reservation Input worksheet and the Catering worksheet.
3. **Troubleshoot** In the Reservation Input worksheet, the Amount to Pay calculation, which multiplies the number of guests by the charge, is incorrect. Identify the error and correct it.
4. Once you have corrected the error, run the Transfer Data macro to make sure the data is calculated correctly and that the macro is transferring the correct data.
5. **Troubleshoot** In the Documentation worksheet, Lourdes pasted a list of defined names used in the workbook, but then she continued to modify the worksheet. Make sure all of the defined names are included in the list and are accurate. Fix any errors you find or replace the list.
6. Unlock the ranges B2:B10 in the Reservation Input worksheet so that the user can enter data only in those cells. Cell B11 is a formula, so it should remain locked.
7. Protect the Reservation Input worksheet. Do not use a password.
8. Make sure that the Developer tab is on the ribbon.
9. Save the workbook to back it up in case you have problems as you work with the ClearInput macro in the next step.
10. **Troubleshoot** In the Reservation Input worksheet, use the Clear Input button to run the ClearInput macro. The macro is not working correctly. Use the Visual Basic for Applications editor to edit the macro as needed so that it performs the following tasks:
    - Select the range B2:B10.
    - Clear the contents of the selected range.
    - Make cell B2 the active cell.

    Test the macro. If the macro still does not run correctly, close the workbook without saving your changes, reopen the workbook, and then edit the macro again.
11. **Troubleshoot** In the Catering worksheet, the PivotTable should show the total number of guests who have registered for each event. The numbers in the Sum of Guests column are incorrect. Update the PivotTable so that it shows the current counts.
12. Save the workbook as **New Frontier School with Macros**, a macro-enabled workbook, to back it up before recording the CateringCounts macro in the next step.

13. Create a macro named **CateringCounts** with the **Ctrl+n** shortcut key and an appropriate macro description that performs the following actions:
    - Select the Catering worksheet.
    - Filter the PivotTable to show only breakfast and lunch events.
    - Export the PivotTable worksheet to a PDF named **Catering Counts** in the location specified by your instructor.
    - Remove the filters from the PivotTable to show all events.
    - In the Reservation Input worksheet, make cell B2 the active cell.
14. Test the CateringCounts macro using the shortcut key. If the macro doesn't work, close the workbook without saving your changes, reopen the workbook, and record the macro again.
15. Create a button below the Transfer Data button on the Reservation Input worksheet, and then assign the CateringCounts macro to the button. Change the default label to a more descriptive one. (*Hint*: Remove cell protection while creating the macro button, and then reapply cell protection.)
16. Run the CateringCounts and ClearInput macros to test the buttons. Revise the macros, if necessary.
17. Remove the Developer tab from the ribbon.
18. Save the workbook as **Final Frontier School with Macros**, a macro-enabled workbook, and then close the workbook.

CHALLENGE

Case Problem 3

Data File needed for this Case Problem: Chairs.xlsx

The Chair Guy During the long winters at Castle Rock Lake, Wisconsin, Alexander Wilson handcrafts wooden Adirondack chairs. In the spring and summer, he sells this stock at local craft fairs and specialty stores. Alexander wants to create an order form to enter and print customer orders. He also wants to save the basic sale information (chair name, style, wood, and color) so he can analyze the chair sales. Alexander started a workbook to enter information about his customer orders. He asks you to finish it by incorporating input validation, cell protection, and macros to help ensure that the collected information is accurate. Complete the following:

1. Open the **Chairs** workbook located in the Excel7 > Case3 folder included with your Data Files, and then save the workbook as **Chair Orders** in the location specified by your instructor.
2. In the Documentation worksheet, enter your name and the date, and then review all of the worksheets in the workbook.
3. In the Order Form worksheet, create appropriate defined names for each cell in the range A5:B13.
4. Create the following validation rules:
    a. Style (cell B10): The list of styles is in the range E2:E8. Enter an appropriate input message and error alert.
    b. Wood (cell B11): The list of woods is in the range E11:E12. Enter an appropriate input message and error alert.
    c. Color (cell B12): The list of colors is in the range G2:G12 Enter an appropriate input message and error alert.
5. Test the validation rules for cells you created in the range B10:B12, making corrections as needed.
6. Create the following input messages:
    a. Customer contact information (range B5:B8): Prompt the user to enter the customer contact information, such as name, address, city, state, Zip, and telephone number or email address.
    b. Chair Name (cell B9): Prompt the user to name the chair.
7. In cell B13, create a comment that explains the pricing for chairs. All pine chairs are $100 and oak chairs are $150.
8. In cell B13, enter a formula to compute the pricing based on the wood selected in cell B11. (*Hint:* You will need to use the IF function for this formula.)

Explore 9. In the Order Form worksheet, insert a WordArt text box, and then enter **The Chair Guy** as the text. Rotate the WordArt so that it is vertical in column C. Change the text fill to a color that complements the other colors used in the worksheet. (*Hint*: On the Insert tab, in the Text group, click the Insert WordArt button, and then select a WordArt style. Use the Drawing Tools Format tab to format the WordArt.)

10. Create the following formulas for the specified cells in the Chair Sale Transfer Area:
    - Cell A22: **=Chair_Name**
    - Cell B22: **=Style**
    - Cell C22: **=Wood**
    - Cell D22: **=Color**
11. In the Order Form worksheet, unlock the input cells, which are in the range B5:B12. Cell B13 has a formula and will be locked.
12. Protect the Documentation, Order Form, and Chair Sales worksheets.
13. In the Order Form worksheet, enter the following data:
    - Customer Name: **Glenn Cole**
    - Address: **1044 Sycamore Lake Road**
    - City, State, Zip: **Castle Rock Lake, WI 43573**
    - Telephone/e-mail: **glenncole@example.com**
    - Chair Name: **Amanda**
    - Style: **Rocking - Child**
    - Wood: **Oak**
    - Color: **Purple**
14. Save the workbook to back it up before you record the macros.
15. Create a macro named **PrintOrder** with the shortcut key **Ctrl+o** that does the following:
    - Set the Order Form print area to the range A1:C20.
    - Set the orientation to landscape and center the print area horizontally.
    - Export to a PDF file.
    - Return the worksheet to its original state.
16. Create a macro named **AddSale** with the shortcut key **Ctrl+s** that does the following:
    - Go to the Chair Sales worksheet, and then remove the cell protection.
    - Make the Order Form worksheet the active sheet.
    - Select the Chair Sale Transfer Area, and copy it to the Clipboard.
    - Return to the Chair Sales worksheet. Select cell A1, and then press the Ctrl+↓ keys to go to the last row with values.
    - On the Developer tab, turn on Use Relative References.
    - Move down one row.
    - Turn off Use Relative References
    - Paste the values in the Clipboard to the Chair Sales worksheet using the Values option.
    - Go to cell A1.
    - Turn on the worksheet protection.
    - Go to the Order Form worksheet, and then make cell B5 the active cell.
17. Record a macro named **ClearOrderInput** with no shortcut key that clears the range B5:B12, which is the Order Form input area, and then make cell B5 the active cell.
18. Test all of the macros by selecting and running the macros.

Explore 19. Remove the cell protection from the Order Form worksheet. Create macro buttons for all three macros using either clip art or shapes. (*Hint*: On the Insert tab, in the Illustrations group, click the button for the picture, shape, or online picture and place on the worksheet. Right-click the object to edit the text or style of the button and assign the macro to the button). Use descriptive labels for each macro button. Place the buttons in the blank area of columns D through G so they will not show up on the printed order.

20. Reset cell protection for the Order Form worksheet.
21. Test all of the macro buttons. Check the Chair Sales worksheet to see how and where new records were added.
22. Save the workbook as **Chair Orders with Macros**, a macro-enabled workbook, and then close the workbook.

CREATE

Case Problem 4

There are no Data Files needed for this Case Problem.

Resale Shoppe Debbie Oboyle opened a resale shop in Anacortes, Washington, in 2015. She sells everything from children's toys to clothes to jewelry to books. She wants to develop an electronic billing/invoicing system for organizing sales by their type (for example, coat) and the intended user (for example, adult). She asks you to follow her plan to create an Excel application that does these tasks. Complete the following:

1. Open a new, blank workbook, and then save it as **Resale** in the location specified by your instructor.
2. Rename the worksheet as **Documentation**, and then enter the company name, your name, the date, and a purpose statement.
3. Insert two additional worksheets, and then rename them as **Invoice** and **Item Information**.
4. In the Item Information worksheet, enter the data for the types of items and the age groups shown in Figure 7-47.

Figure 7-47 **Input data for the Resale Shoppe**

	A	B	C
1	**Item Group**		**Age Group**
2	Toys		Baby
3	Coats		Toddler
4	Shoes		Youth
5	Shirts		Teen
6	Pants		Adult
7	Dresses		
8	Purses		
9	Sheets		
10	Towels		
11	Blankets		
12	Jewelry		
13	Books		

5. In the Invoice worksheet, create the invoice shown in Figure 7-48. Use defined names for the Customer Name, Street Address, City, Associate, Subtotal, Sales Tax, and Total to assist in creating formulas. (*Hint*: Review the steps below before you begin to create the invoice.)
   a. Enter the labels as shown in Figure 7-48.
   b. Change the column widths, and format the labels appropriately.
   c. Use a function to insert the current date.
   d. Insert an input message in the Customer cells with a reminder about what data should be entered in cells C10, C11, and C12.
   e. For each of the four item lines (rows 17–20), use data validation rules to create lists of the different item groups and age groups that you entered in the Item Information worksheet. Use appropriate input messages and error alerts.
   f. In each item's description, insert an input message with a reminder to enter a brief description of the item.
   g. In the Subtotal cell, enter a formula to add the price from each of the four items.
   h. In the Sales Tax cell, enter a formula that uses a defined name to calculate 8.5 percent of the subtotal.
   i. In the Total cell, enter a formula that sums the Subtotal, and the Sales Tax cells.

Figure 7-48 Finished invoice for the Resale Shoppe

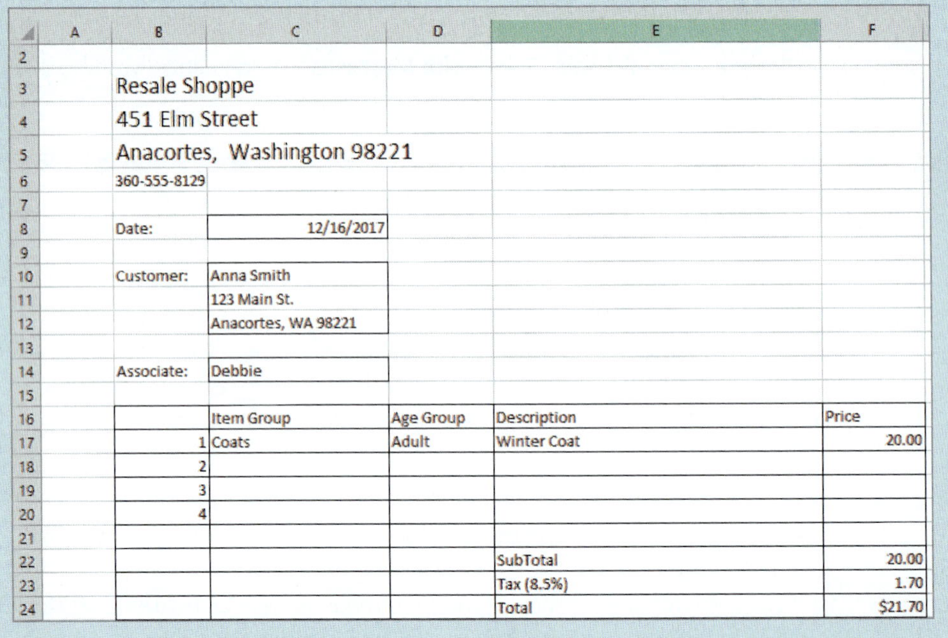

	A	B	C	D	E	F
2						
3		Resale Shoppe				
4		451 Elm Street				
5		Anacortes, Washington 98221				
6		360-555-8129				
7						
8		Date:	12/16/2017			
9						
10		Customer:	Anna Smith			
11			123 Main St.			
12			Anacortes, WA 98221			
13						
14		Associate:	Debbie			
15						
16			Item Group	Age Group	Description	Price
17		1	Coats	Adult	Winter Coat	20.00
18		2				
19		3				
20		4				
21						
22					SubTotal	20.00
23					Tax (8.5%)	1.70
24					Total	$21.70

6. Format the worksheet with fonts, font sizes, font colors, cell styles borders, and shading to make the invoice attractive and easy to read.
7. Protect the worksheet so a user can enter the Customer data in cells C10, C11, and C12, the Associate name in cell C14, and item information in the range C17:F20 data but cannot enter data in any other cells. Do not use a password. Protect Documentation and Item Information worksheets. Do not use a password.
8. Save the workbook.
9. Create a macro named **PrintInvoice** that prints the invoice. Assign a shortcut key, and type an appropriate macro description as you begin recording this macro. Set the print area to the range A1:G25 with landscape orientation, and center the worksheet horizontally. Export to a PDF, and return the worksheet to its original state.
10. On the Invoice worksheet, create a macro button, assign the PrintInvoice macro to the button, and then enter a descriptive label for the button.
11. Create a macro named **ClearInputs** that deletes the values from the range C10:C12,C14,C17:F20. Assign a shortcut key, and type an appropriate macro description as you begin recording this macro. (*Hint*: Use the Delete key to clear a value from a cell.)
12. On the Invoice worksheet, create a macro button, assign the ClearInputs macro to the button, and then enter a descriptive label for the button.
13. Remove the cell protection from the Item Information worksheet. In the Item Information worksheet, paste a list of the defined names with their locations. Below this entry, type a list of the macro names and their shortcut keys. Reapply cell protection to the Item Information worksheet.
14. Apply worksheet protection to the Invoice worksheet.
15. Test the worksheet by entering the data shown in Figure 7-48.
16. Use the PrintInvoice macro button to print the invoice for the data you entered, and then use the ClearInputs macro button to remove the input data.
17. Save the workbook as **Resale with Macros**, a macro-enabled workbook, and then close the workbook.

EXCEL

MODULE 8

Working with Advanced Functions

Analyzing Employee and Product Data

OBJECTIVES

Session 8.1
- Use the IF function
- Use the AND function
- Use the OR function
- Use structured references in formulas

Session 8.2
- Nest the IF function
- Use the VLOOKUP function
- Use the HLOOKUP function
- Use the IFERROR function

Session 8.3
- Use conditional formatting to highlight duplicate values
- Summarize data using the COUNTIF, SUMIF, and AVERAGEIF functions

Case | *MB Hobbies & Crafts*

Vanessa Beals is the managing director for MB Hobbies & Crafts (MBHC), a Texas-based craft and hobby supplier. MBHC has nearly 100 employees employed at its four stores, which are located in Bonham, Bowie, Garland, and Graham. The MBHC product list includes more than 10,000 items for dressmaking, floral crafting, jewelry making, model ship or boat building, quilting, or yarn crafting. Each store has a focus on specific crafts, although all of the stores stock a large selection of supplies for all crafts. For example, Garland stocks a wide range of items from the product list, but its main focus is on quilting supplies.

Vanessa has an Excel worksheet that she uses to track basic employee information, including each employee's ID, name, hire date, birth date, job status, and current salary. She wants to analyze this data in different ways. For example, she wants to send each employee a birthday greeting during their birthday month, create name badges that are color-coded by years of employment, identify part-time employees who are eligible for comp days, and calculate salary increases and bonuses. Vanessa is also developing a product data worksheet for analyzing the store suppliers. So far, the worksheet includes basic data such as part number, category, and description. Vanessa wants to expand the data to include the supplier name for each product and which store specializes in that product. To provide Vanessa with all this information, you'll use a variety of logical and lookup functions.

STARTING DATA FILES

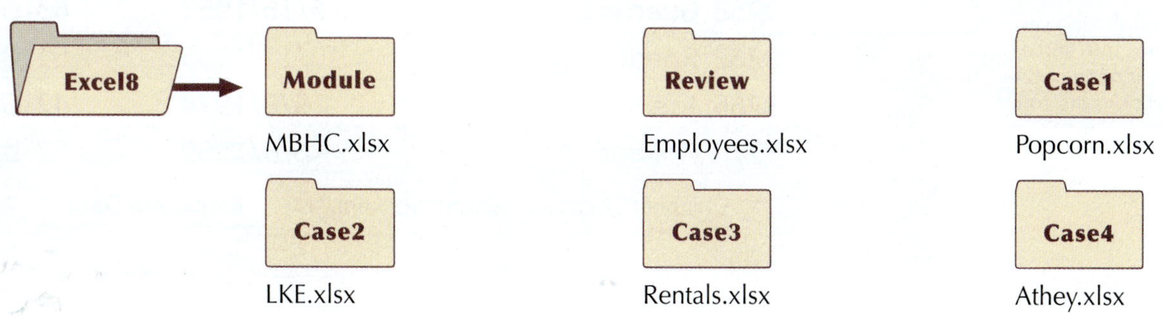

Session 8.1 Visual Overview:

When you create a formula that references all or parts of an Excel table, you can replace a specific cell or range address with a **structured reference**, which is the actual table name or column header.

The IF function is a logical function that evaluates a condition, and then returns one value if the condition is true and a different value if the condition is false.

A **logical condition** is an expression such as I80="PT" that returns either a TRUE or FALSE value.

The **AND function** is a logical function that returns a TRUE value if all of the logical conditions are true and a FALSE value if any of the logical conditions are false.

The **OR function** is a logical function that returns a TRUE value if any of the logical conditions are true and a FALSE value if none of the logical conditions are true.

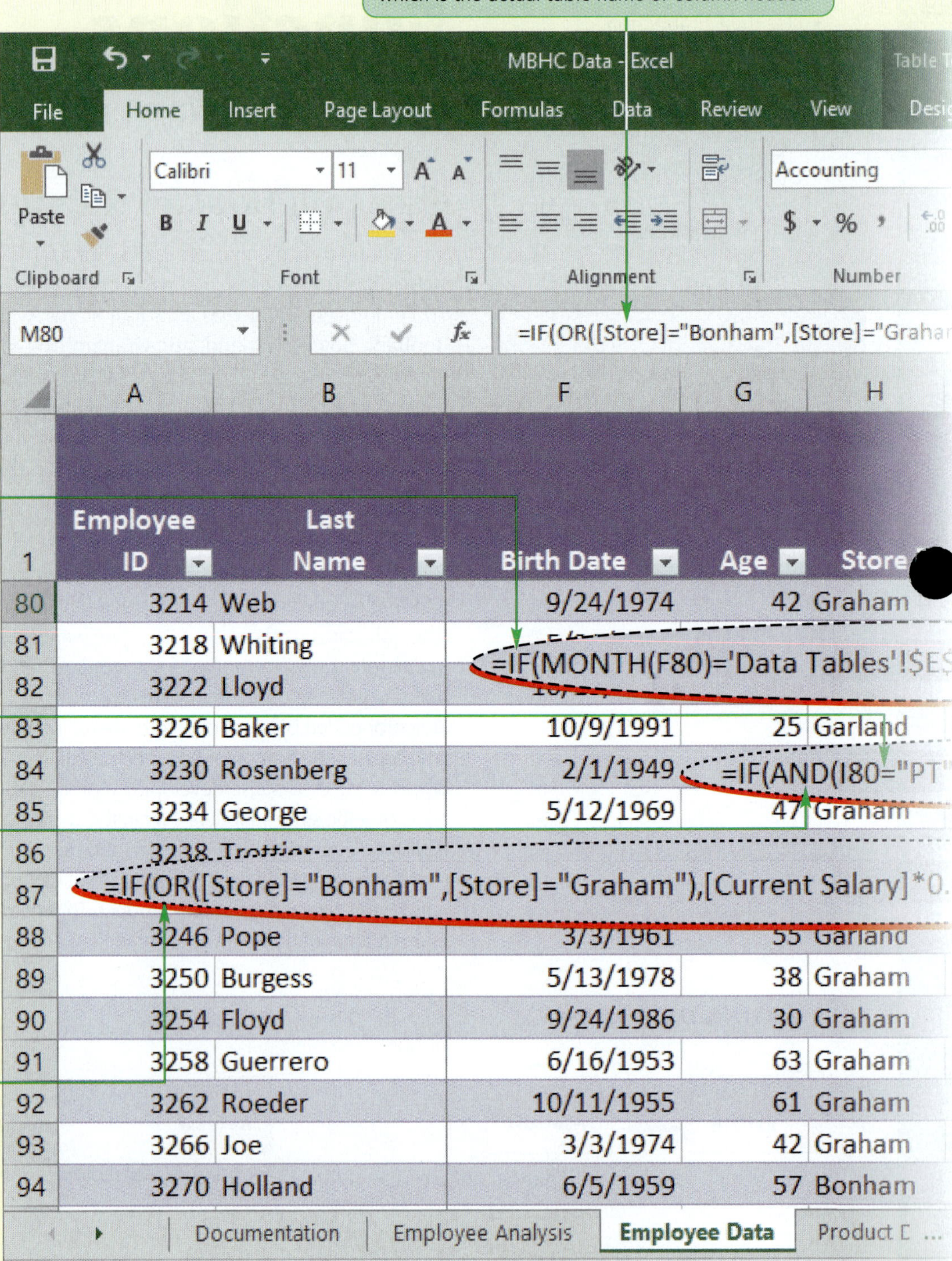

Logical Functions

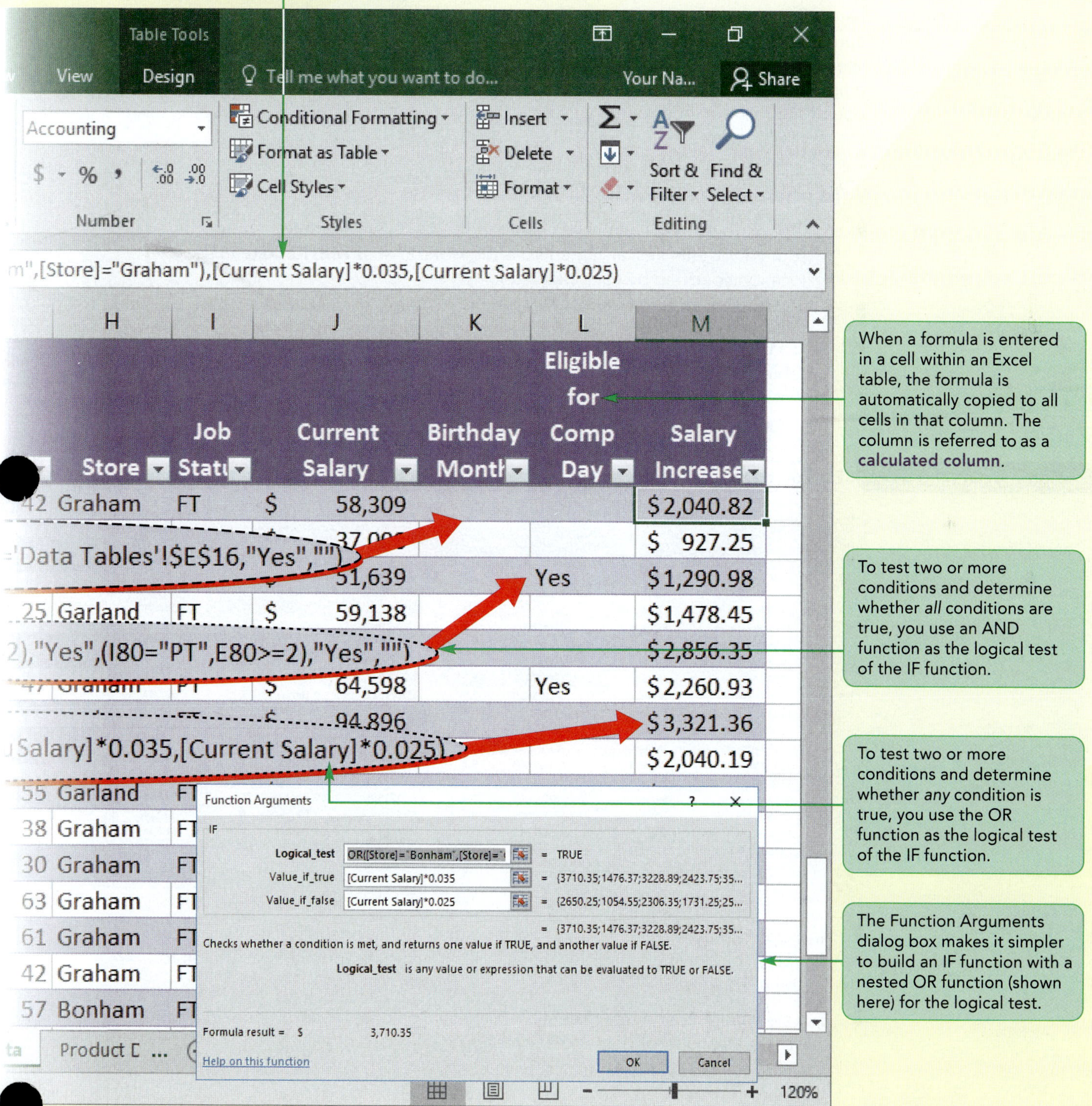
In this formula, the structured reference [Current Salary] references the cells in column J of the EmployeeTbl table.
When a formula is entered in a cell within an Excel table, the formula is automatically copied to all cells in that column. The column is referred to as a calculated column.
To test two or more conditions and determine whether all conditions are true, you use an AND function as the logical test of the IF function.
To test two or more conditions and determine whether any condition is true, you use the OR function as the logical test of the IF function.
The Function Arguments dialog box makes it simpler to build an IF function with a nested OR function (shown here) for the logical test.
m",[Store]="Graham"),[Current Salary]*0.035,[Current Salary]*0.025)
='Data Tables'!$E$16,"Yes","")
2),"Yes",(I80="PT",E80>=2),"Yes","")
Salary]*0.035,[Current Salary]*0.025)
Function Arguments
Checks whether a condition is met, and returns one value if TRUE, and another value if FALSE.
Logical_test is any value or expression that can be evaluated to TRUE or FALSE.
Formula result = $ 3,710.35

Working with Logical Functions

Logical functions such as IF, AND, and OR determine whether a condition is true or false. A condition uses one of the comparison operators <, <=, =, <>, >, or >= to compare two values. You can combine two or more functions in one formula, creating more complex conditions.

Vanessa created a workbook that contains data for each MBHC employee. She stored this information in an Excel table. The table includes each employee's ID, last name, first name, hire date, years of service, birth date, age, store, job status, and current salary. Vanessa wants you to determine if employee birth dates occur in a specified month, determine comp day eligibility of part-time employees, and compute employee salary increases. You will use IF, AND, and OR functions to do this after you open Vanessa's workbook and review the employee data.

To open and review the MBHC workbook:

1. Open the **MBHC** workbook located in the **Excel8 > Module** folder included with your Data Files, and then save the workbook as **MBHC Data** in the location specified by your instructor.
2. In the Documentation worksheet, enter your name and the date.
3. Go to the **Employee Data** worksheet. The worksheet contains an Excel table named EmployeeTbl, which includes each employee's ID, last name, first name, hire date, years of service, birth date, age, store, job status, and current salary. See Figure 8-1.

Figure 8-1 Employee Data worksheet

	A	B	C	D	E	F	G	H	I	J
1	Employee ID	Last Name	First Name	Hire Date	Years of Servic	Birth Date	Age	Store	Job Stat	Current Salary
2	1102	Delosreyes	Lori	7/10/2014	3.5	4/11/1961	55	Bonham	FT	$ 106,010
3	1106	Goode	Bari	11/6/2015	2.2	11/23/1991	25	Graham	FT	$ 42,182
4	1110	Reams	Linda	12/4/2015	2.1	10/15/1966	50	Bonham	FT	$ 92,254
5	1114	Rodriguez	Richard	3/24/2003	14.8	12/8/1964	52	Graham	FT	$ 69,250
6	1118	Peters	Jessica	5/23/2011	6.6	2/15/1962	54	Bonham	FT	$ 102,567
7	1122	Cortez	Nick	8/12/2002	15.4	10/15/1968	48	Bowie	FT	$ 94,517
8	1126	Millard	Melissa	11/6/2015	2.2	3/20/1973	43	Garland	FT	$ 51,791
9	1130	Burns	Brenda	6/10/2010	7.6	4/20/1966	50	Garland	FT	$ 32,530
10	1134	Kimball	Susan	1/20/2016	1.9	3/21/1957	59	Graham	FT	$ 94,502
11	1138	Ford	Charles	5/4/2012	5.7	6/28/1967	49	Bonham	PT	$ 45,671
12	1142	Vazquez	Johnny	7/16/2011	6.5	2/8/1986	30	Graham	FT	$ 70,346
13	1146	Whetstone	William	4/12/2008	9.7	7/13/1986	30	Garland	FT	$ 34,685
14	1150	Arnold	Leroy	3/13/2012	5.8	7/8/1949	67	Bonham	FT	$ 96,944
15	1154	Basile	Santos	8/8/2015	2.4	12/1/1956	60	Bonham	FT	$ 92,091
16	1158	Loftis	Robert	7/17/2015	2.5	7/12/1959	57	Garland	FT	$ 30,150
17	1162	Olson	Ruth	1/8/2015	3.0	3/6/1970	46	Bonham	FT	$ 81,536
18	1166	Gridley	Marjorie	10/4/2013	4.2	10/25/1959	57	Bowie	FT	$ 96,021

Documentation | Employee Analysis | Employee Data | Product Data | Data Tables

Ready

4. Scroll down and to the right. Although the column headers remain visible as you scroll down, the employee ID and last name disappear as you scroll to the right.
5. Select cell **C2**, and then freeze the panes so columns A and B remain on the screen as you scroll across the screen.

Inserting Calculated Columns in an Excel Table

TIP

Calculated columns work only in Excel tables. In a range of data, you must copy and paste the formula or use the AutoFill feature.

An Excel table does not have a fixed structure. When you add a column to an Excel table, the table expands, and the new column has the same table formatting style as the other columns. If you enter a formula in one cell of a column, the formula is automatically copied to all cells in that column. These calculated columns are helpful as you add formulas to an Excel table.

If you need to modify the formula in a calculated column, you edit the formula in any cell in the column, and the formulas in all of the cells in that table column are also modified. If you want to edit only one cell in a calculated column, you need to enter a value or a formula that is different from all the others in that column. A green triangle appears in the upper-left corner of the cell with the custom formula in the calculated column, making the inconsistency easy to find. After a calculated column contains one inconsistent formula or value, any other edits you make to that column are no longer automatically copied to the rest of the cells in that column. Excel does not overwrite custom values.

PROSKILLS

Written Communication: Creating Excel Table Fields

Excel tables should be both easy to use and easy to understand. This requires labeling and entering data in a way that effectively communicates a table's content or purpose. If a field is entered in a way that is difficult to use and understand, it becomes more difficult to find and present data in a meaningful way.

To effectively communicate a table's function, keep the following guidelines in mind when creating fields in an Excel table:

- **Create fields that require the least maintenance.** For example, hire date and birth date require no maintenance after they are entered, unlike age and years of service, whose values change each year. If you need to know the specific age or years of service, use calculations to determine them based on values in the Hire Date and Birth Date columns.
- **Store the smallest unit of data possible in a field.** For example, use three separate fields for city, state, and zip code rather than one field. Using separate fields for each unit of data enables you to sort or filter each field. If you want to display data from two or more fields in one column, you can use a formula to reference the City, State, and zip Code columns. For example, you can use the & operator to combine the city, state, and zip code in one cell as follows: =C2&D2&E2
- **Apply a text format to fields with numerical text data.** For example, formatting fields such as zip codes and Social Security numbers as text ensures that leading zeros are stored as part of the data. Otherwise, the zip code 02892 is stored as a number and displayed as 2892.

Using these guidelines means that you and others will spend less time interpreting data and more time analyzing results. This lets you more effectively communicate the data in an Excel table.

Using the IF Function

In many situations, the value you store in a cell depends on certain conditions. Consider the following examples:

- An employee's gross pay depends on whether that employee worked overtime.
- A sales tax depends on the sales tax rate and the value of the purchase.
- A shipping charge depends on the dollar amount of an order.

To evaluate these types of conditions, you use the IF function. Recall that the IF function is a logical function that evaluates a condition and then returns one value if the condition is true and another value if the condition is false. The value can be text, numbers, cell references, formulas, or functions. The IF function has the syntax

```
IF(logical_test,value_if_true,value_if_false)
```

where `logical_test` is a condition that is either true or false, `value_if_true` is the value returned by the function if the condition is true, and `value_if_false` is the value returned by the function if the condition is false. The IF function results in only one value—either the `value_if_true` or the `value_if_false`.

You will use an IF function to alert Vanessa that an employee has a birth date during a specified month. MBHC employees who have an upcoming birthday receive a birthday card with a gift card to MBHC. A Yes value in the Birthday Month column will indicate that an employee has a birthday during the specified month, and a blank cell will indicate that an employee does not have a birthday during the specified month.

The flowchart shown in Figure 8-2 illustrates Vanessa's logic for determining whether an employee's birthday occurs in a specified month. The flowchart shows that if an employee's birthday month occurs in the specified month (*birthday month = specified month* is True), "Yes" is entered in the cell. If the employee does not have a birthday in the specified month, the cell is left blank.

Figure 8-2 **Flowchart with logic to determine if an employee's birthday is in the specified month**

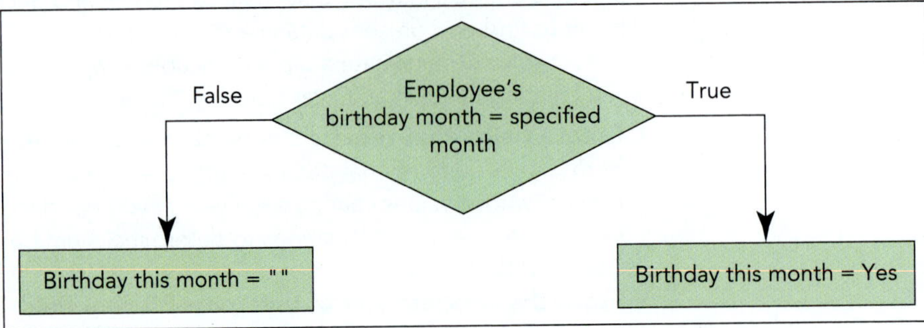

The EmployeeTbl table doesn't include a column that lists only the birthday month; this information is included as part of the employee's complete birth date, which is stored in column F. To extract the month portion of the employee's birth date, you will use the MONTH function. This function is a Date function that returns the month as a number from 1 (January) to 12 (December). The MONTH function has the syntax

```
MONTH(date)
```

where `date` is a date that includes the month you want to extract. Recall that Excel stores dates as a number equal to the number of days between January 1, 1900 and the specified date so they can be used in calculations. For example, January 1, 2017 is stored as the serial number 42736 because it occurs 42,736 days since the start of the Excel calendar. The MONTH function determines the month number from the stored serial number. For example, the birth date of the employee in row 2 of the EmployeeTbl table is 4/11/1961, which is stored in cell F2. The following MONTH function extracts the month portion of this stored date, which is 4:

```
=MONTH(F2)
```

You'll use the MONTH function in the logical test of the IF function, which will check whether the employee's birth month matches the month number entered in cell E16 of the Data Tables worksheet. Vanessa wants to know which employees have birthdays in April, so she entered 4 as the month number in cell E16. The following formula includes the complete IF function to determine if an employee has a birthday in April:

```
=IF(MONTH(F2)='Data Tables'$E$16,"Yes","")
```

The logical test `MONTH(F2)='Data Tables'$E$16` determines if the employee's birth month is equal to the birthday month stored in cell E16 of the Data Tables worksheet. If the condition is TRUE, Yes is displayed in the Birthday Month column; otherwise, the cell is left blank.

You'll add a column to the EmployeeTbl table to display the results of the IF function that determines if an employee's birthday occurs in the specified month.

To determine which employees have birthdays in the specified month:

1. In cell **K1**, enter **Birthday Month** as the column header. The Excel table expands to include this column and applies the table formatting to all the rows in the new column.
2. Make sure cell **K2** is the active cell, and then click the **Insert Function** button next to the formula bar. The Insert Function dialog box opens.
3. Click **Logical** in the Or select a category list, click **IF** in the Select a function box, and then click the **OK** button. The Function Arguments dialog box for the IF function opens.
4. In the Logical_test box, type **MONTH(F2)='Data Tables'!$E$16** and then press the **Tab** key. This condition tests whether the employee's birth month is equal to the month specified in cell E16 of the Data Tables worksheet. The function MONTH returns the month number of the date specified in cell F2. TRUE appears to the right of the Logical_test argument box, indicating this employee has a birthday in the specified month.
5. In the Value_if_true box, type **Yes** and then press the **Tab** key. This argument specifies that if the condition is true (the employee's birth month matches the value in cell E16 of the Data Tables worksheet), display Yes as the formula result. The value to the right of the Value_if_true argument box is Yes because the condition is true. Notice that Excel inserts quotation marks around the text value because you did not include them.
6. In the Value_if_false box, type **""**. This argument specifies that if the condition is false (the employee's birth month does not match the value in cell E16 of the Data Tables worksheet), display nothing in cell K2. The value to the right of the Value_if_false argument box is "", which indicates that cell K2 appears blank if the condition is false. See Figure 8-3.

Figure 8-3 Function Arguments dialog box for the IF function

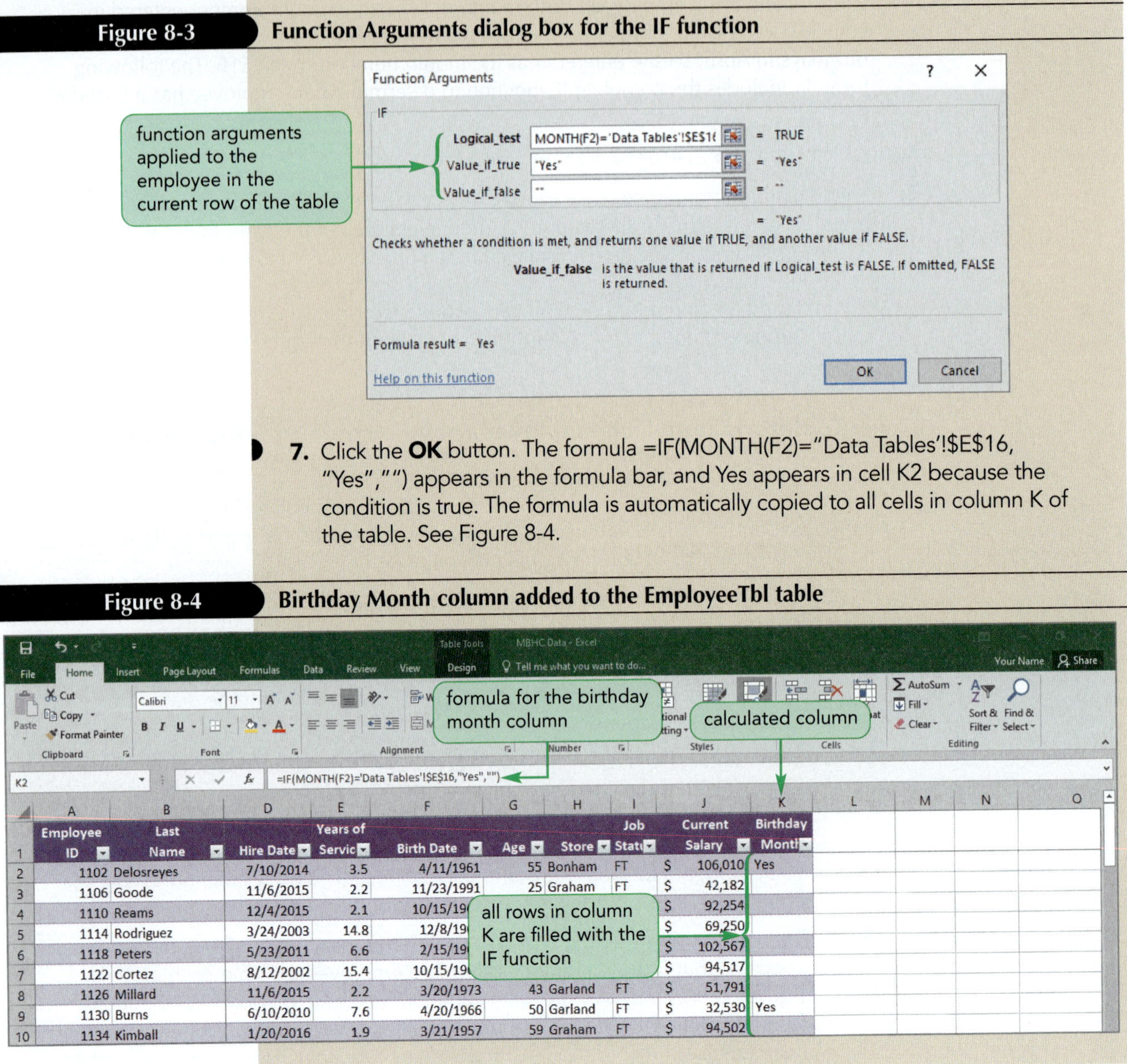

7. Click the **OK** button. The formula =IF(MONTH(F2)="Data Tables'!$E$16, "Yes","") appears in the formula bar, and Yes appears in cell K2 because the condition is true. The formula is automatically copied to all cells in column K of the table. See Figure 8-4.

Figure 8-4 Birthday Month column added to the EmployeeTbl table

Using the AND Function

The IF function evaluates a single condition. However, you often need to test two or more conditions and determine whether *all* conditions are true. You can do this with the AND function. The AND function is a logical function that returns the value TRUE if all of the logical conditions are true and returns the value FALSE if any or all of the logical conditions are false. The syntax of the AND function is

```
AND(logical1[,logical2]...)
```

where *logical1* and *logical2* are conditions that can be either true or false. If all of the logical conditions are true, the AND function returns the logical value TRUE; otherwise, the function returns the logical value FALSE. You can include up to 255 logical conditions in an AND function. However, keep in mind that *all* of the logical conditions listed in the AND function must be true for the AND function to return a TRUE value.

Figure 8-5 illustrates how the AND function is used to determine student eligibility for the dean's list. In this scenario, when students have 12 or more credits (stored in cell B1) *and* their GPA is greater than 3.5 (stored in cell B2), they are placed on the dean's list. Both conditions must be true for the AND function to return the logical value TRUE.

Figure 8-5 **AND function example**

Purpose: To determine dean's list requirements

Logic Scenario: 12 or more semester credits and GPA above 3.5

Formula: AND function with two conditions
`=AND(B1>=12,B2>3.5)`

Data: cell B1 stores number of credits
cell B2 stores student's GPA

Example:

Data		Condition1	Condition2	Results
Cell B1	**Cell B2**	**B1>=12**	**B2>3.5**	**(Dean's List?)**
15	3.6	True	True	True
12	3.25	True	False	False
6	3.8	False	True	False
10	3.0	False	False	False

Vanessa wants you to use an AND function to determine part-time employees' eligibility for comp days. MBHC part-time employees are eligible for comp days if they are part-time employees (PT in Job Status) *and* have worked for the company for two or more years (equal to or greater than 2 in Years of Service). As long as *both* conditions are true, the employee is eligible for comp days. If neither condition is true or if only one condition is true, the employee is not eligible for comp days. Vanessa outlined these eligibility conditions in the flowchart shown in Figure 8-6.

Figure 8-6 **Flowchart illustrating AND logic for the comp day eligibility**

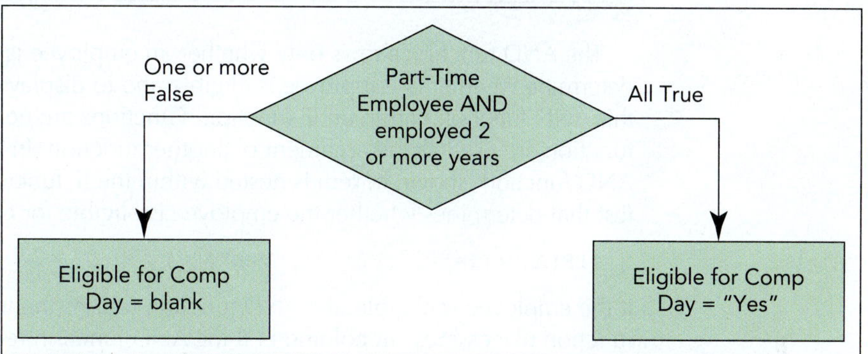

To calculate eligibility of each part-time employee, you need to use the AND function with the IF function. You use the AND function shown in the following formula as the logical test to evaluate whether each employee in the EmployeeTbl table fulfills the eligibility requirements:

```
=AND(I2="PT",E2>=2)
```

This formula tests whether the value in cell I2 (the job status for the first employee) is equal to PT (an abbreviation for part time), and whether the value in cell E2 (the years of service for the first employee) is greater than or equal to 2 (indicating two or more years of employment at MBHC). When an employee is a part-time employee (I2="PT") *and* has worked two or more years at MBHC (E2>=2), the AND function returns the value TRUE; otherwise, the AND function returns the value FALSE. Figure 8-7 shows the result returned by the AND function for four different sets of employee values for job status and years of service.

Figure 8-7 **AND function results for comp day eligibility**

Purpose: To determine eligibility for comp days

Logic Scenario: A part-time employee is eligible for comp days if the employee has part-time (PT) job status and has two or more years of service.

Formula: AND function with two conditions
`=AND(I2="PT",E2>=2)`

Data: cell I2 stores Job Status
cell E2 stores Years of Service

Example:

Data		Condition1	Condition2	Results
Cell I2	Cell E2	I2="PT"	E2>=2	(Comp Day?)
FT	2.5	False	True	False
FT	1.5	False	False	False
PT	2.5	True	True	True
PT	1.5	True	False	False

The AND function shows only whether an employee is eligible for comp days. To determine whether an employee is eligible *and* to display "Yes" in column L, you nest this AND function within an IF function. Functions are nested when the results of one function are used as the argument of another function. In the following formula, the AND function (shown in red) is nested within the IF function and is used as the logical test that determines whether the employee is eligible for comp days:

```
=IF(AND(I2="PT",E2>=2),"Yes","")
```

If the employee is eligible, the AND function returns the logical value TRUE and the IF function places "Yes" in column L. If the AND function returns the logical value FALSE, the IF function displays nothing in the cell.

You'll insert a new column in the EmployeeTbl table, and then enter the formula to determine whether the employee is qualified for comp days.

To determine if part-time employees are eligible for comp days:

1. In cell **L1**, enter **Eligible for Comp Day** as the column header. The Excel table expands to include the new column, and cell L2 is the active cell.
2. AutoFit column L so that the entire heading is visible.
3. Make sure cell **L2** is the active cell, and then click the **Insert Function** button *fx* next to the formula bar. The Insert Function dialog box opens.
4. Click **IF** in the Select a function box, and then click the **OK** button. The Function Arguments dialog box opens.
5. In the Logical_test box, type **AND(I2="PT",E2>=2)** and then press the **Tab** key. This logical test evaluates whether the employee is part time, indicated by PT in cell I2, *and* has worked at MBHC for two years or more. FALSE appears to the right of the Logical_test box, indicating that this condition for the employee in row 2 is false. This employee's job status is full time, so one of the conditions is not true.
6. In the Value_if_true box, type **Yes** and then press the **Tab** key. This argument specifies that if the condition is true (the employee is eligible for comp time as determined by the AND function), the word Yes appears to the right of the Value_if_true box.
7. In the Value_if_false box, type **""**. This argument specifies that if the condition is false (the employee is not eligible for comp time as determined by the AND function), nothing is displayed in cell L2, as specified by "" to the right of the Value_if_false box. See Figure 8-8.

Figure 8-8 Function Arguments dialog box for the IF function with nested AND function

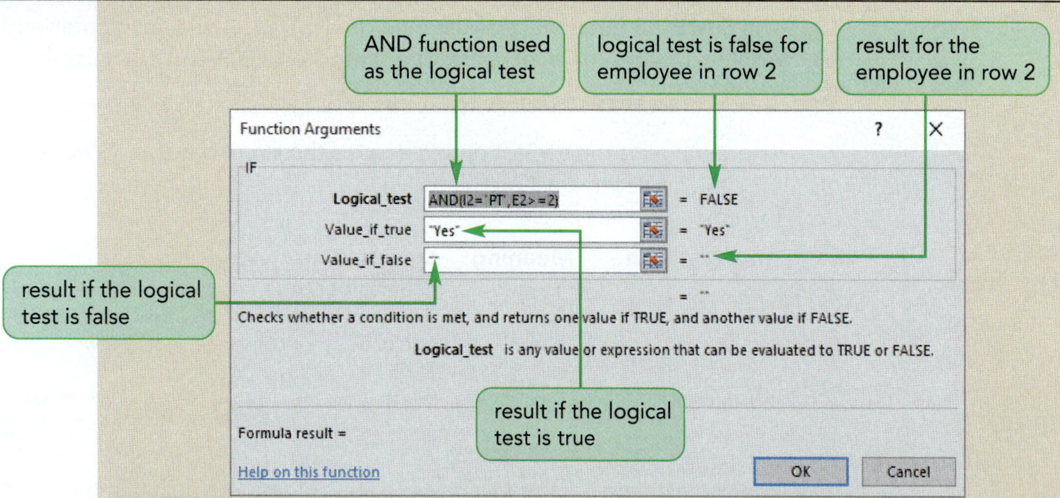

8. Click the **OK** button. The formula with the IF function that you just created is entered in cell L2 and copied to all rows in column L of the table.
9. Select cell **L2**. The formula =IF(AND(I2="PT",E2>=2),"Yes","") appears in the formula bar and nothing appears in cell L2 because the condition is false. See Figure 8-9.

Figure 8-9 **IF function with the AND function to determine comp day eligibility**

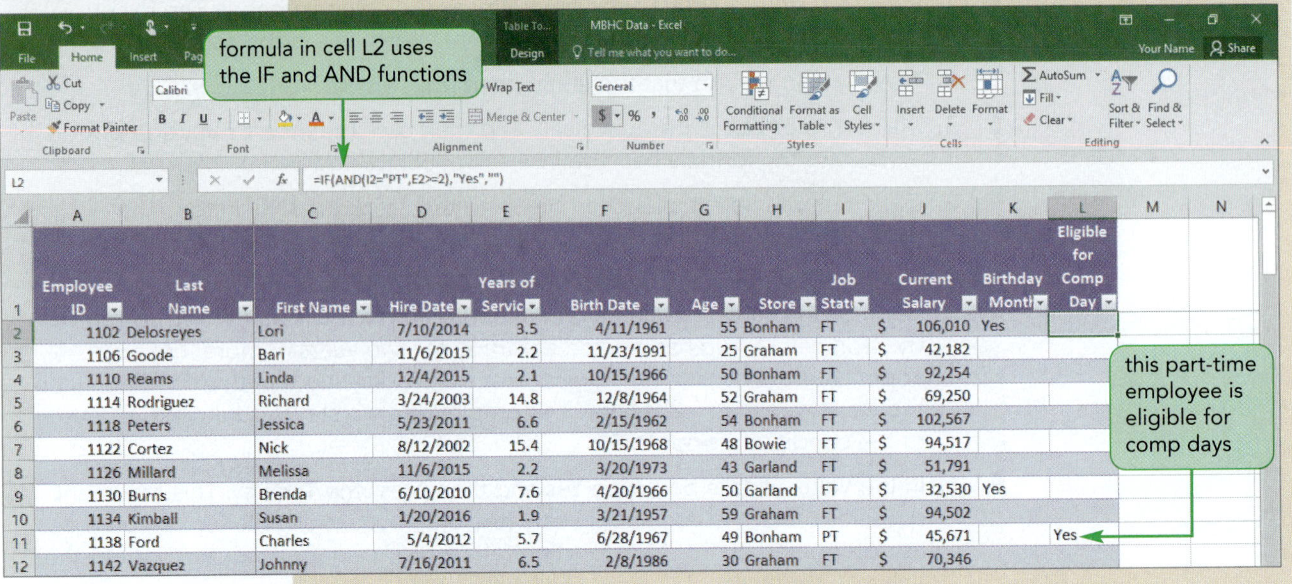

Employee ID	Last Name	First Name	Hire Date	Years of Service	Birth Date	Age	Store	Job Status	Current Salary	Birthday Month	Eligible for Comp Day
1102	Delosreyes	Lori	7/10/2014	3.5	4/11/1961	55	Bonham	FT	$ 106,010	Yes	
1106	Goode	Bari	11/6/2015	2.2	11/23/1991	25	Graham	FT	$ 42,182		
1110	Reams	Linda	12/4/2015	2.1	10/15/1966	50	Bonham	FT	$ 92,254		
1114	Rodriguez	Richard	3/24/2003	14.8	12/8/1964	52	Graham	FT	$ 69,250		
1118	Peters	Jessica	5/23/2011	6.6	2/15/1962	54	Bonham	FT	$ 102,567		
1122	Cortez	Nick	8/12/2002	15.4	10/15/1968	48	Bowie	FT	$ 94,517		
1126	Millard	Melissa	11/6/2015	2.2	3/20/1973	43	Garland	FT	$ 51,791		
1130	Burns	Brenda	6/10/2010	7.6	4/20/1966	50	Garland	FT	$ 32,530	Yes	
1134	Kimball	Susan	1/20/2016	1.9	3/21/1957	59	Graham	FT	$ 94,502		
1138	Ford	Charles	5/4/2012	5.7	6/28/1967	49	Bonham	PT	$ 45,671		Yes
1142	Vazquez	Johnny	7/16/2011	6.5	2/8/1986	30	Graham	FT	$ 70,346		

All part-time employees who qualify for comp days have been identified.

INSIGHT

Using the DATEDIF Function to Calculate Employee Age

In the EmployeeTbl table, the Age column was calculated using the DATEDIF function. The **DATEDIF function** calculates the difference between two dates and shows the result in months, days, or years. The syntax for the DATEDIF function is

```
DATEDIF(Date1,Date2,Interval)
```

where `Date1` is the earliest date, `Date2` is the latest date, and `Interval` is the unit of time the DATEDIF function will use in the result. You specify `Interval` with one of the following interval codes:

Interval Code	Meaning	Description
"m"	Months	The number of complete months between *Date1* and *Date2*
"d"	Days	The number of complete days between *Date1* and *Date2*
"y"	Years	The number of complete years between *Date1* and *Date2*

For example, the following formula calculates an employee's age in complete years:

```
=DATEDIF(F2,'Data Tables'!$E$17,"y")
```

The earliest date is located in cell F2, the birth date. The latest date is in cell E17 in the Data Tables worksheet, which shows the date used to compare against the birth date—as of a cut-off date. The interval "y" indicates that you want to display the number of complete years between these two dates.

The DATEDIF function is undocumented in Excel, but it has been available since Excel 97. To learn more about this function, search the web using "DATEDIF function in Excel" as the search text in your favorite search engine.

Using the OR Function

The OR function is a logical function that returns a TRUE value if any of the logical conditions are true, and returns a FALSE value if all of the logical conditions are false. The syntax of the OR function is

```
OR(logical1[,logical2]...)
```

where `logical1` and `logical2` are conditions that can be either true or false. If any of the logical conditions are true, the OR function returns the logical value TRUE; otherwise, the function returns the logical value FALSE. You can include up to 255 logical conditions in the OR function. However, keep in mind that if any logical condition listed in the OR function is true, the OR function returns a TRUE value.

Figure 8-10 illustrates how the OR function is used to determine eligibility for a 10 percent discount. In this scenario, anyone who is 65 years or older (stored in cell B1) or anyone who is a college student (stored in cell B2) receives a 10 percent discount. At least one condition must be true for the OR function to return the logical value TRUE.

Figure 8-10 **Example of the OR function**

Purpose: To determine who is eligible for a discount

Logic Scenario: Discount is 10 percent for seniors (65 or older) or college students (Status =STU)

Formula: OR function with two conditions
`=OR(B1>=65,B2="STU")`

Data: cell B1 stores Age
cell B2 stores Status (STU, FAC, STF)

Example:

Data		Condition1	Condition2	Results
Cell B1	Cell B2	B1>=65	B2="STU"	(Discount?)
22	STU	False	True	True
67	FAC	True	False	True
65	STU	True	True	True
45	STF	False	False	False

MBHC is considering awarding a 3.5 percent raise to employees working in the original stores (Bonham or Graham) and a 2.5 percent raise for all other employees. The criteria for awarding a salary increase are based on location. If the employee is working in either Bonham or Graham, the employee will receive the 3.5 percent raise. In other words, if either Store equals Bonham or Store equals Graham is True, the condition is true, and the employee will receive the 3.5 percent raise. If the condition is false—meaning the employee works at a store other than Bonham or Graham—the employee receives a 2.5 percent raise. Vanessa outlined the salary increase criteria in the flowchart shown in Figure 8-11.

Figure 8-11 **Flowchart of the OR function to calculate salary increase**

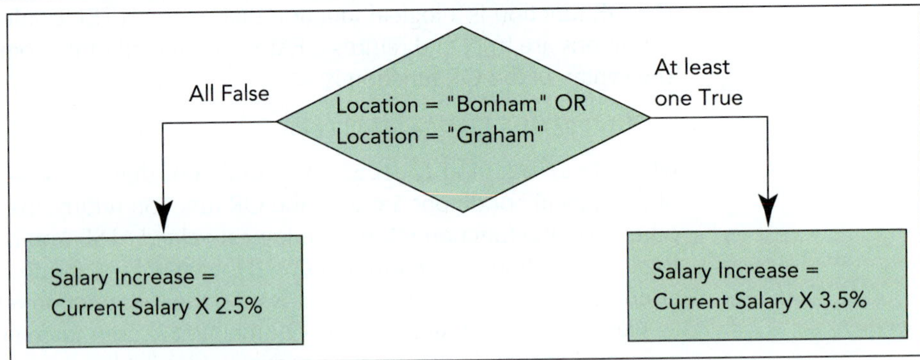

You need to use the OR function to test whether an employee meets the criteria for the 3.5 percent or 2.5 percent salary increase. The following formula uses the OR function to test whether the value in cell H2 (the store for the first employee) is equal to Bonham *or* whether the value in cell H2 is equal to Graham:

```
=OR(H2="Bonham",H2="Graham")
```

If the employee works in the Bonham store *or* the employee works in the Graham store, the OR function returns the value TRUE; otherwise, the OR function returns the value FALSE.

Figure 8-12 shows the results returned using the OR function for four different employee work locations—Bonham, Bowie, Garland, and Graham.

Figure 8-12 **OR function results for four employee work locations**

Purpose: To determine an employee's salary increase percentage

Logic Scenario: Proposed 3.5 percent salary increase to full-time (FT) employees located in Graham or Bonham

Formula: OR function with two conditions
`=OR(F2="Graham",F2="Bonham")`

Data: cell F2 stores Location

Example:

Data	Condition1	Condition2	Results
Cell F2	F2="Graham"	B2="Bonham"	(OR function)
Graham	True	False	True
Bonham	False	True	True
Garland	False	False	False
Bowie	False	False	False

The OR function only determines which raise an employee is eligible for. It does not calculate the amount of the salary increase. To determine the amount of the salary increase, the OR function must be nested within an IF function. In the formula

```
=IF(OR(H2="Bonham",H2="Graham"),J2*0.035,J2*0.025)
```

the logical test of the IF function uses the OR function (shown in red) to determine whether an employee is either working in the Bonham store *or* working in the Graham store. If the OR function returns a TRUE value, the IF function multiplies the Current Salary by 3.5 percent. If the OR function returns a FALSE value, the IF function multiplies the Current Salary by 2.5 percent.

Using Structured References to Create Formulas in Excel Tables

When you create a formula that references all or parts of an Excel table, you can replace the specific cell or range address with a structured reference, the actual table name, or a column header. This makes the formula easier to create and understand. The default Excel table name is Table1, Table2, and so forth unless you enter a more descriptive table name, as Vanessa did for the EmployeeTbl table. Column headers provide a description of the data entered in each column. Structured references make it easier to create formulas that use portions or all of an Excel table because the names or headers are usually simpler to identify than cell addresses. For example, in the EmployeeTbl table, the table name EmployeeTbl refers to the range A2:L101, which is the range of data in the table excluding the header row and the Total row. When you want to reference an entire column of data in a table, you create a column qualifier, which has the syntax

```
Tablename[qualifier]
```

where *Tablename* is the name entered in the Table Name box in the Properties group on the Table Tools Design tab, and *qualifier* is the column header enclosed in square brackets. For example, the following structured reference references the Current Salary data in the range J2:J101 of the EmployeeTbl table (excluding the column header and total row, if any):

```
EmployeeTbl[Current Salary]
```

You can use structured references in formulas. The following formula adds the Current Salary data in the range J2:J101 of the EmployeeTbl table; in this case, [Current Salary] is the column qualifier:

```
=SUM(EmployeeTbl[Current Salary])
```

When you create a calculated column you can use structured references in the formula. A formula that includes a structured reference can be fully qualified or unqualified. In a fully qualified structured reference, the table name precedes the column qualifier. In an unqualified structured reference, only the column qualifier (column header enclosed in square brackets) appears in the reference.

If you are creating a calculated column or formula within an Excel table, you can use either the fully qualified structured reference or the unqualified structured reference in the formula. If you use a structured reference outside the table or in another worksheet to reference an Excel table or portion of the table, you must use a fully qualified reference.

You'll use structured references to calculate the salary increases for MBHC Employees.

To calculate the salary increases using the IF and OR functions:

1. In cell **M1**, enter **Salary Increase** as the column header. The Excel table expands to include the new column, and cell M2 is the active cell.
2. Make sure cell **M2** is the active cell, and then click the **Insert Function** button next to the formula bar. The Insert Function dialog box opens.
3. Click **IF** in the Select a function box, and then click the **OK** button. The Function Arguments dialog box opens.
4. In the Logical_test box, type **OR([Store]="Bonham",[Store]="Graham")** to enter the OR function with structured references. This logical test evaluates whether the employee works in the Bonham store or works in the Graham.
5. Click the **Collapse dialog box** button so you can see the entire function in the Logical_test box. See Figure 8-13.

Be sure to type square brackets and use the exact spelling and location shown. Otherwise, the formula will return an error.

Figure 8-13 Logical_test argument for the OR function

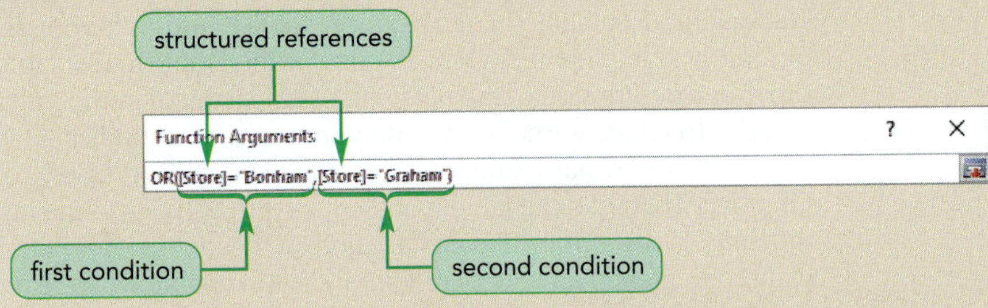

6. Click the **Expand dialog box** button, and then press the **Tab** key. TRUE appears to the right of the Logical_test box because the employee in the active row, row 2, is eligible for the 3.5 percent salary increase.

   Trouble? If Invalid appears instead of TRUE as the logical test results, you probably mistyped the logical test. Compare the function in your Logical_test box to the one shown in Figure 8-13, confirming that you used square brackets around the structured reference [Store] and typed all the text correctly.

7. In the Value_if_true box, type **[Current Salary]*0.035** and then press the **Tab** key. This argument specifies that if the logical test is true (the employee is eligible for the 3.5 percent increase), the amount in the employee's salary cell is multiplied by 3.5 percent. The salary increases for all employees, beginning in row 2, whose logical test is true appear to the right of the Value_if_true box.

8. In the Value_if_false box, type **[Current Salary]*0.025**. This argument specifies that if the logical test is false (the employee is not eligible for the 3.5 percent salary increase), the amount in the employee's salary cell is multiplied by 2.5 percent. The salary increases for all employees, beginning in row 2, whose logical test is false appear to the right of the Value_if_false box. See Figure 8-14.

Figure 8-14 **Function Arguments dialog box for the IF function with an OR function**

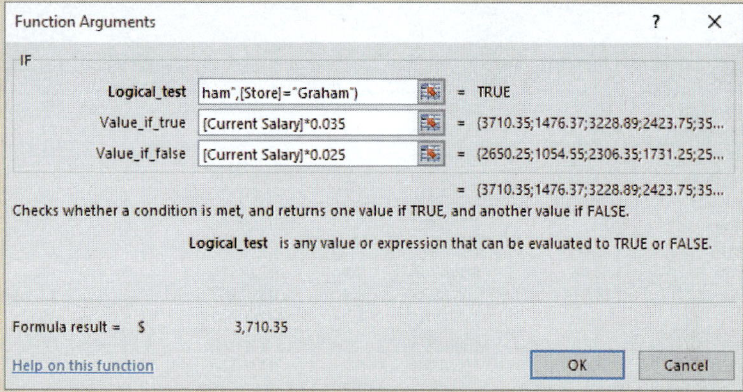

9. Click the **OK** button. The formula =IF(OR([Store]="Bonham",[Store]="Bonham"),[Current Salary]*0.035,[Current Salary]*0.025) appears in the formula bar, and the value 3710.35 appears in cell M2 because the condition is true. The formula is automatically copied to all rows in column M of the table.

TIP

Double-click above the header row to select the column header and data.

10. Position the pointer at the top of cell **M1** until the pointer changes to ⬇, and then click the left mouse button to select the Salary Increase data values.
11. Format the range with the **Accounting** style with two decimal places, and then increase the column width to display all values, if necessary.
12. Select cell **M2** to deselect the column. See Figure 8-15.

Figure 8-15 IF function with the OR function calculates salary increase

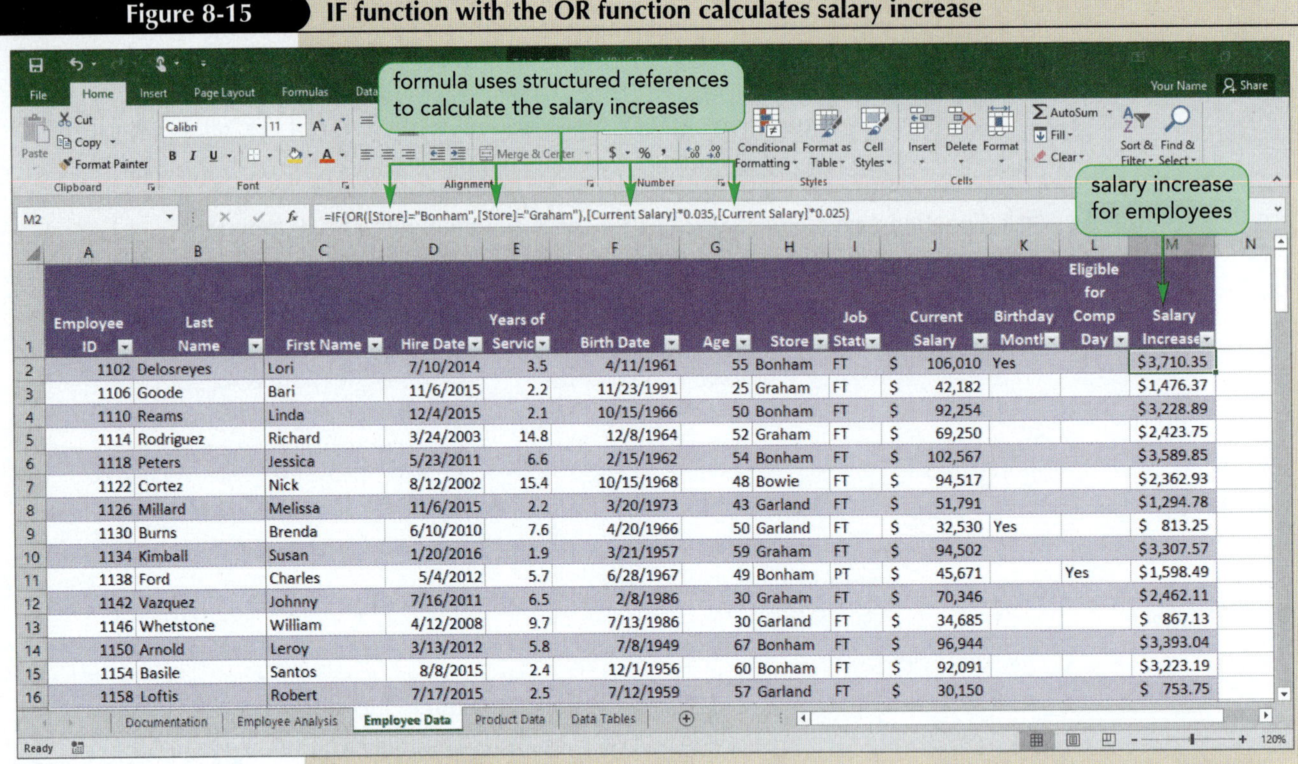

	Employee ID	Last Name	First Name	Hire Date	Years of Servic	Birth Date	Age	Store	Job Statu	Current Salary	Birthday Month	Eligible for Comp Day	Salary Increase
2	1102	Delosreyes	Lori	7/10/2014	3.5	4/11/1961	55	Bonham	FT	$ 106,010	Yes		$3,710.35
3	1106	Goode	Bari	11/6/2015	2.2	11/23/1991	25	Graham	FT	$ 42,182			$1,476.37
4	1110	Reams	Linda	12/4/2015	2.1	10/15/1966	50	Bonham	FT	$ 92,254			$3,228.89
5	1114	Rodriguez	Richard	3/24/2003	14.8	12/8/1964	52	Graham	FT	$ 69,250			$2,423.75
6	1118	Peters	Jessica	5/23/2011	6.6	2/15/1962	54	Bonham	FT	$ 102,567			$3,589.85
7	1122	Cortez	Nick	8/12/2002	15.4	10/15/1968	48	Bowie	FT	$ 94,517			$2,362.93
8	1126	Millard	Melissa	11/6/2015	2.2	3/20/1973	43	Garland	FT	$ 51,791			$1,294.78
9	1130	Burns	Brenda	6/10/2010	7.6	4/20/1966	50	Garland	FT	$ 32,530	Yes		$ 813.25
10	1134	Kimball	Susan	1/20/2016	1.9	3/21/1957	59	Graham	FT	$ 94,502			$3,307.57
11	1138	Ford	Charles	5/4/2012	5.7	6/28/1967	49	Bonham	PT	$ 45,671		Yes	$1,598.49
12	1142	Vazquez	Johnny	7/16/2011	6.5	2/8/1986	30	Graham	FT	$ 70,346			$2,462.11
13	1146	Whetstone	William	4/12/2008	9.7	7/13/1986	30	Garland	FT	$ 34,685			$ 867.13
14	1150	Arnold	Leroy	3/13/2012	5.8	7/8/1949	67	Bonham	FT	$ 96,944			$3,393.04
15	1154	Basile	Santos	8/8/2015	2.4	12/1/1956	60	Bonham	FT	$ 92,091			$3,223.19
16	1158	Loftis	Robert	7/17/2015	2.5	7/12/1959	57	Garland	FT	$ 30,150			$ 753.75

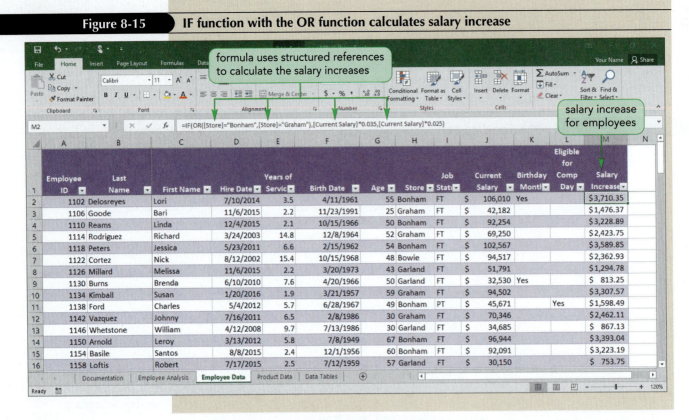

In this session, you used the IF, AND, and OR functions to determine if employees' birth dates occur in a specified month, to determine if part-time employees are eligible for comp days, and to calculate employees' salary increases for next year. Vanessa still needs to calculate the employee bonuses and complete the product data worksheet with the product supplier and specialty store for each product. In the next session, you will create formulas with functions to perform these calculations.

REVIEW

Session 8.1 Quick Check

1. What changes occur in the appearance and size of an Excel table after you enter a new column header named "Phone"?
2. Whenever you enter a formula in an empty column of an Excel table, Excel automatically fills the column with the same formula. What is this called?
3. If an Excel worksheet stores the cost per meal in cell Q5, the number of attendees in cell Q6, and the total cost of meals in cell Q7, what IF function would you enter in cell Q7 to calculate the total cost of meals (cost per meal times the number of attendees) with a minimum cost of $10,000?
4. When does the AND function return a TRUE value?
5. Write the formula that displays the label "Outstanding" in cell Y5 if the amount owed (cell X5) is greater than 0 and the transaction date (cell R5) is after 3/1/2016 (stored in cell R1) but otherwise leaves the cell blank.
6. When you create a formula that references all or parts of an Excel table, what can you use to replace the specific cell or range addresses with the actual table or column header names?
7. If the formula `=IF(OR(B25="NY",B25="CA",B25="TX"),"Select","Ignore")` is entered in cell B26, and `"PA"` is entered in cell B25, what is displayed in cell B26?
8. Write the OR function that represents the following rule—"A potential enlistee in the army is not eligible to enlist if younger than 17 or older than 42." The age is stored in cell B25. Display "Eligible" if the potential enlistee can enlist, and display "Not Eligible" if the potential enlistee cannot enlist.

Session 8.2 Visual Overview:

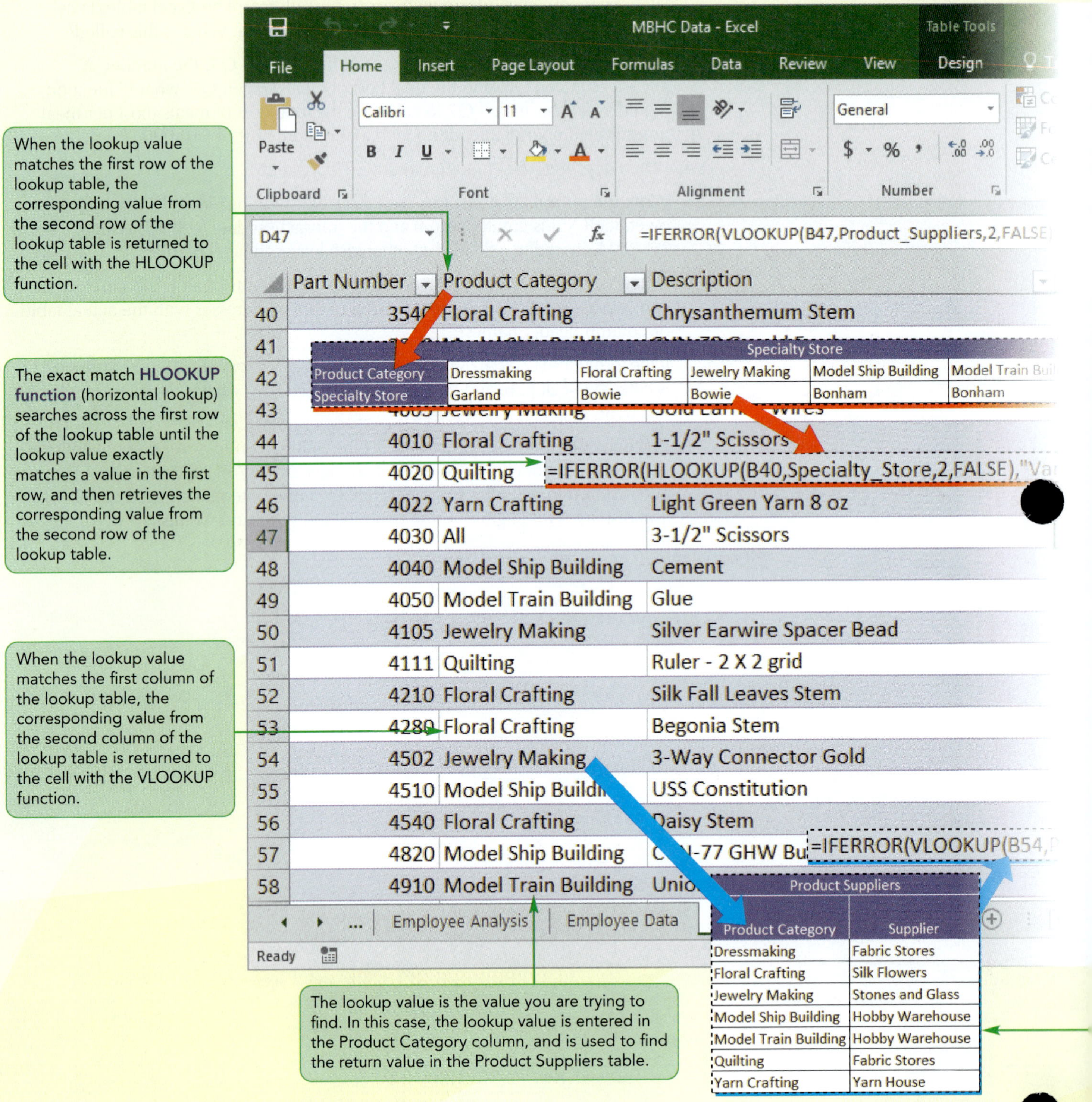

When the lookup value matches the first row of the lookup table, the corresponding value from the second row of the lookup table is returned to the cell with the HLOOKUP function.

The exact match **HLOOKUP function** (horizontal lookup) searches across the first row of the lookup table until the lookup value exactly matches a value in the first row, and then retrieves the corresponding value from the second row of the lookup table.

When the lookup value matches the first column of the lookup table, the corresponding value from the second column of the lookup table is returned to the cell with the VLOOKUP function.

The lookup value is the value you are trying to find. In this case, the lookup value is entered in the Product Category column, and is used to find the return value in the Product Suppliers table.

MBHC Data - Excel

D47 =IFERROR(VLOOKUP(B47,Product_Suppliers,2,FALSE)

	Part Number	Product Category	Description
40	3540	Floral Crafting	Chrysanthemum Stem
44	4010	Floral Crafting	1-1/2" Scissors
45	4020	Quilting	=IFERROR(HLOOKUP(B40,Specialty_Store,2,FALSE),"Va
46	4022	Yarn Crafting	Light Green Yarn 8 oz
47	4030	All	3-1/2" Scissors
48	4040	Model Ship Building	Cement
49	4050	Model Train Building	Glue
50	4105	Jewelry Making	Silver Earwire Spacer Bead
51	4111	Quilting	Ruler - 2 X 2 grid
52	4210	Floral Crafting	Silk Fall Leaves Stem
53	4280	Floral Crafting	Begonia Stem
54	4502	Jewelry Making	3-Way Connector Gold
55	4510	Model Ship Buildi	USS Constitution
56	4540	Floral Crafting	Daisy Stem
57	4820	Model Ship Building	=IFERROR(VLOOKUP(B54,
58	4910	Model Train Building	Unio

Specialty Store

Product Category	Dressmaking	Floral Crafting	Jewelry Making	Model Ship Building	Model Train Bui
Specialty Store	Garland	Bowie	Bowie	Bonham	Bonham

Employee Analysis | Employee Data

Product Suppliers

Product Category	Supplier
Dressmaking	Fabric Stores
Floral Crafting	Silk Flowers
Jewelry Making	Stones and Glass
Model Ship Building	Hobby Warehouse
Model Train Building	Hobby Warehouse
Quilting	Fabric Stores
Yarn Crafting	Yarn House

Lookup Tables and the IFERROR Function

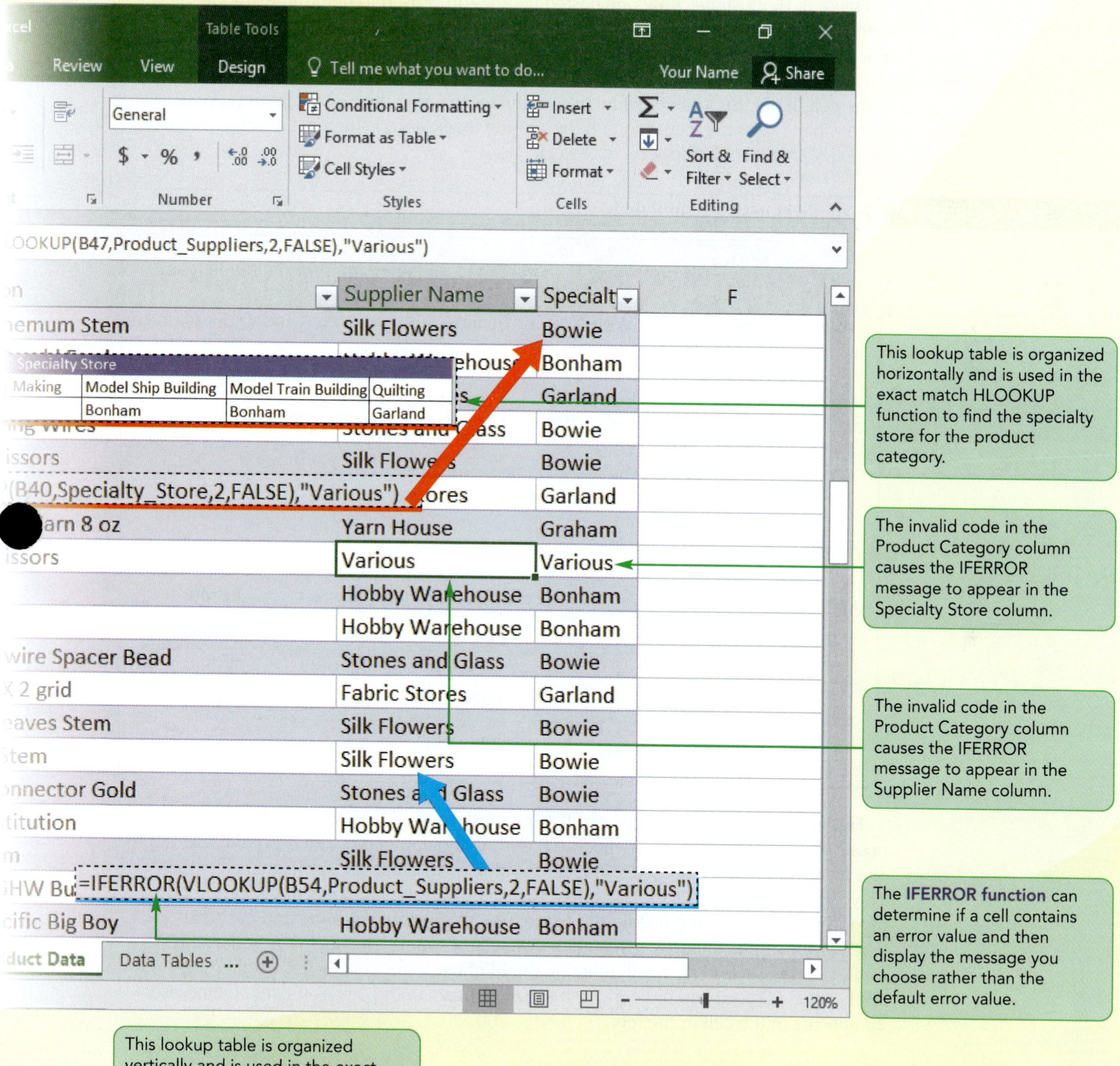
Table Tools
Review
View
Design
Tell me what you want to do...
Your Name
Share
General
Conditional Formatting
Format as Table
Cell Styles
Insert
Delete
Format
Sort & Filter
Find & Select
Number
Styles
Cells
Editing
OOKUP(B47,Product_Suppliers,2,FALSE),"Various")
Supplier Name
Specialt
F
Specialty Store
Making
Model Ship Building
Model Train Building
Quilting
Bonham
Bonham
Garland
(B40,Specialty_Store,2,FALSE),"Various")
=IFERROR(VLOOKUP(B54,Product_Suppliers,2,FALSE),"Various")
Data Tables
120%
This lookup table is organized horizontally and is used in the exact match HLOOKUP function to find the specialty store for the product category.
The invalid code in the Product Category column causes the IFERROR message to appear in the Specialty Store column.
The invalid code in the Product Category column causes the IFERROR message to appear in the Supplier Name column.
The IFERROR function can determine if a cell contains an error value and then display the message you choose rather than the default error value.
This lookup table is organized vertically and is used in the exact match VLOOKUP function to find the supplier for the product category.

Creating Nested IFs

The IF function can choose between only two outcomes. When you want the function to choose from three or more outcomes, you can nest IF functions. A **nested IF function** is when one IF function is placed inside another IF function to test an additional condition. You can nest more than one IF function to test for multiple outcomes.

Figure 8-16 illustrates how one nested IF function is used to determine among three outcomes—whether the home football team won, lost, or tied a game. The first IF function evaluates whether the home team score (stored in cell B1) is greater than the visiting team score (stored in cell B2). If the home team score is higher, Won appears in the cell. If not, the nested IF function evaluates whether the visiting team score is greater than the home team score. If the visiting team score is higher, Lost appears in the cell. Otherwise, Tie appears in the cell.

Figure 8-16 **Example of nested IF functions**

Purpose: To determine the outcome of football games for the home team

Logic Scenario: Display Won, Lost, or Tie based on home team and visitor team scores

Formula: Nested IF functions
`=IF(B1>B2,"Won",IF(B2>B1,"Lost","Tie"))`

Data: cell B1 stores the home team score
cell B2 stores the visitor team score

Example:

Data		Condition1	Condition2	Results
Cell B1	**Cell B2**	**B1>B2**	**B2>B1**	**(Outcome)**
21	18	True	Not evaluated	Won
17	24	False	True	Lost
9	9	False	False	Tie

Figure 8-17 illustrates how nested IF functions are used to determine among four possible outcomes for a driver's license based on the applicant's age (stored in cell B1). The first IF function (highlighted in green) evaluates whether the applicant is less than 16 years old. If the applicant is younger than 16, Too Young appears in the cell. If not, the formula moves to the first nested IF function (highlighted in blue) and evaluates whether the applicant is 45 years old or younger. If so, 30 appears in the cell as the fee. If not, the second nested IF function (highlighted in red) evaluates whether the applicant is 60 years old or younger. If so, 25 appears in the cell as the fee. Otherwise, 20 appears in the cell as the fee.

Figure 8-17 Additional example of nested IF functions

Purpose: To determine the fee for a driver's license

Logic Scenario: Driver's license fee varies by age

Below 16 "Too Young"
16–45 $30
46–60 $25
61 and older $20

Formula: Nested IF functions

```
=IF(B1<16,"Too Young",IF(B1<=45,30,IF(B1<=60,25,20)))
```

Data: cell B1 stores the driver's age

Example:

Data	Condition1	Condition2	Condition3	Results
Cell B1	**B1<16**	**B1<=45**	**B1<=60**	**(Fee)**
15	True	Not evaluated	Not evaluated	Too Young
25	False	True	Not evaluated	30
55	False	False	True	25
65	False	False	False	20

You need to use nested IF functions to determine MBHC employee bonus amounts. MBHC pays employee bonuses based on each employee's years of service. MBHC has three bonus amounts. Employees who have been at the company for 10 or more years will receive a bonus of $500. Employees who have been at the company for 5 years to less than 10 years will receive $250. Employees who have been at the company less than 5 years will receive $100. In this case, you need to nest IF functions to calculate the different series of outcomes for the employee bonuses.

Vanessa created the flowchart shown in Figure 8-18 to illustrate the logic for determining bonus awards. She used different colors to identify each IF function. The flowchart shows that if an employee's years of service is >=10, the bonus amount equals $500 and the IF function (shown in green) is finished. If the employee's years of service is >=5, then the second IF function (shown in blue) is evaluated. If the employee's years of service is >=5, then the bonus amount equals $250 and the IF function is finished. All other employees (years of service is less than 5 years) will receive a bonus of $100.

Figure 8-18 **Flowchart of nested IF functions to determine the bonus amount**

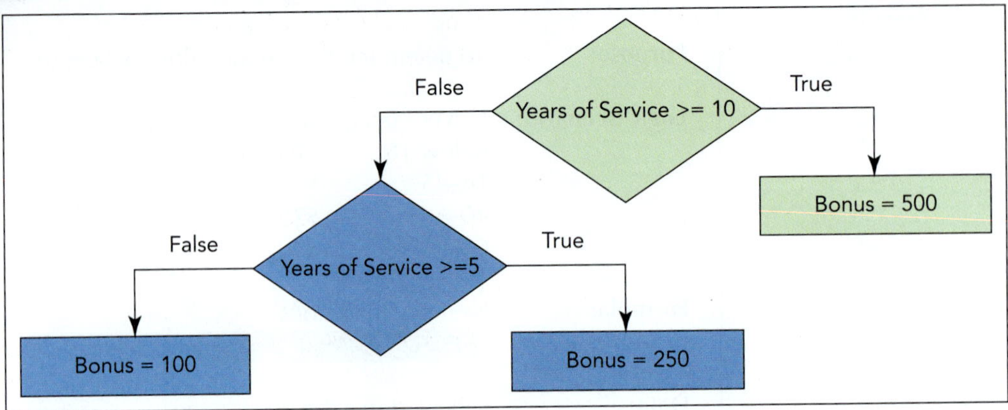

The following formula converts Vanessa's flowchart into a formula with nested IF functions:

```
=IF([Years of Service]>=10,500,IF([Years of Service]>=5,250,100))
```

The first IF function (shown in green) tests whether the value in the Years of Service is greater than or equal to 10. If this condition ([Years of Service]>=10) is true, the formula returns 500 in the Bonus cell. If this condition is false (the Years of Service is < 10), the second IF function (shown in blue) is evaluated. The second IF function tests whether the value in the Years of Service cell is greater than or equal to 5. If this condition ([Years of Service]>=5) is true, the formula returns 250 in the Bonus cell. If this condition is false (the value in the Years of Service cell is less than 5), the formula returns 100 in the Bonus cell.

Problem Solving: Finding and Fixing Errors in Formulas

If formulas in a worksheet are returning errors or not working as expected, you need to find and fix the problems. Two common categories of formula errors in Excel are syntax errors and logic errors. A syntax error is an error in a statement that violates the rules of Excel. A syntax error might occur due to unmatched parentheses or a required argument that is omitted in a function. Logic errors occur in formulas that work but return an incorrect result. Logic errors are often detected by the user because the results seem out of line. A logic error could occur because the formula uses the wrong calculation, the formula references the wrong cell, or the formula uses faulty reasoning, leading to incorrect results.

Some problem-solving approaches can help resolve these types of errors. First, examine the formulas in worksheet cells instead of the results by pressing the Ctrl+~ keys to display the formulas in each cell. Or, you can use the Formula Auditing tools on the Formulas tab to visually identify and trace cells used in a formula. This can help you locate and fix inaccurate cell references and faulty logic.

By carefully evaluating formulas and fixing any problems, you help to ensure that a worksheet is error-free and returns accurate results.

Vanessa wants the EmployeeTbl table to include a column that contains a formula to calculate the bonus amount. Vanessa stored the three bonus amounts (0, 250, and 500) in the Data Tables worksheet cells B17, B18, and B19. You will reference these cells in the formula to calculate the employee bonus. This approach enables you to quickly update the calculated bonus amounts in the Data Tables worksheet without having to edit the bonus formula.

To enter nested IFs to calculate employee bonuses:

1. If you took a break at the end of the previous session, make sure the MBHC Data workbook is open and the Employee Data worksheet is active.
2. In cell **N1**, enter **Bonus Amount** as the column header. The Excel table expands to include the new column, and cell N2 is the active cell.
3. Make sure cell **N2** is the active cell, and then click the **Insert Function** button fx next to the formula bar. The Insert Function dialog box opens.
4. Click **IF** in the Select a function box, and then click the **OK** button. The Function Arguments dialog box opens.
5. In the Logical_test box, type **[Years of Service]>=10** and then press the **Tab** key to enter the logical test using a structured reference. This logical test evaluates whether the employee's years of service is greater than or equal to 10. The FALSE values to the right of the Logical_test box indicate that the years of service for the first few employees is not greater than or equal to 10.

   Trouble? If the value to the right of the Logical_test box is Invalid, you probably mistyped the logical test. Select the text in the Logical_test box, and then repeat Step 5, typing the logical test exactly as shown, being sure to use square brackets around the structured reference.

TIP

If you type a formula directly in a cell, the available structured references appear after you type the opening bracket. Double-click the structured reference to add it to the formula, and then type the closing bracket.

6. In the Value_if_true box, type **'Data Tables'!$B$19** and then press the **Tab** key. The value to the right of the Value_if_true argument box is 500, which is the value in cell B19 of the Data Tables worksheet. This argument specifies that if the logical test is true (the years of service is greater than or equal to 10), display the value stored in cell B19 of the Data Tables worksheet (500 bonus amount). The absolute reference ensures that the formula in each row will refer to cell B19 of the Data Tables worksheet, which contains the bonus amount. Note that values that change, such as the Bonus Amount, are stored in a separate worksheet.
7. In the Value_if_false box, type **IF([Years of Service]>=5,'Data Tables'!$B$18,'Data Tables'!$B$17)** and then press the **Tab** key. This argument is a nested IF function that specifies if the logical condition is true (years of service are greater than or equal to 5), display the value stored in cell B18 of the Data Tables worksheet (250 bonus amount); otherwise, display the value stored in cell B17 of the Data Tables worksheet (100 bonus amount). Again, you used absolute references to ensure that the formula will always refer to cell B18 and cell B17 of the Data Tables worksheet. The values to the right of the Value_if_false box indicate the bonus amounts for the employees in the first few rows. See Figure 8-19.

Figure 8-19 Function Arguments dialog box with a nested IF

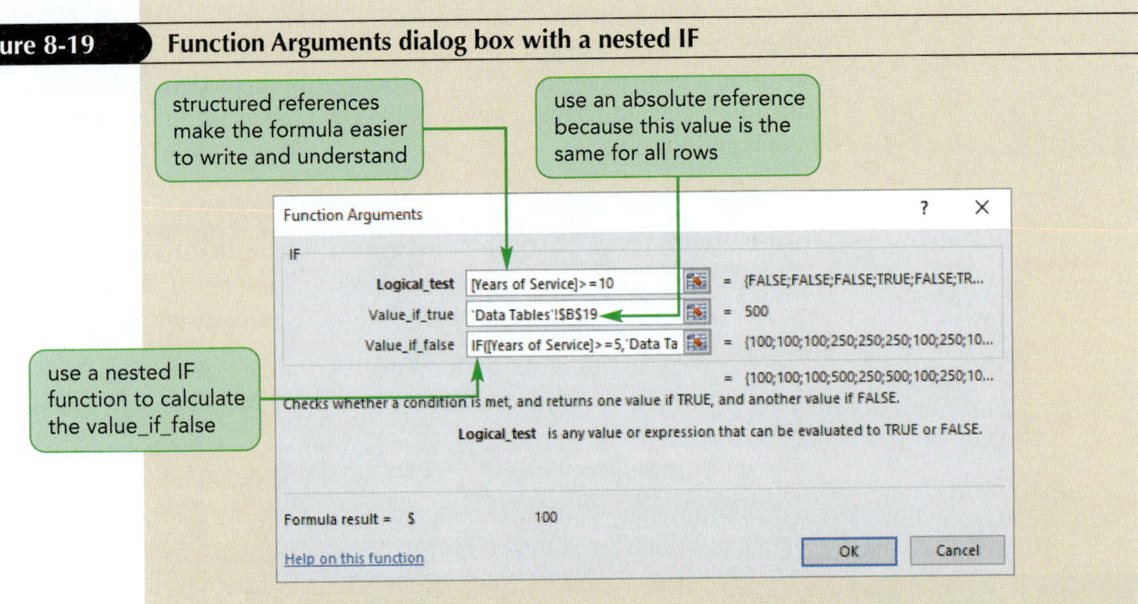
structured references make the formula easier to write and understand
use an absolute reference because this value is the same for all rows
use a nested IF function to calculate the value_if_false
Function Arguments
IF
Logical_test [Years of Service]>=10 = {FALSE;FALSE;FALSE;TRUE;FALSE;TR...
Value_if_true 'Data Tables'!$B$19 = 500
Value_if_false IF([Years of Service]>=5,'Data Ta = {100;100;100;250;250;250;100;250;10...
= {100;100;100;500;250;500;100;250;10...
Checks whether a condition is met, and returns one value if TRUE, and another value if FALSE.
Logical_test is any value or expression that can be evaluated to TRUE or FALSE.
Formula result = $ 100
Help on this function
OK
Cancel

8. Click the **OK** button. The formula =IF([Years of Service]>=10,'Data Tables'!$B$19,IF([Years of Service]>=5,'Data Tables'!$B$18,'Data Tables!$B$17)) appears in the formula bar, and the value 100 appears in cell N2 because this employee has 3.5 years of service. The bonus formula is automatically copied to all other rows in the Bonus Amount column. The references to cells B19, B18, and B17 of the Data Tables worksheet are absolute references and do not change from cell to cell in the Bonus Amount column.
9. Select the Bonus values, and then format the selected range using the **Accounting** format with no decimal places.
10. Select cell **N2** to deselect the column. See Figure 8-20.

Figure 8-20 Nested IF function calculating the employee bonus amounts

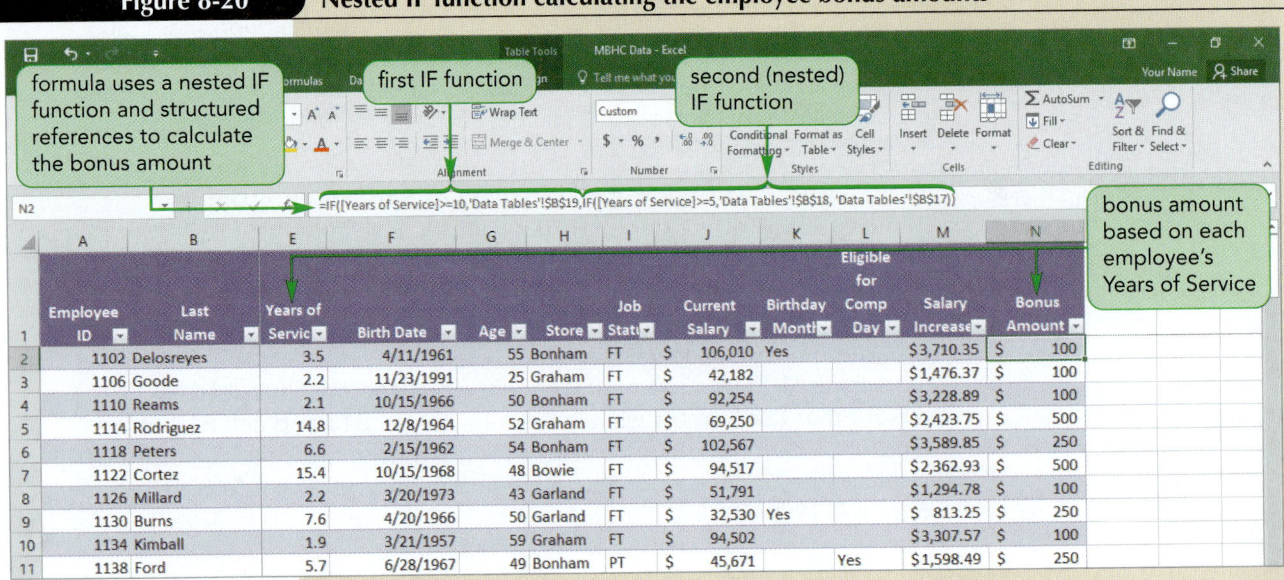
formula uses a nested IF function and structured references to calculate the bonus amount
first IF function
second (nested) IF function
bonus amount based on each employee's Years of Service
=IF([Years of Service]>=10,'Data Tables'!$B$19,IF([Years of Service]>=5,'Data Tables'!$B$18, 'Data Tables'!$B$17))

Employee ID	Last Name	Years of Service	Birth Date	Age	Store	Job Status	Current Salary	Birthday Month	Eligible for Comp Day	Salary Increase	Bonus Amount
1102	Delosreyes	3.5	4/11/1961	55	Bonham	FT	$ 106,010	Yes		$3,710.35	$ 100
1106	Goode	2.2	11/23/1991	25	Graham	FT	$ 42,182			$1,476.37	$ 100
1110	Reams	2.1	10/15/1966	50	Bonham	FT	$ 92,254			$3,228.89	$ 100
1114	Rodriguez	14.8	12/8/1964	52	Graham	FT	$ 69,250			$2,423.75	$ 500
1118	Peters	6.6	2/15/1962	54	Bonham	FT	$ 102,567			$3,589.85	$ 250
1122	Cortez	15.4	10/15/1968	48	Bowie	FT	$ 94,517			$2,362.93	$ 500
1126	Millard	2.2	3/20/1973	43	Garland	FT	$ 51,791			$1,294.78	$ 100
1130	Burns	7.6	4/20/1966	50	Garland	FT	$ 32,530	Yes		$ 813.25	$ 250
1134	Kimball	1.9	3/21/1957	59	Graham	FT	$ 94,502			$3,307.57	$ 100
1138	Ford	5.7	6/28/1967	49	Bonham	PT	$ 45,671		Yes	$1,598.49	$ 250

The Bonus Amount column shows the bonuses for each employee.

INSIGHT

Checking Formulas for Matching Parentheses

A common problem when creating formulas is mismatched parentheses. As you write a formula, you should verify that you enclosed the correct argument, function, or term within the parentheses of the formula you are creating. This is especially important when you develop a complex formula that includes many parentheses, such as a nested IF function. Excel color-codes the parentheses as you build a formula so you can quickly determine whether the formula includes complete pairs of them. You can also verify that the formula includes matching pairs of parentheses by selecting the cell with the formula and then clicking in the formula bar. Press the right arrow key to move the insertion point through the formula one character at a time. When the insertion point moves across one parenthesis, its matching parenthesis is also highlighted briefly. This color-coding helps you ensure that all parentheses in a formula are paired (opening and closing parentheses).

By using cell references to input values rather than including constants in formulas, you make a worksheet more flexible and easier to update. The executive team has increased the bonus for employees with 10 or more years of service from $500 to $750. Vanessa asks you to update this bonus amount so the employee bonuses will be current.

To update the bonus amount for years of service >=10:

1. Go to the **Data Tables** worksheet.
2. In cell **B19**, enter **750**. The new bonus amount is entered in the data table.
3. Go to the **Employee Data** worksheet.
4. In the Bonus Amount column, observe that the bonus amount for all employees who have 10 or more years of service is now $750.

Using LOOKUP Functions

Recall that lookup functions allow you to find values in a table of data and insert them in another worksheet location. For example, you might enter a product table in a worksheet that includes the product ID, product name, and price of all products a company sells. You could then use this product table to build an invoice in another worksheet by entering a product ID and having Excel look up the product name and price, and insert these values in the invoice. The table that stores the data you want to retrieve is called a lookup table.

Both the VLOOKUP and HLOOKUP functions are used to return a value from a lookup table. The VLOOKUP function always searches for a value in the first column of the lookup table. The HLOOKUP function always searches for a value in the first row of the lookup table. Both these functions can retrieve a value from lookup tables designed for *exact match* or *approximate match* lookups. Recall that an exact match lookup occurs when the lookup value must match one of the values in the first column (or row) of the lookup table. An approximate match lookup occurs when the lookup value is found within a range of numbers in the first column (or row) of the lookup table. Which function you use depends on how the data is arranged in the lookup table. If the first column of the lookup table is searched, then use VLOOKUP; if the first row of the lookup table is searched, then use HLOOKUP.

At MBHC, all products have a supplier based on the product category. The supplier for dressmaking and quilting is Fabric Stores, the supplier for floral crafting is Silk Flowers, the supplier for jewelry making is Stones and Glass, the supplier for model ship and train building is Hobby Warehouse, and the supplier for yarn crafting is Yarn House. If a product can be supplied by many sources and is located in all stores it will have a product category of All. You could determine the supplier for a product by using several nested IF functions. However, a simpler approach is to use a lookup function.

You can use the Product Suppliers data shown in Figure 8-21 as an exact match lookup table. The lookup table includes the product categories and their corresponding suppliers. To retrieve the product supplier, Excel moves down the first column in the Product Suppliers lookup table until it finds the category that matches the product category of the product. Then it moves to the second column in the lookup table to locate the supplier, which is then displayed in the cell where the lookup formula is entered or used as part of a calculation. If the product category code doesn't match one of the values in the first column of the Product Suppliers table (spelling or spaces are different), the #N/A error value is displayed. For example, to find the return value for the Floral Crafting lookup value, Excel searches the first column of the lookup table until the Floral Crafting entry is found. Then, Excel moves to the second column of the lookup table to locate the corresponding return value, which is Silk Flowers, in this case.

Figure 8-21 Product Suppliers lookup table used for an exact match lookup

Lookup Value = Floral Crafting

search down the first column until the lookup value exactly matches the value in the first column

Product Suppliers	
Product Category	Supplier
Dressmaking	Fabric Stores
Floral Crafting	Silk Flowers
Jewelry Making	Stones and Glass
Model Ship Building	Hobby Warehouse
Model Train Building	Hobby Warehouse
Quilting	Fabric Stores
Yarn Crafting	Yarn House

return the corresponding value from the second column of the lookup table

Return Value = Silk Flowers

Lookup tables can also be constructed as approximate match lookups. A discount based on the quantity of items purchased where each discount covers a range of units purchased is an example of an approximate match lookup. Figure 8-22 shows the approximate match lookup table for these quantity discounts. In this example, purchases of fewer than 25 units receive no discount, purchases of between 25 and 99 units receive a 2 percent discount, purchases of between 100 and 499 units receive a 3 percent discount, and purchases of 500 or more units receive a 4 percent discount. For example, to find the quantity discount for a purchase of 55 units, Excel searches the first column of the lookup table until it finds the largest value that is less than or equal to 55 (the lookup value), which is 25 in this example. Then, Excel moves to the second column of the lookup table and returns 2 percent as the quantity discount.

Figure 8-22 Approximate match lookup table

Lookup Value = 55
search down the first column until the largest value less than or equal to the lookup value is found
return the corresponding value from the second column of the lookup table
Return Value = 2%

Quantity	Discount Rate
0	0%
25	2%
100	3%
500	4%

Using the VLOOKUP Function to Find an Exact Match

To retrieve the correct value from the lookup table, you use the VLOOKUP function. Recall that the VLOOKUP function searches vertically down the first column of the lookup table for the value you entered and then retrieves the corresponding value from another column of the table. The VLOOKUP function has the syntax

```
VLOOKUP(lookup_value,table_array,col_index_num[,range_lookup])
```

where `lookup_value` is the value, cell reference, defined name, or structured reference you want to search for in the first column of the lookup table; `table_array` is a range reference, a defined name, or the name of an Excel table that is the lookup table; `col_index_num` is the number of the column in the lookup table that contains the value you want to return; and `range_lookup` indicates whether the lookup table is an exact match (FALSE) or an approximate match (TRUE). The `range_lookup` argument is optional; if you don't include a `range_lookup` value, the value is considered TRUE (an approximate match).

You'll use the VLOOKUP function to identify the product supplier because you can search the values in the first column of the lookup table. You can use the range reference (the range A8:B14 on the Data Tables worksheet) or the defined name Product_Suppliers when you reference the lookup table in the VLOOKUP formula to determine the product supplier for a product on the Product Data worksheet:

Range reference `=VLOOKUP(B2,'Data Tables'!$A$8:$B$14,2,FALSE)`

Defined name `=VLOOKUP(B2,Product_Suppliers,2,FALSE)`

Both of these formulas use the VLOOKUP function to search for the product's supplier using the product category, column B in the Product Data worksheet, and the Product Suppliers lookup table in the Data Tables worksheet. The lookup uses the value in column B of the Product Data worksheet to find the matching product category in first column of the Product Suppliers lookup table (the range A8:B14 in the Data Tables worksheet) and then return the corresponding value from the second column of the lookup table, which shows the supplier. The formulas use FALSE as the *range_lookup* argument because you want the lookup value to exactly match a value in the first column of the lookup table.

Vanessa wants you to enter the VLOOKUP function using the defined name to reference the lookup table in the VLOOKUP function so she can easily determine what's included in the function. This is also simpler than entering range references, and you don't need to change the reference to an absolute reference.

To find an exact match in the Product Suppliers table using the VLOOKUP function:

1. Go to the **Product Data** worksheet.
2. In cell **D1**, enter **Supplier Name**. The table expands to include the new column.

3. Make sure cell **D2** is the active cell, and then click the **Insert Function** button f_x next to the formula bar. The Insert Function dialog box opens.
4. Click the **Or select a category** arrow, click **Lookup & Reference**, and then double-click **VLOOKUP** in the Select a function box. The Function Arguments dialog box opens.
5. Drag the Function Arguments dialog box below row 2, if necessary, so you can see the column headers.
6. In the Lookup_value box, type **B2** and then press the **Tab** key. The lookup value is the product category, which is located in column B.
7. In the Table_array box, type **Product_Suppliers** and then press the **Tab** key. Product_Suppliers is the defined name assigned to the range A8:B14 in the Data Tables worksheet. If the Product Suppliers data was entered as a range rather than a defined name, the table_array argument would be entered as 'Data Tables'!A8:B14, and you would need to change the range to absolute references ('Data Tables'!$A$8:$B$14) so the formula would copy correctly to other cells.

For the col_index_num value, be sure to enter the number of the column's position in the table, not its column letter, to avoid receiving #NAME? or #VALUE! as the result.

8. In the Col_index_num box, type **2** and then press the **Tab** key. The number 2 indicates the product supplier is stored in the second column of the Product_Suppliers lookup table.
9. In the Range_lookup box, type **FALSE**. This sets the function to find an exact match in the lookup table. See Figure 8-23.

Figure 8-23 Function Arguments dialog box for VLOOKUP function

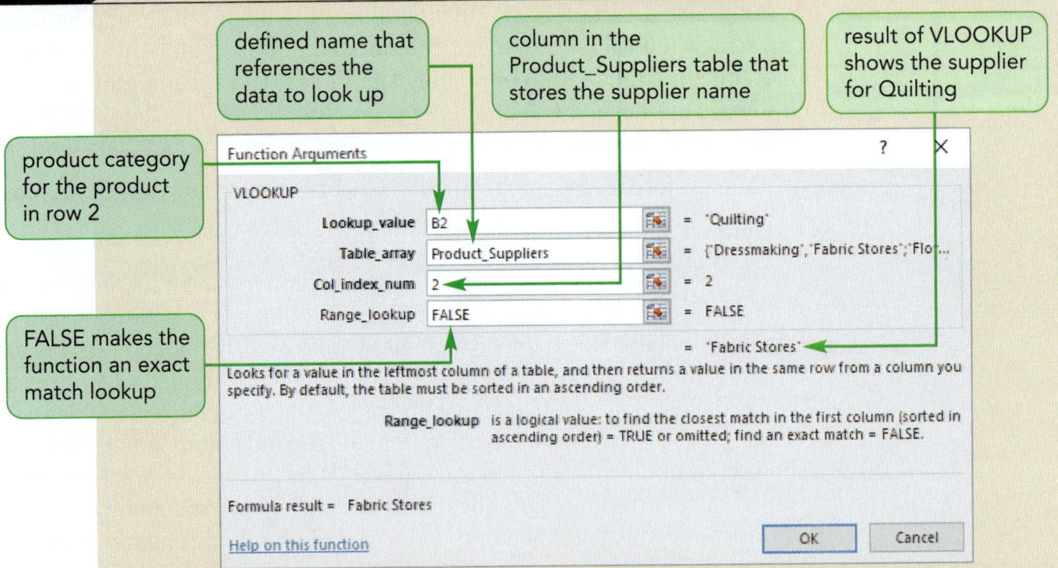

10. Click the **OK** button. The dialog box closes, Fabric Stores appears in cell D2, and the formula =VLOOKUP(B2,Product_Suppliers,2,FALSE) appears in the formula bar. The remaining rows in the Supplier Name column are filled with the VLOOKUP function. If the value in column D does not match a value in the first column of the Product_Suppliers table, an exact match does not exist, and the function returns #N/A in the cell.
11. AutoFit the contents of column D so you can see the full Supplier Name.
12. Select cell **D2** to deselect the column. See Figure 8-24.

Figure 8-24 **Exact match VLOOKUP function to locate the supplier for a product group**

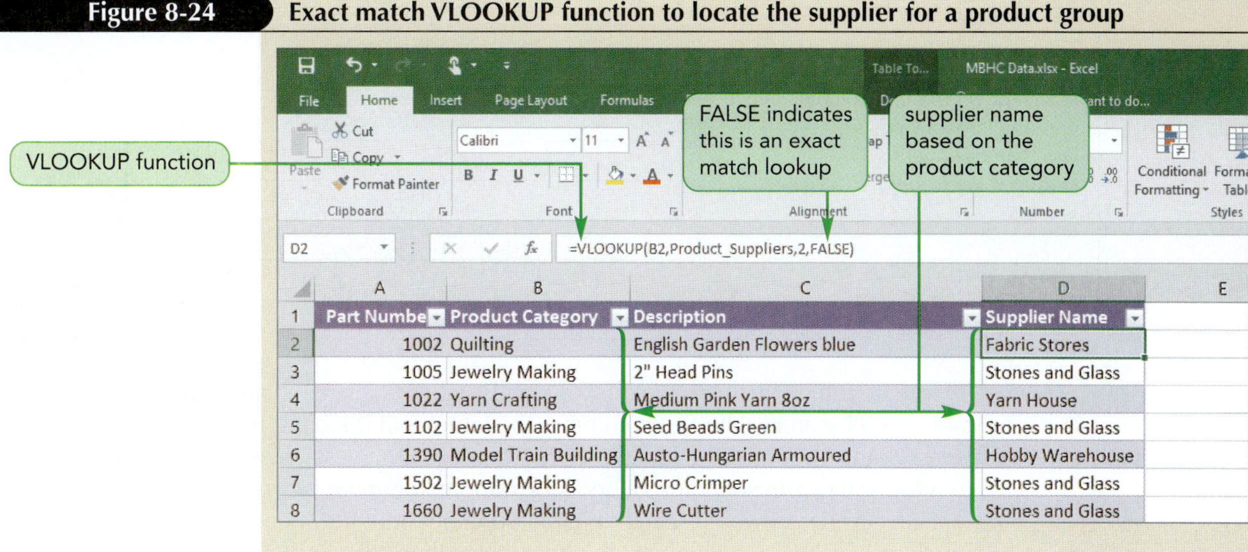

Using the VLOOKUP Function to Find an Approximate Match

You can also use a VLOOKUP function to return a value from a lookup table that is based on an approximate match lookup. The previous lookup used the Product_Suppliers table to return a value only if Excel found an exact match in the first column of the lookup table. The values in the first column or row of a lookup table can also represent a range of values. Quantity discounts, shipping charges, and income tax rates are a few examples of approximate match lookups.

MBHC's management wants all employee name badges to identify employees' years of service by color. Vanessa developed the criteria shown in Figure 8-25 to summarize the colors planned for the name badges.

Figure 8-25 **Criteria for the Name Badge Color lookup table**

Years of Service	Name Badge Color
>=0 and <1	Green
>=1 and <4	Blue
>=4 and <7	Purple
>=7 and <10	Silver
>=10	Gold

In the Name Badge table, you are not looking for an exact match for the lookup value. Instead, you need to use an approximate match lookup to determine which range of values the lookup value falls within. You want to use the lookup table to determine an employee's years of service range and then return the badge color based on the appropriate row. To accomplish this, you must rearrange the first column of the lookup table so that each row in the table represents the *low end* of the years of service range, as shown in Figure 8-26.

Figure 8-26 **Name Badge lookup table for an approximate match lookup**

Lookup Value = 3.5
search down the first column until the largest value less than or equal to the lookup value is found
return the corresponding value from the second column of the lookup table
Return Value = Blue

Name Badge	
Years of Service	Name Badge Color
0	Green
1	Blue
4	Purple
7	Silver
10	Gold

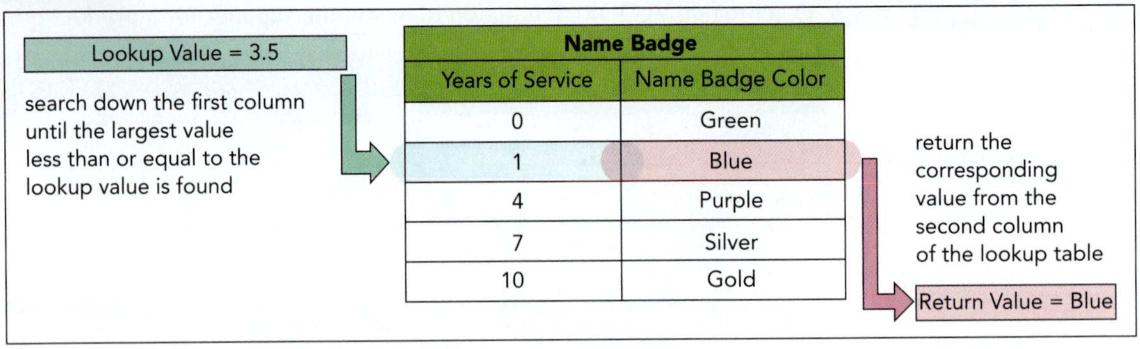

To determine whether a lookup value falls within a range of values in the lookup table, Excel searches the first column of the table until it locates the largest value that is less than or equal to the lookup value. Then Excel moves across the row in the table to retrieve the corresponding value. For example, for an employee working at MBHC for six years, Excel would search the lookup table until the value in the first column is 4 (the largest value in the lookup table that is less than or equal to the lookup value) and retrieve Purple from the second column of that row.

When a lookup table is used with a range of values (approximate match), the values in the first column must be sorted in low-to-high order. When the first column's values are arranged in a different order, Excel may not retrieve the correct value, leading to incorrect results. The setup of the lookup table in an approximate match is critical for a VLOOKUP formula to work properly.

INSIGHT

Setting Up an Approximate Match Lookup Table

Approximate lookup tables are commonly used to find a taxpayer's tax rate in a tax table, find a shipping charge based on the weight of a package in a shipping charges table, or determine a student's letter grade from a table of grading criteria. Setting up the lookup tables for an approximate match lookup can be tricky. Consider the following example, in which an instructor uses Excel to calculate grades. The instructor assigns final grades based on the following grading policy table:

Score	**Grade**
90–100	A
80–89	B
70–79	C
60–69	D
0–59	F

To set up the lookup table so it works in Excel, the leftmost column in the lookup table must (1) represent the lower end of the range for each category, and (2) be sorted in ascending order based on the value in the first column. Otherwise, Excel cannot retrieve the correct result. Following this structure, the lookup table for the instructor's grading policy would be arranged as follows:

Score	**Grade**
0	F
60	D
70	C
80	B
90	A

In the EmployeeTbl table, you will create the formula

```
=VLOOKUP([Years of Service],Name_Badge,2)
```

to determine the color for each employee's name badge, where `[Years of Service]` is the structured reference for the employee's years of service (the lookup value), `Name_Badge` is the defined name that references the lookup table, and `2` specifies the column in the lookup table in which to find the badge color. The fourth argument is not needed because this is an approximate match lookup. You will use an approximate match VLOOKUP formula because each cell in the Years of Service column in the lookup table represents a range of values.

To insert the approximate match VLOOKUP formula:

1. Go to the **Employee Data** worksheet. You will enter this VLOOKUP function in the EmployeeTbl.
2. In cell **O1**, enter **Name Badge Color** as the column heading. A new column is added to the table, and cell O2 is the active cell.
3. AutoFit the contents of column O so you can view the entire column heading in cell O1.
4. Click the **Insert Function** button next to the formula bar. The Insert Function dialog box opens with the Lookup & Reference category active.
5. In the Select a function box, double-click **VLOOKUP**. The Function Arguments dialog box opens.
6. In the Lookup_value box, type **[Years of Service]** and then press the **Tab** key. The lookup value is entered using the column header (structured reference) for the employee's years of service. The value 3.479452055 appears as the lookup value for the current row.
7. In the Table_array box, type **Name_Badge** and then press the **Tab** key. Name_Badge is the defined name assigned to the range D8:E12 in the Data Tables worksheet. If the Name_Badge data was entered as a range reference, the *table_array* argument would be entered as 'Data Tables'!D8:E12, and you would need to change the range to absolute references ('Data Tables'!$D$8:$E$12) so that the formula would copy correctly to other cells.
8. In the Col_index_num box, type **2**. The number 2 indicates the column where the name badge color is stored—the second column of the Name_Badge table. You do not need to enter the optional fourth argument in the VLOOKUP formula because Excel assumes the value to be TRUE and will use an approximate match table lookup. See Figure 8-27.

Figure 8-27 Function Arguments dialog box for the VLOOKUP function

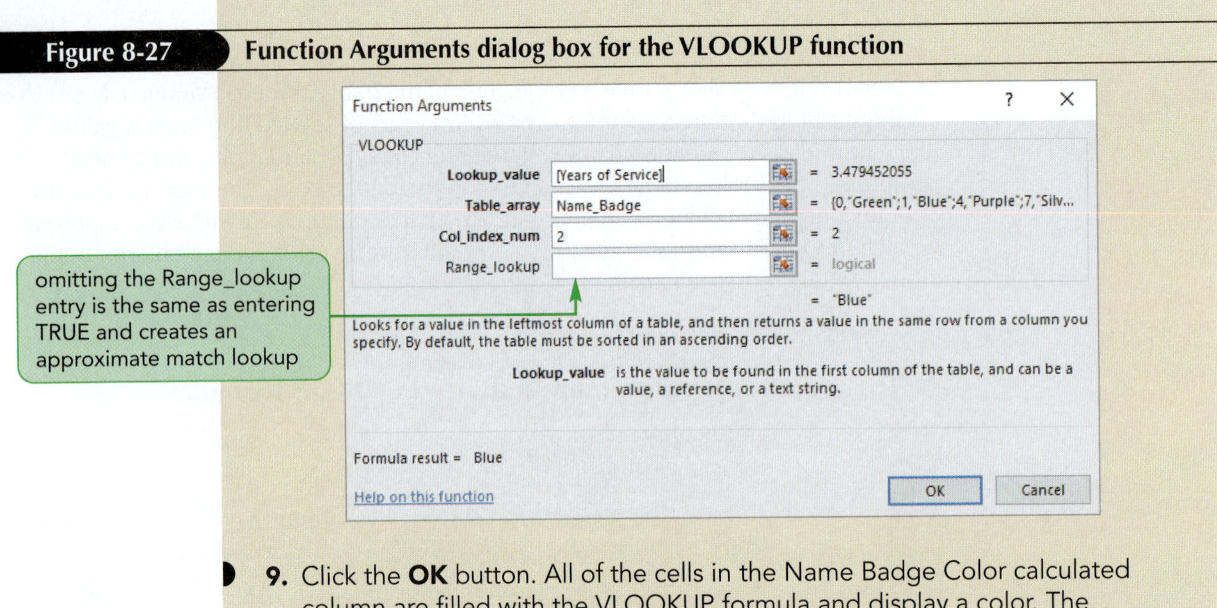
Function Arguments
VLOOKUP
Lookup_value [Years of Service] = 3.479452055
Table_array Name_Badge = {0,"Green";1,"Blue";4,"Purple";7,"Silv...
Col_index_num 2 = 2
Range_lookup = logical
= "Blue"
Looks for a value in the leftmost column of a table, and then returns a value in the same row from a column you specify. By default, the table must be sorted in an ascending order.
Lookup_value is the value to be found in the first column of the table, and can be a value, a reference, or a text string.
Formula result = Blue
Help on this function
OK
Cancel
omitting the Range_lookup entry is the same as entering TRUE and creates an approximate match lookup

9. Click the **OK** button. All of the cells in the Name Badge Color calculated column are filled with the VLOOKUP formula and display a color. The employee in row 2 has 3.5 years of service and will have a Blue badge. This is a good illustration of the approximate match lookup because 3.5 does not equal a value in the first column of the lookup table. Instead, it falls between two values in the table.

10. Select cell **O2** to deselect the column. See Figure 8-28.

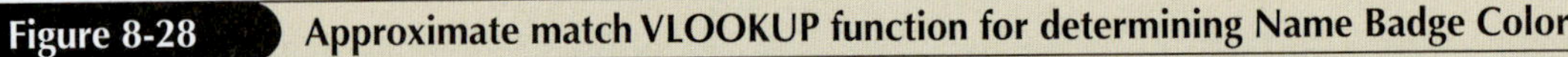

Figure 8-28 Approximate match VLOOKUP function for determining Name Badge Color

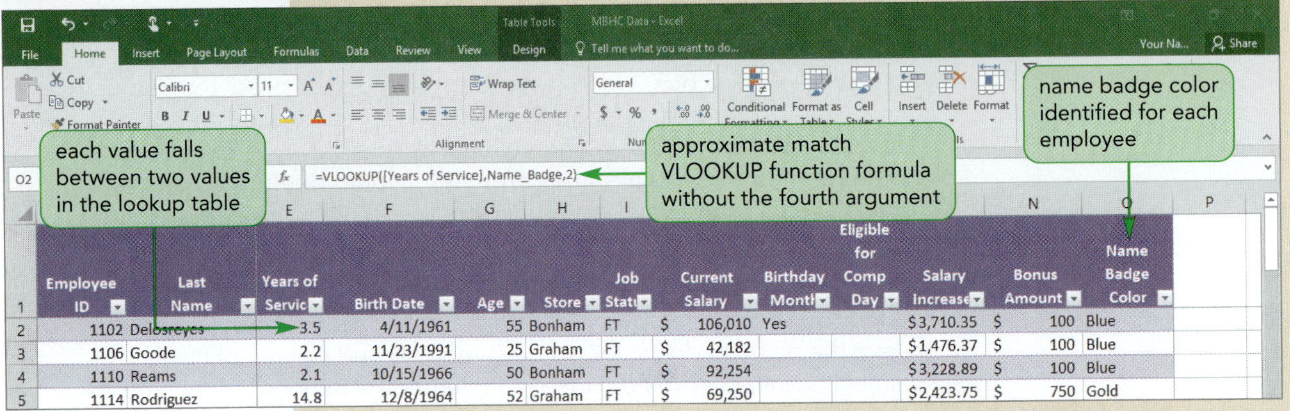
each value falls between two values in the lookup table
approximate match VLOOKUP function formula without the fourth argument
name badge color identified for each employee
=VLOOKUP([Years of Service],Name_Badge,2)

Using the HLOOKUP Function to Find an Exact Match

The HLOOKUP function is very similar to the VLOOKUP function. The HLOOKUP function (horizontal lookup function) searches across the top row of the lookup table until the lookup value is found and then retrieves the value from the same column in the lookup table. The HLOOKUP function has the syntax

```
HLOOKUP(lookup_value,table_array,row_index_num[,range_lookup])
```

where *lookup_value* is the value, cell reference, defined name, or structured reference you want to search for in the first row of the lookup table; *table_array* is the range reference, defined name, or Excel table name of the lookup table; *row_index_num* is the number of the row in the lookup table that contains the value you want to return;

and *range_lookup* indicates whether the lookup table is an exact match (FALSE) or an approximate match (TRUE). The *range_lookup* argument is optional; if you don't include a *range_lookup* value, the value is considered TRUE (an approximate match).

The major difference between the HLOOKUP and VLOOKUP functions is the way the lookup tables are organized. Figure 8-29 shows how the Product Suppliers and Name Badge tables would be arranged for a lookup using the HLOOKUP function.

Figure 8-29 **Lookup tables for the HLOOKUP function**

Product Suppliers							
Product Category	Dress Making	Floral Crafting	Jewelry Making	Model Ship Building	Model Train Building	Quilting	Yarn Crafting
Supplier	Fabric Stores	Silk Flowers	Stones and Glass	Hobby Warehouse	Hobby Warehouse	Fabric Stores	Yarn House

Name Badge					
Years of Service	0	1	4	7	10
Name Badge Color	Green	Blue	Purple	Silver	Gold

With the lookup tables arranged as shown in Figure 8-29, the exact match formula to identify the Supplier on the Product Data worksheet is

```
=HLOOKUP(B2,Product_Suppliers,2,FALSE)
```

and the approximate match formula to calculate the name badge color on the Employee Data worksheet is

```
=HLOOKUP(E2,Name_Badge,2)
```

Vanessa wants you to use the HLOOKUP function to identify the specialty store for each product. Figure 8-30 shows the Specialty Store table in the Data Tables worksheet, which includes the specialty store for each product category. The values in the first row of the horizontal lookup table are compared to the product category that you want to find (lookup value). When the match is found, the corresponding value in one of the rows in the lookup table is returned. For example, to find the return value for product with Jewelry Making as the product category, Excel searches across the first row of the lookup table until it finds the Jewelry Making entry. Then Excel moves down to the second row to locate the corresponding return value, which is Bowie in this case. The table in Figure 8-30 is an exact match lookup because if the product category does not match one of the values in the first row of the lookup table, the #N/A error value is returned.

Figure 8-30 Specialty_Store lookup table for an exact match lookup

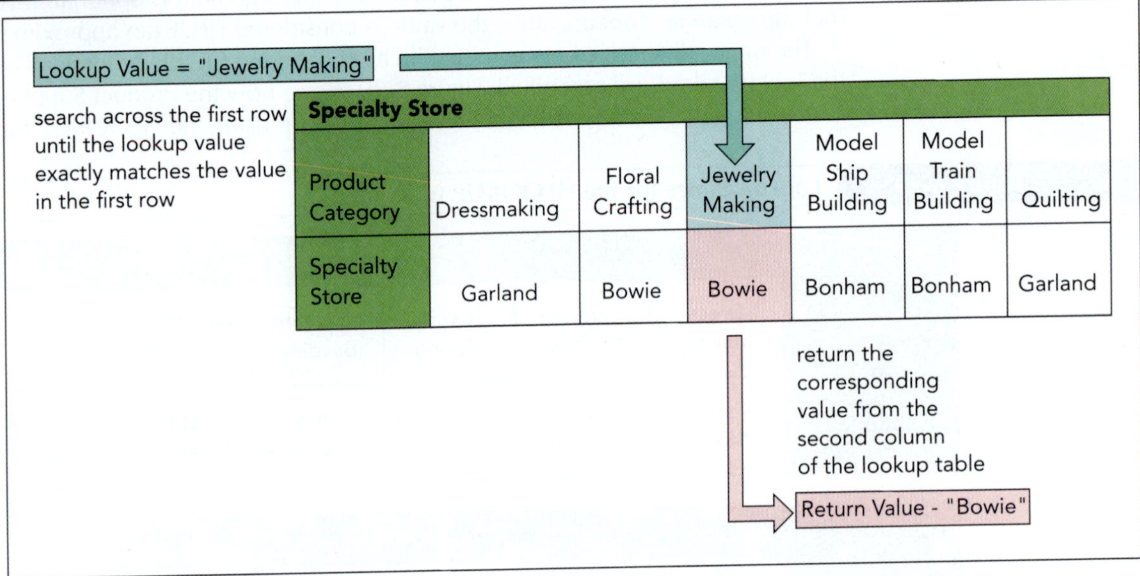

The following formula uses the product category and the Specialty_Store table to determine the specialty store for the product:

```
=HLOOKUP(B2,Specialty_Store,2,FALSE)
```

In this formula, B2 is the cell that stores the product category in the Product Data worksheet, Specialty_Store is the defined name that references the lookup table, 2 specifies the row to find the specialty store, and FALSE indicates that this is an exact match lookup. You will enter this formula to identify the Specialty Store for each product in the ProductTbl table.

To find an exact match in the Specialty_Store table using the HLOOKUP function:

1. Go to the **Product Data** worksheet.
2. In cell **E1**, enter **Specialty Store**. The table expands to include the new column.
3. Make sure cell **E2** is the active cell, and then click the **Insert Function** fx button next to the formula bar. The Insert Function dialog box opens.
4. Click the **Or select a category** arrow and click **Lookup & Reference**, if necessary, and then double-click **HLOOKUP** in the Select a function box. The Function Arguments dialog box opens.
5. If necessary, drag the Function Arguments dialog box below row 2 so you can see the column headers.
6. In the Lookup_value box, enter **B2** and then press the **Tab** key. The lookup value is the product category, which is located in column B.
7. In the Table_array box, type the defined name **Specialty_Store** and then press the **Tab** key. Specialty_Store references the range B3:H4 in the Data Tables worksheet. If the defined name Specialty_Store was not defined, the table_array argument would be entered as 'Data Tables'!B3:H4, and you would need to change the range to absolute references ('Data Tables'!$B$3:$H$4) so the formula would copy correctly to other cells.

8. In the Row_index_num box, type **2** and then press the **Tab** key. The number 2 indicates that the specialty store location is stored in the second row of the Specialty_Store lookup table.
9. In the Range_lookup box, type **FALSE**. This sets the function to find an exact match in the lookup table. See Figure 8-31.

Figure 8-31 Function Arguments dialog box for HLOOKUP function

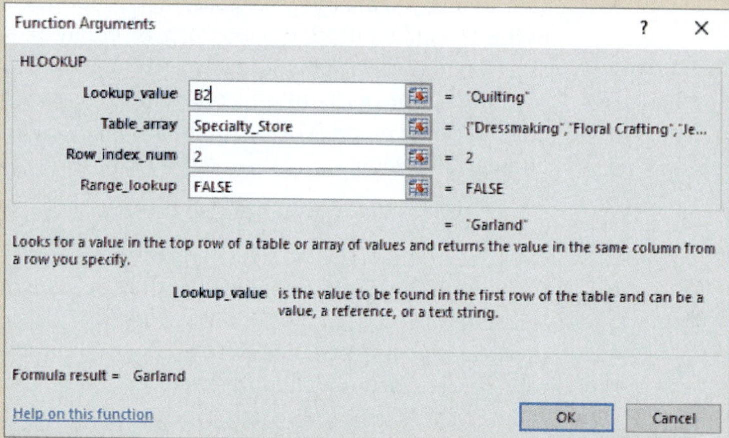

10. Click the **OK** button. The dialog box closes, Garland appears in cell E2, and the formula =HLOOKUP(B2,Specialty_Store,2,FALSE) appears in the formula bar. The remaining rows in the Specialty Store column are filled with the HLOOKUP function.

    Trouble? If #N/A appears in the Specialty Store column, you may have used a VLOOKUP function. If necessary, edit the formula in cell E2 to use HLOOKUP instead of VLOOKUP.

11. Select cell **E2** to deselect the column. See Figure 8-32.

Figure 8-32 Exact match HLOOKUP function for identifying the Specialty Store for each product

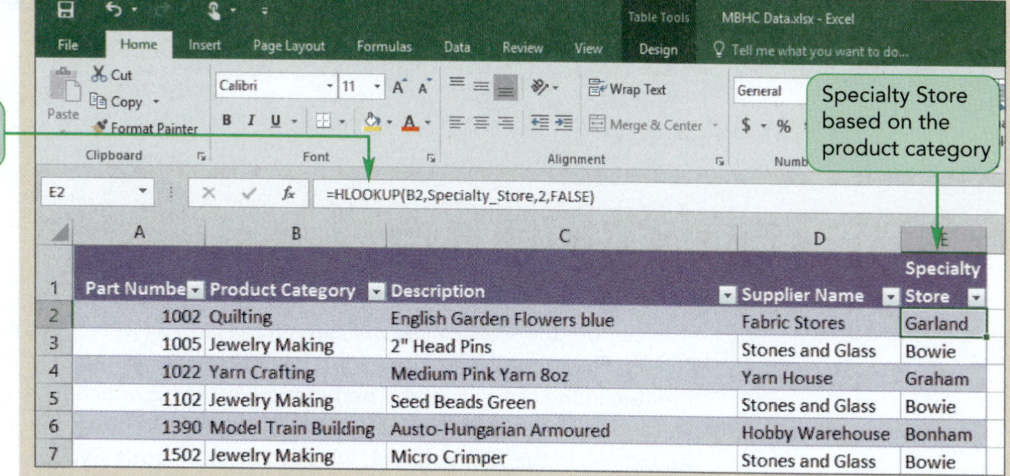

The specialty store for each part is entered in the worksheet.

INSIGHT

Using the INDEX and MATCH Functions to Perform a Lookup

The INDEX function returns a value or the reference to a value from within a table or range. For example, you would use the INDEX function when you know (or can calculate) the position of a cell in a range and you want to return the actual value. The Array form returns the value of a specified cell or array of cells, and has the syntax

`INDEX(array,row_num,column_num)`

where *array* is the range of cells, named range, or table; *row_num* is the row number in the array (if omitted, *column_num* is required); and *column_num* is the column number in the array (if omitted, *row_num* is required). For example, the formula `=INDEX(A1:D6,4,3)` returns the value in cell C4, the cell in the fourth row and third column of the range A1:D6. The Reference form returns a reference to specified cells, and has the syntax

`INDEX(reference,row_num,column_num,area_num)`

where *reference* is one or several ranges and *area_num* specifies which range from the *reference* argument to use. If the *area_num* argument is omitted, the INDEX function will return the result for the first range listed in the reference. For example, the formula `=INDEX((A2:D3,A5:D7),3,4,2)` returns the value in cell D7, the cell in the third row and fourth column of the second reference.

The MATCH function searches for a specified number or text in a range of cells, and then returns the relative position of that data in the range. The MATCH function has the syntax

`MATCH(lookup_value,lookup_array,[match_type])`

where *lookup_value* is the number or text you are looking for, *lookup_array* is the range of cells being searched, and the optional argument *match_type* specifies whether you want to return an exact match or the nearest match. The *match_type* argument can be 1, 0, or –1. You enter 1 to find the largest value less than or equal to the *lookup_value* (the list must be in ascending order), 0 to find the value exactly equal to the *lookup_value* (the list can be in any order), or–1 to find the smallest value greater than or equal to the *lookup_value* (the list must be in descending order). If the *match_type* argument is omitted, it is assumed to be 1.

You can use the Array form of the INDEX function to return the value of the cell identified by the MATCH function in the *lookup_array* argument. For example, consider the following item codes and items entered in the range A1:B6:

	A	B
1	*Item Code*	*Item*
2	SH001	Shirt
3	SW050	Sweater
4	CO200	Coat
5		
6	Sweater	

In cell B6, the `=INDEX(A2:A4,MATCH(A6,B2:B4,0))` formula returns the value SW050. First, the MATCH function looks for an exact match for data in cell A6, which is Sweater, in the range B2:B4. The function returns 2, which is the position of Sweater in the range B2:B4. Then, the Array form of the INDEX function returns the value of the second cell in the range A2:A4, which is the item code SW050.

When you use the INDEX and MATCH functions, the lookup value can be any column in the array. In the VLOOKUP function, it must be in the first column.

Using the IFERROR Function

Error values indicate that some element in a formula or a cell referenced in a formula is preventing Excel from returning a calculated value. Recall that an error value begins with a number sign (#) followed by an error name that indicates the type of error. For instance, the error value #N/A appears in a Product Supplier cell when the VLOOKUP function cannot find the product supplier in the Product_Suppliers lookup table. This error value message is not particularly descriptive or helpful.

You can use the IFERROR function to display a more descriptive message that helps users fix the problem. The IFERROR function can determine if a cell contains an error value and then display the message you choose rather than the default error value; or if no error value exists in the formula, display the result of the formula. The IFERROR function has the syntax

```
IFERROR(expression,valueIfError)
```

where ***expression*** is the formula you want to check for an error, and ***valueIfError*** is the message you want displayed if Excel detects an error in the formula you are checking. If Excel does not detect an error, the result of the ***expression*** is displayed.

You can use the IFERROR function to find and handle formula errors. For example, you can enter the following formula to determine whether an invalid code was entered in the Product Category of the Product Data worksheet and then display a more descriptive message if Excel detects an error:

```
=IFERROR(VLOOKUP(B2,Product_Suppliers,2,FALSE),"Various")
```

Based on this formula, if the value in cell B2 is Quilting, the result of the VLOOKUP formula is Fabric Stores (the corresponding value from the Product_Suppliers table), the first argument in the IFERROR function (shown in red) is executed, and the product supplier is displayed. On the other hand, if cell B2 has an invalid product category, such as All, the VLOOKUP function returns the error value #N/A, the second argument in the IFERROR function (shown in blue) is executed, and Various is displayed.

Vanessa wants to verify that all products in the product data worksheet have a valid product category in the Product Category column. You will check whether any cell in the Product Category column contains an error value.

To check for an error value in the Supplier Name column:

1. In the Product Data worksheet, scroll to row **47**. Notice the error value #N/A in cells D47 and E47, the supplier name and specialty store, respectively.
2. Select cell **D47**. See Figure 8-33.

Figure 8-33 Error value in the Supplier Name and Specialty Store columns

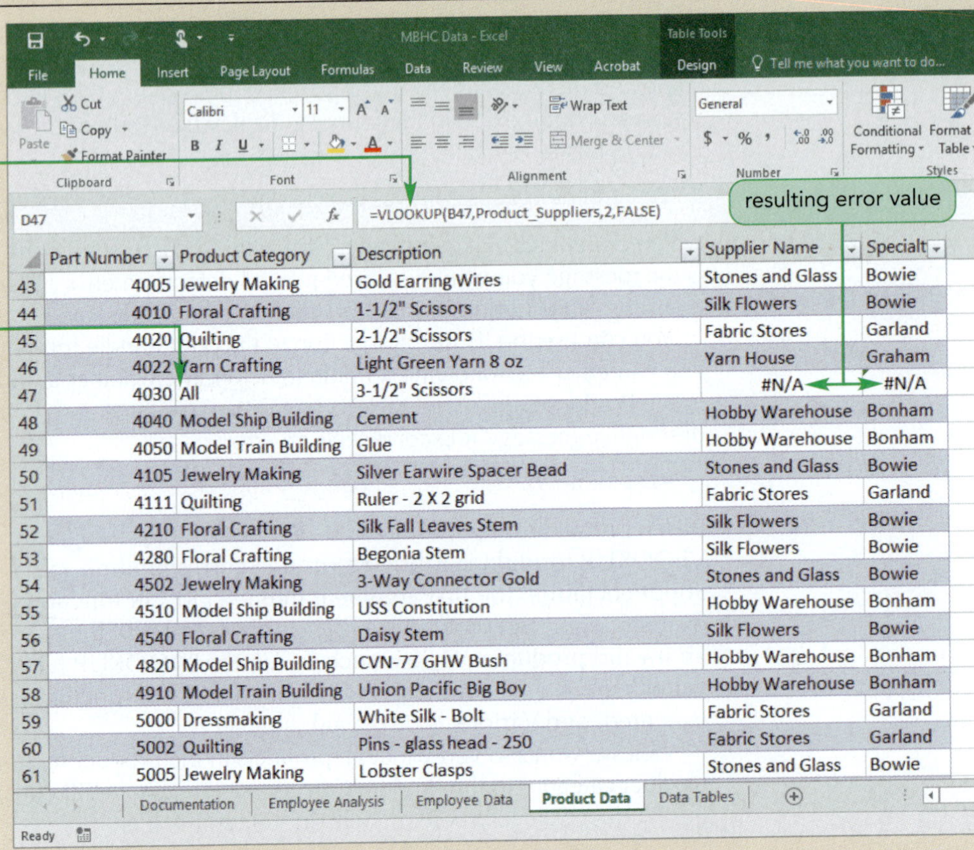

	Part Number	Product Category	Description	Supplier Name	Specialty
43	4005	Jewelry Making	Gold Earring Wires	Stones and Glass	Bowie
44	4010	Floral Crafting	1-1/2" Scissors	Silk Flowers	Bowie
45	4020	Quilting	2-1/2" Scissors	Fabric Stores	Garland
46	4022	Yarn Crafting	Light Green Yarn 8 oz	Yarn House	Graham
47	4030	All	3-1/2" Scissors	#N/A	#N/A
48	4040	Model Ship Building	Cement	Hobby Warehouse	Bonham
49	4050	Model Train Building	Glue	Hobby Warehouse	Bonham
50	4105	Jewelry Making	Silver Earwire Spacer Bead	Stones and Glass	Bowie
51	4111	Quilting	Ruler - 2 X 2 grid	Fabric Stores	Garland
52	4210	Floral Crafting	Silk Fall Leaves Stem	Silk Flowers	Bowie
53	4280	Floral Crafting	Begonia Stem	Silk Flowers	Bowie
54	4502	Jewelry Making	3-Way Connector Gold	Stones and Glass	Bowie
55	4510	Model Ship Building	USS Constitution	Hobby Warehouse	Bonham
56	4540	Floral Crafting	Daisy Stem	Silk Flowers	Bowie
57	4820	Model Ship Building	CVN-77 GHW Bush	Hobby Warehouse	Bonham
58	4910	Model Train Building	Union Pacific Big Boy	Hobby Warehouse	Bonham
59	5000	Dressmaking	White Silk - Bolt	Fabric Stores	Garland
60	5002	Quilting	Pins - glass head - 250	Fabric Stores	Garland
61	5005	Jewelry Making	Lobster Clasps	Stones and Glass	Bowie

3. In row 47, observe that the Product Category is All. This invalid code causes the error messages #N/A because the lookup table does not have a corresponding value.

Vanessa asks you to modify the formulas in the Supplier Name and the Specialty Store columns so that the descriptive error message "Various" appears rather than the error value. The IFERROR function will check for errors in the formula and display the error message you create rather than the error value if it finds an error.

You'll nest the VLOOKUP function within the IFERROR function to display "Various" in the Supplier Name and Special Store columns if Excel detects an error value.

Be sure to type a comma before the error message.

To nest the VLOOKUP function within the IFERROR function:

1. Double-click cell **D47** to enter Edit mode. The formula =VLOOKUP(B47,Product_Suppliers,2,FALSE) appears in the cell and the formula bar. You'll nest this formula within the IFERROR function.
2. Click to the right of = (the equal sign), and then type **IFERROR(** to begin entering the IFERROR function. The first argument in the IFERROR function is the formula you want to use if no error value is found; this is the VLOOKUP function already entered in the cell.
3. Move the insertion point to the right of the entire formula, and then type **,"Various")** to add the text you want to display if an error is found.
4. Press the **Enter** key. The error message "Various" appears in cell D47, and the revised formula is automatically copied to all cells in the column.
5. Double-click cell **E47** to enter Edit mode. The formula =HLOOKUP(B47,Specialty_Store,2,FALSE) appears in the cell and the formula bar. You'll nest this formula within the IFERROR function.
6. Click to the right of = (the equal sign), and then type **IFERROR(** to begin entering the IFERROR function. The first argument in the IFERROR function is the formula you want to use if no error value is found; this is the VLOOKUP function already entered in the cell.
7. Move the insertion point to the right of the entire formula, and then type **,"Various")** to add the text you want to display if an error is found.
8. Press the **Enter** key. The error message "Various" appears in cell E47, and the revised formula is automatically copied to all cells in the column. See Figure 8-34.

Figure 8-34 Various message in the Supplier Name and Specialty Store columns

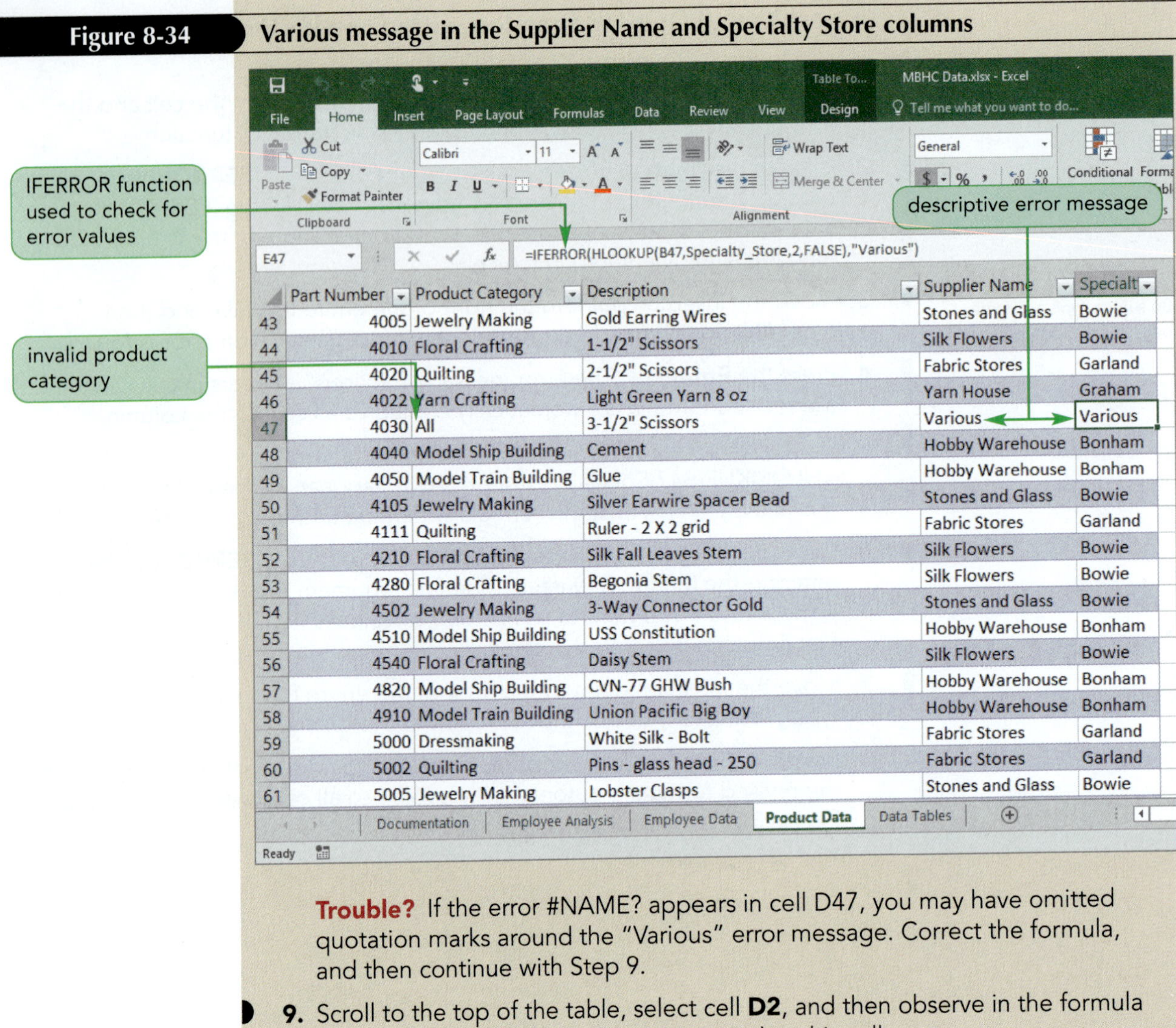

	Part Number	Product Category	Description	Supplier Name	Specialt
43	4005	Jewelry Making	Gold Earring Wires	Stones and Glass	Bowie
44	4010	Floral Crafting	1-1/2" Scissors	Silk Flowers	Bowie
45	4020	Quilting	2-1/2" Scissors	Fabric Stores	Garland
46	4022	Yarn Crafting	Light Green Yarn 8 oz	Yarn House	Graham
47	4030	All	3-1/2" Scissors	Various	Various
48	4040	Model Ship Building	Cement	Hobby Warehouse	Bonham
49	4050	Model Train Building	Glue	Hobby Warehouse	Bonham
50	4105	Jewelry Making	Silver Earwire Spacer Bead	Stones and Glass	Bowie
51	4111	Quilting	Ruler - 2 X 2 grid	Fabric Stores	Garland
52	4210	Floral Crafting	Silk Fall Leaves Stem	Silk Flowers	Bowie
53	4280	Floral Crafting	Begonia Stem	Silk Flowers	Bowie
54	4502	Jewelry Making	3-Way Connector Gold	Stones and Glass	Bowie
55	4510	Model Ship Building	USS Constitution	Hobby Warehouse	Bonham
56	4540	Floral Crafting	Daisy Stem	Silk Flowers	Bowie
57	4820	Model Ship Building	CVN-77 GHW Bush	Hobby Warehouse	Bonham
58	4910	Model Train Building	Union Pacific Big Boy	Hobby Warehouse	Bonham
59	5000	Dressmaking	White Silk - Bolt	Fabric Stores	Garland
60	5002	Quilting	Pins - glass head - 250	Fabric Stores	Garland
61	5005	Jewelry Making	Lobster Clasps	Stones and Glass	Bowie

Trouble? If the error #NAME? appears in cell D47, you may have omitted quotation marks around the "Various" error message. Correct the formula, and then continue with Step 9.

9. Scroll to the top of the table, select cell **D2**, and then observe in the formula bar that the IFERROR formula was copied to this cell.

In this session, you used nested IF functions to determine employee bonuses, you used the VLOOKUP function to calculate the product suppliers and name badge color, and you used the HLOOKUP function to identify the specialty store. You also used the IFERROR function to display a descriptive message in cells where invalid product categories are entered in the ProductTbl table. In the next session, you will use conditional formatting to identify duplicate records, and use the COUNTIF, SUMIF, and AVERAGEIF functions to report on employee salaries.

REVIEW

Session 8.2 Quick Check

1. What is a nested IF function?
2. If cell Y5 displays the value 35, cell Y6 displays the value 42, and cell Y7 contains the following formula, what is displayed in cell Y7?

```
=IF(Y5>Y6,"Older",IF(Y5<Y6,"Younger","Same Age"))
```

3. Explain the difference between an exact match lookup and an approximate match lookup.
4. A customer table includes columns for name, street address, city, state abbreviation, and zip code. A second table includes state abbreviations and state names from all 50 states (one state per row). You need to add a new column to the customer table with the state name. What is the most appropriate function to use to display the state name in this new column?
5. Convert the following criteria used to determine a student's level to a table that can be used in a VLOOKUP function to display the level of each student:

Earned Credits	Level
>=0 and <=30	Freshman
>=31 and <=60	Sophomore
>=61 and <=90	Junior
>=91	Senior

6. In cell X5, the error value #DIV/0! appears when you divide by 0. What IFERROR function can you use with the formula =W5/W25 so that instead of the error value #DIV/0! being displayed, the message "Dividing by zero" appears in the cell?
7. In cell X5, the formula =W5/W25 results in the error value #DIV/0! when W25 stores the value 0. Use the IF function to modify the formula =W5/W25 so that instead of the error value #DIV/0! being displayed when W25 stores 0, the message "Dividing by zero" appears in the cell.
8. Which function could be used with the following Sales Tax Rate table to display the sales tax rate for a customer in one of these four states?

State	CO	NM	OK	TX
Sales Tax Rate	10%	7%	9%	9.5%

Session 8.3 Visual Overview:

Highlighting duplicate values adds formatting to cells that have the same entry. In this instance, duplicate values with a gold fill highlights cells with the same Employee ID.

The Conditional Formatting button provides access to the Duplicate Values conditional format and the Manage Rule option, which opens the Conditional Formatting Rules Manager dialog box.

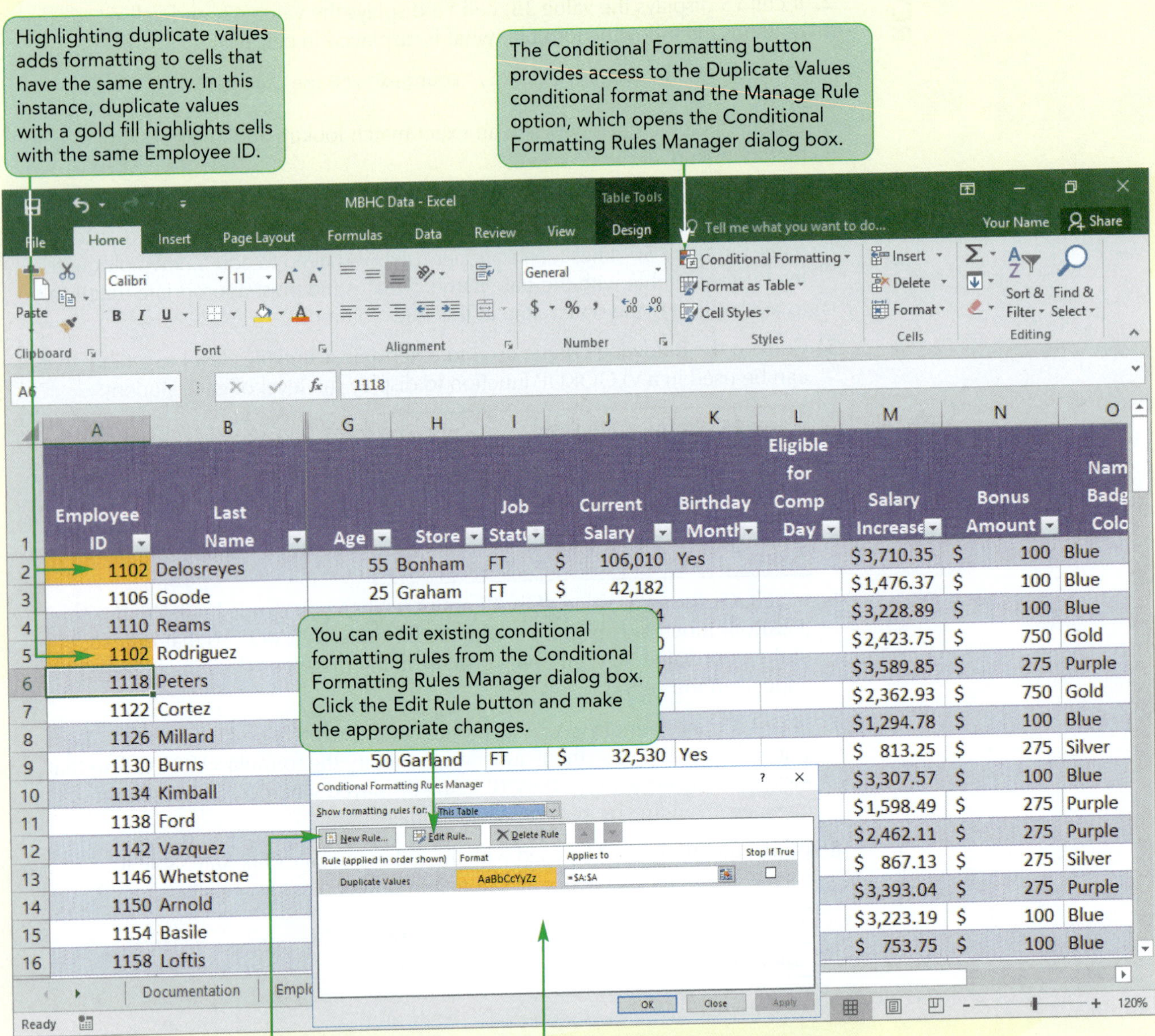

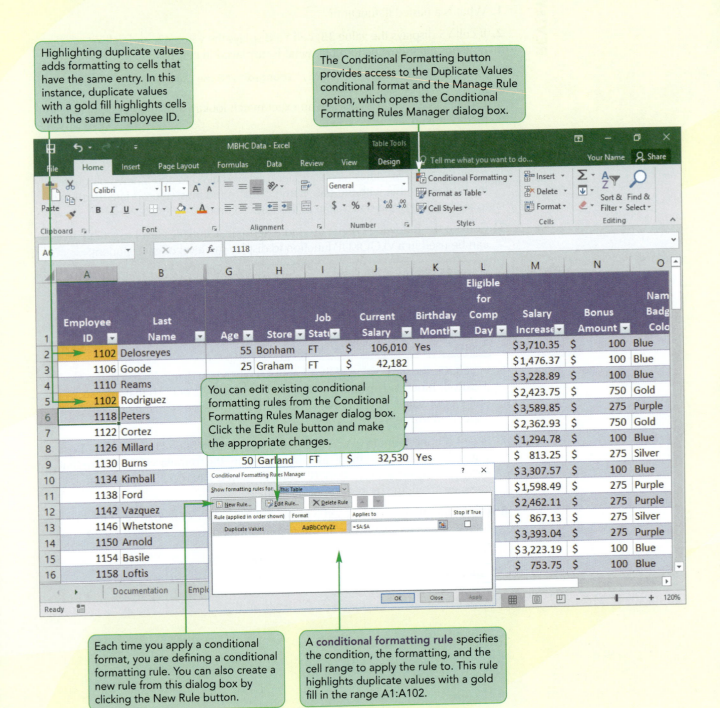

You can edit existing conditional formatting rules from the Conditional Formatting Rules Manager dialog box. Click the Edit Rule button and make the appropriate changes.

Each time you apply a conditional format, you are defining a conditional formatting rule. You can also create a new rule from this dialog box by clicking the New Rule button.

A **conditional formatting rule** specifies the condition, the formatting, and the cell range to apply the rule to. This rule highlights duplicate values with a gold fill in the range A1:A102.

Conditional Formatting and Functions

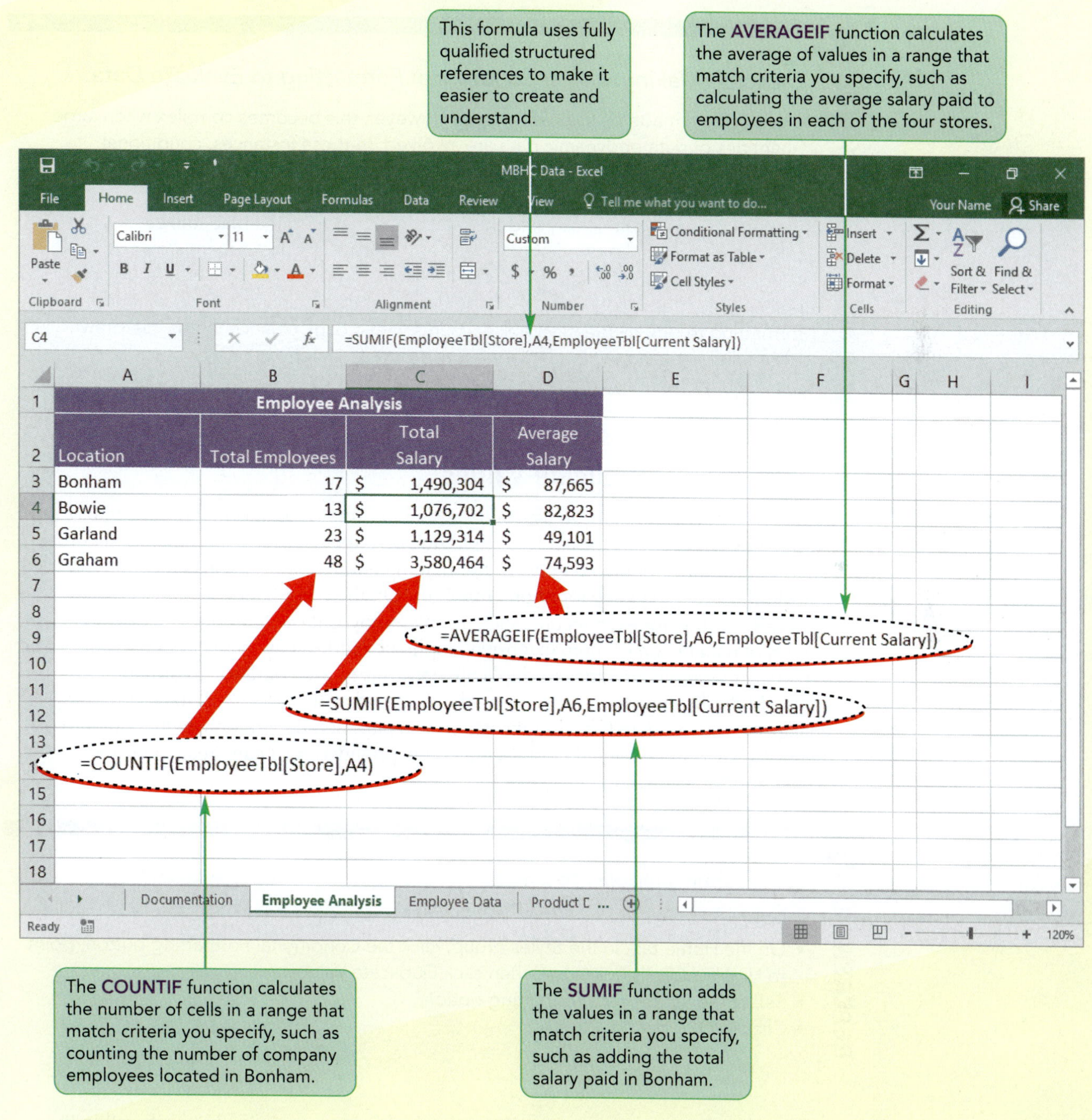
This formula uses fully qualified structured references to make it easier to create and understand.
The AVERAGEIF function calculates the average of values in a range that match criteria you specify, such as calculating the average salary paid to employees in each of the four stores.
MBHC Data - Excel
=SUMIF(EmployeeTbl[Store],A4,EmployeeTbl[Current Salary])
Employee Analysis
Location
Total Employees
Total Salary
Average Salary
Bonham 17 $ 1,490,304 $ 87,665
Bowie 13 $ 1,076,702 $ 82,823
Garland 23 $ 1,129,314 $ 49,101
Graham 48 $ 3,580,464 $ 74,593
=AVERAGEIF(EmployeeTbl[Store],A6,EmployeeTbl[Current Salary])
=SUMIF(EmployeeTbl[Store],A6,EmployeeTbl[Current Salary])
=COUNTIF(EmployeeTbl[Store],A4)
Documentation
Employee Analysis
Employee Data
The COUNTIF function calculates the number of cells in a range that match criteria you specify, such as counting the number of company employees located in Bonham.
The SUMIF function adds the values in a range that match criteria you specify, such as adding the total salary paid in Bonham.

Applying Conditional Formatting

Conditional formatting changes a cell's formatting when its contents match a specified condition. You have already used conditional formatting to highlight cells based on their values and to add data bars that graph the relative values in a range. You can also use conditional formatting to highlight duplicate values in a column of data.

PROSKILLS

Decision Making: Using Conditional Formatting to Evaluate Data

Decisions are made by evaluating data. However, this becomes complex when large quantities of data or dynamic data are involved. In these instances, conditional formatting can be a useful tool to help with your decision making. Conditional formatting is designed to make searching a data range both simple and efficient. For instance, you can quickly find the latest market prices in a real-time stock quote spreadsheet by using conditional formatting to highlight them. You can use conditional formatting to find stocks whose price drops below the target buy price by highlighting the row of any stock that meets the buy criteria. You can use conditional formatting to quickly identify bank accounts with a bank balance that is overdrawn by highlighting accounts with a negative balance. Mastering the art of conditional formatting can help you make better decisions.

Highlighting Duplicate Values

Excel is often used to manage lists of data, such as employee information, inventory, or phone numbers. These types of lists often include data that repeats in different records, such as the employee's state in his or her mailing address, a warehouse location for inventory, or an area code for phone numbers. On the other hand, some of the data is usually unique for each record, such as an employee ID or a product number. As the list of data becomes more extensive, duplicate entries may inadvertently occur. One way to identify unintended duplicate entries is to use conditional formatting to highlight duplicate values in a range with a font and/or fill color. This color coding makes it easier to identify the duplicates so you can then determine whether an entry needs to be corrected. In addition to the colors provided, you can create a custom format for the highlighting.

REFERENCE

Highlighting Duplicate Values

- Select the range in which to highlight duplicate values.
- On the Home tab, in the Styles group, click the Conditional Formatting button, point to Highlight Cells Rules, and then click Duplicate Values.
- Select the appropriate formatting option.
- Click the OK button

Vanessa wants you to use duplicate value highlighting to verify that each cell in the employee ID column has a unique entry. She believes the current employee ID data in the EmployeeTbl table is accurate but wants you to use conditional formatting to ensure that there are no duplicate entries.

To highlight duplicate employee IDs using conditional formatting:

1. If you took a break at the end of the previous session, make sure the MBHC Data workbook is open.
2. Go to the **Employee Data** worksheet, and then select the data in column **A**. Rows 2 through 101 in the Employee ID column are selected.
3. On the Home tab, in the Styles group, click the **Conditional Formatting** button, point to **Highlight Cells Rules**, and then click **Duplicate Values**. The Duplicate Values dialog box opens.
4. Click the **values with** arrow to display a list of formatting options, and then click **Custom Format**. The Format Cells dialog box opens so you can create a format that is not in the list. You'll change the background fill color to red.
5. Click the **Fill** tab, and then, in the Background Color palette, click **red** (the second color in the last row).
6. Click the **OK** button in the Format Cells dialog box, and then click the **OK** button in the Duplicate Values dialog box. Any duplicate values in the ID column appear in a red cell.
7. Scroll the table to ensure that no duplicate values are found.

After you enter a formula, you should test all situations to verify how the formula performs in each case. In this case, you should test the column both with duplicate values and without duplicate values. No duplicate records appear in the EmployeeTbl table, so you'll change the Employee ID of the fourth record from 1114 to 1102, which is the Employee ID of the first employee. The backgrounds of the cells with the duplicate Employee IDs should turn red, which will confirm that the conditional formatting is working as intended. Then, you will return the ID to its original value and confirm that the duplicate value highlighting disappears.

To test the duplicate value conditional formatting:

1. Click cell **A2**, and observe that the employee ID in that cell is 1102.
2. Select cell **A5** in the EmployeeTbl table. Notice that this employee ID is 1114.
3. In cell A5, enter **1102**. The Employee ID changes from 1114 to 1102, and cells A2 and A5 are filled with red because they contain a duplicate Employee ID. See Figure 8-35.

Figure 8-35 Duplicate values highlighted

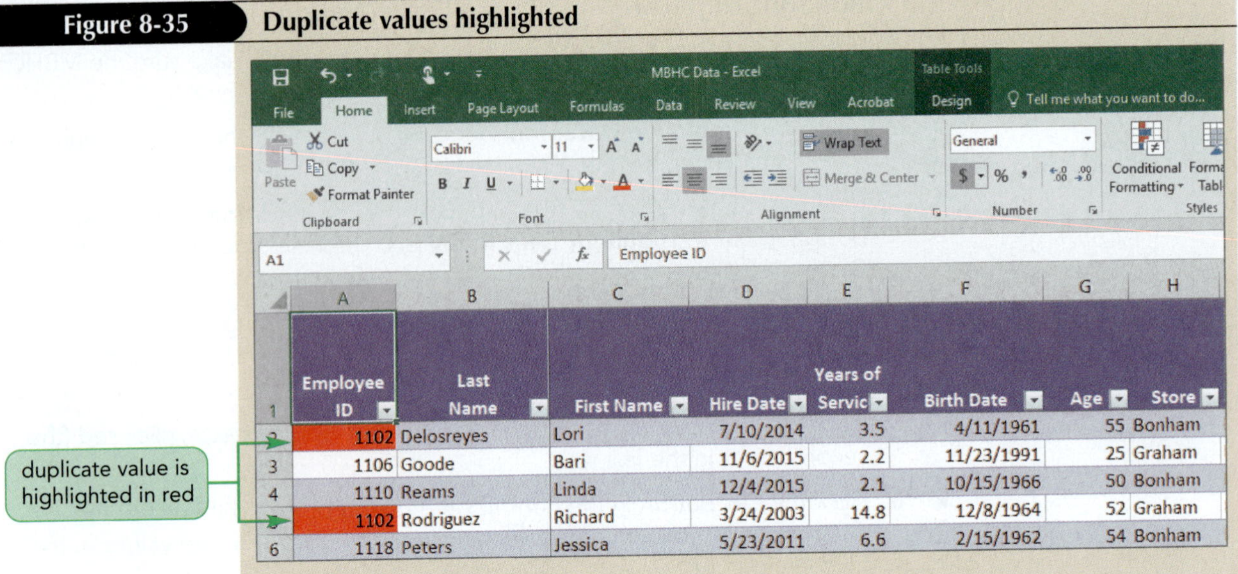
duplicate value is highlighted in red

The conditional formatting correctly identified the duplicate values.

Using the Conditional Formatting Rules Manager

Each time you apply a conditional format, you are defining a conditional formatting rule. A rule specifies the type of condition (such as formatting cells greater than a specified value), the type of formatting when that condition occurs (such as light red fill with dark red text), and the cell or range the formatting is applied to. You can edit existing conditional formatting rules from the Conditional Formatting Rules Manager dialog box.

REFERENCE

Editing a Conditional Formatting Rule

- Select the range with the conditional formatting you want to edit.
- On the Home tab, in the Styles group, click the Conditional Formatting button, and then click Manage Rules.
- Select the rule you want to edit, and then click the Edit Rule button.
- In the Select a Rule Type box, click a rule type, and then make the appropriate changes in the Edit the Rule Description section.
- Click the OK button in each dialog box.

The red background fill makes the cell content difficult to read. Vanessa asks you to use a gold fill color to better contrast with the black text. You'll use the Conditional Formatting Rules Manager dialog box to edit the rule that specifies the formatting applied to duplicate values in the Employee ID column.

To change the duplicate values fill color using the Conditional Formatting Rules Manager:

1. On the Home tab, in the Styles group, click the **Conditional Formatting** button, and then click **Manage Rules**. The Conditional Formatting Rules Manager dialog box opens, listing all the formatting rules for the current selection, which, in this case, is the EmployeeTbl table.
2. Verify that the Show formatting rules for box shows **This Table**. All of the rules currently in effect in the EmployeeTbl table are displayed. You can add new rules and edit or delete existing rules. You also can control which formatting rules are displayed in the dialog box, such as all rules in a specific worksheet or table. See Figure 8-36.

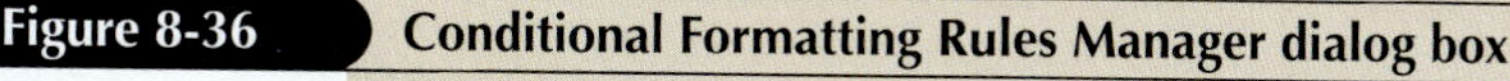

Figure 8-36 Conditional Formatting Rules Manager dialog box

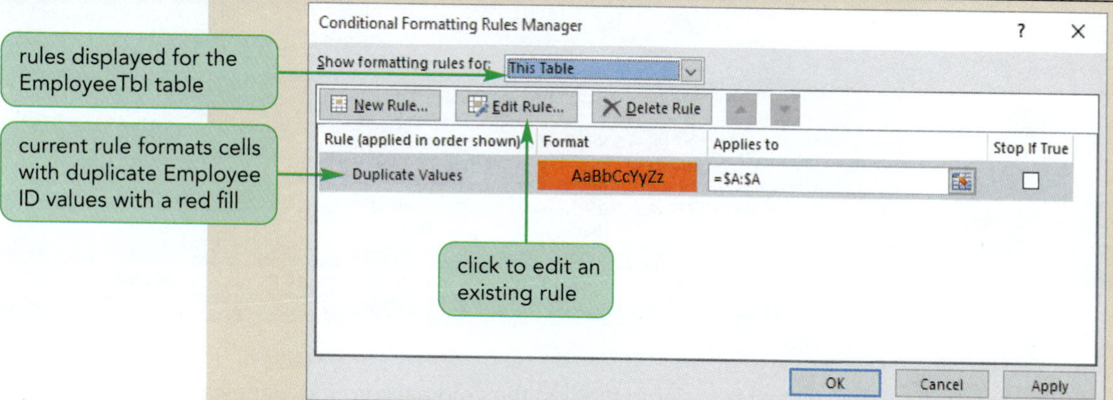

3. Click the **Edit Rule** button. The Edit Formatting Rule dialog box opens. See Figure 8-37.

Figure 8-37 Edit Formatting Rule dialog box

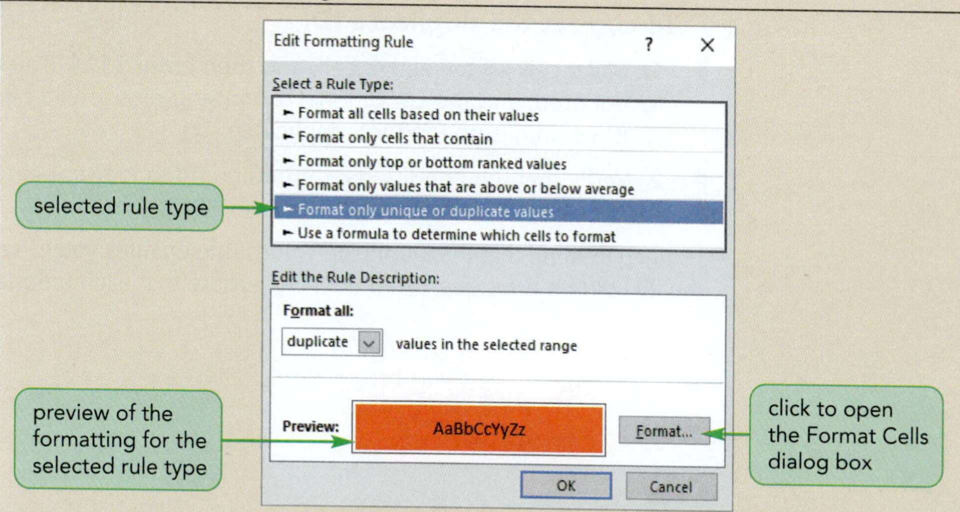

4. Click the **Format** button. The Format Cells dialog box opens.
5. Click the **Fill** tab, if necessary, and then, in the Background Color palette, click **gold** (the third color in the last row).
6. Click the **OK** button in each of the three dialog boxes. The duplicate records in the table are formatted with a gold background color. See Figure 8-38.

Figure 8-38 Edited conditional formatting for duplicate records

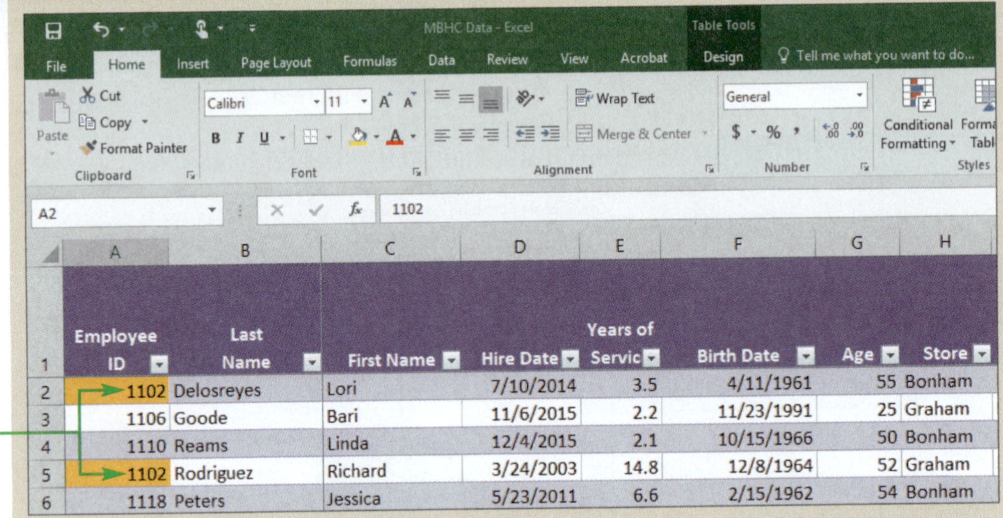

The cell text is easier to read on the gold background. Vanessa wants you to correct the duplicate ID in cell A5 by entering the employee's actual ID number. The conditional format will remain active and apply to any new records that Vanessa adds to the EmployeeTbl table.

To correct the duplicate ID:

1. Make cell **A5** the active cell, and then enter **1114**. The employee's ID is updated, and the conditional formatting disappears because the value in the ID column is no longer a duplicate.
2. Verify that the conditional formatting no longer appears in cell A2.

Keep in mind that the Duplicate Values rule enables you to verify that each entry in the ID column is unique, but it does not ensure that each unique value is accurate.

INSIGHT

Creating a Formula to Conditionally Format Cells

Sometimes the built-in conditional formatting rules do not apply the formatting you need. In these instances, you may be able to create a conditional formatting rule based on a formula that uses a logical expression to describe the condition you want. For example, you can create a formula that uses conditional formatting to compare cells in different columns or to highlight an entire row.

When you create the formula, keep in mind the following guidelines:

- The formula must start with an equal sign.
- The formula must be in the form of a logical test that results in a True or False value.
- In most cases, the formula should use relative references and point to the first row of data in the table. If the formula references a cell or range outside the table, use an absolute reference.
- After you create the formula, enter test values to ensure the conditional formatting works in all situations that you intended.

For example, to use conditional formatting to highlight whether the hire date entered in column D is less than the birth date entered in column F, you need to enter a formula that applies conditional formatting and compares cells in different columns of a table. The following steps describe how to create this formula:

1. Select the range you want to format (in this case, the Hire Date column).
2. On the Home tab, in the Styles group, click the Conditional Formatting button, and then click New Rule.
3. In the Select a Rule Type box, click the "Use a formula to determine which cells to format" rule.
4. In the "Format values where this formula is true" box, enter the appropriate formula (in this case, =D2<F2).
5. Click the Format button to open the Format Cells dialog box, and then select the formatting you want to apply.
6. Click the OK button in each dialog box.

Another example is to highlight the entire row if an employee has 10 or more years of service. In this case, you would select the range of data, such as A2:O101, and then enter =E$2>=10 in the "Format values where this formula is true" box. The other steps remain the same.

Using Functions to Summarize Data Conditionally

The COUNT function tallies the number of data values in a range, the SUM function adds the values in a range, and the AVERAGE function calculates the average of the values in a range. However, sometimes you need to calculate a conditional count, sum, or average using only those cells that meet a particular condition. In those cases, you need to use the COUNTIF, SUMIF, and AVERAGEIF functions. For example, Vanessa wants to create a report that shows the number, total, and average salaries for employees in each store. You will use the COUNTIF, SUMIF, and AVERAGEIF functions to do this.

Using the COUNTIF Function

You can calculate the number of cells in a range that match criteria you specify by using the COUNTIF function, which is sometimes referred to as a **conditional count**. The COUNTIF function has the syntax

```
COUNTIF(range, criteria)
```

where *range* is the range of cells you want to count, and *criteria* is a number, an expression, a cell reference, or text that defines which cells to count.

There are many ways to express the criteria in a COUNTIF function, as shown in Figure 8-39.

Figure 8-39 Examples of COUNTIF function criteria

Formula	Explanation of Formula	Result
=COUNTIF(H2:H101,"Bonham")	Number of employees in Bonham	17
=COUNTIF(H2:H101,H3)	Number of employees in cell H3 (Graham)	48
=COUNTIF(J2:J101,<50000)	Number of employees with salary <50000	22
=COUNTIF(J2:J101, ">=" &J2)	Number of employees with salary >= value in cell J2 (106010)	7

TIP

You can use structured references or cell and range addresses to reference cells within an Excel table.

Vanessa wants to know how many employees are located in Bonham. You can use the COUNTIF function to find this answer because you want a conditional count (a count of employees who meet a specified criterion; in this case, employees located in Bonham). The location information is stored in column H of the EmployeeTbl table. To count the number of employees in Bonham you can use either one of the following formulas:

Range reference `=COUNTIF('Employee Data'!H2:H101,"=Bonham")`

Fully qualified structured reference `=COUNTIF(EmployeeTbl[Store],"=Bonham")`

With either formula, Excel counts all of the cells in the Store column of the EmployeeTbl table that contain the text equal to Bonham. Because Bonham is text, you must enclose it within quotation marks. It is not necessary to enclose numbers in quotation marks.

You will enter this formula using the COUNTIF function in the Employee Analysis worksheet. You will use the Insert Function dialog box to help you build the formula using worksheet and range references to calculate the number of employees who work in Bonham.

To count employees located in Bonham using the COUNTIF function:

1. Go to the **Employee Analysis** worksheet.
2. Select cell **B3**, and then click the **Insert Function** button next to the formula bar. The Insert Function dialog box opens.
3. Click the **Or select a category** arrow, and then click **Statistical**.
4. In the Select a function box, double-click **COUNTIF**. The Function Arguments dialog box opens.
5. In the Range box, type **'Employee Data'!H2:H101** to enter the range to search, and then press the **Tab** key. The range 'Employee Data'!H2:H101 refers to all data values in the range H2:H101 (Store column) in the Employee Data worksheet.

6. In the Criteria box, type **A3**. Cell A3 in this worksheet contains Bonham, which is the criterion you want Excel to use to determine which employee records to count. You could also have typed "=Bonham" or "Bonham" in the criteria box. See Figure 8-40.

Figure 8-40 Function Arguments dialog box for the COUNTIF function

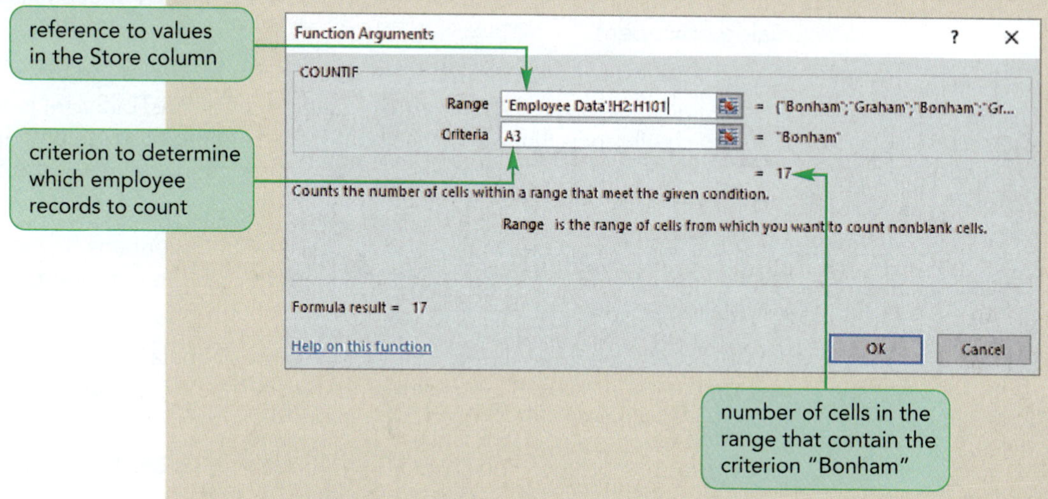

7. Click the **OK** button. Cell B3 remains active. The formula =COUNTIF('Employee Data'!H2:H101,A3) appears in the formula bar, and 17 appears in cell B3, indicating that the company has 17 employees in Bonham. See Figure 8-41.

Figure 8-41 Location summary for Bonham employees

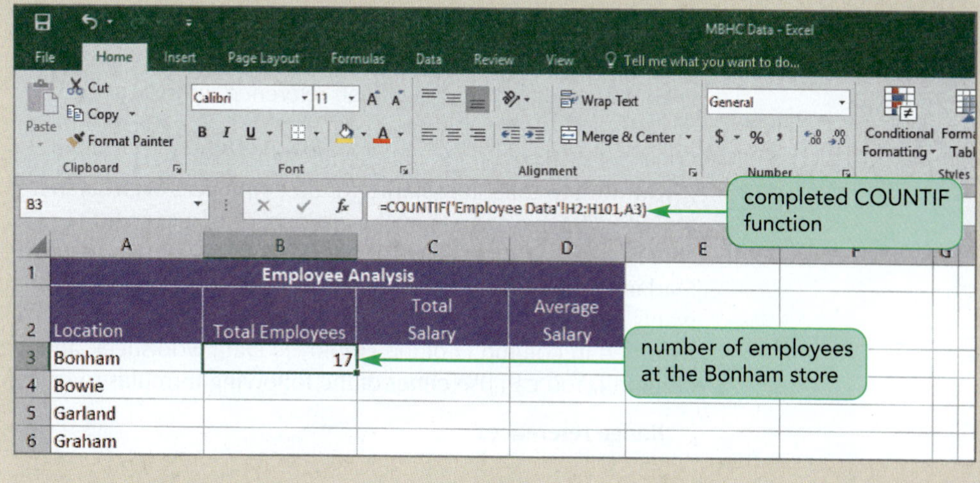

You will enter a similar formula to calculate the number of employees who work in Bowie, Garland, and Graham. This time, however, you will use structured references to specify the range to search.

To count the number of employees who work in Bowie, Garland, and Graham:

1. Select cell **B4**, and then click the **Insert Function** button next to the formula bar. The Insert Function dialog box opens with the Statistical category still selected.
2. In the Select a function box, double-click **COUNTIF**. The Function Arguments dialog box opens.
3. In the Range box, type **EmployeeTbl[Store]** to enter the range to search, and then press the **Tab** key. The range EmployeeTbl[Store] is a structured reference that refers to all data values in the Store column in the EmployeeTbl table (the range H2:H101). The beginning values in the Store column appear to the right of the Range box.
4. In the Criteria box, type **A4**. Cell A4 in this worksheet contains Bowie (the value shown to the right of the Criteria box), which is the criterion Excel will use to determine which employee records to count.
5. Click the **OK** button. Cell B4 remains active. The formula =COUNTIF(EmployeeTbl[Store],A4) appears in the formula bar, and 13 appears in cell B4, indicating 13 employees work in Bowie.
6. Copy the COUNTIF formula in cell B4 to the range **B5:B6**. The total employees for Garland is 22 and Graham is 48.

Using the SUMIF Function

The SUMIF function adds the values in a range that meet criteria you specify. The SUMIF function is also called a **conditional sum**. The syntax of the SUMIF function is

```
SUMIF(range,criteria[,sum_range])
```

where *range* is the range of cells you want to filter before calculating a sum; *criteria* is a number, an expression, a cell reference, or text that defines which cells to count; and *sum_range* is the range of cells to total. The *sum_range* argument is optional; if you omit it, Excel will total the values specified in the *range* argument. For example, if you want to total the salaries for all employees with salaries greater than $50,000 (">50000"), you do not use the optional third argument.

Vanessa wants to compare the total salaries paid to employees in Bonham, Bowie, Garland, and Graham. You can use the SUMIF function to do this because Vanessa wants to conditionally add salaries of employees at a specified location. Store is recorded in column H of the Employee Data worksheet, and the salary data is stored in column J. You can use either of the following formulas to calculate this value:

Range references

```
=SUMIF('Employee Data'!H2:H101,"Bonham",'Employee Data'!J2:J101)
```

Fully qualified structured references

```
=SUMIF(EmployeeTbl[Store],"Bonham",EmployeeTbl[Current Salary])
```

Both of these formulas state that the salary of any employee whose store is Bonham will be added to the total. Using the SUMIF function, you will insert the formula with structured references into the Employee Analysis worksheet.

To sum employee salaries in the Bonham, Bowie, Garland, and Graham stores using the SUMIF function:

1. Select cell **C3**, and then click the **Insert Function** button next to the formula bar. The Insert Function dialog box opens.
2. Click the **Or select a category** arrow, and then click **Math & Trig**.
3. In the Select a function box, double-click **SUMIF**. The Function Arguments dialog box opens.
4. In the Range box, type **EmployeeTbl[Store]** to specify the range of data to filter, and then press the **Tab** key. The range EmployeeTbl[Store] is a structured reference that refers to all data values in the Store column in the EmployeeTbl table (the range H2:H101).
5. In the Criteria box, type **A3** and then press the **Tab** key. Cell A3 in this worksheet contains "Bonham" (shown to the right of the Criteria box), which is the criterion Excel will use to determine which employee records to sum.
6. In the Sum_range box, type **EmployeeTbl[Current Salary]** to indicate that the Current Salary column in the EmployeeTbl table contains the data to sum in the filtered rows. The values to the right of the Sum_range box are the amounts in the filtered Current Salary column. See Figure 8-42.

Figure 8-42 Function Arguments dialog box for the SUMIF function

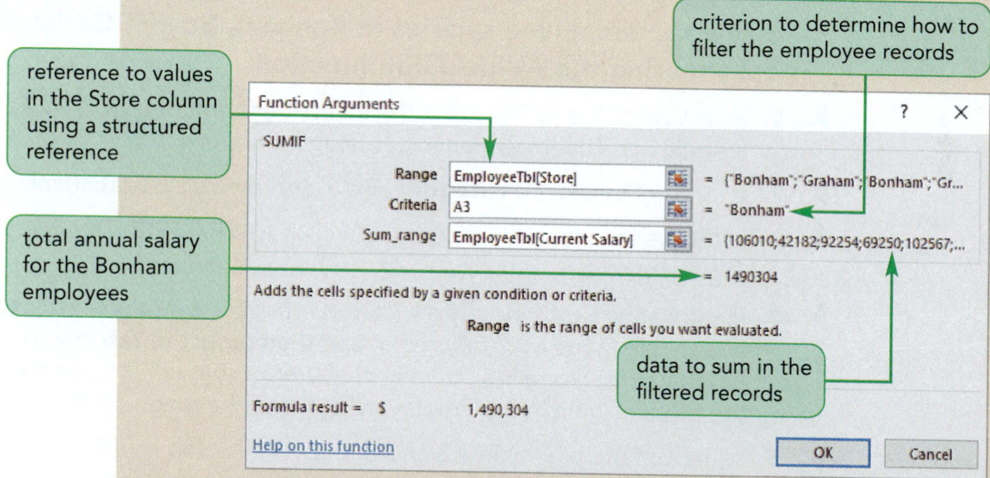

7. Click the **OK** button. Cell C3 is active. The formula =SUMIF(EmployeeTbl[Store],A3,EmployeeTbl[Current Salary]) appears in the formula bar and $1,490,304 appears in cell C3, indicating the total annual salaries paid to Bonham employees.

   Trouble? If Invalid appears in the cell or an error message appears, you probably mistyped some part of the formula. Review the SUMIF formula you entered, and make sure it matches the formula =SUMIF(EmployeeTbl[Store],A3,EmployeeTbl[Current Salary]).

8. Copy the SUMIF formula in cell C3 to the range **C4:C6**. The total Current Salary for employees working in Bowie is $1,076,702, Garland is $1,106,314, and Graham is $3,580,464.

Using the AVERAGEIF Function

The AVERAGEIF function is similar to the SUMIF function. You use the AVERAGEIF function to calculate the average of values in a range that meet criteria you specify. The syntax of the AVERAGEIF function is

```
AVERAGEIF(range,criteria[,average_range])
```

where ***range*** is the range of cells you want to filter before calculating the average, ***criteria*** is the condition used to filter the range, and ***average_range*** is the range of cells to average. The ***average_range*** argument is optional; if you omit it, Excel will average the values specified in the *range* argument.

Vanessa also wants to compare the average salaries paid to employees in Bonham, Bowie, Garland, and Graham. Store is recorded in column H of the Employee Data worksheet, and the current salary data is stored in column J. The formulas to calculate this value are:

Range references

```
=AVERAGEIF('Employee Data'!H2:H101,"Bonham",'Employee Data'!J2:J101)
```

Fully qualified structured references

```
=AVERAGEIF(EmployeeTbl[Store],"Bonham",EmployeeTbl[Current Salary])
```

Both of these formulas state that the current salary of any employee whose store is Bonham will be included in the average. You will enter the formula into the Employee Analysis worksheet using the AVERAGEIF function with structured references.

To average employee salaries in Bonham, Bowie, Garland and Graham using the AVERAGEIF function:

1. Select cell **D3**, and then click the **Insert Function** button *fx* next to the formula bar. The Insert Function dialog box opens.
2. Click the **Or select a category** arrow, and then click **Statistical**.
3. In the Select a function box, double-click **AVERAGEIF**. The Function Arguments dialog box opens.
4. In the Range box, type the structured reference **EmployeeTbl[Store]** to specify the range of data to filter, and then press the **Tab** key. The range EmployeeTbl[Store] is a structured reference that refers to all data values in the Store column in the EmployeeTbl table (the range H2:H101).
5. In the Criteria box, type **A3** and then press the **Tab** key. Cell A3 in this worksheet contains "Bonham" (shown to the right of the Criteria box), which is the criterion Excel will use to determine which employee records to average.
6. In the Average_range box, type **EmployeeTbl[Current Salary]** to indicate that the Current Salary column in the EmployeeTbl table contains the data to average in the filtered rows. See Figure 8-43.

Figure 8-43 Function Arguments dialog box for the AVERAGEIF function

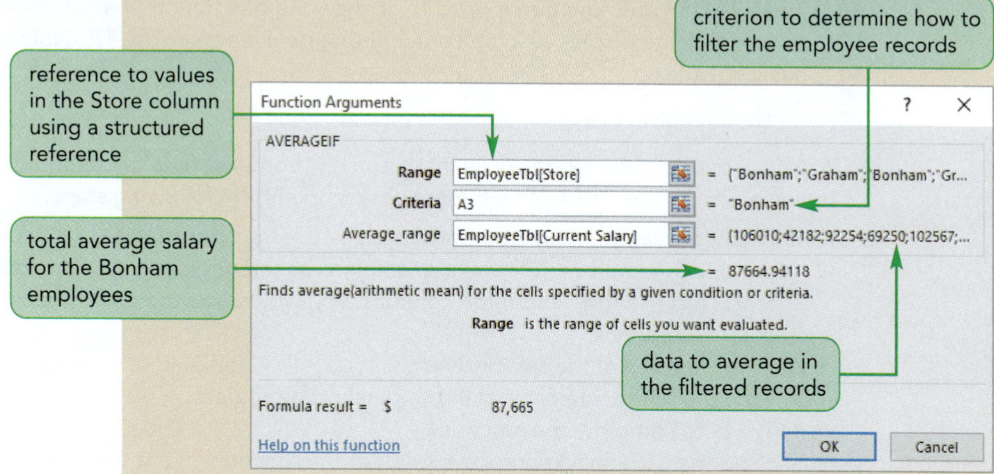

7. Click the **OK** button. Cell D3 remains active. The formula =AVERAGEIF(EmployeeTbl[Store],A3,EmployeeTbl[Current Salary]) appears in the formula bar and $87,665 appears in cell E3, indicating the average current salary paid to Bonham employees.
8. Copy the formula in cell D3 to cell **D4:D6**. MBHC pays an average of $87,665 to employees working in Bonham, $82,823 in Bowie, $50,287 in Garland, and $74,593 in Graham. See Figure 8-44.

Figure 8-44 Completed Location Analysis report

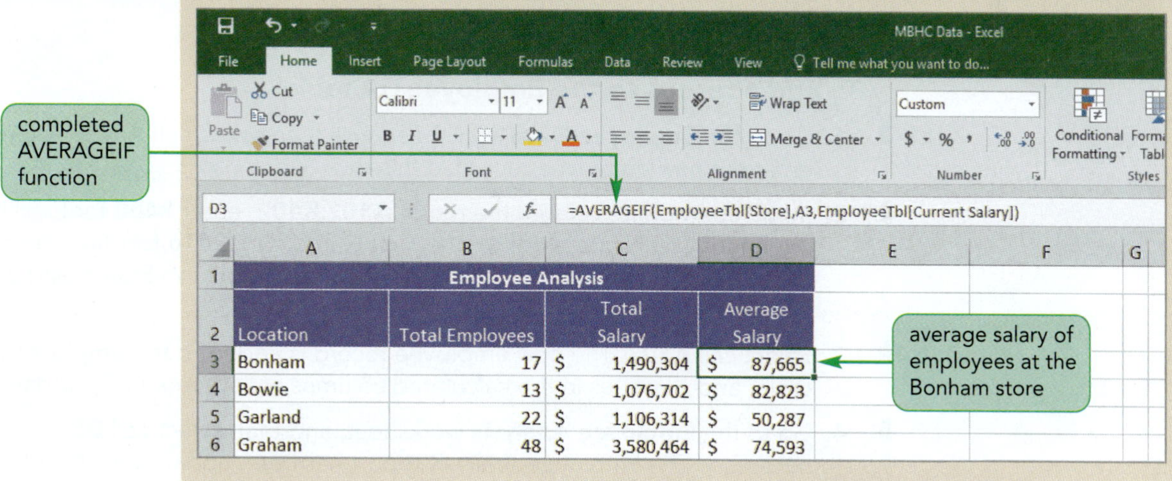

As Vanessa enters new employees or edits the location or current salary values of current employees, the values in the Employee Analysis worksheet will be automatically updated because the formulas reference the EmployeeTbl table.

INSIGHT

Using the TRANSPOSE Function

The **TRANSPOSE function** is used to change the orientation of a range—that is, return a vertical range of cells as a horizontal range, or vice versa. The TRANSPOSE function has the syntax

```
TRANSPOSE(array)
```

where *array* is the range you want to convert from row data to column data (or vice versa). To use the TRANSPOSE function, complete the following steps:

1. Select the range where you want to place the transposed data. Be sure to select the opposite number of rows and columns as the original data. For example, if the range has five rows and three columns, you would select a range that has three rows and five columns.
2. In the first cell of the selected range, type =TRANSPOSE(to begin the function.
3. Type the range reference of the original range of data.
4. Type) to complete the function.
5. Press the Ctrl+Shift+Enter keys to enter the function. (Note that pressing only the Enter key would create incorrect formula results.) Excel places curly brackets { } around the array formula and enters the formula in every cell of the selected range.

Keep in mind that the TRANSPOSE function only copies the data from the cells in the initial range. Any formatting applied to the original range must be reapplied to the new range. However, any changes made to the data in the original range are automatically made to the data in the transposed range. To delete the transposed range, select the entire range, and then press the Delete key.

Vanessa recently hired a new employee, and she asks you to add the new record to the Excel table.

To add a record to the EmployeeTbl table:

1. Go to the **Employee Data** worksheet, and then select cell **A102**. You will enter the new employee record in this row.
2. In the appropriate cells in the range **A102:K102**, enter **3400** for Emp ID, **Joplin** for Last Name, **Jodi** for the First Name, **4/1/2016** for Hire Date, **11/15/1970** for Birth Date, **Garland** for Store, **PT** for Job Status, and **23000** for Current Salary.
3. Select cell **A103**. The new employee record is added to the EmployeeTbl table, and all values in the calculated columns are automatically updated.
4. Go to the **Employee Analysis** worksheet, and then select cell **B5**, if necessary. The Employee Analysis report has been updated to reflect the new employee. The number of employees in Garland is 23, the total salary is $1,129,314, and the average salary is $49,101. See Figure 8-45.

Figure 8-45 **Updated Location Analysis report**

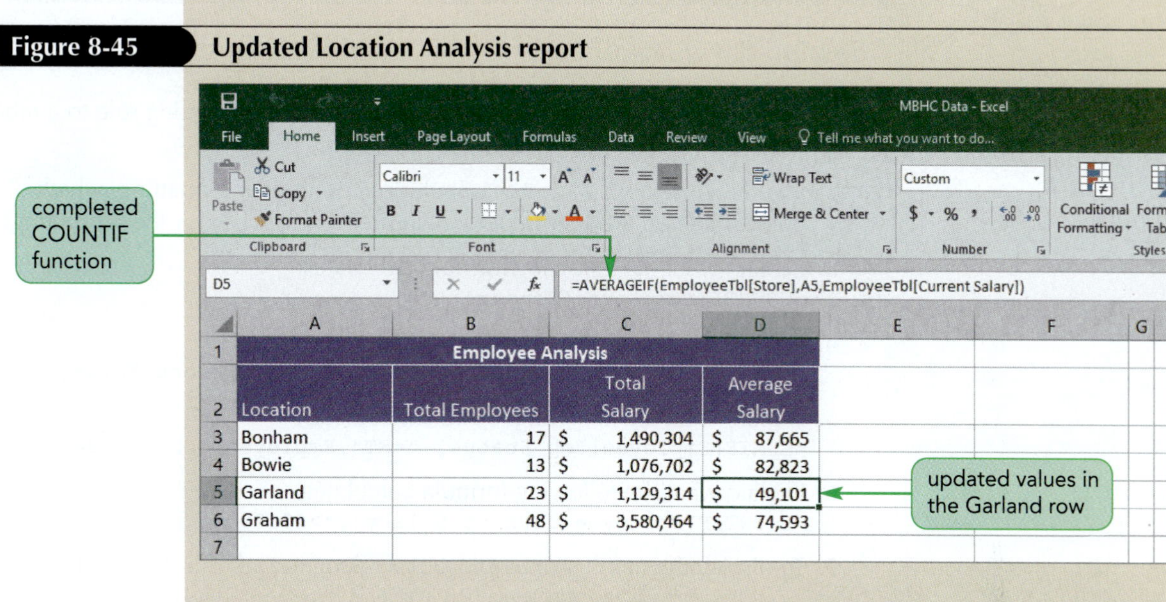

completed COUNTIF function
=AVERAGEIF(EmployeeTbl[Store],A5,EmployeeTbl[Current Salary])
Employee Analysis
Location
Total Employees
Total Salary
Average Salary
Bonham 17 $ 1,490,304 $ 87,665
Bowie 13 $ 1,076,702 $ 82,823
Garland 23 $ 1,129,314 $ 49,101
Graham 48 $ 3,580,464 $ 74,593
updated values in the Garland row

5. Save the workbook, and then close it.

If the employee data had been stored as a range of data instead of an Excel table, the Employee Analysis report would not have automatically updated. Instead, you would have had to modify all the formulas in the report to reflect the expanded range of employee data. Vanessa is pleased with the formulas you added to the Employee Analysis, Employee Data, and Product Data worksheets.

REVIEW

Session 8.3 Quick Check

1. Would you apply the duplicate value conditional formatting rule to a table column of last names? Why or why not?
2. If you receive a worksheet that includes conditional formatting, which dialog box would you use to find out what criteria were used for the formatting?
3. Explain what the following formula calculates:
`=COUNTIF(Employee[Gender],"F")`
4. Explain what the following formula calculates:
`=AVERAGEIF(Employee[Age],">50",Employee[Current Salary])`
5. Explain what the following formula calculates:
`=SUMIF(Employee[Job Status],"=FT",Employee[Current Salary])`
6. Explain what the following formula calculates:
`=COUNTIF(Employee[Current Salary],">100000")`
7. To display the number of employees working in Dallas (DA), which function would you use—the VLOOKUP, COUNTIF, IF, or COUNT function?
8. To identify duplicate values in a column of an Excel table, what Excel feature would you use?

PRACTICE

Review Assignments

Data File needed for the Review Assignments: Employees.xlsx

Vanessa wants you to analyze the MBHC employee data to determine each employee's work anniversary, available comp days, and bonus eligibility. She also wants you to calculate the bonus amount for eligible employees. Complete the following:

1. Open the **Employees** workbook located in the Excel8 > Review folder included with your Data Files, and then save the workbook as **MBHC Employees** in the location specified by your instructor.
2. In the Documentation worksheet, enter your name and the date.
3. In the Employee Data worksheet, rename the Excel table as **EmployeeTbl**.
4. In the Work Anniversary column, enter an IF function. If the month in the employee's hire date matches the month in the Data Tables worksheet (cell B4), **Yes** should appear in the work anniversary column; otherwise, the cell should remain blank. (*Hint*: Remember to use an absolute cell reference to cell B4 because the formula will be copied to the rest of the column.) All employees receive a card on their work anniversary.
5. In the Eligible for Bonus column, enter a formula with IF and OR functions to display the text **No** if the employee's pay grade is **D** or the employee's job status is a part time (**PT**). Leave the cell blank if the employee is eligible for a bonus.
6. In the Comp Days column, enter a formula with nested IFs to display the number of comp days that an employee will receive based on their years of service. The table for Comp Days is on the Data Tables worksheet. (*Hint*: Remember to use absolute references to the cells in the Data Tables worksheet because the formula will be copied to the entire column.)
7. In the Bonus column, enter an IF function with a nested VLOOKUP function to calculate the bonus for each employee based on whether the employee is eligible for a bonus (column M) and his or her Pay Grade. The bonus information for qualifying employees is in a table named Bonus_Table in the Data Tables worksheet. Format the Bonus column with the Accounting format with no decimal places.
8. In the Years of Service column, modify the formula to include the IFERROR function and display the message **Invalid hire date** if an error value occurs. Test the modified formula by changing the date in cell E2 from 7/10/2014 to **17/10/2014**. AutoFit the column.
9. In the Work Anniversary column, which also uses the Hire Date, modify the formula to include the IFERROR function and display the message **Invalid hire date** if an error value occurs. AutoFit the column.
10. Edit the Duplicate Values conditional formatting rule applied to the Employee ID column so that the fill color of the duplicate value is formatted as light blue (the seventh color in the bottom row of the Background Color palette). Test this change by typing **3226** in cell A101.
11. In the Employee Analysis worksheet, enter the COUNTIF function in cells B3 and B4 to count the number of part-time and full-time employees, respectively. (*Hint*: Count the Job Status column in the EmployeeTbl table.)
12. In cells C3 and C4, enter the SUMIF function to calculate the total salaries of part-time employees and the total salaries of full-time employees, respectively. Format the Total Salary column with the Accounting format and no decimal places.
13. In cells D3 and D4, enter the AVERAGEIF function to calculate the average salary of part-time employees and the average salary of full-time employees, respectively. Format the Average Salary column with the Accounting format and no decimal places.
14. Save the workbook, and then close it.

APPLY

Case Problem 1

Data File needed for this Case Problem: Popcorn.xlsx

Ricky's Popcorn Ricky Nolan established Ricky's Popcorn in Hawthorne, Nevada, in 2000. He ships flavored popcorn in standard flavors such as plain and kettle corn and gourmet flavors such as grape and orange. Customers place their orders via the company website and then receive their popcorn in one to three days, depending on the shipping option they choose. Ricky wants to create a professional-looking invoice he can use for each customer transaction. Ricky used Excel to create the invoice layout and wants you to add formulas to calculate the price per item, sales tax, shipping, and invoice total based on existing tables for pricing and shipping. Complete the following:

1. Open the **Popcorn** workbook located in the Excel8 > Case1 folder included with your Data Files, and then save the workbook as **Rickys Popcorn** in the location specified by your instructor.
2. In the Documentation worksheet, enter your name and the date.
3. In the Pricing and Shipping worksheet, assign the defined name **ShippingCost** to the data in the range D3:E7, which can be used for an approximate match lookup. (*Hint*: The lookup table includes only the values, not the descriptive labels.)
4. In the Customer Invoice worksheet, in the Item column (range B16:B26), use data validation to create a list of the items in the Product Pricing table in the Pricing and Shipping worksheet. (*Hint*: Select the entire range before setting the validation rule.)
5. In the Flavor column (range E16:E26), use data validation to create an input message indicating that the popcorn flavor should be entered. The flavors are located below the invoice.
6. In the Price cell (cell G16), use a VLOOKUP function to retrieve the price of the ordered item listed in the Product Pricing table in the Pricing and Shipping worksheet. (*Hint*: Use the defined name ProductPrice that was assigned to the Product Pricing table.) When no item is selected, this cell will display an error message.
7. Modify the formula in the cell G16 by combining the IFERROR function with the VLOOKUP function to display either the price or a blank cell if an error value occurs. Copy the formula down the range G16:G26.
8. In the Total column (range H16:H26), enter a formula to calculate the total charge for that row (Qty × Price). Use the IFERROR function to display either the total charge or a blank cell if an error value occurs.
9. In the Subtotal cell (cell H27), add a formula to sum the Total column. Use the IFERROR function to display either the subtotal or a blank cell if an error value occurs.
10. In the Sales Tax cell (cell H28), enter a formula with an IF function so if the customer's state (cell C12) is **NV**, then calculate 6.85 percent of the subtotal (cell H27); otherwise, use 0 for the sales tax. (*Hint*: The defined name State is assigned to cell C12, and the defined name Sub_Total is assigned to cell H27. Note that the defined name "Sub_Total" is intentionally not spelled as "Subtotal," which is the name of an Excel function.)
11. In the Shipping cell (cell H29), enter a formula that nests the VLOOKUP function in an IF function to look up the shipping cost from the Shipping Cost table in the Pricing and Shipping worksheet based on the subtotal in cell H27. If the subtotal is 0, the shipping cost should display 0. (*Hint*: Use the defined name you created for the Shipping Cost table data.)
12. In the Total Due cell (cell H30), calculate the invoice total by entering a formula that adds the values in the Subtotal, Sales Tax, and Shipping cells.

13. Test the worksheet by using the following order data:
    - Sold to: **Lauri Bradford**
    - Street: **3226 South Street**
    - City, State Zip: **Hawthorne, NV 89415**
    - Date: **12/1/2017**
    - Item 1: **Gourmet (2) 1g**
    - Flavor: **Nacho Cheese**
    - Quantity **2**
    - Item 2: **Plain Tin 1g**
    - Quantity: **1**
14. Save the workbook, and then close it.

TROUBLESHOOT

Case Problem 2

Data File needed for this Case Problem: LKE.xlsx

LKE Distribution LKE Distribution in North Platte, Nebraska, sells everything needed to outfit an office from basic office supplies to high-end office equipment and technology to furniture. Laura Easterling manages the Accounts Receivable (the amount customers owe LKE Distribution). She has entered the billing information in an Excel workbook. She wants you to enter formulas that will help her to analyze the data. Complete the following:

1. Open the **LKE** workbook located in the Excel8 > Case2 folder included with your Data Files, and then save the workbook as **LKE Receivables** in the location specified by your instructor.
2. In the Documentation worksheet, enter your name and the date.
3. In the Invoices worksheet, in cell B1, enter **7/1/2017** as the current date. Note the defined name CurrentDate has been assigned to cell B1.

Troubleshoot 4. The sales rep commission rate varies for each sales rep. In column E, Laura used a VLOOKUP function to look up the commission rate for each sales rep and then multiplied the commission rate by the invoice amount to calculate the commission. Although the first row in column E of the Excel table named Aging displays the correct commission, all the other cells display a number, "-", or #N/A. Find the problem with the formulas in the Commission column and fix it.

5. In column G, enter a formula with an IF function to calculate the days past due. If the number of days since the invoice was sent (CurrentDate – Invoice Date) is greater than 30, calculate the days past due (Current Date – Invoice Date – 30); otherwise, enter 0.
6. Create the following formulas to assign the value in the Invoice Amount column to one of five columns—Current, 1–30 days, 31–60 days, 61–90 days, and Over 90 days:
    a. In Current (column H), if the Days Past Due equals 0, display the invoice amount (column F); otherwise, display a blank cell.
    b. In 1–30 days (column I), if the days past due is greater than or equal to 1 and less than or equal to 30, display the invoice amount (column F); otherwise, display a blank cell.
    c. In 31–60 days (column J), if the number of days past due is greater than or equal to 31 and less than or equal to 60, display the invoice amount (column F); otherwise, display a blank cell.
    d. In 61–90 days (column K), if the number of days past due is greater than or equal to 61 and less than or equal to 90, display the invoice amount (column F); otherwise, display a blank cell.
    e. In Over 90 days (column L), if the number of days past due is greater than or equal to 91 days, display the invoice amount (column F); otherwise, display a blank cell.

7. Copy the Invoices worksheet, and then rename the copied worksheet as **Overdue Accounts**. In the Overdue Accounts worksheet, do the following:
   a. Filter the records so only invoices whose balance is past due are displayed. These are all records with an amount in 1–30 days (column I), 31–60 days (column J), 61–90 days (column K), or Over 90 days (column L).
   b. Sort the filtered data by invoice date (oldest first).
   c. Include a Total row in this table, and display sums for columns I through L.
   d. Hide columns D, E, F, G, and H.
   e. Remove the filter buttons and gridlines from the table. (*Hint*: Use options on View tab and the Table Tools Design tab.)

Troubleshoot 8. In the Invoice Reports worksheet, Laura used the COUNTIF function to count the number of invoices for each sales rep. The formulas she created display only zeros. Fix the formulas in the range B3:B6 so that they display the number of invoices processed by each sales rep.

9. In the Invoice Reports worksheet, complete the Sales Rep Analysis report. In the Commission and Total Amount columns (columns C and D), use the SUMIF function to summarize sales commissions (column E in the Aging table in the Invoices worksheet) and the invoice amount (column F in the Aging table) for each sales rep.
10. In the range B7:D7, enter a formula to calculate the totals. Format these columns appropriately.
11. In the Invoice Reports worksheet, complete the Accounts Receivable Aging report. In the Number of Invoices column, create formulas that count the number of invoices for each group in the Invoices worksheet. (*Hint*: A cell with a zero, not blank as specified in Step 6, will be counted).
12. In the Total Amount column, sum the total amounts for those invoices.
13. Save the workbook, and then close it.

CHALLENGE

Case Problem 3

Data File needed for this Case Problem: Rentals.xlsx

Barrett Furniture Rentals Barrett Furniture Rentals leases furniture by the room to corporations outfitting apartments for temporary stays as well as to homeowners and realtors for staging a house for sale. They offer a variety of grouping for living rooms, dining rooms, bedrooms, and game rooms. Elise Williams, the manager, maintains an Excel worksheet to track furniture rentals. She wants to know the number of rentals and the total rental income for July, August, and September. Elise also wants to know the total number of 6- and 12-month rentals along with the total income for each type of rental. Complete the following:

1. Open the **Rentals** workbook located in the Excel8 > Case3 folder included with your Data Files, and then save the workbook as **Furniture Rentals** in the location specified by your instructor.
2. In the Documentation worksheet, enter your name and the date. In the range A10:D22, review the data definition table. This table describes the different fields used in the Rental Data worksheet.
3. In the Rental Data worksheet, in column G, create a formula that uses the HLOOKUP function to assign a group code (A, B, C, D, or E) from the FurnitureGroups range in the Rental Information worksheet to the furniture listed in column B.
4. In column H, create a formula using the IF and VLOOKUP functions to calculate the rental charges for each set of furniture based on the furniture's group code, the rental period, and the Furniture Rental Charges table. (*Hint*: For the IF function arguments, use one VLOOKUP function for 3 months and another for 9 months. The defined name RentalCharges has been assigned to the Furniture Rental Charges table.)

5. In column I, enter a formula to calculate the insurance charge if the renter has elected insurance coverage (Yes in column E). Use the furniture's group code and the Monthly Insurance column in the RentalCharges table to look up the insurance charge. Remember to multiply the monthly insurance charge by the rental period. If the renter has not elected insurance, the cost is 0.
6. In column J, enter the formula with an IF function to determine the shipping charge for each set of furniture. Use the shipping code (column F) and the shipping charge options Pickup (0) and Truck ($50) to assign shipping costs to rental furniture.
7. In column K, enter a formula to calculate the total cost, which is the sum of the rental charges, the insurance cost, and the shipping cost.
8. Format columns H through K with the Accounting format with no decimal places.
9. In the Rental Report worksheet, complete the Rental Summary report by creating formulas in the range C4:D5 using the COUNTIF and SUMIF functions.
10. In the Rental Data worksheet, enter the following new record:
    - Renter: **Allen**
    - Furniture: **LR-3pc**
    - Rental Date: **9/15/2017**
    - Rental Period: **12**
    - Insurance: **Yes**
    - Shipping Code: **Truck**

Explore 11. Create a PivotTable to display the number of rentals and rental $ by rental month. Rename the worksheet as **Monthly Rentals**. (*Hint*: Select any Rental Date in the PivotTable, and then on the PivotTable Tools Analyze tab, in the Group group, click the Group Field button to open the Grouping dialog box. Use Months as the grouping field.)

12. Save the workbook, and then close it.

CREATE

Case Problem 4

Data File needed for this Case Problem: Athey.xlsx

Athey Department Store Athey Department Store in Fort Dodge, Iowa, has always accepted returns of any product purchased in its store. Mitchell Athey wants to develop a system for handling the returns. A routing slip will allow him to monitor who handled the return at each step. He will also be able to collect the returns data in a worksheet for count of returns in each category. Mitchell has started developing the routing slip, and he wants you to finish creating it. Complete the following:

1. Open the **Athey** workbook located in the Excel8 > Case4 folder included with your Data Files, and then save the workbook as **Athey Routing Slip** in the location specified by your instructor.
2. In the Documentation worksheet, enter your name and the date.
3. Create a defined name for the table on the Return Data worksheet to help you when you create formulas with VLOOKUP functions. (*Hint*: Use a name other than ReturnTbl because this name is already used as the defined name for the table on the Return Data worksheet.)
4. In the Return Routing worksheet, do the following:
    a. In cell B9, use a date function to display the current date.
    b. In cell B11, use an input message to inform the user to enter a product description in this cell.
    c. In cell B14, use a list validation for the Department located on the Return Data worksheet.
    d. In cell B16, use a list validation for the Resolution located on the Return Table worksheet (the range B1:E1).
    e. In cell B20, use an input message to inform the person entering the information to enter their name, initials, or Employee ID in this area.

5. In cell B18, create a formula using nested IF functions and VLOOKUP functions to determine what to do with the returns. Use the lookup table in the Return Data worksheet. Refer to Figure 8-46 for some hints on how to create the formula.

Figure 8-46 Formula for return resolution

If the value in B16 is:	The lookup_ value is:	The table_ array is:	The col_ index_num is:	The range_ lookup is:	Nested IF Function
Destroy	B14	Dept_Returns	2	FALSE	IF(B16="Destroy",VLOOKUP(B14, Dept_Returns,2,FALSE),
Return to Mfg	B14	Dept_Returns	3	FALSE	IF(B16="Return to Mfg",VLOOKUP (B14,Dept_Returns,3,FALSE),
Repack	B14	Dept_Returns	4	FALSE	IF(B16="Repack",VLOOKUP(B14, Dept_Returns,4,FALSE),
Restock	B14	Dept_Returns	5	FALSE	IF(B16="Restock",VLOOKUP(B14, Dept_Returns,5,FALSE),"None"))))

6. Test your routing slip by entering the following information:
   - Product Name: **Deluxe Vacuum**
   - Department: **Electronics**
   - Resolution: **Return to Mfg**
   - Customer Assistant: **01265**
7. Protect all cells in the Return Routing worksheet except those in which you enter data.
8. In the Return Analysis worksheet, complete the following analysis of the Return Data worksheet using COUNTIF:
   a. Compute the total Returns by Department.
   b. Compute the total Returns by Resolution.
9. Save the workbook, and then close it.

MODULE 9

Exploring Financial Tools and Functions

Analyzing a Business Plan

EXCEL

OBJECTIVES

Session 9.1
- Work with financial functions to analyze loans and investments
- Create an amortization schedule
- Calculate interest and principal payments for a loan or investment

Session 9.2
- Perform calculations for an income statement
- Interpolate and extrapolate a series of values
- Calculate a depreciation schedule

Session 9.3
- Determine a payback period
- Calculate a net present value
- Calculate an internal rate of return
- Trace a formula error to its source

Case | *QR Shopper*

Ryan Mitchell is the founder of QR Shopper, a new tech company in Rochester, New York, that is developing a smart grocery-shopping cart to simplify traditional methods of shopping and checking out. The QR Shopper Cart features a tablet and scanner that customers use to scan products directly from the shelf, freeing up time at checkout and taking instant advantage of coupons and specials offered by participating stores.

Ryan has lined up financial backing for the new product, but he still needs additional capital to launch the company. To obtain funding and attract investors, Ryan must present a business plan that details the financial challenges the company will face. The plan will include revenue and expense estimates for the company's first five years of business and estimates of the yearly cash flow and balances. Investors will also want to know what kind of return they will get from investing in this business. Ryan has created a workbook to analyze these financial issues and asks you to perform some of the financial calculations needed to complete the document.

STARTING DATA FILES

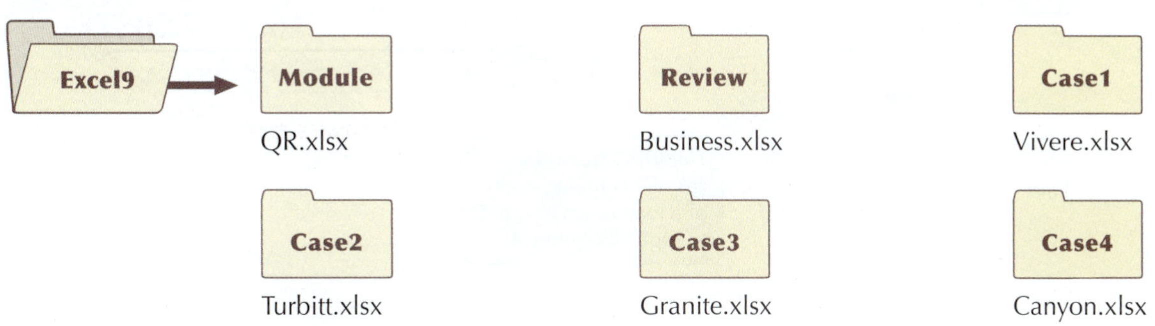

Session 9.1 Visual Overview:

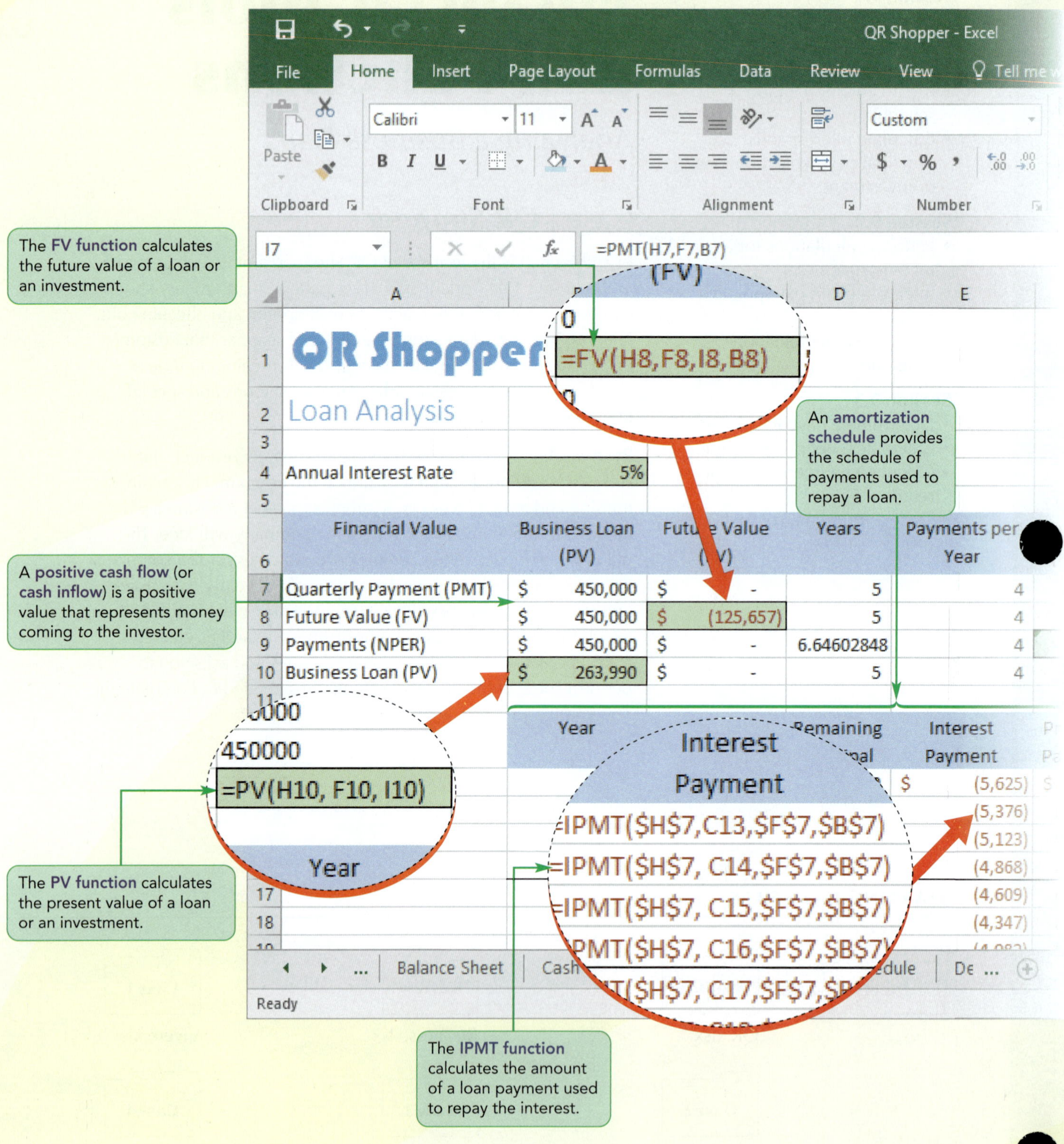

Loan and Investment Functions

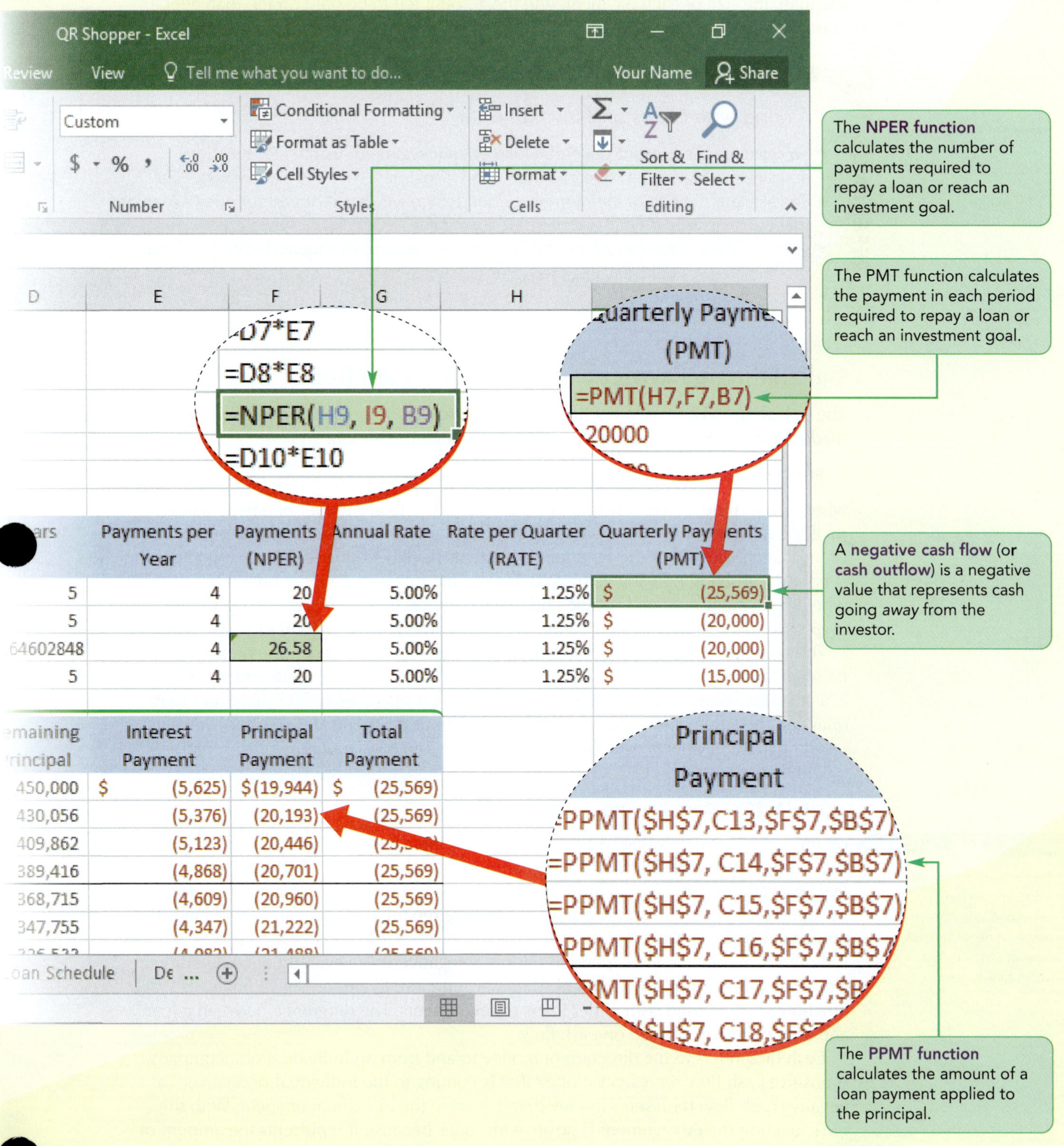

Calculating Borrowing Costs

Excel has a variety of functions related to finance and business. You'll start by exploring functions used to calculate costs associated with borrowing money. You can use these functions to determine the size of a loan, the number of payments needed to repay the loan, the size of each payment, and the amount left to be paid on the loan after a specified length of time has passed.

REFERENCE

Working with Loans and Investments

- To calculate the present value of a loan or an investment, use the PV function.
- To calculate the future value of a loan or an investment, use the FV function.
- To calculate the size of the monthly or quarterly payments required to repay a loan or meet an investment goal, use the PMT function.
- To calculate the number of monthly or quarterly payments required to repay a loan or meet an investment goal, use the NPER function.
- To calculate the interest on a loan or an investment, use the RATE function.

Calculating a Payment with the PMT Function

The following PMT or payment function is used to determine the size of payments made periodically to either repay a loan or reach an investment goal:

```
PMT(rate,nper,pv[,fv=0][,type=0])
```

where *rate* is the interest rate per period, *nper* is the total number of payment periods, *pv* is the present value of the loan or investment, and *fv* is the future value of the loan or investment after all of the scheduled payments have been made. The *fv* argument is optional and has a default value of 0. Finally, the optional *type* argument specifies whether payments are made at the end of each period (*type*=0) or at the beginning (*type*=1). The default is to assume that payments are made at the end of each period.

For example, if Ryan's company borrows $400,000 at 5 percent annual interest to be repaid quarterly over a five-year period, the value of the *rate* argument would be 5%/4, or 1.25 percent, because the 5 percent annual interest rate is divided into four quarters. The value of the *nper* argument is 4×5 (four payments per year for five years), resulting in 20 payments over the five-year period. The PMT function for this loan would be entered as

```
PMT(1.25%, 20, 400000)
```

TIP

The financial functions automatically format calculated values as currency; negative cash flows appear in a red font within parentheses.

returning the negative value –$22,728.16, which indicates that the company would have to pay more than $22,700 each quarter to entirely repay the $400,000 loan in five years at 5 percent annual interest. Note that a default value of 0 is assumed for the *fv* argument because the loan will be completely repaid, which means it will have a future value of 0.

In this example, the PMT function returns a negative value even though you entered a positive value for the *pv* argument. The PMT function, like many Excel financial functions, can be used with either loans or investments. The difference between a loan and an investment is based on cash flow.

Cash flow refers to the direction of money to and from an individual or a company. A positive cash flow represents money that is coming to the individual or received; a negative cash flow represents money that is leaving the individual or spent. With the PMT function the *pv* argument is positive for loans because it represents the amount of money being borrowed (coming to the individual), and the function returns a negative value because it represents money being spent to repay the loan (going away from the individual). Conversely, the *pv* argument is negative when used with investments because it represents money that is invested (or spent), and the PMT function returns a positive value because it represents returns from the investment coming back to the individual. Cash flow, whether positive or negative, has nothing to do with who owns the money. When Ryan's company borrows money, that money still belongs to the lender even as it is being used to establish QR Shopper.

Ryan already has lined up some of the financial backing needed to start QR Shopper. The company also plans to take out a business loan of $450,000 to cover some of the costs for the first few years of business. Ryan wants to know what would be the quarterly payment on a $450,000 loan at 5 percent annual interest to be completely repaid in five years. A good practice is to enter the loan conditions into separate cells rather than including them in the PMT function. This makes the loan conditions visible and allows them to be easily changed for what-if analyses. You will enter the loan conditions in the workbook Ryan created, and then use the PMT function to calculate the quarterly payment.

To calculate a quarterly payment with the PMT function:

1. Open the **QR** workbook located in the **Excel9 > Module** folder included with your Data Files, and then save the workbook as **QR Shopper** in the location specified by your instructor.
2. In the Documentation worksheet, enter your name and the date.
3. Go to the **Loan Analysis** worksheet. Ryan has already entered and formatted much of the content in this worksheet.
4. In cell **B4**, enter **5%** as the annual interest rate of the loan.
5. In cell **B7**, enter **$450,000** as the amount of the business loan.
6. In cell **C7**, enter **0** for the future value of the loan because the loan will be completely repaid by the company.
7. In cell **D7**, enter **5** as the length of the loan in years.
8. In cell **E7**, enter **4** as the number of payments per year, which is quarterly.
9. In cell **F7**, enter the formula **=D7*E7** to calculate the total number of loan payments. In this case, four loan payments per year for five years is 20.
10. In cell **G7**, enter the formula **=$B$4** to display the annual interest rate specified in cell B4.
11. In cell **H7**, enter the formula **=G7/E7** to calculate the interest rate for each payment. In this case, the annual interest rate divided by quarterly payments returns 1.25% as the interest rate per quarter.
12. In cell **I7**, enter the formula **=PMT(H7,F7,B7)** to calculate the payment due each quarter based on the rate value in cell H7, the number of payments specified in cell F7, and the amount of the loan in cell B7. The formula returns ($25,569), a negative value that indicates the company will need to make payments of $25,569 each quarter to pay off the loan in five years. See Figure 9-1.

Be sure to use the interest rate for that payment period rather than the annual interest rate to apply the PMT function correctly.

Figure 9-1 Quarterly payment required to repay a loan

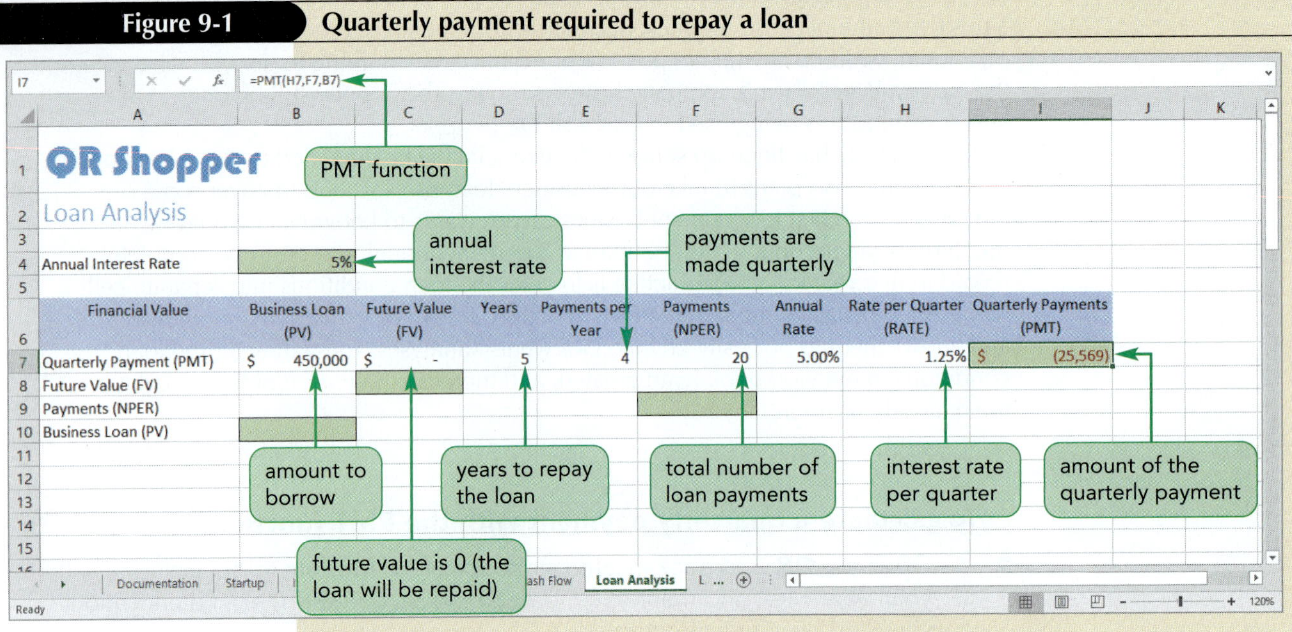

The $25,569 quarterly payments are higher than Ryan anticipated. He was hoping for quarterly payments closer to $20,000. He asks you to determine how much of the loan would be unpaid after five years with quarterly payments of $20,000. You can calculate the amount left on the loan using the FV function.

Calculating a Future Value with the FV Function

So far, you have used the default value of 0 for the future value because the intent was to repay the loan completely. However, when a loan will not be completely repaid, you use the FV function to calculate the loan's future value. The syntax of the FV function is

```
FV(rate,nper,pmt[,pv=0][,type=0])
```

where the `rate`, `nper`, `pmt`, and `type` arguments still represent the interest rate per period, the number of payments, the payment each period, and when the payment is due (beginning or end of the period). The `pv` argument is optional and represents the present value of the loan or investment, which is assumed to be 0 if no value is specified.

The FV function is often used with investments to calculate the future value of a series of payments. For example, if you deposit $100 per month in a new savings account that has a starting balance of $0 and pays 1 percent interest annually, the FV function to calculate the future value of that investment after 10 years or 120 months is

```
FV(1%/12, 10*12, -100)
```

which returns $12,614.99. The extra $614.99, the amount above the $12,000 you deposited, is the interest earned from the money during that 10-year period. Note that the payment value is –100 because it represents the monthly deposit (negative cash flow), and the value returned by the FV function is positive because it represents money returned to the investor (positive cash flow). The `pv` value in this example is assumed to be 0 because no money was in the savings account before the first deposit.

When used with a loan, a positive payment value is included as the present value of the loan. For example, if you borrow $1,200 at 4 percent annual interest and repay the loan at a rate of $100 per month, you would calculate the amount remaining on the loan after one year or 12 months using the function

```
FV(4%/12, 12, -100, 1200)
```

which returns ($26.64), a negative value indicating that you still owe $26.64 on the loan.

Ryan wants to know how much the company would still owe after five years if the quarterly payments were $20,000. You will use the FV function to calculate this future value.

To calculate the future value of the loan:

1. In cell **B8**, enter **$450,000** as the size of the loan.
2. Copy the values and formulas from the range **D7:H7** to the range **D8:H8**.
3. In cell **I8**, enter **–$20,000** as the size of the quarterly payments. Again, the value is negative because it represents money that the company will spend (negative cash flow).
4. In cell **C8**, enter the formula **=FV(H8, F8, I8, B8)** to calculate the future value of the loan based on the rate value in cell H8, the number of payments specified in cell F8, the quarterly payments specified in cell I8, and the present value of the loan entered in cell B8. The formula returns ($125,657), a negative value that indicates the company will still owe the lender more than $125,000 at the end of the five-year period. See Figure 9-2.

Figure 9-2 Future value of a loan

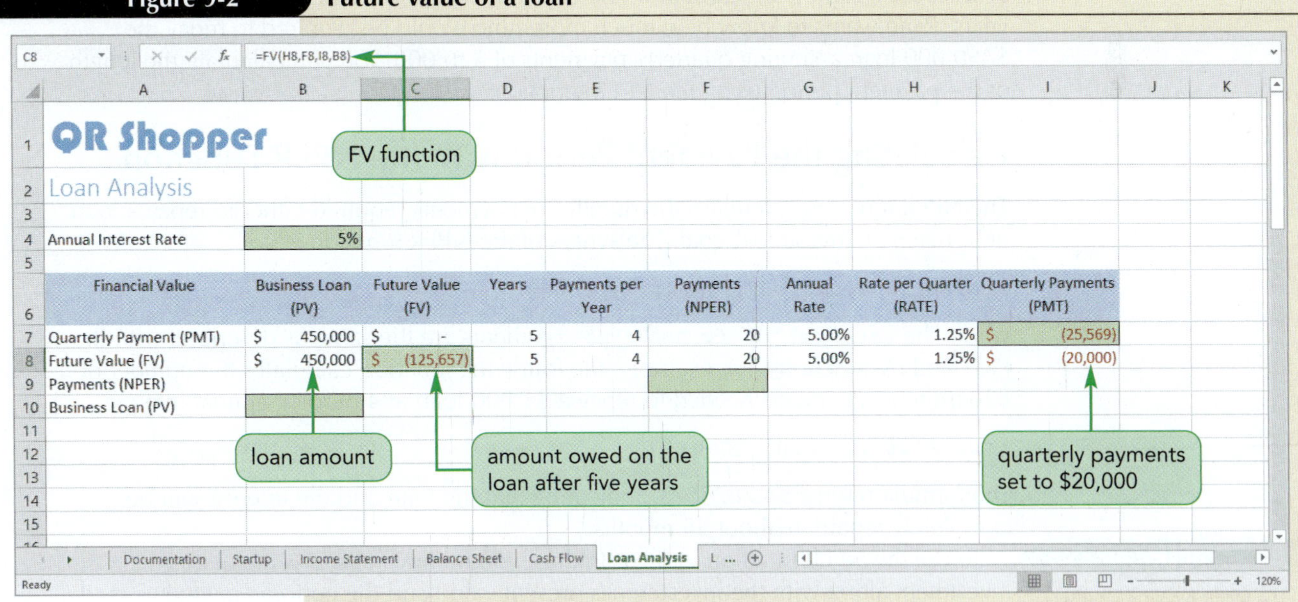

At 5 percent annual interest, more than one-fourth of the original $450,000 loan will still need to be repaid at the end of five years if the quarterly payments are limited to $20,000.

INSIGHT

Calculating Inflation with the FV Function

You can use the FV function to calculate future costs, adjusting for the effects of inflation. To project a future value of an item, use

```
FV(rate,years,0,present)
```

where `rate` is the annual inflation rate, `years` is the number of years in the future for which you want to project the cost of the item, and `present` is the present-day cost. For example, if an item currently costs $15,000 and the inflation rate is 2.3 percent, the cost of the item in eight years is calculated using

```
FV(2.3%, 8, 0, 15000)
```

which returns –$17,992.70. The negative value is based on how Excel handles the FV function with positive and negative cash flows. For the purposes of predicting an inflated value, you can ignore the minus sign and use a value of $17,992.70 as the future cost of the item. Notice that you enter 0 for the value of the `pmt` argument because you are not making payments toward inflation.

The FV function can also be used to express today's dollars in terms of yesterday's dollars by entering a negative value for the `years` value. For example, the following function uses a value of –8 for years

```
FV(2.3%, -8, 0, 15000)
```

returning the value –$12,505.07, indicating that at an annual inflation rate of 2.3 percent, $15,000 today is equivalent to about $12,500 eight years ago.

Because a significant amount of the original loan would still be unpaid after five years, Ryan wants to know how much more time would be required to repay the $450,000 loan assuming quarterly payments of $20,000. You can calculate the length of the payment period using the NPER function.

Calculating the Payment Period with the NPER Function

The NPER function calculates the number of payments required either to repay a loan or to reach an investment goal. The syntax of the NPER function is:

```
NPER(rate,pmt,pv[,fv=0][,type=0])
```

where the `rate`, `pmt`, `pv`, `fv`, and `type` arguments are the same as described with the PMT and FV functions. For example, the following function calculates the number of $20 monthly payments needed to repay a $1,000 loan at 4 percent annual interest:

```
NPER(4%/12, -20, 1000)
```

The formula returns 54.7875773, indicating that the loan and the interest will be completely repaid in about 55 months.

TIP

The NPER function returns the number of payments, not necessarily the number of years.

To use the NPER function for investments, you define a future value of the investment along with the investment's present value and the periodic payments made to the investment. If you placed $200 per month in an account that pays 3 percent interest compounded monthly, the following function calculates the number of payments required to reach $5,000:

```
NPER(3%/12, -200, 0, 5000)
```

The formula returns 24.28, which is just over two years. Note that the `pv` value is set to 0 based on the assumption that no money was in the account before the first deposit.

You will use the NPER function to calculate how long it will take to repay a $450,000 loan at 5 percent interest with quarterly payments of $20,000.

To calculate the number of payments for the loan:

1. Copy the present and future values of the loan in the range **B7:C7** to the range **B9:C9**.
2. In cell **E9**, enter **4** to specify that payments are made quarterly.
3. Copy the annual interest rate, rate per quarter, and size of the quarterly payments values and formulas in the range **G8:I8** to the range **G9:I9**.
4. In cell **F9**, enter the formula **=NPER(H9, I9, B9)** to calculate the required number of payments based on the interest rate per quarter in cell H9, the quarterly payments value in cell I9, and the present value of the loan in cell B9. The formula returns 26.58, indicating that about 27 payments are required to fully repay the loan.
5. In cell **D9**, enter the formula **=F9/E9** to divide the total number of payments by the number of payments per year, which determines the number of years needed to repay the loan. The formula returns 6.646028, indicating that the loan will be repaid in a little more than six and half years.
6. Select cell **F9**. See Figure 9-3.

TIP

If the NPER function returns #NUM!, the loan cannot be repaid because the payments for each period are less than the interest due.

Figure 9-3 Payments required to repay a loan

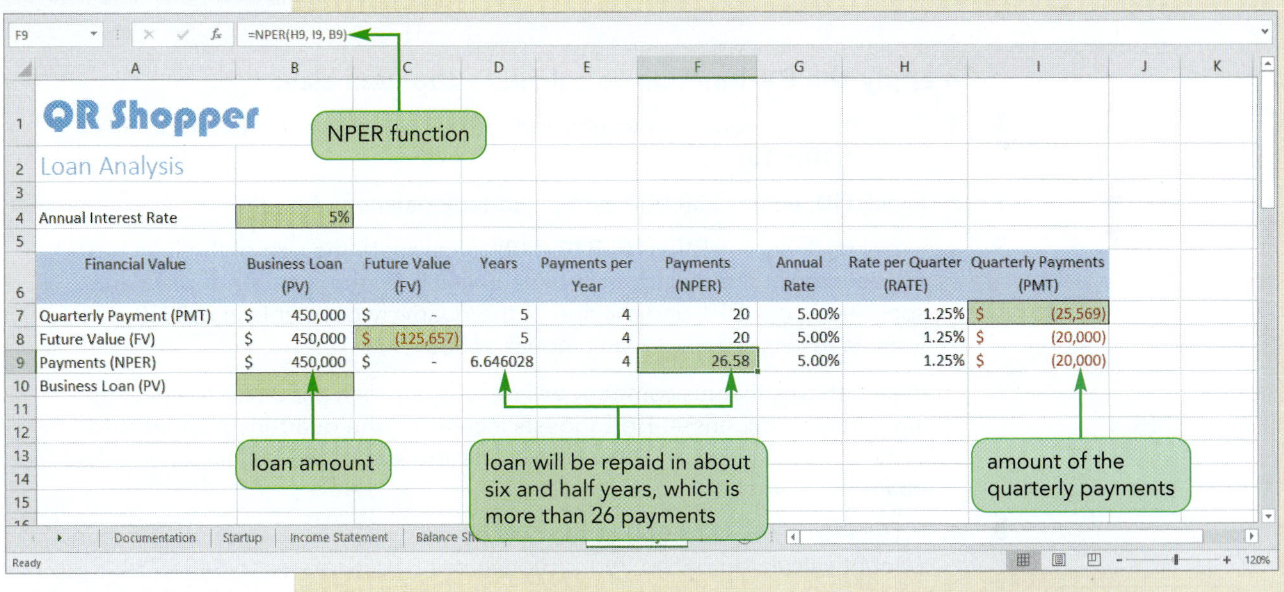

Ryan doesn't want to take more than six years to repay a business loan. He suggests that you calculate the size of the loan that could be repaid within five years at $20,000 per quarter.

Calculating the Present Value with the PV Function

The PV function calculates the present value of a loan or an investment. For a loan, the present value would be the current size of the loan. For an investment, the present value is the amount of money initially placed in the investment account. The syntax of the PV function is

```
PV(rate,nper,pmt[,fv=0][,type=0])
```

where the `rate`, `nper`, `pmt`, `fv`, and `type` arguments have the same meanings they had for the other financial functions.

You can use the PV function to calculate the loan amount that you can afford given a set number of payments and an annual interest rate. For example, if you make $100 monthly payments at 4 percent annual interest for four years (or 48 months), the function to calculate the largest loan you can afford is

```
PV(4%/12, 48, -100)
```

which returns $4,428.88. Note that because you are paying $100 per month for 48 months, the total amount paid back to the lender is $4,800. The $371.12 difference between the total amount paid and the loan amount represents the cost of the loan in terms of the total amount of interest paid.

With investments, the PV function calculates the initial investment amount required to reach a savings goal. For example, if you add $100 per month to a college savings account that grows at 4 percent annual interest and you want the account to reach a future value of $25,000 in 10 years (or 120 months), the following function returns the size of the initial investment:

```
PV(4%/12, 120, -100, 25000)
```

The function returns –$6,892.13, indicating you must start with almost $6,900 in the account to reach the $25,000 savings goal at the end of 10 years.

You will use the PV function to determine the largest loan that Ryan's company can afford given $20,000 quarterly payments made over a five-year period at 5% annual interest.

To apply the PV function to calculate the loan size:

1. Copy the loan condition values and formulas in the range **C7:H7** to the range **C10:H10**.
2. In cell **I10**, enter **–$20,000** as the quarterly payment amount.
3. In cell **B10**, enter **=PV(H10, F10, I10)** to calculate the size of the loan based on the interest rate per quarter value in cell H10, the number of payments specified in cell F10, and the size of the quarterly payments in cell I10. The formula results specify a loan amount of $351,986.

   Ryan believes that his company will need more than $350,000 to cover its initial startup expenses. He suggests increasing the quarterly payments to $23,000 over five years. You will calculate the size of the loan assuming that quarterly payment.
4. In cell **I10**, enter **–$23,000** as the new quarterly payment amount. The loan amount calculated by the PV function in cell B10 increases to $404,784. Ryan believes this amount will be sufficient if he can find additional funding from other sources.
5. Select cell **B10**. See Figure 9-4.

Figure 9-4 Present value of a loan

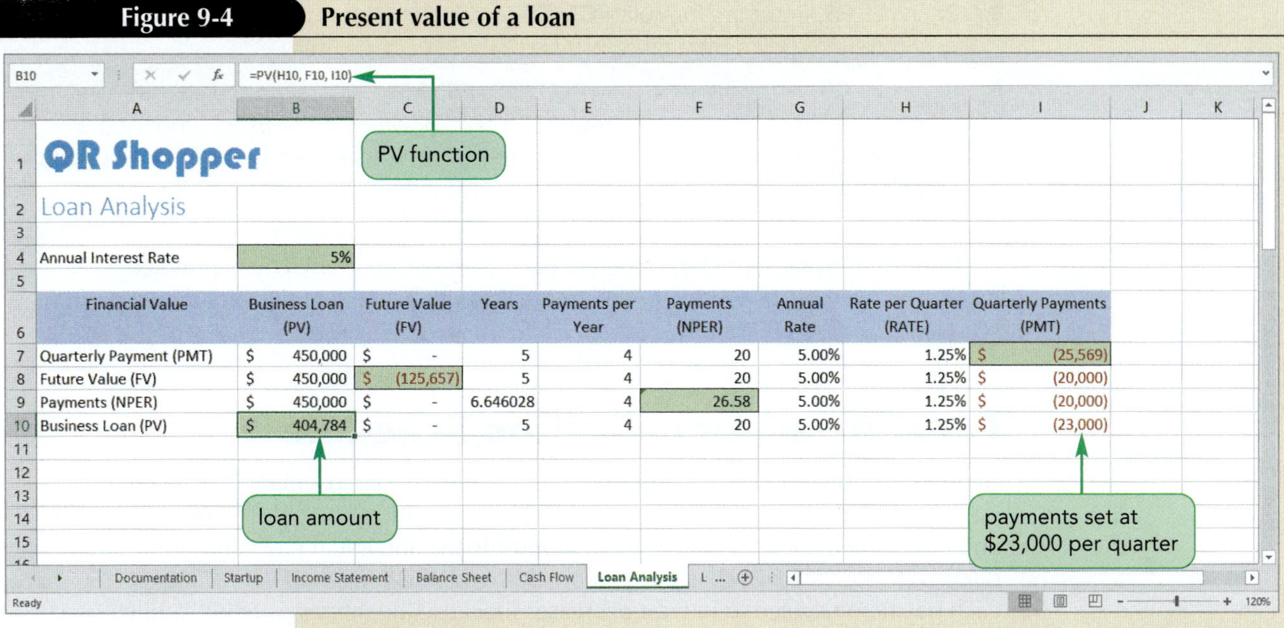

Ryan has settled on a loan amount of $400,000 to be repaid at 5 percent interest in quarterly payments over the first five years of the company's operation. You will enter this loan amount in the Startup worksheet, which Ryan created to detail the company's startup costs and assets.

To enter the loan amount:

1. Go to the **Startup** worksheet.
2. In cell **B26**, enter **400,000** as the loan amount.
3. Explore the rest of the Startup worksheet, noting the expenses and assets for starting up the company as well as other sources of funding.

Ryan wants you to provide more detailed information about the proposed business loan in the Loan Schedule worksheet. You'll start by entering the terms of the loan and calculate the exact value of each loan payment.

To calculate the size of the loan payments:

1. Go to the **Loan Schedule** worksheet.
2. Select cell **A5**, type **=** to begin the formula, go to the Startup worksheet, click cell **B26**, and then press the **Tab** key. The formula **=Startup!B26** entered in cell A5 displays the loan amount of $400,000 from cell B26 in the Startup worksheet.
3. In cell **B5**, enter **5.00%** as the annual interest rate.
4. In cell **C5**, enter **4** as the number of payments per year because Ryan plans to make quarterly payments.
5. In cell **D5**, enter the formula **=B5/C5** to calculate the interest rate per quarter. The formula returns 1.25% as the interest rate.
6. In cell **E5**, enter **5** to indicate that the loan will be repaid in five years.

7. In cell **F5**, enter the formula **=C5*E5** to calculate the total number of payments, which is 20 payments in this instance.
8. In cell **G5**, enter the formula **=PMT(D5, F5, A5)** to calculate the size of each payment. The formula returns –$22,728, which is the exact amount the company will have to spend per quarter to completely repay the $400,000 loan in five years.

Ryan wants to examine how much of each $22,728 quarterly payment is spent on interest charged by the lender. To determine that value, you'll create an amortization schedule.

Creating an Amortization Schedule

An amortization schedule specifies how much of each loan payment is devoted to paying interest and how much is devoted to repaying the principal. The principal is the amount of the loan that is still unpaid. In most loans, the initial payments are usually directed toward interest charges. As more of the loan is repaid, the percentage of each payment devoted to interest decreases (because the interest is being applied to a smaller and smaller principal) until the last few payments are almost entirely devoted to repaying the principal. Figure 9-5 shows a typical relationship between the amount paid toward interest and the amount paid toward the principal plotted against the number of payments.

Figure 9-5 **Interest and principal payments**

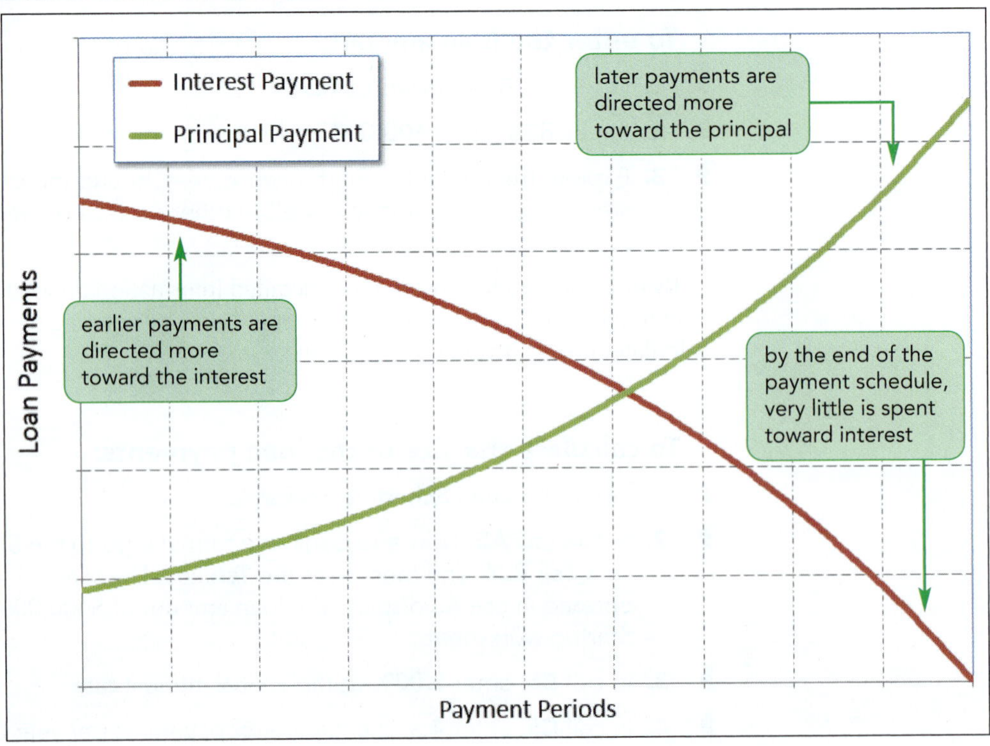

Calculating Interest and Principal Payments

To calculate the amount of a loan payment devoted to interest and to principal, you use the IPMT and PPMT functions. The IPMT function returns the amount of a particular payment that is used to pay the interest on the loan. It has the syntax

```
IPMT(rate,per,nper,pv[,fv=0][,type=0])
```

where the ***rate***, ***nper***, ***pv***, ***fv***, and ***type*** arguments have the same meaning as they do for the PMT and other financial functions. The ***per*** argument defines the period for which the interest is due. For example, the following function calculates how much interest is due in the third payment of the company's $400,000 loan at 5% interest paid quarterly over five years:

```
IPMT(5%/4, 3, 20, 400000)
```

The function returns –$4,554.03, indicating that the company will owe $4,554.03 in interest in the third payment.

The PPMT function calculates the amount used to repay the principal. The PPMT function has the following syntax, which is similar to the IPMT function:

```
PPMT(rate,per,nper,pv[,fv=0][,type=0])
```

The following function calculates the amount of the principal that is repaid with the third payment of the company loan:

```
PPMT(5%/4, 3, 20, 400000)
```

This function returns –$18,174.13. Note that the sum of the interest payment and the principal payment is –$22,728.16, which is the quarterly payment amount returned by the PMT function in cell G5 of the Loan Schedule worksheet. The total amount paid to the bank each quarter doesn't change—the only change is how that amount is allocated between interest and principal.

Ryan asks you to create an amortization schedule for QR Shopper's loan. You'll use the IPMT and PPMT functions to do this. The Loan Schedule worksheet already contains the table in which you'll enter the formulas to track the changing amounts spent on principal and interest over the next five years.

TIP

Use absolute references for the loan conditions so the same values apply to every payment period when you copy the formulas to the rest of the amortization schedule.

To create the amortization schedule for the company's loan:

1. In cell **C9**, enter the formula **=A5** to display the initial principal of the loan.
2. In cell **D9**, enter the formula **=IPMT($D$5, B9, $F$5, $A$5)** to calculate the interest due for the first payment, with $D$5, $F$5, and $A$5 referencing the loan conditions specified in row 5 of the worksheet, and cell B9 referencing the number of the period. The formula returns –$5,000, which is the amount of interest due in the first payment.
3. In cell **E9**, enter the formula **=PPMT($D$5, B9, $F$5, $A$5)** to calculate the portion of the payment applied to the principal in the first period. Excel returns the value –$17,728, which is the amount by which the principal on the loan is reduced after the first payment.
4. In cell **F9**, enter the formula **=D9+E9** to calculate the total payment for the first period of the loan. The formula returns –$22,728, matching the quarterly payment value in cell G5. See Figure 9-6.

Figure 9-6 Initial payment in the amortization schedule

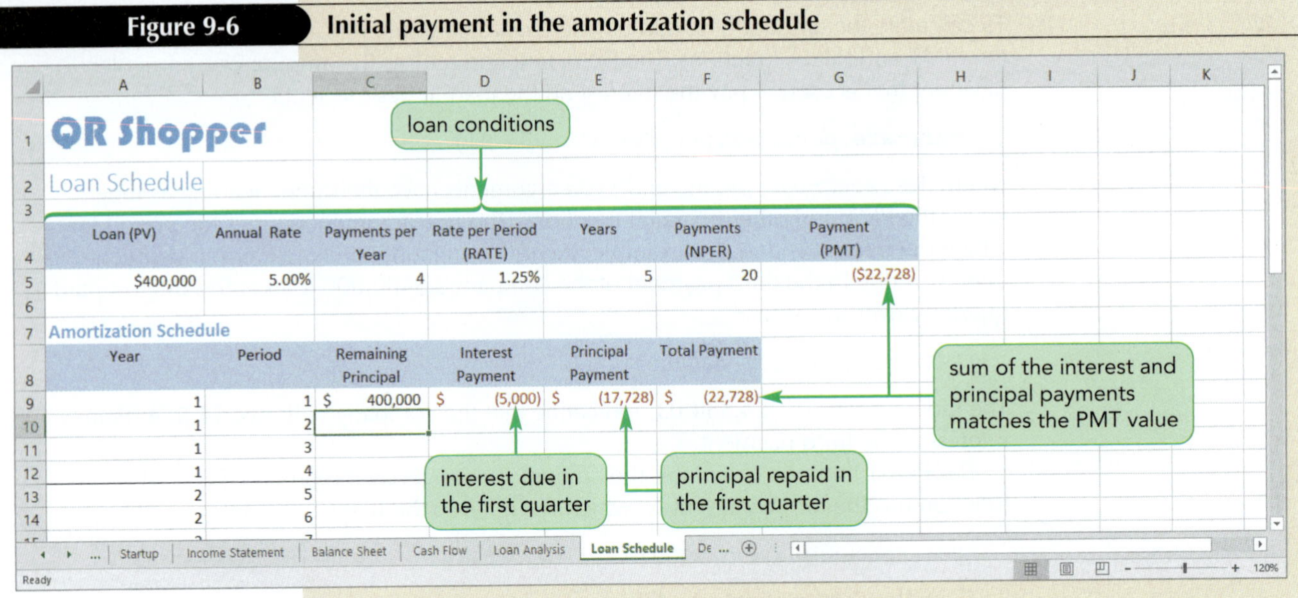

The formulas for the rest of the amortization schedule are similar to that for the first quarter except that the remaining principal in column C must be reduced by the amount paid toward the principal from the previous quarter.

To complete the amortization schedule:

1. In cell **C10**, enter the formula **=C9+E9** to add the remaining principal at the start of the first quarter to the first quarter principal payment. This calculates the principal remaining at the start of the second quarter of the loan, which is $382,272.
2. Copy the formulas in the range **D9:F9** to the range **D10:F10** to calculate the interest, principal, and total payment for the second quarter. The interest due is $4,778, the principal payment is $17,950, and the total payment remains $22,728. The interest due for the second quarter is less than for the first quarter because the remaining principal is lower. As a result, more of the total payment for this quarter is used to reduce the principal.
3. Use the fill handle to copy the formulas in the range **C10:F10** to the range **C11:F28**. The formulas are copied into the rest of the rows of the amortization schedule to calculate the remaining principal, interest payment, principal payment, and total payment for each of the remaining 18 quarters of the loan.
4. Click the **Auto Fill Options** button, and then click the **Fill Without Formatting** option button. The formulas are entered without overwriting the existing worksheet formatting. Notice that in the last quarterly payment at the end of the fifth year, only $281 of the $22,728 payment is used to pay the interest on the loan. The remaining $22,448 is used to repay the principal.
5. In cell **C29**, enter the formula **=C28+E28** to calculate the final balance of the loan after the final payment. The final balance is 0, verifying that the loan is completely repaid at the end of the five-year period. See Figure 9-7.

Figure 9-7 Completed amortization schedule

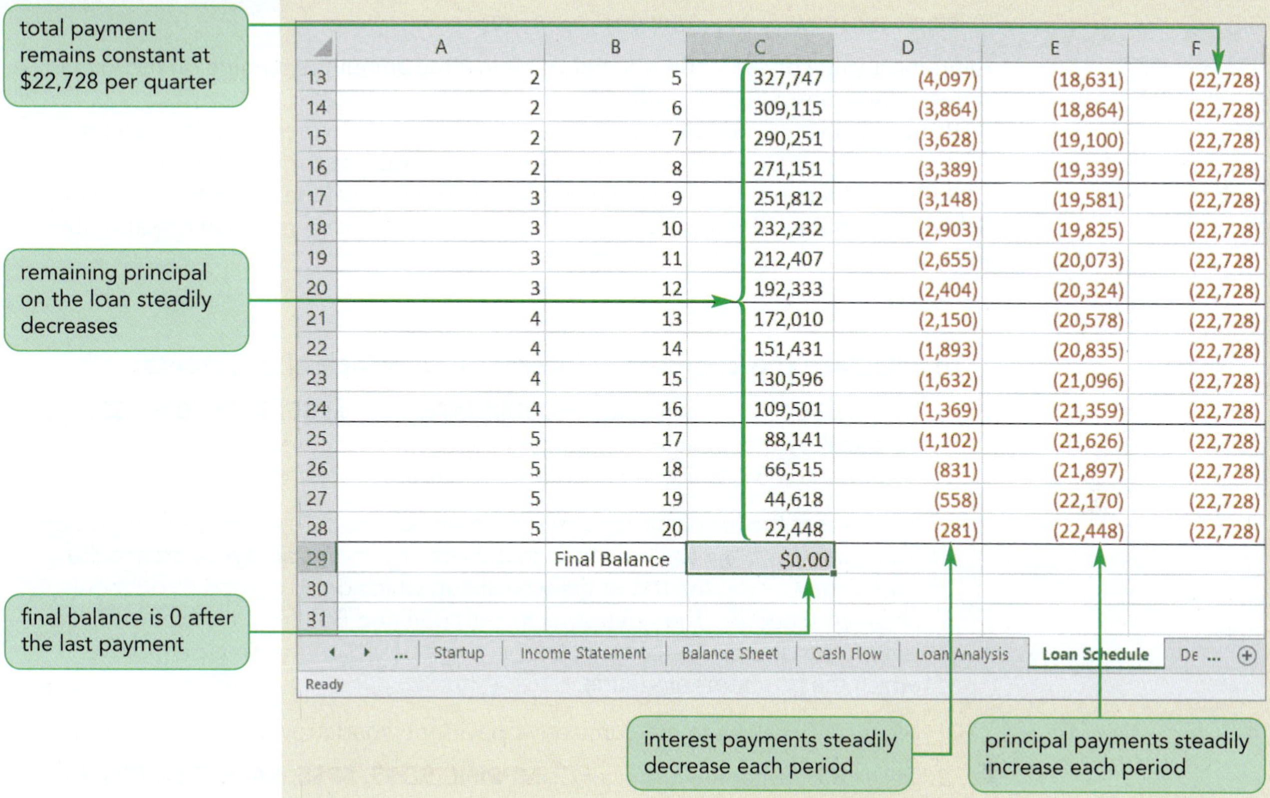

total payment remains constant at $22,728 per quarter

remaining principal on the loan steadily decreases

final balance is 0 after the last payment

	A	B	C	D	E	F
13	2	5	327,747	(4,097)	(18,631)	(22,728)
14	2	6	309,115	(3,864)	(18,864)	(22,728)
15	2	7	290,251	(3,628)	(19,100)	(22,728)
16	2	8	271,151	(3,389)	(19,339)	(22,728)
17	3	9	251,812	(3,148)	(19,581)	(22,728)
18	3	10	232,232	(2,903)	(19,825)	(22,728)
19	3	11	212,407	(2,655)	(20,073)	(22,728)
20	3	12	192,333	(2,404)	(20,324)	(22,728)
21	4	13	172,010	(2,150)	(20,578)	(22,728)
22	4	14	151,431	(1,893)	(20,835)	(22,728)
23	4	15	130,596	(1,632)	(21,096)	(22,728)
24	4	16	109,501	(1,369)	(21,359)	(22,728)
25	5	17	88,141	(1,102)	(21,626)	(22,728)
26	5	18	66,515	(831)	(21,897)	(22,728)
27	5	19	44,618	(558)	(22,170)	(22,728)
28	5	20	22,448	(281)	(22,448)	(22,728)
29		Final Balance	$0.00			
30						
31						

Startup | Income Statement | Balance Sheet | Cash Flow | Loan Analysis | Loan Schedule | De ...

Ready

interest payments steadily decrease each period

principal payments steadily increase each period

Ryan finds it helpful to see how much interest the company is paying each quarter. However, many financial statements also show the amount paid toward interest and principal over the whole year. This information is used when creating annual budgets and calculating taxes.

Calculating Cumulative Interest and Principal Payments

Cumulative totals of interest and principal payments can be calculated using the CUMIPMT and CUMPRINC functions. The CUMIPMT function calculates the sum of several interest payments and has the syntax

```
CUMIPMT(rate,nper,pv,start,end,type)
```

where `start` is the starting payment period for the interval you want to sum and `end` is the ending payment period. This function has no `fv` argument; the assumption is that loans are always completely repaid. Also, note that the `type` argument is not optional. You must specify whether the payments are made at the start of the period (`type`=0) or at the end (`type`=1). For example, to calculate the total interest paid in the second year of the company's loan (quarters 5 through 8), you would enter the function

```
CUMIPMT(5%/4, 20, 400000, 5, 8, 0)
```

which returns –14,978.30 as the total spent on interest in the second year of the loan. To calculate the cumulative total of payments made toward the principal, you use the CUMPRINC function, which has a similar syntax:

```
CUMPRINC(rate,nper,pv,start,end,type)
```

with the *rate*, *nper*, *pv*, *start*, *end*, and *type* arguments having the same meaning as they do for the CUMIPMT function. Thus the following function calculates the total amount spent on reducing the principal of the loan during the 5th to 8th quarters

```
CUMPRINC(7%/4, 20, 300000, 5, 8, 0)
```

returning a value of –$55,708.87, indicating that the amount remaining on the loan is reduced by almost $76,000 during the second year.

Ryan wants you to add the total interest and principal payments for the loan for each of the five years in the amortization schedule. You'll use the CUMIPMT and CUMPRINC functions to calculate these values. The table at the bottom of the Loan Schedule worksheet already has the starting and ending quarters for each year of the loan, which you'll reference in the functions.

To calculate the cumulative interest and principal payments:

1. In cell **B36**, enter the formula **=CUMIPMT($D$5, $F$5, $A$5, B34, B35, 0)** to calculate the cumulative interest payments for the first year. The formula returns –18,659, which is the amount spent on interest the first year.

   Notice that the formula uses absolute references to cells D5, F5, and A5 for the *rate*, *nper*, and *pv* arguments so that these arguments always reference the loan conditions at the top of the worksheet, which don't change throughout the loan schedule. The references to cells B34 and B35 for the *start* and *end* arguments are relative because they change based on the time period over which the payments are made.

   Next you'll calculate the cumulative payments made toward the principal.

2. In cell **B37**, enter the formula **=CUMPRINC($D$5, $F$5, $A$5, B34, B35, 0)** to calculate the principal payments in the first year. The formula returns –$72,253, which is the amount by which the principal will be reduced the first year.

3. Copy the formulas in the range **B36:B37** to the range **C36:F37** to calculate the cumulative interest and principal payments for each of the next four years. Each year, more money is spent reducing the principal. For example, in Year 5, the company will spend $2,772 on interest payments and will reduce the principal by $88,141. See Figure 9-8.

Figure 9-8 Annual cumulative interest and principal payments

C36: =CUMIPMT($D$5,$F$5,$A$5,C34,C35,0) ← CUMIPMT function

	A		B	C	D	E	F
32	Cumulative Interest and Principal Payments per Year						
33			Year 1	Year 2	Year 3		
34		Quarters	1	5	9	13	17
35			4	8	12	16	20
36	Interest		($18,659)	($14,978)	($11,110)	($7,044)	($2,772)
37	Principal		($72,253)	($75,934)	($79,803)	($83,868)	($88,141)
38	Principal Remaining						
39							
40							

cumulative interest payments for Year 1 through Year 5

cumulative principal payments for Year 1 through Year 5

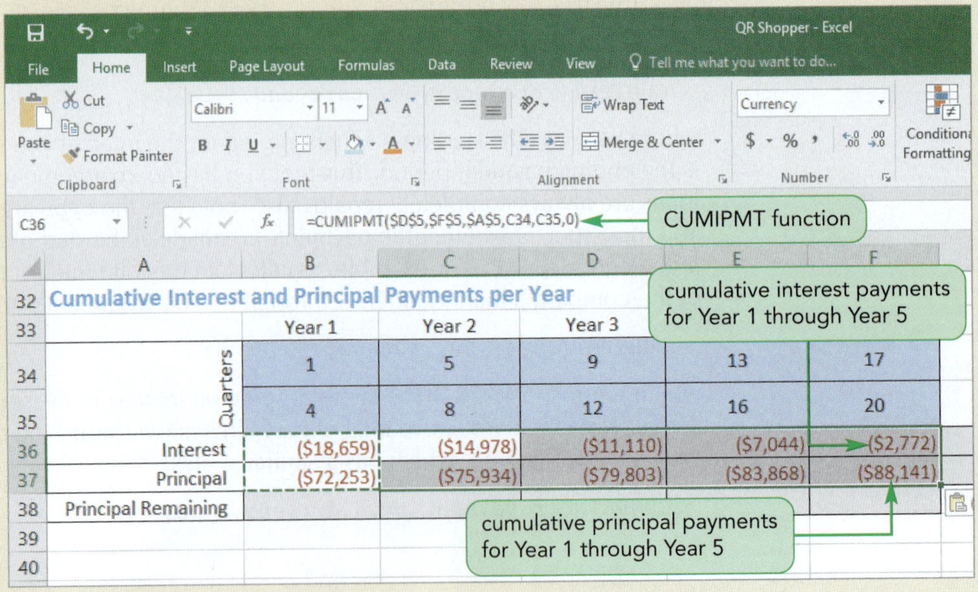

Next you will calculate the total paid on interest and principal through the five years of the loan and the principal remaining at the end of each year.

To complete the cumulative payment table:

1. Select the range **G36:G37**.
2. On the Home tab, in the Editing group, click the **AutoSum** button to calculate the total interest and principal payments over the five years of the loan, which are $54,563 and $400,000, respectively.

   Finally, you will calculate the principal remaining at the end of each year.
3. In cell **B38**, enter the formula **=$A$5+B37** to add the cumulative principal payment to the initial amount of the loan in cell A5. The formula returns $327,747, which is the amount of the loan remaining to be paid after the first year.
4. In cell **C38**, enter the formula **=B38+C37** to calculate the remaining principal at the end of Year 2 by adding the Year 1 principal to the Year 2 principal payments. The formula returns $251,812.
5. Copy the formula in cell **C38** to the range **D38:F38**, calculating the remaining principal at the end of each of the next three years. Note that at end of the fifth year, the principal remaining is zero since the entire loan is paid off.
6. Select cell **A31** to deselect the table. Figure 9-9 shows the final table of cumulative interest and principal payments.

Figure 9-9 Total loan payments

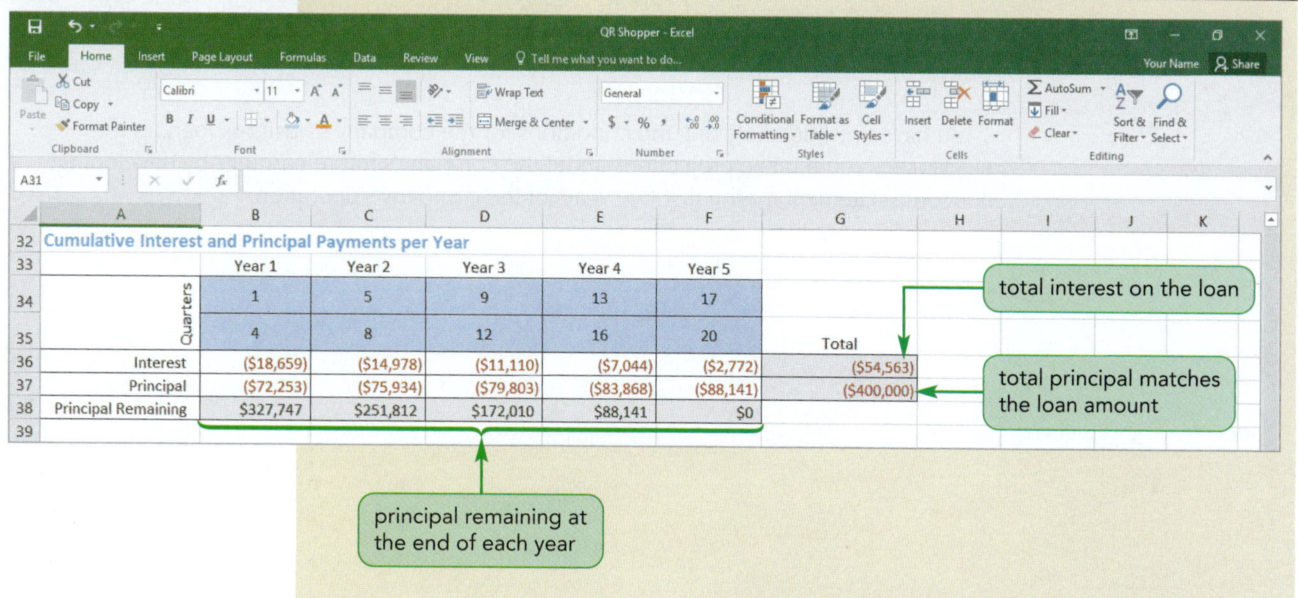

The Loan Schedule worksheet shows that the company will spend almost $55,000 in interest payments to finance this loan. Calculating the total principal payment lets you verify that the loan conditions are set up correctly. If the total payment on the principal does not match the initial amount of the loan, there must be a mistake in the calculations used in the loan schedule.

Written Communication: Writing a Financial Workbook

The goal of all writing is communication. A properly written financial workbook should be simple for others to read and understand. It should also be easily edited to allow exploration of what-if scenarios needed to analyze the impact of different financial conditions on the bottom line. To help ensure that any financial workbook you create meets these goals, keep in mind the following principles:

- Place all important financial variables at or near the top of a worksheet so that they can be easily read by others. For example, place the interest rate you use in calculations in a well-labeled worksheet cell.
- Use defined names with the financial variables to make it easier to apply them in formulas and functions.
- Clearly identify the direction of the cash flow in all of your financial calculations. Most Excel financial functions require a particular direction to the cash flow to return the correct value. Using the wrong sign will turn the calculation of a loan payment into an investment deposit or vice versa.
- Place argument values in worksheet cells where they can be viewed and easily changed. Never place these values directly into a financial formula.
- When values are used in more than one calculation, enter them in a cell that you can reference in all formulas rather than repeating the same value throughout the workbook.
- Use the same unit of time for all the arguments in a financial function. For example, when using the PMT function to calculate monthly loan payments, the interest rate and the number of payments should be based on the interest rate per month and the total months to repay the loan.

A financial workbook that is easy to read and understand is more useful to yourself and others when making business decisions.

You have finished analyzing the conditions for the company's business loan. In the next session, you'll make projections about the company's future earnings by developing an income statement for the first five years of the company's operation.

REVIEW

Session 9.1 Quick Check

1. Explain the difference between positive and negative cash flow. If you borrow $20,000 from a bank, is that a positive or negative cash flow? Justify your answer.
2. What is the formula to calculate how much a savings account would be worth if the initial balance is $1000 with monthly deposits of $75 for 10 years at 4.3 percent annual interest compounded monthly? What is the formula result?
3. You want a savings account to grow from $1,000 to $5,000 within two years. Assume the bank provides a 3.2 percent annual interest rate compounded monthly. What is the formula to calculate how much you must deposit each month to meet your savings goal? What is the formula result?
4. You want to take out a loan for $250,000 at 4.8 percent interest compounded monthly. If you can afford to make monthly payments of only $1,500 on the loan, what is the formula to calculate the number of months required to repay the loan completely? What is the formula result?
5. Rerun your calculations from Question 4 assuming that you can afford only a $1,000 monthly payment. What are the revised formula and resulting value? How do you explain the result?
6. You take out a 10-year loan for $250,000 at 5.3 percent interest compounded monthly. What is the formula to calculate the monthly payment and the resulting value?
7. For the loan conditions specified in Question 6, provide formulas to calculate the amount of the first payment used for interest and the amount of the first payment used to repay the principal. What are the resulting values?
8. For the loan conditions specified in Question 6, what are the formulas to calculate how much interest you will pay in the first year and how much you will repay toward the principal? What are the resulting values?
9. For the loan conditions in Question 6, calculate the total cost of the loan in terms of the total interest paid through the 10 years of the loan.

Session 9.2 Visual Overview:

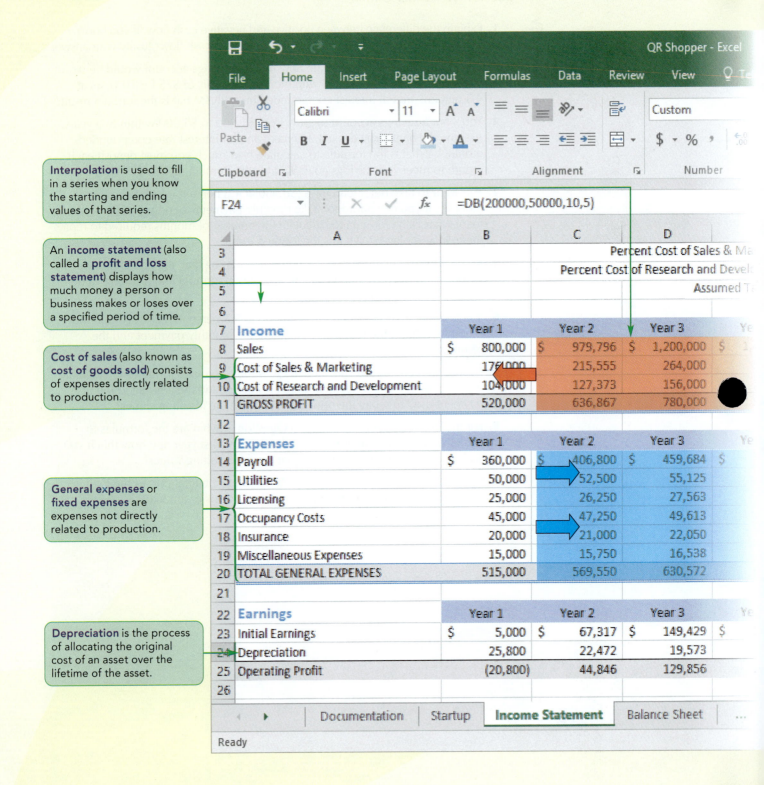

Interpolation is used to fill in a series when you know the starting and ending values of that series.

An **income statement** (also called a **profit and loss statement**) displays how much money a person or business makes or loses over a specified period of time.

Cost of sales (also known as **cost of goods sold**) consists of expenses directly related to production.

General expenses or **fixed expenses** are expenses not directly related to production.

Depreciation is the process of allocating the original cost of an asset over the lifetime of the asset.

QR Shopper - Excel

File | Home | Insert | Page Layout | Formulas | Data | Review | View

Paste | Clipboard | Calibri | 11 | Font | Alignment | Custom | Number

F24 =DB(200000,50000,10,5)

	A	B	C	D
3			Percent Cost of Sales & Ma	
4			Percent Cost of Research and Devel	
5			Assumed T	
6				
7	**Income**	Year 1	Year 2	Year 3
8	Sales	$ 800,000	$ 979,796	$ 1,200,000
9	Cost of Sales & Marketing	176,000	215,555	264,000
10	Cost of Research and Development	104,000	127,373	156,000
11	GROSS PROFIT	520,000	636,867	780,000
12				
13	**Expenses**	Year 1	Year 2	Year 3
14	Payroll	$ 360,000	$ 406,800	$ 459,684
15	Utilities	50,000	52,500	55,125
16	Licensing	25,000	26,250	27,563
17	Occupancy Costs	45,000	47,250	49,613
18	Insurance	20,000	21,000	22,050
19	Miscellaneous Expenses	15,000	15,750	16,538
20	TOTAL GENERAL EXPENSES	515,000	569,550	630,572
21				
22	**Earnings**	Year 1	Year 2	Year 3
23	Initial Earnings	$ 5,000	$ 67,317	$ 149,429
24	Depreciation	25,800	22,472	19,573
25	Operating Profit	(20,800)	44,846	129,856
26				

Documentation | Startup | Income Statement | Balance Sheet | ...

Ready

Income Statement and Depreciation

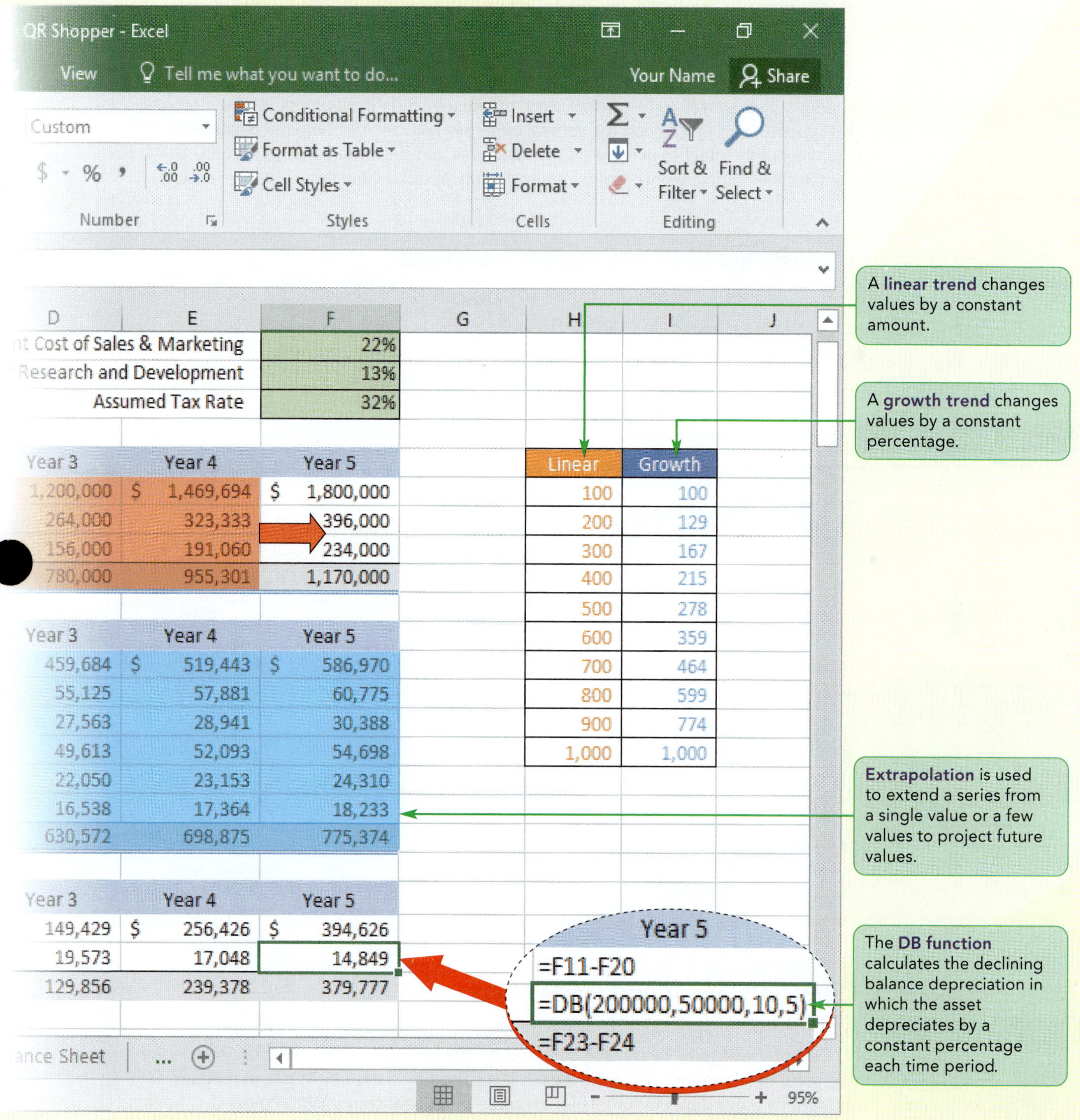

Projecting Future Income and Expenses

A key part of any business plan is a projection of the company's future income and expenses in an income, or profit and loss, statement. Income statements are usually created monthly, semiannually, or annually.

Ryan created the Income Statement worksheet to project the QR Shopper's income and expenses for its first five years of operation. The income statement is divided into three main sections. The Income section projects the company's income from sales of its cart scanner tablets as well as the cost of sales, marketing, and development for those tablets. The Expenses section projects the general expenses incurred by company operations regardless of the number of tablets it manufactures and sells. The Earnings section estimates the company's net profit and tax liability. You'll review this worksheet now.

To view the Income Statement worksheet:

1. If you took a break after the previous session, make sure the QR Shopper workbook is open.
2. Go to the **Income Statement** worksheet, and review the three main sections—Income, Expenses, and Earnings. See Figure 9-10.

Figure 9-10 Income Statement worksheet

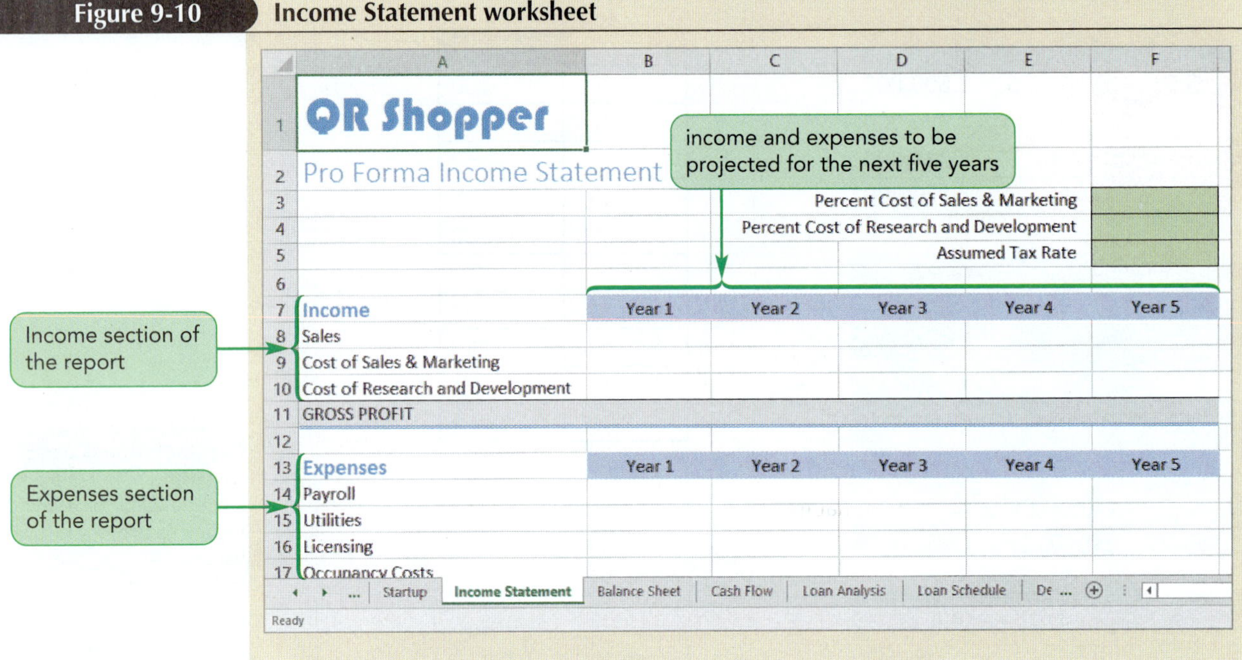

Exploring Linear and Growth Trends

TIP

A growth trend is also called exponential growth in the fields of science, economics, and statistics.

Ryan foresees two possibilities for the company's income in its first five years: (1) Revenue will grow by a constant amount from one year to the next, or (2) revenue will grow by a constant percentage each year. The first scenario, in which revenue changes by a constant amount, is an example of a linear trend. When plotted, a linear trend appears as a straight line. The second possibility, in which revenue changes by a constant percentage rather than a constant amount, is an example of a growth trend. For example, each value in a growth trend might be 15 percent higher than the previous year's value. When plotted, a growth trend appears as a curve with the greatest increases occurring near the end of the series.

Figure 9-11 shows a linear trend and a growth trend for revenue that starts at $800,000 in Year 1 increasing to $1,800,000 by Year 5. The growth trend lags behind the linear trend in the early stages but reaches the same revenue value at the end of the time period.

Figure 9-11 **Linear and growth trends**

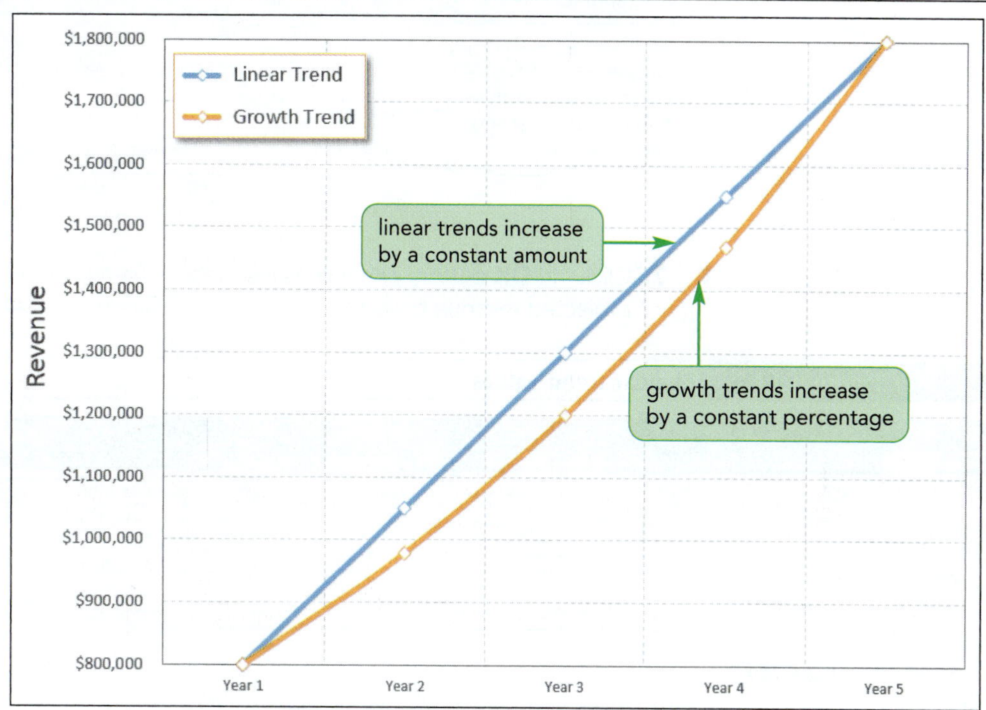

Interpolating from a Starting Value to an Ending Value

Interpolation is the process that estimates values that fall between a starting point and an ending point. You can use AutoFill to interpolate values for both linear and growth trends. Ryan wants you to estimate revenues for the first five years of QR Shopper. He projects that the company's revenue will grow from $800,000 in Year 1 to $1,800,000 in Year 5. He first wants to determine how much revenue will be generated if it grows by a constant amount each year. You'll interpolate the company's revenue for Year 2 through Year 4 using a linear trend.

To project future revenue based on a linear trend:

1. In cell **B8**, enter **$800,000** as the Year 1 revenue.
2. In cell **F8**, enter **$1,800,000** as the Year 5 revenue.
3. Select the range **B8:F8**, which includes the starting and ending revenue values.
4. On the Home tab, in the Editing group, click the **Fill** button, and then click **Series** to open the Series dialog box.
5. Verify that the **Rows** option button in the Series group and the **Linear** option button in the Type group are selected. Excel will fill the series within the same rows using a linear trend.
6. Click the **Trend** check box to insert a checkmark and apply a trend that interpolates between the starting and ending values in the selected range. See Figure 9-12.

Figure 9-12 Series dialog box for interpolation

Series
Series in: Rows, Columns
Type: Linear, Growth, Date, AutoFill
Date unit: Day, Weekday, Month, Year
Trend
Step value: 250000 Stop value:
OK Cancel

fills the series within the same row

applies a trend to interpolate the values between the starting and ending values

fills the series by a constant amount

fills the series by a constant percentage

7. Click the **OK** button. The values inserted in the range C8:E8 show the company's projected revenue based on a linear trend. See Figure 9-13.

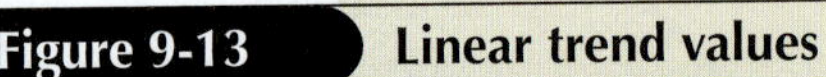

Figure 9-13 Linear trend values

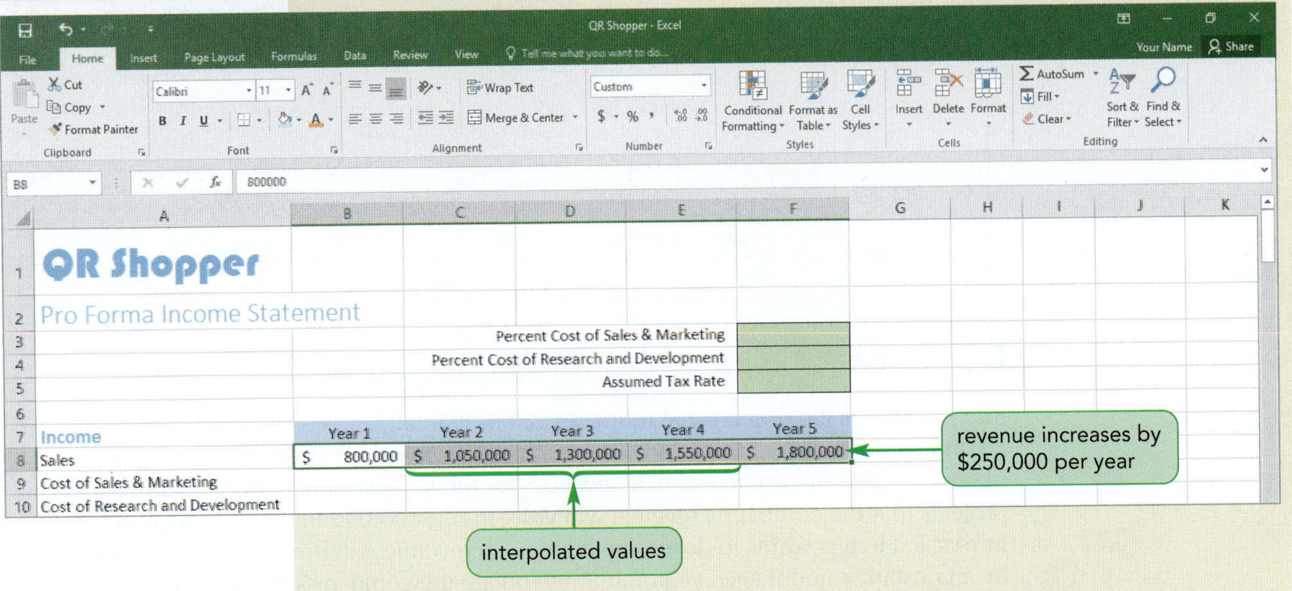

The linear trend projects an increase in the company's revenue of $250,000 per year. Next, you'll fill in the revenue values in Year 2 through Year 4 assuming a growth trend. To interpolate the growth trend correctly, you first must remove the Year 2 through Year 4 values, leaving those cells blank.

Be sure the middle cells in the range are blank so you can interpolate new values.

To project future revenue assuming a growth trend:

1. On the Quick Access Toolbar, click the **Undo** button to remove the interpolated values under the linear trend model.
2. On the Home tab, in the Editing group, click the **Fill** button, and then click **Series** to open the Series dialog box.
3. In the Type section, click the **Growth** option button, and then click the **Trend** check box to select it, applying a growth trend to the interpolated values.
4. Click **OK**. The Year 1 through Year 5 revenue projections are now based on a growth trend. See Figure 9-14.

Figure 9-14 Growth trend values

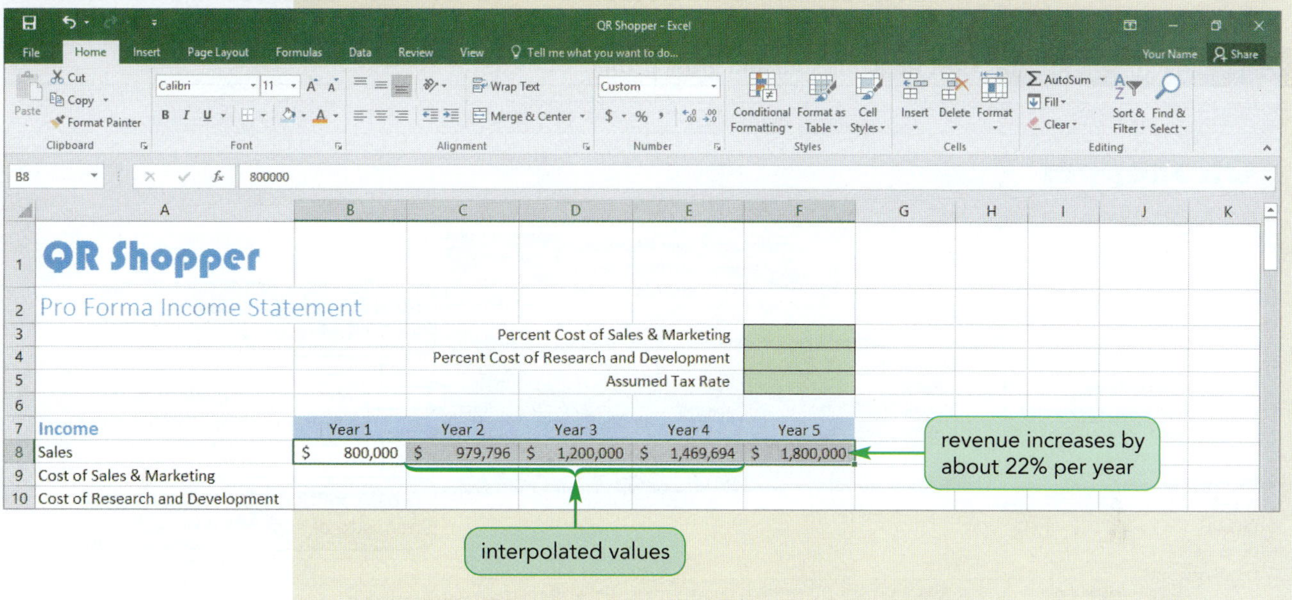

In a growth trend, the values change by a constant percentage each year. You can determine the percent change by dividing one year's revenue value by the previous year's revenue. For the projected QR Shopper revenue, the values grow at a constant rate of about 22.5 percent per year. The largest revenue increase occurs at the end of the five-year period. For example, revenue grows by $179,796 from Year 1 to Year 2, but by $330,306 from Year 4 to Year 5.

Calculating the Cost of Goods Sold

The next part of the income statement displays the cost of sales, also known as the cost of goods sold. QR Shopper needs to purchase the raw material to create the cart scanners, and it also must invest time into the development and upgrade of the software to match changing market conditions. Ryan has estimated for every dollar of sales revenue, the company will need to spend 13 cents on research and development and 22 cents on sales and marketing. As the company's revenue increases, these costs will also increase. The difference between the company's sales revenue and the cost of goods sold is the company's **gross profit**.

Ryan wants you to project the cost of goods sold and the company's gross profit for each of the next five years using the estimates he's provided you.

To project the cost of goods sold and the gross profit:

1. In cell **F3**, enter **22%** as the percent cost of sales and marketing.
2. In cell **F4**, enter **13%** as the percent cost of research and development.
3. In cell **B9**, enter the formula **=B8*$F$3** to multiply the Year 1 revenue by the cost of goods percentage for sales and marketing. Excel returns a value of 176,000, which is the estimated cost of sales and marketing for Year 1.
4. In cell **B10**, enter the formula **=B8*$F$4**. Excel returns a value of 104,000, which is the estimated cost of research and development in Year 1.
5. In cell **B11**, enter the formula **=B8–(B9+B10)**. Excel returns a value of 520,000, which is the estimated gross profit in Year 1.

6. Copy the formulas in the range **B9:B11** to the range **C9:F11** to calculate the cost of goods sold and the gross profit for Year 2 through Year 5. See Figure 9-15.

Figure 9-15 Cost of goods sold and gross profit

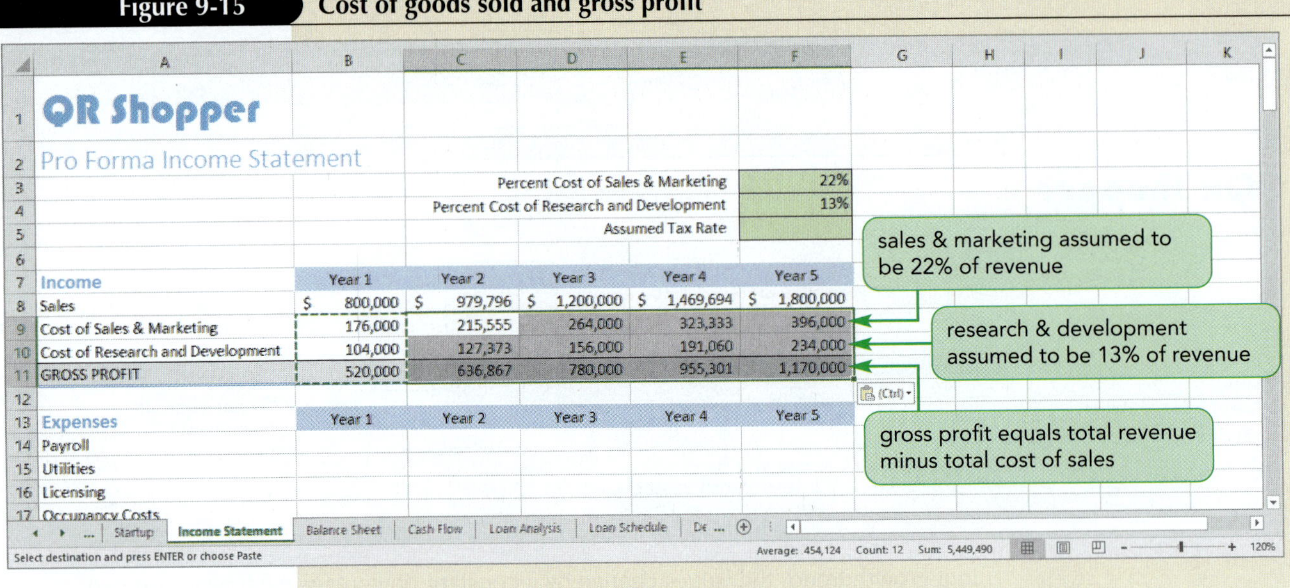

Based on these calculations, the company's gross profit is projected to increase from $520,000 in Year 1 to $1,170,000 in Year 5.

REFERENCE

Interpolating and Extrapolating a Series

To interpolate a series of values between starting and ending values:

- Select the range with the first cell containing the starting value, blank cells for middle values, and the last cell containing the ending value.
- On the Home tab, in the Editing group, click the Fill button, and then click Series.
- Select whether the series is organized in rows or columns, select the type of series to interpolate, and then check the Trend check box.
- Click the OK button.

To extrapolate a series from a starting value:

- Select a range with the first cell containing the starting value followed by blank cells to store the extrapolated values.
- On the Home tab, in the Editing group, click the Fill button, and then click Series.
- Select whether the series is organized in rows or columns, select the type of series to extrapolate, and then enter the step value in the Step value box.
- Click the OK button.

The next section of the income statement contains the projected general expenses for the company. These expenses are not directly related to production. For example, the company must purchase insurance, provide for general maintenance, and pay for office space, regardless of the number of products it sells. Add the Year 1 general expenses to the Income Statement worksheet.

To enter the Year 1 expenses:

1. In the range **B14:B19**, enter the following general expense values: **360,000** in cell B14 for payroll, **50,000** in cell B15 for utilities, **25,000** in cell B16 for licensing, **45,000** in cell B17 for occupancy costs, **20,000** in cell B18 for insurance, and **15,000** in cell B19 for miscellaneous expenses.
2. Click cell **B20**. You will use the SUM function to calculate the total estimated general expenses entered in the range B14:B19.
3. On the Home tab, in the Editing group, click the **AutoSum** button, and then press the **Enter** key. The value 515,000 appears in cell B20, indicating that the general expenses for the first year will be more than $500,000.

Next, you'll project these initial expenses over the next four years. To do that, you'll extrapolate a trend from the Year 1 values.

Extrapolating from a Series of Values

Extrapolation differs from interpolation in that only a starting value is provided; the succeeding values are estimated by assuming that the values follow a trend. As with interpolation, Excel can extrapolate a data series based on either a linear trend or a growth trend. With a linear trend, the data values are assumed to change by a constant amount. With a growth trend, they are assumed to change by a constant percentage. To extrapolate a data series, you must provide a step value representing the amount by which each value is changed as the series is extended. You do not have to specify a stopping value.

Ryan estimates that the company's payroll will increase by 13 percent per year. The other costs will increase by 5 percent per year. These percent increases are equivalent to multiplying each year's expenses by 1.13 and 1.05, respectively. Rather than writing this formula into the worksheet, you'll extrapolate the expenses using the Fill command.

To extrapolate the Year 1 expenses:

1. Select the range **B14:F14** containing the cells in which the Year 1 through Year 5 payroll values will be entered.
2. On the Home tab, in the Editing group, click the **Fill** button, and then click **Series**. The Series dialog box opens.
3. Click the **Growth** option button, and then type **1.13** in the Step value box. See Figure 9-16.

Figure 9-16 Series dialog box for extrapolating a series

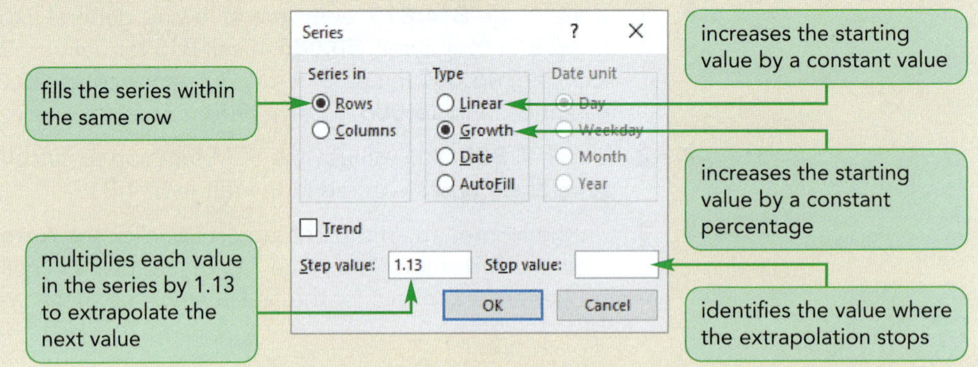
Series
fills the series within the same row
multiplies each value in the series by 1.13 to extrapolate the next value
increases the starting value by a constant value
increases the starting value by a constant percentage
identifies the value where the extrapolation stops
Series in
Rows
Columns
Type
Linear
Growth
Date
AutoFill
Date unit
Day
Weekday
Month
Year
Trend
Step value: 1.13
Stop value:
OK
Cancel

4. Click the **OK** button. The payroll expenses are extrapolated into Year 2 through Year 5, culminated in a Year 5 payroll of $586,970.

   Next, you will extrapolate the other general expenses assuming a growth rate of 5 percent.

5. Select the range **B15:F19**. Do *not* select the row containing the total general expenses.
6. In the Editing group, click the **Fill** button, and then click **Series** to reopen the Series dialog box.
7. Click the **Growth** option button, and then type **1.05** in the Step value box to increase the expenses by 5 percent per year.
8. Click the **OK** button. The expense values from Year 1 are extrapolated into the Year 2 through Year 5 columns. For example, the expense for utilities increases to $60,775 in Year 5.
9. Copy the formula in cell **B20** to the range **C20:F20** to calculate the total general expenses for the company for each of the five years.

TIP

To extrapolate a decreasing trend, use a negative step value for a linear trend, and use a step value between 0 and 1 for a growth trend.

The calculations show that the projected general expenses will rise from $515,000 in Year 1 to $775,374 by the end of Year 5. Next, you want to calculate the company's earnings during each of the next five years. The initial earnings estimate is equal to the company's gross profit minus the total general expenses.

To calculate the company's initial earnings:

1. In cell **B23**, enter the formula **=B11–B20** to subtract the total general expenses from the gross profit for Year 1. The estimate of earnings for the first year is $5,000.
2. Copy the formula in cell **B23** to the range **C23:F23** to project yearly earnings through Year 5. See Figure 9-17.

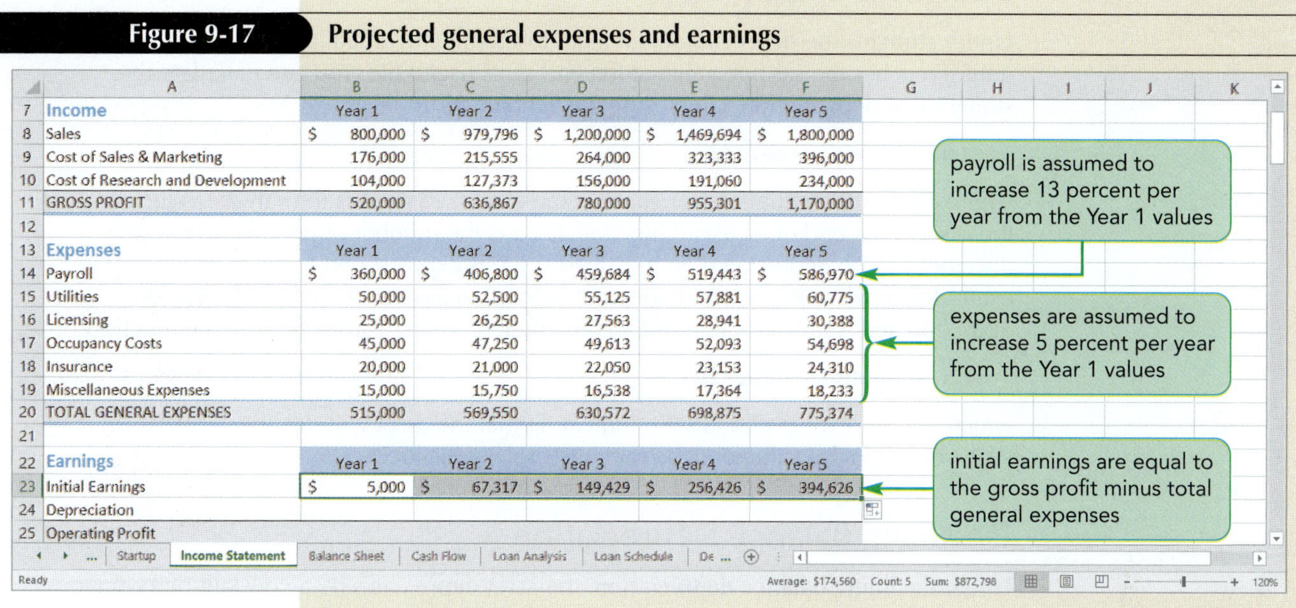

	A	B	C	D	E	F
7	Income	Year 1	Year 2	Year 3	Year 4	Year 5
8	Sales	$ 800,000	$ 979,796	$ 1,200,000	$ 1,469,694	$ 1,800,000
9	Cost of Sales & Marketing	176,000	215,555	264,000	323,333	396,000
10	Cost of Research and Development	104,000	127,373	156,000	191,060	234,000
11	GROSS PROFIT	520,000	636,867	780,000	955,301	1,170,000
12						
13	Expenses	Year 1	Year 2	Year 3	Year 4	Year 5
14	Payroll	$ 360,000	$ 406,800	$ 459,684	$ 519,443	$ 586,970
15	Utilities	50,000	52,500	55,125	57,881	60,775
16	Licensing	25,000	26,250	27,563	28,941	30,388
17	Occupancy Costs	45,000	47,250	49,613	52,093	54,698
18	Insurance	20,000	21,000	22,050	23,153	24,310
19	Miscellaneous Expenses	15,000	15,750	16,538	17,364	18,233
20	TOTAL GENERAL EXPENSES	515,000	569,550	630,572	698,875	775,374
21						
22	Earnings	Year 1	Year 2	Year 3	Year 4	Year 5
23	Initial Earnings	$ 5,000	$ 67,317	$ 149,429	$ 256,426	$ 394,626
24	Depreciation					
25	Operating Profit					

Figure 9-17 Projected general expenses and earnings

The calculations project that the company's annual earnings will increase from $5,000 in Year 1 to $394,626 in Year 5.

Calculating Depreciation of Assets

The financial status of a company is not determined solely by its revenue, expenses, or annual earnings. Its wealth is also tied up in noncash assets such as equipment, land, buildings, and vehicles. These assets are known as **tangible assets** because they are long-lasting material assets not intended for sale but for use only by the company. Not all material assets are tangible assets. For example, assets such as the ingredients a restaurant uses when preparing its dishes are not considered tangible assets because although they are used in the cooking process, they are sold indirectly to the consumer in the form of a finished meal. However, items such as the cooking stove, refrigeration units, deep fryers, and so forth are tangible assets for that restaurant.

Tangible assets wear down over time and lose their value. Because this reduces the company's overall wealth, tax laws allow companies to deduct this loss of value from reported earnings on the company's income statement, reducing the company's tax liability. The loss of the asset's original value doesn't usually happen all at once but is instead spread out over several years in a process known as depreciation. For example, an asset whose original value is $200,000 might be depreciated to $50,000 after 10 years of use. Different types of tangible assets have different rates of depreciation. Some items depreciate faster than others, which maintain their value for longer periods. In general, to calculate the depreciation of an asset, you need to know the following:

- The asset's original cost
- The length of the asset's useful life
- The asset's salvage value, which is the asset's value at the end of its useful life
- The rate at which the asset is depreciated over time

There are several ways to depreciate an asset. This module focuses on straight-line depreciation and declining balance depreciation.

Straight-Line Depreciation

Under **straight-line depreciation**, an asset loses value by equal amounts each year until it reaches the salvage value at the end of its useful life. You can calculate the straight-line depreciation value using the SLN function

```
SLN(cost,salvage,life)
```

where `cost` is the initial cost or value of the asset, `salvage` is the salvage value of the asset at the end of its useful life, and `life` is the number of periods over which the asset will be depreciated. In most cases, life is expressed in terms of years. For example, to calculate the yearly depreciation of an asset with an initial value of $200,000 and a salvage value of $50,000 after 10 years, you would use the function

```
SLN(200000, 50000, 10)
```

which returns a value of $15,000, indicating that the asset will decline $15,000 every year from its initial value until it reaches its salvage value.

Declining Balance Depreciation

Under **declining balance depreciation**, the asset depreciates by a constant percentage each year rather than a constant amount. The depreciation is highest early in the asset's lifetime and steadily decreases as the asset itself loses value. Figure 9-18 compares the yearly straight-line and declining balance depreciation over a 10-year lifetime as an asset declines from its initial value of $200,000 down to $50,000.

Figure 9-18 Straight-line and declining balance depreciation

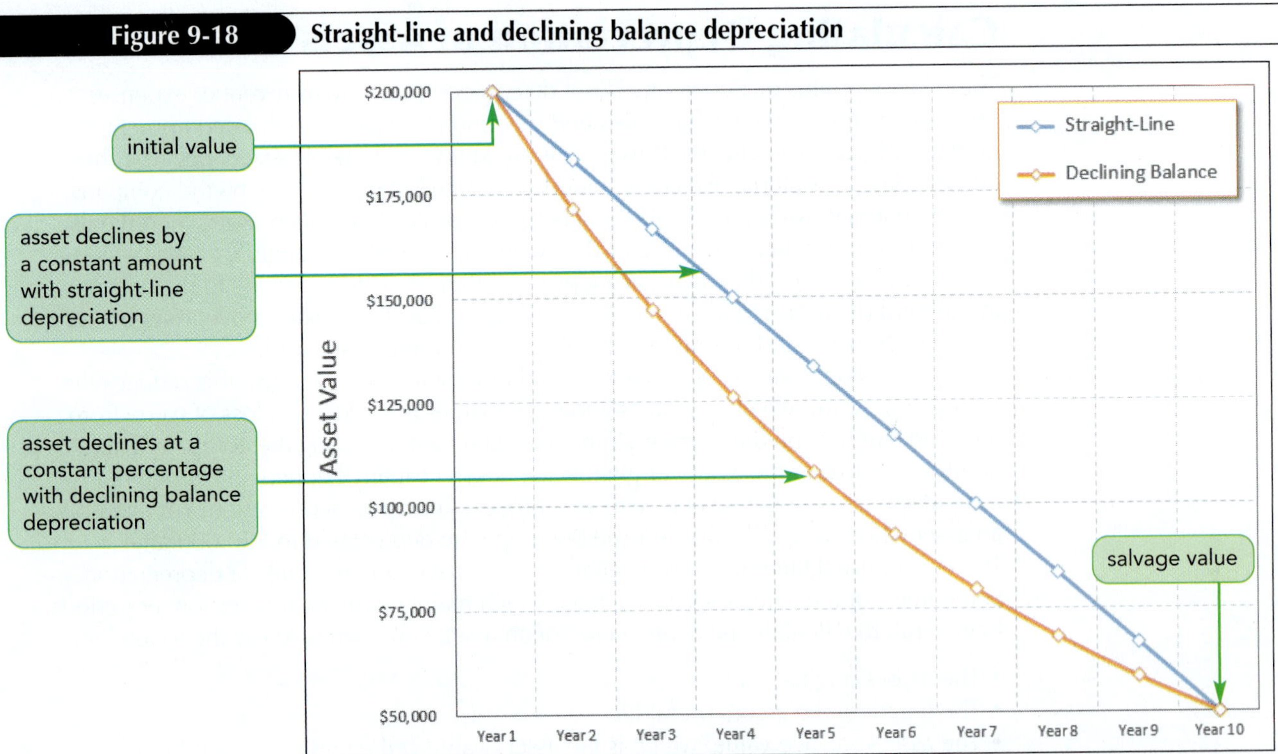

An asset shows a greater initial decline under declining balance depreciation than under straight-line depreciation. Declining balance depreciation is another example of a negative growth trend in which the asset decreases in value by a constant percentage rather than by a constant amount, as is the case with straight-line depreciation.

You can calculate the declining balance depreciation with the DB function

```
DB(cost,salvage,life,period[,month=12])
```

where `cost`, `salvage`, and `life` are again the initial cost, salvage cost, and lifetime of the asset, respectively, and `period` is the period for which you want to calculate the depreciation. If you are calculating depreciation on a yearly basis, then period would contain the year value of the depreciation. For example, to calculate the fourth year of depreciation of a $200,000 asset that declines to a salvage value of $50,000 after 10 years, you would use the function

```
DB(200000, 50000, 10, 4)
```

which returns $17,048.03, indicating that the asset declines in value more than $17,000 during its fourth year of use. By contrast, the asset's depreciation in its fifth year is calculated with the function

```
DB(200000, 50000, 10, 5)
```

which returns $14,848.83. The depreciation is smaller in the fifth year because the asset has a lower value that late into its useful life.

The DB function also supports an optional `month` argument, which is needed when the asset is used for only part of the first year. For example, if you are depreciating the $200,000 asset after using it for only two months in Year 1, you would calculate its depreciation in the fifth year as

```
DB(200000, 50000, 10, 5, 2)
```

which returns $16,681.50. This is a higher depreciation value because the asset has not been subjected to wear and tear for a full five years, making it more valuable going into Year 5.

Ryan estimates that QR Shopper will have $200,000 in tangible assets at its startup. The useful life of these assets is estimated at 10 years with a salvage value of $50,000. You will add this information to the company's startup figures and then apply it to the Depreciation worksheet in the QR Shopper workbook.

To specify the values of the tangible assets:

1. Go to the **Startup** worksheet.
2. In cell **B13**, enter **200,000** as the value of the long-term assets.
3. Go to the **Depreciation** worksheet.
4. In cell **B4**, type **=** to begin the formula, go to the **Startup** worksheet, click cell **B13**, and then press the **Enter** key. The formula =Startup!B13 is entered in cell B4, displaying the $200,000 long-term assets value from the Startup worksheet.
5. In cell **B5**, enter **$50,000** as the asset's estimated salvage value.
6. In cell **B6**, enter **10** as the useful life of the asset.

Next, you'll calculate the depreciation of the company equipment using straight-line depreciation.

To calculate the straight-line depreciation:

1. In cell **B10**, enter the formula **=SLN($B$4, $B$5, $B$6)** to calculate the straight-line depreciation in Year 1 based on the cost value in cell B4, the salvage value in cell B5, and the life value in cell B6. The formula returns a depreciation value of $15,000, indicating the asset will decline in value by $15,000 in Year 1.
2. Copy the formula in cell **B10** to the range **C10:F10** to calculate the straight-line depreciation for the remaining years. Because the straight-line depreciation is a constant amount every year, the formula returns a depreciation value of $15,000 for Year 2 through Year 5.

   Next, you will calculate the cumulative depreciation of the asset from Year 1 through Year 5.
3. In cell **B11**, enter the formula **=B10** to display the depreciation for the first year.
4. In cell **C11**, enter the formula **=B11+C10** to add the Year 2 depreciation to the depreciation from Year 1. The total depreciation through the first two years is $30,000.
5. Copy the formula in cell **C11** to the range **D11:F11** to calculate cumulative depreciation through the first five years. By Year 5, the asset's value will have declined by $75,000.
6. In cell **B12**, enter the formula **=$B$4–B11** to calculate the depreciated asset's value after the first year. The asset's value is $185,000.
7. Copy the formula in cell **B12** to the range **C12:F12**. By Year 5, the asset's value has been reduced to $125,000.
8. Click cell **B10** to deselect the copied range. See Figure 9-19.

Figure 9-19 Straight-line depreciation of the asset

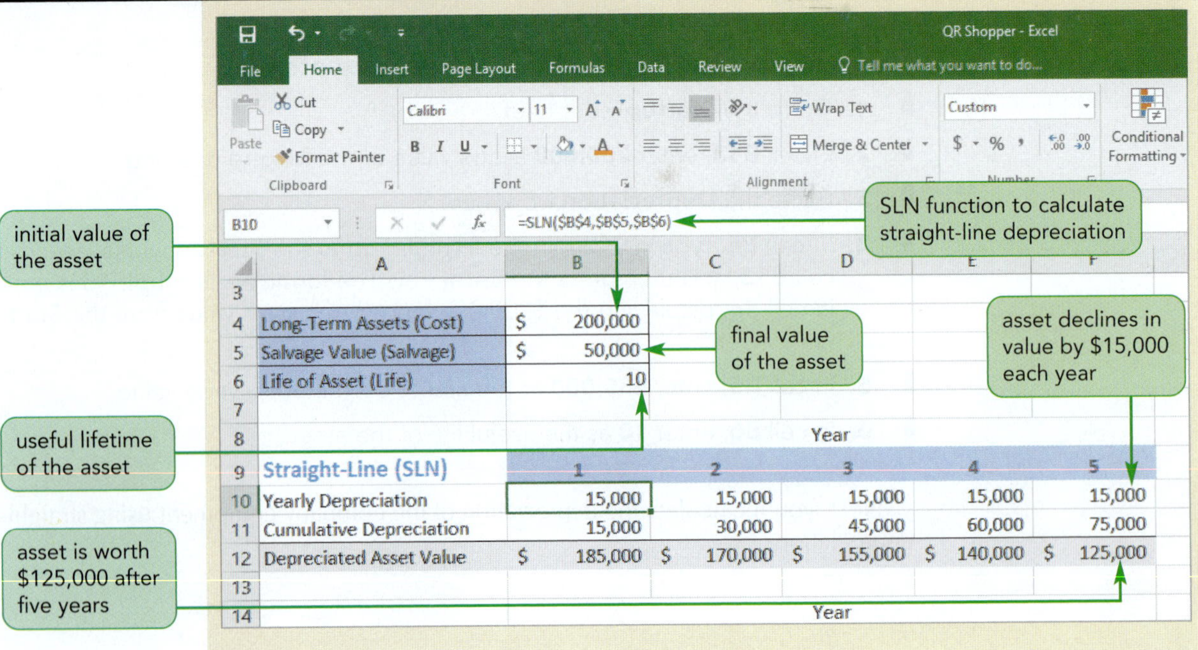

Ryan also wants to explore the depreciation of the company's tangible assets under the declining balance depreciation method.

To calculate the declining balance depreciation:

1. In cell **B16**, enter the formula **=DB($B$4, $B$5, $B$6, B15)** to calculate the declining balance depreciation for Year 1 based on the initial cost of the asset in cell B4, the salvage value in cell B5, the life of the asset in cell B6, and the current period (or year) in cell B15. The formula returns 25,800, which is the amount that the assets will depreciate in Year 1.
2. Copy the formula in cell **B16** to the range **C16:F16** to calculate the depreciation in each of the remaining four years. The depreciation amount decreases each year under the declining balance schedule, dropping to $14,849 in Year 5.
3. Copy the formulas in the range **B11:F12** to the range **B17:F18** to calculate the cumulative depreciation and depreciated value of the asset.
4. Click cell **B16** to deselect the copied range. See Figure 9-20.

Figure 9-20 Declining balance depreciation of the asset

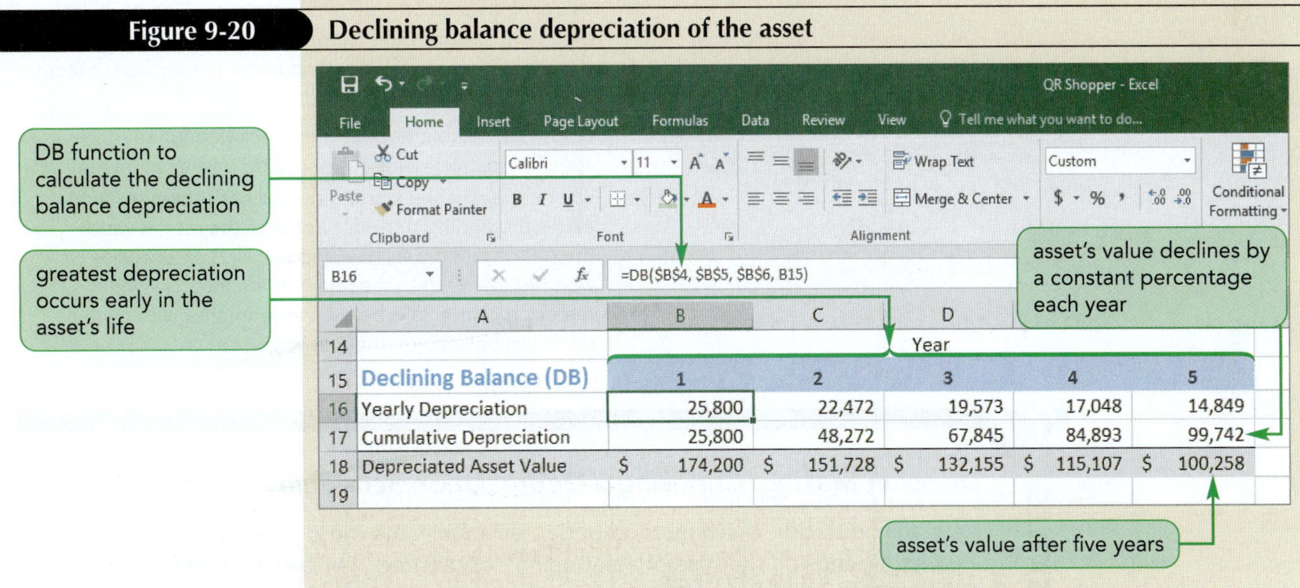

Based on the declining balance depreciation method, the value of the asset declines to $100,258 by the end of Year 5, which is lower than the Year 5 value under the straight-line depreciation model. Figure 9-21 describes several other depreciation functions that can be used to satisfy specialized accounting needs.

Figure 9-21 **Excel depreciation functions**

Function	Description
`SLN(cost,salvage,life)`	Returns the straight-line depreciation in which the asset declines by a constant amount each year, where *cost* is the initial cost of the asset, *salvage* is the salvage value, and *life* is the useful lifetime of the asset.
`DB(cost,salvage,life,period [,month])`	Returns the declining balance depreciation in which the asset declines by a constant percentage each year, where *period* is the year of the depreciation and *month* is an optional argument that defines the number of months that the asset was owned during Year 1.
`SYD(cost,salvage,life,period)`	Returns the sum-of-years' digit depreciation that results in a more accelerated depreciation than straight-line depreciation, but a less accelerated depreciation than declining balance depreciation.
`DDB(cost,salvage,life,period [,factor=2])`	Returns the double-declining balance depreciation that doubles the depreciation under the straight-line method and applies that accelerated rate to the original asset value minus the cumulative depreciation. The *factor* argument specifies the factor by which the straight-line depreciation is multiplied. If no factor is specified, a factor of 2 (for doubling) is assumed.
`VDB(cost,salvage,life,start, end[,factor=2] [,no_switch=FALSE])`	Returns a variable declining depreciation for any specified period using any specified depreciation method, where *start* is the starting period of the depreciation, *end* is the ending period, *factor* is the rate at which the depreciation declines, and *no_switch* specifies whether to switch to the straight-line method when the depreciation falls below the estimate given by the declining balance method.

PROSKILLS

Decision Making: Choosing a Depreciation Schedule

How do you decide which method of depreciation is the most appropriate? The answer depends on the type of asset being depreciated. Tax laws allow different depreciation methods for different kinds of assets and different situations. In general, you want to choose the depreciation method that most accurately describes the true value of the asset and its impact on the company's financial status. In tax statements, depreciation appears as an expense that is subtracted from the company's earnings. So, if you accelerate the depreciation of an asset in the early years of its use, you might be underestimating the company's profits, making it appear that the company is less profitable than it actually is. On the other hand, depreciating an asset slowly could make it appear that the company is more profitable than it really is. For this reason, the choice of a depreciation method is best made in consultation with a tax accountant who is fully aware of the financial issues and the tax laws involved.

Adding Depreciation to an Income Statement

Depreciation is part of a company's income statement because even though the company is not losing actual revenue, it is losing worth as its tangible assets decline in value, and that reduces its tax liability. Ryan wants to add the declining balance depreciation figures from the Depreciation worksheet to the projected income statement to project the company's operating profit, which represents the company's profits before calculating its tax liability.

To add depreciation to the income statement:

1. Go to the **Income Statement** worksheet.
2. In cell **B24**, type **=** to begin the formula, go to the **Depreciation** worksheet, click cell **B16**, and then press the **Enter** key. The formula =Depreciation!B16 is entered and displays the depreciation value 25,800 for Year 1.
3. Copy the formula in cell **B24** to the range **C24:F24** to show the annual depreciation for Year 2 through Year 5.
4. In cell **B25**, enter the formula **=B23–B24** to subtract the depreciation from the company's initial earnings. QR Shopper shows a loss in operating profit in the first year of $20,800.
5. Copy the formula in cell **B25** to the range **C25:F25** to calculate the operating profit for Year 2 through Year 5.

When depreciation is included, the company's operating profit increases throughout the five-year period, culminating in a Year 5 operating profit of $379,777.

Adding Taxes and Interest Expenses to an Income Statement

Interest expenses are also part of a company's income statement. You have already projected the annual interest payments the company will have to make on its $400,000 loan (shown earlier in row 36 of Figure 9-9). Rather than reenter these values, you can reference the calculated values from that worksheet in the income statement. Because those values were displayed as negative numbers, you'll change the sign to match the format of the Income Statement worksheet.

To include the interest expense in the income statement:

1. In cell **B27**, type **=–** (an equal sign followed by a minus sign) to begin the formula.
2. Go to the **Loan Schedule** worksheet, click cell **B36**, which contains the total interest payments in Year 1, and then press the **Enter** key. The formula = –'Loan Schedule'!B36 is entered in the cell, returning the value 18,659.
3. In cell **B28**, enter the formula **=B25–B27** to subtract the interest expense from the operating profit for Year 1. Excel returns a value of –39,459, indicating that the company will lose almost $40,000 pretax for the first year.
4. Copy the formulas in the range **B27:B28** to the range **C27:F28** to calculate the interest payments and pretax profits for the remaining years.

When interest is considered, the company's projected pretax profit is $377,006 in Year 5.

Finally, you need to account for the taxes that the company will pay on the money it makes. Ryan estimates that the company will be subject to a 32 percent tax rate on its pretax income. You will add this tax rate to the Income Statement worksheet and then calculate the company's tax liability. The company will pay taxes only if it makes money, so you will use an IF function to test whether the pretax income is positive before calculating its tax liability. If the pretax profit is negative, the taxes owed will be zero.

To calculate the company's tax liability:

1. In cell **F5** of the Income Statement worksheet, enter **32%** as the tax rate.
2. In cell **B30**, enter the formula **=IF(B28>0, B28*$F$5, 0)** to first test whether the pretax income in Year 1 is greater than 0. If it is, then the pretax income will be multiplied by the tax rate in cell F5. Otherwise, the formula will return 0. Because QR Shopper will show a net loss in its first year of operation, the formula should return a value of 0.
3. In cell **B31**, enter the formula **=B28–B30** to subtract the taxes owed for Year 1 from the pretax income.
4. Copy the formulas in the range **B30:B31** to the range **C30:F31** to calculate the tax liability and after-tax profit for the remaining years.
5. Click cell **B30** to deselect the copied formulas. See Figure 9-22.

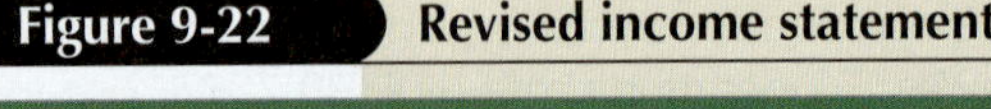
Figure 9-22 Revised income statement

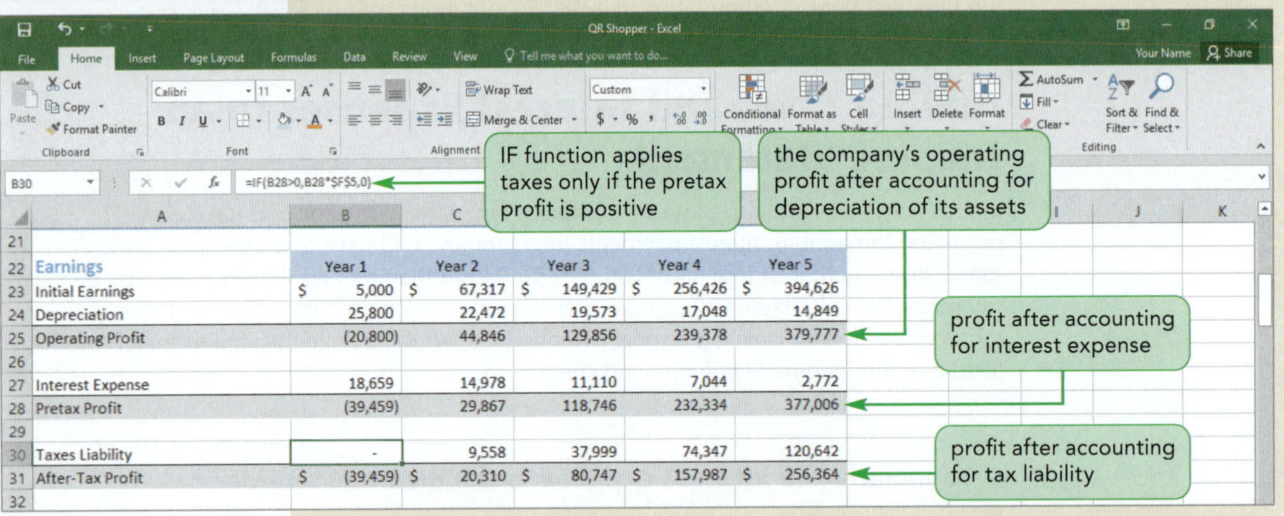

	A	B	C	D	E	F
21						
22	Earnings	Year 1	Year 2	Year 3	Year 4	Year 5
23	Initial Earnings	$ 5,000	$ 67,317	$ 149,429	$ 256,426	$ 394,626
24	Depreciation	25,800	22,472	19,573	17,048	14,849
25	Operating Profit	(20,800)	44,846	129,856	239,378	379,777
26						
27	Interest Expense	18,659	14,978	11,110	7,044	2,772
28	Pretax Profit	(39,459)	29,867	118,746	232,334	377,006
29						
30	Taxes Liability	-	9,558	37,999	74,347	120,642
31	After-Tax Profit	$ (39,459)	$ 20,310	$ 80,747	$ 157,987	$ 256,364
32						

6. Save the workbook.

After accounting for its tax liability, QR Shopper will show an after-tax profit of $256,364 by the end of its fifth year.

With the initial financial planning laid out, the company needs to attract some investors. In the next session, you will evaluate the return on investment that the company will be able to offer investors and the impact it will have on the company's profitability.

REVIEW

Session 9.2 Quick Check

1. The first value in a linear trend is 50 and the fifth value is 475. What are the values of the second, third, and fourth items?
2. The first value in a growth trend is 50 and the fifth value is 475. What are the values of the second, third, and fourth items?
3. By what percent do the values in Question 3 grow?
4. The first value in a series is 100. Extrapolate the next four values assuming a linear trend with a step size of 125.
5. The first value in a series is 100. Extrapolate the next four values assuming that each value grows by 18 percent over the previous value.
6. A new business buys $20,000 worth of computer equipment. If the useful life of the equipment is 10 years with a salvage value of $3,000, provide the formula to determine the depreciation during the first year assuming straight-line depreciation. What is the formula result?
7. Provide the value of the asset in Year 1 through Year 5 using the depreciation schedule in Question 6.
8. Assume a declining balance depreciation for the computer equipment described in Question 6, and provide the formula and result to determine the depreciation in the first year.
9. Provide the value of the asset in Year 1 through Year 5 using the declining balance depreciation schedule in Question 8.

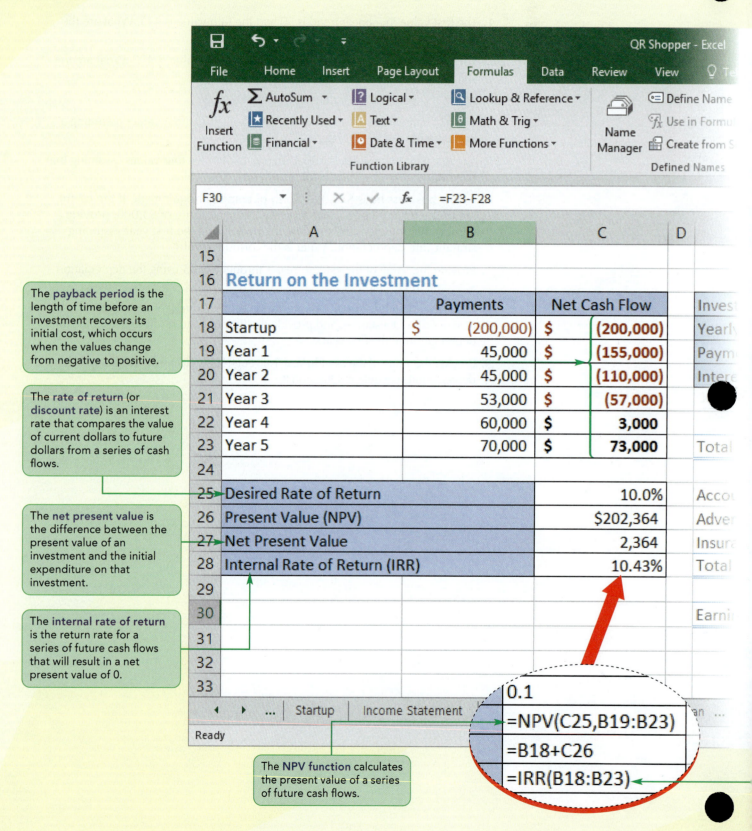

Session 9.3 Visual Overview:

QR Shopper - Excel

File | Home | Insert | Page Layout | Formulas | Data | Review | View

Insert Function | AutoSum | Recently Used | Financial | Logical | Text | Date & Time | Lookup & Reference | Math & Trig | More Functions | Function Library | Name Manager | Define Name | Use in Formula | Create from Selection | Defined Names

F30 | =F23-F28

	A	B	C
15			
16	**Return on the Investment**		
17		Payments	Net Cash Flow
18	Startup	$ (200,000)	$ **(200,000)**
19	Year 1	45,000	$ **(155,000)**
20	Year 2	45,000	$ **(110,000)**
21	Year 3	53,000	$ **(57,000)**
22	Year 4	60,000	$ **3,000**
23	Year 5	70,000	$ **73,000**
24			
25	Desired Rate of Return		10.0%
26	Present Value (NPV)		$202,364
27	Net Present Value		2,364
28	Internal Rate of Return (IRR)		10.43%
29			
30			
31			
32			
33			

Startup | Income Statement

Ready

0.1

=NPV(C25,B19:B23)

=B18+C26

=IRR(B18:B23)

The **payback period** is the length of time before an investment recovers its initial cost, which occurs when the values change from negative to positive.

The **rate of return** (or **discount rate**) is an interest rate that compares the value of current dollars to future dollars from a series of cash flows.

The **net present value** is the difference between the present value of an investment and the initial expenditure on that investment.

The **internal rate of return** is the return rate for a series of future cash flows that will result in a net present value of 0.

The **NPV function** calculates the present value of a series of future cash flows.

NPV and IRR Functions and Auditing

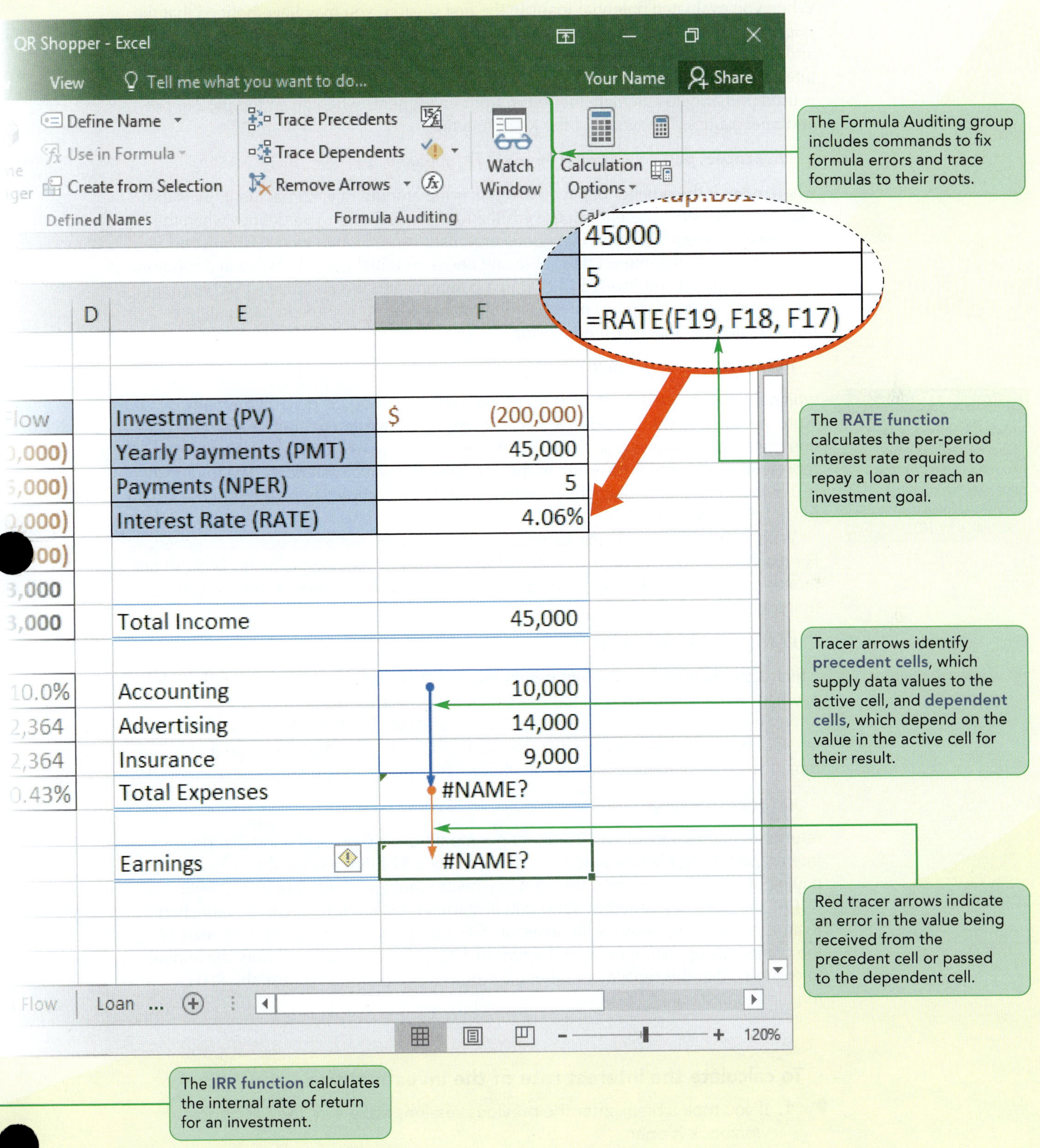
QR Shopper - Excel
View
Tell me what you want to do...
Your Name
Share
Define Name
Use in Formula
Create from Selection
Defined Names
Trace Precedents
Trace Dependents
Remove Arrows
Formula Auditing
Watch Window
Calculation Options
45000
5
=RATE(F19, F18, F17)
D
E
F
Investment (PV)
$ (200,000)
Yearly Payments (PMT)
45,000
Payments (NPER)
5
Interest Rate (RATE)
4.06%
Total Income
45,000
Accounting
10,000
Advertising
14,000
Insurance
9,000
Total Expenses
#NAME?
Earnings
#NAME?
Loan
120%
The Formula Auditing group includes commands to fix formula errors and trace formulas to their roots.
The RATE function calculates the per-period interest rate required to repay a loan or reach an investment goal.
Tracer arrows identify precedent cells, which supply data values to the active cell, and dependent cells, which depend on the value in the active cell for their result.
Red tracer arrows indicate an error in the value being received from the precedent cell or passed to the dependent cell.
The IRR function calculates the internal rate of return for an investment.

Calculating Interest Rates with the RATE Function

When you evaluated potential loans in the first session, you may have noticed that the *pmt*, *fv*, *nper*, and *pv* arguments are matched by the Excel functions PMT, FV, NPER, and PV. The *rate* argument also has a matching RATE function that calculates the interest rate based on the values of the other financial arguments. The RATE function is used primarily to calculate the return from investments when given the *pv*, *fv*, *pmt*, and *nper* values. The syntax of the RATE function is

```
RATE(nper,pmt,pv[,fv=0][,type=0][,guess=0.1])
```

where *nper* is the number of payments, *pmt* is the amount of each payment, *pv* is the loan or investment's present value, *fv* is the future value, and *type* defines when the payments are made. The optional *guess* argument is used when the RATE function cannot calculate the interest rate value and needs an initial guess to arrive at a solution.

For example, if you invest $14,000 in a company and then receive $150 per month for the next 10 years (or 120 months) for a total of $18,000, you can calculate the interest rate from that investment using the function

```
RATE(120, 150, -14000)
```

TIP

Always multiply the RATE function results by the number of payments per year. For monthly payments, multiply the rate value by 12.

which returns an interest rate of 0.43 percent per month or 5.2 percent annually. Note that the *pmt* value is positive because this is an investment and the payments are coming to you (positive cash flow), but the present value –14,000 is negative because it represents money spent investing in the company (negative cash flow). The future value is 0 by default because once the investment has been completely paid out, there are no funds left for the investor.

With loans, the positive and negative signs of the *pmt* and *pv* values are switched. For example, if you can borrow $14,000 and repay it by making payments of $150 per month over the next 10 years, you can calculate the monthly interest rate using the function

```
RATE(120, -150, 14000)
```

which again returns 0.43 percent per month or 5.2 percent annually. Notice that the payment value is negative and the present value is positive.

Not every combination of payments and present value will result in a viable interest rate. For example, if you try to calculate the interest rate for a $14,000 loan that is repaid with payments of $100 per month for 120 months, the function

```
RATE(120, -100, 14000)
```

returns an interest rate of –0.25 percent per month or –3.0 percent annually. The interest rate is negative because you cannot repay a $14,000 loan within 10 years by paying only $100 per month. The total payments would amount to only $12,000.

QR Shopper needs another $200,000 in startup capital before it can be launched. Ryan is considering repaying the investors $45,000 per year for the first five years of the company's operation for a total return of $225,000. He wants to know the annual interest rate that this repayment schedule would represent. You will use the RATE function to find out.

To calculate the interest rate of the investment:

1. If you took a break after the previous session, make sure the QR Shopper workbook is open.
2. Go to the **Startup** worksheet, and then in cell **B31**, enter **200,000** as the amount contributed by investors.

3. Go to the **Investment Analysis** worksheet, which you'll use to analyze the value of investing in QR Shopper.
4. In cell **B6**, type **= –** (an equal sign followed by a minus sign), go to the **Startup** worksheet, click cell **B31**, and then press the **Enter** key. The formula =–Startup!B31 is entered in the cell.

   The formula displays the negative value $(200,000) in the cell. You want to use a negative value because you are examining this investment from the point of view of the investors, who are making an initial payment of $200,000 to the company (a negative cash flow).
5. In cell **B7**, enter **45,000** as the annual payment. The value is positive because this money is being repaid to the investors each year (a positive cash flow from their point of view).
6. In cell **B8**, enter **5** as the total number of payments made to the investors.
7. In cell **B9**, enter the formula **=RATE(B8, B7, B6)** to calculate the interest rate of this repayment schedule based on the number of payments in cell B8, the size of each payment in cell B7, and the present value of the investment in cell B6. See Figure 9-23.

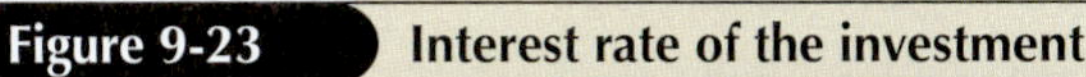

Figure 9-23 Interest rate of the investment

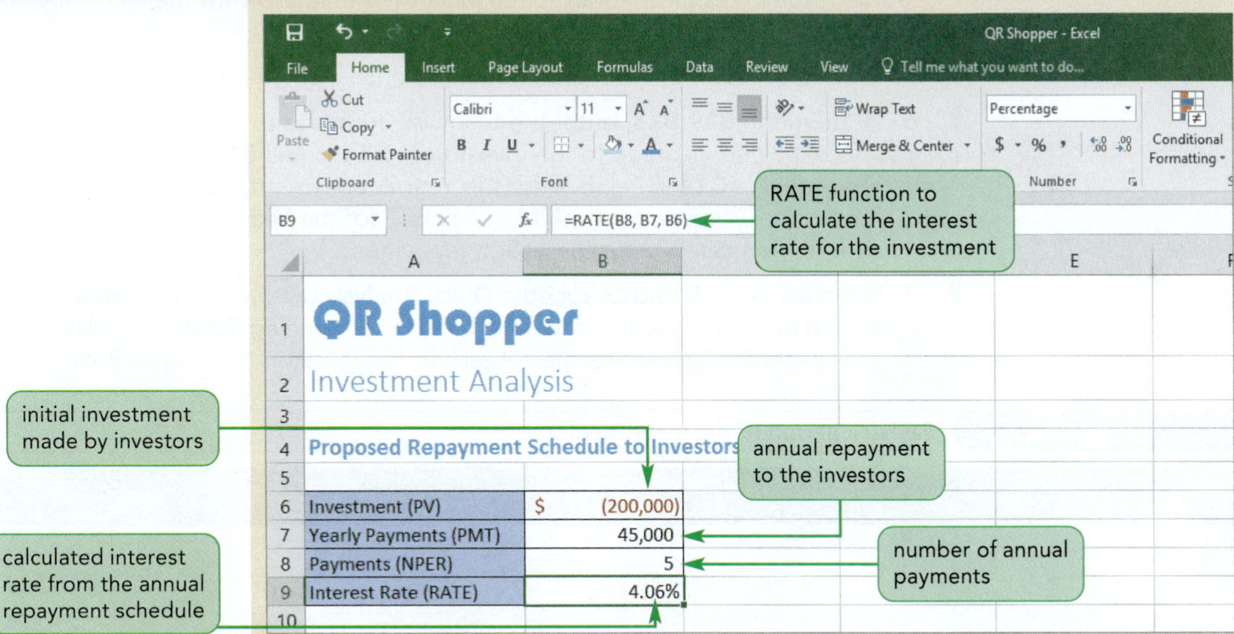

Based on your calculations, the annual interest rate to the investors for this repayment schedule is 4.06 percent. Another way to view this value is that investors could achieve the same return by placing the $200,000 in savings account or fund that pays 4.06 percent annual interest.

Viewing the Payback Period of an Investment

One simple measure of the return from an investment is the payback period, which is the length of time required for an investment to recover its initial cost. For example, a $400,000 investment that returns $25,000 per year would take 16 years to repay the initial cost of the investment.

Ryan doesn't believe he can attract investors if all he can promise is a 4.06 percent annual interest rate. Another possibility is to pay the investors dividends taken from the company's annual profits. Because the company will not show much profit initially, leaving less cash to pay dividends, Ryan is considering the following schedule of dividend payments: Year 1—$0; Year 2—$0; Year 3—$8,000; Year 4—$15,000; and Year 5—$25,000.

Ryan wants you to add these dividends to the repayment of the investors' original $200,000 investment and then calculate the payback period.

To determine the payback period for the investment:

1. In cell **B12**, enter the formula **=$B$7** to reference the annual loan repayment to the investors.
2. Copy the formula in cell **B12** to the range **C12:F12** to apply the same loan repayment to each year.
3. In the range **B13:F13**, enter the following dividends: **0** in cell B13, **0** in cell C13, **8,000** in cell D13, **15,000** in cell E13, and **25,000** in cell F13.
4. Select the range **B14:F14**, and then use **AutoSum** to calculate the total reimbursement to the investors for each of the first five years. The total values range from $45,000 in Year 1 to $70,000 in Year 5.

   Next, you'll add these totals to the initial investment to view the cumulative total payments made to the investors.
5. In cell **B18**, enter the formula **=B6** to reference the initial investment value.
6. In the range **B19:B23**, enter the following formulas to reference the annual payments made to the investors: **=B14** in cell B19 for the Year 1 repayment, **=C14** in cell B20 for the Year 2 repayment, **=D14** in cell B21 for the Year 3 repayment, **=E14** in cell B22 for the Year 4 repayment, and **=F14** in cell B23 for the Year 5 repayment.
7. Select the range **B18:B23**, click the **Quick Analysis** button, click **Totals**, scroll right to the end of the Totals tools, and then click **Running Total** to calculate a column of running totals for the net cash flow to investors. See Figure 9-24.

Figure 9-24 Payback period of the investment

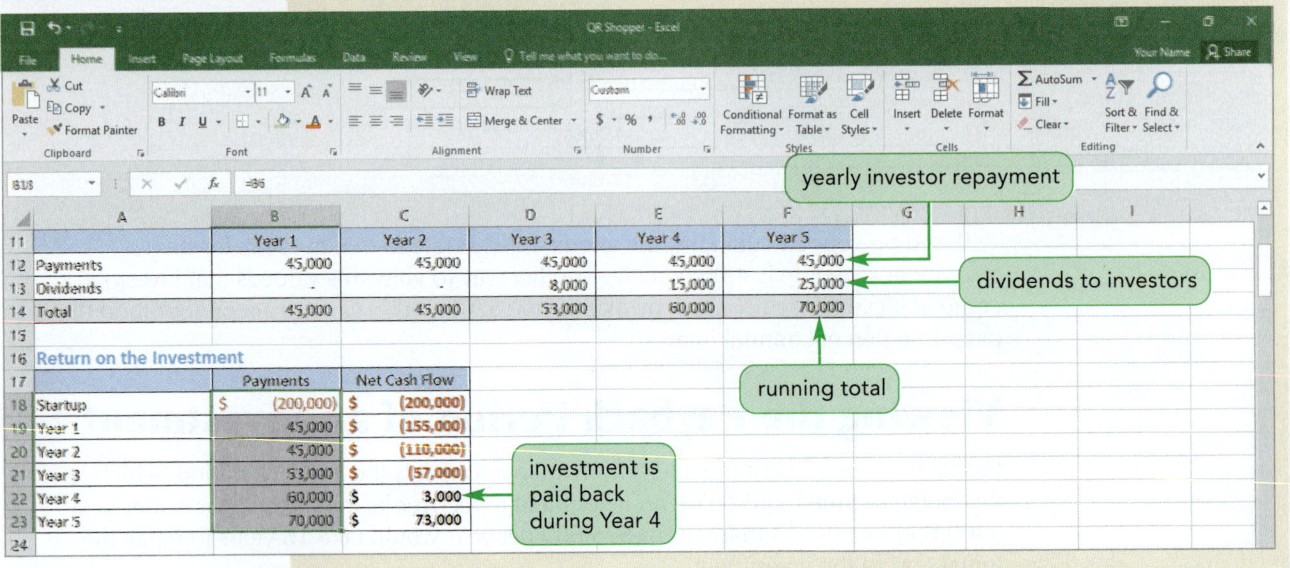

	Year 1	Year 2	Year 3	Year 4	Year 5
Payments	45,000	45,000	45,000	45,000	45,000
Dividends	-	-	8,000	15,000	25,000
Total	45,000	45,000	53,000	60,000	70,000

	Payments	Net Cash Flow
Startup	$ (200,000)	$ (200,000)
Year 1	45,000	$ (155,000)
Year 2	45,000	$ (110,000)
Year 3	53,000	$ (57,000)
Year 4	60,000	$ 3,000
Year 5	70,000	$ 73,000

Based on these calculations, the investors will be repaid for their investments during the fourth year (when the value of the cumulative net cash flow changes to positive). By the end of the fifth year, investors will see a profit of $73,000 on their original investments.

Calculating Net Present Value

The payback period is a quick method of assessing the long-term value of an investment. The major drawback of the payback period is that it does not take into account the time value of money. To understand why, you must explore how time impacts financial decisions.

The Time Value of Money

The **time value of money** is based on the observation that money received today is often worth more than the same amount received later. One reason for this is that you can invest the money you receive today and earn interest on that investment. The time value of money can be expressed in terms of what represents a fair exchange between current dollars and future dollars.

For example, is it better to get $100 today or $105 one year from now? The answer depends on what you could do with that $100 during the year. If you could invest it in an account that pays 6 percent interest per year, the $100 would turn into $106 in one year, making it better to receive the $100 now and invest it; but, if you could earn only 4 percent interest on the $100, it would be better to wait a year and receive the $105.

The interest rate you assume for the present value of your investment is known as the rate of return, or the discount rate. The rate of return defines the time value of money and provides a method of comparing present value to future value.

You can use the PV function to calculate the time value of money under different rates of return. For example, the following PV function calculates the present value of receiving $100 per year for the next five years at a 6 percent annual rate of return:

```
PV(6%, 5, 100)
```

The function returns a negative value of –$421.24, indicating that it would be a fair exchange to spend $421.24 today to receive $100 per year for each of the next five years. In other words, $421.24 today is worth the same as $500 spread out over $100 annual payments over the next five years with a rate of return of 6 percent.

For investments that pay off at the end of the investment period without any intermediate payments, you enter 0 for the payment value and enter the amount returned by the investment as the future value. So, to calculate the present value of receiving $500 at the end of five years at a 6 percent rate of return, you enter the PV function

```
PV(6%, 5, 0, 500)
```

which returns –$373.63, indicating that it would be a fair exchange to spend $373.63 today to receive $500 five years from now.

You also can use the FV function to estimate how much a dollar amount today is worth in terms of future dollars. For example, to determine the future value of $100 in two years when the rate of return is 5 percent, you would enter

```
FV(5%, 2, 0, -100)
```

returning a value of $110.25. The positive cash flow indicates that spending $100 today is a fair exchange for receiving $110.25 two years from now.

Using the NPV Function

The PV function assumes that all future payments are equal. If the future payments are not equal, you must use the NPV (net present value) function to determine what would be a fair exchange. The syntax of the NPV function is

```
NPV(rate,value1[,value2,value3,…])
```

where *rate* is the rate of return, and *value1*, *value2*, *value3*, and so on are the values of future payments from the investment. The NPV function assumes payments occur at the end of each payment period and the payment periods are evenly spaced.

For example, to calculate the present value of a three-year investment that pays $100 at the end of the first year, $200 at the end of the second year, and $500 at the end of the third year with a 6 percent annual rate of return, you would use the NPV function

```
NPV(6%, 100, 200, 500)
```

which returns a value of $692.15, indicating that the $800 paid out by the investment according to the three-year schedule is equal to receiving $692.15 today.

Unlike the PV function, which returns a negative value for the investment's present value, the NPV function returns a positive value. This occurs because the PV function returns a cash flow value that indicates how much you need to invest now (a negative cash flow) to receive money later (a positive cash flow); whereas the NPV function calculates the value of those payments in today's dollars based on your chosen rate of return.

You can receive surprising results when you take into account the time value of money. Consider an investment that has a 6 percent rate of return with these transactions: Year 1—investor receives $250; Year 2—investor receives $150; Year 3—investor receives $100; Year 4—investor pays $150; and Year 5—investor pays $400.

At first glance, this seems to be a bad investment. The investor receives a total of $500 in the first three years but spends $550 in the last two years, yielding an apparent net loss of $50. However, that analysis doesn't take into account the time value of money. When the present value of this transaction is calculated using the NPV function

```
NPV(6%, 250, 150, 100, -150, -400)
```

the value of the investment in current dollars is equal to $35.59, a positive result. The investment is actually profitable because the investor receives the money early and pays it back later using dollars of lesser value.

Choosing a Rate of Return

Determining whether an investment is profitable is based on the assumed rate of return. Choosing an appropriate rate of return is related to the concept of risk—the possibility that the entire transaction will fail, resulting in a loss of the initial investment. Investments with higher risks generally should have higher rates of return. If an investor places $200,000 in a simple bank account (a low-risk venture), he or she would not expect a high rate of return; on the other hand, investing the $200,000 in a startup company is riskier and merits a higher rate of return.

After discussing the issue with financial analysts, Ryan has settled on a 10 percent rate of return, meaning that QR Shopper will return to the investors at least as much as they would get if they had invested $200,000 in an account paying 10 percent annual interest over five years. You'll use that rate of return in the NPV function as you calculate the net present value of the proposed investment in the QR Shopper startup.

To calculate the net present value of the investment:

1. In cell **C25**, enter **10.0%** as the desired rate of return.
2. In cell **C26**, enter **=NPV(C25, B19:B23)** to calculate the net present value of the investment based on the rate value in cell C25 and the return paid to the investors for Year 1 through Year 5 in the range B19:B23. The formula returns $202,364, indicating the present value of the investment is more than $200,000.
3. In cell **C27**, enter **=B18+C26** to add the initial investment to the present value of the investment over the next five years. The net present value is $2,364.

Be sure to add the initial cash flow value to the net present value.

4. Select cell **C26**. See Figure 9-25.

Figure 9-25 Payback period of the investment

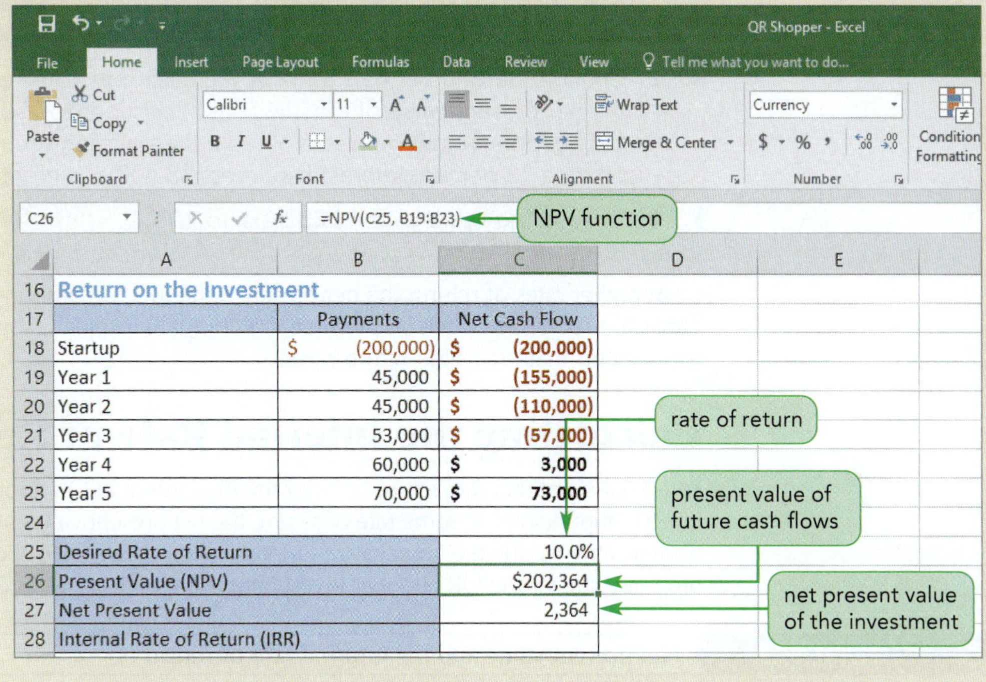

	A	B	C
16	Return on the Investment		
17		Payments	Net Cash Flow
18	Startup	$ (200,000)	$ (200,000)
19	Year 1	45,000	$ (155,000)
20	Year 2	45,000	$ (110,000)
21	Year 3	53,000	$ (57,000)
22	Year 4	60,000	$ 3,000
23	Year 5	70,000	$ 73,000
24			
25	Desired Rate of Return		10.0%
26	Present Value (NPV)		$202,364
27	Net Present Value		2,364
28	Internal Rate of Return (IRR)		

According to these results, the $200,000 investment is worth $2,364 more than the payout obtained by placing the same amount in a savings account that pays 10 percent annual interest. Of course, that assumes QR Shopper is as profitable as Ryan claims.

INSIGHT

Understanding Net Present Value and the NPV Function

The financial definition of net present value is the difference between the present value of a series of future cash flows and the current value of the initial investment. One source of confusion for Excel users is that despite its name, the NPV function does not return the net present value of an investment. Instead, it returns the investment's present value based on the returns that the investment will provide in the future. To calculate the net present value in Excel, the initial cost of the investment must be added to the present value of the returns from the investment using the formula

```
=initial investment + NPV value
```

where ***initial investment*** is the initial cost of the investment and ***NPV value*** is the value of Excel's NPV function applied to future returns. The initial investment is assumed to have a negative cash flow because that investment is being purchased, and it is assumed to be based on current, not future, dollars.

The exception to this formula occurs when the initial investment also takes place in the future. For example, if the initial investment takes place in one year and the returns occur annually after that, then the NPV function will return the net present value without having to be adjusted because the initial investment is also paid with discounted dollars.

In any financial analysis, it is a good idea to test other values for comparison. You will rerun the analysis using return rates of 5 percent and 12 percent.

To view the impact of different rates of return:

1. In cell **C25**, change the value to **5%** to decrease the desired rate of return. The net present value in cell C27 increases to $33,666. The investment is about $33,000 more profitable (in current dollars) than what could be achieved by an account bearing 5 percent annual interest.
2. Change the value of **C25** to **12%**, increasing the desired rate of return. Now the net present value of the investment declines to –$8,372. Investing in QR Shopper would be less profitable than putting the money in an account bearing 12 percent interest by almost $8,400 in current dollars.
3. Change the value of cell **C25** back to **10%**.

At higher rates of return, the net present value of the company investment decreases. That's not surprising when you realize the company project is being compared with investments that offer high return rates.

Calculating the Internal Rate of Return

Your analysis of different return rates for the investment in QR Shopper illustrates an important principle: At some rate of return, the net present value of an investment switches from positive (profitable) to negative (unprofitable.) Figure 9-26 shows the change in net present value for the QR Shopper investment using different rates of return.

Figure 9-26 Net present value and the internal rate of return

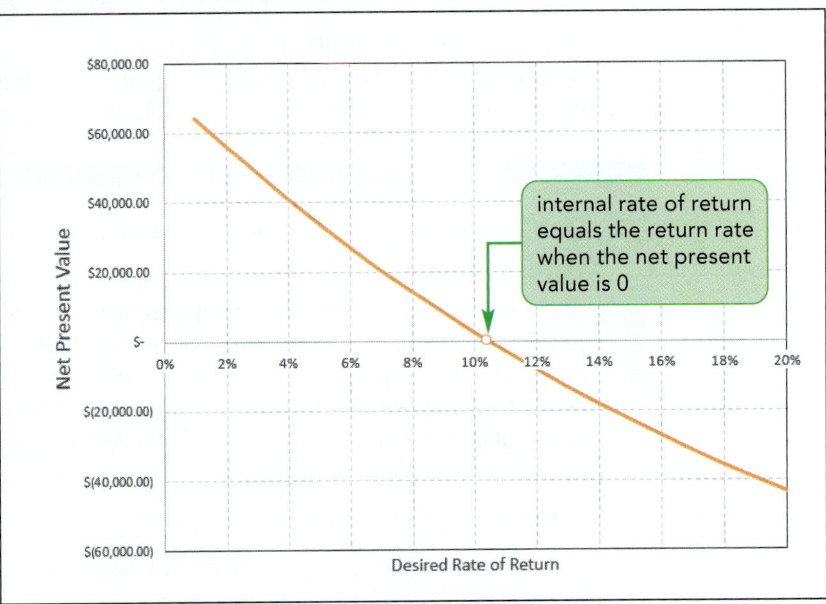

The point at which the net present value of an investment equals 0 is called the internal rate of return (IRR) of the investment. The internal rate of return is another popular measure of the value of an investment because it provides a basis of comparison between investments. Investments with higher internal rates of return are preferred to those with lower IRRs.

Using the IRR Function

The IRR function calculates the internal rate of return for an investment. Its syntax is

```
IRR(values[,guess=0.1])
```

where `values` are the cash flow values from the investment, and `guess` is an optional argument in which you provide a guess for the IRR value. A guess is needed for financial transactions that have several possible internal rates of return. This can occur when the investment alternates between negative and positive cash flows several times during its lifetime. For those types of transactions, an initial guess helps Excel locate the final value for the IRR. Without the guess, Excel might not be able to calculate the IRR. If you don't include a guess, Excel will use an initial guess of 10 percent for the IRR and proceed from there to determine the answer.

TIP

When you enter values directly in the IRR function, you must enclose them in curly braces. This is not necessary if the values are expressed as cell references.

For example, the internal rate of return for a $500 investment that pays $100 in the first year, $150 in the second and third years, and $200 in the fourth year is calculated using the IRR function

```
IRR({-500, 100, 150, 150, 200})
```

which returns a value of 6.96 percent. This indicates that the return for this investment is equally profitable as an account that pays 6.96 percent annual interest.

The order of payments affects the internal rate of return. In the above example, the total amount of money paid back on the investment is $600. However, if the payments were made in the opposite order—$200, $150, $150, and $100—the internal rate of return would be calculated as

```
IRR({-500, 200, 150, 150, 100})
```

which returns a value of 8.64 percent. The increased rate of return is due to the larger payments made earlier with dollars of greater value.

The list of values in the IRR function must include at least one positive cash flow and one negative cash flow, and the order of the values must reflect the order in which the payments are made and the payoffs are received. Like the NPV function, the IRR function assumes that the payments and payoffs occur at evenly spaced intervals. Unlike the NPV function, you include the initial cost of the investment in the values list.

REFERENCE

Calculating the Value of an Investment

- To calculate the net present value when the initial investment is made immediately, use the NPV function with the discount rate and the series of cash returns from the investment. Add the cost of the initial investment (negative cash flow) to the value returned by the NPV function.
- To calculate the net present value when the initial investment is made at the end of the first payment period, use the NPV function with the discount rate and the series of cash returns from the investment. Include the initial cost of the investment as the first value in the series.
- To calculate the internal rate of return, use the IRR function with the cost of the initial investment as the first cash flow value in the series. For investments that have several positive and negative cash flow values, include a guess to aid Excel in finding a reasonable internal rate of return value.

You will calculate the internal rate of return from the investment in QR Shopper.

To calculate the internal rate of return for the investment:

1. In cell **C28**, enter the formula **=IRR(B18:B23)**, where the range B18:B23 contains the initial investment and the returns that investors can expect. The internal rate of return is 10.43 percent.
2. Select cell **C28**. See Figure 9-27.

Figure 9-27 Internal rate of return

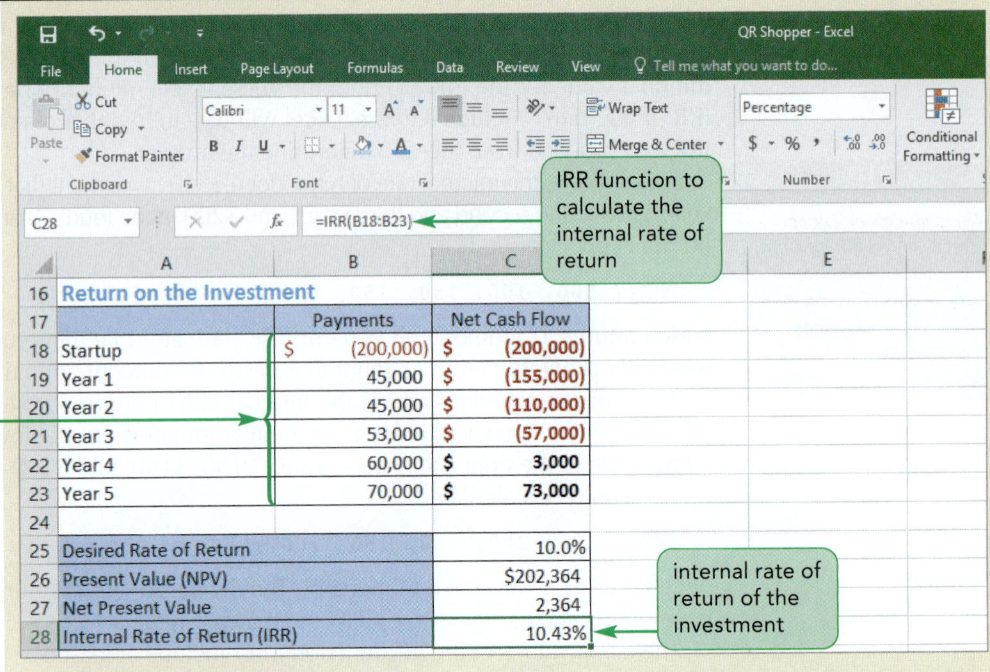

Based on the IRR calculation, Ryan can tell potential company investors that they will receive a 10.43 percent return on their investments. If this analysis is correct, that would seem like a worthwhile return compared to other competing investments.

PROSKILLS

Decision Making: Using NPV and IRR to Compare Investments

Businesses often have several investment options. In general, they want investments that have positive net present values or internal rates of return that are higher than a specified rate. In comparing two investments, businesses usually want to select the investment with the higher net present value or the higher internal rate of return.

If they rely on the net present value, they can receive contradictory results depending on the value specified for the desired rate of return. For example, consider the following two returns from an initial investment of $1,000. Option 1 has a higher net present value when discount rates are greater than 9 percent, while Option 2 has a higher net present value when the discount rate is 9 percent or less.

Options	Investment	Year 1	Year 2	Year 3	Year 4
Option 1	–$1,000	$350	$350	$350	$350
Option 2	–$1,000	0	0	0	$1,600

Using the internal rate of return instead of the net present value can also lead to contradictory results. This often occurs when an investment includes several switches between positive and negative cash flows during its history. In those situations, more than one internal rate of return value could fit the data.

To choose between two or more investments, it is a good idea to graph the net present value for each investment against different possible rates of return. By comparing the graphs, you can reach a decision about which investment is the most profitable and under what conditions.

Exploring the XNPV and XIRR Functions

Both the NPV and IRR functions assume that the cash flows occur at evenly spaced intervals such as annual payments in which the cash receipts from an investment are returned at the end of the financial year. For cash flows that appear at unevenly spaced intervals, you use the XNPV and XIRR functions.

The XNPV function, which calculates the net present value of a series of cash flows at specified dates, has the syntax

```
XNPV(rate,values,dates)
```

where `rate` is the desired rate of return, `values` is the list of cash flows, and `dates` are the dates associated with each cash flow. The series of values must contain at least one positive and one negative value. The cash flow values are discounted starting after the first date in the list, with the first value not discounted at all. Figure 9-28 shows an investment in which the initial deposit of $300,000 on September 1 is returned with eight payments spaced at irregular intervals over the next two years for a total of $340,000. The net present value of this investment is $7,267.04 based on a 7.2 percent rate of return. Note that the net present value is not $40,000 (the difference between the deposit and the total payments) because the investment is paid back over time with dollars of lesser value.

Figure 9-28 **Net present value calculated over irregular time intervals**

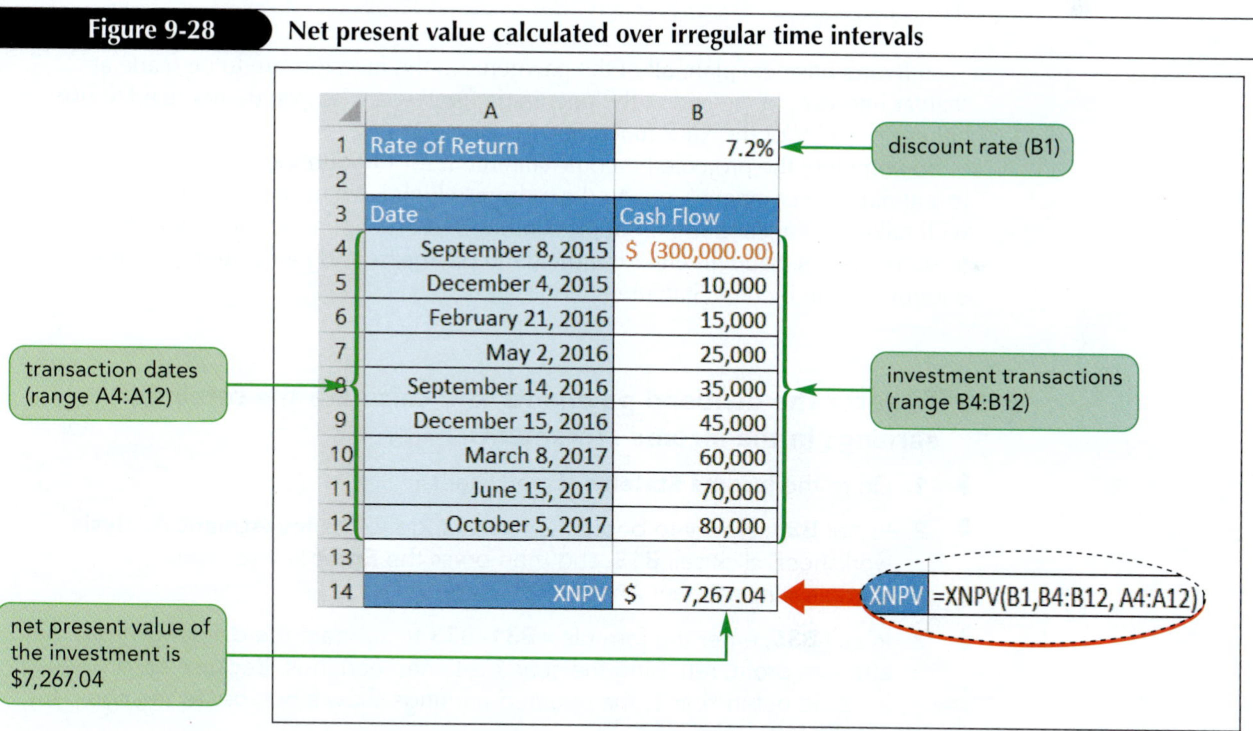

Likewise, the XIRR function calculates the internal rate of return for a series of cash flows made at specified dates. It has the syntax

```
XIRR(values,dates[,guess=0.1])
```

where `values` is the list of cash flow values, `dates` are the dates of each cash flow, and `guess` is an optional argument to help Excel arrive at an answer. Figure 9-29 shows the internal rate of return for the transaction presented in Figure 9-28. This investment's internal rate of return is 9 percent.

Figure 9-29 **Internal rate of return calculated over irregular time intervals**

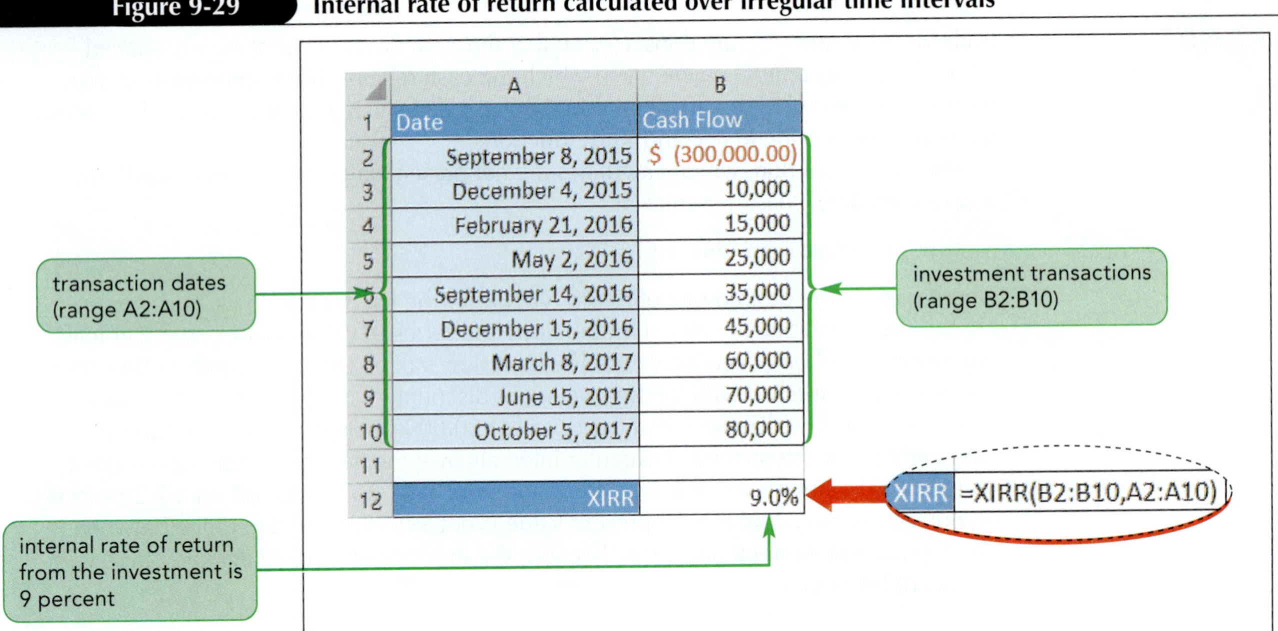

	A	B
1	Date	Cash Flow
2	September 8, 2015	$ (300,000.00)
3	December 4, 2015	10,000
4	February 21, 2016	15,000
5	May 2, 2016	25,000
6	September 14, 2016	35,000
7	December 15, 2016	45,000
8	March 8, 2017	60,000
9	June 15, 2017	70,000
10	October 5, 2017	80,000
11		
12	XIRR	9.0%

In Ryan's business plan, all of the payments to the investors are to be made at regular intervals, at the end of the upcoming fiscal years, so you do not need to use either the XNPV or the XIRR function.

To complete the projected income statement for QR Shopper, Ryan wants you to estimate the company's retained earnings, which is the money that the company will make after accounting for depreciation, interest expenses, taxes, and dividends to shareholders. You will enter the dividend payments and calculate the retained earnings in the Income Statement worksheet.

To enter the dividend payments and calculate the retained earnings in the income statement:

1. Go to the **Income Statement** worksheet.
2. In cell **B33**, type **=** to begin the formula, go to the **Investment Analysis** worksheet, click cell **B13**, and then press the **Enter** key to insert the formula ='Investment Analysis'!B13 into cell B33.
3. In cell **B35**, enter the formula **=B31–B33** to subtract the dividends from the after-tax profit, returning the Year 1 retained earnings. Because no dividends are paid out in Year 1, the retained earnings show a net loss to the company of $39,459.

   Next, you will calculate the net earnings for the remaining four years.
4. Select the range **B33:B35** and copy it to the range **C33:F35**.
5. Click cell **F35** to deselect the copied range. Figure 9-30 shows the projected retained earnings for QR Shopper from Year 1 through Year 5.

Figure 9-30 Final income statement

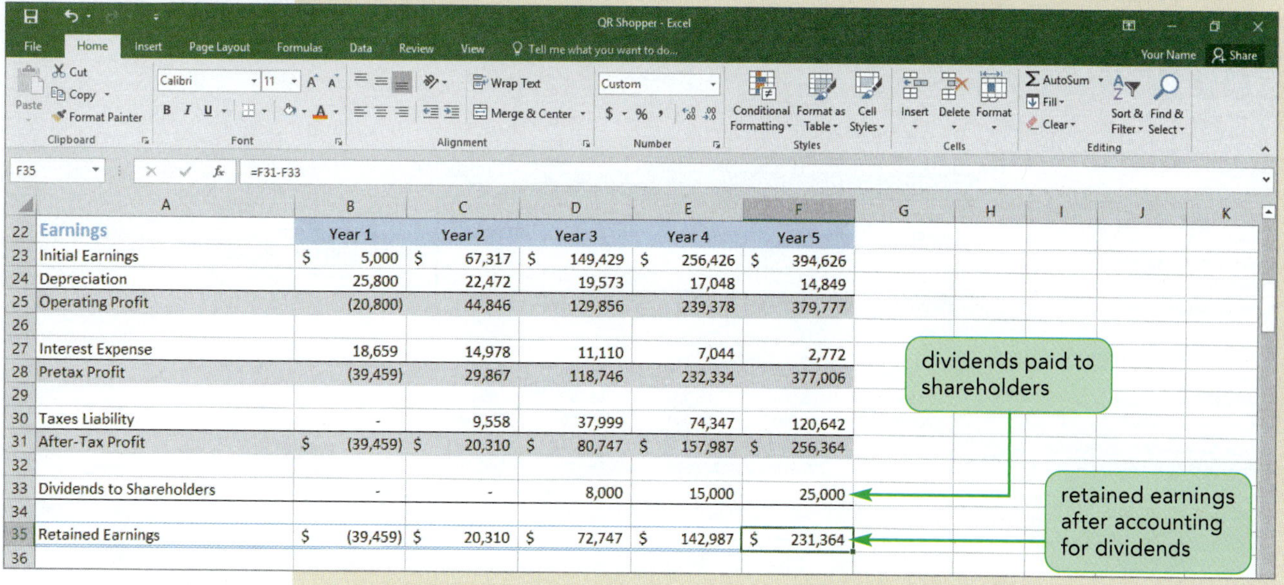

F35 =F31-F33

	A	B	C	D	E	F
22	Earnings	Year 1	Year 2	Year 3	Year 4	Year 5
23	Initial Earnings	$ 5,000	$ 67,317	$ 149,429	$ 256,426	$ 394,626
24	Depreciation	25,800	22,472	19,573	17,048	14,849
25	Operating Profit	(20,800)	44,846	129,856	239,378	379,777
26						
27	Interest Expense	18,659	14,978	11,110	7,044	2,772
28	Pretax Profit	(39,459)	29,867	118,746	232,334	377,006
29						
30	Taxes Liability	-	9,558	37,999	74,347	120,642
31	After-Tax Profit	$ (39,459)	$ 20,310	$ 80,747	$ 157,987	$ 256,364
32						
33	Dividends to Shareholders	-	-	8,000	15,000	25,000
34						
35	Retained Earnings	$ (39,459)	$ 20,310	$ 72,747	$ 142,987	$ 231,364
36						

dividends paid to shareholders

retained earnings after accounting for dividends

Based on these calculations, the retained earnings of the company will grow to annual total of $231,364 in Year 5 after accounting for depreciation, interest expenses, taxes, and owed dividends. At the end of the fifth year, the company has completely repaid its $400,000 loan and completely repaid its investors.

Auditing a Workbook

In designing this workbook, Ryan created several worksheets with interconnected values and formulas. The initial financial conditions entered in the Startup worksheet impact the company's loan repayment schedule. The values in the Depreciation worksheet are used in the Income Statement to access the company's yearly pretax profits. The dividends in the Investment Analysis worksheet are used to calculate the annual retained earnings. This interconnectedness gives Ryan the ability to view the impact of changing one or more financial assumption on a wide variety of financial statements.

The downside of this approach is that it can become a bit overwhelming to trace the value of a cell in one worksheet through the myriad of cells in other worksheets that contribute to its value. The QR Shopper workbook also contains a balance sheet and a cash flow schedule. The Balance Sheet worksheet projects the company's expected assets, liabilities, and equity for the next five years. This sheet provides a picture of what a business owns in both cash and tangible assets and what it owes to banks and investors. The Cash Flow worksheet projects the amount of cash that the company will generate and use in its first five years of operation.

Unfortunately, these worksheets contain errors. Ryan has asked you to locate the source of those errors and fix them, knowing that the source of the error could be located almost anywhere within the workbook. You'll start by reviewing the Balance Sheet worksheet to see if you can locate the errors.

To review the Balance Sheet worksheet:

1. Go to the **Balance Sheet** worksheet. Several cells display the #NAME? error value. See Figure 9-31.

Figure 9-31 Error values in the Balance Sheet worksheet

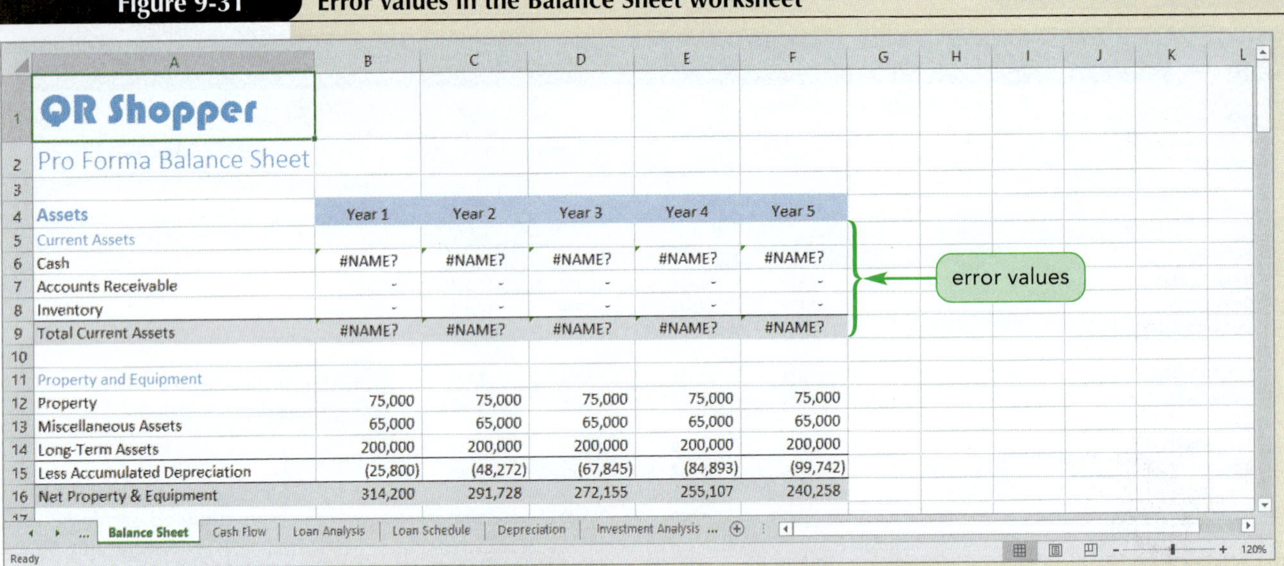

	A	B	C	D	E	F
1	QR Shopper					
2	Pro Forma Balance Sheet					
3						
4	Assets	Year 1	Year 2	Year 3	Year 4	Year 5
5	Current Assets					
6	Cash	#NAME?	#NAME?	#NAME?	#NAME?	#NAME?
7	Accounts Receivable	-	-	-	-	-
8	Inventory	-	-	-	-	-
9	Total Current Assets	#NAME?	#NAME?	#NAME?	#NAME?	#NAME?
10						
11	Property and Equipment					
12	Property	75,000	75,000	75,000	75,000	75,000
13	Miscellaneous Assets	65,000	65,000	65,000	65,000	65,000
14	Long-Term Assets	200,000	200,000	200,000	200,000	200,000
15	Less Accumulated Depreciation	(25,800)	(48,272)	(67,845)	(84,893)	(99,742)
16	Net Property & Equipment	314,200	291,728	272,155	255,107	240,258

2. Go to the **Cash Flow** worksheet. Several cells display the #NAME? error value.

The source of the error is unclear at first. Is the mistake in the Balance Sheet worksheet or elsewhere? Are there multiple errors or one error source for all of the error values? To help trace an error back to its source, Excel auditing tools help you explore the interconnectedness of the formulas and values within a workbook.

Tracing an Error

In tracing an error value to its source, you need to work with dependent and precedent cells. A dependent cell is one whose value depends on the values of other cells in the workbook; a precedent cell is one whose value is used by other cells. A cell can be both a dependent cell and a precedent cell. For example, if cell C15 contains the formula =C13+C14, then cell C15 is a dependent cell, relying on cells C13 and C14 for its value. Any error values in cell C13 or cell C14 would also appear in cell C15. If cell C16 contains the formula =C15/10, then cell C15 acts a precedent for that cell, and errors in cell C13 or cell C14 would also impact cells C16 through C15.

To locate the source of an error value, you select any cell containing the error value and trace that error back through the line of precedent cells. If any of the precedent cells displays an error value, you need to trace that cell's precedents and so on until you reach an error cell that has no precedents. That cell is the source of the error values in all of its dependent cells. After correcting the error, if other errors still exist, repeat this process until you have removed all of the errors from the workbook.

REFERENCE

Tracing Error Values

- Select the cell containing an error value.
- On the Formulas tab, in the Formula Auditing group, click the Error Checking button arrow, and then click Trace Error.
- Follow the tracer arrows to a precedent cell containing an error value.
- If the tracer arrow is connected to a worksheet icon, double-click the tracer arrow, and open the cell references in the worksheet.
- Continue to trace the error value to its precedent cells until you locate a cell containing an error value that has no precedent cells with errors.

You will use Excel's auditing tools to trace the #NAME? error values in the Balance Sheet worksheet back to their source or sources, and then correct the errors.

To trace the error in the Balance Sheet worksheet:

1. Go to the **Balance Sheet** worksheet, and then click cell **F9**. You'll start tracing the error from this cell.
2. On the ribbon, click the **Formulas** tab.
3. In the Formula Auditing group, click the **Error Checking button arrow**, and then click **Trace Error**. A tracer arrow is attached to cell F9. See Figure 9-32.

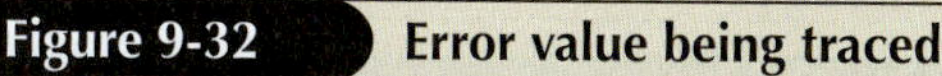

Figure 9-32 Error value being traced

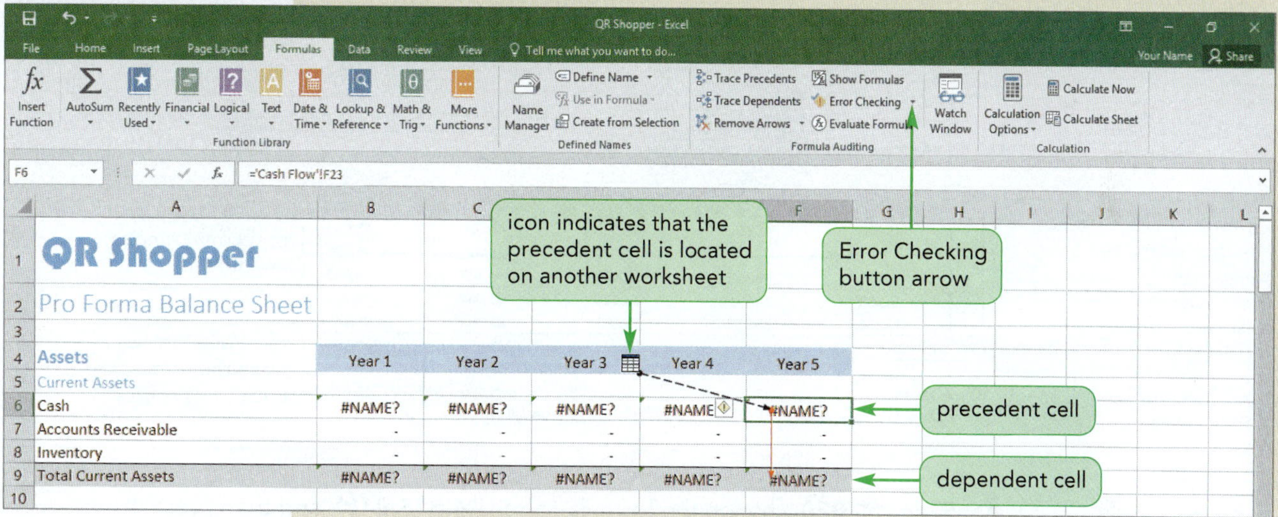

The tracer arrow provides a visual clue to the source of the error. A blue tracer arrow indicates that no error has been received or passed. A red tracer arrow indicates that an error has been received from the precedent cell or passed to the dependent cell. In this case, a red tracer arrow points from cell F6 to cell F9, indicating that cell F6 is the source of the error in cell F9. However, cell F6 also has a precedent cell. A black dashed tracer arrow points from a worksheet icon, indicating that the precedent cell for the value in cell F6 is in another worksheet in the workbook. You'll follow the tracer arrow to that sheet.

To continue tracing the error to its source:

1. Double-click the **tracer arrow** that connects the worksheet icon to cell F6. The Go To dialog box opens, listing a reference to cell F23 in the Cash Flow worksheet.
2. In the Go to box, click the reference to cell **F23**, and then click the **OK** button. Cell F23 in the Cash Flow worksheet is now the active cell. Notice that the #NAME? error appears throughout this worksheet, too.
3. On the Formulas tab, in the Formula Auditing group, click the **Error Checking button arrow**, and then click **Trace Error** to trace the source of the error in cell F23.

The tracer arrows pass through several cells in row 23 before going to cell B23 and settling on cell B20. Cell B20 has a single precedent indicated by the blue arrow and the blue box, which surrounds the range that is the precedent to the formula in cell B20. Because blue is used to identify precedent cells that are error free, the source of the error must be in cell B20 of the Cash Flow worksheet, which is selected.

4. Review the formula for cell B20 in the formula bar. Notice that the function name in the formula is entered incorrectly as SUMM, which is why the #NAME? error code is displayed in cell B20. See Figure 9-33.

Figure 9-33 Source of the error value

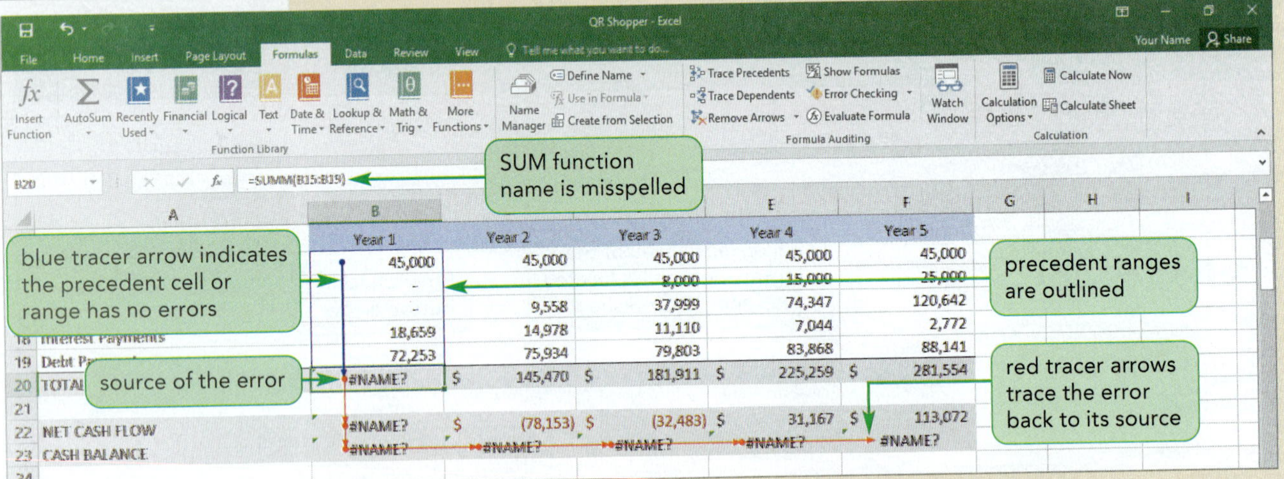

5. In cell **B20**, change the formula to **=SUM(B15:B19)**, and then press the **Enter** key. After you edit the formula, the #NAME? error values disappear from the worksheet. Also, the color of the tracer arrows changes from red to blue because they no longer connect to cells containing errors.

   Trouble? If the tracer arrows already disappeared from your workbook, it's not a problem. Excel removes tracer arrows automatically. Continue with Step 7.

6. On the Formulas tab, in the Formula Auditing group, click the **Remove Arrows** button to remove all of the tracer arrows from the worksheet.

7. Go to the **Balance Sheet** worksheet, and verify that no error values appear on that sheet.

8. Click the **Remove Arrows** button, if necessary, to remove the tracer arrows from the worksheet.

TIP

To restore the tracer arrows that have disappeared, retrace the formulas in the workbook.

You can use the auditing tools to track any cell formula whether or not it contains an error. To trace the precedents of the active cell, click the Trace Precedents button in the Formula Auditing group on the Formulas tab. To locate cells that are dependent upon the active cell, click the Trace Dependents button.

Evaluating a Formula

Another way to explore the relationship between cells in a workbook is by evaluating formulas using the Evaluate Formula tool. From the Evaluate Formula dialog box, you can display the value of different parts of the formula or "drill down" through the cell references in the formula to discover the source of the formula's value. This is helpful for subtle worksheet errors that are not easily seen and fixed.

On a balance sheet, the value of the company's total assets should equal the value of the total liabilities and equity. Checking that these totals match is a basic step in auditing any financial report. In the Balance Sheet worksheet, the total assets in row 16 balance the total liabilities and equity in row 34 for Year 1 through Year 4. However, in Year 5 these values do not match. The company's Year 5 total assets shown in cell F18 are $392,949, but the Year 5 total liabilities and equity shown in cell F34 is $481,090. Because the values differ, an error must occur somewhere in the workbook. You'll use the Evaluate Formula tool to evaluate the formula in cell F34 to locate the source of the error.

To evaluate the formula in cell F34 of the Balance Sheet worksheet:

1. Select cell **F34**, which contains the total liabilities and equity value for Year 5.
2. On the Formulas tab, in the Formula Auditing group, click the **Evaluate Formula** button. The Evaluate Formula dialog box opens with the formula in cell F34 displayed. See Figure 9-34.

Figure 9-34 Evaluate Formula dialog box

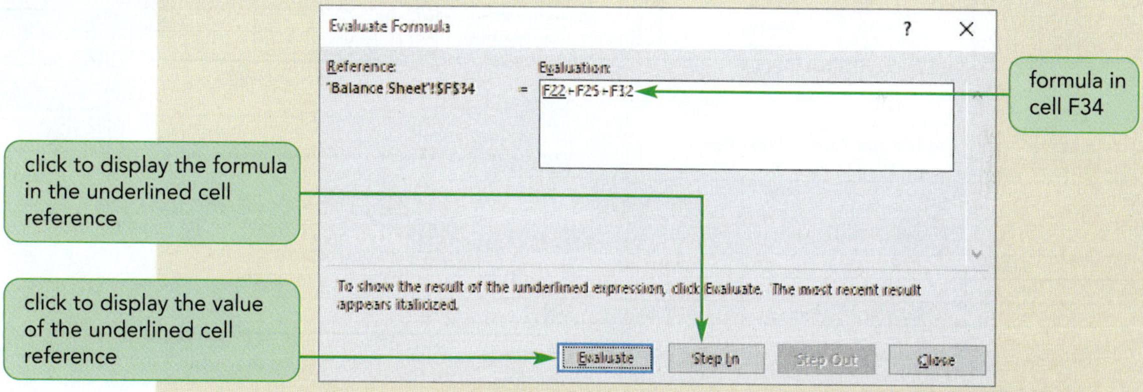

From this dialog box, you can evaluate each component of the formula in cell F34. To display the value of the underlined cell reference, click the Evaluate button. If the underlined part of the formula is a reference to another formula located elsewhere in the workbook, click the Step In button to display the other formula. Likewise, the Step Out button hides the nested formula.

3. Click the **Evaluate** button. The selected cell reference F22 is replaced with the current liabilities for Year 5 (0). Cell F25 is now the underlined reference.
4. Click the **Step In** button to view the formula in cell F25. The formula ='Loan Schedule'!E38 appears below the original formula, indicating that cell F25 gets its value from cell E38 in the Loan Schedule worksheet. See Figure 9-35.

Figure 9-35 Stepping into a formula

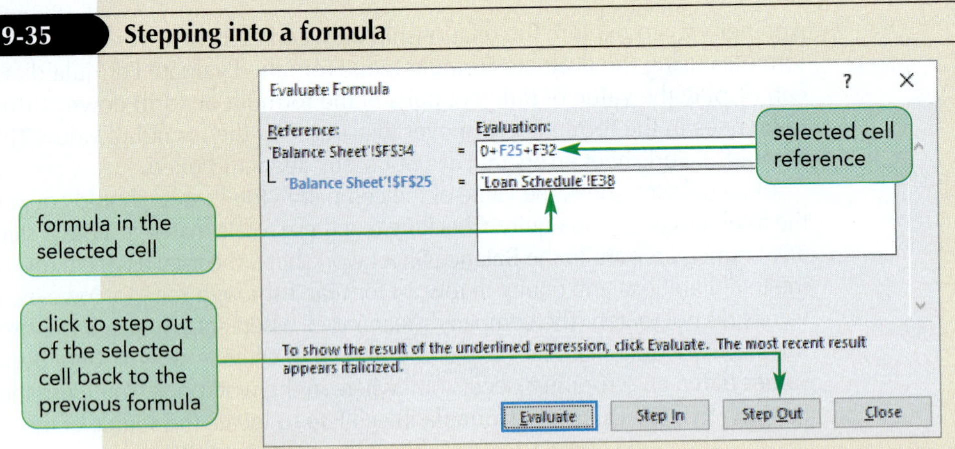

5. Click the **Step In** button to evaluate the formula in cell E38 of the Loan Schedule worksheet. See Figure 9-36.

Figure 9-36 Finding the source of the error

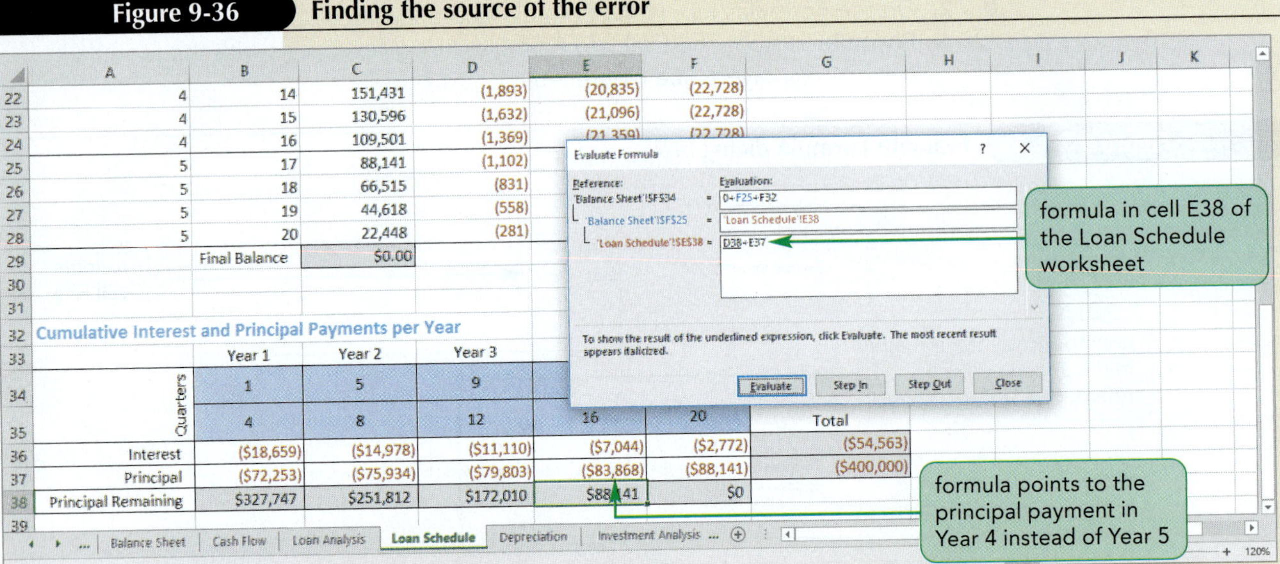

You've located the source of the problem. As shown in Figure 9-36, cell E38 in the Loan Schedule worksheet is the Principal Remaining value for Year 4 of the loan payment schedule. However, it should be pointing to cell F38, which contains the Year 5 value, because you are examining liabilities and assets for Year 5.

6. Click the **Step Out** button to hide the nested formula and redisplay the Balance Sheet worksheet.
7. Click the **Close** button to close the Evaluate Formula dialog box and return to the Balance Sheet worksheet with cell F25 selected.
8. In cell **F25**, change the formula from ='Loan Schedule'!E38 to **='Loan Schedule'!F38**. The total liabilities and equity value in cell F34 changes to $392,949, matching the total assets value in cell F18. The balance sheet is in balance again.

Using the Watch Window

Workbooks can contain dozens of worksheets with interconnected formulas. When you change a value in one worksheet, you may want to view the impact of that change on cell values in other worksheets. Moving among worksheets can be slow and clumsy if the values you want to follow are spread across many worksheets. Rather than jumping to different worksheets, you can create a **Watch Window**, which is a window that displays values of cells located throughout the workbook. When you change a cell's value, a Watch Window allows you to view the impact of the change on widely scattered dependent cells. The window also displays the workbook, worksheet, defined name, cell value, and formula of each cell being watched.

Ryan wants to know what would happen if the government increased the tax rate from 32 percent to 38 percent. You'll create a Watch Window to display the company's Year 5 retained earnings, the Year 5 net worth value, and the Year 5 cash balance value.

To use the Watch Window to display values from multiple cells:

1. Go to the **Income Statement** worksheet, and scroll to the top of the sheet.
2. On the Formulas tab, in the Formula Auditing group, click the **Watch Window** button. The Watch Window opens.
3. Click the **Add Watch** button. The Add Watch dialog box opens.
4. Click cell **F35** in the Income Statement worksheet, and then click the **Add** button. The Year 5 retained earnings value in cell F35 of the Income Statement worksheet is added to the Watch Window.
5. Click the **Add Watch** button, go to the **Balance Sheet** worksheet, click cell **F36**, and then click the **Add** button. The Year 5 net worth value from cell F36 of the Balance Sheet worksheet is added to the Watch Window.
6. Click the **Add Watch** button, go to the **Cash Flow** worksheet, click cell **F23**, and then click the **Add** button. The Year 5 cash balance in cell F23 of the Cash Flow worksheet is added to the Watch Window.

TIP
You can assign defined names to watched cells to make the Watch Window easier to interpret.

Now you can see the impact on these three values when the tax rate changes from 32 percent to 38 percent.

To modify the tax rate value:

1. Scroll to the top of the Income Statement worksheet, and then click cell **F5**.
2. Change the assumed tax rate value from 32% to **38%**. The Watch Window shows the impact of increasing the tax rate. See Figure 9-37.

Figure 9-37 Watch Window under a 38% tax rates

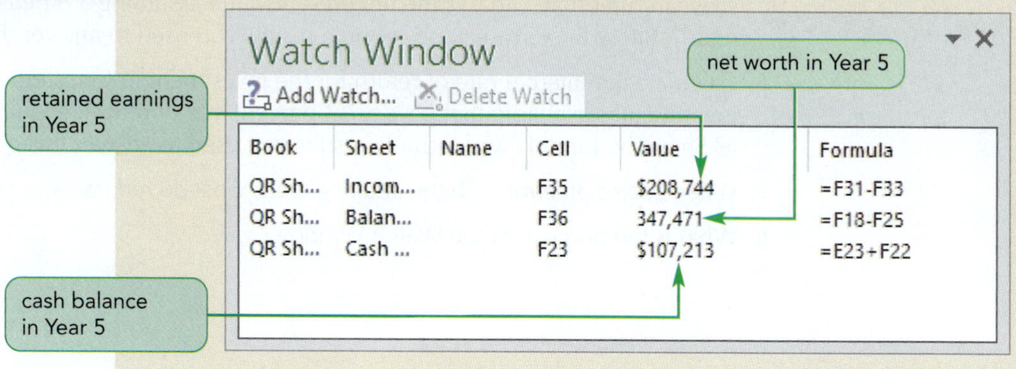

From the Watch Window you can observe the effect of the revised tax rate throughout the workbook. The Year 5 retained earnings amount in the Income Statement worksheet changes from $231,364 to $208,744—a drop of about $23,000. The Year 5 net worth value in the Balance Sheet worksheet changes from $392,949 to $347,471—a drop of about $45,000. Finally, the Year 5 cash balance in the Cash Flow worksheet changes from $152,690 to $107,213—also a drop of about $45,000. With operating margins so tight in the tech field, any increase in the tax rate and the resulting losses are a great concern. Ryan will study this more closely and perhaps revise the business plan to deal with this possibility.

You will restore the tax rate to its original values.

To restore the tax rate:

1. In cell **F5**, change the tax rate value back to **32%**.
2. Close the Watch Window.
3. Save the workbook, and then close it.

You have completed the financial analysis of Ryan's initial business plan for QR Shopper. He will continue to revise his plan and discuss the venture with his financial analysts, lawyers, and other consultants.

REVIEW

Session 9.3 Quick Check

1. If you take out a loan for $200,000 that must be repaid in 10 years with quarterly payments of $7,200, what is the formula to calculate the annual interest rate of the loan? What is the result?
2. If the annual rate of return is 5 percent, is $95 today worth more than, less than, or the same as $100 a year from now? Show the formula and formula results you used to answer this question.
3. You receive $50 at the end of Year 1 from an investment, $75 at the end of Year 2, and $100 at the end of Year 3. If the rate of return is 6 percent, what is the present value of this investment? Show the formula and formula results you used to answer this question.
4. You spend $350 on an investment that pays $75 per year for the next six years. If you make the investment immediately, what is the net present value of the investment? Assume a 6 percent rate of return. Show the formula and formula results you used to answer this question.
5. Suppose that instead of spending $350 immediately on an investment, you spend $350 one year from now and then receive $75 per year for the next six years after that. What is the net present value assuming a 6 percent rate of return? Show the formula and formula results you used to answer this question.
6. Calculate the internal rate of return for the investment in Question 4. If another investment is available that pays a 7.3 percent rate of return, should you take it? Show the formula and formula results you used to answer this question.
7. When tracing an error with the auditing tools, what do red tracer arrows indicate?
8. What is the purpose of the Watch Window?

PRACTICE

Review Assignments

Data File needed for the Review Assignments: Business.xlsx

Ryan has some new figures for the business plan for QR Shopper. He has received slightly better conditions on the business loan, which means that the company needs less money from investors to fund the company. He has also modified the depreciation schedule for the business's tangible assets. Ryan wants you to make the necessary changes in the workbook to calculate the company's financial data for the next five years. Complete the following:

1. Open the **Business** workbook located in the Excel9 > Review folder included with your Data Files, and then save the workbook as **Business Plan** in the location specified by your instructor.
2. In the Documentation worksheet, enter your name and the date.
3. In the Loan Scenarios worksheet, in cell B4, enter the **4.85%** annual interest rate that the company has secured for a business loan.
4. Calculate the following possible loan scenarios:
   a. In row 7, for a $425,000 business loan that is repaid in 10 years at a 4.85 percent interest rate with quarterly payments, use the PMT function in cell I7 to calculate the quarterly payments.
   b. In row 8, for a $425,000 loan at a 4.85 percent interest rate with quarterly payments of $10,000 made over 10 years, use the FV function in cell C8 to calculate the principal at the end of 10 years.
   c. In row 9, for a $425,000 loan at a 4.85 percent interest rate that is completely repaid with quarterly payments of $10,000, use the NPER function in cell F9 to calculate the number of quarterly payment periods and then in cell D9, calculate the number of years required to repay the loan.
   d. In row 10, for quarterly payments of $12,000 for 10 years at a 4.85 percent interest rate, use the PV function in cell B10 to calculate the largest loan the company could completely repay in 10 years.
5. In the Startup Plan worksheet, in cell B25, enter **425,000** as the size of the loan that QR Shopper will take out to fund the startup costs of the business.
6. In the Amortization Schedule worksheet, in the range A5:F5, enter the conditions for a $425,000 loan at a 4.85 percent interest rate with quarterly payments to be repaid in 10 years. Reference the loan value from cell B25 in the Startup Plan worksheet. In cell G5, use the PMT function to calculate the amount of the quarterly payments required to repay the loan.
7. In the range C9:F48, complete the amortization schedule as follows:
   a. Use absolute references to the loan conditions in row 5 of the worksheet for your formulas.
   b. Use the PPMT function to calculate the principal payment for each quarter.
   c. Use the IPMT function to calculate the interest payment for each quarter.
   d. Reduce the principal owed for each new quarter by the amount paid in the previous quarter.
   e. Verify that the loan is completely repaid by displaying the value of the remaining principal in cell C49.
8. Calculate the cumulative interest and principal payments per year as follows:
   a. In the range B55:F55, use the CUMPRINC function to calculate the cumulative principal payments in each of the first five years of the loan. Include absolute references to the loan conditions in row 5 as part of your calculations.
   b. In the range B56:F56, use the CUMIPMT function to calculate the cumulative interest payments in each of the first five years of the loan.
   c. In cells G55 and G56, calculate the total principal payments and interest payments in the first five years of the loan.
   d. In the range B57:F57, calculate the remaining principal at the end of each of the first five years of the loan.
9. In the Profit and Loss worksheet, in the range C8:E8, project the company's income and expenses for the next five years by interpolating the Year 2 through Year 4 revenue assuming a growth trend.

10. In cell F3, enter **20%** as the percent cost of marketing and in cell F4, enter **10%** as the percent cost of R&D. In the range B9:F10, use those percentages to calculate the Year 1 through Year 5 cost of sales. In the range B11:F11, calculate the gross profit by subtracting the cost of market and R & D from the annual projected revenue.
11. In the range C14:F14, extrapolate the Year 2 through Year 5 payroll expenses by assuming the payroll grows by 12 percent per year. In C15:F17, extrapolate the other expenses by assuming they grow by 5 percent per year from the initial Year 1 values. In the range C18:F18, calculate the total expenses for Year 2 through Year 5.
12. In the range B21:F21, calculate the company's initial earnings for each year, equal to the gross profit minus the total general expenses.
13. In the Startup Plan worksheet, in cell B12, enter **225,000** as the long-term tangible assets that will need to be depreciated.
14. In the Depreciation worksheet, in cell B4, reference the long-term assets' value from cell B12 in the Startup Plan worksheet. In cell B5, enter **35,000** as the assets' salvage value. In cell B6, enter **15** as the useful lifetime of the assets.
15. In the range B10:F10, calculate the yearly straight-line depreciation of the long-term assets using the SLN function. In the range B11:F11, calculate the cumulative depreciation through the first five years. In the range B12:F12, calculate the depreciated value of the assets at the end of each of the first five years.
16. In the range B16:F16, use the DB function to calculate the yearly declining balance of the assets. In the range B17:F17, calculate the cumulative depreciation of the assets. In the range B18:F18, calculate the depreciated value of the assets at the end of each year.
17. In the Profit and Loss worksheet, in the range B22:F22, enter formulas to reference the declining balance depreciation values in the range B16:F16 of the Depreciation worksheet. Calculate the company's operating profit in B23:F23 range by subtracting the yearly depreciation from the yearly initial earnings.
18. In the range B25:F25, enter formulas for the yearly interest expenses that reference the cumulative interest payments in the range B56:F56 of the Amortization Schedule worksheet. Enter the interest expenses as positive values by changing the sign of value. In the range B26:F26, calculate the company's pretax profit by subtracting the interest expenses from the operating profit.
19. In cell F5, enter **33%** as the assumed tax rate. In the range B28:F28, use an IF function to calculate the company's tax liability for each of the first five years assuming the tax rate in cell F5. If the company's pretax profit is negative, set the tax burden to $0; otherwise, multiply the assumed tax rate by the pretax profit. In the range B29:F29, calculate the company's after-tax profit by subtracting the taxes owed from the pretax profit.
20. In the Startup Plan worksheet, in cell B30, enter **$160,000** as the amount the company hopes to attract from investors.
21. In the Investment worksheet, in cell B6, enter a reference to cell B30 in the Startup Plan worksheet as a negative cash flow. In cells B7 and B8, enter values to show that the company repay investors **$35,000** per year for **5** years. In cell B9, use the RATE function to calculate the interest of the proposed repayment schedule.
22. In the range B12:F13, enter the annual payment and dividend schedule using cell references to cell B7 to enter the yearly payments and dividends of **$4,000** in Year 2 and Year 3 and **$15,000** in Year 4 and Year 5. In the range B14:F14, calculate the total sum paid to the investors each year.
23. In the range B18:C23, determine the payback period, and calculate the net cash flow to the investors.
24. In cell C25, enter **12%** as the desired rate of return for the investors. In cell C26, use the NPV function to calculate the present value of the Year 1 through Year 5 payments from the range B19:B23 using the desired rate of return specified in cell C25. In cell C27, calculate the net present value of their investment in the company by adding the startup payment to the present value of the Year 1 through Year 5 repayments.
25. In cell B28, use the IRR function to calculate the internal rate of return of their investment.
26. In the Profit and Loss worksheet, in the range B31:F31, enter references to the yearly dividend values paid to the shareholders as specified in the range B13:F13 of the Investment worksheet. In the range B33:F33, calculate the company's retained earnings by subtracting the dividends from the after-tax profit.

27. An error is somewhere in the workbook. Starting with cell F18 in the Balance sheet, trace the #REF error in the workbook back to its source, and correct it.
28. Save the workbook, and then close it.

APPLY

Case Problem 1

Data File needed for this Case Problem: Vivere.xlsx

Vivere Studio John Barnes is owner of Vivere Studio, a startup animation studio located in Citrus Height, California. John is looking to upgrade the company's digital equipment and computers for some upcoming projects. He can either buy this new equipment or lease it. The equipment will cost $23,000 to purchase. John has learned that he can sell the equipment back to the store after three years for about 92 percent of its depreciated value. To lease the same equipment will cost John an initial security deposit of $1,500, which will be returned after three years as long as the equipment is still in good condition. The monthly lease fee is $320. John wants you to determine the present value of both of buying versus leasing the equipment. Complete the following:

1. Open the **Vivere** workbook located in the Excel9 > Case1 folder included with your Data Files, and then save the workbook as **Vivere Studio** in the location specified by your instructor.
2. In the Documentation worksheet, enter your name and the date.
3. In the **Buy vs. Lease** worksheet, in cell B4, enter **$23,000** as the current price of the digital equipment.
4. The digital equipment has a salvage value of $8,000 after 120 months, or 10 years. In the range B5:B6, enter the salvage value and the salvage time (in months).
5. Digital equipment depreciates at reduced rate. In cell B7, enter **0.8** as the depreciation factor.
6. John decides to purchase an optional service maintenance contract that covers the next three years. In cell B10, enter **$660** as the value of this contract.
7. In cell B11, enter **3.5%** as the sales tax John will have to pay on the equipment. Enter this tax rate. In cell B12, enter a formula to calculate the tax on sale amount by multiplying the sales tax rate by the current price of the equipment.
8. In cell B13, enter **92%** as the resale percent (which means that the store will agree to repurchase the digital equipment at 92% of its depreciated value after three years).
9. If John decides to lease this equipment, he will have to pay a $1,500 security deposit and a monthly payment of $320. Enter these values in the range B16:B17.
10. In cell E4, enter a formula that shows the current value of the digital equipment entered in cell B4.
11. In the range E5:E40, calculate the value of the equipment as it depreciates each year. To calculate the depreciated values, subtract the depreciation amount from the value of the equipment in the previous month. To calculate the depreciation amount, use the DDB function for the double-declining method using the depreciation values entered in the range B4:B7 and the corresponding period value in column D.
12. In cell F4, enter as a negative the cash flow the cost of purchasing the equipment plus the cost of the service contract in cell B10 and the cost of sales tax in B12.
13. For Month 1 through Month 36, John will not have to make any payments on the equipment. Enter **0** as the cash flow values in the range F5:F40.
14. After Month 36, John will sell the equipment back to the store. In cell F41, enter as a positive cash flow the final depreciated value of the equipment in cell E40 multiplied by the resale percentage in cell B13.
15. In cell G4, enter as a negative cash flow the cost of the security deposit on the digital equipment entered in cell B16.
16. In the range G5:G40, enter as a negative cash flow the monthly lease payments in cell B17.
17. After the term of the lease is over, John will return the digital equipment and receive his security deposit back. In cell G41, enter the value of the security deposit from cell B16 as a positive cash flow.

18. To calculate the time value of money, John will assume a 4.80 percent discount rate. Enter this value into cell B20. To express this as a monthly percentage, in cell B21, enter a formula to divide the value of cell B20 by 12.
19. In cell B22, enter a formula to calculate the net present value of buying the digital equipment by adding the initial investment in cell F4 to the present value of the cash flows in the range F5:F41. Use the NPV function with the monthly discount rate in cell B21 as the rate of return to calculate the present value of the cost of the buying the digital equipment for the next three years of use.
20. In cell B23, enter a formula to calculate the net present value of leasing by adding the initial investment from cell G4 to the present value of the cash flows in the range G5:G41. Again, use cell B21 as the discount rate, and calculate the present value of leasing the equipment for the next three years.
21. In cell B24, enter an IF function that displays the text BUY if the present value of buying the equipment is greater than the present value of leasing the equipment; otherwise display the text LEASE.
22. Save the workbook.
23. If the digital equipment depreciates more than expected, John will have to sell it back to the company for less money. Change the value depreciation factor in cell B7 to **1.5** (resulting in faster depreciation and a lower buy-back value). Determine whether your choice of buying versus leasing changes under this scenario.
24. Save the revised workbook as **Vivere Studio 2**, and then close it.

APPLY

Case Problem 2

Data File needed for this Case Problem: Turbitt.xlsx

Turbitt Farm Ian Turbitt owns a small farm located near Jackson, Ohio. He is considering purchasing or leasing a harvester for the farm. If he purchases the harvester, he will have to take out a loan and pay interest until he completely repays the loan or resells the harvester. However, taking out a farm loan has advantages, including reducing the amount of farm income subject to taxes. You will explore the financial and tax benefits of owning versus leasing for Ian. Complete the following:

1. Open the **Turbitt** workbook located in the Excel9 > Case2 folder included with your Data Files, and then save the workbook as **Turbitt Farm** in the location specified by your instructor.
2. In the Documentation worksheet, enter your name and the date.
3. Ian wants to get a $410,000 harvester for the farm. He can afford a down payment of $75,000 on the equipment. In the Buy vs. Lease worksheet, in the range B7:B8, enter this information, entering the down payment as a negative cash flow.
4. Ian believes that he will be able to resell the harvester for $275,000 after five years. The harvester itself has a salvage value of $175,000 after 10 years. In the range B9:B11, enter this data.
5. The cost of insurance and housing for the harvester is $2,500 per year. The maintenance, labor, and fuel and oil costs are $3,000, $5,500, and $9,000 annually. In the range B14:B17, enter this data as a negative cash flow. In cell B18, calculate the sum of the annual cost of ownership, also as a negative cash flow.
6. Ian can secure a loan for the harvester at a 5.3 percent annual interest rate with annual payments made once at the beginning of each year over a five-year period. Calculate the following values:
   a. In cell B21, enter the annual interest rate of the loan.
   b. In cell B22, enter the length of the loan in years.
   c. In cell B23, enter the amount of loan by calculating the sum of the values in B7 and B8.
   d. In cell B24, use the PMT function to calculate the annual loan payment. (*Hint*: The value of the type attribute should reflect the fact that the loan is paid at the beginning of each year.)
7. Ian can negotiate a lease agreement in which he pays $45,000 a year for five years. In the range B27:B28, enter these parameters, entering the annual lease payment as a negative cash flow.
8. In cell B31, enter the discount rate for the time-value of money, which Ian estimates at 4.4 percent.

9. In the range B32:B33, enter the marginal tax rate that Ian owes as 45 percent and the self-employment tax rate of 15.9 percent.
10. Lease payments are due at the end of each year and apply forward to the next year. In the range E8:I8, enter the annual lease payments for Year 0 through Year 4 using the value in cell B28.
11. In the range F9:J9, enter the Year 1 through Year 5 cost of ownership of the harvester using the value in cell B18.
12. In the range F10:J10, multiply the sum of the lease payments and ownership costs by the marginal tax rate in cell B32, and then multiply this value by –1 to calculate the reduction in taxes owed as a positive cash flow.
13. In the range E12:J12, add the lease payment, the ownership cost, and the reduction in taxes owed for each year to calculate the annual cash flow under the lease agreement for Year 0 through Year 5.
14. In cell E14, add the value of cell E12 to the net present value of the cash flows in the F12:J12 range using the discount rate in cell B31 to calculate the present value of the lease agreement.
15. In cell E18, enter the cost of the down payment in Year 0 using the value in cell B8. In cell J19, enter the income from reselling the harvester using the value in cell B9. The down payment should appear as a negative cash flow and the resell value should appear as a positive cash flow. In the range E20:J20, calculate the sum of the down payment and resell values for Year 0 through Year 5.
16. In the range F22:J22, enter the yearly loan payment cost using the value from cell B24.
17. In the range F25:J25, enter the annual cost of ownership for Year 1 through Year 5 using the value in cell B18.
18. In the range F26:J26, calculate the interest paid for Year 1 through Year 5 on the loan. Use the IPMT function with the loan terms in cells B21, B22, and B23 and the year values in cells F17 through J17 for the period of the loan.
19. In range F27:J27 calculate the depreciation of the harvester for Year 1 through Year 5. Use the DB function with the cost, salvage, and life values in cells B7, B10, and B11, and the year values in cells F17 through J17 to specify the period of the depreciation. Add a negative sign before the depreciation values so that they are treated as negative cash flows.
20. In the range F28:J28, calculate the total deductions Ian can take each year by adding the cost of ownership, interest on loan, and annual depreciation for Year 1 through Year 5. Change the sign of the sum by multiplying it by –1 so that the values appear as a positive cash flow.
21. In the range F29:J29, multiply the total deductions for each year by the marginal tax rate in cell B32 to calculate the reduction in taxes owed.
22. In cell E31, enter the value of the harvester using the value from cell B7. In the range F31:J31, calculate the yearly value of the harvester by adding that year's depreciation (in row 27) to the previous year's harvester value.
23. When Ian sells the harvester at the end of Year 5, he will owe taxes if he sells it for more than its depreciated value. In cell J32, insert an IF function that tests whether the resale price (cell J19) is greater than the depreciated value (cell J31). If the condition is true, return the difference of the resale price and the depreciated value multiplied by the difference between the marginal tax rate (cell B32) and the self-employment tax rate (cell B33). If the condition is false, return a value of 0.
24. In the range F34:J34, calculate Ian's overall tax reduction for Year 1 through Year 5 by subtracting the taxes owed on the harvester resale (row 32) from the reduction in taxes owed (row 29). Note that only in Year 5 will Ian owe any taxes on the harvester resale. These values represent how much less Ian will owe in taxes each year due to owning and operating the harvester.
25. In the range E36:J36, calculate Ian's net cash flow for Year 0 through Year 5 by adding the profit/loss on the harvester (row 20), the annual loan payments (row 22), the cost of ownership (row 25), and the overall tax reduction (row 34).
26. In cell E38, add the value of cell E36 to the net present value of the cash flows in the range F36:J36 using the discount rate in cell B31 to calculate the present value of buying the harvester.
27. The values in cells E14 and E38 represent what the leasing plan and the buying plan will cost Ian in current dollars. In cell B3, enter an IF function that displays the text BUY if cell E38 is greater than cell E14; otherwise, display the text LEASE.
28. Save the workbook, and then close it.

CHALLENGE

Case Problem 3

Data File needed for this Case Problem: Granite.xlsx

Hawthorne Granite Anita Garcia is a project analyst at Hawthorne Granite, a mining company in central Michigan. The company is considering investing in a granite quarry near the town of Mount Pleasant, Michigan. Anita wants you to examine the current value of the project assuming that the quarry will have an initial startup cost of $7.7 million with growing revenue through its first 10 years of existence and declining revenue for the next 15 years as the granite deposits become more difficult and less economical to extract. The company will also have to clean up the site after 25 years of operation to restore it to its original condition. The current cleanup cost is $8.2 million, but Anita wants the Year 25 value, assuming a 3.2 percent annual inflation rate. You will use the financial data supplied by Anita to estimate the profitability of the project. Complete the following:

1. Open the **Granite** workbook located in the Excel9 > Case3 folder included with your Data Files, and then save the workbook as **Granite Quarry** in the location specified by your instructor.
2. In the Documentation worksheet, enter your name and the date.
3. In the Project Analysis worksheet, enter the following initial assumptions for the project:
   - In cell B5, enter **$7.70** as the startup costs for the project (in millions).
   - In cell B6, enter **31.0%** as the operational costs percentage.
   - In cell B7, enter **$8.20** as the cleanup cost in current dollars (in millions).
   - In cell B8, enter **25** as the years of operation.
   - In cell B9, enter **3.2%** as the annual inflation rate.

Explore 4. In cell B12, use the FV function to calculate the final cleanup cost in 25 years, using the inflation rate in cell B9, the number of years in cell B8, a payment value of 0, and the present value of the cleanup cost in cell B7. Change the sign of the result so it appears as a positive value.

5. In cell G6, enter the startup cost of the mine using the value in cell B5.
6. Enter the following projected annual income values that the quarry will generate:
   a. In cell E7, enter **$0.50** million as the projected earnings for Year 1.
   b. In cell E16, enter **$12** million as the projected earnings for Year 10.
   c. In cell E26, enter **$2** million as the projected earnings for Year 20.
   d. In cell E31, enter **$1** million as the projected earnings for Year 25.
7. Do the following to fill in the missing income values:
   a. Interpolate the rising income values between E7 and E16 assuming a growth trend.
   b. Interpolate the declining income values between E16 and E26 assuming a growth trend.
   c. Interpolate the declining income values between E26 and E31 assuming a linear trend.
8. In the range F7:F31, calculate the annual cost of goods by multiplying the income value for each year by the operational cost percentage in cell B6.
9. Anita estimates the quarry will have $1.2 million in fixed costs in Year 1. Enter this value in cell G7.
10. Anita projects that fixed costs will grow at a rate of 4 percent per year. Extrapolate the Year 1 fixed cost value through Year 20 in the range G8:G26.
11. From Year 21 to Year 25, Anita projects that fixed costs will decline by 10 percent per year (so that each year's fixed cost is 90 percent of the previous year). Extrapolate the Year 21 fixed-cost values through Year 25 in the range G27:G31.
12. In cell G32, enter the cleanup cost using the value you calculated in cell B12.
13. In the range H6:H32, calculate the quarry's gross profit by subtracting the sum of the annual cost of goods and fixed costs from the quarry's annual income.
14. In the range I6:I32, calculate the cumulative gross profit for each year by adding the sum of the previous year's gross profit values.

15. Create an area chart of the range D5:D32,I5:I32 to show the cumulative profit of the quarry, showing the year in which the initial investment is paid back. Format the chart to make it easier to read, and then resize the chart to cover the range K5:P20.
16. In cell B13, calculate the total income from the quarry by adding all of the values in column E. In cell B14, calculate the total cost of the quarry by adding all of the values in columns F and G. Note that by the raw totals, the quarry appears to lose money over its history.

Explore 17. Do the following to calculate the rate of return from the quarry:

   a. In cell A17, enter **1.0%** as your guess for the rate of return. In cell B17, calculate the internal rate of return using the profit values in column H and your guess in cell A17.
   b. In cell A18, enter **10.0%** as your guess for the rate of return. In cell B18, calculate the internal rate of return using the cash flow values in column H and your guess in cell A18.

Explore 18. When a cash flow switches from positive to negative several times during its history, more than one internal rate of return is possible. To see how this is possible, you will do the following to calculate the net present value for different possible discount rates:

   a. In the range A21:A39, enter the discount rates from **1%** to **10%** in steps of 0.5%.
   b. In the range B21:B39, add the value of cell H6 to the present value of the cash flows in the H7:H32 range using the NPV function with the corresponding discount rate in column A.

19. Create a line chart of the values in the range A20:B39, using the percentages in the range A21:A39 as category levels. Format the chart to make it easier to read.
20. Resize the chart to cover the range K22:P39. The net present value crosses the *x*-axis twice, resulting in two possible internal rates of return depending on the initial guess of the rate of return.
21. Save the workbook, and then close it.

TROUBLESHOOT

Case Problem 4

Data File needed for this Case Problem: Canyon.xlsx

Canyon Properties Katherine Boniver owns and operates Canyon Properties, a real estate company in Flagstaff, Arizona. Katherine is examining the financial details involved with purchasing a vacation home in the city. Canyon Properties will retain the home for 10 years, receiving yearly income from rentals that will cover the expenses and will eventually repay the cost of the initial investment. Her assistant created a workbook to perform the initial financial analysis, but the workbook contains several errors. You will locate and fix the errors and complete the workbook. Complete the following:

1. Open the **Canyon** workbook located in the Excel9 > Case4 folder included with your Data Files, and then save the workbook as **Canyon Properties** in the location specified by your instructor.
2. In the Documentation worksheet, enter your name and the date.

Troubleshoot 3. A #REF error value appears through the workbook. In the Financial Statements worksheet, starting from cell L11, trace the error back to its source and correct it.

Troubleshoot 4. Starting from cell K11 on the Depreciation worksheet, trace the second error back to its source and correct it. Verify that there are no error values left in the workbook.

5. In the Home Info worksheet, enter the following initial conditions for the vacation home:
   a. In cell B5, enter **10** as the number of years that company will hold the property.
   b. In cell B6, enter **3.70%** as the annual inflation rate.
   c. In cell B7, enter **2.10%** as the property tax rate the company will have to pay each year.
   d. In cell B8, enter **29.50%** as the tax rate the company will have to pay on the income it generates from renting the home.
   e. In cell B9, enter **38.30%** as the tax rate the company will have to pay upon selling the vacation home in 10 years.

6. In cell B12, use the FV function to calculate the future value of the home, given the annual inflation rate in cell B6, the number of years the home will be owned in cell B5, and the present value of the home in cell B4 (use 0 for the payment value in the function). Change the sign of the future value so it appears as a positive number.
7. In cell B13, show the depreciated value of the vacation home in Year 10, using the value Katherine has already calculated in cell K11 of the Depreciation worksheet.
8. The taxable gain on the property is the difference between its Year 10 future value in cell B12 and its depreciated value in cell B13. In cell B14, calculate the value of the taxable gain.
9. In cell B15, calculate the resale tax based on the tax rate on the sale applied to the taxable gain.
10. In the Financial Statements worksheet, complete the worksheet to project the income and expenses from the vacation home for each of the next 10 years by doing the following:
    a. In cell C6, enter **$36,000** as the Year 1 rental income from the property.
    b. In range the D6:L6, extrapolate the Year 2 income through Year 10 assuming a growth rate of 4 percent per year.
    c. In the range C8:C10, enter **1,200** for the Year 1 property taxes, **3,200** for the Year 1 maintenance costs, and **2,500** for the Year 1 miscellaneous costs.
    d. In the range D8:L10, extrapolate the Year 2 property taxes, maintenance costs, and miscellaneous costs through Year 10 assuming a growth rate of 3.5 percent per year.
    e. In the range C12:L12, calculate the total expenses for each year by summing the property taxes, maintenance costs, miscellaneous expenses, and deprecation for Year 1 through Year 10.
    f. In the range C13:L13, calculate the pretax income for each year by subtracting the total expenses from the rental income.
    g. In the range C15:L15, calculate the income taxes owed by the company each year by multiplying the pretax income by the rental income tax rate. Use an IF function so that if the pretax income is negative, the income tax is 0.
    h. In the range C16:L16, calculate the after-tax income for each year by subtracting the taxes owed from the pretax income.
11. At the end of Year 10, the company will sell the vacation home based on its anticipated future value. Calculate the finances associated with selling the property as follows:
    a. In cell L18, enter the income from the home sale using the value in cell B12 of the Home Info worksheet.
    b. In cell L19, enter the taxes owed on the home sale using the value in cell B15 of the Home Info worksheet.
    c. In cell L20, subtract the taxes owed on the home sale from the home sale income to calculate the net income from the sale of the home.
12. In the C22:L22 range, determine the yearly net income by adding the after-tax income to the resale net income (note that only in Year 10 is there resale income).
13. Complete the financial statement by calculating the yearly cash flow as follows:
    a. In Year 0, the company will purchase the vacation home. In cell B24, enter as a negative cash flow the cost of the home using the present value from cell B4 in the Home Info worksheet.
    b. To calculate the cash flow for each year, add the total net income in row 22 to the depreciation values in row 11 for Year 1 through Year 10.
14. In the Home Info worksheet, do the following to analyze the profitability of this investment:
    a. In cell B18, enter **10.00%** as the discount rate that Katherine wants to assume.
    b. In cell B19, calculate the net present value of the investment, and add the initial expenditure in Year 0 from cell B24 of the Financial Statements worksheet to the net present value of the net cash flow values in the range C24:L24 of the Financial Statements worksheet. Use the assumed discount rate in cell B18.
    c. In cell B20, calculate the internal rate of return from the investment using the cash flow values in the range B24:L24 of the Financial Statements worksheet.
15. Save the workbook, and then close it.

MODULE 10

Performing What-If Analyses

Maximizing Profits with the Right Product Mix

EXCEL

OBJECTIVES

Session 10.1
- Explore the principles of cost-volume-profit relationships
- Create a one-variable data table
- Create a two-variable data table

Session 10.2
- Create and apply different Excel scenarios with the Scenario Manager
- Generate a scenario summary report
- Generate a scenario PivotTable report

Session 10.3
- Explore the principles of a product mix
- Run Solver to calculate optimal solutions
- Create and apply constraints to a Solver model
- Save and load a Solver model

Case | *Coltivare Tool*

Irena Rostov manages production and sales in the lawn mower division at Coltivare Tool, a manufacturer of lawn and garden equipment based in Chesterfield, Missouri. Irena wants to use Excel to analyze the profitability of the company's line of power lawn mowers to determine the number of mowers the company must produce and sell in the second quarter to be profitable. She is interested in whether the company can increase its net income by reducing the selling price of the mowers in order to increase the sales volume. Your analysis for Irena will focus on the four most popular models the company sells. As part of your analysis, you will also study whether the company can increase its profits by promoting one model over another. In the process, you'll try to find the best product mix—one that maximizes profits subject to the limitations of customer demand, available parts, and manufacturing capability.

STARTING DATA FILES

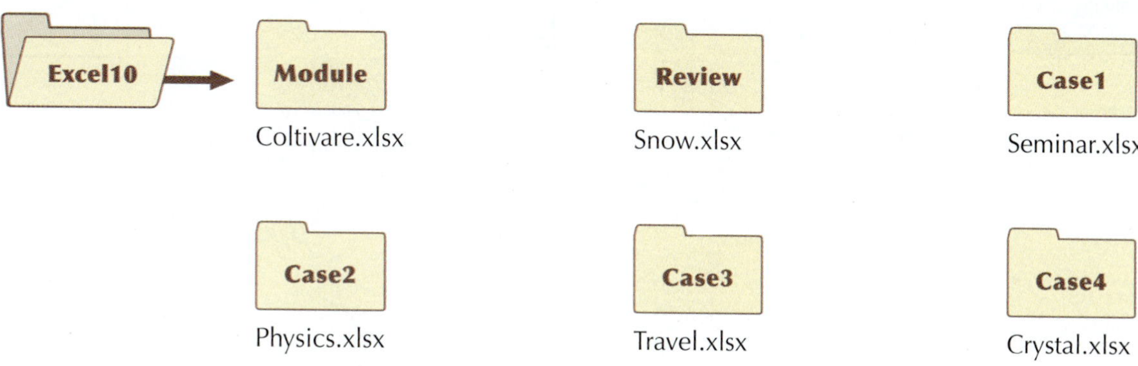

Session 10.1 Visual Overview:

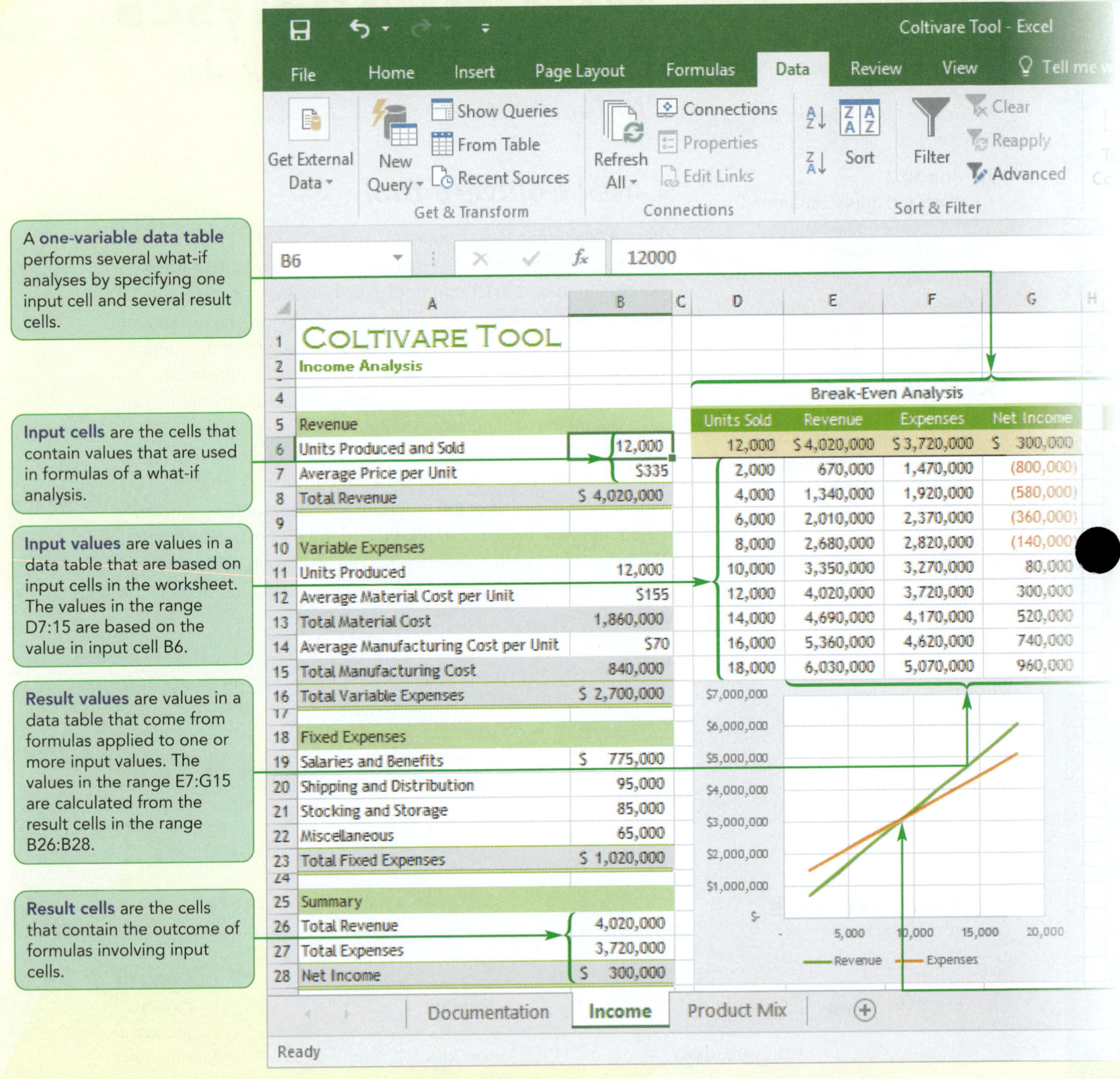

Data Tables and What-If Analysis

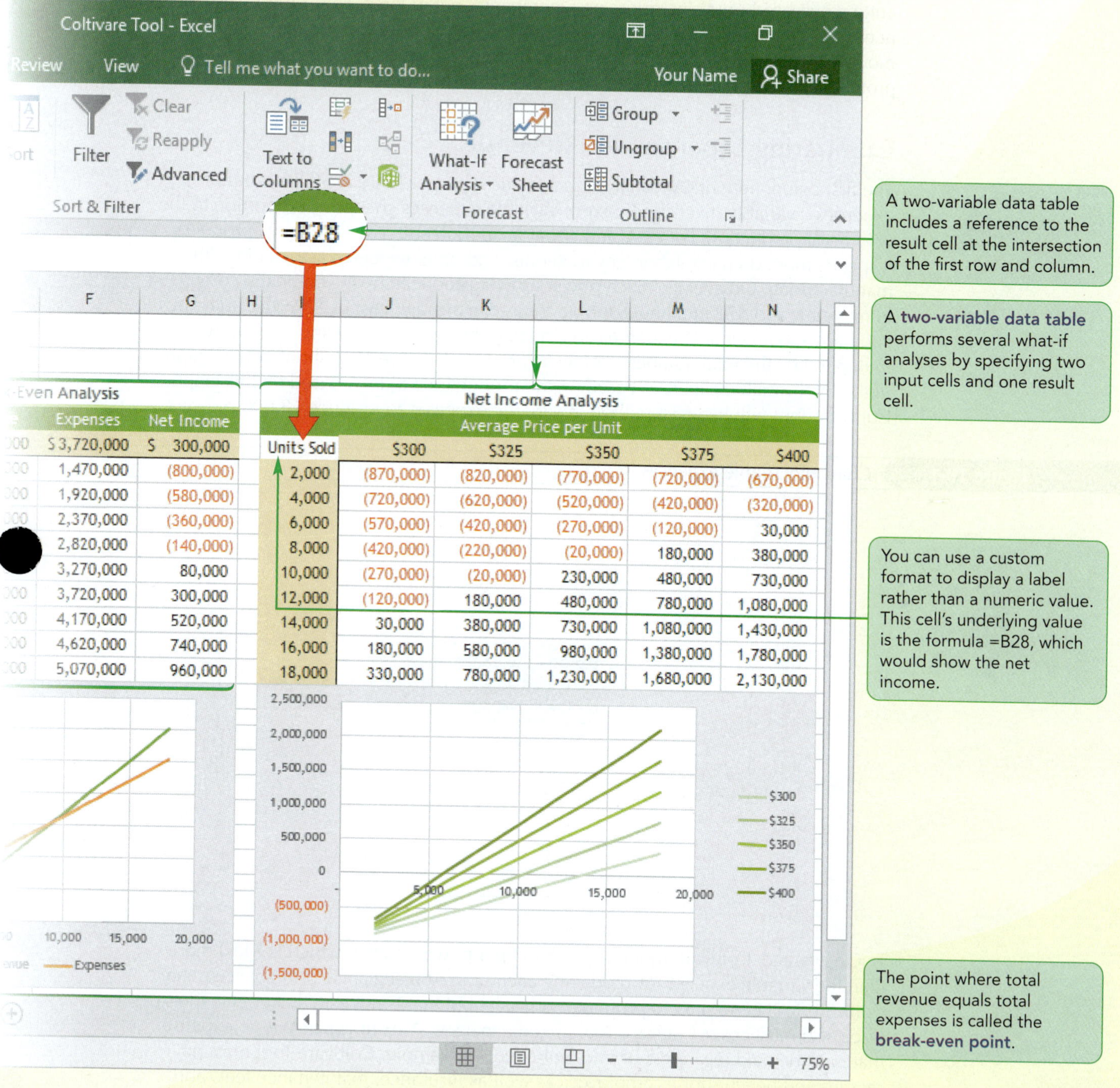
Coltivare Tool - Excel
Review
View
Tell me what you want to do...
Your Name
Share
Clear
Reapply
Filter
Advanced
Sort & Filter
Text to Columns
What-If Analysis
Forecast Sheet
Forecast
Group
Ungroup
Subtotal
Outline
=B28
A two-variable data table includes a reference to the result cell at the intersection of the first row and column.
A two-variable data table performs several what-if analyses by specifying two input cells and one result cell.
Net Income Analysis
Average Price per Unit
You can use a custom format to display a label rather than a numeric value. This cell's underlying value is the formula =B28, which would show the net income.
Expenses
Net Income
The point where total revenue equals total expenses is called the break-even point.
75%

Units Sold	$300	$325	$350	$375	$400
2,000	(870,000)	(820,000)	(770,000)	(720,000)	(670,000)
4,000	(720,000)	(620,000)	(520,000)	(420,000)	(320,000)
6,000	(570,000)	(420,000)	(270,000)	(120,000)	30,000
8,000	(420,000)	(220,000)	(20,000)	180,000	380,000
10,000	(270,000)	(20,000)	230,000	480,000	730,000
12,000	(120,000)	180,000	480,000	780,000	1,080,000
14,000	30,000	380,000	730,000	1,080,000	1,430,000
16,000	180,000	580,000	980,000	1,380,000	1,780,000
18,000	330,000	780,000	1,230,000	1,680,000	2,130,000

Understanding Cost-Volume Relationships

Cost-volume-profit (CVP) analysis is a branch of financial analysis that studies the relationship between expenses, sales volume, and profitability. CVP analysis is an important business decision-making tool because it can help predict the effect of cutting overhead or raising prices on a company's net income. For example, Irena needs to determine a reasonable price to charge for Coltivare Tool's line of power mowers. She needs to know how much to charge to break even and how much added profit Coltivare Tool could realize by increasing (or even decreasing) the sales price.

Comparing Expenses and Revenue

The first component of CVP analysis is cost, or expense. There are three types of expenses—variable, fixed, and mixed. **Variable expenses** change in proportion to the volume of production. For each additional lawn mower that the company produces, it spends more on parts, labor, raw materials, and other expenses associated with manufacturing. On average, each power mower produced by the company costs $155 in materials and $70 in manufacturing, for a total average cost of $225 per unit. The company's total variable expenses are equal to the cost of producing each mower multiplied by the total number of mowers produced. Figure 10-1 shows a line graph of the total variable expenses based on the production volume. Based on this graph, Coltivare Tool will incur $4 million in variable expenses to produce 18,000 mowers.

Figure 10-1 **Chart of variable expenses**

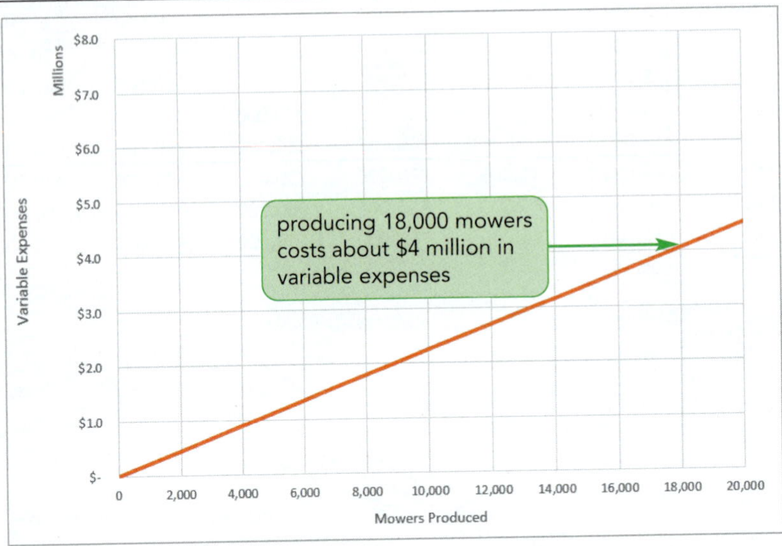

On average, Coltivare Tool charges $335 per power mower, which is $110 more than the variable expense for producing each unit. At first glance, it might seem that Coltivare Tool earns a $110 profit on each sale, but that is not exactly correct. The sales price also must cover Coltivare Tool's fixed expenses. A **fixed expense** is an expense that must be paid regardless of sales volume. For example, Coltivare Tool must pay salaries and benefits for its employees as well as insurance, maintenance fees, and administrative overhead. Irena tells you that the lawn mower division of Coltivare Tool has more than $1 million in fixed expenses, which must be paid even if that division doesn't produce or sell a single mower.

You can estimate Coltivare Tool's total expense for its line of power mowers by adding the company's variable and fixed expenses. The graph in Figure 10-2 shows the company's total expenses for a given number of mowers produced each year. As you can see, if the company produces 18,000 mowers, its total expense would be more than $5 million. Of this about $1 million represents fixed expenses and $4 million is from variable expenses related to the actual production of the mowers.

Figure 10-2 **Chart of total expenses**

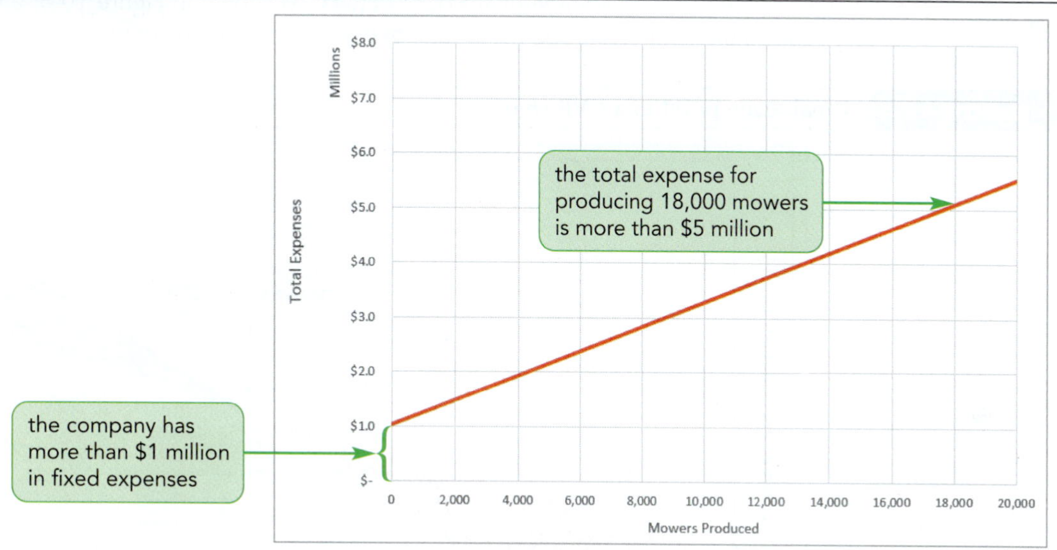

A third type of expense is a **mixed expense**, which is an expense that is part variable and part fixed. For example, if the salespeople at Coltivare Tool receive bonuses based on sales volume, their compensation would be an example of a mixed expense to the company. Each salesperson would have a fixed salary with extra income as the volume of sales increases. In the analysis you'll prepare for Irena, you will not consider any mixed expenses.

Coltivare Tool is selling most of what it produces, so the company should bring in more revenue as it increases production. Figure 10-3 shows the increase in revenue in relation to the increase in sales volume. For example, selling 18,000 mowers at an average price of $335 per mower would generate about $6 million in revenue.

Figure 10-3 **Chart of revenue**

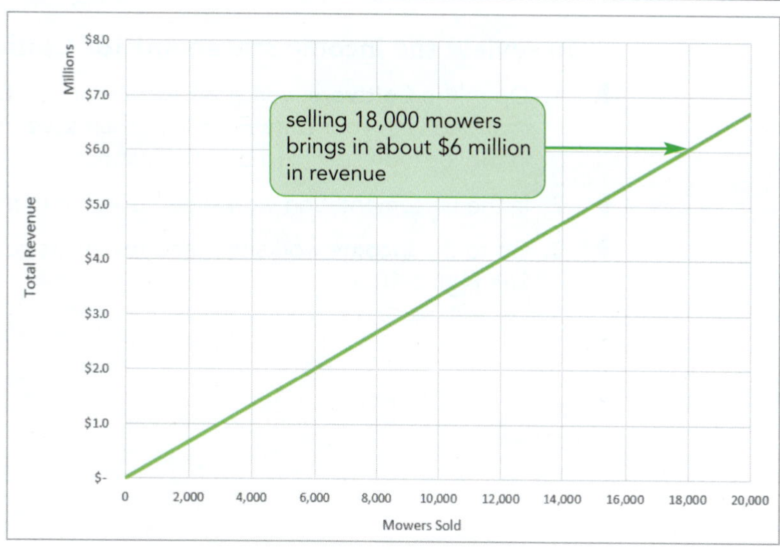

Exploring the Break-Even Point

The point where total revenue equals total expenses is called the **break-even point**. For this reason, CVP analysis is sometimes called **break-even analysis**. The more mowers that Coltivare Tool sells above the break-even point, the greater its profit. Conversely, when sales levels fall below the break-even point, the company loses money.

You can illustrate the break-even point by graphing revenue and total expenses against sales volume. The break-even point occurs where the two lines cross. This type of chart is called a **cost-volume-profit (CVP) chart**. As shown in Figure 10-4, a CVP chart shows the relationship between total expenses and total revenue.

Figure 10-4 Break-even point in a CVP chart

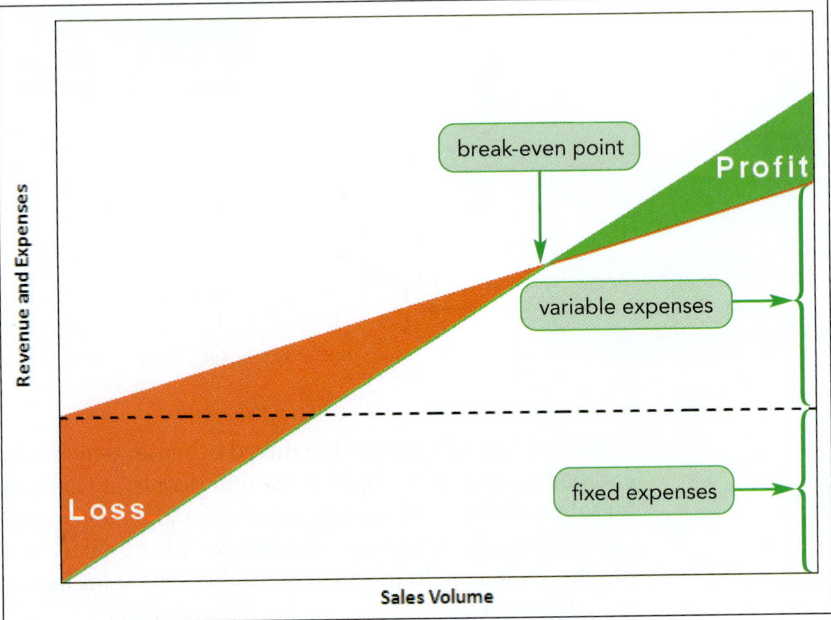

Irena has prepared an income statement for the power mower division of Coltivare Tool that includes projected revenue, variable expenses, and fixed expenses based on the previous year's sales. You'll review the worksheet with this data. Later, you will use this data to calculate the company's break-even point.

To review the income statement for Coltivare Tool:

1. Open the **Coltivare** workbook located in the **Excel10 > Module** folder included with your Data Files, and then save the workbook as **Coltivare Tool** in the location specified by your instructor.
2. In the Documentation worksheet, enter your name and the date.
3. Go to the **Income** worksheet and review its contents and formulas. See Figure 10-5.

Figure 10-5 Revenue and expenses from Coltivare Tool's mower division

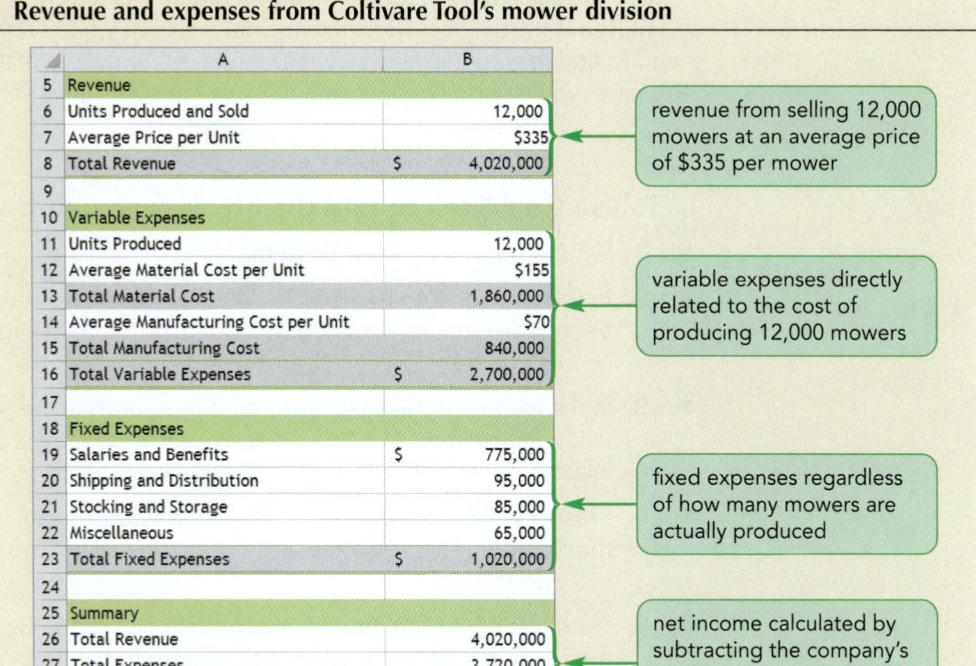

	A	B	
5	Revenue		
6	Units Produced and Sold		12,000
7	Average Price per Unit		$335
8	Total Revenue	$	4,020,000
9			
10	Variable Expenses		
11	Units Produced		12,000
12	Average Material Cost per Unit		$155
13	Total Material Cost		1,860,000
14	Average Manufacturing Cost per Unit		$70
15	Total Manufacturing Cost		840,000
16	Total Variable Expenses	$	2,700,000
17			
18	Fixed Expenses		
19	Salaries and Benefits	$	775,000
20	Shipping and Distribution		95,000
21	Stocking and Storage		85,000
22	Miscellaneous		65,000
23	Total Fixed Expenses	$	1,020,000
24			
25	Summary		
26	Total Revenue		4,020,000
27	Total Expenses		3,720,000
28	Net Income	$	300,000

revenue from selling 12,000 mowers at an average price of $335 per mower
variable expenses directly related to the cost of producing 12,000 mowers
fixed expenses regardless of how many mowers are actually produced
net income calculated by subtracting the company's total expenses from its revenue

As itemized in the Income worksheet, the company projects that it will sell 12,000 mowers at an average price of $335 per mower, generating more than $4 million in revenue. The variable expenses involved in producing 12,000 mowers are $2.7 million. The company's fixed expenses are $1.02 million. Based on this sales volume, Coltivare Tool would generate $300,000 in revenue.

Finding the Break-Even Point with What-If Analysis

What-if analysis lets you explore the impact of changing different values in a worksheet. You can use such an analysis to explore the impact of changing financial conditions on a company's profitability. Irena wants to know what the impact would be if the number of mowers Coltivare Tool produces and sells rises to 15,000 or falls to 9000.

To perform what-if analysis for different sales volumes:

1. In cell **B6**, enter **15,000** to change the units produced and sold value. Under this sales volume, the net income of the company shown in cell B28 increases to $630,000.
2. In cell **B6**, enter **9,000**. If the units produced and sold drop to 9000 units, the net income shown in cell B28 becomes –$30,000. The company will lose money with that low of a sales volume.
3. In cell **B6**, enter **12,000** to return to the original units produced and sold projection.

Irena wants to know how low sales can go and still maintain a profit. In other words, what is the sales volume for the break-even point? One way of finding the break-even point is to use Goal Seek. Recall that Goal Seek is a what-if analysis tool that can be used to find the input value needed for an Excel formula to match a specified value. In this case, you'll find out how many mowers must be sold to set the net income to $0.

To use Goal Seek to find the break-even point:

1. On the ribbon, click the **Data** tab.
2. In the Forecast group, click the **What-If Analysis** button, and then click **Goal Seek**. The Goal Seek dialog box opens with the cell reference in the Set cell box selected.
3. In the Income worksheet, click cell **B28** to replace the selected cell reference in the Set cell box with $B$28. The absolute reference specifies the Net Income cell as the cell whose value you want to set.
4. Press the **Tab** key to move the insertion point to the To value box, and then type **0**. This specifies that the goal is to set the net income value in cell B28 to 0.
5. Press the **Tab** key to move the insertion point to the By changing cell box, and then click cell **B6** in the Income worksheet to enter the cell reference $B$6. The absolute reference specifies that you want to reach the goal of setting the net income to 0 by changing the units produced and sold value in cell B6.
6. Click the **OK** button. The Goal Seek Status dialog box opens once Excel finds a solution.
7. Click the **OK** button to return to the worksheet. The value 9,273 appears in cell B6, indicating that the company must produce and sell about 9,273 mowers to break even. See Figure 10-6.

Figure 10-6 **Sales required to break even**

	A	B
5	Revenue	
6	Units Produced and Sold	9,273
7	Average Price per Unit	$335
8	Total Revenue	$ 3,106,364
9		
10	Variable Expenses	
11	Units Produced	9,273
12	Average Material Cost per Unit	$155
13	Total Material Cost	1,437,273
14	Average Manufacturing Cost per Unit	$70
15	Total Manufacturing Cost	649,091
16	Total Variable Expenses	$ 2,086,364
17		
18	Fixed Expenses	
19	Salaries and Benefits	$ 775,000
20	Shipping and Distribution	95,000
21	Stocking and Storage	85,000
22	Miscellaneous	65,000
23	Total Fixed Expenses	$ 1,020,000
24		
25	Summary	
26	Total Revenue	3,106,364
27	Total Expenses	3,106,364
28	Net Income	$ -

producing and selling 9,273 mowers results in a net income of $0

8. In cell **B6**, enter **12,000** to return to the original units produced and sold projection.

Irena wants to continue to analyze the company's net income under different sales assumptions. For example, what would happen to the company's net income if sales increased to 16,000 mowers? How much would the company lose if the number of sales fell to 8,000 mowers? How many mowers must the company sell to reach a net income of exactly $50,000? You could continue to use Goal Seek to answer these questions, but a more efficient approach is to use a data table.

Working with Data Tables

A data table is an Excel table that displays the results from several what-if analyses. The table consists of input cells and result cells. The input cells are the cells whose value would be changed in a what-if analysis. The result cells are cells whose values are impacted by the changing input values. In Excel, you can use one-variable data tables and two-variable data tables.

Creating a One-Variable Data Table

In a one-variable data table, you specify one input cell and any number of result cells. The range of possible values for the input cell is entered in the first row or column of the data table, and the corresponding result values appear in the subsequent rows or columns. One-variable data tables are particularly useful in business to explore how changing a single input value can impact several financial measures.

Figure 10-7 shows a one-variable data table that is used to determine the impact of different interest rates on a $315,000 loan's monthly payment, total payments, and cost. In this worksheet, cell B3 containing the interest rate is the input cell, and the cells in the range B8:B10 are the result cells. Possible input values for cell B3, ranging from a 4 percent interest rate to a 6 percent rate, are entered in the first column of the data table. The next three columns of the table show the result values based on these interest rates.

Figure 10-7 **One-variable data table example**

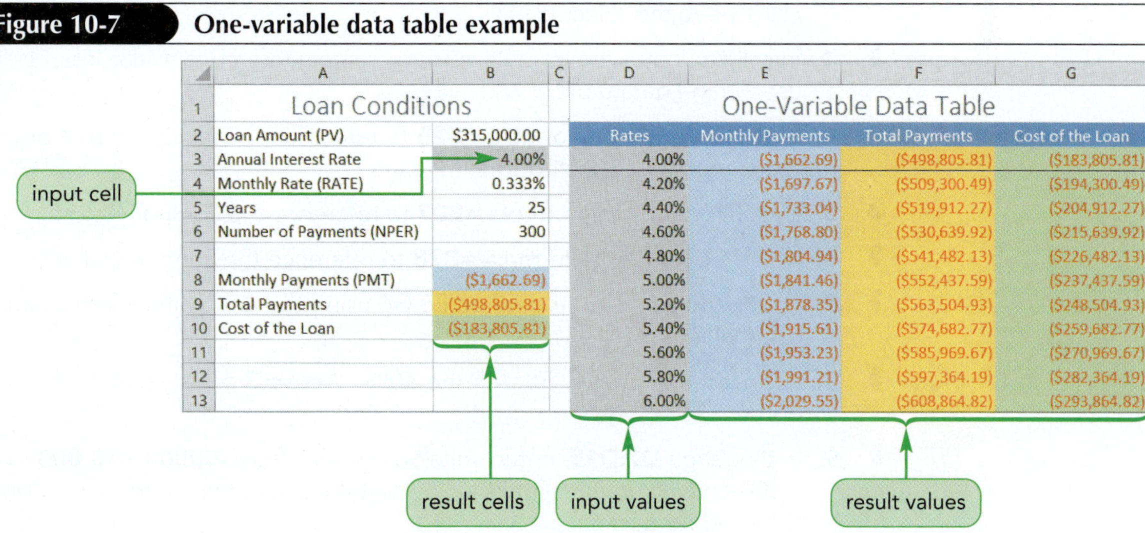

	A	B	C	D	E	F	G
1	Loan Conditions			One-Variable Data Table			
2	Loan Amount (PV)	$315,000.00		Rates	Monthly Payments	Total Payments	Cost of the Loan
3	Annual Interest Rate	4.00%		4.00%	($1,662.69)	($498,805.81)	($183,805.81)
4	Monthly Rate (RATE)	0.333%		4.20%	($1,697.67)	($509,300.49)	($194,300.49)
5	Years	25		4.40%	($1,733.04)	($519,912.27)	($204,912.27)
6	Number of Payments (NPER)	300		4.60%	($1,768.80)	($530,639.92)	($215,639.92)
7				4.80%	($1,804.94)	($541,482.13)	($226,482.13)
8	Monthly Payments (PMT)	($1,662.69)		5.00%	($1,841.46)	($552,437.59)	($237,437.59)
9	Total Payments	($498,805.81)		5.20%	($1,878.35)	($563,504.93)	($248,504.93)
10	Cost of the Loan	($183,805.81)		5.40%	($1,915.61)	($574,682.77)	($259,682.77)
11				5.60%	($1,953.23)	($585,969.67)	($270,969.67)
12				5.80%	($1,991.21)	($597,364.19)	($282,364.19)
13				6.00%	($2,029.55)	($608,864.82)	($293,864.82)

Using the table, you can quickly see that a 5 percent interest rate results in a $1,841.46 monthly payment, total payments of $552,437.59, and a loan cost of $237,437.59. You can also observe how quickly the loan cost rises with an increasing interest rate. For example, when the annual interest rate increases one percentage point from 5 percent to 6 percent, the total cost of the loan increases by about $56,500.

REFERENCE

Creating a One-Variable Data Table

- In the upper-left cell of the table, enter a formula that references the input cell.
- In either the first row or the first column of the table, enter input values.
- For input values in the first row, enter formulas referencing result cells in the table's first column; for input values in the first column, enter formulas referencing result cells in the table's first row.
- Select the table (excluding any row or column headings).
- On the Data tab, in the Forecast group, click the What-If Analysis button, and then click Data Table.
- If the input values are in the first row, enter the cell reference to the input cell in the Row input cell box; if the input values are in the first column, enter the cell reference to the input cell in the Column input cell box.
- Click the OK button.

Irena wants to examine the impact of changing sales volume on the company's revenue, total expenses, and net income. You'll create a one-variable data table to do this. The first step is to set up the data table so that the first row of the table starts with a reference to the input cell in the worksheet, followed by references to one or more result cells.

To set up the one-variable data table to examine the impact of changing sales volume:

1. In cell **D4**, enter **Break-Even Analysis**, merge and center the range D4:G4, and then format the text with the Heading 3 cell style.
2. In the range **D5:G5**, enter the labels **Units Sold**, **Revenue**, **Expenses**, and **Net Income**, center the text in the selected cells, and then apply the **Accent 2** cell style to the selected cells.
3. In cell **D6**, enter the formula **=B6** to create a reference to the input cell to be used in the data table.
4. In cell **E6**, enter the formula **=B26** to reference the result cell that displays the company's expected total revenue.
5. In cell **F6**, enter the formula **=B27** to reference the company's total expenses.
6. In cell **G6**, enter the formula **=B28** to reference the company's net income.
7. Format the values in the range E6:G6 using the Accounting format with no decimal places.
8. Format the range D6:G6 with the **40% - Accent3** cell style and a bottom border.
9. In the range **D7:D15**, enter Units Sold values from **2,000** to **18,000** in 2,000-unit increments, and then format the selected cells with the Comma style and no decimal places.
10. Select cell **D6**. See Figure 10-8.

Figure 10-8 Setup for the one-variable data table

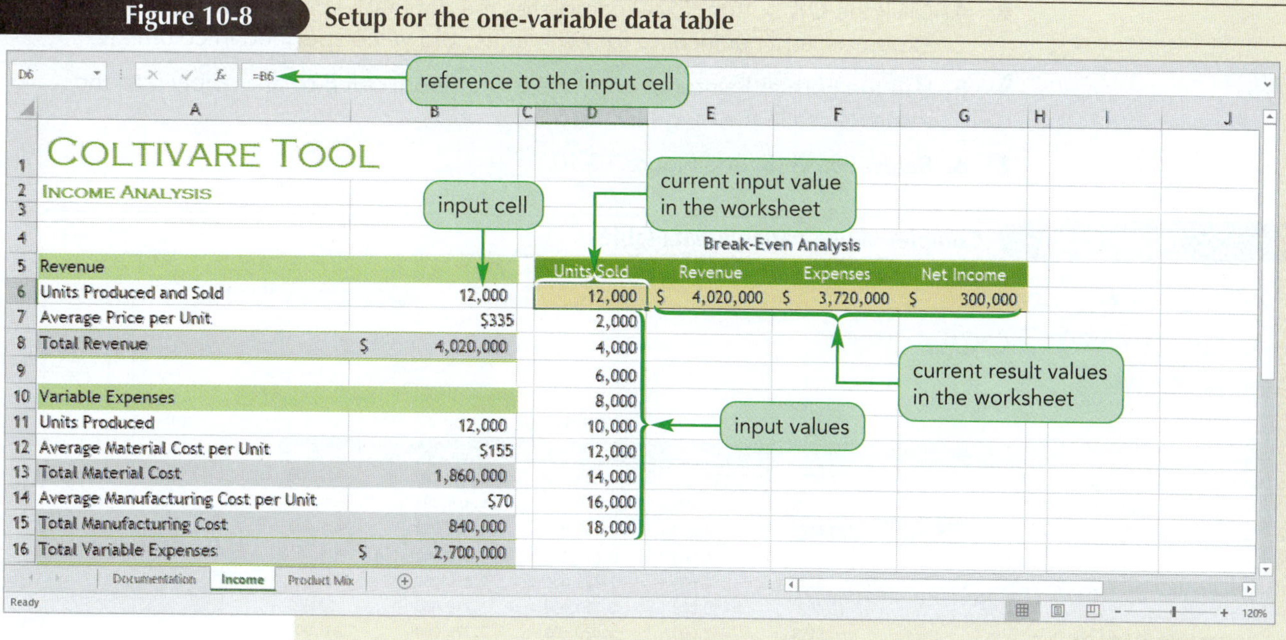

You'll complete the table with the result values. To do this, you must identify the row input cell or the column input cell. The **row input cell** is used when the input values have been placed in the first row of the data table, and the **column input cell** is used when the input values are placed in the data table's first column. In the Income worksheet, the input values are in the first column, so you'll use the column input cell option. If you had oriented the table so that the input values were in the first row, you would use the row input cell option.

To complete the one-variable data table:

1. Select the range **D6:G15** containing the cells for the data table.
2. On the Data tab, in the Forecast group, click the **What-If Analysis** button, and then click **Data Table**. The Data Table dialog box opens.
3. Press the **Tab** key to move the insertion point to the Column input cell box, and then click cell **B6** in the Income worksheet. The absolute reference $B$6 is entered in the Column input box. See Figure 10-9.

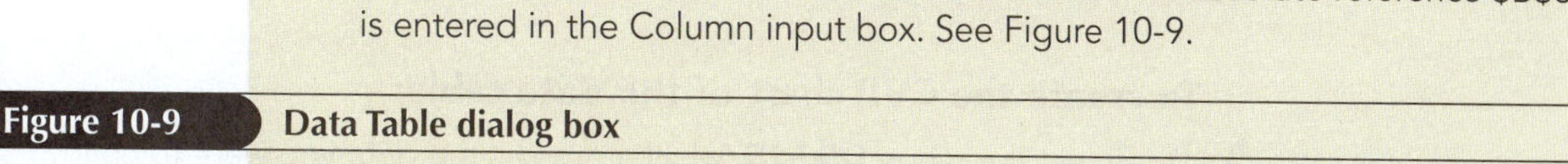

Figure 10-9 Data Table dialog box

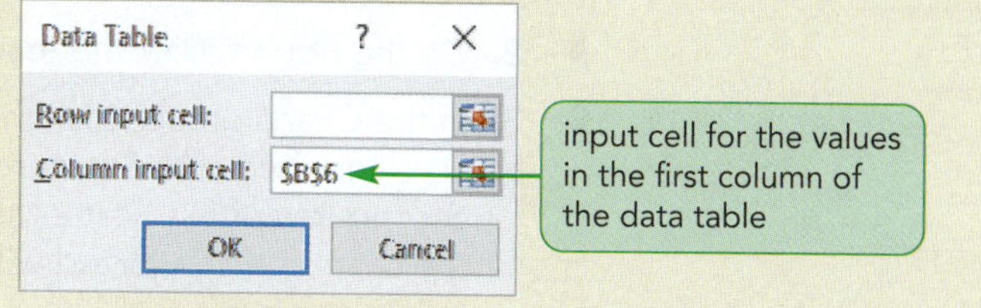

4. Click the **OK** button. Excel completes the data table by entering the revenue, expenses, and net income for each units sold value specified in column D.
5. Use the Format Painter to copy the format from cell **B26** and apply it to the result values in the range **E7:G15**.
6. Select cell **G15**. See Figure 10-10.

Figure 10-10 Completed one-variable data table

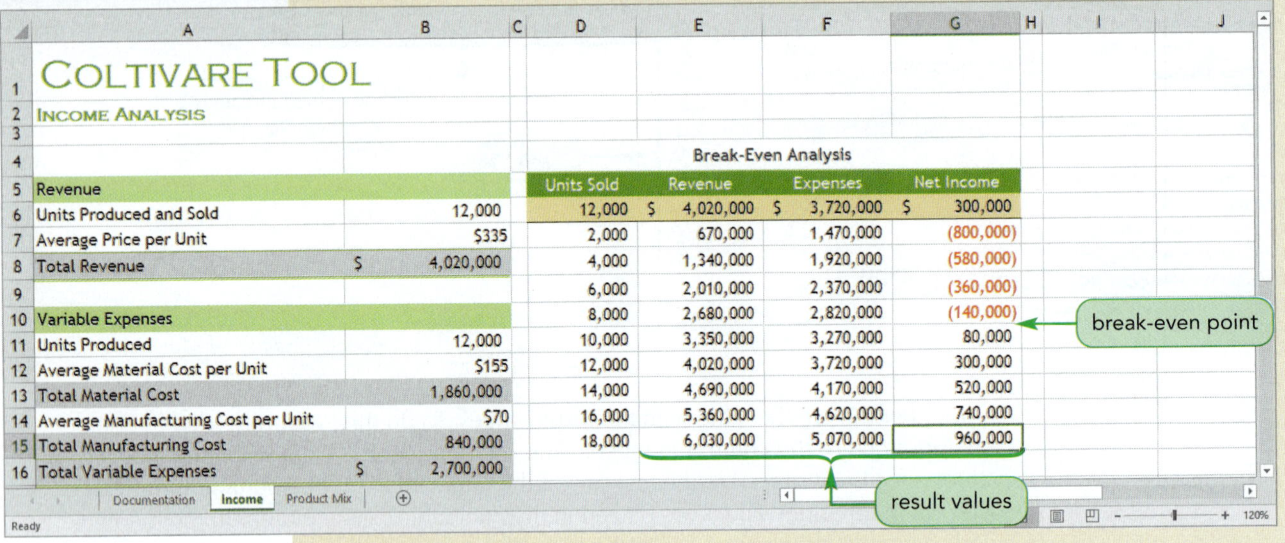

	A	B	C	D	E	F	G
1	COLTIVARE TOOL						
2	INCOME ANALYSIS						
3							
4					Break-Even Analysis		
5	Revenue			Units Sold	Revenue	Expenses	Net Income
6	Units Produced and Sold	12,000		12,000	$ 4,020,000	$ 3,720,000	$ 300,000
7	Average Price per Unit	$335		2,000	670,000	1,470,000	(800,000)
8	Total Revenue	$ 4,020,000		4,000	1,340,000	1,920,000	(580,000)
9				6,000	2,010,000	2,370,000	(360,000)
10	Variable Expenses			8,000	2,680,000	2,820,000	(140,000)
11	Units Produced	12,000		10,000	3,350,000	3,270,000	80,000
12	Average Material Cost per Unit	$155		12,000	4,020,000	3,720,000	300,000
13	Total Material Cost	1,860,000		14,000	4,690,000	4,170,000	520,000
14	Average Manufacturing Cost per Unit	$70		16,000	5,360,000	4,620,000	740,000
15	Total Manufacturing Cost	840,000		18,000	6,030,000	5,070,000	960,000
16	Total Variable Expenses	$ 2,700,000					

The data table shows the results of several what-if analyses simultaneously. For example, if sales were 10,000 units, the company's revenue would be $3,350,000, but the total expenses would be $3,270,000, yielding a net income of $80,000.

Charting a One-Variable Data Table

The data table provides the results of several what-if analyses, but the results are often clearer if you include a CVP chart along with the table. The chart gives a better picture of the relationship between sales volume, revenue, and expenses. You'll use a scatter chart to map out the revenue and total expenses against the total number of units sold.

To create the CVP chart of the data table:

1. Select the range **D5:F15**, which contains the data you want to chart.
2. On the ribbon, click the **Insert** tab.
3. In the Charts group, click the **Insert Scatter (X, Y) or Bubble Chart** button, and then click **Scatter with Straight Lines** (the second option in the second row of the Scatter section). Each point in the data table is plotted on the chart and connected with a line. The break-even point occurs where the two lines cross.

4. Move and resize the chart so that it covers the range D16:G28.
5. Change the fill color of the chart area to **Gray - 25%, Background 2**, and then change the fill color of the plot area to **white**.
6. Next to the chart, click the **Chart Styles** button, click **Color**, and then click **Color 3** (the third option in the Colorful list).
7. Click cell **G15** to deselect the chart. See Figure 10-11.

Figure 10-11 Completed CVP chart

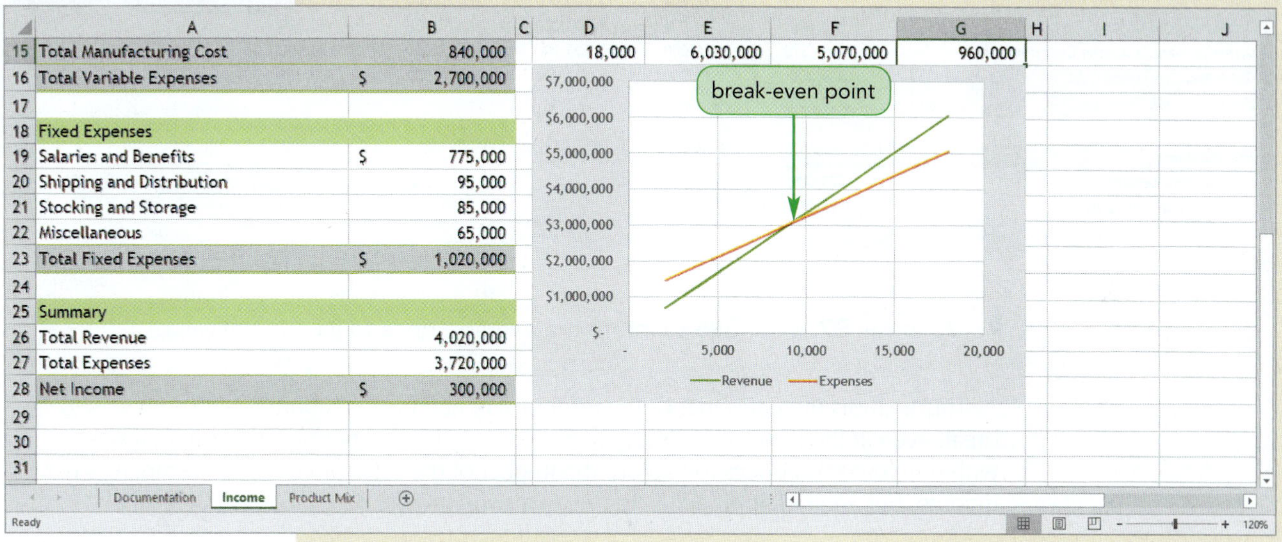

Modifying a Data Table

Because data tables are dynamic, changes in the worksheet are automatically reflected in the data table values. This includes changes to cells that are not part of the data table but are involved in the values displayed in the result cells. Coltivare Tool is considering lowering its prices to be more competitive with other manufacturers. Irena asks you to perform another what-if analysis using an average sales price of $300. Changing the value in the Income worksheet will affect other results in the sheet, including the what-if analysis displayed in the one-variable data table and the break-even chart.

To view the impact of changing the sales price:

1. In cell **B7**, enter **300** to change the average price per unit from $335 to $300. At this lower sales price, the break-even point moves to somewhere between 12,000 and 14,000 units. You can see this reflected in both the data table and the CVP chart. See Figure 10-12.

Figure 10-12 Data table for the $300 price

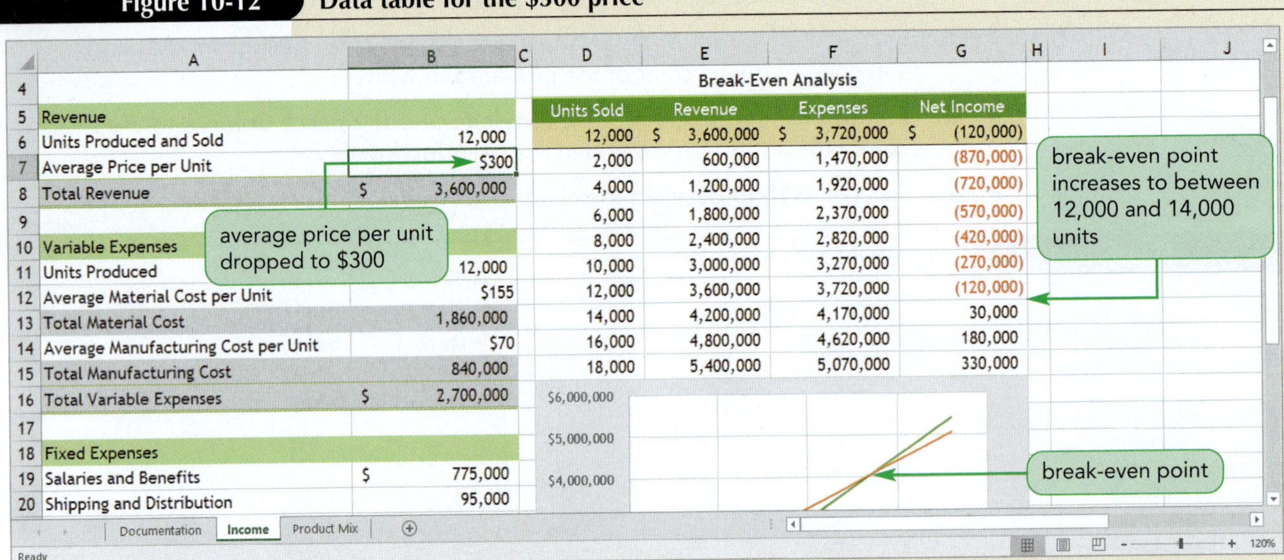

2. In cell **B7**, enter **335** to return the average price to its original value.

This analysis indicates that Coltivare Tool will need to sell about 14,000 mowers to break even at the lower sales price. You could continue to perform what-if analyses with different sales prices to explore the impact of the sales price on the company's net income, but another approach is to create a two-variable data table.

INSIGHT

Directly Calculating the Break-Even Point

A CVP chart is a useful visual tool for displaying the break-even point. You can also calculate the break-even point directly by using the following formula:

$$\textit{break-even point} = \frac{\textit{fixed expenses}}{\textit{sales price per unit} - \textit{variable expenses per unit}}$$

For example, with a sales price of $300, fixed expenses of $1,020,000, and variable expenses of $225 per unit, the following equation calculates the break-even point at 13,600 units produced and sold:

$$\textit{break-even point} = \frac{1{,}020{,}000}{300 - 225} = 13{,}600$$

Creating a Two-Variable Data Table

A two-variable data table lets you view the relationship between two input cells and one result cell. Figure 10-13 shows a two-variable data table that examines the impact of the interest rate and the length of the mortgage on the monthly payment.

Figure 10-13 Two-variable data table example

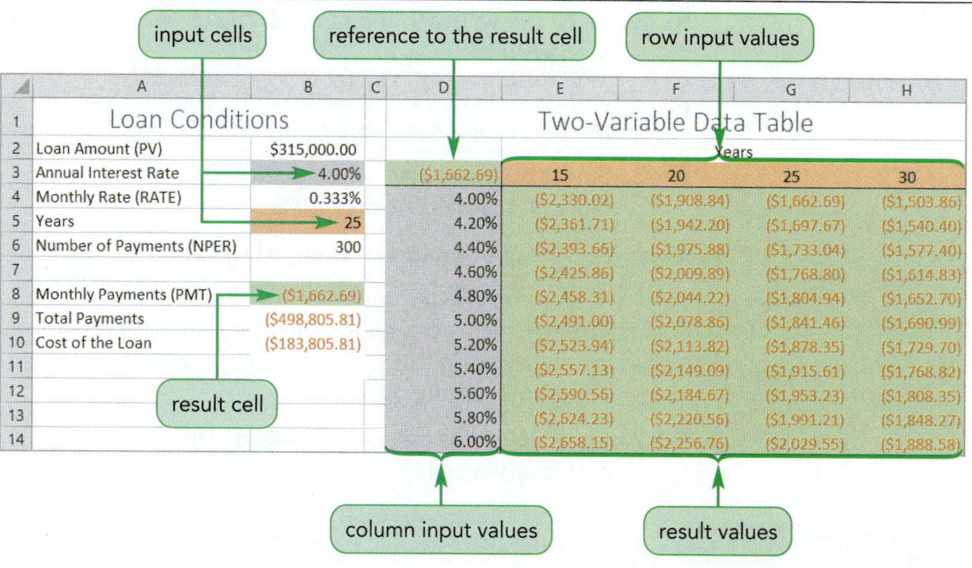

	A	B	C	D	E	F	G	H
1	Loan Conditions			Two-Variable Data Table				
2	Loan Amount (PV)	$315,000.00				Years		
3	Annual Interest Rate	4.00%		($1,662.69)	15	20	25	30
4	Monthly Rate (RATE)	0.333%		4.00%	($2,330.02)	($1,908.84)	($1,662.69)	($1,503.86)
5	Years	25		4.20%	($2,361.71)	($1,942.20)	($1,697.67)	($1,540.40)
6	Number of Payments (NPER)	300		4.40%	($2,393.66)	($1,975.88)	($1,733.04)	($1,577.40)
7				4.60%	($2,425.86)	($2,009.89)	($1,768.80)	($1,614.83)
8	Monthly Payments (PMT)	($1,662.69)		4.80%	($2,458.31)	($2,044.22)	($1,804.94)	($1,652.70)
9	Total Payments	($498,805.81)		5.00%	($2,491.00)	($2,078.86)	($1,841.46)	($1,690.99)
10	Cost of the Loan	($183,805.81)		5.20%	($2,523.94)	($2,113.82)	($1,878.35)	($1,729.70)
11				5.40%	($2,557.13)	($2,149.09)	($1,915.61)	($1,768.82)
12				5.60%	($2,590.56)	($2,184.67)	($1,953.23)	($1,808.35)
13				5.80%	($2,624.23)	($2,220.56)	($1,991.21)	($1,848.27)
14				6.00%	($2,658.15)	($2,256.76)	($2,029.55)	($1,888.58)

The two input cells are cell B3 and cell B5, which show the interest rate and the number of years before the loan is repaid, respectively. The first column of the data table displays a range of interest rate values for the first input cell, and the first row of the data table shows a range of years for the second input cell. The result cell is cell B8—the monthly payment. The data table is set up with a formula that displays the result cell value in cell B8. The rest of the table shows how different combinations of interest rate and years affects the monthly loan payment. For example, a 30-year loan at 5 percent interest would require a monthly payment of $1,690.99 (cell H9).

REFERENCE

Creating a Two-Variable Data Table

- In the upper-left cell of the table, enter a formula that references the result cell.
- In the first row and first column of the table, enter input values.
- Select the table (excluding any row or column headings).
- On the Data tab, in the Forecast group, click the What-If Analysis button, and then click Data Table.
- Enter the cell reference to the first row input values in the Row input cell box; enter the cell reference to the first column input values in the Column input cell box.
- Click the OK button.

Irena wants you to examine the impact of the sales price and the yearly sales volume on the net income from selling the Coltivare Tool line of power mowers. You'll create a two-variable data table to do this.

To set up the two-variable data table:

1. In cell **I4**, enter **Net Income Analysis**, merge and center the range **I4:N4**, and then format the merged range with the **Heading 3** cell style.
2. In cell **I5**, enter **Average Price per Unit**, and then merge and center the range **I5:N5**.

3. Copy the values in the range **D7:D15**, and then paste them into the range **I7:I15**.
4. In the range **J6:N6**, enter **$300** through **$400** in increments of $25. The prices are entered in the range.
5. Select the nonadjacent range **I7:I15,J6:N6**, and then change the fill color to **Gold, Accent 3, Lighter 60%**.
6. Add a right border to the range **I7:I15** and a bottom border to the range **J6:N6**.

   In two-variable data tables, the reference to the result cell is placed in the upper-left corner of the table at the intersection of the row and column input values. In this case, you'll enter a formula in cell I6 that references the company's net income.
7. In cell **I6**, enter the formula **=B28**. The current net income value $300,000 is displayed in cell I6. See Figure 10-14.

Figure 10-14 Setup for the two-variable data table

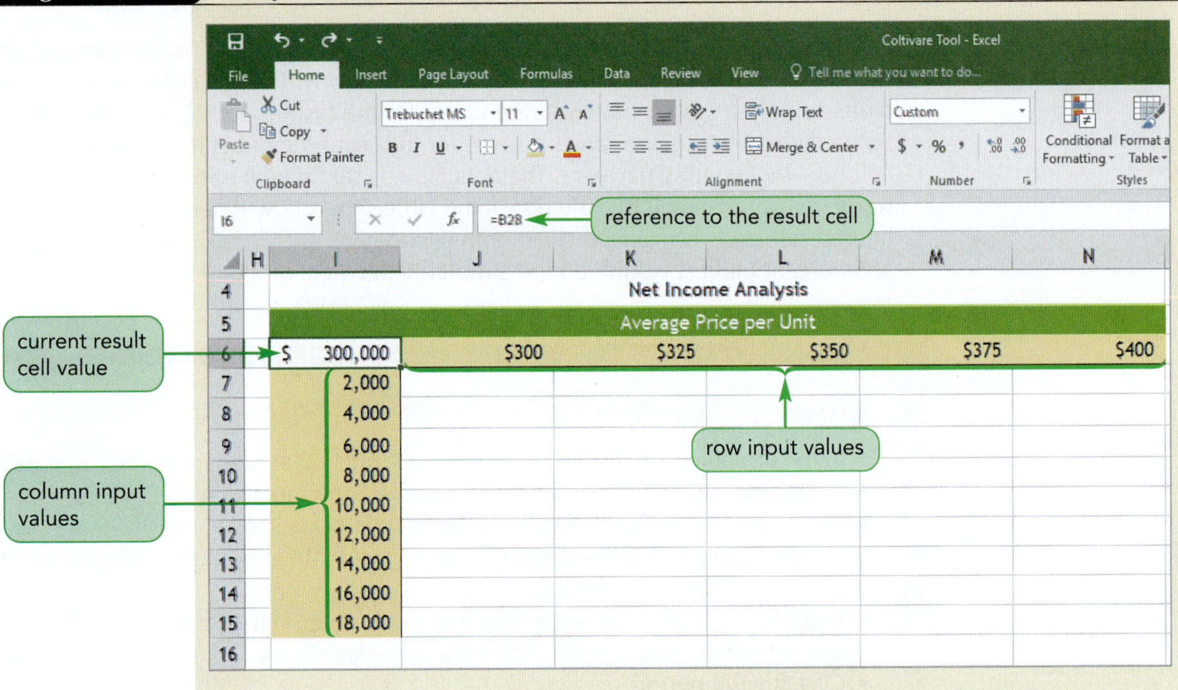

The two-variable data table is completed using the same Data Table command used with the one-variable data table, except that you specify both the row input cell (using the values in the first row of the table) and the column input cell (using the values in the table's first column.)

To display the result values:

1. Select the range **I6:N15** containing the row input values, the column input values, and the reference to the result cell.
2. On the ribbon, click the **Data** tab. In the Forecast group, click the **What-If Analysis** button, and then click **Data Table**. The Data Table dialog box opens.

3. In the Row input cell box, type **B7** to reference the average price per unit value from the income statement.
4. In the Column input cell box, type **B6** to reference the number of units produced and sold value from the income statement.
5. Click the **OK** button. The data table values appear in the range J7:N15.
6. Use the Format Painter to copy the formatting from cell **G15** to the range **J7:N15**.
7. Click cell **J7** to deselect the highlighted range. See Figure 10-15.

Figure 10-15 **Result values in the two-variable data table**

	I	J	K	L	M	N
4			Net Income Analysis			
5			Average Price per Unit			
6	$ 300,000	$300	$325	$350	$375	$400
7	2,000	(870,000)	(820,000)	(770,000)	(720,000)	(670,000)
8	4,000	(720,000)	(620,000)	(520,000)	(420,000)	(320,000)
9	6,000	(570,000)	(420,000)	(270,000)	(120,000)	30,000
10	8,000	(420,000)	(220,000)	(20,000)	180,000	380,000
11	10,000	(270,000)	(20,000)	230,000	480,000	730,000
12	12,000	(120,000)	180,000	480,000	780,000	1,080,000
13	14,000	30,000	380,000	730,000	1,080,000	1,430,000
14	16,000	180,000	580,000	980,000	1,380,000	1,780,000
15	18,000	330,000	780,000	1,230,000	1,680,000	2,130,000
16						
17						
18						
19						
20						

The break-even points for different combinations of price and units sold are easy to track because negative net income values are displayed in red and positive net income values are displayed in black. For example, if the average price per unit is set to $300, Coltivare Tool must sell between 12,000 and 14,000 mowers to break even. However, if the price is increased to $400, the break-even point falls between 4000 and 6000 mowers.

Formatting the Result Cell

The reference to the result cell in the table's upper-left corner might confuse some users. To prevent that, you can hide the cell value using the custom format `"text"`, where `text` is the text you want to display in place of the cell value. In this case, you'll use a custom format to display "Units Sold" instead of the value in cell I6.

To apply a custom format to cell I6:

1. Right-click cell **I6**, and then click **Format Cells** on the shortcut menu (or press the **Ctrl+1** keys). The Format Cells dialog box opens.
2. If necessary, click the **Number** tab, and then in the Category box, click **Custom**.

Be sure to use opening and closing quotation marks around the custom text.

3. In the Type box, select any text, and then type **"Units Sold"** (including the quotation marks) as the custom text to display in the cell. See Figure 10-16.

Figure 10-16 Format Cells dialog box

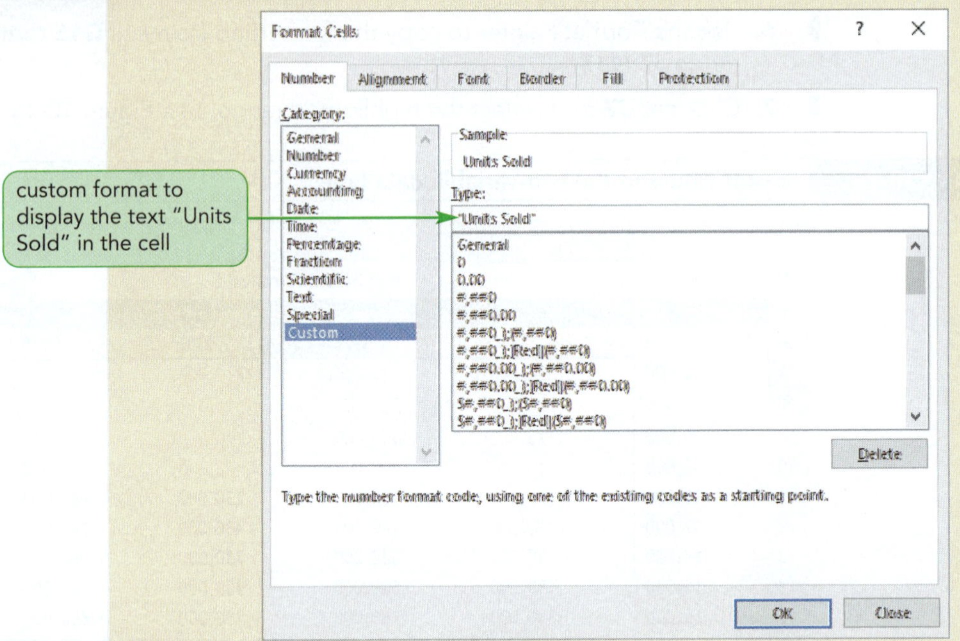

TIP

You can also hide the reference to the result cell by applying the same font and fill color to the cell.

4. Click the **OK** button. The text "Units Sold" appears in cell I6 even though the cell's underlying formula is =B28.

Trouble? If "Units Sold" does not appear in cell I6, you probably didn't include the quotation marks in the custom format. Repeat Steps 1 through 4, making sure that you include both opening and closing quotation marks.

Charting a Two-Variable Data Table

You can chart the values from a two-variable data table using lines to represent the different columns of the table. Irena wants you to create a scatter chart based on the two-variable data table you just created.

To create a chart of the two-variable data table:

1. Select the range **I7:N15**. You'll plot this range on a scatter chart. You did not select the unit prices in row 5 because Excel would interpret these values as data values to be charted, not as labels.
2. On the ribbon, click the **Insert** tab. In the Charts group, click the **Insert Scatter (X, Y) or Bubble Chart** button, and then click the **Scatter with Straight Lines** chart subtype (the second chart in the second row of the Scatter section).

3. Move and resize the chart so that it covers the range **I16:N28**.
4. Remove the chart title, and then position the chart legend to the right of the chart.
5. Change the fill color of the chart area to **Gray - 25%, Background 2**, and then change the fill color of the plot area to **white**. See Figure 10-17.

Figure 10-17 **Chart of net income values**

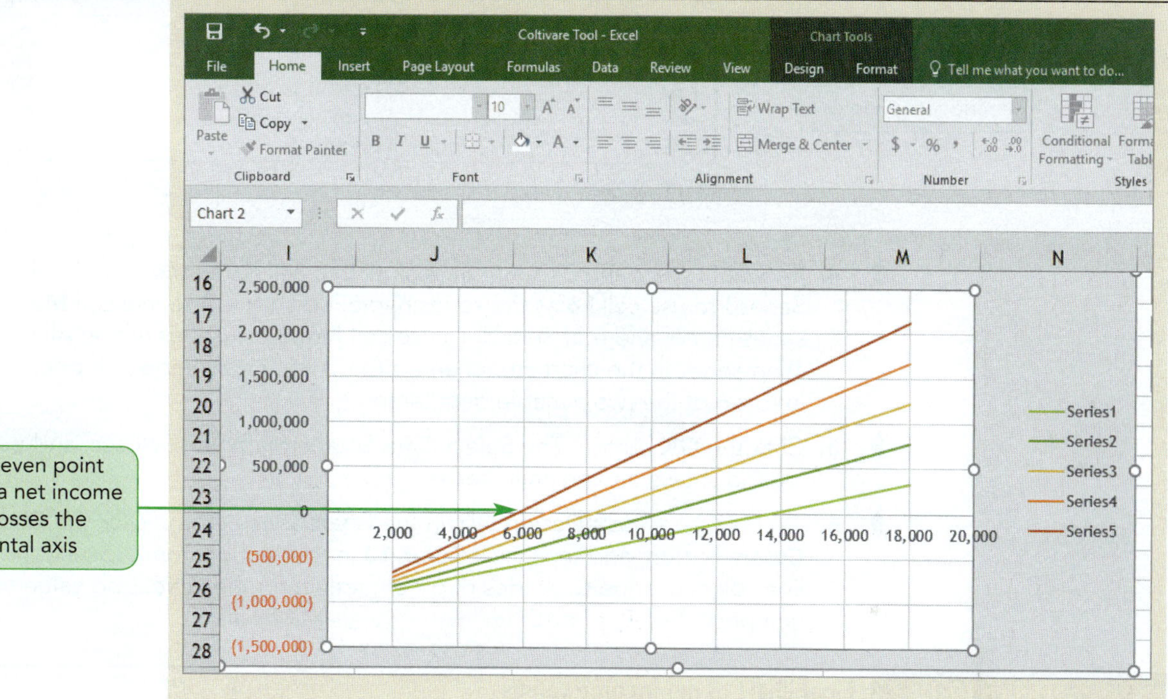

The chart shows a different trend line for each of the five possible values for unit price. However, the prices are not listed in the chart, and Excel uses generic series names (Series1, Series2, Series3, Series4, and Series5). To use the unit prices rather than the generic names in the chart, you must add the unit price values as series names.

To edit the chart series names:

1. On the Chart Tools Design tab, in the Data group, click the **Select Data** button to open the Select Data Source dialog box.
2. In the Legend Entries (Series) box, click **Series1**, and then click the **Edit** button. The Edit Series dialog box opens.
3. Within the insertion point in the Series name box, click cell **J6** to insert the reference =Income!$J$6, and then click the **OK** button. The Select Data Source dialog box reappears with the Series1 name changed to $300. See Figure 10-18.

Figure 10-18 Select Data Source dialog box

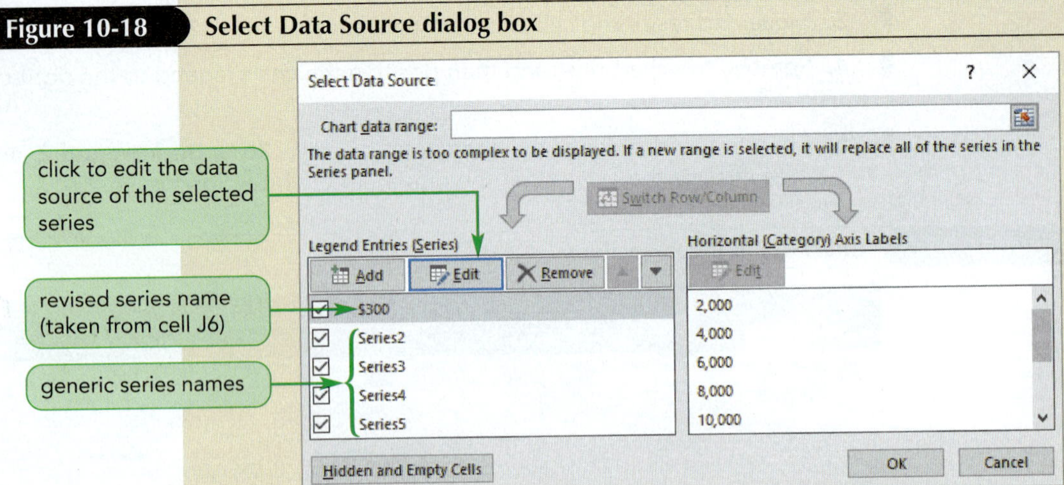

4. Repeat Steps 2 and 3 to edit Series2 to use cell **K6** as the series name, edit Series3 to use cell **L6** as the series name, edit Series4 to use cell **M6** as the series name, and edit Series5 to use cell **N6** as the series name. All of the chart series in the chart are renamed to match the average unit price values in row 6 of the two-variable data table.
5. Click the **OK** button. The Select Data Source dialog box closes, and the legend shows the renamed series.
6. On the Chart Tools Design tab, in the Chart Styles group, click the **Change Colors** button, and then click **Color 13** in the Monochromatic section. The line colors change to shades of green, reflecting the increasing value of the unit price. See Figure 10-19.

Figure 10-19 Final chart of net income values

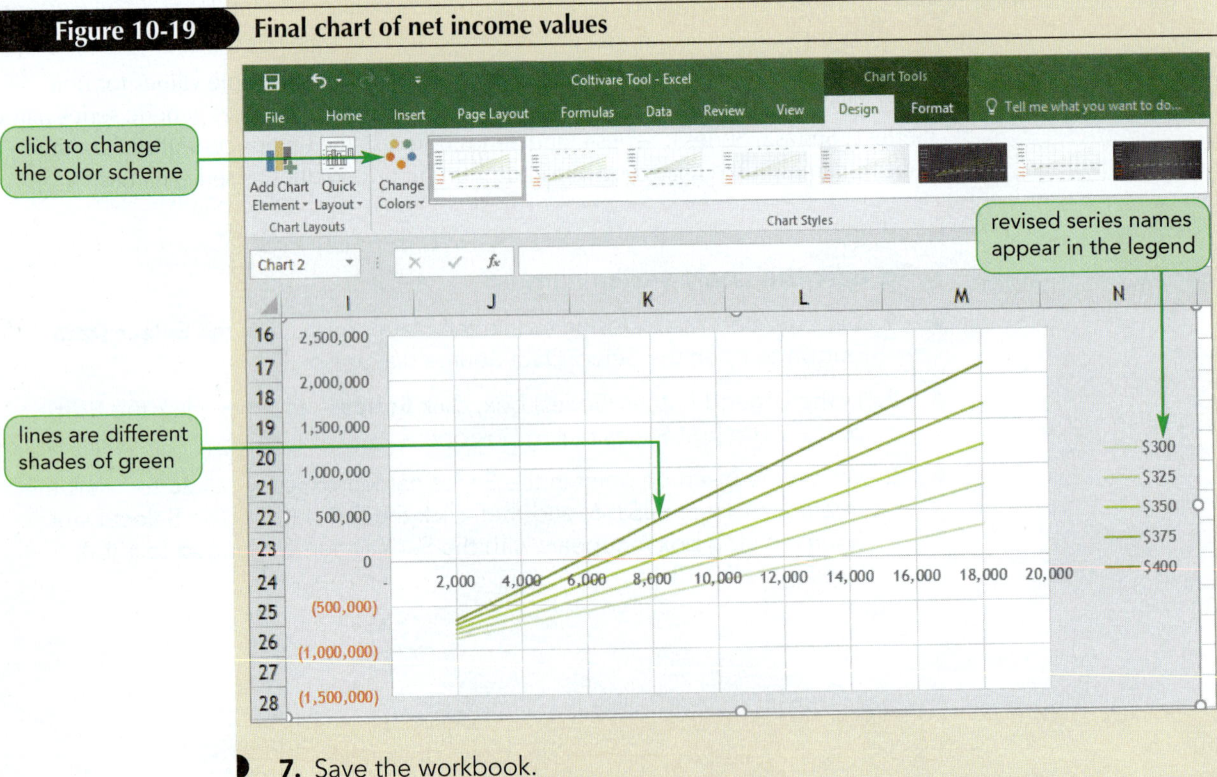

7. Save the workbook.

The chart shows how different unit prices will affect the relationship between sales volume and net income. The horizontal axis represents the break-even point. For example, the $325 line (the second lowest of the five lines) crosses the horizontal axis near 10,000, indicating that with an average cost of $325, the company will have to sell about 10,000 mowers to break even. At that same sales volume of 10,000 mowers but with an average sales price of $375, the company will generate a net profit of about $500,000.

INSIGHT

Data Tables and Arrays

If you examine the cells in the two-variable data table you just created, you can see that every cell displays a different value even though it has the same formula: {=TABLE(B7, B6)}. This formula is an **array formula**, which performs multiple calculations in a single step, returning either a single value to one cell or multiple values to several cells. Array formulas are always enclosed within curly braces.

One example of an array formula that returns a single value is {=SUM(B1:B10*C1:C10)}. This formula multiplies each cell in the range B1:B10 by the matching cell in the same row of the range C1:C10. The sum of those 10 products is then calculated and returned. To create this array formula, enter the formula =SUM(B1:B10*C1:C10), and then press the Ctrl+Shift+Enter keys. Excel treats the formula as an array formula, adding the curly braces for you.

The TABLE function is an array function that returns multiple values to multiple cells. Other such functions include the TREND, MINVERSE, MMULT, and TRANSPOSE functions. To calculate multiple cell values, select the range, type the array formula, and then press the Ctrl+Shift+Enter keys to enter the formula. Excel applies the array formula to all of the selected cells.

Array formulas are a powerful feature of Excel. They can perform complex calculations within a single expression and extend a single formula over a range of cells. Use Excel Help to learn more about array formulas and the functions that support them.

So far, you have used what-if analysis with Goal Seek and data tables to analyze how much Coltivare Tool can charge for its mowers and what impact sales volume has on the company's profitability. In the next session, you will use other what-if analysis tools to examine the impact of more than two factors on a financial outcome.

REVIEW

Session 10.1 Quick Check

1. Describe the difference between a variable expense and a fixed expense.
2. When does the break-even point occur?
3. What is a data table? What is an input cell? What is a result cell?
4. What is a one-variable data table? What is a two-variable data table?
5. How many result cells can you display with a one-variable data table? How many result cells can you display with a two-variable data table?
6. Cell E5 contains the formula =B10. You want to display the text "Profits" instead of the formula's value. What custom format would you use?
7. What is an array formula?

Session 10.2 Visual Overview:

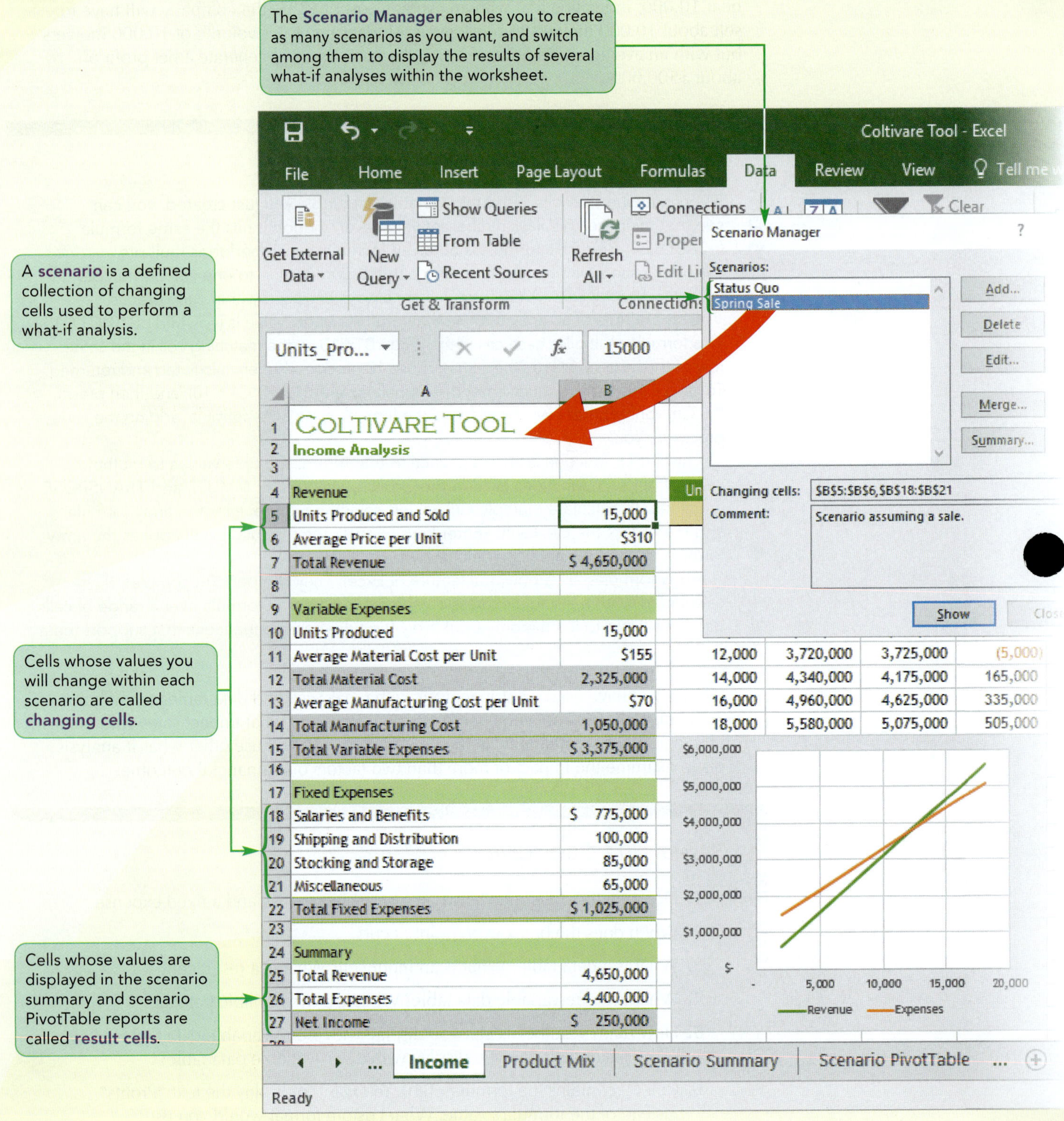

What-If Scenarios

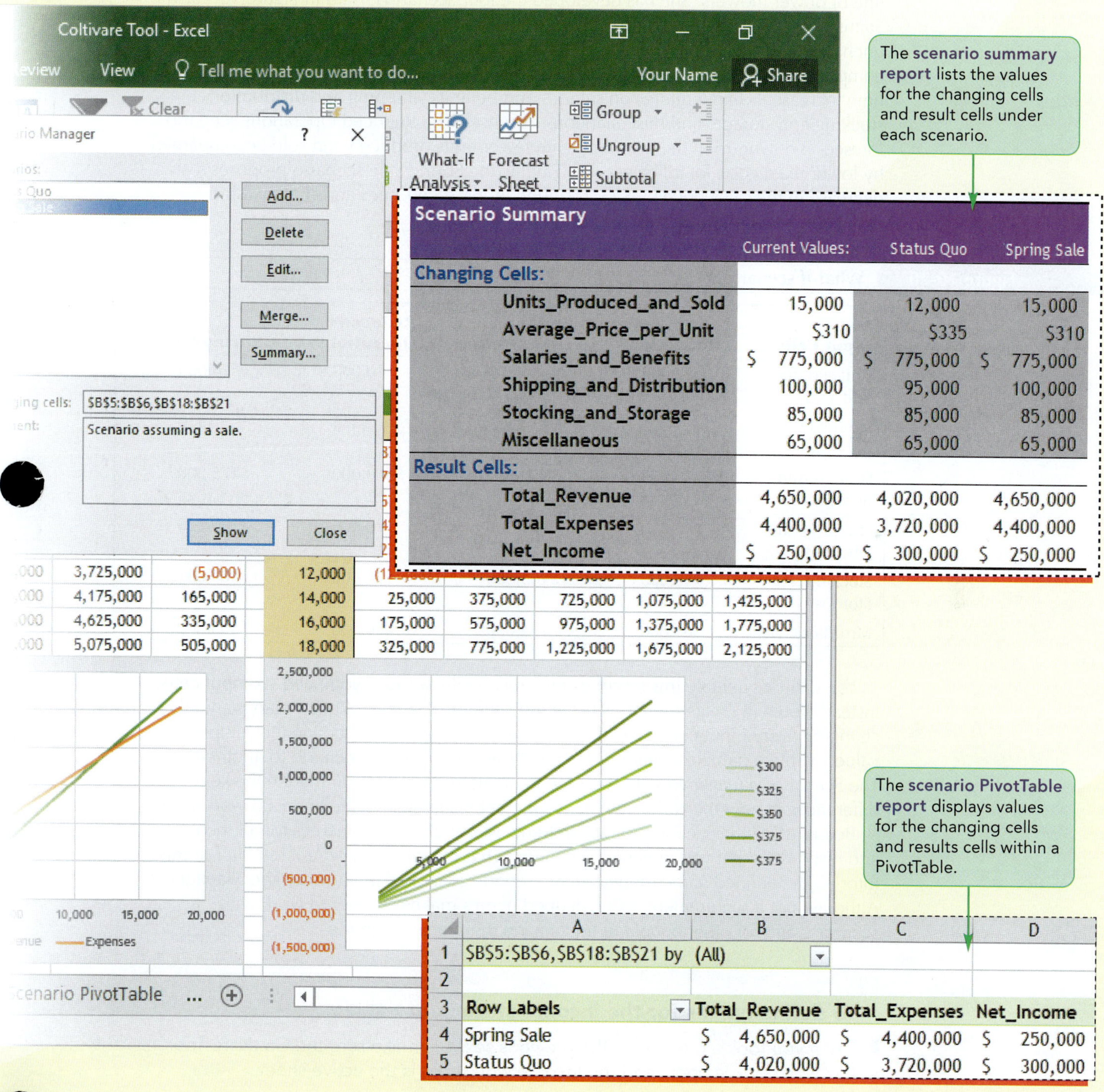

Developing Financial Scenarios with the Scenario Manager

Many financial analyses explore the impact of several input values on several different results. Because data tables are limited to two input cells, you must create a scenario to perform a what-if analysis with more than two input cells.

Irena wants to explore other ways of increasing the profitability of Coltivare Tool's line of power mowers. She has developed the four scenarios listed in Figure 10-20. The Status Quo scenario assumes that the fixed expenses, units sold, and unit prices remain unchanged for the coming year. The Expanded Operations scenario assumes that the company will increase the total number of units produced and sold while at the same time increase its expenditures on salaries and benefits, shipping and distribution, stocking and storage, and miscellaneous expenses. The Reduced Operations scenario foresees a downturn in the economy with fewer units produced and sold accompanied by lower fixed costs for all categories. Finally, the Spring Sale scenario proposes a decrease in the sales price by $25, resulting in increased sales and slightly more expenditures for shipping and distribution.

Figure 10-20 What-if scenarios

Input Cells	Status Quo	Expanded Operations	Reduced Operations	Spring Sale
Units Produced and Sold	12,000	14,200	10,000	16,000
Average Price per Unit	$335	$335	$335	$310
Salaries and Benefits	$775,000	$950,000	$650,000	$775,000
Shipping and Distribution	$95,000	$125,000	$75,000	$100,000
Stocking and Storage	$85,000	$105,000	$70,000	$85,000
Miscellaneous	$65,000	$85,000	$50,000	$65,000

You cannot generate this report using a data table because you need six input cells. Instead, you will create scenarios using the Scenario Manager. Rather than manually changing every input cell value, the Scenario Manager lets you define those input values within a named scenario and quickly switch from one scenario to another. The Scenario Manager can also be used to create reports that summarize the key differences in how the various scenarios impact result cells in the financial worksheet.

Before using the Scenario Manager, Irena asks you to define names for all the input and result cells that you intend to use in the what-if analysis. As you'll see later in this tutorial, the defined names appear in the reports generated by the Scenario Manager. Although not a requirement, using defined names makes it easier to work with scenarios and for other people to understand the scenario reports.

To define names for the income statement values:

1. If you took a break after the previous session, make sure the Coltivare Tool workbook is open, and the Income worksheet is the active sheet.
2. In the Income worksheet, select the nonadjacent range **A6:B7,A19:B22,A26:B28**. You'll define names for each of these cells.

3. On the ribbon, click the **Formulas** tab. In the Defined Names group, click the **Create from Selection** button. The Create Names from Selection dialog box opens.
4. Click the **Left column** check box to insert a checkmark, if necessary, and then click any other check boxes that have a checkmark to deselect them.
5. Click the **OK** button. The cell values in column B are named using the labels in the corresponding cells in column A.
6. Select cell **A1** to deselect the range.

Now that you've defined the names used in the worksheet, you'll create scenarios based on the values shown in Figure 10-20.

Defining a Scenario

Scenarios are defined using the Scenario Manager. Each scenario includes a scenario name, input or changing cells, and the values of each input cell. The number of scenarios you can create is limited only by your computer's memory.

REFERENCE

Defining a Scenario

- Enter the data values in the worksheet for the scenario.
- On the Data tab, in the Forecast group, click the What-If Analysis button, and then click Scenario Manager.
- Click the Add button in the Scenario Manager dialog box.
- In the Scenario name box, type a name for the scenario.
- In the Changing cells box, specify the changing cells.
- Click the OK button.
- In the Scenario Values dialog box, specify values for each input cell, and then click the Add button.
- Click the OK button.

You'll start by creating the Status Quo scenario, whose values match those currently entered in the workbook.

To add the Status Quo scenario:

1. On the ribbon, click the **Data** tab. In the Forecast group, click the **What-If Analysis** button, and then click **Scenario Manager**. The Scenario Manager dialog box opens. No scenarios are defined yet.
2. Click the **Add** button to open the Add Scenario dialog box.
3. In the Scenario name box, type **Status Quo**, and then press the **Tab** key. The cell reference in the Changing cells box is selected.

TIP

Scenarios are limited to a maximum of 32 changing cells.

The Scenario Manager refers to input cells as "changing cells" because these worksheet cells contain values that are changed under the scenario. Changing cells can be located anywhere in the worksheet. You can type the range names or locations of changing cells, but it's faster and more accurate to select them with the mouse.

The changing cells for each of the four scenarios are:

- Cell B6: Units Produced and Sold
- Cell B7: Average Price per Unit
- Cell B19: Salaries and Benefits
- Cell B20: Shipping and Distribution
- Cell B21: Stocking and Storage
- Cell B22: Miscellaneous

You'll specify the changing cells for the Status Quo scenario.

To specify the changing cells for the Status Quo scenario:

1. With the Changing Cells box still active, select the nonadjacent range **B6:B7,B19:B22**. Absolute references for the range appear in the Changing cells box. These are the input cells.
2. Press the **Tab** key to select the default text in the Comment box, and then type **Scenario assuming no change in values.** in the Comment box. See Figure 10-21.

Figure 10-21 Edit Scenario dialog box

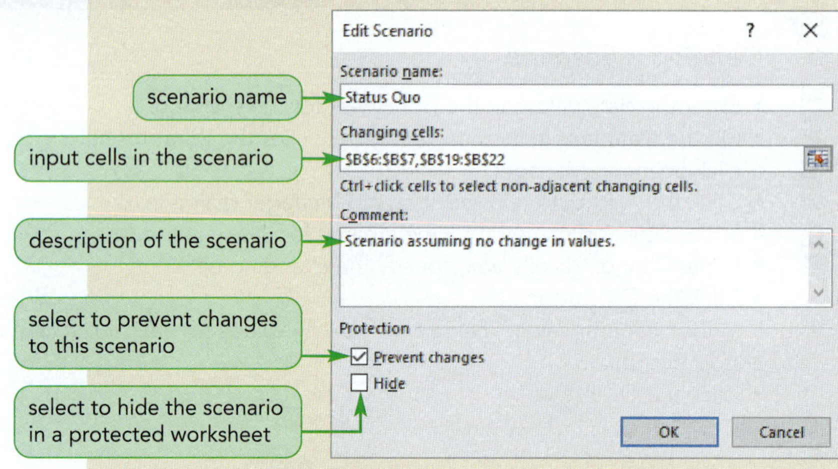

3. Click the **OK** button. The Scenario Values dialog box opens so you can enter values for each changing cell you entered in the Changing cells box in the Edit Scenario dialog box. The Status Quo scenario values already appear in the dialog box because these are the current values in the workbook. See Figure 10-22.

Figure 10-22 Scenario Values dialog box

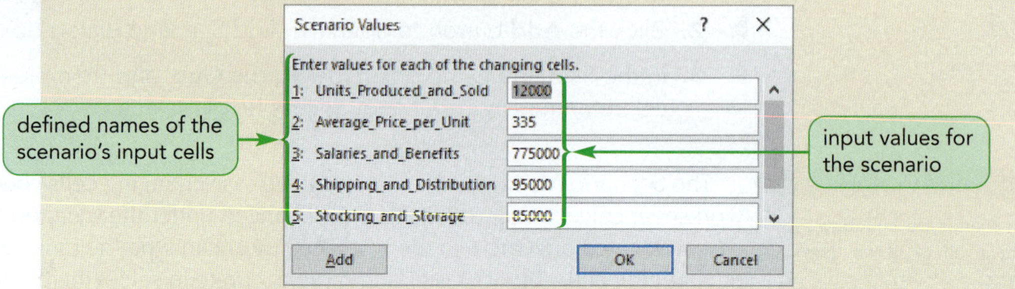

4. Click the **OK** button. The Scenario Manager dialog box reopens with the Status Quo scenario listed in the Scenarios box as shown in Figure 10-23.

Figure 10-23 Scenario Manager dialog box

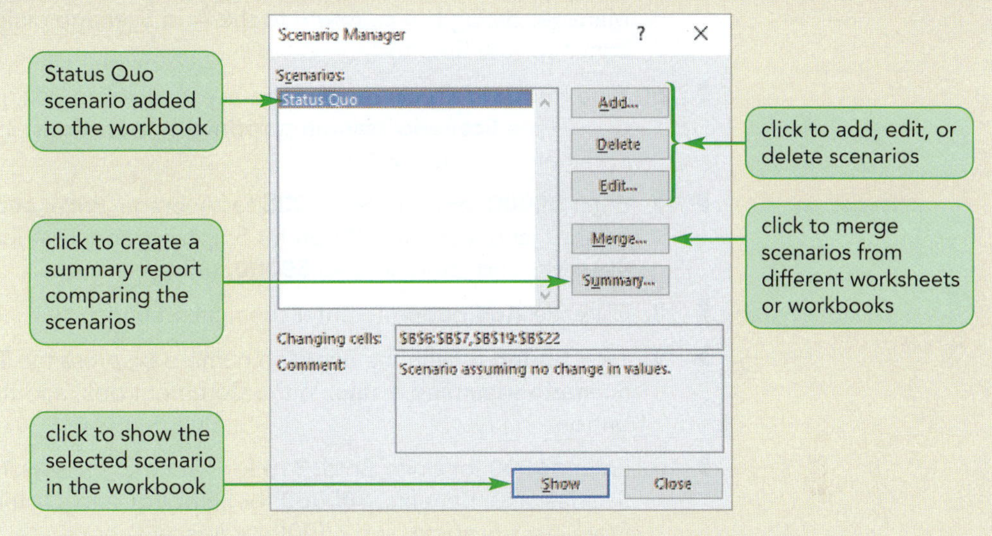

You'll use the same process to add the remaining three scenarios that Irena is interested in—Expanded Operations, Reduced Operations, and Spring Sale.

To add the remaining scenarios:

1. Click the **Add** button to open the Add Scenario dialog box.
2. In the Scenario name box, type **Expanded Operations**, press the **Tab** key twice to go the Comment box, and then type **Scenario assuming expanded operations.** in the Comment box.

   Note that the nonadjacent range you selected for the Status Quo scenario appears in the Changing cells box. Because you want to use the same set of changing cells, you didn't edit the range.
3. Click the **OK** button to open the Scenario Values dialog box for the Expanded Operations scenario.
4. Enter the following values, pressing the **Tab** key to move from one input box to the next: **14200** for Units_Produced_and_Sold, **335** for Average_Price_per_Unit, **950000** for Salaries_and_Benefits, **125000** for Shipping_and_Distribution, **105000** for Stocking_and_Storage, and **85000** for Miscellaneous.

   Be sure you enter the values for the scenario; do not simply accept the default values currently in the worksheet.

   Trouble? If the Scenario Manager dialog box reopens, you probably pressed the Enter key instead of the Tab key. Make sure that the Expanded Operations scenario is selected in the Scenarios box, click the Edit button, and then click the OK button to return to the Scenario Values dialog box. Enter the remaining values in the scenario, being sure to press the Tab key to move to the next input box.

5. Click the **Add** button. The Add Scenario dialog box reopens so you can enter the next scenario.

   Trouble? If the Scenario Manager dialog box reopens, you clicked the OK button instead of the Add button. Click the Add button in the Scenario Manager dialog box to return to the Add Scenario dialog box, and then continue with Step 6.

6. Type **Reduced Operations** in the Scenario name box, press the **Tab** key twice, type **Scenario assuming reduced operations.** in the Comment box, and then click the **OK** button.
7. Enter **10000** for Units_Sold, **335** for Average_Price_per_Unit, **650000** for Salaries_and_Benefits, **75000** for Shipping_and_Distribution, **70000** for Stocking_and_Storage, and **50000** for Miscellaneous.
8. Click the **Add** button to enter the final scenario.
9. Type **Spring Sale** in the Scenario name box, press the **Tab** key twice, type **Scenario assuming a sale.** in the Comment box, and then click the **OK** button.
10. Enter **16000** for Units_Sold, **310** for Average_Price_per_Unit, **775000** for Salaries_and_Benefits, **100000** for Shipping_and_Distribution, **85000** for Stock_and_Storage, and **65000** for Miscellaneous.
11. Click the **OK** button. The Scenario Manager dialog box reappears with all four scenarios listed.

Now that you've entered all four of the scenarios, you can view their impact on the Coltivare Tool income statement.

Viewing Scenarios

You can view the effect of each scenario by selecting that scenario in the Scenario Manager dialog box. You switch from one scenario to another by clicking the Show button in the Scenario Manager dialog box. You do not have to close the dialog box to switch scenarios. You'll start by viewing the results of the Expanded Operations scenario.

To view the impact of the Expanded Operations scenario:

1. In the Scenario Manager dialog box, click **Expanded Operations** in the list of scenarios. The changing cells and the comment for the selected scenario appear at the bottom of the Scenario Manager dialog box.
2. Click the **Show** button. The values in the Income worksheet change to reflect the scenario.
3. Click the **Close** button. The Scenario Manager dialog box closes. The income statement for Coltivare Tool is updated to show expanded operations with increased fixed expenses. See Figure 10-24.

TIP

You can double-click a scenario name in the Scenario Manager dialog box to view that scenario.

Figure 10-24 Income statement under the Expanded Operations scenario

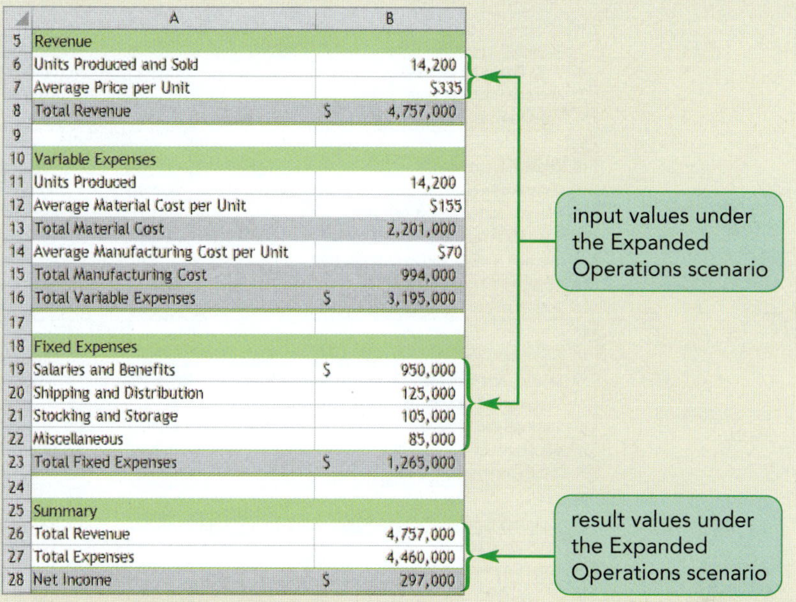

	A	B	
5	Revenue		
6	Units Produced and Sold		14,200
7	Average Price per Unit		$335
8	Total Revenue	$	4,757,000
9			
10	Variable Expenses		
11	Units Produced		14,200
12	Average Material Cost per Unit		$155
13	Total Material Cost		2,201,000
14	Average Manufacturing Cost per Unit		$70
15	Total Manufacturing Cost		994,000
16	Total Variable Expenses	$	3,195,000
17			
18	Fixed Expenses		
19	Salaries and Benefits	$	950,000
20	Shipping and Distribution		125,000
21	Stocking and Storage		105,000
22	Miscellaneous		85,000
23	Total Fixed Expenses	$	1,265,000
24			
25	Summary		
26	Total Revenue		4,757,000
27	Total Expenses		4,460,000
28	Net Income	$	297,000

Trouble? If the values in your income statement do not match those in the figure, you might have entered the values for the scenario incorrectly. You'll learn how to edit a scenario shortly.

Excel automatically changes the values of the six input cells to match the scenario. Under the Expanded Operations scenario, the company's net income in cell B28 decreases from the current value of $300,000 to $297,000. You'll review the other scenarios.

To view the impact of the remaining scenarios:

1. On the Data tab, in the Forecast group, click the **What-If Analysis** button, and then click **Scenario Manager** to open the Scenario Manager dialog box.
2. In the Scenarios box, double-click **Reduced Operations** to update the worksheet, and then click the **Close** button to close the Scenario Manager dialog box. Under the Reduced Operations scenario, the net income value shown in cell B28 drops to $255,000.
3. Repeat Steps 1 and 2 to update the worksheet with the Spring Sale scenario. Under the Spring Sale scenario, with the reduced unit price of each mower, the company would generate a net income of $335,000. Figure 10-25 shows the income statements for the Reduced Operations and Spring Sale scenarios.

Figure 10-25 Income statements under the Reduced Operations and Spring Sale scenarios

	A	B	
5	Revenue		
6	Units Produced and Sold		10,000
7	Average Price per Unit		$335
8	Total Revenue	$	3,350,000
9			
10	Variable Expenses		
11	Units Produced		10,000
12	Average Material Cost per Unit		$155
13	Total Material Cost		1,550,000
14	Average Manufacturing Cost per Unit		$70
15	Total Manufacturing Cost		700,000
16	Total Variable Expenses	$	2,250,000
17			
18	Fixed Expenses		
19	Salaries and Benefits	$	650,000
20	Shipping and Distribution		75,000
21	Stocking and Storage		70,000
22	Miscellaneous		50,000
23	Total Fixed Expenses	$	845,000
24			
25	Summary		
26	Total Revenue		3,350,000
27	Total Expenses		3,095,000
28	Net Income	$	255,000

Reduced Operations

	A	B	
5	Revenue		
6	Units Produced and Sold		16,000
7	Average Price per Unit		$310
8	Total Revenue	$	4,960,000
9			
10	Variable Expenses		
11	Units Produced		16,000
12	Average Material Cost per Unit		$155
13	Total Material Cost		2,480,000
14	Average Manufacturing Cost per Unit		$70
15	Total Manufacturing Cost		1,120,000
16	Total Variable Expenses	$	3,600,000
17			
18	Fixed Expenses		
19	Salaries and Benefits	$	775,000
20	Shipping and Distribution		100,000
21	Stocking and Storage		85,000
22	Miscellaneous		65,000
23	Total Fixed Expenses	$	1,025,000
24			
25	Summary		
26	Total Revenue		4,960,000
27	Total Expenses		4,625,000
28	Net Income	$	335,000

Spring Sale

Notice that when you substitute a new scenario for the Status Quo scenario, all worksheet values and charts are automatically updated. For example, under the Spring Sale scenario, the one-variable and two-variable data tables changed to reflect the new values of the input and result cells. The break-even point for the Spring Sale scenario is close to 12,000 units.

Editing a Scenario

After you create a scenario, you can edit its assumptions to view other possible outcomes. When you edit a scenario, the worksheet calculations are automatically updated to reflect the new scenario.

The Spring Sale scenario results in the highest net income, but it relies on the company selling 16,000 mowers at an average price of $310 to generate a net income of $335,000. Irena is unsure whether the company can meet that sales goal at that sales price. She asks you to modify the Spring Sale scenario, reducing the total sales to 15,000 units to see how this impacts the company's profitability.

To edit the Spring Sale scenario:

1. On the Data tab, in the Forecast group, click the **What-If Analysis** button, and then click **Scenario Manager** to reopen the Scenario Manager dialog box.
2. In the Scenarios box, click **Spring Sale** if it is not already selected, and then click the **Edit** button to open the Edit Scenario dialog box. You don't need to make any changes in this dialog box.
3. Click the **OK** button to open the Scenario Values dialog box.
4. Change the Units_Sold value from **16000** to **15000**, and then click the **OK** button to return to the Scenario Manager dialog box.

5. Click the **Show** button, and then click the **Close** button. The Income worksheet updates to reflect the revised scenario, which results in net income decreasing from $335,000 to $250,000. See Figure 10-26.

Figure 10-26 **Revised Spring Sale scenario**

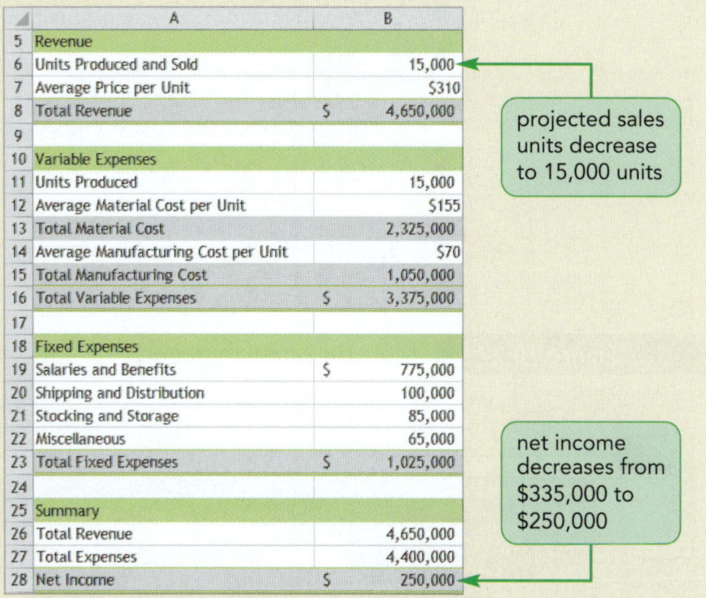

	A	B	
5	Revenue		
6	Units Produced and Sold		15,000
7	Average Price per Unit		$310
8	Total Revenue	$	4,650,000
9			
10	Variable Expenses		
11	Units Produced		15,000
12	Average Material Cost per Unit		$155
13	Total Material Cost		2,325,000
14	Average Manufacturing Cost per Unit		$70
15	Total Manufacturing Cost		1,050,000
16	Total Variable Expenses	$	3,375,000
17			
18	Fixed Expenses		
19	Salaries and Benefits	$	775,000
20	Shipping and Distribution		100,000
21	Stocking and Storage		85,000
22	Miscellaneous		65,000
23	Total Fixed Expenses	$	1,025,000
24			
25	Summary		
26	Total Revenue		4,650,000
27	Total Expenses		4,400,000
28	Net Income	$	250,000

projected sales units decrease to 15,000 units
net income decreases from $335,000 to $250,000

6. Open the Scenario Manager dialog box, and then double-click **Status Quo** in the Scenarios box to return the Income worksheet to the original values. Leave the Scenario Manager dialog box open.

Creating Scenario Summary Reports

Although scenarios can help you make important business decisions, repeatedly switching scenarios can become time consuming. To compare the results from multiple scenarios on a single worksheet, you can create a report either as an Excel table or as a PivotTable. Irena wants you to create both types of reports with the four scenarios you generated for Coltivare Tool, starting with a summary report that appears in an Excel table.

REFERENCE

Creating a Scenario Summary Report or a Scenario PivotTable Report

- On the Data tab, in the Forecast group, click the What-If Analysis button, and then click Scenario Manager.
- Click the Summary button.
- Click the Scenario summary or Scenario PivotTable report option button.
- Select the result cells to display in the report.
- Click the OK button.

To create a scenario summary report, you must identify which result cells you want to include in the report. Irena is interested in the following result cells—cell B26 (Total Revenue), cell B27 (Total Expenses), and cell B28 (Net Income). You'll display these values along with the values of the input cell defined by the scenario in your report.

To create the scenario summary report:

1. In the Scenario Manager dialog box, click the **Summary** button. The Scenario Summary dialog box opens, allowing you to create a scenario summary report or a scenario PivotTable report. You want to create a scenario summary report.
2. Verify that the **Scenario summary** option button is selected.
3. Make sure that the reference in the Result cells box is selected, and then in the Income worksheet, select the range **B26:B28** to enter the range reference for the result cells you want to display in the report.
4. Click the **OK** button. The scenario summary report is inserted in the workbook as a new worksheet.
5. Move the **Scenario Summary** worksheet to the end of the workbook. See Figure 10-27.

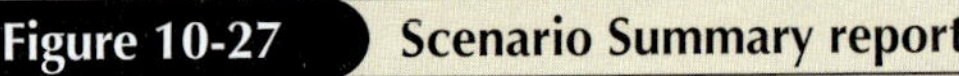

Figure 10-27 Scenario Summary report

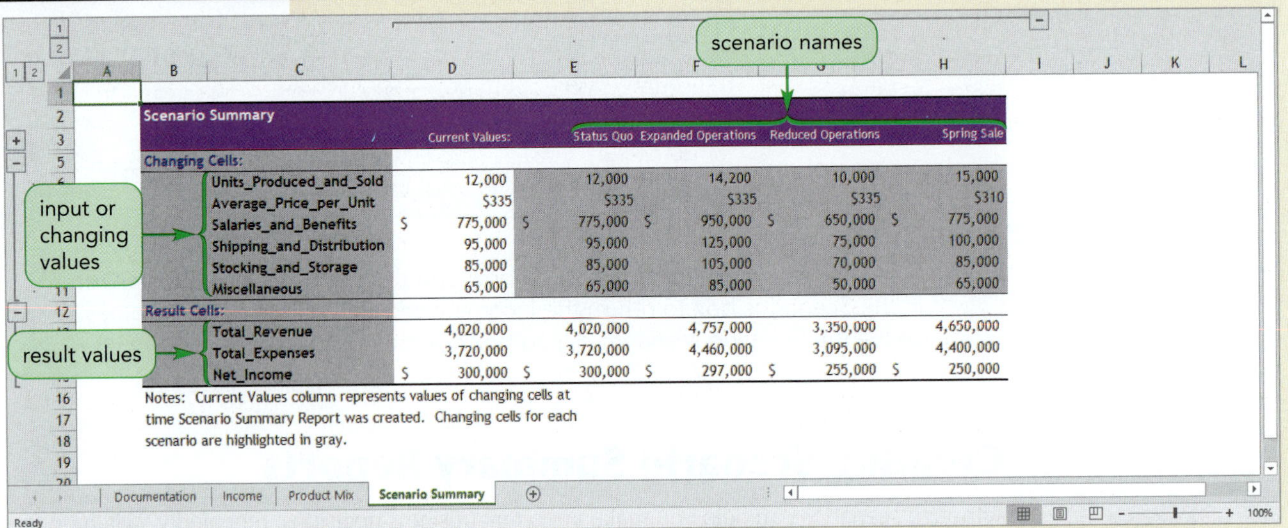

TIP

Use the outline tools to hide and expand different parts of the scenario summary report.

The scenario summary report displays the values of the changing cells and result cells under each scenario. Each scenario is listed by name, and the current worksheet values are also displayed. Note that the report uses the defined names you created earlier to identify the changing and result cells. The defined names make the report simpler to interpret.

Next, Irena wants you to compare the scenarios using a PivotTable report. As the name implies, a Scenario PivotTable report displays the results from each scenario as a PivotTable field in a PivotTable.

To create the Scenario PivotTable report:

1. Go to the **Income** worksheet, and then open the Scenario Manager dialog box.
2. Click the **Summary** button to open the Scenario Summary dialog box, and then click the **Scenario PivotTable report** option button.

3. Click the **OK** button. The Scenario PivotTable sheet is inserted in the workbook and contains the scenario values in a PivotTable.
4. Move the **Scenario PivotTable** worksheet to the end of the workbook, and then change the zoom level of the worksheet to **120%**. See Figure 10-28.

Figure 10-28 Scenario PivotTable report

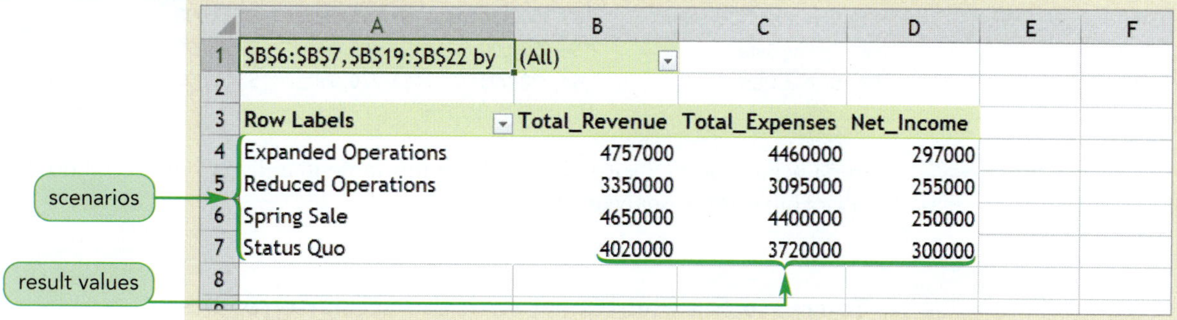

	A	B	C	D	E	F
1	$B$6:$B$7,$B$19:$B$22 by	(All)				
2						
3	Row Labels	Total_Revenue	Total_Expenses	Net_Income		
4	Expanded Operations	4757000	4460000	297000		
5	Reduced Operations	3350000	3095000	255000		
6	Spring Sale	4650000	4400000	250000		
7	Status Quo	4020000	3720000	300000		
8						

Irena wants you to edit the scenario PivotTable to make it easier to read but not filter it. Then, she wants you to generate a PivotChart of revenue, expenses, and net income under each scenario.

To edit and format the PivotTable report:

1. In the PivotTable Fields pane, in the VALUES box, click the **Total_Revenue** button, and then click **Value Field Settings**. The Value Field Settings dialog box opens.
2. Click the **Number Format** button to open the Format Cells dialog box, click **Currency** in the Category box, change the number of decimal places to **0**, and then click the last entry **($1,234)** in the Negative numbers box to display negative currency values in a red font enclosed in parentheses.
3. Click the **OK** button in the Format Cells dialog box, and then click the **OK** button in the Value Field Settings dialog box. The number format is applied to the Total_Revenue cells.
4. Repeat Steps 1 through 3 for the Total_Expenses and the Net_Income buttons in the Values box to apply the same number format.
5. In the PivotTable Fields pane, in the FILTERS box, click the **$B$6:$B$7,$B...** button, and then click **Remove Field**. You will not filter the PivotTable.
6. In cell **A1**, enter **Scenario PivotTable**, and then format the text with the **Title** cell style. See Figure 10-29.

Figure 10-29 Formatted PivotTable report

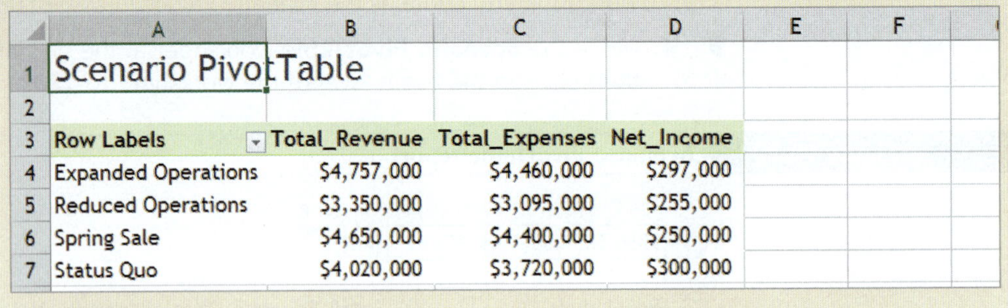

	A	B	C	D	E	F
1	Scenario PivotTable					
2						
3	Row Labels	Total_Revenue	Total_Expenses	Net_Income		
4	Expanded Operations	$4,757,000	$4,460,000	$297,000		
5	Reduced Operations	$3,350,000	$3,095,000	$255,000		
6	Spring Sale	$4,650,000	$4,400,000	$250,000		
7	Status Quo	$4,020,000	$3,720,000	$300,000		

Irena wants you to display the results of this table in a PivotChart. You'll do this from the PivotTable Tools Analyze tab.

To create the PivotChart with the scenario results:

1. Click cell **A3** to select the PivotTable.
2. On the ribbon, click the **PivotTable Tools Analyze** tab. In the Tools group, click the **PivotChart** button to open the Insert Chart dialog box.
3. If it is not already selected, click the **Clustered Column** chart type (the first chart subtype in the Column section), and then click the **OK** button.
4. Move and resize the embedded chart so that it covers the range **A8:D19**.
5. On the ribbon, click the **PivotChart Tools Analyze** tab. In the Show/Hide group, click the **Field Buttons** button to hide the field buttons in the chart. See Figure 10-30.

Figure 10-30 Scenario PivotChart

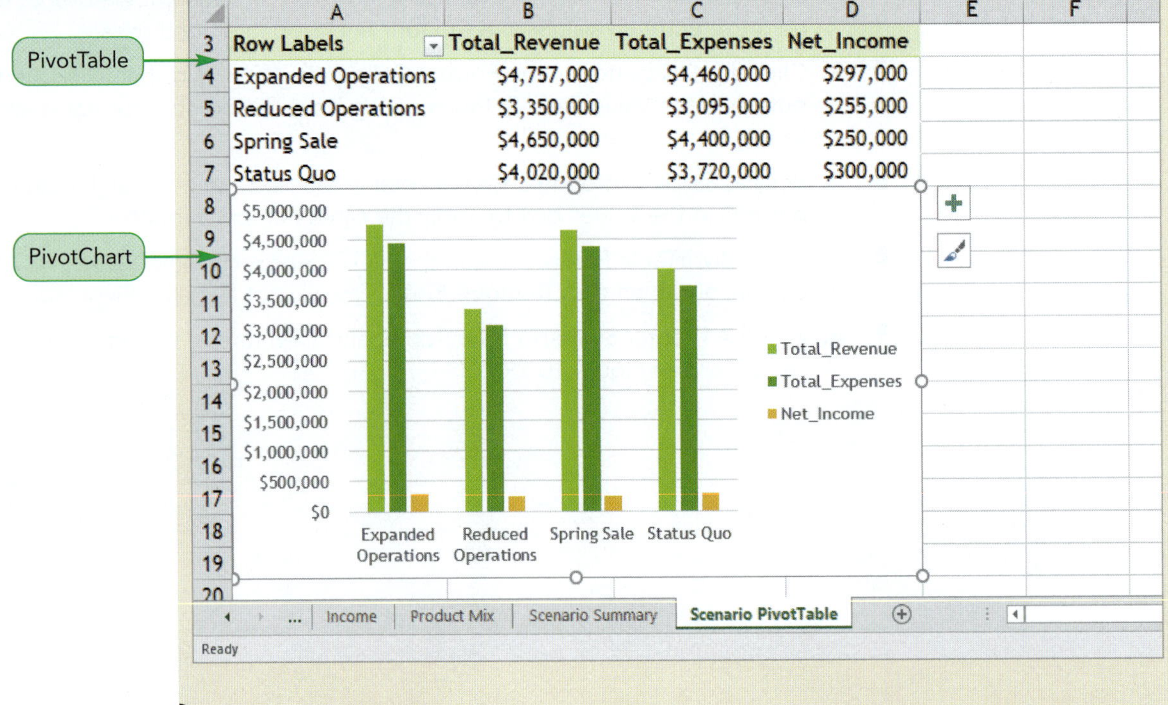

6. Save the workbook.

Based on the income statements from the different scenarios, Irena can expect a net income from the power mower sales ranging from $250,000 to $300,000 per year.

PROSKILLS

Teamwork: Merging Scenarios

In a business, several workbooks often track the same set of figures and evaluate the same set of scenarios. Colleagues can share scenarios by merging the scenarios from multiple workbooks into one workbook. The Scenario Manager dialog box includes a Merge button that you can use to merge scenarios from different workbooks. The scenarios merge into the active sheet. It's easier to merge scenarios if all of the what-if analyses on the different worksheets and workbooks are identical. All of the changing cells from the merged scenario must correspond to changing cells in the active workbook and worksheet. By sharing scenarios, a team can more easily explore the impact of different financial situations, ensuring that the entire team is always working from a common set of assumptions and goals.

In this session, you used scenarios to examine the impact of different financial scenarios on the profitability of Coltivare Tool's line of power mowers. In the next session, you'll explore how by emphasizing different power mower models within its lineup, Coltivare Tool can increase the profitability of its operations.

REVIEW

Session 10.2 Quick Check

1. What is one advantage of scenarios over data tables?
2. What should you do before creating a scenario report to make the entries on the report easier to interpret?
3. What are changing cells in a scenario?
4. Where do you define result cells in the Scenario Manager?
5. How do you display a scenario in the active worksheet?
6. How do you create a scenario PivotTable report?

Session 10.3 Visual Overview:

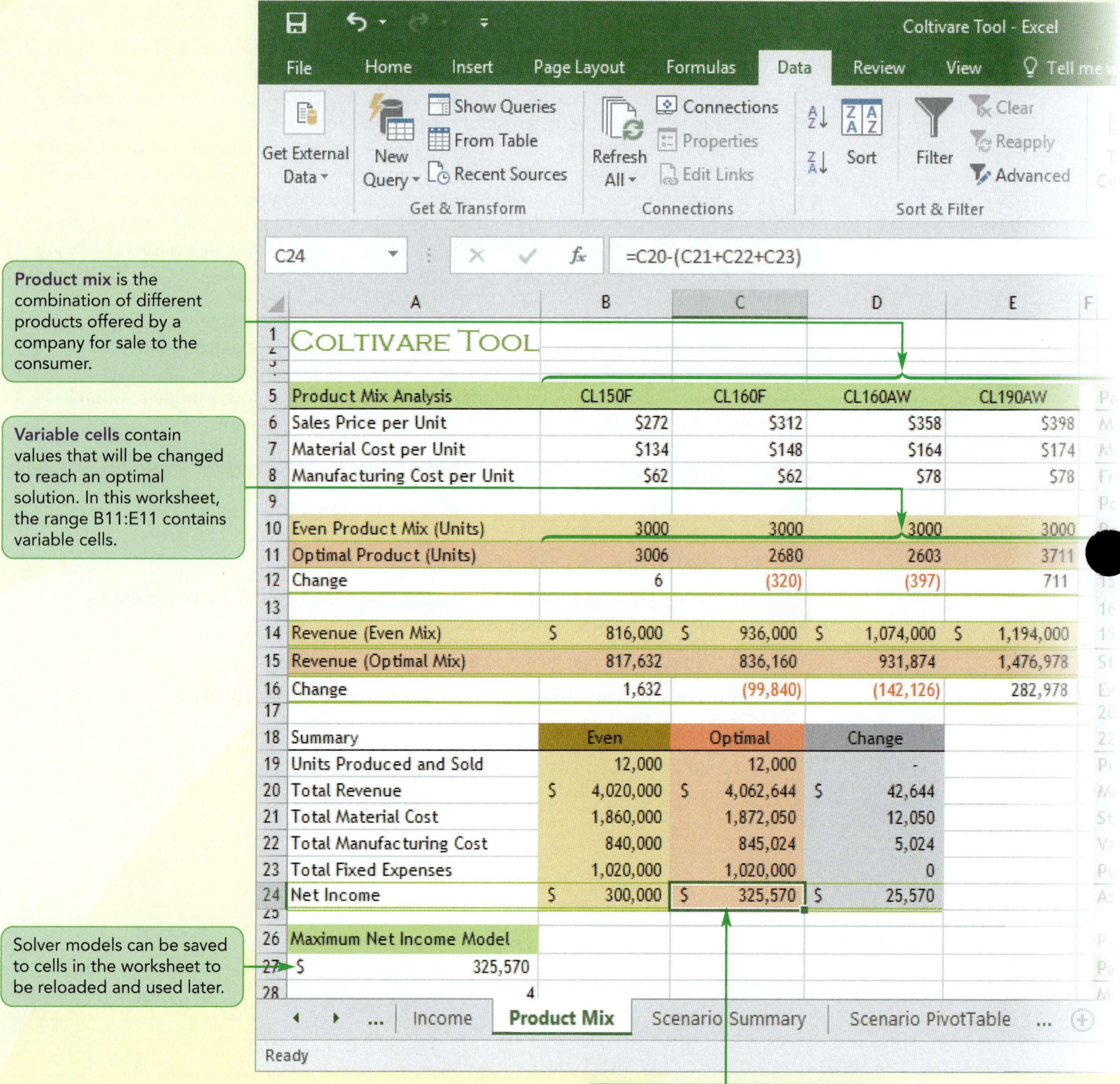

	A	B	C	D	E
5	Product Mix Analysis	CL150F	CL160F	CL160AW	CL190AW
6	Sales Price per Unit	$272	$312	$358	$398
7	Material Cost per Unit	$134	$148	$164	$174
8	Manufacturing Cost per Unit	$62	$62	$78	$78
10	Even Product Mix (Units)	3000	3000	3000	3000
11	Optimal Product (Units)	3006	2680	2603	3711
12	Change	6	(320)	(397)	711
14	Revenue (Even Mix)	$ 816,000	$ 936,000	$ 1,074,000	$ 1,194,000
15	Revenue (Optimal Mix)	817,632	836,160	931,874	1,476,978
16	Change	1,632	(99,840)	(142,126)	282,978
18	Summary	Even	Optimal	Change	
19	Units Produced and Sold	12,000	12,000	-	
20	Total Revenue	$ 4,020,000	$ 4,062,644	$ 42,644	
21	Total Material Cost	1,860,000	1,872,050	12,050	
22	Total Manufacturing Cost	840,000	845,024	5,024	
23	Total Fixed Expenses	1,020,000	1,020,000	0	
24	Net Income	$ 300,000	$ 325,570	$ 25,570	
26	Maximum Net Income Model				
27	$ 325,570				
28	4				

Product mix is the combination of different products offered by a company for sale to the consumer.

Variable cells contain values that will be changed to reach an optimal solution. In this worksheet, the range B11:E11 contains variable cells.

Solver models can be saved to cells in the worksheet to be reloaded and used later.

The **objective cell** contains a value to maximize, minimize, or set to a specific value. In this worksheet, cell C24 is the objective cell.

Optimal Solutions with Solver

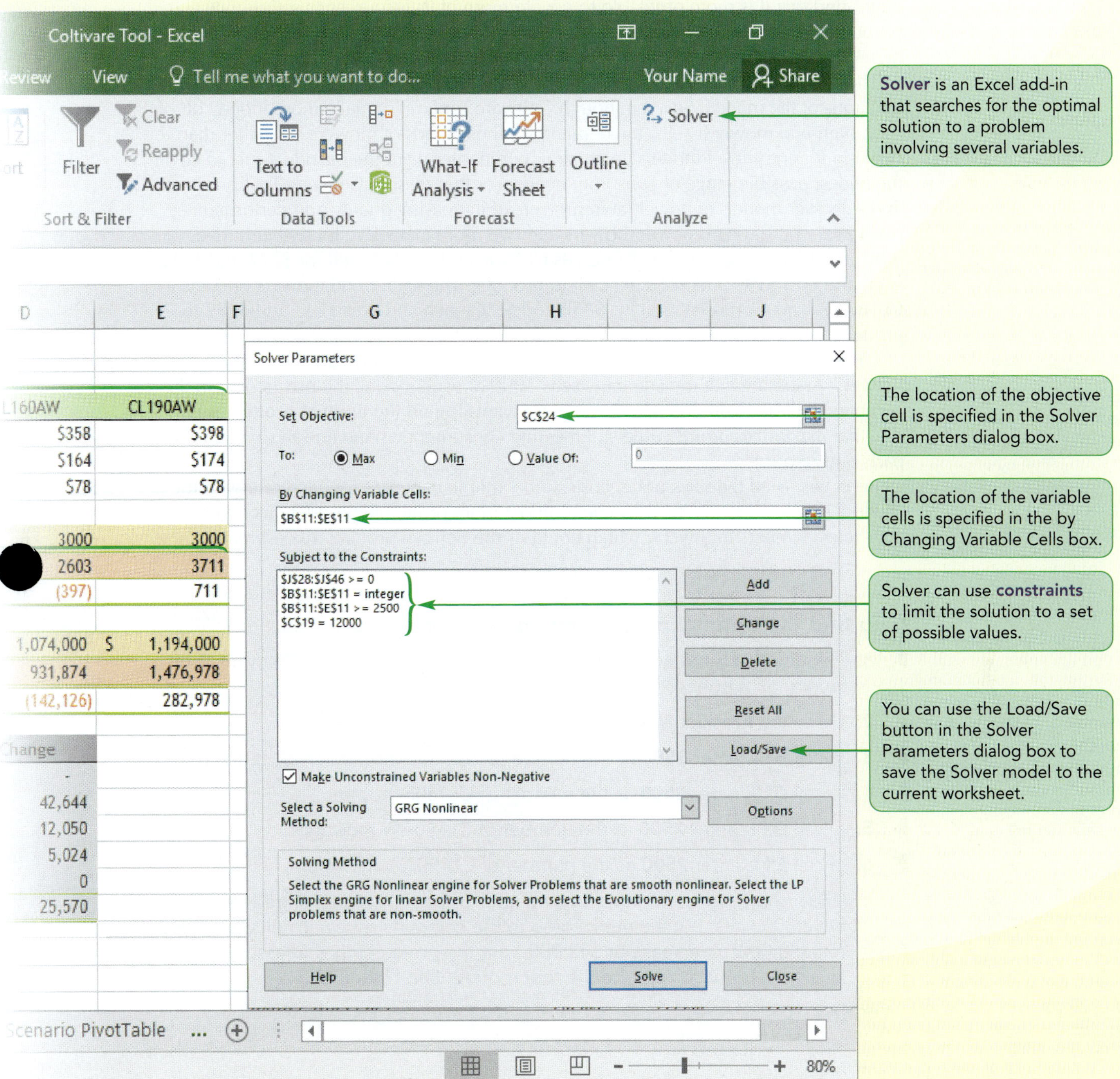

Introducing Product Mix

The combination of products offered by a company is known as the company's product mix. Not all products are alike; one product may differ from another in its sales price, its production costs, and its attractiveness to the consumer. Because of this, a company might find that it is more profitable to devote more of its resources to selling one product over another. For example, Coltivare Tool might make a larger profit on each high-end mower it sells compared to its profit margin on less expensive mowers.

The challenge for the company is to maximize its profits while still meeting the demands of the market. So even though Coltivare Tool might make more money off of each high-end mower it sells, the demand for those kinds of mowers is smaller than the demand for entry-level models. In general, companies want their product mix to cover the widest possible range of consumer needs. For that reason, Coltivare Tool produces and sells four models of power lawn mowers of increasing quality and performance: two lower-end standard power mowers and two more expensive four-wheel-drive mowers. The lower-end mowers (models CL150F and CL160F) sell for $272 and $312 each and cost $196 and $210 per unit to produce. The higher-end mowers (models CL160AW and CL190AW) sell for $358 and $398 each and cost $242 and $252 to produce.

Under the Status Quo scenario, Irena estimates the company can sell 12,000 mowers. Assuming that the company sells 3000 of each model, the net income to the company will be $300,000. However, Irena wants to find the **optimal product mix**, one that maximizes profits while still meeting consumer demand and the availability of parts and resources.

Irena has listed the sales price, costs, and variable expenses for each model in the Product Mix worksheet. She asks you to find a more profitable product mix by entering new sales numbers in row 11, which contains the optimal product mix estimates.

To find the optimal product mix by trial and error:

1. If you took a break after the previous session, make sure the Coltivare Tool workbook is open.
2. Go to the **Product Mix** worksheet.
3. In cell **B11**, enter **3500** as the number of CL150F mowers produced and sold.
4. In cell **C11**, enter **3500** as the number of CL160F mowers.
5. In cell **D11**, enter **2500** as the number of CL160AW mowers.
6. In cell **E11**, enter **2500** as the number of CL190AW mowers.

   Under this product mix, the total number of mowers is unchanged, remaining at 12,000 units; but the net income to the company shown in cell C24 drops to $258,000, a decrease of $42,000 from the product mix that assumes equal levels of production among the four models. See Figure 10-31.

Figure 10-31 Comparison of product mixes

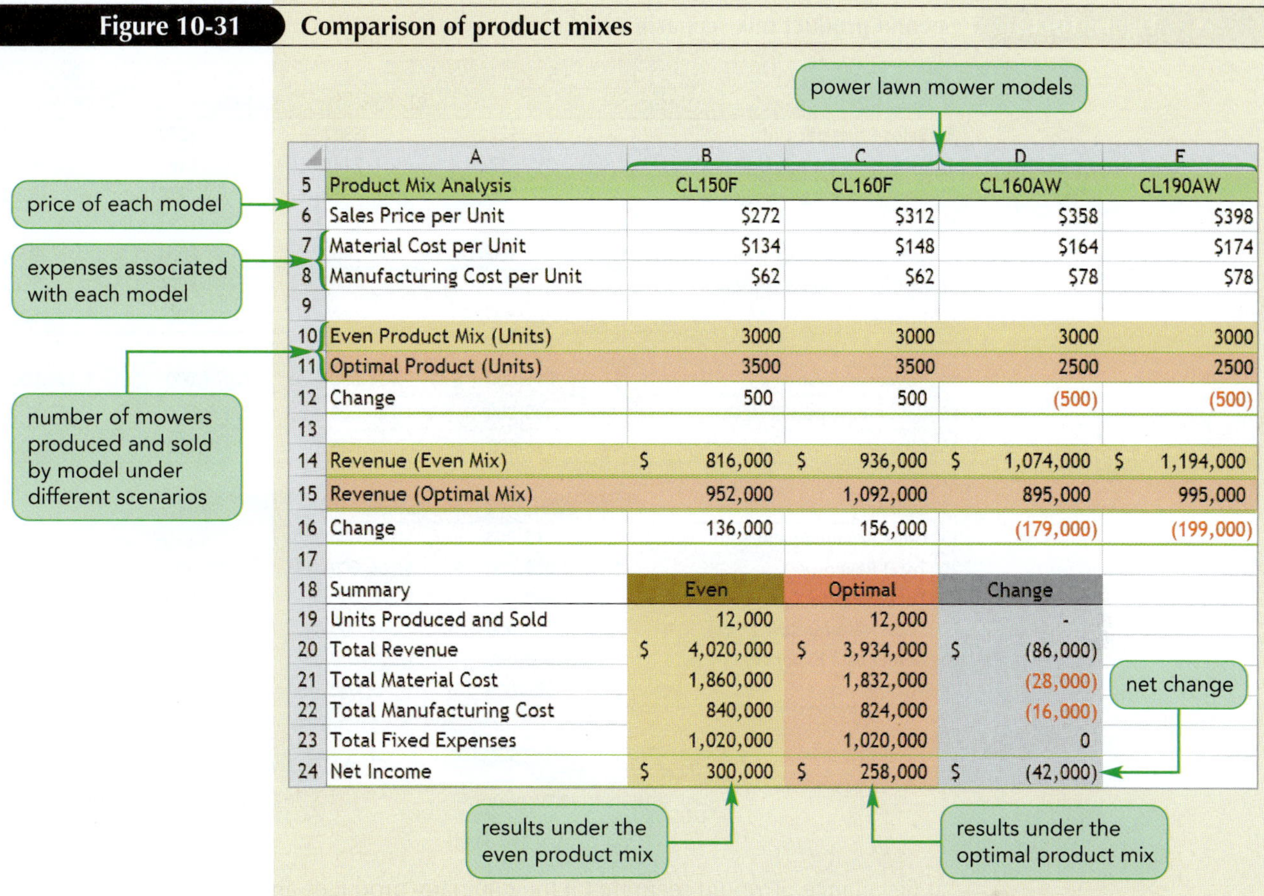

	A	B	C	D	E
5	Product Mix Analysis	CL150F	CL160F	CL160AW	CL190AW
6	Sales Price per Unit	$272	$312	$358	$398
7	Material Cost per Unit	$134	$148	$164	$174
8	Manufacturing Cost per Unit	$62	$62	$78	$78
9					
10	Even Product Mix (Units)	3000	3000	3000	3000
11	Optimal Product (Units)	3500	3500	2500	2500
12	Change	500	500	(500)	(500)
13					
14	Revenue (Even Mix)	$ 816,000	$ 936,000	$ 1,074,000	$ 1,194,000
15	Revenue (Optimal Mix)	952,000	1,092,000	895,000	995,000
16	Change	136,000	156,000	(179,000)	(199,000)
17					
18	Summary	Even	Optimal	Change	
19	Units Produced and Sold	12,000	12,000	-	
20	Total Revenue	$ 4,020,000	$ 3,934,000	$ (86,000)	
21	Total Material Cost	1,860,000	1,832,000	(28,000)	
22	Total Manufacturing Cost	840,000	824,000	(16,000)	
23	Total Fixed Expenses	1,020,000	1,020,000	0	
24	Net Income	$ 300,000	$ 258,000	$ (42,000)	

Next, you'll try a different product mix to see if you can increase the company's net income by producing more of the all-wheel-drive models.

7. In the range **B11:E11**, enter the following values: **2500**, **2500**, **3500**, and **3500**. Under this product mix, the net income increases by $42,000 to a total net income of $342,000. See Figure 10-32.

Figure 10-32 Second product mix scenario

	A	B	C	D	E
5	Product Mix Analysis	CL150F	CL160F	CL160AW	CL190AW
6	Sales Price per Unit	$272	$312	$358	$398
7	Material Cost per Unit	$134	$148	$164	$174
8	Manufacturing Cost per Unit	$62	$62	$78	$78
9					
10	Even Product Mix (Units)	3000	3000	3000	3000
11	Optimal Product (Units)	2500	2500	3500	3500
12	Change	(500)	(500)	500	500
13					
14	Revenue (Even Mix)	$ 816,000	$ 936,000	$ 1,074,000	$ 1,194,000
15	Revenue (Optimal Mix)	680,000	780,000	1,253,000	1,393,000
16	Change	(136,000)	(156,000)	179,000	199,000
17					
18	Summary	Even	Optimal	Change	
19	Units Produced and Sold	12,000	12,000	-	
20	Total Revenue	$ 4,020,000	$ 4,106,000	$ 86,000	
21	Total Material Cost	1,860,000	1,888,000	28,000	
22	Total Manufacturing Cost	840,000	856,000	16,000	
23	Total Fixed Expenses	1,020,000	1,020,000	0	
24	Net Income	$ 300,000	$ 342,000	$ 42,000	

changed units per model

increasing sales of all-wheel-drive mowers…

…results in an increase in net income

At first glance, it would seem that if the company produces and sells more all-wheel-drive mowers, it will maximize its profits. Is this always the case, and can the company successfully market those kinds of mowers? Perhaps there are other combinations that are even more profitable. To find the best combination of models produced and sold among all possible combinations, you can use Solver.

Finding an Optimal Solution Using Solver

Solver finds the numeric solution to a problem involving several input values. For example, Solver can be used to find the combination of input values that maximizes profits. It also can be used to find a set of input values that minimizes costs, or it can act like Goal Seek and find the input values required to match a given result.

Activating Solver

Solver is an **add-in**, which is a program that adds commands and features to Microsoft Office applications such as Excel. You might need to activate Solver before you can use it.

REFERENCE

Activating Solver

- On the Data tab, confirm whether Solver appears in the Analyze group. If it appears, Solver is already active. If it does not appear, continue with the rest of these steps.
- Click the File tab, and then click the Options button in the navigation bar.
- Click Add-ins in the left pane, click the arrow next to the Manage box, and then click Excel Add-ins.
- Click the Go button to open the Add-Ins dialog box.
- Click the Solver Add-in check box, and then click the OK button.
- Follow the remaining prompts to install Solver, if it is not already installed.

You will check whether Solver is already active on your version of Excel. If the Solver button does not appear on the Data tab in the Analyze group, the Solver add-in needs to be activated. If you are working on a network, you might need your instructor or network administrator to activate Solver for you. If you are working on a stand-alone PC, you can activate Solver yourself.

To activate the Solver add-in:

1. On the ribbon, click the **Data** tab, and then look for the Analyze group and the Solver button. If you see the Solver button, as shown in Figure 10-33, Solver is active and you should read but not perform the rest of the steps in this section. If you don't see the Solver button, continue with Step 2.

Figure 10-33 **Solver button in the Analyze group on the Data tab**

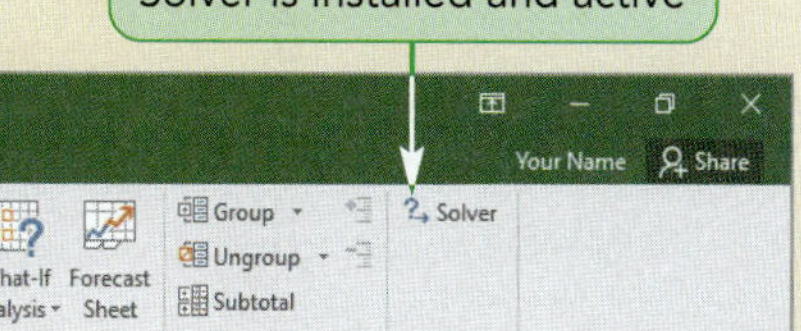

TIP

You can also open the Excel Options dialog box by right-clicking the ribbon, and then clicking Customize the Ribbon on the shortcut menu.

2. Click the **File** tab, and then click the **Options** button in the navigation bar to open the Excel Options dialog box.
3. In the left pane, click **Add-ins**. Information about all of the add-ins currently installed within Excel appears in the right pane.
4. If necessary, click the **Manage box arrow** at the bottom of the dialog box, and then click **Excel Add-ins**.
5. Click the **Go** button. The Add-ins dialog box opens and displays a list of all of the available Excel add-ins. Although these add-ins are available, they might not have been activated.
6. Click the **Solver Add-in** check box to insert a checkmark.

   Trouble? If you don't see Solver in the list of available add-ins, you may have to reinstall Excel on your computer. See your instructor or technical resource person for help.
7. Click the **OK** button. Solver is activated, and its button is added to the Data tab in the Analyze group.

Now that Solver is activated, you can use it to find the optimal product mix.

INSIGHT

Excel Add-Ins

Solver is only one of the available Excel add-ins. Other add-ins provide the ability to perform statistical analyses, generate business reports, and produce interactive maps. You can also create your own add-in using the Visual Basic for Applications (VBA) macro language. The process for activating add-ins is the same as the process you used to activate the Solver add-in. Most third-party add-ins provide detailed instructions for their installation and use.

Setting the Objective Cell and Variable Cells

Every Solver model needs an objective cell and one or more variable cells. An objective cell is a result cell that is maximized, minimized, or set to a specific value. A variable cell is an input cell that changes so that the objective cell can meet its defined goal.

In the Product Mix worksheet, cell C24, which displays the optimal net income, is the objective cell whose value you want to maximize. The cells in the range B11:E11, which contain the number of mowers produced and sold by the company under the optimal product mix, are the variable cells whose values you want Solver to change in order to reach that optimal net income.

REFERENCE

Setting Solver's Objective and Variable Cells

- On the Data tab, in the Analyze group, click the Solver button.
- In the Set Objective box, specify the cell whose value you want to set to match a specific objective.
- Click the Max, Min, or Value Of option button to maximize the objective cell, minimize the objective cell, or set the objective cell to a specified value, respectively.
- In the By Changing Variable Cells input box, specify the changing cells.

You will start Solver now and define the objective cell and the variable cells.

To set up the Solver model:

1. On the Data tab, in the Analyze group, click the **Solver** button. The Solver Parameters dialog box opens with the insertion point in the Set Objective box.
2. Click cell **C24** in the Product Mix worksheet.
3. Verify that the **Max** option button is selected. This option tells Solver to find the maximum value possible for cell C24.
4. Click the **By Changing Variable Cells** box, and then select the range **B11:E11** in the Product Mix worksheet. The absolute reference to this range tells Solver to modify the product mix values stored in these cells in order to maximize the value in cell C24. See Figure 10-34.

TIP

Changing cells can contain only constant values, not formulas.

Figure 10-34 Solver Parameters dialog box

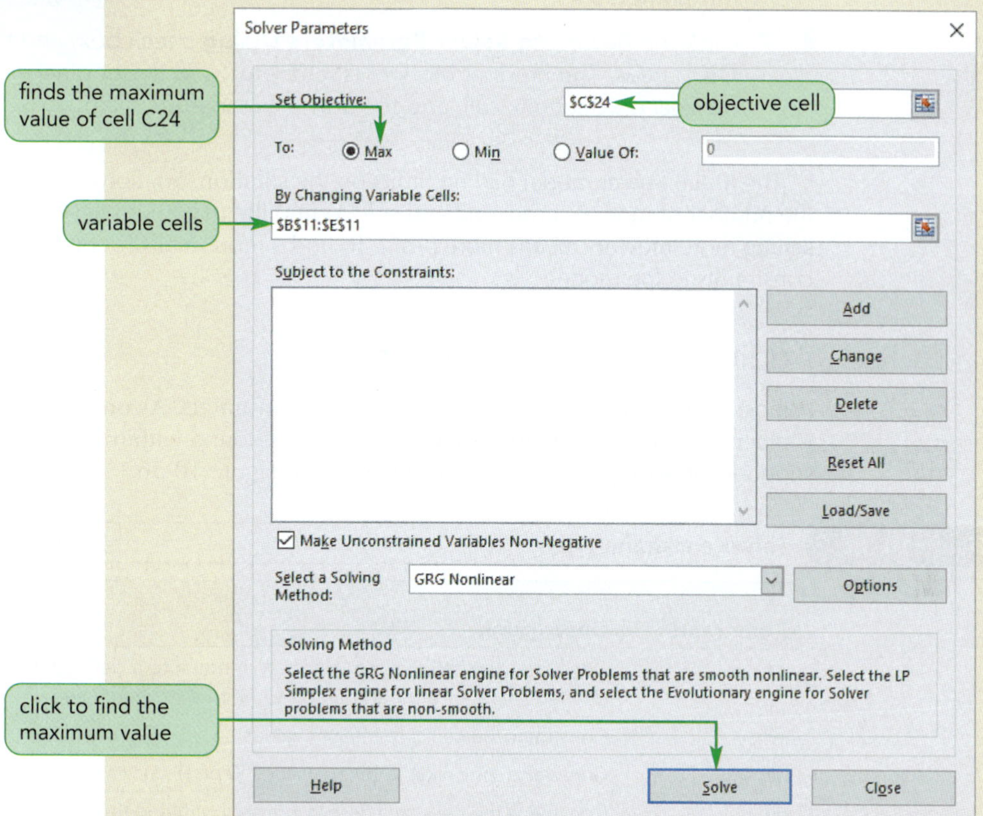
finds the maximum value of cell C24
objective cell
variable cells
click to find the maximum value

5. Click the **Solve** button. Solver finds the maximum net income and the optimal product mix by evaluating different product mix combinations. The Solver Results dialog box opens, showing that Coltivare Tool should produce and sell billions of mowers to maximize its net income—a nice idea, but hardly practical. See Figure 10-35.

Figure 10-35 Impractical Solver results

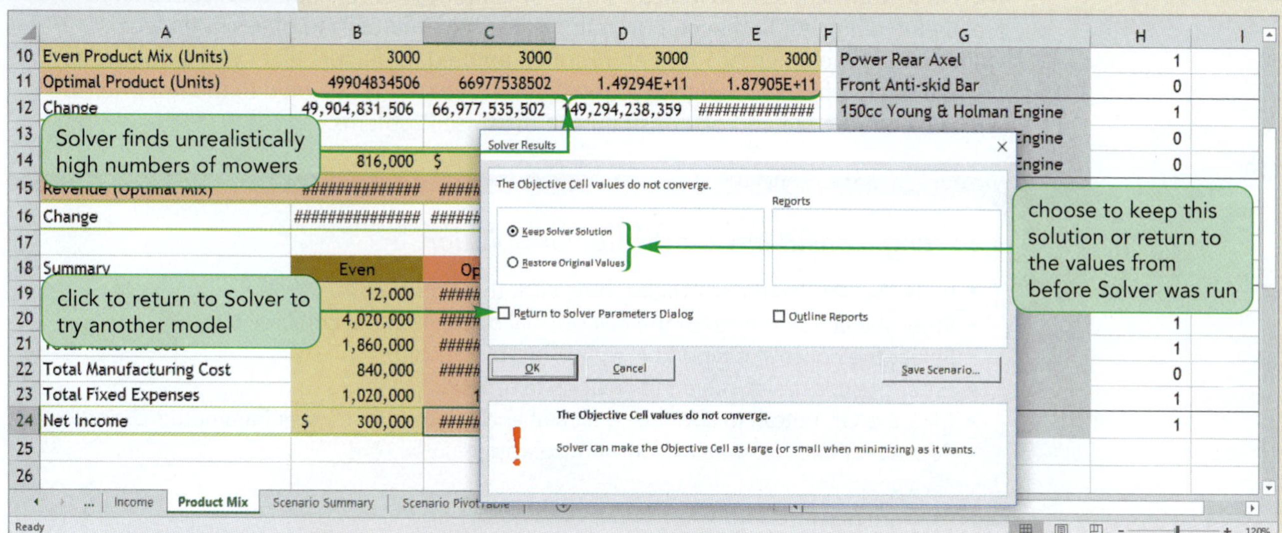
Solver finds unrealistically high numbers of mowers
choose to keep this solution or return to the values from before Solver was run
click to return to Solver to try another model

6. Click the **Restore Original Values** option button to reset the original product mix numbers.
7. Click the **Return to Solver Parameters Dialog** check box, and then click the **OK** button. The Product Mix worksheet returns to the original values for the optimal product mix cell, and the Solver Parameters dialog box reappears.

The initial Solver model had no limits on the solution. So, Solver kept increasing the number of mowers produced and sold to find the maximum net income because selling more mowers means more profit. To find a more realistic solution, you must add constraints to the model.

Adding Constraints to Solver

Almost every Solver model needs one or more constraints. A constraint is a limit that is placed on the solution applied to the result cells found within the worksheet. Solver supports the six types of constraints described in Figure 10-36.

Figure 10-36 Solver constraint types

Constraint	Description
<= , = , >=	Constrains the cell(s) to be less than or equal to a defined value, equal to a defined value, or greater than or equal to a defined value
int	Constrains the cell(s) to integer values
bin	Constrains the cell(s) to binary values (0 or 1)
dif	Constrains the cells to different integers within in the range 1 to *n* where *n* is the number of cells in the constraint

For example, you can use the <= constraint to limit the total number of mowers produced and sold to a reasonable number, or you can use the = constraint to specify the exact number of mowers produced and ultimately sold. Other constraints are used for special types of data.

The bin, or binary, constraint limits cells to values of 0 or 1 and is often used to indicate the presence or absence of a thing. For example, binary constraints could be used in a work schedule to indicate when an employee is scheduled to work a shift. Finally the dif, or All Different, constraint is used to limit cells to different integer values within the range of 1 to *n* and is often applied for factors that need to follow a defined order when 1 is assigned to the first factor and *n* is assigned to the last one. You will use both the bin and dif constraints in the Case Problems.

REFERENCE

Setting Constraints on the Solver Solution

- In the Solver Parameters dialog box, click the Add button.
- Enter the cell reference of the cell or cells containing the constraint.
- Select the constraint type (<=, =, >=, int, bin, or dif).
- Enter the constraint value in the Constraint box.
- Click the OK button to add the constraint and return to the Solver Parameters dialog box.
- Repeat for each constraint you want to add.

Irena wants to set the total number of mowers sold to exactly 12,000 so that she can compare the optimal product mix results to the results of the current product mix, which also is based on 12,000 mowers produced and sold. You will add an = constraint to Solver.

To add the units sold constraint to Solver:

1. In the Solver Parameters dialog box, click the **Add** button. The Add Constraint dialog box opens with the insertion point in the Cell Reference box.
2. Click cell **C19** in the Product Mix worksheet to enter the absolute cell reference to the Optimal Units Produced and Sold value.
3. Click the **arrow** next to the constraint type box (the center box), and then click **=** in the list to specify an equal to constraint.
4. In the Constraint box, type **12000**. This constraint limits cell C19 to be equal to 12,000. See Figure 10-37.

TIP

Constraints can be applied only to adjacent ranges. For a nonadjacent range, apply separate constraints to each part of the range.

Figure 10-37 Add Constraint dialog box

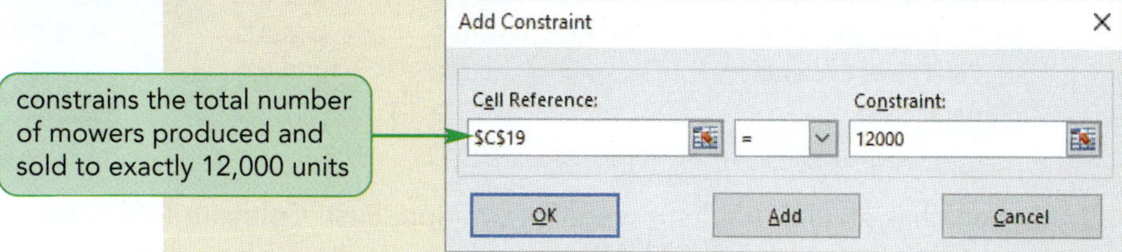

5. Click the **OK** button. The Solver Parameters dialog box reappears with the constraint $C$19 = 12000 added to the Subject to the Constraints box.
6. Click the **Solve** button. The Solver Results dialog box opens, indicating that the solution that Solver found satisfies the objective and constraints. Solver's solution, shown in the Product Mix worksheet, is that the company should produce only CL190AW lawn mowers. See Figure 10-38.

Figure 10-38 Solver results with one constraint

	A	B	C	D	E
5	Product Mix Analysis	CL150F	CL160F	CL160AW	CL190AW
6	Sales Price per Unit	$272	$312	$358	$398
7	Material Cost per Unit	$134	$148	$164	$174
8	Manufacturing Cost per Unit	$62	$62	$78	$78
9					
10	Even Product Mix (Units)	3000	3000	3000	3000
11	Optimal Product (Units)	0	0	0	12000.00005
12	Change	(3,000)	(3,000)	(3,000)	9,000
13					
14	Revenue (Even Mix)	$ 816,000	$ 936,000	$ 1,074,000	$ 1,194,000
15	Revenue (Optimal Mix)	-	-	-	4,776,000
16	Change	(816,000)	(936,000)	(1,074,000)	3,582,000
17					
18	Summary	Even	Optimal	Change	
19	Units Produced and Sold	12,000	12,000	0	
20	Total Revenue	$ 4,020,000	$ 4,776,000	$ 756,000	
21	Total Material Cost	1,860,000	2,088,000	228,000	
22	Total Manufacturing Cost	840,000	936,000	96,000	
23	Total Fixed Expenses	1,020,000	1,020,000	0	
24	Net Income	$ 300,000	$ 732,000	$ 432,000	

under this solution the production is limited to the CL190AW model

total mowers sold fixed at 12,000 units

noninteger value for units sold

Irena has several problems with this solution. First, Coltivare Tool cannot limit its production to only the CL190AW mower because there is not enough demand for only that model. Second, Coltivare Tool wants to diversify its offerings by producing and selling a variety of power lawn mowers to attract a wide range of customers.

To fix this problem, you will add the following constraint that the company must produce at least 2500 units of each model. Also, because the company cannot produce fractions of lawn mowers, you'll add the additional constraint that the number of mowers produced and sold must be an integer value.

To add constraints to the model:

1. Click the **Restore Original Values** option button, verify that the **Return to Solver Parameters Dialog** check box is selected, and then click the **OK** button to return to the Solver Parameters dialog box.
2. Click the **Add** button. The Add Constraint dialog box opens with the insertion point in the Cell Reference box.
3. Select the range **B11:E11** in the Product Mix worksheet, select **>=** as the constraint type, and then enter **2500** in the Constraint box, specifying that each value in the range B11:E11 must be greater than or equal to 2500.
4. Click the **Add** button to add the constraint to the Solver model. The Add Constraint dialog box remains open so you can add another constraint.
5. Select the range **B11:E11** in the Product Mix worksheet, and then select **int** as the constraint type. The word "integer" is added to the Constraint box, specifying that each value in the range B11:E11 must be an integer.

6. Click the **OK** button to add the constraint to the model and return to the Solver Parameters dialog box. The Subject to the Constraints box now lists three constraints.

7. Click the **Solve** button. The Solver results appear in the Product Mix worksheet. See Figure 10-39.

Figure 10-39 Solver results with three constraints

	A	B		C		D		E
5	Product Mix Analysis	CL150F		CL160F		CL160AW		CL190AW
6	Sales Price per Unit	$272		$312		$358		$398
7	Material Cost per Unit	$134		$148		$164		$174
8	Manufacturing Cost per Unit	$62		$62		$78		$78
9								
10	Even Product Mix (Units)	3000		3000		3000		3000
11	Optimal Product (Units)	2500		2500		2500		4500
12	Change	(500)		(500)		(500)		1,500
13								
14	Revenue (Even Mix)	$	816,000	$	936,000	$	1,074,000	$ 1,194,000
15	Revenue (Optimal Mix)		680,000		780,000		895,000	1,791,000
16	Change		(136,000)		(156,000)		(179,000)	597,000
17								
18	Summary	Even		Optimal		Change		
19	Units Produced and Sold		12,000		12,000		-	
20	Total Revenue	$	4,020,000	$	4,146,000	$	126,000	
21	Total Material Cost		1,860,000		1,898,000		38,000	
22	Total Manufacturing Cost		840,000		856,000		16,000	
23	Total Fixed Expenses		1,020,000		1,020,000		0	
24	Net Income	$	300,000	$	372,000	$	72,000	

the company must produce at least 2,500 units of each model

net income increases by $72,000 under this product mix

8. Click the **Return to Solver Parameters Dialog** check box to remove the checkmark.

9. Click the **OK** button. The Solver Results dialog box closes, and the Solver solution remains in the worksheet.

As you can see in the Product Mix worksheet, Solver's solution is a product mix in which Coltivare Tool produces and sells 4500 CL190AW mowers and 2,500 of each of the other three models. With this product mix, the company will show a net income of $372,000, which is an increase of $72,000 over the current product mix.

Although this product mix is the most profitable to the company, production is limited by the number of available parts. In the range G27:J46, Irena included a table that tracks the parts each model requires, the quantity of each part currently available, and the number of parts remaining after the proposed production run. Figure 10-40 shows the parts usage under the optimal product mix you just found using Solver.

Figure 10-40 Parts remaining after the proposed product mix

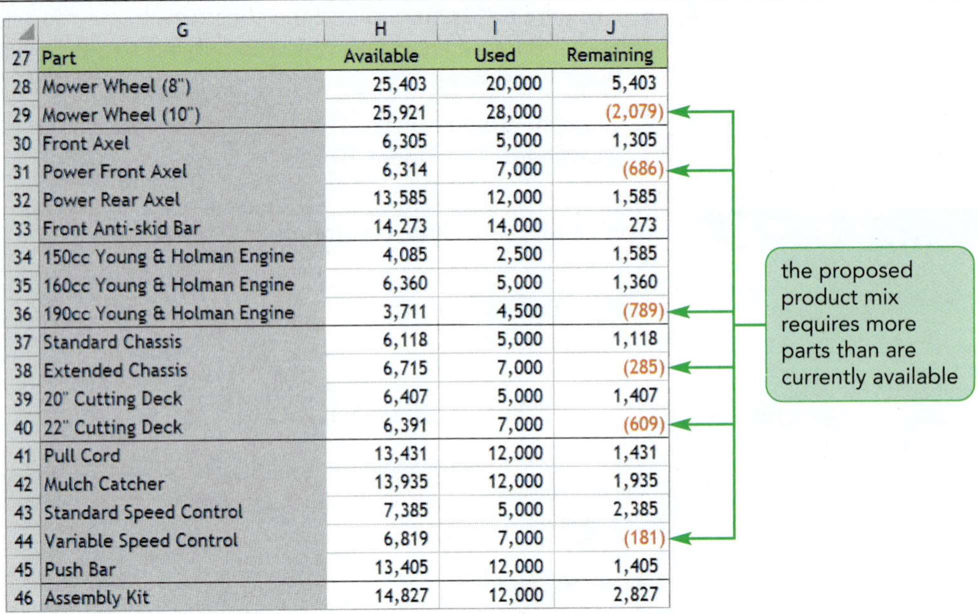

	G	H	I	J
27	Part	Available	Used	Remaining
28	Mower Wheel (8")	25,403	20,000	5,403
29	Mower Wheel (10")	25,921	28,000	(2,079)
30	Front Axel	6,305	5,000	1,305
31	Power Front Axel	6,314	7,000	(686)
32	Power Rear Axel	13,585	12,000	1,585
33	Front Anti-skid Bar	14,273	14,000	273
34	150cc Young & Holman Engine	4,085	2,500	1,585
35	160cc Young & Holman Engine	6,360	5,000	1,360
36	190cc Young & Holman Engine	3,711	4,500	(789)
37	Standard Chassis	6,118	5,000	1,118
38	Extended Chassis	6,715	7,000	(285)
39	20" Cutting Deck	6,407	5,000	1,407
40	22" Cutting Deck	6,391	7,000	(609)
41	Pull Cord	13,431	12,000	1,431
42	Mulch Catcher	13,935	12,000	1,935
43	Standard Speed Control	7,385	5,000	2,385
44	Variable Speed Control	6,819	7,000	(181)
45	Push Bar	13,405	12,000	1,405
46	Assembly Kit	14,827	12,000	2,827

the proposed product mix requires more parts than are currently available

Coltivare Tool cannot manufacture the mowers in the proposed product mix because it lacks enough 10" wheels, power front axels, 190cc engines, extended chassis, 22" cutting decks, and variable speed controls. Irena asks you to add one more constraint that limits the company to produce a mower only when it has all of the required parts.

To add a constraint limiting the product mix to the available parts:

1. In the range **B11:E11**, change the product mix values to **3000** for each model of lawn mower.
2. On the Data tab, in the Analyze group, click the **Solver** button. The Solver Parameters dialog box opens showing the current Solver model.
3. Click the **Add** button to open the Add Constraint dialog box.
4. Select the range **J28:J46**, which contains the number of parts remaining after the production run, select **>=** as the constraint type, and then type **0** in the Constraint box to force all of the values in the range J28:J46 to be greater than or equal to 0. Solver will use parts as needed until none are remaining.
5. Click the **OK** button. The complete Solver model appears in the Solver Parameters dialog box. See Figure 10-41.

Figure 10-41 **Final Solver model**

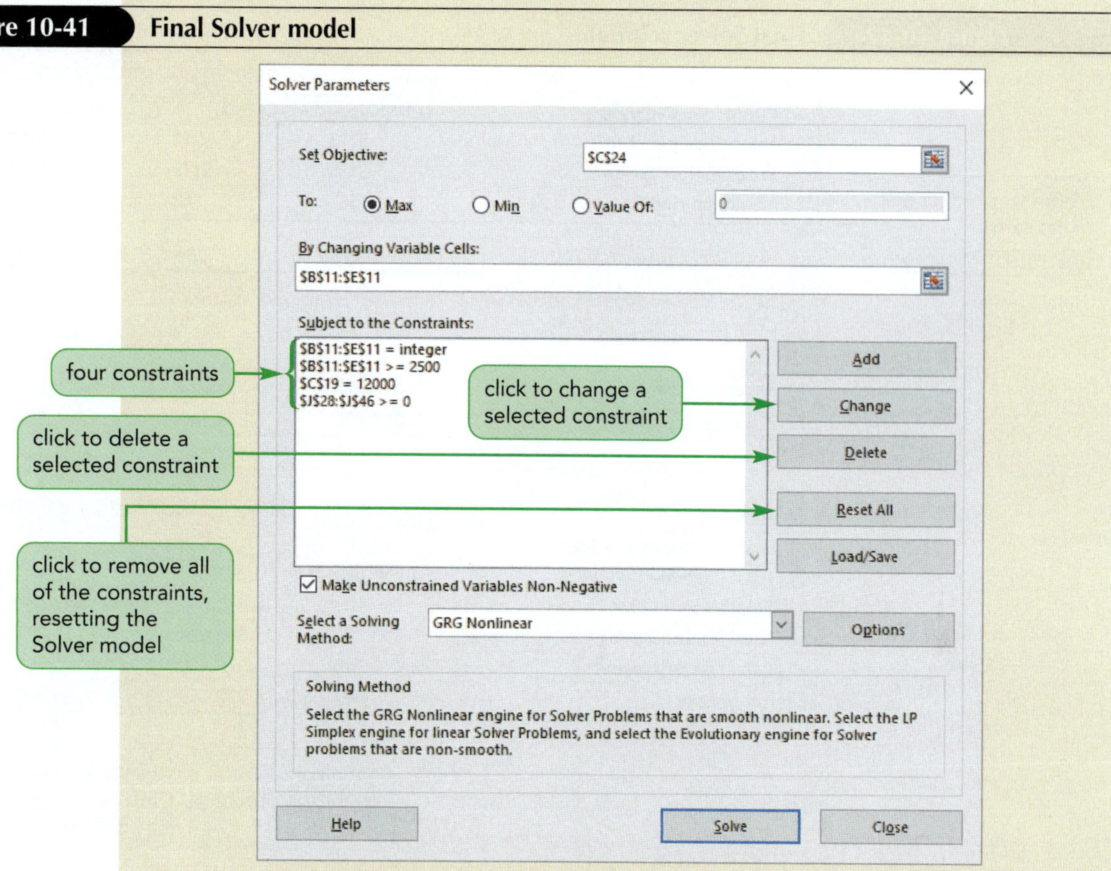

6. Click the **Solve** button, click the **OK** button in the Solver Results dialog box, and then click the **Close** button in the Solver Parameters dialog box to accept the Solver solution.
7. Scroll to the top of the Product Mix worksheet to see the Solver results. See Figure 10-42.

Figure 10-42 Final Solver solution

	A	B	C	D	E
5	Product Mix Analysis	CL150F	CL160F	CL160AW	CL190AW
6	Sales Price per Unit	$272	$312	$358	$398
7	Material Cost per Unit	$134	$148	$164	$174
8	Manufacturing Cost per Unit	$62	$62	$78	$78
9					
10	Even Product Mix (Units)	3000	3000	3000	3000
11	Optimal Product (Units)	3006	2680	2603	3711
12	Change	6	(320)	(397)	711
13					
14	Revenue (Even Mix)	$ 816,000	$ 936,000	$ 1,074,000	$ 1,194,000
15	Revenue (Optimal Mix)	817,632	836,160	931,874	1,476,978
16	Change	1,632	(99,840)	(142,126)	282,978
17					
18	Summary	Even	Optimal	Change	
19	Units Produced and Sold	12,000	12,000	-	
20	Total Revenue	$ 4,020,000	$ 4,062,644	$ 42,644	
21	Total Material Cost	1,860,000	1,872,050	12,050	
22	Total Manufacturing Cost	840,000	845,024	5,024	
23	Total Fixed Expenses	1,020,000	1,020,000	0	
24	Net Income	$ 300,000	$ 325,570	$ 25,570	

optimal product mix that satisfies all four constraints

net income under the optimal product mix

optimal product mix increases net income by $25,570

8. Scroll through the worksheet to verify that all four constraints are met, including the constraint that manufacturing the mowers in the proposed product mix will not exceed the number of available parts.

These results show that if Coltivare Tool can produce and sell 3006 CL150F mowers, 2680 CL160F mowers, 2603 CL160AW mowers, and 3711 CL190AW mowers, the company will generate a net income of $325,570, which is an increase of $25,570 over the current product mix. Irena will examine these figures to determine whether sufficient demand exists to support this product mix.

Exploring the Iterative Process

Solver arrives at optimal solutions through an **iterative process**, in which Solver starts with an initial solution and uses that as a basis to calculate a new solution. If that solution improves the value of the objective cell, it will be used to generate the next solution; if it doesn't, Solver tries a different set of values. Each step, or iteration, in this process improves the solution until Solver reaches the point where any new solutions are not significantly better than the solution from the previous step. At that point, Solver will stop and indicate that it has found an answer.

One way to think about this process is to imagine a terrain in which you want to find the highest point. The iterative process accomplishes this by following the terrain upward until a peak is scaled. The challenge with this approach is that you might simply find a nearby peak that is not the overall highpoint in the area. Solver refers to the overall highpoint as the **global optimum** while a nearby high point is the **local optimum**.

To find the global optimum, you may want to rerun Solver using different initial values and then compare the solutions to determine which result represents the overall best solution. Solver also supports the following iterative methods:

TIP

For simple expressions, the Simplex LP method will always find the global optimum solution; however, that may not be the case with more complex expression.

- The **Simplex LP method**, which is used for simple linear expressions involving only the operations of addition, subtraction, multiplication, and division
- The **GRG Nonlinear method**, which is used for complicated expressions involving nonlinear functions such as some exponential and trigonometric functions
- The **Evolutionary method**, which is used for complicated expressions that involve discontinuous functions that jump from one value to another

If Solver fails to find a solution or you are not sure if its solution is the global optimum, you can try each method and compare the results to determine which solution is the best.

Creating a Solver Answer Report

TIP

You cannot display sensitivity and limits reports when the Solver model contains integer constraints.

You can evaluate the solution the Solver produced through three different reports—an answer report, a sensitivity report, and a limits report. The **answer report** is probably the most useful because it summarizes the results of a successful solution by displaying information about the objective cell, changing cells, and constraints as well as the initial and final values in the worksheet. The **sensitivity report** and **limits report** are often used in science and engineering to investigate the mathematical aspects of the Solver solution, allowing you to quantify the reliability of the solution.

Irena wants you to create an answer report to provide information on the process used to determine the optimal product mix. To ensure that the answer report includes information on the entire process, you'll reset the quantities to their original values.

To create an answer report for the optimal product mix:

1. In the range **B11:E11**, enter **3000** for each model to set the product mix to an even distribution of production and sales among the four mower models.
2. On the Data tab, in the Analyze group, click the **Solver** button to open the Solver Parameters dialog box, and then click the **Solve** button to run Solver using the conditions you specified earlier.
3. In the Solver Results dialog box, click **Answer** in the Reports box, and then verify that the **Keep Solver Solution** option button is selected.
4. Click the **Outline Reports** check box so that Solver returns its report using Excel's outline tools. See Figure 10-43.

Figure 10-43 Solver Results dialog box with the answer report selected

Solver Results
Solver found a solution. All Constraints and optimality conditions are satisfied.
Reports
Answer
Keep Solver Solution
Restore Original Values
Return to Solver Parameters Dialog
Outline Reports
OK
Cancel
Save Scenario...
Reports
Creates the type of report that you specify, and places each report on a separate sheet in the workbook
select to display an answer report summarizing the results
select to display the answer report with Excel's outline buttons
click to save the Solver solution as a scenario

TIP

Answer reports are named Answer Report 1, Answer Report 2, and so on; the newest report has the next highest number.

5. Click the **OK** button to accept the solution and generate the answer report in a separate sheet called Answer Report 1.
6. If necessary, click the **Close** button to close the Solver Parameters dialog box.
7. Drag the **Answer Report 1** worksheet to the end of the workbook, and then rename the worksheet as **Product Mix Report**.

   The answer report is long. With the outline tools turned on, some of the report is hidden.

8. Click the last three expand outline buttons [+] to view more detailed information about the variable cells and the constraints used in the solution. See Figure 10-44.

Figure 10-44 Solver answer report

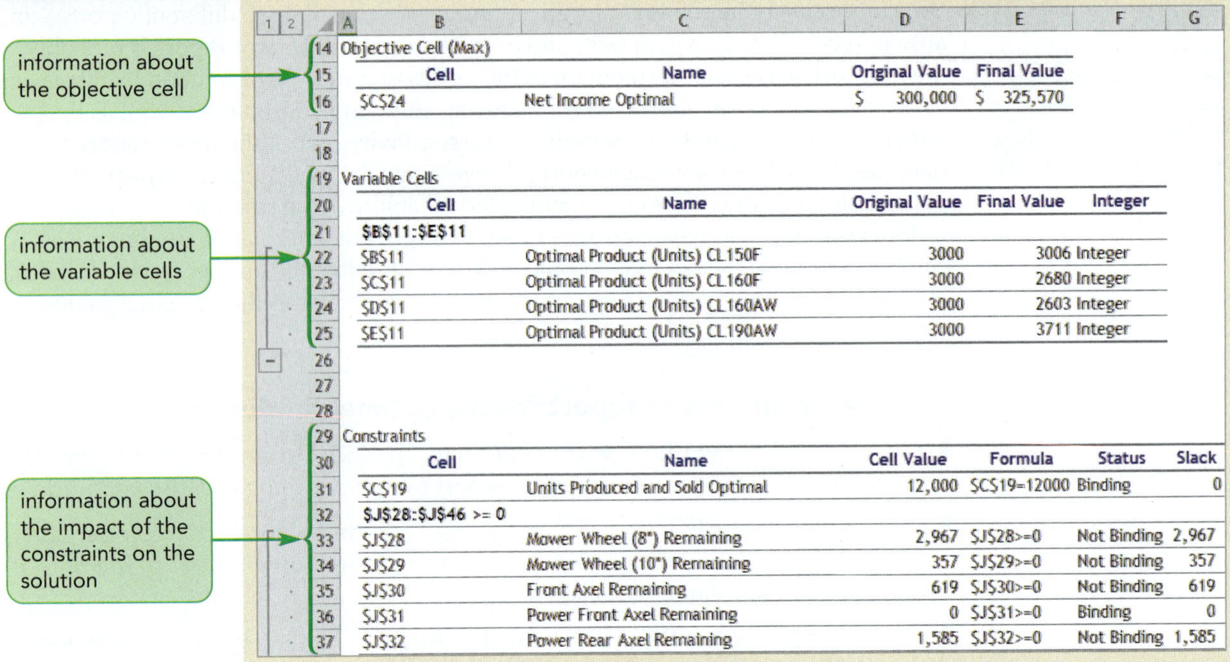

information about the objective cell

information about the variable cells

information about the impact of the constraints on the solution

	A	B	C	D	E	F	G
14	Objective Cell (Max)						
15		Cell	Name	Original Value	Final Value		
16		$C$24	Net Income Optimal	$ 300,000	$ 325,570		
17							
18							
19	Variable Cells						
20		Cell	Name	Original Value	Final Value	Integer	
21		$B$11:$E$11					
22		$B$11	Optimal Product (Units) CL150F	3000	3006	Integer	
23		$C$11	Optimal Product (Units) CL160F	3000	2680	Integer	
24		$D$11	Optimal Product (Units) CL160AW	3000	2603	Integer	
25		$E$11	Optimal Product (Units) CL190AW	3000	3711	Integer	
26							
27							
28							
29	Constraints						
30		Cell	Name	Cell Value	Formula	Status	Slack
31		$C$19	Units Produced and Sold Optimal	12,000	$C$19=12000	Binding	0
32		$J$28:$J$46 >= 0					
33		$J$28	Mower Wheel (8") Remaining	2,967	$J$28>=0	Not Binding	2,967
34		$J$29	Mower Wheel (10") Remaining	357	$J$29>=0	Not Binding	357
35		$J$30	Front Axel Remaining	619	$J$30>=0	Not Binding	619
36		$J$31	Power Front Axel Remaining	0	$J$31>=0	Binding	0
37		$J$32	Power Rear Axel Remaining	1,585	$J$32>=0	Not Binding	1,585

The answer report is divided into the following sections:

- The Title section (not shown in Figure 10-44) identifies the worksheet containing the Solver model, the date on which the report was created, and whether Solver found a solution.
- The Solver Engine section (not shown) provides technical information about how long Solver took to find a solution.
- The Solver Options section (not shown) lists the technical options used by Solver in arriving at a solution.
- The Objective Cell section provides the original and final value of the objective cell.
- The Variable Cells section lists the original and final values of the variable cells used in the solution.
- The Constraints section lists the constraints imposed on the solution by Solver.

The status of each constraint is listed as either Binding or Not Binding. A **binding constraint** is a constraint that must be included in the Solver model and is a limiting factor in arriving at the solution. The other possibility is a **nonbinding constraint**, which is a constraint that did not need to be included as part of the Solver model. For example, the constraint that the number of units produced and sold be equal to 12,000 is a binding constraint that limited the solutions available to Solver. On the other hand, the constraint in the range B11:E11 that the company produce and sell at least 2,500 of each model turned out to be nonbinding. Once Coltivare Tool was limited to producing exactly 12,000 mowers and was limited by the available parts on hand to manufacture those mowers, the optimal product mix would have resulted in the company producing at least 2,500 of each mower model anyway.

The last column in the Constraints section shows the slack for each constraint. The **slack** is the difference between the value in the cell and the value at the limit of the constraint, showing how close the constraint came to be a binding constraint. A binding constraint always shows a slack of 0, while nonbinding constraints show a nonzero value. For example, the slack for cell J28, the number of 8" wheels remaining in stock, is 2,967. This indicates that when Solver found the optimal product mix, there were still 2,967 of those wheels in stock, ready to be used. As a result, the availability of 8" wheels was not a limiting factor in the solution.

PROSKILLS

Decision Making: Choosing a What-If Analysis Tool

Part of performing an effective what-if analysis is deciding which what-if analysis tool to use. Each tool has its own set of advantages and disadvantages. Data tables are best used when you want to perform several what-if analyses involving one or two input cells and you need to display the analysis in a tabular format. Data tables can also be easily displayed as charts, providing a visual picture of the relationship between your input values and the result values. For what-if analyses involving more than two input cells, you must create a scenario. Scenario summary tables and scenario PivotTables can be used to obtain a quick snapshot of several possible outcomes, and scenarios can be merged and shared among several workbooks. Data tables and scenarios can provide a lot of information, but they cannot easily deliver a single solution or "best outcome." If you need to maximize or minimize a value, you must use Solver. You can also use Solver to set a calculated cell to a specific value. However, if you don't need to specify any constraints on your solution, it is generally quicker and easier to use Goal Seek.

Saving and Loading Solver Models

Sometimes you might want to apply several Solver models to the same data. For example, in addition to knowing what product mix maximizes the company's net income, Irena wants to know what product mix minimizes the company's total cost spent on materials. To determine this, you would create another Solver model. However, creating a new model in the worksheet overwrites the previous model. If you later wanted to rerun the first model, you would have to reenter its parameters. However, you can store the Solver parameters within worksheet cells that you can later retrieve and use to reload and run that Solver model.

REFERENCE

Saving and Loading a Solver Model

- Open the Solver Parameters dialog box.
- Click the Load/Save button.
- Select an empty range containing the number of cells specified in the dialog box, and then click the Save button.
- Select the range containing the saved model, and then click the Load button.

Before running the second Solver problem for Irena, you'll store the parameters of the current model that maximizes the company's net income.

To save the current Solver model:

1. Return to the **Product Mix** worksheet.
2. On the Data tab, in the Analyze group, click the **Solver** button to open the Solver Parameters dialog box.
3. Click the **Load/Save** button. The Load/Save Model dialog box opens, specifying that you need to select an empty range with eight cells to store the model.
4. Select the range **A27:A34** in the Product Mix worksheet. You'll store the Solver parameters in this range.
5. Click the **Save** button. The information about the Solver model is entered in the range A27:A34, and the Solver Parameters dialog box reappears.
6. Click the **Close** button to close the Solver Parameters dialog box.
7. In cell **A26**, enter **Maximum Net Income Model**, and then format the text with the **40% - Accent2** cell style. See Figure 10-45.

Be sure the range of cells you select to save the Solver parameters is empty so you don't overwrite other information on the worksheet.

Figure 10-45 Saved Solver model

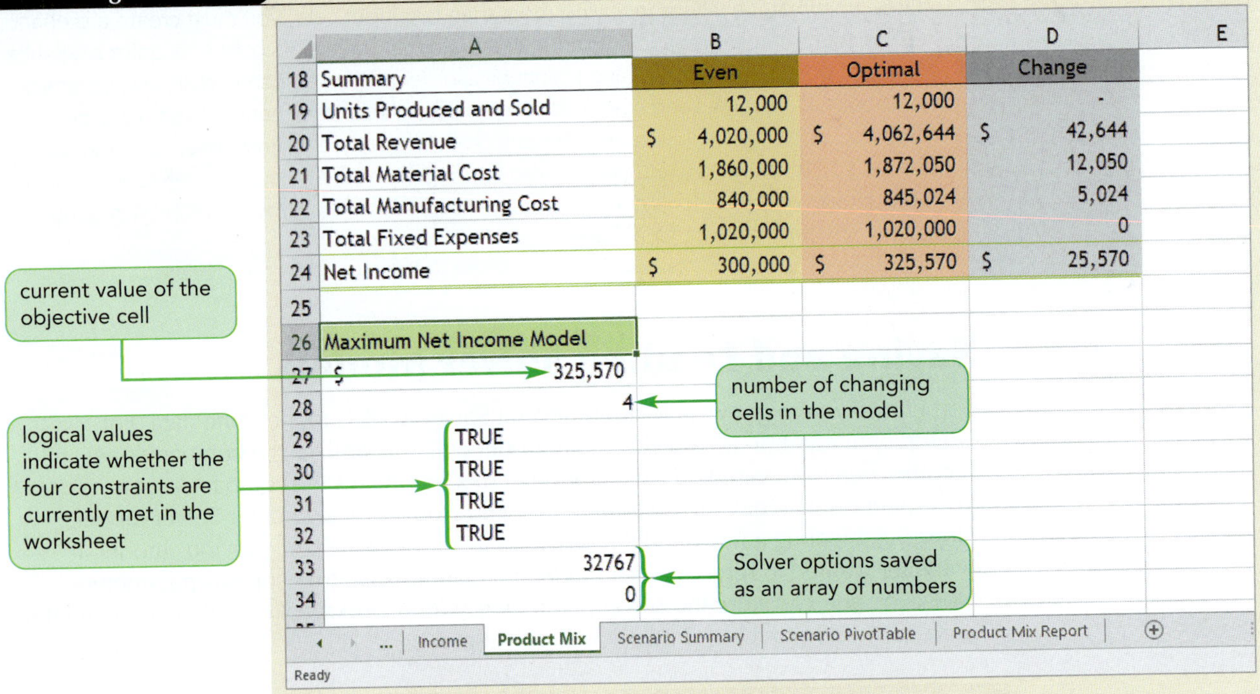
A
B
C
D
E
18 Summary
Even
Optimal
Change
19 Units Produced and Sold
12,000
12,000
-
20 Total Revenue
$ 4,020,000
$ 4,062,644
$ 42,644
21 Total Material Cost
1,860,000
1,872,050
12,050
22 Total Manufacturing Cost
840,000
845,024
5,024
23 Total Fixed Expenses
1,020,000
1,020,000
0
24 Net Income
$ 300,000
$ 325,570
$ 25,570
25
26 Maximum Net Income Model
27 $ 325,570
28 4
29 TRUE
30 TRUE
31 TRUE
32 TRUE
33 32767
34 0
Income
Product Mix
Scenario Summary
Scenario PivotTable
Product Mix Report
Ready
current value of the objective cell
number of changing cells in the model
logical values indicate whether the four constraints are currently met in the worksheet
Solver options saved as an array of numbers

The first parameter in cell A27 displays $325,570, which is the value of the objective cell under this model. The second parameter in cell A28 displays 4, indicating the number of variable cells in the model. The next four cells display TRUE, which correspond to the constraints in the model. TRUE indicates that the values currently in the worksheet satisfy the constraints. If you later change some of the worksheet data so that it violates a constraint, the Solver parameter cells will display FALSE. The cells provide a quick visual check that all of the model's conditions are still being met as the worksheet is modified. The final two cells, cells A27 and A28, are used to store the technical options for the iterative process by which Solver arrives at a solution (refer to the section titled, "Exploring the Iterative Process").

Now that you have saved this Solver model, you can create a second model to determine the product mix that minimizes the material cost of producing and selling these mowers. Irena wants to know what product mix would result in the lowest material cost given that the company still wants to produce 12,000 mowers and still wants to make at least 2500 of each model. The objective cell for this model is cell C21 instead of cell C24.

To determine the product mix that minimizes the total material cost:

1. In the range **B11:E11**, change the values back to **3000**.
2. Open the Solver Parameters dialog box.
3. With the Set Objective box selected, click cell **C21** in the Product Mix worksheet, the cell containing the total material cost under the Optimal product mix.
4. Click the **Min** option button. You want Solver to find the minimum value for cell C21. The changing cells and constraints you used to find the maximum net income remain unchanged for this model.
5. Click the **Solve** button. Solver finds the product mix that minimizes the total material cost.
6. Click the **OK** button to close the Solver Results dialog box and view the solution. See Figure 10-46.

Figure 10-46 Solver solution to minimize the total material cost

	A	B	C	D	E
5	Product Mix Analysis	CL150F	CL160F	CL160AW	CL190AW
6	Sales Price per Unit	$272	$312	$358	$398
7	Material Cost per Unit	$134	$148	$164	$174
8	Manufacturing Cost per Unit	$62	$62	$78	$78
9					
10	Even Product Mix (Units)	3000	3000	3000	3000
11	Optimal Product (Units)	3618	2687	2500	3195
12	Change	618	(313)	(500)	195
13					
14	Revenue (Even Mix)	$ 816,000	$ 936,000	$ 1,074,000	$ 1,194,000
15	Revenue (Optimal Mix)	984,096	838,344	895,000	1,271,610
16	Change	168,096	(97,656)	(179,000)	77,610
17					
18	Summary	Even	Optimal	Change	
19	Units Produced and Sold	12,000	12,000	-	
20	Total Revenue	$ 4,020,000	$ 3,989,050	$ (30,950)	
21	Total Material Cost	1,860,000	1,848,418	(11,582)	
22	Total Manufacturing Cost	840,000	835,120	(4,880)	
23	Total Fixed Expenses	1,020,000	1,020,000	0	
24	Net Income	$ 300,000	$ 285,512	$ (14,488)	

product mix to minimize the total material cost

minimum total material cost based on the constraints

optimal total material cost is $11,582 less than the material cost under the Even product mix

The minimum material cost to the company is $1,848,418, which is $11,582 less than the material cost under the Even product mix. This is the optimal solution based on the constraints that the company must produce exactly 12,000 mowers, produce at least 2500 units of each model, and not exceed the available parts. You will save this model in the Product Mix worksheet.

To save the model to minimize material costs:

1. In cell **A36**, enter **Minimum Material Cost Model**, and then format the text with the **40% - Accent2** cell style.
2. Open the Solver Parameters dialog box, and then click the **Load/Save** button. The Load/Save Model dialog box opens.
3. Select the range **A37:A44** in the Product Mix worksheet to specify the eight cells in which to save the model.
4. Click the **Save** button. The current Solver model is saved in the Product Mix worksheet.
5. Click the **Close** button to close the Solver Parameters dialog box.

You have two Solver models saved in the Product Mix worksheet—the Maximum Net Income model and the Minimum Material Cost model. You can quickly reload each of these Solver models in the worksheet from the Solver Parameters dialog box.

Irena wants the final version of the worksheet to display the Solver model that maximizes net income for the company. You'll load and run the Maximum Net Income model.

To load the Maximum Net Income model and run it:

1. In the range **B11:E11**, enter **3000** as the initial units produced and sold for each of the four mower models.
2. Open the Solver Parameters dialog box, and then click the **Load/Save** button to open the Load/Save Model dialog box.
3. In the Product Mix worksheet, select the range **A27:A34** containing the parameters of the Maximum Net Income model.
4. Click the **Load** button to load the Solver parameters from the worksheet. The Load Model dialog box opens, asking whether you want to replace the current model or merge the new model with the current model.
5. Click the **Replace** button. The Solver Parameters dialog box appears. The parameters for the Maximum Net Income model have replaced the parameters for the Minimum Material Cost model.
6. Click the **Solve** button. Solver runs the Maximum Net Income model, and then the Solver Results dialog box opens.
7. Click the **OK** button to keep the Solver solution, and then, if necessary, click the **Close** button to close the Solver Parameters dialog box.
8. Save the workbook, and then close it.

TIP

To combine the Solver model with the model currently used in the worksheet, click the Merge button.

By saving the Solver model parameters to cells on the worksheet, you can create as many models as you need to effectively analyze the data. You can then load and apply these different models to your analysis as new data is entered.

You have finished analyzing how Coltivare Tool can maximize its profits from its line of power mowers by modifying the product mix. Through the use of data tables, Excel scenarios, and Solver models, you provided Irena with several pricing and production options to increase the company's net income for the upcoming year.

REVIEW

Session 10.3 Quick Check

1. What is an add-in?
2. What are three options for the objective cell using Solver?
3. What is an objective cell? What is a variable cell?
4. What are the six types of constraints you can put on a cell in a Solver model?
5. What is an iterative process?
6. What is the difference between a binding constraint and a nonbinding constraint?
7. In the Solver report, what is meant by the term "slack"?
8. How do you save several Solver models on a single worksheet?

PRACTICE

Review Assignments

Data File needed for the Review Assignments: Snow.xlsx

Coltivare Tool also produces and sells a line of snow blowers. As you did with the company's line of power lawn mowers, Irena wants you to perform a what-if analysis on the company's income statement for its snow blower line. She wants you to create one-variable and two-variable data tables to determine the break-even point for sales and use Scenario Manager to explore the impact on the profitability of the line under different possible scenarios. Finally, she wants you to calculate the product mix that will result in the maximum net income to the company. Complete the following:

1. Open the **Snow** workbook located in the Excel10 > Review folder included with your Data Files, and then save the workbook as **Snow Blowers** in the location specified by your instructor.
2. In the Documentation worksheet, enter your name and the date.
3. In the Income Statement worksheet, in the range D6:G6, enter formulas that reference Units Sold value in cell B6 and the Revenue, Expenses, and Net Income values in the range B26:B28.
4. Create a one-variable data table in the range D7:G16 using Units Sold values that range from 1,000 to 10,000 in increments of 1,000.
5. Create a cost-volume-profit chart of the revenue and expenses values in the one-variable data table. Resize the chart so that it covers the range D17:G28. Format the chart so that it is easy to read and displays the break-even point.
6. In the range I6:N16, create a two-variable data table in which possible units sold values are placed in the range I7:I16 containing values from 1,000 up to 10,000 in 1,000-unit increments. Place the possible average unit price in the range J6:N6 containing values from $400 to $600 in $50 increments. Have the data table display the net income for each combination of units sold and average price. Format the formula in cell I6 to display the text "Units Sold" rather than the net income value.
7. Create a scatter chart of the net income values from the two-variable data table, displaying each average sales price as a different line in the chart. Format the chart appropriately; make sure that the chart legend identifies each line by the average sales price value listed in row 4. Resize the chart so that it covers the range I17:N28.
8. Use the Scenario Manager to display the financial impact of the different scenarios listed in Figure 10-47.

Figure 10-47 Snow blowers what-if scenarios

Input Cells	Status Quo	Increased Production	Reduced Production	Winter Sale
Units Produced and Sold	6,000	7,000	5,000	7,500
Average Price per Unit	$515	$515	$515	$485
Salaries and Benefits	$625,000	$750,000	$515,000	$725,000
Shipping and Distribution	$105,000	$125,000	$90,000	$115,000
Stocking and Storage	$90,000	$100,000	$75,000	$90,000
Miscellaneous	$75,000	$85,000	$55,000	$60,000

9. Create a scenario summary report of the four scenarios proposed by Irena, displaying their impact on total revenue, total expenses, and net income. Move the worksheet to the end of the workbook.
10. Create a Scenario PivotTable report of the four scenarios displaying the total revenue, total expenses, and net income under each scenario, formatted using the Currency style with no decimal places. Remove the filter from the PivotTable, and in cell A1 enter **Scenario Report** as the sheet title, formatting using the Title cell style.
11. Add a PivotChart of the PivotTable displaying the data as a clustered column chart positioned over the range A8:D20. Format the chart to make it easy to read and interpret.
12. The Product Line worksheet lists five snow blower models produced and sold by Coltivare Tool. Use Solver to find the product mix that maximizes the value in cell C24 by changing the values in the range B11:F11 under the following constraints:
    - The total snow blowers produced and sold as indicated in cell C19 must be 6000.
    - At least 700 of each model, as specified in the range B11:F11, must be produced and sold.
    - The values in the range B11:F11 must be integers.
    - The values in the range K29:K48 must be greater than or equal to zero because Coltivare Tool cannot produce more snow blowers than the available parts.
13. Enter **Maximum Net Income** in cell A26 formatted using the Accent2 cell style. Save the Solver model you just created to the range A27:A34.
14. Change the values in the range B11:F11 to **1200** units of each model, and then rerun Solver to find the product mix that minimizes the total material cost in cell C21 subject to the same constraints you used for the Maximum Net Income model.
15. Enter **Minimum Material Cost** in cell A36 formatted using the Accent2 cell style. Save the Solver model to the range A37:A44.
16. Restore the values in the range B11:F11 to **1200** units of each model is produced. Load the Maximum Net Income model into Solver, and then run Solver. Create an answer report, and then move the Answer Report worksheet to the end of the worksheet.
17. In the Product Line worksheet, in the merge cell C26, enter notes indicating which snow blower parts are a binding constraint on the Maximum Net Income solution.
18. Save the workbook, and then close it.

APPLY

Case Problem 1

Data File needed for this Case Problem: Seminar.xlsx

Paget Integrated Solutions Constance Paget is the owner of Paget Integrated Solutions, a Web technology consulting firm based in Seattle, Washington. Paget is planning a seminar on Web applications with a popular guest speaker to take place in Houston, Texas, next spring. She wants your help in generating a budget for the seminar that will incorporate the fixed, variable, and mixed costs to determine under what conditions the seminar will be profitable for her company. Complete the following:

1. Open the **Seminar** workbook located in the Excel10 > Case1 folder included with your Data Files, and then save the workbook as **Seminar Budget** in the location specified by your instructor.
2. In the Documentation worksheet, enter your name and the date.
3. Constance hopes to attract 100 people to the seminar at a cost of $120 per person. In the Budget worksheet, enter these values in the range B5:B6. Calculate the total revenue in cell B7.
4. Each participant will receive training materials worth $35 and a goodie bag worth $15. Enter these values into the range B10:B11. Calculate the total variable costs in cell B12 based on the number of attendees entered in cell B5.

5. There are several fixed costs associated with the seminar. Providing an Internet hotspot for the attendees will cost $50. The seminar speaker's fee is $900 plus a $500 travel allowance and a $140 lodging stipend. Constance estimates $350 in miscellaneous expenses. Enter these values in the range B15:B19. Calculate the total fixed costs in cell B20.
6. The company must rent a conference room large enough to accommodate the number of attendees. The lookup table in the range D5:E10 contains the room charges for seminars of 0 to 50 people, 50 to 100 people, 100 to 150 people, 150 to 200 people, and beyond 200 people. For example, a room that fits 0 to 50 people will cost the company $400. In cell B23, calculate the room rental cost by looking up the room rental fee based on the number of attendees to the seminar. (*Hint*: Use the VLOOKUP function with an approximate match lookup.)
7. The more people attending the seminar, the less the hotel will charge per person to cater the seminar meals. In cell B24, calculate the total catering charge by using the lookup table in range D13:E16 to determine the cost per person, and then multiply that value by the number of attendees.
8. The company also needs to pay for the hotel support staff. The larger the seminar, the higher the support staff fee. The lookup table in the range D19:E23 contains the staff fees for groups of different sizes. For example, a seminar of 0 to 50 people will incur a $60 staff fee. In cell B25, calculate the support staff charge for the number of attendees to the seminar.
9. In cell B26, calculate the total mixed costs from the room rental, meal catering, and support staff. In cell B28, calculate the balance from the conference by subtracting the sum of the variable, fixed, and mixed costs from the total revenue.
10. Use Goal Seek to determine what number of attendees will result in a balance of $0. Enter your conclusion in the merged cell A30, indicating how many attendees are needed to break even for a registration fee of $120. Change the value in cell B5 back to **100**.
11. Create a one-variable data table of different seminar budgets. In cell G6, display the value of cell B5. In cell H6, display the value of B7. In cell I6, display the sum of cells B12, B20, and B26. In cell J6, display the value of cell B28. In the range G7:G21, enter the number of possible attendees ranging from 20 to 300 in increments of 20. Complete the data table, showing the total revenue, total costs, and balance for each seminar size.
12. Create a CVP chart of the Total Revenue and Total Costs values in the one-variable table. Format the table so that it is easy to read, and resize it to cover the range G23:J34.
13. Constance wants to investigate the impact of different registration fees and number of attendees on the seminar balance. In cell L6, display the value of cell B28, formatted to display the text "Attendees". In the range L7:L21, enter attendee values ranging from 20 to 300 in increments of 20. In the range M6:P6, enter registration fees of $75 to $150 in increments of $25. In the range L6:P21, complete the two-variable data table using the number of attendees and the registration fee as the input values.
14. Create a chart of the balances versus the number of attendees with each registration fee displayed as a separate line. Format the chart so that it is easy to interpret, and resize it to cover the range L23:P34 of the worksheet.
15. Create scenarios for the other possible values for the input cells listed in Figure 10-48.

Figure 10-48 Seminar what-if scenarios

Changing Cell	Seminar 1	Seminar 2	Seminar 3
Attendees	100	150	75
Registration Fee	$120	$85	$140
Training Material Cost	$35	$30	$40
Goodie Bag Cost	$15	$10	$20
Speaker Fee	$900	$750	$950
Speaker Travel	$500	$420	$500
Speaker Lodging	$140	$125	$120

16. Create a scenario summary report of the Seminar 1, Seminar 2, and Seminar 3 scenarios, showing the balance from each seminar as the result. Move the sheet to the end of the workbook.
17. Constance knows that as the registration fee for the seminar increases, the number of attendees willing to pay decreases, as shown in the range T5:X18 in the Budget worksheet. In cell B5 of the Budget worksheet, change the number of attendees from a constant value to the following formula that projects the number of attendees for a given registration fee based on the value in cell B6. (*Hint*: Look at the formulas in the range S6:S18 to learn how to translate this equation into an Excel formula.)

$$attendees = 600 \times e^{-\left(\frac{registration\ fee}{75}\right)}$$

18. Use Solver to determine the registration fee in cell B6 that will maximize the balance value in cell B28 with the constraint that the registration fee should be an integer. Run Solver with an initial registration fee of $100.
19. Add your conclusion regarding the registration fee that results in the highest ending balance to the company to the merged cell A30. Be sure to include the registration fee, the number of attendees, and the resulting maximum balance in your summary.
20. Save the workbook, and then close it.

APPLY

Case Problem 2

Data File needed for this Case Problem: Physics.xlsx

Physics 212 Professor Ian Roche teaches Physics 212 at Welles-Ryan College in Lewiston, Maine. Professor Roche and his teaching assistants have recently scored the semester final exam for the 204 students in the class. He wants to use Excel to determine an appropriate grading curve. Professor Roche wants roughly the top 15 percent of his students to receive an A, the next 40 percent to receive a B, the next 35 percent to receive a C, and the bottom 10 percent to receive a D. The professor has already created a workbook that contains the student scores and the start of a grading scale. He wants you to use the Scenario Manager and Solver to determine appropriate cutoff points for each grade. Complete the following:

1. Open the **Physics** workbook located in the Excel10 > Case2 folder included with your Data Files, and then save the workbook as **Physics Grades** in the location specified by your instructor.
2. In the Documentation worksheet, enter your name and the date.
3. In the Grade List worksheet, summarize each student's final exam score by adding the following calculations:
   a. In cell B3, count the number of numeric values in column N.
   b. In cell B4, calculate the average score in column N.
   c. In cell B5, display the minimum score in column N.
   d. In cell B6, use the QUARTILE.INC function to display the score for the 1st quartile from column N.
   e. In cell B7, use the MEDIAN function to display the median exam score from column N.
   f. In cell B8, use the QUARTILE.INC function to display the score for the 3rd quartile from column N.
   g. In cell B9, display the maximum exam score in column N.
4. The range D5:E8 will contain the lower and upper range for each grade, as follows:
   a. In the range D5:D8, enter the values **0**, **70**, **80**, and **90** to indicate that the lowest value Ds, Cs, Bs, and As are 0, 70, 80, and 90 points, respectively.
   b. In the range E5:E7, enter formulas that return a value one point less than the lowest value for the next grade to calculate the upper limit for each grade. For example, the formula to enter in cell E5 is **=D6–1**.
   c. In cell E8, enter **100** as the upper limit for an A.

5. In the range F5:F8, enter the letter grades **D**, **C**, **B**, and then **A**, associated with each range of exam values.
6. In column O, calculate each student's grade with the VLOOKUP function, using the student's exam score in column N as the lookup value, the range D4:F8 as the lookup table, and the third column of that table as the return value. Use an approximate match to perform the lookup.
7. In the range G5:G8, use the COUNTIF function to count the number of exam grades in column O within each of the four possible class grades, using the letter grades from F5 through F8 as the criteria.
8. In cell G9, calculate the total number of grades given, confirming that it matches the class size value listed in cell B3.
9. In the range H5:H8, enter formulas to calculate the percentage of the students who received each grade. In cell H9, add the total percentage of the four grades, confirming they add up to 100 percent.
10. In cell I5, enter **10%** as the goal percentage of students who should receive a D. In the range I6:I8, enter **35%**, **40%**, and **15%** as the goal percentages for grades C through A, respectively. In cell I9, add the four goal percentages, confirming that they add up to 100 percent.
11. In cell J5, enter the formula **=ABS(H5–I5)** to calculate the absolute value of the difference between the observed percentage of Ds and the predicted percentage. Copy the formula to the range J6:J8 to calculate the absolute percentage differences for the other grades. In cell J9, add the values in the range J5:J8. This value represents the total absolute difference between the observed distribution of grades and the grading curve that Professor Roche wants.
12. Use the Scenario Manager to enter the three grading curves described in Figure 10-49, using the cells in the range D6:D9 as in the input cells.

Figure 10-49 **Physics 212 grading curves**

Changing Cell	Standard	Curved	Low Curve
Lower Range for C	70	60	50
Lower Range for B	80	70	60
Lower Range for A	90	80	70

13. View each scenario in the worksheet, and note which scenario results in the lowest value for the absolute difference in cell J9.
14. Using the scenario chosen in the last question as a starting point, set up Solver to find the optimal grading scale by doing the following:
    - Minimize the value of cell J9 by changing the cells in the range D6:D8.
    - Add the constraint that all of the values in the range D6:D8 must be integers.
    - Add constraints that cell D6 (the lowest C) must fall between 50 and 70, cell D7 (the lowest B) must fall between 60 and 80, and cell D8 (the lowest A) must fall between 75 and 100.
    - Use the Evolutionary method to arrive at a solution.
15. Run Solver to find the optimal solution that minimizes the total absolute difference. Note that the Evolutionary method may take a minute to arrive at a solution.
16. Save the grading scale that Solver found as a fourth scenario named **Optimal Grading Curve**.
17. Create a scenario summary report of the four scenarios you created showing the ranges D5:E8 and H5:H8 as the result cells.
18. Move the answer report to the end of the workbook, and rename the sheet as **Grading Curves**.
19. Save the workbook, and then close it.

CHALLENGE

Case Problem 3

Data File needed for this Case Problem: Travel.xlsx

Fiocco Snowboards Anita Park is a sales rep for Fiocco Snowboards of Provo, Utah. She is planning a trip to Colorado to meet with stores that sell the company's products. After landing in Denver, Anita will visit nine stores over a three-day period. She wants to reduce the time she spends on the road, so she has asked you to come up with a travel route that minimizes the distance traveled between the nine cities. In a worksheet, Anita identified each store with an ID number ranging from 1 to 9 and entered the longitude and latitude of the cities she will visit, the travel distance between each city, and a map of the city locations. You will use this data to find the best route for Anita's trip. Complete the following:

1. Open the **Travel** workbook located in the Excel10 > Case3 folder included with your Data Files, and then save the workbook as **Travel Route** in the location specified by your instructor.
2. In the Documentation worksheet, enter your name and the date.
3. In the Sales Map worksheet, in cell B6, enter **9** to specify Denver as the first stop in her route.
4. In cell C6, use an exact match VLOOKUP function to retrieve the city name from the lookup table in the range J6:K14. In cells D6 and E6, also use VLOOKUP functions to retrieve the city's longitude and latitude.
5. For your initial values, assume that Anita goes to Leadville from Denver. In cell F6, enter **2** for the store ID. In cell G6, use an exact match VLOOKUP function to retrieve the city name.
6. In cell H6, use an exact match VLOOKUP function to retrieve the distance between Denver and Leadville using the lookup table in the range J17:T26. (*Hint*: Use cell B6 as the lookup value, and add two to the value in cell F6 for the column index number.)
7. In cell B7, display the value of cell F6 because Anita will use the ending city from the previous stop as the starting point for the next leg of her trip.
8. Copy the formulas in the range C6:E6 into the range C7:E7 to display the city name and location for the start of the second leg of her trip.
9. In cell F7, enter **3** as the destination (Telluride) of the second leg of the trip. Copy the formulas in the range G6:H6 into the range G7:H7 to display the city name and travel distance for the end of the second leg. (There will not be a value because you haven't specified this location yet.)
10. Copy the formulas and values in the range B7:H7 into the range B8:H14.
11. In cell F14, enter **9** because Anita intends to return to Denver at the end of her trip. The values in the table represent the initial conditions for the route you will find.
12. In cell H15, enter a formula to calculate the total driving distance in the range H6:H14.

Explore 13. Use Solver as follows to find a route that will minimize the total travel distance:
   a. Minimize the value in cell H15 by changing the values in the range F6:F13 containing each destination to find the minimum driving distance. (You don't change cell F14 because Anita ends her trip in Denver.)
   b. Add a constraint to the model that all of the values in the range F6:F13 are different. This will have the effect inserting the integers 1 through 8 one time each into the selected cells.
   c. Change the Solving method to Evolutionary, and then run the model. (Note that it may take a minute for Solver to find the minimum travel distance.) When Solver is complete, the route map will show the complete path that Anita will take to visit the nine stores.

Explore 14. Save the Answer and Population report for Solver method so that Anita can study the method that Solver used to arrive at a solution. Move the worksheets to the end of the workbook.

15. Save the workbook, and then close it.

CHALLENGE

Case Problem 4

Data File needed for this Case Problem: Crystal.xlsx

Crystal Screen Michael Boyle is a manager at the Crystal Screen movie theater in Oakland Park, Florida. One of his jobs is to create the weekly work schedule for the movie ushers. The theater employs 16 ushers—14 are full-time and two are part-time. The theater needs eight ushers to work each weekday, 11 on Saturday, and 10 on Sunday. Michael is currently working on the usher schedule for the second week in August. Michael tries to accommodate all time-off requests while maintaining the required staff. He has been developing a workbook to automatically generate the work schedule. The workbook already contains the names of the ushers and their time-off requests. He asks you to determine which ushers will be working which days. Complete the following:

1. Open the **Crystal** workbook located in the Excel10 > Case4 folder included with your Data Files, and then save the workbook as **Crystal Screen** in the location specified by your instructor.
2. In the Documentation worksheet, enter your name and the date.
3. You will use the numbers 0 and 1 to indicate which shifts each employee is working. For example, 0 indicates an employee is not working that day, whereas 1 indicates that employee is scheduled to work. In the Schedule worksheet, in the range D5:J19, enter **0** in each cell to indicate that you have not yet scheduled any shift for any employee.
4. In the range K5:K19, enter formulas to calculate the total number of shifts for each employee.
5. In the range L5:L19, calculate the total number of hours worked by each employee. Each shift is eight hours.
6. In the range D21:J21, enter the number of shifts required per day. The theater requires eight shifts on weekdays, 11 shifts on Saturday, and 10 shifts on Sunday.
7. In the range D22:J22, enter a formula that calculates the total number of shifts actually scheduled for the employees on each day.
8. In the range D23:J23, enter a formula to subtract the attendants required value from the attendants actually scheduled value. A negative number indicates that not enough employees have been scheduled to cover the day's shifts.
9. In cell D25, calculate the total shortfall in shifts by entering a formula to total the values in the range D23:J23.

Explore 10. Create a Solver model that sets the value of cell D25 to 0 (indicating that all shifts are covered) by changing the values in the range D5:J19 under the following constraints:
   - Add a binary constraint to force every value in the range D5:J19 to be either a 0 or a 1.
   - Add a constraint to limit the total hours worked by each full-time employee to less than or equal to 40.
   - Add a constraint to limit the total hours worked by each part-time employee to less than or equal to 24.
   - Add a constraint to require that the difference values in the range D23:J23 all equal 0.
   - Based on the entries in the range C5:C19, add constraints so that employees are not scheduled to work shifts on days when they are unavailable to work.

Explore 11. Run the Solver model using the Evolutionary method. (Note that Solver might take a minute to arrive at a solution.) Confirm that the schedule generated by Solver fulfills all of the requirements—all shifts are covered each day, no employee works more hours than allowed by his or her full- or part-time status, and no employee works on a requested day off.

Explore 12. Because of increased movie attendance on the weekends, Michael wants to know whether he can schedule 11 employees on Sunday instead of 10. Revise the work schedule information, set the values in the range D5:J19 to **0**, and then rerun Solver to determine whether the schedule can be revised to accommodate an extra Sunday shift. Write your analysis of the Solver results as a comment in the merged cell A21.

13. Restore the workbook to the original schedule where only 10 ushers are needed on Sunday.
14. Save the workbook, and then close it.

MODULE 11

Analyzing Data with Business Intelligence

Creating a Sales Report for a Music Store

OBJECTIVES

Session 11.1
- Retrieve data using the Query Editor
- Create and edit a query
- Chart trends and forecast future values

Session 11.2
- Explore database concepts
- Explore the Data Model in the Power Pivot
- Construct a PivotTable based on several data tables

Session 11.3
- Create a hierarchy of fields
- Drill down into a field hiearchy
- Explore data with Power View
- Visualize data with Power Map

Case | *World Rhythm*

Gabriel Cardoso is an account manager at World Rhythm, a music store chain that specializes in musical instruments imported from around the globe. From its humble origins in a small shop in Brooklyn, New York, World Rhythm has expanded to a chain of large stores located across the East Coast and Midwest. Gabriel is working on a sales report that analyzes customer preferences and projects future sales trends for the chain. To create this report, Gabriel asks for your help in importing data from a variety of sources into an Excel workbook and using **Business Intelligence** (**BI**)—a suite of Excel tools used to discover relationships that may be hidden within a dataset.

STARTING DATA FILES

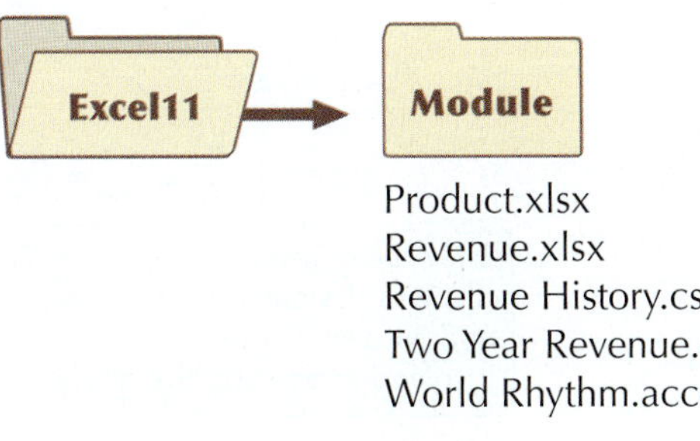

Review
Sales.xlsx
Sales History.csv
WR Data.accdb

Case1
Coronado.xlsx
Creamery Tables.accdb

Case2
Food.xlsx
Foodborne Illness.accdb

Case3
Forctis.xlsx
Forctis Products.csv
Forctis Sales.csv
Forctis Stores.csv

Case4
Aviary.xlsx
Bird Data.csv
Migration Data.csv

Session 11.1 Visual Overview:

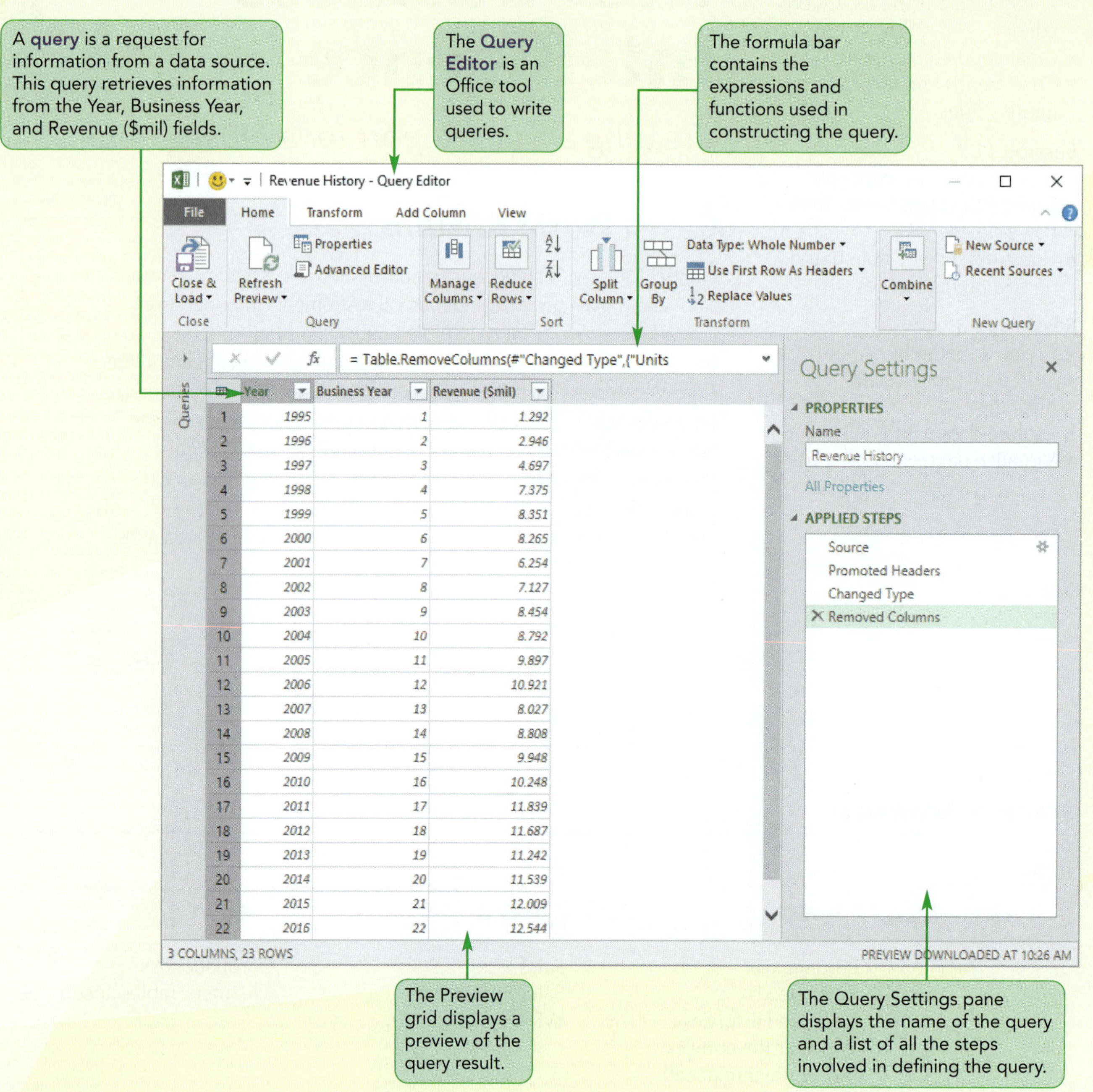
A query is a request for information from a data source. This query retrieves information from the Year, Business Year, and Revenue ($mil) fields.
The Query Editor is an Office tool used to write queries.
The formula bar contains the expressions and functions used in constructing the query.
Revenue History - Query Editor
File
Home
Transform
Add Column
View
Close & Load
Refresh Preview
Properties
Advanced Editor
Manage Columns
Reduce Rows
Split Column
Group By
Data Type: Whole Number
Use First Row As Headers
Replace Values
Combine
New Source
Recent Sources
Close
Query
Sort
Transform
New Query
= Table.RemoveColumns(#"Changed Type",{"Units
Queries
Year
Business Year
Revenue ($mil)
Query Settings
PROPERTIES
Name
Revenue History
All Properties
APPLIED STEPS
Source
Promoted Headers
Changed Type
Removed Columns
3 COLUMNS, 23 ROWS
PREVIEW DOWNLOADED AT 10:26 AM
The Preview grid displays a preview of the query result.
The Query Settings pane displays the name of the query and a list of all the steps involved in defining the query.

Queries and Trendlines

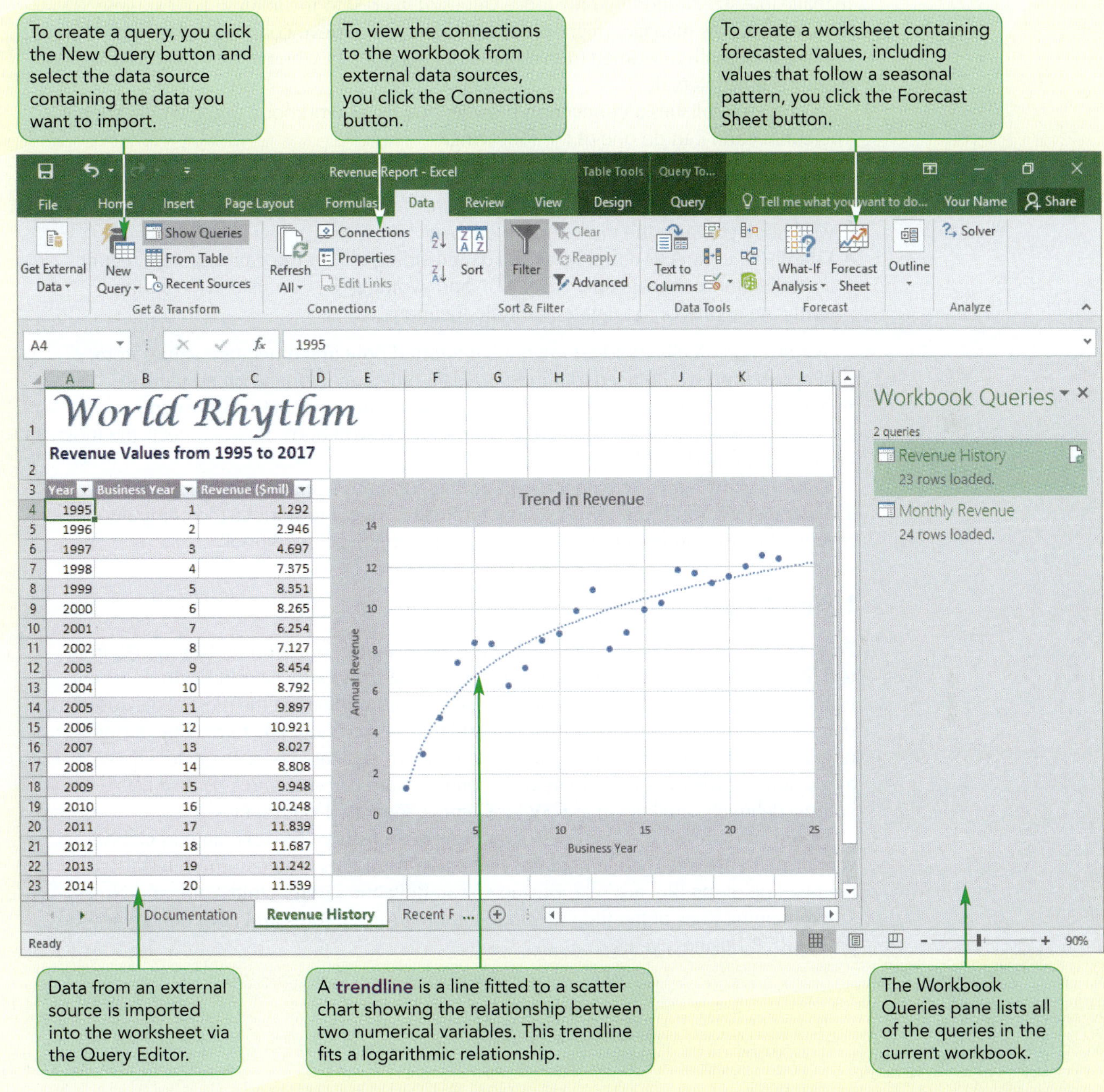
To create a query, you click the New Query button and select the data source containing the data you want to import.
To view the connections to the workbook from external data sources, you click the Connections button.
To create a worksheet containing forecasted values, including values that follow a seasonal pattern, you click the Forecast Sheet button.
RevenueReport - Excel
Table Tools
Query To...
File
Home
Insert
Page Layout
Formulas
Data
Review
View
Design
Query
Tell me what you want to do...
Your Name
Share
Get External Data
New Query
Show Queries
From Table
Recent Sources
Get & Transform
Refresh All
Connections
Properties
Edit Links
Sort
Filter
Clear
Reapply
Advanced
Sort & Filter
Text to Columns
Data Tools
What-If Analysis
Forecast Sheet
Forecast
Outline
Solver
Analyze
A4
1995
World Rhythm
Revenue Values from 1995 to 2017
Year
Business Year
Revenue ($mil)
Trend in Revenue
Annual Revenue
Business Year
Workbook Queries
2 queries
Revenue History
23 rows loaded.
Monthly Revenue
24 rows loaded.
Documentation
Revenue History
Ready
90%
Data from an external source is imported into the worksheet via the Query Editor.
A trendline is a line fitted to a scatter chart showing the relationship between two numerical variables. This trendline fits a logarithmic relationship.
The Workbook Queries pane lists all of the queries in the current workbook.

Writing a Data Query

In many reports, the data you want to use in your Excel workbook is located in an external file or data source. To access that data, you create a query, which is a request for information from that data source. Because data sources often contain thousands or even millions of records, a query will typically include commands to pare down the data to a manageable size, importing only those values of interest to the analyst. For example, a human resources manager might construct a query to retrieve company salary records, limiting the search to women from a particular department who were hired within a specified time interval.

A query establishes a connection between the Excel workbook and the data source. The connection can do one of the following:

- Import the data once, creating a "snapshot" of the data at a specific moment in time.
- Establish a "live connection" that will be updated periodically, ensuring that the workbook contains the most current data.
- Establish a connection, but leave the data residing within the data source, creating a smaller, more manageable workbook and avoiding the confusion of creating duplicate copies of the data in multiple locations.

For example, a climatologist might be interested only in temperature values from past epochs and would need to import the data only once. On the other hand, a financial analyst would probably want to establish a live connection between his or her workbook and a stock market data source so the workbook always reflects the most current values and trends.

Gabriel wants you to create a report on the company's annual revenue from its 23-year history. You'll use Power Query to create a query to retrieve the company's revenue history and import the data directly into the Excel workbook.

Using Power Query

Power Query is a BI tool used for writing queries to almost any kind of data source, from text files to websites to large database structures. The data for the World Rhythm's revenue history is stored in a text file. Text files are the simplest and one of the most widely used data storage formats, containing only text and numbers without any formatting, formulas, or graphics. The data is usually organized in columns separated by a character known as a **delimiter**. The most commonly used delimiters are commas and tabs. Text files with comma delimiters are known as **CSV** (or **Comma Separated Values**) files.

Figure 11-1 shows the first lines of the Revenue History CSV text file that Gabriel wants you to access. The file contains five columns of data. The column titles, listed in the first line of the file, are Year, Business Year, Revenue ($mil), Units Sold, and Notes. The remaining lines of the file contain the annual sales figures and commentary for the previous 23 business years.

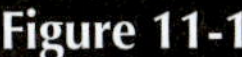

Figure 11-1 First lines of the Revenue History CSV file

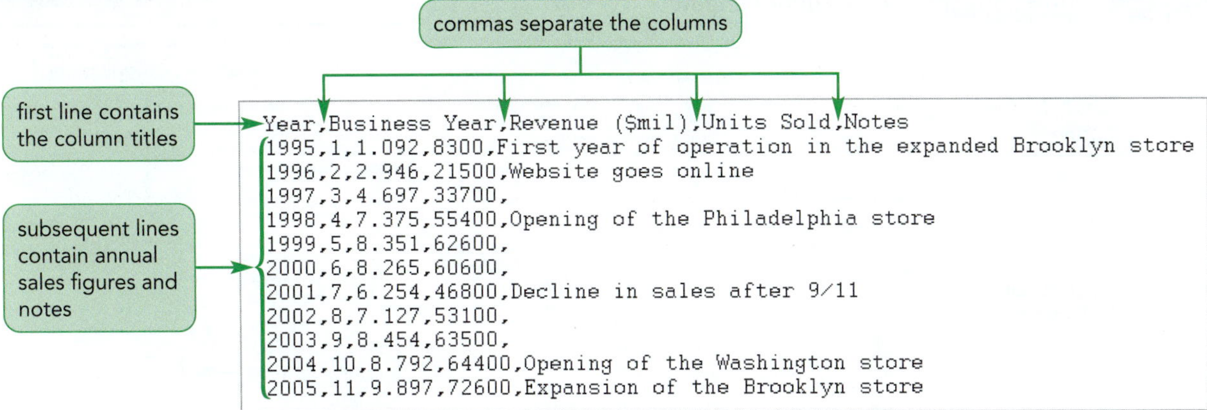

REFERENCE

Constructing a Query

- On the Data tab, in the Get & Transform group, click New Query.
- On the New Query menu, select a data source category, click the type of file or the data source, and then import the data source file.
- In the Query Editor, click toolbar commands to transform the data from the data source.
- In the Query Settings pane, edit the steps in the query.
- On the Home tab, in the Close group, click the Close & Load arrow button, and then click Close & Load To.
- In the Load To dialog box, select how to load the data, and then click the Load button.

You will use Power Query to connect to the data values in the Revenue History CSV file.

To create a query to the revenue history data:

1. Open the **Revenue** workbook located in the **Excel11 > Module** folder included with your Data Files, and then save the workbook as **Revenue Report** in the location specified by your instructor.
2. Go to the **Documentation** worksheet, and then enter your name and the date.
3. Go to the **Revenue History** worksheet. You will place the company's past revenue values in this worksheet.
4. On the ribbon, click the **Data** tab, and then in the Get & Transform group, click the **New Query** button. The New Query menu opens.
5. On the menu, point to **From File** to open a menu of file categories, and then click **From CSV**. The Import Data dialog box opens with CSV (Comma delimited) specified as the file format.
6. Navigate to the **Excel11 > Module** folder included with your Data Files, click the **Revenue History** CSV file, and then click the **Import** button. Power Query opens the Query Editor window, previewing the data from the Revenue History CSV file. See Figure 11-2.

TIP

To use the Query Editor tools with a table in the workbook, select the table, and then click the From Table button in the Get & Transform group on the Data tab.

Figure 11-2 Query Editor window

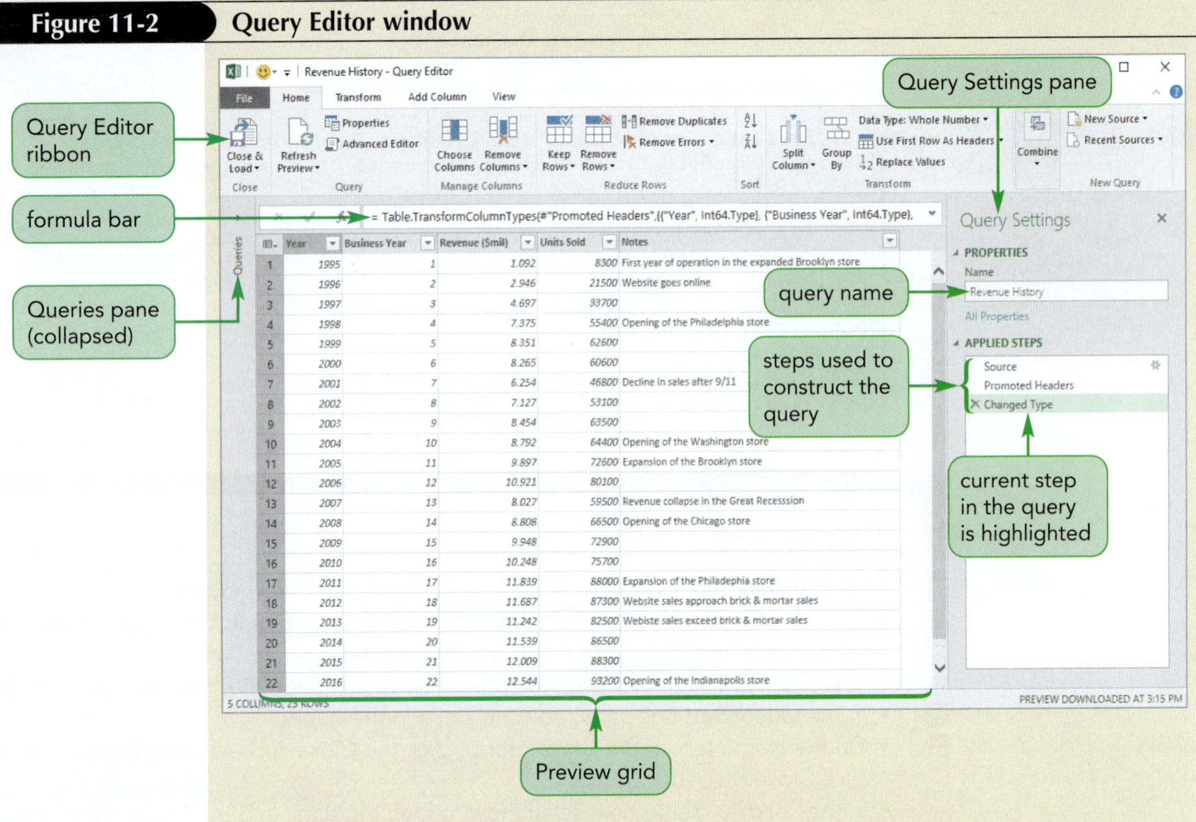

Trouble? If you don't see the formula bar in the Query Editor, click the View tab on the ribbon, and then click the Formula Bar check box.

> **TIP**
>
> To rename the query, select its name in the Name box in the Query Settings pane, and then type a new name.

The query is named Revenue History, matching the name of the data file. Power Query, recognizing the file format as CSV, has already located the values from the separate columns and applied the first three steps in constructing the query. Gabriel asks you to review those initial steps.

To view the first three steps in the query:

1. In the Query Settings pane, in the APPLIED STEPS box, click **Source**. The Source step establishes the connection to the Revenue History.csv file. The Preview grid displays the contents of the file. Note that the column titles are in the first row, and the default column names are Column1 through Column5.
2. In the APPLIED STEPS box, click **Promoted Headers**. The Promoted Headers step moves the five column titles from the first row to the column headers.
3. In the APPLIED STEPS box, click **Changed Type**. The Changed Type third step applies data formats to the values in the five columns, displaying numeric data in italics to distinguish them from text data. In this case, the Year, Business Year, Revenue ($mil), and Units Sold values are all treated as numeric data.

You can modify a query step by selecting the step and editing the command in the formula bar. You can delete the step by clicking the Delete button [X] to the left of the step title. Be aware, however, that editing or deleting a query step might cause subsequent steps to fail.

INSIGHT

M: The Language of Power Query

All steps in Power Query are written in the language **M**, which is a **mashup query language** used to extract and transform data. Each expression in M is applied as a function that creates or acts upon the connection to the data source. For example, the following Csv.Document() function retrieves the contents of the Revenue CSV file located in the Excel folder of the user's MAIN computer, using a comma symbol as the delimiter to separate one column of data from the next:

```
=Csv.Document(File.Contents("\\MAIN\Excel\Revenue.csv"),
[Delimiter=",",Encoding=1252])
```

You can view and edit all of the M commands in a query by clicking the Advanced Editor button in the Query group on the Home tab of the Query Editor window.

Retrieving Data into an Excel Table

You can retrieve the query data into an Excel table in the current workbook, placing it within a current worksheet or a new sheet. Gabriel wants you to load the revenue data into the Revenue History worksheet.

To load the query data into an Excel table:

1. On the Home tab, in the Close group, click the **Close & Load button arrow**, and then click **Close & Load To**. The Load To dialog box opens.

   Trouble? If Excel automatically loaded the data into a new worksheet, you clicked the Close & Load button. Cut and paste the Excel table into cell A3 of the Revenue History worksheet, and read but do not perform Steps 2 through 4.

2. Verify that the **Table** option button is selected, and then click the **Existing worksheet** option button.
3. If necessary, enter **$A$3** in the cell reference box so that the upper-left corner of the table will be placed in cell A3 of the active sheet.
4. Click the **Load** button. After a few seconds, the data is loaded into a new table on the Revenue History worksheet. See Figure 11-3.

Figure 11-3 Query retrieved into an Excel table

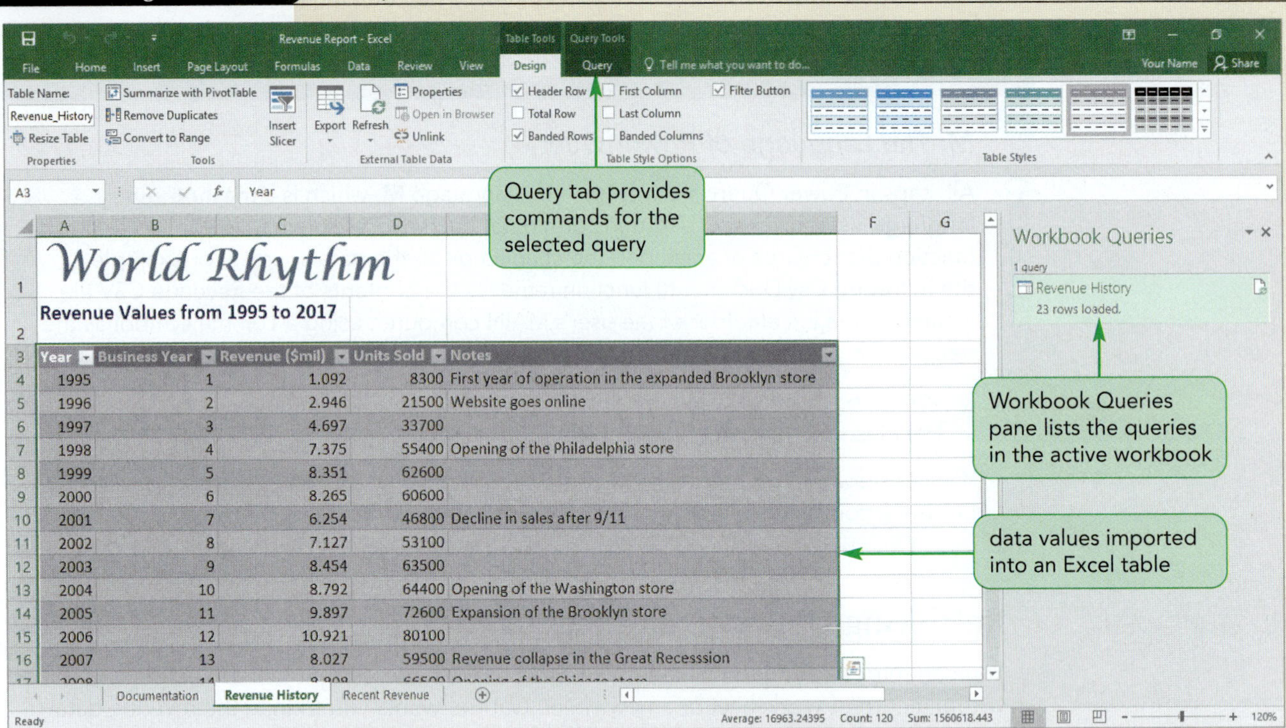

When the Revenue_History table is selected, the ribbon displays the Table Tools Design tab and the Query Tools Query tab, which contains commands for editing the selected query. The Workbook Queries pane also appears, listing all of the queries in the active workbook.

Editing a Query

Gabriel wants you to edit the Revenue History query, removing the Units Sold and Notes columns so he can focus on the revenue data. To edit a query, point to that query in the Workbook Queries pane. A box opens, displaying information about the selected query and options for modifying the query.

To edit the existing Revenue History query:

1. In the Workbook Queries pane, point to **Revenue History**. A box appears with information about the query. See Figure 11-4.

Figure 11-4 Revenue History box

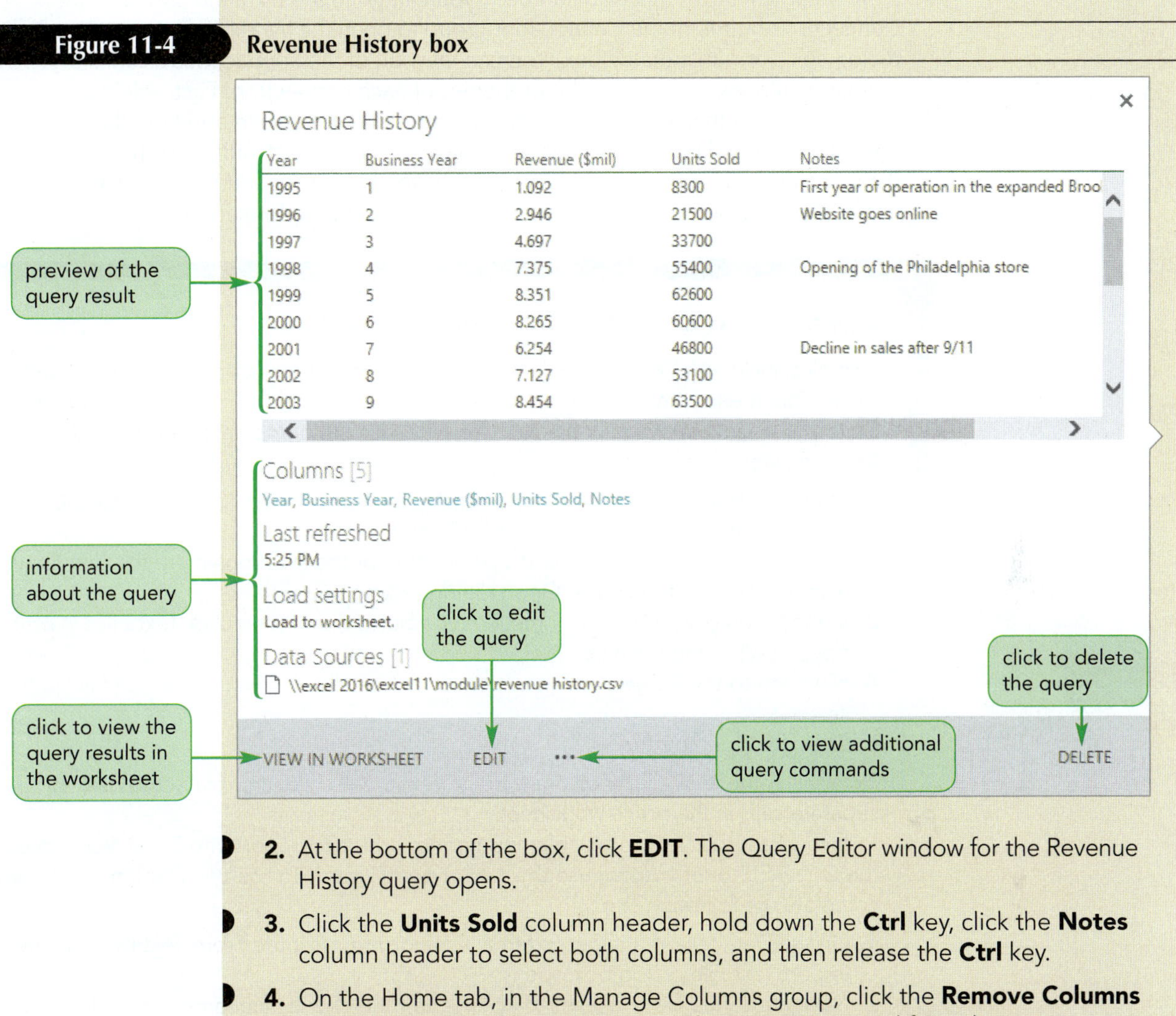

2. At the bottom of the box, click **EDIT**. The Query Editor window for the Revenue History query opens.
3. Click the **Units Sold** column header, hold down the **Ctrl** key, click the **Notes** column header to select both columns, and then release the **Ctrl** key.
4. On the Home tab, in the Manage Columns group, click the **Remove Columns** button. The Units Sold and Notes columns are removed from the query, leaving only the Year, Business Year, and Revenue ($mil) columns.
5. On the Home tab, in the Close group, click the **Close & Load** button. The edited query is loaded, and the Excel table now shows only the first three columns from the data source.

Note that removing columns from a query does not affect the data in the data source; it only affects the data that was imported into Excel.

Refreshing Query Data

Loading data from a query into Excel creates a snapshot of that data. If the values in the data source change, the connection can be refreshed to show the most current information. You can refresh a query by clicking the Refresh button in the Load group on the Query tab.

To automatically refresh a data query, you can go to the Data tab and click the Connections button in the Connections group to open the Workbook Connections dialog box. From that dialog box, you can view all of the connections established in your workbook and modify the properties of each connection. First, select a connection, and then click the Properties button to define when and how the connection should be refreshed. You can have Excel automatically refresh external data on a periodic schedule or whenever the workbook is opened. In this way, you can ensure that your workbook contains timely and accurate information.

INSIGHT

Opening Text and CSV Files Directly in Excel

Text files, including TXT and CSV files, are file types that are supported by Microsoft Excel. That means that you can open them directly in Excel without using the Query Editor. To open a text or CSV file in Excel, importing all of the data, complete the following steps:

1. On the ribbon, click the File tab to display Backstage view, and then click Open in the navigation bar (or press the Ctrl+O keys).
2. On the Open screen, click the Browse button or the location where the text file you want to open is stored. The Open dialog box appears.
3. In the Open dialog box, click the file type button, and then click Text Files (*.prn; *.txt; *.csv) as the file type.
4. Navigate to the file you want to open, and then click its filename in the file list to select it.
5. Click the Open button.

Excel will retrieve all of the columns in the text or CSV file, and place the data in separate cells in the active worksheet.

If you want to select some columns and not others to import into Excel, you can use the Query Editor or you can use the Text Import Wizard. To use the Text Import Wizard, complete the following steps:

1. On the Data tab, in the Get External Data group, click the From Text button. The Import Text File dialog box opens.
2. Navigate to the file you want to open, and then click its filename in the file list to select it.
3. Click the Import button. The Text Import Wizard starts.
4. In Step 1 of the Text Import Wizard, choose to import data from a fixed-width or delimited format and which row to start the import, and then click the Next button.
5. In Step 2, select the type of delimiter used in the file, and then click the Next button.
6. In Step 3, select which columns to include and which columns to omit in the text import, specify the data type of each column, and then click the Finish button. The Import Data dialog box opens.
7. Select where to place the data in an existing worksheet or a new worksheet, and then click the OK button.

Once the text data is imported, Excel establishes a connection between the text file and the Excel workbook. If you update the text file, you can refresh the data connection so that it shows the most current data values.

The Text Import Wizard is the older standard for importing text data into Excel. For sophisticated tasks involving more manipulation of the imported data, you should use the Query Editor.

Transforming Data with Queries

A data source is not usually organized in the way you need it for your report. As you have seen, you can use the Query Editor to remove columns from the data source. The Query Editor also includes tools to create new columns, group data values, and calculate summary statistics. This capability is particular useful for large datasets in which the analyst is interested in only overall measures and not individual values.

Gabriel has another CSV file that contains daily orders from the past two years from World Rhythm's customers. Although Gabriel limited his survey to 93 products from five stores, the file still contains information on more than 14,000 transactions. To make the data a more manageable size, Gabriel wants to see only the monthly totals. You will access this data file now.

To write a query to access the Two Year Revenue data source:

1. In the Revenue Report workbook, click the **Recent Revenue** sheet tab, and then click cell **A3** if necessary to make it the active cell.
2. On the Data tab, in the Get & Transform group, click the **New Query** button.
3. Point to **From File**, and then click **From CSV**. The Import Data dialog box opens.
4. Click the **Two Year Revenue** CSV file located in the **Excel11 > Module** folder, and then click the **Import** button. The Query Editor opens and applies the first three steps of the query.

   The data in the Two Year Revenue file includes 11 columns of data, which is more information than Gabriel needs. You'll remove all of the columns except the OrderDate and Revenue columns.
5. Click the **OrderDate** column heading, hold down the **Ctrl** key, click the **Revenue** column heading, and then release the **Ctrl** key. The two columns are selected in the Preview grid.
6. On the Home tab, in the Manage Columns group, click the **Remove Columns button arrow** to open a menu of remove options, and then click **Remove Other Columns**. All of the columns that were not selected are removed. Only the OrderDate and Revenue columns remain in the query.

   Trouble? If you deleted the selected columns rather than the other columns, delete the last step listed in the Query Settings pane, and then repeat Steps 5 and 6.

Be sure to click the Remove Columns button arrow, and not the Remove Columns button; otherwise, you will delete the selected columns.

Adding a New Column

You can add columns to a query to display other data. Gabriel wants to know the monthly revenue totals, not the daily revenue totals as is currently displayed in the Preview grid. To do this, you'll first create a new column named Month to display the date of the last day in each month—that is, 1/31/2016 for January, 2/29/2016 for February, and so forth.

To create a new column with the end-of-month dates:

1. If necessary, click the **OrderDate** column heading to select only the OrderDate column in the Preview grid.
2. On the ribbon, click the **Add Column** tab, and then in the From Date & Time group, click the **Date** button. A menu opens with date options.

3. On the menu, point to **Month**, and then click **End of Month**. The EndOfMonth column is added to the Preview grid.
4. Right-click the **EndOfMonth** column heading, and then click **Rename** on the shortcut menu.
5. Type **Month** to replace the selected column heading, and then press the **Enter** key. The column is now named Month. See Figure 11-5.

Figure 11-5 Month column created in the data query

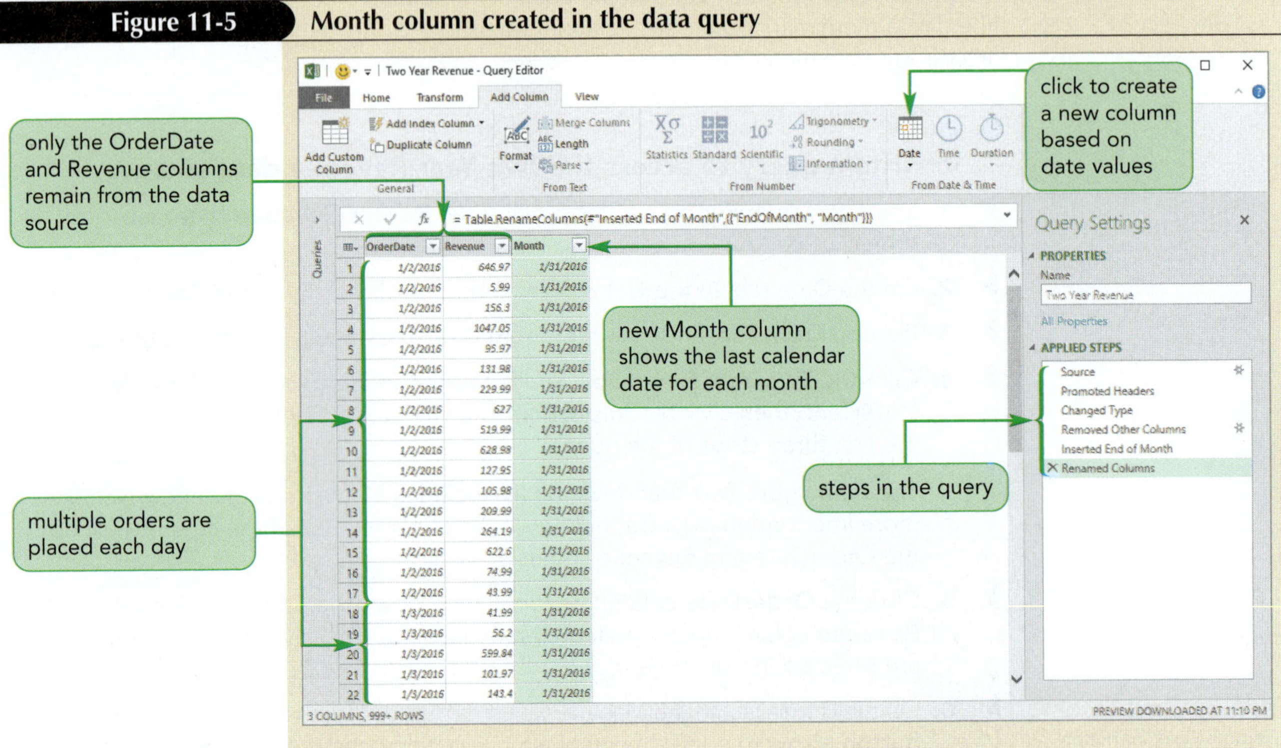

Grouping Values in a Query

In a query, you can group the data by the values within one of the columns. When you create a grouping, the query editor adds a new column to summarize the numeric values within each group by calculating the

- Sum, average, median, minimum, or maximum of the data values
- Count of rows within each group
- Count of rows with distinct values within each group

Gabriel wants to see the total revenue within each month. You will group the query by the values in the Month column and create a new column containing the sum of the Revenue values within each month.

To calculate the monthly revenues:

1. On the ribbon, click the **Transform** tab, and then in the Table group, click the **Group By** button. The Group By dialog box opens.
2. If necessary, click the **Group by** box, and then click **Month**. This will group the values by the dates in the Month column.

3. In the **New column name** box, double-click **Count**, and then type **Monthly Revenue** as the new name.
4. Click the **Operation** box, and then click **Sum** in the list of possible operations. This operation will total the values for the column you select.
5. Click the **Column** box, and then click **Revenue** as the column to sum within the Month group. See Figure 11-6.

Figure 11-6 Group By dialog box

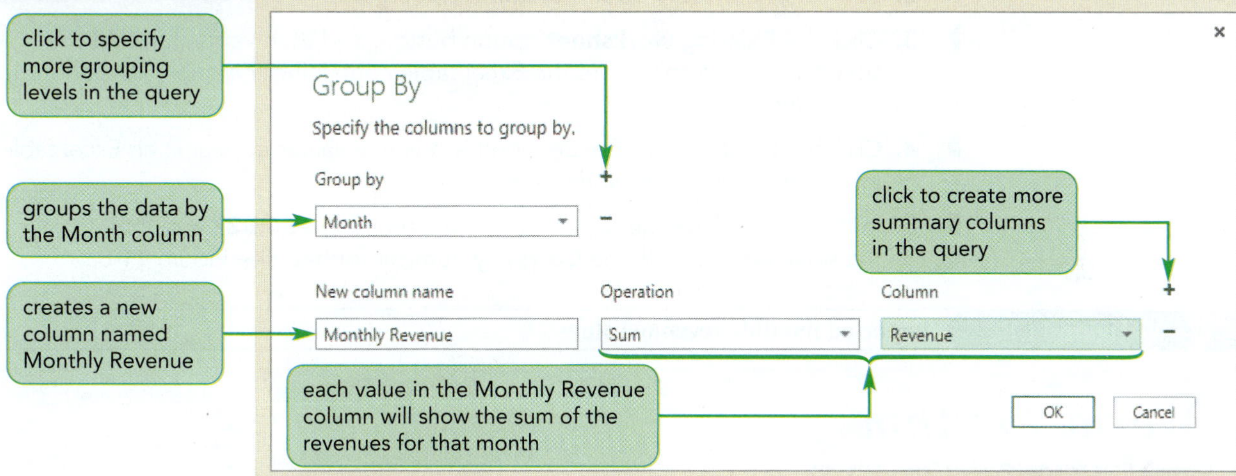

6. Click the **OK** button. The values in the data query are grouped in a new column named Monthly Revenue.
7. In the Query Settings pane, in the Name box, change the query name to **Monthly Revenue**. See Figure 11-7.

Figure 11-7 Final Monthly Revenue query

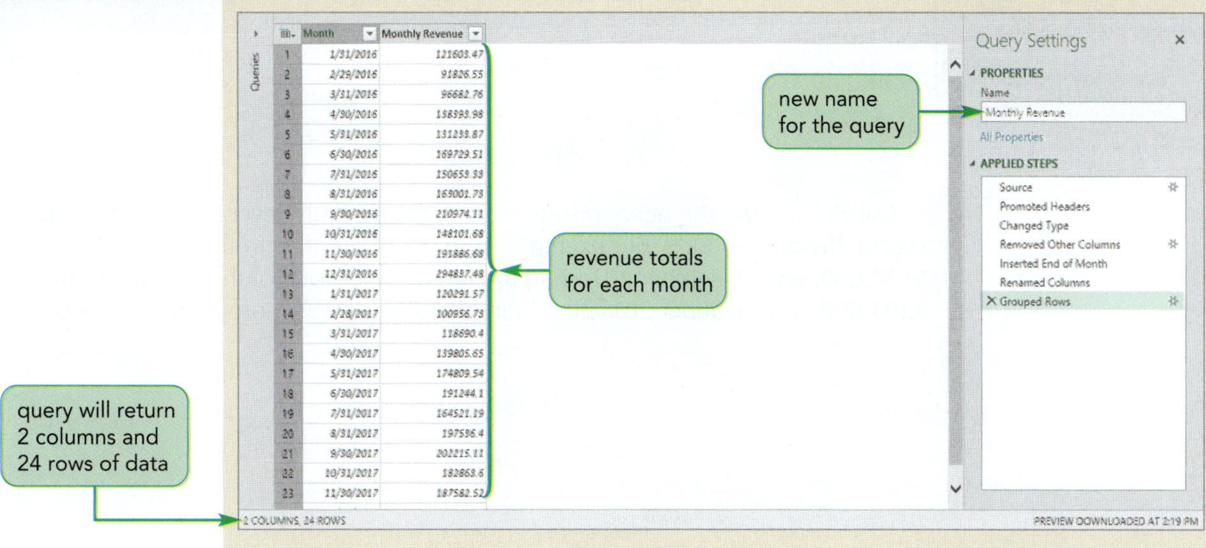

	Month	Monthly Revenue
1	1/31/2016	121603.47
2	2/29/2016	91826.55
3	3/31/2016	96682.76
4	4/30/2016	138393.98
5	5/31/2016	131233.87
6	6/30/2016	169729.51
7	7/31/2016	150653.33
8	8/31/2016	169001.73
9	9/30/2016	210974.11
10	10/31/2016	148101.68
11	11/30/2016	191886.68
12	12/31/2016	294837.48
13	1/31/2017	120291.57
14	2/28/2017	100956.73
15	3/31/2017	118690.4
16	4/30/2017	139805.65
17	5/31/2017	174809.54
18	6/30/2017	191244.1
19	7/31/2017	164521.19
20	8/31/2017	197596.4
21	9/30/2017	202215.11
22	10/31/2017	182863.6
23	11/30/2017	187582.52

The query is now ready to be loaded into the Revenue Report workbook. Note that the query will return 2 columns and 24 rows of data. This amount of data is more manageable than the 14,000 records stored in the data source.

To close and load the Monthly Revenue query:

1. On the ribbon, click the **Home** tab. In the Close group, click the **Close & Load button arrow**, and then click **Close & Load To**. The Load To dialog box opens.
2. Verify that the **Table** option button is selected.
3. Click the **Existing worksheet** option button, and then verify that **$A$3** is specified for the cell where the Excel table containing the query data should be loaded.
4. Click the **Load** button. The 24 monthly revenue values appear in an Excel table in the Recent Revenue worksheet.
5. In the Recent Revenue worksheet, select the range **B4:B27** and then format the selected cells with the **Currency** number format. See Figure 11-8.

Figure 11-8 Imported monthly revenue values

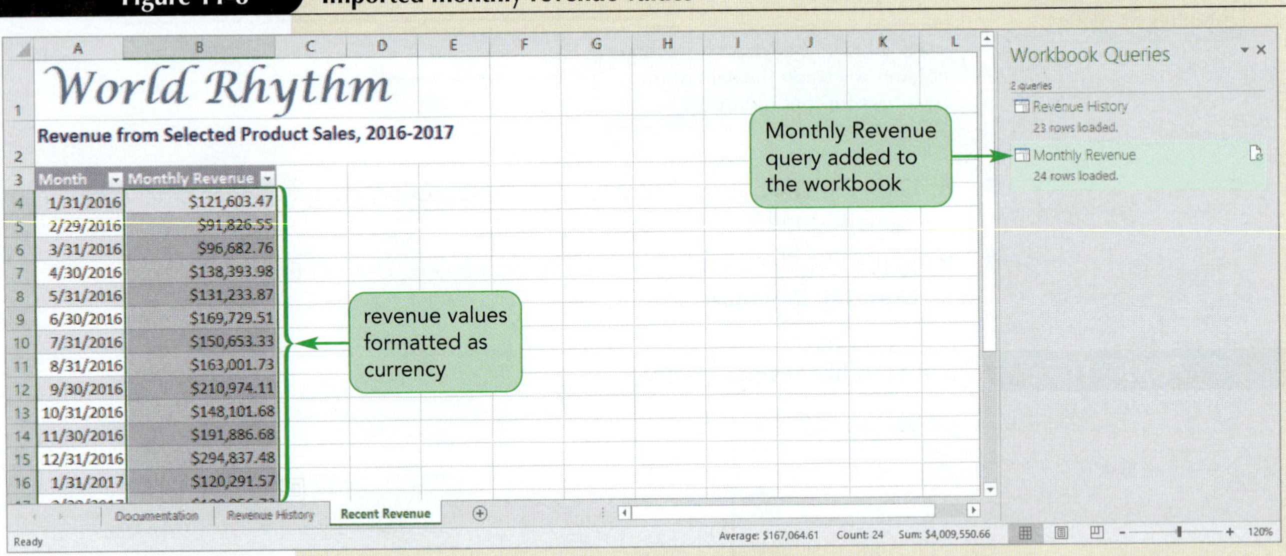

Gabriel can use the query results to track the monthly revenue of the 93 selected World Rhythm products. For example, January 2016 sales brought in more than $120,000, and December 2016 had the largest sales total of the year at almost $295,000. In December 2017, the monthly revenue was more than $320,000.

INSIGHT

Moving a Data Source

The connection between a workbook and a data source can be lost when one or the other is moved to a new location. If the files are no longer stored in the original location, the data can no longer be refreshed. To update the path between the workbook and the data source, do the following:

1. Open the query in the Query Editor.
2. Double-click the first step in the query that defines the location of the data source.
3. Specify the new location of the data source.
4. Save the query.

After saving the query, you can refresh the query within Excel and verify that it can again connect to the data source without error.

Gabriel wants to chart the annual revenue figures for the past 23 years and the monthly revenue figures for the past two years, looking for trends in the data.

Charting Trends

When examining the relationship between two data fields, such as monthly revenue and date of purchase, analysts often want to find trends in the data. One way to identify a trend is by adding a trendline to a scatter chart of the data.

REFERENCE

Adding and Editing a Trendline

To add a trendline:

- Create a scatter chart of the data.
- Select the chart, click the Chart Elements button, click the arrow next to the Trendline check box, and then select the type of trendline.

To edit a trendline:

- Double-click the trendline in the scatter chart to open the Format Trendline pane.
- In the Format Trendline pane, select the option button for the type of trendline to fit to the data.
- Project future values along the same trend by entering the number of future values in the Forward box.
- Display the equation of the trendline by clicking the Display Equation on chart check box.
- Display the R^2 value by clicking the Display R-squared value on chart check box.

Gabriel wants you to create a scatter chart showing the company's annual revenue from the past 23 years with trendline indicating the general pattern of revenue growth. He is interested in learning whether revenues have grown by a constant amount each year or are showing signs of leveling off.

To create a scatter chart of the company's annual revenue:

1. Go to the **Revenue History** worksheet, and then select the range **B3:C26**.
2. On the ribbon, click the **Insert** tab. In the Charts group, click the **Insert Scatter (X, Y) or Bubble Chart** button, and then click **Scatter** (the first chart in the gallery). A scatter chart plotting Revenue vs. Business Year appears in the worksheet.
3. Move and resize the chart so that it covers the range **E3:L19**.
4. Add the axis title **Annual Revenue ($mil)** to the vertical axis and the axis title **Business Year** to the horizontal axis.
5. Change the chart title to **Trend in Revenue**. The chart shows that the company's revenue has gone up and down over the years, but the general trend is upward.
6. Click the **Chart Elements** button, and then click the **Trendline** check box. A straight line is added to the chart. See Figure 11-9.

Figure 11-9 Linear trendline added to the scatter chart

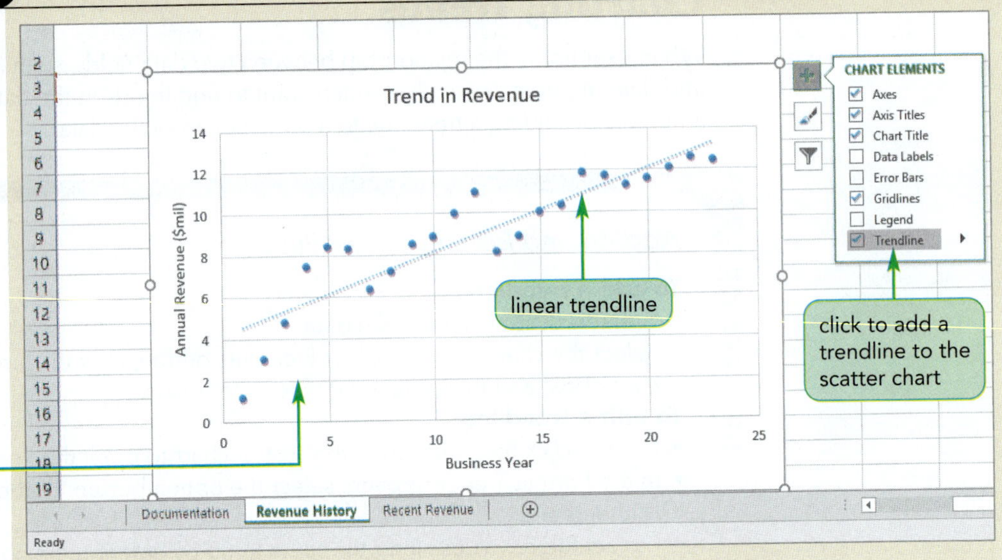

You can add various types of trendlines to a chart. These include the following trendlines types:

- **Exponential** for data values that rise or fall at increasingly higher rates
- **Linear** for straight-line trends that increase or decrease by a constant amount
- **Logarithmic** for trends that increase or decrease quickly and then level out
- **Moving Average** to smooth out data by charting the average of consecutive data points
- **Polynomial** for trends that fluctuate between peaks and valleys
- **Power** for trends that increase or decrease by a constant multiple

TIP

Power and Exponential trendlines cannot be used if the data contains zero or negative values.

The straight line in the chart you created for Gabriel is for a linear trend, based on the assumption that revenue increases by a constant amount each year. However, the linear trendline overestimates the revenue in the early years. Gabriel thinks that a logarithmic trendline would be more appropriate because the revenues increase rapidly at the beginning and then appear to level off.

To change the linear trendline to a logarithmic trendline:

1. With the chart still selected, click the **Chart Elements** button [+], and then click the **Trendline** check box. The linear trendline disappears from the chart.
2. Click the **arrow** that appears next to the Trendline check box to display a list of trendline options, and then click **More Options**. The Format Trendline pane opens.
3. In the Trendline Options section, click the **Logarithmic** option button. The logarithmic trendline appears on the chart.
4. Scroll down the Format Trendline pane to the Forecast options, type **2** in the Forward box, and then press the **Enter** key. The trendline extends to forecast the company's annual revenue for the next two periods, or years. See Figure 11-10.

Figure 11-10 Revenue estimated using a logarithmic trend

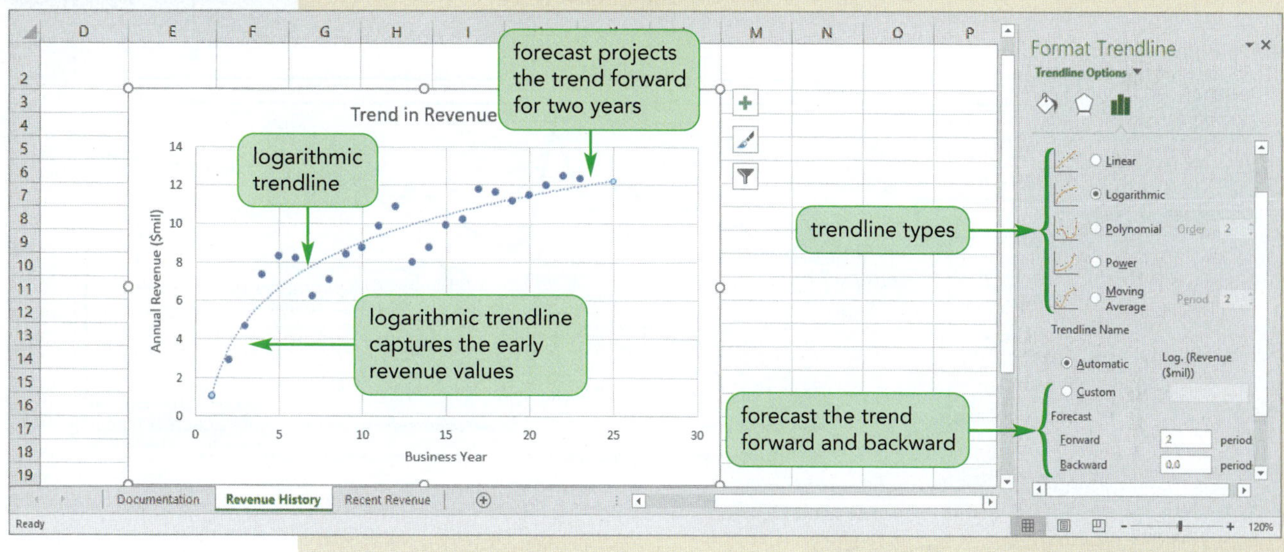

The logarithmic trendline follows the general growth of the company's annual revenue better than the linear trend. Based on this analysis, Gabriel estimates the company's total annual revenue will remain at or above $12 million for each of the next two years.

Creating a Forecast Sheet

Forecast sheets are another Excel tool used for modeling data and forecasting future values. One advantage of forecast sheets is that they can be used to analyze **seasonal data** in which the values follow a periodic pattern throughout the calendar year.

REFERENCE

Setting Forecast Sheet Options

- In the Create Forecast Worksheet dialog box, expand Options.
- To add a seasonal trend to the forecasts, in the Seasonality group, click the Set Manually option, and then enter the number of periods in one season.
- To set the confidence interval for the forecasted values, enter a value in the Confidence Interval input box.
- To set the extent of the forecast, enter the ending date in the Forecast End box.

Gabriel wants to create a forecast sheet to track the seasonal changes in monthly revenue and project next year's monthly revenue.

To generate a forecast sheet of the monthly revenue:

1. Go the **Recent Revenue** worksheet, and then, if necessary, select the range **A3:B27**.
2. On the ribbon, click the **Data** tab, and then in the Forecast group, click the **Forecast Sheet** button. The Create Forecast Worksheet dialog box opens, showing a preview of the forecasted values. See Figure 11-11.

Figure 11-11 Create Forecast Worksheet dialog box

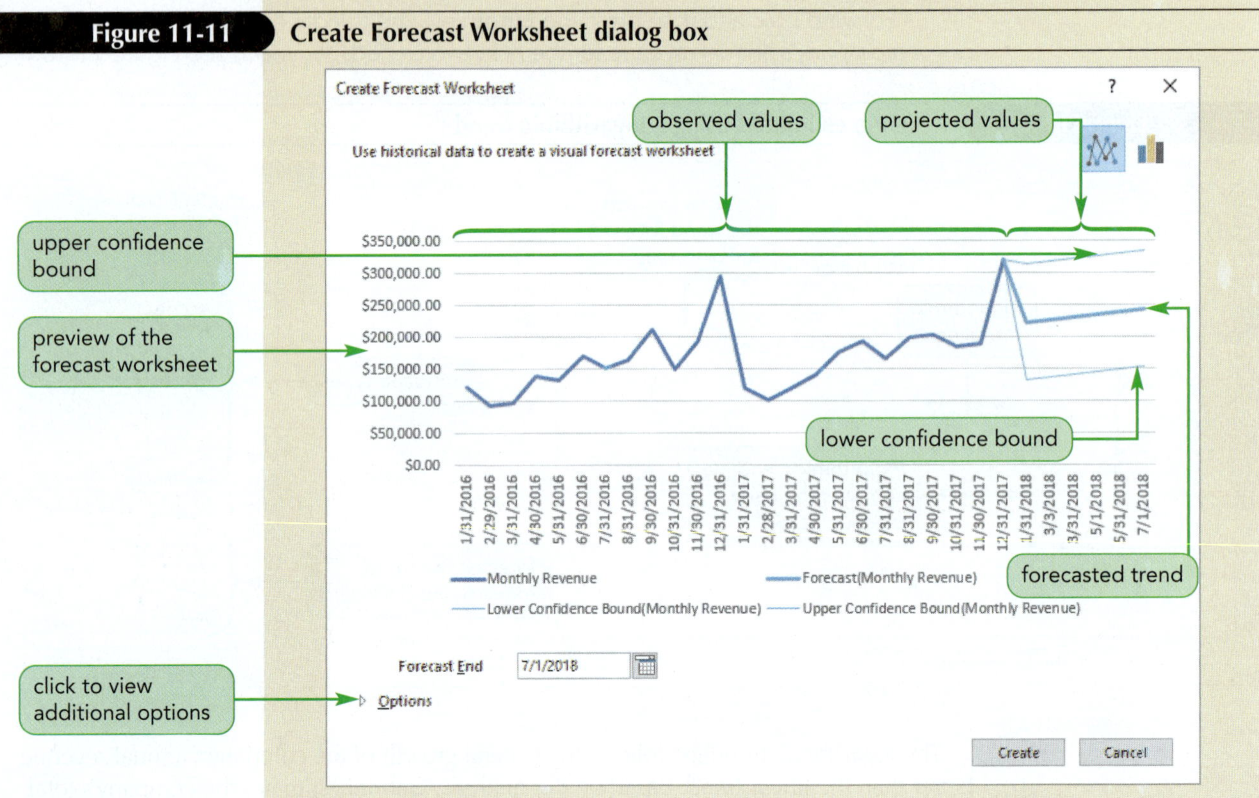

> **TIP**
> To change the confidence interval percentage, expand Options, and then enter a new value in the Confidence Interval box.

Excel uses two years of monthly revenue figures to project the revenue trend up to July 1, 2018. The trend is bracketed by upper and lower confidence bounds, which provide a measure of the uncertainty of the forecast. The default is to create 95 percent confidence intervals, indicating a region in which one is 95 percent confident that the actual values will appear. The fact that the upper and lower bounds are so far apart in Figure 11-11 indicates a large measure of uncertainty in the estimate of each month's revenue.

However, Gabriel notes that the revenue data shows an obvious seasonal pattern with the highest sales totals occurring in November and December and low sales in January through March. The forecasted values have not picked up this trend. You will revise the forecast to account for seasonal variability.

To create a seasonal forecast of the monthly revenue:

TIP

You need at least two complete years of data to project a seasonal trend for the next year.

1. In the Create Forecast Worksheet dialog box, click the **Options** menu title below the graph. The dialog box expands to display the forecast options.
2. In the Seasonality group, click the **Set Manually** option button, and then enter **12** in the Set Manually box. This specifies a seasonal pattern that will repeat itself every 12 months.
3. In the Forecast End box, change the date to **12/31/2018** to forecast a complete year's worth of monthly revenue. When the revenue follows a seasonal pattern, the confidence bands are much smaller than when no seasonality was assumed. See Figure 11-12.

Figure 11-12 Seasonal trend added to the forecast

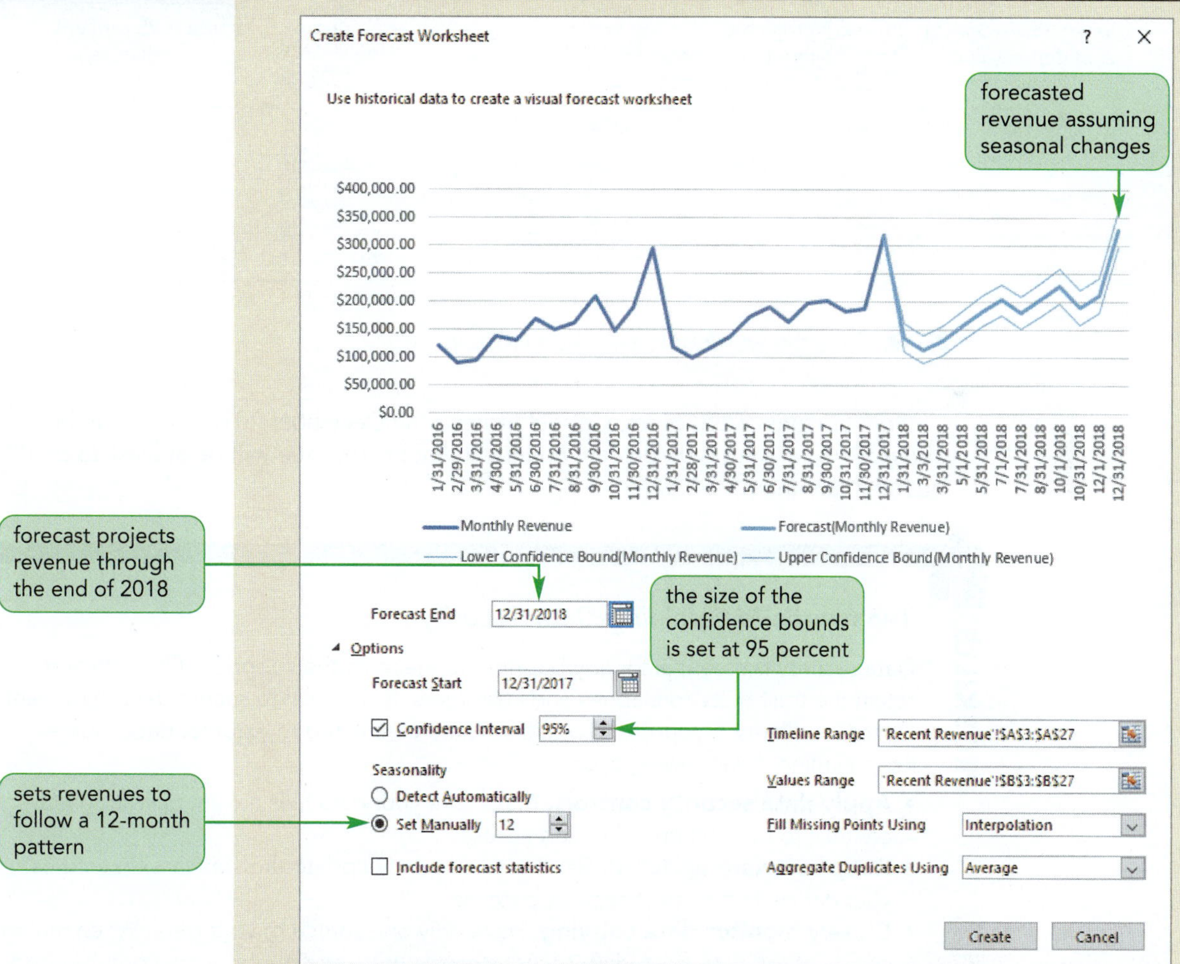

4. Click the **Create** button. The forecast worksheet is added to the workbook.
5. If the FORECAST SHEET dialog box opens, read the message, and then click the **Got it!** button.
6. Rename the forecast worksheet as **Monthly Revenue Forecasts** and then move it to the end of the workbook.
7. Resize the forecast chart to cover the range C2:E24.

8. Scroll to the bottom of the worksheet to view the forecasted revenue for the next 12 months as well as the lower and upper confidence bounds on those estimates. See Figure 11-13.

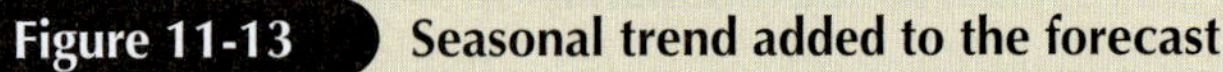

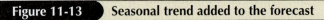

Figure 11-13 Seasonal trend added to the forecast

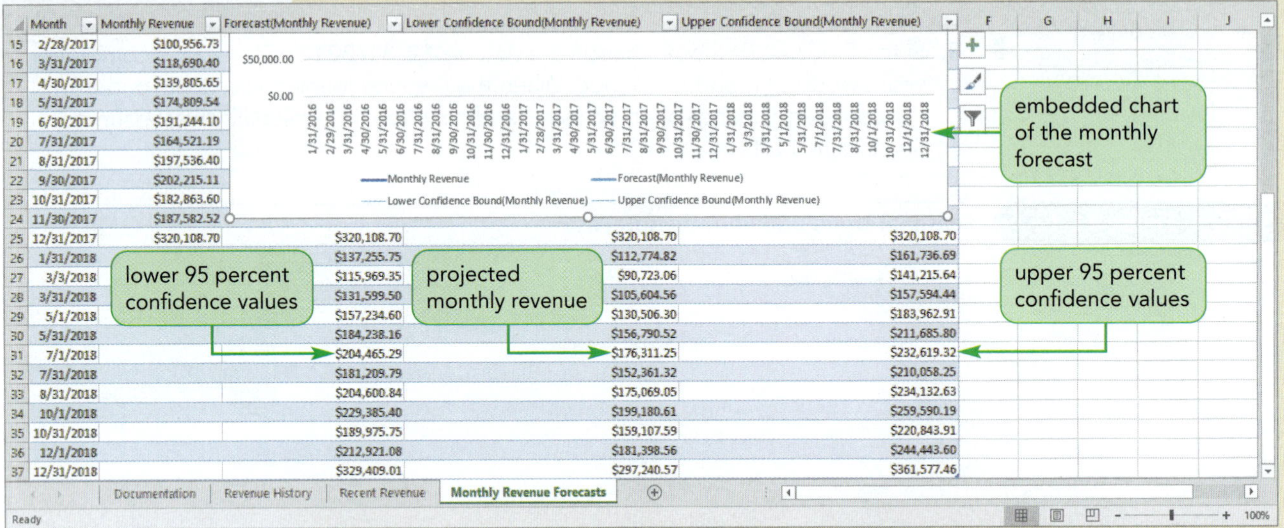

	Month	Monthly Revenue	Forecast(Monthly Revenue)	Lower Confidence Bound(Monthly Revenue)	Upper Confidence Bound(Monthly Revenue)
15	2/28/2017	$100,956.73			
16	3/31/2017	$118,690.40			
17	4/30/2017	$139,805.65			
18	5/31/2017	$174,809.54			
19	6/30/2017	$191,244.10			
20	7/31/2017	$164,521.19			
21	8/31/2017	$197,536.40			
22	9/30/2017	$202,215.11			
23	10/31/2017	$182,863.60			
24	11/30/2017	$187,582.52			
25	12/31/2017	$320,108.70	$320,108.70	$320,108.70	$320,108.70
26	1/31/2018		$137,255.75	$112,774.82	$161,736.69
27	3/3/2018		$115,969.35	$90,723.06	$141,215.64
28	3/31/2018		$131,599.50	$105,604.56	$157,594.44
29	5/1/2018		$157,234.60	$130,506.30	$183,962.91
30	5/31/2018		$184,238.16	$156,790.52	$211,685.80
31	7/1/2018		$204,465.29	$176,311.25	$232,619.32
32	7/31/2018		$181,209.79	$152,361.32	$210,058.25
33	8/31/2018		$204,600.84	$175,069.05	$234,132.63
34	10/1/2018		$229,385.40	$199,180.61	$259,590.19
35	10/31/2018		$189,975.75	$159,107.59	$220,843.91
36	12/1/2018		$212,921.08	$181,398.56	$244,443.60
37	12/31/2018		$329,409.01	$297,240.57	$361,577.46

9. Save the workbook, and then close it.

From the forecasted values, Gabriel projects the December 2018 revenue to be about $297,240 and is 95 percent confident that the revenue will be at least $329,409 but not more than $361,577.

PROSKILLS

Teamwork: Maintaining Data Security

Data security is essential for any business to maintain the integrity of its data and retain the trust of its colleagues and customers. It is critical to secure data to prevent lapses in security. If your Excel workbooks are connected to external data sources, keep in mind the following tips:

- **Apply data security controls.** Make sure your data files are set up with password controls to prohibit unauthorized access.
- **Keep software updated.** Be sure to diligently update the software that stores your data with the latest security patches.
- **Closely monitor data copying.** Have only one source of your data. When multiple copies of the data exist, data security, consistency, and integrity are compromised.
- **Encrypt your data.** Use data encryption to prevent hackers from gaining unauthorized access to sensitive information.

Maintaining data security requires that everyone with access to your data files knows how to retrieve and process that data appropriately. In the end, your data will be only as secure as the work habits of the people who access it.

You have completed the revenue estimates and projections using data retrieved with the Query Editor. In the next session, you'll perform analyses that involve combining data from several data sources.

REVIEW

Session 11.1 Quick Check

1. What three ways might a connection to data source be handled in Excel?
2. What is a delimiter?
3. What is a CSV file?
4. How do you undo an action in the Query Editor?
5. What is the M language, and how is it applied?
6. What trendline should you add to a chart for data that increases or decreases quickly and then levels out?
7. What does a 95 percent confidence boundary tell you about forecasted values?

Session 11.2 Visual Overview:

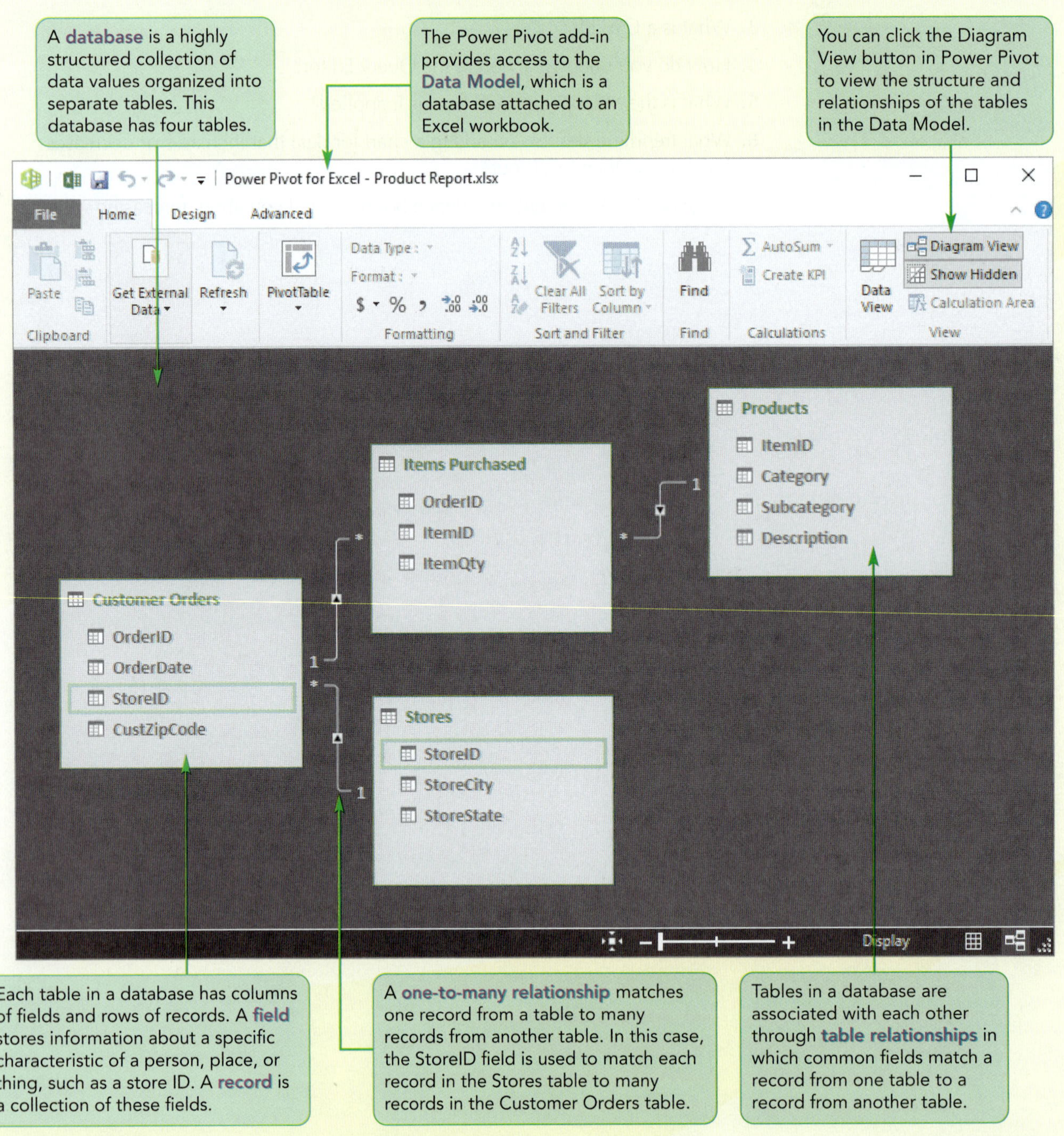
A database is a highly structured collection of data values organized into separate tables. This database has four tables.
The Power Pivot add-in provides access to the Data Model, which is a database attached to an Excel workbook.
You can click the Diagram View button in Power Pivot to view the structure and relationships of the tables in the Data Model.
Power Pivot for Excel - Product Report.xlsx
File
Home
Design
Advanced
Paste
Clipboard
Get External Data
Refresh
PivotTable
Data Type :
Format :
Formatting
Clear All Filters
Sort by Column
Sort and Filter
Find
AutoSum
Create KPI
Calculations
Data View
Diagram View
Show Hidden
Calculation Area
View
Products
ItemID
Category
Subcategory
Description
Items Purchased
OrderID
ItemID
ItemQty
Customer Orders
OrderID
OrderDate
StoreID
CustZipCode
Stores
StoreID
StoreCity
StoreState
Display
Each table in a database has columns of fields and rows of records. A field stores information about a specific characteristic of a person, place, or thing, such as a store ID. A record is a collection of these fields.
A one-to-many relationship matches one record from a table to many records from another table. In this case, the StoreID field is used to match each record in the Stores table to many records in the Customer Orders table.
Tables in a database are associated with each other through table relationships in which common fields match a record from one table to a record from another table.

Power Pivot and the Data Model

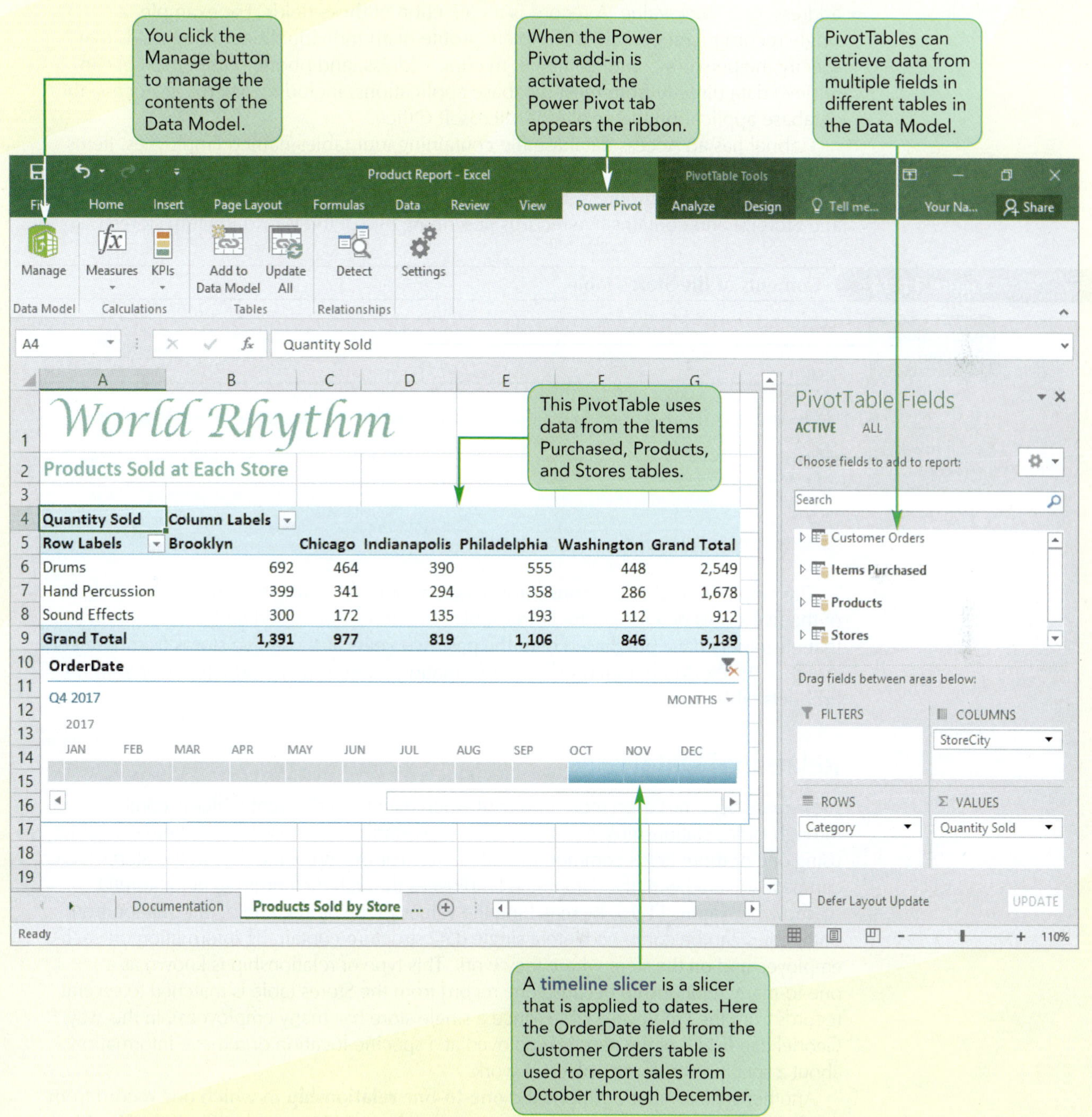

Introducing Databases

A database is a highly structured collection of data values organized into separate tables. Each table in a database is arranged in columns and rows, which are also referred to as fields and records. A field stores information about a specific characteristic of a person, place, or thing such as an individual's last name, a company address, or a stock value. A record is a collection of these fields. For example, a single record might contain a complete profile of an individual, including fields that specify the person's complete name, mailing address, and phone number. Excel can retrieve data directly from most database applications, including Microsoft Access, the database application that is part of Microsoft Office.

Gabriel has an Access database file containing four tables named Employees, Items Purchased, Products, and Stores. The Stores table shown in Figure 11-14 has eight fields named StoreID, StoreAddress, StoreCity, StoreState, StoreZIP, StorePhone, StoreManager, and StoreEst and contains five records describing five of the World Rhythm stores.

Figure 11-14 **Contents of the Stores table**

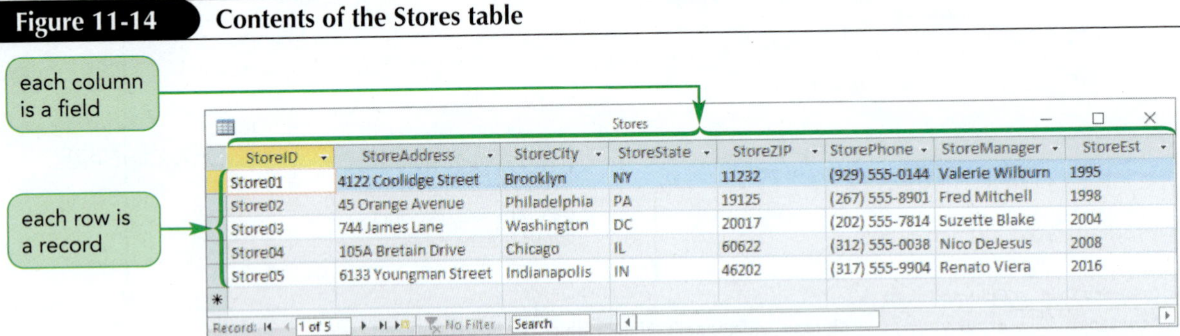
each column is a field
each row is a record

Stores

StoreID	StoreAddress	StoreCity	StoreState	StoreZIP	StorePhone	StoreManager	StoreEst
Store01	4122 Coolidge Street	Brooklyn	NY	11232	(929) 555-0144	Valerie Wilburn	1995
Store02	45 Orange Avenue	Philadelphia	PA	19125	(267) 555-8901	Fred Mitchell	1998
Store03	744 James Lane	Washington	DC	20017	(202) 555-7814	Suzette Blake	2004
Store04	105A Bretain Drive	Chicago	IL	60622	(312) 555-0038	Nico DeJesus	2008
Store05	6133 Youngman Street	Indianapolis	IN	46202	(317) 555-9904	Renato Viera	2016

Record: 1 of 5 No Filter Search

The Employees table contains information about World Rhythm employees at each of the five stores entered in the Stores table. The Items Purchased table lists the items that customers have purchased over the past two years at those five stores from a select group of 93 World Rhythm products. Information about those products is stored in the Products table.

Relational Databases

A database becomes even more powerful when data from different tables is combined through table relationships. A table relationship establishes an association between tables using one or more fields common to both tables. For example, the data in the Stores table can be associated with the data in the Employees through the common field StoreID. As shown in Figure 11-15, by matching the values of the StoreID field, information from both tables can be combined into a single data structure containing information on each employee and on the store where they work. This type of relationship is known as a one-to-many relationship because one record from the Stores table is matched to several records from the Employees table (since a single store has many employees). In this way, Gabriel can list all of the people employed at a specific location or retrieve information about a specific employee's place of work.

Another type of relationship is the **one-to-one relationship** in which one record from the first table can be matched to only one record from the second table. If the World Rhythm database had a Payroll table containing salary data for its employees, it would have a one-to-one relationship with the Employees table because each employee would have a single payroll record.

Figure 11-15 Two tables related based on a common field

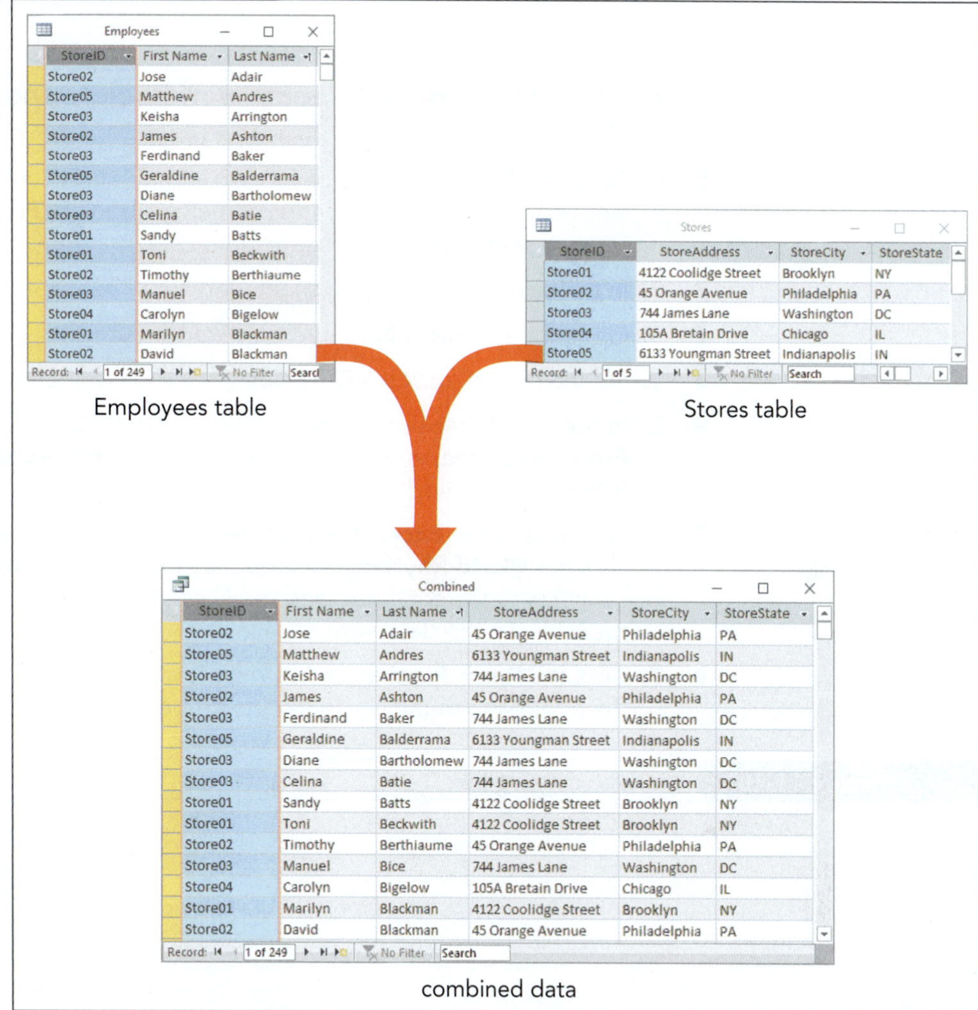

Databases in which tables can be joined through the use of common fields are known as **relational databases**. Because the tables can be joined through common fields, it is unnecessary to duplicate the same piece of information in multiple tables. For example, the price of a product needs be entered in only one table rather than in several tables. By removing duplication, relational databases make it easier to manage large datasets and improve data quality and integrity.

Querying an Access Database

TIP

To use a different database, on the Data tab, in the Get & Transform group, click the New Query button, point to From Other Sources, and then click From ODBC.

To extract specific information from a database, you use Power Query and the Query Editor. Power Query supports almost all of the popular database applications, including Microsoft Access, SQL Server, Oracle, IBM DB2, and MySQL. You then use the Query Editor to create a query that extracts data from any one table within those databases, or you can create a query that extracts data from several tables.

Gabriel wants to use the data from the World Rhythm database in another report he is preparing that describes sales of individual products from the World Rhythm stores.

To connect the Product Report workbook to the World Rhythm database:

1. Open the **Product** workbook located in the **Excel11 > Module** folder included with your Data Files, and then save the workbook as **Product Report** in the location specified by your instructor.
2. In the Documentation worksheet, enter your name and the date.
3. Go to the **Products Sold by Store** worksheet.
4. On the ribbon, click the **Data** tab.
5. In the Get & Transform group, click the **New Query** button, point to **From Database**, and then click **From Microsoft Access Database**. The Import Data dialog box opens.
6. Navigate to the **Excel11 > Module** folder included with your Data Files, click the **World Rhythm** database file, and click the **Import** button. Excel connects to the database, and the Navigator dialog box opens, listing all of the tables in the database.
7. Click the **Items Purchased** table. A preview of the selected table appears in the right pane of the Navigator dialog box. See Figure 11-16.

Figure 11-16 Navigator dialog box

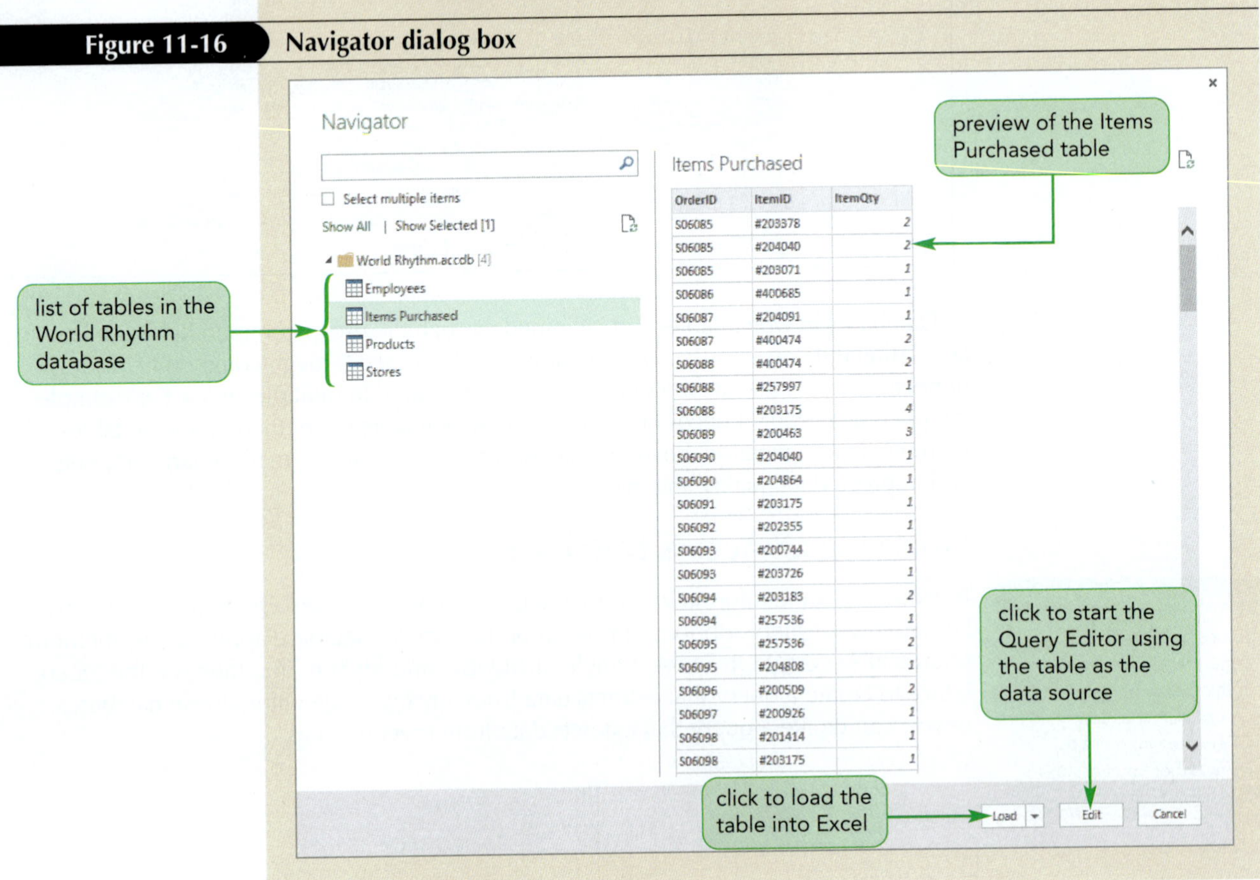

The Items Purchased table has three fields. The OrderID field identifies in which order the product was purchased, the ItemID field identifies the product, and the ItemQty provides the quantity of the product purchased on that order. Though not shown in the dialog box, this table has 21,418 records—one for each product purchase from the World Rhythm stores over the past two years. Gabriel wants you to load this large table into the Data Model.

Exploring the Data Model

The Data Model is a database attached to an Excel workbook that provides many of the tools found in database programs such as Microsoft Access. Because the Data Model is part of the workbook, its contents are immediately available to PivotTables, PivotCharts, and other Excel tools. Data stored in the Data Model is compressed, resulting in a smaller file than if the data were stored in an Excel table. Compressing the data also means that queries run faster and PivotTables load more quickly. However, the Data Model contents are not visible in the workbook. To view them, you must use Power Pivot, an Excel add-in for managing database tables and defining table relationships. You use the Query Editor to establish a connection between the data source and the Data Model.

Gabriel wants you to connect the Items Purchased table in the World Rhythm database to the Data Model.

To load Items Purchased table into the Data Model:

1. In the Navigator dialog box, click the **Load button arrow**, and then click **Load To**. The Load To dialog box opens.
2. Click the **Only Create Connection** option button. This creates a connection to the Items Purchased table but does not load that data into an Excel table in the workbook.
3. Click the **Add this data to the Data Model** check box. See Figure 11-17.

Figure 11-17 Loading data to the Excel Data Model

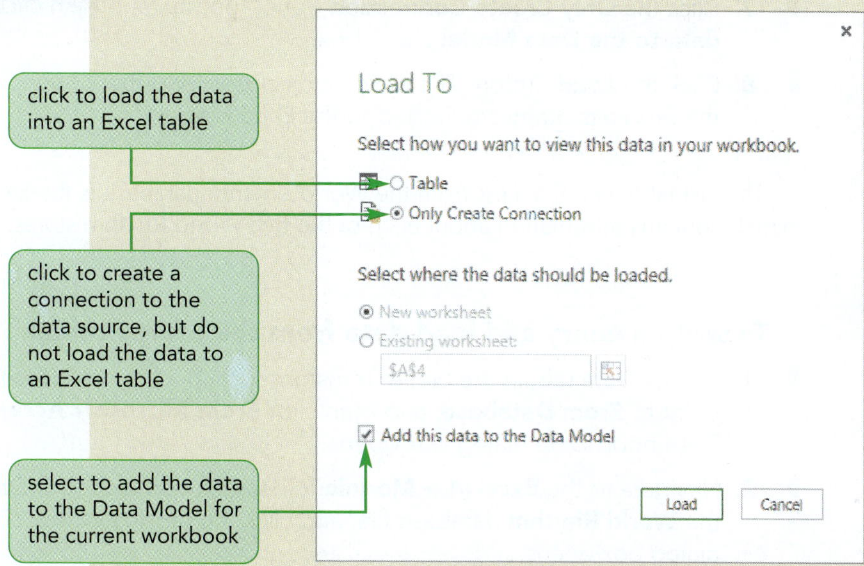

4. Click the **Load** button to establish the connection to the Data Model. When the data loading is complete, the Items Purchased query appears in the Workbook Queries pane with 21,418 rows loaded, but you do not see any actual data in the worksheet.

   Trouble? If you see an Excel table containing the Items Purchased data, delete the table and the query, and then recreate the query and repeat Steps 1 through 4, making sure to load the table only to the Data Model and not to an Excel table.

You can also create a query based on a table's data by clicking the Edit button in the Navigator dialog box to open the Query Editor. Gabriel wants the Data Model to include data from the Products table.

To write a query and load data from the Products table:

1. On the Data tab, in the Get & Transform group, click the **New Query** button, point to **From Database**, and then click **From Microsoft Access Database**. The Import Data dialog box opens.
2. Navigate to the **Excel11 > Module** folder included with your Data Files, select the **World Rhythm** database file, and click the **Import** button. The Navigator dialog box opens.
3. Click the **Products** table, and then click the **Edit** button. The Query Editor opens.
4. Select the **ItemID**, **Category**, **Subcategory**, and **Description** columns.
5. On the Home tab, in the Manage Columns group, click the **Remove Columns button arrow**, and then click **Remove Other Columns**. Only the selected columns remain in the query.
6. On the Home tab, in the Close group, click the **Close & Load button arrow**, and then click **Close & Load To**. The Load To dialog box opens.
7. Click the **Only Create Connection** option button, and then click the **Add this data to the Data Model** check box.
8. Click the **Load** button. The dialog box closes, and the 93 rows of data from the Products query are loaded to the Data Model.

The last table you'll access from the World Rhythm database is the Stores table, which contains information about each of the five World Rhythm stores.

To write a query and load data from the Stores table:

1. On the Data tab, in the Get & Transform group, click the **New Query** button, point to **From Database**, and then click **From Microsoft Access Database**. The Import Data dialog box opens.
2. Navigate to the **Excel11 > Module** folder included with your Data Files, select the **World Rhythm** database file, and click the **Import** button. The Navigator dialog box opens.
3. Click the **Stores** table, and then click the **Edit** button. The Query Editor opens.
4. Select the **StoreID**, **StoreCity**, and **StoreState** columns.

5. On the Home tab, in the Manage Columns group, click the **Remove Columns button arrow**, and then click **Remove Other Columns**. Only the selected columns remain in the query.
6. On the Home tab, in the Close group, click the **Close & Load button arrow**, and then click **Close & Load To**. The Load To dialog box opens.
7. Click the **Only Create Connection** option button, and then click the **Add this data to the Data Model** check box.
8. Click the **Load** button. The dialog box closes, and the five rows of data are loaded from the Stores table to the Data Model.

You have added three queries to the Product Report workbook. The last query will retrieve the customer orders data stored in the Two Year Revenue CSV file that you worked with in the previous session. Using the data in this workbook, Gabriel will be able to track when and where each product was purchased in the last two years.

To create the query for the customer order data:

1. On the Data tab, in the Get & Transform group, click the **New Query** button, point to **From File**, and then click **From CSV**. The Import Data dialog box opens.
2. Navigate to the **Excel11 > Module** folder included with your Data Files, click the **Two Year Revenue** CSV file, and then click the **Import** button. The file opens in the Query Editor.

   Gabriel wants to import the OrderID, OrderDate, StoreID, and CustZipCode columns. However, Power Query has imported the CustZipCode values as numbers, rather than as text so that a zip code like 07920 is retrieved as 7920 with the leading 0 removed. To correct this problem, you'll first remove the step that changed the data types of the data values.
3. In the Query Settings pane, in the APPLIED STEPS box, click the **delete** icon ☒ next to the Changed Type step. The step is removed, and the values in the CustZipCode column are once again treated as text rather than numbers.
4. Select the **OrderID**, **OrderDate**, **StoreID**, and **CustZipCode** columns.
5. On the Home tab, in the Manage Columns group, click the **Remove Columns button arrow**, and then click **Remove Other Columns**. Only the four selected columns remain in the query.
6. Click the **OrderDate** column header to select that column. Gabriel wants these values to be treated as dates.
7. On the ribbon, click the **Transform** tab. In the Any Column group, click the **Data Type** button, and then click **Date**.
8. In the Query Settings pane, in the Name box, rename the query as **Customer Orders**. See Figure 11-18.

Figure 11-18 Final Customer Orders query

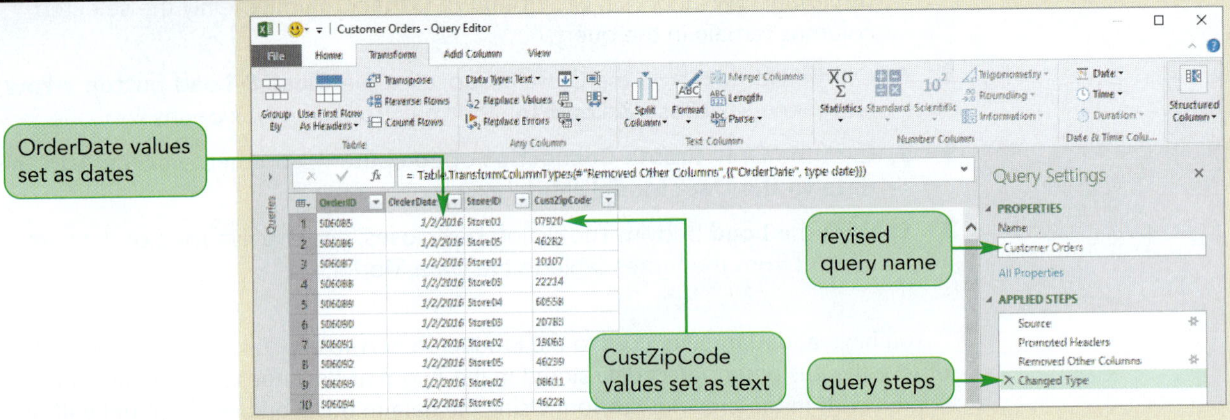

9. On the ribbon, click the **Home** tab. In the Close group, click the **Close & Load button arrow**, and then click **Close & Load To**. The Load To dialog box opens.
10. Click the **Only Create Connection** option button, click the **Add this data to the Data Model** check box, and then click the **Load** button.

The Customer Orders query loads 14,324 to the Data Model, representing all of the customer orders over the two-year period.

PROSKILLS

Written Communication: Designing a Database

Databases are great tools to organize information, track statistics, and generate reports. When used with Excel, a properly designed database can provide valuable information and help you make informed financial decisions. Whether you are creating a database in the Data Model or Microsoft Access, keep in mind the following guidelines:

- **Split data into multiple tables.** Keep each table focused on a specific topical area. Link the tables through one or more common fields.
- **Avoid redundant data.** Key pieces of information, such as a customer's address or phone number, should be entered in only one place in your database.
- **Use understandable field names.** Avoid using acronyms or abbreviations that may unclear or confusing.
- **Maintain consistency in data entry.** Include validation rules to ensure that rules such as abbreviate titles (for example, Mr. instead of Mister) are always followed.
- **Test the database on a small subset of data before entering all of the data.** The more errors you weed out early, the easier it will be to manage your database.

A badly designed or improperly used database will end up creating more problems rather than solving them.

With all of the queries loaded into the Data Model, you are ready to use Power Pivot to view the query data and set up relationships between all four tables.

Transforming Data with Power Pivot

Power Pivot is a BI tool for combining multiple data sources within a single data structure, including the ability to define relationships between data tables, and constructing formulas to summarize and filter data values. Because Power Pivot is an add-in, you must install it before using it to work with the contents of the Data Model. You can have Excel install the Power Pivot add-in by attempting to view the contents of the Data Model. If Power Pivot is not already installed, Excel will install it for you.

To install Power Pivot:

1. On the Data tab, in the Data Tools group, click the **Manage Data Model** button. If Power Pivot is not installed, a dialog box opens, prompting you to enable the Data Analysis add-ins.
2. If prompted, click the **Enable** button. If it is not already present, the Power Pivot tab appears on the ribbon, and the Power Pivot window opens showing the contents of the Data Model. See Figure 11-19.

Figure 11-19 The Data Model viewed in Power Pivot

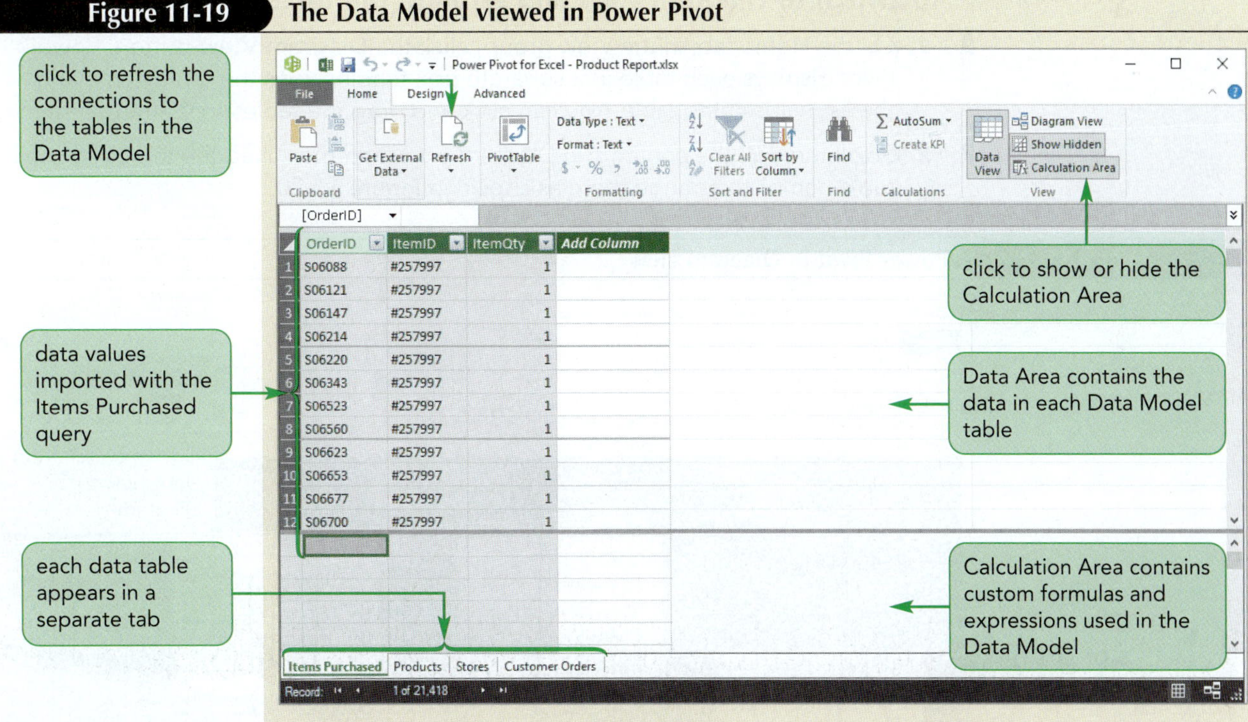

The Power Pivot window places each table in the Data Model on a separate tab. The Data Area displays the contents of each table, and the Calculation Area is used for writing customized functions and expressions used with the data in the Data Model.

TIP

To add a selected Excel table to the Data Model, click the Add to Data Model button in the Tables group on the Power Pivot tab.

To view the contents of the Data Model:

1. Scroll through the rows in the Items Purchased tab to review the contents of that table.
2. Click the **Products** tab to view the data returned by the Products query.
3. Click the **Stores** tab, and then review the contents of the table generated by the Stores query.

4. Click the **Customer Orders** tab, and then review contents of the table generated by the Customer Orders query.

Exploring the Data Model in Diagram View

So far, you have looked at the Data Model in **Data view**, which shows the contents of each table in the Data Model in a separate tab. Data view is useful when you want to view the contents of each table in the Data Model. You can also look at the Data Model in **Diagram view**, which shows the structure of each table, including the table fields. Diagram view is useful when you want to work with the general database structure of the tables in your model. From Diagram view, you can quickly define the relationships that connect the tables.

Gabriel wants you to switch to Diagram view so you can define the relationships between the tables in the Data Model.

To switch to Diagram view and arrange the tables:

1. On the Home tab, in the View group, click the **Diagram View** button. Power Pivot displays each table in a separate box that includes the table name and the list fields in the table. You can click and drag the tables to rearrange them.
2. Scroll through the contents in Diagram view, and then drag the tables by their table names to arrange them as shown in Figure 11-20.

Figure 11-20 Power Pivot in Diagram view

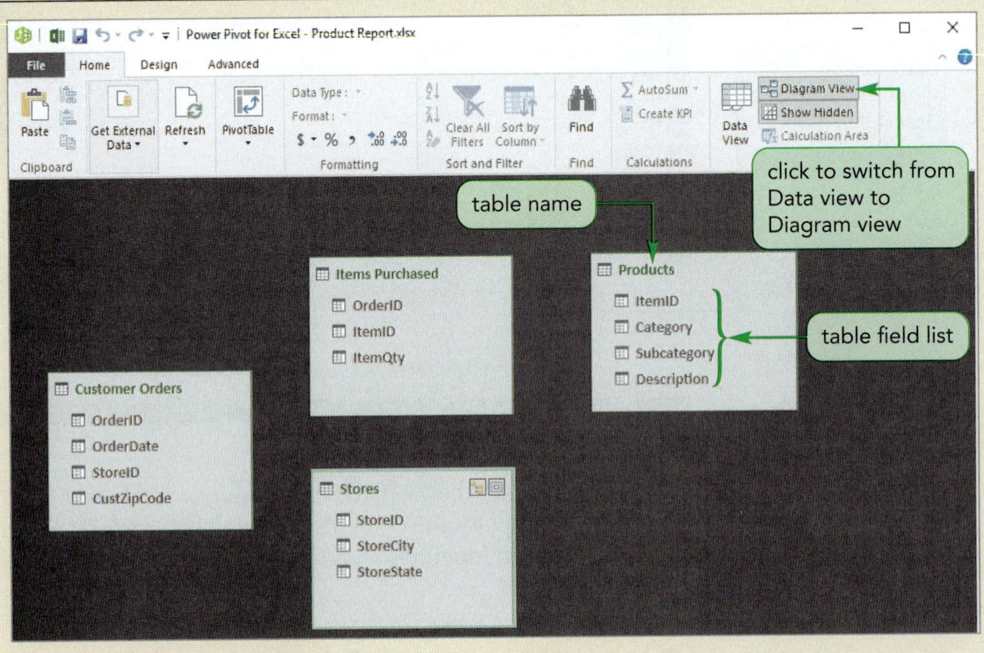

Managing Table Relationships

To create a relationship between two tables, you drag a common field from one table to the other. The relationship is indicated by a line connecting the two tables. One of the tables in a relationship often acts as a lookup table for the other. This usually occurs in one-to-many relationships in which the "many" table is retrieving specific information from a single record in the "one" table. For example, the Stores table can act as a lookup table for the Customer Orders table, providing specific information about the store at which the customer made his or her purchase. In this case, data from the Stores table is flowing toward the Customer Orders table. Diagram View indicates the direction of the data by adding an arrow icon to the connecting line, pointing in the direction of the data flow.

You need to establish relationships between the four tables in the Data Model. All customer orders are in the Customer Orders table, but information about the store that handled that order are in the Stores table. The common field in those two tables is the StoreID field. Likewise, the Items Purchased table shares the common field OrderID with the Customer Orders table, and the Products table shares the common field ItemID with the Items Purchased table. You will use these common fields to establish the table relationships.

TIP

To define table relationships in Excel, click the Relationships button in the Data Tools group on the Data tab.

To define the table relationships in Diagram view:

1. Drag the **StoreID** field name in the Customer Orders table box to cover the **StoreID** field name in the Stores table box. Power Pivot adds a connecting line between the Customer Orders table and the Stores table.

   Note that this is a one-to-many relationship, as indicated by the * character next to the Customer Orders table (there are many customer orders from each store) and the 1 character next to the Stores table (each store is listed only once). The arrow icon points from the Stores table to the Customer Order table, indicating the Stores table acts as the lookup table for customer orders.

2. Drag the **OrderID** field name in the Customer Orders table box to cover the **OrderID** field name in the Items Purchased table box. The connecting line again indicates a one-to-many relationship—but here the Customer Orders table is the lookup table because a single customer order might contain many different items purchased.

3. Drag the **ItemID** field name in the Items Purchased table box to cover the **ItemID** field name in the Products table box. This connection is also a one-to-many relationship with the Products table acting as the lookup table for the Items Purchased table, supplying specific information about each product. See Figure 11-21.

Figure 11-21 Table relationships established in Power Pivot

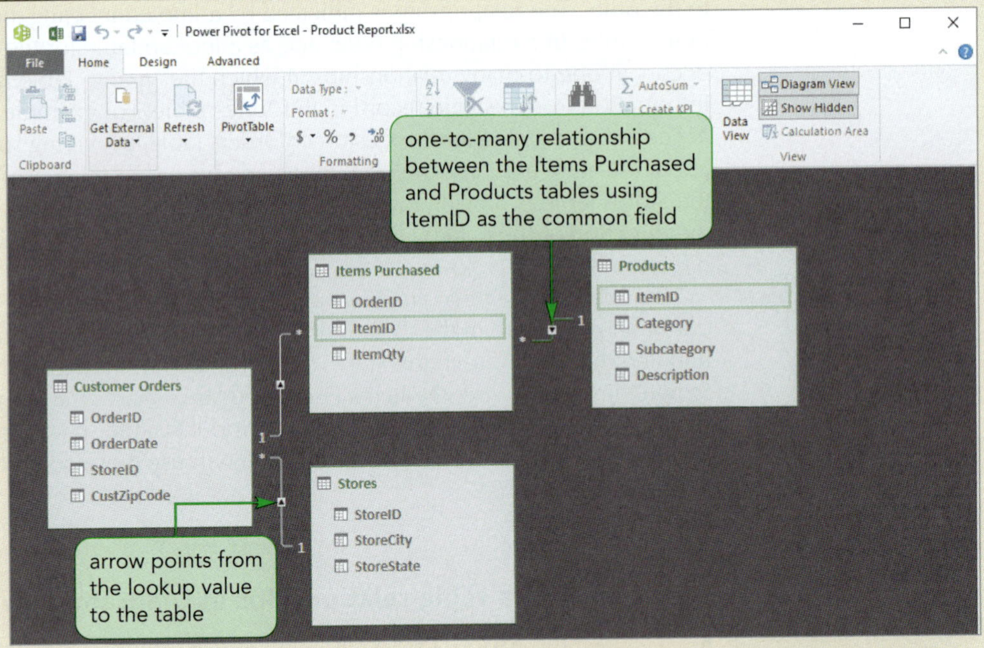

4. Close the Power Pivot window and return to the Excel workbook, and then close the Workbook Queries pane if it is open.
5. If Excel displays a Security Warning bar indicating that the external connections have been disabled, click the **Enable Content** button, and then click the **Yes** button to make this workbook a trusted document on your network.

With the table relationships defined, you are ready to analyze the customer orders data, pulling information from any of the four tables in the Data Model.

Creating a PivotTable from the Data Model

So far, you have created PivotTables from a single data source, usually an Excel table. With Power Pivot and the Data Model, you can create PivotTables based on information contained in multiple tables drawn from a variety of data sources. Note that for a PivotTable to use multiple tables, the tables must be added to the Data Model and have table relationships defined based on common fields.

Gabriel wants you to create a PivotTable that shows the breakdown of product categories sold at the five stores over the past two years. To create this PivotTable, you'll use the Data Model as the data source.

To create a PivotTable based on the Data Model:

1. In the Products Sold by Store worksheet, make sure cell **A4** is the active cell.
2. On the ribbon, click the **Insert** tab, and then in the Tables group, click the **PivotTable** button. The Create PivotTable dialog box opens.
3. Verify that the **Use this workbook's Data Model** option button is selected, the **Existing Worksheet** option button is selected, and **'Products Sold by Store'!$A$4** appears in the Location box. See Figure 11-22.

Figure 11-22 Create PivotTable dialog box

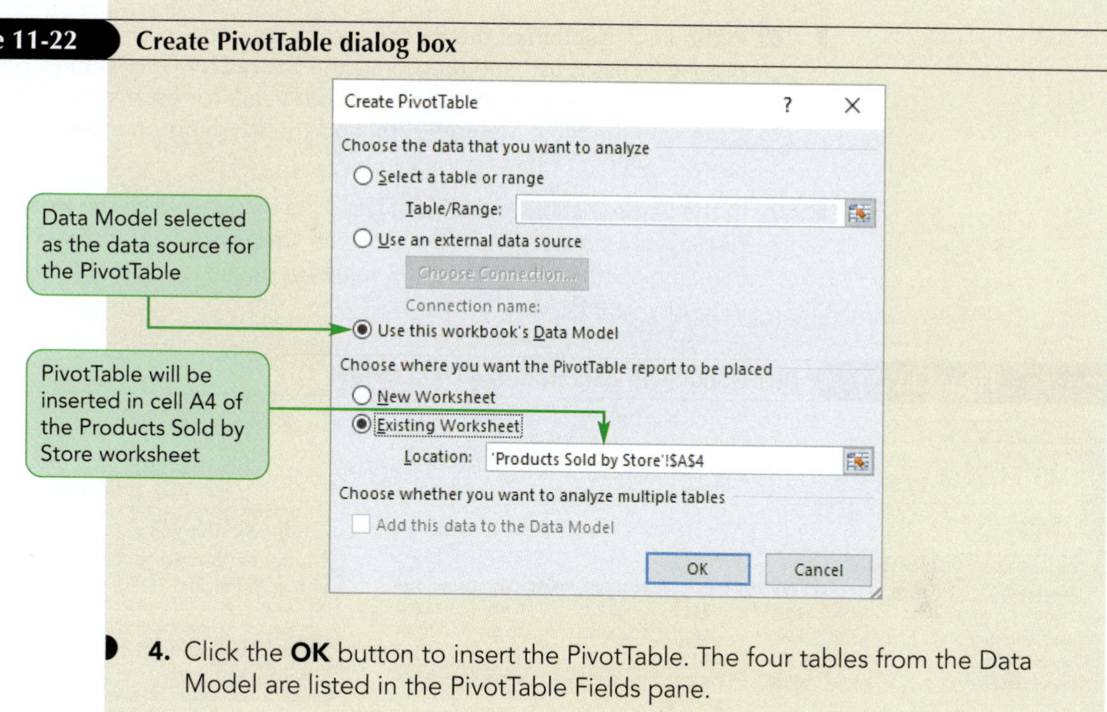

4. Click the **OK** button to insert the PivotTable. The four tables from the Data Model are listed in the PivotTable Fields pane.

Working with Fields from Multiple Tables

The PivotTable Fields pane lists all of tables in the Data Model in the fields section. To view the fields within each table, you click the table name. To add a field to the PivotTable, you drag the field name from any of the tables to the FILTERS, COLUMNS, ROWS, or VALUES boxes in the PivotTable fields pane. Because you established table relationships, fields from one table will be automatically matched to corresponding records in another table.

Gabriel wants the PivotTable to shows the sum of the quantity of products sold at each store. To do this, you will add the following to the PivotTable: the ItemQty field from the Items Purchased table, the StoreCity field from the Stores table, and the Category field from the Products table.

To create a PivotTable of the products sold by store:

1. In the PivotTable Fields pane, click **Items Purchased** to display the table's field list.
2. In the field list, drag the **ItemQty** field to the VALUES box. The PivotTable displays the Sum of ItemQty field, showing that 29,979 items were sold during the two-year period.
3. On the PivotTable Tools Analyze tab, in the Active Field group, click the **Field Settings** button. The Value Field Settings dialog box opens so you can format the Sum of ItemQty field value.
4. In the Custom Name box, enter **Quantity Sold**.
5. Click the **Number Format** button to open the Format Cells dialog box, click **Number** in the Category box, reduce the number of decimal places to **0**, click the **Use 1000 Separator(,)** check box, and then click the **OK** button in each dialog box. The PivotTable shows the formatted value.

6. In the fields section of the PivotTable Fields pane, click the **Stores** table to display its fields list, and then drag the **StoreCity** field to the COLUMNS box. The PivotTable shows the Quantity Sold value for each store. The Brooklyn store sold the most items (7,570), and the Washington store sold the fewest items (4,988).
7. In the fields section of the PivotTable Fields pane, click the **Products** table to display its fields list, and then drag the **Category** field to the ROWS box. The PivotTable shows Quantity Sold value for each store broken out by product category. See Figure 11-23.

Figure 11-23 PivotTable with data from the Data Model

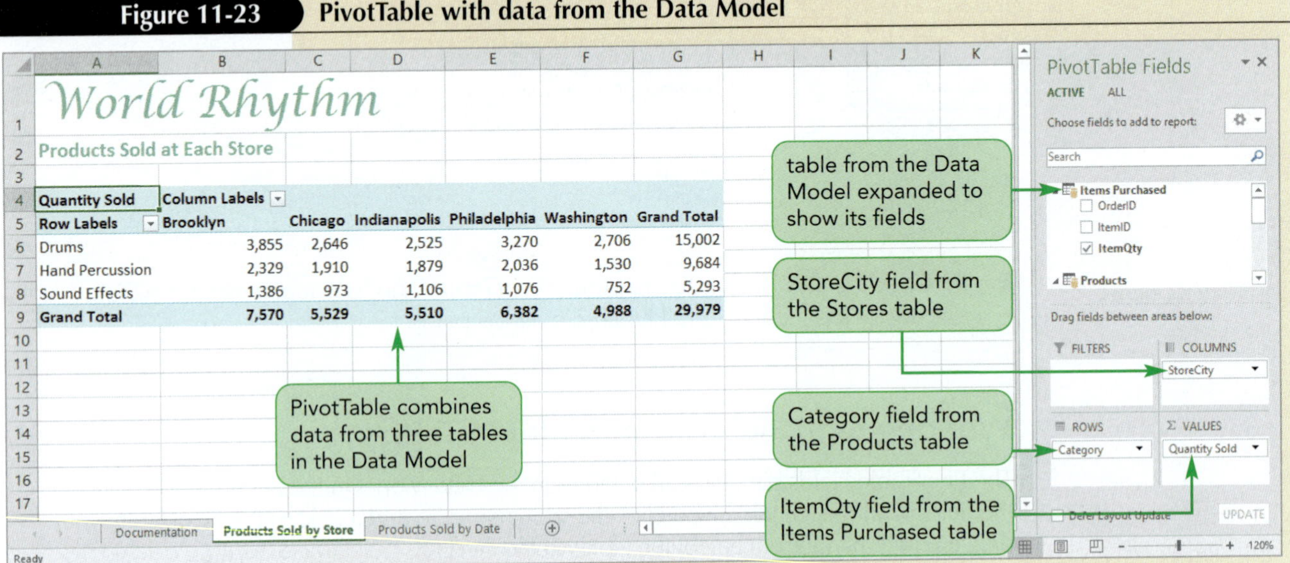

From the PivotTable, Gabriel learns that almost half of the products sold were in the Drums category, Hand Percussion instruments were the next biggest sellers, followed by Sound Effect instruments. The highest combination of product category and store occurred at the Brooklyn store, which sold 3,855 drums.

INSIGHT

Data Cubes and Cube Functions

A PivotTable is a multidimensional array of values known as a **Data Cube**. Data Cubes differ from database tables by storing summary measures from combinations of fields rather than individual records and fields. The Data Cube is part of an **OLAP** (**Online Analytic Processing**) database, built to optimize structured data for querying and reporting. For example, the government stores demographic information in OLAP databases to make it easy to construct cross-tabulations of various ethnic and socioeconomic groups.

One advantage of Power Pivot is that you can treat the Data Model as a Data Cube and extract information using **Cube functions** without having to construct a PivotTable. The following formula uses the CUBEVALUE function to access the workbook's Data Model, returning the quantity of drums sold in Chicago:

```
=CUBEVALUE("ThisWorkbookDataModel","[Sum of ItemQty]",
"[StoreCity].[Chicago]","[Category].[Drums]")
```

This formula returns 2,646, which matches the value of cell C6 shown in Figure 11-23 found at the intersection of the Drums row and the Chicago column in the PivotTable. Excel supports seven Cube functions, which can be used to calculate a wide variety of summary statistics.

You can also treat an existing PivotTable as a Data Cube and extract information using the GETPIVOTDATA function. The following formula also returns 2,646, the number of drums sold by the Chicago store:

```
=GETPIVOTDATA("[Measures].[Sum of ItemQty]",$A$4,
"[Stores].[StoreCity]","[Stores].[StoreCity].&[Chicago]",
"[Products].[Category]","[Products].[Category].&[Drums]")
```

Unlike the CUBEVALUE function, the PivotTable must exist for the GETPIVOTDATA function to return a value. However, because the function does not rely on the Data Model, it can be used with any PivotTable in the workbook.

Adding a Timeline Slicer

A **timeline** is a slicer that is applied to date fields. Using the timeline, you can summarize the data for ranges of time intervals from years down to minutes and seconds.

Gabriel wants to see how these customer orders break down by date. One way of doing this is by creating a timeline based on the OrderDate field in the Customer Orders table.

To create a timeline for the OrderDate field:

1. On the PivotTable Tools Analyze tab, in the Filter group, click the **Insert Timeline** button. The Insert Timelines dialog box opens.
2. Click the **ALL** tab to display a list of all the date and time fields in the Data Model, which, in this Data Model, is only the OrderDate field in the Customer Orders table.
3. Click the **OrderDate** check box. You want to create a timeline based on the date of the customer order.
4. Click the **OK** button. The OrderDate timeline appears in the worksheet.
5. Move and resize the timeline box to cover the range **A10:G16**.

The timeline is laid out as a horizontal scrollbar grouped by months over the two-year period in which Gabriel has sampled sales data. You can filter the timeline so that it shows the sales for specified time intervals. Gabriel wants to see the product sales during December of 2017.

TIP

You can click the down arrow in the upper-right corner of the timeline box and select another interval.

To filter the timeline:

1. Drag the timeline scroll bar until you see DEC 2017 in the timeline box.
2. Click the blue box directly below DEC, deselecting all of the other months in the timeline. During December 2017, the company sold 2,300 items with 607 items sold from the Brooklyn store, 474 from Chicago, 333 from Indianapolis, 529 from Philadelphia, and 357 from Washington. See Figure 11-24.

Figure 11-24 Timeline slicer showing December 2017 sales

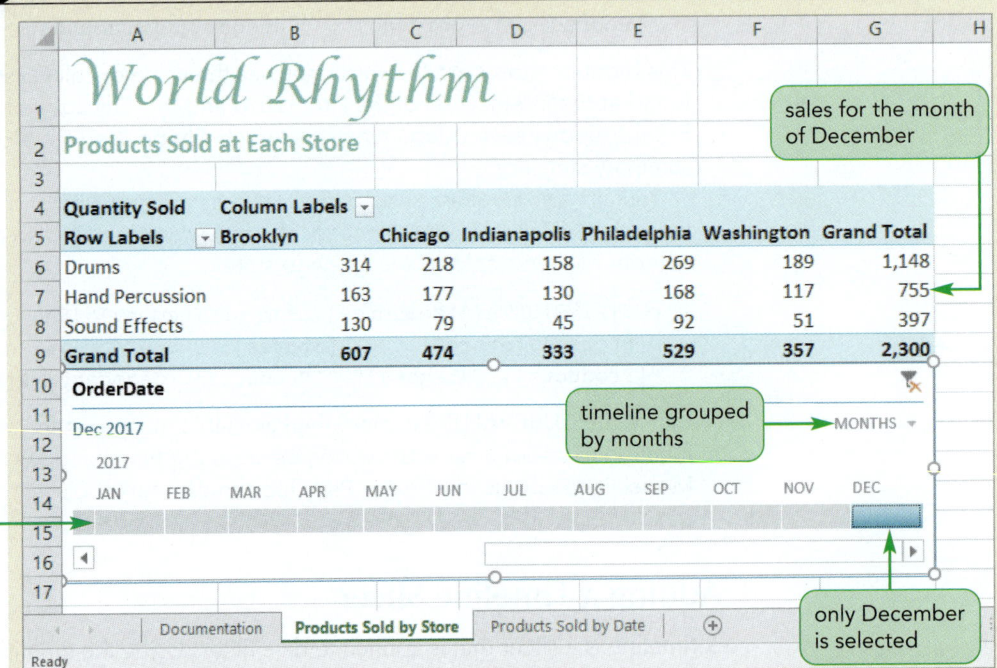

3. Drag the left border of the DEC box so that it covers the months of OCT through DEC. The PivotTable displays World Rhythm total sales for October through December 2017, which includes 5,139 items in the Drums, Hand Percussion, and Sound Effects categories.
4. Click the **Clear Filter** button in the upper-right corner of the timeline (or press the **Alt+C** keys) to restore the timeline to display of the dates in the sample.
5. Save the workbook.

Timelines can also be established for nonadjacent intervals by holding down the Ctrl key and clicking each interval and then releasing the Ctrl key. In this way, Gabriel could create a timeline limited to December sales of each year.

In this session, you loaded data from an Access database into the Data Model and then analyzed data from fields spread across multiple tables in a PivotTable. In the next session, you'll continue to explore the BI tools by examining how to create interactive reports and maps of the World Rhythm sales data.

REVIEW

Session 11.2 Quick Check

1. What are fields and records?
2. What is a relational database?
3. What is a one-to-many relationship?
4. What is the Data Model? What are some advantages of placing your data in the Data Model?
5. Describe how to create a table relation in Power Pivot in Diagram view.
6. How you do use multiple tables within the same PivotTable?
7. How do you add a timeline to a PivotTable?

Session 11.3 Visual Overview:

Power View sheets are organized around **data visualizations**, which are the tables, charts, and maps that present data in a visual way.

Power View is an add-in that visualizes data, looking for patterns within the data.

Tables and fields from the Data Model are accessible to Power View.

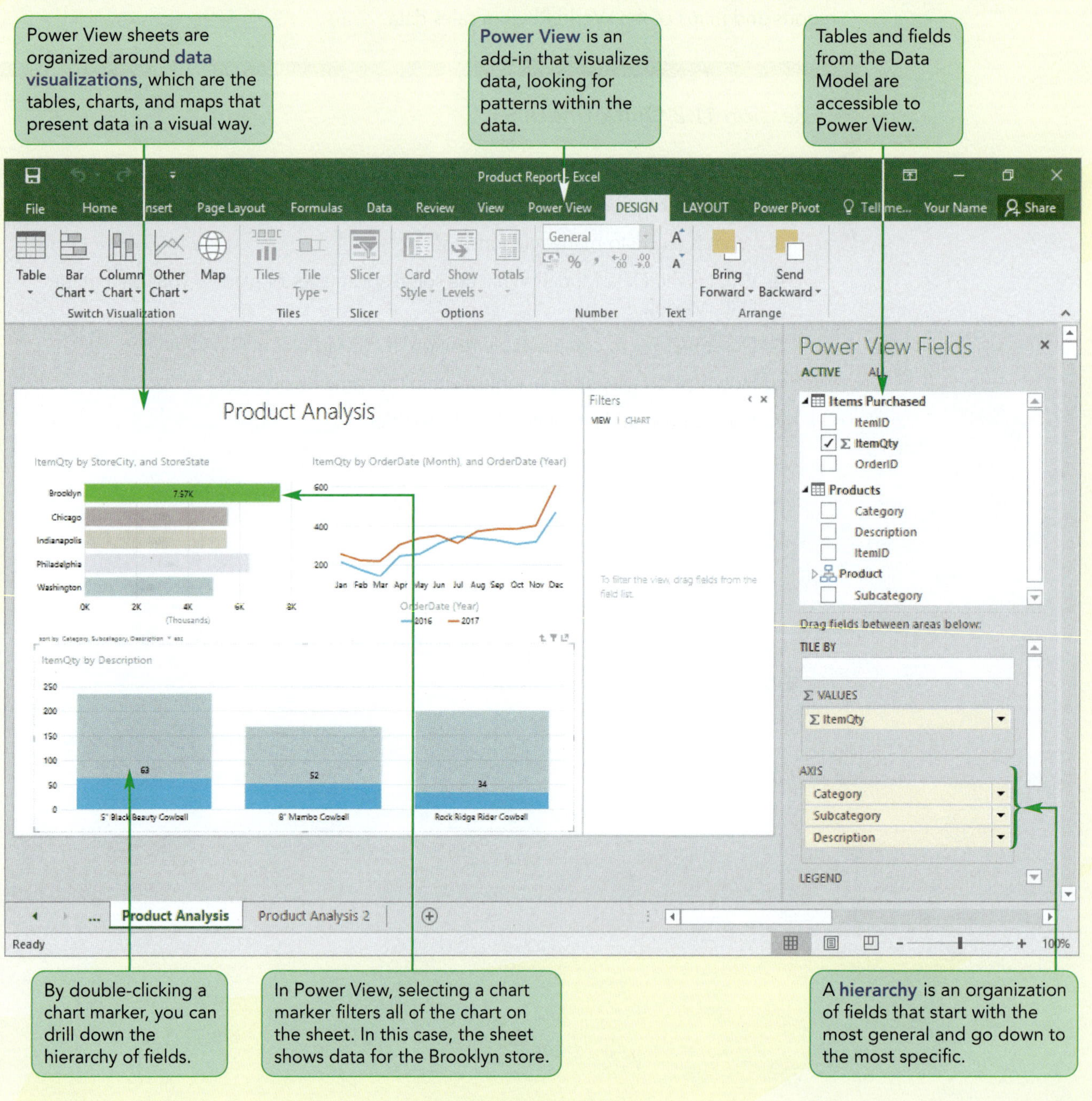

By double-clicking a chart marker, you can drill down the hierarchy of fields.

In Power View, selecting a chart marker filters all of the chart on the sheet. In this case, the sheet shows data for the Brooklyn store.

A **hierarchy** is an organization of fields that start with the most general and go down to the most specific.

Power View and Power Map

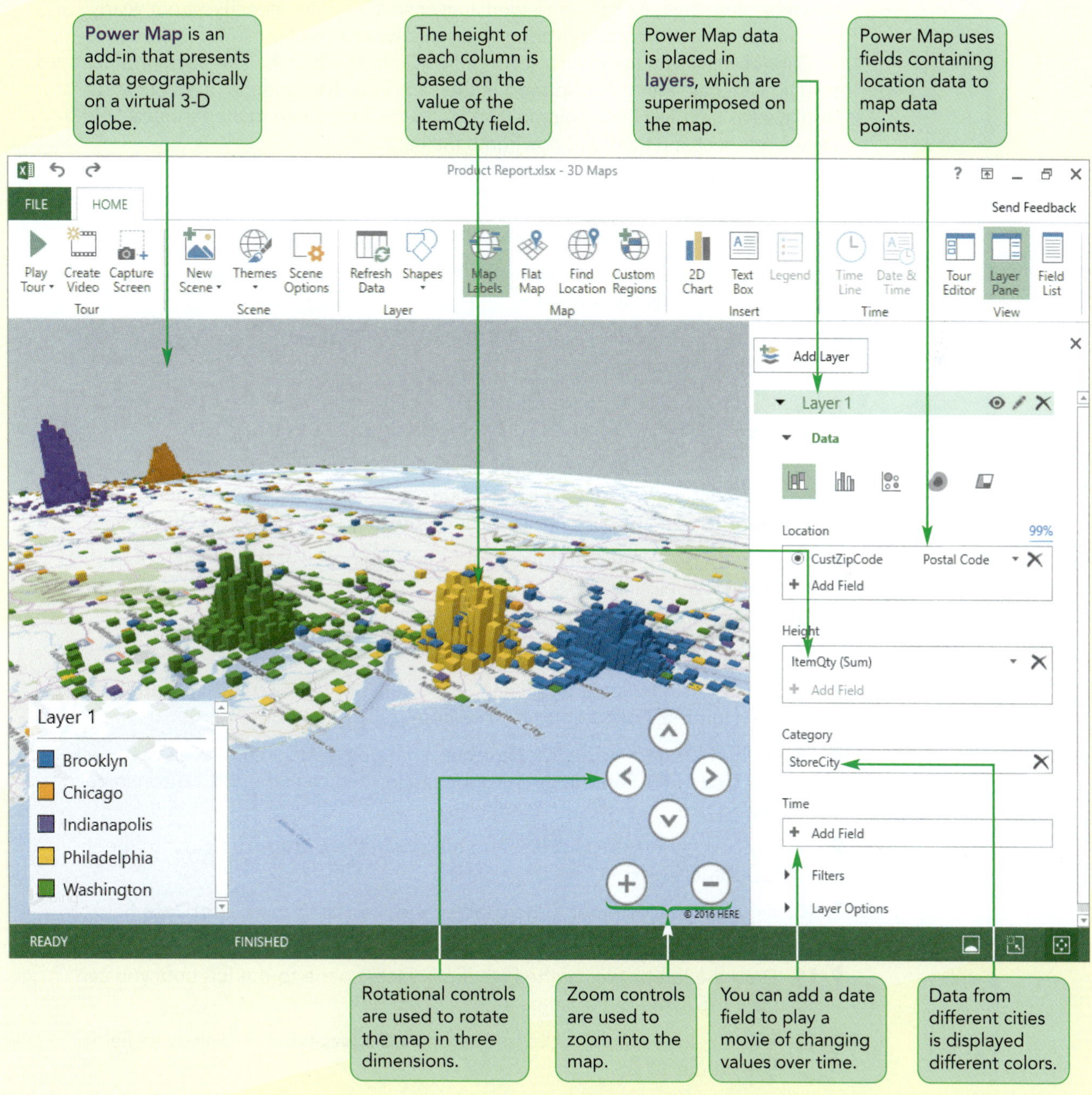

Drilling Down into Data

At the end of the previous session, you used a timeline slicer to summarize data across selected time intervals. Another way to perform such an analysis is by **drilling down** into data, which means going from a general overview of all of the data values to a more specific view with finer and finer detail. Date fields are often used for drilling down because the data can be viewed at ever smaller time intervals—from yearly summaries down to reports covering spans of days or even hours.

Gabriel wants you to create a second PivotTable in which he can track product sales by date with date intervals displayed in the PivotTable row and the product category displayed as the PivotTable column. You'll add this PivotTable to the Products Sold by Date worksheet and then drill down into the data.

To create the PivotTable of product sales by date:

1. If you took a break at the end of the previous session, make sure the Product Report workbook is open.
2. Go to the **Products Sold by Date** worksheet, and then verify that cell **A4** is the active cell.
3. On the ribbon, click the **Insert** tab, and then in the Tables group, click the **PivotTable** button. The Create PivotTable dialog box opens.
4. Verify that the **Use this workbook's Data Model** option button is selected, the **Existing Worksheet** option button is selected, and **'Products Sold by Date'!$A$4** appears in the Location box, and then click the **OK** button.
5. Expand the **Items Purchased** table to display its fields, and then drag the **ItemQty** field into the VALUES box.
6. On the PivotTable Tools Analyze tab, in the Active Field group, click the **Field Settings** button. The Value Field Settings dialog box opens.
7. In the Custom Name box, change the value to **Item Quantity**, and then click the **Number Format** button. The Format Cells box opens.
8. In the Category box, click **Number**, change the decimal places to **0**, click the **Use 1000 Separator** check box, and then click the **OK** button in each dialog box.
9. Expand the **Products** table, and then drag the **Category** field into the COLUMNS box.
10. Expand the Customer Orders table, and then drag the **OrderDate** field to the ROWS box.
11. Drag the left border of the PivotTable Fields pane to the left until you can view the name of the fields in the ROWS box.
12. In the fields section, click the **Customer Orders** table to display its fields. See Figure 11-25.

Figure 11-25 PivotTable sales by year and product category

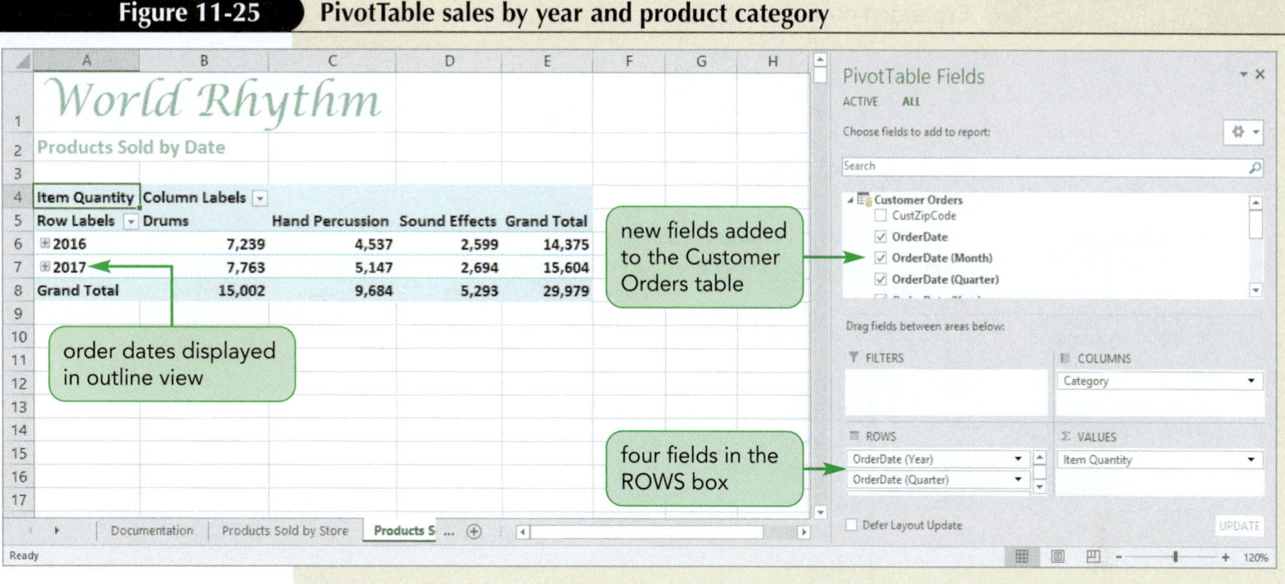

Outlining a PivotTable with a Date Field

When you add a date field to a PivotTable, Excel automatically generates three new fields containing the date's year, month, and quarter values. In this case, Excel added three new fields to the Customer Orders table named OrderDate (Month), OrderDate(Quarter), OrderDate(Year) containing the month, quarter, and year values for each customer order. The ROWS area now contains four fields—the three new fields and the OrderDate field—arranged in order from the most general (years) down to the most specific (dates). Finally, the order dates in the PivotTable row are displayed in outline view so you can view totals for individual years, quarters, months, and dates.

Gabriel asks you to expand the outline to view the sales on January 2, 2016.

To expand the outline for order dates:

1. Click the **Expand Outline icon** [+] next to the 2016 row label to show the sales for each of the four quarters in that year.
2. Click the **Expand Outline icon** [+] next to the Qtr1 label, and then click the **Expand Outline icon** [+] next to the Jan label to drill the outline down to the individual January dates. The company sold 2,343 items in the first quarter of 2016 of which 889 were sold in January and specifically 41 were sold on January 2. Of those 41 items, 21 were drums, 11 were hand percussion instruments, and 9 were sound effect instruments. See Figure 11-26.

Figure 11-26 Expanded outline of the order dates

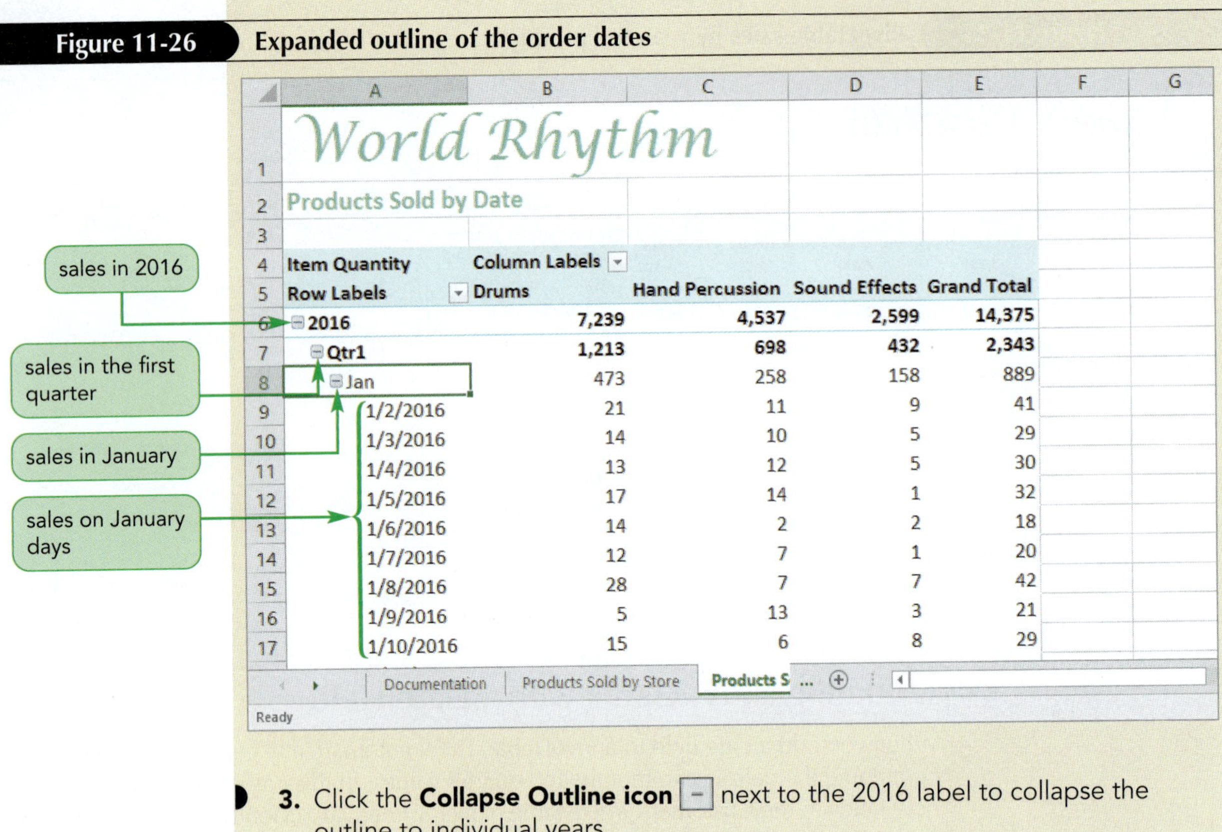

3. Click the **Collapse Outline icon** [-] next to the 2016 label to collapse the outline to individual years.

Outline view is helpful but a bit unwieldy, displaying subcategories that may not be of interest. For example, if Gabriel wants to see only the 2016 first-quarter sales, the PivotTable does not need to show sales for other years or other quarters. To display only specific categories, you can create a hierarchy.

Creating a Hierarchy of Fields

A hierarchy is an organization of fields that start with the most general and go down to the most specific. A Year, Month, and Date field is one example of a hierarchy. Another example is a hierarchy of products that range from a general classification down to individual product names. You define hierarchies within Power Pivot in Diagram view.

REFERENCE

Creating a Hierarchy of Fields

- View the Data Model in Diagram view in the Power Pivot window.
- Click the Create Hierarchy button in the table box to create a hierarchy for the table.
- Specify a name for the hierarchy.
- Drag fields into the hierarchy, arranged in order from the most general down to the most specific.

Gabriel wants you to create a hierarchy for the newly created OrderDate fields that were generated for the PivotTable and that are not part of the Data Model. You'll also create a hierarchy of fields relating to each product's category, subcategory, and description.

To create hierarchies of the new date fields and the product fields:

1. On the ribbon, click the **Power Pivot** tab, and then in the Data Model group, click the **Manage** button to return to Power Pivot.
2. On the Home tab, in the View group, click the **Diagram View** button, if necessary, to switch the Data Model to Diagram view.
3. Point to the **Customer Orders** table box, and then click the **Create Hierarchy** button in the upper-right corner of the table box. Excel creates a new entry in the Customer Orders field list named *Hierachy1*.
4. With the name still selected, type **Date** as the new hierarchy name, and then press the **Enter** key. The Date hierarchy is created. You will add fields to the hierarchy, starting with the most general field and ending with the most specific.
5. Drag the **OrderDate (Year)** field down and on top of the Date hierarchy entry. When you release the mouse button, the OrderDate (Year) field drops into the hierarchy.
6. Drag the **OrderDate (Quarter)** field below the OrderDate (Year) field in the hierarchy.
7. Drag the **OrderDate (Month)** field below the OrderDate(Quarter) field in the hierarchy.
8. Scroll up and drag the **OrderDate** field to the bottom of the hierarchy. The fields in the Date hierarchy start with the most general and end with the most specific. See Figure 11-27.

Figure 11-27 Fields added to the Date hierarchy

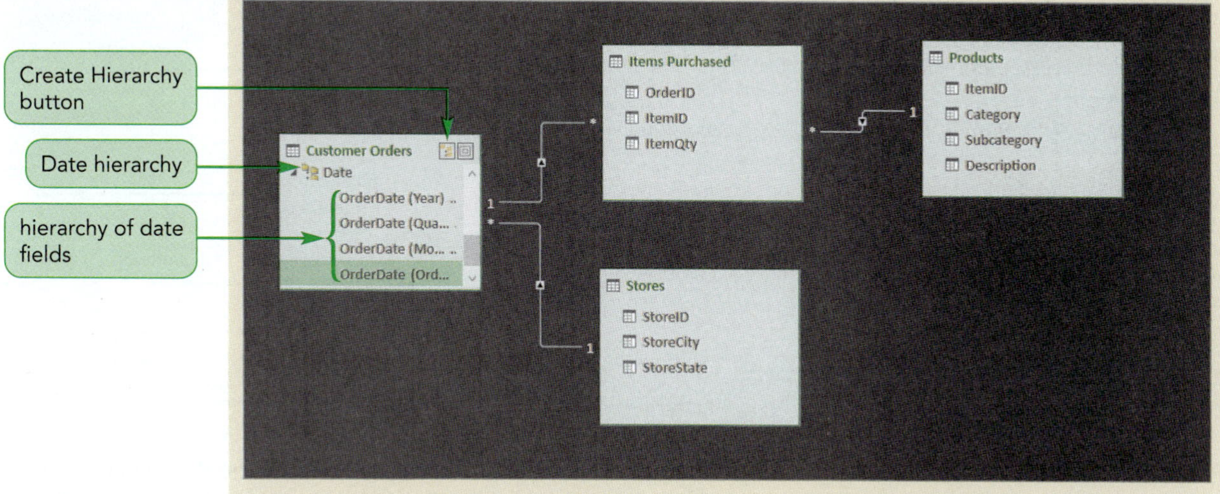

Next, you'll create a hierarchy for each product's category, subcategory, and description.

To create the Product hierarchy:

1. Select the **Products** table box, click the **Create Hierarchy** button, type **Product** as the new hierarchy name, and then press the **Enter** key.
2. Drag the following fields into the hierarchy in the order listed: **Category**, **Subcategory**, and **Description**.

3. Close the Power Pivot window, and return to the Excel workbook.
4. If you are prompted to enable the external data connection in a Message Bar, click the **Enable Content** button.

The Date and Product hierarchies you created are part of the Customer Orders and Products tables. You can add them to the PivotTable as you would any other field. Gabriel wants you to replace the fields in the ROWS and COLUMNS boxes with the Date and Product hierarchies.

To add the Date and Product hierarchies to the PivotTable:

1. In the PivotTable Fields pane, drag the **Category** field out of the COLUMNS box, removing it from the PivotTable.
2. Drag the **OrderDate(Year)**, **OrderDate(Quarter)**, **OrderDate(Month)**, and **OrderDate** fields out of the ROWS box to remove them from the PivotTable.
3. In the field section, click the **Customer Orders** table to display its field list, and then drag the **Date** hierarchy to the ROWS box.
4. Click the **Products** table to display its field list, and then drag the **Product** hierarchy to the COLUMNS box. See Figure 11-28.

Figure 11-28 **Date and Product hierarchies added to the PivotTable**

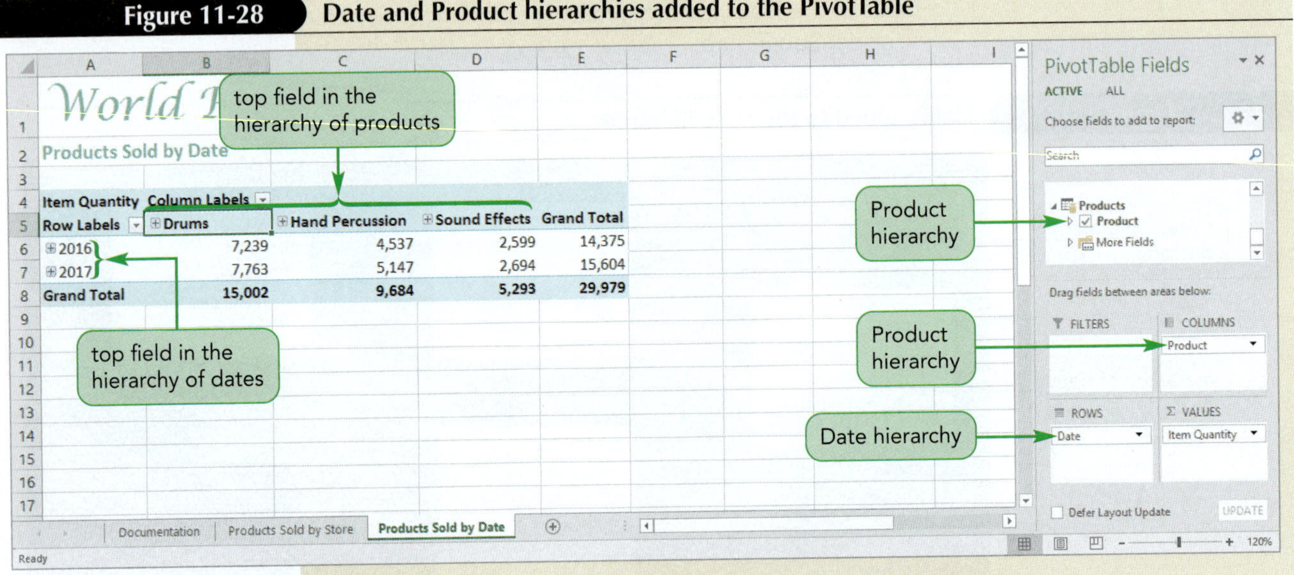

Using the hierarchies you created, you can drill down into the data to find sales figures for any specific product on any date. Gabriel wants to track the sale of Bata drums, which are double-headed drums used for religious ceremonies by the native cultures in Nigeria. You will drill into the PivotTable to track the sales of this type of drum during January of 2016.

To drill into the PivotTable to track Bata drum sales:

TIP

To view the PivotTable data in outline form, click the Expand buttons in front of the column or row labels.

1. Click cell **B5**, which contains the Drums label. You want to drill down this product category.
2. On the ribbon, click the **PivotTable Tools Analyze** tab, and then in the Active Field group, click the **Drill Down** button. The column labels change from the instrument categories to the drum subcategories.
3. With the Bata Drums label selected, click the **Drill Down** button again. The column labels change to the three sizes of Bata drums sold by World Rhythm—Large, Medium, and Small. The best-selling drum for 2016 and 2017 is the Small Bata drum with 174 total units sold.
4. Click cell **A6** to select the 2016 label, and click the **Drill Down** button. The PivotTable displays the sales totals for the four quarters of 2016.
5. With the Qtr1 label selected, click the **Drill Down** button to display the sales for January, February, and March, and then click the **Drill Down** button again to display the daily sales for January of 2016. Bata drums were sold only on five days in that month. See Figure 11-29.

Figure 11-29 Individual Bata drum sales in January of 2016

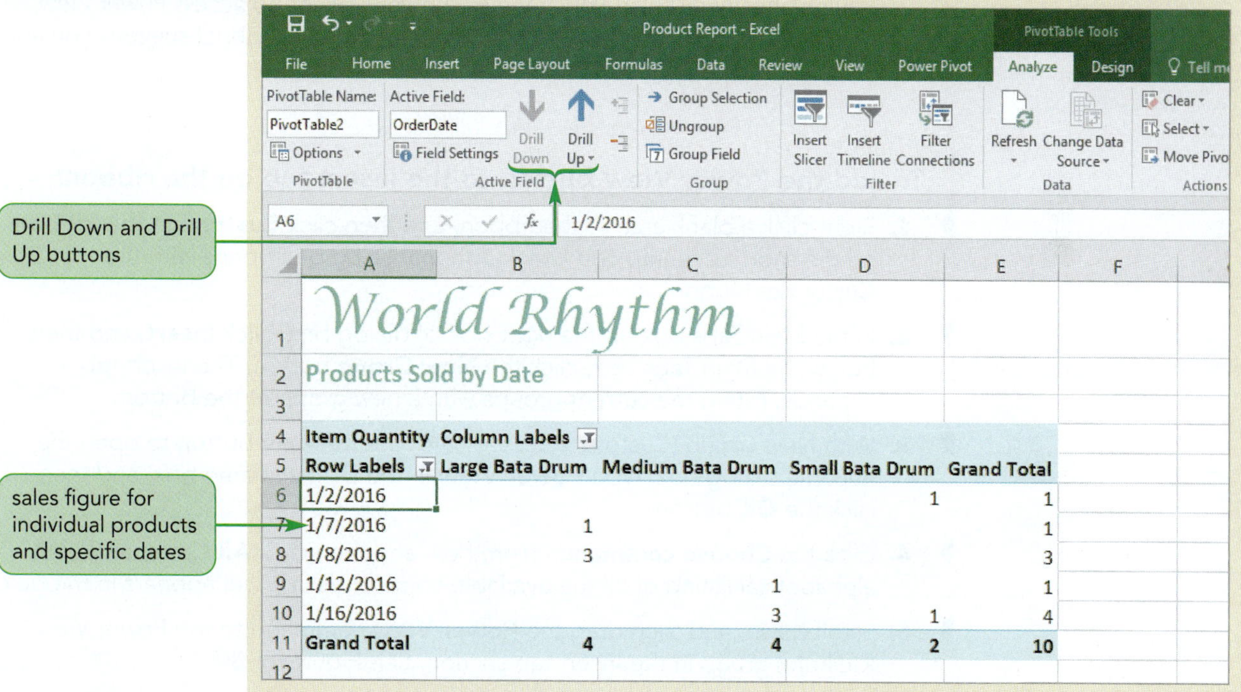

Drill Down and Drill Up buttons
sales figure for individual products and specific dates
World Rhythm
Products Sold by Date
Item Quantity Column Labels
Row Labels | Large Bata Drum | Medium Bata Drum | Small Bata Drum | Grand Total
1/2/2016 | | | 1 | 1
1/7/2016 | 1 | | | 1
1/8/2016 | 3 | | | 3
1/12/2016 | | 1 | | 1
1/16/2016 | | 3 | 1 | 4
Grand Total | 4 | 4 | 2 | 10

6. On the PivotTable Tools Analyze tab, in the Active Field group, click the **Drill Up** button three times to return to the more general Year level of data.
7. Click cell **B5** to select the Large Bata Drum label, and then click the **Drill Up** button twice to return to the more general instrument categories.

You can continue to drill up and down the PivotTable to explore other connections between the sales date and the products sold. However, the PivotTable doesn't contain information about the stores that sold the product or the customers who bought it. Gabriel wants to create a single sheet that shows how the data are interconnected. One way of doing this is with Power View.

Visualizing Data with Power View

Power View is a BI tool for visually exploring the data from Power Pivot and is chiefly used for finding hidden relationships within the data. Power View is an example of a **dashboard**, which is a data visualization tool containing interactive tables, charts, key performance indicators, and live maps. The term *dashboard* evokes the idea of an automobile dashboard that presents a lot of important information to the driver, except that the Power View dashboard is customizable and can present data in a wide variety of forms.

Excel automatically installed Power View with PowerPivot. To access Power View, you need to add the button to start Power View to the ribbon. Gabriel suggests you add the button to a new group on the Insert tab.

To add the Power View button to the Insert tab on the ribbon:

1. Right-click a blank area of the ribbon, and then click **Customize the Ribbon** on the shortcut menu. The Excel Options dialog box opens with the Customize Ribbon category selected.
2. In the Main Tabs box on the right side of dialog box, click **Insert**, and then below the Main Tabs box, click the **New Group** button. The Insert tab expands, listing the current groups with a new group at the bottom.
3. With New Group (Custom) selected, click the **Rename** button to open the Rename dialog box, type **Power View** in the Display name box, and then click the **OK** button.
4. Click the **Choose commands from** box, and then click **All Commands**. An alphabetical listing of all the available commands in Excel appears in the box.
5. Scroll down, and then drag the **Power View** command to the Power View (Custom) group in the Insert tab section. See Figure 11-30.

Figure 11-30 Customize Ribbon options

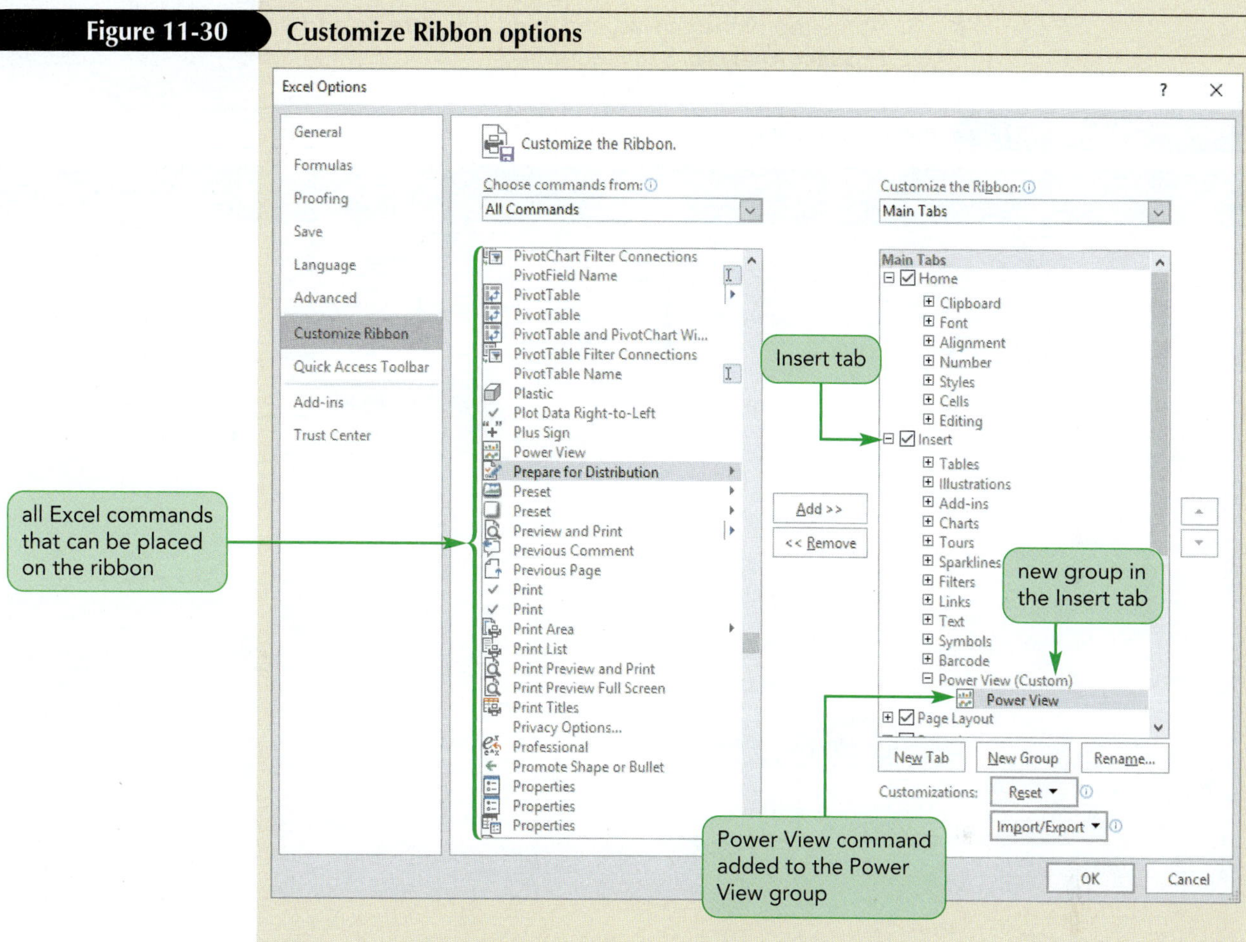

6. Click the **OK** button. The Excel Options dialog box closes.
7. On the ribbon, click the **Insert** tab, and then verify that the Power View group appears on the tab and includes the Power View button.

With the Power Viewer button added to the ribbon, you can create Power View sheets. The Power View dashboard has three main areas. The canvas displays a Power View sheet containing charts, tables, maps, and other visual elements. The Filters area contains the filters used to limit the data to specific categories of interest. The Power View Fields lists the tables and fields used in the visual elements placed on the canvas.

Keep in mind that Power View is intended for data discovery, not data presentation. Because it has minimal tools for formatting tables and charts, you should recreate any charts you plan to present using the Excel charting tools. You will create the Power View sheet for Gabriel now.

To create a Power View sheet:

1. On the Insert tab, in the Power View group, click the **Power View** button. A blank Power View sheet named Power View1 is added to the workbook.

   Trouble? If you are prompted to install or update Silverlight, click the Install Silverlight link, follow the instructions on the Microsoft website to complete the installation, return to the Product Report workbook, and then click the Reload button.

2. Rename the Power View1 sheet as **Product Analysis**.

3. At the top of the canvas, click the **Click here to add a title** text, and then type **Product Analysis**. See Figure 11-31.

Figure 11-31 Power View sheet

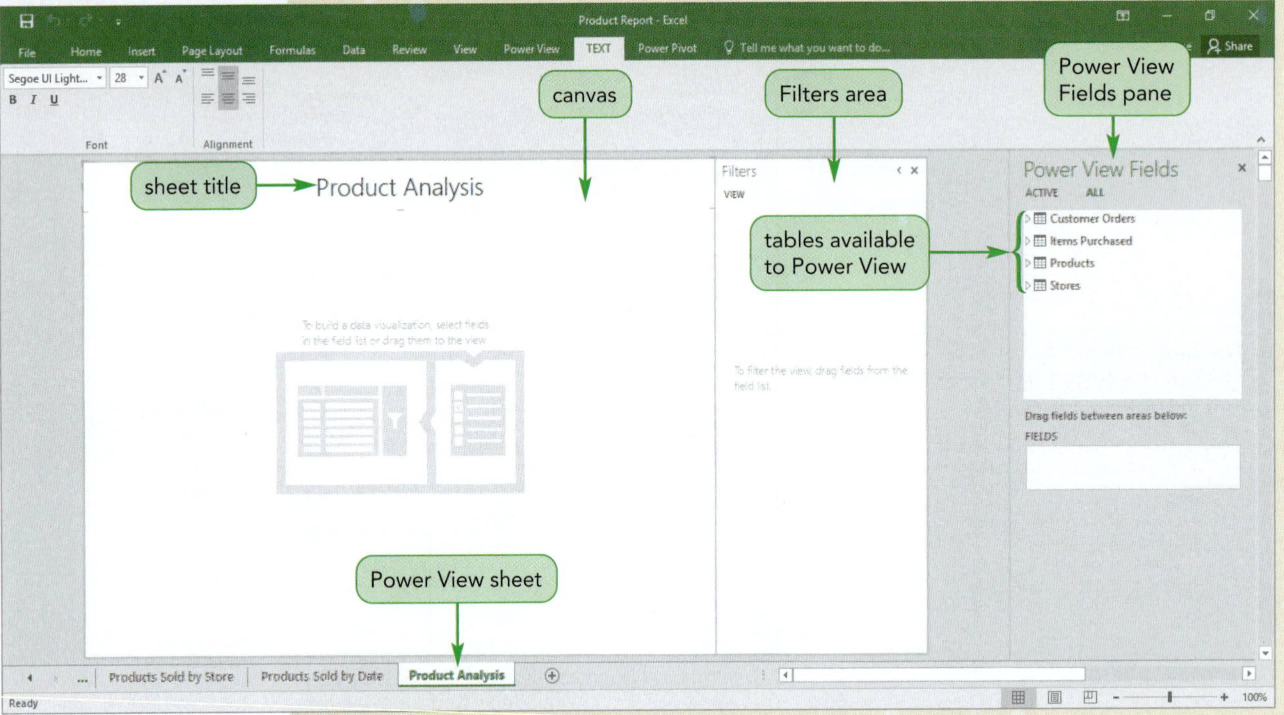

Creating a Data Visualization

Power View sheets are organized around **data visualizations**, which are the tables, charts, and maps that present data in a visual way. Every data visualization is based on fields that are placed from the Field List onto the canvas. The fields are initially displayed in a table that you can then change to a chart or map.

Fields that can be used in mapping, such as StoreCity and StoreState, appear in the FIELDS box with the globe icon. Numeric fields that can be measured, such as ItemQty, are displayed with the sigma icon Σ. By default, Excel displays the sum of the ItemQty field. You can choose a different function by clicking the field's box arrow in the FIELDS areas and clicking a different summary function.

Gabriel want you to add the StoreCity, StoreState, and ItemQty fields to the Power View sheet so you can display the total items sold for each city. Then he wants you to change this table to a bar chart with labels displaying sales for each city.

To display the total items sold by each store in a bar chart:

1. In the Power View Fields pane, click the **Expand arrow** ▷ next to the **Stores** table to display its fields, and then click the **StoreCity** and **StoreState** check boxes. The selected fields are added to the FIELDS box, and the sheet contains a table listing five World Rhythm stores.
2. In the Power View Fields pane, expand the **Items Purchased** table, and then click the **ItemQty** check box. The table expands to include the total items sold for each city. See Figure 11-32.

Figure 11-32 Items sold by city and state

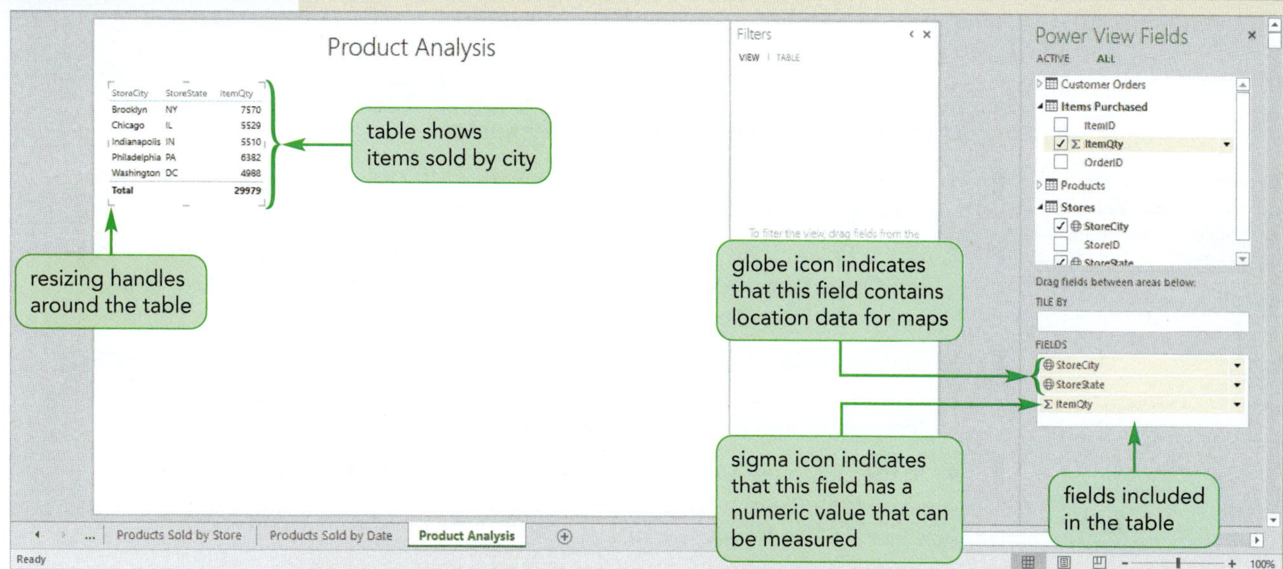

3. On the DESIGN tab, in the Switch Visualization group, click the **Bar Chart** button, and then click **Stacked Bar** as the chart type. The table data changes to a stacked bar chart.

TIP

To view detailed information about a chart element, such as a bar, position the pointer over the element.

4. Drag the resizing handles around the bar chart until the chart covers the upper-left quarter of the sheet.
5. On the ribbon, click the **LAYOUT** tab. In the Labels group, click the **Legend** button, and then click **None** to remove the legend.
6. In the Labels group, click the **Data Labels** button, and then click **Show**. The ItemQty values appear on the bars in the chart. See Figure 11-33.

Figure 11-33 Bar chart of items sold by city and state

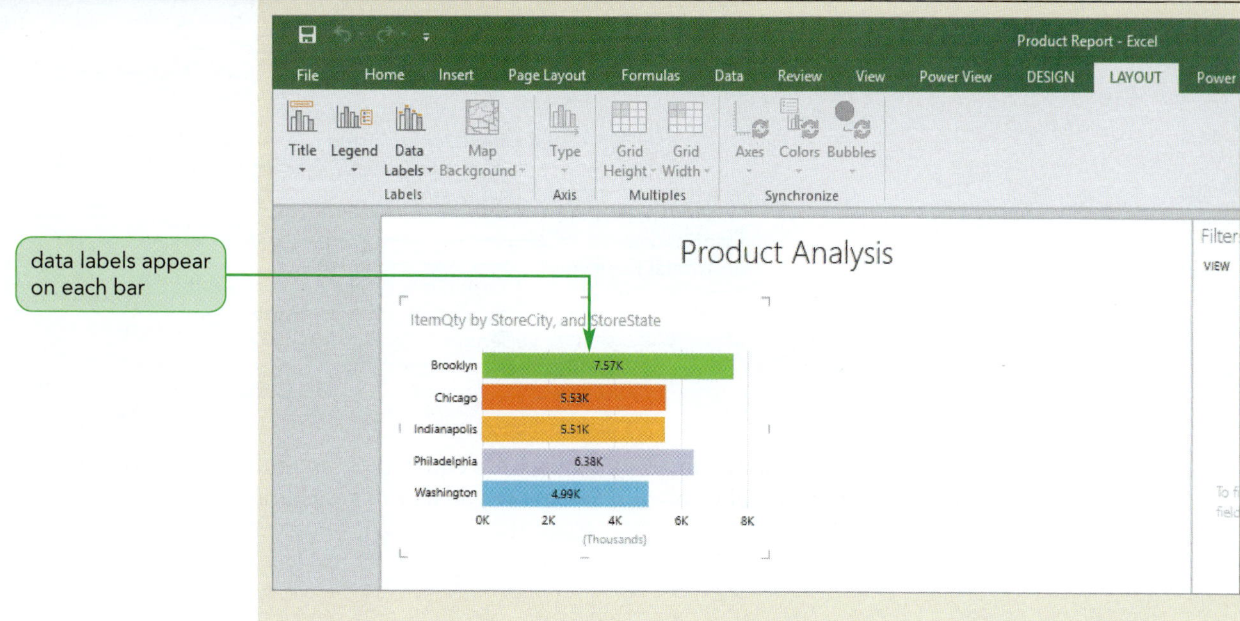

The chart clearly shows that the Brooklyn store sold the most items over the past two years, about 7,570 units. The Washington store sold the least, about 4,990 units. Next, Gabriel wants you to add a line chart that tracks the monthly sales for 2016 and 2017.

Be sure to deselect the bar chart so that fields are added as a new data visualization.

To create a line chart of monthly sales:

1. Click a blank area of the Power View sheet to deselect the bar chart. The resizing handles disappear from the bar chart.
2. In the Power View Fields pane, expand the **Customer Orders** table, select the **OrderDate (Month)** field, expand the **Items Purchased** table, and then select the **ItemQty** field.
3. On the DESIGN tab, in the Switch Visualization group, click the **Other Chart** button, and then click **Line**. The line chart that appears shows the total sales for each month over the two-year period.
4. In the Customer Orders table, select the **OrderDate (Year)** field. The OrderDate(Year) field is added as a chart legend, and the chart shows a separate line for each year.
5. Resize the chart to cover the upper-right quarter of the Power View sheet.
6. On the ribbon, click the **LAYOUT** tab. In the Labels group, click **Legend**, and then click **Show Legend at Bottom**. The legend moves to below the chart. See Figure 11-34.

Figure 11-34 Line chart of units sold versus month and year

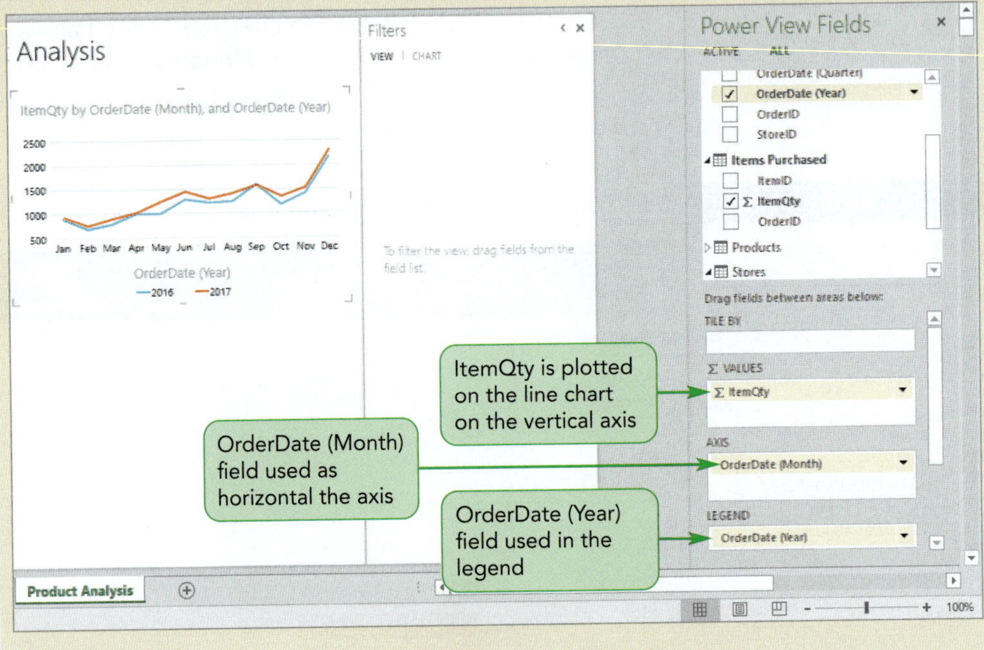

The line chart shows that 2017 sales were equal to or larger than the 2016 sales for every month. Gabriel wants you to explore whether this was true for every store.

Filtering Charts in a Power View Sheet

You could have easily created the bar and line charts using the usual Excel charting tools. However, the charts you created in Power View are linked, so that every marker on one chart acts as a filter for every other chart or map on the canvas.

Gabriel wants you to filter the line chart values based on the store selected in the bar chart.

To filter the line chart:

TIP

You can also drop a category field into the Filters area and then select the category of values to view in the charts.

1. In the bar chart, click the top bar to select the Brooklyn bar and gray out the other bars. The line chart is filtered to show only the sales in Brooklyn store. Except for July, the Brooklyn store showed a significant increase in sales from 2016 to 2017.
2. Click each of the bars representing the **Chicago**, **Philadelphia**, and **Washington** stores to select that store and deselect the others.
3. Click the **Indianapolis** bar. The Indianapolis store constantly underperformed in 2017, with its December sales significantly lagging. See Figure 11-35.

Figure 11-35 Line chart filtered

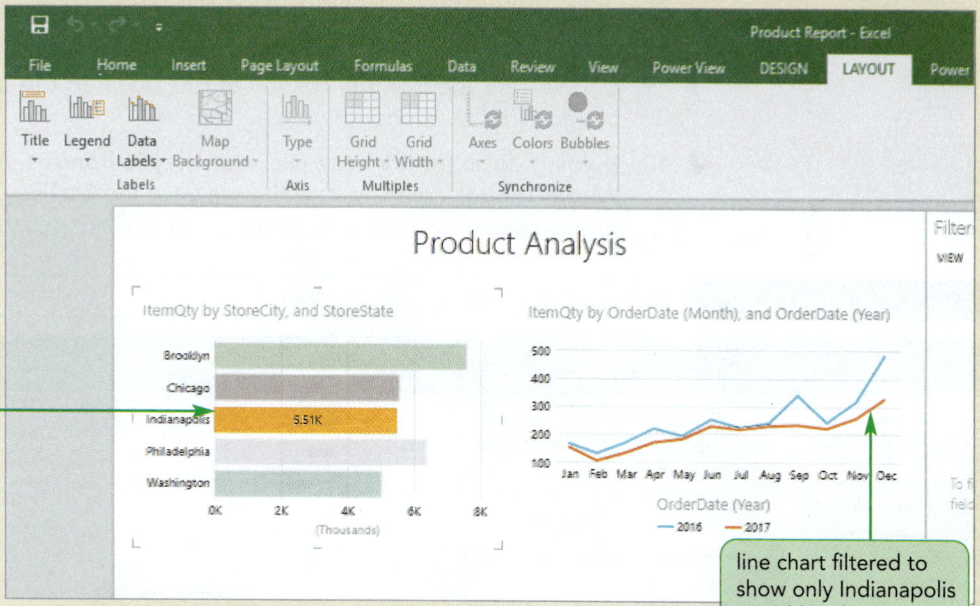

4. Click the **Indianapolis** bar to remove the filter from the Power View sheet and show the sales from all five stores.

Another way to filter the charts in a Power View sheet is to drill down into a chart. You can drill down into charts when the chart element contains a hierarchy of fields. Drilling down does not affect the other charts on the canvas—they will still display the total sales for all products. Only filtering modifies the other charts and maps. Gabriel wants you to add a stacked column chart of sales broken down by the hierarchy of product fields and then drill down the product fields.

To create the stacked column chart and drill down product sales:

1. Click an empty area of the Power View sheet to deselect the current chart.
2. Click the **ItemQty** field from the expanded Items Purchased table and the **Category** field from the expanded Products table.
3. On the DESIGN tab, in the Switch Visualization group, click the **Column Chart** button, and then click **Stacked Column** to create a column chart showing the sales broken down by product category.
4. Resize the stacked column chart so that it covers the bottom half of the sheet.
5. Drag the **Subcategory** field and then the **Description** field from the Products table to the AXIS area box within the Power View Fields pane.
6. On the ribbon, click the **LAYOUT** tab. In the Labels group, click the **Data Labels** button, and then click **Show** to display the sales within each instrument category.
7. In the column chart, click the **Drums** column. Because column chart is linked to the bar and line charts, all three charts are filtered to show only the drum sales across the five stores and for each month in 2016 and 2017.
8. Double-click the **Drums** column to drill down into the subcategories of drums. The column chart shows sales totals for 11 types of drums. Bongos are the largest seller with about 3,140 units sold over the past two years.
9. Double-click the **Bongos** column to drill down to the sales of the six types of bongos sold by World Rhythm.
10. Holding down the **Ctrl** key, click the **Acrylic Bongos**, **Natural Style**, and **Wood Bongos** columns, and then release the **Ctrl** key. The charts are filtered to show sales for the selected three types of bongos. See Figure 11-36.

Figure 11-36 **Drilling down into sales by product**

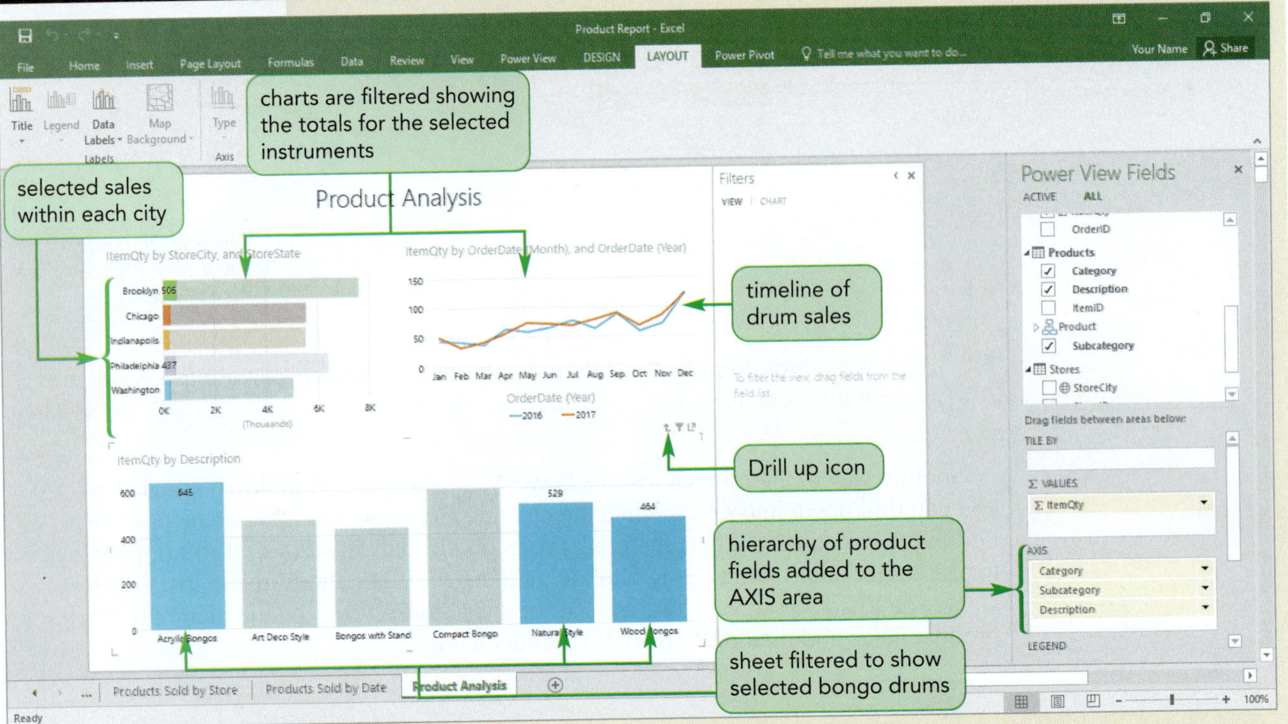

11. Point to the upper-right corner of the column chart, and then click the **Drill up** icon [t] twice to return to the top level of the hierarchy.

Next, you'll create a Power View sheet that shows sales data for each store displayed in pie charts.

Creating Multiple Charts

In Power View, you can create multiple versions of the same chart that are arranged horizontally or vertically across the canvas. The charts share a common format and are linked, so that any filtering or drilling you do in one chart also appears in the other charts.

Gabriel wants you to create a report in which product sales are displayed in pie charts with a separate chart for every store. You will do this in a new Power View Sheet.

To add multiple pie charts to a Power View sheet:

1. On the ribbon, click the **Insert** tab. In the Power View group, click the **Power View** button to insert a new sheet.
2. Rename the sheet as **Product Analysis 2**, and then add the title **Product Analysis 2** at the top of the sheet.
3. In the Power View Fields pane, select **Category** from the Products table, and then select **ItemQty** in the Items Purchased table. The two fields are added to the canvas.
4. On the DESIGN tab, in the Switch Visualization group, click the **Other Chart** button, and then click **Pie** to transform the data into a pie chart.

   Each color is the pie chart represents a different product category. Gabriel wants the entire hierarchy of product fields to be represented in the pie colors.
5. Point the **Subcategory** field in the Products table, click the **down arrow** that appears, and then click **Add as Color** on the menu. The Subcategory field is added to the COLOR area of the pie chart.
6. Repeat Step 5 to add the **Description** field to the COLOR area below the Category and Subcategory categories.
7. Point to the **StoreCity** field in the Stores table, click the **down arrow** that appears, and then click **Add to Vertical Multiples** on the menu. The pie chart is duplicated for every store, and the charts are displayed vertically on the canvas.
8. Drag the resizing handles so that the multiple pie charts fill the canvas.
9. On the ribbon, click the **LAYOUT** tab. In the Labels group, click the **Legend** button, and then click **Show Legend at Bottom**. The legend moves below the pie charts. See Figure 11-37.

TIP

You cannot add data labels to pie slices, but you can point to each slice to view its raw count and category name.

Figure 11-37 Multiple pie charts in Power View

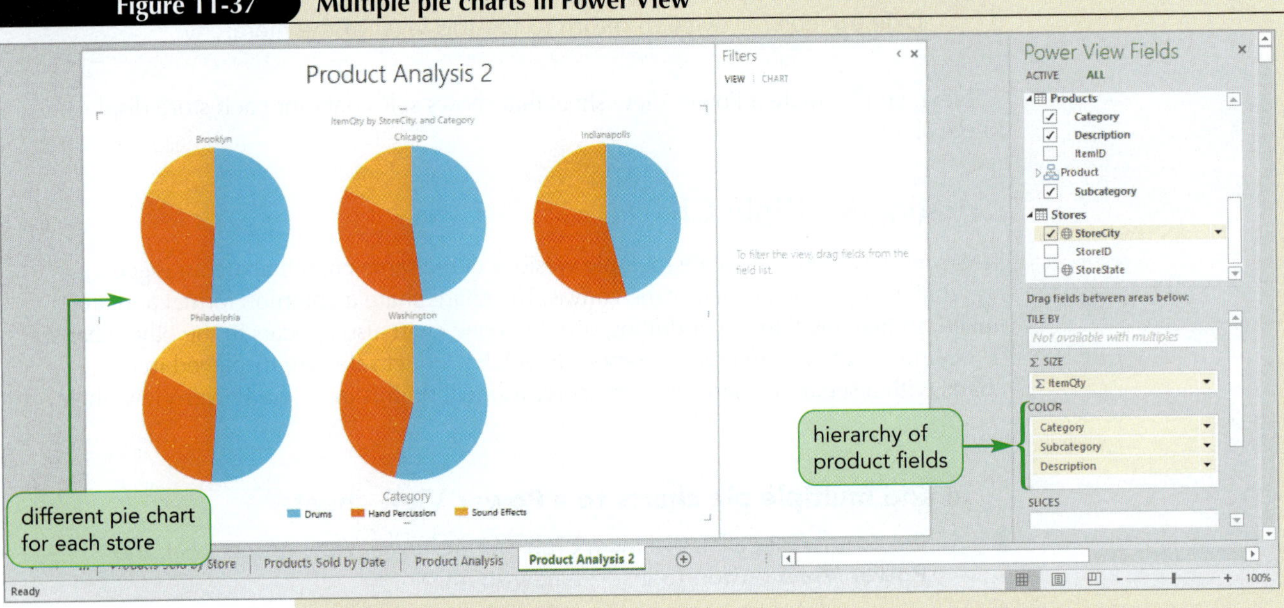

Excel lays out the charts vertically, filling each column in the allotted space and then going to the next column for the next set of charts. You can define a different chart grid by clicking the LAYOUT tab and selecting the grid layout from the Grid Height and Grid Width buttons in the Multiples group.

Gabriel notes that the breakdown of the product sales at the five stores is very similar with the Washington, DC, store perhaps selling a higher percentage of drums. He asks you to explore whether the breakdown of products is consistent from one year to the next.

To drill down and filter a column chart showing sales by year:

1. Click an empty area of the canvas to deselect the multiple pie chart visualization. The FIELDS box in the Power View Fields pane is empty, confirming you deselected the chart.
2. Click the **OrderDate (Year)** field in the Customer Orders table, and then click the **ItemQty** field in the Items Purchased table. The table of values added to the canvas is selected.
3. On the DESIGN tab, in the Switch Visualization group, click the **Column Chart** button, and then click **Stacked Column**.
4. Move the column chart to the bottom-right corner of the canvas, and then resize it so that you can easily view the columns and values.

   Next, you will drill down into the pie charts to display the breakdown of bongo drum sales by year and store.
5. In any of the five pie charts, double-click the slice representing **Drums** to display pie charts for drum categories.
6. In any of the five pie charts, double-click the slice representing **Bongos** (in the upper-right corner of each pie chart) to display pie charts for different categories of Bongo drums.

7. In the column chart, click the **2017** column to filter the charts to display only that year's data. Within each pie slice, the portion of the slice from 2017 sales is highlighted while the portion resulting from 2016 is grayed out. See Figure 11-38.

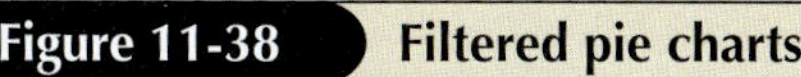

Figure 11-38 Filtered pie charts

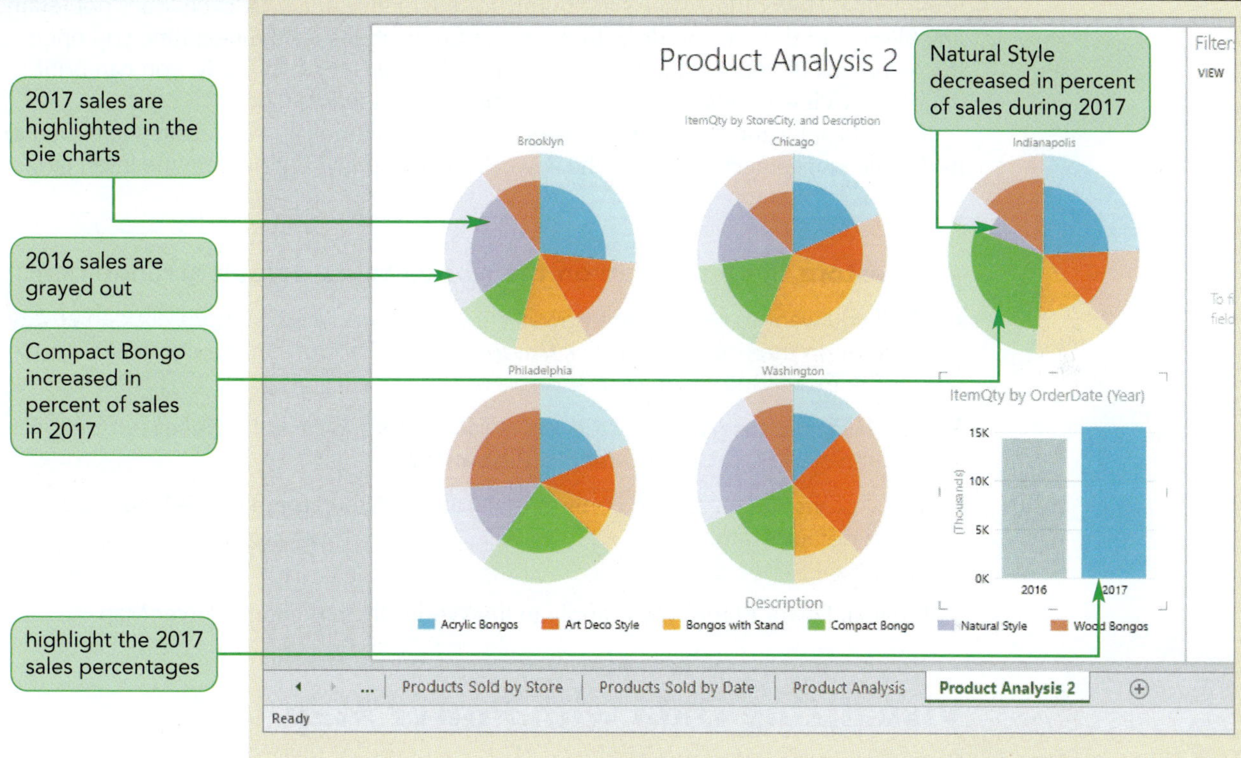

The filtered pie charts provide useful information to Gabriel about how the sales percentages per store have changed from 2016 to 2017. With filter pie charts, the size of a slice increases relative to other slices if its percentage goes up while the slice decreases as the percentage goes down. For example, the percentage of Compact Bongo drums sold at the Indianapolis store increased during 2017, as indicated by the larger area given to it relative to area of the 2016 portion. On the other hand, sales of Natural Style bongos decreased in Indianapolis during 2017 relative to the 2016 levels.

PROSKILLS

Written Communication: Data Visualization Best Practices

Data Visualization with Power View is an important tool for research and discovering trends and relationships. When choosing a data visualization for your audience, you want your pictures to tell a story; but be careful not to let the picture distort the data. Always consider what information the reader needs. Choose a visualization that presents the information readers need without cluttering a chart with secondary details.

Successful data visualizations will give readers an *aha* moment as they intuitively grasp an important facet of your data and its implications. Your primary goal is to ensure that what readers take away from a Power View sheet is clear, accurate, and meaningful.

You have completed your work with Power View. Before you continue, you'll save the workbook.

To close the Power View sheet and save the workbook:

1. Click the **Documentation** sheet tab to go to the Documentation sheet, closing the Power View sheet.
2. Save the workbook, but leave it open.

Note that Power View sheets are purely for interactive analysis. Excel does not retain any filtering or drilling you do with the data visualizations for the next time you open the workbook. If you want to preserve data explorations for later study, you can print your Power View sheets using the Print command on the File tab.

If you do not want to work with Power View in the future, you can restore the ribbon to its default arrangement, removing the Power View group and button from the Insert tab.

To restore the Insert tab on the ribbon to its default arrangement:

1. If you want to remove the Power View group and button, right-click an empty spot on the ribbon, and click **Customize the Ribbon** on the shortcut menu. The Excel Options dialog box opens.
2. Make sure **Insert** is selected in the Main tabs list, click the **Reset** button, and then click **Reset only selected Ribbon Tab**.
3. Click the **OK** button to confirm that you want to change of the Insert tab to its default state.

The final Power BI tool you'll apply to the World Rhythm data is Power Map.

Visualizing Data with Power Map

Power Map is a 3-D visualization tool for charting data against a virtual globe. Using Power Map, you can often discover insights into data that might be hidden in other charts and diagrams. Like Power View, Power Map is an add-in that was installed when you activated PowerPivot.

A Power Map map is not displayed as sheet within the workbook. Instead, it opens within a new window containing its own ribbon and menu commands. However, like the Data Model, a Power Map map is attached within the workbook and can be accessed at any time using the Power Map tools.

The Power Map window is organized into four sections: The Tour Editor contains the list of maps in the Power Map window, each of which is called a **tour**. The Map pane displays the map of the data and includes controls to rotate and zoom in or out of the map. The Field Lists window contains the list of tables and fields that can be applied to the map. The Layer pane contains the fields used to construct a layout of graphic objects over the map. A single map can contain multiple layers.

Gabriel wants to see a map showing the location of the customers who purchased products from World Rhythm over the past two years. You will create a 3-D map using Power Map to display customer zip codes, which are stored in the CustZipCode field in the Customer Orders table.

To use Power Map to display customer locations by zip codes:

1. On the ribbon, click the **Insert** tab, and then in the Tours group, click the **3D Map** button. The Power Map window opens, showing a world map and a list of tables and fields in the Data Model.
2. In the Field List box, drag the **CustZipCode** field from the Customer Orders table into the Location box in the Layer pane. Power Map begins to populate the map with a marker for each location of a World Rhythm customer. See Figure 11-39. Note that your map might differ slightly from the map shown in the figure.

Figure 11-39 Map of World Rhythm customers

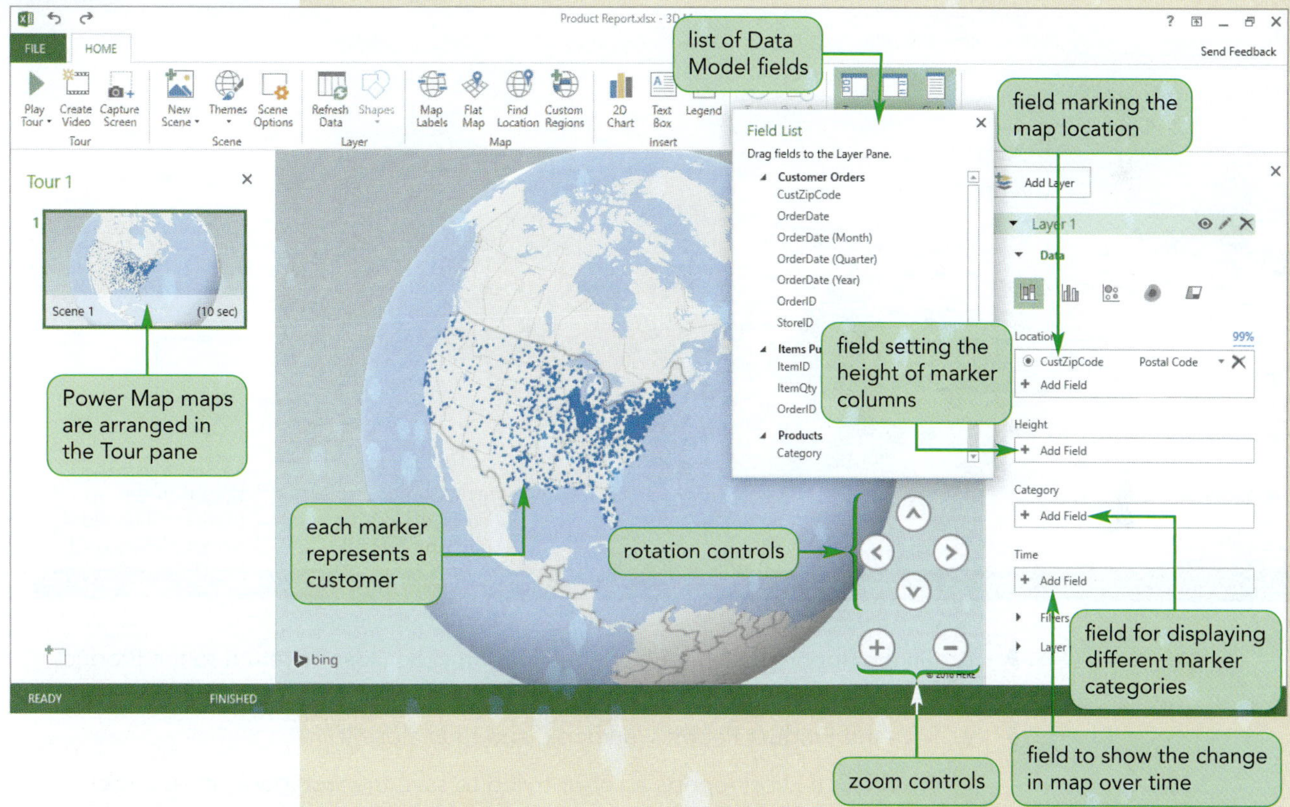

Gabriel asks you change the markers representing each customer to columns whose heights represents the total number of items ordered by customers at each zip code.

3. Drag the **ItemQty** field from the Items Purchased table into the Height box in the Layer pane.
4. Drag the **StoreCity** field from the Stores table into the Category box in the Layer pane to display the stores handling the customer orders in different colors.
5. Click the **Zoom in** button ⊕ to zoom into the map.

TIP

To view the map in a full screen, click the Play Tour button in the Tour group on the Home tab.

6. Use the rotational controls to rotate the map view in three dimensions, moving the viewpoint to above the Eastern seaboard of the United States, looking toward the northwest and use the zoom controls to zoom into the map.
7. Resize the Layer 1 box so that you can view more of the map, and then click the **Tour Editor** and **Field List** buttons in the View group on the HOME tab to close both the Tour Editor pane and the Field List box. See Figure 11-40.

Figure 11-40 Customer locations from the five World Rhythm stores

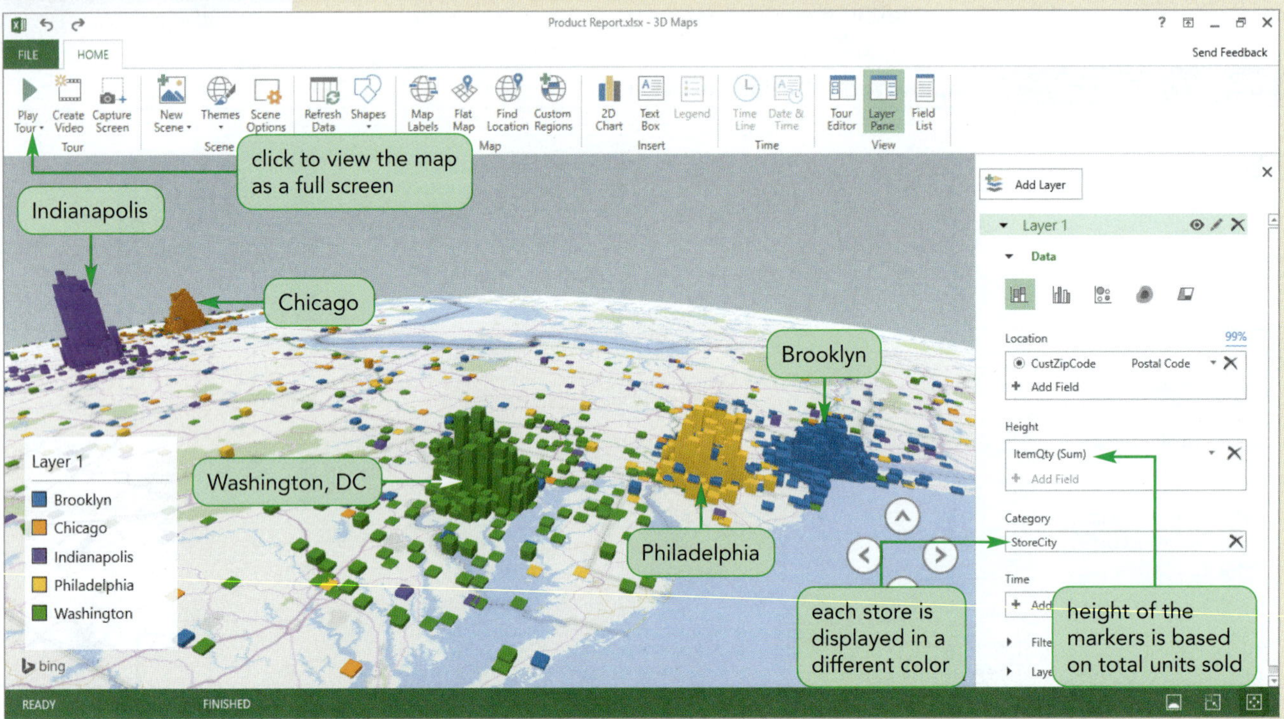

8. On the ribbon, click the **FILE** tab, and then click **Close** to return to the Product Report workbook.
9. Save the Product Report workbook, and then close it.

Trouble? If Excel reports an error trying to save the workbook, close Excel and then restart it. Repeat Steps 1 through 9 to create and save the Power Map map.

TIP

To use geographic regions such as countries, states, or counties as markers, select the Region visualization in the Layer pane.

Most items are sold to customers near locations of the five World Rhythm stores, though many items still are sold to customers across the country. Although the Indianapolis store had the lowest sales, it has the highest columns, which means that sales are more concentrated in the Indianapolis area. On the other hand, even though Brooklyn store had the highest sales, its customer base is more widespread geographically.

You have finished extracting data from a variety of data sources and finding patterns and relationships within those data. Gabriel will use your work as a foundation for his report about World Rhythm sales and the preferences of its customers.

REVIEW

Session 11.3 Quick Check

1. What does Excel do automatically when a date field from the Data Model is added to a PivotTable?
2. What is a hierarchy? How do you add a hierarchy to a data table within the Data Model?
3. How do you drill down into a PivotTable?
4. How do you customize the ribbon in Excel?
5. What is Power View?
6. What happens when you select a chart marker within a Power View sheet?
7. What is Power Map?

PRACTICE

Review Assignments

Data Files needed for the Review Assignments: Sales.xlsx, Sales History.csv, WR Data.accdb

Gabriel wants you to create a workbook examining sales data drawn from several data sources. In this report, he wants to analyze two-year sales data from three product categories—cymbals, drum sets, and gongs. You will write a query to retrieve the data and combine the data within Power Pivot. You will then create a PivotTable to summarize the results, a Power View sheet for data exploration, and a Power Map to present the data geographically. Complete the following:

1. Open the **Sales** workbook located in the Excel11 > Review folder included with your Data Files, and then save the workbook as **Sales Report** in the location specified by your instructor.
2. In the Documentation worksheet, enter your name and the date.
3. In the Sale History worksheet, construct a query to retrieve the Year, Business Year, and Units Sold columns from the **Sales History** CSV file located in the Excel11 > Review folder. Load the data into an Excel table, starting at cell A4 of the Sales History worksheet.
4. Format the Units Sold data in Comma style with no decimal places.
5. Create a scatter chart of Units Sold versus Business Year, and then resize and move it to cover the range D4:K18 in the Sales History worksheet. Add a logarithmic trendline to the chart, projecting the next five years of sales for the company. Remove the chart legend.
6. In the Current Sales worksheet, use the Query Editor to access the **WR Data** Access database file located in the Excel11 > Review folder. Create a query that accesses the Customer Transactions table, and then do the following:
   a. Remove all of the columns except for the Date and Revenue columns.
   b. Change the format of the Date column from Text to Date.
   c. Create a new column named **Month** containing the end-of-month date for each record in the table.
   d. Group the table by the values of the Month column, creating a new column named **Monthly Revenue** containing the sum of the values in the Revenue column.
   e. Name the query **Monthly Revenue**.
   f. Close and load the 2 columns and 24 rows from the query as a table into the Current Sales worksheet starting at cell A4.
   g. Format the Monthly Revenue values as currency with no decimal places.
7. Create a forecast sheet of the Month and Monthly Revenue values through 12/31/2018, assuming a 12-month seasonal trend in the data and a 95 percent confidence interval around the forecasts. Name the sheet containing the forecasted values as **Forecasted Revenue**, and move it after the Current Sales worksheet. Format the sheet so that the chart and values are easy to read and interpret.
8. Use the Query Editor to create queries that load the following data from the **WR Data** Access database file located in the Excel11 > Review folder into the Data Model (but only create a connection to the data; do *not* create an Excel table):
   a. From the Customer Transactions table, retrieve the OrderID, Date, StoreID, and CustZip columns. Change the data type of the Date column from Text to Date.
   b. From the Items table, retrieve the ItemID, Category, Subcategory, and Instrument columns.
   c. From the Product Purchases table, retrieve the OrderID, ItemID, and ItemRevenue columns.
   d. From the Stores table, retrieve the StoreID, StoreCity, and StoreState columns.

9. In Power Pivot, connect the Customer Transactions table to the Product Purchases table through the OrderID field, connect the Product Purchases table to the Items table through the ItemID field, and then connect the Customer Transactions table to the Stores table through the StoreID field.
10. Insert a PivotTable in cell A4 of the Sales Summary worksheet. Place the Date field from the Customer Transactions table in the Rows area. Place the sum of the ItemRevenue field from the Product Purchases table in the Values area. Change the name of the field to **Revenue**, and display the values in Currency format with no decimal places.
11. Return to Power Pivot. In the Items table, create the Products hierarchy containing the Category, Subcategory, and Instrument fields in that order. In the Customer Transactions table, create the Dates hierarchy containing the Date (Year), Date (Quarter), Date (Month), and Date fields.
12. Return to the PivotTable. Replace the fields in the Rows area with the Dates hierarchy. Place the Products hierarchy in the Columns area. Drill down the PivotTable to show only the October, November, and December 2017 sales for the four instruments within the Drum Sets category and Hi-Hat subcategory.
13. Create Power View sheet named **Sales Analysis** and then do the following:
    a. Add the sheet title **Sales Analysis**.
    b. Create a bar chart in the upper-left quarter of the sheet showing the sum of the ItemRevenue field by StoreCity. Add labels to the bar chart displaying the sales values.
    c. Create a line chart in the upper-right corner of the sheet displaying ItemRevenue versus Date (Month) with Date (Year) as the legend to show different lines for different years.
    d. Create a column chart showing the value of the ItemRevenue field with the Category, Subcategory, and Instrument fields in the AXIS area. Add labels to the column chart displaying the sales values.
    e. Drill down into the column chart to display the five types of drum sets.
    f. Filter the sheet to show the sales revenue from only the Hi-Hat subcategory of drum sets.
    g. Using the Print command on the File tab, print the current appearance of the Power View sheet scaled to a single page.
14. Create a Power View sheet titled **Store Analysis**, and then do the following:
    a. Create a pie chart using ItemRevenue in the Size area and the Category, Subcategory, and Instrument fields in the COLOR area.
    b. Add the StoreCity field to the Vertical Multiples area to create different pie charts for every store. Resize the visualization to fit the entire sheet.
    c. Drill into the pie charts to show the breakdown of drum set sales by subcategory (Crash, Hi-Hat, Ice Bell, Special, and Splash).
    d. Print a copy of the Power View sheet showing your data exploration scaled to a single page.
15. Add the following Power Map to the workbook to show the location of the customers for this line of World Rhythm products:
    a. Use the CustZip field as the map location.
    b. Use the ItemRevenue field to set the height of each map marker.
    c. Use the StoreCity field as the category to set the color of the markers.
    d. Rotate and zoom into the map to better show relative heights of the markers as viewed from the west of Chicago.
16. Close the Power Map window, and then save and close the Excel workbook.

APPLY

Case Problem 1

Data Files needed for this Case Problem: Coronado.xlsx, Creamery Tables.accdb

Coronado Creamery George Brown is the owner of Coronado Creamery, an ice cream shop located near Coronado Beach outside of San Diego, California. He is considering expanding his successful business but wants to analyze sales data from the shop's last four years of operation. He wants to explore how customer preferences for different dessert products have changed during that time and what factors influence the size of customer traffic. Complete the following:

1. Open the **Coronado** workbook located in the Excel11 > Case1 folder included with your Data Files, and then save the workbook as **Coronado Creamery** in the location specified by your instructor.
2. In the Documentation worksheet, enter your name and the date.
3. In the Monthly Sales worksheet, construct a query to retrieve data from the Daily Orders table in **Creamery Tables** Access database file located in the Excel11 > Case1 folder, and then do the following:
   a. Remove all of the columns except for the Date and Orders columns.
   b. Change the format of the Date column from Date/Time to Date.
   c. Add a column containing the last day of each month from the dates in the Date column, and then rename the column as **Month**.
   d. Group the data by the Month column, adding a new column named **Average Monthly Orders** that displays the average of the values in the Orders column.
   e. Change the name of the query to **Average Monthly Orders** and then load the query data to an Excel table starting at cell A4 in the Monthly Sales worksheet.
   f. Format the average monthly order values in the range B5:B52 to one decimal place.
4. Use the data in the range A4:B52 to create a forecast sheet that projects the average daily sales through 12/31/2018, assuming a 12-monthly seasonal pattern and a 90 percent confidence interval for the forecast. Name the worksheet **Forecasted Sales** and then resize the forecast chart to cover the range C2:E21. Move the Forecasted Sales worksheet after the Monthly Sales worksheet.
5. Construct queries to the Daily Orders, Products List, and Product Orders tables located in the **Creamery Tables** Access database file, only creating a connection to the data source and adding the data to the Data Model.
6. Go to the Data Model in Power Pivot, and link the Daily Orders table to the Product Orders table through the Date field. Link the Product Orders table to the Product List table through the ProductType field.
7. Insert the following PivotTable in cell A4 of the Daily Orders worksheet using the Data Model to show average customer orders by date and product type:
   a. Place the Customer Orders field from the Product Orders table in the Values area of the table. Change the value field settings so that the average of the field is displayed using a number format with no decimal places.
   b. Place the Date field from the Daily Orders in the Rows area. Excel generates the Date (Year), Date (Quarter) and Date (Month) fields, outlining the PivotTable.
   c. Place the Product Name column from the Product List table in the Columns area.
   d. Use the Grand Totals button in the Layout group on the PivotTable Tools Design tab to turn off grand totals for both rows and columns.
   e. Expand the Date outline for each of the four years to show the quarterly sales averages.

8. George wants to examine how the average number of orders placed each day varies throughout the year and the week. Insert a Power View sheet with the title **Product Report** and then create the following data visualizations to explore how average sales change throughout the year and the week:
   a. In the upper-left quarter of the sheet, create a line chart of the average of the Orders field from the Daily Orders table plotted against the Date (Month) field. Add a legend using the Date (Year) field so that separate lines are plotted for each year. (*Hint*: Display the average customer order by selecting Average from the list of measures in the Values area.)
   b. Compare weekday and weekend sales by creating a stacked bar chart of the average of the Orders field with the Weekend field from the Daily Orders table as the chart axis. Show data labels on the chart. Place the chart in the upper-right quarter of the sheet.
   c. George wants to examine how the average orders vary by product and year. In the bottom half of the sheet, create a column chart of the average of the Customer Orders field from the Product Orders table and the Product Name field from the Product List table in the chart axis. Show data labels on the chart. Show multiple copies of this chart by adding the Date (Year) field from the Daily Orders table to the Vertical Multiples area.
   d. Print a copy of your Power View sheet scaled to a single page.
9. George wants to explore whether weather plays a role in sales. Insert a Power View sheet with the name and title **Weather Effects**, and then create the following visualizations:
   a. In the lower-left corner of the sheet, construct a bar chart that displays the average of the Orders field against the Weather field from the Daily Orders table. Show data labels on the chart.
   b. In the right half of the sheet, construct a scatter chart with the MaxTemp field from the Daily Orders table as the *x*-value, the Orders field as the *y*-value, the Date field in the Details area, and the Weather field in the Color area. (Because of the size of the dataset, Power View shows only a representative sample in the scatter chart.)
   c. Print a copy of the Power View sheet scaled to a single page.
10. Save the workbook, and then close it.

APPLY

Case Problem 2

Data Files needed for this Case Problem: Food.xlsx, Foodborne Illness.accdb

Food Safety Monitors Leah Simpson is a researcher at Food Safety Monitors, a nonprofit advocacy group to help prevent the spread of foodborne illness from tainted foods and inadequate preparation. She has asked your help in developing an Excel workbook that tracks incidents of food poisoning from the past seventeen years. Leah wants to explore the relationship between the type of foodborne illness, the food consumed, and the meal location. She also wants to compare the rate of foodborne illnesses between states during the 17-year period. Complete the following:

1. Open the **Food** workbook located in the Excel11 > Case2 folder included with your Data Files, and then save the workbook as **Food Safety Monitors** in the location specified by your instructor.
2. In the Documentation worksheet, enter your name and the date.
3. In the Annual Incidents worksheet, create the following query to extract the annual incidents of foodborne illnesses:
   a. Connect to the **Foodborne Illness** Access database file located in the Excel11 > Case2 folder, and then select the Illness table.
   b. Remove all of the columns from the query except the Date and Illnesses columns.
   c. Add a column named **Year** containing the year value for each record. (*Hint*: In the Add Column tab, click the Date button, and then select Year as the value to create.)

d. Group the data by the Year column, creating a new column named **Foodborne Illnesses** that contains the sum of the Illnesses field.

e. Change the name of the query to **Annual Illnesses**.

f. Load the query data into an Excel table starting with cell A4 in the Annual Incidents worksheet.

g. In the range B5:B21, format the values to add a thousands separator and display no decimal places.

4. Create a scatter chart of Foodborne Illnesses vs. Year in the range C4:J21, and add a trendline to the chart with an exponential curve. Format the chart to make it easy to read and interpret.
5. Create queries to the contents of the following tables in the Foodborne Illness Access database: Food Lookup, Genus Species Lookup, Genus Subspecies Lookup, Illness, and Meal Location Lookup. Have each query create a connection to the data and load the data in the Data Model, but do not create Excel tables in the workbook. (*Hint*: To quickly load all five database tables, click the Select multiple items check box in the Navigator dialog box, and then select each table to load into the Data Model.)
6. In Power Pivot, use common fields to link the Illness table to the Genus Species Lookup, Genus Subspecies Lookup, Meal Location Lookup, and Food Lookup tables.
7. Leah wants detailed information on the annual incidents of different types of foodborne illnesses. In the Incidents by Year worksheet, insert a PivotTable at cell A4 displaying the sum of the Illnesses field from the Illness table broken down by the Genus Species field from the Genus Species Lookup table in the COLUMNS area and the Date field from the Illness table in the ROWS area. Format the Sum of Illnesses value using a thousands separator and no decimal places.
8. Leah also wants to know the food origin of these illnesses. In the Incidents by Food Group worksheet, create a PivotTable starting in cell A4 that displays the sum of the Illnesses field broken down by the Genus Species field in the COLUMNS area and the Food Group field in the ROWS area. Format the Sum of Illnesses value using a thousands separator with no decimal places.
9. Leah wants a breakdown of the illness by meal location. In the Incidents by Location worksheet, create a PivotTable that shows the sum of the Illnesses field broken down by the Genus Species field (COLUMNS area) and the Meal Location field (ROWS area). Format the Sum of Illnesses value using a thousands separator with no decimal places.
10. Insert a Power View sheet with the sheet name and title **Foodborne Illnesses**, and then add the following data visualizations:

    a. In the top half of the sheet, create a column chart of the Illnesses field with the Genus Species and Genus Subspecies fields in the chart axis. Show data labels on chart.

    b. In the lower-left corner, create a column chart of the Illnesses field plotted against the Food Group field. Show data labels on the chart.

    c. In the lower-right corner, create column chart of the Illnesses field plotted against the Meal Location field. Show data labels on the chart.

11. Verify that you can filter the Power View sheet by any of the genus species, food groups, or meal locations. Also, verify that you can drill into the column chart of the genus species to view illness by the genus subspecies.
12. Leah wants to know which states have the highest annual average of foodborne illnesses. Create a Power Map selecting the Region visualization (the last visualization option in the first row of the Layout Pane). Place the State field in the Location box and the Illnesses field in the Value box. Change the summary measure of the Illnesses field from Sum to Average. States with higher averages of foodborne illness will appear in a dark shade on the map.
13. Save the workbook, and then close it.

CHALLENGE

Case Problem 3

Data Files needed for this Case Problem: Forctis.xlsx, Forctis Sales.csv, Forctis Stores.csv, Forctis Products.csv

Forctis Sport Ray Stohler is a sales analyst at Forctis Sport, a chain of sporting goods stores located in the western United States. Ray is working on a sales report that will detail customer purchases of Forctis Sport's line of cycling products. He has CSV files with two years of sales data. Ray wants you to compare website sales with brick-and-mortar store sales over that period. He also wants you to explore whether growing interest in women's cycling apparel is reflected in clothing sales at the company. Complete the following:

1. Open the **Forctis** workbook located in the Excel11 > Case3 folder included with your Data Files, and then save the workbook as **Forctis Sport** in the location specified by your instructor.
2. In the Documentation worksheet, enter your name and the date.
3. In the Sales Trend worksheet, use the Query Editor to connect to the **Forctis Sales** CSV file located in the Excel11 > Case3 folder, and then do the following:
   a. Remove all columns except the Sales Date and Revenue columns.
   b. Create a column named **Month** that stores the end-of-month date for each transaction.
   c. Group the data by the Month column, creating a new column named **Monthly Revenue** that displays the sum of the revenue values for each of the 24 months in the data.
   d. Change the name of the query to **Monthly Revenue** and then load the query to an Excel table, starting in cell A4 of the Sales Trend worksheet.
   e. Format the monthly revenue values in the range B5:B28 as currency with no decimal places.
4. In the Sales Trend worksheet, insert a scatter chart with straight lines of the data in the range A4:B28 resized to cover the range C4:L22. Format the chart so that it is easy to read and interpret.
5. Add a linear trendline to the chart to highlight the general trend of the monthly sales over the past two years, even with the seasonal variation in sales.
6. Based on the data in the range A4:B28, create a forecast sheet named **Revenue Forecast** that projects monthly sales up to 12/31/2020 assuming a 12-month seasonal period and including a 95 percent confidence interval for the projections. Resize the forecast chart to cover the range C2:E23. Note that the increasingly wider confidence band around the projected values indicates that the forecast is less precise farther into the future. Move the worksheet after the Sales Trend sheet.
7. Create the following queries, only creating a connection and loading the data in the Data Model:
   a. Access the **Forctis Sales** CSV file. Delete the Changed Type step that the Query Editor generates, and then insert a new step that sets the data type of the Sales Date column to Date, the Units Sold column to Whole Number, and the Revenue column to Decimal Number. Retrieve all of the columns in the file.
   b. From the **Fortis Stores** CSV file, retrieve all of the columns except Street, Phone, and Manager.
   c. From the **Forctis Products** CSV file, retrieve all of the columns except the Unit Price column.
8. Define the following table relationships: Connect the Forctis Sales and Forctis Stores table through the StoreID field. Connect the Forctis Sales and Forctis Products through the ProductID field.

9. In the Product Revenue worksheet, starting in cell A4, insert a PivotTable that displays the sum of the Revenue field from the Forctis Sales table broken down by the Sales Date field in the ROWS area and the Group field in the COLUMNS area. Format the revenue values as currency with no decimal places.
10. Open to the Data Model in Power Pivot, and then create the following hierarchies in the specified order:
    a. In the Forctis Sales table, create the **Date** hierarchy containing the Sales Date (Year), Sales Date (Quarter), Sales Date (Month), and Sales Date fields.
    b. In the Forctis Stores table, create the **Location** hierarchy containing the StoreType, Region, State, and City State fields.
    c. In the Forctis Products table, create the **Product** hierarchy containing the Group, Subgroup, and Product Description fields.
11. Insert a PivotTable in cell A4 of the Products and Locations worksheet, breaking down the total revenue by the Product hierarchy (COLUMNS area) and the Location hierarchy (ROWS area). Drill down into the table so that it displays sales of men's and women's jackets for the three Colorado stores. Format the sum of the Revenue field as currency with no decimal places.
12. Insert a Power View sheet with the name and title **Sales Report** and then add the following visualizations:
    a. In the left half of the sheet, display a table containing the StoreType, Region, City State, and Revenue fields from the Forctis Stores and Forctis Sales tables. Format the revenue values as currency with no decimal places. (*Hint*: Select any revenue value in the Revenue column, and then apply the Currency format from the Number group on the DESIGN tab.)
    b. In the upper-right quarter of the sheet, insert a bar chart displaying the values of the Revenue field with all of the fields in the Location hierarchy from the Forctis Stores table in the AXIS area of the chart to enable the user to drill down into the chart from StoreType down to City State. Show data labels on the chart.
    c. In the bottom-right quarter of the sheet, insert a column chart displaying sales revenue with all of the fields from the Product hierarchy in AXIS area. Show data labels on the chart.
    d. Drill down into the bar chart to show the revenue values broken down by the four sales regions (Midwest, Mountain, Pacific, and Southwest) for brick-and-mortar stores. Use the column chart to filter the table and bar chart, showing the revenue from only clothing sales.
    e. Print the Power View sheet in its current form scaled to a single page.
13. Ray wants to explore how sales have been impacted by the company's website. Insert a Power View sheet, rename the sheet as **Website Sales**, add the title **Website Sales**, and then do the following:
    a. In the upper-left quarter of the sheet, create a line chart of revenue with the Sales Date (Year) field on the chart axis and the StoreType field as the chart legend. Place the legend below the line chart.
    b. In the upper-right quarter of the sheet, create a pie chart of revenue with the slice colors defined by the Product hierarchy in the Forctis Products table. Place the legend below the chart.
    c. In the bottom half of the sheet, create multiple column chart versions of the sales revenue with the StoreType field as chart axis and the Sales Date (Year) field defining the vertical multiples. Show data labels on the chart.
    d. In the pie chart, click the Clothing slice so that the sheet compares website and brick-and-mortar store sales only for Forctis Sport's line of cycling clothing.
    e. Print the Power View sheet in its current form scaled to a single page.

Explore 14. Insert a Power View sheet with the name and title **Clothing Sales**. This sheet will explore clothing sales by gender. Drag the Gender field from the Forctis Products table into the Filters Area. From the list of Gender categories, select only the Men and Women check boxes to display data only on items specifically designed for men and women. Add the following visualizations to the Clothing Sales sheet:

a. In the top half of the sheet, insert a column chart displaying sales revenue. Add the Subgroup and Product Description fields to the chart axis, and add data labels to the chart columns.

b. In the bottom-right quarter, insert a line chart plotting revenue against the Sales Date (Year) field with the Gender field as the chart legend to show different lines for men's and women's clothing sales over the past two years.

c. In the bottom-left quarter, insert a pie chart of revenue with the pie slice colors set by the Gender field. Create separate pie charts for each year by adding the Sales Date (Year) field to the Vertical Multiples area.

d. In the column chart, click the **Shoes** subgroup to filter the other charts to show only shoe sales.

e. Print the Power View sheet in its current form scaled to a single page.

Explore 15. Create the following Power Map of the sales data to determine where most of the Forctis customers are located:

- Use the CustState field, containing each customer's state of residence, as the marker location in the map.
- Change the map visualization to Region so that Power Map fills in markers based on state borders.
- Use the sum of the sales revenue as the marker value so that states with larger customer bases are highlighted in darker colors.
- Click the 2D Chart button in the Insert group on the HOME tab to add a column chart showing the states with the largest number of Forctis Sport customers.

16. Close the Power Map window, and then save and close the Excel workbook.

CHALLENGE

Case Problem 4

Data Files needed for this Case Problem: Aviary.xlsx, Bird Data.csv, Migration Data.csv

Aviary Unlimited Dixie Eberle is a researcher at Aviary Unlimited, a nonprofit company dedicated to preservation of endangered bird species. Part of her research is tracking migratory routes. She has compiled migration data from eight turkey vultures (*Cathartes aura*) tracked with GPS monitors for one year. She wants you to import this data into Excel and analyze the migration data, learning what route the birds followed during the year and how far each bird traveled in its journeys. Complete the following:

1. Open the **Aviary** workbook located in the Excel11 > Case4 folder included with your Data Files, and then save the workbook as **Aviary Unlimited** in the location specified by your instructor.
2. In the Documentation worksheet, enter your name and the date.
3. Create a query that retrieves the data on the eight birds in the **Bird Data** CSV file located in the Excel11 > Case4 folder. Remove the Species, Tracking, and Tracker columns. Create only a connection to the data and load it into the Data Model.

Explore 4. Create a query that retrieves the detailed information on each bird's movements from 9/1/2016 to 8/31/2017 in the **Migration Data** CSV file located in the Excel11 > Case 4 folder. Within the query, create a new column named **Date** that contains only the date value from the DateTime column. (*Hint*: Select the DateTime column, click the Date button in the From Date & Time group on the Add Column tab, and then click Date Only.) Drag the Date column to between the Tag and DateTime columns to reorder the columns. Create only a connection to the data source and load it into the Data Model.

5. Define the table relation between the Bird Data and Migration Data tables using Tag as the common field.
6. In the Migration Distance worksheet, insert a PivotTable in cell A4, displaying the sum of the distance in miles traveled by the birds broken down by the Tag field in the COLUMNS area and the Date field in the ROWS area. Expand the ROWS outline to show the monthly distance totals for each bird. Display the sum using a thousands separator with no decimal places.
7. Create a line PivotChart of the monthly distance totals, covering the range K4:T25. Format the chart so that it is easy to read and interpret.
8. In the Wingspan Analysis sheet, insert a PivotTable in cell A4, displaying the sum of the migration distance broken down by the Wingspan filed in the ROWS area. Use the Report Layout button in the Layout group on the PivotTable Tools Design tab to change the report layout to tabular form and remove grand totals from the PivotTable. Format the distance values using a thousands separator with no decimal places.
9. Dixie wants a scatter chart comparing distance and wingspan, but Excel does not allow scatter charts with PivotTables. Copy the data from the PivotTable, and paste the values only into the range D4:E12 of the worksheet. Format the values to make them easier to read. Insert a scatter chart of the wingspan and distance data covering the range A15:E29. Format the chart appropriately.
10. Add a trendline to the scatter chart assuming a Power trend between wingspan and total annual distance flown. Project the trendline curve backward 0.9 units and forward 0.6 units to project the total migration distance for birds with 60 in and 70 in wingspans.
11. Create a Power Map map using the Latitude and Longitude fields from the Migration Data table to show the migration paths.
12. Add the Speed Class field from the Migration Data table to the Category area. Add the Speed (MPH) field from the Migration Data table to the Height area, and then set the height of the columns to the average value.

Explore 13. In the Layer pane, expand the Layer Options section, and then use the Color boxes to change the category markers for 0–9 mph to Green, for 10–24 mph to Yellow, and for 24+ mph to Red.

Explore 14. Drag the DateTime field from the Migration Data table to the Time area in the Layer pane to create an animation of the bird migration. Click the Play button on the bar to play the animation. Play the animation again, noticing that the markers are not replaced by subsequent markers as the animation is played.

Explore 15. In the Layer pane, next to the Time box, click the Clock button, and then click "Data shows for an instant" to have each marker replaced by the subsequent location of the bird in its migratory flight. Replay the animation of the turkey vulture migration.

16. Close the Power Map window, and then save and close the Excel workbook.

MODULE **12**

Collaborating on a Shared Workbook

EXCEL

Working with a Team on a Financial Report

OBJECTIVES

Session 12.1
- Share a workbook with multiple users
- Track changes made to a workbook
- Accept and reject workbook edits
- Merge multiple workbooks into one file
- Save and share workbooks on the cloud

Session 12.2
- Set workbook properties and tags
- Encrypt a document file
- Mark a workbook as final
- Link and embed an Office document
- Customize the Excel working environment
- Save a workbook as a PDF file

Case | *Cooking Craft*

Cooking Craft, based in Warwick, Rhode Island, manufactures quality cookware and kitchen appliances. By law, the company must publish an annual financial report for its stockholders. Marta Filipovic and her team in the financial department are responsible for creating the Excel workbook that summarizes the financial status of the company. The report will go through several drafts and revisions as different members of the team review and edit its content. Marta asks you to help manage this collaboration so that all edits and comments can be tracked as the report moves from its initial draft to its final form. As part of the finished report, you will combine the final form of the workbook with other Office documents.

STARTING DATA FILES

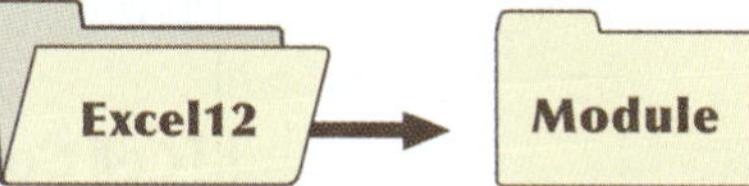

Module
Cooking.xlsx
Financial.xlsx
Garza Edits.xlsx
Hawkes.docx
Income.xlsx
Paris.xlsx
Team.xlsx

Review
Brussels.xlsx
Cash.xlsx
Cash Flow.xlsx
Garza Review.xlsx
Notes.docx
Projected.xlsx
Section.xlsx

Case1
Sandwich.xlsx
Shop1.xlsx
Shop2.xlsx
Shop3.xlsx
Shop4.xlsx

Case2
Agape.xlsx
Donor.docx

Case3
Menu.xlsx
Review.docx

Case4
Soul.xlsx

Session 12.1 Visual Overview:

A **shared workbook** is a workbook that can be edited by more than one user at the same time.

Cells with changes listed in the tracking log are marked with a color border.

The highlighted change is displayed in a comment box labeled with the name of the person who made the edit, the date and time of the edit, and a description of the edit.

Each comment in a shared workbook is labeled with the name of the person who made the comment.

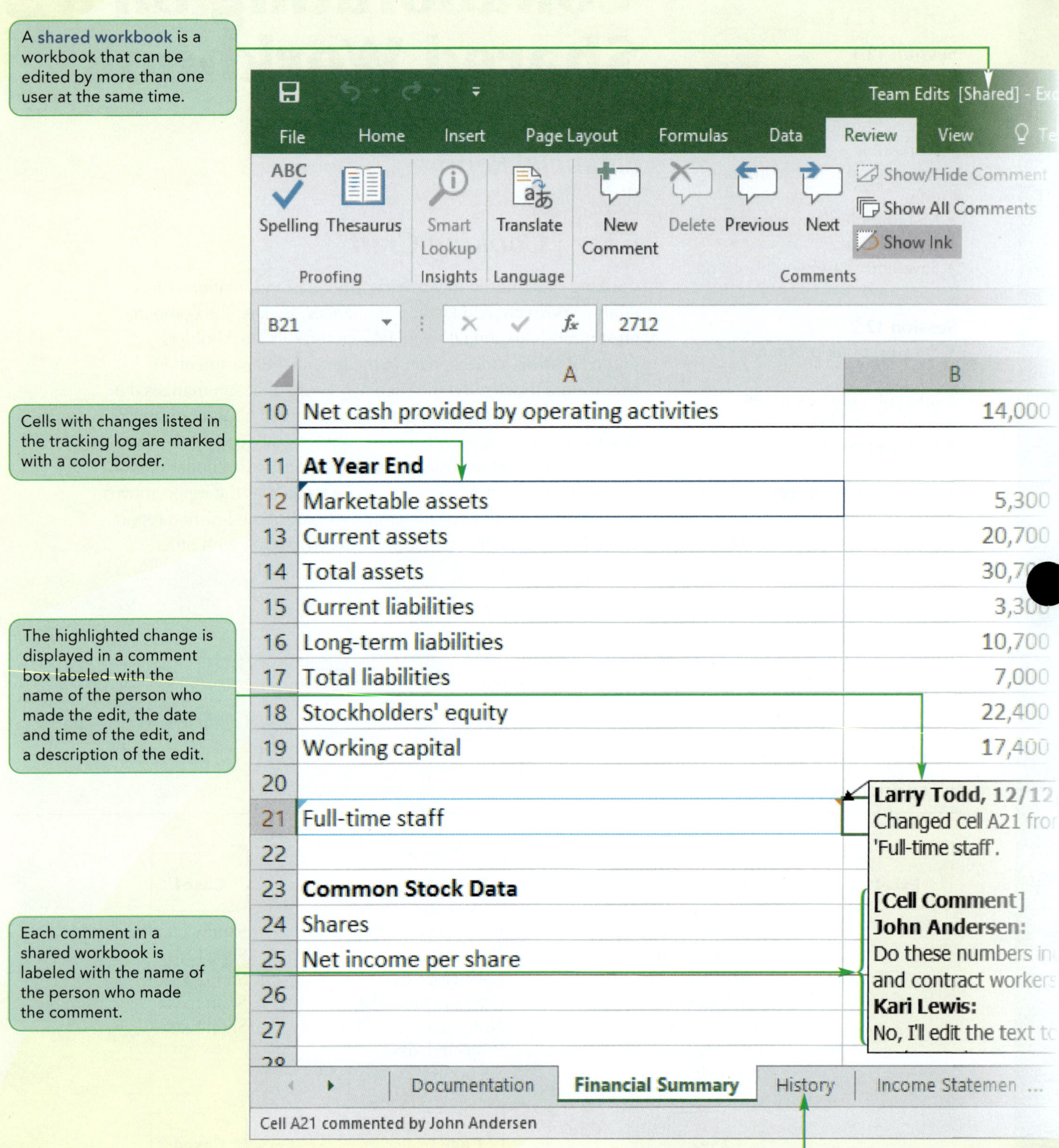

A list of the changes made to the workbook are stored in a **tracking log**, which can be displayed in a History worksheet.

Collaborating on a Workbook

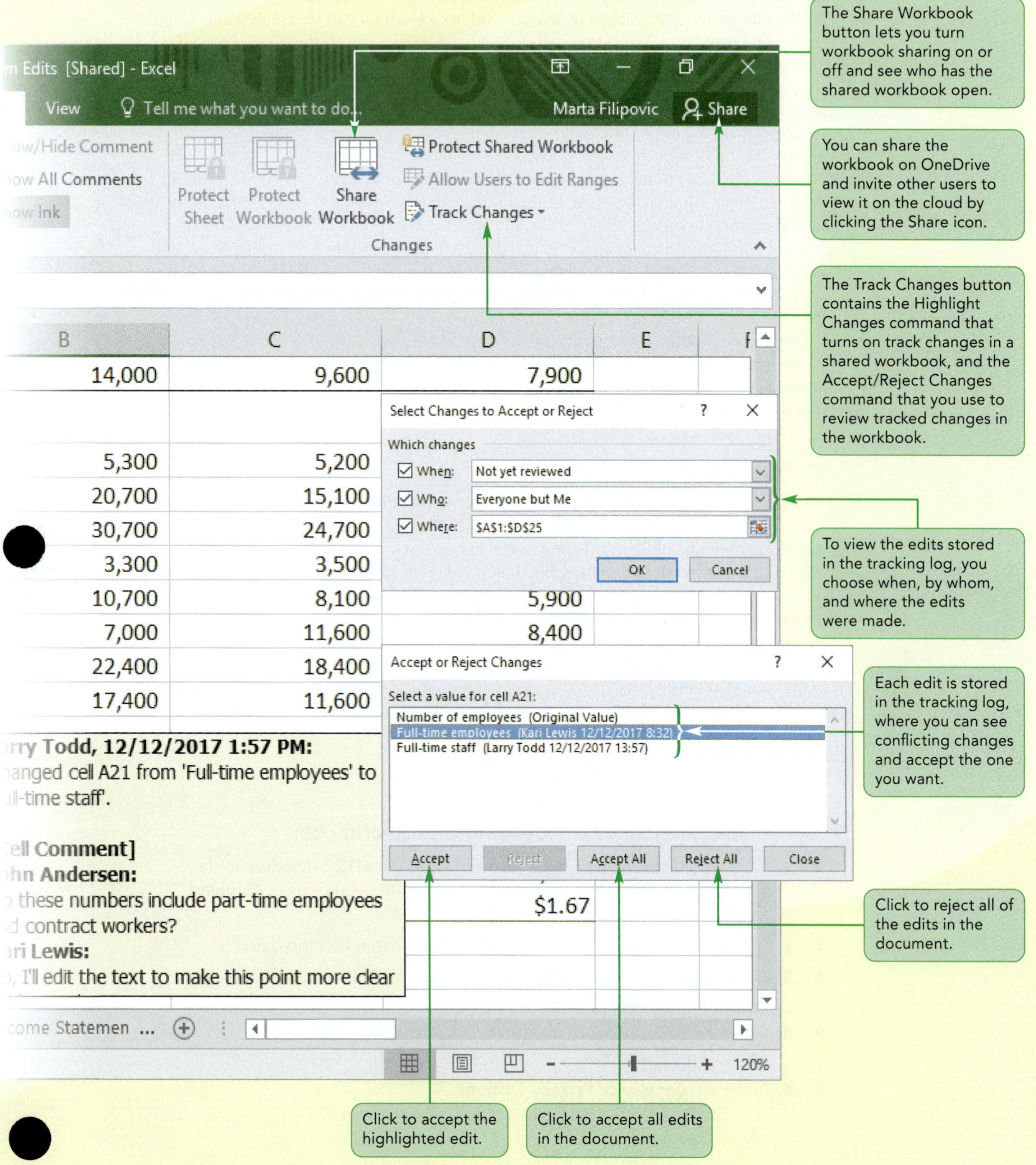

Sharing a Workbook Among Multiple Users

Many documents are the combined efforts of multiple authors, with each person providing input and content from his or her area of expertise. Excel facilitates such collaboration through the use of shared workbooks, which can be created and edited by several users.

Team members can work on the same document either simultaneously or sequentially, where the next person continues working on the document after the previous person has finished his or her tasks. A shared Excel workbook tracks the changes made by different people so everyone can examine when and where each change was made.

There are limits to what can be performed when working on a shared workbook. You can enter numbers and text, edit cells, move data, insert new rows and columns, and perform other usual editing tasks. However, you cannot delete worksheets or ranges, insert ranges, merge or split cells, edit charts, or use drawing tools. In general, you can do anything in a shared workbook that does not drastically change the layout or content to such an extent that Excel can no longer reconcile your edits with the edits made by other users.

Shared workbooks are usually stored in shared folders located on either a local network or the Internet. This location on the Internet is also referred to as the **cloud**. These secure locations are established to prevent unauthorized users from viewing the document's contents.

Setting Privacy Options

Once you have saved your workbook in a secure location, you can begin the process of sharing it. Excel workbooks are not shared by default. When a workbook includes review comments, hidden cells or worksheets, or document properties containing descriptive information about the file that are likely to contain personal information, you cannot share the workbook unless you change the workbook's privacy options. Note that privacy options are set for the active workbook, not for all Excel workbooks, so you need to reset the privacy options in each workbook you want to share.

Marta saved the first draft of the financial report in an Excel workbook. The workbook contains worksheets describing the company's financial status during the previous three years. She wants to share this workbook with her colleagues. You'll verify that the privacy options are set to allow Excel to save and share the workbook with other users.

To enable sharing for the Cooking Craft workbook:

1. Open the **Cooking** workbook located in the **Excel12 > Module** folder included with your Data Files, and then save the workbook as **Cooking Craft** in the location specified by your instructor.
2. In the Documentation worksheet, enter your name and the date.
3. On the ribbon, click the **File** tab, and then click **Options** in the navigation bar. The Excel Options dialog box opens.
4. In the left pane, click **Trust Center**, and then in the right pane, click the **Trust Center Settings** button. The Trust Center dialog box opens.
5. In the left pane, click **Privacy Options**.

6. In the Document-specific settings section, verify that the **Remove personal information from file properties on save** check box is either not selected or not selected and grayed out so that Excel will share and save the workbook without having to remove any personal information.
7. Click the **OK** button in each dialog box to return to the workbook. The privacy options are reset for the workbook.

Enabling Workbook Sharing

To make it possible for other users to access and edit the same document simultaneously, you need to share the workbook. You do this using the Share Workbook command. Marta wants to share the Cooking Craft workbook with other employees. You'll turn on workbook sharing so she can do this.

TIP

To password-protect and share a workbook, click the Protect and Share Workbook button in the Changes group on the Review tab.

To share the Cooking Craft workbook:

1. On the ribbon, click the **Review** tab. In the Changes group, click the **Share Workbook** button. The Share Workbook dialog box opens with the Editing tab active.
2. Click the **Allow changes by more than one user at the same time.** check box to insert a checkmark. This allows others to access and edit this workbook. Notice that your name appears as the exclusive user in the Who has this workbook open now box.
3. Click the **OK** button. A dialog box opens, indicating that the workbook will be saved.
4. Click the **OK** button. The workbook is saved, and "[Shared]" appears on the title bar next to the workbook name.
5. Close the workbook.

Tracking Changes in a Workbook

Once a workbook has been shared, Excel will track the changes made to the workbook, recording the name of the user who made the changes and when the changes were saved. You can use the Share Workbook dialog box to monitor who else is accessing the document and when they first started editing the file. For example, Marta shared her workbook with John Andersen, who also began to edit the workbook. Figure 12-1 shows the Share Workbook dialog box listing who is accessing the workbook.

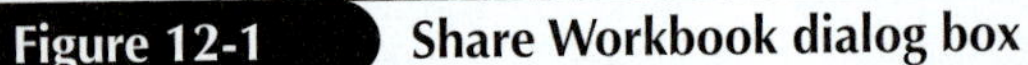

Figure 12-1 Share Workbook dialog box

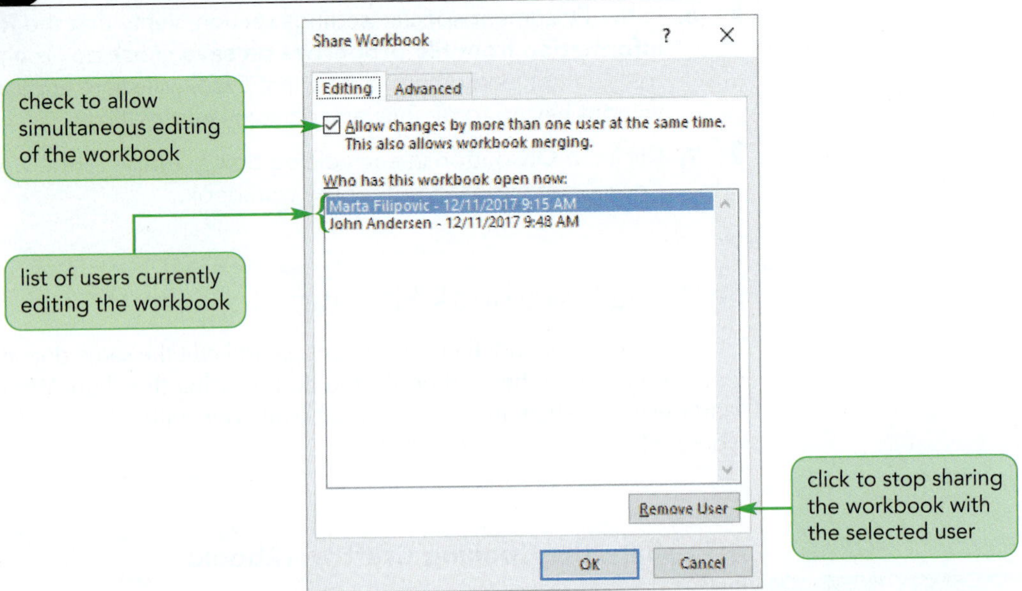

When two or more people edit a workbook simultaneously, Excel will notify each user of the changes saved by others. Consider the situation shown in Figure 12-2, in which Marta Filipovic and John Andersen are editing the same workbook at the same time. John edits the value in cell B5, and then saves the workbook. When Marta saves the workbook a little later, John's edit appears as a comment attached to the changed cell, notifying Marta what John did. Excel removes these comments automatically when the workbook is closed but saves the edit history for 30 days.

Figure 12-2 **Two users simultaneously editing a shared workbook**

Marta and John edit the workbook simultaneously.

	A	B	C	D	E
1	Cooking Craft				
2	Income Statement				
3				(in thousands, except per share data)	
4	Period Ending	Dec 31, 2017	Dec 31, 2016	Dec 31, 2015	
5	Revenue	$ 40,000	$ 32,100	$ 25,800	
6	Cost and expenses				
7	Cost of goods sold	3,600	3,700	3,300	
8	Marketing and selling	13,500	12,300	10,400	
9	Research and development	7,400	6,400	4,900	
10	General and administrative	6,600	5,800	4,100	
11	Total cost and expenses	31,100	28,200	22,700	

John enters a new value in cell B5 and saves his workbook.

	A	B	C	D	E
1	Cooking Craft				
2	Income Statement				
3				(in thousands, except per share data)	
4	Period Ending	Dec 31, 2017	Dec 31, 2016	Dec 31, 2015	
5	Revenue	$ 41,200	$ 32,100	$ 25,800	
6	Cost and expenses				
7	Cost of goods sold	3,600	3,700	3,300	
8	Marketing and selling	13,500	12,300	10,400	
9	Research and development	7,400	6,400	4,900	
10	General and administrative	6,600	5,800	4,100	
11	Total cost and expenses	31,100	28,200	22,700	

When Marta saves her workbook, a comment notifies her of John's edit.

	A	B	C	D	E
1	Cooking Craft				
2	Income Statement				
3				(in thousands, except per share data)	
4	Period Ending	Dec 31, 2017			
5	Revenue	$ 41,200	$		
6	Cost and expenses				
7	Cost of goods sold	3,600			
8	Marketing and selling	13,500			
9	Research and development	7,400	6,400	4,900	
10	General and administrative	6,600	5,800	4,100	
11	Total cost and expenses	31,100	28,200	22,700	

John Andersen, 12/11/2017 10:24 AM:
Changed cell B5 from ' $40,000.00 ' to ' $41,200.00 '.

Conflicts can occur when multiple users edit the same workbook. In this example, no conflict occurs as long as Marta does not also edit cell B5. However, suppose John saves his workbook with a value of $41,200 in cell B5, and then Marta, unaware of John's edit, enters $41,800 in the same cell. When Marta saves the workbook, the Resolve Conflicts dialog box opens, flagging the conflict between her edit and John's earlier edit in cell B5 (see Figure 12-3). From this dialog box, Marta can resolve the conflict by choosing which value to accept. Note that the Resolve Conflicts dialog box opens only when users edit the same cell while working on the document simultaneously. It will not appear if one user edits a cell and the other user leaves that cell unchanged. All users have equal authority to resolve conflicts, but only the person who first saves the workbook that has a conflict sees the Resolve Conflicts dialog box.

Figure 12-3 Resolve Conflicts dialog box

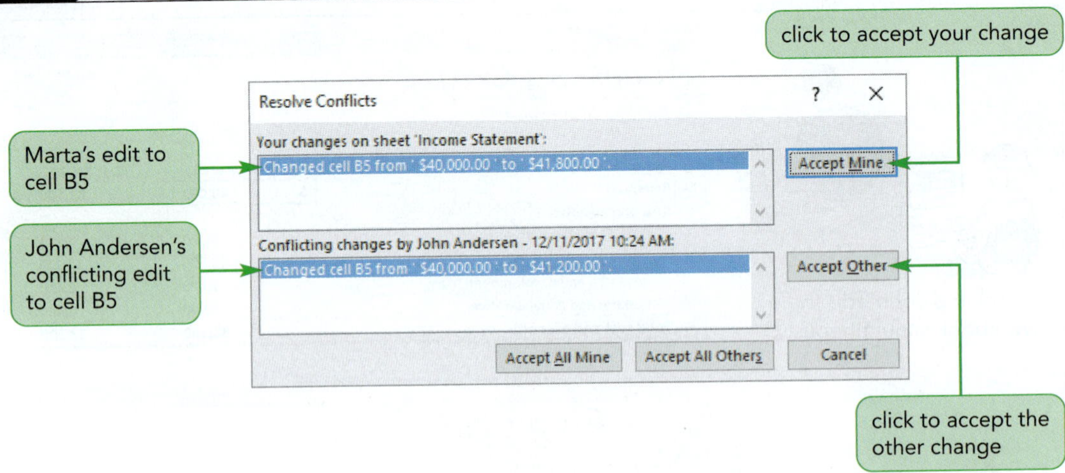

Since saving the shared version of the Cooking Craft workbook, Marta has sent the document to her colleagues for their input and edits. You'll open the current version of the shared workbook.

To open the shared workbook:

1. Open the **Team** workbook located in the **Excel12 > Module** folder included with your Data Files.
2. Save the workbook as **Team Edits** in the location specified by your instructor.
3. In the Documentation worksheet, enter your name and the current date. Note that these edits will be saved in the tracking log.

   Trouble? If Excel reports that the file is locked, click the Notify button, wait until Excel notifies you that the file is no longer locked for editing, and then click the Read/Write button in the next dialog box that opens.

Reviewing Comments in a Shared Workbook

Comments are a powerful collaboration tool, giving team members the ability to offer insights and make suggestions about the workbook and its content. The running conversation among users about a cell is displayed within a single comment box connected to that cell. Each comment in the comment box is identified by the user who entered it.

John Andersen, Kari Lewis, and Larry Todd all added comments about how to improve Marta's workbook. You'll review their suggestions.

To review comments in the shared workbook:

1. On the ribbon, click the **Review** tab. In the Comments group, click the **Next** button. The next—or, in this case, the first—comment in cell D4 of the Financial Summary worksheet is selected. It contains responses to Marta's query about whether to expand the report scope to five years. John and Larry suggest leaving the report as is; Kari prefers the five-year report. See Figure 12-4.

Figure 12-4 User comments attached to cell D4

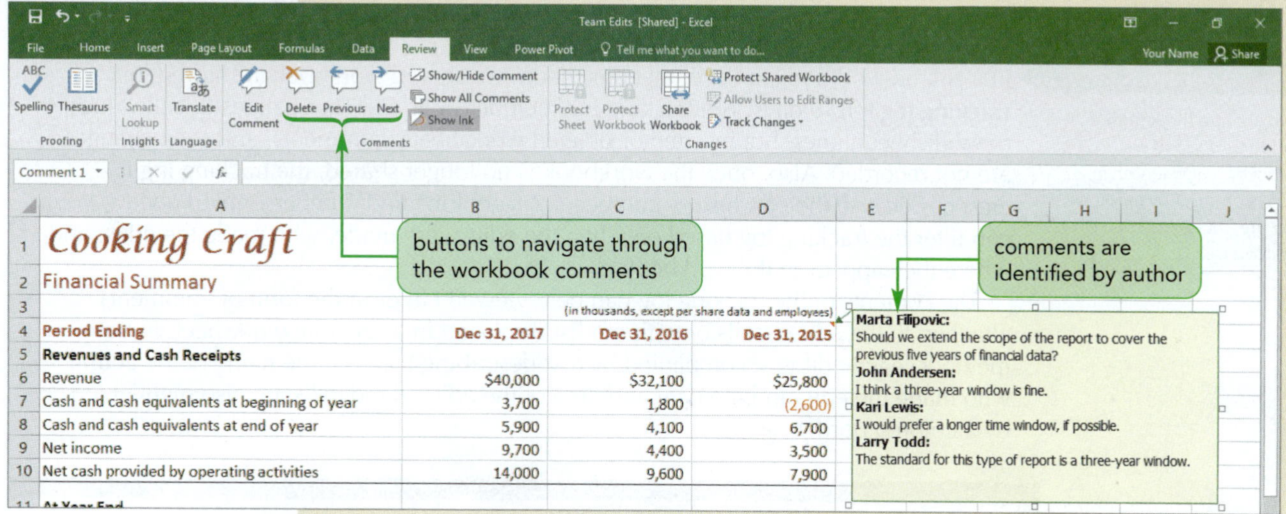

2. Click the **Next** button again. Excel moves through the workbook, searching within each sheet from left to right and then top to bottom, starting from the first sheet and continuing through the last. The next comment appears in cell A21, which is selected. In this comment, John asked whether the number of employees reported in the worksheet includes part-time employees. Kari responded that it doesn't.
3. Click the **Next** button again. Larry's comment in cell B25 regarding the Net income per share value is displayed along with John's response.
4. Click the **Next** button again. A dialog box opens, indicating Excel reached the end of the workbook and asking whether you want to continue reviewing comments from the beginning of the workbook.
5. Click the **Cancel** button to end the comment review.

To keep the workbook uncluttered, you can delete comments that have been addressed, leaving only the ones that still need follow-up. You have reviewed all of the comments in the workbook, and none require additional changes. Marta asks you to remove the comments from the workbook.

To delete the comments from the shared workbook:

1. In the Financial Summary worksheet, select cell **A1**. You want to review the comments, starting at the beginning of the worksheet.
2. On the Review tab, in the Comments group, click the **Next** button to go to the first comment in the workbook located in cell D4.
3. In the Comments group, click the **Delete** button. The list of comments attached to cell D4 is deleted.
4. Repeat Steps 2 and 3 for the other two comments in the workbook. When no comments remain in the workbook, the Delete, Previous, and Next buttons in the Comments group are grayed out.
5. Select cell **A1** to return to the beginning of the report.

Now that you have reviewed the comments, you'll examine what changes Marta's colleagues have made to the workbook.

Reviewing Changes Using the Tracking Log

TIP

To change the length of the tracking log history, specify a new length in days on the Advanced tab in the Share Workbook dialog box.

In a shared workbook, a list of all edits made to a shared workbook are stored in a **tracking log** for 30 days. The tracking log includes edits such as changes to cell values or worksheet names, but inserted or deleted worksheets, comments, and style changes are not recorded. Also, once the workbook is no longer shared, the tracking log is erased. Because the edit history can become very long and cumbersome to review, you can filter the tracking log based on when the edits were made, who made the edits, and where they appear in the workbook.

The contents of the tracking log can be reviewed either in the form of comments attached to the edited cells or within a list displayed in a separate worksheet. In both methods, each edit is accompanied by text describing the edit, the name of the author who made the edit, and the date and time of the edit. Edited cells are also highlighted by a colored border.

REFERENCE

Reviewing Tracked Changes in a Shared Workbook

- On the Review tab, in the Changes group, click the Track Changes button, and then click Highlight Changes.
- Specify when, who, and where in the Highlight which changes section.
- Click the Highlight changes on screen check box to see edits in comments.
- Click the List changes on a new sheet check box to view the tracking log.
- Click the OK button.
- Point to the highlighted cells to see the edits and/or view the tracking log in the History worksheet.

Marta wants you to highlight and review the edits in the Team Edits workbook as comments attached to the changed cells.

To highlight and review the changes to the shared workbook:

1. On the Review tab, in the Changes group, click the **Track Changes** button, and then click **Highlight Changes**. The Highlight Changes dialog box opens. You'll review all of the changes made by everyone but yourself.

TIP

To review only changes that are of interest to you, always specify when and who made the changes.

2. Click the **When** box arrow, and then click **All**. This specifies that you'll review changes made at any time in the workbook.
3. Click the **Who** box arrow, and then click **Everyone but Me**. This limits your review only to edits made by other people.
4. If necessary, click the **Highlight changes on screen** check box to insert a checkmark, and then if necessary, click the **List changes on a new sheet** check box to remove the checkmark. The tracked changes will be displayed in comments in the worksheets. See Figure 12-5.

Figure 12-5 Highlight Changes dialog box

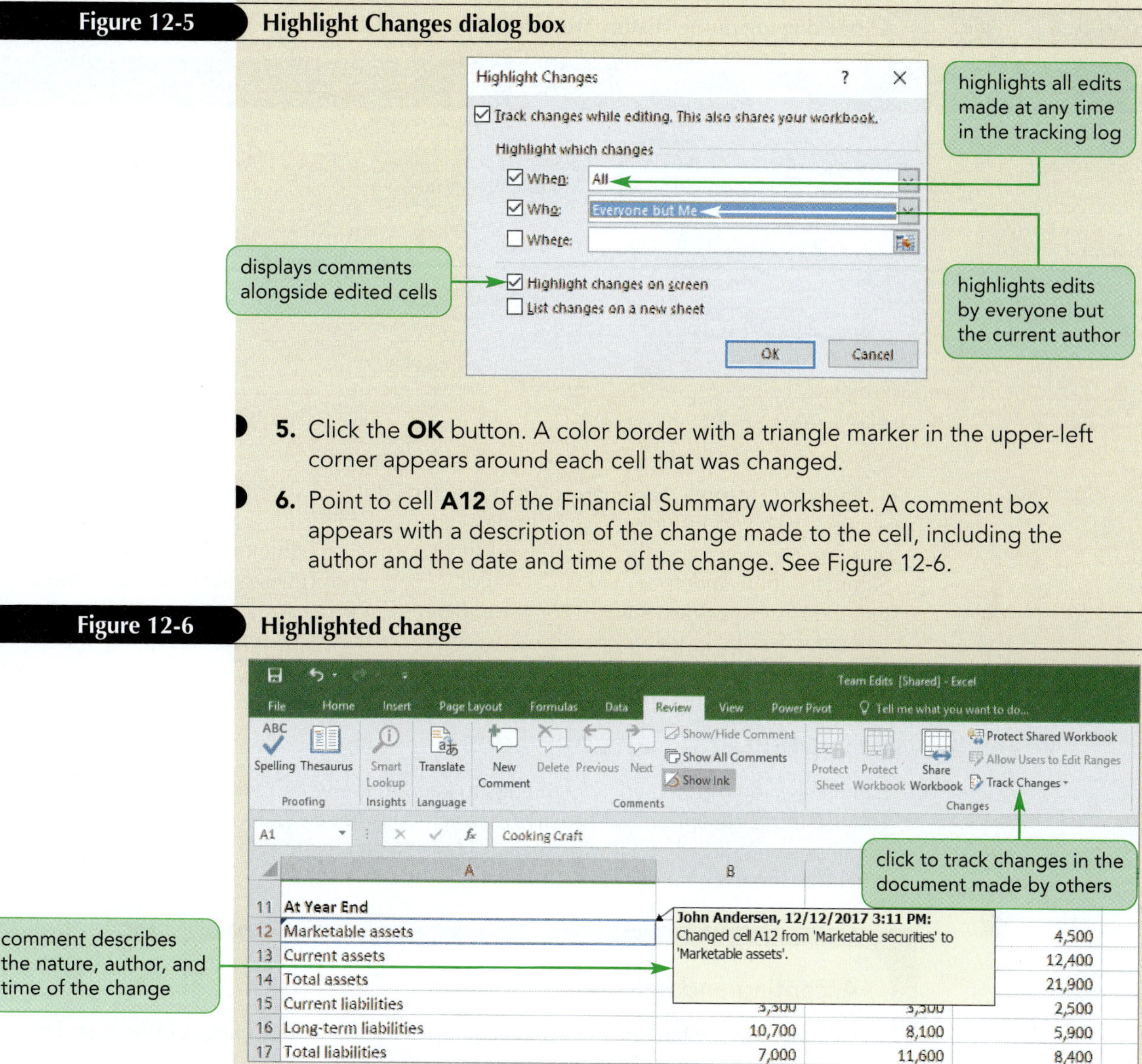

5. Click the **OK** button. A color border with a triangle marker in the upper-left corner appears around each cell that was changed.
6. Point to cell **A12** of the Financial Summary worksheet. A comment box appears with a description of the change made to the cell, including the author and the date and time of the change. See Figure 12-6.

Figure 12-6 Highlighted change

Examining all of the sheets in a workbook to locate the highlighted changes can be time consuming, especially in workbooks with many worksheets. A quicker approach is to review the list of all changes from the tracking log in a separate worksheet. Marta wants you to display the contents of the tracking log. You'll list these changes on a new worksheet.

To list the edits on a separate worksheet:

1. On the Review tab, in the Changes group, click the **Track Changes** button, and then click **Highlight Changes**. The Highlight Changes dialog box opens.
2. Click the **List changes on a new sheet** check box to insert a checkmark.
3. Click the **OK** button. The History worksheet is added to the end of the workbook, detailing the history of the six changes made to the document in chronological order along with who made each change, where it was made, and what kind of change it was. See Figure 12-7.

Figure 12-7 Tracking log in the History worksheet

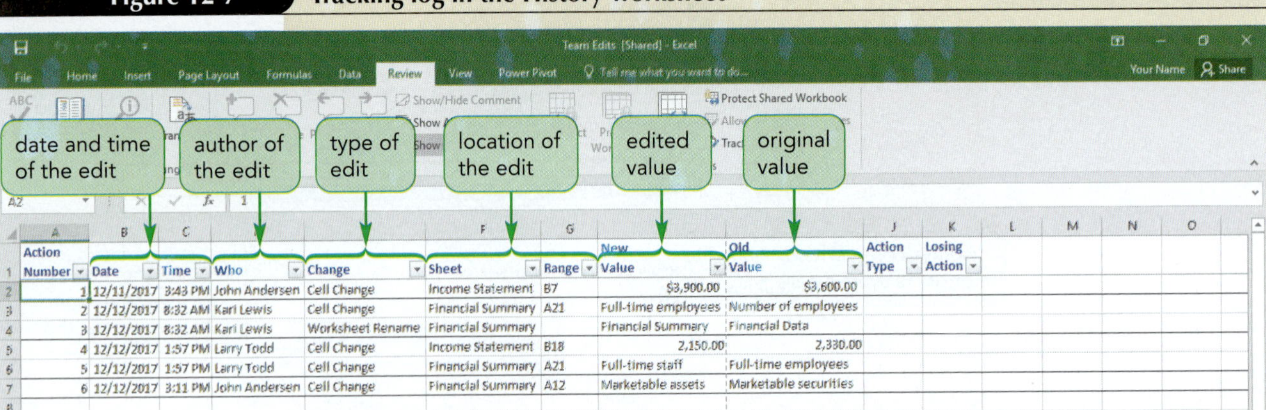

Action Number	Date	Time	Who	Change	Sheet	Range	New Value	Old Value	Action Type	Losing Action
1	12/11/2017	3:43 PM	John Andersen	Cell Change	Income Statement	B7	$3,900.00	$3,600.00		
2	12/12/2017	8:32 AM	Kari Lewis	Cell Change	Financial Summary	A21	Full-time employees	Number of employees		
3	12/12/2017	8:32 AM	Kari Lewis	Worksheet Rename	Financial Summary		Financial Summary	Financial Data		
4	12/12/2017	1:57 PM	Larry Todd	Cell Change	Income Statement	B18	2,150.00	2,330.00		
5	12/12/2017	1:57 PM	Larry Todd	Cell Change	Financial Summary	A21	Full-time staff	Full-time employees		
6	12/12/2017	3:11 PM	John Andersen	Cell Change	Financial Summary	A12	Marketable assets	Marketable securities		

The history ends with the changes saved on 12/12/2017 at 3:11 PM.

From the History worksheet, you can see that a total of six edits were made to the workbook by various users. Five edits have changed cell values, and one edit, made by Kari Lewis, changed the second worksheet name from Financial Data to Financial Summary. John Andersen made the last edit at 3:11 PM on December 12, 2017. Note that the History worksheet exists only for the current Excel session. It is automatically deleted when the workbook is closed or when you start rejecting or accepting the changes from the tracking log.

Accepting and Rejecting Edits

Ultimately, you must decide which edits to keep in the workbook and which to reject. You use the same options for specifying which edits to accept or reject uses the same options as you did when viewing the workbook's tracking log. Changes appear in the order that the team made them.

REFERENCE

Accepting and Rejecting Edits

- On the Review tab, in the Changes group, click the Track Changes button, and then click Accept/Reject Changes.
- Specify when, by whom, and where changes are to be reviewed.
- Click the OK button.
- Click the Accept, Reject, Accept All, or Reject All button to accept and reject changes.
- Click the Close button.

Marta wants to keep some edits but not others. You'll accept and reject edits based on her preferences.

To accept or reject edits in the workbook:

1. On the Review tab, in the Changes group, click the **Track Changes** button, and then click **Accept/Reject Changes**. The Select Changes to Accept or Reject dialog box opens.

   Trouble? If a dialog opens, indicating that this action will save the workbook, click the OK button.

2. Make sure **Not yet reviewed** appears in the When box, and **Everyone but Me** appears in the Who box. See Figure 12-8.

Figure 12-8 Select Changes to Accept or Reject dialog box

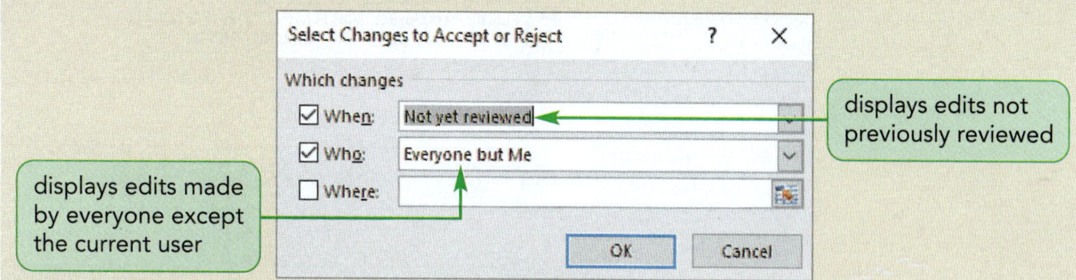

3. Click the **OK** button. The Accept or Reject Changes dialog box opens, listing the first of six edits made in the workbook. The first edit is in the Income Statement worksheet. In cell B7, John Andersen changed the cell value from $3,600.00 to $3,900.00. See Figure 12-9.

Figure 12-9 Accept or Reject Changes dialog box

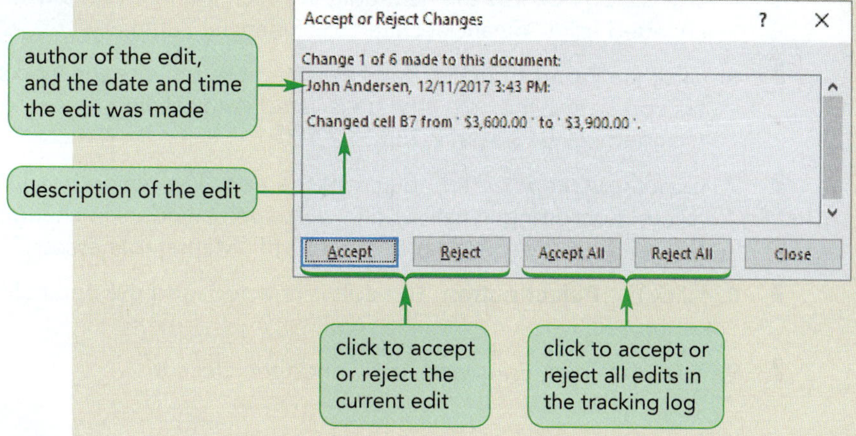

TIP

You can accept or reject all the changes to the workbook at one time by clicking the Accept All or Reject All button.

4. Click the **Accept** button. The edit is accepted, and the dialog box lists the next change—cell A21 in the Financial Summary worksheet contains two conflicting edits. See Figure 12-10.

Figure 12-10 Multiple edits to the same cell

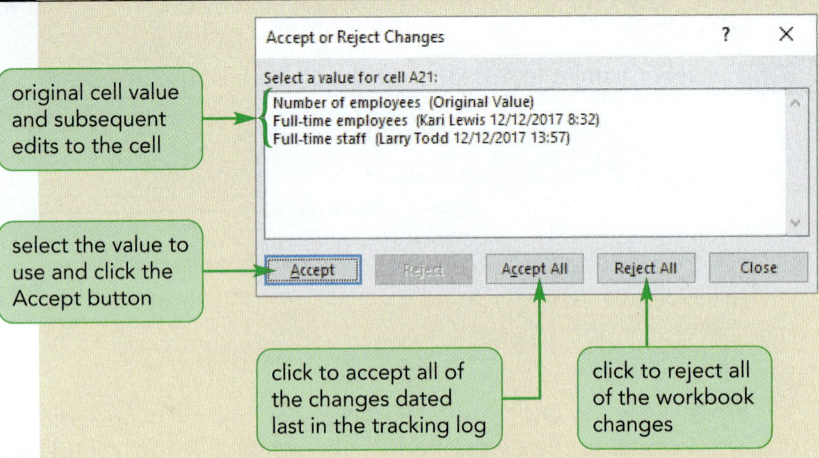

Be sure to select which of the multiple edits made to the cell you want to apply before clicking the Accept button.

5. In the Select a value for cell A21 box, click **Full-time employees**, and then click the **Accept** button. This accepts Kari Lewis's edit and rejects the original text and Larry Todd's later edit.

   The dialog box lists the next edit, in which the name of a worksheet was changed from "Financial Data" to "Financial Summary."

6. Click the **Accept** button. Kari Lewis's edit to rename the worksheet is accepted, and the next change is listed in the dialog box in which Larry Todd changed cell B18 from 2,330 to 2,150.
7. Click the **Accept** button to accept the edit. The dialog box lists the sixth and last edit occurring in cell A12, in which John Andersen changed the text of the cell from "Marketable securities" to "Marketable assets."
8. Click the **Reject** button. The edit is rejected, and the original text is restored to the cell.
9. Save the Team Edits workbook, and then close it.

The Team Edits workbook is reviewed and ready for Marta to work with.

INSIGHT

Action Types and Losing Actions

The choices you make about conflicting edits become part of the tracking log and are displayed in the Action Type and Losing Action columns of the History worksheet. When two edits conflict, the Action Type column will display "Won" for the edit that is kept and "Undo" or "Result of rejected action" for rejected edits. The row numbers in the Losing Action column identify the rows in the History worksheet containing information about the edits that weren't kept, including any deleted data. This way, you can always view not only the edits that have been made to the workbook, but also how conflicting edits were resolved.

Merge and Compare Workbooks

Another way to collaborate on a document is to provide a separate copy of the same shared file to multiple users. Each user works on his or her copy and then returns the edited workbook. The different versions of the workbook can then be merged so that the changes in the copies can be compared and conflicting edits can be resolved. The following conditions must be met to merge two or more workbooks:

- The copies must originate from the same shared file to enable the tracking history.
- The copies must have different filenames.
- The copies must either have the same password or not be password-protected.
- The length of time spent editing the copies cannot exceed the length of the tracking history (30 days by default), or important changes might be lost.

REFERENCE

Merging Workbooks

- Customize the Quick Access Toolbar to display the Compare and Merge Workbooks button.
- Open the workbook into which you want to merge the workbooks.
- Click the Compare and Merge Workbooks button on the Quick Access Toolbar.
- Select the workbook that you want to merge into the current document, and then click the OK button.

The Compare and Merge Workbooks button does not appear on the ribbon. Before you can compare and merge two workbooks, you will add the Compare and Merge Workbooks button to the Quick Access Toolbar.

To add the Compare and Merge Workbooks button to the Quick Access Toolbar:

1. On the Quick Access Toolbar, click the **Customize Quick Access Toolbar** button, and then click **More Commands**. The Excel Options dialog box opens with the options to customize the Quick Access Toolbar displayed.
2. Click the **Choose commands from** arrow, and then click **Commands Not in the Ribbon**. The box displays an alphabetical list of all the commands that do not appear on the ribbon.
3. Click **Compare and Merge Workbooks** from the list of commands, and then click the **Add** button. The Compare and Merge Workbooks command button is added as the last command in the Customize Quick Access Toolbar box.
4. Click the **OK** button. The Compare and Merge Workbooks button appears on the Quick Access Toolbar.

Marta's supervisor, Armando Garza, was away on an overseas business trip and did not access the shared file on the company network. Instead, he edited a copy of the workbook and emailed his edited version to Marta. Marta wants to include Armando's edits in the final report, so you'll merge and compare Marta's and Armando's workbooks. First, you open the workbook into which you want to place the result of merging the two documents, which in this case is Marta's workbook. Then, you use the Compare and Merge Workbooks button to open Armando's workbook and merge it with Marta's file.

To merge Marta's workbook with Armando's workbook:

1. Open the **Financial** workbook located in the **Excel12 > Module** folder included with your Data Files, and then save it as **Financial Report**. This is Marta's version of the report, including all of the edits suggested by her team that she accepted.
2. In the Documentation worksheet, enter your name and the date.
3. On the Quick Access Toolbar, click the **Compare and Merge Workbooks** button. A dialog box opens, indicating the workbook will be saved.
4. Click the **OK** button to save the current workbook. The Select Files to Merge Into Current Workbook dialog box opens.
5. Select the **Garza Edits** workbook located in the **Excel12 > Module** folder included with your Data Files.
6. Click the **OK** button. The two workbooks are merged, and all of the edits and comments from both workbooks appear in the Financial Report file.
7. Go to the **Financial Summary** worksheet, click cell **A2**, and then point to the cell. The comment that Armando added to that cell is displayed. Armando thinks the workbook is in good shape and has made a few minor text edits.
8. On the ribbon, click the **Review** tab, if necessary. In the Comments group, click the **Delete** button. The comment in cell A2 is deleted. The workbook contains no other comments.

Next, you'll review the edits in the merged workbook. You have already reviewed the changes in Marta's workbook, so you need to review only the changes that Armando made in his copy.

To review Armando's changes in the merged workbook:

1. On the Review tab, in the Changes group, click the **Track Changes** button, and then click **Accept/Reject Changes**. The Select Changes to Accept or Reject dialog box opens.
2. Verify that **Not yet reviewed** is selected in the When box.
3. Click the **Who** arrow, and then click **Armando Garza**. Only the changes that Armando made will be displayed.
4. Click the **OK** button. Armando made ten changes, all dealing with the text labels of items in the workbook. The first change listed is in the Cash Flow worksheet in cell A7, where Armando changed the capitalization used in the cell.
5. Click the **Accept** button to accept the change.

   You could continue to review each change one at a time, or you could accept or reject all of the changes. Marta wants you to accept all of Armando's edits.
6. Click the **Accept All** button. All of Armando's edits are accepted, and the dialog box closes.

Now that you have reviewed and accepted Armando's edits and have finished the process of accepting or rejecting edits from other users, you can remove workbook sharing. Before removing workbook sharing, be sure that you are finished collaborating with your team. Once workbook sharing is removed, the contents of the tracking log are erased, and there is no way to retrieve the history of edits made to the workbook.

To turn off workbook sharing:

1. On the Review tab, in the Changes group, click the **Share Workbook** button. The Share Workbook dialog box opens.
2. On the Editing tab, click the **Allow changes by more than one user at the same time** check box to remove the checkmark.
3. Click the **OK** button in the Share Workbook dialog box. A dialog box opens, warning that the workbook will no longer be shared, the change history will be erased, and anyone else editing the workbook will not be able to save his or her changes.
4. Click the **Yes** button. Workbook sharing is turned off, and control of the workbook is once again exclusive to the current user.

   Next, you'll remove the Compare and Merge Workbooks button from the Quick Access Toolbar.
5. On the Quick Access Toolbar, right-click the grayed-out **Compare and Merge Workbooks** button, and then click **Remove from Quick Access Toolbar** on the shortcut menu. The button no longer appears on the Quick Access Toolbar.

Collaborating on the Internet

Colleagues and clients can be located almost anywhere in the world. In such cases, it is often more convenient to use the Internet to share work rather than a local network. The Internet supports a wide collection of file-hosting sites that allow document sharing. Among the most popular are OneDrive, Dropbox, Google Docs, Amazon Cloud Drive, and iCloud.

Microsoft OneDrive offers a specified amount of free storage for new users with the option to purchase additional storage space. One advantage of OneDrive is that its tools and features are integrated into Microsoft Office applications and the Windows operating system. You can sign up for the Microsoft file-hosting service when you install Windows or Microsoft Office.

With the Cooking Craft franchise expanding across the country, and with plans to introduce stores into other countries and regions, Marta will use a file-hosting service to share her workbooks with colleagues and clients located across the country and across the world.

Saving a Workbook to OneDrive

Once you have subscribed to a file-hosting service, you can save files to that account using the same process as for saving files to your computer or local network folder. Many hosting services include folders for private and publically shared files, and you can usually create your own folders.

To save a workbook to OneDrive, you perform the following general steps:

1. Sign in to your Microsoft account.
2. Start Excel, and then on the ribbon, click the File tab, and then click Save As in the navigation bar.
3. On the Save As screen, select your OneDrive account.
4. Navigate to the folder on OneDrive in which you want to save the workbook.
5. Click the Save button.

Other file-hosting services require different methods to save and access files. In most cases, you access your folders using a program supplied by the file-hosting service, which makes those folders appear as local folders installed on your computer.

Viewing a Workbook on the Web

Once a workbook has been saved to OneDrive, you can access the workbook from Excel (as you would if the workbook had been saved locally) or through a web browser. If you using a web browser, you can edit the workbook using the Excel Online website accessed through your Office account. Figure 12-11 shows how the Financial Report workbook that you have been developing for Marta would appear if it were saved to a OneDrive account and then edited using in Excel Online website. Keep in mind that the web is a dynamic medium whose content is constantly being updated and changed, so, the most current version of the Excel Online might differ from that shown in the figure.

Figure 12-11 Financial Report workbook in Excel Online

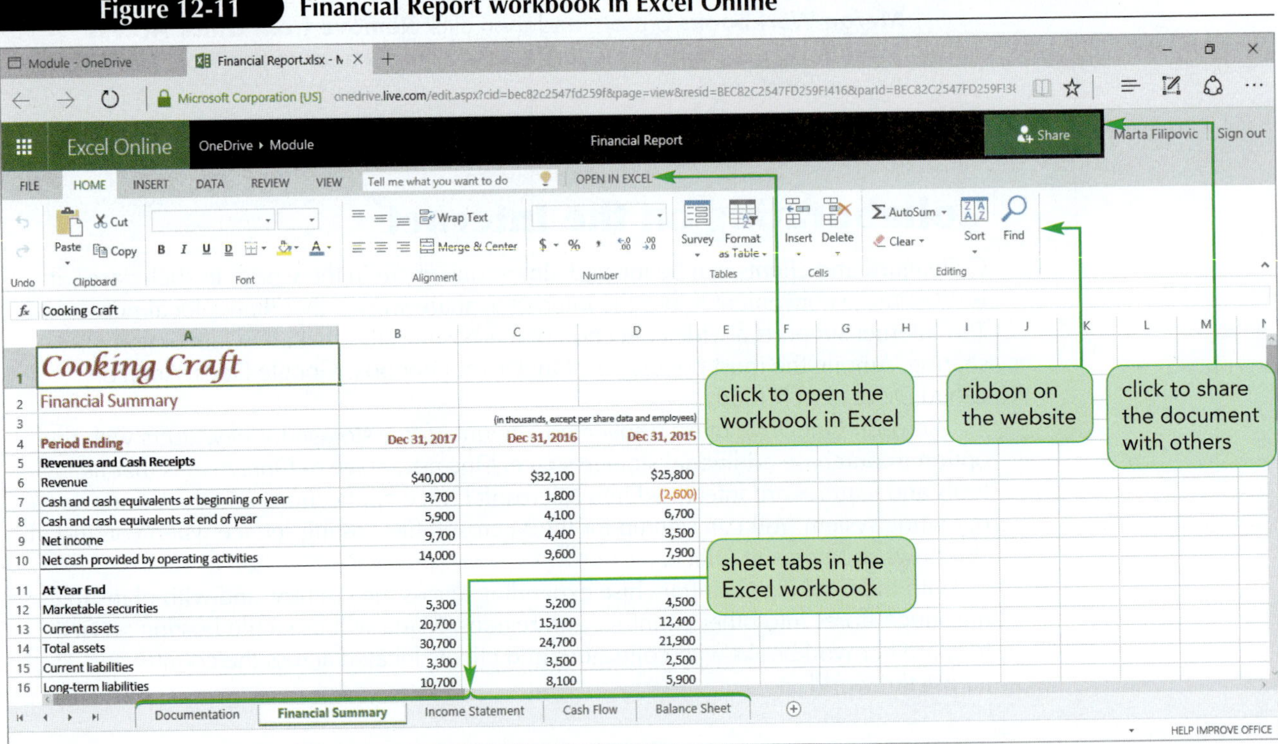

Excel Online includes most of the tools for editing a workbook that are in the Excel desktop application such as the ribbon, sheet tabs, and command buttons. For example, you can rename and reorder worksheets, format cells, and enter formulas into existing cells. If you need more editing tools than the website provides, you can simply reopen and edit the workbook in the Excel desktop application; however, the Excel Online website makes it simple for users to view and edit workbooks while traveling using tablet devices or mobile phones.

Sharing Workbooks on OneDrive

Most file-hosting services make it easy to share documents with others and provide different levels of access to the document content. For example, you might give some users only the ability to view a workbook but give other users the ability to view, edit, and create new content within the workbook. You should avoid storing personal or confidential information in a file that you save in a publically accessible folder because then anyone can access your data.

TIP

A shared workbook with the editing history saved to the tracking log cannot be edited from Excel Online.

You can share workbooks you store in OneDrive by performing the following steps in Excel:

1. Click the Share button at the right edge of the Excel ribbon to display the Share panel.
2. If prompted, save your workbook to a folder on your OneDrive account.
3. Once saved, Excel will display the Share panel.
4. Invite people by entering their email addresses and specifying whether each person can edit the document or only view it.
5. Click the Share button to send the email invitation.

Figure 12-12 shows how Marta might use the Share panel to send an invitation to her colleagues to access her workbook stored on OneDrive. The email message her colleagues receive will include a link to the shared workbook on the file-hosting service. Any sharing privileges are applied only to that workbook and not to other files or folders.

Figure 12-12 **Share panel for the Financial Report workbook**

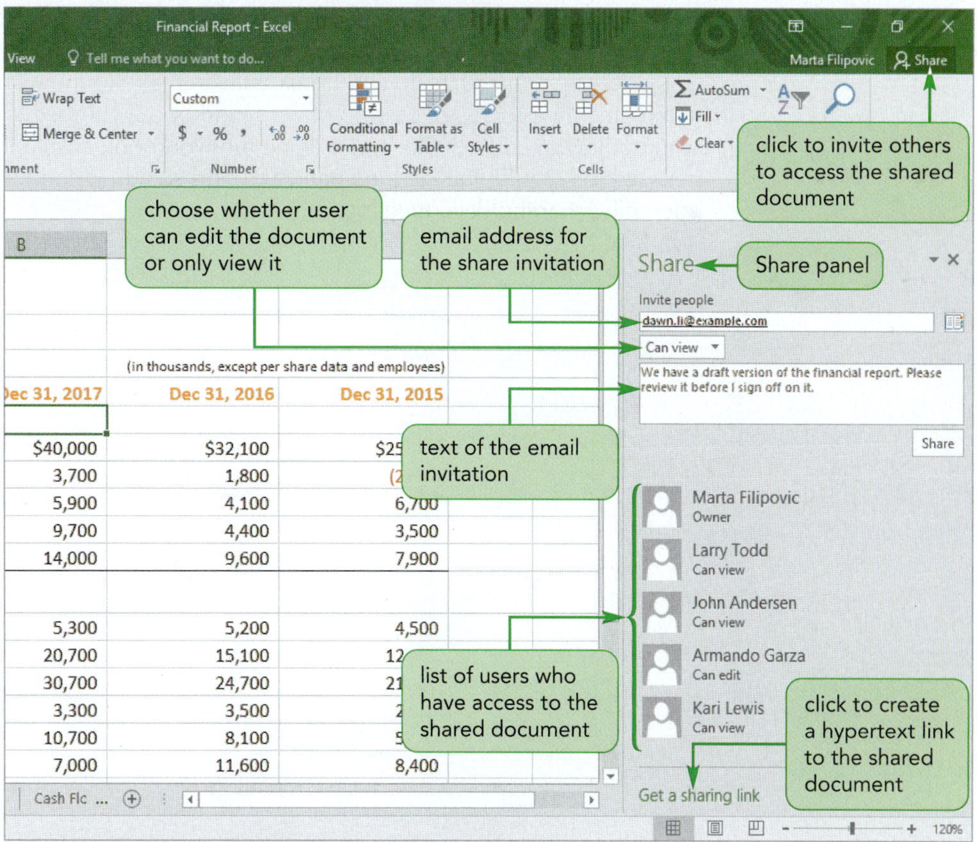

You can remove sharing from your workbook at any time by reopening the Share screen and editing the list of recipients, removing users who should no longer have access to the file.

PROSKILLS

Teamwork: Improving the Collaborative Process

The collaborative tools in Excel make it simpler for groups to share the work of writing, editing, and finishing a financial report. But no tool, however useful, can overcome problems associated with colleagues who cannot work together effectively. Keep in mind the following to improve the collaborative process:

- Project goals should be stated in advance, with all team members clearly understanding what is expected of them. Team members should feel comfortable requesting clarification of those goals at any time in the process.
- Identify the strengths and weaknesses of each team member, and adjust the project accordingly.
- Start work on the project at the earliest possible date.
- Constantly monitor the progress of the project, staying up to date on what has been done and what needs to be done. Communicate the status of the project with progress reports to each team member.
- Make it easy for team members to suggest new ideas and voice objections.
- Finish your tasks on time, and meet your project goals.
- Treat each team member with respect. Do not allow personal grudges or differences to influence the successful completion of the project.

By successfully managing the group dynamic, you can make the Excel collaborative tools even more effective and useful.

Marta's supervisor has no additional edits to make to the workbook. You have completed the process of sharing Marta's workbook with her colleagues, merging her workbook with another file, and making the workbook available on OneDrive. In the next session, you'll finalize the financial report so that it can be distributed before the upcoming shareholders' meeting.

REVIEW

Session 12.1 Quick Check

1. What is a shared workbook?
2. How does Excel resolve two different edits made to the same worksheet cell simultaneously?
3. How long does Excel store edits in the tracking log?
4. What are some edits that are not included in a tracking log?
5. Can any two workbooks be merged? Explain why or why not.
6. List two advantages of saving workbooks to a file hosting service.
7. What is the advantage of using OneDrive?

Session 12.2 Visual Overview:

The Info screen provides information about the current workbook.

You can click the Protect Workbook button to mark the workbook as final and to password-protect the workbook.

You can click the Check for Issues button to run the Document Inspector, the Compatibility Checker, and the Accessibility Checker to verify that the workbook is accessible to users with special needs.

The Document Inspector checks the workbook for hidden properties or personal information.

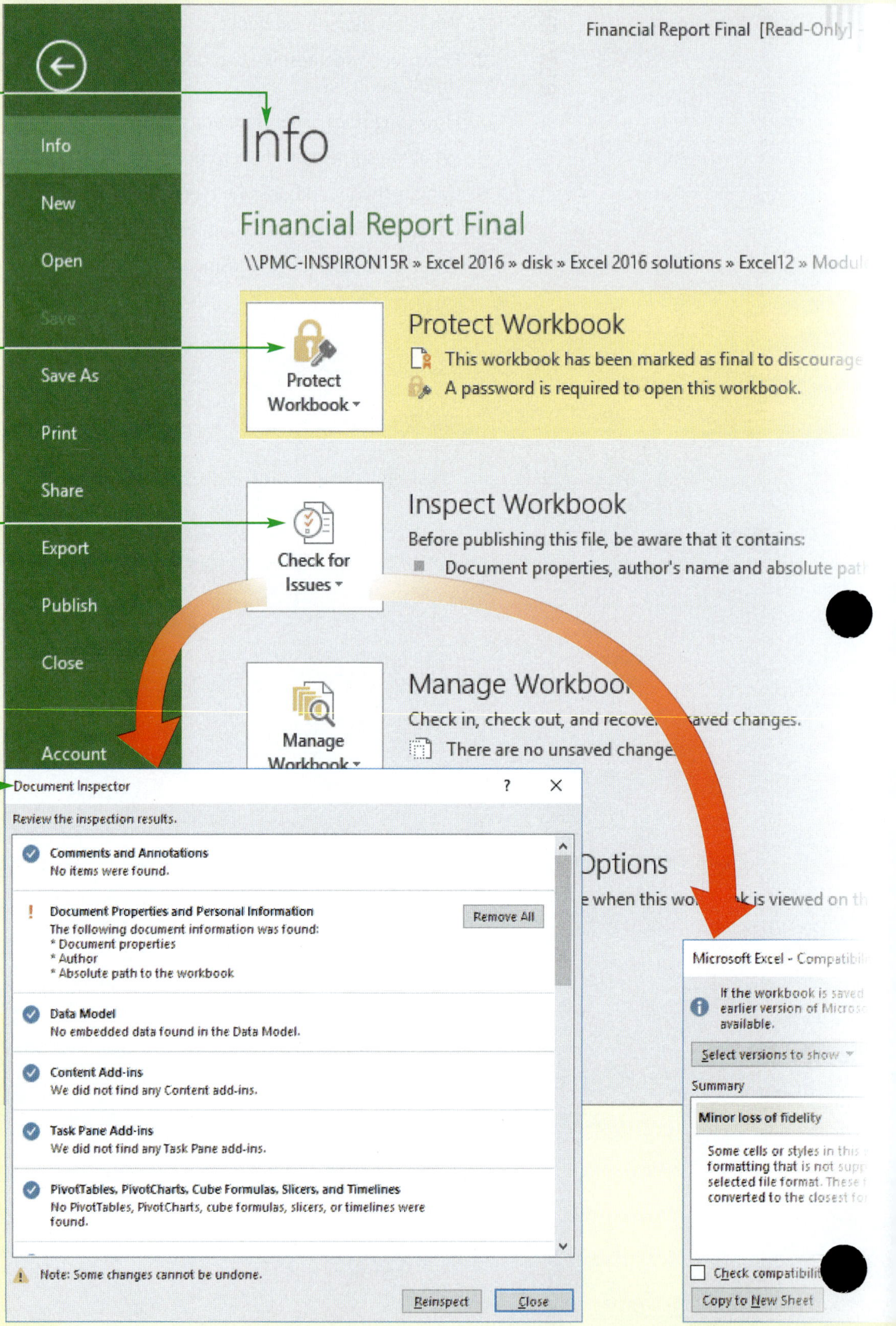

Financial Report Final [Read-Only]

Info
New
Open
Save
Save As
Print
Share
Export
Publish
Close
Account

Info

Financial Report Final

\\PMC-INSPIRON15R » Excel 2016 » disk » Excel 2016 solutions » Excel12 » Modul

Protect Workbook

Protect Workbook ▾

This workbook has been marked as final to discourage

A password is required to open this workbook.

Check for Issues ▾

Inspect Workbook

Before publishing this file, be aware that it contains:

Document properties, author's name and absolute pat

Manage Workbook ▾

Manage Workboo

Check in, check out, and recove aved changes.

There are no unsaved change

Options

e when this wo k is viewed on th

Document Inspector

Review the inspection results.

Comments and Annotations
No items were found.

Document Properties and Personal Information
The following document information was found:
* Document properties
* Author
* Absolute path to the workbook

Remove All

Data Model
No embedded data found in the Data Model.

Content Add-ins
We did not find any Content add-ins.

Task Pane Add-ins
We did not find any Task Pane add-ins.

PivotTables, PivotCharts, Cube Formulas, Slicers, and Timelines
No PivotTables, PivotCharts, cube formulas, slicers, or timelines were found.

Note: Some changes cannot be undone.

Reinspect Close

Microsoft Excel - Compatibil

If the workbook is saved
earlier version of Micros
available.

Select versions to show

Summary

Minor loss of fidelity

Some cells or styles in this
formatting that is not supp
selected file format. These
converted to the closest fo

Check compatibili

Copy to New Sheet

Finalizing a Workbook

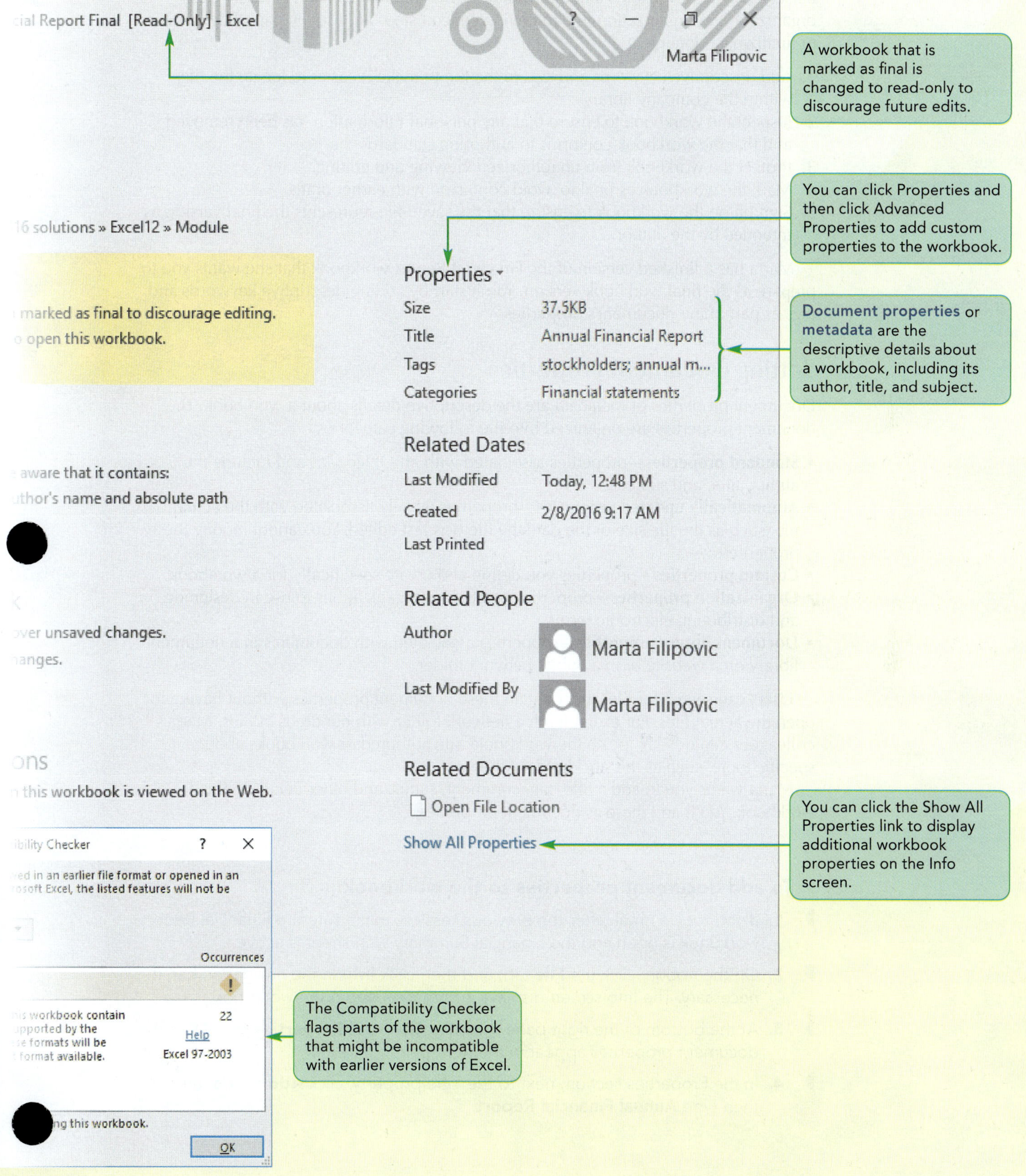

Preparing the Final Workbook

After a workbook has been reviewed and revised to the team's satisfaction, it can be set as the final version. Although what constitutes a final version can vary from organization to organization, the following general steps are usually part of the process of finalizing a document:

1. Add descriptive keywords and tags to the file to make it easier to locate the file within the company library.
2. Inspect the workbook to ensure that any personal information has been removed and that the workbook conforms to authoring standards.
3. Protect the workbook from unauthorized viewing and editing.
4. Mark the workbook as final to avoid confusion with earlier drafts.
5. Sign off on the workbook to ensure that the saved file represents the final version as intended by the author.

Marta has a finished version of the Financial Report workbook that she wants you to prepare as the final workbook version. You'll start by adding descriptive keywords and tags as part of the document's properties.

Setting Document Properties

Document properties or metadata are the descriptive details about a workbook. The document properties are organized into the following categories:

- **Standard properties**—properties associated with all Office files and include the author, title, and subject.
- **Automatically updated properties**—properties usually associated with the actual file, such as the file size or the date the file was last edited. You cannot modify these properties.
- **Custom properties**—properties you define and create specifically for a workbook.
- **Organization properties**—properties created for organizations to use in designing and distributing electronic forms.
- **Document library properties**—properties associated with documents in a document library on a website or in a public network folder.

Users can search for files that contain these document properties without having to open the actual files. For example, in a network folder with hundreds of files, Marta's colleagues can quickly locate the workbooks she authored or workbooks about a specific topic, such as the stockholders' meeting.

Marta wants you to add a title, tag, comment, status, and other details to the workbook. You'll add these as document properties.

To add document properties to the workbook:

1. If you took a break after the previous session, make sure the Financial Report workbook is open and the Financial Summary worksheet is active.
2. On the ribbon, click the **File** tab, and then click **Info** in the navigation bar, if necessary. The Info screen displays information about the workbook.
3. At the bottom of the right pane, click the **Show All Properties** link. All of the document properties appear in the right pane.
4. In the Properties section, next to the Title property, click **Add a title**, and then type **Annual Financial Report**.

5. Next to the Tags property, click **Add a tag**, and then type **stockholders; annual meeting**. Notice that you typed a semicolon to separate the two tags.
6. Next to the Comments property, click **Add comments**, and then type **Final draft of the financial report to be presented at the April meeting in Phoenix**.
7. Next to the Status property, click **Add text**, and then type **Final draft**.
8. Next to the Categories property, click **Add a category**, and then type **Financial statements**.
9. Next to the Subject property, click **Specify the subject**, and then type **Cooking Craft financial report**.
10. Next to the Company property, click **Specify the company**, and then type **Cooking Craft**.
11. In the Related People section, next to the Author property, click **Add an author**, and then type your name to add yourself as an author of the document. See Figure 12-13.

Figure 12-13 Info screen showing the document properties

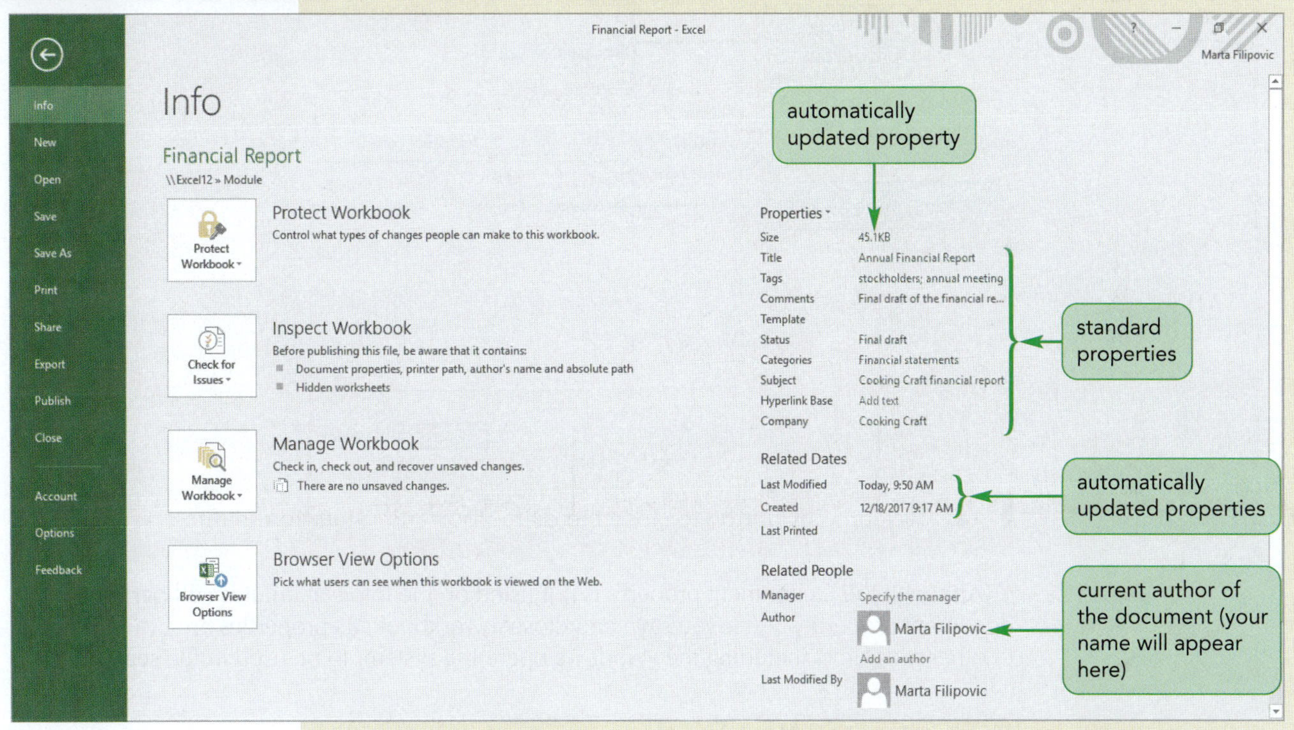

If none of the listed properties fit your needs, you can create a custom property. You can either select custom properties from a list of property names or provide your own name. The value associated with the property can be text, a date, a number, or Yes or No. Marta wants to identify the department that created this workbook. Because no department tag appears in the document properties list, you'll add a custom property.

To add the Department custom property:

1. On the Info screen, at the top of the right pane, click **Properties**, and then click **Advanced Properties**. The Financial Report Properties dialog box opens.
2. Click the **Custom** tab. You enter the custom properties for the workbook here. The Name box includes some common properties that you might want to add to a workbook.
3. In the Name box, click **Department**. The Department property is selected, and the data type is set as Text. You do not need to change this.
4. In the Value box, type **Finance** as the property value.
5. Click the **Add** button. The Department property is added to the Properties box. See Figure 12-14.

Figure 12-14 Financial Report Properties dialog box

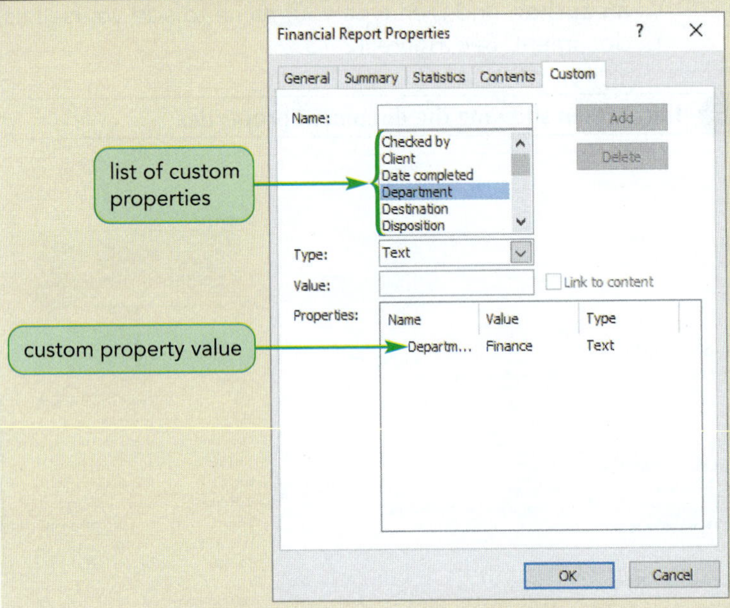

6. Click the **OK** button to close the dialog box and return to the Info screen.

Although the Department property is not listed on the Info screen, it is still part of the document properties. After you save and close a workbook, its properties are available to other programs, including the Windows operating system, to be used in file searches.

Inspecting a Workbook

The next step in finalizing a workbook is to review its contents for sensitive or personal information that you don't want distributed to others. Personal information can appear in comments and annotations, document properties and metadata attached to the workbook, headers and footers, or hidden worksheets and cells. To determine whether a workbook contains sensitive or personal information, you use the Document Inspector, which searches the workbook to locate data and text that you may want removed.

Marta asks you to use the Document Inspector to inspect the workbook and remove any personal information.

To inspect the Financial Report workbook:

1. On the Info screen, click the **Check for Issues** button, and then click **Inspect Document**. A dialog box opens, reminding you to save the workbook.
2. Click the **Yes** button. The Document Inspector dialog box opens.
3. Make sure all of the check boxes are selected, and then click the **Inspect** button. Note that the inspector checks the content of the workbook for hidden properties or personal information in all of the selected categories. The inspection results appear in the dialog box. See Figure 12-15.

Figure 12-15 Document Inspector dialog box

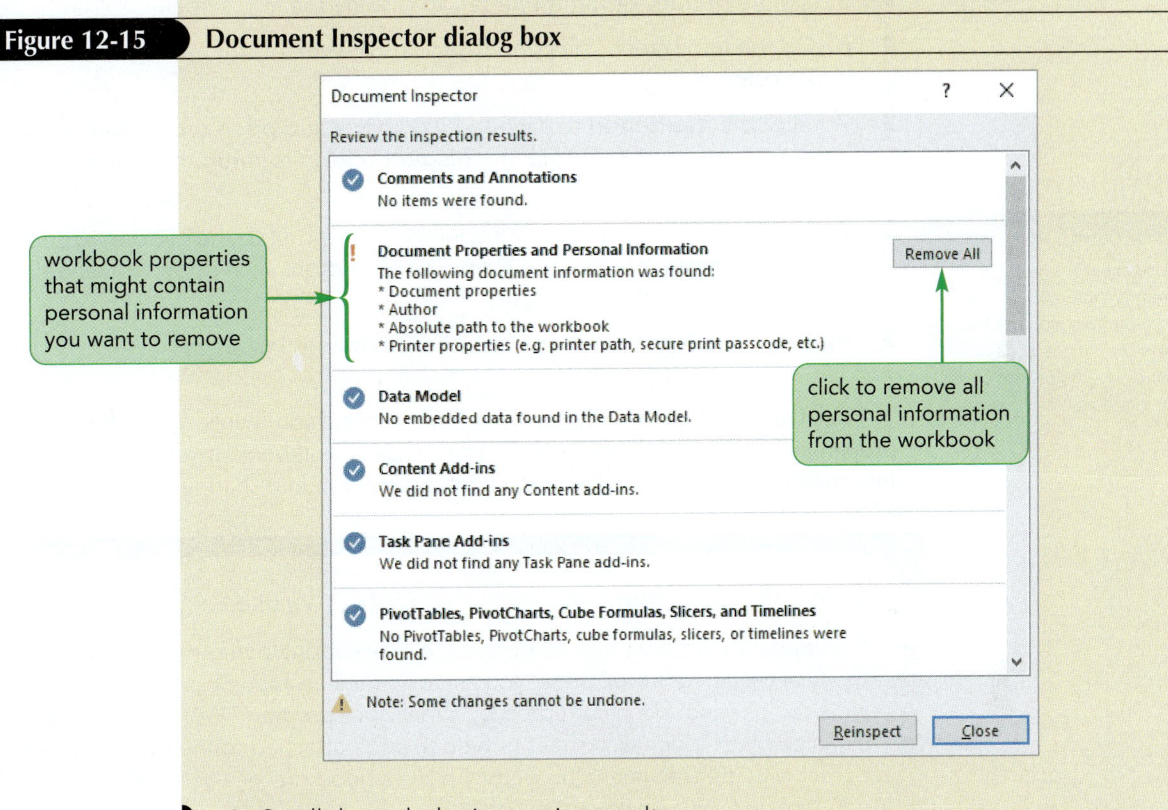

4. Scroll through the inspection results.

The Document Inspector located two instances where personal or sensitive information might appear in the workbook. The first relates to issues with document properties and personal information, including the names of the document authors. The second is a hidden worksheet. Marta is fine with releasing the workbook with the list of the document authors, but she uses hidden worksheets to conceal source data and documentation that is useful to her but could be irrelevant or confusing to others. Before Marta finalizes the workbook, you'll remove the hidden sheet.

To review the hidden worksheet, and then remove it:

1. Click the **Close** button to close the Document Inspector dialog box.
2. Right-click any sheet tab in the workbook, and then click **Unhide** on the shortcut menu. The Unhide dialog box opens, displaying a list of all the hidden sheets in the workbook. In this case, the only hidden sheet is the Notes worksheet.

3. With the **Notes** sheet name selected, click the **OK** button. The Notes worksheet appears between the Documentation and Financial Summary worksheets. The worksheet contains Marta's to-do list for the project, which is not relevant for colleagues and does not need to be part of the final report.

   Rather than just deleting the Notes worksheet, you'll hide it again, and then delete it using the Document Inspector.
4. Right-click the **Notes** sheet tab, and then click **Hide** on the shortcut menu. The worksheet is again hidden from view.
5. On the ribbon, click the **File** tab to display the Info screen.
6. On the Info screen, click the **Check for Issues** button, and then click **Inspect Document**.
7. Click the **Yes** button to save the workbook and open the Document Inspector dialog box, and then click the **Inspect** button to rerun the Document Inspector.
8. Scroll down the Document Inspector dialog box to the Hidden Worksheets section, and then click the **Remove All** button. All hidden worksheets are removed from the workbook.
9. Click the **Close** button to close the Document Inspector.

TIP

Use caution when you remove information and data from a workbook with the Document Inspector because you cannot undo the removal.

Note that the Document Inspector will not remove comments, annotations, document properties, and personal information from a shared workbook. If you need to remove this information, be sure to run the Document Inspector *before* sharing the workbook.

INSIGHT

Using the Document Inspector to Detect Viruses

In addition to ensuring that no personal or inappropriate information is included in the final version of a workbook, you can use the Document Inspector to verify that the workbook has not been corrupted by a malicious program. Workbook viruses are often signaled by a hidden worksheet or hidden code attached to the file, which you can detect with the Document Inspector. This is a good practice to follow for any workbook you receive from an unknown source.

Another concern when finalizing a workbook is whether anyone working with an earlier version of Excel will have trouble reading the workbook contents. To determine whether a workbook is compatible with those older versions, you can inspect the document for compatibility. The Compatibility Checker flags any content, formatting, or element in the workbook that cannot be transferred to earlier versions of Excel, indicating the severity of the problem. The most serious differences between current and older versions of Excel include:

- **Worksheet size**—Current Excel versions support worksheets that are 16,384 columns by 1,048,576 rows; versions earlier than Excel 2007 have a maximum worksheet size of 256 columns by 65,536 rows.
- **International dates**—Current Excel versions support international date formats such as Hebrew Lunar, Japanese Lunar, and Chinese; versions earlier than Excel 2007 do not.
- **Sparklines**—Current Excel versions support sparklines; versions earlier than Excel 2007 do not.
- **Charts**—Current Excel versions support several charts not supported in earlier Excel versions.

In addition to these differences, more minor issues might involve the font formats and color styles used in older Excel versions. In those cases, Excel will attempt to duplicate the formats as closely as possible when saving a new file to an older Excel version.

Marta wants to know whether the Financial Report workbook will be compatible with older versions of Excel. You'll use the Compatibility Checker to determine this.

To run the Compatibility Checker on the Financial Report workbook:

1. On the ribbon, click the **File** tab to open the Info screen.
2. Click the **Check for Issues** button, and then click **Check Compatibility**. The Compatibility Checker dialog box opens, displaying the results of the compatibility test. See Figure 12-16.

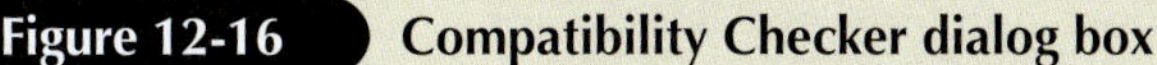

Figure 12-16 Compatibility Checker dialog box

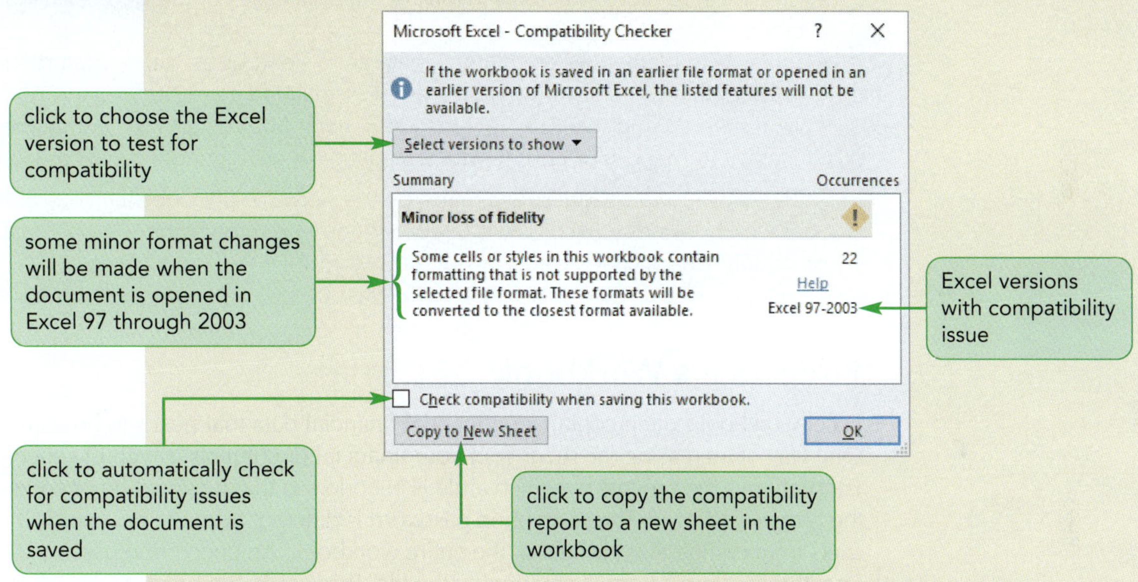
Microsoft Excel - Compatibility Checker
If the workbook is saved in an earlier file format or opened in an earlier version of Microsoft Excel, the listed features will not be available.
Select versions to show
Summary
Occurrences
Minor loss of fidelity
Some cells or styles in this workbook contain formatting that is not supported by the selected file format. These formats will be converted to the closest format available.
22
Help
Excel 97-2003
Check compatibility when saving this workbook.
Copy to New Sheet
OK
click to choose the Excel version to test for compatibility
some minor format changes will be made when the document is opened in Excel 97 through 2003
Excel versions with compatibility issue
click to automatically check for compatibility issues when the document is saved
click to copy the compatibility report to a new sheet in the workbook

The Compatibility Checker finds only a minor issue involving formatting changes between the current document and versions of Excel 97, 2000, 2002, and 2003. Marta does not see a need to make changes to the workbook at this time.

3. Click the **OK** button to close the Compatibility Checker.

TIP

To save the compatibility report to a worksheet, click the Copy to New Sheet button.

You can have Excel automatically check the compatibility of the workbook each time you save by clicking the Check compatibility when saving this workbook check box in the Compatibility Checker dialog box.

PROSKILLS

Written Communication: Making Your Workbook Accessible

The workplace should be an inclusive environment regardless of each employee's disabilities and special needs. One way of testing whether your workbooks meet this goal is the Accessibility Checker. To run the Accessibility Checker, click the Check for Issues button on the Info screen, and then click Check Accessibility. Excel will review the contents of your workbook and flag any issues that might prove challenging to users with disabilities. Many of these issues are focused on users with visual impairments who may need to use a screen reader to interpret the content of your workbook aurally. Issues that the Accessibility Checker flags include:

- Embedded clip art and images without alternate text
- Embedded video clips without closed captioning
- Data tables without a header row, making it difficult to interpret the table contents
- Hypertext links lacking meaningful text and ScreenTips
- Complicated table structures involving multiple cases of merged cells and nested tables
- Tables with blank rows or columns that can mislead users with screen readers into thinking that the end of the table has been reached
- Worksheets using the default names of Sheet1, Sheet2, and so on that provide no useful information for people with disabilities in navigating through the workbook

By following the suggestions made by the Accessibility Checker, you can make your workbooks more accessible to colleagues who might otherwise be unable to contribute to the final product.

Protecting a Workbook

Excel workbooks often contain confidential financial data that needs to be secured. One way of increasing the security of your financial documents is with file encryption. **Encryption** is the process by which a file is encoded so that it cannot be opened without the proper password. The encryption password is different from the passwords that prevent users from editing a worksheet or the entire workbook. An encryption password prevents unauthorized users from even opening the file. Passwords can be up to 255 characters and can include numbers, symbols, uppercase letters, and lowercase letters.

Marta wants to protect the final version of the Financial Report workbook before sending it to different Cooking Craft department heads to ensure that only authorized users can view the data. You'll do this by encrypting the workbook.

To encrypt the workbook:

1. Save the workbook as **Financial Report Final** in the location specified by your instructor.
2. On the ribbon, click the **File** tab to return to the Info screen.
3. Click the **Protect Workbook** button, and then click the **Encrypt with Password**.
4. In the Password box, type **cookingcraft** (in all lowercase letters), and then click the **OK** button.

Type the password carefully to avoid a misspelling, which will make the file difficult or impossible to reopen.

5. In the Reenter password box, type **cookingcraft**, and then click the **OK** button. A password is now required to open this workbook.

6. Save and close the workbook, and then reopen it. The Password dialog box opens, preventing the workbook from opening without the correct password.
7. In the Password box, type **cookingcraft** and then click the **OK** button. The workbook opens.

   Trouble? If the workbook doesn't open, you might have mistyped the password. Repeat Step 7. If the workbook still doesn't open, you might have typed a different password in Steps 4 and 5. There is no simple way to recover a mistyped password from an encrypted document. Open the Financial Report workbook, and then repeat Steps 1 through 7 to resave the Financial Report Final workbook with the correct password.

Marking a Workbook as Final

Marking a workbook as final makes the workbook read-only, discouraging a user from making any changes to it. A workbook marked as final has the editing, typing, and proofing commands turned off. As a result, a user can only view the contents of the file and cannot modify it unless he or she removes the final status from the document.

Even though Marta's workbook has been encrypted, it can still be edited by anyone who knows the password. Marta wants to discourage this from happening. You'll mark the workbook as the final version of the report.

To mark Marta's workbook as final:

1. On the ribbon, click the **File** tab to return to the Info screen.
2. Click the **Protect Workbook** button, and then click **Mark as Final**. A dialog box opens indicating that the workbook will be marked as final and then saved.
3. Click the **OK** button. A second dialog box opens, indicating that the file has been marked as final and its status property is now Final.
4. Click the **OK** button. A read-only version of the workbook is opened, as indicated by "[Read-Only]" in the title bar. The Message Bar also indicates that the workbook has been marked as final.
5. Click a blank cell in the active worksheet, and try to enter some text to confirm that you cannot edit the workbook.
6. Close the workbook.

Marking a workbook as final does not completely prevent anyone from editing the document. Depending on your Excel setup, the Message Bar might include the Edit Anyway button, which a user can click to edit the workbook despite its final status. You can also remove the final status by clicking the Protect Workbook button on the Info screen and then clicking Mark as Final to deselect the command.

Signing Off on a Workbook

A final way to ensure that a document has not been changed by an unauthorized user is with a digital signature, which can be thought of as an electronic version of a written signature. Digital signatures provide a way for the author to authenticate the document by "signing off" on it. Because a workbook marked with a digital signature cannot be altered without removing the signature, the presence of a digital signature lets users know that the workbook comes from a trusted source and has not been altered since it was originally signed.

To add a digital signature to a document, you need a **digital ID** or **digital certificate**, which is an attachment to a document that authenticates the source of the signature. If you do not have a digital certificate, you can get one from a third-party source known as a **certificate authority (CA)**. The CA acts like a notary public, verifying signatures and tracking those that have expired or been revoked.

Marta will work with the company's IT department to obtain a digital certificate and then finalize the Financial Report workbook herself. Once she has obtained a digital certificate, the digital signature can be either inserted directly into the workbook where it is visible to other users or added as an invisible signature that can be viewed only through the Info page or on the workbook's status bar.

To create a visible signature, you select a cell in the workbook, and then click the Add a Signature Line button in the Text group on the Insert tab. The Signature Setup dialog box shown in Figure 12-17 opens so you can enter the name of the signer, the signer's work title and email address, and instructions to the signer.

Figure 12-17 Signature Setup dialog box

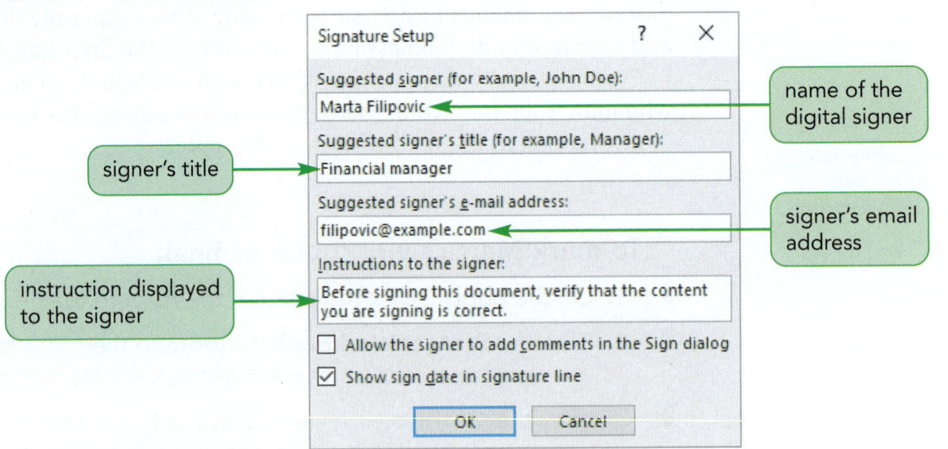

Once the signature has been set up, Excel displays a visible representation of the signature line. To sign off on the document, double-click the signature line and type a name in the signature box. If you have a touch device, you can sign the box or insert an image of the signature. Click the Sign button to display the signature in the document. See Figure 12-18.

Figure 12-18 Signed workbook

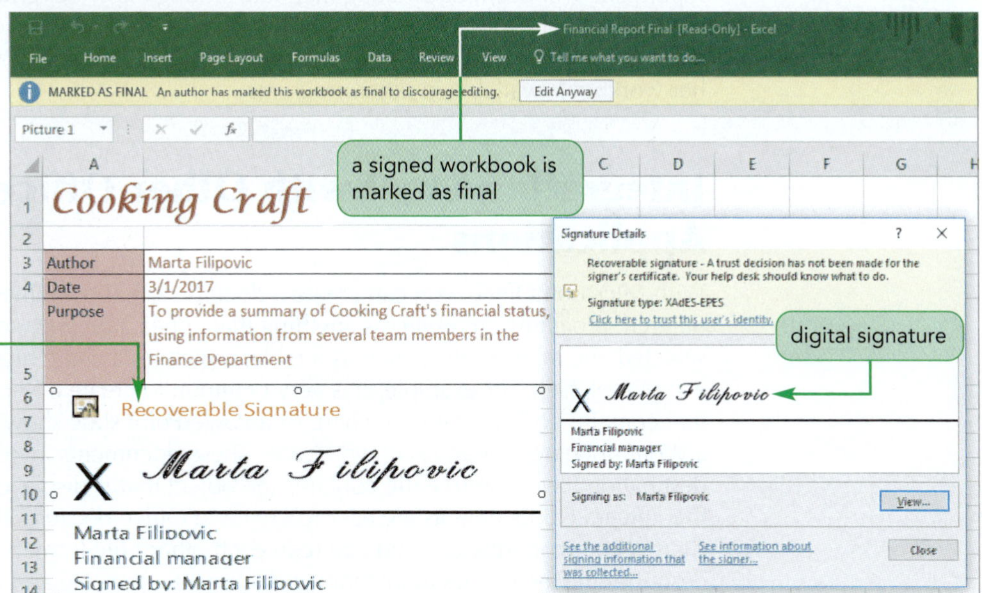

TIP

To create an invisible signature, click the Protect Workbook button on the Info page and click Add a Digital Signature.

After the document has been signed, it will be marked as final, and further editing will be discouraged. If additional edits are made to the document, the digital signature is no longer valid, and this fact is noted on the workbook's Info screen. By creating and signing off with a digital signature, Marta lets other users know that she has signed off on and supports this workbook and that subsequent changes to her workbook by other users will not be attributed to her.

INSIGHT

Creating Digital Certificates

If you cannot obtain a digital certificate from a third party, you can create your own **self-signed certificate**, which is a certificate created and signed by the person it certifies. Because a self-signed certificate is not created and maintained by a trusted authority, it lacks the safeguards associated with third-party certificates. For example, you would never use a self-signed certificate on an e-commerce site or with any transaction that involves personal information such as credit card or Social Security numbers.

Self-signed certificates are useful for developers who create sample documents and applications and don't want to pay hundreds of dollars a year for a third-party certificate. They can also be used with projects that don't involve personal or confidential information in which all of the parties involved are well known to each other.

To create a self-signed certificate with Microsoft Office, go to the Program Files > Microsoft Office > root > Office16 folder and run the SELFCERT.exe program. You will be asked to provide a name for the certificate (usually your own name). The certificate will then be available to your Excel workbooks for digital signing. Note that a self-signed certificate authenticates the document only for the local computer and not for other computers or networks.

If you want to remove or edit your certificate, use the Windows Certification Manager by running the certmgr.msc program from the Search the web and Windows or Ask me anything box (Windows 10) or the Windows Run command (Windows 8). The Certification Manager will list all of the third-party and self-signed certificates installed on your computer and provide commands to edit or remove them.

Now that Marta has completed the process of reviewing and editing the financial report, she will begin distributing that data among the wider group of Cooking Craft employees. Some of these users do not work with Excel. Because they prefer to receive this type of information in Word documents or PowerPoint slides, you'll need to make her workbook available in other programs.

Integrating Excel with Other Office Applications

With Microsoft Office, you can create a document that combines objects from several different programs. An **object** is anything that appears on your screen that can be selected and manipulated, such as a table, a picture, a chart, a cell, a worksheet, or even Excel itself. For example, it is very common to create a Microsoft Word document that contains an Excel table or chart, or a PowerPoint slide show that displays part of a Word document or an Excel workbook. These documents involve source files and destination files. A **source file** contains the object that is displayed in the **destination file**. Integrated documents are easy to create in Office because all Office programs share a common interface and can read each other's file formats. Figure 12-19 describes the three ways to integrate a document—copying and pasting, linking, and embedding. Each method has advantages and disadvantages.

Figure 12-19 Integration methods

Method	Description	When to Use
Copying and pasting	Inserts an object into a file	You want to exchange the data between the two files only once. If the source file changes, that change is not reflected in the destination file.
Linking	Displays an object in the destination file, but only stores the location of the source file	You need to ensure that the data will be current and identical in both the source and destination files. Any changes made to the source file will be reflected in the destination file.
Embedding	Displays and stores an object in the destination file	You want the object to become a part of the destination file. Any changes made in the source file are not reflected in the object.

You can copy text, values, cells and ranges, and even charts and graphics from one program and paste them in another program using the Windows copy and paste features. When you paste an object from the source file, it becomes part of the destination file, but the pasted object is static and has no connection to the source file. If you want to change the pasted object, you must do so within the destination file. For example, an Excel table pasted into a Word document can be edited only in the Word document. Any changes made in the original Excel workbook have no impact on the Word document. For this reason, pasting is used only for one-time exchanges of information.

Object Linking and Embedding

If you want to create a live connection between the source file and the destination file, you must use object linking and embedding. **Object linking and embedding (OLE)** refers to the technology that allows one to copy and paste objects, such as graphics files, cells and ranges, and charts, so that information about the program that created the object is included with the object itself.

The objects are inserted into the destination file as either linked objects or embedded objects. A **linked object** is stored within the destination file and remains connected to the source file. If you make a change to the source file, that change will be reflected in the destination file. On the other hand, an **embedded object** is stored within the destination file and is no longer part of the source file. In the case of an embedded chart, the destination file will store not only the chart image but also any data values on which the chart is based. Figure 12-20 illustrates the difference between linking and embedding.

Figure 12-20 **Embedding contrasted with linking**

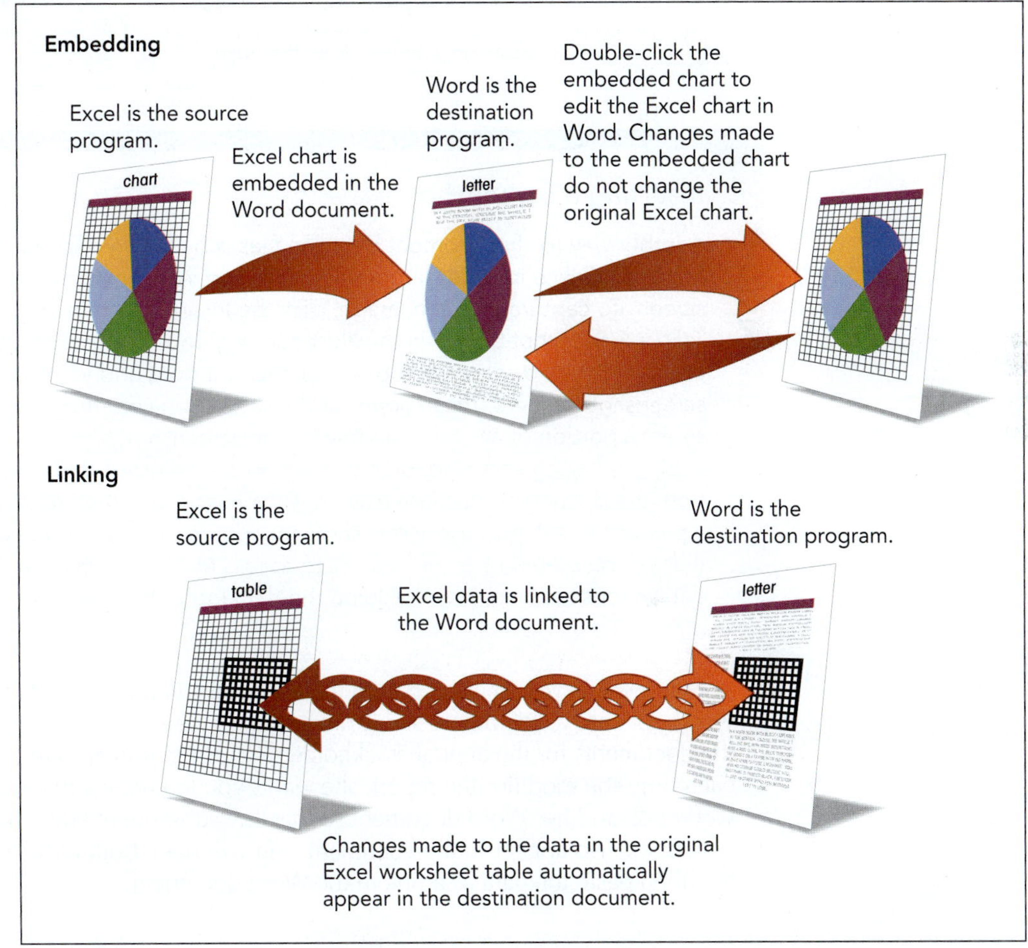

When you paste an object into an Office document, you have the choice of either keeping the formatting applied in the source document or using the formatting styles defined in the destination document. Figure 12-21 summarizes some of the different paste options available in Microsoft Office.

Figure 12-21 Paste options

Icon	Paste Option
	Keep the formatting applied to the object in the source file.
	Use the styles used in the destination file.
	Link to the source file and keep the formatting from the source file.
	Link to the source file and keep the styles used in the destination file.
	Paste the object as a graphic image.
	Paste only the text from the object.

INSIGHT

Inserting a Screenshot

Another way to share content between files is by taking a screenshot of the open file. Microsoft Office includes a tool to capture and insert images from your computer screen. To capture a screen image, click the Insert tab on the ribbon, and then click the Take a Screenshot button in the Illustrations group. If you have more than one window open, a gallery displays thumbnails of each window, and you can choose to take a screenshot of one of these open windows. You can click the Screen Clipping button to select a portion of an open window for the screenshot.

Unlike linking and embedding, inserting a screenshot does not insert the actual data from the document. Because a screenshot inserts only the image of that document as a picture, you should use screenshots for content that is not going to change. For data that will be edited or to allow users to access Microsoft Office tools to manipulate the data, choose linking or embedding the data rather than inserting a screenshot.

Marta wants you to insert part of the financial summary from the Financial Report workbook into a staff memo she is preparing for Gail Hawkes, who is coordinating the documents for the annual stockholders' meeting. Rather than pasting the data each time she modifies the report, she wants you to create a link between her Excel workbook and her Word document so that any subsequent edits she makes to the workbook also appear in the document. You will open both files, copy the Excel data, and then paste the data as a link in the Word document.

To link the Word document to the table in the Excel workbook:

1. Open the **Hawkes** Word document located in the **Excel12 > Module** folder included with your Data Files, and then save the document as **Hawkes Memo** in the location specified by your instructor.
2. At the top of the page, enter your name in the From line and enter the date in the Date line.
3. Open the **Income** workbook located in the **Excel12 > Module** folder included with your Data Files, and then save the workbook as **Income Report** in the location specified by your instructor.
4. In the Documentation worksheet, enter your name and the date.
5. Go to the **Income Statement** worksheet, and then copy the range **A3:D15**.

6. Return to the **Hawkes Memo** Word document, and then click to the left of the paragraph mark below the letter's second paragraph.

   Trouble? If you do not see paragraph marks at the end of each paragraph, you need to show the nonprinting characters. On the Home tab, in the Paragraph group, click the Show/Hide ¶ button.

7. On the Home tab, in the Clipboard group, click the **Paste button arrow** to display the list of paste options.
8. Point to each paste option to see a Live Preview of the table as it would appear in the Hawkes Memo document.
9. Click the **Link & Keep Source Formatting (F)** button. Note that the pasted table maintains the formatting styles used in the Income Report workbook. See Figure 12-22.

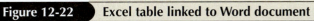

Figure 12-22 **Excel table linked to Word document**

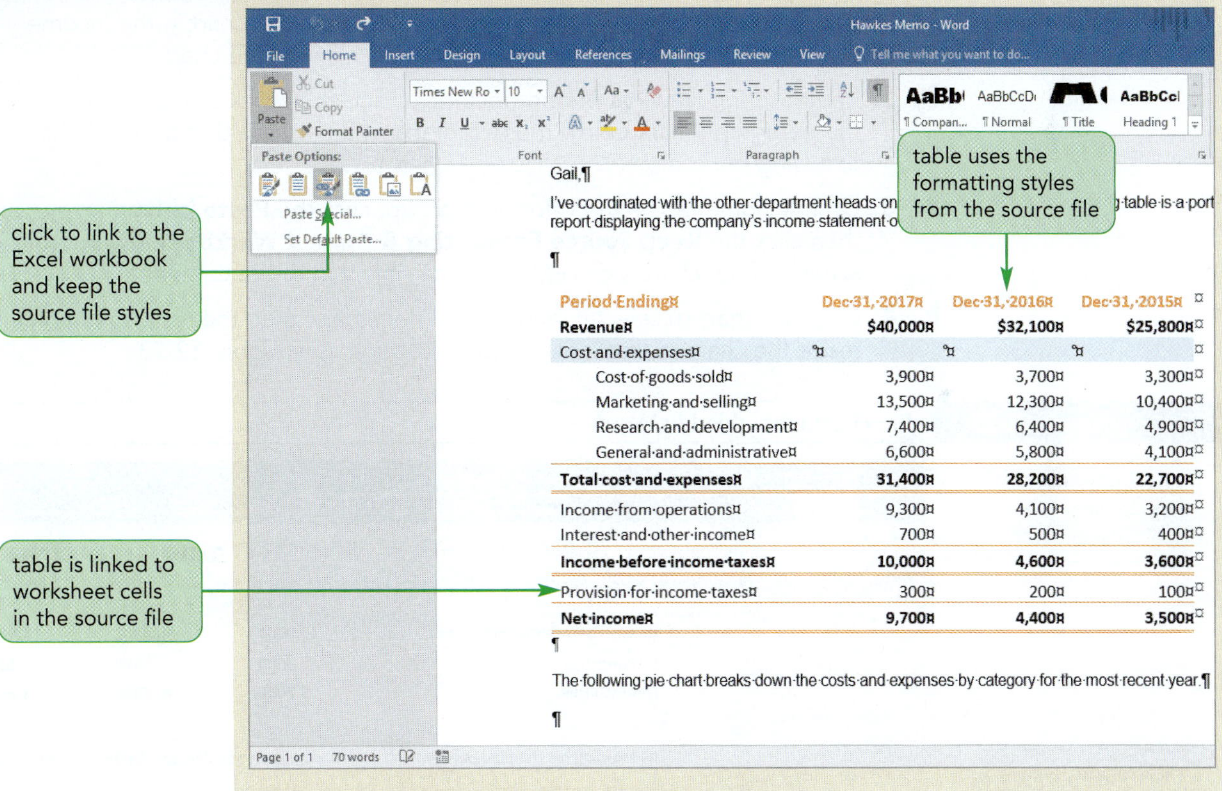
Hawkes Memo - Word
click to link to the Excel workbook and keep the source file styles
table uses the formatting styles from the source file
table is linked to worksheet cells in the source file
Gail,
The following pie chart breaks down the costs and expenses by category for the most recent year.

Period Ending	Dec 31, 2017	Dec 31, 2016	Dec 31, 2015
Revenue	$40,000	$32,100	$25,800
Cost and expenses			
Cost of goods sold	3,900	3,700	3,300
Marketing and selling	13,500	12,300	10,400
Research and development	7,400	6,400	4,900
General and administrative	6,600	5,800	4,100
Total cost and expenses	31,400	28,200	22,700
Income from operations	9,300	4,100	3,200
Interest and other income	700	500	400
Income before income taxes	10,000	4,600	3,600
Provision for income taxes	300	200	100
Net income	9,700	4,400	3,500

Word updates a linked object every time you open the Word document or any time the Excel source file changes while the Word document is open. Marta wants to edit one of the cell titles in the Income Statement worksheet. You'll make her suggested edit and confirm that the table in the Hawkes Memo document changes to match.

To update the linked object:

1. Return to the **Income Report** workbook, and then press the **Esc** key to deselect the range A3:D16.
2. In cell **A14**, type **Pretax income** and then press the **Enter** key.

3. Save the workbook.
4. Return to the **Hawkes Memo** document, right-click the table, and then click **Update Link** on the shortcut menu. Notice that the text linked to cell A14 of the source file changes to "Pretax income."

Marta also wants her memo to include the pie chart from the Income Report workbook that details the source of the company's costs and expenses. She is confident that the pie chart is accurate, so you will embed the chart in the memo. Embedding is done with the same tools used to paste a link to the source object. However, the pie chart and the data it is based on are both stored in the destination document, so changes to the embedded chart will not affect the original chart in the workbook. You'll embed the pie chart from the Income Report workbook now.

To embed the pie chart:

1. Return to the **Income Report** workbook, click the pie chart in the Income Statement worksheet to select it, and then copy the pie chart.
2. Return to the **Hawkes Memo** document, and then click to the left of the paragraph mark below the paragraph in the memo that begins "The following pie chart...").
3. On the Home tab, in the Clipboard group, click the **Paste button arrow**, and then click the **Keep Source Formatting & Embed Workbook (K) button**. A copy of the chart is embedded as an object in the document.
4. Click the chart to select it, and then, if necessary, drag the resizing handles to resize the chart so that it fits on the first page. See Figure 12-23.

Figure 12-23 Pie chart embedded in Word

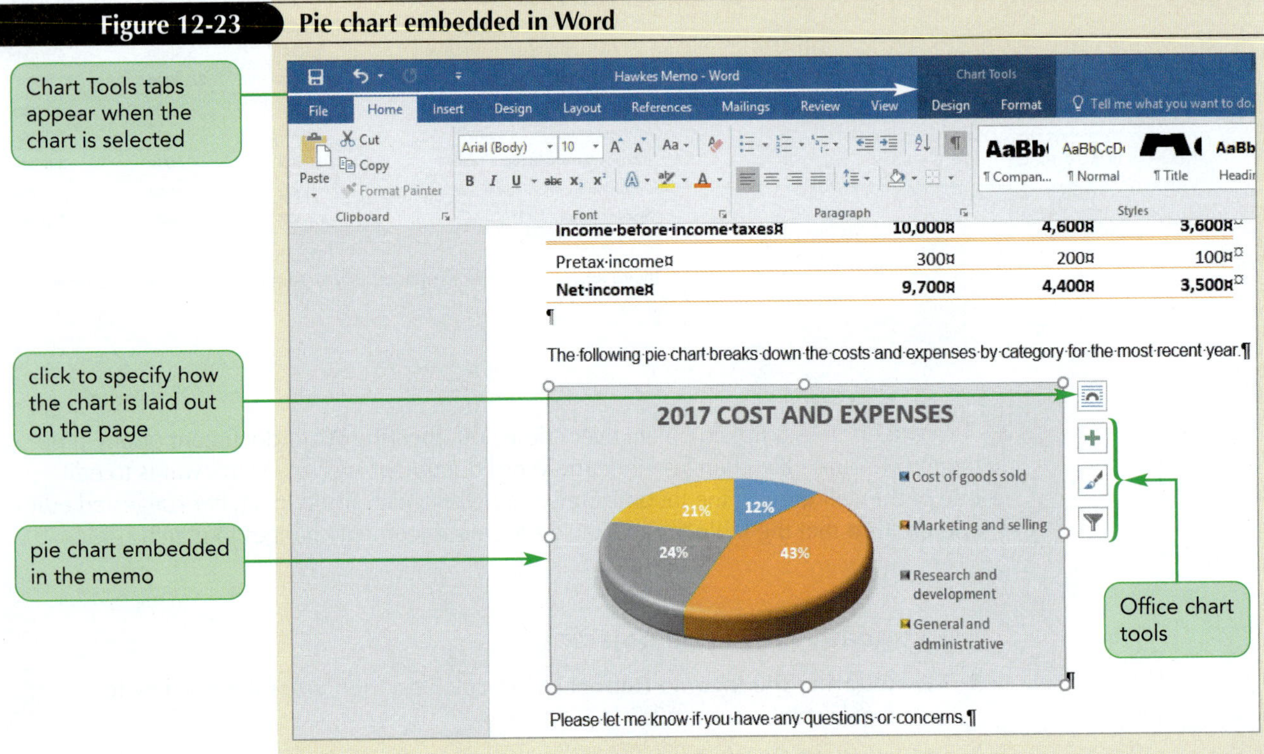

All of the chart tools that are available within Excel are also available with a linked chart or an embedded chart. You'll use the chart tools to change the style of the chart.

To change the chart style:

1. With the embedded chart still selected, click the **Chart Styles** button to the right of the chart.
2. In the Style gallery, click the **Style 3** pie chart style. Word applies the style to the chart. See Figure 12-24.

Figure 12-24 Chart with new chart style

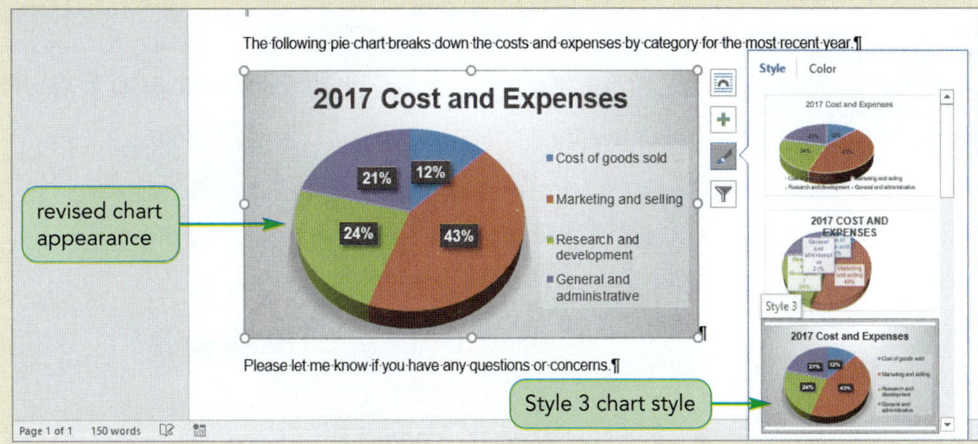

3. Return to the **Income Report** workbook, verify that the appearance of the chart is unaffected, and then return to the **Hawkes Memo** document.

Changing the style of the pie chart has no impact on the chart in the source file because both the embedded chart and the data that it is based on are stored in the memo document. You can view and edit the underlying data to alter the chart's appearance.

To view the data embedded with the chart:

1. Right-click the pie chart, and then click **Edit Data** on the shortcut menu. A spreadsheet window containing the entire contents of the embedded window opens. Notice that even those cells and worksheets that are not used in the chart are still embedded in the document. See Figure 12-25.

Figure 12-25 Embedded chart data

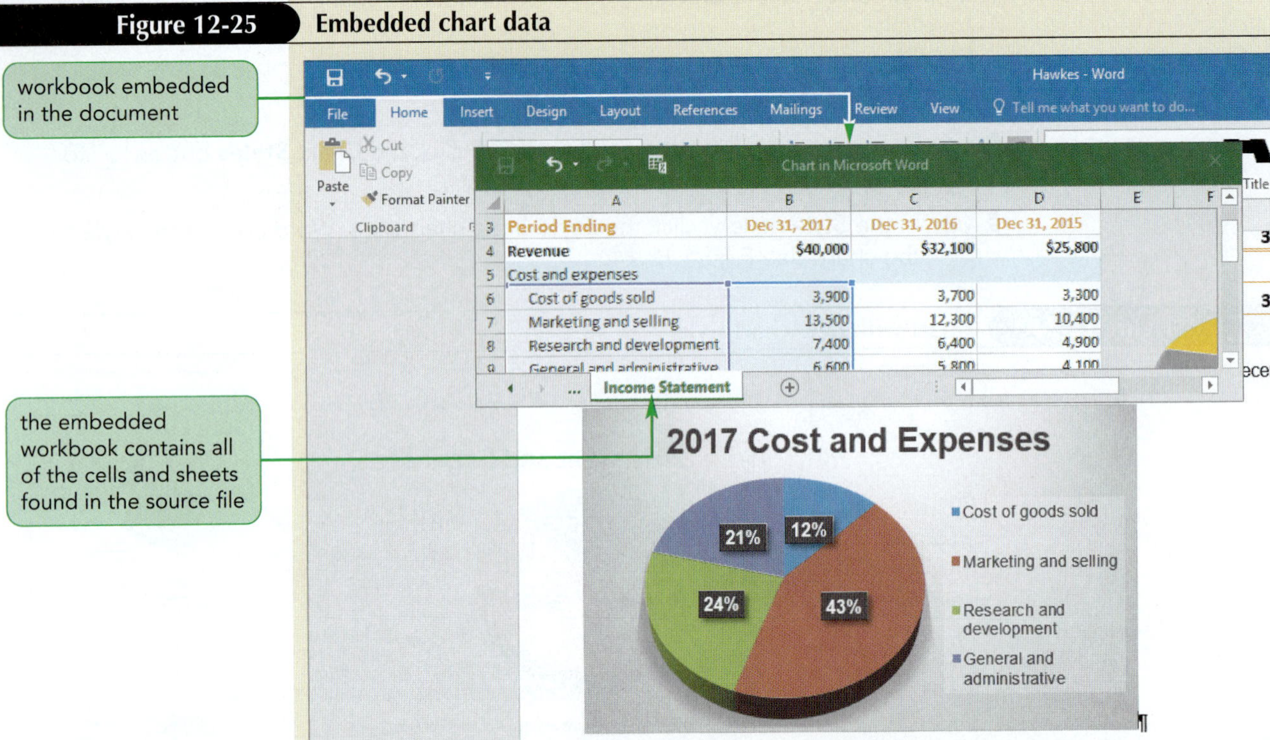

2. In cell **B6**, enter **4,900** to change the embedded data from 3,900. The percentage of the cost of goods sold changes from 12% to 15%.
3. In cell **B6**, enter **3,900** to change the value back to its original.
4. Close the spreadsheet window.
5. Save the Hawkes Memo document, and then close Microsoft Word.

An embedded object such as a chart includes not only the chart sheet but also the other worksheets in the workbook. One disadvantage of embedded objects is that they tend to greatly increase the size of the destination file. You should embed an object only when file size is not an issue and when you need the object's entire contents to be embedded in the destination file.

INSIGHT

Inserting Objects

Another way of embedding one Office object inside another that doesn't involve linking to a source file is to click the Object button in Text group on the Insert tab in any Office program. Office will display a list of objects that can be embedded in the document, including Excel worksheets, Word documents, and PowerPoint slides and presentations. Once embedded in the document, all of the tools and commands associated with the object are available for use.

The advantage of directly embedding the object is that you do not have to maintain two separate files. However, files with several embedded objects are much larger in size and may work more slowly.

Customizing Excel for Your Work Style

Although it is common to collaborate on documents and reports, everyone has his or her own working style. Excel provides options for customizing the Excel environment to meet your own needs and preferences. You have already seen some of these choices in the Excel Options dialog box. You'll examine some of the other customization features of Excel now.

Excel screen elements fall into three general categories:

- Elements that are part of the Excel program
- Elements that are part of the Excel workbook window
- Elements that are part of the Excel worksheet

The difference between these categories is important because it affects under what conditions those elements can be modified. For example, any modifications to the elements that are part of the workbook window are applied to any open workbook. Screen elements that are part of the worksheet are modified only in that worksheet and not in other worksheets and workbooks. Finally, screen elements that are part of the Excel program will be modified across all open workbooks and worksheets. Figure 12-26 lists the screen elements you can customize and the category to which they belong.

Figure 12-26 **Excel screen elements**

Display Location	Screen Element
Excel window	Formula bar
	ScreenTips
	Chart element names on hover
Workbook	Horizontal scroll bar
	Vertical scroll bar
	Sheet tabs
Worksheet	Row and column headers
	Gridlines

Sometimes when Marta presents her workbooks at conferences and talks, she wants to limit the view to only the workbook or worksheet contents to avoid filling the screen with distractions. She asks you to temporarily hide those distracting elements from the viewer. You'll make this change by customizing the Excel display options.

To hide Excel screen elements:

1. Return to the **Income Report** workbook in Excel.
2. On the ribbon, click the **File** tab, and then click **Options** in the navigation bar. The Excel Options dialog box opens.
3. In the left pane, click **Advanced**.
4. Scroll down to the Display section, and then click the **Show formula bar** check box to remove the checkmark.
5. Scroll down to the Display options for this workbook section, and make sure that the workbook name **Income Report** appears in the box.
6. Click the **Show horizontal scroll bar**, **Show vertical scroll bar**, and **Show sheet tabs** check boxes to remove the checkmarks.

7. Scroll down to the Display options for this worksheet section, and make sure that the worksheet name **Income Statement** appears in the box.

8. Click the **Show row and column headers** and **Show gridlines** check boxes to remove the checkmarks. See Figure 12-27.

Figure 12-27 Advanced Excel options

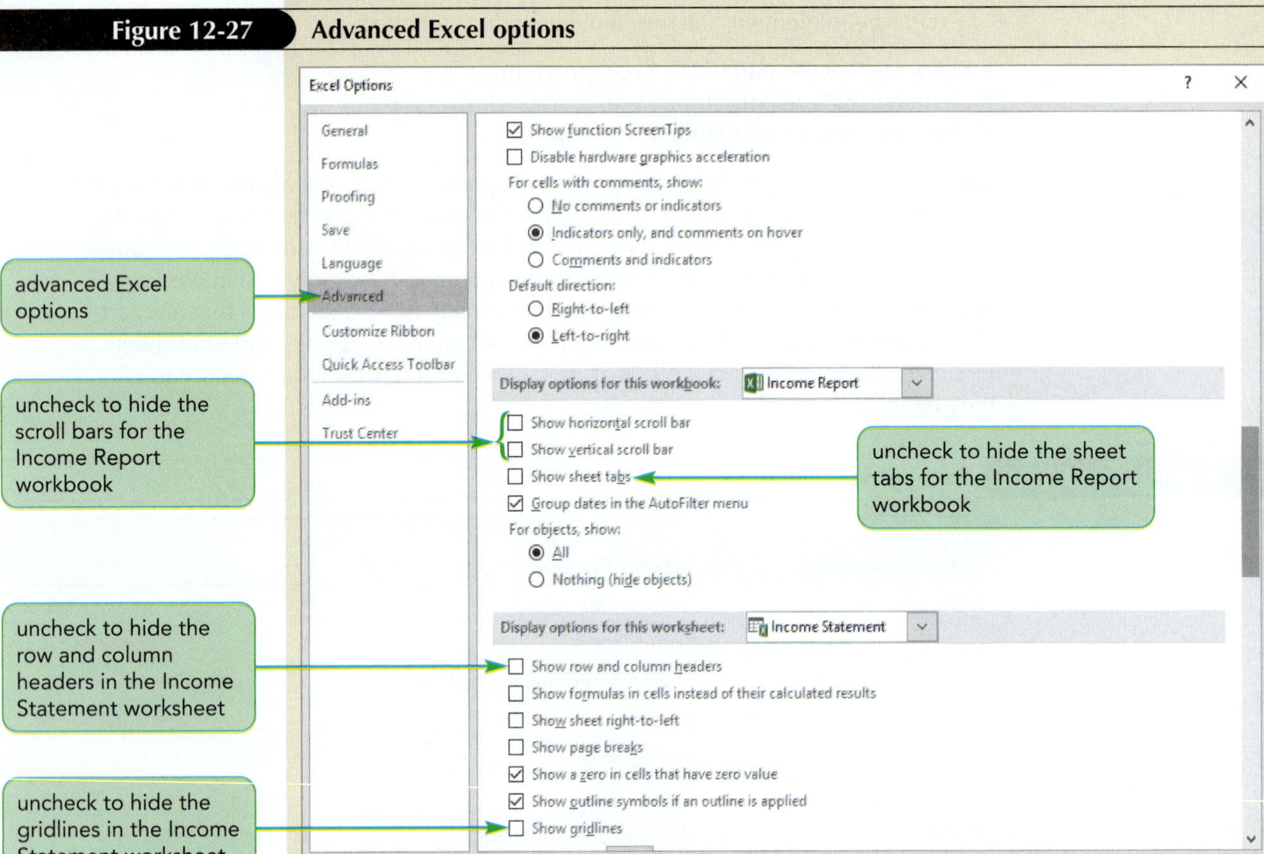

9. Click the **OK** button to apply the new options and close the dialog box. The contents of the Income Statement worksheet appear with many Excel screen elements hidden from view. See Figure 12-28.

Figure 12-28 Hidden screen elements

formula bar hidden

row and column headings hidden

scroll bars hidden

sheet tabs hidden

worksheet gridlines removed

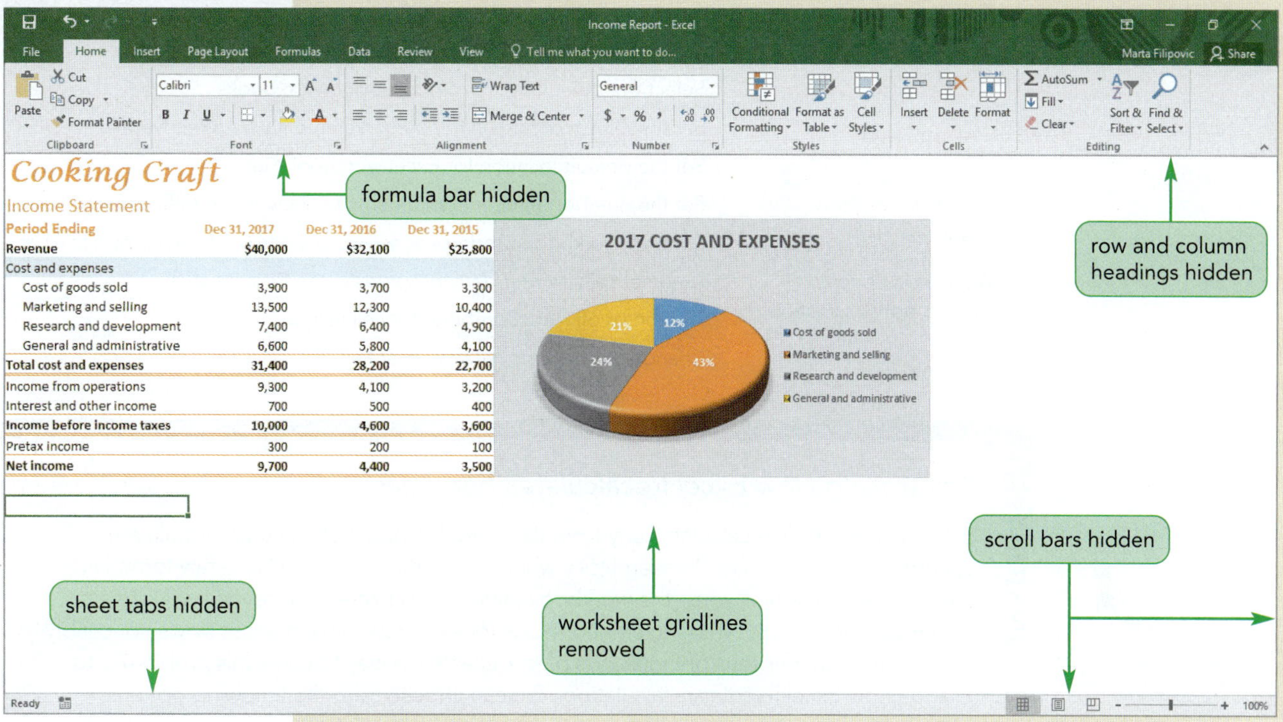

To redisplay the hidden screen elements, you will return to the Excel Options dialog box and select the check boxes for those elements.

To redisplay the workbook and worksheet screen elements:

1. On the ribbon, click the **File** tab, and then click **Options** in the navigation bar to reopen the Excel Options dialog box.
2. In the left pane, click **Advanced**.
3. Click the **Show formula bar**, **Show horizontal scroll bar**, **Show vertical scroll bar**, **Show sheet tabs**, **Show row and column headers**, and **Show gridlines** check boxes to insert checkmarks and redisplay those screen elements.
4. Click the **OK** button. The workbook window returns to its default view with all screen elements displayed.
5. Save and close the Income Report workbook, but keep Excel open.

The Excel Options dialog box provides many customization options for controlling how Excel works on your computer. For example, you can change the default font setting, which is 11-point Calibri. Or, you can change the default number of worksheets in new workbooks from one to another number. Figure 12-29 lists other features you can customize.

Figure 12-29 Excel customization options

Excel Options	Customization Option
Formulas options	Turn on and off Formula AutoComplete
Save options	Select the default file format for saving workbooks
	Set the length of time in minutes to create an AutoRecover file
	Set the default location for Excel workbook files
Advanced options, Display section	Set the number of recent documents to show in the Office menu
	Show all workbook windows as separate icons on the Windows taskbar
Advanced options, Editing options section	Automatically format percent values in the Percent style
	Turn on or off AutoComplete for cell values
	Change the behavior of the Enter key

INSIGHT

Controlling How Excel Recalculates Formulas

Excel automatically recalculates any formula when the input cells to that formula are changed. This process works seamlessly when the workbook is small and few formulas are involved. However, when the workbook increases in size—think several worksheets with thousands of rows with multiple formulas for each row—this process slows noticeably as Excel recalculates tens of thousands of formulas. One way to solve this problem is to change how Excel handles recalculation. You can choose from the following options:

- **Automatic**—all dependent formulas are recalculated every time a change is made to their input cells.
- **Automatic except for data tables**—automatic recalculation is done for all dependent formulas except for formulas within data tables created with the Data Tables feature.
- **Manual**—no recalculation is done except when manually requested by the user.

To manually recalculate the contents of the workbook, press the F9 key, or click the Calculate Now button in the Calculation group on the Formulas tab. You can define calculation options on the Formulas tab in the Excel Options dialog box or by clicking the Calculation Options button in the Calculation group on the Formulas tab.

Another way to speed up a large workbook is to reduce the number of iterative calculations used in performing what-if analyses involving goal seeking. You can set this value using the Enable iterative calculation check box on the Formulas tab in the Excel Options dialog box.

Cooking Craft has a few stores operating in Europe, and several more opening in Asia and South America. Marta wants you to examine how Excel could be customized to help her collaborate with colleagues and clients in different countries.

Developing a Workbook for International Clients

Businesses increasingly need their employees to develop reports and analysis for international customers. If you are creating a workbook that will be viewed by clients in another country, you may need to check on the standards for rendering times, dates, currency, and numbers for use in the country of interest. For example, countries differ in terms of how they use blank spaces, commas, and periods to mark decimal places and number groups. Figure 12-30 shows how the same number will be represented in several different countries.

Figure 12-30 International number formats

Style	Description	supported in
5,308,421.64	Thousands grouped by a comma, decimals marked with a period	English Canada, China, Ireland, Israel, Japan, Korea, Malaysia, New Zealand, Taiwan, Thailand, United Kingdom, United States
5 308 421,64	Thousands grouped by a space, decimals marked with a comma	Albania, Belgium, Brazil, Denmark, France, French Canada, Finland, Germany, Greece, Italy, Netherlands, Poland, Portugal, Romania, Sweden, Switzerland
5.308.421,64	Thousands grouped by a period, decimals marked with a comma	Brazil, Denmark, France, Germany, Greece, Italy, Netherlands, Portugal, Romania, Spain, Sweden
53,08,421.64	Thousands above 9,999 marked in two-digit groups with a comma, decimals marked with a period	India
5'308'421.64	Thousands grouped with an apostrophe, decimals marked with a period	Switzerland
5'308'421,64	Thousands grouped with an apostrophe, decimals marked with a comma	Germany, Greece, Italy, Romania

The number format used by Excel is set by the computer's operating system. If you are running Windows, you can use the Language section of the Control Panel to change the symbols used for the thousands separator and decimal marks, as well as set the parameters for other number formats. However, in some cases, you might want to only temporarily change the number format for a particular workbook. You can make such a change using the advanced Excel options.

Marta has an income statement for the new Cooking Craft store in Paris. She wants to change the number format to match the format used in France.

To change the number format style used by Excel:

1. Open the **Paris** workbook located in the **Excel12 > Module** folder included with your Data Files, and then save the file as **Paris Income** in the location specified by your instructor.
2. In the Documentation worksheet, enter your name and the date.
3. Go to the **Income Statement** worksheet. Note that all of the numbers are expressed using the default number formats set in your operating system. For this data, Marta wants to replace the thousands separator with a period and the decimal point with a comma.
4. On the ribbon, click the **File** tab, and then click **Options** in the navigation bar. The Excel Options dialog box opens.
5. In the left pane, click **Advanced**.
6. In the Editing options section, click the **Use system separators** check box to remove the checkmark so that Excel does not use the number format defined by the operating system.
7. Select the symbol in the **Decimal separator** box, and then type **,** (a comma).

TIP

You can set the language Excel uses for grammar, spell checking, and sorting in the Language options in the Excel Options dialog box.

8. Select the symbol in the Thousands separator box, and then type **.** (a period). See Figure 12-31.

Figure 12-31 Decimal and thousands separators specified

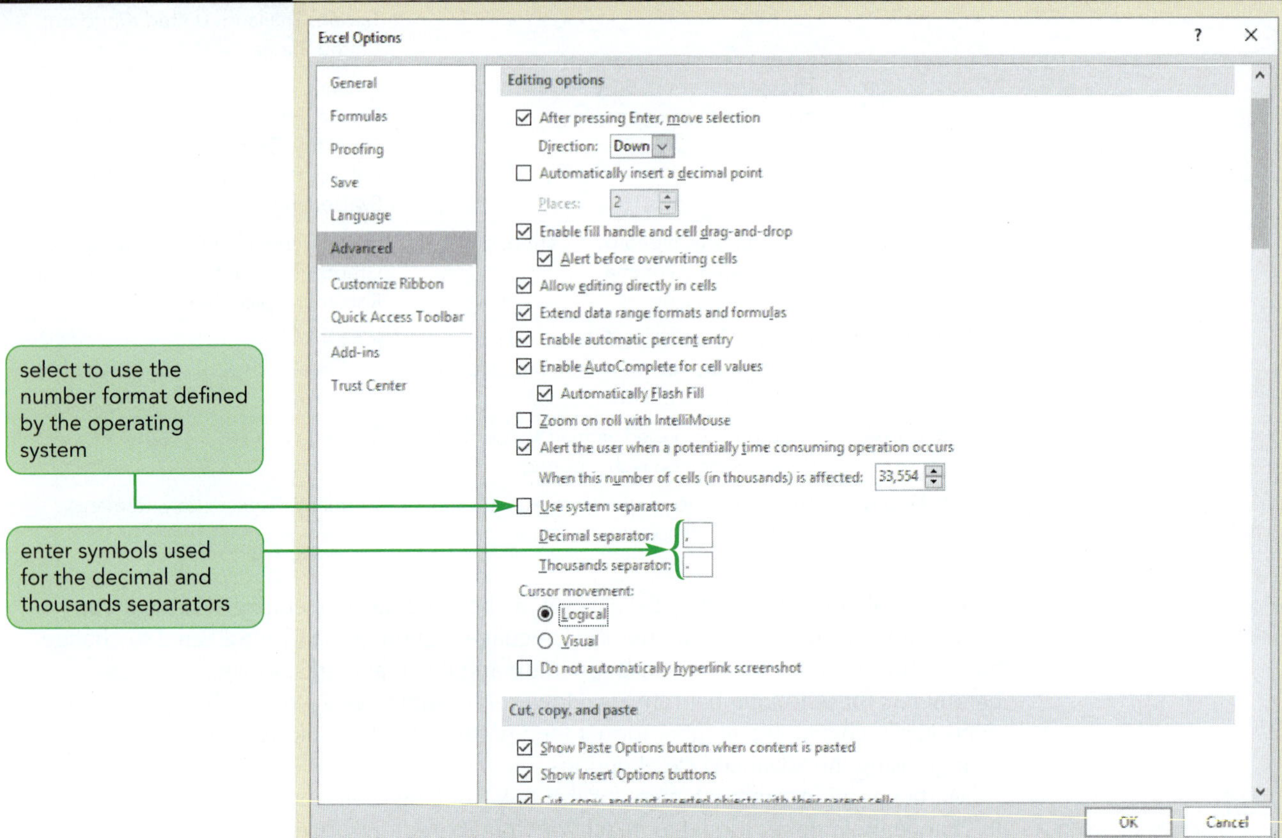

9. Click the **OK** button. In the worksheet, a period is now used for the thousands separator, and a comma is used for the decimal separator. See Figure 12-32.

Figure 12-32 Numbers displayed in French format

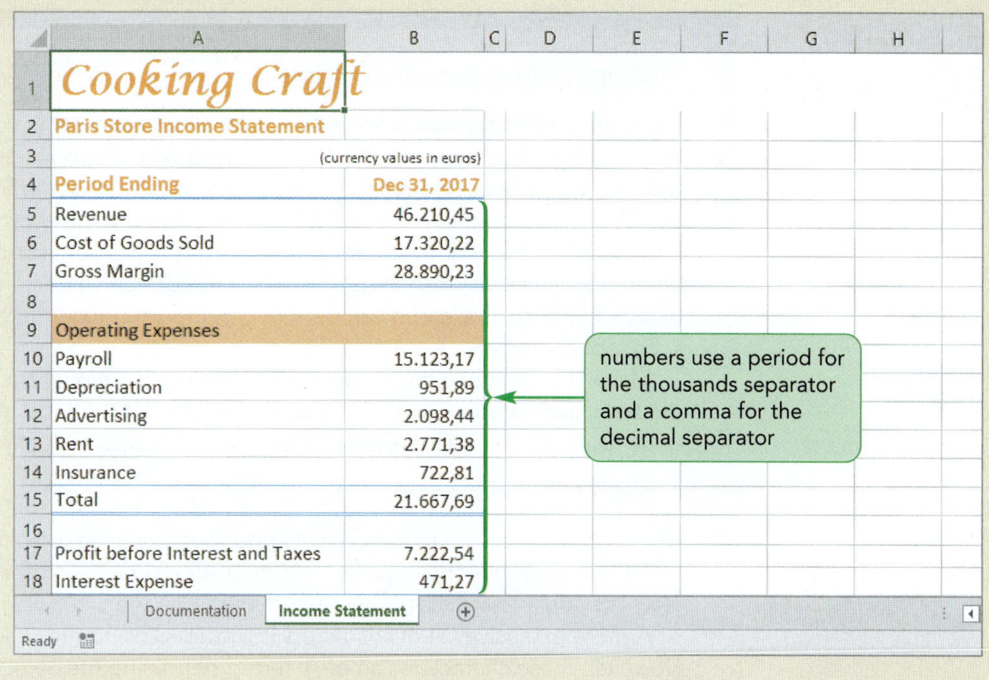

Marta also wants to be clear that the currency values in the Income Statement are expressed in euros, not dollars. You'll make this formatting change to the revenue and net profit values in the worksheet.

To express the currency values in euros:

1. Select the nonadjacent range **B5,B22**. The two cells are selected.
2. On the Home tab, in the Number group, click the **Accounting Number Format button arrow** $, and then click **Euro**. The euro symbol appears with the values in cells B5 and B22. See Figure 12-33.

Figure 12-33 Euro currency symbol

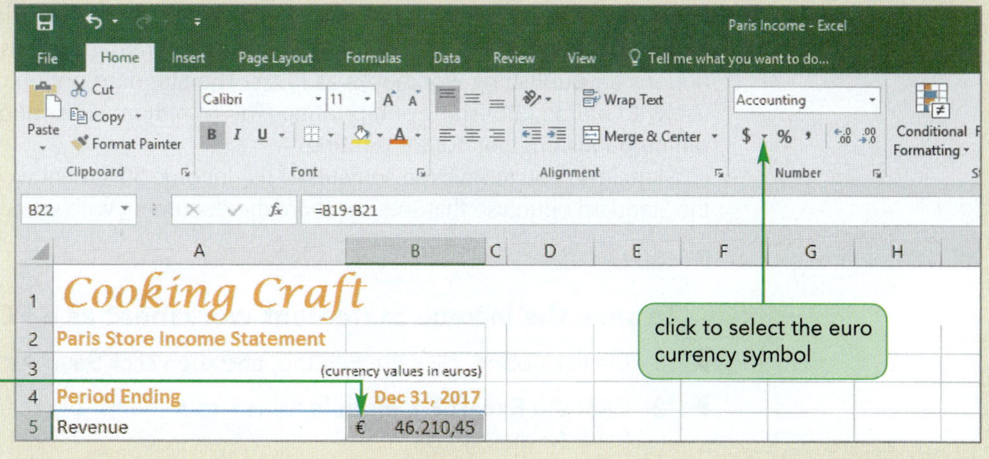

3. Save the workbook.

Excel also includes currency symbols for the English pound (£) and Chinese yuan (¥), which you can select by clicking the Account Number Format button arrow.

INSIGHT

Utilizing International Symbols

If you are creating a document for an international audience, you might need to insert international symbols into the text. One way of quickly doing this is with the Symbol dialog box. To open the Symbol dialog box, click the Symbol button in the Symbols group on the Insert tab. Microsoft Office organizes symbols into different topical categories. For example, you can click the Subset list box to display a gallery of currency symbols from across the world. European characters that include accent or tilde marks such as è and õ can be found in the Latin Extended-A or Latin Extended-B subset of characters.

Many keyboard shortcuts exist for inserting international characters. One form of the keyboard shortcut involves holding down the Alt key and typing the character code using your numeric keypad. This character code is usually written as

```
Alt+character_code
```

where *character_code* is an ASCII code that identifies the character you wish to insert. For example, the keyboard shortcut Alt+0232 inserts the è character. You can view the codes associated with each character in the Symbol dialog box.

A more extensive list of characters is provided using the Unicode character set. However, these characters can be inserted only using the Symbol dialog box. Excel does not support keyboard shortcuts for these characters.

The Excel option to set the symbol for the decimal and thousands separator applies to the entire Excel working environment. This means that any workbook will now show numbers in the French number format until you change the Excel options back to the default operating system settings. Marta doesn't want to change her number formats permanently. Instead, she wants only a hard-copy version of this data using the euro currency and number formatting. She asks you to save a version of this file as a PDF.

Saving a Worksheet as a PDF File

PDF (Portable Document Format) is a file format developed by Adobe Systems for displaying formatted documents containing text, graphics, and complicated layouts. PDFs are often used for collaborative work because Adobe Reader software is free and available on a wide variety of devices and operating systems. Excel provides two options for publishing workbooks as PDFs. The Standard option optimizes the PDF for use with online publishing and printing. The Minimum size option is used strictly for online publishing but not for printing.

Marta asks you to save the contents of the Income Statement worksheet as a PDF using the Standard option so that she can share the document with users who do not have Excel.

To save the Income Statement worksheet as a PDF file:

1. On the ribbon, click the **File** tab, and then click **Save As** in the navigation bar.
2. Click the **Excel12 > Module** folder from the list of recent folders to open the Save As dialog box.

3. In the File name box, type **Paris Income Statement**.
4. Click the **Save as type** box, and then click **PDF** in the list of file types.
5. Verify that the **Standard** option button is selected, and then click the **Save** button. The worksheet is saved as a PDF file.
6. If the Paris Income Statement PDF file is not already open on your screen, open the **Paris Income Statement** PDF file in a browser or PDF reader. See Figure 12-34.

Figure 12-34 PDF version of the Paris report

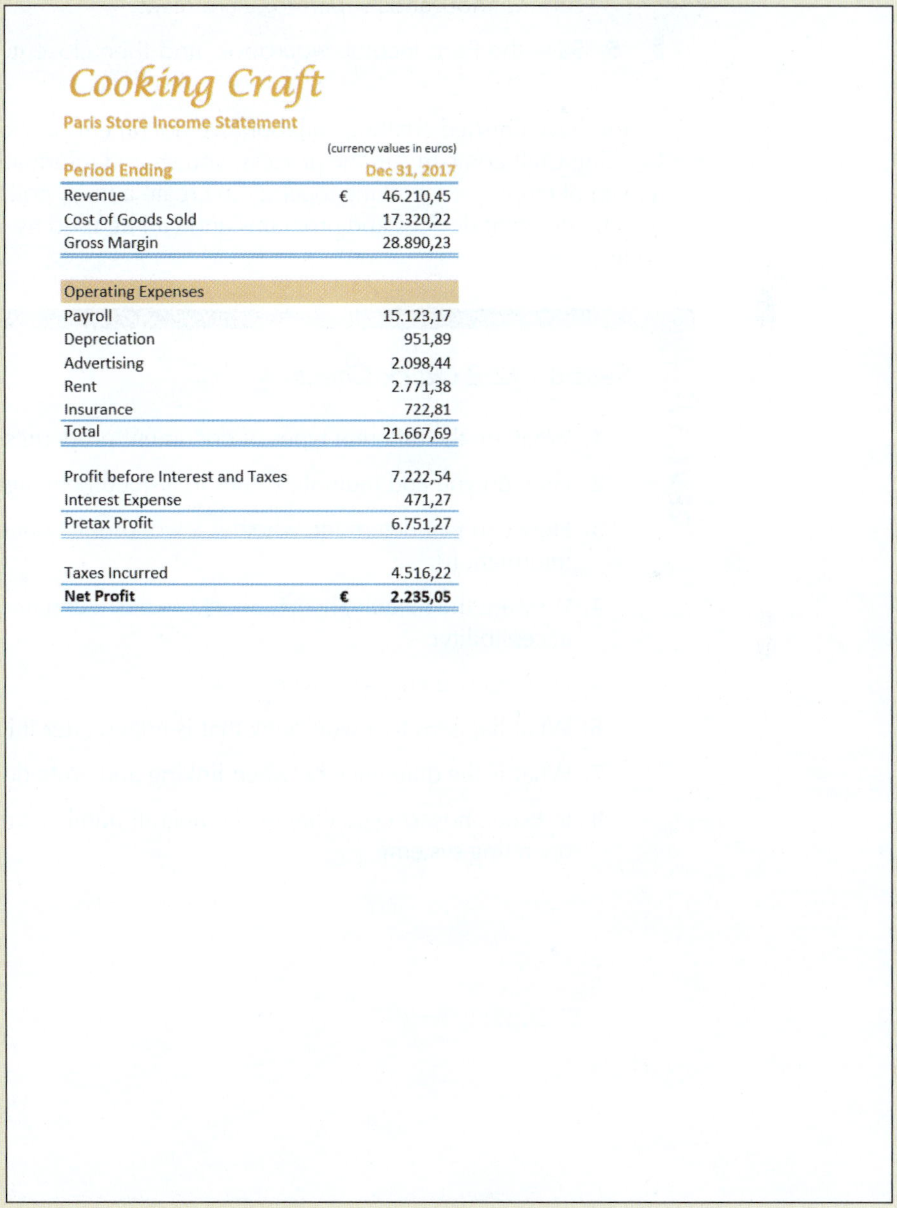

Cooking Craft

Paris Store Income Statement

(currency values in euros)

Period Ending		Dec 31, 2017
Revenue	€	46.210,45
Cost of Goods Sold		17.320,22
Gross Margin		28.890,23
Operating Expenses		
Payroll		15.123,17
Depreciation		951,89
Advertising		2.098,44
Rent		2.771,38
Insurance		722,81
Total		21.667,69
Profit before Interest and Taxes		7.222,54
Interest Expense		471,27
Pretax Profit		6.751,27
Taxes Incurred		4.516,22
Net Profit	**€**	**2.235,05**

7. Close the PDF document, and return to the Excel workbook.

Before finishing your work, Marta wants you to change the numeric formats back to their default operating system settings.

To restore the number format to the system settings:

1. On the ribbon, click the **File** tab, and then click **Options** in the navigation bar. The Excel Options dialog box reopens.
2. In the left pane, click **Advanced**.
3. In the Editing options section, click the **Use system separators** check box.
4. Click the **OK** button. The system separators—a period decimal separator and comma thousands separator—are reset.
5. Save the Paris Income workbook, and then close it.

You have finished creating collaborative documents in Excel for Marta and the Cooking Craft company. In the process, you shared information in several ways among a team of employees working together to create a final, polished document that can be read by different devices and programs and can be used by international customers and colleagues.

REVIEW

Session 12.2 Quick Check

1. What are the different types of document properties?
2. How do you add multiple values to a document tag?
3. How can you determine whether a workbook contains sensitive or personal information?
4. Why are the default Sheet1, Sheet2 worksheet names not good for accessibility?
5. How do you encrypt a workbook?
6. What happens to a workbook that is edited after it is digitally signed?
7. What is the difference between linking and embedding?
8. In Excel, how do you change the default number format set by the computer's operating system?

PRACTICE

Review Assignments

Data Files needed for the Review Assignments: Projected.xlsx, Section.xlsx, Cash.xlsx, Garza Review.xlsx, Cash Flow.xlsx, Notes.docx, Brussels.xlsx

Marta needs to provide a projected income statement and projected cash flow schedule for the coming year for the stockholders' meeting. She already created the initial workbook, but she wants you to send it out for review and then reconcile the edits made by her colleagues. After Marta has a final draft, she wants you to add document properties, encrypt the workbook, and mark it as final. Complete the following:

1. Open the **Projected** workbook located in the Excel12 > Review folder included with your Data Files, and then save the workbook as **Projected Statements** in the location specified by your instructor. In the Documentation worksheet, enter your name and the date.
2. In the Projected Income worksheet, add the following comment to cell B5: **Do you think that this is a reasonable estimate for next year's revenue?**
3. Share the workbook, enabling changes by more than one user at a time, and then save and close the workbook.
4. Open the **Section** workbook located in the Excel12 > Review folder, and then save the workbook as **Section Edits** in the location specified by your instructor. In the Documentation worksheet, replace the author and the date with your name and the current date.
5. In the Income Projections worksheet, delete the comments that were added to cell B5.
6. Display the contents of the tracking log for everyone's changes to the workbook but yours. Print the History worksheet on a single page.
7. Accept or reject the following edits made by the team to the workbook:
   a. In cell B5 of the Income Projections worksheet, accept Larry Todd's recommended projection for the coming year's net revenue.
   b. In cell B7, accept John Andersen's edit for the cost of goods sold.
   c. In cell B10, accept John Andersen's edit for the general and administrative costs.
   d. Accept John Andersen's renaming of the Income Statement sheet and the Cash Flow Statement sheet.
   e. In cell B15, reject Kari Lewis's edit.
   f. Reject Larry Todd's edits to the worksheet names, leaving the worksheets names as Projected Income Statement and Projected Cash Flow Schedule.
8. Save the Section Edits workbook, and then close it.
9. Open the **Cash** workbook located in the Excel12 > Review folder, and then save the workbook as **Cash and Income Report** in the location specified by your instructor. In the Documentation worksheet, enter your name and the date.
10. Add the Compare and Merge Workbooks button to the Quick Access Toolbar, and then merge the contents of the current workbook with the **Garza Review** workbook located in the Excel12 > Review folder to incorporate the edits and comments from Armando Garza. Accept all of Armando's changes to the workbook. Save the document. Remove the Compare and Merge Workbooks button from the Quick Access Toolbar.
11. Save the workbook again as **Cash and Income Report Final**, and then remove the workbook from shared use.
12. Add the following properties to the workbook:
    - Title: **Financial Projections**
    - Tags: **projections; stockholders**
    - Comments: **Financial projections for the stockholders' conference**
    - Status: **Final Draft**
    - Categories: **Conference Reports**
    - Subject: **Stockholders' Report**

- Company: **Cooking Craft**
- Author: your name

13. Insert the Department custom property using Text as the type and **Finance** as the value.
14. Encrypt the document using the password **cookingcraft**.
15. Mark the document as final, and then close the workbook.
16. Open the **Cash Flow** workbook located in the Excel12 > Review folder. Marta wants to share the cash flow projections in this workbook with her supervisor, Denise Mitchell.
17. Using Microsoft Word, open the **Notes** document located in the Excel12 > Review folder included with your Data Files, enter your name on the From line and the date on the Date line, and then save the document as **Notes on Cash Flow**.
18. In the Cash Flow workbook, in the Cash Projections worksheet, copy the range A2:B39, and then in the blank line after the opening paragraph in the Notes on Cash Flow document, paste a link and keep the source formatting, which in this case is the Cash Flow workbook.
19. Save and close the Cash Flow workbook and the Notes on Cash Flow document.
20. Open the **Brussels** workbook located in the Excel12 > Review folder, and then save the workbook as **Brussels Income**. In the Documentation worksheet, enter your name and the date.
21. In the Income Statement worksheet, format the currency values in cells B5 and B22 with the euro currency symbol.
22. Set the Excel options to use a period as the thousands separator and a comma as the decimal separator.
23. Save the Income Statement worksheet as a Standard PDF file with the filename **Brussels Income Statement**.
24. Save the Brussels Income workbook, and then close it.
25. Restore the Excel options to use the operating system settings for number formats.

APPLY

Case Problem 1

Data Files needed for this Case Problem: Sandwich.xlsx, Shop1.xlsx, Shop2.xlsx, Shop3.xlsx, Shop4.xlsx

Sandwich Kite Travon Lee is the financial manager at Sandwich Kite, a chain of sub sandwich shops located in the Southeastern United States. Travon is working on a sales report detailing the monthly sales figures from four stores in the state of Georgia. Each store manager has sent Travon an Excel workbook containing his or her store's monthly sales totals, and Travon wants to compare and merge these documents into a single workbook. Complete the following:

1. Open the **Sandwich** workbook located in the Excel12 > Case1 folder included with your Data Files, and then save the file as **Sandwich Kite** in the location specified by your instructor.
2. In the Documentation worksheet, enter your name and the date.
3. Go to the Income Statements worksheet, and then merge the contents of the **Shop1**, **Shop2**, **Shop3**, and **Shop4** workbooks located in the Excel12 > Case1 folder into the Sandwich Kite workbook. You can select all four workbooks in the Select Files to Merge Into Current Workbook dialog box by holding down the Ctrl key and clicking each filename.
4. Review the comments in the range B4:E4 of the Income Statements worksheet, and then delete the comments from the worksheet.
5. In the Income Statements worksheet, enter formulas to do the following:
   - In the range B6:E6, display the sales for each store.
   - In the range B9:E9, display the cost of sales for each store.
   - In the range B10:E10, calculate the gross profit (Total Sales – Total Cost of Sales).
   - In the range B33:E33, calculate the total expenses for each store.

- In the range B35:E35, calculate the net operating income (Gross Profit – Total Expenses).
- In column F, calculate the total values of each category in the income statement across all four stores.

6. In cell A1 of the Income Statements worksheet, add the following comment: **Data compiled from workbooks provided by Andrew Ferentz, Ryan Seward, Sarah Tollinger, and Diego Melendez.**
7. Remove the document from shared use.
8. On the Info screen, add the following names to the list of document authors: your name, **Andrew Ferentz**, **Ryan Seward**, **Sarah Tollinger**, and **Diego Melendez**.
9. Add the following properties to the workbook—Monthly Income as the title; income statement as the tag; Data compiled from the four stores in Georgia as the comment; Final as the status; and Sandwich Kite as the company.
10. Add the custom Checked by property to the workbook using your name as the property value.
11. Add the custom Date completed property to the workbook using Date as the data type and the current date as the property value.
12. Encrypt the workbook with the password **sandwich** and mark it as final.
13. Save the Income Statements worksheet as a PDF file with the filename **Sandwich Kite Georgia**.
14. Close any open files.

APPLY

Case Problem 2

Data Files needed for this Case Problem: Agape.xlsx, Donor.docx

Agape Center Kevin Hale is the fundraising coordinator for the Agape Center, a collection of family apartments in Michigan provided at no cost to families with children in long-term care at one of the many Michigan children's hospitals. As the annual major fundraising drive approaches, Kevin needs to compile a mailing list of past contributors. He has created a workbook with names and addresses and had his assistants review the workbook and correct errors they found. You'll review his shared workbook and reconcile the edits made by his assistants. Kevin will send a final draft of the workbook to other members of the fundraising team who are creating the form letters and mailing labels as part of the funding drive. Complete the following:

1. Open the **Agape** workbook located in the Excel12 > Case2 folder included with your Data Files, and then save the workbook as **Agape Center** in the location specified by your instructor.
2. In the Documentation worksheet, enter your name and the date.
3. Display the tracking log for all edits made to the workbook except yours in a new sheet. Print the History worksheet with the tracking log in landscape orientation scaled to fit on a single page.
4. Review the changes made by Kevin's assistants, accepting or rejecting the following edits:
   - Accept Ingrid Drake's edit to cell I44
   - Accept Paul Ingres's edit to cell D27
   - Accept Paul Ingres's edit to cell D174
   - Reject Ingrid Drake's edit to cell B64
   - Accept Ingrid Drake's edit to cell C123
   - Accept Maria Cassidy's edits to cells I164 and I98
5. Remove the workbook from shared use.
6. Add the following names as the workbook authors—your name, **Paul Ingres**, **Ingrid Drake**, and **Maria Cassidy**.
7. Add the following document properties to the workbook—**Agape Center** as the title; **Donor list for the annual fundraiser** as the comment; **Final** as the status; **fundraiser** as the category; and **Donor list** as the subject.
8. In the custom properties, add the Checked by property using Text as the type, and **Kevin Hale**, **Paul Ingres**, **Ingrid Drake**, **Maria Cassidy** as the value.

9. Add the Date completed property, use Date as the value type, and then enter the current date as the value.
10. Create a new custom property named **Approved** with the value type set to Yes or no, and then select the value Yes.
11. Run the Compatibility Checker on the workbook to find any issues that Kevin's colleagues will encounter if they are running older versions of Excel. Copy the report results to a new worksheet.
12. Start Word, open the **Donor** document located in the Excel12 > Case2 folder included with your Data Files, and then save the document as **Donor Memo** in the location specified by your instructor.
13. In the From: and Date: lines of the memo, enter your name and the date.
14. In the Agape Center workbook, sort the table of donors in descending order of donation. Copy the information on all donors who donated $1,000 or more.
15. In the Donor Memo document, paste the selected range after the initial paragraph of the memo as a picture. Close the document, saving your changes.
16. In the Agape Center workbook, encrypt the workbook with the password **agape**.
17. Mark the workbook as final, and then close it.

CHALLENGE

Case Problem 3

Data Files needed for this Case Problem: Menu.xlsx, Review.docx

Menu Query Jerry Padgett runs a website called Menu Query that provides nutritional advice and information taken from the menus of different restaurants. Jerry and several coworkers review and update the menu information. Jerry has created a sample workbook describing some of the menu items from the restaurant La Marie. He wants your help with reconciling the different edits to that workbook by his colleagues. He also wants you to link the workbook to a Word document containing a full review of La Marie. Complete the following:

1. Open the **Menu** workbook located in the Excel12 > Case3 folder included with your Data Files, and then save the workbook as **Menu Query** in the location specified by your instructor.
2. In the Documentation worksheet, enter your name and the date.
3. Review the edits made by Stephanie Larson and Barbara Kaufmann, accepting their edits. In case of a conflict, accept Stephanie Larson's edits.
4. Save the Menu Query workbook.
5. Display the contents of the tracking log on the History worksheet, showing everyone's edits, including your edits, and showing your own actions accepting or rejecting the other edits made to the document. Print the log on a single sheet in landscape orientation.
6. Remove sharing from the workbook.

Explore 7. In the La Marie Menu worksheet, several menu items should contain international symbols. Use the Symbol dialog box to make the following edits:
   - In cell A6, change Eclair to Éclair.
   - In cell A11, change Creme Brulee to Créme Brûlée.
   - In cell A15, change Napoleon to Napoléon.
   - In cell A29, change Provencal to Provençal.
   - In cell A31, change Entrees to Entrées.
8. Display the price values in column B as currency using the euro currency symbol. Enlarge the column as necessary.
9. Add the following properties to the document—your name as an author as well as the names **Jerry Padgett**, **Stephanie Larson**, and **Barbara Kaufmann**; enter **La Marie Review** as the title; and **Menu Query** as the company.

10. Add the custom property Checked by with the Text value type and the value **Stephanie Larson, Barbara Kaufmann**. Add the custom property Date completed using the Date value type and the current date as the value.

Explore 11. Jerry wants you to link a review of the restaurant that he saved in a Word document to the workbook. On the Insert tab, in the Text group, use the Object button to open the Object dialog box. On the Create from File tab, browse to select the **Review** document file located in the Excel12 > Case3 folder included with your Data Files, and then click the Link to file check box. Click the OK button, and then place the Word document object in the Documentation worksheet with its upper-left corner in cell D3.

12. Use the Compatibility Checker to check the workbook for compatibility with earlier versions of Excel. Copy the results of the report to a new sheet in the workbook.

Explore 13. Run the Accessibility Checker to check for issues that might affect users with special needs. The Accessibility Checker will note that inserting an object (in this case, the linked Word document) without also providing alternate text may make the document inaccessible for some users. In the Documentation worksheet, right-click the embedded Word document, and then click Format Object on the shortcut menu. In the Alt Text tab, type **Restaurant review of La Marie** as the alternate text, and then click the OK button.

14. Run the Accessibility Checker again, if necessary, to verify that no accessibility issues occur in the workbook.

15. Mark the workbook as final, and then save and close the workbook.

CHALLENGE

Case Problem 4

Data File needed for this Case Problem: Soul.xlsx

Soul Camping Libby Hudson is a financial coordinator for Soul Camping, a new company that manufactures solar panels and devices for hikers and campers. Libby and her team are developing a workbook containing projected income and cash flow for the company's next five years. Libby has to reconcile the different edits made by her team and report the results in a finalized document. Because of the sensitive nature of this information, Libby wants to digitally sign the final version to ensure that no unauthorized changes are made to her team's projections. Complete the following:

1. Open the **Soul** workbook located in the Excel12 > Case4 folder included with your Data Files, and then save the workbook as **Soul Camping** in the location specified by your instructor.
2. In the Documentation worksheet, enter your name and the date.
3. Review and delete all of the comments within the workbook.
4. Display a list of all changes made by users other than yourself to the workbook on the History worksheet, and then print the sheet.
5. Review the edits made to the document, accepting or rejecting the changes as follows:
   - Accept Bill Enders's values for the range B12:F12 in the Balance Sheet worksheet.
   - Accept Bill Enders's edits in cell A2 of the Balance Sheet, Income Statement, and Cash Flow worksheets.
   - Accept the original values for the sales estimates in the range B5:F5 of the Income Statement worksheet.
   - Accept Bill Enders's changes to the names of the Income Statement, Cash Flow, and Balance Sheet worksheets.
   - Accept the original values for the tax liability estimates in the range B27:F27 of the Income Statement worksheet.
   - Accept the original values for the long-term asset values in the range B14:F14 of the Balance Sheet worksheet.
   - Reject Kat Wagner's change of the sheet names for the company's income statement, cash flow statement, and balance sheet.
   - Accept Deidre Templeton's edit of cell A27 on the Income Statement worksheet.

6. Remove sharing from the workbook.
7. Add the following names to the list of authors of the workbook: your name, **Bill Enders**, **Kat Wagner**, and **Deidre Templeton**.
8. Set the value of the Title property to **Projected Financial Statements**. Set the value of the Company property to **Soul Camping**.
9. Add the custom property Department with the Text data type and the value **Finance**.

Explore 10. Go to the Program Files > Microsoft Office > root > Office16 folder and run the **SELFCERT.exe** program to create your own self-signed certificate. Use your name as the certificate name. (If you have trouble accessing this program, ask your instructor or technical resource person about creating your own digital certificate.)

Explore 11. In the Documentation worksheet, select cell A7. On the Insert tab, in the Text group, use the Add a Signature Line button to insert a digital signature. Use your name as the suggested signer, **Financial analyst** as the suggested signer's title, and your email address as the suggested signer's email address. Click the OK button.

Explore 12. Double-click the signature line in the Documentation worksheet, type your name as the signer, and then click the Sign button. Click the Yes button if you are prompted to use the certificate even though it cannot be verified. Click the OK button to confirm that the digital signature is saved with the document. Notice that the signed document is automatically marked as final and changed to a read-only document.

13. Save the workbook, and then close it.

APPENDIX A

Working with Text Functions and Creating Custom Formats

Cleaning Data in a Spreadsheet

EXCEL

OBJECTIVES

- Open a workbook in Compatibility Mode
- Use the LEN function
- Use the LEFT function
- Apply the Paste Values command
- Use the PROPER function
- Use the CONCATENATE function
- Apply the Text to Columns command
- Use the UPPER function
- Use the SUBSTITUTE function
- Apply a special format to phone numbers
- Create custom formats for numbers and dates
- Use the Compatibility Checker

Case | *Billings Cooking Club*

Several home chefs with a strong interest in all things cooking in Billings, Montana, started the Billings Cooking Club in 2014. Club members range from ages 19 to 75 and reside in four local communities—Billings, Ballantine, Huntley, and Laurel. Each month, the club meets at the local banquet hall where they sample food prepared by four members who are selected by random drawing. At the last meeting, the members elected new officers who want to analyze information about the club's current members and determine the potential for new members.

The club has a workbook with data about the current members, but the data was entered by volunteers and is not well organized or consistently entered. Shirley McGregor, the newly elected secretary, wants to clean up the data so she can analyze it more effectively. You will help her organize the data.

STARTING DATA FILES

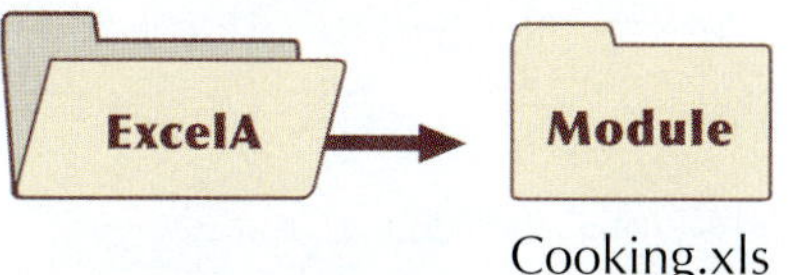

Cooking.xls

Review — Youth.xlsx

Case1 — Club.xlsx

Case2 — House.xlsx

Opening and Saving Workbooks Created in Earlier Versions of Excel

When you open a workbook that was created in Excel 2003 or earlier, it opens in Compatibility Mode. **Compatibility Mode** keeps the workbook in the older file format with the .xls file extension, making the workbook accessible for users who do not have the current version of Excel installed. The words "[Compatibility Mode]" appear in the title bar, indicating the file is not in the latest Excel format. You can work in Compatibility Mode. However, to have access to all the latest features and tools in Excel 2016, you must convert the workbook to the current file format, which has the .xlsx file extension. This is the file format you have used to save workbooks in the modules.

The workbook Shirley received from the previous secretary was created in Excel 2003. Shirley wants you to convert the workbook to the current format.

To save the workbook in the current Excel file format:

1. Open the **Cooking** workbook located in the **ExcelA > Module** folder included with your Data Files. The workbook opens in Compatibility Mode because the workbook was created in an earlier version of Excel. See Figure A-1.

Figure A-1 Workbook in an earlier Excel file format

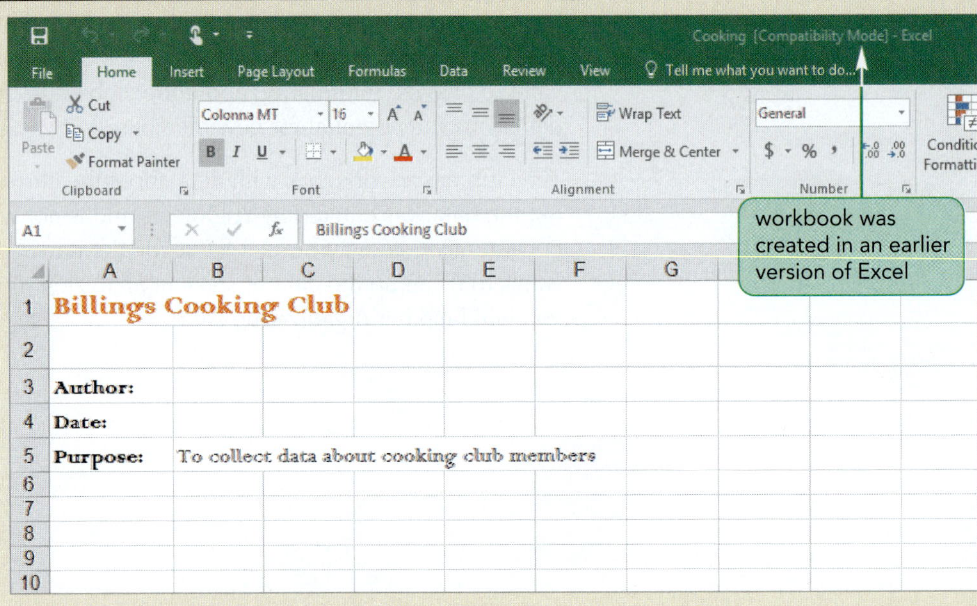

2. On the ribbon, click the **File** tab to open Backstage view, and then click the **Save As** command in the navigation bar.
3. Click the **Browse** button to open the Save As dialog box.
4. In the File name box, type **Cooking Club**. The Save as type box shows that the current file format is Excel 97-2003 Workbook, which is the earlier file format. You'll change this to the latest file format.
5. Click the **Save as type** button, and then click **Excel Workbook**. This is the file format for Excel 2007, 2010, 2013, and 2016.
6. Click the **Save** button. The workbook is saved with the new name and file type.

As you can see from the title bar, the workbook remains in Compatibility Mode. You can continue to work in Compatibility Mode, or you can close the workbook and then reopen it in the new file format. You will open the workbook in the current file format.

To open the Cooking Club workbook in the current file format:

1. Close the Cooking Club workbook.
2. Open the **Cooking Club** workbook. The text "[Compatibility Mode]" no longer appears in the title bar, indicating that the workbook is in the current version file format of Excel.
3. In the Documentation worksheet, enter your name and the date.

The Members worksheet contains data about the club members. Before working with this data, Shirley wants you to convert it to an Excel table.

To create an Excel table from the list of member information:

1. Go to the **Members** worksheet.
2. On the ribbon, click the **Insert** tab.
3. In the Tables group, click the **Table** button. The Create Table dialog box opens with the range $A$1:$G$45 selected, and the My table has headers check box is checked.
4. Click the **OK** button to create the Excel table. Note that filter arrows appear in the column heading cells.
5. On the Table Tools Design tab, in the Properties group, enter **MemberTbl** in the Table Name box to rename the table.
6. In the Table Styles group, select **Table Style Medium 7** as the table style.
7. Select any cell in the Excel table.

Using Text Functions

If you receive a workbook from a coworker or obtain data from other software packages, you often have to edit (sometimes referred to as *clean* or *scrub*) and manipulate the data before it is ready to use. To help users edit and correct the text values in their workbooks, Excel provides Text functions. Text, also referred to as a text string or string, contains one or more characters and can include spaces, symbols, and numbers as well as uppercase and lowercase letters. You can use Text functions to return the number of characters in a string, remove extra spaces, and change the case of text strings. Figure A-2 reviews some of the common Text functions available in Excel.

Figure A-2 **Text functions**

Function	Syntax	Description	Example
LEFT	=LEFT(*text,nbr chars*)	Returns a specified number of characters at the left of the string	=LEFT("Michael",3) returns Mic
RIGHT	=RIGHT(*text,nbr chars*)	Returns a specified number of characters at the right of the string	=RIGHT("Michael",3) returns ael
MID	=MID(*text,start nbr,nbr chars*)	Returns a specified number of characters from a string, starting at a position you specify	=MID("Net Income",5,3) returns Inc
UPPER	=UPPER(*text*)	Converts all lowercase characters in a string to uppercase	=UPPER("kim") returns KIM
LOWER	=LOWER(*text*)	Converts all uppercase characters in a string to lowercase	=LOWER("KIM") returns kim
PROPER	=PROPER(*text*)	Capitalizes the first letter of each word in a string	=PROPER("JASON BAKER") returns Jason Baker
LEN	=LEN(*text*)	Returns the number of characters in a string	=LEN("Judith Tinker") returns 13
SEARCH	=SEARCH(*find_text,within_text, start_nbr*)	Returns the number of the character at which the find_text is first found reading from left to right	=SEARCH("Main","1234 Main St.",1) returns 6
TEXT	=TEXT(*value, format_text_code*)	Formats numbers within text using a specific number format	="Total Revenue " & TEXT(SUM(D5:D75),"$#,0.00") returns Total Revenue $1,052.00
TRIM	=TRIM(*text*)	Removes all spaces from a string except for single spaces between words	=TRIM(" Mary Eck") returns Mary Eck

Using the LEN and LEFT Functions

The Zip column in the Members worksheet includes zip codes in both five-digit and 10-digit formats. Shirley wants only the five-digit component of the zip code. You can use the LEN and LEFT functions nested in an IF function to convert all of the zip codes to the shorter form. The IF function uses the LEN function to test whether the zip code has 10 digits. If true (the zip code has 10 digits), the LEFT function displays the first five digits in the cell. If false (the code does not have 10 digits), all the digits in the cell are displayed.

The **LEN function** returns the number of characters (length) of the specified string. Cell C6 stores the text "Laurel, mt" so the formula

```
=LEN(C6)
```

returns 10, which is the number of characters, including spaces, in "Laurel, mt." You will use the LEN function to determine how many characters are in each cell of the Zip column.

The **LEFT function** returns a specified number of characters from the beginning of the string. To extract the five-digit zip code from the zip code 59006-0999 stored in cell D5, you use the following formula to return 59006:

```
=LEFT(D5,5)
```

The following formula shows the LEN and LEFT functions nested in an IF function to display a five-digit zip code:

```
=IF(LEN([Zip])=10,LEFT([Zip],5),[Zip])
```

Before you enter the IF function to extract the five-digit zip code, you need to prepare the worksheet. First, you need to insert a new column to the left of the Phone # column. Then, you will copy the zip code data into the new column, pasting the data as values so you can use the data in a formula. The results of the formula will appear in the new column as well.

To extract the five-digit zip code from the Zip column:

1. Select cell **E2**. You'll insert the table column to the left of this column.
2. On the ribbon, click the **Home** tab.
3. In the Cells group, click the **Insert button arrow**, and then click **Insert Table Columns to the Left**. A new column named Column1 is inserted with the Text number format, which is the same format as the Zip column (column D). The columns in the worksheet automatically adjust as you add new columns. For example, the phone number in cell F2 changed to 4.063E+09. You will adjust column widths later, so you don't need to be concerned about these automatic adjustments.
4. Select the range **E2:E45**. Because the range is formatted as Text, you cannot enter a formula in a cell. You need to change the formatting of the selected range.
5. On the Home tab, in the Number group, click the **Dialog Box Launcher**. The Format Cells dialog box opens with the Number tab displayed.
6. In the Category box, click **General**, if necessary and then click the **OK** button. Now, you can enter the formula in cell E2.
7. Select cell **E2**, and then click the **Insert Function** button f_x next to the formula bar. The Insert Function dialog box opens.

8. Click **Logical** in the Or select a category list, click **IF** in the Select a function box, and then click the **OK** button. The Function Arguments dialog box opens.
9. In the Logical_test box, type **LEN([Zip])=10**. The logical test tests whether the number of characters in the current cell of the Zip column equals 10.
10. In the Value_if_true box, type **LEFT([Zip],5)**. This argument specifies that if the condition is true, the first five characters from the cell are displayed.
11. In the Value_if_false box, type **[Zip]**. This argument specifies that if the condition is false, all the characters from the cell are displayed. See Figure A-3.

Figure A-3 IF function with LEN and LEFT functions

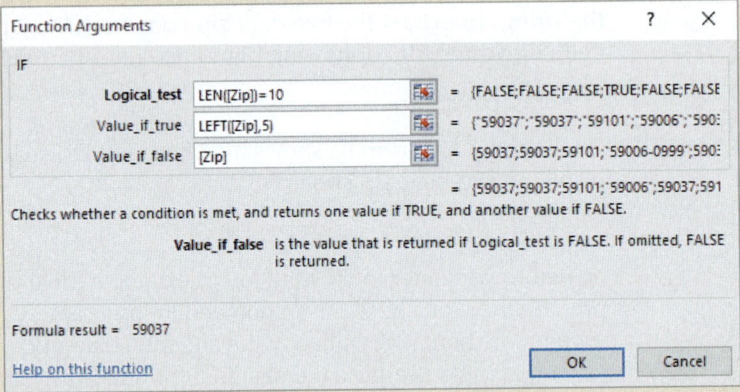

12. Click the **OK** button. The formula =IF(LEN([Zip])=10,LEFT([Zip],5),[Zip]) appears in the formula bar, and the value 59037 appears in cell E2 because the condition is false. The results are automatically copied to all rows in column E of the table. Each cell in column E displays the five-digit zip code. See Figure A-4.

Figure A-4 Table column with five-digit zip codes

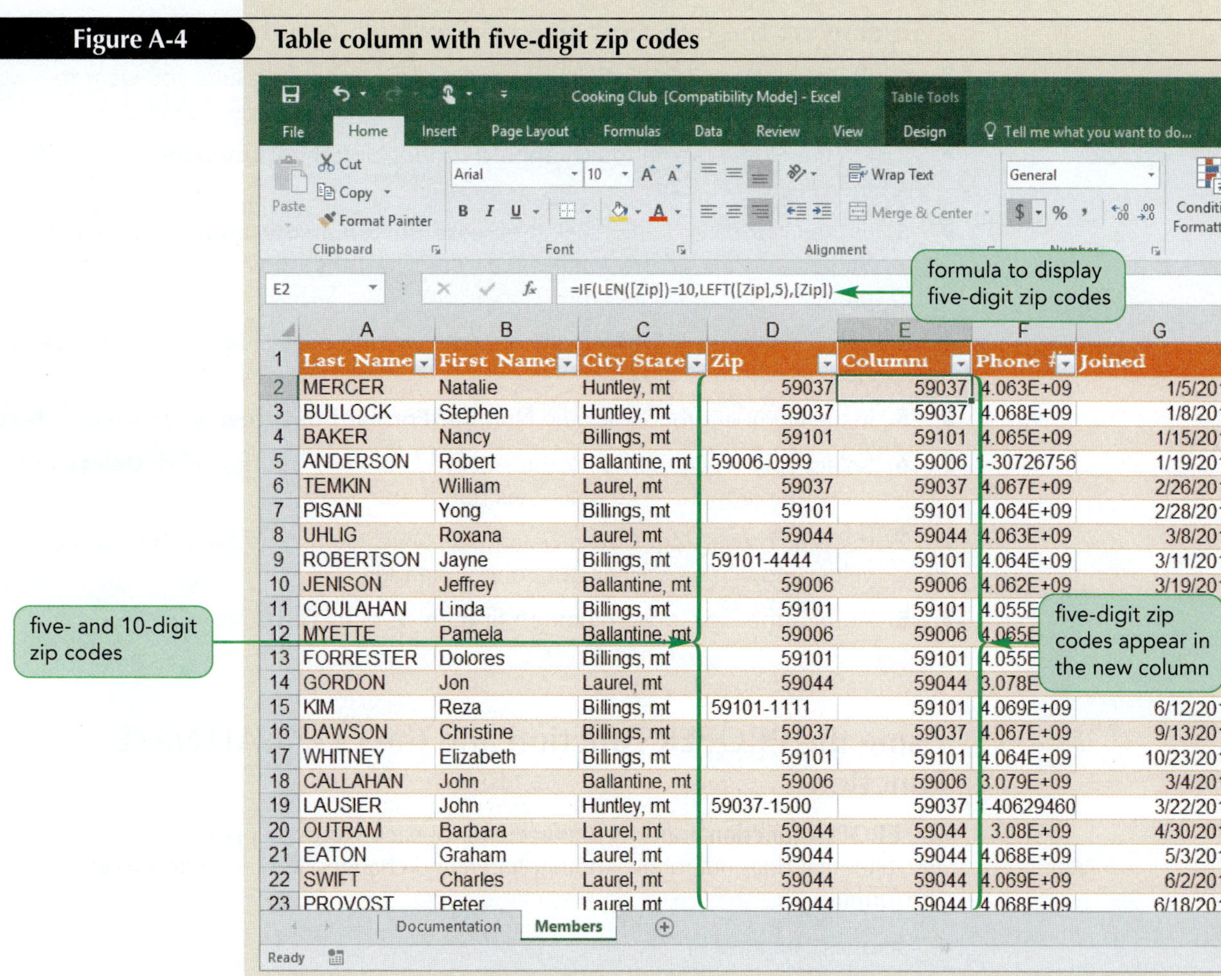

	A	B	C	D	E	F	G
1	Last Name	First Name	City State	Zip	Column1	Phone #	Joined
2	MERCER	Natalie	Huntley, mt	59037	59037	4.063E+09	1/5/201
3	BULLOCK	Stephen	Huntley, mt	59037	59037	4.068E+09	1/8/201
4	BAKER	Nancy	Billings, mt	59101	59101	4.065E+09	1/15/201
5	ANDERSON	Robert	Ballantine, mt	59006-0999	59006	-30726756	1/19/201
6	TEMKIN	William	Laurel, mt	59037	59037	4.067E+09	2/26/201
7	PISANI	Yong	Billings, mt	59101	59101	4.064E+09	2/28/201
8	UHLIG	Roxana	Laurel, mt	59044	59044	4.063E+09	3/8/201
9	ROBERTSON	Jayne	Billings, mt	59101-4444	59101	4.064E+09	3/11/201
10	JENISON	Jeffrey	Ballantine, mt	59006	59006	4.062E+09	3/19/201
11	COULAHAN	Linda	Billings, mt	59101	59101	4.055E	
12	MYETTE	Pamela	Ballantine, mt	59006	59006	4.065E	
13	FORRESTER	Dolores	Billings, mt	59101	59101	4.055E	
14	GORDON	Jon	Laurel, mt	59044	59044	3.078E	
15	KIM	Reza	Billings, mt	59101-1111	59101	4.069E+09	6/12/201
16	DAWSON	Christine	Billings, mt	59037	59037	4.067E+09	9/13/201
17	WHITNEY	Elizabeth	Billings, mt	59101	59101	4.064E+09	10/23/201
18	CALLAHAN	John	Ballantine, mt	59006	59006	3.079E+09	3/4/201
19	LAUSIER	John	Huntley, mt	59037-1500	59037	-40629460	3/22/201
20	OUTRAM	Barbara	Laurel, mt	59044	59044	3.08E+09	4/30/201
21	EATON	Graham	Laurel, mt	59044	59044	4.068E+09	5/3/201
22	SWIFT	Charles	Laurel, mt	59044	59044	4.069E+09	6/2/201
23	PROVOST	Peter	Laurel, mt	59044	59044	4.068E+09	6/18/201

13. If necessary, left-align the new zip code data in column E.

Using the Paste Values Command

You now have two columns with zip codes (columns D and E). You need to keep only the column that displays the five-digit zip code. However, the data in column E is dependent on column D. If you delete column D, column E will display the #REF! error value. Therefore, before you delete column D, you need to convert the data in column E, which is based on a formula, to values. The easiest way to do that is to copy and paste the formula results, but not the actual formula, in the same column using the Paste Values command. Then, you can delete column D.

To convert the five-digit zip code formula results to values:

1. Select the range **E2:E45**, which contains the formula results you want to convert to values.
2. On the Home tab, in the Clipboard group, click the **Copy** button, and then select cell **E2**.
3. In the Clipboard group, click the **Paste button arrow**, and then click the **Values** button. The values are pasted over the original formulas, replacing them.
4. Select the range **E2:E45**. You need to format these values as text, in case any zip codes start with zeros.
5. In the Number group, click the **Number Format box arrow**, and then click **Text**.
6. Select column **D**, right-click the selected column, and then click **Delete** on the shortcut menu. The column is removed.
7. In cell **D1**, enter **Zip Code**. Column D, which stores the five-digit zip code values, now has a descriptive column header.
8. AutoFit the Zip Code column to fit the five-digit zip codes.

Using the PROPER Function and the CONCATENATE Function

The **PROPER function** converts the first letter of each word to uppercase, capitalizes any letter that does not follow another letter, and changes all other letters to lowercase. The formula

```
=PROPER("MERCER")
```

changes the word "MERCER" to "Mercer". You will first use the PROPER function to convert the last name so that the first letter is capitalized.

The **CONCATENATE function** joins, or concatenates, two or more text values. The syntax of the CONCATENATE function is

```
=CONCATENATE(text1,text2,...)
```

where `text1`, `text2`, and so on, are constants or cells storing text or numbers. The CONCATENATE function joins these values to produce a single string. For example, if the last name "MERCER" is in cell A2 and the first name "Natalie" is in cell B2, you can use the formula

```
=CONCATENATE(A2,B2)
```

to join the contents of the two cells (last name and first name) to display the full name in cell C2. However, this formula returns "MERCERNatalie" in cell C2. To include a comma and a space between the two names, you must change the formula to

```
=CONCATENATE(PROPER(A2),", ",B2)
```

which uses two functions, two values, and a string constant (a comma and a space enclosed in quotation marks) to display "Mercer, Natalie" in the cell.

Shirley wants to combine the Last Name and First Name columns into one column and use standard capitalization for the names. You will use a formula that includes the PROPER function and the CONCATENATE function to do this.

To combine the names in one column with standard capitalization:

1. Select cell **C2**, and then insert a table column to the left. A new column named Column1 is inserted to the left of the City State column.
2. In cell **C2**, type **=CONCATENATE(PROPER([Last Name]),", ",[First Name])** and then press the **Enter** key. The formula is entered for every record in column C and displays the member's last name and first name with standard capitalization separated by a comma.
3. AutoFit column C to accommodate the longest entry. Each cell in column C displays the member's name in the form *Last name, First name* with the first letter of each name capitalized. Notice that the Joined column is no longer wide enough to display some of the entries; you will resize the column later. See Figure A-5.

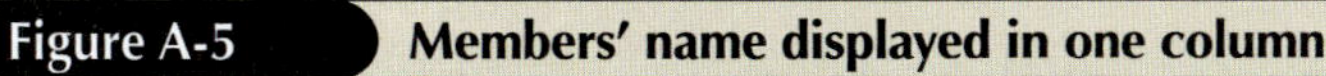

Figure A-5 Members' name displayed in one column

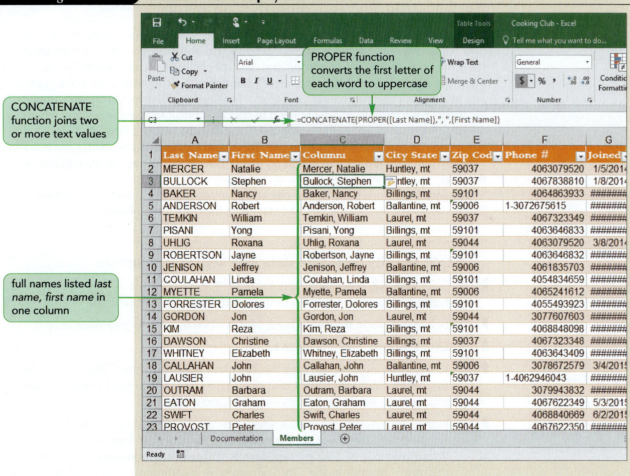

Now that the Members' name data is stored in column C, you no longer need the data in column A (Last Name) and column B (First Name). Because the results in column C are based on a formula, you need to convert the formula in column C to values before you delete the other columns.

To paste the formula results as values and delete the original data:

1. Select the range **C2:C45**, and then copy the range to the Clipboard.
2. Select cell **C2**, and then paste the values from the Clipboard to column C.
3. Press the **Esc** key.
4. In cell **C1**, enter **Member** as the column header.
5. Delete columns **A** and **B**. The Member column remains in the Excel table.

Applying the Text to Columns Command

When multiple pieces of data are stored in one cell, you can separate each piece of data into a different column by using the Text to Columns command. This command starts the Convert Text to Column Wizard. You specify how to split the data based on how the data is stored. You can select what **delimits**, or separates, the data, such as a tab, a semicolon, a comma, or a space. For fixed-width data, you specify break locations. For example, you might need to specify a break location in a string where the first character identifies the warehouse location, characters 2 through 4 identify the aisle, and characters 5 through 8 identify the actual location on the shelf. Each entry in a fixed-width field is the same length no matter how many characters are entered in the field.

The Members worksheet has the city and state separated by a comma delimiter. Shirley wants you to split the city and state data into different columns.

To split the city and state data into separate columns:

1. Select cell **C2**, and then insert a table column to the left. A new column named Column1 is inserted to the left of the Zip Code column.
2. Select the range **B2:B45**. These cells contain the values you want to split.
3. On the ribbon, click the **Data** tab.
4. In the Data Tools group, click the **Text to Columns** button. The Convert Text to Columns Wizard - Step 1 of 3 dialog box opens. You select how the data is organized in this step—delimited or a fixed width.
5. In the Original data type area, verify that the **Delimited** option button is selected, and then click the **Next** button. The Convert Text to Columns Wizard - Step 2 of 3 dialog box opens. You select the delimiter character in this step. The data in the City State column is separated by a comma.
6. Click any check box with a checkmark in the Delimiters section to remove the checkmark, and then click the **Comma** check box to insert a checkmark. The Data preview box shows the City and State data in separate columns. See Figure A-6.

Figure A-6 Convert Text to Columns Wizard – Step 2 of 3 dialog box

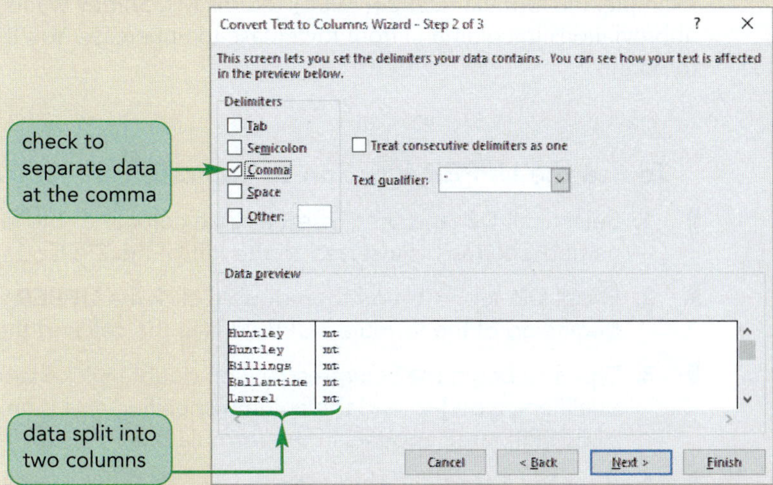

7. Click the **Next** button. The Convert Text to Columns Wizard - Step 3 of 3 dialog box opens so you can set the data format for each column. The Data preview box shows that each column is set to the General number format, which is what you want.
8. Click the **Finish** button. Cities remain in column B; states move to column C.
9. In cell **B1**, enter **City** and then in cell **C1**, enter **State**.
10. AutoFit the widths of columns B and C. See Figure A-7.

Figure A-7 City and State displayed in separate columns

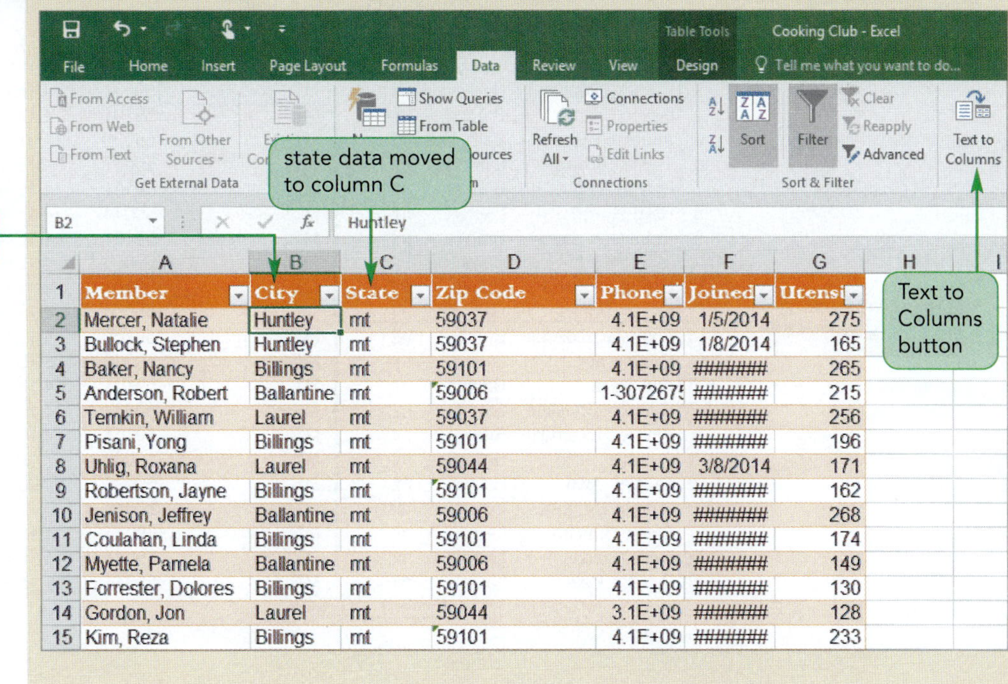

	A	B	C	D	E	F	G
1	Member	City	State	Zip Code	Phone	Joined	Utensi
2	Mercer, Natalie	Huntley	mt	59037	4.1E+09	1/5/2014	275
3	Bullock, Stephen	Huntley	mt	59037	4.1E+09	1/8/2014	165
4	Baker, Nancy	Billings	mt	59101	4.1E+09	#######	265
5	Anderson, Robert	Ballantine	mt	59006	1-3072675	#######	215
6	Temkin, William	Laurel	mt	59037	4.1E+09	#######	256
7	Pisani, Yong	Billings	mt	59101	4.1E+09	#######	196
8	Uhlig, Roxana	Laurel	mt	59044	4.1E+09	3/8/2014	171
9	Robertson, Jayne	Billings	mt	59101	4.1E+09	#######	162
10	Jenison, Jeffrey	Ballantine	mt	59006	4.1E+09	#######	268
11	Coulahan, Linda	Billings	mt	59101	4.1E+09	#######	174
12	Myette, Pamela	Ballantine	mt	59006	4.1E+09	#######	149
13	Forrester, Dolores	Billings	mt	59101	4.1E+09	#######	130
14	Gordon, Jon	Laurel	mt	59044	3.1E+09	#######	128
15	Kim, Reza	Billings	mt	59101	4.1E+09	#######	233

Using the UPPER Function to Convert Case

The **UPPER function** converts all letters of each word in a text string to uppercase. For example, the formula `=UPPER("mt")` returns MT. Shirley wants you to change state abbreviations in column D from lowercase to uppercase. You'll use the UPPER function to do this.

To use the UPPER function to capitalize the state abbreviations:

1. Select cell **D2**, and then insert a table column to the left. A new column named Column1 is inserted to the left of the Zip Code column.
2. In cell **D2**, type =**U** and then double-click the **UPPER** function in the list. The beginning of the formula =UPPER(is in the cell and the formula bar.
3. Type **[** to begin the column specifier, double-click **State** in the list of column qualifiers, type **]** to end the column specifier, and then type **)**. The formula =UPPER([State]) appears in the formula bar.
4. Press the **Enter** key. The state abbreviation appears in all uppercase letters in column E. See Figure A-8.

Figure A-8 UPPER function converted state abbreviations to uppercase

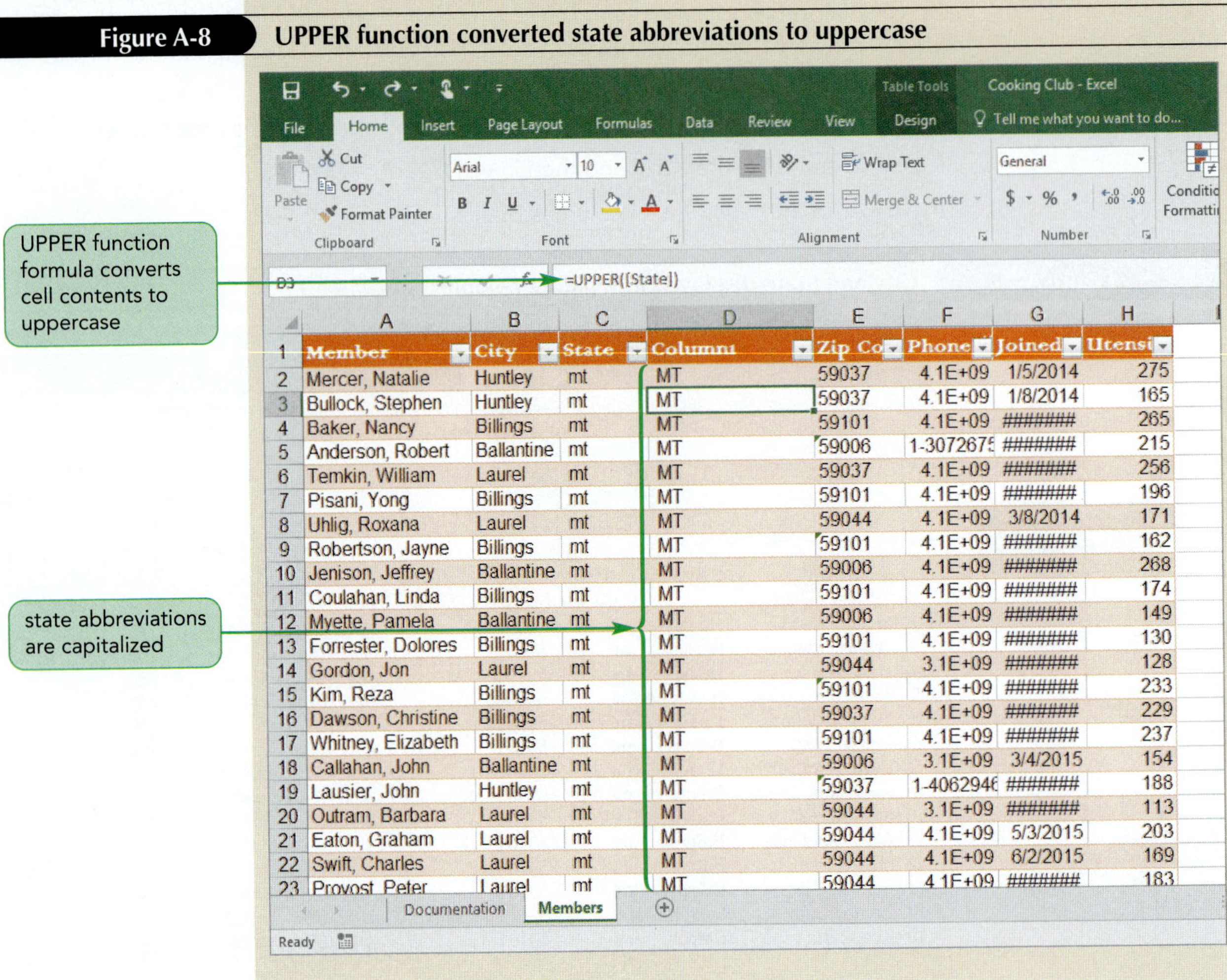

You want to keep only the data in column D. Because the results of column D are based on a formula, you again will convert the formula in column D to values before you delete column C.

To paste the state abbreviations as values:

1. Select the range **D2:D45**, and then copy the range to the Clipboard.
2. Select cell **D2**, and then paste the values from the Clipboard. Verify that the formula bar displays a value and not a formula.
3. Press the **Esc** key.
4. Delete column **C**.
5. In cell **C1**, enter **State**. The column is renamed with a more descriptive header.

Using the SUBSTITUTE Function

The **SUBSTITUTE function** replaces existing text with new text. The SUBSTITUTE function has the syntax

```
SUBSTITUTE(text,old_text,new_text,instance_num)
```

where `text` is a string constant or reference to a cell containing text you want to replace, `old_text` is the existing text you want to replace, `new_text` is the text you want to replace `old_text` with, and `instance_num` specifies which occurrence of `old_text` you want to replace. If you omit `instance_num`, every instance of `old_text` is replaced. The formula

```
=SUBSTITUTE("164-45-890","-","")
```

returns 16445890.

The entries for the phone numbers in column E are inconsistent. Sometimes they are a 10-digit value, and other times they are preceded with 1- (which Shirley wants you to remove from the Phone # column). You'll enter a formula with the SUBSTITUTE function to remove the preceding 1- from this data.

To remove the preceding 1- from the phone number data and paste the values:

1. Select cell **F2**, and then insert a table column to the left. A new column named Column1 is inserted to the left of the Joined column.
2. AutoFit column E (Phone # column) so you can see that some phone numbers are preceded by 1-.
3. Click the **Insert Function** button *fx* next to the formula bar. The Insert Function dialog box opens.
4. Click the **Or select a category** arrow, click **Text** to display the Text functions, and then scroll down to and double-click **SUBSTITUTE** in the Select a function box. The Function Arguments dialog box opens.
5. In the Text box, type **E2**. The text in cell E2 is displayed.

6. In the Old_text box, type **"1-"**. The text you want to remove is enclosed in quotation marks.
7. In the New_text box, type **""**. You want to replace the old text with nothing. You do not need to enter anything in the Instance_num box because you want to replace every instance of 1-.
8. Click the **OK** button. All of the phone numbers are changed to 10-digit numbers, and wherever necessary, the preceding 1- is replaced with an empty string (a blank, or nothing).
9. AutoFit column F, and then select cell **F2**. See Figure A-9.

Figure A-9 **SUBSTITUTE function removed 1-from the phone numbers**

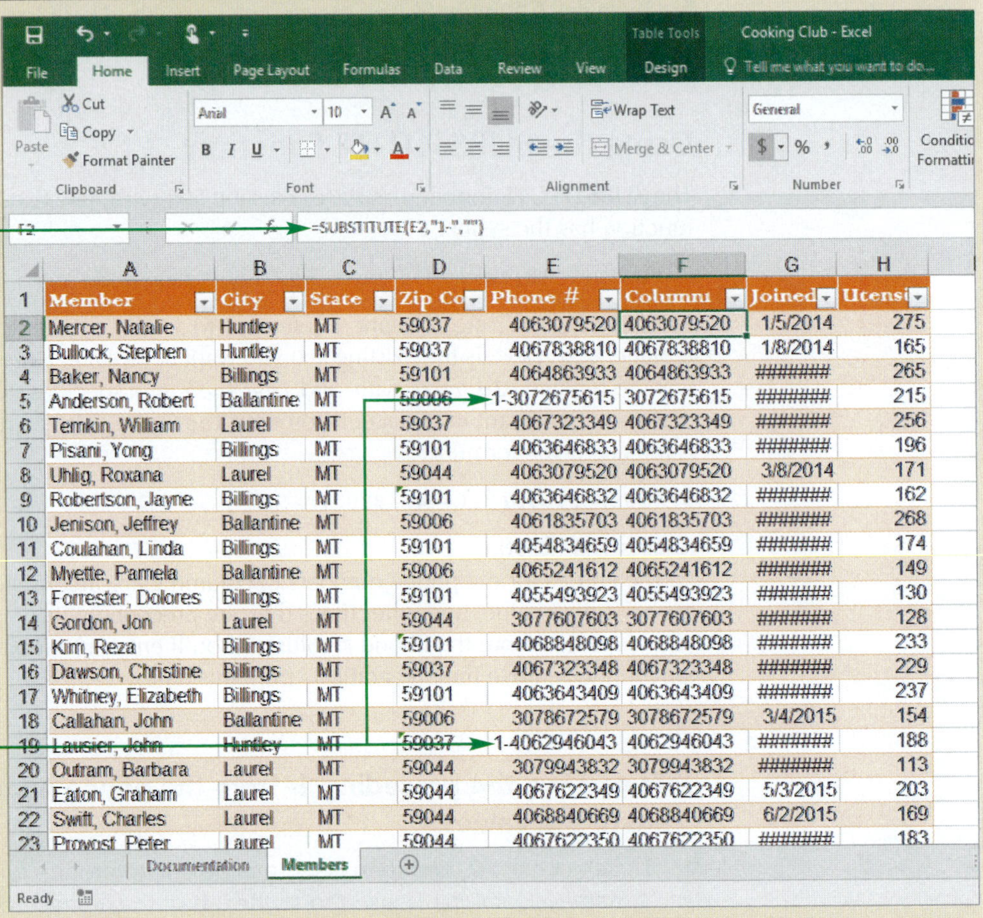

SUBSTITUTE function replaces 1- with an empty string, converting the phone number to 10 digits

=SUBSTITUTE(E2,"1-","")

some phone numbers have a preceding 1-

	A	B	C	D	E	F	G	H
1	Member	City	State	Zip Co	Phone #	Column1	Joined	Utensi
2	Mercer, Natalie	Huntley	MT	59037	4063079520	4063079520	1/5/2014	275
3	Bullock, Stephen	Huntley	MT	59037	4067838810	4067838810	1/8/2014	165
4	Baker, Nancy	Billings	MT	59101	4064863933	4064863933	########	265
5	Anderson, Robert	Ballantine	MT	59006	1-3072675615	3072675615	########	215
6	Temkin, William	Laurel	MT	59037	4067323349	4067323349	########	256
7	Pisani, Yong	Billings	MT	59101	4063646833	4063646833	########	196
8	Uhlig, Roxana	Laurel	MT	59044	4063079520	4063079520	3/8/2014	171
9	Robertson, Jayne	Billings	MT	59101	4063646832	4063646832	########	162
10	Jenison, Jeffrey	Ballantine	MT	59006	4061835703	4061835703	########	268
11	Coulahan, Linda	Billings	MT	59101	4054834659	4054834659	########	174
12	Myette, Pamela	Ballantine	MT	59006	4065241612	4065241612	########	149
13	Forrester, Dolores	Billings	MT	59101	4055493923	4055493923	########	130
14	Gordon, Jon	Laurel	MT	59044	3077607603	3077607603	########	128
15	Kim, Reza	Billings	MT	59101	4068848098	4068848098	########	233
16	Dawson, Christine	Billings	MT	59037	4067323348	4067323348	########	229
17	Whitney, Elizabeth	Billings	MT	59101	4063643409	4063643409	########	237
18	Callahan, John	Ballantine	MT	59006	3078672579	3078672579	3/4/2015	154
19	Lausier, John	Huntley	MT	59037	1-4062946043	4062946043	########	188
20	Outram, Barbara	Laurel	MT	59044	3079943832	3079943832	########	113
21	Eaton, Graham	Laurel	MT	59044	4067622349	4067622349	5/3/2015	203
22	Swift, Charles	Laurel	MT	59044	4068840669	4068840669	6/2/2015	169
23	Provost, Peter	Laurel	MT	59044	4067622350	4067622350	########	183

10. Select the range **F2:F45**, and then copy this range to the Clipboard.
11. Select cell **F2**, paste the values from the Clipboard, and then press the **Esc** key.
12. Delete column **E**.
13. In cell **E1**, enter **Phone #** to identify the data in the column.
14. AutoFit column # as needed to display its entire contents.

Using Special Formats

Four commonly used formats, referred to as special formats, are available—two zip code formats (five-digit and 10-digit), a phone number format (with the area code in parentheses and a hyphen between the prefix and the last four digits), and a Social Security number format (a nine-digit number with hyphens after the third and fifth digits). Using these special formats allows you to type a number without punctuation, yet still display that number in its common format.

Shirley wants you to display the phone number using the common format of area code in parentheses and a hyphen between the prefix and the last four digits.

To format the phone numbers with the Phone Number format:

1. Select the range **E2:E45**. Notice the green triangle in the upper-left corner for the cells in this range.
2. Point to any triangle to display the Error Alert button, click the **Error Alert button arrow**, and then click **Convert to Number** in the list of options.
3. With the range E2:E45 still selected, on the Home tab, in the Number group, click the **Dialog Box Launcher**. The Format Cells dialog box opens with the Number tab active.
4. In the Category box, click **Special**. Four special formats appear in the Type list—Zip Code, Zip Code + 4, Phone Number, and Social Security Number.
5. In the Type box, click **Phone Number**. See Figure A-10.

Figure A-10 Special category on the Number tab

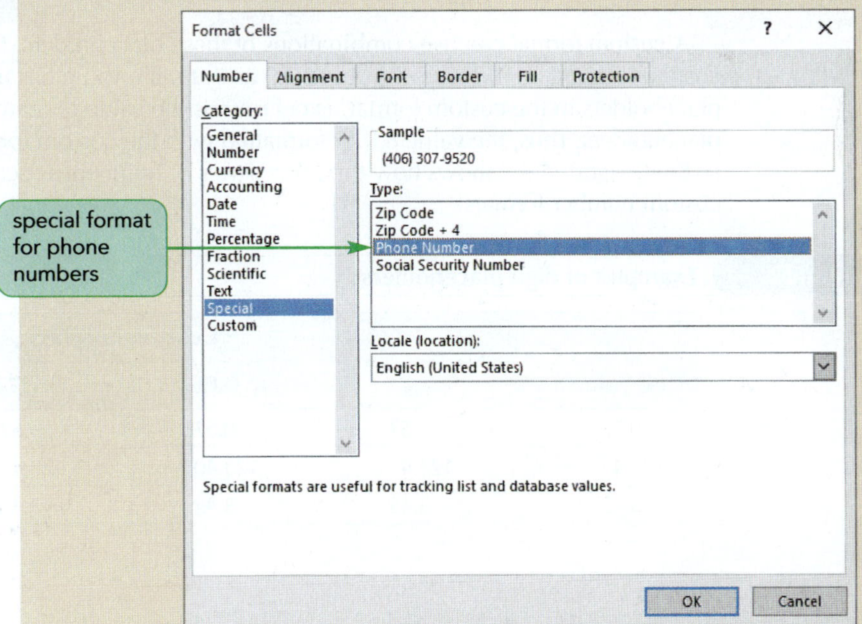

6. Click the **OK** button. The phone numbers are formatted in a standard telephone format.

Creating Custom Formats

TIP

Any custom format you create is stored only in the workbook in which it was created. To use it in another workbook, you must reenter it.

Excel supplies a generous collection of formats and styles to improve the appearance and readability of worksheets. However, sometimes you will need a format and style to accommodate a specific requirement. In these cases, you can create your own formats, called **custom formats**. Custom formats use **format codes**, a series of symbols, to describe exactly how Excel should display a number, date, time, or text string. You can use format codes to display text strings and spaces and determine how many decimal places to display in a cell.

Creating a Custom Number Format

Each number is composed of digits. In displaying these digits, Excel makes special note of **insignificant zeros**, which are zeros whose omission from the number does not change the number's value. For example, the number 0.1 is displayed in the General number format, but changes to 0.10 when the cell is formatted as a number. To format a value, Excel uses the **placeholders** shown in Figure A-11 to represent individual digits.

Figure A-11 **Description of digit placeholders**

Placeholder	Description
#	Displays only significant digits; insignificant zeros are omitted
0 (zero)	Displays significant digits as well as insignificant zeros
?	Replaces insignificant zeros with spaces on either side of the decimal point so that decimal points align when formatted with a fixed-width font, such as Courier

A custom format can use combinations of these placeholders. For example, the custom format #.00 displays the value 8.9 as 8.90. If a value has more digits than placeholders in the custom format, Excel rounds the value to match the number of placeholders. Thus, the value 8.938 formatted with the custom format #.## is displayed as 8.94. Figure A-12 shows how the same series of numbers appears with different custom number formats.

Figure A-12 **Examples of digit placeholders**

	Custom Formats			
Cell Value	#.##	0.00	?.??	#.#0
0.57	.57	0.57	.57	.57
123.4	123.4	123.40	123.4	123.40
3.45	3.45	3.45	3.45	3.45

Number formats also include the decimal point separator (.), the thousands separator (,), and the fraction separator (/). You can use the thousands separator to separate a number in groups of 1,000 or to scale a number by a multiple of 1,000.

The fraction separator displays decimal values as fractions. The general syntax is

```
placeholder/placeholder
```

where *`placeholder`* is one or more of the custom format placeholders. Excel displays the fraction that best approximates the decimal value. You can also specify the denominator for the fraction to convert the decimals to halves, quarters, and so forth. Figure A-13 provides examples of the thousands and fraction separators.

Figure A-13 **Examples of thousands and fraction separators**

Value	Custom Format	Appearance
12000	#,###	12,000
12000	#,	12
12200000	0.0,,	12.2
5.4	# #/#	5 2/5

You can combine all of the numeric format codes in a single custom format. If you don't specify a numeric code for data values, Excel uses the General format code, which hides all insignificant zeros.

Shirley wants utensils rental displayed as a number with two decimal positions followed by the letter "p" to indicate paid. You'll create a custom format for the utensils rental costs.

To create a custom format for the utensils rental cost:

1. Select the range **G2:G45**.
2. On the Home tab, in the Number group, click the **Dialog Box Launcher**. The Format Cells dialog box opens with the Number tab displayed.
3. In the Category box, click **Custom**. You will enter a custom format to display the numbers to the nearest thousand.
4. In the Type box, select the text **General**, and then type **.00?p?** as the custom format code. See Figure A-14.

Figure A-14 Custom category on the Number tab

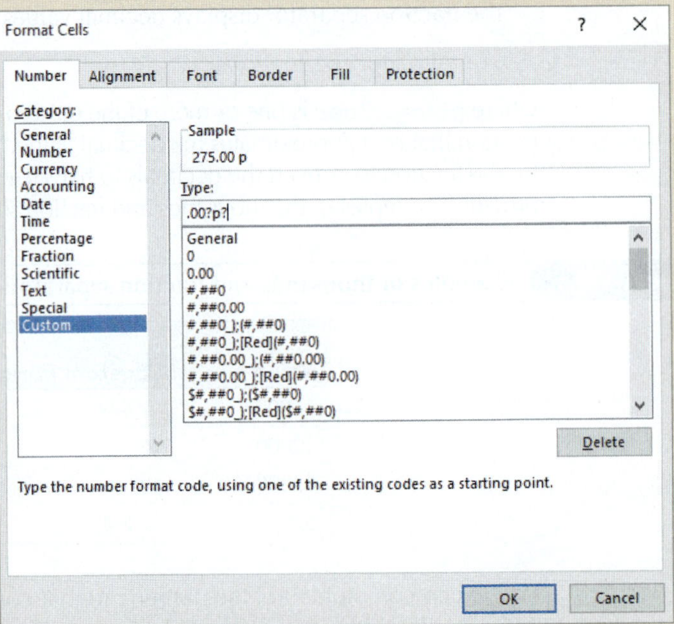

Trouble? If you return to the worksheet, you double-clicked General in the Type list of custom formats. Repeat Step 4, making sure you select the text General in the Type box.

5. Click the **OK** button. The utensils rental costs are displayed as a number with two decimal positions followed by the letter "p" to indicate paid. Because you used the custom format, this text is treated as a number even though it has a letter character (the character is ignored).

Creating a Custom Date Format

When you have dates, times, or both in a workbook, you can use a predefined date and time format to display this information in a readable format. Although the predefined time and date formats are usually fine, you can also create your own custom date formats. Figure A-15 describes the format codes used for dates and times.

Figure A-15 Date and Time format codes

Symbol	To Display
m	Months as 1 through 12
mm	Months as 01 through 12
mmm	Months as Jan through Dec
mmmm	Months as January through December
d	Days as 1 through 31
dd	Days as 01 through 31
ddd	Days as Sun through Sat
dddd	Days as Sunday through Saturday
yy	Years as 00 through 99
yyyy	Years as 1900 through 9999
h	Hours as 1 through 24
mm	Minutes as 01 through 60 (when immediately following h, mm signifies minutes; otherwise, months)
ss	Seconds as 01 through 60

Shirley wants the date values in the Joined column to show the name of the month followed by the year (for example, 7/22/2016 should be displayed as July 2016). You need to apply the custom format code *mmmm yyyy* to do this.

To apply a custom date format to the Joined dates:

1. Select the range **F2:F45**.
2. On the Home tab, in the Number group, click the **Dialog Box Launcher**. The Format Cells dialog box opens with the Number tab active.
3. In the Category box, click **Custom**.
4. In the Type box, select the current format, and then type **mmmm yyyy**. The Sample box shows an example of the custom format you entered.
5. Click the **OK** button, and then click cell **A1** to deselect the range. See Figure A-16.

Figure A-16 **Final formatted workbook**

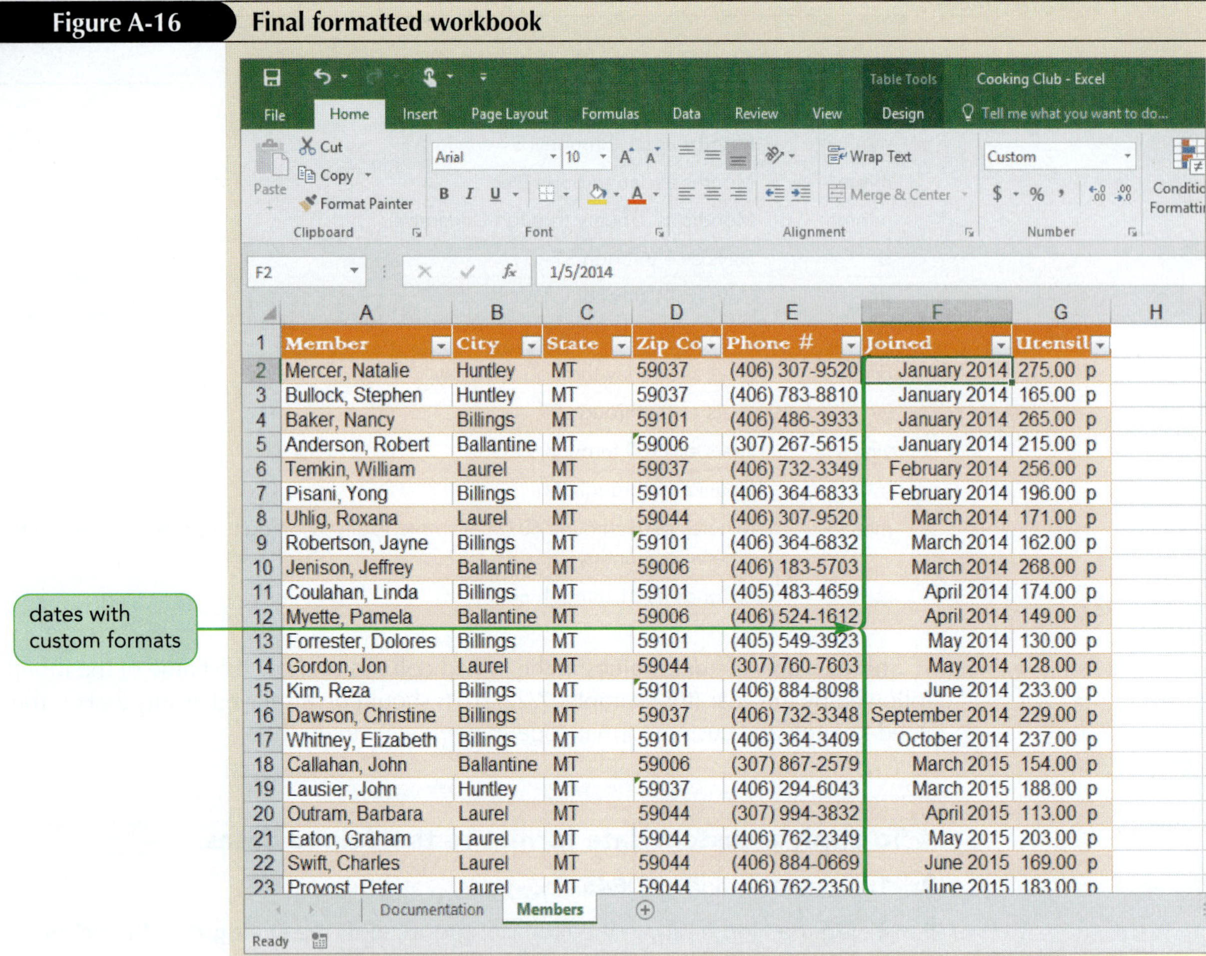

	A	B	C	D	E	F	G	H
1	Member	City	State	Zip Co	Phone #	Joined	Utensil	
2	Mercer, Natalie	Huntley	MT	59037	(406) 307-9520	January 2014	275.00 p	
3	Bullock, Stephen	Huntley	MT	59037	(406) 783-8810	January 2014	165.00 p	
4	Baker, Nancy	Billings	MT	59101	(406) 486-3933	January 2014	265.00 p	
5	Anderson, Robert	Ballantine	MT	59006	(307) 267-5615	January 2014	215.00 p	
6	Temkin, William	Laurel	MT	59037	(406) 732-3349	February 2014	256.00 p	
7	Pisani, Yong	Billings	MT	59101	(406) 364-6833	February 2014	196.00 p	
8	Uhlig, Roxana	Laurel	MT	59044	(406) 307-9520	March 2014	171.00 p	
9	Robertson, Jayne	Billings	MT	59101	(406) 364-6832	March 2014	162.00 p	
10	Jenison, Jeffrey	Ballantine	MT	59006	(406) 183-5703	March 2014	268.00 p	
11	Coulahan, Linda	Billings	MT	59101	(405) 483-4659	April 2014	174.00 p	
12	Myette, Pamela	Ballantine	MT	59006	(406) 524-1612	April 2014	149.00 p	
13	Forrester, Dolores	Billings	MT	59101	(405) 549-3923	May 2014	130.00 p	
14	Gordon, Jon	Laurel	MT	59044	(307) 760-7603	May 2014	128.00 p	
15	Kim, Reza	Billings	MT	59101	(406) 884-8098	June 2014	233.00 p	
16	Dawson, Christine	Billings	MT	59037	(406) 732-3348	September 2014	229.00 p	
17	Whitney, Elizabeth	Billings	MT	59101	(406) 364-3409	October 2014	237.00 p	
18	Callahan, John	Ballantine	MT	59006	(307) 867-2579	March 2015	154.00 p	
19	Lausier, John	Huntley	MT	59037	(406) 294-6043	March 2015	188.00 p	
20	Outram, Barbara	Laurel	MT	59044	(307) 994-3832	April 2015	113.00 p	
21	Eaton, Graham	Laurel	MT	59044	(406) 762-2349	May 2015	203.00 p	
22	Swift, Charles	Laurel	MT	59044	(406) 884-0669	June 2015	169.00 p	
23	Provost, Peter	Laurel	MT	59044	(406) 762-2350	June 2015	183.00 p	

6. Save the workbook.

Using the Compatibility Checker

When you save an Excel 2007, 2010, 2013, or 2016 workbook in an earlier format, the **Compatibility Checker** alerts you to any features that are not supported by earlier versions of Excel. You can click the Cancel button and redo the worksheet using a different approach, or you can click the Continue button to save the workbook in the earlier format. If you save the workbook in an earlier format, unsupported features will be lost.

You'll save a copy of the workbook in the Excel 2003 format.

To convert the workbook to the Excel 2003 file format:

1. On the ribbon, click the **File** tab to open Backstage view, and then click **Save As** in the navigation bar. The Save As screen appears.
2. Click the **Browse** button to open the Save As dialog box, navigate to the location specified by your instructor, and then change the filename to **Cooking Club 2003**.
3. Click the **Save as type** button, and then click **Excel 97-2003 Workbook**. This is the earlier Excel file format you want to use.
4. Click the **Save** button. The Compatibility Checker dialog box opens, alerting you to features not supported by earlier versions of Excel. See Figure A-17.

Figure A-17 Compatibility Checker with error message

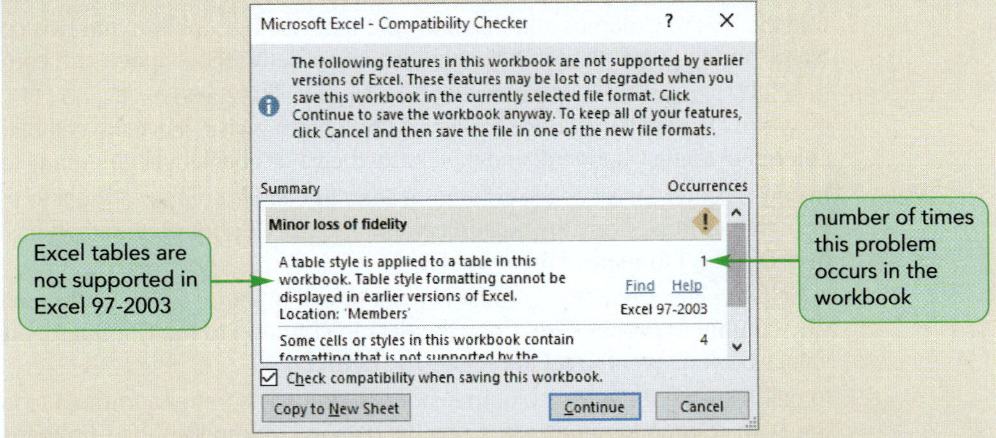

5. Read the message, and then click the **Continue** button. The workbook is saved in the earlier file format with the .xls file extension.
6. Close the workbook.

The workbook data is clean, and the workbook is formatted as Shirley requested. She'll be able to analyze this data for the club.

PRACTICE

Review Assignments

Data File needed for the Review Assignments: Youth.xlsx

The Billings Cooking Club also has a youth division for members 6 to 18 years of age. Shirley has a second workbook to store the information collected about these members. Shirley asks you to clean and format the data. Complete the following:

1. Open the **Youth** workbook located in the ExcelA > Review folder included with your Data Files, and then save the workbook in Excel Workbook format as **Youth Cooking** in the location specified by your instructor.
2. In the Documentation worksheet, enter your name and the date.
3. In the Members worksheet, rename the table **MembersTbl**.
4. Insert a blank column to the left of column B to store the first name, and leave the last name in column A.
5. Use the Text to Columns command to split the Member column into two columns named **Last Name** and **First Name**. (*Hint*: You will have two delimiters—space and comma.)
6. In cell H1, enter **Status** as the column header. In cell **H2**, use the IF and LEFT functions to display the word **Discard** if the address begins with PO; otherwise, leave the cell blank. Copy the data in column H to the Clipboard, and then paste the values back over column H to remove the formulas.
7. In cell I1, enter **Street** as the column header. In cell I2, enter a formula to trim the extra spaces from the address. Copy the data in column I to the Clipboard, and then paste the values back over column I to remove the formulas.
8. In cell J1, enter **Cty** as the column header. In cell J2, enter a formula to convert the data in the City column to proper case. Copy the data in column J to the Clipboard, and then paste the values back over column J to remove the formulas.
9. In cell K1, enter **St** as the column header. In column K, enter a formula to convert the data in the State column to uppercase. Copy the data in column K to the Clipboard, and then paste the values back over column K to remove the formulas.
10. In cell L1, enter **City State** as the column header. In column L, combine the city and state data from columns J and K into one column using the format *City, State*.
11. Format the data in the Phone column (column F) with the Phone Number format.
12. You can now delete columns C (Address), D (City), and E (State).
13. Save the workbook, and then close it.

APPLY

Case Problem 1

Data File needed for this Case Problem: Club.xlsx

First Thursday Book Club The First Thursday book club started in 1997 and has 15 members who meet at the main library in Hot Springs, Arkansas, on the first Thursday of each month. At each meeting, club members select one of the top five books on *The New York Times* nonfiction bestseller list to read and discuss at the next meeting. Each book must have at least two readers. At the next meeting, members discuss their selection with others who chose the same book. Fred Arnett, the secretary of the club, has begun compiling a list of the group's members. You will clean and format the data in the worksheet before he continues working on the project. Complete the following:

1. Open the **Club** workbook located in the ExcelA > Case1 folder, and then save the workbook in the Excel Workbook format as **Book Club** in the location specified by your instructor.
2. In the Documentation worksheet, enter your name and the date.
3. In the Members worksheet, rename the table **MemberTbl**.
4. Apply the Phone Number format to the data in the Telephone column.
5. Split the data in the Name column into two columns. Store the first names in column B and the last names in column C. Change the column headers to **First Name** and **Last Name**, respectively.
6. In the Member Since column, apply a custom format that displays only the year.
7. Member ID is formed from the first initial of the last name, birth month and day. Fred wants to send a birthday card for members with a birthday in the month of the meeting. The birth month is the two numbers after the letter. Use the MID function in column G (name it **Birth Month**) to separate those numbers.
8. The last two numbers in the Member ID is the day of the member's birthday. Use the RIGHT function in column H (name it **Birth Day**) to separate that value.
9. Save the workbook, and then close it.

APPLY

Case Problem 2

Data File needed for this Case Problem: House.xlsx

Tidy House Every two weeks, Tierra Waggoner collects payroll information for the employees who work at her housekeeping business in Terre Haute, Indiana. The worksheet with the information is sent to a payroll service that generates the paychecks. Tierra has started to collect the information, but she needs you to clean up the data before she sends it to the payroll service. Complete the following:

1. Open the **House** workbook located in the ExcelA > Case2 folder included with your Data Files, and then save the workbook in the Excel Workbook format as **Housekeeping** in the location specified by your instructor.
2. In the Documentation worksheet, enter your name and the date.
3. In the Employee Hours worksheet, create an Excel table named **EmployeeTbl** with a blue table style.
4. Split the data in the Name column into two columns. Store the first name data in column A and the last name data in column B. Change the column headers to **First Name** and **Last Name**, respectively.
5. Split the data in the City, State Zip column into three columns. Store the city data in column D, the state data in column E, and the zip codes in column F. (*Hint*: First split the data into four columns: City, comma, State, Zip. Then, delete the column with the comma.) Change the column headers to **City**, **State**, and **Zip**, respectively.
6. Use functions as needed to change the data in the City and State columns to use standard capitalization. (*Hint*: Remember to copy the data as values and remove any unnecessary columns.)
7. Apply the Social Security Number format to the data in the SS Number column.
8. Use a function to change the data in the Type of Work column so that it is all lowercase. (*Hint*: Remember to copy the data as values and remove any unnecessary columns.)
9. Apply a custom format to the data in the Hourly Rate column that shows two decimal places.
10. Apply a custom format to the data in the Overtime Hours column so that full hours display only significant digits and partial hours display two digits whether significant or insignificant. (*Hint*: Refer to Figure A-11 to see a description of the digit placeholders used in custom formats for values.)
11. Save the workbook, and then close it.

APPENDIX **B**

EXCEL

Advanced Filters, Database Functions, and Summary IFS Functions

Filtering and Summarizing Database Information

OBJECTIVES

- Use advanced filters
- Create a criteria range
- Use Database functions
- Summarize data using the COUNTIFS, SUMIFS, and AVERAGEIFS functions

Case | ***Sally's Lawn & Snow Service***

Sally's Lawn & Snow Service, located in Wellsville, New York, provides commercial and residential lawn care and snow removal services. Sally Chambers, the owner of the company, has been tracking the landscape maintenance and snow removal equipment at its main garage on Field Street and its secondary locations on Broad and Oak Streets. Sally has developed a replacement plan for the company's equipment based on the following criteria:

- Outdated equipment that can no longer be serviced with an "end-of-use date" of today, which is 10/31/2017. This would flag outdated equipment that is past its use date, has exceeded its maximum service, and needs to be replaced.
- Active equipment that has a value of less than $1,000 and with an "end-of-use date" one year from today (10/31/2018). This would allow enough time to budget to replace the equipment before it has reached its end of use.

Sally also wants to know the average value of the equipment and to review a summary of the equipment's life as well as its total and average values. You will use advanced filters to generate the list of equipment that is eligible for replacement and then use Database functions and other functions to calculate the summary information.

STARTING DATA FILES

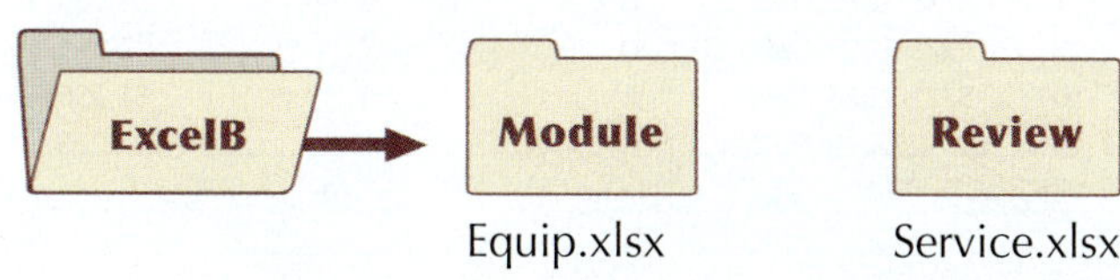

Equip.xlsx

Service.xlsx

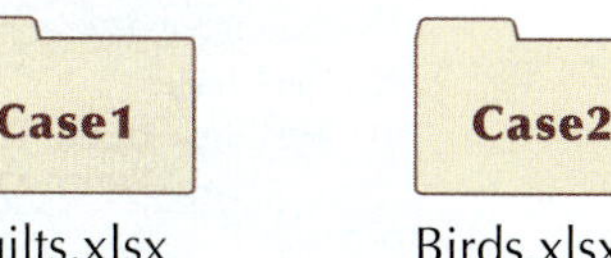

Quilts.xlsx

Case2

Birds.xlsx

Using Advanced Filters

Advanced filtering displays a subset of the rows in an Excel table or a range of data that match the criteria you specify. With advanced filtering, you specify the filter criteria in a separate range. Advanced filtering enables you to perform Or conditions across multiple fields, such as the criteria Sally wants you to use to find equipment that is eligible for replacement. You can also use advanced filtering to create complex criteria using functions and formulas. For example, Sally could use advanced filtering to find all equipment that is past its use date, has exceeded its maximum service, and needs to be replaced.

Sally created a workbook that contains an Excel table named Equipment to store the data for all of the equipment. For each piece of equipment, she has listed the description, date acquired, life (in years), end-of-use date (calculated using the date acquired and life), garage location, status, times serviced, maximum service, and current value. You will open Sally's workbook and filter the equipment data to identify which equipment is eligible for replacement.

To open and review Sally's workbook:

1. Open the **Equip** workbook located in the **ExcelB > Module** folder included with your Data Files, and then save the workbook as **Sallys Equipment** in the location specified by your instructor.
2. In the Documentation worksheet, enter your name and the date.
3. Go to the **Equipment** worksheet, scroll up to row 4, and then review the equipment table, which Sally named EquipTbl. See Figure B-1.

Figure B-1 EquipTbl table in the Equipment worksheet

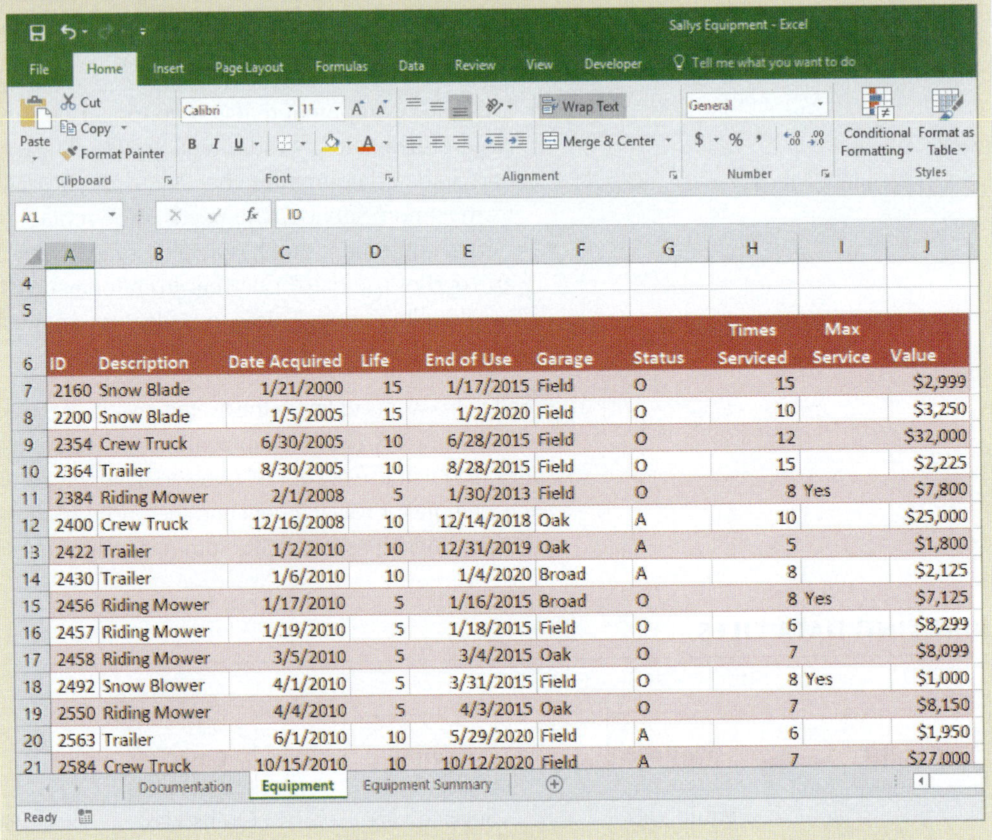

ID	Description	Date Acquired	Life	End of Use	Garage	Status	Times Serviced	Max Service	Value
2160	Snow Blade	1/21/2000	15	1/17/2015	Field	O	15		$2,999
2200	Snow Blade	1/5/2005	15	1/2/2020	Field	O	10		$3,250
2354	Crew Truck	6/30/2005	10	6/28/2015	Field	O	12		$32,000
2364	Trailer	8/30/2005	10	8/28/2015	Field	O	15		$2,225
2384	Riding Mower	2/1/2008	5	1/30/2013	Field	O	8	Yes	$7,800
2400	Crew Truck	12/16/2008	10	12/14/2018	Oak	A	10		$25,000
2422	Trailer	1/2/2010	10	12/31/2019	Oak	A	5		$1,800
2430	Trailer	1/6/2010	10	1/4/2020	Broad	A	8		$2,125
2456	Riding Mower	1/17/2010	5	1/16/2015	Broad	O	8	Yes	$7,125
2457	Riding Mower	1/19/2010	5	1/18/2015	Field	O	6		$8,299
2458	Riding Mower	3/5/2010	5	3/4/2015	Oak	O	7		$8,099
2492	Snow Blower	4/1/2010	5	3/31/2015	Field	O	8	Yes	$1,000
2550	Riding Mower	4/4/2010	5	4/3/2015	Oak	O	7		$8,150
2563	Trailer	6/1/2010	10	5/29/2020	Field	A	6		$1,950
2584	Crew Truck	10/15/2010	10	10/12/2020	Field	A	7		$27,000

Understanding the Criteria Range

The **criteria range** is an area in a worksheet, separate from a range of data or an Excel table, used to specify the criteria for the data to be displayed after the filter is applied to the range or Excel table. The criteria range consists of a header row that lists field names from the table's header row and at least one row with the specific filtering criteria for each field. The criteria range specifies which records from the data range will be included in the filtered data.

Criteria placed on the same row are considered to be connected with the logical operator And. That means all criteria in the same row must be met before a record is included in the filtered data. Figure B-2 shows an And criteria range filter to retrieve all equipment that has reached its maximum service and is at its end of use on October 31, 2017.

Figure B-2 **Example of an And filter specified in a criteria range**

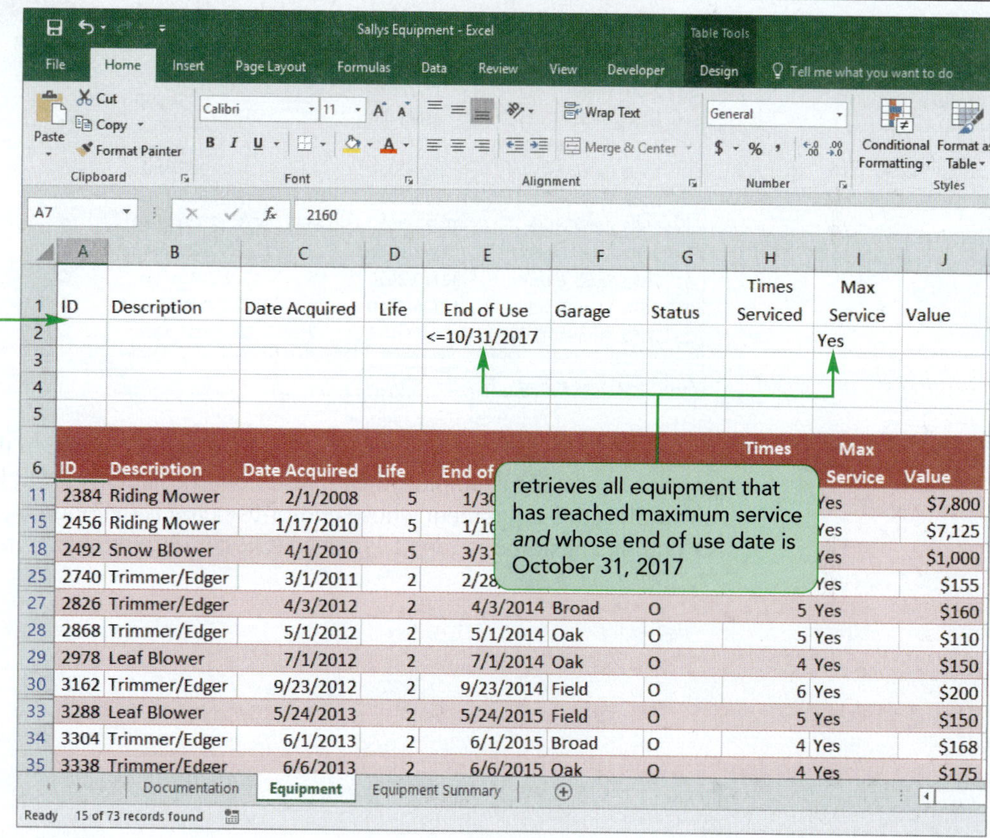

Criteria placed on separate rows of the criteria range are treated as being connected by the logical operator Or. That means records that meet all the criteria on either row in the criteria range will be displayed. Figure B-3 shows an example of the Or filter to retrieve equipment that is active or stored in the Oak garage.

Figure B-3 **Example of an Or filter specified in a criteria range**

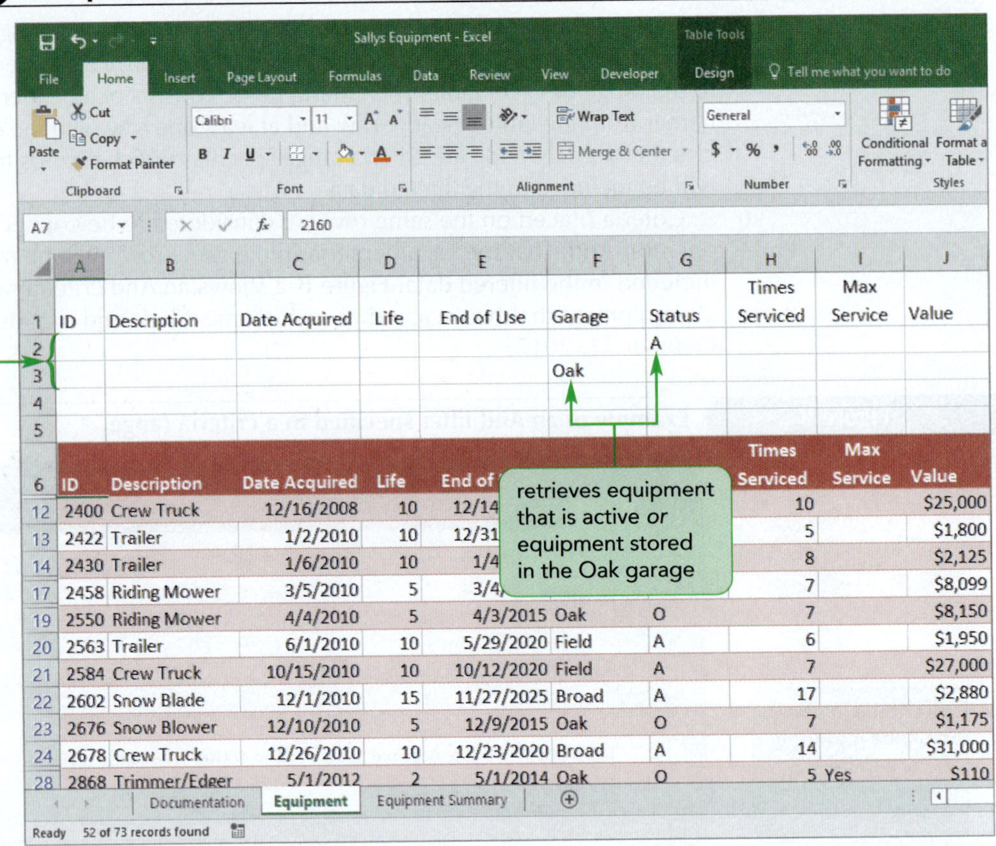
criteria for the Or condition are entered on different rows
retrieves equipment that is active *or* equipment stored in the Oak garage

You can combine the logical operators by placing criteria on the same row and on separate rows. For example, you can use both the AND and OR logical operations to show all active equipment whose end-of-use date is October 31, 2017 (And condition) or equipment stored in the Oak garage (OR condition), as shown in Figure B-4.

Figure B-4 **Example of an Or filter combined with an And filter**

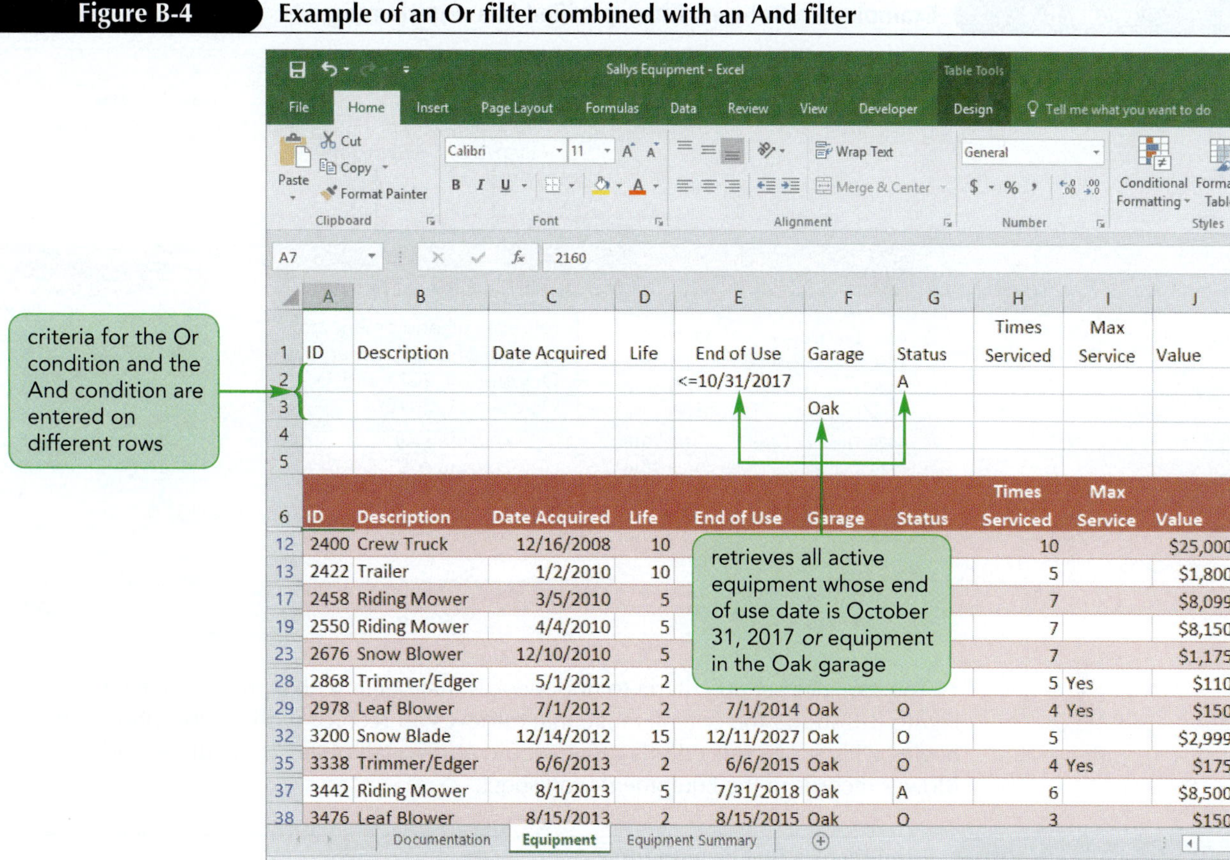
criteria for the Or condition and the And condition are entered on different rows
retrieves all active equipment whose end of use date is October 31, 2017 *or* equipment in the Oak garage

To specify criteria between a range of values in the same field, you use the same field name repeated in separate cells within the same row to match a range of values (Between criteria). Figure B-5 shows a criteria range to retrieve all equipment whose end-of-use date is between October 31, 2017 and October 31, 2018.

Figure B-5 Example of a Between filter specified in a criteria range

	A	B	C	D	E	F	G	H	I	J
1	ID	Description	Date Acquired	Life	End of Use	End of Use	Status	Times Serviced	Max Service	Value
2					>=10/31/2017	<=10/31/2018				
3										
4										
5										
6	ID	Description	Date Acquired	Life	End of Use	Garage	Status	Times Serviced	Max Service	Value
37	3442	Riding Mower	8/1/2013					6		$8,500
65	4606	Leaf Blower	12/30/2015					2		$160
66	4620	Leaf Blower	1/1/2016					2		$150
68	4680	Trimmer/Edger	3/2/2016					1		$175
69	4688	Leaf Blower	3/31/2016					2		$110
70	4694	Trimmer/Edger	4/6/2016	2	4/6/2018	Field	A	2		$120
71	4712	Leaf Blower	4/28/2016	2	4/28/2018	Oak	A	1		$150
72	4752	Trimmer/Edger	6/28/2016	2	6/28/2018	Broad	A	1		$205
80										
81										
82										

Documentation | Equipment | Equipment Summary

Ready 8 of 73 records found

retrieves all equipment at the end of use *between* October 31, 2017 and October 31, 2018

You can also set up criteria to find records that begin with a group of characters. Figure B-6 shows the criteria range that retrieves all records with a description that begins with Snow. This criteria range would retrieve all of the Snow Blade and Snow Blower records in the Equipment worksheet.

Figure B-6 Example of a Begins with filter

retrieves all equipment with a description that *begins with* Snow

	A	B	C	D	E	F	G	H	I	J
1	ID	Description	Date Acquired	Life	End of Use	Garage	Status	Times Serviced	Max Service	Value
2		Snow								
3										
4										
5										
6	ID	Description	Date Acquired	Life	End of Use	Garage	Status	Times Serviced	Max Service	Value
7	2160	Snow Blade	1/21/2000	15	1/17/2015	Field	O	15		$2,9
8	2200	Snow Blade	1/5/2005	15	1/2/2020	Field	O	10		$3,2
18	2492	Snow Blower	4/1/2010	5	3/31/2015	Field	O	8	Yes	$1,0
22	2602	Snow Blade	12/1/2010	15	11/27/2025	Broad	A	17		$2,8
23	2676	Snow Blower	12/10/2010	5	12/9/2015	Oak	O	7		$1,1
26	2790	Snow Blower	3/15/2012	5	3/14/2017	Field	O	6		$1,3
32	3200	Snow Blade	12/14/2012	15	12/11/2027	Oak	O	5		$2,9
40	3560	Snow Blade	12/2/2013	15	11/28/2028	Field	A	4		$2,7
50	4254	Snow Blade	11/29/2014	15	11/25/2029	Oak	A	3		$2,9
51	4256	Snow Blade	11/30/2014	15	11/26/2029	Field	A	3		$3,1
52	4266	Snow Blower	12/5/2014	5	12/4/2019	Oak	A	3		$1,1

Documentation | Equipment | Equipment Summary

Ready Filter Mode

INSIGHT

Using the NOT Function

Sometimes you will want to perform a specific action when a cell is *not* this or that (for example, a cell value is NOT equal to 10, and so on). In those instances, you can use the IF function in combination with the NOT and OR functions to run a test, then take one action if the result is TRUE, and (optionally) take another action if the result of the test is FALSE. The logical argument can consist of a single cell reference that contains a Boolean value or an expression that will reduce to a TRUE or FALSE value. The following examples show the NOT function used in formulas:

- NOT(TRUE) returns the value FALSE.
- NOT(FALSE) returns the value of TRUE.
- NOT(7<10) returns the value FALSE, because 7 is less than 10.
- NOT(H2=2) returns the value TRUE, assuming that the cell H2 contains any value other than 2.

Creating a Criteria Range

Typically, you place a criteria range above the data range to keep it separate from the data. If you place a criteria range next to the data range, the criteria might be hidden when the advanced filtering causes rows to be hidden. You can also place a criteria range in a separate worksheet, particularly if you need to use several criteria ranges in different cells to perform calculations based on various sets of filtered records.

You will place the criteria range in rows 1 through 4 of the Equipment worksheet to make it easier to locate. Because the field names in the criteria range must exactly match the field names in the Excel table or range except for capitalization, you should copy and paste the field names instead of retyping them. In row 2, you will enter an And criteria range with the criteria for equipment that has reached maximum service and whose end-of-use date is today's date. In row 3, you will enter the Or criteria for active equipment that has a value of less than $1,000 and whose end-of-use date is one year before today's date.

To create the criteria range to find equipment that meets the replacement plan:

1. Point to the left side of cell **A6** until the pointer changes to ➡, and then click the mouse button. The column headers in row 6 are selected.
2. Copy the field names to the Clipboard.
3. Select cell **A1**, and then paste the field names. The field names for the criteria range appear in row 1.

4. Press the **Esc** key to remove the copied data from the Clipboard.

   Now, you will enter the first set of criteria.

5. In cell **E2**, enter **<=10/31/2017**. This condition retrieves all equipment whose end-of-use date is older than or equal to today's date (10/31/2017).

6. In cell **G2**, enter **O**. This condition retrieves all outdated equipment.

7. In cell **I2**, enter **Yes**. This condition retrieves equipment that has reached its maximum service.

   The And condition is complete. Next, you will enter the second set of criteria for the OR condition.

8. In cell **E3**, enter **<=10/31/2018**. The condition retrieves all equipment whose end-of-use date is at least one year after today's date (10/31/2017).

9. In cell **G3**, enter **A**. This condition retrieves all active equipment.

10. In cell **J3**, enter **<1000**. This condition retrieves all equipment with a value of less than $1,000. The criteria in row 3 retrieve active equipment with a value of less than $1,000 and within a year of its end of life. See Figure B-7.

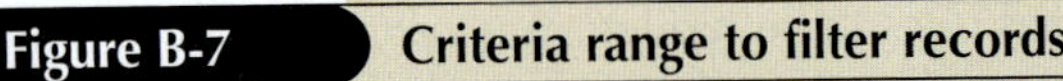

Figure B-7 **Criteria range to filter records**

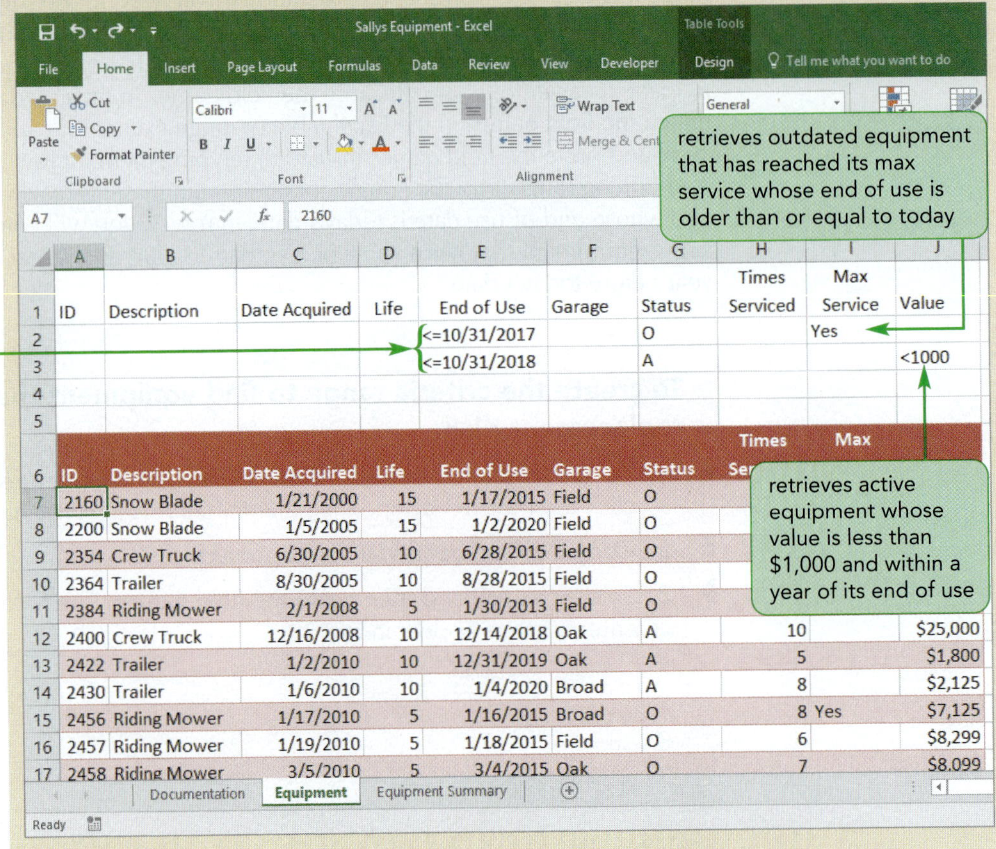

	A	B	C	D	E	F	G	H	I	J
1	ID	Description	Date Acquired	Life	End of Use	Garage	Status	Times Serviced	Max Service	Value
2					<=10/31/2017		O		Yes	
3					<=10/31/2018		A			<1000
4										
5										
6	ID	Description	Date Acquired	Life	End of Use	Garage	Status	Times Serviced	Max Service	Value
7	2160	Snow Blade	1/21/2000	15	1/17/2015	Field	O			
8	2200	Snow Blade	1/5/2005	15	1/2/2020	Field	O			
9	2354	Crew Truck	6/30/2005	10	6/28/2015	Field	O			
10	2364	Trailer	8/30/2005	10	8/28/2015	Field	O			
11	2384	Riding Mower	2/1/2008	5	1/30/2013	Field	O			
12	2400	Crew Truck	12/16/2008	10	12/14/2018	Oak	A	10		$25,000
13	2422	Trailer	1/2/2010	10	12/31/2019	Oak	A	5		$1,800
14	2430	Trailer	1/6/2010	10	1/4/2020	Broad	A	8		$2,125
15	2456	Riding Mower	1/17/2010	5	1/16/2015	Broad	O	8	Yes	$7,125
16	2457	Riding Mower	1/19/2010	5	1/18/2015	Field	O	6		$8,299
17	2458	Riding Mower	3/5/2010	5	3/4/2015	Oak	O	7		$8,099

Now that the criteria range is established, you can use the Advanced Filter command to filter the Equipment table. You can filter the records in their current location by hiding rows that don't match your criteria, as you have done with the Filter command. Or, you can copy the records that match your criteria to another location in the worksheet. Sally wants you to filter the records in their current location.

To filter the Equipment table in its current location:

1. Select any cell in the EquipTbl table to make the table active.
2. On the ribbon, click the **Data** tab.
3. In the Sort & Filter group, click the **Advanced** button. The Advanced Filter dialog box opens.
4. Make sure the **Filter the list, in-place** option button is selected and the range **$A$6:$J$79** appears in the List range box. The range $A$6:$J$79 is the current location of the EquipTbl table, which is the table you want to filter in its current location.
5. Make sure the Criteria range box displays **$A$1:$J$3**. This range references the criteria range, which includes the field names.
6. Make sure the **Unique records only** check box is unchecked. Every record in the EquipTbl table is unique. You would check this option if the table contained duplicate records that you did not want to display. See Figure B-8.

Figure B-8 **Advanced Filter dialog box**

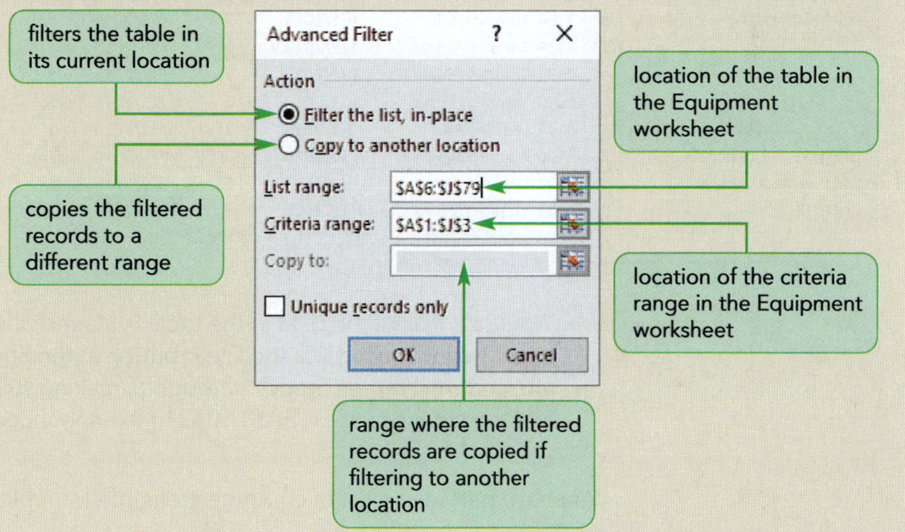

7. Click the **OK** button, and then scroll through the worksheet. The list is filtered in its current location, and 28 equipment records (as shown in the status bar) match the criteria. See Figure B-9.

Figure B-9 **Filtered Equipment data**

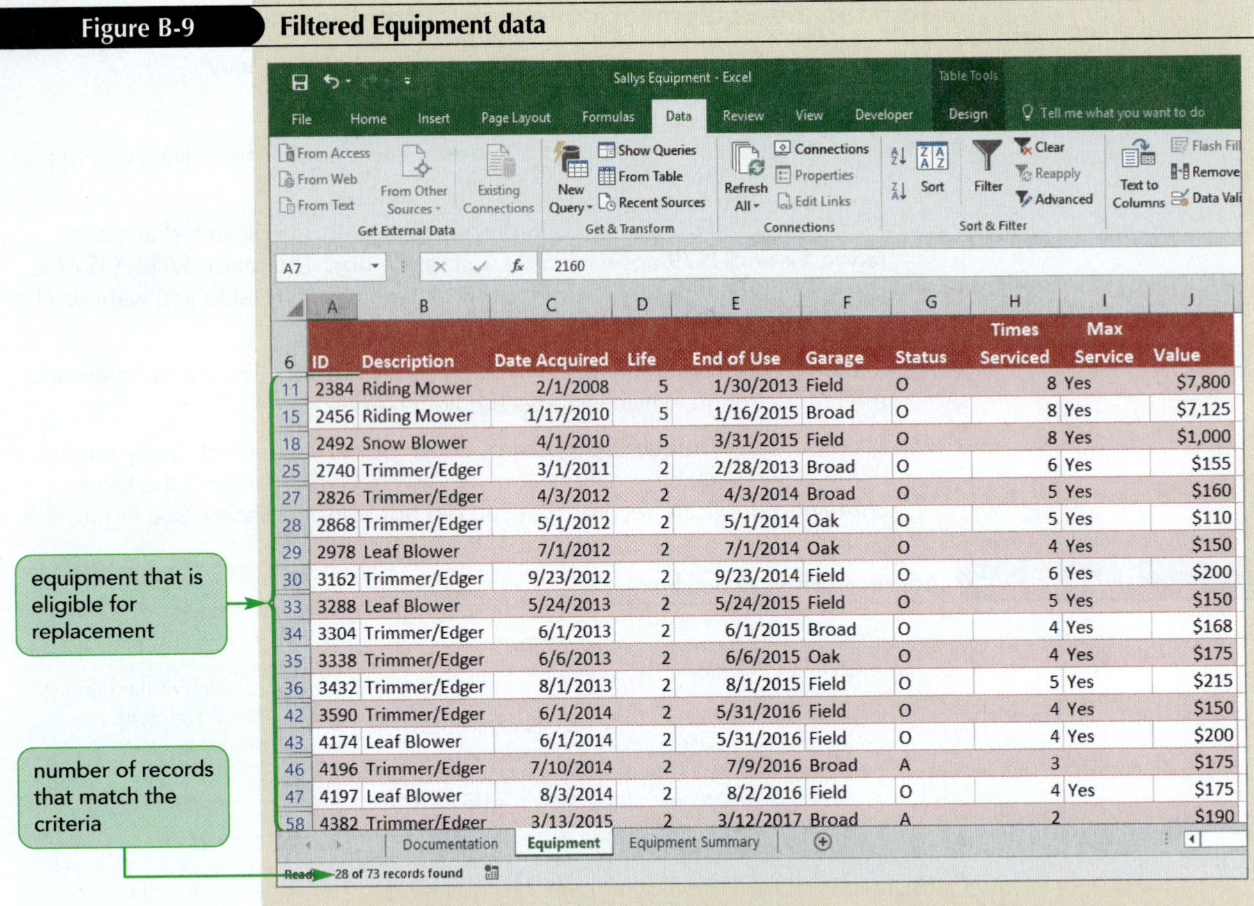

6	ID	Description	Date Acquired	Life	End of Use	Garage	Status	Times Serviced	Max Service	Value
11	2384	Riding Mower	2/1/2008	5	1/30/2013	Field	O	8	Yes	$7,800
15	2456	Riding Mower	1/17/2010	5	1/16/2015	Broad	O	8	Yes	$7,125
18	2492	Snow Blower	4/1/2010	5	3/31/2015	Field	O	8	Yes	$1,000
25	2740	Trimmer/Edger	3/1/2011	2	2/28/2013	Broad	O	6	Yes	$155
27	2826	Trimmer/Edger	4/3/2012	2	4/3/2014	Broad	O	5	Yes	$160
28	2868	Trimmer/Edger	5/1/2012	2	5/1/2014	Oak	O	5	Yes	$110
29	2978	Leaf Blower	7/1/2012	2	7/1/2014	Oak	O	4	Yes	$150
30	3162	Trimmer/Edger	9/23/2012	2	9/23/2014	Field	O	6	Yes	$200
33	3288	Leaf Blower	5/24/2013	2	5/24/2015	Field	O	5	Yes	$150
34	3304	Trimmer/Edger	6/1/2013	2	6/1/2015	Broad	O	4	Yes	$168
35	3338	Trimmer/Edger	6/6/2013	2	6/6/2015	Oak	O	4	Yes	$175
36	3432	Trimmer/Edger	8/1/2013	2	8/1/2015	Field	O	5	Yes	$215
42	3590	Trimmer/Edger	6/1/2014	2	5/31/2016	Field	O	4	Yes	$150
43	4174	Leaf Blower	6/1/2014	2	5/31/2016	Field	O	4	Yes	$200
46	4196	Trimmer/Edger	7/10/2014	2	7/9/2016	Broad	A	3		$175
47	4197	Leaf Blower	8/3/2014	2	8/2/2016	Field	O	4	Yes	$175
58	4382	Trimmer/Edger	3/13/2015	2	3/12/2017	Broad	A	2		$190

Trouble? If all of the data in the table is filtered, the list range or criteria range might be incorrect. Click the Clear button in the Sort & Filter group on the Data tab, and then repeat Steps 1 through 6, making sure the list range is $A$6:$J$79 and the criteria range is $A$1:$J$3 in the Advanced Filter dialog box.

You have provided a list of equipment eligible for replacement.

INSIGHT

Copying Filtered Records to a New Location

The advanced filtering command does more than filter data in a range or an Excel table. You can also copy data in a table to another worksheet location. If you want to filter the data and then copy the filtered data to a different location, you can select the Copy to another location option button in the Action section of the Advanced Filter dialog box. From the Advanced Filtering dialog box, you can choose to copy any of the following:

- All the columns from the original table in their current order to another worksheet location.
- A subset of columns from the original table to another worksheet location.
- A subset or all the columns from the original table and change the sequence of columns in the new worksheet location.
- A unique list of values from the original table into another worksheet location. For example, you can retrieve a unique list of equipment names from a table that repeats the equipment names many times.

Then you can specify the first cell of the range where you want to copy the filtered records in the Copy to box. Excel copies the filtered records to the location beginning at the cell you specified in the Copy to box. All cells below this cell will be cleared when the Advanced Filter is applied.

Sally asks you to display all of the records in the Equipment table. You do this by clearing the filter.

To show all of the records in the Equipment table:

1. On the Data tab, in the Sort & Filter group, click the **Clear** button. All of the records in the EquipTbl table are redisplayed.

Using Database Functions to Summarize Data

Database functions (or **Dfunctions**) perform summary data analysis, such as sum, average, and count, on an Excel table or data range based on criteria specified in a criteria range. Figure B-10 describes the Database functions. Although you can often use the SUMIF, AVERAGEIF, and COUNTIF functions; the Total row of an Excel table; and PivotTables to achieve the same results as Database functions, some situations require Database functions. For example, the type of summary analysis, the placement of the summary results, or the complexity of the criteria might require using Database functions.

Figure B-10 Database functions

Function	Description
DAVERAGE	Returns the average of the values that meet specified criteria
DCOUNT	Returns the number of cells containing numbers that meet specified criteria
DCOUNTA	Returns the number of nonblank cells that meet specified criteria
DMAX	Returns the maximum value in the search column that meets specified criteria
DMIN	Returns the minimum value in the search column that meets specified criteria
DSTDEV	Returns the estimate of standard deviation based on a sample of entries that meet the specified criteria
DSUM	Returns the sum of the values in the summary column that meet specified criteria

Sally needs to know the average value of the equipment by garage and by status. The status of the equipment indicates whether or not the equipment is in use (active) or whether the equipment is not in use but available if needed (outdated). To generate this information, you must set up a criteria range to retrieve the appropriate records for each calculation. Consequently, a Database function is a good approach.

Database functions use a criteria range to specify the records to summarize. In a Database function, the criteria range is used as one of the arguments of the function. The general syntax for any Database function is

```
DatabaseFunctionName(table range, column to summarize,
criteria range)
```

where `table range` refers to the cells where the data to summarize is located, including the column header; `column to summarize` is the column name of the field to summarize entered within quotation marks; and `criteria range` is the range where the criteria that determine which records are used in the calculation are specified.

REFERENCE

Using a Database Function

- Select the database function you want to use.
- Enter the table name or range of data you want to use in the database function.
- Indicate the column in the table name or range of data that you want to summarize.
- Enter the criteria range containing the criteria for selection as the field name followed by the value to use from a table on the formula worksheet.

You will use Database functions to summarize the average equipment value for each garage by status. First, you will set up a criteria range. Although the criteria range often includes all fields from the table, even those not needed to select records, you do not have to include all field names from the table when setting up a criteria range. In this case, you will use only the fields needed to specify the criteria.

You will create three criteria ranges to complete the Average Value of Equipment section in the Equipment Summary sheet.

To create criteria ranges for the active and outdated equipment for the Broad, Field, and Oak garages:

1. Go to the **Equipment Summary** worksheet. The appropriate column headers for the criteria range have already been copied from the Equipment worksheet.
2. In cell **G6**, enter **Broad** and then in cell **H6**, enter **A**. These criteria will find all active equipment at the Broad garage.
3. In cell **J6**, enter **Broad** and then in cell **K6**, enter **O**. These criteria will find all outdated equipment at the Broad garage.
4. In cell **G10**, enter **Field** and then in cell **H10**, enter **A**. These criteria will find all active equipment at the Field garage.
5. In cell **J10**, enter **Field** and then in cell **K10**, enter **O**. These criteria will find all outdated equipment at the Field garage.
6. In cell **G14**, enter **Oak** and then in cell **H14**, enter **A**. These criteria will find all active equipment at the Oak garage.
7. In cell **J14**, enter **Oak** and then in cell **K14** enter **O**. These criteria will find all outdated equipment at the Oak garage. See Figure B-11.

Figure B-11 Criteria ranges for the active and outdated equipment in all garages

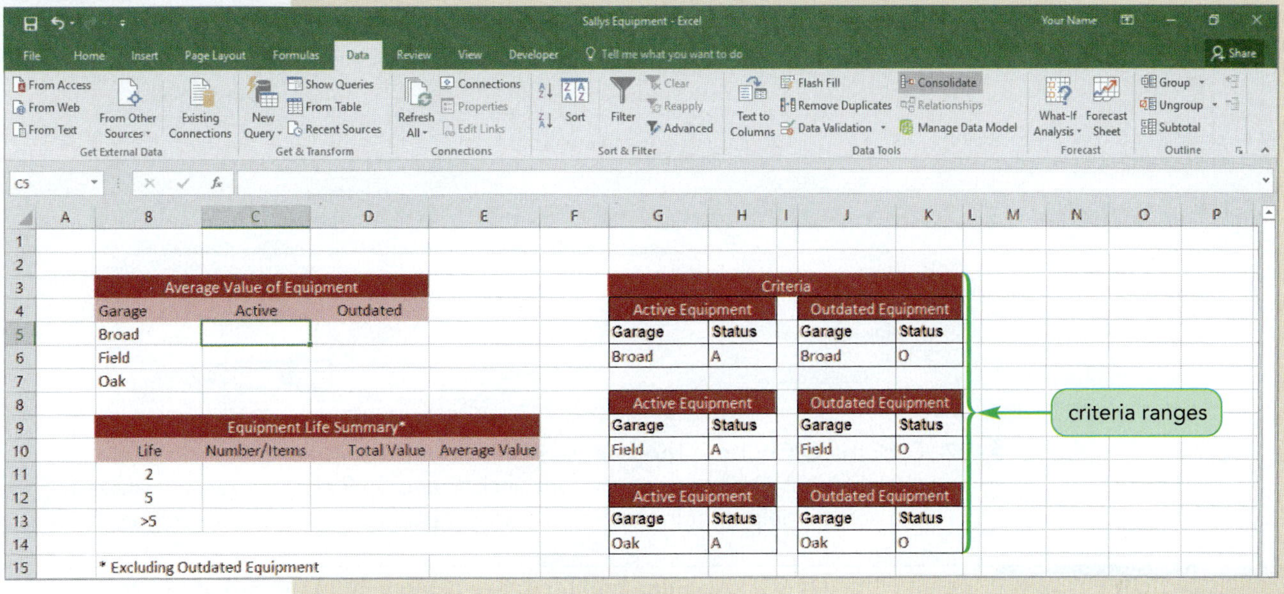

Average Value of Equipment		
Garage	Active	Outdated
Broad		
Field		
Oak		

Equipment Life Summary*			
Life	Number/Items	Total Value	Average Value
2			
5			
>5			

* Excluding Outdated Equipment

Criteria			
Active Equipment		Outdated Equipment	
Garage	Status	Garage	Status
Broad	A	Broad	O
Active Equipment		Outdated Equipment	
Garage	Status	Garage	Status
Field	A	Field	O
Active Equipment		Outdated Equipment	
Garage	Status	Garage	Status
Oak	A	Oak	O

criteria ranges

The criteria ranges are complete, so you can use the DAVERAGE function to calculate the average value of active equipment by garage. The first two arguments are the same for each garage. The third argument, the criteria range, is different for each garage so you can average a different subset of each garage's equipment.

To find the average value of the active equipment for the Broad and Field garages:

1. Select cell **C5**, and then click the **Insert Function** button f_x next to the formula bar. The Insert Function dialog box opens.
2. Click the **Or select a category** arrow, and then click **Database** in the list of functions.
3. In the Select a function box, select **DAVERAGE**, if necessary, and then click the **OK** button. The Function Arguments dialog box opens.
4. In the Database box, type **Equipment!$A$6:$J$79** to enter the range to search, and then press the **Tab** key. In this case, Equipment!$A$6:$J$79 refers to all of the data values in the range A6:J79 of the Equipment worksheet.

   Trouble? If the error "Invalid" appears to the right of the Database box, you probably mistyped the range to search. Make sure you typed ! (an exclamation mark) before the criteria range.
5. In the Field box, type **"Value"** and then press the **Tab** key. The field specifies the table column that contains the data to be averaged.
6. In the Criteria box, type **G5:H6** to specify the criteria for active equipment in the Broad garage. See Figure B-12.

TIP

You could also use the EquipTbl reference in the Database box named Equipment to reference all of the equipment.

Figure B-12 DAVERAGE Function Arguments dialog box

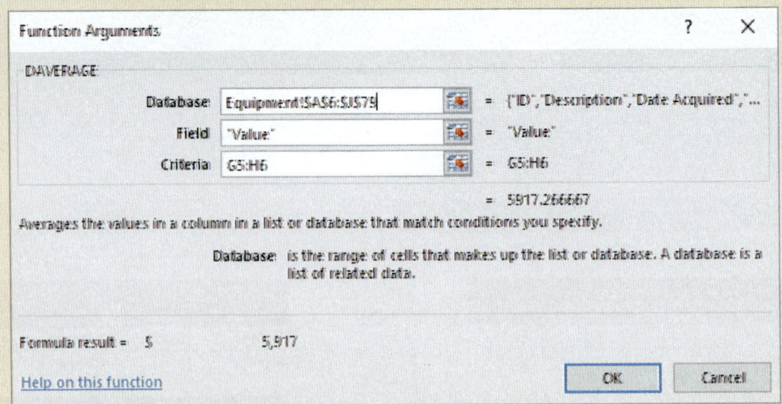

7. Click the **OK** button. The formula =DAVERAGE(Equipment!$A$6:$J$79, "Value",G5:H6) appears in the formula bar, and $5,917, the average value of the active equipment in the Broad garage appears, in cell C5. See Figure B-13.

Figure B-13 Result of the DVAGERAGE function for active equipment in the Broad garage

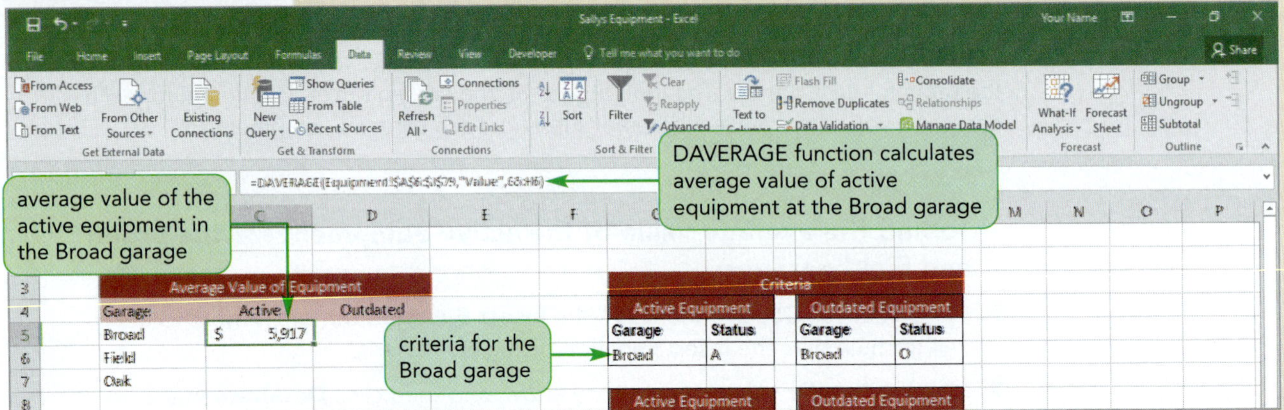

8. Select cell **C6**, and then click the **Insert Function** button next to the formula bar.

9. Repeat Step 3 to open the DAVERAGE Function Arguments dialog box, and then repeat Steps 4 and 5 to enter the first two arguments for the DAVERAGE function, specifying all of data values in the EquipTbl table and the field name.

10. In the Criteria box, type **G9:H10** to specify the active equipment in the Field garage.

11. Click the **OK** button. The formula =DAVERAGE(Equipment!$A$6:$J$79,"Value", G9:H10) appears in the formula bar, and $5,529, the average value of the active equipment in the Field garage, appears in cell C6.

12. Select cell **C7**, and then click the **Insert Function** button next to the formula bar.

13. Repeat Step 3 to open the DAVERAGE Function Arguments dialog box, and then repeat Steps 4 and 5 to enter the first two arguments for the DAVERAGE function, specifying all of data values in the EquipTbl table and the field name.

14. In the Criteria box, type **G13:H14** to specify the active equipment in the Oak garage.
15. Click the **OK** button. The formula =DAVERAGE(Equipment!$A$6:$J$79, "Value",G13:H14) appears in the formula bar, and $6,145, the average value of the active equipment in the Oak garage, appears in cell C7.

To calculate the average equipment value for the outdated equipment in the Broad, Field, and Oak garages, you will copy the formulas in the range C5:C7 to cells D5 and D7 and then edit the third argument.

To find the average equipment value for outdated equipment for the Broad, Field and Oak garages:

1. Copy the formula in cell **C5** to cell **D5.**
2. Select cell **D5**, and then change the criteria range (the third argument) from H5:I6 to **J5:K6**. The formula =DAVERAGE(Equipment!$A$6:$J$79, "Value",J5:K6) appears in the formula bar, and $2,126, the average value of outdated equipment in the Broad garage, appears in cell D5.
3. Copy the formula from cell **C6** to cell **D6**.
4. Select cell **D6**, and then change the criteria range (the third argument) from H9:I10 to **J9:K10**. The formula =DAVERAGE(Equipment!$A$6:$J$79, "Value",J9:K10) appears in the formula bar, and $4,283, the average value of outdated equipment in the Field garage, appears in cell D6.
5. Copy the formula from cell **C7** to cell **D7**.
6. Select cell **D7**, and then change the criteria range (the third argument) from H13:I14 to **J13:K14**. The formula =DAVERAGE(Equipment!$A$6:$J$79, "Value",J13:K14) appears in the formula bar, and $2,358, the average value of outdated equipment in the Oak garage, appears in cell D7. See Figure B-14.

Figure B-14 Average equipment values

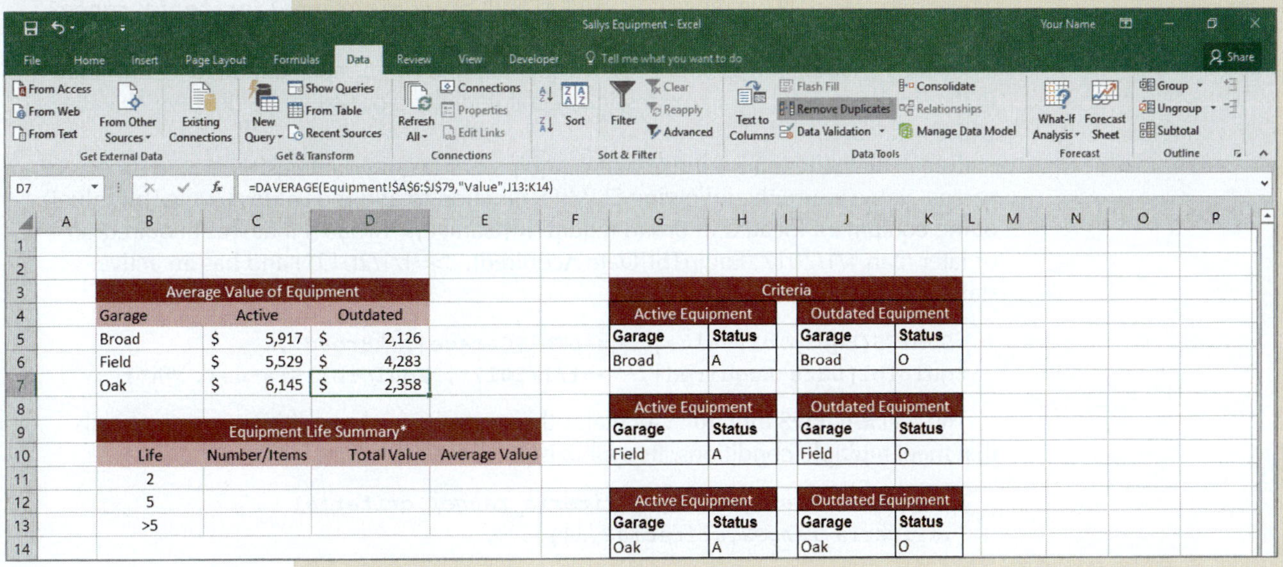

D7 =DAVERAGE(Equipment!$A$6:$J$79,"Value",J13:K14)

Average Value of Equipment		
Garage	Active	Outdated
Broad	$ 5,917	$ 2,126
Field	$ 5,529	$ 4,283
Oak	$ 6,145	$ 2,358

Equipment Life Summary*			
Life	Number/Items	Total Value	Average Value
2			
5			
>5			

Criteria

Active Equipment		Outdated Equipment	
Garage	Status	Garage	Status
Broad	A	Broad	O

Active Equipment		Outdated Equipment	
Garage	Status	Garage	Status
Field	A	Field	O

Active Equipment		Outdated Equipment	
Garage	Status	Garage	Status
Oak	A	Oak	O

Summarizing Data Using the COUNTIFS, SUMIFS, and AVERAGEIFS Functions

Sally wants you to summarize the years of service for the company's equipment. She needs to know the total and average values of the active equipment based on the life of the equipment.

TIP

You can also count the number of blank cells in a range using the COUNTBLANK function. Remember to allow iterative calculations in the options.

The COUNTIFS, SUMIFS, and AVERAGEIFS functions are similar to the COUNTIF, SUMIF, and AVERAGEIF functions except the latter functions enable you to specify only one condition to summarize the data, whereas the former functions enable you to summarize the data using several conditions.

The **COUNTIFS function** counts the number of cells within a range that meet multiple criteria. Its syntax is

```
COUNTIFS(criteria_range1,criteria1[,criteria_range2,criteria2,…])
```

where *criteria_range1*, *criteria_range2*, and so on represent up to 127 ranges (columns of data) in which to evaluate the associated criteria; and *criteria1*, *criteria2*, and so on represent up to 127 criteria in the form of a number, an expression, a cell reference, or text that define which cells will be counted. Criteria can be expressed as a number such as 50 to find a number equal to 50; an expression such as ">10000" to find an amount greater than 10,000; text such as "A" to find a text value equal to A; or a cell reference such as B4 to find the value equal to the value stored in cell B4. Each cell in a range is counted only if all of the corresponding criteria specified in the COUNTIFS function are true.

To count the number of pieces of Active (A) equipment in the Broad garage (Broad) and with a value more than $500, you can use the COUNTIFS function.

```
=COUNTIFS(EquipTbl[Status], "A", EquipTbl[Garage], "Broad",
EquipTbl[Value], ">500")
```

The criteria are treated as if they are connected by an AND function, so all conditions must be true for a record to be counted.

The SUMIFS and AVERAGEIFS functions have a slightly different syntax. The **SUMIFS function** adds values in a range that meet multiple criteria using the syntax

```
SUMIFS(sum_range,criteria_range1,criteria1
[,criteria_range2,criteria2,…])
```

where *sum_range* is the range you want to add; *criteria_range1*, *criteria_range2*, and so on represent up to 127 ranges (columns of data) in which to evaluate the associated criteria; and *criteria1*, *criteria2*, and so on represent up to 127 criteria in the form of a number, an expression, a cell reference, or text that define which cells will be added.

To calculate the total value of active equipment acquired after 2017 in the Broad garage, you can use the following SUMIFS function to add the values (EquipTbl[Value]) of the equipment located in Broad (EquipTbl[Garage], "Broad") that was acquired on or later than 1/1/2017 (EquipTbl[Date Acquired], ">=1/1/2017") and has an active status (EquipTbl[Status], "A"):

```
=SUMIFS(EquipTbl[Value],EquipTbl[Garage], "Broad",
EquipTbl[Date Acquired], ">=1/1/2017", EquipTbl[Status], "A")
```

The **AVERAGEIFS function** calculates the average of values within a range of cells that meet multiple conditions. Its syntax is

```
AVERAGEIFS(average_range,criteria_range1,criteria1
[,criteria_range2,criteria2,…])
```

where *average_range* is the range to average; *criteria_range1*, *criteria_range2*, and so on represent up to 127 ranges in which to evaluate the associated criteria; and *criteria1*, *criteria2*, and so on represent up to 127 criteria in the form of a number, an expression, a cell reference, or text that define which cells will be averaged.

To calculate the value of active equipment that has a two-year life, you can use the following AVERAGEIFS function to average the values (EquipTbl[Value]) of active equipment (EquipTbl[Status], "A") having two years of life (EquipTbl[Life], "2"):

```
=AVERAGEIFS(EquipTbl[Value], EquipTbl[Status], "A",
EquipTbl[Life], "2")
```

One of the first items you need for the Years' Service Summary report is a count of equipment with a two-year life. You will use the COUNTIFS function to compute statistical information for the active equipment in both garages.

To calculate the total amount of active equipment with a life of two, five, and greater than five years:

1. Select cell **C11**, and then click the **Insert Function** button next to the formula bar. The Insert Function dialog box opens.
2. Click the **Or select a category** arrow, and then click **Statistical**.
3. In the Select a function box, click **COUNTIFS**, and then click the **OK** button. The Function Arguments dialog box opens.
4. In the Criteria_range1 box, enter **EquipTbl[Status]** and then press the **Tab** key. This criterion selects the status of the equipment in the EquipTbl.
5. In the Criteria1 box, type **"A"** to specify active equipment, and then press the **Tab** key. The first condition is complete, and 43 appears as the total count in the middle of the Function Arguments dialog box.
6. In the Criteria_range2 box, enter **EquipTbl[Life]** and then press the **Tab** key. This criterion selects equipment in the table.
7. In the Criteria2 box, type **"2"** to select equipment with a life of two years, and then press the **Tab** key. The second condition is complete, and 15 appears as the total count. See Figure B-15.

TIP

You could also use the worksheet reference 'Equipment'!G7:G79 to reference all of the equipment.

Figure B-15 COUNTIFS Function Arguments box

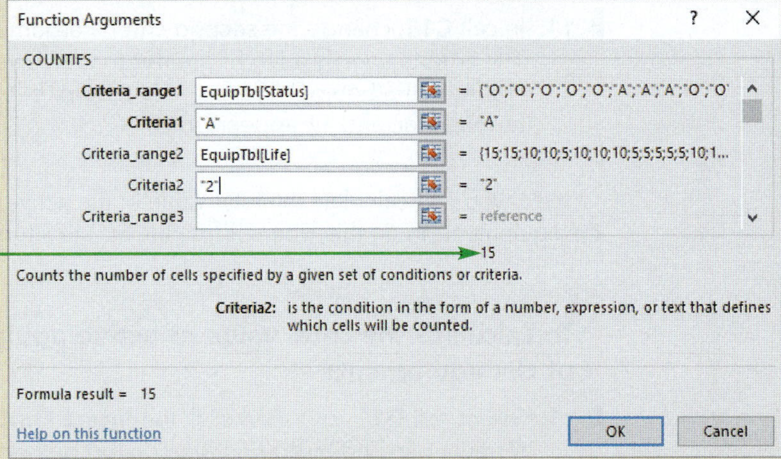

8. Click the **OK** button. The formula =COUNTIFS(EquipTbl[Status],"A", EquipTbl[Life], "2") appears in the formula bar, and the value 15 appears in cell C11. See Figure B-16.

Figure B-16 Summary of the equipment with a two-year life

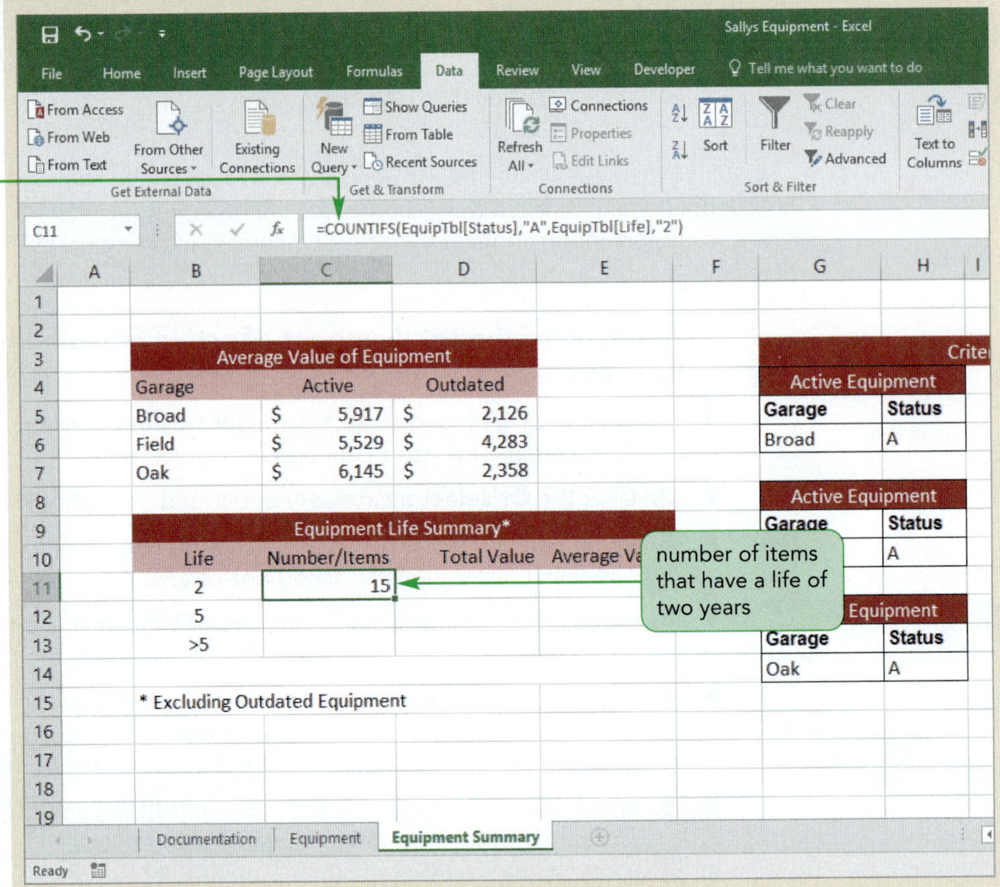

9. Copy the formula from cell **C11** to the range **C12:C13.**
10. In cell **C12**, change the second criteria argument from "2" to **"5"**. The criteria specify a life of five years. The formula =COUNTIFS(EquipTbl[Status],"A", EquipTbl[Life], "5") appears in the formula bar, and 11 appears in cell C12.
11. In cell **C13**, change the second criteria argument from "2" to **">5"**. The criteria specify a life of greater than five years. The formula =COUNTIFS(EquipTbl[Status], "A",EquipTbl[Life], ">5") appears in the formula bar, and 17 appears in cell C13.

Next, you will calculate the total value of the active equipment based on the life of the equipment. To do this, you will use the SUMIFS function.

To calculate the total value of active equipment based on the life of the equipment:

1. Select cell **D11**, and then click the **Insert Function** button next to the formula bar. The Insert Function dialog box opens.
2. Click the **Or select a category** arrow, and then click **Math & Trig**.
3. In the Select a function box, click **SUMIFS**, and then click the **OK** button. The Function Arguments dialog box opens.

4. In the Sum_range box, type **EquipTbl[Value]** to enter the range of data to sum, and then press the **Tab** key.
5. In the Criteria_range1 box, enter **EquipTbl[Status]** and then press the **Tab** key. This will include the status for all equipment in the EqupTbl table.
6. In the Criteria1 box, type **"A"** to specify active equipment, and then press the **Tab** key. The first condition is complete.
7. In the Criteria_range2 box, enter **EquipTbl[Life]** for the range referencing the life of the equipment, and then press the **Tab** key.
8. In the Criteria2 box, type **"2"** to specify the life of the equipment. All conditions are complete. See Figure B-17.

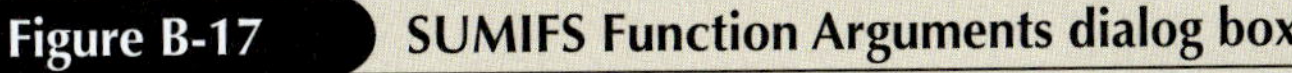

Figure B-17 SUMIFS Function Arguments dialog box

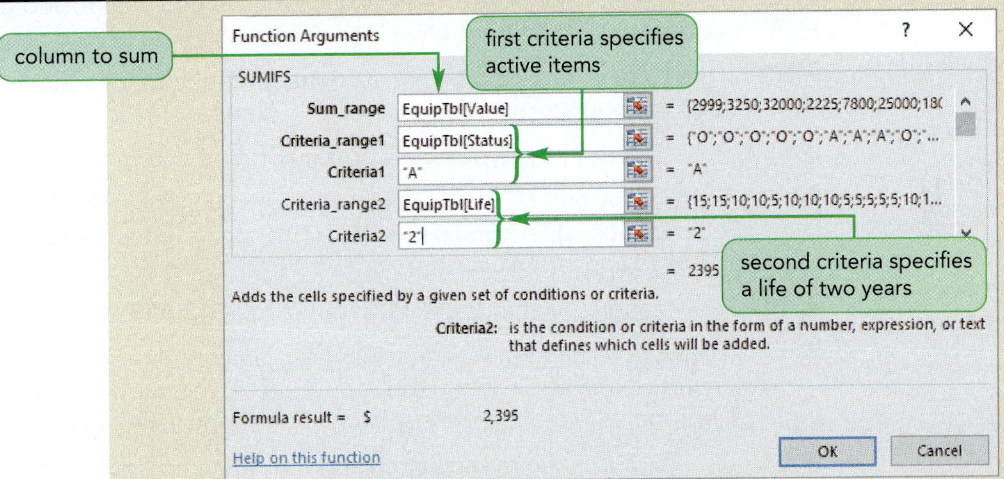

9. Click the **OK** button. The formula =SUMIFS(EquipTbl[Value],EquipTbl[Status],"A", EquipTblLife],"2") appears in the formula bar, and $2,395 appears in cell D11.
10. Copy the formula from cell **D11** to the range **D12:D13**.
11. In cell **D12**, change the second criteria argument from "2" to **"5"**. The formula =SUMIFS(EquipTblValue],EquipTblStatus],"A",EquipTblLife],"5") appears in the formula bar, and $54,378 appears in cell D12.
12. In cell **D13**, change the second criteria argument to **">5"**. The formula =SUMIFS(EquipTblValue],EquipTblStatus], "A",EquipTblLife],">5") appears in the formula bar, and $194,805 appears in cell D13.

Next, you will calculate the average value of active equipment based on the life of the equipment. You will use the AVERAGEIFS function to do this.

To calculate the average value of active equipment based on the life of the equipment:

1. Select cell **E11**, and then click the **Insert Function** button *fx* next to the formula bar. The Insert Function dialog box opens.
2. Click the **Or select a category** arrow, and then click **Statistical**.
3. In the Select a function box, click **AVERAGEIFS**, and then click the **OK** button. The Function Arguments dialog box opens.
4. In the Average_range box, type **EquipTbl[Value]** to enter the range to be averaged, and then press the **Tab** key.
5. In the Criteria_range1 box, enter **EquipTbl[Status]** for the range referencing the status of the equipment, and then press the **Tab** key.
6. In the Criteria1 box, type **"A"** to specify active equipment, and then press the **Tab** key. The first condition is complete.
7. In the Criteria_range2 box, enter **EquipTbl[Life]** for the range referencing the life of the equipment, and then press the **Tab** key.
8. In the Criteria2 box, type **"2"** to specify a life of two years for the equipment.
9. Click the **OK** button. The formula =AVERAGEIFS(EquipTbl[Value], EquipTbl[Status],"A",EquipTbl[Life],"2") appears in the formula bar, and $160 appears in cell E11.
10. Copy the formula from cell **E11** to the range **E12:E13**.
11. In cell **E12**, change the second criteria argument from "2" to **"5"**. The formula =AVERAGEIFS(EquipTbl[Value],EquipTbl[Status],"A", EquipTbl[Life], "5") appears in the formula bar, and $4,943 appears in cell E12.
12. In cell **E13**, change the second criteria argument to **">5"**. The formula =AVERAGEIFS(EquipTbl[Value],EquipTbl[Status],"A", EquipTbl[Life], ">5" appears in the formula bar, and $11,459 appears in cell E13.

13. Select cell **E13**. See Figure B-18.

Figure B-18 **Completed Equipment Life Summary**

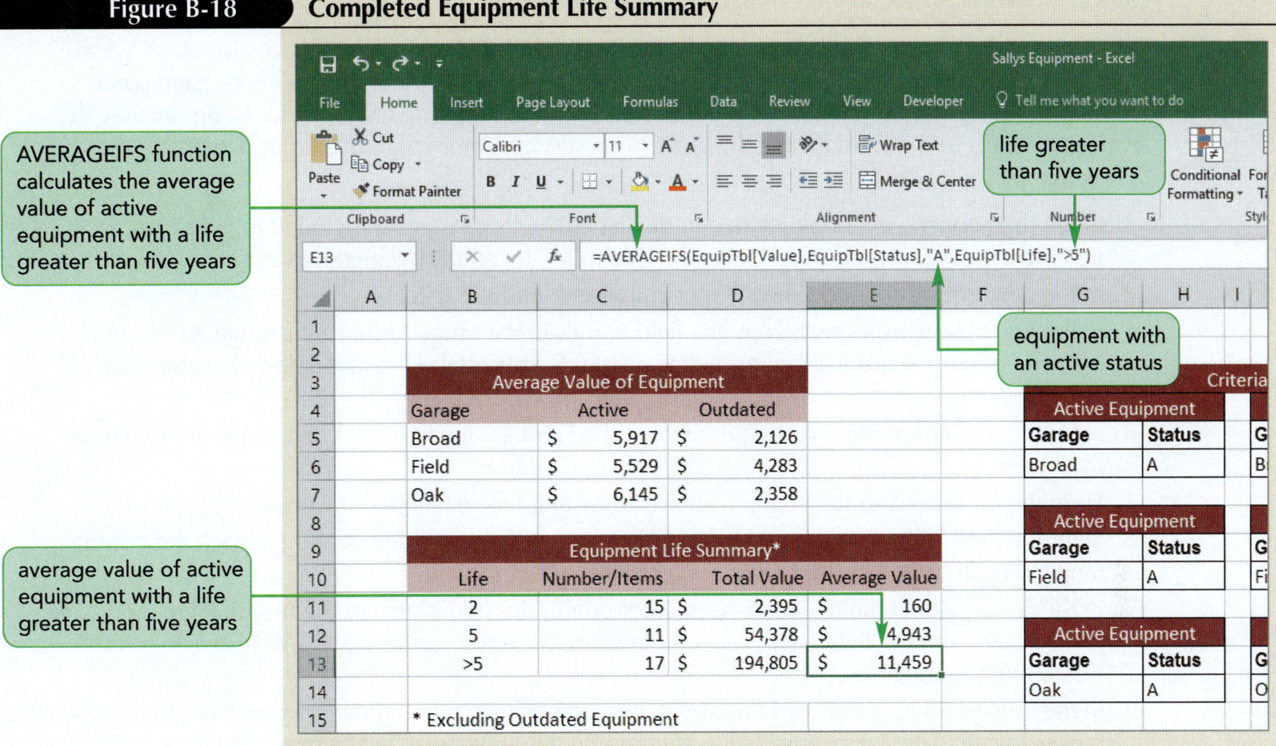

14. Save the workbook, and then close it.

The Equipment Summary worksheet is complete. In this appendix, you used advanced filtering techniques to evaluate the equipment. You also used the DAVERAGE and AVERAGEIFS functions to calculate the average value of equipment broken down by garage and status.

PRACTICE

Review Assignments

Data File needed for the Review Assignments: Service.xlsx

The replacement plan analysis was helpful to Sally. But before Sally makes any decisions on which equipment is to be replaced, she wants an additional analysis about how many times each piece of equipment has been serviced. You will perform advanced filtering tasks that focus on items with service contracts in the Field garage that have been serviced more than five times. Complete the following:

1. Open the **Service** workbook located in the ExcelB > Review folder included in your Data Files, and then save the workbook as **Sallys Service** in the location specified by your instructor.
2. In the Documentation worksheet, enter your name and the date.
3. In the Equipment worksheet, copy the field names in the range A6:J6 to the range A1:J1, and make sure row 1 has the same formatting as row 6. This establishes the criteria for advanced filtering.
4. Enter the And criteria to select equipment at the Field garage that has been serviced more than five times.
5. Enter the Or criteria to select any Trimmer/Edger that has reached Max Service.
6. Filter the data in the EquipTbl table based on the criteria you entered. (*Hint*: Check the criteria range to make sure that the proper range is selected.)
7. In the Equipment Summary worksheet, enter criteria for equipment at the Broad, Field, and Oak garages and whether they have reached Max Service in the ranges G5:H6, G9:H10, G14:H15, J5:K6, J9:K10, and J14:K15.
8. In the range C5:D7, enter the DAVERAGE function using the criteria you entered in the criteria ranges to calculate the average value of equipment that has reached its max service at each garage and that has available service at each garage.
9. In the range C11:C13, enter the COUNTIFS function using EquipTbl Status equal to A and the specified Times Serviced values. For example, cell C11 Times Serviced < 5 cell C12 will have Times Serviced = 5, and cell C13 will have Times Serviced > 5.
10. In the range D11:D13, enter the SUMIFS function using EquipTbl Status equal to A and the specified Times Serviced values.
11. In the range E11:E13, enter the AVERAGEIFS function using EquipTbl Status equal to A and the specified Times Serviced values.
12. Save the workbook, and then close it.

APPLY

Case Problem 1

Data File needed for this Case Problem: Quilts.xlsx

Broadway Quilt Guild Broadway Quilt Guild includes an active group of quilters who meet monthly to complete quilting projects. Each year, guild members work together to make 6 to 10 quilts to raffle. The proceeds of the raffle along with the quilt are donated to a local charity. Vesta Reed, the president of the guild, has created a worksheet to track the quilts and the raffle proceeds. She wants you to analyze this information. Complete the following:

1. Open the **Quilts** workbook located in the ExcelB > Case1 folder included with your Data Files, and then save the workbook as **Guild Quilts** in the location specified by your instructor.
2. In the Documentation worksheet, enter your name and the date.
3. In the Quilts worksheet, use advanced filtering to display donation totals in 2016 that were greater than $300.
4. Sort the filtered data by donation total from highest to lowest.
5. Make a copy of the Quilts worksheet, and rename it **New Quilts**. In the New Quilts worksheet, remove all filtering and clear the criteria entered in the range A2:E3.
6. In the New Quilts worksheet, use advanced filtering to display queen-sized quilts completed in 2016 or quilts created for the Halfway House charity.
7. In the Summary worksheet, in the range B4:B8, use the DAVERAGE function for the data in the Quilts worksheet in the range A5:E48, the Donation Total field, and the corresponding criteria in the range E2:I3 to calculate the average donation for each charity.
8. In the Summary worksheet, in the range B14:F18, use the COUNTIFS function with the QuiltTbl Size and Donation Total to complete the Count of Quilts by Type and Donation Total table.
9. Save the workbook, and then close it.

CHALLENGE

Case Problem 2

Data File needed for this Case Problem: Birds.xlsx

Third Street Bird Watchers Daniel Yates is the recorder for the Third Street Bird Watchers in Pueblo, Colorado. The group conducted a backyard bird count during the first three days in November. He has created a worksheet to capture the data that the group collected and wants you to analyze the information to determine who counted the most birds and the most unique birds. Complete the following:

1. Open the **Birds** workbook located in the ExcelB > Case2 folder included with your Data Files, and then save the workbook as **Bird Watchers** in the location specified by your instructor.
2. In the Documentation worksheet, enter your name and the date.
3. In the Bird Count worksheet, enter the And criteria to select the bird sightings on 11/3/2017 of more than two birds.
4. Add an Or criteria to display the Blue Jay records.
5. Filter the data in the Bird Count worksheet.
6. **Explore** In the Analysis worksheet, in the range B2:B4, use the DCOUNT function using the bird count data in the range A6:D105 of the Bird Count worksheet to count the values in the Count field using the corresponding criteria in the range E2:G3 to count the birds identified on each of the three dates. (*Hint*: The formula for 11/1/2017 uses the range E2:E3 for the criteria.)
7. In the range B11:B16, use the COUNTIFS function to count the number of birds identified by each bird watcher.
8. In the range C11:C16, use the SUMIFS function to tally the total count of birds for each watcher during the three days.
9. Save the workbook, and then close it.

APPENDIX C

Working with Enhanced Formatting Tools

Formatting Seasonal Calendars for a Waterpark

OBJECTIVES

- Create a custom cell style
- Create a custom table style
- Create a conditional format to highlight cells
- Create a color scale conditional format
- Create an icon set conditional format
- Insert and modify a SmartArt graphic
- Modify the image properties of a picture
- Create and save a theme

Case | *Waves World*

Waves World is a waterpark based in Rapid City, South Dakota. Emma Drake is an event coordinator at the park. She is creating a workbook with calendars of events for the upcoming season and daily projections of park attendance. She wants to use advanced formatting tools in Excel to present the calendars in a visually striking way, highlighting the calendar days in which special events occur and showing how attendance changes throughout the summer months. She has asked your help in developing the workbook.

EXCEL

STARTING DATA FILES

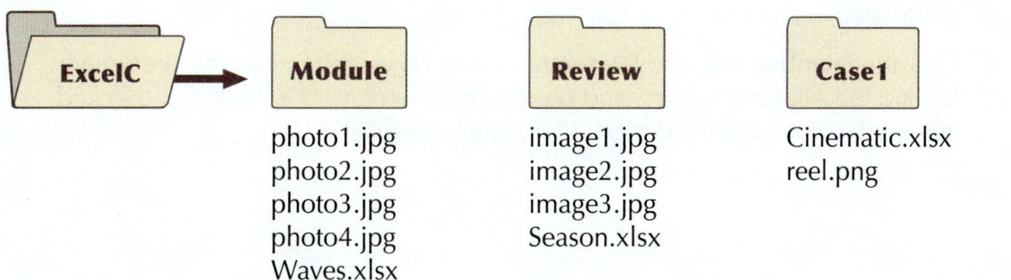

Creating a Custom Cell Style

A **custom cell style** is a cell style created by a user that can be added to a workbook. Custom cell styles are created using the same formatting tools that you have used with individual cells. After a cell contains all the formatting you want to include in the custom cell style, you save the cell style with a new name. This name will appear in the Cell Styles gallery alongside the built-in styles.

REFERENCE

Creating a Cell Style

- Select a cell that contains the formatting you want to use in the custom cell style.
- On the Home tab, in the Styles group, click the Cell Styles button, and then click New Cell Style.
- In the Style name box, type a name for the style.
- In the Style Includes (By Example) section, check the style elements that you want to be part of the custom style.
- Click the Format button, and then select any other formatting options you want to include in the custom style.
- Click the OK button in each dialog box to add the custom cell style to the Cell Styles gallery.

Emma wants to use custom styles to create a unifying look for her workbook containing calendars for the upcoming waterpark season. The workbook contains four worksheets in addition to the Documentation worksheet. The Events of Note sheet lists special events that will take place in the upcoming season. The Operation Calendar sheet provides information on the days in which the park is open. The Attendance Calendar sheet projects the daily attendance at the park from May through September. Finally, the Events Calendar sheet marks the days in which special events occur at the park.

Emma asks you to create a custom cell style named CalTitle that will format the calendar titles displayed on the three calendar worksheets.

To create the CalTitle cell style:

1. Open the **Waves** workbook located in the **ExcelC > Module** folder included with your Data Files, and then save the workbook as **Waves World** in the location specified by your instructor.
2. In the Documentation worksheet, enter your name and the date.
3. Go to the **Operation Calendar** worksheet, and then select the merged cell **A7**.
4. On the Home tab, in the Styles group, click the **Cell Styles** button to open the Cell Styles gallery, and then click **New Cell Style**. The Style dialog box opens.
5. In the Style name box, type **CalTitle**.
6. Click the **Number**, **Fill**, and **Protection** check boxes to remove the checkmarks, leaving the Alignment, Font, and Border style elements checked. The checked items are included in the custom style. See Figure C-1.

Figure C-1 Style dialog box

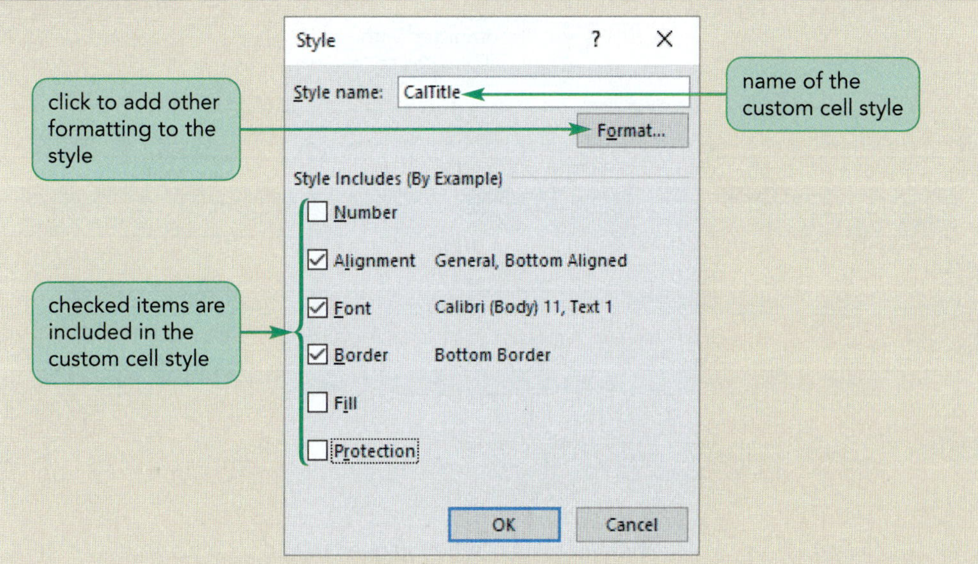

7. Click the **Format** button. The Format Cells dialog box opens.
8. Click the **Alignment** tab, click the **Horizontal** arrow, and then click **Center**.
9. Click the **Font** tab, click **Bold** in the Font style box, and then click **14** in the Size box.
10. Click the **Border** tab, click the **double line** in the Style box, and then click the **Outline** preset.
11. Click the **OK** button in each dialog box to create the custom style and return to the workbook.

Custom styles appear at the top of the Cell Styles gallery. You will use the Cell Styles gallery to apply the CalTitle cell style to the active cell, which is cell A7.

To apply the CalTitle cell style:

1. On the Home tab, in the Styles group, click the **Cell Styles** button to open the Cell Styles gallery.
2. In the Custom section, click **CalTitle**. The custom style is applied to the selected cell, cell A7.
3. Apply the **CalTitle** cell style to the month titles of all the five calendars on the Operation Calendar, Attendance Calendar, and Events Calendar worksheets.
4. Go to the **Operation Calendar** worksheet, and then click cell **A1**. Figure C-2 shows the reformatted titles for the first two calendars on the worksheet.

Figure C-2 CalTitle cell style applied

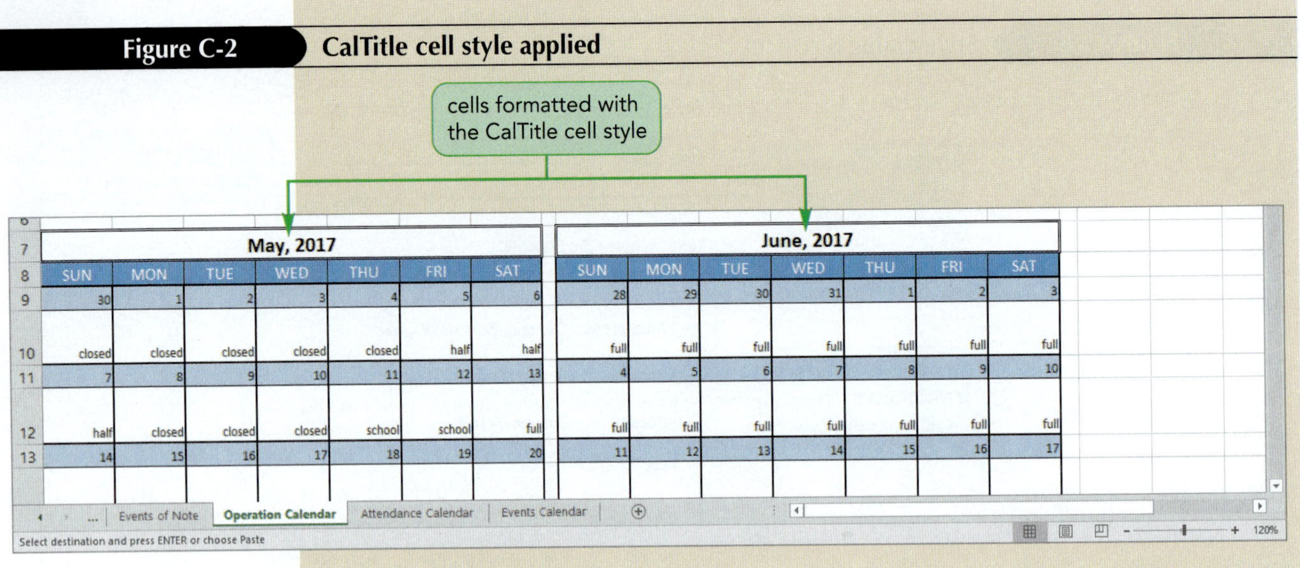

Modifying a cell style changes the appearance of any cell formatted with that style. You can use styles to make global changes to the workbook's appearance without having to select and reformat individual cells. Emma wants you to modify the CalTitle cell style, changing the font color to a dark blue and removing the font bolding.

To modify the CalTitle cell style:

1. On the Home tab, in the Styles group, click the **Cell Styles** button. The Cell Styles gallery opens.
2. In the Custom section, right-click **CalTitle**, and then click **Modify** on the shortcut menu. The Style dialog box for the CalTitle cell style opens.
3. Click the **Format** button. The Format Cells dialog box opens.
4. Click the **Font** tab, click the **Color** arrow, and then click **Blue, Accent 5** (the second-to-last theme color).
5. In the Font style box, click **Regular** to change the font style from Bold to Regular.
6. Click the **OK** button in each dialog box. The CalTitle cell style is updated and applied to every calendar title in the workbook.

Creating a Custom Table Style

You can also create custom table styles. A **table style** is a style definition that describes the appearance of different elements of an Excel table. To create a table style, you format any of 13 table elements, including the header row, the first and last columns, the first and last rows, and the stripes used in banded rows or columns. Any element left unformatted in a custom table style uses Excel's default style.

Emma wants you to format the data in the Events of Note worksheet as an Excel table.

To apply a table style to an Excel table:

1. Go to the **Events of Note** worksheet, click cell **A4**, and then press the **Ctrl+Shift+End** keys. The entire range of the events is selected.
2. On the Home tab, in the Styles group, click the **Format as Table** button to open the gallery, and then click **Table Style Medium 2** (the second table style in the first row in the Medium section). The Format As Table dialog box opens.
3. Make sure the range **$A$4:$C$22** is specified as the data for your table and the **My table has headers** check box is checked, and then click the **OK** button. The selected range is converted to an Excel table with the table style applied.
4. On the Table Tools Design tab, in the Table Style Options group, click the **First Column** check box to insert a checkmark. The first column of the table (in column A) is formatted in bold. See Figure C-3.

Figure C-3 Table style applied to the events list

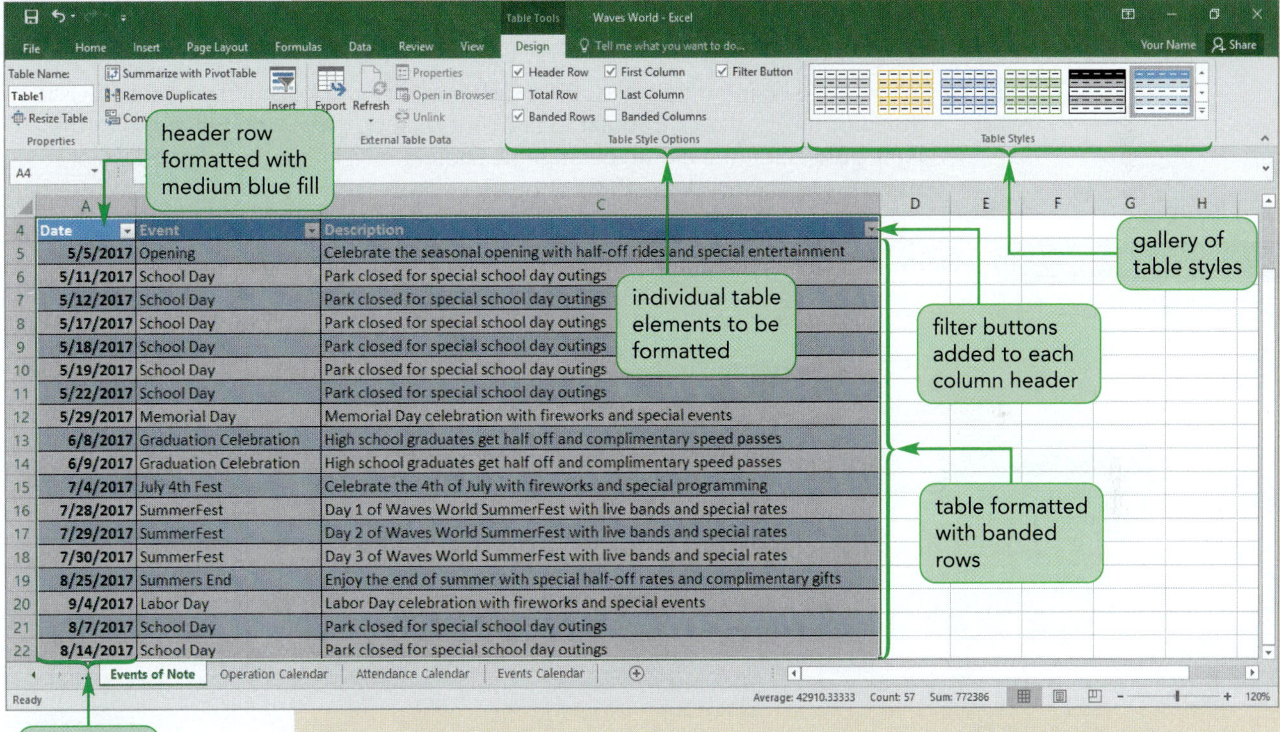

Emma wants you to format the Excel table in the Events of Note worksheet so that table headers have a dark green fill and the first column has a light gold fill. You'll make these changes to the table style, save them as a custom style, and then apply the custom style to the Excel table.

To create and apply the custom table style:

1. On the ribbon, click the **Home** tab. In the Styles group, click the **Format as Table** button, and then click **New Table Style**. The New Table Style dialog box opens. The Table Element box lists the 13 table elements you can format. The Preview box shows the formatted table.
2. In the Name box, type **EventTable** as the name of the custom table style.

3. In the Table Element box, click **Header Row**, and then click the **Format** button. The Format Cells dialog box opens.
4. Click the **Fill** tab, and then in the Background Color palette, click the **green** color (the last color in the first row).
5. Click the **OK** button to return to the New Table Style dialog box. You can see the header row formatting in the Preview box.
6. In the Table Element box, click **First Row Stripe**, verify that **1** is entered in the Stripe Size box, and then click the **Format** button.
7. On the Fill tab, click the **white** color (the first color in the first row) in the Background Color palette, click the **Font** tab, click the **Color** arrow, click **Black, Text 1** from the first row, and then click the **OK** button.
8. In the Table Element box, click **Second Row Stripe**, and then verify that **1** is entered in the Stripe Size box.
9. Click the **Format** button, click the **Fill** tab, click the **light green** color (the last color in the third row) in the Background Color palette, and then click the **OK** button. The second color used in the banded rows will be light green.
10. In the Table Element box, click **First Column**, click the **Format** button, and click the **Font** tab, and click **Regular** in the Font style box, click the **Fill** tab, click the **light gold** color (the eighth color in the second row) in the Background Color palette, and then click the **OK** button. See Figure C-4.

TIP

You can create banded rows that cover more than one row with a color by increasing the value in the Stripe Size box.

Figure C-4 Modify Table Style dialog box

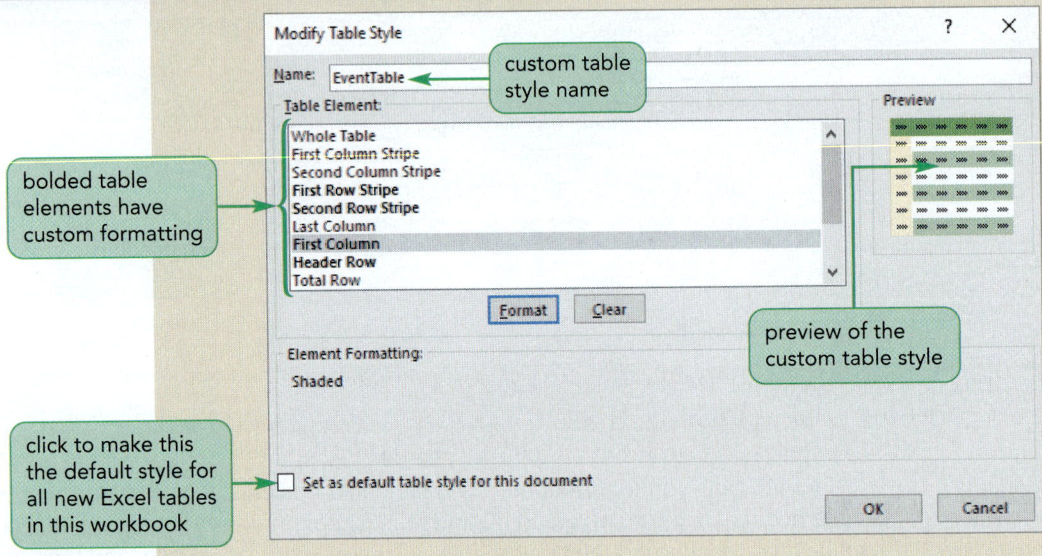

11. Click the **OK** button. The EventTable style is added to the Table Styles gallery.
12. With the Excel table still selected, click the **Format as Table** button, and then click the **EventTable** table style in the Custom section at the top of the Style gallery. The table is formatted with the custom table style.

TIP

To make a table style available in every workbook, create the style in a blank workbook named book.xltx in the xlstart folder.

Exploring Conditional Formats

Emma wants to present the information in the three calendar worksheets in a visually interesting and informative way. You'll start by formatting the calendars in the Operation Calendar worksheet that describe each day of operation at the waterpark from May through September.

Highlighting Cells

Emma added a legend to the worksheet that indicates how she wants the different days colored. Although you could edit the fill colors of selected cells to match the legend, it is more efficient to highlight the cells using conditional formatting based on the text entries in each date. You'll start by highlighting the days on which the waterpark is closed.

To the highlight closed dates:

1. Go to the **Operation Calendar** worksheet, click the **Name Box** arrow, and then click **Operation_Dates**. All of the cells in the worksheet containing the calendar days are selected.
2. On the Home tab, in the Styles group, click the **Conditional Formatting** button, point to **Highlight Cells Rules**, and then click **Text that Contains**. The Text That Contains dialog box opens. Instead of typing text, you'll use the closed entry from the legend.
3. Scroll up and click cell **C4**, click the **with** box, and then click **Custom Format**. The Format Cells dialog box opens.
4. On the Fill tab, click the **gray** color (the first color in the third row) in the Background Color palette, and then click the **OK** button in each dialog box to return to the worksheet.
5. Select cell **A1**, and then scroll the worksheet to verify that only days containing the text "closed" have a gray fill.

To highlight the other operational days, you'll repeat this process for the remaining entries in the legend.

To highlight the remaining element families:

1. Click the **Name Box** arrow, and then click **Operation_Dates** to select all of the cells containing dates in the worksheet.
2. Click the **Conditional Formatting** button, point to **Highlight Cells Rules**, and then click **Text that Contains** to open the Text That Contains dialog box.
3. Click cell **D4**, click the **with** box, and then click **Custom Format** to open the Format Cells dialog box.
4. On the Fill tab, click the **light gold** color (the eighth color in the second row) in the Background Color palette, and then click the **OK** button in each dialog box. Days containing the text "school" have a light gold fill.
5. Repeat Steps 2 through 4, clicking cell **E4** and selecting the **light blue** color (the fifth color in the second row) so that days containing the text "half" have a light blue fill.

6. Repeat Steps 2 through 4, clicking cell **F4** and selecting the **medium green** color (the last color in the first row) so that days containing the text "full" have a medium green fill.
7. Select cell **A1** to deselect the range, and then reduce the zoom level to **60%** so you can all five calendar tables. See Figure C-5.

Figure C-5 Conditional format applied to the days of operation

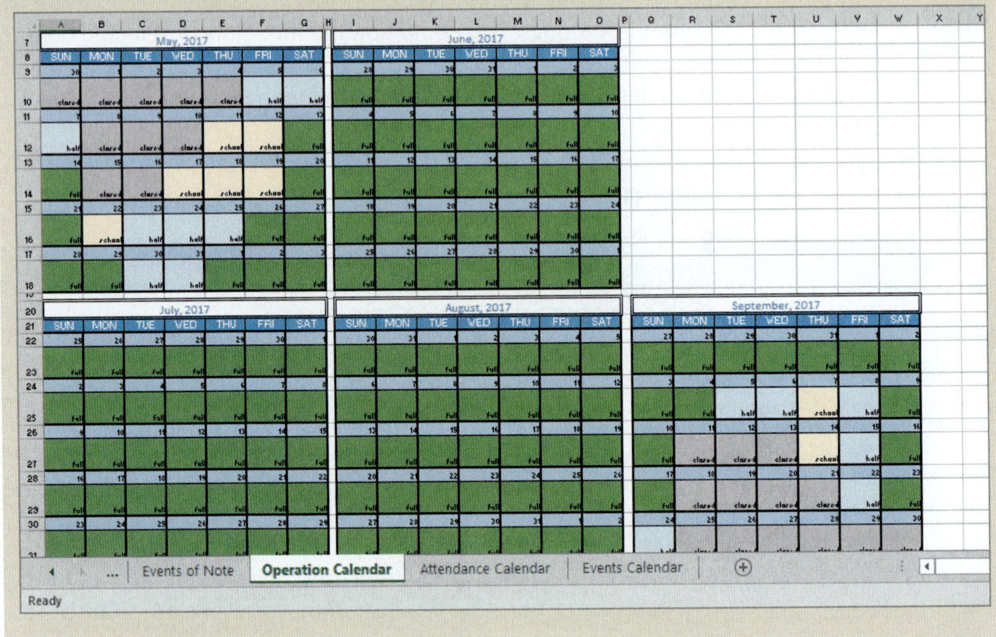

Emma wants you to hide the text in the operation days to make the calendars easier to read. Instead of changing the font color to match the background color to hide the text, you'll apply a custom format that prevents Excel from displaying a cell's value by changing the format code to ;;; (three semicolons).

To hide the operation status in the calendars:

1. Click the **Name Box** arrow, and then click **Operation_Dates** to select all of the calendar dates.
2. On the Home tab, in the Number group, click the **Dialog Box Launcher**. The Format Cells dialog box opens with the Number tab displayed.
3. In the Category box, click **Custom**, select the text in the Type box, type **;;;** (three semicolons), and then click the **OK** button. All of the text strings in the calendar days are hidden.
4. Zoom the worksheet back to **120%**.

Modifying a Conditional Formatting Rule

As with cell styles, you can modify a conditional formatting rule to change the look of cells formatted with that rule. Emma wants you to change the color of the half days to a light green fill color.

To modify a conditional formatting rule:

1. On the Home tab, in the Styles group, click the **Conditional Formatting** button, and then click **Manage Rules**. The Conditional Formatting Rules Manager dialog box opens.
2. Click the **Show formatting rules for** arrow, and then click **This Worksheet** to show all of the conditional formatting rules for the current worksheet.
3. In the Rule list, click **Cell Value contains =$E$4** to select the rule for half days at the waterpark, and then click the **Edit Rule** button. The Edit Formatting Rule dialog box opens.
4. Click the **Format** button to open the Format Cells dialog box, and then on the Fill tab, click the **light green** color (the last color in the third row) in the Background Color palette.
5. Click the **OK** button in each dialog box to return to the worksheet.
6. Select cell **E5** to select the legend entry for half, and then change its fill color to **light green** to match the conditional format. See Figure C-6.

TIP

To delete a rule, select the rule in the Rule list, and then click the Delete Rule button.

Figure C-6 Modified conditional format

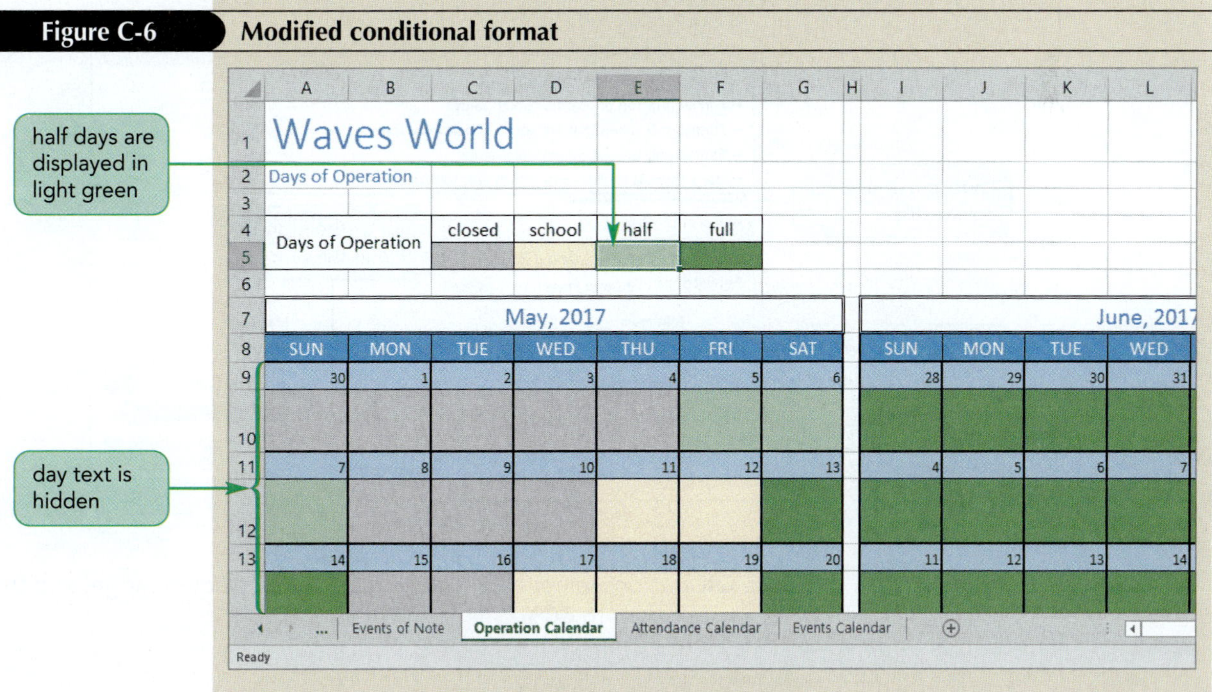

The highlight cells rule you created changes the fill color when cells have a specific value. You can also create a spectrum of fill colors based on a range of possible cell values.

Working with Color Scales

A **color scale** is a conditional format in which the fill color is based on a range of cell values where larger values have progressively darker or lighter shades of color. You'll create a color scale for the Attendance Calendar worksheet that projects the number of people attending the waterpark on each day of the season.

To highlight how attendance changes throughout the season, Emma wants the background fill to grow increasingly darker for days with the largest attendance.

To apply a color scale to the attendance calendar:

1. Go to the **Attendance Calendar** worksheet, click the **Name Box** arrow, and then click **Attendance_Dates** to select the calendar days on the worksheet.
2. On the Home tab, in the Styles group, click the **Conditional Formatting** button, point to **Color Scales**, and then click **More Rules**. The New Formatting Rule dialog box opens.
3. Verify that **2-Color Scale** is selected in the Format Style box.
4. In the Minimum column, click the **Color** box, and then click the **white** color (the first color in the first row).
5. In the Maximum column, click the **Color** box, and then click **Green, Accent 6** (the last color in the first row). The Preview box shows the color scale. See Figure C-7.

Figure C-7 **Edited color scale rule**

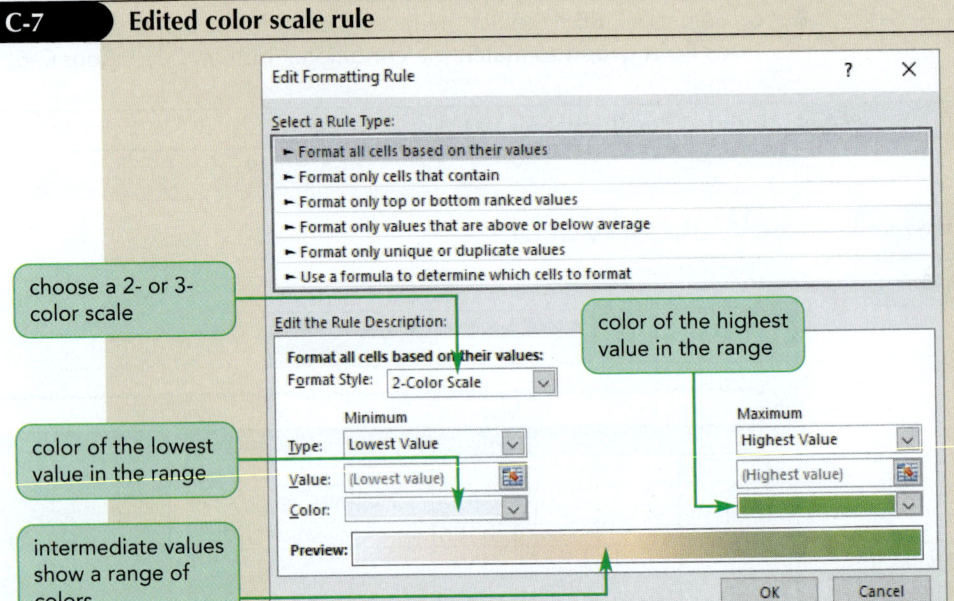

6. Click the **OK** button, select cell **A1** to deselect the selected range, and then zoom the worksheet to **60%**. See Figure C-8.

Figure C-8 Color scales added to the calendar days

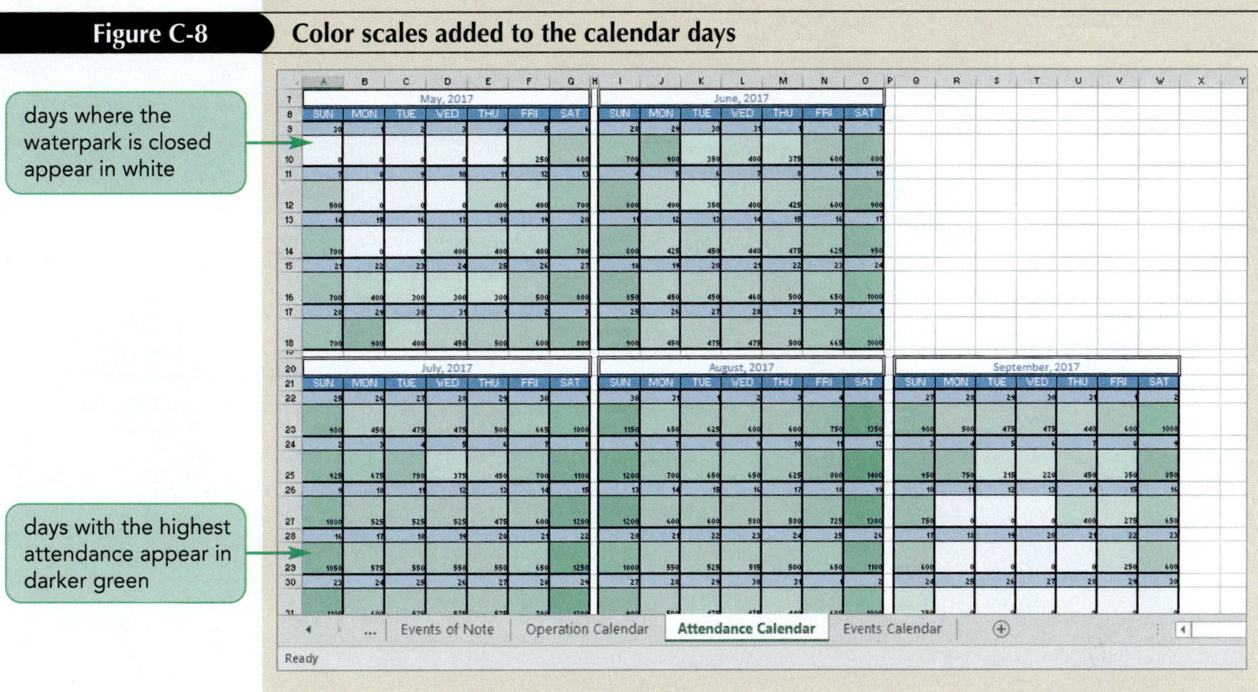

The color scale displays cells with the highest values in dark green and the lowest values in white. You'll add a legend to the worksheet so that readers understand what the colors mean.

To add a color scale legend:

1. Zoom the worksheet to **120%**, and then scroll to the top of the worksheet.
2. Right-click cell **A4**, click **Format Cells** on the shortcut menu to open the Format Cells dialog box, click the **Fill** tab, and then click the **Fill Effects** button. The Fill Effects dialog box opens.
3. In the Colors section, click the **Color 2** arrow, and then click the **Green, Accent 6** color (the last color in the first row) in the palette.
4. In the Shading styles box, click the **Vertical** option button.
5. In the Variants box, click the first color variant in the first row, in which the color shades darken from left to right. See Figure C-9.

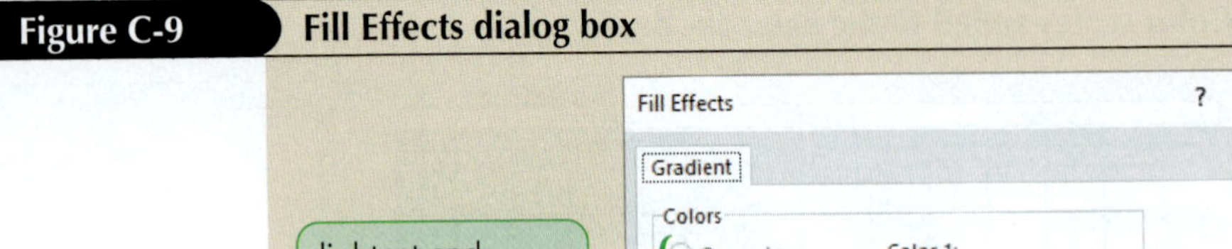

Figure C-9 **Fill Effects dialog box**

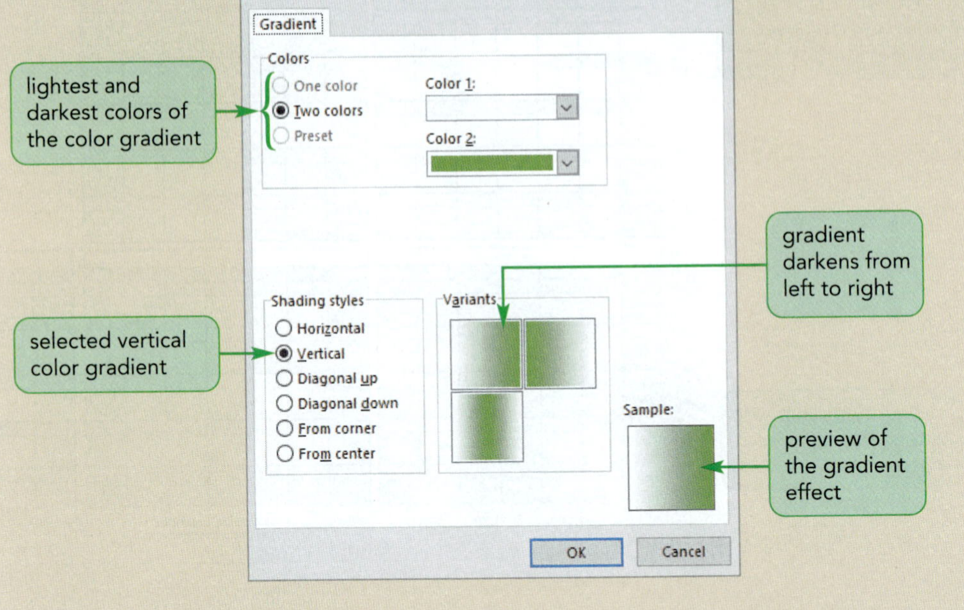

6. Click the **OK** button in each dialog box to return to the worksheet. The vertical gradient fill effect appears in the merged cell A4. See Figure C-10.

Figure C-10 **Gradient fill added to the legend**

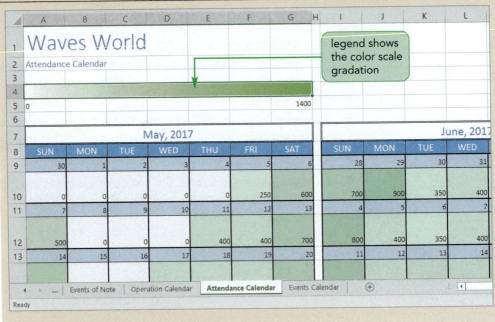

	A	B	C	D	E	F	G	H	I	J	K	L
1	Waves World											
2	Attendance Calendar											
3												
4												
5	0						1400					
6												
7	May, 2017								June, 2017			
8	SUN	MON	TUE	WED	THU	FRI	SAT		SUN	MON	TUE	WED
9	30	1	2	3	4	5	6		28	29	30	31
10	0	0	0	0	0	250	600		700	900	350	400
11	7	8	9	10	11	12	13		4	5	6	7
12	500	0	0	0	400	400	700		800	400	350	400
13	14	15	16	17	18	19	20		11	12	13	14

Working with Icon Sets

An **icon set** is a conditional format in which different icons are displayed in a cell based on the cell's value. Icon sets are useful for identifying extreme values or tracking changing values. For example, up and down arrow icons can be used to mark rising and falling stock prices.

You'll use icon sets for the Events Calendar worksheet, which marks the dates on which special events occur at the waterpark. Emma has marked special event days with a value of 1, and she wants you to replace those values with a star.

To apply an icon set to the calendar dates:

1. Go to the **Events Calendar** worksheet, click the **Name Box** arrow, and then click **Event_Dates** to select the calendar dates on the worksheet.
2. On the Home tab in the Styles group, click the **Conditional Formatting** button, point to **Icon Sets**, and then click **3 Stars** from the Ratings group.
3. Scroll down the worksheet so that you see stars in all dates that have a value of 1.
4. In the Styles group, click the **Conditional Formatting** button, and then click **Manage Rules**. The Conditional Formatting Rules Manager dialog box opens.
5. Verify that **Current Selection** appears in the Show formatting rules for box.
6. In the Rule list, click **Icon Set**, and then click the **Edit Rule** button. The Edit Formatting Rule dialog box opens.

   According to the rule description, the full star icon appears in cells with a value greater than or equal to 67 percent. The half star icon appears in cells with a value less than 67 percent but greater than or equal to 33 percent. The empty star icon appears in all other cells in the range. In this case, you want to display the full star icon for cells with a value equal to 1.
7. In the row for the full star icon, click the **Value** box and change the value to **1**, and then click the **Type** box and select **Number**. The full star will appear in cells with a number value of 1.
8. In the row for the half star icon, click the **Value** button and change the value to **0**, and then click the **Type** box and select **Number**.
9. Click the **Show Icon Only** check box to insert a checkmark, which hides the cell values. See Figure C-11.

TIP

When possible, apply the conditional formatting rule to the cells with the legend and the worksheet values so any edits you make affect both.

Figure C-11 Edited icon set rule

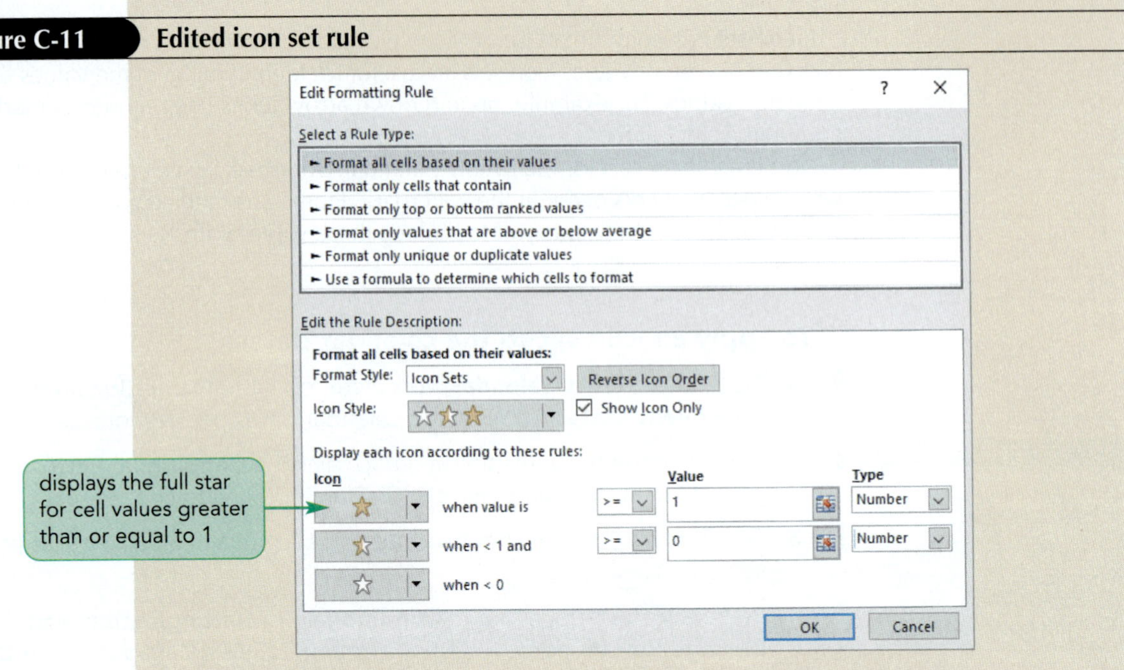

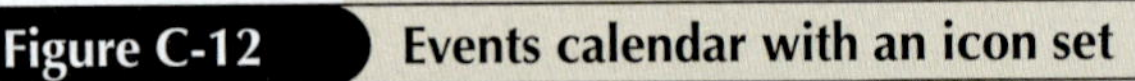

10. Click the **OK** button in each dialog box to return to the worksheet.
11. Select cell **A1**, and then zoom the worksheet to **60%**. The full star icon appears for dates on which special events occur. The other dates still show periods because the icon set rule applies only to numeric values. See Figure C-12.

Figure C-12 Events calendar with an icon set

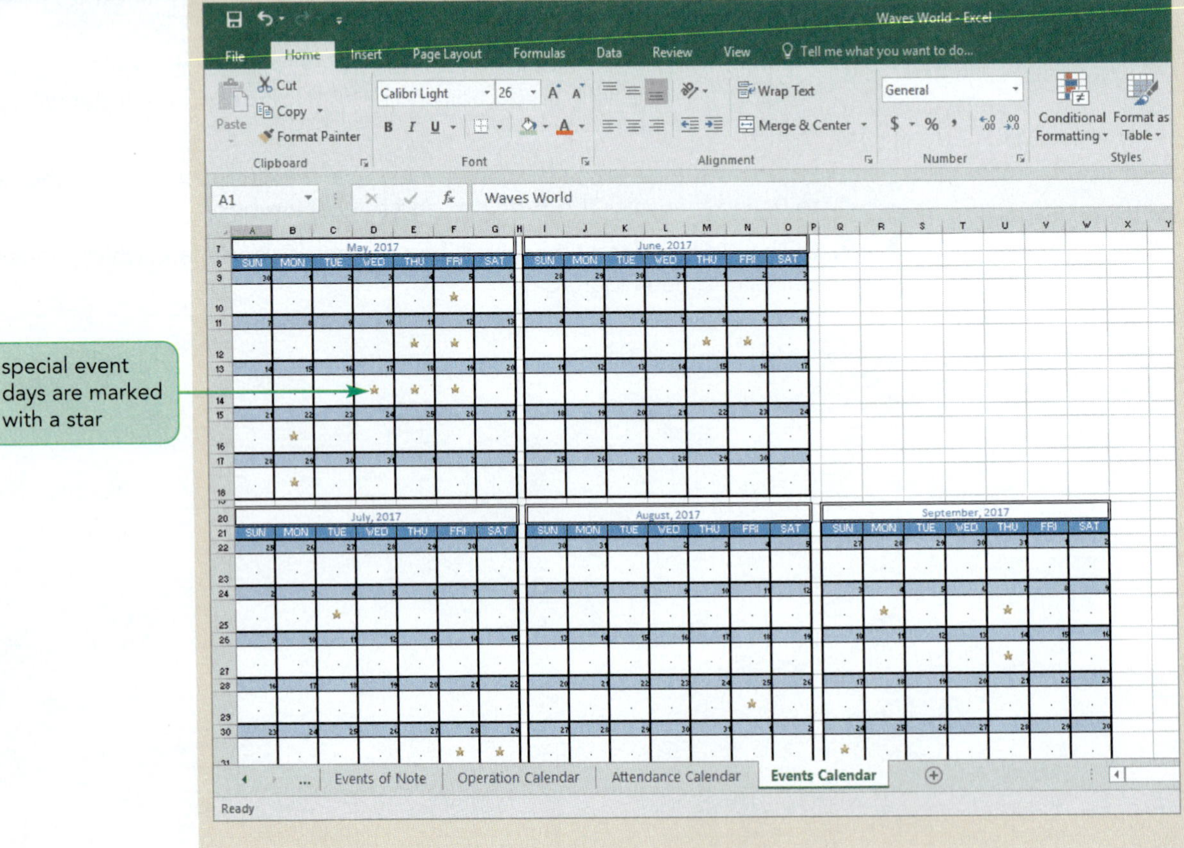

Using Formulas to Apply Conditional Formatting

All of the conditional formats you have used so far are based on the cell's value. You can also base the format on a function of the cell's value. For example, you can highlight cells with dates that fall on a weekend differently from cells with dates that fall on a weekday. To highlight a cell based on a formula, click the Conditional Formatting button in the Styles group on the Home tab, click New Rule to open the New Formatting Rule dialog box, and then click "Use a formula to determine which cells to format" in the Select a Rule Type box. In the Edit the Rule Description section of the dialog box, enter a formula that begins with an equal sign and uses a logical function that returns a true or false value. If the formula's value is true, the conditional formatting is applied; if its value is false, the formatting is not applied. For example, the following formula will format the cell only if the value in cell A3 is less than the value in cell A4:

```
=IF(A3<A4, true, false)
```

A more compact way of writing the same formula is:

```
=A3<A4
```

Conditional formatting formulas can use relative, absolute, and mixed references. When applying a conditional format formula to a range of cells, write the formula for the active cell in the selected range. Excel will modify the references to match the new location of each cell in the range.

You can use formulas when defining conditional formatting rules for data bars, color scales, and icon sets. You enter the formula as a function of the selected cell using a logical function. For example, to display different icons based on the cell's value relative to the average value in the range A1:A10, enter the following formula in the Value box for the conditional formatting rule:

```
=AVERAGE(A1:A10)
```

As with formulas stored within cells, Excel will adjust the relative references as the format is copied across the selected range.

Working with Pictures and SmartArt Graphics

SmartArt graphics are professionally designed business graphics included with Microsoft Office. For example, you can use SmartArt graphics to create flow charts, organization charts, and production cycle charts as well as other illustrations. Emma wants you to use SmartArt graphics to add graphic images to the Documentation worksheet.

To insert a SmartArt Graphic:

1. Go to the **Documentation** worksheet.
2. On the ribbon, click the **Insert** tab. In the Illustrations group, click the **SmartArt** button. The Choose a SmartArt Graphic dialog box opens.
3. Click **List** in the left pane, and then click the **Picture Caption List** icon (the third icon in the first row) in the center pane. See Figure C-13.

Figure C-13 Choose a SmartArt Graphic dialog box

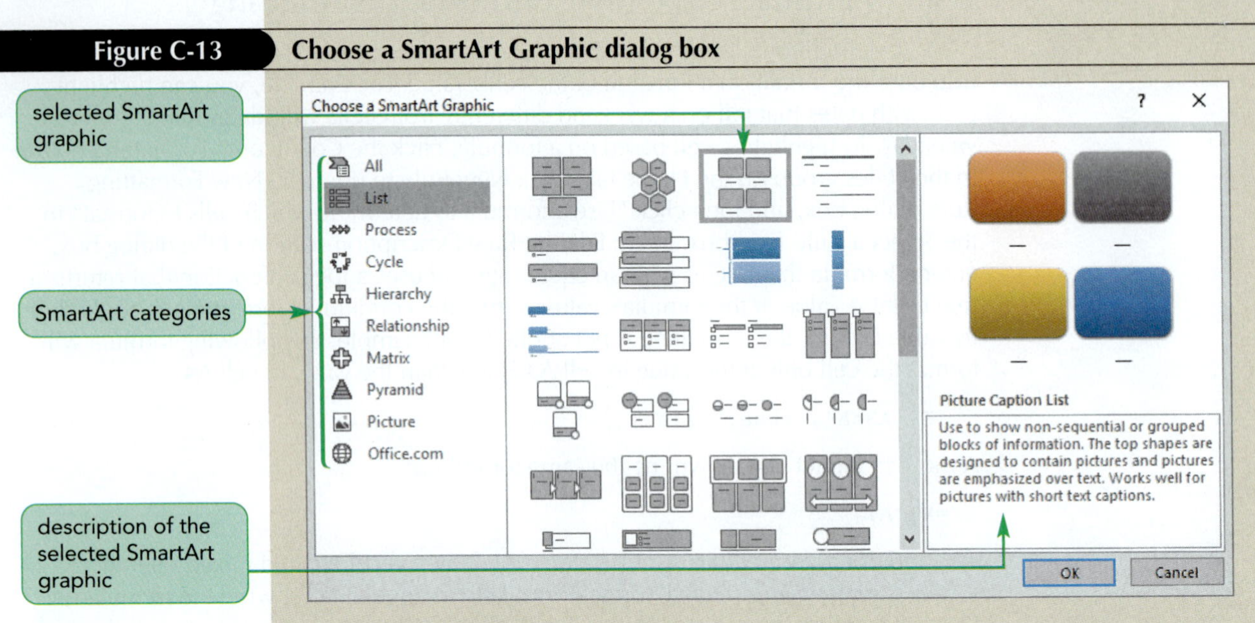

4. Click the **OK** button. The SmartArt graphic is inserted in the Documentation worksheet. The Text pane is displayed along its left side, and the SmartArt Tools contextual tabs appear on the ribbon. See Figure C-14.

Figure C-14 SmartArt graphic inserted in the worksheet

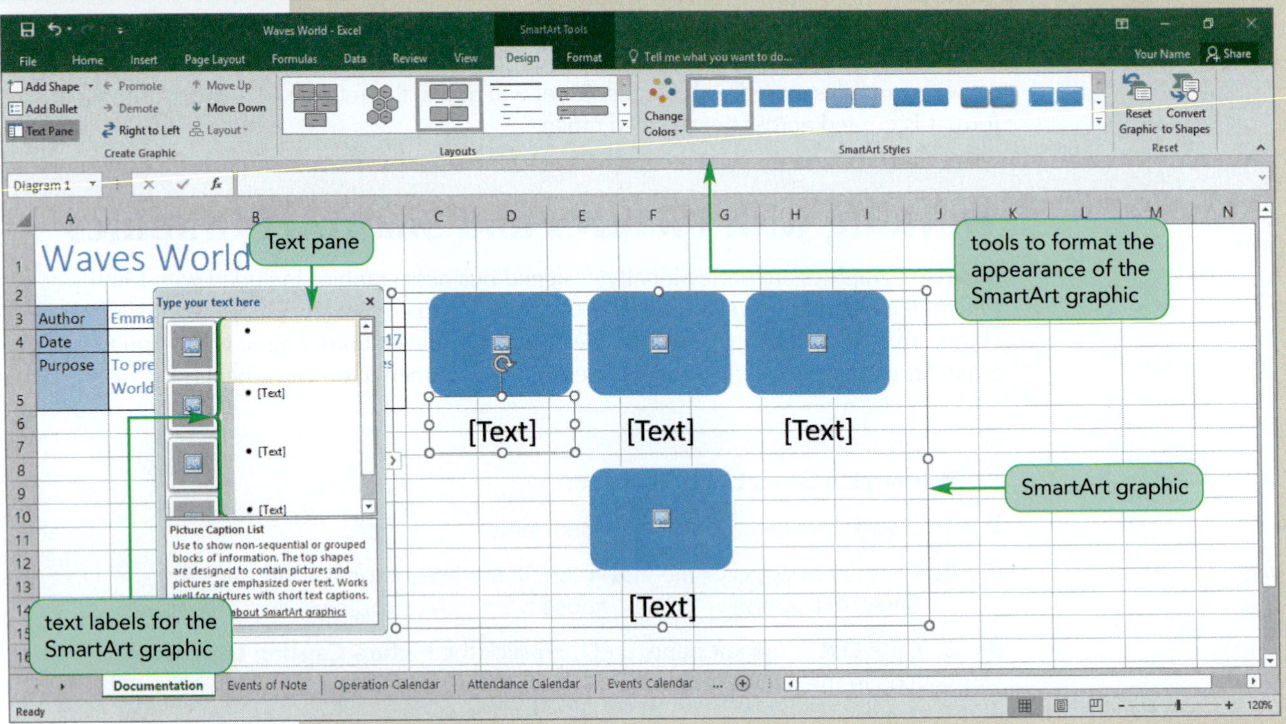

Trouble? If you do not see the Text pane, you need to display it. Click the Text Pane button in the Create Graphic group on the SmartArt Tools Design tab.

You can modify the SmartArt graphic in a variety of ways, including adding captions and images.

INSIGHT

Inserting Images and Shapes

If you don't want to use SmartArt graphics, you can also insert graphics from image files saved on your computer or the web. To insert an image, click the Pictures or Online Pictures button in the Illustrations group on the Insert tab. Select the image you want to use, and insert it into the worksheet. You can then use the sizing handles to set the image size. Excel has drawing tools to modify the image's brightness, contrast, sharpness, and softness. You can also modify the image's color and create transparent sections of the image.

You can also insert ready-made shapes such as circles, squares, and arrows. Click the Shapes button in the Illustrations group, and then select the shape you want to use. You can format a shape by modifying its line and fill colors and adding special visual effects such as drop shadows.

Adding Text Labels to SmartArt Graphics

You enter or edit text for each element of the SmartArt graphic in the Text pane. As you type the text, the font size changes so that the label fits within its graphic element. Font sizes also increase or decrease as needed when the SmartArt graphic is resized. The Text pane uses the following rules for editing the SmartArt graphic text:

- Press the Enter key to add a new row of text to the Text pane and a new element to the SmartArt graphic.
- Press the Tab key to demote the text to the next lower level.
- Press the Backspace key to promote the text to the next higher level.
- Hold down the Shift key as you press the Enter key to insert text on a new line at the same level.
- Press the ↓ and ↑ keys to move between the entries in the Text pane without inserting new text.

Emma wants you to insert the labels "South Dakota's Best Waterpark" in the SmartArt graphic with each word associated with a different graphic box.

To enter text into the SmartArt graphic:

1. With the first entry selected in the Text pane, type **South** as the text label.
2. Click the second text label entry, and then type **Dakota's** for the second text label.
3. Click the third text label entry, and then type **Best** for the text label.
4. Click the fourth text label entry, and then type **Waterpark** for the fourth and last label.

Applying SmartArt Styles

You can format a SmartArt graphic to achieve a unique look that fits the workbook's purpose. As with other Excel elements, you can use a style to format the SmartArt graphic. A **SmartArt style** is a collection of formats you can use to change a SmartArt graphic's appearance. You can also apply formatting to change the color and outline style of the graphic. You can rotate the graphic elements to give them a 3-D look.

Emma wants the SmartArt graphic to have a "chiseled" 3-D look and change the color to green. You'll format the SmartArt graphic.

To format the SmartArt graphic:

TIP

To restore a SmartArt graphic to its original appearance, click the Reset Graphic button in the Reset group on the SmartArt Tools Design tab.

1. On the SmartArt Tools Design tab, in the SmartArt Styles group, click the **More** button, and then click the **Inset** style (the second style in the first row) in the 3-D section of the gallery. The style is applied to the graphic.
2. In the SmartArt Styles group, click the **Change Colors** button, and then click **Colored Fill – Accent 6** (the second option) in the Accent 6 section. The graphic color changes to olive green. See Figure C-15.

Figure C-15 Formatted SmartArt graphic

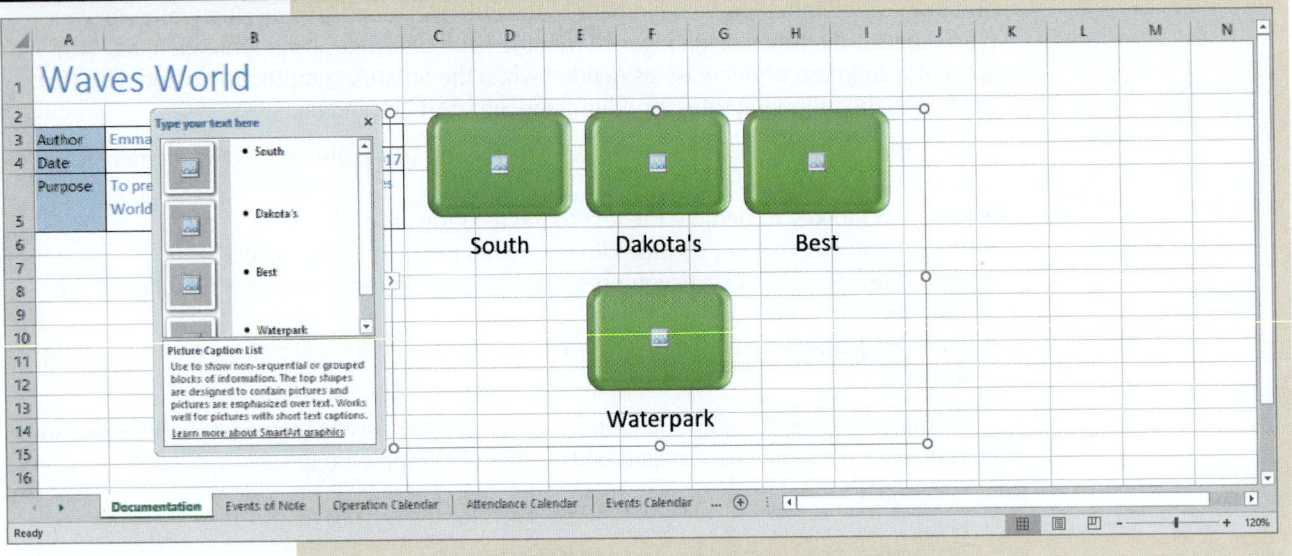

Inserting and Editing Pictures

Pictures or other images can enhance a worksheet or object such as a SmartArt graphic. Emma has four graphic images that she wants you to place within the four boxes of the SmartArt graphic.

To fill the SmartArt with pictures:

1. Click the top-left box in the SmartArt graphic. A selection box appears around the selected box element.
2. On the ribbon, click the **SmartArt Tools Format** tab. In the Shape Styles group, click the **Shape Fill button arrow**, and then click **Picture**. The Insert Pictures window opens.
3. Click the **From a file** button to open the Insert Picture dialog box, navigate to the **ExcelC > Module** folder included with your Data Files, click the **photo1** JPEG file, and then click the **Insert** button. The box is filled with the photo1 image.
4. Repeat Steps 1 through 3, clicking the next shape and adding the **photo2**, **photo3**, and **photo4** JPEG files into the remaining three boxes. See Figure C-16.

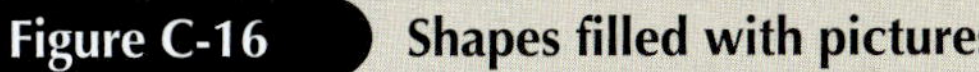
Figure C-16 **Shapes filled with pictures**

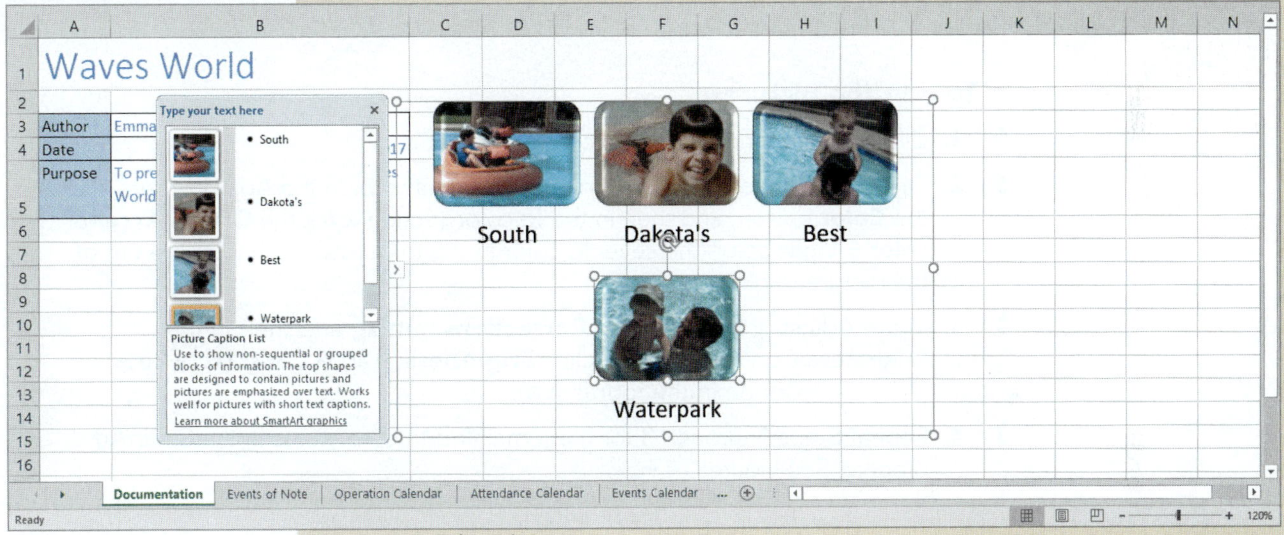

Photos courtesy of Patrick Carey

Next, you will format the appearance of these four images. With the Excel imaging tools, you can recolor pictures and change the picture's contrast and brightness levels. For pictures inserted into a workbook as separate graphic objects (as opposed to fills), you can change the picture's shape, add a graphical border, and apply special effects such as rotating the picture in three dimensions and adding a drop shadow.

REFERENCE

Editing a Picture

- Select the picture image, and then click the Picture Tools Format tab on the ribbon.
- To change the color tint, brightness, or contrast of the picture, click the Color button or the Corrections button in the Adjust group.
- To add an artistic effect to the picture, click the Artistic Effects button in the Adjust group.
- To apply a style to the picture, select an effect in the Styles gallery in the Picture Styles group.
- To add a graphical border or a special effect, click the Picture Border or Picture Effects button, respectively, in the Pictures Styles group.
- To crop or resize the picture, click the Crop button or enter values in the Size boxes in the Size group.
- To restore the picture to its original appearance, click the Reset Picture button in the Adjust group.

Emma wants you to recolor the graphic images, giving them a green tint. You'll also increase the brightness and contrast of the images.

To edit the pictures:

1. Click the first SmartArt graphic box to select it.
2. On the ribbon, click the **Picture Tools Format** tab. In the Adjust group, click the **Color** button, and then in the Recolor section, click the **Green, Accent color 6 Light** color (the seventh color in the third row) to change the tint of the picture to olive green.
3. In the Adjust group, click the **Corrections** button, and then in the Brightness/Contrast section, click **Brightness: +20% Contrast: +20%** (the fourth option in the fourth row).
4. Repeat Steps 1 through 3 for the remaining three pictures in the SmartArt graphic. See Figure C-17.

Figure C-17 Pictures with color tint and increased brightness and contrast

Photos courtesy of Patrick Carey

You have formatted the color, brightness, and contrast in the pictures. Next, you'll resize and position the SmartArt graphic.

INSIGHT

Creating Text Boxes

Excel worksheets are not always a good document format for inserting a lot of text. Although you can merge cells to create big text blocks, that might not work well with other rows and columns in the worksheet. Another option is to insert a text box. **Text boxes** are objects in which you can type that are placed on top of the worksheet and can be sized to any width or height. You create a text box using the Text Box button in the Text group on the Insert tab. You can format the content of text boxes using the font and alignment options on the Home tab. You can also format the border and fill color of the text box itself using the tools on the Drawing Tools Format tab. Text boxes can be oriented horizontally on the page, or you can rotate it so that the text is at right angles to the rest of the worksheet content.

Resizing a SmartArt Graphic

The layout and size of objects within a SmartArt graphic automatically change based on the dimensions of the graphic. Currently the SmartArt graphic you created is laid out in two rows with three boxes in the first row. Emma suggests that you resize the SmartArt graphic so that all four boxes are on a single row and located below row 6 in the Documentation worksheet.

To resize and move the SmartArt graphic:

1. With the SmartArt graphic still selected, move the pointer over the graphic border until it changes to ✥, and then drag the graphic below row 6.
2. Drag the middle-right resizing handle to the right, increasing the width of the SmartArt graphic until all four boxes are on a single row.
3. Drag the lower-right resizing handle to column E to decrease the size of the SmartArt graphic while retaining its proportions.
4. Click cell **A1** to deselect the graphic. Figure C-18 shows the resized and moved graphic as it appears in the Documentation sheet.

Figure C-18 **Resized and moved SmartArt graphic**

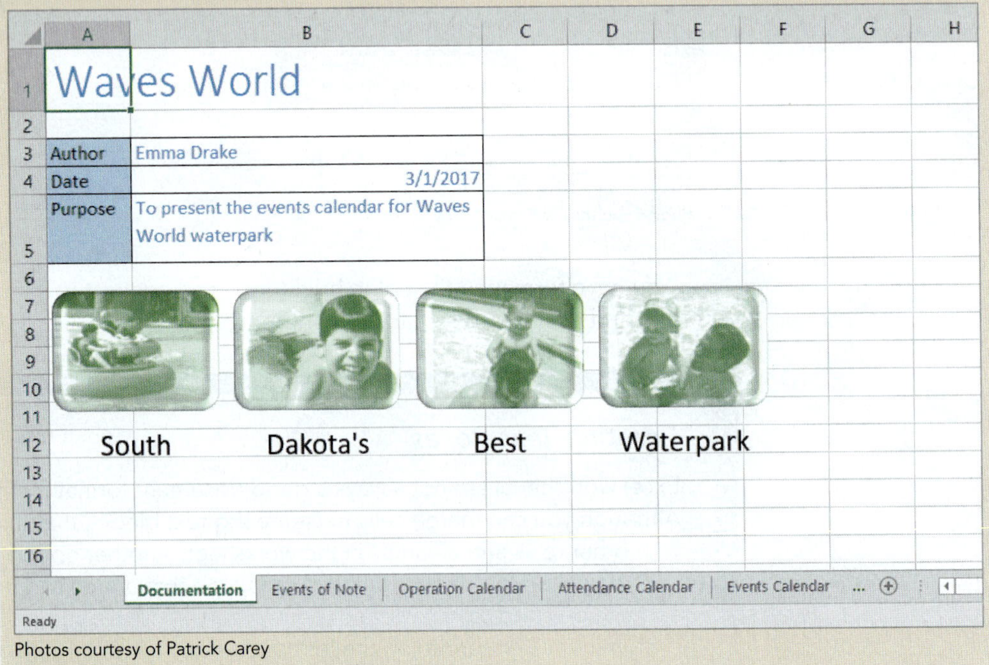

Photos courtesy of Patrick Carey

Note that objects, such as SmartArt graphics and pictures, are moved and resized along with the worksheet cells. So, if you insert a cell, column, or row within the object, the object will be repositioned to the right or down to compensate for the new worksheet content. You can change this default behavior by right-clicking the object, clicking Size and Properties on the shortcut menu, and then choosing one of the following options in the Properties section of the Format Shape pane: (a) move and size the object with the worksheet cells, (b) move but don't resize with the cells, or (c) don't move and don't resize the object with the cells.

PROSKILLS

Decision Making: Choosing a Graphic Image Type

Excel supports most graphic file formats, so you have a choice of formats for the pictures you import into workbooks. The most common picture format is the **Joint Photographic Experts Group** format, commonly known as **JPEG**. JPEGs are produced by most digital cameras and can support up to 16.7 million colors (which is more colors than the human eye can distinguish). JPEGs can also be compressed to save file space without greatly affecting image quality. You will most often use JPEGs with photo images.

Another popular format is the **Portable Network Graphics** format, or **PNG**. Like JPEGs, PNG graphics allow for picture compression for smaller file sizes. PNG is a better choice than JPEG for storing images that contain line art or text. PNG also supports transparency, allowing graphic images in which sections of the background will appear through the graphic. You will use PNGs for photo images, line art images, and images that require the use of transparency.

For better quality photos, choose the **Tagged Image File Format**, or **TIFF**. Although TIFFs provide higher-quality photos, the image files tend to be much larger as well, which increases the workbook's size.

Finally, you can also import logos and formatted documents in **Encapsulated PostScript format**, or **EPS**. Written in the PostScript language, EPS files provide perhaps the highest quality format for clip art files but require access to a PostScript printer to view the results; otherwise, EPS files are not viewable.

Working with Themes

To quickly change the appearance of a workbook, you can change its theme. Office supports many built-in themes. If a workbook uses only theme colors and fonts, you can switch between themes without editing the styles of individual cells and ranges. Emma wants you to use a different theme for the Waves World workbook.

To apply a different theme to the Waves World workbook:

1. On the ribbon, click the **Page Layout** tab. In the Themes group, click the **Themes** button to open the Themes gallery, and then click **Facet**. The workbook's theme changes from the default Office theme to the Facet theme.
2. View each worksheet in the workbook to see the impact of the Facet theme on the workbook, and note that the fonts and colors changed to reflect that theme.
3. Go to the **Operation Calendar** worksheet, and change the zoom level to **60%** so you can view all of the calendars under the new theme. See Figure C-19.

Figure C-19 Operation Calendar sheet viewed under the Facet theme

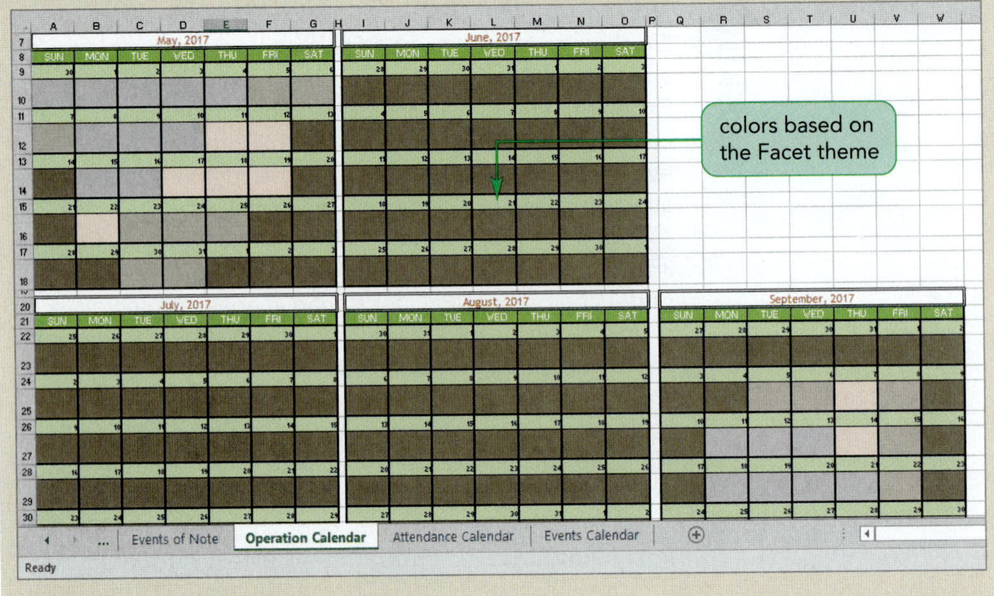

4. Restore the zoom level to **120%**.

Modifying a Theme's Fonts and Colors

If the built-in themes do not meet your needs, you can create a custom theme by selecting different fonts, colors, and effects. You can choose from a list of built-in theme fonts, colors, and effects, or you can create your own collection.

REFERENCE

Creating and Saving a Theme

- On the Page Layout tab, in the Themes group, click the Themes button, and then click a theme to apply it.
- In the Themes group, click the Fonts button, the Colors button, or the Effects button, and then click the theme fonts, colors, or effects you want to use in the custom theme.
- In the Themes group, click the Themes button, and then click Save Current Theme.
- Type a filename in the File name box, and then click the Save button.

A font can be defined for either the theme's heading text or for the body text. The default font under the Facet theme is Trebuchet MS for both the heading and body text. Emma wants to change theme's fonts and colors. You'll change the heading font to Impact and the body font to Times New Roman.

To change the heading and body font for the Facet theme:

1. On the Page Layout tab, in the Themes group, click the **Fonts** button. The Fonts gallery lists heading/body font options. Instead of selecting one of these options, you'll create a custom set of fonts.
2. Click **Customize Fonts**. The Create New Theme Fonts dialog box opens.
3. Click the **Heading font arrow**, and then click **Impact** to select the Heading font for the theme.
4. Click the **Body font arrow**, and then click **Times New Roman** to select the Body font for the theme.
5. In the Name box, type **Wave Fonts** as the name for the custom theme font choices. See Figure C-20.

Figure C-20 Create New Theme Fonts dialog box

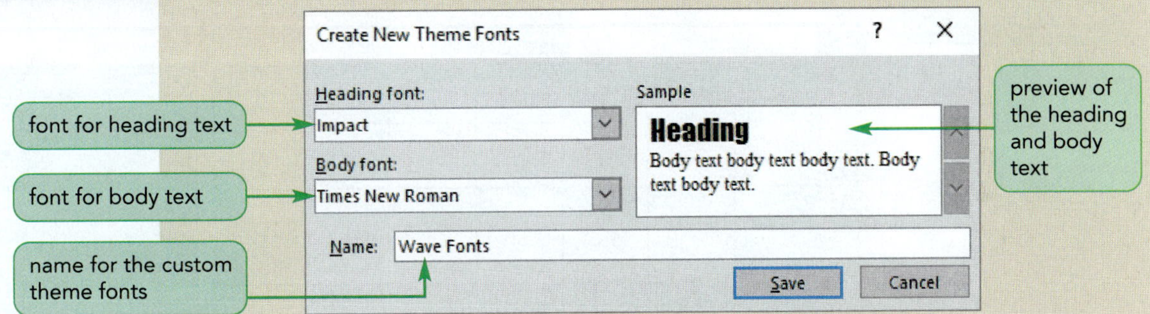

6. Click the **Save** button. Wave Fonts is added as a font option for heading and body text and applied to the workbook.

The heading text in cell A1 changes to the Impact font, and the body text located everywhere else in the worksheet changes to the Times New Roman font. You can also change the theme colors used in the workbook. Emma wants you to select a different set of theme colors for the workbook.

TIP

You can click Customize Colors in the Colors gallery to select custom colors in the Create New Theme Colors dialog box.

To select different theme colors for the workbook:

1. On the Page Layout tab, in the Themes group, click the **Colors** button. The Colors gallery shows the color options available for the current theme.
2. Click **Blue Green**. The workbook changes to the new theme colors. See Figure C-21.

Figure C-21 Operation Calendar worksheet with custom theme fonts and colors

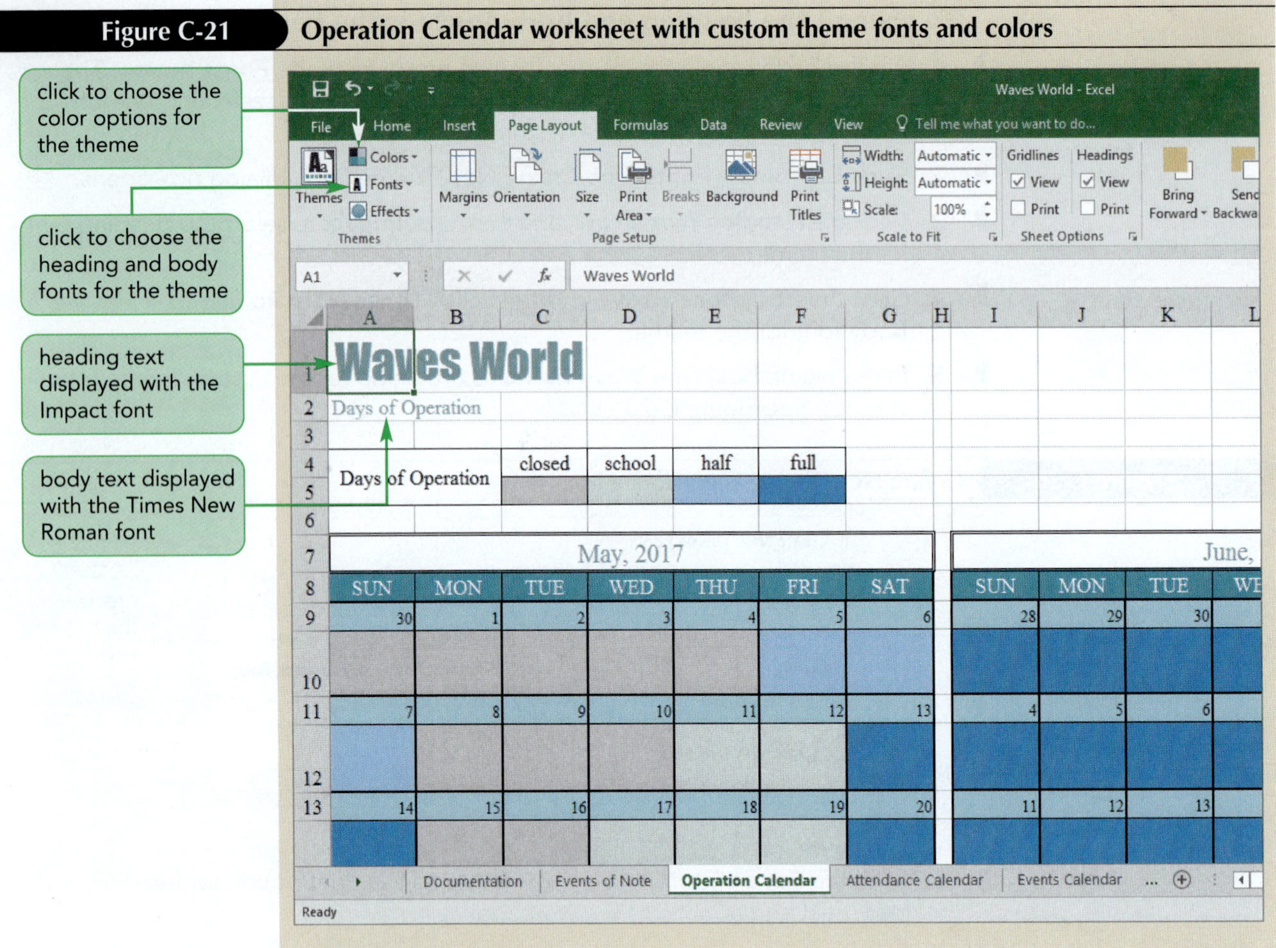

Saving a Custom Theme

When you are satisfied with the look of the custom theme, you can save it as a permanent file to be used in formatting other workbooks. You can save theme files in the default theme folders on your computer or in another folder you choose. Files stored in the default theme folders appear in the Themes gallery, which is not the case when you save the theme file elsewhere. All theme files have the .thmx file extension.

To save the current theme and delete Wave Fonts:

1. On the Page Layout tab, in the Themes group, click the **Themes** button, and then click **Save Current Theme**. The Save Current Theme dialog box opens, displaying the default Office theme folders.
2. Save the custom theme with the filename **Waves** in the location specified by your instructor.

   You no longer need Wave Fonts because you saved the Waves theme. You can delete these theme fonts.
3. In the Themes group, click the **Fonts** button.
4. In the Custom section of the Fonts gallery, right-click the **Wave Fonts** entry, and then click **Delete** on the shortcut menu. A dialog box opens to confirm that you want to delete these theme fonts.
5. Click the **Yes** button to confirm the deletion. The theme fonts are deleted.
6. Save the workbook, and then close it.

Excel, Word, and PowerPoint use the same file format for theme files, so you can share custom themes that you create in Excel with other Office files. For example, Emma could create a consistent look and feel for all of her Office files by designing a theme with the fonts, colors, and effects she wants. If Emma later modifies and resaves the custom theme file, the changes will automatically be reflected in every Excel, Word, and PowerPoint document that uses the theme.

Improving Accessibility with Alternative Text

Workbooks need to be accessible to all users, including those users who have special visual needs. You can improve the accessibility of workbook content by adding alternative text that will be read by screen readers and other aural devices in place of graphics, charts, and tables.

To add alternative text to a graphic or chart, complete the following steps:

1. Right-click the object and then on the shortcut menu, click Format Chart Area, Format Picture, Format Object, or Format Shape, matching the object that you want to add alternative text to.
2. In the Formatting pane, click the Size & Properties button, and then click the Alt Text menu entry.
3. Enter a title and description that provides a summary of the contents of the object.

You can also add alternative text to Excel tables, which provides a title and description that summarizes the table's content. To add alternative text to an Excel table, complete the following steps:

1. Right-click the table, and then on the shortcut menu, click Table and Alternative Text.
2. Enter a title and description that provides a summary of the table's contents.

Adding accessible content is an essential aspect to designing workbooks that are not just informative but also are inclusive of all people.

The Waves World workbook is complete. Emma is pleased with the design and graphic elements you added. She plans to produce other workbooks for the company containing information about the upcoming season.

PRACTICE

Review Assignments

Data Files needed for the Review Assignments: ***season.xlsx, image1.jpg, image2.jpg, image3.jpg***

Emma created another workbook of calendar data for Waves World. This workbook contains calendars listing the size of the staff (administrative, half, or full), the daily high temperature, and the hours of operation (closed, three quarter, half, or full.) She wants you to format these tables, add graphical elements to the workbook, and create a unified design theme. Complete the following:

1. Open the **Season** workbook located in the ExcelC > Review folder included with your Data Files, and then save the workbook as **Season Calendar** in the location specified by your instructor.
2. In the Documentation worksheet, enter your name and the date.
3. Create a new custom cell style named **WavTitle** with the following formatting:
   - Font—14-point bold in white
   - Fill—Light blue background color (the fifth theme color in the first row of the palette)
   - Alignment—Text centered horizontally
   - Border—Thick outline
4. Apply the WavTitle cell style to the titles above each monthly calendar in the Staff Calendar, Temperature Calendar, and Hours Calendar worksheets. (*Hint*: You can group the sheets to speed up the process of applying the WavTitle cell styles.)
5. In the Events Table worksheet, add a new table style named **WavTable** with the following formatting:
   - Header row—white text on a light blue background (the fifth theme color) and a thick outline border
   - First row stripe—two stripes high, light blue background fill (the fifth color in the second row of the color palette)
   - Second row stripe—two stripes high, white background fill
6. Apply the WavTable table style to the table in the Events Table worksheet.
7. In the Staff Calendar worksheet, which indicates the staffing at the waterpark for the upcoming season, select the Staff_Dates range from the Name box, and then apply the following conditional formatting rules:
   a. Highlight cells that contain the text "admin" with a medium gray fill color (first color in the third row of the color palette).
   b. Highlight cells that contain the text "half" with a light green fill color (last color in the second row).
   c. Highlight cells that contain the text "full" with a medium green fill color (last color in the first row).
8. In the Temperature Calendar worksheet, which contains the daily high temperature for each day of the upcoming season, select the Temperature_Dates range from the Name box, and then apply a color scale that ranges from white to Orange, Accent 2 (the sixth color in the first row).
9. Format cell A4 with a fill effect that uses a gradient fill ranging from white to Orange, Accent 2 to indicate the range of colors in the table.
10. In the Hours Calendar worksheet, which contains the how many hours the park is open each day, select the Hours_Dates range from the Name box, apply the following rules, and show only the icon to the selected range:
    - When the value is ≥ 80 percent, display a full black circle.
    - When the value is between 60 percent and 80 percent, display a three-quarter black circle.
    - When the value is between 40 percent and 60 percent, display a half circle.
    - When the value is between 20 percent and 40 percent, display a quarter circle.
    - Otherwise, display an empty circle.

11. In the Documentation worksheet, insert a SmartArt graphic, click Picture in the left pane, and then choose Picture Accent Blocks (the third graphic in the fourth row). Add the captions **South Dakota's**, **Best**, and **Waterpark** to the three blocks and display the **image1**, **image2**, and **image3** JPEG image files located in the ExcelC > Review folder as the block images.
12. Move the SmartArt graphic so the three image blocks wrap around the lower-right corner of cell B5.
13. Change the brightness of the three pictures to +40% and the contrast to –40%.
14. Apply the Wisp theme to the workbook.
15. Change the theme fonts to Arial Black for the heading font and Garamond for body font.
16. Change the theme colors to Orange Red.
17. Save the revised workbook theme as **CalTheme** in the location specified by your instructor.
18. Save the workbook, and then close it.

APPLY

Case Problem 1

Data Files needed for this Case Problem: *Cinematic.xlsx, reel.png*

Cinematic Movie Theater Halley Iverson is the financial manager at the Cinematic Movie Theater in Springfield, Illinois. She is creating a workbook that details the daily attendance figures at the theater, comparing those values to attendance from the previous year. Halley has asked for your help in adding special formatting to the report to highlight how attendance varies throughout the year and between years. Complete the following:

1. Open the **Cinematic** workbook located in the ExcelC > Case1 folder included with your Data Files, and then save the workbook as **Cinematic Theater** in the location specified by your instructor.
2. In the Documentation worksheet, enter your name and the date.
3. Create a new cell style named **Cinematic** that sets the font to 24-point Impact in white and changes the fill to a fill effect of the Blue, Accent 1 theme color radiating out from the center to the Orange, Accent 2 theme color.
4. Apply the Cinematic cell style to cell A1 of each worksheet.
5. Create a new cell style named **CinemaSub** that sets the font to 14-point Arial Black in the orange theme color.
6. Apply the CinemaSub cell style to cell A2 of the 2017 Attendance, 2016 Attendance, and Monthly Totals worksheets.
7. In the 2017 Attendance worksheet, create a color scale for the daily attendance figures in the range B6:M36 that displays the lowest attendance days with a light blue fill and the highest attendance days with a dark blue fill.
8. Add conditional formatting to the daily attendance figures in the range B6:M36 that highlights the day with the highest attendance with a bold yellow font and a solid yellow border.
9. Repeat Steps 7 and 8 for the attendance figures in the 2016 Attendance worksheet.
10. In the Monthly Totals worksheet, for the table in the range A4:D17, create a table style name **MonthTable** with the following properties, and then apply it to the range:
    - Display the text in the header row and the first column in a white font on a blue fill.
    - Display the first row stripe with a light blue fill.
    - Display the second row stripe with a light gold fill.
11. For the Difference values in the range D5:D17, add an icon set that displays a green up arrow for any year attendance increased compared to the previous year, a yellow horizontal arrow for any year attendance was unchanged, and a red down arrow for any year the attendance decreased.

12. In the Documentation worksheet, insert the **reel** PNG picture file located in the ExcelC > Case1 folder included with your Data Files.
13. Make the following changes to the picture:
    a. Resize the picture to cover the range C1:E5.
    b. Recolor the picture with Orange, Accent color 2 Light.
    c. From the Artistic Effects button in the Adjust group of the Picture Tools Format tab, apply the Pencil Sketch effect (the fourth effect in the first row of the Artistic Effects gallery) to the picture.
14. Save the workbook, and then close it.

CHALLENGE

Case Problem 2

Data File needed for this Case Problem: *Bronco.xlsx*

Bronco Design Peter Hampstein owns FPS owns Bronco Design, a website design firm located in Erie, Pennsylvania. The company just received a contract to create a new website for Kinman Brothers Grocery store, a local chain of stores in northwestern Pennsylvania. The website must be ready to go live in six weeks. To keep the project on schedule, Peter wants to create a Gantt chart (a graphical representation of a project with each phase represented as a horizontal bar, with vertical lines superimposed that indicate the current date to show the progress of the project versus time). Peter asks you to develop an Excel workbook containing the Gantt chart. Complete the following:

1. Open the **Bronco** workbook located in the ExcelC > Case2 folder included with your Data Files, and then save the workbook as **Bronco Design** in the location specified by your instructor.
2. In the Documentation worksheet, enter your name and the date.
3. In the Production Schedule worksheet, in the range A7:A14, enter formulas to calculate the percentage of each task that has been completed given the task's start and stop dates and the current date in cell D5. (*Hint*: The percentage equals the number of days from the current date shown in cell D5 to the task's start date in column C divided by the number of days allotted to complete each task.)
4. Replace the percentages in the range A7:A14 with the 5 Quarters icon set, and then edit the icon set as follows:
    - Display the full circle when the cell's value is greater than or equal to 1.
    - Display the three-quarter circle when the cell's value is from 0.75 up to 1.
    - Display the half circle when the cell's value is from 0.5 up to 0.75.
    - Display the quarter circle when the cell's value is from 0.25 up to 0.5.
    - Display an empty circle when the cell's value is less than 0.25.
    - Show only the icons in the selected range and not the cell values.

Explore 5. Create a conditional formatting rule that places a blue right border in the Gantt chart cells that fall on the current date as specified in cell D5. To create the rule, select the range E7:AU14, click the Conditional Formatting button, click New Rule, and then in the dialog box, click the "Use a formula…" option. Create the highlight rule for the cells in the range using the formula

```
=IF(E$4=$D$5,TRUE,FALSE)
```

which tests whether the date values in the fourth row of the table are equal to current date value in cell D5. If the function returns the value true, the cell should display a blue right border.

Explore 6. Create a conditional formatting rule that highlights the cells in the Gantt chart corresponding to the dates each task is performed. To create this rule, create a second highlight rule for the cells in the range E7:AU14 using the formula:

```
=IF(AND(E$4>=$C7,E$4<=$D7),TRUE,FALSE)
```

which tests whether the dates in the fourth row of the table fall between the dates specified in column C and D. If the formula returns the value true, the cell should have a horizontal gradient fill effect starting with a light green color at the top and ending with a dark green color at the bottom.

Explore 7. In the Production Tasks worksheet, insert the Continuous Block Process SmartArt graphic located in the Process category, and then type the eight task names from the Production Schedule worksheet into eight blocks on the SmartArt graphic, pressing the Enter key to create a new block.

8. Format the SmartArt graphic as follows:
   a. Set its size to 3.75 inches high by 7 inches wide using the options in the Size group on the SmartArt Tools Format tab.
   b. Change its color to Colorful Range – Accent Colors 2 to 3 using the Change Colors button in the SmartArt Styles group on the SmartArt Tools Design tab.
   c. Apply the Cartoon style located in the 3-D section of the SmartArt Styles gallery.
9. Move the SmartArt graphic under the Kinman Brothers Grocery Website Task List title so that it covers column A through column K.
10. Save the workbook, and then close it.

INDEX

C

D

E

F

G

Q

R

S

T

X

Z